Principles of Inland Transportation

Principles of
Inland Transportation

FOURTH EDITION

STUART DAGGETT

Late Professor of Transportation
University of California

Harper & Brothers   Publishers   New York

Library of Congress catalog card number: 55–6348

CONTENTS

Exhaustion of Lake Superior Deposits. Labrador Deposits. Coal. New
York Barge Canal and St. Lawrence River

PART IV. RELATIONS BETWEEN THE CARRIERS AND THE USERS OF TRANSPORTATION SERVICE

PART V. RATES

PART VI.   COMPETITION

PART VII.   RELATIONS OF CARRIERS
WITH EACH OTHER

PART VIII. PROBLEMS AND PRACTICE
OF REGULATION

Safety Regulations. Service. Consolidation, Merger, and Acquisition of
Control. Rates and Tariffs. Discrimination. Securities. Summary

I L L U S T R A T I O N S

xv

Preface to the First Edition

The author does not underestimate the difficulty of describing all major forms of transportation in the United States within the limits of a volume of moderate size. Yet he includes the automobile and the inland waterway and the tramway and the airplane, nevertheless, as well as the railroad, in his discussion, because he is persuaded that these different mechanisms of transport are so closely connected with one another in the common task of moving people and goods, that it is no longer possible to understand the activities of any one of them without being cognizant, in some degree, of the work of the others also. Nor is it even true that the underlying principles of transport still find their best expression in the field of any single agency.

Many interesting problems of price-fixing in the transportation world today are presented by the experience of the street railway companies; some of the most disputed calculations of cost relate to our rivers and canals; and the influence of transport upon settlement can be observed in connection with the tramway and the automobile at least as well as in connection with the railroad.

The obvious danger in extending the scope of a treatise upon transportation to cover several forms of machinery and organization, instead of only one, is that the resulting work may lack unity. The analysis may seem to be concerned with a variety of subjects, instead of with one subject under a variety of aspects. It may be that the present volume will produce such an effect. The author can only urge in his defense his belief in the essential unity in principle and in purpose of the different forms of transport, and his conviction that at the present moment more can be expected from an attempt to see the transport problem as a whole, than from continued preoccupation with its various parts.

The rest of the author's apology, if a preface is to be interpreted as an apology, must concern itself with quite another matter—namely, with the inclusion of a considerable amount of economic geography in a book devoted to transportation. It is true that the two subjects are linked together in treatises upon the principles of economics, but for many years the discussions of railroad economics, which constitute most of the recent study of the science of transportation, have concerned themselves primarily with those sides of the railroad question which have been discussed in national or state legislatures, or with problems of labor or finance which confront the railroad because it is a corporation or an employing agency, not because it is concerned with transport.

Now it is easy to understand why excellent books have been produced upon these aspects of the railroad question; but, on the other hand, it is not unreasonable to observe that transport, in its essence, is neither corporation finance, nor big business, nor any other of a number of incidental things; but that, in the main, it is the process of moving articles and people along established routes between defined termini. If this is the fact, then it is proper that attention should be drawn both to the facilities which traffic uses and to the flow of traffic which carriers are organized to promote, as well as to the more traditional and publicly contentious questions with which legislators have been concerned. This is all that the present treatise seeks to do.

Most of the information offered to the reader has been drawn directly from official sources. The author is indebted to many people for courtesies extended in the course of the preparation of this work. He will not attempt to enumerate all the instances in which he has received friendly assistance, but he wishes to express his appreciation of the coöperation of the staffs of the Interstate Commerce Commission and the Department of Commerce at Washington, and of the offices of the United States commercial *attachés* at London, Paris, and Berlin. It would have been difficult to complete the chapters upon the English, French, and German railways without the connections which the last-named offices were able to supply. Acknowledgment should at the same time be made of facilities provided by the Ministry of Transport in England, and by the Ministries of Public Works in France and in Germany, which have made possible convenient access to published and, in France, also to unpublished, material bearing upon the transportation problem in these countries.

STUART DAGGETT

Preface to the Fourth Edition

Upon his achievement of emeritus status in 1951, Professor Daggett continued working upon this final edition of his monumental volume, *Principles of Inland Transportation*. Fortunately, the manuscript had been completed and galley proofs checked when he became incapacitated by his final illness on August 27, 1954. Death occurred on December 22, 1954.

Since I have had no connection with the preparation of this volume, I am unable to make the customary acknowledgments for assistance rendered, except during the period of Professor Daggett's illness. Professor John Hugh Jones of the faculty of Civil Engineering cheerfully and efficiently checked the page proofs and prepared the index. Miss Elinor M. Alexander and Miss Isabel H. Jackson of the University Library were most helpful in checking citations. To these three, and no doubt many others who must remain anonymous, appreciation is expressed for facilitating the preparation and processing of the book.

This fourth edition of *Principles of Inland Transportation* is a complete revision. It is the product of several years of painstaking research and writing by the ranking scholar in the field. The text has been entirely rewritten to incorporate the most recent evidence and analysis, together with numerous instructional aids. Professor Daggett included a great deal of material and many suggestions in footnotes for the assistance of beginning instructors. It was his hope, also, that the use of footnotes for this type of detail would make the body of the text more readable to students.

Professor Daggett's physician has stated that it would have been mental and physical bondage for Stuart Daggett to have given up systematic scholarly pursuits. On the very day when his final illness overtook him, he was at the University at work on his collection of materials on the St. Lawrence Seaway. His life to the end of his career truly exemplified the lines from Chaucer's *The Canterbury Tales,* which were

engraved on a copper plaque presented to him by colleagues and friends
in March, 1951:

> Sownynge in moral virtu was his speche,
> And gladly wolde he lerne and gladly teche.

E. T. GRETHER

Berkeley, California
January, 1955

Part

I

Introductory

The Transportation System of the United States

Elements in a Modern Transportation System

The principal elements of a transportation plant in a modern country are the following:

1. Inland and coastal waterways, including canals, improved or canalized rivers, lakes, bays, and parts of the ocean used for coastwise navigation.

2. A road system, in most cases originally constructed for the use of draft animals, but frequently reconstructed and enlarged for motor vehicles.

3. A railroad system.

4. Pipe lines for the transportation of petroleum and its products.

5. Interurban, suburban, and urban railways, generally driven by electric power.

6. Air routes with proper landing places.

This list does not exhaust the mechanical aids which man today employs for inland movements, but it does include the more essential.[1]

If, now, we examine the relative importance of these different forms of machinery and their location in the United States, we have the following details:

Inland Waterways

The earliest medium of communication to be developed in a country is apt to be its waterways, and this has been true of the United States.

Coastwise traffic is important in this country because of the length of coastline, the excellence of harbors, and the presence of large centers of

---

[1] The kinds of equipment mentioned in the text supply facilities for horizontal movements. This is, of course, what is commonly meant by transportation. It would not be unreasonable, though impracticable for various reasons, to refer also to vertical movements. If this were done the passenger elevators in city buildings might rank high with respect to the number of passengers handled.

population attracted to the coasts or within easy reach of harbors. In the interior of the United States the most important water route is unquestionably that supplied by the Great Lakes. Next to the Great Lakes comes the Mississippi River and its tributaries, and after that a long list of rivers and artificial waterways which are of less significance individually, but which in the aggregate perform a transportation service of considerable magnitude. The artificial waterways on the list include the New York State Barge Canal system, the Cape Cod Canal, and the various coastal canals that make up what is known as the Intercoastal Waterway. Among the important rivers outside the Mississippi system may be mentioned the Hudson River; the Black Warrior, Warrior, and Tombigbee rivers in Alabama; the James, Columbia, Willamette, Hoquiam, and Snohomish rivers in Oregon and Washington; and short sections of the Delaware, the Potomac, and the Taunton rivers emptying into the Atlantic ocean.

According to figures compiled by the Chief of Engineers of the United States Army, the ton-miles assignable to various segments of the inland waterway system of the United States were, in 1950, as in Table 1.

TABLE 1.   Traffic on Inland Waterways of the
United States, 1951

Division	Ton-Mileage (000)
Great Lakes	119,983,804
Mississippi River and tributaries	36,754,185
Rivers, canals, and connecting channels, excluding Great Lakes and Mississippi River system	25,478,135
Total	182,216,124

SOURCE: United States War Department, *Annual Report of the Chief of Engineers,* Part II, *Commercial Statistics,* 1951, p. xxxvii.

The Chief of Engineers reports, in addition to the items in the preceding table, 186,759,124 tons of coastwise, including intercoastal, traffic and a large amount of so-called internal, intraport, and local water business. Statistics do not show ton-mileage in these categories. It must be large in coastal and intercoastal transportation, although the average length of haul in other groups is relatively small.

Roads

The road system of the United States consists of more than three million miles of highway, a mileage so great that if it measured a single continuous road, that road would encircle the earth at its equator more than one hundred times. The greater part of this system is, of course, local.

The network includes, however, state administered highways measuring 599,000 miles (1952), or more than the steam railroad mileage of the country. Of these, 540,000 miles are surfaced.[2] In addition, there is a large amount of county and city construction of a relatively permanent character which state governments have not financed.

There are no exact tonnage or passenger statistics of road traffic because private carriers handle a large proportion of the total business and do not report the amount of traffic which they carry. Most highway travel is by truck or by automobile. In 1952 there were 42,682,591 passenger automobiles registered in the United States, 230,641 buses, and 9,035,754 trucks. Conclusions with respect to road transport are estimates attempting to measure the use of this equipment. The information upon which such estimates rest includes: (1) ton and ton-mileage and passenger and passenger-mileage statistics furnished to state and federal regulatory bodies by motor vehicle common carriers; (2) figures of registration from state motor vehicle departments and federal agencies; (3) information concerning the capacity of vehicles, their average loading, and the average mileage traveled by day or month or year. Much of this last type of data is derived from motor vehicle surveys conducted by state and city governments and by the United States Bureau of Public Roads. The earlier surveys were of roads outside of municipalities; but since 1944 special attention has been paid to the use of city streets. There are also studies of particular commodity movements such as those of livestock, fruits, vegetables, cotton, and assembled automobiles that provide useful data. The record of cases brought before the Interstate Commerce Commission often contains material of this sort, and the Commission has published the results, also, of general and informing studies. As federal regulation develops we shall know more of the characteristics of interstate motor vehicle transport by common and by certain types of contract carriers; but it is not yet clear how reliable statistics relative to private motor vehicle carriage can be obtained.

Among the estimates of intercity truck traffic which have been prepared by responsible organizations have been the following:

Source of Estimate	Ton-Miles (000)
1. United States Bureau of Public Roads, 1925	8,178,000
2. Bureau of Railway Economics, 1928	10,276,000
3. Federal Coordinator of Transportation, 1932	29,976,800
4. Presidential Committee of Six, 1937	43,380,000
5. Interstate Commerce Commission, 1946	66,061,000
6. Interstate Commerce Commission, 1951	133,000,000

[2] U. S. Department of Commerce, Bureau of Public Roads, *Highway Statistics*, 1952, p. 115.

The progression in the figures given is partly due to changes in the method of estimating, but it also reflects an undoubted increase in the volume of intercity truck movements that has taken place during the past 25 years. For our purposes we may use the last estimate prepared by the Interstate Commerce Commission because it is the most recent and because it is also, probably, the best which present circumstances permit.

Railroads

The railroads of a modern country constitute the major portion of its facilities for inland freight transportation.

The United States railway system, on December 31, 1950, comprised the mileage shown in Table 2. Carriers are divided by the Interstate Com-

TABLE 2. United States Railway System—Miles of Line
Owned and Operated, 1951

	Eastern District	Southern District	Western District	Total
Class I Carriers				
Number of roads	49	29	49	127
Line owned	32,108	39,077	112,366	183,551
Line operated	53,328	45,887	126,759	225,974
All Carriers				
Number of roads	344	189	243	776
Line owned	51,291	46,953	125,183	223,427
Line operated	55,223	49,240	132,136	236,599

SOURCE: Interstate Commerce Commission, *Annual Report on the Statistics of Railways in the United States,* 1951, Table 2.

merce Commission for statistical purposes into three classes, based upon the amount of their annual operating revenues: Class I, including companies with revenues above $1,000,000; Class II, companies with revenues from $100,000 to $1,000,000; and Class III, companies with revenues below $100,000. The mileage operated by Class I carriers comprises 96 percent of all the mileage in the country. The Class I companies, moreover, control all the principal routes and are responsible for 99 percent of the ton- and passenger-mileage. For most practical purposes the 649 line haul carriers with revenues below $1,000,000 may be disregarded in discussing the railroad systems of the United States, and attention may be concentrated upon the 127 larger organizations.

Comparison with Foreign Railroads

The railway mileage of the principal countries, in the last year for which figures are generally available, is shown in Table 3. It will be

TABLE 3.   Railway Mileage in the United States and in
Other Principal Countries

	Date	Railway Mileage	Railway Mileage per 100 Square Miles of Territory	Railway Mileage per 10,000 Inhabitants
United States	1951	236,999	6.03	15.07
Canada	1950	42,978	1.20	37.00
Germany (Federal Rep.)	1950	10,097	12.83	2.22
India	1950	33,885	39.15	1.05
Australia	1951	26,979	1.10	31.91
Argentina	1949	26,568	3.10	16.65
France	1948	41,272	14.04	1.02
Brazil	1949	22,380	6.66	4.40
Italy	1950	13,441	7.15	2.08
Great Britain	1950	19,471	20.57	2.05
Union of South Africa	1951	13,328	3.50	15.04

SOURCE: *Statesman's Yearbook*. There are elements of inaccuracy in tables such as
that given in the text, but the broad conclusions that may be drawn from the table
given are probably defensible.

observed that the mileage of railroads in the United States is more
than five times that in Canada or in Australia, countries of comparable
area, and that it is nearly three times that reported by Germany,
France, Great Britain, and Italy combined. The size of our railway net is
of course due to the great distances to be traversed in this country, as
well as to an abundance of capital available for investment and to a
farsighted readiness to spend money on improved forms of transportation. It should be noticed, however, that the railway mileage per 100
square miles of country served is less in the United States, in spite of the
impressive aggregate, than in the more thickly settled countries of Great
Britain, Germany, and France. In this matter the United States takes its
place, on the whole, with certain other countries of large area and
moderate density of population such as Australia, Canada, the South
African Union, and the Argentine Republic.

In 1951 Class I railroads in the United States carried 484 million passengers and 2,791 million tons of revenue freight. Revenue passenger and
ton-mileage figures were, respectively, 34,613 million and 646,620 million.
These numbers would be raised slightly by the addition of statistics for
rail carriers of Classes II and III, for electric carriers, and for express and
mail. This is a smaller number of passengers and passenger miles than was
handled in the same year by motor vehicles, including private automobiles,
but more ton miles than that accomplished by motor carriers of freight.

Electric Railways

Electric railways reporting to the Interstate Commerce Commission are separately treated in the Commission's tabulations. They do a comparatively small volume of business, and the results of their operations are not published in detail.

Interurban, Suburban, and Urban Railways

The present treatise is not concerned with urban and suburban transportation, except incidentally in connection with motor transport. Statistics are accordingly omitted from the tabulations that are presented in this chapter.

Pipe Lines

In addition to its inland waterways and highways and railroads, the United States possess a considerable mileage of pipe lines, used principally for the transportation of crude petroleum and its products. These lines carry a substantial quantity of traffic. In 1951 there were 76 companies which reported to the Interstate Commerce Commission, operating 83,523 miles of trunk lines and 47,629 miles of gathering lines, or a total of 131,116 miles in all. The volume of freight transported was stated in terms of barrels,[3] not in tons, but when the conversion is made it would appear that the trunk pipe lines alone performed a service that exceeded 50 billion ton-miles.

Pipe lines do not serve the public in the general way that characterizes railroad operations. Most systems are owned by, or are affiliated with, large producing organizations; indeed, over half of the large companies advised the Rayburn Committee of 1933 that they carried no oil except that purchased or produced by members of the group with which they were affiliated. But whether oil is carried for few or for many shippers the volume that moves through pipes has given concern to the railroads because much of it is diverted from the railroad routes. These matters will be considered in later chapters.

Air Routes

Air service in the United States is still a small contributor in the carriage of either freight or passengers, although its possibilities are not to be overlooked. During the year 1952 domestic air trunk lines in this country flew 458 million miles, carrying 17 million passengers and, in addition, mail, express, and baggage. The tons of freight handled are not separately stated in the statistical reports of the Civil Aeronautics Board;

---

[3] On the basis of 310.8 pounds of crude and 277.2 pounds of gasoline to the barrel.

but mail, express, and revenue freight ton-mileage and passenger-mileage were respectively, in round numbers, 300 million and 12 million.

Conclusion

Tables 4 and 5, prepared by the Interstate Commerce Commission, bring together the statistics of passenger and freight movements by agencies of inland transport in the United States with which this chapter has been concerned. For convenience, the data for passengers and for freight will be stated separately. It is evident from these figures that more

TABLE 4. Volume of Intercity Freight Traffic in the United States, 1951 and 1952

Agency	Ton-Miles (billions)		Percent	
	1951	1952	1951	1952
Railways steam and electric, including mail and express	655.4	623.5	55.9	54.9
Highways Motor transportation of property	182.5	184.1	15.6	16.2
Inland waterways including Great Lakes	182.2	170.0	15.5	15.0
Pipe lines (oil)	152.1	157.5	13.0	13.9
Airways (domestic revenue service), including express and mail	.3	.4	.03	.04
Total	1,172.5	1,135.5	100.0	100.0

SOURCE: Interstate Commerce Commission, *Annual Report*, 1953.

than half of the freight hauling is still done by the railroads and by carriers on the inland waterways. Of the water routes the Great Lakes are the most important and the Mississippi River is next in line. Pipe lines and highways follow, while the air service is very small.

The predominance of the private automobile in transporting passengers is overwhelming.

It is hoped that the enumeration in the present chapter will give the reader some initial conception of the size and relative importance of the principal transportation agencies in daily use in the United States. Few

TABLE 5.   Volume of Intercity Passenger Traffic in the United States, 1951 and 1952

Agency	Passenger-Miles (billions)		Percent	
	1951	1952	1951	1952
Railways steam and electric	35.3	34.7	7.9	7.2
Highways Motor carriers of passengers	22.3	21.1	5.0	4.4
Private automobiles	379.3	410.3	84.5	85.5
Inland waterways, including Great Lakes	1.3	1.4	.3	.3
Airways, domestic revenue service	10.6	12.6	2.3	2.6
Total	448.6	480.1	100.00	100.00

SOURCE: Interstate Commerce Commission, *Annual Report,* 1953.

people visualize the extent of modern transportation facilities, and probably still fewer have their attention called to the relative position of the different groups. The railroad is and will long be our principal carrier of freight, but it is no longer our chief carrier of passengers, and its work is supplemented even in the movement of freight by other machinery of no mean importance.

REFERENCES

General Treatises

Bigham, Truman C., and Roberts, Merrill J., *Transportation, Principles and Problems,* New York, McGraw-Hill, 1952.

Fair, Marvin L., and Williams, Ernest W., *Economics of Transportation,* New York, Harper, 1950.

Healy, Kent T., *The Economics of Transportation in America,* New York, Ronald, 1940.

Johnson, Emory R., *Transport Facilities, Services and Policies,* New York, Appleton-Century-Crofts, 1947.

Landon, Charles E., *Transportation, Principles, Practices, Problems,* New York, Sloane, 1951.

Locklin, D. Philip, *Economics of Transportation,* Chicago, Irwin, 1947.

Westmeyer, Russell E., *Economics of Transportation*, New York, Prentice-Hall, 1952.

Special and Miscellaneous

Automobile Manufacturers' Association, *Motor Truck Facts*, Detroit, annual.

National Automobile Chamber of Commerce, *Facts and Figures of the Automobile Industry*, annual.

United States Army, *Annual Report of the Chief of Engineers*, Part II, *Commercial Statistics*, compiled by the Statistical Division, Board of Engineers for Rivers and Harbors.

United States Department of Commerce, Civil Aeronautics Board, Economic Bureau, Accounting and Rate Division, *Annual Airline Statistics, United States Certified Air Carriers*.

United States Department of Commerce, Bureau of Public Roads, *Highway Statistics*, annual.

United States Interstate Commerce Commission, *Annual Report on the Statistics of Railways in the United States*.

United States Interstate Commerce Commission, Bureau of Transport Economics and Statistics, *Volume of Intercity Freight Traffic, Public and Private, by Kinds of Transportation, 1939–1949*, September, 1950.

United States Interstate Commerce Commission, *Monthly Comment on Transportation Statistics*.

The Effects of Improved Transportation upon Industrial Society

Before proceeding to discuss the history and characteristics and the problems associated with the different types of transport we may, perhaps, consider the general significance of the transportation facilities which most modern countries in the world possess. What services do these facilities perform? Wherein is a country benefited by efficient transport and wherein does it suffer when it lacks the equipment to carry persons and property from place to place?

Nature of Advantages Received

If we ask ourselves what contribution the new mechanical devices for transport have made to modern life, the answer must be that they have rendered movements more regular and calculable, safer, more rapid, and more cheap. It is hardly necessary to produce evidence to support these statements if we recall that in England and France as late as the early nineteenth century the chief reliance for passenger travel was the horse and the stagecoach, and for freight the pack train and the wagon. Railroads move freight today at speeds of approximately 17 miles per hour, at a cost of little over 1 cent per ton per mile, and subject to damage which is less than 1 percent of the freight rate. The speed of early nineteenth-century wagons probably did not exceed 3 or 4 miles per hour, costs ranged from 6½ cents to over 20 cents per ton-mile, and damages were certainly greater than in railroad transportation of the present day, though by how much it is impossible to say. The difference between pre-railroad and modern passenger movements is less, but it is still great.

If we ask further why the transport characteristics mentioned are desirable it must be replied that regular, safe, cheap, and rapid transport minimizes the effect of space relationships and makes it easier for people to coöperate in accomplishing the purposes which most of them have in mind. A treatise on transportation assumes that coöperation for these purposes is desirable, and this is generally true in economic matters, whatever controversies may arise in other fields.

Effects of Improvements in the Speed of Transportation

Speaking more specifically of improved transportation, we may repeat that among the most significant results have been those caused by the reduction in time in which transportation service has been performed. Thus an early writer said:

The extent of soil by which great cities are supplied with perishable articles of food is necessarily limited by the speed of transport. A ring of country immediately about a great capital, is occupied by market-gardens and other establishments for supplying the vast population collected in the city with their commodities. The width of this ring will be determined by the speed with which the articles in question can be transported. It cannot exceed such a breadth as will enable the products raised at its extreme limit to reach the center in such a time as may be compatible with their fitness for use.

It is evident that any improvement in transport which will double its speed will double the radius of this circle; an improvement which will treble its speed will increase the same radius in a threefold proportion. Now, as the actual area or quantity of soil included within such a radius is augmented, not in the simple ratio of the radius itself, but in the proportion of its square, it follows that a double speed will give a fourfold area of supply, a triple speed a ninefold area of supply, and so on. How great the advantages, therefore, are, which in this case attend increased speed, are abundantly apparent.[1]

This early discussion points to one aspect of the advantages of greater speed in the movement of goods. There are, however, additional considerations. Thus, other things being equal, more rapid movement reduces the time that goods spend in transit. Insofar as the carrier is concerned, this means less capital equipment or equipment employed for shorter periods; there is economy except to the extent that higher speed requires more expensive installations and is associated with a greater operating cost.[2]

---

[1] D. Lardner, *Railway Economy*, London, 1850, pp. 13–14. The quotation in the text properly refers to the speed with which articles can be transported. It should be remembered that this is not the same as vehicle speed, because a fast vehicle with low carrying capacity will require a number of trips to transfer any given quantity of goods.

[2] Railroads have studied the effects of increasing the speed of trains and have reached some general conclusions. Thus a committee of the American Railway Engineering Association reported in 1944 that:
1. High speed is damaging to track. Heavier tracks should be installed when speeds are to be increased.
2. Fuel and water consumption and power requirements are enlarged as speed rises. The power needed grows approximately with the square of the speed.

Apart from the effect of greater speed upon the use of carriers' equipment, an improvement in transport performance may affect production from the beginning of the process to the final sale of a transported good. It can do this by reducing the time during which the commodity is acquiring utility without change in form. If it does this it will reduce the expenses which are attributable to time and which may be estimated, perhaps, by applying an interest rate to the value of the commodity which is being shipped. A shortening of production time will also make it easier for the manufacturer and the merchant to gauge the market. It will, therefore, lessen the number of mistakes. These results are ordinarily desirable and it is an achievement of modern transport when they are brought about.[3]

With respect to passengers, greater speed brings greater comfort by shortening the period during which travelers are confined in the cramped quarters of a carriage or of a train. While many people travel for pleasure, most displacements are means to an end, not ends in themselves, so that the more quickly they are made the larger is the convenience to the public. Speed of passenger travel has its business aspects, in that modern

---

3. Higher speed adds to the maintenance of equipment at least in proportion to the additional power used.
4. As train speeds increase, more trains, each of a smaller tonnage, are necessary to handle a given volume of freight.
    One inference from the above findings is that it is better to increase the speed of rail freight transport by minimizing the number of transfers and by decreasing terminal delays than by increasing route speeds.
    Special high-speed passenger trains must, apparently, in spite of the foregoing, depend upon route speed. Railroads recognize the extra cost of such trains but install them because they appeal to the traveling public. (See American Railway Engineering Association, *Proceedings of the 44th Annual Convention,* 1944, vol. 45, pp. 29–31; *ibid., 41st Annual Convention,* 1940, vol. 41, pp. 150–151; *Railway Age,* December 11, 1948, pp. 48–51.)
    [3] The discussion in the text assumes two things. The first is that an "improvement in transport performance" means a decrease in transfer time and not merely a lessening in the time of transit. This may not be true. Rapid but infrequent trains may not get goods to market quickly, and if the production flow is regular, goods will have to wait. The second is that a reduction in transfer time will shorten the entire production process. It may not do this because the length of the process may be fixed by climatic or price considerations. If coal can be mined only in July and will be consumed only in December, then no improvement in transport will shorten the period during which the coal is held. It will be stored at point of origination or destination if it is not kept in railroad cars. Likewise, if goods are shipped in the afternoon there may be no advantage in delivering them before the opening of next morning's trade.
    Ashton presents an interesting diagram expressing the character of the demand for speed and indicating the equilibrium point with an assumed demand and a scheduled cost at varying speeds, all other costs being left out of the account. The peculiarity of the demand curve is that the demand begins at a low point where the speed is low and rises with the offering of faster service instead of beginning, as does the usual demand curve, with a high demand per unit for the first few units that are supplied. (See Herbert Ashton, "The Time Element in Transportation," *American Economic Review,* May, 1947.)

systems of distribution are based on the assumption that the manufacturer will be able to keep in touch with his market over a wide area through visits by himself or his representatives. The commercial traveler is a product of the railway and the business executive has taken to the air. Rapid transit tends to equalize the supply of labor in different places, lessening unemployment and standardizing wages. It has also its social aspects, for not only does increased speed of travel encourage freer movement of people, lessening differences and breaking down prejudices, but modern facilities for the carriage of passengers tend to diffuse population, to encourage the growth of suburban communities, and to do something in this way to offset the tendency to concentration which has been strengthened by the possibility of shipping goods at high speed and low cost.

Effects of Reduction in the Cost of Transporting Passengers

In addition to the improvement in speed, we have already said that modern transportation has brought about a considerable decrease in the cost of transportation. This decrease has had the following effects:

Where the transportation of passengers is concerned, it has been the general experience that a decline in the fare charged has stimulated movements, both by encouraging habitual travelers to travel more and by bringing the cost of travel within the reach of more moderate incomes. This effect is most clear when pleasure travel is concerned, for the extent of commercial traveling is dependent upon complicated conditions relating to the sale of goods or of ultimate services, which had best be omitted in the present discussion. We indicate the tendency of travel to expand as fares decrease by saying that the demand for passenger transportation is elastic. To this statement the important qualification should be made that a reduction in fares will have little effect upon the volume of travel when such travel involves the passenger in incidental expenses not affected by the change in the passenger tariffs which is supposed to have taken place. Thus, on the whole, reduction on long hauls involving at least temporary changes of residence for the passenger, together with heavy accessory expenses, will have less effect in increasing traffic than will a corresponding decline in fares over short distances.

Effects of Reductions in the Cost of Transporting Goods

We have seen that increased speed in freight transport is desirable, in part because it lowers cost. A reduction in the cost of carriage for any other reason would have the same effect. It would enable consumers, that is to say, to enjoy the benefit of goods which are not to be had in their immediate neighborhood because of climatic or soil conditions, because of lack of raw material or power, because of lack of skill, or generally, because the cost of production is relatively great. Consumers in such districts cannot obtain the goods in question without transport. But better transportation permits communities to obtain goods from more distant places, provided that the costs are not too great. And the less the cost of movement, the more easily can payment be arranged.[4]

To the direct advantage mentioned in the preceding paragraph, should be added possibilities associated with the division of labor. We mean here, by division of labor, the specialized application of units of land, labor, and capital in any area to the growth or production of selected products. Division of labor does not need transport if enough goods are locally consumed. But if the local market is inadequate, specialized production will produce a surplus which must be sent elsewhere. In doing this there will be a cost of carriage which must be covered by the price. The lower the expense of transportation, the smaller the final price, the more numerous the customers, the greater the possible specialization, and the more important are the production savings which division of labor can bring about.

When a community produces and exports those goods in which its specialized effort is most effective, it will cease or reduce its output of other articles, even if such articles can be locally produced. These, instead, will be secured by exchange. Thus, given ideal conditions and several or many producing areas, each community will concentrate upon the products which it can best supply and exchange these commodities with other centers. It will not provide, comprehensively, for its entire demand. These are, probably, the most important sequences which improved transportation has brought about. We shall discuss practical applications of the principle of division of labor in later chapters of this text.

Output of Goods vs. Increase in Leisure

It is to be observed that a reduction in the cost of carriage or an increase in the division of labor would be significant even though no increase in ultimate output should take place. In the absence of an increase in output, more effective means of production would result in an increase in leisure for the working population. People would be able to maintain their customary standard of living at the expense of fewer hours of daily work, and would have time free for rest, recreation, or for forms of activity usually classed as unproductive.

The characteristic result of modern technique has not been an increase in leisure but a rise in the standard of living and a greater consumption of goods. Producers have tended to maintain their former level of effort,

---

[4] If goods are perishable, a reduction in the cost of transport, alone, may not enlarge their market or multiply the sources of their supply. But if they are not perishable, or if they can be adequately protected while en route, it is quite possible that halving the cost of transportation may quadruple the area which is accessible to a community.

and have found themselves, accordingly, in possession of larger quantities of goods, which they have sold in the market place to provide for themselves a more amply supply of those commodities which they have themselves desired to consume. Prices have declined, of course, in the face of such a policy, both in terms of goods obtainable for a day of human labor, and also in terms of money value; but since the decline in price has stimulated consumption, producers have still found their own net purchasing power increased, while the supply of commodities at the disposal of the general public has been notably enlarged.

There is some reason to believe, however, that in some communities, as in England and in the United States, the emphasis upon leisure has increased. The causes include (1) the attainment of a more favorable standard of living for manual workers; (2) the monotony of tasks where the processes of production are minutely divided; and (3) the technique of bargaining in which gains in working conditions appear to be obtainable without sacrifice of or at the same time as increases in the level of pay. The relation of transport to division of labor and of division to the efficiency of production is not changed, however, by an alteration in the final goals which producers have in mind.

Competition and Prices

Another way in which lowered costs of transportation may reduce prices, apart from the encouragement they offer to the division of labor, is through the increased competition which arises as marketing areas become broader. We shall have excellent examples of this in later chapters of this book which deal with railroad rates and service. The wider the market, the more generally does competition exist, and the less can any producer depend upon local fortuitous advantages of either production or distribution. Service must be met with service, and price with price. Of course, better transportation in individual cases may cause some increases in price as well as some decreases, but even here the more uniform standard of charges remains an advantage in itself.

Experience shows that prices of commodities are most likely to be reduced by changes in the rates charged for their transportation, first, when the commodity is of low value and the average haul is long, so that the rate constitutes a material portion of the selling price of the goods; second, when the commodity in question is produced under conditions of free competition; third, when the demand for the article is inelastic; and lastly, when the costs of production per unit other than transportation grow less as the supply increases. Extreme examples of commodities produced under some of these conditions are steel, textiles, and rough lumber.

On the other hand, if the supply of any commodity is limited, or even if the supply is of a character which cannot be rapidly increased, the effect of reduction in the cost of transportation is more likely to be an increase in the net revenue secured by the producer, not a decrease in the price charged to the consumer. This is true, at least over short periods of time, for grain, coal, and monopolized articles of all descriptions. In France, between 1840 and 1872, the price of oysters is said to have multiplied ninefold, because the construction of railroads opened new markets for the seacoast towns, while the supply of these bivalves only slowly increased; this phenomenon may serve as an example of the principle referred to.[5]

It is, however, true that noteworthy reductions in price may occur even when conditions appear at first sight to be likely to lead to increased producers' profit, as has happened in the production of coal in the United States, or in the case of agricultural supplies which are placed on the market under conditions of increasing cost, and yet have been powerfully affected with respect to price by changes in the art of transportation. In these instances the direct saving in costs of production through the decline in the railroad charge has been sufficient to lower the market price, in spite of contrary influences relating to the production of the article itself.

Equalization of the Supply of Goods

Still another advantage growing out of our modern transportation system relates to the stabilization of the supply of consumable commodities at any given point, particularly of products of the soil. The output of articles of this type depends not only upon acreage planted and available labor supply, but also upon conditions of temperature, rainfall, and insect pests, which are only slightly within human control. It is thus more variable than the supply of manufactured goods is likely to be, and it is not inconceivable that a persistent drought may cause an entire crop failure over a considerable area. Since the products of agriculture form the basis of our food supply, the seriousness of such a condition is apparent.

Fortunately, it rarely happens that a failure of crops is world-wide; and transportation was able to rid the world of a recurrent scourge, famine, when it enabled consumers in less favored localities to draw quickly and cheaply upon the temporarily more abundant resources of their neighbors. Moreover, even when famine has not threatened, transportation has equalized prices in different areas by the movements which it has brought about.

Data brought together by the United States Department of Agriculture in 1911 illustrate the wide range of sources of supply of the most ordinary articles of current consumption, and show, by inference, how slight the

[5] Alfred de Foville, *La Transformation des Moyens de Transport et Ses Conséquences Économiques et Sociales,* Paris, Guillaumin, 1880, p. 228.

effect of failure of any one of these sources is likely to be. To quote the report:

For season of 1910, the quotations of Florida tomatoes appeared in the produce reports of Chicago, New York, and Kansas City, early in the winter and continued to about the middle of June, when Texas tomatoes began to appear. These were followed, in the Chicago market, by shipments from Mississippi, and about the first week of July by the produce of more northern fields. Among the states which contributed tomatoes to the Chicago trade in 1910, besides Florida, Mississippi, and Texas, were California, Tennessee, Missouri, and, of course, Illinois. New York's supply also came from a large number of states, among which were California, Florida, Texas, Mississippi, Tennessee, Virginia, North Carolina, South Carolina, New Jersey, Maryland, and Delaware, while some were imported from Cuba.

The supplies of peaches, strawberries, cantaloupes, string beans, and other products were also drawn from a wide range of territory. In 1910 there were at the same time quoted in New York City strawberries from Florida, Louisiana, Virginia, Maryland, and the Carolinas, and while some of these Southern berries were still in the market, supplies came in from New Jersey and New York. The cantaloupes used in New York, in the latter part of June and the first of July, 1910, were coming from Florida, Georgia, and the Carolinas, and also from Arizona and the Imperial Valley of California. A few weeks later melons from Maryland, Delaware, Virginia, and New Jersey met, on the same market, those from New Mexico, Nevada, and Colorado.

In April and May of the same year the asparagus sold in New York City was grown, some near the Pacific coast and some in the regions along the Atlantic. Peaches from Texas and other Western states were included with those from Eastern states in the receipts at New York.[6]

It is evident enough that the range of sources of supply referred to in the report just quoted not only provided the cities of Chicago and New York with seasonable commodities over a longer season than these cities could have counted upon had they been forced to rely upon nearby producers, but also equalized prices by limiting the effects on price of a chance falling off in the output of any single producing region. The quotation refers to conditions in 1910; but a similar statement might be made in 1953.

Attempts to Measure the Benefits Derived from Efficient Transportation

From time to time attempts are made to measure the benefits which improvements in transport facilities bring to the communities in which they are installed. This is not quite the same thing as an effort to calculate the advantages of a transportation system, for such attempts generally assume the presence of some kind of more or less primitive transport, the

[6] United States Department of Agriculture, *Yearbook,* 1911: "Reduction of Waste in Marketing," by Frank Andrews.

value of which is ignored, and seek only to estimate the gains which may be expected from improvement of this plant. In spite of this weakness, which tends toward understatement, and in spite of the contrary influence of a conscious purpose in most instances to maximize the gains to be expected, calculations of benefit from transport possess considerable interest.

Benefits Measured by Gross Earnings

There is one type of estimate that is free from the first objection mentioned in the preceding paragraph. This estimate is based upon the theory that the benefits from a transport system are defined by the gross earnings of the agencies which undertake the task of carriage. This conclusion follows from the assumption that the sum which purchasers of a service are willing to pay measures the satisfaction which they expect to secure from the service they are to enjoy. The fundamental defect of the assumption is, however, that while its gross earnings may indicate the minimum utility which we may impute to a business, such a yardstick will not measure total utility. Most users of a transport system get more than the equivalent of the rate or fare out of the services which they are able to buy, and this is true even when transportation is sold in the open market without the restraining influence of government control.

Benefits Measured by Differences in Cost

When we consider the reduction in cost of transport attributable to the introduction of an improved plant, we pass from the attempt to calculate the gain derived from a transport system as a whole to an attempt to measure the importance attributable to an improvement in that system. Most estimates are of this sort, probably because conclusions as to public policy can be based upon the information which they yield. Thus a government seldom needs to inquire into the total significance of an existing facility, but it may often have a lively interest in the probable results of an improvement in the apparatus for transport with which a community may happen, at a given time, to be equipped.

The usual first step in ascertaining the gain from an improvement is to determine the consequent reduction in the cost of transporting a selected unit, say a ton, a stated distance, say a mile. The next step is to multiply the unit saving so arrived at by a number representing the volume of service to be performed in a given period of time. The product may serve as an expression of the total saving which the improvement in transport will produce.

At this point two possibilities present themselves. In selecting the multiplier by which the unit saving is to be increased reference will doubtless be made to experience. But experience may suggest two sets of figures.

We may, that is to say, multiply the unit saving by the ton-mileage performed by the transport system before the improvement is effected, or we may multiply by the actual or expected ton-mileage after the existing transport system has been transformed. The first of these alternatives makes no allowance for the probable increase in business that the improvement will produce, and for this reason, as well as because of the usual desire to produce as large an estimate of gain as possible, it has rarely, if ever, been employed. The second, on the other hand, is very commonly resorted to. Its defect is that it exaggerates the social importance of better transport, instead of minimizing it as in the previous instance. This is because it neglects the fact that patrons who ship at lower rates made possible by new and lower costs do not gain to an extent measured by the difference between the old conditions and the new, but only to a lesser extent, varying in individual cases.[7]

[7] The following simple calculation may illustrate the principle referred to in the text. Suppose a bridge has been constructed at such expense that a toll of $1.00 per ton is required to provide interest and funds for amortization. Over the bridge pass 1,000 tons daily at the dollar rate. Suppose, now, that a new bridge is built beside the first, of better design and material, which makes lower costs possible. An analysis of the effects of a reduction in tolls from $1.00 to 50 cents which, for the sake of clearness, is divided into steps, yields the following results:

Rate	Tonnage	Increase in Tonnage	Saving to the Public					
			On Original 10,000 Tons	On New Increments				
				A	B	C	D	E
$1.00	10,000	—	—	—	—	—	—	—
.90	11,000	A — 1,000	$1,000	$ 50	—	—	—	—
.80	14,000	B — 3,000	1,000	100	150	—	—	—
.70	18,000	C — 4,000	1,000	100	300	$200	—	—
.60	23,000	D — 5,000	1,000	100	300	400	$250	—
.50	30,000	E — 7,000	1,000	100	300	400	500	$350
Totals			$5,000	$450	$1,050	$1,000	$750	$350
Grand total			$8,600					

According to the figures given the result of operations over the new bridge is a decrease in toll from $1.00 to 50 cents per ton, an increase in tonnage from 10,000 tons to 30,000 tons, and a saving in social cost of $8,600 daily, from which should be deducted enough to amortize the investment in the old bridge which has been displaced. In explanation of the calculation it may be pointed out that the third column in the table sets forth the increase in tonnage caused by each decrease in rate. The value of the service to the shippers of the original 10,000 tons may be assumed to be at least $1.00 per ton, as movement actually occurred at this rate, so that on this tonnage each successive reduction of 10 cents per ton provides a gain of $1,000. The next additional 1,000 tons did not move at a rate of $1.00, but first offered itself at a rate of 90 cents —the value of service to the shippers of these goods may be taken at the midway point between $1.00 and 90 cents or 95 cents, and the saving to them of the first reduction

Benefits Measured by Total Expenditure for Transport

Finally, the advantages of improved transport are sometimes measured by comparing the total community outlay for transportation after the change with the total outlay before an improvement has taken place. It is here assumed that if, and only if, the outlay has been reduced a gain can be said to have occurred, and that the amount of the reduction is also the amount of the gain. This was a method used by J. B. Say, a French economist in the nineteenth century. Such a procedure leads to results which are as inaccurate as those criticized in the preceding paragraph. For better facilities for carriage are important because of their indirect effect upon processes of production as well as because of their direct effect upon transport. The use of new sources of supply of raw material, better access to labor, and the advantages of concentration and specialization are to be desired even when the expenditures for transportation are concomitantly increased. Indeed, it seems quite likely that modern industrial societies usually pay more in the aggregate for transport than do primitive ones, but in spite of this fact, or rather because of this fact, better transportation is significant because by its operation community costs of production are notably reduced.

Government Support Based upon the Theory of Social Benefit

The preceding comments indicate that the benefits of better transport, while undeniably great, are difficult to measure in exact terms. On most occasions precision is unimportant; but it may be well to bear the obvious pitfalls in mind when proposals are made to install transport machinery that is not likely to pay its way and government subsidies or direct government investment are advocated because of the indirect benefits which the new facilities will produce. It is always possible in such a case that the argument for government support is sound. On the other hand, there are always three difficulties which must be faced. In the first place, as we have just seen, the calculation of the indirect benefits which will follow new transport is difficult to make. In the second place, the building of better routes is not the only way of advancing the national welfare, nor necessarily the best when a country is already reasonably well supplied. And finally, it should not be forgotten that state resources are derived from individual contributions. A government, in collecting taxes, reduces the ability of the

will be 5 cents, or the difference between 95 cents and 90 cents. This particular group of shippers will, however, benefit to the full extent from all subsequent, additional reductions. In the same way it is possible to indicate the difference between the actual payments made by the shippers of each other category, the sum of all savings serving as a measure of the total social gain from the improvement. This total is $8,600, not $15,000, as it would be if the maximum gain of 50 cents were applied to the total tonnage of 30,000 moving after the improvement had been installed.

taxpayer to develop capital equipment from which social benefits also may be obtained, and the direct and indirect gains from state aid to or state construction of transport must be balanced against the direct and indirect losses which the restrictions of private enterprise entail.[8]

Political and Social Effects

This is a treatise upon the economics of transportation, and the case for the railroad and for other forms of transportation by the use of mechanical power might perhaps be closed at this point. It is an adequate statement when we observe, as we have done in the foregoing pages, that modern means of transportation have increased the supply of goods, have lowered and equalized prices, and have rendered a direct service in the quick, inexpensive, and comfortable transportation of passengers which may yield as real a pleasure to those who take advantage of it as that derived from the contemplation of art or the consumption of much-prized material goods.

We should not be unmindful, however, even in a discussion of this sort, that quick, cheap, and reliable transportation has political and cultural effects as well as economic ones. No country the size of the United States could be held together were it not for the ease of movement within its boundaries. No modern city could exist without the facilities which transport brings. Transportation makes for homogeneity of type, for the sympathy which comes from knowledge, and for the ease of coöperative action in noneconomic as well as in economic matters which comes from uniformity in customs, a common point of view, and a likeness in environment. We talk the same language, we read the same books, we wear, in general, the same sort of clothes, we eat similar foods, and in spite of individual differences we achieve a unity of spirit which, while doubtless the result of many factors, is to an important degree a consequence of modern transportation. If we add to this the military power which results from transportation and which helps to render us secure, the importance of modern transportation machinery is made still more manifest.

[8] The question of social benefit is well discussed in Bonavia, *The Economics of Transport*, 1947. He observes that improved transport may have some disadvantages as well as some advantages. It is said, for instance, that transportation has imposed a certain drab uniformity of outlook on the population and that it has concentrated population where there is no provision for decent living. It has been argued, on the other hand, that short-distance transport has been more improved, at least in recent years, than long-distance carriage, so that the separate individuality of local communities has been emphasized rather than reduced. These are matters which it would be interesting to discuss.

Bonavia also remarks that the state is interested in securing output of a kind whose social net returns are higher than its private net returns. He points out and illustrates, however, the difficulty in establishing and comparing social and private returns in different enterprises.

REFERENCES

General Treatises

d'Avenel, Georges, *L'Évolution des Moyens de Transport*, Paris, Flammarion, 1919.

Bigham, Truman C., and Roberts, Merrill J., *Transportation, Principles and Problems*, New York, McGraw-Hill, 1951.

Fair, Marvin L., and Williams, Ernest W., *Economics of Transportation*, New York, Harper, 1950.

de Foville, Alfred, *La Transformation des Moyens de Transport et Ses Conséquences Économiques et Sociales*, Paris, Guillaumin, 1880.

Gilfillan, S. C., *The Sociology of Invention*, Chicago, Follatt, 1935.

Landon, Charles E., *Transportation, Principles, Practices, Problems*, New York, Sloane, 1951.

Lardner, Dionysius, *Railway Economy:* A Treatise on the New Art of Transport, Its Management, Prospects, and Relations, London, 1850.

Locklin, D. Philip, *Economics of Transportation*, Chicago, Irwin, 1947.

Pigou, A. C., *Wealth and Welfare*, London, Macmillan, 1912.

Schulz, Bruno, *Die volkswirthschaftliche Bedeutung der Eisenbahnen*, Jena, Fischer, 1922.

Willey, Malcolm M., and Rice, Stuart A., *Communication Agencies and Social Life*, New York, McGraw-Hill, 1933.

Other Books

Clark, J. M., *Standards of Reasonableness in Local Freight Discrimination*, New York, Columbia, 1910.

Cleveland, F. A., and Powell, F. W., *Railroad Promotion and Capitalization*, New York, Longmans, 1909.

Healy, Kent T., *The Economics of Transportation in America*, New York, Ronald, 1940.

McPherson, Logan G., *The Working of the Railroads*, New York, Holt, 1907.

Picard, Alfred, *Les Chemins de Fer*, Paris, Dunod et Pinat, 1918.

Pratt, Edwin A., *A History of Inland Transport and Communication in England*, London, Paul Kegan, 1912.

Sax, Emil, *Die Verkehrsmittel in Volks- und Staatswirthschaft*, Wien, Hölder, 1878.

Ulrich, Franz, *Das Eisenbahntarifwesen in Allgemeinen*, Berlin, Guttentag, 1886.

Periodicals

Ashton, Herbert, "The Time Element in Transportation," *American Economic Review*, May, 1947.

Knapp, Martin A., "Social Effects of Transportation," *Annals of the American Academy of Political and Social Science*, January, 1939.

Special and Miscellaneous

Dupuit, M., *"De la Mesure de l'Utilité des Travaux Publics,"* Annales des Ponts et Chaussées, 2d ser., vol. 8, 1844.

Dupuit, M., *"De l'Influence des Peages sur l'Utilité des Voies de Communication,"* Annales des Ponts et Chaussées, 2d ser., vol. 17, 1849.

Part

II

Survey of Agencies

C H A P T E R 3

Inland Waterways

Let us now return to the elements in a modern transportation system which we enumerated in Chapter 1, and let us carry our discussion of inland waterway, highway, motor, and air transport some steps beyond a mere listing and comparison of size. We may now have some little history in each case, and some additional description and analysis, although there will still remain problems, when we shall have completed this chapter and the three which follow, that will require consideration in later chapters of this book. We shall begin with the subject of inland waterways for reasons of convenience and because of the early importance which this type of facility assumed.

General Characteristics of Water Transportation

The essential advantage of the waterway from the point of view of transport is that it offers less resistance to traction at moderate speeds than does the road. Natural waterways, moreover, such as rivers, lakes, and ocean routes adjacent to the land, are navigable to some extent without preliminary expenditure of capital and labor. Communities which, by choice or accident, locate near such water routes are accordingly likely at an early stage to develop more or less elaborate systems of transportation which accelerate their growth and increase their economic strength.

The disadvantages of water routes are, however, no less obvious than their advantages. Water freezes in many latitudes at certain seasons of the year; the flow of streams varies, also, even when temperature is moderate, so that constant use of natural routes cannot be guaranteed, because of drought or flood. Quite as significant are other facts. Rivers, and to a lesser degree lakes, may be obstructed by bars, falls, or other obstacles; normal depths may be sufficient for small craft but insufficient for the larger boats required for economical handling of passengers and freight; and water routes may not connect the points between which people and

29

goods must move, or may connect them only by long detours. Ocean harbors need improvement, and coastal and intercoastal shipping is subject to interference in time of war. The history of inland waterway improvement is the story of attempts to minimize or to offset the disadvantages of water transportation by canalization, capital investment, legislative preference, and regulation. The limit of any development is reached when the necessary expenditure for control becomes so great that it overcomes the advantages which water carriage appears, at first, to present.

Varieties of Water Transport

The first chapter listed ocean routes adjacent to the land, lakes, rivers, and canals and connecting channels as elements of the inland waterways system of the United States.[1] We will now discuss the segments of this system at greater length.

Canals and Connecting Channels

Canal projects in the United States have been of the following sorts:
1. *Short channels around the falls of rivers.* The first canal construc-

---

[1] Beginning in 1947, the Chief of Engineers of the United States Army classified inland waterways, with respect to tonnage handled, in a different way (*Commercial Statistics,* 1949, p. xix). The revised classification and the tables based upon it supply no ton-mile data and are otherwise inconvenient for the purposes of the text. They are not, therefore, used in Chapter 1. The classification is an improvement, however, in some respects, and is the subject of this note.

According to the revised arrangement the tonnage handled upon inland waterways is now characterized as lakewise, coastwise, internal, intraport, and coastal. The Board of Engineers gives the following detailed explanation of the terms used:

"Coastwise" refers to any movement which includes a carriage over the oceans or the Gulf of Mexico. A movement between any two points, both of which are located on the Great Lakes system is termed "Lakewise." All other domestic traffic represents movements over inland waterways exclusively, and is referred to as "Internal," "Local," or "Intraport."

The term "Internal" is applied to movements between two separate and distinct areas, communities, localities, points, or ports, whereas the names "Local" and "Intraport" pertain to movements between two piers within the same area. Thus, a shipment between two seaports via a connecting river, canal, or channel is called internal traffic, as is a movement between two river ports or between a river port and a seaport. Shipments from Memphis to New Orleans, from New York to Albany, from Pittsburgh to Cincinnati, from San Francisco to Oakland or Stockton, from Portland, Oregon, to Longview, and from Houston to Chicago are all classified as internal traffic. From New Orleans to Mobile via the Gulf Intracoastal Canal would be internal, but via the Gulf of Mexico it would be coastwise.

Chesapeake Bay and Puget Sound are considered as inland waterways, and traffic between any two places located on these waterways is counted as internal. A movement between Philadelphia, Pa., and Norfolk, Va., may be either internal, if the Chesapeake and Delaware Canal and Chesapeake Bay are utilized, or coastwise if the vessel uses the open waters of the Atlantic Ocean; carriage from Seattle to Tacoma is internal.

There is a relatively small tonnage of merchandise moving between ports in the Great Lakes system and inland ports via either the Illinois Waterway or the New York State Barge Canal. These movements are classed as internal because the equipment used is controlled by the lesser depths of water available on the inland waterways."

tion was of this sort. Improvements of this kind are useful, and they are inexpensive in most cases.

2. *Connection of adjacent natural waterways.* Canals for this purpose are usually longer and more costly than projects on a single stream although they, too, when properly planned, may be very helpful.

3. *Canals linking river or river and lake systems.* Still a third type of canal is that which seeks to join two great systems as, for example, the Great Lakes with the Mississippi River or the American rivers emptying into the Atlantic Ocean with the Great Lakes or with the Mississippi River and its tributaries.

The reason why so little was accomplished during the early decades of the nineteenth century in the way of waterway connection between the Atlantic Seaboard and the Mississippi Valley was that the Appalachian Mountains lay athwart all routes except one, and that the cost of lock construction over the mountains was prohibitive. The result was that, except in New York State, the most ambitious projects stopped at the mountains on either side, leaving the intermediate transit to be accomplished by road or by rail.[2]

[2] We should, perhaps, refer to two projects in a little more detail. These are:

1. The Chesapeake and Ohio Canal Company. This enterprise began with the organization of the Potomac Canal Company in 1786 to open the channel of the Potomac to Cumberland and to join Cumberland with the Ohio by means of a road. In 1823, when the Erie Canal was approaching completion, the plans for improvement of the Potomac were replaced by plans for canal construction with the Ohio. The route recommended made use of the Youghiogeny and Monongahela rivers. It proposed to reach the Ohio at Pittsburgh. This ambitious undertaking was never finished, but a canal was built from Georgetown, near Washington, to Cumberland on the Potomac, under the direction of the Chesapeake and Ohio Canal Company. The canal was begun in 1828 and was completed to Cumberland in 1851. It was closed in 1924 (A. B. Hulbert, *Historic Highways of America,* Cleveland, A. H. Clark, Vol. 13, 1904; J. L. Ringwalt, *Development of Transportation Systems in the United States,* Philadelphia, 1888).

2. The Pennsylvania State Works. These works were authorized by act of the state legislature of Pennsylvania in February, 1826, and were opened in March, 1834. They were designed to afford a connection between the city of Philadelphia and the West comparable with that which New York enjoyed by use of the Hudson River and the Erie Canal. As finally constructed, the works were composed of four sections:

a. The Philadelphia and Columbia Railroad. This line commenced at the intersection of Vine and Broad streets, Philadelphia, and terminated at Columbia on the Susquehanna, a distance of 81.6 miles.

b. The eastern and Juniata divisions of the Pennsylvania Canal, extending from Columbia to Hollidaysburg, a distance of 172 miles.

c. The Allegheny Portage Railroad. This railroad began at Hollidaysburg, rose 1,398.71 feet in 10.1 miles by means of inclined planes, crossed the summit of the mountains, and then, by the use of inclined planes upon the western side, descended to Johnstown, Pennsylvania. The total distance was 36.69 miles.

d. The western division of the Pennsylvania Canal from Johnstown through Pittsburgh to the Monongahela River, a distance of 104 miles.

The entire distance between Philadelphia and Pittsburgh by way of the Pennsylvania State Works was 394 miles. The canals were 4 feet deep, 28 feet wide at the

Erie Canal

There is no question but that the Erie Canal was the most important canal undertaken in the United States before 1855. It ran from a point near Albany on the Hudson to a point near Buffalo on Lake Erie, and therefore falls within the class of improvements designed to connect river systems emptying into the Atlantic with the Great Lakes. It was later extended to Oswego, on Lake Ontario.

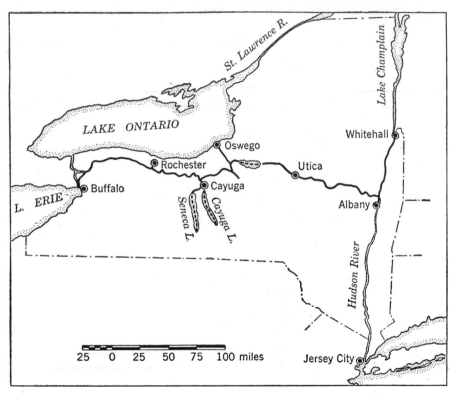

FIGURE 1.   The New York Barge Canal.

bottom, and 40 feet wide at the water line. The locks were 90 feet long and from 15 to 17 feet wide.

Service over the Allegheny Portage was discontinued in 1854. In 1857, the Portage Railroad, together with the Philadelphia and Columbia Railroad and the canal property between Columbia and Pittsburgh, was purchased by the Pennsylvania Railroad from the commonwealth of Pennsylvania (S. K. Farrington, *Railroading from the Head End*, New York, Doubleday, 1943).

The Pennsylvania State Works have attracted rather more attention from historians than they deserve, but they afford useful evidence of the interest of seaboard cities in trans-Appalachian trade at the time when they were built. (See A. L. Bishop, *The State Works of Pennsylvania*, New Haven, Transactions of the Connecticut Academy of Arts and Sciences, 1907.)

CONSTRUCTION AND IMPROVEMENT. The original dimensions of the Erie Canal were the same as those adopted for the Pennsylvania canals, namely, a depth of 4 feet and widths of 28 feet at the bottom and 40 feet at the water line. Between 1836 and 1872 the depth was increased to 7 feet and the widths to 56 and 70 feet; and again in 1903 the people of New York State authorized enlargement to a depth of 12 feet, a width at the bottom of 75 feet, and a width at the water line of 123 feet. This last-mentioned change gave a channel which was approximately as deep as the controlling depth of the Hudson River at Waterford. There was also, in 1903, a very considerable rebuilding of the original canal. In 1930, proposals were made to transform the enterprise into a ship canal, with a depth of 20 or 25 feet from Lake Erie or Lake Ontario to the Hudson River. It was hoped to persuade the federal government to undertake this work, but Congress would not go so far. Congress did, however, agree to appropriate and New York State agreed to receive federal monies to improve the Erie Canal from the Hudson River at Waterford to Three Rivers Point, where a branch of the Canal diverged to Lake Ontario, and to improve the Oswego branch from Three Rivers Point to Lake Ontario. Construction proceeded under this agreement until 1942. The war then caused the suspension of federal assistance; but, after the war, operations were resumed. The Canal now has a channel of 14 feet from Waterford to Three Rivers Point and thence over the Oswego Canal to Lake Ontario; the minimum depth over lock sills, however, remains at 12 feet and a planned clearance of 20 feet has not yet been attained. The degree of completion of the federal projct was, in 1950, 78 percent.[3] Locks and channels will accommodate a boat 300 feet long, with a beam of 43½ feet, a height no greater than 15 feet, and a draft not exceeding 11½ feet.

TRAFFIC OVER THE NEW YORK CANALS. It is evident from the foregoing that the Erie Canal was not only opened in the first quarter of the nineteenth century, but that it has been and still is a recognized portion of the water navigation system of New York.

The great natural advantage which the Erie Canal enjoys from an engineering point of view is, first, that its route lies through the only practicable gap in the Appalachian range between Maine and Georgia and, second, that central New York State, through which the Canal passes, is well supplied with lakes and rivers which either can be used directly or can serve as a source of water supply.

These advantages made the construction of the Erie Canal possible. What made it immediately profitable was the fact that it opened on the west upon a splendid natural highway—the Great Lakes—and that it

[3] United States Army, *Annual Report of the Chief of Engineers,* 1950, Part I, vol. 1, p. 256.

was able to draw to itself the trade of western New York, northwestern Pennsylvania, Ohio, and Indiana through the lake system and subsidiary canals which were presently built between the Lakes and the Ohio River. On the east lay the industrial seaboard and on the west the agricultural states of the northern Mississippi Valley. The two were complementary one to the other and exchanged products readily as soon as facilities were built. Under these conditions traffic over the New York canals grew steadily until 1872–73 and then again, after the panic of 1873, until 1880.

After 1880 canal traffic declined. This was partly because of shifts in the location of sources of production upon which the Erie Canal relied, and partly because of railroad and later of motor competition. Canal service was and is slow, seasonal, subject to interruption, and unable to seek out and develop new types of business operating at a distance from its route. It is definitely more expensive than modern railroad carriage if capital and maintenance costs are included in the calculation. In 1950 the total tonnage over the New York canals was 4,615,613 tons, or less than the movement 90 years before. The principal westbound commodity is now petroleum. Eastbound, grain, pulpwood, molasses, paper, and chemicals account for most of the cargoes. During World War II a good deal of bauxite was transported; this traffic disappeared when the war was over because of the surplus stocks of aluminum on hand at the close of hostilities. During the war, also, heavy eastbound shipments of petroleum replaced the customary westbound petroleum movements, but the normal westbound flow was resumed after the reinstallation of coastwise shipping. Eastbound grain traffic fell off in 1943 and 1944 because wheat was diverted to the Canadian route for the sake of greater speed, but the grain carriage has since been resumed. On the whole, the war record of the New York canals was disappointing. It is evident that the New York canals do not now, in peace or in war, handle the volume of business for which they are designed, and there seems to be no immediate prospect for any large increase. This should not, however, lessen our appreciation of the part which they played in earlier years.[4]

[4] According to the Federal Coordinator of Transportation, costs of canal transport include the expense of maintaining the canal, interest and amortization of the capital invested, and the direct costs of movement. These costs are now substantially higher by canal than by rail. Thus in 1936 the total expense of moving grain from Buffalo to Albany was estimated by the Coordinator to be 14.7 mills per ton per mile by canal and only 8.3 mills by rail. Between New York and Buffalo the relative figures were 11.8 mills and 9.6 mills on sugar, 11.6 mills and 6.4 mills on sulphur, and 11.6 mills and 6.7 mills on iron and steel. Taking general merchandise, the weighted cost for all canal movements was $4.03 per ton in 1936, while the cost of moving the same goods between the same destinations by rail was $2.57.

The estimates which we have just quoted are drawn from the report of an impartial and official observer. The general conclusion that barge canal transport is more expensive than rail transport when capital and maintenance expenditures are taken into account is not seriously disputed. But partisans of canals do reply that it is no more

Mississippi River

Historically, the Mississippi River provided a means for long-distance transportation in a territory devoid of roads and remote from the sea. In doing this, the river linked northern and southern settlements which early developed products that could be profitably exchanged, and it supplied an east-west water route through its Ohio and Missouri River branches which was useful to the westward moving pioneer. These characteristics lent the Mississippi great importance during the first half of the nineteenth century.

Up to 1817, the principal craft used on Western rivers were the flat-boat, the ark, and the raft for downstream navigation, and the keelboat or barge for upstream transit.[5] Steamboat navigation upon the Mississippi began with the steamboat *Enterprise*, which left Pittsburgh in September, 1811, and reached New Orleans in January, 1812. Regular steam service is usually dated, however, from 1817 when the steamboat *Washington* made the trip from Louisville to New Orleans and return in 41 days, the voyage upstream consuming 25 days.[6] Thereafter the steamer rapidly displaced the keelboat and the barge, although the flatboat continued to be used until the Civil War.

---

proper to charge the cost of maintaining the barge canal against its users than it would be to include the cost of maintaining highways in computing the cost of moving freight over the public roads. Highways, except toll roads, are, of course, generally free, although there is a respectable body of opinion to the effect that motor trucks pay, or should pay, for the public facilities which they use.

There is some sentiment in favor of the imposition of tolls upon boats using the New York Canal system. Such tolls were levied until 1882, and were removed principally in an attempt to check the diversion of traffic from the canal to the railroad route. The arguments for the charging of tolls are: (1) that the canals cost the State of New York large sums annually, of which the greater part is for interest and amortization of capital investment; (2) that 90 percent of the tonnage is interstate; and (3) that subsidized barge canal transportation diverts traffic from a more economical (railroad) to a less economical (canal) route. On the other hand, it is replied: (1) that the net cost to the state is exaggerated and that it amounts, in any case, to but a small part of the state's annual outlays; (2) that the canal serves shippers indirectly by preventing railroad charges from increasing; (3) that canal shipments originate at or are destined to points in New York State although they may have one terminus in other states; and (4) that tolls on the canal will divert traffic to the St. Lawrence River, not to competing railroad lines.

The present constitution of the State of New York prohibits the imposition of tolls on persons or property transported on the canals. A bill proposing the elimination of this restriction passed the State Assembly in 1936, with railroad support, but it was not finally approved, and there is little real likelihood that New York will withdraw the financial support which it now gives to barge canal transportation.

[5] For further details consult J. L. Ringwalt, *Development of Transportation Systems in the United States*, Philadelphia, 1888; B. H. Meyer, *History of Transportation in the United States Before 1860*, Washington, D. C., Carnegie Institution, 1917; and F. H. Dixon, *A Traffic History of the Mississippi River System*, Washington, D. C., Government Printing Office, 1909.

[6] Dixon, *op. cit.*, pp. 12–13.

From the 1850's until the early 1880's, steamboat transportation on the lower Mississippi was the chief agency upon which the people of the Mississippi Valley depended for the carriage of freight and passengers. Through boat lines connected Cincinnati, Louisville, and St. Louis with New Orleans; there was an equally important trade from Memphis, Greenville, and Vicksburg to New Orleans; and branch services ran up the Red, Arkansas, White, Ouachita, Yazoo, and other streams.[7] Likewise upon the Ohio and its tributaries, the Cumberland, Tennessee, and Monongahela Rivers and to a less degree upon the upper Mississippi, an extensive commerce was carried on.

Diversion of River Traffic to the Railroads

The decline in the importance of the Mississippi began even before the Civil War with the diversion of increasing proportions of produce from the northern part of the Mississippi Valley to the east and west route to the Atlantic seaboard. During the years 1854 to 1858 western produce represented only 18 per cent of the total receipts at New Orleans as compared with 61 per cent in the early days of river commerce. The same type of change occurred in the South, where traffic left the river for the rail. The following table shows the receipts of cotton at New Orleans from 1873 to 1904:

TABLE 6.   Receipts of Cotton at New Orleans

Year	Receipts by Rail (bales)	Receipts by River (bales)	Percentage of all Receipts by River
1873	438,495	968,877	68.8
1875	406,076	750,080	64.8
1880	627,577	1,087,522	63.4
1885	1,018,261	680,376	40.1
1890	1,722,473	425,828	19.8
1899	1,935,177	343,450	15.1
1904	1,833,755	192,842	9.5

SOURCE: F. H. Dixon, *A Traffic History of the Mississippi River System*, Washington, D. C., Government Printing Office, 1909, p. 59.

The decline in the percentage of river receipts of cotton at New Orleans from 68.8 in 1873 to 40.1 in 1885 and to 9.5 in 1904 was due in part to direct competition of parallel railroads and in part to a change in the location of cotton-producing areas analogous to the extension of grain districts to areas more remote from the river lines. Generally speaking, also

[7] *Preliminary Report of the Inland Waterways Commission*, 1908, p. 133.

river transportation was slow, subject to interruption on the upper reaches by ice, handicapped by floods, droughts, and variations in depth, poorly organized and insufficiently equipped with terminal facilities. Railroads refused to quote through rates with the water lines, and they reduced their water-competitive rates to noncompensatory levels, recouping their losses elsewhere.[8] These various reasons explain the fact that during the last part of the nineteenth century and for at least 20 years prior to 1917 there was no common carriage of consequence upon the Mississippi. The question today is whether it is possible to restore the Mississippi to something like its old commercial importance; and whether, if such a policy is successful, the results will justify the very considerable expenditures which will be incurred. Government aid will be necessary, for private investors will not improve the route, although they will operate when a satisfactory route has been provided.

Physical Improvement of the Mississippi and Its Tributaries

Herbert Hoover, when he was Secretary of Commerce, visualized a river system composed of a north-south trunk line 1,500 miles in length, reaching from New Orleans to Chicago and there connecting with the Great Lakes System; and crossing this, a great east-west trunk line, 1,000 miles in length, from Pittsburgh through Cairo to Kansas City. The addition of feeding lines on the upper branches and tributaries of the Mississippi, the Ohio, and the Missouri rivers would produce, as Hoover saw it, 9,000 miles of connected waterways. The map reproduced on page 39 shows the segments of this Mississippi River system which is included in the federal government's current developmental plan.[9]

[8] United States, Office of the Federal Coordinator of Transportation, *Public Aids to Transportation,* vol. 3, 1939, p. 18.

[9] The effective and project depths in different portions of the Mississippi River and in some of its important tributaries were, in 1949, as follows:

Segment of River	Effective Depth	Project Depth
Mississippi River		
New Orleans to mouth of passes	Not less than 35 feet	40 feet
Baton Rouge to, but not including, New Orleans	Not less than 35 feet	35 feet
Mouth of Ohio to, but not including, Baton Rouge	Not less than 9 feet	12 feet
Mouth of Missouri to mouth of Ohio	9 feet. Occasional dredging in a few localities	9 feet
Minneapolis to mouth of Missouri	9 feet	9 feet
Illinois Waterway		
Mouth of Illinois River to Lockport	9 feet	9 feet

The principal portions are as follows:

OHIO RIVER. This stream flows through a highly industrialized part of the United States, and the volume of traffic which may conceivably make use of an improved waterway in the Ohio area is so great that large sums of money can reasonably be spent to deepen and to maintain the river channel.[10] Present structures consist of 46 low dams, each with a lock of 110 by 600 feet, which maintain a 9-foot depth from Pittsburgh to the mouth of the Ohio. In most cases these dams have sections which can be lowered to the bottom of the river when desired. Work has been done also on tributaries of the Ohio such as the Allegheny and the Monongahela.[11]

The obvious importance of the Ohio River, the local character of much

Lockport to Damen Ave., Chicago (Chicago Sanitary Canal)	22	feet	9 feet
Damen Ave. to Lake St., Chicago (Chicago River)	21	feet	9 feet
Calumet-Sag Canal from junction with Chicago Sanitary Canal to Blue Island, and the Little Calumet and Calumet Rivers to Turning Basin No. 5	9	feet	9 feet
Ohio River			
Pittsburgh to Cairo	9	feet	9 feet
Missouri River			
Kansas City to mouth	6½	feet	9 feet
Kansas City to Omaha	6	feet	9 feet
Omaha to Blair	4½	feet	9 feet
Blair to mouth of Big Sioux River	3½	feet	9 feet

NOTE: The Missouri River depths as given are available during the season of navigation only—March 15 to November 30.

[10] In its original condition river navigation on the Ohio was obstructed by snags, rocks, and bars composed of sand and gravel, as well as by the falls at Louisville. The minimum depth over bars at extreme low water was about 1 foot in the upper sections and about 2 feet in the lower section. In some of the intervening pools, however, the depth was as great as 30 feet. The slope of the river is comparatively uniform except at Louisville, where there is a low-water drop of 26 feet in a distance of 2 miles. In 1830 a canal was completed around the falls of the Ohio. Other work in early years was confined to the removal of obstructions, the building of contracting works to secure a low-water depth of 3 feet, and the canalization of the river from Marietta to Pittsburgh. In 1907 a project for the systematic improvement of the Ohio to produce a low-water depth of 9 feet was approved.

[11] United States Army, *Annual Report of the Chief of Engineers,* 1950, pp. 1678–1681. The cost of locks and dams, including the cost of some dams which have been replaced or eliminated was, up to 1949, $128,554,241. See also United States Army, Corps of Engineers, *Transportation in the Mississippi and Ohio Valleys,* Transportation Series no. 2, 1929, p. 12.

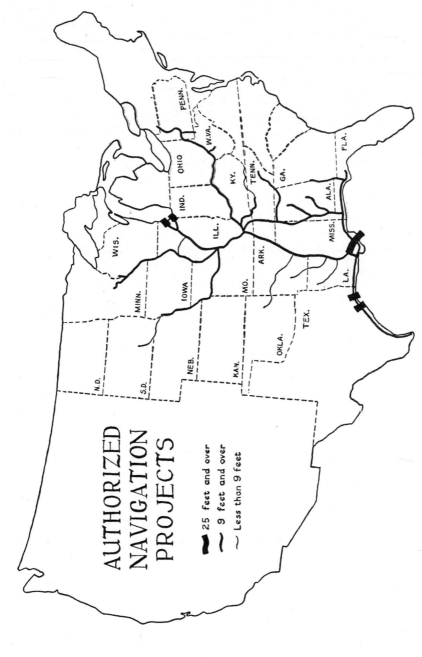

FIGURE 2. Project Depths of the Mississippi River System and Connecting Waterways.

of its traffic, and perhaps also, the fact that navigation upon this river has been continuously in private hands, has protected projects for the development of the Ohio from the criticism which similar undertakings have encountered elsewhere. Complaints in recent years have been directed less to the construction plans employed than to the failure of government dams to defend river communities against the ravages of the flood of 1936 and to the high expense of installing a navigation channel in particular tributaries such as the Tennessee.

LAKES-TO-THE-GULF WATERWAY. The central feature of the Hoover plan, and the second of the major improvements to be finished was the 9-foot waterway between New Orleans and Chicago. A channel of this depth was already available as early as 1920 between New Orleans and Cairo, although this part of the river has been straightened and still further improved in later years. The greater part of the new expenditures have been for work north of Cairo. Here the route of the Lakes-to-the-Gulf waterway proceeds by way of the Chicago River, the Chicago Sanitary and Ship Canal, the Des Plaines River, the Illinois River, and the Mississippi.[12]

UPPER MISSISSIPPI EXTENSION. In addition to the Ohio River and the Lakes-to-the-Gulf Waterway, the Hoover plan, as now approved, calls for the development of the Upper Mississippi and of the Missouri Rivers. Both of these extensions have encountered difficulties because of the lack of sufficient water in the upper reaches of these streams.

The government engineers who prepared plans for a 9-foot channel between Minneapolis and Alton (near St. Louis), Illinois, were of the opinion that neither ordinary processes of regulation and dredging nor even the building of large storage reservoirs at appropriate points could be relied upon to maintain a 9-foot depth in the Upper Mississippi during periods of low water. The solution which they adopted required the construction of a multiplicity of dams across the river, creating a succession of pools, in each of which a 9-foot level could be established. These dams were to be low, so as not to flood adjacent country, and they were to be numerous, in order that slack water areas could be made contiguous. In all, there are now 26 dams, each with a lock to permit the passage

---

[12] See W. M. Smith, "Engineering Features of the Illinois Waterway," *American Society of Civil Engineers,* March, 1937.

The State of Illinois originally undertook to canalize the Des Plaines and Illinois rivers so as to connect the Chicago Drainage Canal at Lockport with the navigable waters of the Illinois River near Utica, a distance of 60 miles. The project included the construction of 5 locks with a total lift of 126 feet. The State spent $20,000,000 on this undertaking and then asked the federal government to provide an additional 6 or 7 millions to complete the work. Congress took over the state enterprise through a clause in the Rivers and Harbors Act approved July 3, 1930, and the 9-foot channel to the Lakes was finished at federal expense. The responsibility of establishing and maintaining a 9-foot channel from Utica to Cairo fell from the beginning on the national government.

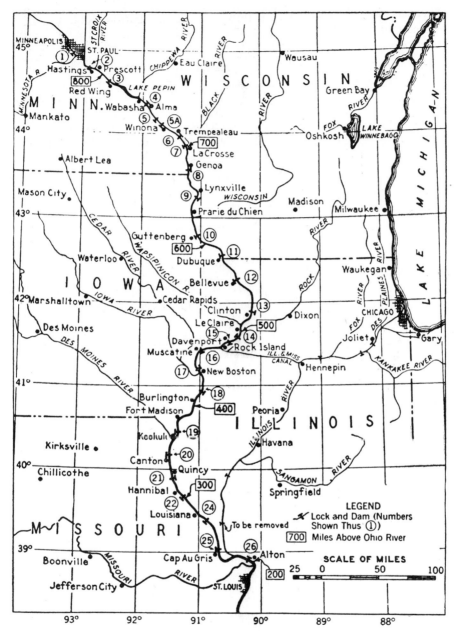

FIGURE 3. Upper Mississippi with Canalization Improvements and Connecting Waterways. (United States Army, Office of Division Engineers, Upper Mississippi Division.)

of vessels, in a stretch of 651 miles, or one dam for every 23 miles. The cost up to 1949 had been $209,750,000, including a short extension above Anthony Falls, Minnesota. In that year the project was about 74 percent complete.[13] A system of this sort is of little use for flood control, because the dams are not constructed for storage, and it will produce little power; the engineers in charge, however, cite as incidental advantages the preservation of wild life and fish refuges and the possibility of recreational use of the pools by residents of adjacent regions.

MISSOURI RIVER. On the Missouri River the government has undertaken to provide a 9-foot channel from Kansas City to the mouth of the river, to be obtained by revetment of banks, construction of permeable dikes to contract and stabilize the waterway, cutoffs to eliminate long bends, closing of minor channels, removal of snags, and dredging as required. The length of the section here under improvement is 386.2 miles. The project was about 85 percent complete at the close of the fiscal year 1949. On June 30, 1949, the controlling depth of the river was 6 feet.[14] Above Kansas City and as far as Sioux City (376.3 miles) a similar improvement is proposed and was, in 1949, 65 percent complete. The controlling depth in 1949 was 6 feet as far as Omaha and less beyond.

The difficulties in securing and in maintaining project depths are in principal part responsible for the construction of the Fort Peck dam in Montana, 1,070 miles above Sioux City. This earth dam, twice as high and considerably longer than the Gatun dam at the Panama Canal, is designed to hold back some 19 million acre-feet of water for release in low-water seasons. As a by-product it will permit the generation of power, though no power is expected at the beginning of its operation. The Fort Peck project and, indeed, the entire plan for the development of the Missouri River for purposes of navigation, has been bitterly criticized as a waste of public funds in view of the comparatively small traffic which the Missouri River is likely to attract.[15] On the other hand, Major General Lytle Brown, Chief of Engineers, United States Army, has made the cautious statement that the dam can probably be justified on the basis of combined benefits for navigation, power, flood control, and irrigation.[16]

Federal Operation upon the Mississippi River—The Inland Waterways Corporation

Federal operation upon the Mississippi and Warrior rivers was first

[13] United States Army, *Annual Report of the Chief of Engineers*, 1950, pp. 1437–1443.

[14] United States Army, *Annual Report of the Chief of Engineers*, 1950. The estimated cost of completion was $151,200,400.

[15] Henry E. Riggs, "The Fort Peck Dam and Navigation," *Railway Age*, October 31, 1936, pp. 622–626.

[16] Lytle Brown, "Waterways and Improvements in the United States," *Civil Engineering*, October, 1935, pp. 613–617.

authorized in June, 1918, under the stress of war conditions. In the following month the Director General of Railroads appointed a federal manager and instructed him to commandeer and put in operation as soon as possible all available equipment on the lower Mississippi and Warrior rivers capable of being used for the transportation of freight, and also to proceed with the construction of a new fleet. On termination of federal transportation control after the First World War, government facilities upon these two rivers were transferred to the Secretary of War [17] and in 1924 Congress authorized the Secretary to incorporate the "Inland Waterways Corporation" for their administration. [18] Later, in 1939, the Corporation was moved from the Department of War to the Department of Commerce. The Secretary of Commerce appointed the president of the Corporation and was responsible, in a general way, for the direction of the enterprise. [19]

EXTENT OF FEDERAL SERVICES. The Mississippi River service of the federal barge lines in 1952 was between St. Paul and New Orleans, and the barges also touched at Dubuque, Clinton, Rock Island, Burlington, St. Louis, Cairo, Memphis, Helena, Vicksburg, and Baton Rouge. The barge line made no attempt to serve the smaller river landings. The route to Chicago left the Mississippi slightly above St. Louis and proceeded by way of the Illinois River and its connections to Chicago. There was service upon the Missouri River between St. Louis and Omaha, and barges operated from Port Birmingham, on the Warrior River, to the Tombigbee, thence to the Alabama River, thence into the Mobile River, Mobile Bay, Mississippi Sound, Lake Borgne, and through the Lake Borgne Canal to the Mississippi River and New Orleans harbor. Units between St. Louis and New Orleans left both termini twice a week. [20] The scheduled time was

---

[17] 41 Stat. 458, 1920.

[18] 43 Stat. 360, 1924.

[19] After 1928 the Corporation operated principally under the so-called "Denison Act." It exercised some authority also under the Transportation Act of 1920. Thus under Section 201 of the latter law it could (1) construct and operate terminal facilities and (2) make loans to state and local governments and to transportation companies for terminal developments, subject to conditions determined by the Corporation. The Corporation, in addition, exercised powers originally delegated to the Secretary of War under Section 500 of the same statute for the purpose of promoting inland waterway transportation. These powers enabled it to investigate a good many subjects which interest those who use or operate water facilities, including the subjects of floating equipment and terminals, and to prepare and distribute statistics and other data relative to inland waterway transportation. (See United States, Select Committee to Investigate the Executive Agencies of the Government, *Preliminary Report,* 75th C., 1st S., Sen. Rep. 1275, 1937, chap. 8.

[20] Barge services during World War I were confined to the Mississippi River between New Orleans and St. Louis and to the Intracoastal Waterway and the Mobile, Tombigbee, and Black Warrior rivers from New Orleans to Birminghamport, Alabama, near Birmingham.

In 1924 Congress directed the Secretary of War to initiate service above St. Louis as soon as such service was feasible. The directive was carried out in 1926.

7 days down stream and 15 days up stream. There was a biweekly service between St. Louis and Chicago and between St. Louis and the Twin Cities. There was one sailing every 17 days between New Orleans and Port Birmingham, Alabama. The service was slower than that which the railroads offered and it was not suited to all kinds of freight; the amount of tonnage was, however, considerable, although less than was expected a few years earlier.

PROPOSALS FOR DISCONTINUANCE OF GOVERNMENT OPERATION. The Inland Waterways Corporation was not financially successful.[21] The reasons are, of course, a subject for debate. The following facts doubtless contributed: (1) an inadequate volume of business; (2) the construction of expensive terminals which were not fully utilized;[22] (3) the handling of merchandise traffic. Most of the Corporation's shipments were in bulk, but the Corporation paid more attention to merchandise than did the private lines;[23] (4) unsatisfactory relations with railroads; (5) poor overall management. The management in later years improved.

Whatever the reason, the Corporation was short of money. It followed that part of the floating equipment of the company became worn out and obsolete and that extensive repairs were required upon the rest.[24] Another result was that the Corporation withdrew from the operation of a number of terminals at one time leased from municipal owners, in order to cut its loss. Finally, the possibility of liquidating the government enterprise was seriously discussed,[25] and sale to private parties was accomplished in 1953.

[21] Prior to 1930 there were annual losses except in two years. From 1930 to 1939 the corporation reported profits, but after 1939 it operated in the red. The Company's accounts have been elaborately discussed. (See, *inter alia,* House Doc. 234, 80th C., 1st S.; Hearings before the Subcommittee of the Committee on Appropriations, 81st C., 1st S., on the Independent Offices Appropriation Bill for 1950, Part 2, 1949, p. 1158.)

So far as tonnage is concerned, the Inland Waterways Corporation has had some good years, but its figures of tons handled compared unfavorably, during its life, with the tonnage reported for all traffic on the Mississippi River. This was particularly true of the later period. Thus, between 1937 and 1949 the tonnage transported by the Corporation rose from 2,109,854 to 2,705,394 tons, or 24 percent; but the total number of tons moved upon the Mississippi River on the stretch between Minneapolis and the Passes at the mouth of the river grew from 28,307,790 to 59,322,908 tons, or 110 percent.

[22] See United States House of Representatives, Hearings before the Select Committee on Small Business pursuant to H. Res. 18, 80th C., 1st S., 1947, testimony Ingersoll, p. 533.

[23] United States House of Representatives, Hearings before a subcommittee of the Committee on Interstate and Foreign Commerce on H. R. 328, H. R. 4978, and H. R. 429, 81st C., 2d S., 1949, testimony Schwartz, Ingersoll.

[24] United States House of Representatives, subcommittee of the Committee on Appropriations, Hearings on the Government Corporations Appropriation Bill for 1949, 80th C., 2d S., testimony Ingersoll, p. 369.

[25] See *Traffic World,* August 1, 1953.

Private Lines

In addition to past government services there are a number of private corporations operating upon the Mississippi River system. The Engineering Department of the United States Army prepared a list of these private operators in 1951 from which it appears that 780 companies then offered transportation upon the Mississippi River and its tributaries or upon the Gulf Intercoastal Waterway, including some companies which functioned on both streams. This is a large number. Most of the companies which the Engineers report are small organizations. Many of them operate a single boat and most of them have fleets of less than five. They dredge, tow, and handle logs, gravel, sand, cement, construction materials, oil well supplies, etc., as opportunity may appear. There are also large corporations or companies which are controlled by large corporations which operate good-sized fleets.[26]

[26] The principal private carriers which operate upon the Mississippi are of three sorts:

1. *Common carriers of freight.* In 1951 the Engineer's Department of the United States Army reported 29 carriers which operated upon the Mississippi River System and the Gulf Intracoastal Waterway as common carriers of freight, in addition to the Inland Waterways Corporation.

a. Among these larger companies were the American Barge Line Company and the Mississippi Barge Line Company. The first operates from Pittsburgh to Chicago, to points on the Upper Mississippi, to New Orleans, to Houston, Texas, and to intermediate points via the Ohio, the Mississippi River, and the Gulf Intracoastal Waterway. The Mississippi Valley Barge Line operates between Pittsburgh, Cincinnati, and New Orleans, with connections to St. Louis and services upon the Allegheny, Kanawha and Monongahela rivers.

b. Other private common carriers include the following:

(1) *Ohio River Company.* Subsidiary to West Virginia Coal and Coke Company. Handles coal, steel, petroleum, mostly on the Ohio River and its tributaries.

(2) *Union Barge Line.* Subsidiary to Dravo Corporation, a contracting and engineering company. Handles steel, coal, sulfur, petroleum products, machinery, grain, etc., over the Mississippi River system and connecting waterways.

(3) *Central Barge Company.* Handles coal, grain, iron, steel, etc., on the Mississippi River between Minneapolis and New Orleans, on the Illinois River, and on the Ohio River and its tributaries.

(4) A miscellaneous list of 24 companies—some of which provide only towage while others undertake both towing and transportation—with fleets which range from a single boat to a maximum of 63 boats and barges. Some of these companies do a strictly local business, but others operate over considerable stretches of the Mississippi River and the Gulf Intracoastal systems.

Common carriers must, in principle, accept all traffic which is presented for shipment. River lines are charged, however, with quoting high rates upon undesirable traffic and with failing to supply adequate equipment and service for certain hauls and types of goods.

2. *Contract carriers.* There are a few companies that were classified, in 1951, as contract carriers. In most cases these lines own a combination of towboats and barges and supply service, as required, in the movement of bulk freight. Typical commodities are logs and pulpwood, stone, sand, steel, iron ore and pig iron, and crude oil.

3. *Industrial corporations.* A number of large industrial organizations own and operate power boats and barges upon the Mississippi River system for their own con-

FIGURE 4. Towboat "Sam Clemens" on the Mississippi River Moving South past St. Louis on the Way to Houston, Texas. (Black Star.)

It is a fact that the bulk of transportation upon the Mississippi River System has been and is supplied by private companies, in spite of the considerable development of the Inland Waterways Corporation. This is true of common carrier service; the predominance of private enterprise is still greater when industrial and contract river carriers are taken into the account.

Traffic upon the Mississippi and Its Tributaries

Speaking generally of Mississippi River transportation, the tonnage carried may be summarized as follows:

The tonnage moved upon the Ohio River reached a total, in 1950, of 48,589,227 tons. Most of this was coal, petroleum, and steel or steel products, along with strictly local movements such as those of gravel and sand. The tonnage upon the Monongahela, a tributary of the Ohio, was 28,509,901 tons. Almost all of this was bituminous coal from the West Virginia mines. The tonnage upon the Missouri, in 1950, amounted to 1,609,304 tons, of which the greater part was gravel, sand, and stone. This small volume was due, in part at least, to the incomplete physical development of the Missouri River.

On the main body of the Mississippi the most important shipments northbound, in 1950, were crude and refined petroleum and residual oils, coal, aluminum ore, sulfur, lumber, sugar, coffee, and rubber. Petroleum movements naturally resulted from the production and refining of petroleum in the great oil districts in Oklahoma and Texas. Sugar, rubber, and coffee were, mainly, imported. South-bound the river carried grain, principally corn and wheat, and the barges were loaded also with cement, oilseed, lumber, and miscellaneous manufactures from the north, of which iron and steel products were relatively important. There was, in addition, a heavy movement of oil. In earlier years a good deal of merchandise was transported, including less-than-bargeload consignments.

The tonnage on the Mississippi River from Minneapolis to the Mouth of the Passes was, in 1950, 66,922,594 tons. That on the entire Mississippi System, including tributaries and eliminating duplications, was 138,144,871 tons.

---

venience. Oil companies like the Humble and Texas companies use barges for the movement of petroleum and also for the handling of steel, cement, machinery, and supplies. The Wheeling, Weirton, and Jones & Laughlin corporations carry coal and coke, scrap steel, and steel products. Construction companies such as the Dravo Company and the Material Service Corporation transport sand, gravel, coal, gasoline, and equipment. There is no record of the volume of this business, but the total must be very large. It makes use of the river but it is not subject to regulation.

See United States Army, Corps of Engineers, *Transportation Lines on the Mississippi River System and the Gulf Intracoastal Waterway*, Transportation Series no. 4, 1951.

Great Lakes

The character of Great Lakes movements will be fully described in chapter 7, and its regulation will be considered in chapter 32. Figures quoted in chapter 1 show that the Great Lakes now carry a larger tonnage than any other inland waterway. Prior to the opening of the Erie canal, however, the Lakes possessed no great importance, for Western settlements before 1825 were attracted by the Ohio River rather than by the Lakes, and except in Ohio there was no large group of settlers north

FIGURE 5.   The Great Lakes.

of the watershed which separates the rivers emptying into the Lakes from those emptying into the Mississippi. In fact, even in Ohio the communities upon the Lake Erie shore were few and unimportant.[27] This means that the foundations for Lake commerce were lacking until the completion of the Erie Canal on the east and of the Ohio canals on the south made Lake Erie a link in a route which neither began nor ended on her shores.

The real use of the Great Lakes began with the working of the iron ore deposits of Lake Superior and with the extension of wheat production to districts west and northwest of Duluth. For such traffic, Lakes Superior, Huron, and Erie afforded a route as direct as that supplied by rail, while the depth of water and the freedom for maneuvering in these inland seas made it possible to perfect a type of bulk steam carrier that reduced the cost of transportation to extremely low figures.

St. Mary's Falls Canal.   There are three points upon the Great

[27] F. L. Paxson, *History of the American Frontier,* Boston, Houghton Mifflin, 1924.

Lakes system where it has been necessary to spend large sums in order to facilitate transportation. The first of these is in the narrows between Lake Superior and Lake Huron, the second is in the St. Clair and Detroit rivers between Lake Huron and Lake Erie, and the third is at the Falls of Niagara, between Lake Erie and Lake Ontario.

Previous to 1855, the passage of freight to and from Lake Superior necessitated a portage of one mile around the St. Mary's rapids, and traffic was relatively light.[28] The first ship canal, built on the American side of the river, was opened in 1855, and in 1895 a canal on the Canadian side was added. The original American canal had a depth at low water of 10 feet. Locks in the Canadian canal are now 18.25 feet deep,[29] and the minimum depth in the largest of the American locks is 31 feet and in its approaches 27 feet.[30]

ST. CLAIR AND DETROIT RIVERS. There are no locks in the rivers and lake between Lake Huron and Lake Erie, but the federal government has established a minimum channel depth of 25 feet in Lake St. Clair and a minimum of 21 feet in the St. Clair and Detroit rivers.[31]

WELLAND CANAL. The third critical point in lake navigation is between Lake Erie and Lake Ontario. The Welland Canal around Niagara Falls was opened in 1929 with a depth of 8 feet. This was subsequently increased to 14 feet and then to 23 feet where it now stands. The depth over lock sills is 30 feet, allowing a deepening of the channel without reconstruction of the locks.[32] This and the controlling depths established elsewhere in the Great Lakes permits the operation of vessels with a capacity of 16,000 tons. The most favored type of lake freighter is 600 feet long, with a capacity of 11,000 tons, although the average vessel is, of course, of considerably smaller dimensions.

ST. LAWRENCE RIVER. There are pending proposals to deepen the St. Lawrence River between Montreal and Lake Ontario to 27 feet, with corresponding improvement of other lake channels, in order to permit the free passage of large ships between the Atlantic Ocean and the head of Lake Superior. These plans go back to the treaty of 1932 between Canada and the United States providing for the construction of a deep waterway between the Ocean and the Great Lakes. There are arguments both for and against the enterprise. The project was still active in 1954.

[28] United States Department of Commerce, Bureau of Foreign and Domestic Commerce, *Inland Water Transportation in the United States,* 1923, p. 53.

[29] *Canada Yearbook,* 1950, p. 768.

[30] United States Army, *Report of the Chief Engineer,* 1949, pp. 2083, 2086–2087.

[31] The minimum in the St. Clair and Detroit rivers is 21 feet upbound and 25 feet downbound. *Ibid.,* pp. 2021–2032.

[32] *Canada Yearbook,* 1951, p. 759.

Shipping Companies on the Great Lakes

Most of the larger vessels operating upon the Lakes are steel steam freighters, generally between 3,000 and 7,000 net registered tons, engaged in the carriage of bulk coal, ore, and grain. This traffic will be described in chapter 7. In addition to these ships there are some tankers and oil barges, some automobile carriers, and a very large number of small miscellaneous craft of various sorts.

The major ships referred to are in two groups from the point of view of organization and ownership.[33] The larger group consists of ships owned and operated by independent corporations in fleets which range from 1 or 2 to 17 or 18 vessels averaging 4,000 or 5,000 net registered tons.[34]

A second group is composed of vessels controlled and operated by manufacturing and mining companies. Most of these industrial organizations are steel corporations, but the list includes also mining companies, the Ford Motor Company, and the International Harvester Company.[35]

[33] Prior to 1915, Lake ships owned by railroad companies formed a third group. The federal act of 1912 forbade railroads to hold an interest in any common carrier by water with which they competed (37 Stat. 566, 1912; 54 Stat. 909, 1940). The Interstate Commerce Commission interpreted this statute to apply to Lake carriers and the railroads were therefore compelled to surrender their Lake subsidiaries except in the case of a few car-ferry operations.

[34] The independent companies operating Lake fleets for the carriage of bulk coal, ore, steel, scrap, grain, and stone, in 1951, included the following:

Name of Company	Number of Ships	Net Tonnage
American Steamship Co.	17	84,825
Buckeye Steamship Co.	13	48,049
Columbia Transportation Co.	18	75,603
Great Lakes Steamship Co.	15	73,385
Interstate Steamship Co.	34	184,239
Midland Steamship Co.	7	30,808
Nicholson Transit Co.	14	34,685
Pioneer Steamship Co.	16	78,558
Reiss Steamship Co.	9	45,414
Wilson Transportation Co.	10	53,876
Total	153	709,442
Other independent companies	46	175,255
Grand total	199	884,697

This list includes the Great Lakes Steamship Company and the Interlakes Steamship Company in which industrial companies hold a small or undetermined interest.

[35] The industrial companies operating Lake fleets for the carriage of bulk coal, ore, steel, scrap, grain, and stone, in 1951, included the following:

It is not possible to state the total industrial interest in Great Lakes shipping with precision, but this interest probably amounts to more than 45 percent of the tonnage devoted to the carriage of bulk coal, ore, steel, scrap, grain, and stone.

Extent of Traffic upon the Great Lakes

This subject will be again discussed in chapter 7. The construction of canals and the deepening of channels at the points mentioned in previous pages now enable shipping lines on the Great Lakes to operate large ships from Duluth and Fort William to Lake Erie ports, and in this way to reduce the ton-mile cost of transporting commodities such as ore and grain to a figure far below that which any other inland waterway in the United States can hope to attain. Instead of being driven from the field as the Erie Canal has been, the Lakes have increased their tonnage. There have been, however, fluctuations up and down.

Coastal and Intercoastal Transportation

This category of water transport includes carriage between American ports over the ocean or the Gulf of Mexico. It makes use of ocean routes, characteristically adjacent to the land, although intercoastal movements travel considerable distances over the open sea. Historically, coastwise transportation is relatively old. It was important during the colonial period and has been significant at all times since. Participation is limited to American vessels.

Coastal and intercoastal water transport compete with railroad and motor service. From a broad point of view the business is an important complement to land operations both for the carriage of freight between

Name of Company	Number of Ships	Net Tonnage
United States Steel Co.	69	404,165
Bethlehem Steel Co.	13	65,585
Cleveland Cliff Iron Co.	22	105,813
M. A. Hanna Co.	3	19,940
Inland Steel Co.	5	32,308
National Steel Corp.	7	38,426
Jones & Laughlin Steel Co.	4	24,138
Shenango Furnace Co.	3	19,798
Ford Motor Co.	2	13,252
International Harvester Co.	2	11,967
Total	130	735,392

The Pittsburgh Coke and Chemical Company also owns a substantial interest in the Great Lakes Steamship Company.

ocean ports and for transport between inland cities that can be served by rail-water or motor-water hauls. The traffic can be divided into three parts. The first class includes shipments along the Pacific Coast and between that coast and Atlantic and Gulf harbors by way of the Panama Canal. Reports to the Interstate Commerce Commission show that carriers in this trade had, in 1949, the highest individual and group earnings of all carriers in inland water transport. They also had responsibility for the longest hauls. A second class of operations takes place between Atlantic and Gulf seaports or between harbors on either of these seaboards. Some companies engage in both intercoastal business via the Canal and in other coastal traffic, and some of these send ships, also, to foreign ports. A third category consists of tugs, barges, and other craft employed in intra-port and local carriage. The units are relatively small and the distances traveled are short. The service is partly, though not entirely, complementary to ocean transportation. Intraport and local movements constitute, nevertheless, an important part of waterway operation.

The total tonnage of coastal and intercoastal tonnage declined during World War II because the United States government requisitioned most of the ships which were available, as well as for other reasons. Attention has been paid, since 1945, to the revival of the business; but efforts have met, so far, with only moderate success. It must be recognized that the costs of ship operation on coastal and intercoastal routes are much higher than they were before the war. They now appear to be higher than the cost of competing railroad service. The difference may be reduced, to some extent, by changed methods of cargo handling and, possibly, by the redesign of vessels.[36] The water lines have asked the government to protect them by forcing the railroads to raise the level and to alter the structure of existing railroad rates; the federal government has not been willing, however, to accede to this request.

REFERENCES

General Treatises

Dunbar, Seymour, *A History of Travel in America,* Indianapolis, Bobbs-Merrill, 1915.

Fair, Marvin L., and Williams, Ernest W., *Economics of Transportation,* New York, Harper, 1950.

Gephart, W. F., *Transportation and Industrial Development in the Middle West,* Columbia University Studies in History, Economics, and Public Law, vol. 34, no. 1, 1909.

[36] United States Senate, Committee on Interstate and Foreign Commerce, *Merchant Marine Study and Investigation,* Sen. Rep. 2494, 81st C., 2d S., 1950, pp. 14–17. See also United States Interstate Commerce Commission, *Problems in the Regulation of Domestic Transportation by Water,* Ex Parte 165, Report of C. S. Morgan, 1946.

Johnson, E. R., *Transport Facilities, Services, and Policies,* New York, Appleton-Century-Crofts, 1947.

Locklin, D. Philip, *Economics of Transportation,* Chicago, Irwin, 1947.

Meyer, B. H., *History of Transportation in the United States Before 1860,* Washington, D. C., Carnegie Institution, 1917.

Ringwalt, J. L., *Development of Transportation Systems in the United States,* Philadelphia, Author, 1888.

Other Books

Ambler, C. H., *A History of Transportation in the Ohio Valley,* Glendale, Cal., A. H. Clark, 1932.

Bishop, Avard Longley, *The State Works of Pennsylvania,* Transactions of the Connecticut Academy of Arts and Sciences, New York, Longmans, 1924.

Bogart, E. L., *Internal Improvements and State Debt in Ohio,* New York, Longmans, 1924.

Dixon, F. H., *A Traffic History of the Mississippi River System,* Washington, D. C., Government Printing Office, 1909.

Hartsough, Mildred L., *From Canoe to Steel Barge in the Upper Mississippi,* Minneapolis, University of Minnesota, 1934.

Hunter, Louis Clair, *Steamboats on the Western Rivers, An Economic and Technological History,* Cambridge, Mass., Harvard, 1949.

Whitford, Noble E., *History of the Barge Canal of New York State,* Supplement to the Annual Report of the State Engineer and Surveyor for the year ended June 30, 1921, Albany, 1921.

Periodicals

Angel, Arthur D., "The Great Lakes–St. Lawrence Project," *Land Economics,* August, 1950.

Hunter, L. C., "The Invention of the Western Steamboat," *Journal of Economic History,* vol. 3, 1943.

Sumner, John D., "An Analysis of Mississippi River Traffic 1918–1930," *Journal of Land and Public Utility Economics,* February, 1932.

Special and Miscellaneous

Appleton, John B., *The Declining Significance of the Mississippi as a Commercial Highway in the Middle of the Nineteenth Century,* Bulletin of the Geographical Society of Philadelphia, October, 1930.

Bureau of Railway Economics, *An Economic Survey of Inland Waterway Transportation in the United States,* Special Series No. 56, Washington, D. C., 1930.

National Resources Planning Board, *Transportation and National Policy,* Part II, section II, *Coastwise, Intercoastal, and Great Lakes Shipping,* prepared by the Division of Economics and Statistics, United States Maritime Commission, 1942.

National Resources Planning Board, *Transportation and National Policy,* Part II, section IV, *Inland Water Transport,* prepared under the direction of Julian L. Schley, 1942.

United States Army, *Annual Report of the Chief of Engineers,* Part II, *Commercial Statistics,* compiled by the Statistical Division, Board of Engineers for Rivers and Harbors.

United States Army, Corps of Engineers, *Transportation Lines on the Mississippi River System and the Gulf Intercoastal Waterway,* Transportation Series no. 4, 1951.

United States Board of Investigation and Research, *The National Traffic Pattern,* U. S. Congress, 79th C., 1st S., Sen. Doc. 83, 1944.

United States Inland Waterways Commission, *Preliminary Report of the Inland Waterways Commission,* U. S. Congress, 60th C., 1st S., Sen. Doc. 325, 1908.

United States, Office of the Federal Coordinator of Transportation, *Public Aids to Transportation,* vol. 3, 1939.

The History of American Railways

Early Experiments with Steam Power for Transportation

The term *railroad* connotes two things, of which only one is specifically referred to in the name. Of these the first is the use of parallel supports known as "rails," upon which vehicles are made to run, and the second is some form of mechanical power. For the most part we are indebted to England for early experiment with both of these devices. Mechanical power in the form of steam was tried in England during the early years of the nineteenth century, notably by Richard Trevithick and George Stephenson.

Richard Trevithick gained his first experience in working and repairing pumping engines in the tin mines of Cornwall, England. In 1803 he built a steam carriage which was tried upon the public road in one of the Cornish mining towns. Somewhat altered and improved, this engine was successfully exhibited in London. In 1804, Trevithick built a locomotive to run on rails, which proved able to draw 10 tons of bar iron, together with necessary carriages, water, and fuel, 9 miles at the rate of 5½ miles an hour.

George Stephenson, like Trevithick, worked as a young man with the pumping engines then used in England to keep mines clear of water, though his experience was with the coal mines of Northumberland rather than with the tin mines of Cornwall. He also operated a winding engine used to draw up coal from the pit. In 1812, when he was 31 years of age, he was appointed engine-wright in one of the more important collieries of his district. During the years 1813 to 1815, Stephenson interested his principals in the project of constructing a locomotive engine, mounted on wheels and driven by steam, which should replace horses in hauling the coal taken out of the mine from the mine to tidewater. Stephenson's first engine of this type in 1814 drew 8 loaded carriages of 30 tons weight each at a speed of about 4 miles an hour on an ascending gradient of 1 in 450. His second engine, in 1815, was even more successful.[1]

During the decade prior to 1825 a number of steam locomotives, more or less resembling those of Stephenson, were used by collieries in England. They were slow, heavy, complicated machines, strange to modern eyes; but they were more powerful than horse transport and were fairly well suited to the conditions into which they were introduced.

Development of the Permanent Way

Meanwhile in England considerable progress had been made in improving the surface over which certain kinds of vehicles were drawn. Apart from the general improvement of the roads, there were districts in which it proved profitable to build long stretches of narrow tracks made of stone or wood in order to reduce the cost of traction. These stretches were known as "way leaves," because in establishing them it was necessary to get permission or "leaves" for rights of way over private land, and they were serviceable for the haul of commodities like coal, particularly when the shape of the land made it possible to secure a downgrade on the loaded and an upgrade on the light or return haul between the mines and tidewater.

During the last of the eighteenth and the first part of the nineteenth centuries way leaves, or tramways, to use a word more descriptive of the whole undertaking, multiplied, especially in the mining districts near Newcastle, and in other mining sections of England, Scotland, and Wales. When the steam engine became sufficiently developed to suggest its use in transportation it was employed to pull cars upon these local roads. Indeed, it was the supporting power of iron rails as well as the opportunity for economy arising out of a regular and abundant supply of freight that made the use of engines in mining operations profitable from the beginning. There was some question as to whether the adhesion of smooth wheels to a smooth rail would give sufficient tractive power, but experience soon showed that fears on this score were groundless.

Stockton and Darlington Railway

It was at this stage in the perfection of English mechanical transport that persons in the northeastern part of England carried through a larger undertaking which helped to open people's eyes to the possibilities of the railroad. This undertaking was the construction of a railway from Stock-

---

[1] Samuel Smiles, *Lives of the Engineers: George and Robert Stephenson,* London, Murray, 1904; Nicolas Wood, *A Practical Treatise on Railroads,* Longman, Orine, etc., 3d ed., 1838. Besides the names of Trevithick and Stephenson, those of Joseph Cugnot, a Frenchman, and Oliver Evans, an American, should be mentioned. The experiments of Cugnot and Evans preceded those of Trevithick and Stephenson, but they led to no practical results.

ton, the port of the River Tees, to Darlington, a distance of 12 miles westerly as the road was eventually laid down. The main purpose in improving communication between Darlington and Stockton was to facilitate the exporting of coal by avoiding the windings of the river. Men in Stockton, and at least one element in Darlington, proposed a canal to handle coal shipments, but in the end the advocates of a railway, led by an energetic Quaker named Edward Pease, prevailed and a railroad line was built.[2]

FIGURE 6. "Locomotion No. 1"—Stockton and Darlington Railway, 1825. (E. L. Ahrons, *The British Steam Railway Locomotive,* The Locomotive Publishing Co., Ltd., London, 1927.)

The Stockton and Darlington Railroad was opened on September 27, 1825. George Stephenson was the company's engineer and responsible for most of the technical decisions made in the course of the construction of the road. These included the question as to whether rails should be of wood or of wrought or cast iron, what the weight of the rail should be, what the gauge, and, most important, what the motive power should be.

Fortunately, George Stephenson had a locomotive engine at a nearby colliery, and when the question of motor power arose he was able to put this machine through its paces before the directors of the Stockton and Darlington Company, and to convince them that the steam locomotive was reliable, powerful, and cheap. This demonstration was confirmed at

[2] *The Diaries of Edward Pease, the Father of English Railways,* London, Headley, 1907.

the opening of the railroad, when a locomotive which Stephenson built for the purpose attained a speed of 15 miles an hour and hauled a load, including passengers, coal, and merchandise, weighing about 90 tons.

The Stockton and Darlington Railway differed from most of the colliery roads which had preceded it in that it was designed to serve many shippers as a common carrier, not to handle the business of a single mine. Like some of the early American and continental railroads, it was originally intended to be free to all persons who chose to place their wagons and horses or engines upon it, provided they paid the established tolls, although it was not long after business had begun before the company found it necessary to take over the entire operation of the line.

The Stockton and Darlington was also, perhaps, the earliest railway to transport passengers by locomotive power. However, passengers were not hauled by the company's locomotives for some years after the opening of the line, but by private coaching companies which used horses, and availed themselves of the convenience of the railroad only with regard to its right of way. The beginning of regular passenger service can better be associated with the construction of the Liverpool and Manchester Railroad than with that of the Stockton and Darlington, as the latter was essentially a coal carrier.

Liverpool and Manchester Railroad

The next important railway in England was the Liverpool and Manchester line, opened in 1830. With this company we have an undertaking (1) which contemplated from the first the carriage of passengers and miscellaneous merchandise, not, as in the case of coal railroads, the carriage of a single kind of freight; and (2) upon which locomotive engines were used from the beginning.

There is no reason to suppose that the Liverpool and Manchester Railroad was constructed because of the success of the Stockton and Darlington. In the first place, the greatest success of this last-named carrier came in the years subsequent to the opening of the longer line; and in the second place, the Stockton and Darlington was only one of many English enterprises in which the locomotive engine was rendering useful service in 1825. It is, however, a fact that the promoters of the Liverpool and Manchester took pains to acquaint themselves with what had been accomplished along the River Tees, and that they employed George Stephenson, the expert for the Stockton and Darlington, as their engineer. These two circumstances establish a connection between the Stockton and Darlington and the Liverpool and Manchester railroads which lends continuity to the story of English railroad development.

It is of less importance to describe the local engineering difficulties which were encountered in the course of building a line from Liverpool to Manchester than to point out, first, that the controversy which arose over the best form of motor power to employ upon it was the cause of several important improvements in the locomotive engine, and second, that the attention of the country was so fixed upon this enterprise that its success finally established in England the position of the steam-driven vehicle upon the iron road.

Principles of Railroad Economics Formulated as Early as 1850

During the twenty years after 1830 something like 12,000 miles of railway were built in England and in the principal European countries. Both in England and on the Continent, railway transportation proved itself superior to existing roads and waterways with regard to regularity of movement, ease of terminal handling, adaptation of routes to the needs of business, and in the provision of facilities for freight traffic, including responsibility for loss and damage to freight as well as the more obvious matters of speed and capacity.

Not only this, but the art of railroad operation had advanced so far by 1850 that certain general principles relating to railroad economics were then recognized. Thus we find the following statements of general application in Lardner's volume, published in 1850:

"1.   *The greatest railroad revenue is to be anticipated from the carriage of freight, not from the carriage of passengers.*" This principle, which was contrary to the expectation of the promoters of many of the early railway lines, and to the experience of railroads like the Liverpool and Manchester during the first year of its operation, is now accepted without dispute. Rail carriers in the United States earn more than nine times as much from freight as from passengers. In 1846 and 1847 the percentage of total revenue contributed by the goods traffic on European railroads was nearly 50 per cent of the whole, and was rapidly increasing.

"2.   *In the field of passenger business the greatest income and the steadiest income is to be obtained from traffic which pays relatively low rates per person carried.*"   It has always been the practice in European countries to separate passengers into three or more classes according to the fares paid and the accommodations provided, class one including those passengers who pay the highest rates and occupy the most luxurious places, class two coming next in line, and classes three and four following. Lardner pointed out in 1850 that while the average fare paid by first-class passengers on the principal English lines in 1847 was 2.385d and that paid by third-class passengers was only 0.992d, yet the total earnings from third-class passengers were nearly equal to the earnings of first-class service. It may be added that what was merely a tendency in Lardner's time has since become an accomplished fact.

"3.   *Railroad expenses do not vary in proportion to the volume of business handled.*" This is an important principle to which we shall return in the course of our discussion of railway rates. Lardner did not assign proportions to the fixed and variable expenses of a railroad, but he did point out that large elements in each type of railroad expense, including outlays for direction and management, way and works, locomotive power, and transportation, were independent of traffic, varying with time and with the action of the weather; or, if not altogether independent of traffic, they did not vary proportionately to it, as in the case of station expenses and of that part of the wear and tear of locomotive engines which resulted from the haulage of the weight of cars, apart from the weight of their contents.

Besides enunciating these general principles, Lardner was able, as early as 1850, to make a number of very practical recommendations, stressing the importance of heavy loading, the avoidance of empty hauls, the limitation of the number of trains run, especially of express trains, the provision for mixed carriage of passengers, instead of carriages designed exclusively for service of first, second, or third classes, and suggesting that traffic as far as possible be segregated according to destination.

Early Interest in the United States

The first rail- or tramroads built in the United States were probably quite unaffected by the British experience. These were short lines constructed for industrial purposes to haul granite or other heavy loads. The rails used by these undertakings were sometimes of iron and sometimes of wood, and the motive power was the horse. In addition, there were certain more elaborate suggestions which came to nothing. Oliver Evans submitted to the consideration of the Lancaster Turnpike Company in September, 1804, a statement of the costs and profits of a steam carriage to carry 100 barrels of flour 50 miles in 24 hours, and offered to build such a carriage at a very low price. And John Stevens is known, among other things, for his proposal in 1812 to construct a railway between Lake Erie and Albany supported on pillars raised from three to five or six feet above the surface of the ground. On such a railway, with steam power, he estimated that a train of 160 tons could be drawn at a rate of 4 miles an hour.[3] Proposals of this sort, and occasional demonstrations that steam power could actually be used for transport, doubtless attracted some attention but they led to nothing practical.

As early as 1825, however, we find a definite attempt in the United States to obtain information concerning English practice. It was in this year that the Pennsylvania Society for the Promotion of Internal Improvements in the Commonwealth sent one William Strickland to Europe to

---

[3] J. L. Ringwalt, *Development of Transportation Systems in the United States*, Philadelphia, 1888, pp. 65, 70.

collect information relating to the construction of canals, roads, railways, bridges, steam engines, and various industrial arts. The Society admonished Mr. Strickland that the utility of railways was appreciated in the United States but that nothing was known with certainty of the mode of constructing them or of their cost. Rails and locomotive machinery were to receive his particular attention, and he was authorized to procure a model of the most approved locomotive machine at the expense of the Society. It was in October of the same year that the trials of the famous *Rocket* occurred at Rainhill in England, and word of the success of Stephenson's engine soon reached the United States, notably increasing public interest in railway transportation.

Desire of Atlantic Seaboard Cities for Cheap Transportation to the Mississippi Valley

It is evident that prior to 1830 many minds in this country were concerned with the subject of steam locomotion. Perhaps the principal difficulty in 1830 was less that of inventing a workable engine than that of securing capital with which to make experiments upon a large scale. Fortunately this difficulty was soon to be overcome. In Great Britain the fact which attracted practical men to the use of new transportation devices was the pressing need for better communication between the towns of Liverpool and Manchester. In the United States the deciding element was the desire to afford the principal cities of the Atlantic coast facilities for reaching the expanding markets of the Mississippi Valley. This was the influence that caused the construction of the Erie Canal and of the Pennsylvania State Works, and it was this which led to the incorporation of the Baltimore and Ohio Railroad.

Baltimore and Ohio Railroad

Like Philadelphia and New York, Baltimore had at first intended to rely largely upon canal construction for her connection with the West. But by the early part of 1827, men of financial standing in the city had become convinced of two things: first, that the cost of a canal across the mountains would be prohibitive, and second, that a railroad was possible. A committee of citizens reported in February, 1827, that while the available facts with regard to railroad systems were not as extensive as they desired, they had gleaned from the documents that they examined upon the subject enough to leave no doubt in their minds that these roads were far better adapted to the situation and circumstances of Baltimore than a canal across the mountains would be. The committee therefore recommended that measures be taken to construct a double railroad between the city of Baltimore and some suitable point on the Ohio River by the most eligible and direct route, and that a charter to incorporate a company to execute the work be obtained as early as practicable. The Baltimore and Ohio Railroad, organized in conformity with this recommendation, was chartered in February, 1827. Actual construction was begun on July 4, 1828. The first division of the road from Baltimore to Ohio reached Cumberland in November, 1842; Wheeling, West Virginia, in December, 1852; and St. Louis in 1857. While not the first railroad in the United States, or even the first railroad upon which a steam locomotive was tried, the beginning of the American railroad system is generally associated with the foundation of this company. It is at least correct to say that the Baltimore and Ohio Railroad was the first railroad of any considerable length, designed for the purpose of general passenger and freight traffic between terminals then considered to be widely separated, which was proposed and commenced in the United States; and that the first locomotive built in the United States, that of Peter Cooper, was successfully operated upon it on August 28, 1830.

Railroad Construction in the United States, 1830–1860

Between 1830 and the Civil War, the total mileage in operation in the United States in different years was as follows:

Year	Mileage
1833	380
1835	1,098
1840	2,818
1845	4,633
1850	9,021
1855	18,374
1860	30,626

During this period of thirty years the principal developments in the railroad net of the United States were as follows:

LOCAL SERVICE.   In spite of the fact that the Baltimore and Ohio Railroad was conceived by its promoters as part of a through route, a large proportion of the early American railroads was organized to render local service. Indeed, much railroad transportation, even at the present time, is over short distances, and it was natural that American roads should accommodate local traffic long before they could handle through business by longer hauls.

The densest rail network in the country before the Civil War lay in New England, where by 1845 there were 710 miles of railroad with terminals in Boston, besides some outlying companies in Massachusetts, Maine, New Hampshire, Vermont, and Connecticut. Of the Boston roads, the most important were the Boston and Lowell to the north, the Boston and Providence to the south, the Boston and Worcester to the west, and the Eastern Railroad to the northeast. The railroads in central New York were also local in purpose, although they eventually combined into an effective through route between Albany and Buffalo. Other local lines were built in eastern Pennsylvania, in New Jersey, and in the states south of the Potomac River, connecting large towns with each other and with the surrounding country. Such, for instance, in the South, were the railroads completed between Richmond and Fredericksburg (1837), between Columbia and Charlotte (1852), and between Atlanta and Montgomery (1853).

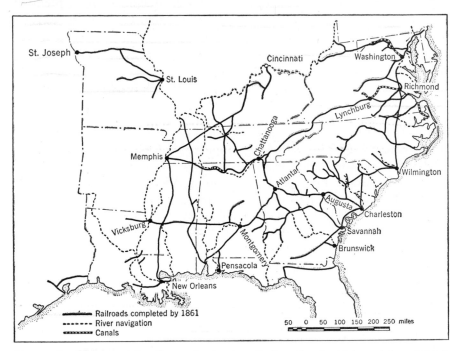

FIGURE 7. Transportation Routes in the Ante-Bellum South. (Adapted from Ulrich B. Phillips, *A History of Transportation in the Eastern Cotton Belt to 1860*, Columbia University Press, New York, 1908.)

SOUTHERN STATES. The beginning of construction in the South was contemporaneous with the building of the Baltimore and Ohio Railroad. Indeed, the Charleston and Hamburg was chartered in December, 1827, and the Baltimore and Ohio only in February of the same year. Construction on the latter railroad was begun in 1828; on the former, in 1831. The first 13 miles of the Baltimore and Ohio were opened in 1830, and the first 62 miles of the Charleston and Hamburg in 1832. At the time the Charleston and Hamburg reached Hamburg, 136 miles from Charleston, in 1833, it was the longest railway in the world.

The Charleston and Hamburg Railroad was designed to admit Charleston to the trade of the interior city of Augusta, in competition with Savannah, Georgia. The terminal, Hamburg, was therefore located on the Savannah River, opposite Augusta. Parallel with this railroad, but some distance from it to the southwest, lay the Central of Georgia Railroad from Savannah to Macon, which was begun in 1836 and completed in 1843, under the stimulus of Charleston competition. A branch of the Central of Georgia reached Augusta in 1854. These were the first two railroads which were undertaken south of the Potomac. In September, 1845, the Charleston and Hamburg was extended to Atlanta, Georgia, where it was joined a month later by the railroad from Savannah.

Southern railway construction may perhaps best be regarded as local in character, analogous to projects in the northeast. Yet the railroads from Charleston and Savannah to Atlanta were also the beginning of an east-and-west system which reached, like the trunk lines of the North, from the Atlantic seaboard into the Mississippi Valley. The necessary connection with the Ohio River was accomplished by the building of the Western and Atlantic, begun in 1838 and completed to Chattanooga in 1851. At a later date rails were laid from Chattanooga to Memphis (1856), from Atlanta via Montgomery and Meridian to Vicksburg, and from Chattanooga northeast through the mountains to Lynchburg and Richmond, Virginia (1858). These were the most noteworthy through railroads. The northeast-and-southwestern lines, later united into the Seaboard Air Line, the Atlantic Coast Line, and the Southern Railway, which are the outstanding features of our southeastern railways at the present time, were developed by the consolidation of local lines, most of which were built with very little apprecation of their importance to through movements. The advantages of a connection with the Mississippi Valley were, however, expressly recognized by the east-and-west construction which has been described.

NORTHEASTERN RAILWAYS. In the territory north of the Ohio and Potomac rivers, construction prior to the Civil War followed the influences which have been dwelt upon in describing the reasons for the building of the Baltimore and Ohio. Characteristically, the great systems here ran east and west; and while these lines served important local purposes, their greatest significance lay in the access which they afforded centers of population on the Atlantic coast to the fertile valleys of the Mississippi and its tributaries.

Apart from local projects, the principal railroad routes before 1860 in the area bounded by the Atlantic seaboard, the St. Lawrence River, and the Great Lakes upon the east and north, and the Mississippi, Ohio, and Potomac rivers upon the west and south, with the dates of completion, were as follows:

1842. The Baltimore and Ohio Railroad was completed from Baltimore to Cumberland, and the Boston and Albany road from Boston to Albany in this year. The Boston and Albany, originally incorporated as the Western Railroad, was promoted with the conscious intent of securing for Boston a share of the western trade. It reached the western boundary of Massachusetts in 1841, and in 1842, after the completion of connecting lines out of Albany, it was able to render service from Boston to the Hudson River and, in connection with the Erie Canal and with local lines in New York, to Lake Erie. The Western Railroad was in part financed by the state of Massachusetts.[4]

1851. In the spring of 1851 the Erie Railroad was completed from New York Harbor to Dunkirk on Lake Erie. The opening of the Hudson River Railroad between New York and Albany in the fall of the same year gave New York City access to a rail route through central New York which Boston had been using for nine years.

1852. In this year the Pennsylvania Railroad entered Pittsburgh. The Pennsylvania was incorporated in 1846 to provide continuous rail connection with the West in lieu of the combined rail and water facilities of the Pennsylvania State Works. It made use at first of the rail portions of the State Works, including the inclined planes and Portage Railroad over the Alleghenies. The first through cars from Philadelphia to Pittsburgh were run on December 10, 1852.[5]

1853. The opening of a stretch of railroad between Cleveland and Toledo completed continuous rail connections between Buffalo and Chicago.[6] This was the first New York-to-Chicago line. The same year saw the extension of the Baltimore and Ohio to Wheeling, West Virginia, on the Ohio River; and the incorporation of the New York Central, bringing the separate companies between Albany and Buffalo under a common control.[7]

1857. The Baltimore and Ohio reached St. Louis in 1857.[8]

[4] The names of the local lines in New York State, which together afforded through rail connection between Albany and Buffalo, and the dates on which they were opened, are as follows: Mohawk and Hudson (Albany to Schenectady), 1831; Utica and Schenectady, 1836; Tonawanda (Rochester to Batavia), 1837; Auburn and Syracuse, 1838; Syracuse and Utica, 1839; Auburn and Rochester, 1841; Tonawanda (Batavia to Attica), 1842; Attica to Buffalo (the last lap of the through line), 1842. The Hudson River Railroad from New York to East Albany was opened in 1851.

[5] Sipes, *The Pennsylvania Railroad,* Philadelphia, 1875.

[6] *Poor's Manual,* 1868–1869. The companies operating between Buffalo and Chicago were the following: Buffalo and State Line; Erie and Northeast; Michigan Central; Michigan Southern; Cleveland and Toledo; and Cleveland, Painesville, and Ashtabula.

[7] *Ibid.* The companies which consolidated into the New York Central system in 1853 were the following: Albany and Schenectady; Schenectady and Troy; Utica and Schenectady; Syracuse and Utica; Syracuse and Utica Direct; Rochester and Syracuse; Buffalo and Lockport; Mohawk Valley; Rochester, Lockport, and Niagara Falls; and Buffalo and Rochester.

[8] W. P. Smith, *The Book of the Great Railway Celebration of 1857,* New York, Appleton-Century-Crofts, 1858.

1858. The western connection of the Pennsylvania Railroad, the Pittsburgh, Fort Wayne, & Chicago, secured entrance to the city of Chicago in 1858, thus opening the route between Philadelphia and Lake Michigan.[9] The Pittsburgh, Fort Wayne, & Chicago was leased to the Pennsylvania in 1869.

During 1858, also, the Canadian Grand Trunk Railway reached Sarnia on the St. Clair River between Lakes Huron and Erie, opening, in connection with railroads across the Michigan peninsula, a new route from the Atlantic seaboard at Portland, Maine, to Chicago.

Most of the east-and-west lines which connected the Atlantic seaboard with the Mississippi Valley prior to the outbreak of the Civil War lay in the Northern states. Whether North or South, however, the construction of such lines made it possible for the distributing centers upon the ocean to sell their manufactured goods in all that range of states which bordered upon the Mississippi and its eastern tributaries, while at the same time the agricultural products of the West now found an outlet to the east as well as to the south, which was essential to their success. At the same time, though this was not the impelling motive for railroad construction, the closer linking of the East and West produced political and social effects of the first magnitude.

MISSISSIPPI VALLEY. Railroad construction in the Mississippi Valley was naturally less extensive before the Civil War than railroad construction farther east. This was because population was less dense and industry not so far advanced. Apart from the western extensions of the trunk lines and a series of short railroads connecting the Ohio River with the Great Lakes, the most important work undertaken in the Mississippi Valley before 1860 was, first, the building of the Illinois Central, and, second, the beginning of lines which were eventually to reach out from Chicago and St. Louis to connections with the Missouri River and with the transcontinental railroads operating to the Pacific Coast.

The Illinois Central was incorporated in 1851. Its purpose was to develop the interior communities of Illinois by providing them cheap transportation to the Mississippi River. To this end the railroad was planned with one terminus at Cairo at the junction of the Ohio and Mississippi rivers, and other termini at Galena on the northwest border of the state and at Chicago on Lake Michigan. In order to facilitate construction, representatives and senators from Illinois induced the national legislature to grant, in 1850, nearly three million acres of public land to the state of Illinois; land which the state turned over to the railroad company when the latter had received its charter. Similar grants of land were made to the states of Mississippi and Alabama in order to secure political sup-

---

[9] Pennsylvania Railroad Company, *Twelfth Annual Report,* February 7, 1859.

port. The construction of the Illinois Central was begun in December, 1851, and the railroad was formally opened to Cairo in September, 1856.

Finally, westward construction included railroads from St. Louis toward Kansas City; and the beginning outside of Chicago of what later became the Chicago, Burlington, & Quincy; the Chicago, Rock Island, & Pacific; the Chicago and Northwestern; the Chicago, Milwaukee, & St. Paul; and the Chicago and Alton railway systems. The first railway in Illinois from Lake Michigan to the Mississippi was the Chicago and Rock Island, opened in February, 1854. The second, made up of the Galena and Chicago (later part of the Chicago and North Western) and the Illinois Central, was opened early in 1855. The so-called Granger railroads will be considered later in this chapter.

If the reader will consult the preceding pages with the aid of a modern railroad map, he will be able to understand the general trend of railroad construction in the United States during the first thirty years following the successful inauguration of the Baltimore and Ohio. Before passing to the construction of the transcontinental lines to the Pacific coast which were the achievement of the next generation, we may pause to consider some of the similarities and contrasts between the early railroad development in the United States and that in the European countries, including England, which we have previously described.

Early American Railroad Practices the Result of Independent Initiative

To a much greater degree than on the continent of Europe, American practice in railroad construction and operation was the result of independent initiative. This was partly because of mere distance. It was not so easy to command the services of English engineers in Maryland as it was in Austria or in France. Nor were English standards as applicable in the United States as they were in the more densely settled countries of Europe. Whereas European engineers inclined to a permanent type of construction, American railroads were often best built when most cheaply built, with light rails, sharp curves, and steep grades. Only such roads could expect to earn interest on their investment, in view of the scant population of the country and the pioneer character of many of the early enterprises. It is true that two American engineers were present at the tests of Rainhill, England, and that three English locomotives were immediately ordered after these tests for the Carbondale and Honesdale Railroad (Delaware and Hudson). But these locomotives proved too heavy for the American track and were presently abandoned. English locomotives were also operated upon the Camden and Amboy Railroad in New Jersey, the Newcastle and Frenchtown, and on some other lines; and when somewhat modified to meet local conditions, the English machines gave satisfactory service for many years.

In spite of English precedent and the partial use of English material, the early years of American railroading were marked by continuous experiments, for which lines like the Baltimore and Ohio provided laboratory facilities. It was said of this company in 1935 that its reports had gone forth as a textbook, and that its road and workshops had been a lecture room to thousands who were then practicing and improving upon its experience.

The Charleston and Hamburg and the Baltimore and Ohio both experimented with cars propelled by sails, and with treadmill locomotives operated by horse power. Upon the Baltimore and Susquehanna two cars were joined together by shafts of timber, and the horses, which were hitched between, were kept from falling by a broad belt of leather passed under their bodies and attached to the shafts. The first use of an American locomotive upon any American railroad was upon the Baltimore and Ohio on August 28, 1830. On January 4, 1831, this same company offered $4,000 for the most approved engine which should be delivered for trial on the road on or before June 1 of the same year. A new machine which met all specifications was built at York, Pennsylvania, and entered into regular use following the trial.

This, with the locomotive placed upon the Charleston and Hamburg in November, 1830, probably marks the definite adoption of steam as tractive power upon the American railroad system, and it was also an important step in establishing the independence of the United States with regard to its mechanical railroad equipment.

Mechanical Improvements

The following five improvements associated with early American railroad development deserve mention:

1. The four-wheel bogie or swivel truck, first placed under the front end of the locomotive and later used in connection with freight and passenger cars.

2. The spark arrester, made imperative by the fact that the original American locomotives were nearly all wood burners.

3. The use of equalizing beams, distributing the weight of locomotives equally over the driving wheels in spite of inequalities in the track.

4. The use of steel springs, first under the locomotives and tenders, and then under freight cars.

5. The introduction of eight-wheel cars. Up to 1834, the cars in use upon railroads had only four wheels and were but little larger than a stage coach. By the ingenuity of Ross Winans of the Baltimore and Ohio, large eight-wheel cars were devised and constructed and put upon the road for transportation of passengers. It has been said that in perhaps no other improvement in the operation of railroads was the Baltimore

and Ohio more conspicuous even at this early day, than in the entire organization and perfection of the eight-wheel car.

Permanent Way

Extensive experiments were also carried out in the fourth and fifth decades of the nineteenth century with respect to the permanent way. Piling, granite blocks, granite sills, broken stone, and longitudinal timbers were all tried as a means of support for the rail; and strap rails, or flat iron bars resting upon timbers, were frequently used before the English edge rail finally demonstrated its superiority. The object sought was durability without so great rigidity as to produce excessive wear upon rolling stock.

Variation in Gauges

There was even less uniformity with regard to gauge in the United States than there had been in England. As a matter of fact, it is extremely difficult to defend any particular spacing of railroad rails as ideally correct. The most important effect of any gauge is that produced upon the design of the locomotive, particularly with respect to the width of the locomotive fire box. But the desirable width of such a fire box itself depends upon the quantity and character of traffic to be hauled, the standard speed, the kind of fuel, the presence or absence of labor-saving devices for supplying fuel to the fire, and upon a number of other things as well. It is not surprising that different American railroad engineers favored different gauges, ranging mostly between 4' 8½" and 6'. In the end, the advantage of uniformity was seen to outweigh the mechanical gain from the adoption of a nonstandard gauge in any special case, and the principal lines adopted gauges which were at least sufficiently similar to permit of the indiscriminate circulation of cars.

Early Opposition to the Steam Railroad

As in England, the introduction of railways in the United States provoked opposition from persons interested in other forms of transportation, and from those who disliked or disbelieved in the possibilities of railway travel. The list of those hostile to the railroad included, of course, innkeepers, the proprietors of turnpike roads, and stagecoach and wagon carriers. Still more important opposition came from the canal interests. It was argued that railroads were complicated machines compared with canals, and more likely to get out of order. This was also true, it was said, of the equipment used. Many a farmer was able to build a boat on his own land that would do for a canal, but few or none could make a locomotive carriage. A canal was accessible anywhere, a railroad nowhere except by special arrangement. On a canal every boatman could choose his own speed; by rail every traveler must move at the same speed. The cost of transportation on a canal was only a third of the cost of transport by rail, and the canal was also cheaper than a railroad to build and maintain.

Speaking against the construction of a railroad from Boston to the Hudson River, a member of the Massachusetts legislature exclaimed in 1827:

> It [the railroad] was premature, it would cost an enormous sum of money, and would be worth little or nothing. He begged the House to pause, to have mercy on the people, to have some compassion. In the winter the snow would be in some places 10 feet deep, and so make the railroad useless. . . . How would turkeys, butter and eggs look after coming over it together in the same car? There was nothing else to bring. He called upon the House to wait before they began the work, till they saw a reasonable chance of getting their money's worth. If they must have a magnificent project, he would go the whole length, and would try to bring Heaven down to Earth, or Earth to Heaven.[10]

Arguments of this sort found ready listeners, and even legislators who thought that the railroad was a superior device were ready to handicap the rail carrier in order to protect the government's investment in canals. This was why railroads in New York State which ran parallel or nearly parallel to a canal owned by the state were required as late as 1848 to pay tolls on all property carried except the baggage of passengers.[11]

State and Local Aid

On the whole the introduction of railways met with less opposition in the United States than in England, doubtless because the canal and stage interests in this country were less powerful, and the large landowners less influential with the legislature. The new methods of transportation had, of course, to demonstrate their usefulness, as was quite proper, but in most instances there was no deliberate attempt to handicap them in the interest of some other means of travel.

Indeed, our early railroads secured a considerable amount of state and city, and later, federal support. This aid took a variety of forms. It included contributions of cash, materials, equipment, labor, and securities by states, local governments, and individuals. State and local bodies also lent large sums, not all of which were repaid. Sometimes railroad bonds were guaranteed; sometimes tax exemptions or banking or lottery privileges were accorded, and in many instances communities made subscriptions to railroad stock. Among the companies benefiting from this sort of assistance were the Baltimore and Ohio, which received a subscription of

---

[10] T. W. Van Metre, *Early Opposition to the Steam Railroad,* New York, Columbia School of Business, 1929, p. 23.

[11] This law was repealed in 1851.

$3,500,000 from the state of Maryland and nearly as much ($3,000,000) from the City of Baltimore; the Western Railroad of Massachusetts, which obtained a loan of $4,000,000 from the State of Massachusetts; the Richmond and Danville, which was granted perpetual exemption from taxation by the state of Virginia; and the Georgia Railroad and Banking Corporation, which was given banking rights by the state of Georgia. State and local authorities also gave rights of way, terminal facilities, rights in city streets, and privileges on other public property which, together, were important. The loans and subscriptions previously mentioned were sometimes regarded as investments; more generally, each local unit expected that railroad construction would provide it with freer access to sources of supply, widen its markets, and raise the value of city lands. The diversion of traffic from other routes was, usually, prominently in mind.[12]

There was some federal support to railroad enterprise as early as 1830 when a tariff act provided a 25 percent drawback of the duties on railroad iron imported and used for railroad purposes. Federal aid first became important, however, in 1850, with the beginning of the grants of federal land; it continued with an expansion of the federal land grant policy and with federal loans for Pacific railroad construction in 1862 and 1864. The federal land grants were given, principally, to Western but also to Southern railroad companies. The policy is discussed in chapter 35. In all, the federal grants amounted to 183,187,000 acres, all voted before 1871.

General Tests to Be Applied to Subsidies

The general tests which may be applied to any system of state aid are four: (1) Is the assistance accurately measured to the need? (2) Is the aid made available at the moment when help is most necessary? (3) Does the state aid lead to railroad building which is economically unjustifiable? (4) Are the subsidies larger than the communities which offer them can afford?

American practice shows very little attempt to meet tests such as these. What happened was that promoters appealed to public bodies for as much assistance in railroad building as they thought the temper of the public would support, and that legislatures or city councils gave upon application whatever loose assets they had unpledged, or voted such privileges as they thought might prove of value. This procedure conveyed to the railroads many gifts which were of little immediate use because they could not be applied directly or sold for cash except at a heavy discount while the construction process was going on. Land grants, particu-

---

[12] The early period of state and local aid to railroads is well described in F. A. Cleveland and F. W. Powell, *Railroad Promotion and Capitalization in the United States,* New York, Longmans, 1909.

larly, were of little service in financing railroad building, although they increased the reward for successful enterprise after the railroads had been built. Railroad subsidies were unnecessarily expensive to American governments for this reason, to say nothing of the fact that privileges were often granted, the ultimate value of which it was difficult to foresee. The need for railroads in the early days was so great, however, that very little mileage was built which did not find some good use.

Government Construction

In some instances state or local governments actually undertook to build railroads. Instances of this sort, besides the Pennsylvania State Works, were the Western and Atlantic, built by the state of Georgia from Atlanta, Georgia, to Chattanooga, Tennessee; the Michigan Central, begun and partially completed by the state of Michigan; and a railroad from Meridosia to Springfield, Illinois, constructed by the state of Illinois. The state of North Carolina bought the Raleigh and Gaston Railroad on a foreclosure sale in 1845, but subsequently released it to a private company in 1851. None of these undertakings was profitable, and none of them remained permanently in state control.

Railroad Mileage in the United States, 1861–1951

The miles in operation in the United States from 1861 to 1951 are indicated in the following table, at 5-year intervals.

Year	Miles of Line in Operation
1861	31,286
1865	35,085
1870	52,922
1875	75,096
1880	93,262
1885	128,320
1890	167,191
1895	184,628
1900	198,964
1905	225,196
1910	249,992
1915	264,378
1920	263,821
1925	261,871
1930	262,215
1935	254,347
1940	246,739
1945	240,156
1951	236,599

SOURCE: *Poor's Manual* prior to 1890; Interstate Commerce Commission thereafter.

A large part of railroad construction after the Civil War served to complete systems and main lines which had already been begun. It must be remembered, however, that the entire framework of the railway system west of the Mississippi River had still to be laid down.

Granger Roads

Among the first railways completed after the Civil War were the Granger roads, running from Chicago north and northwest into the grain-growing districts of Illinois, Iowa, and Wisconsin. These carriers afforded connection between the eastern trunk lines and the transcontinental railways terminating at Omaha and St. Paul. The most important companies in the Granger group were the Chicago and North Western; the Chicago, Burlington, & Quincy; the Chicago, Milwaukee, & St. Paul; the Chicago, Rock Island, & Pacific; and the Chicago and Alton. The Chicago and North Western reached Council Bluffs, Iowa, in 1867, and the Chicago and Alton was open to St. Louis in the same year. The second railroad to connect Chicago and Council Bluffs was the Rock Island, opened in June, 1869. The third was the Chicago, Burlington, & Quincy, which reached Burlington, Iowa, in 1867, and Council Bluffs late in 1869. Still another line from Chicago to the Missouri River was that of the Chicago, Milwaukee, & St. Paul, which was organized under the name of the Milwaukee and St. Paul Railway in 1858. It completed the first line opened from Chicago to St. Paul in 1867, and reached Council Bluffs in the late 1870's. The company's present name dates from February, 1874.

Transcontinental Railways

Transcontinental railways represent the second great type of railroad construction which followed the Civil War. The agitation for a transcontinental railway dates back at least as far as 1845, but the movement obtained no support until after the discovery of gold in California, and the migration of a considerable population to the Pacific Coast.

The dates at which the various through lines to the Pacific Coast were opened are as follows:

1869. The Union Pacific Railroad and the Central Pacific Railroad of California met at Promontory Point, west of Ogden.

1881. The Atchison, Topeka, & Santa Fe, starting at Atchison, Kansas, reached a connection with the Southern Pacific running south from San Francisco and Goshen, California, at Deming, Arizona. This afforded a second through route from the East to San Francisco Bay.

1882. In this year the Southern Pacific made connection with the Texas and Pacific at a point 523 miles west of Fort Worth. The eastern end of the Texas and Pacific in 1882 was at Gouldsboro, opposite New Orleans.

1883. The Galveston, Harrisburg, & San Antonio was completed from Houston to the Rio Grande River near El Paso. The acquisition during the same twelve months of three smaller companies, the Texas and New Orleans, the Louisiana Western, and Morgan's Louisiana and Texas Railroad, connecting Houston and New Orleans, created, together with the Southern Pacific west from El Paso, a new through line from the Gulf to the Pacific coast under a single control.[13]

In the same year the Northern Pacific was opened from Northern Pacific Junction, Minnesota, 23 miles from Duluth, to Wallula Junction, Washington Territory, reaching also by connecting lines St. Paul and Duluth upon the east and Portland and Tacoma upon the west.

1884. The Oregon Railway and Navigation Company, operating a railroad from Portland up the south bank of the Columbia River, connected with the Oregon Short Line Railroad, a subsidiary of the Union Pacific, on November 25, 1884, completing a fifth transcontinental route between the Mississippi River and the Pacific Ocean.[14]

1886. The line of the Canadian Pacific was opened from Montreal to Port Moody on Vancouver Sound on June 28, 1886, and a branch to Vancouver was opened on June 1, 1888.

1893. The Great Northern Railway is, as its name implies, the most northerly transcontinental railroad in the United States. It was completed from St. Paul to Puget Sound (Everett) on January 5, and was opened for traffic on June 18, 1893.

Since 1893 there have been three additional transcontinental lines placed in operation. The first was the San Pedro, Los Angeles, and Salt Lake, which began operation from Salt Lake City to Los Angeles on May 1, 1905; the second was the Chicago, Milwaukee, & St. Paul from the Missouri River to Tacoma and Seattle, opened for freight traffic on August 1, 1909; and the third was the Western Pacific, running from San Francisco to Salt Lake City, which began its through business as a freight carrier on December 1, 1909, and regular passenger service on August 22, 1910.

Completion of American Railway System

The completion of the principal transcontinental railway routes by 1893, and the prior connection of these lines with Chicago through the Granger companies, fitted in the last members of the framework of the American railway system as we know it today. It is a sufficiently accurate generalization to say that railroad building in the United States since 1893 has been concerned with the filling out of the outlines sketched before that time. This does not mean that later construction has been

---

[13] *Poor's Manual,* 1884, pp. 835–836.
[14] *Ibid.,* p. 916.

unimportant. On the contrary, regarded from the point of view of quantity of mileage built, the amount of construction since 1893 now exceeds the construction before that date. The fact to remember is that the railroad net of the United States had, by 1893, assumed a character which it later retained and that the competence of railroad transportation had been thoroughly established. The full discussion of railroad problems in later chapters of the text makes it unnecessary to deal further with railroad history at this point, important as the subject would be, if considered by itself.[15]

Future Outlook for New Construction

During the next fifteen or twenty years we may again see an expansion of railway facilities. But if this expansion occurs it will probably take the form in the United States of more cars, more numerous and more powerful locomotives, better arranged and more ample terminals, and a larger supply of second, third, and fourth tracks and sidings upon existing routes that pay, rather than that of a substantial increase in main-track mileage. There are few cities in this country of any importance today, and few districts which promise to yield large quantities of freight, which are not now served by at least one railway line. Nor are there many railways— possibly none at all—which find in a lack of main-track mileage the limiting factor that prevents an increase in the tonnage they are prepared to haul. The reason why the existing railway system of the United States finds it difficult from time to time to handle the freight and the passengers which it is called upon to accommodate is, first, that congestion occurs at terminals, and, secondly, that motive power in many localities or the supply of freight cars, needs to be increased. To remedy such

[15] The reader should be reminded that the railroad, as an instrument of transport, has a long and striking technological history that includes much more than the mere laying of railroad track. This is, moreover, still continuing. During the last few years alone railroads have added not less than 50 percent to the service life of steel rail while reducing its liability to breakage. The life of cross ties has been trebled and the maintenance of track has been largely mechanized. Railroads have adopted new types of power. In 1940, Diesel locomotives moved 5 percent of the car miles in passenger service and less than 1 percent of the car miles in freight service. In 1953 the percentages were 70 and 65. The rail companies now have air-conditioned passenger cars; they have used new materials in passenger equipment and they have employed some striking new designs. There has been improvement in the range, flexibility, and interrelations of automatic signals and in the use of telephonic and radio instead of telegraphic communications. Centralized traffic control has been introduced; this control enables a single track line to carry a volume of traffic which a double track line could formerly accommodate. New devices have been installed in switching yards, such as the electropneumatic car retarder. The items mentioned are only late additions to a list of technical accomplishments that covers a period of more than a hundred years. (See *The American Railroad in Laboratory*, published by the American Railway Association in 1933; also United States Senate, Committee on Interstate and Foreign Commerce, *Study of Domestic Land and Water Transportation*, Hearings before a subcommittee pursuant to S. Res. 50, 81st C., 2d S., 1950, testimony Parmelee, pp. 53–54.)

FIGURE 8. "Sunset Limited" Train Crossing the Rio Grande on the Way to El Paso. (Courtesy of the Southern Pacific.)

shortages will require the fresh investment of capital, but only occasionally the building of new lines.

Another reason why the next few years are unlikely to witness any considerable change in the framework of the American railroad system is to be found in the rapidly developing use of the passenger automobile, the motor truck, and the airplane. The place of the automobile in our modern transportation system will be discussed in the following chapter. We shall content ourselves here by observing that it has already assumed an appreciable portion of the burden that has hitherto rested upon the railroad industry alone, and that it is probably destined to play a still greater part. This is likely to lessen the amount of railroad construction as well as to change the character of the work which railroads are called upon to do.

Current Railroad Problems

During recent years the development of other means of transport, the alternations of periods of prosperity and depression, and the effects of two major wars have forced upon railroad managers problems which they have not yet been able successfully to solve. Much of the later discussion in this book will be concerned with these problems. The difficulties which the railroads have faced have not so far, on the whole, prevented the smooth running of their systems, but economic, legal, and political pressure has threatened their investment and this is rightly regarded as a major national concern. What the best organization of the railroad plant may be, what its relations with other agencies of transportation, on what terms it should seek to attract capital, what its responsibilities should be for national defense, and how far users of transport service everywhere should and can be compelled to pay the total cost of facilities which they enjoy are uncertain. It is now too early in our discussion to generalize with respect to railroad problems, but we shall return to the subjects that have just been mentioned as opportunity appears.

REFERENCES

General Treatises

Adams, Charles Francis, *Railroads: Their Origin and Problems,* New York, Putnam, 1878.

Bigham, Truman C., and Roberts, Merrill J., *Transportation, Principles and Problems,* New York, McGraw-Hill, 1952.

Carter, Charles F., *When Railroads Were New,* New York, Simmons-Boardman, 1926.

Fair, M. L., and Williams, Ernest W., *Economics of Transportation,* New York, Harper, 1950.

Farrington, S. Kip, *Railroading from the Head End,* Garden City, N. Y., Doubleday, 1943.

Flint, Henry M., *The Railroads of the United States: Their History and Statistics,* Philadelphia, John E. Potter, 1868.

Haney, Lewis Henry, *A Congressional History of Railways in the United States,* Bulletin of the University of Wisconsin, no. 211, Madison, Wis., 1908.

Healy, Kent T., *The Economics of Transportation in America,* New York, Ronald, 1940.

Holbrook, Stewart H., *The Story of American Railroads,* New York, Crown, 1947.

Johnson, E. R., *Transport Facilities, Services and Policies,* New York, Appleton-Century-Crofts, 1947.

Landon, Charles E., *Transportation,* New York, Sloane, 1951.

Lardner, Dionysius, *Railway Economy: A Treatise on the New Art of Transport, Its Management, Prospects, and Relations,* London, 1850.

Meyer, B. H., *History of Transportation in the United States Before 1860,* Washington, D. C., Carnegie Institution, 1916.

Moody, John, *The Railroad Builders,* New Haven, Yale, 1921.

Parmelee, Julius, *The Modern Railway,* New York, Longmans, 1940.

Ringwalt, J. L., *Development of Transportation Systems in the United States,* Philadelphia, 1888.

Sax, Emil, *Die Verkehrsmittel in Volks- und Staatswirthschaft,* Wien, Holder, 1876.

Van Metre, T. W., *Transportation in the United States,* Chicago, Foundation Press, 1939.

Other Books

Adams, Charles Francis, and Adams, Henry, *Chapters of Erie and Other Essays,* Boston, Osgood, 1871.

Barger, Harold, *The Transportation Industries, 1889–1946, A Study of Output, Employment, and Productivity,* New York, National Bureau of Economic Research, 1951.

Brown, C. E., *A State Movement in Railroad Development: The Story of North Carolina's First Effort to Establish an East and West Trunk Line Railroad,* Chapel Hill, N.C., University of North Carolina, 1908.

Cleveland, F. A., and Powell, F. W., *Railroad Promotion and Capitalization in the United States,* New York, Longmans, 1909.

Hungerford, Edward, *Story of the Baltimore & Ohio Railroad,* New York, Putnam, 1928.

Kistler, T. M., *The Rise of Railroads in the Connecticut River Valley,* Northampton, Mass., Smith College Studies in History, 1938.

Overton, Richard C., *Burlington West,* Cambridge, Mass., Harvard, 1941.

Pease, Edward, *The Diaries of Edward Pease,* London, Headley, 1907.

Phillips, U. B., *A History of Transportation in the Eastern Cotton Belt to 1860,* New York, Columbia, 1908.

Reizenstein, Milton, *The Economic History of the Baltimore & Ohio Railroad, 1827–1853,* Baltimore, Johns Hopkins, 1897.

Riegel, R. E., *The Story of the Western Railroads*, New York, Macmillan, 1926.

Smiles, Samuel, *Lives of the Engineers*, London, Murray, 1861–1862.

Turnbull, A. D., *John Stevens, An American Record*, New York, Appleton-Century-Crofts, 1928.

Warren, J. G. H., *A Century of Locomotive Building by Robert Stephenson & Co., 1823–1923*, Newcastle-upon-Tyne, A. Reif, 1923.

Special and Miscellaneous

Sketch of the Rise and Progress of the Internal Improvements and of the Internal Commerce of the United States; with a Review of the Charges of Monopoly Made Against Railroad Corporations, in Poor's *Manual of the Railroads of the United States*, 1881, pp. i–lxxxi.

United States Interstate Commerce Commission, Bureau of Transport Economics and Statistics, *Study of Railroad Motive Power*, File no. 66-A-11, Statement no. 5025, 1950.

United States, Office of the Federal Coordinator of Transportation, *Public Aids to Transportation*, Vol. 2, 1938.

United States Pacific Railway Commission, *Report and Testimony*, 50th C., 1st S., Sen. Exec. Doc. 51, Ser. 2505–2509, Washington, D. C., 1887–1888.

United States, Senate, *Railroad Consolidation in the Eastern Region*, 76th C., 3d S., Sen. Rep. 1182, 1940.

United States Senate, *Report of the Select Committee on Transportation— Routes to the Seaboard*, 43d C., 1st S., Sen. Rep. 307, 1881 (Windom Committee).

United States Senate, *Report of the Senate Select Committee on Interstate Commerce*, 49th C., 1st S., Sen. Rep. 46, 1886 (Cullom Committee).

Highway Transportation

Road transport is old transport. Road routes and movements over these routes are traceable to very early periods in the history of man. The road system of a modern state antedates its railroads, and perhaps even its inland waterways; for some form of smoothed way over the land is necessary in comparatively primitive stages of commercial and industrial development. Experiments with power, also, are not new, although during many centuries the horse supplied the major tractive effort required for highway travel.

Steam-Driven Vehicles on the English Roads

It is not generally known that between 1831 and 1838 there were not far short of a dozen companies in England formed to operate lines of steam coaches upon the public roads. Most of these services were in London, or ran between the capital and nearby cities; but successful coaching companies were also to be found in Glasgow, Gloucester, Southampton, and other English and Scotch towns. In 1831 a Select Committee came to the following conclusions with respect to steam road vehicles:

1. That carriages can be propelled by steam on common roads at an average rate of ten miles per hour.
2. That at this rate they have conveyed upwards of fourteen passengers.
3. That their weight, including engine, fuel, water, and attendants, may be under three tons.
4. That they can ascend and descend hills of considerable inclination with facility and safety.
5. That they are perfectly safe for passengers.
6. That they are not (or need not be if properly constructed) nuisances to the public.
7. That they will become a speedier and cheaper mode of conveyance than carriages drawn by horses.
8. That as they admit of greater breadth of tyre than other carriages and as the roads are not acted upon so injuriously as by the feet of horses in

common draught, such carriages will cause less wear of roads than coaches drawn by horses.

9. That rates of toll have been imposed on steam carriages which would prohibit their being used on several lines of road were such charges permitted to remain unaltered.[1]

Technological and Legal Obstacles to Early Automobile Development

The favorable findings of the Select Committee of 1831 indicate that English road transport was then expected to develop, and it is a fact that automotive engineers before 1850 made valuable contributions to the art of steam engine construction.[2] But road carriages had to be made light in weight before they could be widely used, and the technique of steel manufacture was insufficiently advanced to produce light, strong vehicles. There were no rolling mills in 1831, tubes were formed from hammered sheet iron by welding or riveting, and engine parts were forged and turned by hand. Railroads and steamboats suffered less than road engines from this condition, because weight is less of a handicap to vehicles operated upon water or upon rails; but the steam car for common highways found it difficult to compete with other forms of transport until the methods of the iron and steel industry had been improved.

Early English steam automobiles were forced to contend with unfavorable legislation as well as with imperfect materials. In the first place, the steam coaches had to pay heavier taxes than the government demanded from the railroads. The railroads paid a mileage duty of ⅛ penny per passenger per mile, and were sometimes permitted to compound for this tax at a favorable rate. The coach paid turnpike tolls, stagecoach duties calculated upon the licensed capacity of the vehicle, mileage duties payable according to the number of miles which the coach ran, and other minor taxes. The aggregate was much more than the sum which the railroad was obliged to meet. Finally, the coach owner suffered from many annoying restrictions in the operation of his machine. Most of these regulations were local; but mention may be made of a parliamentary statute in 1865 which prescribed: (1) that the maximum speed of steam road vehicles should be reduced from ten to four miles per hour (two miles an hour in towns and villages); (2) that the number of persons required to operate the locomotive should be increased to three; (3) that a man should precede each machine with a red flag; and (4) that motor vehicles should be forbidden to blow off steam.[3] Regulations of this sort were sufficient in themselves to drive steam coaches from English roads.

[1] H. O. Duncan, *The World on Wheels*, Paris, Author, 1926.

[2] This was particularly true of boiler construction. The boiler of the Hancock steam carriage, for instance, was superior to those of Stephenson's competitors at Rainhill, both because of its greater heating surface and because it was built to operate at pressures of 100 pounds per square inch. The boiler of the *Rocket* itself was intended to withstand pressures of only 50 pounds per square inch.

[3] This legislation was repealed in 1896. It was inspired by a complete misconception of the essential nature of automobile transport.

Daimler and Levassor

The significant beginnings of modern road transport are associated with the invention and development of the internal combustion gasoline engine rather than with the English experiments which have been described.

The internal combustion engine using gasoline or petroleum spirits was patented by a German named Gottfried Daimler in 1884. Daimler was a trained mechanic. He attended the Polytechnic School in Stuttgart from 1857 to 1859. In 1861 he went to England for two or three years; later he was shop superintendent of the Karlsruhe Machine Construction Company, and in 1872 he took over the direction of the Deutz Gas Motor factory near Köln. It was in Köln that he produced his first gas motor. Daimler fitted his engine to a bicycle, and afterwards to boats, one of which ran on the river Seine during the Paris Exposition of 1887. In this engine a Frenchman named Levassor became interested. Levassor was a member of the firm of Panhard and Levassor, manufacturers of woodworking machinery. The firm secured the French rights to Daimler's invention in 1887. Levassor himself devised the ingenious system of clutch, gears, and differential for the application of power to driving wheels which characterizes the automobile today, and the motor vehicle may be said to have been born.

Motor Vehicles in the United States

The statistics of factory sales and of registration of privately owned motor vehicles in the United States go back to 1895. For stated years they are as follows: [4]

Year	Factory Sales	Registration
1895	4	4
1905	25,000	78,000
1915	969,930	2,490,932
1920	2,227,349	9,239,161
1925	4,265,830	19,940,724
1930	3,355,986	26,531,999
1935	3,946,934	26,229,743
1940	4,472,286	32,035,424
1945	725,215	30,638,429
1950	8,003,056	48,600,505
1951	6,765,263	51,326,438

Of this number of 51,326,438, representing the total registration of privately owned automobiles in the United States in 1951, 42,525,217 were passenger cars, 143,290 were buses, and 8,657,931 were trucks.

[4] In addition to the totals given in the text there were, in 1951, 157,374 passenger cars, 87,171 buses, and 377,823 trucks which were owned by public authorities. There were also an unreported number of military vehicles.

There are no statistics of numbers of passengers handled or of tons of freight moved, and such estimates as are possible have been discussed in chapter 1. The value of the annual output of cars, buses, and trucks in 1951 is reported by the Automobile Manufacturers' Association to have been $9,737,254,000 and the total national investment in automobiles probably considerably exceeds $30 billion. The depreciated capital investment of the steam railroads of the United States was, in 1951, about $25 billion. The last sum covers costs of rights of way and roadbed, with which motor vehicles are not directly concerned.[5]

Classification of Motor Vehicles

Motor vehicles may be classified according to their physical characteristics or according to the nature of their use. The former division distinguishes the passenger automobile, carrying from two to seven persons, the motor bus, and the motor truck. The latter separates the car used in the service of its owner and the vehicle operated in the service of third parties, either as a common or as a contract carrier. The temptation in discussing motor vehicle operation is to dwell chiefly upon those types of automobile and truck service which are comparable with the service which the railroad undertakes. This is justifiable for some purposes, for the commercial operator conducts a large and rapidly growing business, the main features of which it is important to understand. But it must not be forgotten that the motor passenger car and the truck operate today primarily for their owners. This is a matter of common knowledge in so far as passenger cars are concerned. But it is also true of trucks, as we shall see in later pages of this chapter. Indeed, the fact that an individual or a company may, with a comparatively small investment, control his transportation in complete detail instead of adjusting himself to the standard requirements necessarily imposed upon a carrier which serves others than himself, is one of the major reasons for the appeal which the motor vehicle makes to the shipper of goods.[6]

Private Passenger Cars

Of the vehicles on the road today, the greater part are privately owned passenger cars. The proportion appears to run between 80 and 90 percent.

---

[5] Automobile Manufacturers' Association, *Automobile Facts and Figures,* annual.

[6] Most of the information which we possess with respect to the use of privately owned automobiles comes from personal observation, from surveys, usually conducted by state or federal governments, and from testimony and exhibits in official investigations. During the 1930's and especially between 1936 and 1939 most states undertook basic surveys of road traffic outside of cities. On completion of these surveys automatic recording instruments were widely installed upon main highways. These and annual summer counts have supplied information of value on the composition and volume of traffic in later years, although not in the detail covered in the basic surveys. In addition to the sources just mentioned, there have been so-called motor vehicle allocation

Buses throughout the country, in 1951, were responsible for about 1 percent of all vehicle miles, and trucks and combinations for about 19 percent.[7] The characteristics of private passenger cars may be summarized under the heads of load, average length of haul, speed, and type of use.

LOAD.   The average load of passenger cars is small. For the country as a whole, the Bureau of Public Roads estimated the number of occupants per car, in 1948, as between 1.75 and 2.00.[8]

AVERAGE TRIP.   The average trip is also low. It is under, and probably much under, 30 miles. This may be compared with a rail average, in 1949, of 63 miles. Passenger cars are most frequently used for trips to and

---

studies and road use surveys. The former were originally designed to reveal the incidence of motor vehicle taxation with respect to vehicle type and place of ownership (rural, urban). Road use surveys, similarly, were expected to show the distribution of the benefit of highway expenditures between different sorts of vehicles and different kinds of use. There was much reliance upon sampling in these later surveys; sections of the motor vehicle population were sought out at their homes or places of business and were asked to state the amount, character, and location of their driving during the previous year (*Public Roads,* October-November-December, 1946, p. 264). Other special surveys, covering urban traffic, were introduced after 1944 (*ibid.,* October-November-December, 1945, p. 16). To all this we may add official data as to the number of cars registered and taxes paid and, for commercial operators, some statistics gathered by state and federal regulatory commissions or presented in litigation before these bodies, and a variety of local or specialized studies of one kind or another. It will be observed that information on privately owned and operated automobiles is irregular and varied rather than uniform, systematic, and comprehensive; and that it cannot always be up to date. It is difficult to avoid these handicaps; yet we probably have, in spite of them, a picture of the kind and use of the private automobile in the United States which is reasonably correct.

[7] Thomas S. Dimmick and Mary E. Kipp, "Traffic Trends on Rural Roads in 1946," *Public Roads,* March, 1948. In Connecticut in 1934, 85.5 percent of all vehicles counted were privately owned passenger cars, and in Rhode Island in the same year the proportion was 90.3 percent (L. E. Peabody, "Digest of Report on Connecticut Traffic Survey," *Public Roads,* 1936, p. 225. See also "Some Characteristics of Highway Traffic in Rhode Island," *ibid.,* p. 238). In California, in 1946, 85 percent of all vehicle miles were produced by passenger cars, 1 percent by buses, and 14 percent by trucks (Joint Fact-finding Committee on Highways, Streets, and Bridges, *A Study for the California Legislature,* "Engineering Facts and a Future Program," by G. Donald Kennedy, 1946, p. 62). In the same year privately owned passenger cars, including taxicabs, accounted for 82 percent of all vehicle miles on highways in the United States. Buses throughout the country, in 1946, were responsible for about 1 percent of all vehicle miles, and trucks and combinations for about 16 percent. (See Dimick and Kipp, *op. cit.*)

[8] Speaking only of passenger cars, the average number of passengers per car in California, in 1922, was 2.02 in summer and 1.84 in winter. In Ohio the average was 2.3 and in Illinois it was 2.7, ranging from 2.3 persons per car where the proportion of business traffic was large to 3.5 where business traffic was less considerable. In New Hampshire the average number of persons per car was 1.9 for business and 3.2 for pleasure use. Referring again to California, 790,508 cars entered this state at quarantine stations between January and June, 1946, carrying 2,134,338 passengers, or an average of 2.7 passengers per car. In 1941 the corresponding average had been 2.8 (Joint Fact Finding Committee on Highways, Streets, and Bridges, *op. cit.,* p. 80). In the city of Sacramento, an elaborate survey in 1948 showed an average of 1.9, including a figure of 1.6 in the case of social and recreational travel.

from places of business, local markets, and places of gathering. Very little distance is involved in transport of this sort.[9]

AVERAGE SPEED. The average speed of all vehicles was, in 1952, 49.6 miles per hour on the open highways with lesser speeds in and near urban areas. There were, however, many instances of higher speeds, and the average has increased.[10] It appears that automobile speed is controlled by the density of route traffic in thickly populated sections and by the extent of delay at intersections; while elsewhere it is affected by surfacing, marking, and alignment of highways, and by the effective separation of high-speed and low-speed drivers.[11] It is also affected by

[9] In Connecticut, in 1922, the average automobile journey was 45.1 miles and in Ohio it was 38 miles. But more recent reports covering twelve states show averages ranging from 11.7 to 18.7 miles (United States, Office of the Federal Coordinator of Transportation, *Public Aids to Transportation,* vol. 4, 1940, p. 15). An elaborate survey in California, in 1946, reported that 64 percent of all trips observed were for distances less than 10 miles. The average was greater, but still under 30 miles (Joint Fact Finding Committee, *op. cit.,* p. 59). A report by the Bureau of Public Roads, in 1939, showed similar facts in eleven scattered states (United States House of Representatives, *Toll Roads and Free Roads,* 76th C., 1st S., House Doc. 272, 1939, p. 12).

[10] The average speed of automobiles has been the subject of frequent observation. The result of 347 speed studies conducted by the Public Roads Administration in 1947, which included reports on 105,449 vehicles on main rural highways in fourteen states, showed that the average speed of all vehicles observed was, for the year ended December 31, 1947, 46.8 miles per hour. The average for passenger cars was 47.8 miles, that for buses, 47.4 miles, and that for trucks, 42.2 miles. In 1952 the corresponding speeds were 50.9, 52.2, and 44.9. Speeds are highest in Pacific and Mountain states and lowest in Connecticut, Maine, and New Jersey (United States Federal Works Agency, Public Roads Administration, *Traffic Speed Trends,* Informational Memorandum, May 3, 1948). In California, the speed on unrestricted portions of the State Highway system averaged, in 1946, about 45 miles per hour, with about 15 percent of the drivers averaging 53 miles per hour. The speed in and near urban areas was, however, less. On a modern 4-lane divided highway (not a freeway) in San Diego, the average speed was 30 miles per hour, and on congested downtown streets in San Francisco the average speed during hours of heavy traffic dropped as low as 10 to 15 miles per hour (Joint Fact Finding Committee, *op. cit.*). The effect of city congestion was similarly emphasized by a street traffic survey of the city of Detroit, in 1936–37, which recorded variations of passenger automobile speeds by hours in the downtown area. In this district speeds varied from 26 miles per hour at 6 A.M. to 15 miles per hour at 9 A.M., obviously with relation to the number of vehicles in the streets (*Street Traffic, City of Detroit, 1936–37,* prepared and published by and under the direction of Michigan State Highway Department, in cooperation with the Detroit Police Department and the Works Progress Administration).

[11] A state-wide speed survey in Connecticut showed average speeds on different types of highway in June, 1948, as follows:

Types of Highway	*Average Speed in Miles per Hour*
2-lane, 2-way highways	40.6
4-lane, undivided highways, intersections at grade	41.6
4-lane, divided highways, intersections at grade	42.6
4-lane, divided highways, passenger vehicles only (parkways)	48.5

SOURCE: Connecticut State Highway Department, *Highway Speed Study,* prepared by Traffic Section, Division of Highway Control, Hartford, 1948.

characteristics of individual drivers and by the length of trips which travelers undertake.[12]

TYPE OF USE. Attempts have been made to distinguish business uses from other uses of private passenger cars, and even to separate nonbusiness uses into trips for social and for recreational purposes.[13] Common observation indicates, well enough, that private passenger vehicles are used in all these various ways. The heavy travel which fills rural roads on week ends is evidence of pleasure use, and the distribution of traffic on city streets through successive weekday hours show the importance of the private automobile in carrying persons to and from their jobs.[14] But little reliance can be placed on distinctions between business and pleasure employment, especially on rural roads, and attempts to separate social and recreational uses are particularly uncertain. Traffic studies do, however, demonstrate one important fact. This is that most highway travel has a city either as a point of origin or destination. The attraction of any given city varies directly with the size of its population but, in any case, the number of trips which both begin and end in a rural area is comparatively small.[15]

[12] Investigations by the Public Roads Administration have shown that, on an average, persons traveling long distances drive faster and generally have newer cars than local travelers; young persons drive somewhat faster than older persons; men drive somewhat faster than women; and the newer vehicles are driven faster than older vehicles (United States Federal Works Agency, Public Roads Administration, *Highway Development Administration, and Finance,* Part II of a discussion of highway practice in the United States, presented at the 45th annual meeting, American Road Builders' Association, Chicago, July 16–24, 1948, p. 16).

Highway administrations appreciate the fact that high speeds multiply the number of accidents and, especially, that they increase the seriousness of accidents which occur. On the other hand, more cars can pass over a given highway when speeds are uniform and high than can pass when speeds are uniform and low. It is desirable, for this reason, that high speeds should be made possible. The evidence seems to show that further improvement can be made with proper segregation and construction, without unduly increasing the risk to the traveling public.

[13] Estimates by the Bureau of Public Roads, based upon data for 1941, are to the effect that, in the country at large, 18 percent of travel in 1941 consisted of driving to work; 4 percent of the travel was for shopping, 37 percent, for business trips, 15 percent, for social purposes, and 26 percent, for recreation (Joint Fact Finding Committee, *op. cit.,* 1946).

[14] In the Los Angeles area during the last war, 80 percent of the half-million war plant employees got to work by automobile. One large aircraft plant found that 92 percent of its personnel rode an average of 11 miles daily from home to work in their own cars (*ibid.,* p. 74).

[15] In Michigan, in 1947, on rural trunk lines and county roads, 89 percent of all travel consisted of trips that had one or both terminals in an urban place; trips from one rural place to another made up only 11 percent of the whole. On rural trunk lines alone, 95 percent of the travel was made up of city-to-city, city-to-country, or country-to-city driving; only 5 percent consisted of trips between rural points. On county roads, trips to or from cities made up 74 percent of the travel (*Highway Needs in Michigan, An Engineering Analysis,* Michigan Good Roads Federation, Highway Study Committee. Coöperating, Public Roads Administration, Federal Works Agency; Consultants, Automotive Safety Foundation, Washington, D. C.; Staff work by Planning and Traffic Division, Michigan State Highway Department, 1947).

It also appears that, entering cities, a high proportion of traffic is destined for the downtown area. Appreciation of these facts is doubtless responsible for emphasis upon urban highway improvement in federal aid programs of recent years and also for the conclusion that highways which are relocated to bypass cities do not, effectively, reduce congestion upon urban roads.

Motor Bus

This vehicle functions as a common, contract, or private carrier, but it differs from the railroad and from the street and interurban electric car in that it travels upon public roads and not upon a track which it constructs. It differs from the private passenger car in size and because, in most categories, it furnishes transportation for sale and not for the owner's use. In discussing bus operation, we may distinguish between the city and the intercity carrier.

The City Omnibus

In city traffic, the characteristic vehicle is the motor driven bus seating from 31 to 45 persons. These buses approximate street cars in capacity and may exceed them in rate of acceleration and in speed.

ADVANTAGES OF THE CITY BUS. The advantages of the bus over the street railway car are chiefly in cheapness of installation and in flexibility of operation. The bus line lays no track and so saves an important element in expense. The first cost of motor power is, also, likely to be less than that of an electric installation, unless the passenger movement is very heavy. Bus lines are, therefore, especially adapted to lightly settled areas and for pioneering work. It is true that, in a certain measure, bus line construction is cheap because the taxpayer builds the road over which the bus operates, but this is not the whole story, and even if it were, the competitive advantage of the bus, as matters stand, would still be real.

Besides being cheap to install the bus is also flexible in operation; it is not tied to one street or even to one position in a street. Buses are able to avoid fires, parades, or other obstructions by detours. They can deliver passengers at the curb. A bus in movement can pass a bus that is loading or unloading passengers or one that has broken down. While tastes differ, many people find the city bus pleasanter to ride in than the street railway car. And the absence of tracks facilitates the movement of private passenger automobiles and of trucks when buses are not present.

DISADVANTAGES OF THE BUS. The chief disadvantage of the city bus is that it relies upon a decentralized power plant. It is not possible in a bus system as in an electric railway system to transfer power that is not, at a given moment, utilized by one unit of equipment to other units upon the line. Each vehicle must be equipped to handle peak demands upon

all segments of its route. For this and other reasons the cost of bus power
is relatively large in districts of dense traffic and uneven terrain. The bus
also requires more skill of the driver and it can more easily cause or suffer
damage. The bus uses the street less effectively than does the electric
train, although not less effectively than the single electric car.

Trolley Bus

The trolley bus presents a compromise between the gasoline driven
vehicle and the electric car. It is an instrument which derives its power
from overhead wires, as does the traditional street car, but operates with
a body similar to that of the gasoline coach. The trolley bus uses no
track; it has less freedom of action than the standard bus, but it has,
nevertheless, a possibility of lateral movement which enables it to draw
up at a curb and to avoid obstacles upon a city street. It has the advantage
of a central power supply. The field for efficient employment of the trolley
bus is in areas where the density of traffic is too great for the city bus but
not sufficient to justify the use of electric trains, or possibly of electric cars.

Interurban Bus Lines

In addition to the slow, capacious, city omnibus, large, fast motorbuses
are in operation upon many interurban routes. These buses compete
actively with railroad lines. Their equipment is being constantly improved. Some of the latest types of vehicles have smoking compartments,
toilets, facilities for furnishing lunches, reclining chairs for night travel,
and reading lights. Coaches are heated with hot water during the winter
months and cooled with electric fans during the summer months, and
there is space for carrying 75 to 150 pounds of baggage per passenger.
Some further problems of this service will be discussed in chapter 25.

ADVANTAGES OF INTERURBAN BUSES. Like the city bus, the interurban motor service enjoys the advantage of the small investment which it
requires for operation as compared with the expenditure necessary to
install railroad or interurban electric service, the advantage of the ease
with which routes can be altered and established, and that of the frequency of service made possible by the fact that the unit of bus operation
is the single car, not the train. A bus can receive and discharge passengers
at any point en route. Its city terminals are sometimes, though not always,
more conveniently located than those of the railroad company, and for
hauls of moderate length, in fair weather, travel by bus is as agreeable
as that by rail.

DISADVANTAGES OF INTERURBAN BUSES. The disadvantage of the bus
is that it is subject to interference from other traffic, which reduces speed
and increases the likelihood of accident. Nor can the bus maintain or
police its route according to railroad standards. Again, the bus is lighter

than the railroad car, is less stable, affords less freedom of movement to passengers, and is generally unable to supply sleeping and dining facilities. It handles a substantial volume of long-distance traffic, but at a lower price.

In 1951, 166 Class I intercity bus carriers reporting to the Interstate Commerce Commission carried 306,450,217 passengers and registered a total of approximately 18,000,000,000 intercity passenger miles. This is to be compared with 214,000,000 passengers and 29,000,000,000 passenger miles [16] reported by Class I railroad carriers.

Motor Trucks

The principal uses of the freight automobile, or motor truck, include the following:

1. A very large proportion of truck use is local in character. Trucks are employed upon the farm and in movements from farm to local markets. Farmer owned vehicles bring cotton to the gin, tobacco to the auction floor, and milk to the loading platforms of milk routes. In cities, a local use is found in the delivery service of retail stores, including butcher, bakery, dairy, and grocery, as well as department stores.

2. Another type of service is the haul of perishable commodities such as milk, eggs, vegetables, and fruit from producing territory into the larger cities. Most population centers are dependent upon trucks for their supply of fluid milk. The success of the motor truck in capturing the fruit and vegetable traffic is shown by the fact that, in 1951, 47.7 percent of the fruits and vegetables unloaded in twelve principal cities in the United States came in by truck as compared with 52.3 percent by rail.[17]

3. In certain parts of the Middle West, there are truck operators who specialize in the transportation of livestock from farms to packing or rail-

[16] Excluding commutation travel.

[17] The proportions were 25.8 percent at Chicago, 24.2 percent at St. Louis, 35.2 percent at New York, 44.3 percent at New Orleans (excluding truck shipments originating in Louisiana), 52.9 percent at Philadelphia, 79.2 percent at Atlanta; and at Los Angeles 87.7 percent of the fruits and vegetables reported to the Department of Agriculture reached the city by means of a truck haul (Automobile Manufacturers' Association, *Automobile Facts and Figures,* 1952).

Truck service in the case of fruits and vegetables is not limited to the final haul which terminates at the consuming market, nor are the vehicles used for fruits and vegetables restricted to the handling of these commodities alone. Thus, in California, the truck movement is seasonal. It may start with the cantaloupe crop in the Imperial Valley where the peak season continues for a few weeks; then the equipment may be transferred to the Los Angeles district to take care of the transportation of citrus fruit or hay and grain; from there to the Bakersfield district for the cotton crop; thence to Fresno for the grain and raisin crop; and thence on to other districts successively to meet the peak production of other crops until, within the course of a year, a large amount of transportation equipment has made practically a complete round of the state and is back again at the starting point (*Motor Bus and Truck Investigation,* I.C.C. Docket no. 18,300, testimony Boston, p. 2044).

shipping centers. Hauls of 60 to 80 miles are common. The trucks which carry outbound hogs, cattle, and sheep are filled with return loads of merchandise, agricultural machinery, fertilizer, and other freight shipped from industrial centers to small towns along the motor routes. In 1951, 45 percent of the sheep and lambs, 75 percent of the cattle, 79 percent of the calves, and 80 percent of the hogs received at stockyards in the United States were hauled to public markets by truck instead of entering by rail.

4. An equally specialized service is that of hauling household goods. Well over half of the furniture shipped from Michigan now goes by truck—uncrated, but protected by pads. This method saves time, labor, and lumber, and makes possible door to door delivery.[18] Vans constructed for the purpose often move long distances. They offer the advantage of speedy transportation and reduction in breakage, because they eliminate intermediate handling of the freight.

5. Still other important uses of the truck are in the haulage of cotton, automobiles, coal, construction materials such as lumber, gravel, and cement, oil and oil-field supplies, and motion picture properties. Some interesting figures presented in a report by an examiner of the Interstate Commerce Commission in 1932 [19] showed a particularly heavy movement of coal in certain areas.[20] Truck traffic in some instances had repercussions upon local systems of distribution because many truck haulers engaged in the retail coal business in order to provide themselves with freight.[21]

AVERAGE LOAD. Characteristically, trucking is conducted in small units. According to the Bureau of Public Roads the average load was 2.43 tons for single-unit trucks and 10 tons for truck and trailer combina-

---

[18] *Highway Needs in Michigan, op. cit.*

[19] *Report on Coordination of Motor Transportation,* Sen. Doc. 43, 72d C., 1st S., 1932, p. 49. See also United States Department of Commerce, Office of Domestic Commerce, Transportation Division, Industry Report, Domestic Transportation, *An Evaluation of Motor Truck Transportation,* May-August, 1948.

[20] According to the examiner's report, about 33 percent of the coal received annually at Reading, Pennsylvania, 50 percent of the total anthracite used at Lebanon, and 40 percent of that used at Harrisburg were then being moved to these points by motor truck. In southern Indiana, in 1931, coal was being trucked from the mines to points within a radius of 50 miles, and the Chicago, Burlington and Quincy Railroad estimated that it had lost to the trucks an annual coal traffic of 250,000 tons. In 1945, in 29 states, 90 million tons out of a production of 620 million tons moved from the mines by truck. Of this truck transport, 47.1 million tons were shipments from the mines to railroad sidings, 1.4 million tons were carried from the mines to waterways, and 41.5 million tons went directly to destination (Automobile Manufacturers' Association, *Motor Trucks,* 1947. See also United States Interstate Commerce Commission, Bureau of Transport Economics and Statistics, *Monthly Comment on Transportation Statistics,* April 13, 1951, p. 5).

[21] *Railway Age,* February 6, 1932, p. 254.

tions, in the year 1949.[22] The combined average is nearer the second than the first of these figures because approximately 60 percent of the freight ton-miles are carried by truck and trailer combinations or by three-axle trucks.[23] It appears that the loaded and empty weights of single-unit trucks have not much changed since before World War II; the loaded and empty weights of truck combinations have, however, rather notably increased. Most truck-railroad competition is to be credited to these heavier vehicles.[24]

AVERAGE HAUL. Characteristically, also, the typical motor haul is short. It is true that the average length of haul on the lines of individual Class I intercity motor carriers was, in 1949, 218 miles, while the comparable railroad average was only 229 miles. But the proportion which the number of Class I motor carriers reporting to the Commission bears to the total number of trucks upon the road is small, and it is unlikely that the cited figure represents anything like the practice of the average truck upon the road.[25]

This does not mean, however, that long-distance trucking does not

[22] During the summer of 1949 the highway departments of 46 states, in coöperation with the Public Roads Administration, conducted a survey to obtain data concerning the volume and composition of traffic and the weight of trucks and truck combinations on rural roads for the determination of trends in traffic. Rural roads, in this connection, were main highways which were not urban roads. A total of 253,316 trucks and truck combinations were counted during the period of the survey, of which 110,000 were weighed. The final report showed that the average weight of single truck units was 2.95 tons for empty and 5.38 tons for loaded trucks observed. The indicated average load, on this basis, was 2.43 tons, which is the figure cited in the text. Strictly speaking, this average was an estimate only, because the same trucks were not observed loaded and empty. It was, however, a suggestion upon which a conclusion can, probably, be based. The report also showed that the average weight of combinations was 10 tons unloaded and 20 tons loaded, indicating a usual load of 10 tons (United States Bureau of Public Roads, Highway Transport Research Branch, "Traffic Trends on Rural Roads in 1949." *Public Roads,* December, 1950).

[23] United States Senate, Committtee on Interstate and Foreign Commerce, *Study of Domestic Land and Water Transportation,* Hearings before a subcommittee pursuant to S. Res. 50, 81st C., 2d S., 1950, testimony Mackie, p. 140.

[24] *Ibid.,* testimony MacDonald, p. 1016.

[25] Reference may be made to the following:

1. State surveys of the 1930's reported a predominance of short hauls. These reports concluded that in Connecticut 79.5 percent, in California 60.7 percent, in Maine 80.5 percent, in Ohio 71.6 percent, and in Cook County, Ill., 75.8 percent of trips of loaded trucks observed on rural roads were for less than 30 miles.

2. The investigations of the National Interregional Highway Committee in 1943 (78th C., 2d S., House Doc. 379, 1944) indicated that 75.4 percent of the truck traffic on which the Committee had information was intrastate. It is not necessarily true that intrastate movements are shorter than interstate movements but the distances covered are likely to be shorter, on the whole.

3. Tables and maps showing the density of highway traffic usually reveal a heavy traffic on mileage adjacent to cities and a rapidly decreasing density as the distance from cities increases. It would seem evident, from this, that most motor vehicles move within a restricted range. These maps do not distinguish between trucks and passenger cars; they may, however, provide a suggestion with respect to trucking hauls.

exist. On the contrary, there is a good deal of traffic moved between widely separated points of origin and destination. The Interstate Commerce Commission stressed the development of long-distance motor carriage in its annual report for 1951. It observed that the longest hauls were between the Midwest and the Pacific Coast. Among the commodities, the Commission named household goods, fresh fruits and vegetables, and fresh meats and packing house products. It is common knowledge that trucks carry meat from Ogden to Los Angeles, fish from Seattle to Los Angeles, citrus from Texas and Florida to Chicago, and many other goods between distant cities. These movements are important and they may be multiplied. But they do not represent motor traffic as a whole.[26]

Advantages of Motor Truck Service

A primary advantage of motor trucks in the field of transportation is that operating units are small requiring, for each unit, only a small investment of capital. This permits a great variety of equipment and of use, adapting equipment and types of service to the particular needs of shippers who rely on motor service for transportation and to varying conditions at different places and at different times. The adjustment is most exact in the case of owner-operated vehicles, but it is important in the case of contract carriers and apparent, to some extent, where common carriers are concerned.[27]

[26] See United States Board of Investigation and Research, *The National Traffic Pattern*, 79th C., 1st S., Sen. Doc. 83, 1945, pp. 65–66; Association of American Railroads, "Report of Subcommittee on Motor Transport of the Railroad Committee for the Study of Transportation," *Highway Motor Transportation*, August, 1945.

[27] The specialization in truck equipment takes the following general forms:
1. Adaptation in strength and size and form of vehicles to different kinds of shipments.
2. Construction to permit easier loading and unloading.
3. Protection of consignments on the road to ensure better condition upon arrival. This protection may reduce expenses in packaging which shippers, otherwise, would be compelled to incur.
4. Provision for greater speed, reducing time in transit.

The United States Board of Investigation and Research made the following remarks upon this subject in 1944:

"The first truck . . . was little more than a converted automobile carriage with a heavier axle and springs and a strengthened frame . . . In those early days there was a distinct line of demarcation between heavy-duty and light-duty trucks. . . . It was not until 1929 that the first signs appeared that even in the lower-tonnage classification the industry was headed toward specialization to meet each specific set of operating requirements.

"Today, even in the 1½ ton field there is almost no such thing as a standard truck. Though standard 1½ ton chassis are still listed the variety of options available to the purchaser are so great that the individual operator can almost purchase a truck in this as well as in the higher tonnage classifications to his own specifications. . . .

"The manufacture of bodies for trucks is a separate industry in itself . . . A variety of specialized operating conditions has made it seemingly impossible to standardize on anything—the hauling of perishable merchandise, the transportation of liquids, the

Multiplication of operating truck units produces, indeed, two effects: In the case of trailers, which are containers only, the advantage of the motor vehicle is found, principally, in adaptation of form. When trucks are driven by their own power, greater frequency of service becomes also possible without prohibitive expense, because it is possible to dispatch five trucks at 12-minute intervals as easily as to dispatch the same trucks together at the beginning of every hour.[28] A truck-trailer combination with two units only should probably be included in this class.

In addition to advantages in frequency of service and in specialization of equipment, motor trucks have advantages over rail operations in certain other ways. Thus, in many instances, the truck has easier access to the points of origin and destination of shipments than has the railroad car. This is essentially because the road mileage of the country reaches more places than does the railroad mileage. It follows that a trucker can, more often than a railroad, pick up consignments at the place of business of the shipper and deliver them to the place of business of the consignee. The railroad may not be able to do this except, by itself, operating trucks; and if the railroad adopts this policy, it is under the handicap that freight must be rehandled in transfer to and from the railroad trains.[29]

Trucks may also, under certain circumstances, deliver consignments

---

collection of garbage, the hauling of produce to market, the transportation of cattle and horses, the movement of household goods, street flashing and road oiling, dairy and bakery deliveries, long distance hauling, special trucks for utilities and railroads, and so forth.

"As a result, trucks today are no longer just 'trucks.' Those manufacturers who have been able to survive and succeed have done so largely on the strength of painfully acquired knowledge of transportation requirements in hundreds if not thousands of occupations and have become capable of engineering and building vehicles designed for each specific use" (United States Transportation and Research Board, *Report on Technological Trends in Transportation,* Washington, D. C., 1945).

[28] The frequency of service which trucks supply is an advantage to jobbers because it permits them to adjust the volume of their receipts currently to the volume of their sales. They are relieved from the necessity of storage or, at least, of as much storage as would be necessary if inbound movements were widely spread and sales occurred in something like a steady flow. Frequency of service regularizes inbound movements to the market and this is a gain if sales are regular. It is even an advantage when sales are irregular if the irregularity in disposing of commodities can be matched by selection from a frequent service which coincides with consumer needs. Frequency of transit is of advantage to the producer for similar reasons, although in a slightly different way.

[29] There may be as much rehandling in truck as in railroad shipments under certain conditions. In the first place, shippers' warehouses are frequently located on railroad sidings. In such cases the railroad has as good or a better access to terminal points than the truckers can secure. And in the second place, truck hauls are often divided into two parts. One portion is a gathering or dispersing movement. The other is a line haul movement between termini. Truck hauls which are so divided require two or more handlings of freight; this may be as expensive as railroad service and as damaging to goods. In spite of these qualifications, truckers often handle freight directly, without break of bulk, which railroads would find it necessary to tranship. The contrast is clearest in the case of short and least certain in the case of longer hauls.

more promptly than these consignments can be delivered by rail. This is most likely:

1. When the frequency of service by truck is greater than the frequency by rail. It may be added that frequency of service during critical periods during the day or night has an independent importance when, for business reasons, it is desired to have shipments arrive at a designated time.

2. When rail shipments do and truck shipments do not require rehandling at terminals.

3. When full truckloads can be loaded through to destinations and full carloads cannot be so handled. Intermediate transfer and switching is expensive. The average truckload is smaller than the average carload or trainload, so that these conditions can be expected to occur.

4. When the highway route is shorter than the rail route. This is frequently true in the case of short hauls, especially when the same truck performs a gathering and a line haul service.

5. When the highway is less congested than the railroad route.

Highway transport is by no means always faster than railroad transport. There is no doubt, however, but that under favorable circumstances a higher journey speed and often a higher route speed can be attained.

And finally, perhaps because of the newness of the service, the flexibility of its operating organization, the relatively small size of the standard vehicle, and the greater ability of the highway as compared with the rail line to accommodate special movement, the truck can render emergency rush services which a railroad may find it impossible to undertake.

The advantages of motor truck service may be, and often are, overbalanced by the advantages of other forms of transport. It seems clear, however, that under many conditions and for many types of transport, motor truck operation meets a present need which no other form of machinery can supply.[30]

Common Carrier Truck Service

The most important advantages of the motor truck as compared with the rail car are independent of the kind of ownership to which the truck is subject. It is well to remember, however, that the trucking business is conducted in at least three distinct ways. Some trucks are common carriers, serving all who apply; some are contract carriers, limiting themselves to a particular clientele; and some are owned by the shipper of the freight which they transport.

[30] The competitive advantages and disadvantages of truck transportation were summarized by the Federal Coordinator of Transportation in 1934 and 1935 (*Merchandise Traffic Report,* 1934, and *Freight Traffic Report,* 1935), and by the United States Board of Investigation and Research in 1945 (*The National Traffic Pattern,* 79th C., 1st S., Sen. Doc. 83, pp. 67–71).

The available data do not enable us to state with any precision what part of the motor truck service is performed by regularly organized companies engaged in common or contract carriage and what part by shippers who own both the trucks and the commodities which they transport. Some of the older truck surveys did, however, secure information of this sort. Thus in Connecticut in 1934, 74.4 percent of the trucks counted were carrying freight for their owners, 18 percent were contract, and 8 percent were common carriers. In Arkansas in 1935 the percentages were 85.2, 10.1, and 4.7; in California in 1935 they were 79.0, 18.2, and 1.9. These and other similar figures may not now represent the facts. But it seems probable that the commercial trucking companies handle a good deal less than half of the total trucking business and that common carrier service by truck takes care of only a portion of this fraction, whatever it may be.

In later chapters we shall discuss the use of the truck in terminal service, the competition of motor vehicles generally with the railroad plant, and the manner and extent to which state and federal regulation has been extended to the highway carriage of passengers and goods. Let us now leave the subject of road transportation for the moment, however, to consider the development of facilities for air travel—the last of the major instrumentalities which we shall undertake to describe.

REFERENCES

General Treatises

Bigham, Truman C., and Roberts, Merrill J., *Transportation, Principles and Problems,* New York, McGraw-Hill, 1952.

Dearing, Charles L., *American Highway Policy,* Washington, D. C., Brookings Institution, 1941.

Duncan, H. O., *The World on Wheels,* Paris, Author, 1926.

Fair, Marvin L., and Williams, Ernest W., *Economics of Transportation,* New York, Harper, 1951.

Johnson, E. R., *Transport Facilities, Services, and Policies,* New York, Appleton-Century-Crofts, 1947.

Landon, C. E., *Transportation—Principles, Practices, Problems,* New York, Sloane, 1951.

Locklin, D. Philip, *Economics of Transportation,* Chicago, Irwin, 1947.

Owen, W., *Automotive Transportation, Trends and Problems,* Washington, D. C., Brookings Institution, 1949.

Walker, G., *Road and Rail—An Enquiry into the Economics of Competition and State Control,* London, Allen & Unwin, 1947.

Wilson, G. L., *Coordinated-Motor-Rail-Steamship Transportation,* New York, Appleton-Century-Crofts, 1930.

Other Books

Dearing, Charles L., *Automobile Transportation in the War Effort,* Washington, D. C., Brookings Institution, 1942.

Edwards, Ford, *Principles of Motor Transportation,* New York, McGraw-Hill, 1933.

Mason, Linton W., *Local Trucking,* New York, McGraw-Hill, 1951.

Stocker, H. E., *Motor Traffic Management,* New York, Prentice-Hall, 1942.

Taff, C. A., *Commercial Motor Transportation,* Chicago, Irwin, 1950.

Wyatt, Horace M., *The Motor Industry, Its Growth, Its Methods, Its Prospects, and Its Products, with an Indication of the Uses to Which Motor Vehicles of All Kinds Are, or Could Be, Advantageously Applied,* London, Pitman, 1917.

Periodicals

Dimmick, Thomas B., "Traffic Trends on Rural Roads in 1949," *Public Roads,* December, 1950.

Hilts, H. E., "Planning the Interregional Highway System," *Public Roads,* June, 1941.

Hitchcock, S. T., and Burrage, R. H., "Some Travel and Parking Habits Observed from Parking Stations," *Public Roads,* June, 1950.

Long, John C., "Motor Transport and Our Radial Frontier," *Journal of Land and Public Utility Economics,* January, 1926.

Plimpton, R. E., "Distribution Advances with the Motor Truck," *Journal of Land and Public Utility Economics,* August, 1931.

Paxson, F. L., "The Highway Movement, 1916–1935," *American Historical Review,* January, 1946.

St. Clair, G. P., "Trends in Motor Vehicle Transportation, 1936 to 1945," *Public Roads,* July–September, 1946.

Special and Miscellaneous

Automobile Manufacturers' Association, *Automobile Facts and Figures,* Detroit, annual.

Automobile Manufacturers' Association, *Motor Truck Facts,* Detroit, annual.

Bureau of Railway Economics, *An Economic Survey of Motor Vehicle Transportation in the United States,* Washington, D. C., 1933.

Labutut, Jean, and Lane, Wheaton J., eds., *Highways in Our National Life: A Symposium,* Princeton, Princeton University, 1950.

National Resources Planning Board, *Transport and National Policy,* Part II, section III, *The Motor Transport Industry,* by C. S. Morgan, E. V. Breitenbach, and J. C. Riley, 1942.

United States Bureau of Agricultural Economics, *Transportation of Selected Agricultural Commodities to Leading Markets by Rail and Motortruck, 1939–1950,* by Ezekiel Limmer, 1951.

United States Board of Investigation and Research, *The National Traffic Pattern,* 79th C., 1st S., Sen. Doc. 83, 1945.

United States Board of Investigation and Research, *Comparison of Rail, Motor, and Water Carrier Costs,* 79th C., 1st S., Sen. Doc. 84, 1945.

United States Board of Investigation and Research, *Report on Technological Trends in Transportation,* 79th C., 1st S.; Sen. Doc. 76, 1945.

United States Department of Commerce, Bureau of Public Roads, *Highway Statistics,* annual.

United States Department of Commerce, Bureau of Public Roads, *Toll Roads and Free Roads,* 76th C., 1st S., House Doc. 272, 1939.

United States Department of Commerce, Office of Domestic Commerce, Transportation Division, Industry Report, Domestic Transportation, *An Evaluation of Motor Truck Transportation,* May–August, 1948.

United States Federal Trade Commission, *Report on Motor Vehicle Industry,* 76th C., 1st S., House Doc. 468, Ser. 10, 346, 1939.

United States Federal Works Agency, Public Roads Administration, *Highway Development, Administration, and Finance,* Part II of a discussion of highway practice in the United States, presented at the 45th annual meeting, American Road Builders' Association, Chicago, 1948.

United States Interstate Commerce Commission, 140 I.C.C. 685, *Motor Bus and Motor Truck Operation,* 1928; 182 I.C.C. 263, *Coordination of Motor Transportation,* 1932. (See also 72d C., 1st S., Sen. Doc. 43.)

United States, Office of the Federal Coordinator, *Freight Traffic Report,* 1935.

United States, Office of the Federal Coordinator, *Merchandise Traffic Report,* 1934.

United States, Office of the Federal Coordinator, *Public Aids to Transportation,* 1940.

CHAPTER 6

Air Transportation

Early History

Air transport is new transport, for it is only recently that men have learned to fly. Yet flight is a phenomenon which men have long observed, and the notion that, in some way or other, human beings might propel themselves through the air has provoked experiment during many hundreds of years. Roger Bacon in the thirteenth century wrote that "there may be made some flying instrument, so that a man sitting in the middle of the instrument and turning some mechanism may put in motion some artificial wings which may beat the air like a bird flying." And Leonardo da Vinci, about 1500, drew designs for gliders and for planes or helicopters, as we should term them now, to be actuated by manpower much as Bacon had imagined.

Balloons

The simplest flying instrument to construct is not the airplane but the balloon; and it was in the building of lighter-than-air craft that success in flying was first attained. The first balloons were floated by two Frenchmen, brothers named Montgolfier, during the last years of the eighteenth century. The bags were inflated with hot air; but this unsatisfactory support was soon replaced by gas, and a hydrogen-filled balloon actually crossed the English Channel in 1785. Vehicles of essentially the same character are still made today, and they are useful for certain purposes. But the fact that round balloons can be neither steered nor efficiently propelled makes them unsuitable for transport, and modern lighter-than-air machines differ greatly from those with which the Montgolfiers and their immediate successors were familiar.

Zeppelin Dirigibles

The type of balloon best suited for commercial use is the so-called "rigid dirigible" or "Zeppelin," which takes its name from a German nobleman, Count Zeppelin, who first launched such a ship in 1900, constructed after his own ideas. The peculiarity of a "Zeppelin" is its long, cylindrical hull, built of rigid horizontal girders braced by cross-bridges of metal work. The hull of a "Zeppelin" is covered by a skin, but lifting power is obtained from a number of smaller gas-inflated sacs or balloons introduced into compartments into which the hull is divided. Engines placed below the hull operate propellers that drive the apparatus forward, while fins and rudders direct its course. Vessels of this kind may be built to almost any desired size. The last large rigid airship, the *Hindenburg*, used in aerial commercial navigation was 813 feet long, 135 feet 2 inches in maximum diameter, and had a normal gas capacity of 6,710,000 cubic feet. Its cruising range at speeds of 78 miles per hour was 8,700 miles. The gas cells of the Hindenburg could support a weight of 471,800 pounds; most of this lifting power was necessarily utilized, however, to keep the vessel itself, with fuel and equipment, in the air, so that the net or pay load was only 42,000 pounds.[1]

Advantages and Disadvantages of Dirigible Airships

There is no question but that airships are to be credited with some remarkable achievements, both in regular commercial service and in exploratory flights. Thus, in 1917, the German *L 57* flew to East Africa and back, covering 4,200 miles in 96 hours. Two years later the British *R 34* flew to America in 108 hours, remained there four days, and then flew back to England in 75 hours. The total distance was 6,400 miles, and the elapsed time 183 hours. In 1924 the *Los Angeles* traveled from Friedrichshafen to Lakehurst, United States, in 80¾ hours. In 1926 the *Norge* flew with Amundsen over the North Pole. In 1929 the *Graf Zeppelin* circumnavigated the globe in 21 days.

But the safety record of the airship has been unsatisfactory, largely because lower speed and lesser weight per unit of volume make it more subject to accident from wind pressure than is the airplane, and also because the stresses to which airships are subject seem still to be incompletely understood. Modern airplanes, moreover, have been built with range and useful load capacity approximating that of the *Hindenburg* and with cruising speeds exceeding 300 miles per hour. Such planes can transport more freight between given points than can an airship in any stated period of time, and it is not clear that the operation will be more expensive. The large rigid dirigible does not appear, today, to possess transport advantages over the airplane which would justify its use. Its ability to remain suspended in the air, even when stationary, may, however, open opportunities for military, industrial, and scientific employment of some importance.

[1] *Aviation*, April, 1936, p. 15.

Figure 9. Airship "Hindenburg." (Wide World Photos, Inc.)

Gliders

Far more important than the airship is the modern airplane. The history of the airplane began with experiments in gliding. With properly designed apparatus it is possible to soar, as a bird soars, with outstretched wings, supported by air currents; or one may rely upon air resistance to convert an abrupt descent into a lengthened glide which permits the flyer to land safely at some distance from an elevated starting point. No power save that of the wind and gravitation is necessary for these feats. A glider is a plane without an engine, used to soar or to glide.[2] Achievements with light supporting surfaces have been extraordinary. Thus fliers have remained aloft 56 hours and 15 minutes consecutively; they have reached an altitude of 42,100 feet above the starting point; and they have traveled to a landing place 358 miles from the place of departure.[3] Such results cannot be counted upon, but they can be attained under favorable conditions, with a carefully learned technique. It is unlikely that gliders will be used for independent transport. It is possible, however, to launch gliders from an airship or airplane, and gliders can be towed by powered aircraft. It has been said that, with proper design, a plane can tow a gross load equal to its own gross weight at a loss of 25 percent of its commercial cruising speed. This would give a capacity of three times that which the tow plane alone could carry. Power plane units would also be more continuously in use, if gliders were attached, because they would not be immobilized while freight was being loaded or unloaded.[4]

History of Airplanes

The power driven airplane developed from the glider. The airplane is only a glider with an engine attached; yet the addition of power transformed the device from a model or toy into an instrument of carriage. This transformation could not occur until gliders had been constructed which were reasonably stable, and until engines were available which produced a large amount of power for each pound of weight. Both of these conditions were first satisfied toward the end of the nineteenth century; so that it was at this time that the real history of heavier-than-air flying began.

It is not certain who first designed a power plane, nor even who first operated one successfully. This is partly because national patriotism leads

[2] Perhaps the best known of the older gliding experiments were those of Otto Lilienthal who, between 1891 and 1896, accomplished glides as long as 800 feet from a starting point 100 feet above the ground. The record of these attempts later attracted the attention of the Wright brothers, and stimulated them in their efforts to produce a power-driven plane. Lilienthal was by no means the first, however, to use a glider.

[3] *Aircraft Year Book,* 1952, pp. 432–434.

[4] United States Transportation and Research Board, *Technological Trends in Transportation,* Washington, D. C., 79th C., 1st S., Sen. Doc. 76, 1945.

many different nations to claim priority for their inventors, and partly because first flights are brief and it is not always demonstrable that the planes which are referred to really left the ground.[5] In the United States, however, it is clear that two bicycle manufacturers, Wilbur and Orville Wright, were the first who designed and flew heavier-than-air machines with passengers considerable distances across country. The Wrights conducted a long series of experiments which culminated in short, successful flights in December, 1903. In 1908 they were able to produce a plane which could carry two men, aggregating 350 pounds in weight, for one hour continuously, maintaining an average speed of 40 miles an hour on a cross-country flight, to and fro, covering a distance of 10 miles. Wilbur Wright exhibited a similar machine in Europe in the same year. He found that other planes were being built and flown in Europe, but that his own model was, in many respects, superior. He gave exhibitions while abroad, instructed pupils in the art of flying, and sold several planes before his return to the United States.

Airplane history subsequent to 1908 may be divided into three periods. Between 1908 and 1914 there was development of the gasoline engine, but only slow progress in the airplane itself. These were the years when Curtiss, Blériot, Santos Dumont, Farman, and the Wrights attracted public attention by their flights. The World War, 1914–1918, caused effort to be concentrated upon high-speed military aircraft but prevented the extension of the commercial use of aviation. It was after 1918, and to a great extent after 1925, that the air transport industry was organized and the technical improvement of the airplane for purposes other than war occurred. It is this last period which we shall now discuss.

Statistics of Air Transport in the United States

We may measure the extent of the airplane industry in the United States by recording the number of operators, the number of planes used, the miles flown, the number of passengers carried, and the ton-miles of mail, express, and freight. Table 7, which presents this information,

[5] Early candidates for the honor of originating the airplane include W. S. Henson and J. Stringfellow. These were Englishmen who seem to have demonstrated, between 1847 and 1849, that a properly designed, power-propelled model could be made to fly (A. E. Berriman, *Aviation*, New York, Doubleday, 1913). They do not appear to have flown themselves. In France, in 1890, Clement Ader is reported to have flown 150 feet in a birdlike monoplane which he designed (A. F. Zahn, *Aerial Navigation*, New York, Appleton-Century-Crofts, 1911). In the United States, in 1896, S. P. Langley constructed a model airplane with a wing spread of 13 feet and a 5-pound boiler and launched it over the Potomac River, where it flew with entire success. A full-sized plane that Langley built in 1903 was injured in an attempt to launch it into the air. Some believe and some deny that the Langley plane would have flown properly if the launching difficulties could have been overcome. (See *New York Times*, September 30, 1928, for a statement by Dr. Abbott, Secretary of the Smithsonian Institution, in this controversy.)

TABLE 7.   Summary of Scheduled Air Carrier Operation (Domestic)

Year	Number of Operators	Planes in Service	Revenue Miles Flown (000)	Passengers Carried (000)	Mail Ton-Miles (000)	Express and Freight Ton-Miles (000)
1926	13	—	4,318	6	—	—
1930	43	—	32,645	385	—	—
1935	26	—	55,918	679	4,133	1,098
1940	19	—	110,101	2,803	10,118	3,476
1945	20	421	208,969	7,494	65,092	22,197
1952	35	1,078	458,563	25,019	69,333	160,820

SOURCE: United States Department of Commerce, Civil Aeronautics Administration, *Statistical Handbook of Civil Aviation,* 1953.

suggests several reflections. The first of these is that, in magnitude, air transport does not compare with any of the other branches with which we have to deal. Thirty-five operating companies, 1,078 planes, 25,019,000 passengers, and 160,820,000 ton-miles of express and freight hardly entitle the air transport industry to rank with the railroad, the motor vehicle, or the inland waterway. Nor has the increase in business during recent years, although striking in the last decade, been so great as to indicate that airplane carriage will soon equal, in accomplishment, the other forms of transport. Yet the air industry is already significant because it supplies a service which differs in quality from that afforded by any other means of transport. Our interest in it is, moreover, heightened by the belief that the limits of this special service are far from being reached.

Improvement in Airplane Equipment and Performance

Airplane equipment and performance have greatly improved in recent years. Among the major changes related to airplane structure and equipment is the increase in the load per unit of wing area in the airplane, making it possible to attain higher speeds and to carry greater payloads. Another advance has been in the design of engines which, along with better lubricants, higher octane fuels, and superior supercharging, has enlarged the delivery of power without proportionate increase in weight. For very high speeds and at high altitudes jet propulsion has been found efficient. A third change has been in the improvement of cowling around the airplane engine, to reduce air resistance. A fourth is related to the use of multiple-engined planes and to the growth in size of aircraft generally. Up to a certain point the operating costs of large aircraft for the same horse power appear to be less than for smaller planes per unit of revenue load because crews, ground help, the weight of instruments, and some other factors do not increase as fast as does revenue-producing capacity. Propellers with variable pitch, retractable landing gear, and flaps on airplane wings have increased efficiency while pressurized and air-conditioned cabins have permitted operations at high altitudes. There should be mentioned also developments in facilities exterior to the airplane. These include the use of radar and of radio and electronic techniques permitting blind landing and serving as a substitute for light beacons on the airways. Better and longer runways, better illumination at airports, and devices for fog dispersal are of obvious importance to air navigation.[6] Progress of these various sorts has decreased the costs per ton- and passenger-mile of airplane operation and have raised the standards of performance.

Modern planes can fly higher, they can remain longer in the air, and they are less subject to engine failure than were their predecessors. They can also fly faster. The record for an airplane flying with a useful load of 1,000 kilograms was 104.7 miles per hour in 1925, but it was already 325.7 miles per hour in 1938. The United Air Lines carried passengers from coast to coast, in 1927, in single-engine mail and passenger planes that required 33 hours to make the trip, stopping 14 times. In 1951 the same company sent four-engine Douglas planes across the continent, with one stop only, in 10 hours and 10 minutes.[7] These are examples chosen more or less at random. Progress has also been made in size of aircraft. In 1928 the Boeing Company was using single-motor biplanes between San Francisco and Chicago, capable of carrying 16,000 pounds pay load and equipped to accommodate two passengers. In 1951 the Trans World Airlines used, in part for the same service, Lockheed Constellations which could carry 57 passengers and, in addition, 6,000 pounds of cargo. Such changes have attracted public attention and have inspired confidence in the future of air carriage.

Air-Mail Transport

In describing the extent of traffic which aircraft have been able to command, it is desirable to separate mail traffic from other forms of business.

Air-mail carriage has been undertaken in most important American and European countries, and has improved maximum dispatch for long-

---

[6] United States Transportation and Research Board, *op. cit.*

[7] Special planes without commercial load can travel, of course, much faster than the speeds indicated in the text. Thus a Lockheed P-80 plane, early in 1946, flew the 2,470 miles from Long Beach, California, to La Guardia Field, New York, in 4 hours, 13 minutes, and 26 seconds. The average speed of this plane was 580.936 miles per hour and the altitude was, generally, between 35,000 and 41,000 feet (*Aircraft Year-book,* 1950, p. 450).

FIGURE 10. Stratocruiser over San Francisco Bay. (Courtesy of United Airlines.)

distance communications. Service began in the United States on May 15, 1918, when the Post Office Department established a line between New York and Washington, 218 miles. The distance was too short to permit of any substantial saving in time, and the service was discontinued. In 1919, this beginning was followed by the inauguration of service on sections of the transcontinental route, and on September 8, 1920, through service was attempted between New York and San Francisco. At first, flights were made only during the day, the mails being turned over to the railway mail service at night; but on July 1, 1924, a through day-and-night service was begun. After the beginning on air mail in 1918 the system expanded from 218 miles originally installed between New York and Washington to a total of 102,464 miles in 1947.

The amount of time which is saved by the use of air-mail transport depends upon the length of the route, the character of alternative means of transportation, and the schedules by which business operations are controlled. Thus air carriage may be unimportant on short hauls, or even on longer routes where rail service transports consignments during the hours between the close of one business day and the beginning of another; it will be more important on long hauls, such as those across the continent of the United States, and still more in transportation across the ocean or in regions where modern rail movements are not possible. Actually, present schedules between San Francisco and New York offer a saving of approximately 3½ days over the rail times, while airplanes reach the Philippines from San Francisco in 3 days as compared with the 20 days required by water. On the other hand, air service between Boston and New York offers slight advantage in time over rail service, and the original line between New York and Washington was, for a while, discontinued.

Air-Mail Rates

In the United States the postage rate for air mail service has varied. The first price was 24 cents an ounce, including special delivery. This was soon reduced to 16 cents and in 1919, when business still failed to respond, it was announced that letters would be carried by air without any additional charge, but that letters carrying the normal postage should be specially marked for air-mail service if it was desired that they should be sent by plane. In 1924, special airplane postage rates were again introduced, this time upon a zone basis at 8 cents, or later at 5 cents, per ounce. Since 1924 the rate for domestic air mail has repeatedly changed, being sometimes raised and sometimes lowered. In 1949 the rate of postage was 6 cents for each ounce or fraction thereof, on air-mail packages weighing 8 ounces or less, for first-class mail carried by air within the continental United States, including Alaska, and between continental United States and Hawaii, Puerto Rico, the Virgin Islands, Canton Island, the Canal Zone, and any other place where United States mail services were in operation. Six cents was also charged within or between the territories just named. Rates to and from foreign countries varied with the country involved. Legislation in 1948 provided, in addition, for parcel post air rates at a somewhat lower charge.[8]

Volume and Character of Air Mail

Under these various rates the weight of domestic air mail dispatched increased from 2,818 tons in 1928 to 9,777 tons in 1937 and to 85,431 tons in 1952. Mail ton-mileage, or tonnage multiplied by the average distance hauled, increased from 6,366,266 in 1937 to 68,714,690 in 1952.[9] Compared with the volume of mail carried by the railroads this tonnage is still small, although its importance is probably greater than the figures indicate. Railroad mails have not been weighed in this country since the adoption of the space system of railway mail payment, but in 1917 the tonnage was about 10,000 tons per day and the comparison of this figure with the 85,431 tons carried by air in the course of the year 1952 supplies a sufficiently violent contrast to make exact comparisons unnecessary.

As for the type of correspondence which is forwarded by air, the United States Post Office reports that the first air consignments were highly miscellaneous. They included thousands of souvenir post cards, candy, samples, flowers, live chicks, a suit of clothes that cost possibly fifteen dollars and carried eighteen dollars postage—in short, curiosity and publicity material. This traffic, however, rapidly declined, and in its place a more permanent business developed. Banking mail is now important. After the bankers in the line of patronage come the transportation and shipping people. The great steamship companies have much correspondence passing between the Atlantic and Pacific coasts, of which a portion goes by air. Import and export houses, manufacturing concerns doing nation-wide business, publishers, and advertising agencies are among the other users.

It is, of course, possible that further reductions in rates would increase and diversify the use of air mail, though it is not certain how large the increase would be. There have been a number of proposals for decrease in air postal charge; [10] the difficulty is that domestic air mail does not pay

[8] Current air-mail rates are given in the *United States Official Postal Guide*. The Act of 1948 (62 Stat. 1260, 1948) set up a schedule of air rates but authorized the Postmaster General to adjust rates at his discretion.

[9] See annual reports of the Postmaster General. The figures given in the text are for domestic air mail only. Poundage statistics (ton-mileage) have been separately supplied.

[10] It has been suggested that the Post Office Department might, as a matter of policy, ship all first-class mail by air, or at least all nonlocal first-class mail, without any extra charge at all (*Airports and Airlines,* February, 1932), and attention is called to the fact that some European countries carry air mail without surcharge (Parker Van

its way and that a reduction in postage would quite certainly increase the deficit that is incurred.

Air Express

If the amount of air mail is small, the same can be said of express and freight. This does not mean, of course, that these services may not become large in the course of time.

During the week beginning September 7, 1947, 56 percent of the revenue ton-mileage of express and freight handled by 13 large certificated carriers arose out of shipments of auto parts and accessories; agricultural and horticultural products (including cut flowers); apparel; textiles and dry goods; printed matter, including newspapers and magazines; machinery and machine parts; and electrical appliances and parts. Such items also as motion picture films, money, jewelry and other valuables, news photos, drugs, transcription records and radio parts, foods, furs, samples, and personal baggage are seen frequently in air express compartments of air liners.[11]

The first recorded air express transportation was in 1910. In 1919 an attempt was made to fly a full plane load of express from New York to Chicago, but because of adverse weather conditions the cargo was transferred to rail for the final portion of the trip. In September, 1927, the American Railway Express Company entered into contracts with all the airlines then prepared to carry express, and in March, 1929, these contracts were assumed by the Railway Express Agency and have since been renewed and enlarged upon.[12]

The Express Company, now the Railway Express Agency, is a corporation whose stock is owned by railroads. It assumes responsibility for pickup and delivery services, collects all shipping charges, arranges the routing, supervises transfers, and performs the accounting functions necessary to keep a record of business and to make proper allocation of costs and accurate distribution of funds among the various air lines. International service began on August 1, 1934. The express agency now handles air express on planes of domestic companies whose lines extend into Canada

---

Zandt, "3 Cents Air Mail?" *Aviation,* December, 1938). The Post Office Department has estimated an additional 146,000,000 ton-miles of domestic mail which movement by air would expedite. The Department believes that the institution of a policy of moving first-class mail by air whenever the postal service would benefit thereby would increase the volume of air mail by something over eight times in pounds and over five times in ton-miles (*Survival in the Air Age, A Report by the President's Air Policy Commission,* 1948, p. 104). A more moderate proposal is that air-mail postage rates be reduced from time to time until they become only one cent higher than the normal first-class letter rate.

[11] United States Civil Aeronautics Board, *Air Forwarder Case,* 1948.

[12] *Ibid.*

and Alaska; it has also concluded contracts with air lines to Central and South America, Europe, Africa, and Asia. From the revenue received from air express on domestic business, the agency deducts out-of-pocket expenses, many of which are enumerated in the contract, and the remainder is divided monthly—87½ percent to the air carrier, and 12½ percent to the Railway Express Agency. On plane-load shipments the agreements provide that the air carrier shall receive 85 percent of the gross revenue less insurance costs or actual losses suffered, and that the remainder of 15 percent shall go into the general fund for distribution on the 87½ percent—12½ percent basis. Air express agreements may be terminated by either party by the giving of 6 months' written notice. There is obviously, through this procedure, a high degree of coördination in air express service.[13]

Air Freight

The difference between air express and air freight is chiefly in the quality of service rendered. Freight cannot be distinguished from express by size or content of package nor, always, by the time of transit or character of planes used. It is true, however, that freight shipments ordinarily yield priority to air express. Deliveries between airport and city are less frequent, and services in pickup and delivery may be limited to business days and hours. Nor is the same effort made to expedite air freight in case of flight interruption.[14]

[13] Under present arrangements the rates for air express are set in tariffs filed by the Railway Express Agency with the Civil Aeronautics Board. Rates in these tariffs are determined, however, by air carriers operating through a traffic committee. The Civil Aeronautics Board has criticized this procedure on the ground that it requires the Railway Express Agency to incur costs but gives to the air carriers power to control revenues.

A copy of the Air Express Agreement, as of 1936, is printed in testimony submitted to Congress in 1943 (United States Senate, Committee on Interstate Commerce, 78th C., 1st S., Hearings on S. 942, pp. 16–25). This agreement has been changed in some respects since 1943; the document still describes, on the whole, the relations between the parties.

[14] The statements in the text understate the difficulty in distinguishing between air express and air freight. There was no distinction prior to 1944, when the American Airlines filed the first air freight tariff. Since that time definition has seemed to be necessary in order to determine the limits of the authority of the Railway Express Agency to transport cargo under its agreements with air carriers and the right of newly organized airlines which operate under certificates that permit them to carry property but not to handle express. The decisions of the Civil Aeronautics Board in these matters discuss terminology, but without much illumination. The real problem is that of distributing a total business among competing agencies. (See *Air Freight Case*, 10 C.A.B. 572, 1949; *Air Freight Forwarder Case*, 9 C.A.B. 473, 1948; Peter W. Wilson, "Air Freight and Air Express," *Law and Contemporary Problems*, Winter, 1950.

Mr. Patterson, of United Air Lines, has said that in his opinion, deferred air freight services have possibilities only where distances are great or where surface competition is poor. He regards the distinction between air freight and air express as artificial and

There was no segregation of air freight prior to July 1, 1945. Air freight, however, as distinguished from air express, has increased rapidly during the last few years.[15] The possible growth of the business is very great, depending upon relative rates and upon a balancing of air freight movements so that empty plane mileage can be cut down.[16] The Civil Aeronautics Board, indeed, has declared that the air potential is not less than a billion ton-miles annually. This assumes that the airlines will capture a substantial portion of the volume now moving by railway express at first-class rates for distances over 300 miles.[17]

Air Cargo

Most airlines carry both passengers and freight. Beginning in or about 1946 a group of new companies, some of which operated at first as contract carriers and others as nonscheduled carriers [18] undertook to carry freight alone, a practice referred to as "air cargo" operation.[19] These

---

likely to disappear (L. S. Lyon and L. C. Sorrell, *Prospects and Problems in Aviation,* Chicago, Chicago Association of Commerce, 1945, pp. 42–43).

[15] Express and freight ton-mileage since July 1, 1945, in domestic scheduled air carrier operation, has been as follows:

Year	Express Ton-Miles	Freight Ton-Miles
1945 (six months)	20,509,753	1,168,534
1946	23,788,392	14,822,325
1947	28,766,659	35,911,554
1948	30,092,833	71,283,727
1949	27,773,669	95,227,983
1952	41,317,560	119,502,241

SOURCE: United States Civil Aeronautics Board, *Statistical Handbook of Civil Aviation,* 1953.

[16] The difficulty in balancing flows has led the Civil Aeronautics Board to install what are called "directional" rates. A directional rate is a rate which is lower on shipments that move against the current of traffic than on shipments which move with the current. There is unused capacity in the former case that can be utilized at low cost. On this ground the Civil Aeronautics Board, in 1950, authorized air carriers to charge directional rates which were only 60 percent of the standard minima on described hauls over specified distances (Order Serial no. E-4048, Docket no. 1705, April 10, 1950). This authorization was changed to a direction in 1952. The 60 percent was not, however, prescribed.

[17] 10 C.A.B. 572, 1949. Air freight rates are lower than the charges on air express. Express rates to the public have averaged, until recently, about 61 cents per ton per mile as compared with an average of approximately 28 cents for air freight. During the period of competition for air freight which began in 1947, the certificated air carriers filed specific and all commodity rates on air freight which went as low as 13 cents and the noncertificated carriers made similar reductions. These last-mentioned rate levels were, however, too low, and they have since been increased. It has been difficult to estimate the cost of transporting air freight, because cargo is, most generally, carried in the same planes which accommodate passengers and express.

[18] See Chap. 33.

[19] Stephen Ailes, "The Position of the Freight Carrier Before the Civil Aeronautics Board," *Law and Contemporary Problems,* Winter, 1950.

companies were granted experimental authority to undertake scheduled operations on a common carrier basis in June, 1947.[20] In 1947 and 1948 they reported a ton-mileage of 45 million each year at a time when the certificated carriers accomplished first, 36 million, and second, 71 million ton-miles.[21] In 1950 their ton-mileage was somewhat less, or 38 million ton-miles out of a larger total. The reduction can probably be explained by the diversion of air cargo planes to the service of the Military Department. Most of the air cargo traffic is now handled by scheduled planes.

There is still debate concerning the relative economy of all-cargo and what are referred to as "combination" airplanes,[22] but the vigorous initiative of the air cargo operators and the fact that they do not ask for subsidies has made a considerable impression on the industry.[23]

Air Passenger Traffic

Although the volume of air mail is still moderate, and merchandise movements by air are insignificant in amount, examination of the figures reveals at least an impressive increase in the number of passengers carried in the United States. Statistics already given on page 103 show an increase in the number of air travelers carried by American lines from 6,000 in 1926 to 679,000 in 1935, and from 2,803,000 in 1940 to 25,019,742 in 1952.[24] Changes in the first of these periods can be explained by large additions to route mileage and to reductions in the average charge. Increase in air travel during the later years is more largely due to improve-

[20] 9 C.A.B. 344, 1948.

[21] C.A.B. Air Freight Case, Dockets nos. 810 and 731, Orders Serial E-3085, 1949.

[22] A combination plane is one which carries both passengers and freight.

[23] In 1942 several of the larger airlines organized a joint research project to survey air cargo possibilities (John H. Frederick, *Commercial Air Transportation*, Chicago, Irwin, 1946, p. 565). In 1947 the Civil Aeronautics Board approved an agreement between 17 certified air carriers providing for the establishment and operation of *Air Cargo, Inc.*, a corporation which had for its primary purpose the consolidation of existing ground facilities at the major airports for the handling of air freight by member air carriers (C.A.B. Orders Serial no. E-1086, 1947). Air Cargo arranged pick-up and delivery contracts for the airlines which, by 1949, covered about 200 cities. It also operated a freight terminal at Detroit on a consolidated basis (United States Senate, Committee on Interstate and Foreign Commerce, *Air-Line Industry Investigation*, Hearings pursuant to S. Res. 50, 81st C., 1st S., 1950). The Board made it clear, then and later, that any air carrier which held an operating certificate should be allowed to participate in Air Cargo, Inc., as a matter of right (9 C.A.B. 468, 1950). In 1950 there were 19 members of Air Cargo, of which 4 were local service lines (*Traffic World*, April 22, 1950).

[24] The staff of the Civil Aeronautics Administration expects a volume of 40,000,000 air passengers in 1960. (See Wilfred Carsel, Chief Research and Analysis Branch, and Jesse Sternberger, Transportation Economist, Office of Airports, Civil Aeronautics Administration, *The Boom in Airline Passenger Traffic*, published by the University of Illinois, Bureau of Economic and Business Research, 1952. See also United States Civil Aeronautics Administration, *Airline Passengers*, December, 1951. This last study explains the methods which the Civil Aeronautics Administration uses in estimating future volume.)

ments in the quality of air service, to the cumulative effect of vigorous advertising, and to a general recognition by the community that air flight is a usable, though somewhat expensive method of traveling from one location to another.

More recently experiments have been made with coach service in order to attract customers who will be satisfied with less luxurious transport at lower rates.[25] The first experiment was made by the Capital Airlines, in 1948, between New York and Chicago. Other companies, at first, hesitated to follow, but experiments multiplied in and after 1949.[26] In 1950, air coach service accounted for about 13 percent of the total passenger-miles flown in all domestic airline operations during the year.[27] A good deal of business has been diverted from the railroads,[28] and some from the regular air-line service, a fact which the Civil Aeronautics Board has noted with some concern.[29] Profitability from the carriers' point of view will depend upon the load factor which air coaches can secure.

Comparative Rates by Air and Rail

No schedules of passenger rates will long remain unchanged. Table 8, however, compares the cost of rail and standard airplane passenger transportation upon a few selected routes in the United States in October, 1951. The air lane first-class fares listed in Table 8 are, in most cases, close to 6 cents per mile. They are in all cases higher than the rail fares between the same points of origin and destination, although the difference generally disappears if one compares the cost of air travel with that of the highest-class service which the railroads offer. Thus the expense of the rail journey from New York to Chicago was $40.89 for the rail haul alone, in October, 1951. This was $3.21 less than the cost by air; but if we add to the rail rate $12.50 for a roomette and $5.00 for accommodation in an extra-fare train, the rail expense became $58.39,

---

[25] United States Senate, Committee on Interstate and Foreign Commerce, *Air-Line Industry Investigation, op. cit.,* testimony Carmichael, pp. 715–717; Fischgrund, pp. 277, 281, 935–936; Ramspeck, p. 384; Hellman, p. 942–949. Actually, the prices charged are less, in many cases, than the railroad coach rate (*Railway Progress,* August, 1950).

[26] See United States Civil Aeronautics Board, *Annual Report,* 1950, pp. 26–27.

[27] United States Civil Aeronautics Board, *Statistical Handbook of Civil Aviation,* 1950, p. 50.

[28] There is the usual discussion with respect to the nature of air coach traffic. Some limited inquiries suggest that something like a third of coach passengers would have traveled by regular fare airplanes if coach service had not been available in 1949, another third would have gone by railroad, and a quarter would not have traveled at all. (See *Aviation Week,* January 9, 1950; *Railway Progress,* August, 1950.)

[29] When the Civil Aeronautics Board approved Capital's air coach service it set up four conditions: (1) Air coaches must operate between major cities with a heavy traffic flow. (2) The planes must have more seats than are generally used on such equipment. (3) Flights must be conducted at off-hours. (4) All extra services must be eliminated (*Railway Progress, op. cit.*).

TABLE 8.   Comparative Fares by Air and Rail, October, 1951

| Point of Origin | Point of Destina- tion | Rail | | | | Air | Air Mile- age | Rate per Mile |
		First Class	Pull- man *a*	Extra Fare	Total Rail			
		(dol- lars)	(dol- lars)	(dol- lars)	(dol- lars)	(dol- lars)		(cents)
Cleveland	Nashville	22.17	9.65	—	31.82	28.95	469	6.0
Columbus	St. Louis	19.29	6.60	—	25.89	28.78	397	7.2
Wash- ington	Cincinnati	24.91	8.20	—	33.11	25.50	423	6.0
St. Louis	Cincinnati	15.54	5.60	—	21.14	19.90	310	6.4
Chicago	New Orleans	32.90	12.50	—	45.40	54.65	892	6.1
Chicago	Miami	50.87	20.25	—	71.12	78.80	1267	6.2
San Fran- cisco	Los An- geles	16.57	6.60	—	23.17	21.05	348	6.0
San Fran- cisco	Seattle	32.37	13.90	—	46.27	42.50	699	6.1
New York	Chicago	40.89	12.50	5.00	58.39	44.10	719	6.1
New York	San Fran- cisco	109.28	40.50	15.00	164.78	157.85	2654	5.9

a Pullman fares include cost of "roomette" when available—otherwise lower berth.

which was $14.29 more than was charged by air. It is also to be remembered that air fares sometimes include meals and that taxi service to the airport is sometimes provided. On the other hand, the absorption of taxi fares by the air line is not a real saving when passengers are forced to use taxis because of the remote location of the airport. Moreover, while rail Pullman accommodation is expensive, passengers must sleep somewhere, and hotel rooms will be paid for unless a round trip is completed in a single day. Airplanes, finally, usually limit the baggage carried free to 40 pounds per passenger, while rail carriers generally haul 150 pounds without extra charge. These irregularities make it difficult to generalize with respect to the comparative costs of rail and airplane journey. It is probably still true that the cost of first-class airplane travel is so great as to restrict it to persons of more than comfortable circumstances or to cases where the money value of the time saved can be calculated with some precision. Opinions differ among air operators as to how far this condition can be changed. If companies can obtain sufficient traffic from a wealthy or a business public, the present first-class fares may prove profitable; but it is likely that still more must be done in the future than has been done in the past to lower the cost of air transport if air service for passengers is to become a major facility in the United States.

Intercontinental Flights

Among the more spectacular developments in passenger service should be counted the opening of routes between the United States and Central and South America; the establishment of routes across the Pacific Ocean; and the organization of travel across the Atlantic.

Central and South America

Passengers were carried by air between Key West and Havana as early as 1920. Regular service between these points was undertaken by Pan American Airways in 1927, and by the end of 1951 this company had extended its operations to Mexico City, to the Canal Zone, down the west coast of South America to Chilean ports, across the Andes to the Argentine, and back along the east coast of Brazil to the Caribbean.[30] The achievement was extraordinary because of the distances covered, the number of governments from which franchises and contracts had to be obtained, and the investment in airports, lighting, weather service, and other requirements for successful flying which the company had itself to provide. Other lines, of course, now serve most segments of this route.

Transpacific Aviation

Transpacific commercial aviation began in 1936 when the Pan American Airways undertook to carry passengers regularly between Alameda, California, and Canton, China, a distance of 8,678 miles. The opening of this route was the result of nearly 6 years of preparation, including experimental flights during the last 19 months. The first crossing from San Francisco to Honolulu was made by a Pan American clipper, April 16–17, 1935; and between this time and October 21, 1936, when the passenger service started, there were no less than 51 crossings on the San Francisco-Honolulu route and 23 round trips between California and the Philippines. Mail transport began in November, 1935; express in February, 1936; and passengers were accepted in October, 1936. Planes now reach Honolulu in less than 10 hours and Hong Kong in 2 days and 14 hours flying time, touching at the Wake Island group, Guam, and Manila. It has been pointed out that the shortest line from San Francisco to Hong Kong or Shanghai is by way of Fairbanks, Alaska and Harbin or Vladivostok, Manchuria,[31] following a "great circle"; but this would avoid Hawaii and the Philippine Islands, and there would be political difficulties to overcome. The first ships used were four-motored clippers designed to

[30] See "Pan American Airways," *Fortune*, April, 1936.

[31] J. Parker Van Zandt, *The Geography of World Air Transport*, Washington, D. C., Brookings Institution, 1944.

carry 18 passengers, a crew of 7, and mail and baggage. The present planes are so-called "Strato" clippers—airplanes which carry 56 passengers [32] and a crew of 7. Clippers cruise at altitudes between 11,000 and 21,000 feet. Speed varies with height and with the wind; the average annual cruising speed is 255 miles per hour.

Transatlantic Aviation

Transatlantic air connections by heavier-than-air craft are more recent than those across the Pacific, but they have passed through the stages of adventurous pioneer flights, careful exploration of the possibilities of commercial service, and actual commencement of operations. Transatlantic flying appeals to a larger market than transpacific, but it has serious climatic obstacles to overcome. This is principally because the cold water and air masses from the Labrador Stream meet and merge with the warm waters and air masses of the Gulf Stream southeast of the Newfoundland bank, and give rise in these latitudes to storms of unusual frequency and intensity.[33]

EXTREME NORTHERN ROUTE.   There are, it is true, several ways of avoiding the weather handicaps associated with the route which follows the present steamship lines. One method is to fly far to the north. Such a northern line might conceivably pass by way of Halifax, Nova Scotia, St. John's, Newfoundland, and Valencia, Ireland; or it might lie still farther north and pass through Greenland, Iceland, and the Faroe and Orkney islands. A route through Iceland to Norway and Sweden is, actually, operated by the Pan American Airways. The mileages by these northern routes are less than by the southern and the distances between landing places are relatively short. There is also less fog, and there is some reason to believe that storm hazards may be reduced. On the other hand temperatures in the far north are low and failure of equipment would lead to irreparable disaster.[34]

STRATOSPHERE FLYING.   It may be possible to avoid the climatic difficulties of the North Atlantic area by going high into the air. This, at least, is the assumption of those who are interested in what is known as "stratosphere flying." By the term *stratosphere* is meant that portion of the earth's surrounding atmosphere which lies at altitudes above 35,000

[32] The accommodation is for 61 passengers in day flights and 56 passengers in night flights between California and Hawaii. For flights west of Hawaii, 47 passengers are accommodated.

[33] Col. J. Monroe Johnson, "Transoceanic Flying," *Air Commerce Bulletin,* April 13, 1938, pp. 235–239.

[34] Reference to a globe will show that short-line distances from many points in the United States to destinations in eastern Europe are by routes which pass close to the North Pole. The polar route has not yet attracted commercial flyers; we are advised, however, by military authorities that aerial attacks by Russia, if they should occur, would come by such a path.

feet. The characteristics of this area have been to some extent explored by specially prepared balloons, and by instruments of various sorts. It is known to be intensely cold, and the air at high altitudes is too rarefied to support life. Passenger planes which fly at great heights, even though they may not reach the stratosphere itself, require specially built cabins to maintain constant temperature and air pressure, and they have to overcome technical difficulties in navigation not encountered at lower elevations; but they can travel at higher speeds and they may, perhaps, meet with less wind interference. It still is uncertain what air conditions prevail at the high levels of the air, and extremely high velocities may exist. Captain Stevens, who took part in the stratosphere flights in 1934 and 1936 sponsored by the *National Geographic Magazine* and the United States Army Air Corps, thinks that winds may be encountered at great altitudes. Other observations, however, indicate that storms which aviators fear may fade out in the upper levels. Experimental flying at heights above 20,000 feet has shown storms with tops as high as 30,000 or 35,000 feet, but most disturbances of any size are reported to be at considerably lower levels. While severe weather conditions involving a good deal of turbulence and heavy icing may be found all the way up to the base of the stratosphere, the probabilities are that a plane crossing the ocean at 25,000 feet could avoid most of them by inconsiderable detours.[35]

Transatlantic Air Service

German planes, in 1938, were making regular though still experimental trips between the Azores and Port Washington, Long Island. Meanwhile the Pan American was conducting trial flights between the United States and Europe by way of the Azores, Lisbon, Marseilles, and Southampton, and English aircraft were developing the possibilities of the direct route between New York and Ireland by way of Montreal. The initial schedule provided for a service of 22 hours elapsed time to Lisbon. In August, 1952, Pan American planes were leaving New York daily and were arriving at London by way of Newfoundland and Ireland about 14 hours later. The same route was followed by planes of the Trans World Airlines and by those of several foreign lines. Pan American planes also left New York for Lisbon four times a week by way of the Azores, with an additional service to Dakar.

International Agreements

Transoceanic flying as well, indeed, as international air transport generally, requires agreement between nations for the admission of foreign planes. Actually, a number of agreements are in force. Thus, by compact

[35] D. W. Tomlinson, "On Top," *Aviation*, December, 1936.

with the United Kingdom, American planes may use the facilities of airports and may pick up and deliver passengers and cargo at London, Prestwick, Hong Kong, Singapore, Bermuda, and on the Gold Coast and in Nigeria. Similar privileges are given English planes at New York, Chicago, Detroit, Miami, San Francisco, and five other cities.[36] Compacts with other countries have opened a number of additional foreign termini to American aircraft, including Paris, Marseilles, and French possessions in Africa, the West Indies, and the Far East; Lisbon, Copenhagen, Barcelona, Geneva, Cairo, Athens, Bombay, Sydney and Melbourne, and various other places. Typically, such arrangements grant the right to receive and deliver traffic to and from the contracting parties at designated points. They also permit transit along routes which the contracting countries reserve the right to describe, and they provide for the recognition by one nation of licenses and certificates of airworthiness issued by the other. Appropriate local laws relating to entry, clearance, immigration, customs, and quarantine must be complied with. Sometimes, as in the United Kingdom, there are paragraphs relating to the rates which will be charged and to other matters.

In December, 1944, at Chicago, representatives of a number of countries signed an International Air Transport Agreement, according to which each contracting state would grant to other contracting states the following freedoms of the air in respect to scheduled international air services:

1. The privilege to fly across its territory without landing.
2. The privilege to land for nontraffic purposes.
3. The privilege to put down passengers, mail, and cargo taken on in the territory of the state whose nationality the aircraft possessed.
4. The privilege to take on passengers, mail, and cargo destined for the territory of the state whose nationality the aircraft possessed.
5. The privilege to take on passengers, mail, and cargo destined for the territory of any other contracting state and the privilege to put down passengers, mail, and cargo coming from any such territory.

The agreement also provided that each contracting state might specify routes and landing places for foreign planes within its jurisdiction.

The Chicago agreement was ratified by some of the signatories, but not by all. The United States was one of the countries which accepted the Air Transport Agreement but, in 1946, it gave notice of denunciation, effective July 25, 1947. Our relations with foreign countries depend, therefore, with respect to international air transport, upon bilateral understandings. It would seem that the first four of the five freedoms mentioned in the Chicago agreement are essential to any large international

[36] 60 Stat. 1499, 1946.

air traffic. The fifth freedom would make for freer international exchange, but it encounters determined opposition from national and local groups.

Advantages of Air Service

It is perhaps now desirable to summarize the advantages and disadvantages of the airplane for commercial use as compared with older forms of transportation.

The first and by far the greatest advantage of aircraft is speed. Commercial airplanes readily attain speed of 200 miles per hour, whereas railroad trains rarely exceed 60 miles per hour and steamships 25 miles per hour. As against this, it is to be recalled that aircraft termini cannot be located in the center of cities, so that a considerable delay must be allowed for at each end of a trip for transporting freight or passengers between landing stations and city destinations. Terminal delays may be reduced by organization, but they are always of some importance.

In addition to its speed, the airplane shares with the auto bus the advantage of being able to render frequent service. Comparing the train with the airplane, the train as a traffic unit is large. There must, therefore, be wider intervals of delay for the accumulation of loads between successive shipments than in the case of the airplane. The airplane is a small unit, and a flow of urgent traffic can be accommodated by a constant succession of departures from the airdrome, with consequent time economy.

Finally, the airplane enjoys a great financial advantage in being spared the expense of a track. The expenses standing in lieu thereof are less, viz., the cost of landing grounds, wireless installations, radar, weather reporting services, and marking, lighting, and signaling of routes, especially at night or in fog.

The advantages of air transport which have just been enumerated will be realized to an increasing degree as new types of equipment, new methods of air navigation, and more skilled and experienced business managements develop. It has been properly remarked that the industry is dynamic and that its possibilities cannot easily be foretold.[37]

Disadvantages of Air Service

The fundamental disadvantage of the airplane is that it is a poor weight carrier. To secure high speed or long range the commercial load must be kept low. It follows that the investment in equipment per ton- or passenger-mile is great. The expense is further increased because airplanes require great strength and power combined with extreme lightness, and their useful life is short. The fuel cost of air service is greater than the fuel cost per railway passenger car mile, due presumably to the greater power employed; the wages paid air crews are also higher, on the average,

[37] I. R. Barnes, "The Economic Role of Air Transportation," *Law and Contemporary Problems,* Winter-Spring, 1946.

than the sums which railroads pay to engine and train crews, and the number of employees per unit of passenger and freight capacity is relatively large. From the point of view of the passenger, noise, restricted space, and the possibility of air sickness reduce the comfort of air service. On short hauls, the gain in transfer speed is slight.[38]

RELIABILITY. More serious than temporary discomfort to the passenger are the questions of reliability and safety. Up to the present time, air service is still inferior to rail in these respects. The Civil Aeronautics Board has announced that the percentage of trips started in domestic service which were actually completed was 95.48 during 1943 and 94.98 during the calendar year 1944. There has been no great variation in this percentage during the past eight or nine years. This degree of reliability would not be considered satisfactory in railroad service, although it represents a considerable achievement by air. And if we compare the number of air trips completed with those scheduled instead of with those commenced the percentage of performance becomes still less. Nor can too great stress be laid upon rapid improvement in the regularity of air transport because the lives of pilots in all cases and those of passengers in many are involved. A railroad train cannot deviate from its prescribed route, and it can stop without disaster except in the rare cases in which the roadbed is washed away; but a plane can be blown off its course, and sudden cessation of forward movement will cause it to be destroyed. Air operators must consider weather conditions with respect, and for a long time to come transportation through the air would be less reliable than transportation over the ground.

SAFETY. In order to be popular, air service must be safe. "You have an engine which makes lots of noise," says the potential customer. "You go up in the air, and you may be killed." Air carriers, on the other hand, deny that, with proper precaution, air transportation presents unusual risks; and they point to the small number of serious accidents in air travel during recent years as evidence of the truth of their assertion.

There were 35 passengers killed in scheduled domestic air transport in the United States in the year 1940. In 1944 the number was 48, after a considerable increase in business. In 1948 it was 83, and in 1951 it was 142. These figures do not include accidents in pleasure flying, crop dusting, photographing, instructing, and in other types of aeronautical work,

---

[38] W. A. Patterson, President, United Air Lines, said in 1945 that the airplane could claim no material speed advantage over the private intercity bus or train for trips under 100 miles (L. S. Lyons and L. C. Sorrell, *Prospects and Problems in Aviation,* Chicago, Chicago Association of Commerce, 1945).

Bonavia adds that the "distributive capacity" of the airplane is small. He means by this that the air line operates only a single unit, the plane, while the railroad uses trains upon the road but breaks up the trains into units of single cars at termini for distribution of shipments among consignees. In this the air line resembles the shipping company. The motor operator comes in between (Michael R. Bonavia, *The Economics of Transport,* New York, Pitman, 1947).

in which casualties were more numerous, but only loss of life of regularly operated common carrier routes. Ninety-six deaths in the carriage of 17,347,000 passengers, as in 1950, is a better record than we had a few years ago. With a reported death rate of 1.1 deaths per 100 million passenger miles it means that a passenger might have expected, beginning in 1950, to travel approximately 91 million miles by airplane on scheduled routes before he was killed. At a steady speed of 200 miles per hour he could accomplish such a trip in 19,042 days, or in approximately 52 years; but this is more time than most people expect to spend in airplane travel in the course of their natural lifes.

How the record of accidents in air transport compares with the experience of other carriers is difficult to say because available data are not in all respects comparable. The National Safety Council published in its report for 1951, however, a comparison of the number of deaths in air travel with the deaths in other forms of transport. The Council's figures are reproduced in Table 9. The figures compiled by the National Safety

TABLE 9.   Comparison of Accidents in Land Travel, 1951

Agency of Transportation	Passenger Miles (000,000)	Passenger Fatalities	
		Deaths	Death Rate per 100 Million Miles
Passenger automobiles and taxis	860,000	21,000	2.4
Buses	60,000	130	0.22
Railroad passenger trains	34,660	150	0.43
Scheduled air transport companies	10,950	142	1.3

SOURCE: National Safety Council, *Accident Facts*, 1952, p. 77.

Council show that the accident record of the scheduled airplane carriers was, in 1951, unfavorable as compared with that of bus lines and of railroads, but favorable as compared with that of private passenger automobiles, with respect to fatal accidents. The differences are marked, although it should be said that travelers by rail or bus have less advantage over travelers by air with regard to fatal than with respect to nonfatal injuries. An aircraft mishap is generally serious, whereas the passenger on a railroad or on a bus is likely to escape alive when an accident occurs. It is also true, as we have said, that the gross risk is slight; and examination of the data for a series of years will show that fatal airplane accidents have become less frequent.

Causes of Accidents

Some information is available as to causes of airplane accidents, although less than we should like. Thus the Civil Aeronautics Board reports that, in 1950, there were no accidents in scheduled air carrier operation that were attributable to airport terrain. On the other hand, 10 percent of the accidents were chargeable to weather, 10 percent to power plant, and 23 percent to pilot error. The balance was due to other causes, or the reasons had not been determined.

Many of the causes which have produced accidents in the past can be and are being slowly eliminated. Attention to design and quality of material, together with better knowledge of the stresses to which planes are subject, will lessen the number of airplane failures. Better weather reporting systems, better lighting of airways, and the increased use of instruments which permit operators to fly "blind" and to land under conditions of low visibility will reduce the number of casualties due to weather. The problem of controlling failures due to personnel is more difficult, although insurance companies have made some interesting studies of this subject and have published conclusions that may prove helpful.[39] The encouraging fact is that progress toward safety is being made, although the need for further improvement is too clear to be overlooked.

REFERENCES

General Treatises

Fair, Marvin L., and Williams, Ernest W., *Economics of Transportation,* New York, Harper, 1950.
Frederick, John H., *Airport Management,* Chicago, Irwin, 1949.

[39] Age of pilots, according to the Committee on Aviation of the Actuarial Society of America, does not seem to be a significant factor in airplane accident experience. Physical defects may, of course, be important, but the Department of Commerce formerly granted licenses to pilots with slight defects, and the mortality of pilots with defects which the Department waived was no greater than that among pilots who had no defects which required a waiver. Practice in flying helps to prevent accidents, at least until an experience of 400 or 500 hours in the air has been obtained. Further experience does not seem to decrease mortality rates much—indeed, the mortality rate among pilots with an experience of 2000 hours or more is relatively high, perhaps because they undertake more than usually difficult assignments. Pilots who have had one accident are more likely to have another than are pilots with a clear record to have their first mishap. One might expect that a slight mishap would teach the necessity of care, so that a pilot who had escaped would be less likely to suffer accident than one who had not just missed serious injury or death. The fact seems to be that the first accident is apt to be caused by faults of inattention or of judgment which persist. While individual pilots may maintain a perfect record after a single crash, any large group composed of pilots who have at some time come to grief will possess accident-producing characteristics which are not present in the same degree in a group of the same size composed of pilots who have never had an accident (Actuarial Society of America, "Report of the Committee on Aviation," *Transactions,* 1936, p. 228; 1940, p. 264).

Frederick, John H., *Commercial Air Transportation,* Chicago, Irwin, 1951.

Johnson, Emory R., *Transport Facilities, Services and Policies,* New York, Appleton-Century-Crofts, 1947.

Locklin, D. Phillip, *Economics of Transportation,* Chicago, Irwin, 1947.

Puffer, Claude E., *Air Transportation,* Philadelphia, Blakiston, 1941.

Smith, Henry Ladd, *Airways: The History of Commercial Aviation in the United States,* New York, Knopf, 1942.

Smith, Henry Ladd, *Airways Abroad: The Story of American World Air Routes,* Madison, Wis., University of Wisconsin, 1950.

Westmeyer, Russell E., *Economics of Transportation,* New York, Prentice-Hall, 1952.

Wilson, G. L., and Bryan, L. A., *Air Transportation,* New York, Prentice-Hall, 1949.

Wolfe, T., *Air Transportation—Traffic and Management,* New York, McGraw-Hill, 1950.

Other Books

Allen, Hugh, *The Story of the Airship,* Chicago, R. R. Donnelley, 1943.

Allen, Hugh, *The Story of the Airship (Non-Rigid),* Chicago, R. R. Donnelley, 1942.

Cunningham, William Glenn, *The Aircraft Industry: A Study in Industrial Location,* Los Angeles, Lorrin L. Morrison, 1951.

Dollfus, Charles, *Histoire de l'Aéronautique: Texte et Documentation de Charles Dollfus et Henri Bouché,* Paris, L'Illustration, 1932.

Gill, Frederick W., and Bates, Gilbert L., *Airline Competition: A Study of the Effects of Competition on the Quality and Price of Airline Service and the Self Sufficiency of the United States Domestic Airlines.* Boston, Division of Research, Graduate School of Business Administration, Harvard, 1949.

Janes, *All the World's Aircraft,* London, Sampson, Low, Marston, annual.

Langley, S. P., *Researches and Experiments in Aerial Navigation,* Washington, D. C., Government Printing Office, 1908.

Leyson, Captain Burr W., *Wings Around the World,* New York, Dutton, 1948.

Lilienthal, Anna Rothe, and Lilienthal, Gustav, *Die Lilienthals,* Stuttgart und Berlin, Cotta, 1930.

Lyon, L. S., and Sorrell, L. C., *Prospects and Problems in Aviation,* Chicago, Chicago Association of Commerce, 1945.

Ogburn, William, *The Social Effects of Aviation,* Boston, Houghton Mifflin, 1946.

Wright, Wilbur, and Wright, Orville, *Miracle at Kitty Hawk: The Letters of Wilbur and Orville Wright,* edited by Fred C. Kelly, New York, Farrar, 1951.

Periodicals

Ailes, Stephen, "The Position of the Freight Carrier Before the Civil Aeronautics Board," *Law and Contemporary Problems,* Winter-Spring, 1950.

Barnes, Irston R., "The Economic Role of Air Transportation," *Law and Contemporary Problems,* Winter-Spring, 1946.

Bryan, Otis F., "Technological Developments in Air Transport," *Social Science,* October, 1945.

Drew, J. L., and Passen, A., "Air Cargo: A New Force in Marketing," *Journal of Air Law and Commerce,* Winter, 1947.

Frederick, John H., and Hudson, William J., "Sources of Feeder Airline Business," *Journal of Air Law and Commerce,* April, July, October, 1942.

Hinton, W., "First Transatlantic Flight," *Annals of the American Academy,* May, 1927.

Isard, W., and Isard, C., "Economic Implications of Aircraft," *Quarterly Journal of Economics,* February, 1945.

Neal, George C., "The Status of Non-Scheduled Operations Under the Civil Aeronautics Act of 1938," *Law and Contemporary Problems,* Winter-Spring, 1948.

Nicholson, Joseph L., "Possibilities for Lower Airline Costs," *Law and Contemporary Problems,* Winter-Spring, 1946.

Stevens, Captain Albert W., "Exploring the Stratosphere," *National Geographic Magazine,* October, 1934.

Stevens, Captain Albert W., "The Scientific Results of the World-Record Stratosphere Flight," *National Geographic Magazine,* May, 1936. (See also note in *National Geographic Magazine,* October, 1935.)

Special and Miscellaneous

Actuarial Society of America, *Transactions, Reports of Committee on Aviation.*

Aeronautical Chamber of Commerce of America, *Aircraft Yearbook,* New York, annual.

United States Civil Aeronautics Administration, *Economic Aspects of America's Air Navigation Program,* Washington, D. C., Supt. of Docs., 1949.

United States Congress, Joint Committee to Investigate Dirigible Disasters, *Hearings . . . Pursuant to House Con. Res. 15,* 73d C., 1st S., Ser. 9748, 1933.

United States Department of Commerce, Bureau of Foreign and Domestic Commerce, Industry Report, Domestic Transportation, *Postwar Service Standards in Air Passenger Transportation,* August-September, 1946, prepared by Melville A. Brenner.

United States Department of Commerce, Bureau of Foreign and Domestic Commerce, *National Air Cargo Survey,* prepared by James C. Nelson.

United States Federal Aviation Commission, *Report,* 74th C., 1st S., Sen. Doc. 15, January, 1935.

United States, President's Air Policy Commission, *Survival in the Air Age: A Report,* Washington, D. C., Government Printing Office, 1948.

Warner, E. P., *The Early History of Air Transportation,* James Jackson Cabot Professorship Lecture, Northfield, Vt., Norwich University, 1937.

Warner, E. P., *Technical Development and Its Effect on Air Transportation,* James Jackson Cabot Professorship Lecture, Northfield, Vt., Norwich University, 1938.

Part

III

Transportation Geography

The Great Lakes

The magnitude of the transportation machinery provided for a nation like the United States seems calculated to accommodate a population and a volume of raw materials and finished goods in almost daily motion. It is difficult, of course, to analyze this movement, for the reason that neither

FIGURE 11.   Relief Map of the United States.

passengers nor goods are stopped and counted in the course of transit within the country as they would be if they crossed national boundaries and became subject to customs regulations. There is difficulty also in segregating the local or gathering and distributing movements of commodities from the currents of traffic which flow, ofter for long distances, between sources of supply and consuming markets. These handicaps make an exact statement of the flow of inland traffic impossible, but they do not prevent a reasonable approximation that will indicate in a general way the nature of the transportation which occurs.

Recapitulation of the Volume of Freight Traffic of the United States

We have already [1] estimated the annual freight movements in the United States in 1952 as follows:

	Ton-Miles (billions)
Railroads	623.5
Inland waterways	170.0
Pipe lines	157.5
Intercity trucks	184.1
Airways	.4
Total	1135.5

The Interstate Commerce Commission does not distinguish between different forms of inland waterways in transmitting the above information, but the United States Army Engineers assign 119.9 billion ton-miles to the Great Lakes and 36.7 billion to the Mississippi River.[2]

Commodities Handled

The commodities carried by the various means of transportation mentioned in the table may be described as follows:

1. *Railroads.* Common observation suggests that the variety of products carried by the railroad system of the United States is so great as to defy summarization. This is not, however, the fact, as statistics published by the Interstate Commerce Commission show that most railroad tonnage consists of comparatively few classes of articles. The commodities carried by Class I railroads in the United States [3] are grouped in Table 10.

Nearly 70 per cent of the entire tonnage originating on railroads of the United States in 1951 consisted of coal, iron and steel, clay, gravel and stone, grain, lumber, petroleum and products, fertilizers, and cement. If we add fruits, paper, automobiles, ores other than iron ores, and canned goods, the proportion was nearly 76 per cent. More than one fifth of the balance of carload tonnage was provided by brick, cotton, sugar, and livestock. Miscellaneous parcel freight, which represents the greatest variety

[1] See p. 9.

[2] United States Army, *Annual Report of the Chief of Engineers,* Part II, *Commercial Statistics,* 1951, p. xviii.

[3] The Interstate Commerce Commission divides the railroads which report to it into classes according to volume of earnings. Class I includes all railroads with gross earnings of $1,000,000 a year or more.

TABLE 10. Revenue Freight Originated on Class I Railroads of the
United States During the Year Ending December 31, 1951

Article	Tonnage	
Coal	439,470,666	
Iron, iron ore, and steel	154,356,980	
Clay, gravel, and stone	139,242,629	
Grain, flour, and meal	84,801,677	
Lumber, logs, ties, pulpwood	74,542,566	
Petroleum and products	46,889,745	
Fertilizers	46,249,166	
Cement and asphalt	36,433,641	
Total		1,021,987,070
Fruit, including citrus, and vegetables	27,909,717	
Paper and paper board	29,067,334	
Automobiles and parts	12,836,797	
Ores, not including iron ore	12,273,865	
Canned goods	11,077,807	
Total		93,157,520
Other carload tonnage	351,878,013	351,878,013
Total, carload		1,467,022,603
Less-than-carload tonnage	10,378,920	10,378,920
Grand total, carload and less-than-carload tonnage		1,477,401,523

SOURCE: United States Interstate Commerce Commission, *Statistics of Railways,*
1951.

in shipments, accounted for less than 1 per cent of the total originating
tonnage.

2. *Inland waterways, including the Great Lakes, the Mississippi River,
and rivers and inland canals not comprised in either system.*

Great Lakes. The chief commodities handled on the Great Lakes are
iron ore, coal, and grain, with lesser amounts of stone, wood products,
petroleum and petroleum products, and package freight.

Mississippi River. Crude and refined petroleum, sugar and molasses,
iron and steel and manufactured products, grain, cotton, bananas, and
coffee move in quantities upon the Mississippi. Much sand, gravel, and
rock is also carried, but for short distances.

Other waterways include (1) the Warrior River in Alabama; (2) the
Columbia, Willamette, Sacramento, and San Joaquin rivers on the
Pacific Coast; (3) the Hudson River; (4) the New York State Barge
Canal; and (5) a number of rivers of minor importance, mostly emptying

into the Atlantic Ocean or the Gulf of Mexico. The most important of these miscellaneous waterways are the New York State Barge Canal and the Hudson River. Both handle much the same range of commodities, including grain, pulpwood and paper, petroleum and petroleum products, with some iron, molasses, and chemicals. The traffic on other rivers varies, but fuel oil, grain, logs and lumber, coal, sand, and gravel constitute the bulk of the tonnage.

3. *Pipe lines*. This facility transports predominantly crude petroleum and gasoline. Other petroleum products move by rail and truck. Natural gas pipe lines are not here considered.

4. *Intercity trucks*. The statistics of motor truck traffic are extremely incomplete. The business includes the carriage of building materials; perishable goods such as milk, eggs, vegetables, and fruit; livestock; household goods; gasoline; cotton; and the miscellaneous freight supplied by retail and wholesale distributing establishments. This traffic has been described in chapter 5.

5. *Airways*. Aircraft tonnage consists of mail and some express and high-grade freight. The volume of the traffic is slight.

The reader is referred to commercial atlases, to the publications of the United States government, and to other standard sources of information for the location of places within the United States where the articles mentioned in the preceding pages are produced.[4] The evident localization which he will observe is partly determined by climatic and soil conditions. Thus grain is mostly grown in the fertile, open Mississippi Valley; citrus fruit in protected areas in California, Florida, and Texas; and cotton in the Southern states in which the summer temperature reaches an average of 77 degrees. Another cause for localization is the chance occurrence of geological deposits. This is why most of our iron ore is mined near Lake Superior, why most coal comes from the Appalachian and the Eastern regions, and why the greater part of our petroleum originates in what are known as the Mid-Continent and California fields. Still other causes for concentration are conditions of labor supply or the availability of other factors which will be more fully discussed in chapter 22. For whatever cause, production is not evenly spread over the United States, but is concentrated in definite areas; and the articles extracted or grown or prepared in these favored spots then flow out in great streams to the communities where the products are consumed.

Inland Waterway Routes: Rivers and Canals

We have already considered the location of the principal river and

[4] There is a brief but convenient summarization of United States resources and their distribution in the report of the United States Board of Investigation and Research upon the National Traffic Pattern (79th C., 1st S., Sen. Doc. 83, 1945, pp. 145–151).

canal routes in the United States, and the reader is referred back to chapter 3 to refresh his memory in this field. The position of rivers is determined by nature, and while it is possible, within limits, to transform a stream which is not navigable into one which ships can navigate, it is not possible to create a major facility for water transport without prerequisites which only nature can provide. This is why the Mississippi River and its tributaries are and have been, since population settled in the West, the main reliance of those persons who desired to avail themselves of the advantages of river transport. Natural advantages also account for the success of the Erie Canal, artificial as a work of this sort may seem to be. For if the Appalachian range had not been broken in prehistoric times, and if glacial action had not carved the beds of the lakes now found in the Mohawk Valley, it would have been no more possible to build a canal through New York State than it now is to build one through Pennsylvania. The peculiarities of the Mississippi and of the Erie routes we have already explained.

Great Lakes Route

The significance of the Great Lakes, however, deserves further elaboration.

The Great Lakes route runs for most purposes from the head of Lake Superior at Fort William or Duluth to Buffalo on Lake Erie. Lake Michigan ports lie upon a branch of this route. Little traffic passes beyond Buffalo to Lake Ontario, and the St. Lawrence River cannot yet be classed as a major highway from the seacoast to the interior, although its importance is probably destined to increase.

The importance of the Great Lakes route is due in large part to the particular location of iron-, coal-, and grain-producing areas in the United States and Canada. The greatest iron deposits of the country lie west and south of Lake Superior. The greatest iron-using and the greatest coal-producing parts of the United States lie south and east of Lakes Erie and Michigan. The three lakes of Erie, Huron, and Superior provide an east-and-west connection which makes movements of coal and iron cheap between these points of origin and destination. Not only this, but since the grain fields in Canada and in the northern Mississippi Valley are the most important on the American continent, the lakes supply a convenient road for grain to American and Canadian markets, while they also bring this product toward the seaboard and facilitate its export. The principal return shipments over the Great Lakes route consist of the anthracite and bituminous coal of Pennsylvania and other Eastern and Southern states.

Canals at St. Mary's Falls

Representative statistics concerning Great Lakes freight movements are collected at St. Mary's Falls, at the entrance to Lake Superior on the east. At this point are two lock canals, one American and one Canadian, which we have already mentioned in chapter 3. The American canal can accommodate boats with a maximum draft of 27 feet and with a capacity approaching 20,000 tons, although few vessels in use reach these limits.[5] The canals are operated free of tolls. All waterborne traffic passing between Lakes Superior and Huron must pass through one or the other of the two canals; and since the greater part of the Lakes traffic has origin or destination in Lake Superior, the canal statistics provide an unusually satisfactory picture of the business of the Lakes as a whole.

Table 11 presents the figures for the American and Canadian canals combined.

TABLE 11.   St. Mary's Falls Canals, 1950
(Freight Traffic)

Article	Tons
Eastbound	
Iron ore	79,923,358
Wheat and flour	5,765,958
Barley, rye, oats, corn, and flaxseed	2,367,990
Pulpwood, paper, wood pulp	557,730
Other	576,148
Total	89,191,184
Westbound	
Coal	13,507,682
Limestone	965,384
Petroleum and products	935,725
Automobiles and trucks	75,710
Other	1,464,721
Total	16,949,222

SOURCE: United States Army, *Annual Report of the Chief of Engineers,* Part II, *Commercial Statistics,* 1950.

American Grain Shipments

The most important Lake shipping points for American grain are Duluth-Superior on Lake Superior, and Chicago and Milwaukee on Lake Michigan.

[5] United States Army, Corps of Engineers, *Transportation Lines on the Great Lakes,* Transportation Series no. 3, 1946. See also United States Army, *Report of the Chief of Engineers,* Part II, *Commercial Statistics,* 1950.

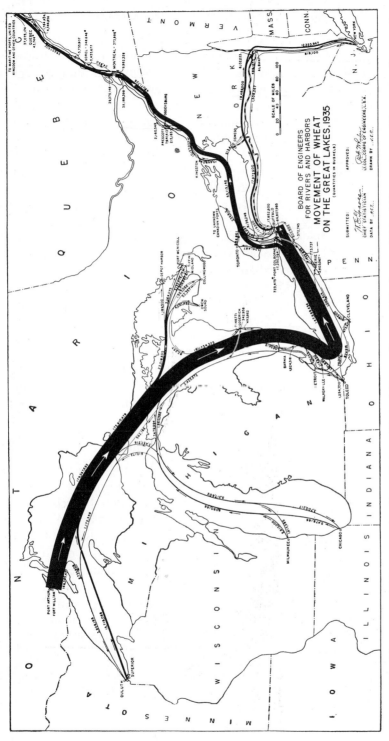

FIGURE 12.   Movement of Wheat on the Great Lakes.   (United States Corps of Engineers, United States Army, *Transportation on the Great Lakes*, 1937.)

Grain, and particularly wheat, moves from the Dakotas, Montana, and Minnesota to Duluth-Superior; and from Illinois, Indiana, Iowa, and portions of Missouri, Kansas, South Dakota, Minnesota, and Wisconsin it moves to Chicago and Milwaukee. From these points, and especially from Duluth-Superior, grain moving to North Atlantic ports of the United States goes chiefly by lake to Buffalo, although some is unloaded at Erie, Toledo, and other Lake ports; some continues to Oswego in Lake Ontario and is there placed in barges for movement through the New York State Barge Canal; and some is transferred at Georgian Bay points where it joins the Canadian flow. Buffalo is important because it is a convenient intermediate stop. Large lake carriers cannot go directly to Montreal because of navigation difficulties on the upper St. Lawrence. A shift of cargo must be made somewhere. Moreover, the shipping capacity for grain at the head of the Lakes exceeds the receiving capacity at Montreal and Quebec, and intermediate storage must be arranged. Buffalo contributes to this need. The main strength of Buffalo's position, however, and this is especially true for American grain, is the fact that it is well equipped with rail connections to the Atlantic seaboard and to points within the large consuming area south of Lakes Erie and Ontario. Outbound rail and barge movements to Middle Atlantic and New England states, milling and local sales, and vessel transport by lake and river to Montreal and to other Canadian ports dispose of most of the grain and wheat that it receives. Of this the rail is several times as important as the water shipment.

Canadian Grain Shipments

The greatest grain tonnage on the Great Lakes is from Canadian, not from American ports of origin. The Lakes shipments of wheat from Duluth-Superior amounted, roughly, to 108 million bushels in 1951.[6] But in 1948–49 lake shipments of Canadian wheat from Fort William–Port Arthur were 160 million bushels and in 1950–51 they were 142 million bushels.[7] This disparity is explained by the competition of Gulf routes for the American production in Kansas, Nebraska, Oklahoma, and Texas, by the indirect character of the water routes from points in Illinois and Indiana, and by the excellent rail facilities which Chicago and Milwaukee command. In recent years the influence of Mississippi barge lines has diverted some American traffic from the Lakes, though it has not much affected the routing of grain grown in the Northwest.

[6] American statistics for Lake grain movements are reported in tons. This tonnage is reduced to bushels, in the text, on the basis of 60 pounds to the bushel.

[7] Canada, Dominion Bureau of Statistics, Agricultural Division, *Report on the Grain Trade of Canada*. See also *Canada Yearbook,* 1950.

Movement of Canadian Crop

The greater part of the Canadian crop is grown in the prairie provinces of Saskatchewan, Alberta, and Manitoba, all west of Lake Superior. Not all is commercially disposed of; but most of the grain marketed passes through Fort William and Port Arthur at the head of Lake Superior and is there reshipped to Eastern destinations for local consumption or for export. By far the largest movement is of wheat.

Canadian wheat consigned to eastern Canadian cities followed, in 1948–49, either of two main routes from Fort William–Port Arthur. The greater portion was shipped by lake to ports on Georgian Bay or upon the eastern shore of Lake Huron. From these termini the movement continued by rail, either to ports on the St. Lawrence River, such as Montreal, accessible to ocean ships, or directly to export centers such as St. Johns and Halifax. A diverted segment was delivered by rail to Port Colborne, Kingston, Toronto, and other harbors on Lakes Erie and Ontario.

In addition to the Georgian Bay movement, wheat was carried by vessel through the Lakes from Fort William and Port Arthur to points on Lakes Erie and Ontario and on the St. Lawrence River. Ships carrying these shipments picked up a portion of the diverted segment which had passed through Georgian Bay. Much of the vessel-borne Canadian wheat coming down the Lakes from Fort William and Port Arthur was distributed locally at points along the route—much Georgian Bay wheat was also so distributed—but a large part continued, waterborne, to river and coastal points from which it could be exported.

A third flow of Canadian wheat is that to American ports. The amount varies. In 1948–49, the year to which our previous figures apply, 14,-441,266 bushels, or about 9 percent of the shipments from Fort William–Port Arthur were so delivered. During World War II, however, and in the early 1930's, the proportions ranged from 22 to 51 percent. Canadian wheat that is to be unloaded at an American port may be sent from Fort William–Port Arthur to Duluth-Superior. It will enter the American flow at the latter destination. It may be shipped down the Lakes, however, to Buffalo or to some other American port where it can be sooner or later reshipped either to American or to Canadian destinations for local consumption or for export. The attractiveness of the American market will be different at different times, as will be the relative supply of shipping at United States and Canadian harbors. The large routing of Canadian wheat through United States ports during the last war was probably caused by a shortage in Canadian ocean ships. The permanent factor in the situation is the circumstance that Canadian grain matures somewhat later than does American grain and continues to flow to lower Lake ports for approximately two weeks after the closing of the St. Lawrence—

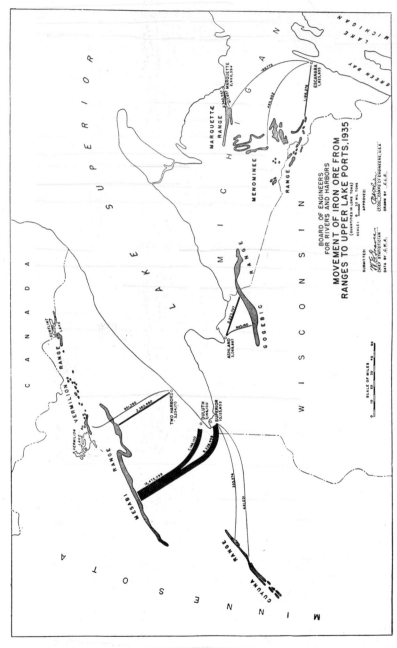

FIGURE 13. Movement of Iron Ore to Upper Lake Ports. (United States Corps of Engineers, United States Army, *Transportation on the Great Lakes*, 1937.)

FIGURE 14. Bulk Freighter Loading Iron Ore, Duluth. (Courtesy of United States Steel.)

usually during the last week in October. This wheat may be stored until spring, for which American ports contribute facilities, or it may be shipped out by rail. In the latter case New York becomes the export point that is most relied upon, and American harbors upon the Lakes will receive Canadian grain in quantity for this purpose.[8]

Iron Ore Shipments

The ore shipments by way of the Great Lakes reach water after a rail haul which varies from 12 to 120 miles. The Marquette field in Michigan, which finds its outlet at Marquette on Lake Superior is the nearest to deep water, and the Mesabi range is the most distant. All the ranges empty upon Lake Superior except the Menominee, for which Escanaba on Lake Michigan is convenient. Including Escanaba, the shipments of iron ore from American ports on Lakes Superior and Michigan in 1953 were as follows:

*Iron Ore Shipments from Principal
American Ranges Season, 1953*

Range	Gross Tons
Minnesota ranges	
Mesabi	74,341,704
Vermilion	1,298,545
Cuyuna	2,696,452
Total Minnesota	78,336,701
Michigan—Wisconsin ranges	
Gogebic	4,375,757
Marquette	5,571,922
Menominee	4,538,063

Grand total U.S. ranges 92,822,443

SOURCE: The Lake Superior Iron Ore Association.

Direction of Iron Ore Movements

Passing out upon the Lakes, the iron ore cargoes proceed east, in specially designed freighters, through Lake Huron and the St. Clair and Detroit rivers to American harbors on the south shore of Lake Erie; or in smaller volume they turn south through Lake Michigan to Calumet and Indiana Harbor and Gary at the extreme end of the Lake.

Ore Receipts at Principal Lake Ports

In 1951 the most important receiving harbors and the incoming tonnage at each were those listed in the following table:

[8] A Canadian shipping and coasting act prohibits the shipping of Canadian grain of any kind through the port of Buffalo when the grain is destined to Montreal unless the upper Lake carrier that transports it from Fort William–Port Arthur to Buffalo is of Canadian registry.

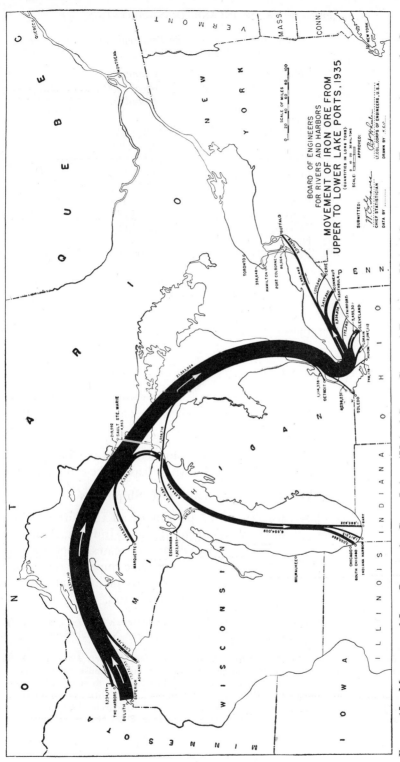

FIGURE 15. Movement of Iron Ore on the Great Lakes. (United States Corps of Engineers, United States Army, *Transportation on the Great Lakes*, 1937.)

Iron Ore Receipts at the Principal
American Ports, 1951

Harbor	Tonnage (tons of 2000 pounds)
Lake Erie Ports	
Cleveland	14,934,555
Conneaut	12,264,308
Ashtabula	10,117,755
Lorain	8,056,776
Buffalo	7,020,071
Erie	4,336,185
Detroit	3,573,644
Toledo	3,554,681
Huron	2,153,100
Tonawanda	299,219
Total	66,310,294
Lake Michigan ports	
Chicago	11,473,084
Indiana Harbor	7,506,746
Gary	7,360,427
Total	26,340,257
Grand total	92,650,551

SOURCE: United States Army, *Annual Report of the Chief of Engineers,* Part II, *Commercial Statistics, 1951.*

Between 85 and 90 percent of the ore shipped from the Lake Superior district is delivered to companies which own or lease Lake Superior mines.[9]

Final Destination of Lake Ore Shipments

In 1953, 181 blast furnaces, or 77 percent of all the furnaces in the United States, were located in Michigan, Illinois, Indiana, New York, Pennsylvania, and Ohio; and these relied, in most cases, upon the Great Lakes for their supply of ore.[10] It follows that Lake Superior ores arriving at lower Lake ports are either used at these ports or are, naturally, forwarded by rail to destinations in these industrial states.

[9] United States Department of Commerce, *The St. Lawrence Survey,* 1941, by N. R. Danielian, Director, Part III, p. 245. See also Temporary National Economic Committee, *Hearings,* Part 18, *Iron and Steel Industry,* 1939.

[10] American Iron and Steel Institute, *Annual Statistical Report, 1953,* p. 29. Blast furnaces and steel making plants usually operate together because of the economy secured by carrying molten material directly from blast furnace to steel mill, eliminating the necessity of reheating. There is also the use of blast furnace gas to be considered. (See United States Board of Investigation and Research, *The Economics of Iron and Steel Transportation,* 79th C., 1st S., Sen. Doc. 80, 1945, p. 38.)

Little or no ore received at the Lake Michigan ports of South Chicago, Indiana Harbor, and Gary is reforwarded.

Most of the ore received at the various Lake Erie ports is reforwarded, although some of it is locally used and some of it is stored for various periods of time.[11]

There are three facts which study will make apparent.

The first fact is that the principal destinations of Lake Erie ore are in the Pittsburgh, Valleys, Steubenville, Wheeling, and Massillon districts. All of these districts lie close to the boundary line separating the states of Ohio and Pennsylvania. Broadly considered, they may all be characterized as part of the Pittsburgh region.

Lake Erie ore transfers which do not move to the vicinity of Pittsburgh are either used in the neighborhood of Buffalo, or they are shipped to the southeast or to points near the steel works at Bethlehem, Pennsylvania; or they are forwarded to the southwest to points in southern Ohio or northern Kentucky near the Ohio River. This is the second fact.

The third fact is that lower Lake harbors specialize, to some degree, in their reshipments. Thus, most of the ore from Conneaut goes to the Pittsburgh district; most of that from Buffalo, to Tonawanda, North Tonawanda, and Lackawanna, which are in the immediate vicinity of Buffalo; most of that from Erie, to Eastern Pennsylvania and Maryland;

[11] The following figures are based upon a flow map published by the Lake Superior Ore Association, showing the distribution of outbound ore shipments from Lake Erie ports during the year 1951.

Movement of Iron Ore from Lower Lake Ports, 1951

(thousands of gross tons)

District of Destination	Lower Lake Port from Which Ore is Shipped							
	Cleveland	Conneaut	Ashtabula	Lorain	Erie	Buffalo	Toledo and Huron	Total
Pittsburgh	2,267	9,820	5,449	—	—	—	397	
Valleys	3,720	7,444	2,432	2,469	—	—	—	
Steubenville	2,329	—	2,318	—	—	—	963	
Wheeling	—	—	—	333	—	—	—	
Massillon	85	—	53	223	—	—	258	
Buffalo	—	—	34	—	58	—	—	
Eastern Pa. and Md.	53	—	47	—	3,203	27	—	
Johnstown, Pa.	889	—	390	—	95	—	—	
Other	661	—	31	—	—	114	2,915	
Total	10,004	17,264	10,754	3,025	3,356	141	4,533	40,077

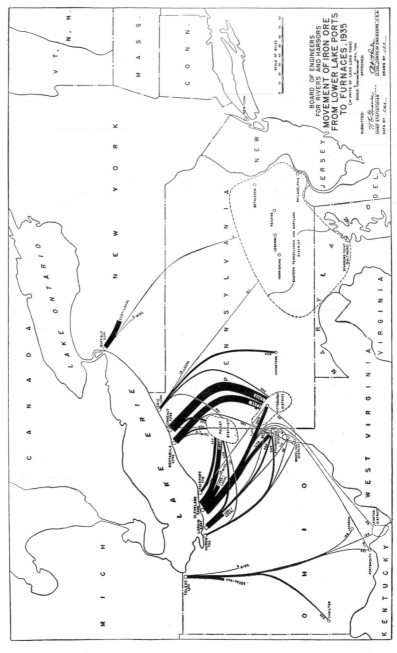

FIGURE 16. Iron Ore Shipments from Lower Lake Ports. (United States Corps of Engineers, United States Army, *Transportation on the Great Lakes*, 1937.)

and most of that from Toledo and Huron, to "other" destinations, which means in this case the Ohio and Kentucky centers which have just been mentioned.

Exhaustion of Lake Superior Deposits

There is some question as to how long and in what volume the flow of iron ore will continue upon the Lakes. The main source of iron production in the United States at the present time are the ranges in Minnesota, Michigan, and northern Wisconsin, previously referred to in the text. These ranges have massive deposits, and they are, also, relatively inexpensive to operate because two-thirds of their output is mined by the so-called "open pit" method of extraction. Between 1939 and 1946 the Lake Superior mines produced 621,725,857 gross tons, or an average of 77,-716,000 tons of crude ore annually. This is 81 percent of all crude ore mined in the United States during these eight years. The Lake Superior output was a major contribution to the war effort; but one result was a decline in estimated reserves from 1,351,705,144 tons in 1939 to 1,138,-347,704 in 1946, or about 16 percent. At the average rate of production mentioned, the figures would indicate an exhaustion of the deposits in 15 years. No such exhaustion is really anticipated because the accelerated output of the war years is not likely to be repeated and because additional tonnage is being added to the reserve estimates each year.[12] Yet it is probable that open pit operations will decline in the Superior region and that greater attention will be paid there to the development of poorer ores. This will include experiments with "taconite"—a source of iron which presents problems of its own. Lake Superior operators may succeed in continuing production at higher costs without much loss of trade and if they do, the volume of Lake ore shipments may be maintained. Higher costs and prices may, on the other hand, reduce consumption, and there is some possibility that imported ore may satisfy a part of the demand which the ranges now supply.[13]

[12] The reserves for the Superior mines were, in 1915, estimated at 1,683,820,532 tons. Since 1915 the mines have produced, approximately, this amount of ore, and yet the current reserves are estimated at more than a billion tons.

So-called "possible" reserves have been estimated at what appears to be fantastic figures. The term possible reserve is used for ore that is not proven but the existence of which is indicated by the formation and by the presence of ore that cannot be moved under present conditions and methods. In 1926 the reserves of low-grade ores and taconite in the Superior region were set at 72,160,000,000 long tons in addition to an "actual" reserve of 2,646,225,000 tons. (See Olin R. Kuhn, *Engineering and Mining Journal*, July, 1926, p. 90. See also United States Department of Commerce, *The St. Lawrence Survey*, 1941, Part III, p. 246.)

[13] See United States Senate, Committee on Foreign Relations, Hearings before a subcommittee, 80th C., 1st S., on S. J. R. 111, 1947, testimony Brown, p. 188.

Labrador Deposits

The foreign deposits which are now attracting attention are those in Canada, across the Labrador-Quebec boundary, 300 to 400 miles north of the Gulf of St. Lawrence. The extent of these deposits is not yet accurately determined. It is known, however, (1) that the supply of ore is large; (2) that the ore is largely "lump" ore of premium grade of a sort used in open hearth furnaces in the United States and Europe; (3) that it can be mined by "stripping"; and (4) that transportation costs will not be excessive.[14] Some of this ore could reach United States consumers in Pennsylvania and Ohio under present conditions and more could be shipped if the St. Lawrence Waterway were improved, as is proposed, to a depth of 27 feet. This Labrador ore could compete with Superior ores and especially with the lower-grade or more expensively handled products which the ranges may be forced to mine. It would be carried up the St. Lawrence River, from east to west, in a direction opposite to that of the usual flow.

Coal

Coal furnishes the chief return cargo for the ore carriers operating to the lower lakes. Bituminous coal reaches Lake Erie at Toledo, Erie, Sandusky, Conneaut, Lorain, Huron, Ashtabula, Fairport, and Cleveland; it proceeds, for the most part, through the Detroit River and Lake Huron, with some deliveries at local points, to destinations on Lake Michigan, Lake Superior, and at intermediate points. Some is shipped eastward to Buffalo. In 1951, out of 31,521,741 short tons of bituminous coal shipped from Lake Erie ports, 9,787,879 were taken by Detroit, 5,720,277 tons by Duluth-Superior, 2,613,116 by Milwaukee, 1,246,800 by Chicago and Indiana Harbor, and 1,860,798 tons by Buffalo. These cargoes aggregated 21,228,870 tons. In addition, some anthracite was forwarded from Lake Erie ports, mostly to Duluth-Superior and to Milwaukee.[15]

The northwestern market for Lake coal includes Wisconsin, Minnesota, Iowa, Michigan, the Dakotas, Montana, and some points even farther west, as well as a large strip of Canadian territory along the adjacent border. This territory requires coal for railroads, homes, iron and copper mines, and growing manufacturing industries. After severe storms, which often delay and sometimes entirely interrupt rail traffic for days at a time,

[14] Department of Mines and Resources, Bureau of Mines, Ottawa, Canada, 1946. Printed in Hearings before a subcommittee of the Committee on Foreign Relations, op. cit., testimony Danielian, pp. 469, 499, 1947.

[15] United States Army, Annual Report of the Chief of Engineers, Part II, Commercial Statistics, 1951. See also studies published by the Corps of Engineers, United States Army, on Ports, Port and Terminal Facilities, and Transportation on the Great Lakes.

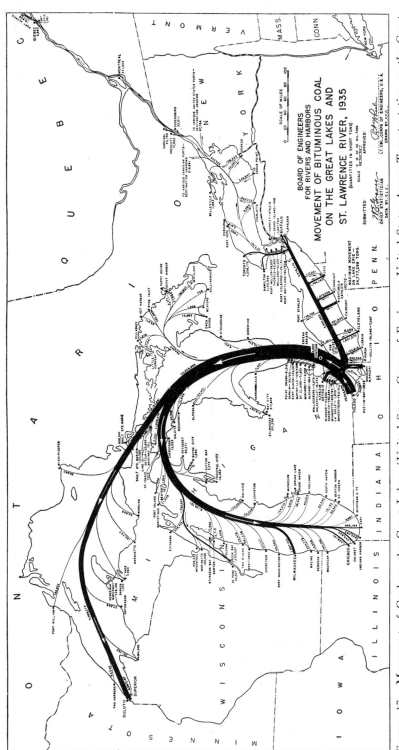

FIGURE 17.   Movement of Coal on the Great Lakes. (United States Corps of Engineers, United States Army, *Transportation on the Great Lakes*, 1937.)

the docks are called upon to meet a sudden and extraordinary demand for coal from all quarters. If the coal supply for the Northwest were to come by rail from the points of production as required, very great difficulty would be experienced in supplying, from current production, the concentrated demands that occur here during the periods when rail transportation, due to climatic conditions, is at its worst.

A railway storage depot such as the docks afford has the flexibility necessary to meet emergencies. As the business has increased, the docks have been called upon more and more to stock coal for consumers. This is particularly true in normal times in the case of railroad companies, whose coal occupies a considerable portion of the dock storage space. Railroads stock their coal early, but take it from the docks only as they require it.

New York Barge Canal and St. Lawrence River

The New York State Barge Canal and the Hudson River serve to some extent as an eastern extension of the Great Lakes route; and the St. Lawrence Deep Waterway would be, if completed, a still more effective portion of this highway. The experts for the International Joint Commission of 1921 expected that grain, some flour, iron ore for Atlantic seaboard furnaces, some lumber, sulfur, and automobiles, together, of course, with other products in smaller quantities, would move eastward from lake to river when the St. Lawrence River and the approaches to the Welland Canal were dredged to depth of 25 or 30 feet.[16] Sugar, manganese, fruit, vegetable oils, rubber, and clay were mentioned as possible westbound quantity movements. This and other forecasts are, however, only prospects, as the actual movement by the St. Lawrence is small. We have already mentioned the character of present shipments over the New York Barge Canal. For most purposes the area of the Great Lakes terminates at the eastern end of Lake Erie, where it connects with the trunk line railroads across Pennsylvania and New York.

REFERENCES

General Treatises

Beasley, Norman, *Freighters of Fortune: The Story of the Great Lakes,* New York, Harper, 1930.
Curwood, James Oliver, *The Great Lakes,* New York, Putnam, 1909.
Jackman, W. T., *Economic Principles of Transportation,* Toronto, University of Toronto, 1935.

Special and Miscellaneous

American Iron and Steel Institute, *Annual Statistical Report.*
Canada, Census and Statistics Office, *The Canada Yearbook,* Ottawa.

[16] The present depth of the Welland Canal is 23 feet.

Canada, Dominion Bureau of Statistics, Agricultural Branch, *Report on the Grain Trade of Canada.*

Canada, *Report of the Royal Grain Inquiry Commission,* 1925.

National Resources Planning Board, *Transportation and National Policy,* Part II, Section II, *Coastwise, Intercoastal, and Great Lakes Shipping,* prepared by the Division of Economics and Statistics, United States Maritime Commission, 1942.

United States, Board of Investigation and Research, *The Economics of Iron and Steel Transportation,* 79th C., 1st S., Sen. Doc. 80, 1945.

United States, War Department, *Annual Report of the Chief of Engineers, Commercial Statistics,* compiled by the Statistical Division of the Board of Engineers for Rivers and Harbors.

United States, War Department, Corps of Engineers, United States Army, *Transportation on the Great Lakes,* Transportation Series No. 1, prepared by the Board of Engineers for Rivers and Harbors, 1937.

United States, War Department, Corps of Engineers, United States Army, *Transportation Lines on the Great Lakes,* 1946.

References on St. Lawrence Deep Sea Waterway

Angel, Arthur D., "The Great Lakes–St. Lawrence Project," *Land Economics,* August, 1950.

Menefee, Ferdinand N., *The St. Lawrence Seaway,* Ann Arbor, Mich., Edward Brothers, 1940.

Schwietert, A. H., and Lyon, L. S., *The Great Lakes–St. Lawrence Seaway and Power Project,* Chicago, Chicago Association of Commerce and Industry, 1952.

Truman, Harry S., *St. Lawrence Seaway and Power Project,* communication from the President transmitting the application to the International Joint Commission, dated June 30, 1952, for approval of certain works in connection with the St. Lawrence seaway and power project, 82d C., 2d S., Department of State publication, 1952.

United States House of Representatives, Committee on Public Works, *Great Lakes–St. Lawrence Basin,* Hearings on H. J. Res. 92, 80th C., 1st S., 1947.

United States Senate, Subcommittee of Committee on Foreign Relations, *Great Lakes–St. Lawrence Basin,* Hearings on S. J. Res. 104 approving agreement between United States and Canada relating to Great Lakes–St. Lawrence Basin, 79th C., 2d S., 1946.

United States Senate, Subcommittee of Committee on Foreign Relations, *St. Lawrence Seaway Project,* Hearings on S. J. Res. 111, 80th C., 1st S., 1947.

United States Senate, Committee on Foreign Relations, Report to accompany S. J. Res. 111 (minority views included), 80th C., 1st S., 1948, Sen. Rep. 810.

United States, Department of Commerce, Bureau of Foreign and Domestic Commerce, Industry Report, Domestic Transportation, *An Economic Appraisal of the St. Lawrence Seaway Project,* prepared by Transportation Division, Paul M. Zeiss, Acting Chief, August–November, 1947.

Motor Vehicle, Air, and Pipe Line Routes

We may now proceed to consider the major land routes of the United States—that is to say, the railroad, motor vehicle, and pipe line routes. Air routes will be added to the list, although the airplane, like the ship, prefers only an occasional contact with the land. We shall discuss motor vehicles, airplanes, and pipe lines first, because their routes are simple or are relatively easy to explain. Railroad routes will be described in the following chapter.

Motor Vehicle Routes

The total road mileage of the United States in 1950 was over 3 million miles. The length of surfaced mileage was much less than this, and the surfaced mileage under state control, as distinguished from county and local roads and roads in national parks, forests, and reservations, was still less, or 542,011 miles.[1] The surfaced mileage under state control is, however, more extensive than the sum of pipe line and air routes or than the length of the single-track railroad mileage of the United States.

Highway Pattern

The highway system of the United States has no general pattern. There are, however, main thoroughfares which may be plotted separately and these are indicated upon the following map.

The map shows the so-called National System of Interstate Highways as of 1951. The National System was recognized in the federal Act of 1944. It is supposed to consist of highways of national as distinguished from those of localized importance. For some purposes it is desirable to have a road network which can accommodate long-distance as well as

---

[1] United States Department of Commerce, Bureau of Public Roads, *Highway Statistics,* 1950. See also Joint Committee on the Economic Report, *Highways and the National Economy,* 81st C., 2d S., 1950, p. 21.

FIGURE 18. National System of Interstate Highways. (Public Roads Administration, Federal Works Agency.)

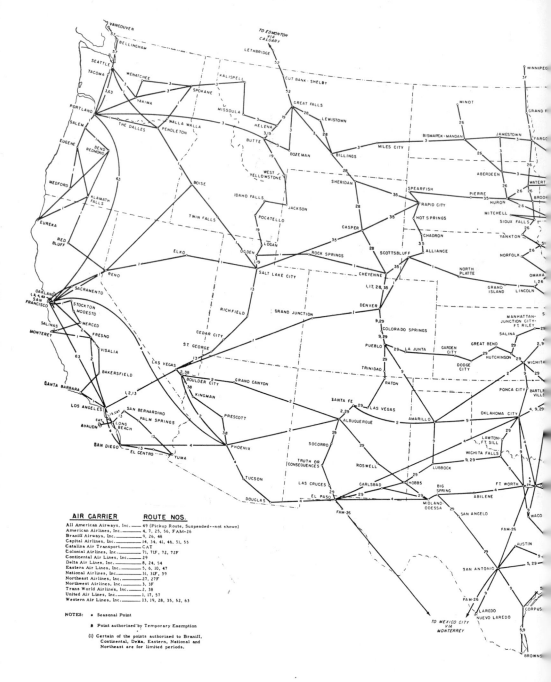

FIGURE 19. United States Air Transportation System: Routes Permanen

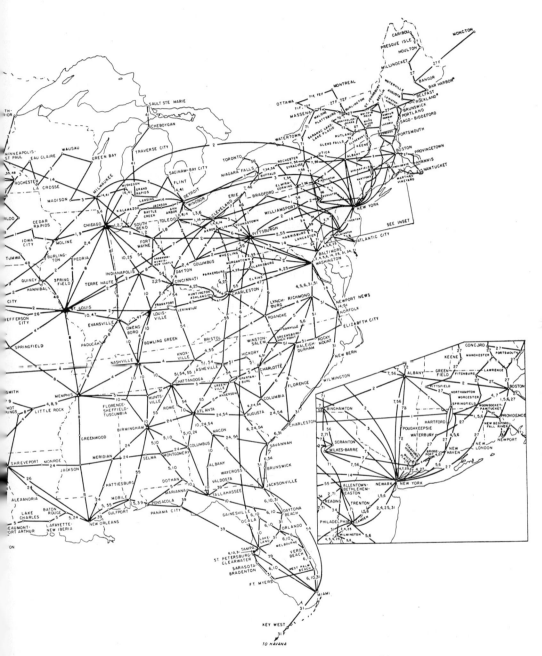

Certificated, 1953. (Bureau of Air Operations, Civil Aeronautics Board.)

short-distance carriage. Motor transport is, characteristically, over short distances and the highways of the country facilitate a massive and widely distributed volume of local traffic.[2] There are, however, long-haul movements. Thus, in 1950, one regular-route general commodity carrier was already operating from coast to coast. Single-line transportation of general freight was common from north to south, and special long-haul service was provided for traffic such as household goods and frozen food. The routes indicated upon the map show the facilities for this interregional communication. It is to be observed that the routes on the map follow, in a general way, the lines of the trunk line railroads. This is natural, because long-distance motor movement, like long-distance air transport, adjusts itself to a preëxisting distribution of population and industry. These routes do and will, nevertheless, provide the paths over which passenger and commodity flows will carry on.

Air-Line Routes

Air-line routes resemble those of the National System of Interstate Highways in that they connect centers of population which were established many years ago. The resemblance is clear if we compare the map of page 149 with the map of page 150. In doing this we should remember that the air-line chart shows all air routes permanently certificated, while the highway map indicates only the principal interstate highways, omitting all roads which are not of primary interstate and interregional concern. There is some cross-route flying, but not of major amount.

Air-Line Companies

Air-line companies operate over the routes set up by the federal government and between airports established by federal and local administrations. These companies may be divided into three major groups.

The first group consists of four companies which operate from the Atlantic to the Pacific Coast of the United States. These are American Airlines, United Air Lines, Trans World Airlines, and Northwest Airlines.

Running across the east to west trunk lines are a number of routes from north to south. Such are the Continental Air Lines and the Braniff Airways from Denver to El Paso, Fort Worth, and Galveston. In this class, also, are Mid-Continent Airlines from Bismarck, North Dakota, to Houston and New Orleans, the Chicago and Southern Air Lines from Chicago to New Orleans, and Western Air Lines from Seattle to Yuma and San Diego, and from Calgary to Los Angeles.

Finally, there are companies which may be described as regional, although their operations, in each case, may cover many states. The largest

[2] See chap. 2.

of these is the so-called Eastern Air Lines. The territory of this company is roughly bounded by lines connecting St. Louis, New York, Miami, and San Antonio. Delta Air Lines serves a similar, though not identical, area in the Southeast. North of the Ohio River, between Chicago and New York, and reaching into Michigan is Pennsylvania Central Airlines Corporation (now Capital Airlines), and there are the Colonial Airlines and the Northeast Airlines that serve New England, New York, and Pennsylvania. At one time the Pennsylvania Central and the Northeast Airlines planned to merge; but the project was abandoned.[3]

Character of Air Movements

The lines of operation of air companies show, after a fashion, the direction and limits of commercial air transport in the United States. Some additional information can, however, be supplied.

INTENSITY. The intensity of commercial air traffic is greatest (1) from Washington through New York along the Atlantic Coast as far north as Boston; (2) on the routes between Chicago and New York; and (3) between Chicago and St. Louis, Chicago and St. Paul, and Chicago and Omaha. Even a cursory glance at the schedules of airplane operations shows how greatly the frequency of service offered by lines in these areas exceeds that offered by companies in the South and East.

LENGTH OF HAUL. There are few air movements for distances less than 100 miles. The use of airplanes for distances between 100 and 400 miles is, however, very great. It is the observation of the Civil Aeronautics Board that the largest percentage of any community's traffic is with its nearest neighbor of similar or greater size except in cases where the attractions of New York or Chicago are overwhelming. Thus Atlanta deals with Jacksonville, Birmingham, and Augusta; Cincinnati with Cleveland, Detroit, and Louisville; and Denver with Kansas City, Los Angeles, and San Francisco. At the same time there is a large volume of very long-distance traffic, which often and understandably exceeds air transfers between nearer points for which air connection has been established.

The map reproduced on page 154 shows the direction and relative volume of air passenger movements in the United States in the month of September, 1948. The map is too condensed to show details; the heavy concentration of air movements between New York and Chicago and between Los Angeles and San Francisco is, however, evident. There is also a noticeable amount of travel between the Atlantic and the Pacific Coasts, between Los Angeles and Seattle, and between the New York area and Miami. Not all traffic moves between the extreme termini of the route

[3] *Moody's Manual, Industrials,* 1948, p. 2863.

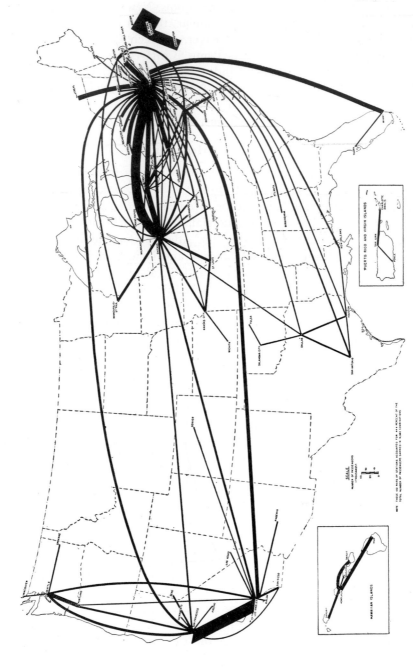

FIGURE 20. Passenger Originations and Destinations Between the 100 Top-Ranking Pairs of Stations, 1948. (Bureau of Economic Regulation, Civil Aeronautics Board.)

which the map shows that it frequents.[4] Yet much of it is through business, especially, as we have said, when one of the termini is a major town.[5]

There is no recent comprehensive record of air freight transport, but
information collected for the year 1935 showed an even greater concentration of traffic in the Northeast than now occurs in the case of passengers
and an even greater predominance of exchanges between large cities.[6]

Feeder Services

These should be mentioned in discussing air movements but the volume
of this carriage is small. It is by no means clear that the pickup and
delivery of passengers and freight at air terminals or even the connection
of these terminals with communities within moderate distances can be as
well handled by air as by surface carriage. It is admitted that the business

[4] United States Civil Aeronautics Board, *Airline Travel Distances, December,* 1948.
[5] The figures in the following table are taken from the Civil Aeronautics Board, *Air-
line Traffic Survey,* for March, 1949.

Number of Tickets Sold for Passage Between San Francisco
and Various Indicated Cities in March, 1950

Base Point	Cities on Route Between San Francisco and New York	Distance from San Francisco (miles)	Number of tickets sold
San Francisco	Sacramento	79	1,966
	Salt Lake	600	1,371
	Cheyenne	970	53
	Omaha	1,434	230
	Chicago	1,856	2,434
	Cleveland	2,163	235
	New York	2,577	4,801
			13,090

The number of through passengers in this illustrative case is obviously very large, but
the intermediate traffic is also considerable.

According to the Civil Aeronautics Board, the volume of air travel between cities
varies with population, distance, including relations between ground and air distance,
producing power, and general area density. The mere listing of factors is not especially
informing. The Civil Aeronautics Board tries, however, to develop a formula. This
formula would give precise results if all significant variables could be included and
their influence measured in quantitative terms. At present the margin of error is probably rather wide. (See United States Department of Commerce, Civil Aeronautics Administration, *Effective Community Air Traffic Potential,* June, 1950.

[6] W. L. McMillen, "Air Express Service in the United States," *Journal of Land and
Public Utility Economics,* August, 1935, November, 1935, and February, 1936. See also
United States Civil Aeronautics Authority, Bureau of Economic Regulation, Accounts
and Analyses Division, *Station to Station Airline Traffic Survey,* August, 1939, and
September, 1940.

is not commercially profitable. The question is as to how far it shall be subsidized. Feeder traffic does not constitute a considerable part of air-line transportation.

Pipe Lines

The mileage of pipe lines reporting to the Interstate Commerce Commission was, as of December 31, 1951, 131,152 miles, of which 80,996 miles were trunk and the rest were gathering lines. Most of the system is devoted to the carriage of crude petroleum; but in recent years pipes have been laid down for the transportation of refined petroleum, principally gasoline. Pipe lines for the movement of natural gas are not included in these figures.[7]

In conveying oil, operators make use of steel pipes, laid on or near the surface of the ground, through which crude or refined oil is forced by pumps driven by internal combustion engines, by electric power, or by steam. Most main trunk pipes are from 8 to 16 inches in diameter; gathering pipe lines range from 2 to 8 inches.[8] Distances between pumping stations vary greatly, but stations are rarely more than 50 miles apart. Spacing depends upon terrain, viscosity of the oil, and the ability of pipes to withstand pressure. During later years pipe lines and their equipment have been considerably improved. Better and larger pipes are now being made and more efficiently installed. There is telephone equipment for communication along the line, improved methods of maintenance, including the development of light, mobile equipment, more accurate metering, and electric welding. These, together with other advances in the art, make it possible to render better service at lower costs. Modern pipe lines employ a telephonic dispatching system, and they organize their maintenance work as carefully as railroads do.

[7] The pipe line mileage of companies reporting to the Interstate Commerce Commission was, in 1950 and 1951, as follows:

	Mileage	
	1950	1951
Crude oil trunk lines	64,622	64,992
Refined oil trunk lines	16,374	18,531
Crude oil gathering lines	47,593	47,629
Total	128,589	131,152

It was estimated, in 1944, that pipe lines reporting to the Interstate Commerce Commission were the following proportions of all pipe line mileages: crude oil trunk lines, 85 percent; refined oil lines, 65 percent; gathering lines, 77 percent (American Petroleum Institute, *Petroleum Facts and Figures,* 1947, p. 142).

[8] Interstate Commerce Commission, Bureau of Transport Economics and Statistics, *A Review of Statistics of Oil Pipe Lines, 1921–1941,* 1942, p. 27. See also United States Department of the Interior, Petroleum Administration for Defense, *Transportation of Oil,* 1951.

PIPE LINE OPERATION.   Speaking of the operation of the Great Lakes Pipe Line Company, the general superintendent of this company says:

All gasoline movements through the system are controlled by a chief dispatcher located in Kansas City. The dispatching is done over telephone by three shift dispatchers under the chief dispatcher. . . .

The actual movements through the line of different specification gasolines are in the care of the chief dispatcher who may have as many as three products spotted at intervals throughout the system, with deliveries of certain quantities to be made at different terminals along the line. The dispatcher knows within a few hundred feet or less where each product is located, and by means of charts and maps showing capacity and mileage, can at all times trace its movements. The dispatcher has control of all pumping speeds, and designates tankage and movements through the system. Check samples are reported to him from all intermediate points, and in the final calculations on a delivery, he will know its arrival within minutes.

From the same source we take the following description of the handling of a particular shipment in a gasoline pipe line:

A typical movement through the system is as follows: Assuming a receipt of 50,000 barrels of "X" gasoline at Muskogee for delivery to Chicago. The Muskogee station will deliver to Okmulgee through a 4-inch line at the rate of 4200 barrels per day, and the front end of this product will arrive in Okmulgee in 14.3 hours.

Due to the difference in pumping capacities between Okmulgee and Muskogee stations, namely, 4200 and 13,000 per day, it will be necessary to store some of the gasoline, which in this case is 162.3 hours of pumping. After this has been done, the product is started north to Barnsdall at the rate of 13,000 barrels per day, and the front end of the stream arrives in Barnsdall in 24 hours.

Here it is again stored and accumulated to overcome the capacity ratio of 13,000 barrels to 25,000 barrels per day, or a wait of 30.6 hours is necessary. Pumping is then started north at the rate of 25,000 barrels per day through the 8-inch line and the progress of the batch is noted every hour.

It passes Kansas City in 67 hours after leaving Barnsdall and reaches Des Moines in 128 hours.

At Des Moines reverse capacity of 25,000 to 13,000 barrels per day is encountered and while it is possible to start the movement east immediately, for the purpose of checking pumpings and determining an over and short on this movement, the first 15,000 barrels are stored in tankage, after which the stream is switched and pumping is started to the east from the first tank at the rate of 13,000 barrels per day and reaches Chicago in 109.4 hours, or in all, a time interval of 473.6 hours from Muskogee.

All during this time interval, dispatchers have full control of movement. Just ahead of this movement and after this movement, other products from different receiving points are handled in the system by means of storage accumulation at the different stations . . . waiting their turn in the line.[9]

It will be observed that the description of pipe line operation in the preceding section refers to a gasoline pipe line. The majority of pipe lines

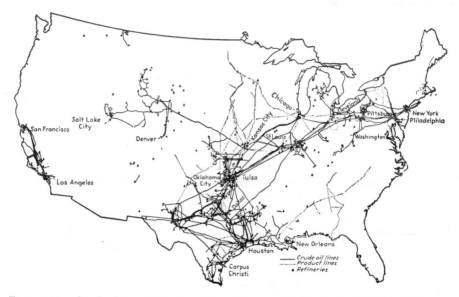

FIGURE 21. Crude Oil and Products Pipe Lines and Refineries in the United States, 1948. (By permission from *Petroleum Production Engineering,* by L. C. Uren. Copyright, 1950. McGraw-Hill Book Company, Inc.)

are built to carry crude oil only. We have, however, already observed that a considerable mileage exists for the carriage of gasoline. The location of these "product" lines can be distinguished on the chart.[10]

[9] F. E. Richardson, "Efficient and Economical Operation of System Depends on Simplicity of Organization," *Oil and Gas Journal,* September 29, 1932, p. 112.

For a technical description of oil pipe line equipment and operation, see *Oil Pipe Line Transportation Practices,* issued by the Bureau of Industrial and Business Extension Training, Division of Extension, University of Texas, and the State Board for Vocational Education, Trade and Industrial Division, Austin, Texas, in coöperation with and validated by the Topical Committee on Vocational Training, American Petroleum Institute, Division of Production, 1944.

[10] Among the longer gasoline lines are those of the Plantation Pipe Line Company (controlled by the Standard Oil Company) from Baton Rouge, La. to Greensboro, N.C., the Phillips Petroleum Company line from the Panhandle of Texas through Oklahoma, Kansas, Missouri, and Illinois to East Chicago, Ind., and the Great Lakes Pipe Line Company line from Ponca City and Tulsa, Okla. by way of Kansas City and Des Moines to Minneapolis and Chicago, with a branch from Kansas City to Omaha and to Grand Forks, N.D. Also important are lines like those of the Atlantic Refining Company and its subsidiaries from Philadelphia to Pittsburgh and from Philadelphia

ROUTES.   The location of crude pipe lines is determined, on the one hand by the occurrence of productive oil wells, and on the other by the position of refineries or of storage points to which oil is brought from the fields. The situation of refineries, in turn, is controlled by various technical and business considerations.

The principal petroleum-producing regions of the United States are (1) the Midcontinent district, including portions of the states of Texas, Oklahoma, Kansas, Louisiana, Arkansas, New Mexico, and Missouri; (2) the California district, including producing wells in the state of California; (3) the Gulf Coast district, including portions of Texas and Louisiana adjacent to the Gulf of Mexico; (4) the Appalachian district, including the western portion of the states of New York, Pennsylvania, West Virginia, eastern portions of Ohio, northern Kentucky, and Tennessee; (5) the Rocky Mountain district, including Wyoming, Montana, Colorado, Utah, northern New Mexico, and Alaska; (6) the Lima-Indiana district, including western Ohio, Indiana, and Michigan; and (7) the Illinois-Indiana district, including parts of southwestern Indiana and southeastern Illinois.[11]

Crude petroleum moves by pipe line from producing areas to the important Texas and Oklahoma inland refining centers, such as West Tulsa and Oklahoma City; to refineries or loading facilities located at Texas Gulf ports; northeastwardly to refining centers at Arkansas City, Coffeyville, Kansas City, Chicago, Cincinnati, Cleveland, Toledo, etc.; or to other refineries scattered throughout the East and Middle West. The crude oil moved by pipe line to the Texas ports is either refined at these points or reshipped in tank vessels to the great Eastern refinery centers at or near New York, Boston, Philadelphia and Baltimore. Some of it is transhipped

---

to Rochester and Buffalo and those of the Shell Oil Company from the Mississippi River near St. Louis to Lima, Dayton, and Columbus.

The most extensive crude oil pipe line system is that of the Standard Oil Company of Indiana. The route operated by this company through its subsidiary, the Stanolind Pipe Line Company, runs from Oklahoma southwest as far as Pecos, Tex., northeast to Chicago, and northwest from the vicinity of Kansas City through Kansas, Nebraska, and Wyoming to a point near Billings, Mont. Other long lines owned by the Texas Sinclair, Humble, Shell, and other companies and their subsidiaries connect Tulsa with Chicago and eastern points, and still others bring oil from Oklahoma and Texas fields to Gulf ports and refineries or from California wells to refineries or shipping points on the Pacific Coast. During World War II two exceptionally large lines, the so-called Big Inch and Little Big Inch, were built from Texas through Arkansas, Missouri, Illinois, Indiana, Ohio, and Pennsylvania to New Jersey. These last rendered good service until the conclusion of the war, when they were transferred to the carriage of natural gas.

[11] United States, Office of the Federal Coordinator, *Freight Traffic Report,* 1935, vol. 2, p. 55. Uren gives a slightly different classification, combining districts 4, 6, and 7 into an "Eastern District" and assigning all of New Mexico to the Mid-Continent District (L. C. Uren, *Petroleum Production Engineering,* New York, McGraw-Hill, 1950). The difference is not important for our present purpose.

at Atlantic coast points and forwarded, still as crude oil, by pipe line to interior refineries. Crude petroleum produced in the California fields moves in large quantities by pipe line to the refining centers or transhipment ports at or near San Francisco, Los Angeles, and Port San Luis; a considerable amount of California crude is also refined at the interior refineries at Bakersfield and Lebec, California.

Crude petroleum produced in the Rocky Mountain region is refined for the most part at the refineries located in the Caspar, Graybull, and Rawlins-Pasco districts in Wyoming, or at smaller refining centers in Wyoming, Montana, Utah, and Colorado. The crude produced at the wells in the Gulf Coast district is either refined at the refineries located within the area or moved to Texas and Louisiana Gulf ports where it is either refined or transhipped as crude to the Eastern Seaboard refineries. The crude petroleum produced in the Lima-Indiana, in the Illinois-Indiana, and in the Appalachian districts is usually refined at nearby refineries in these respective fields; some of it, however, is shipped to refineries upon the Atlantic seaboard.

Refined petroleum products are usually distributed in the sections of the United States in which the refineries are located or within a reasonable distance from such refineries, with the notable exception of the products refined in the Tulsa, Oklahoma, and Borger, Texas, area, which may be transported long distances by gasoline pipe lines. Gasoline may also be carried through the Plantation Pipe Line from Baton Rouge as far as North Carolina. There is also some pipe line movement of gasoline westward from refineries in New Jersey.

Diversion of Oil Traffic from the Railroads

Most crude petroleum moves today by pipe line or by water. The tonnage of crude delivered to refineries by railroads is absolutely and proportionately very small.[12] The reason is that crude oil moves in volume

[12] The Bureau of Mines reports the domestic receipts of crude oil at refineries in the United States as follows:

Deliveries	1937 (million barrels)	1951 (million barrels)
By pipe line		
Intrastate	569.6	1,127.0
Interstate	276.7	629.4
Total	846.3	1,756.4
By boat		
Intrastate	78.5	145.9
Interstate	201.8	256.9
Total	280.3	402.8

to a limited number of destinations and that the cost of pumping under these conditions is less than the cost of railroad carriage. The diversion from one agency to another may here be looked upon as permanent.

The situation is more complicated with respect to refined oil. There has been an evident shift in recent years from rail to pipe line carriage. Calculations prepared by the Interstate Commerce Commission a few years ago concluded that the railroads, in 1946, were carrying only 46.8 percent of the crude oil and 37.1 percent of the refined petroleum tonnage which they would have been transporting if their share of the entire movement had remained equal to that of 1928.[13] And since 1946 the railroad proportion of refined oils has still further fallen off. It is not yet possible, however, to guess what the ultimate equilibrium will be.[14] Meanwhile pipe lines not only divert traffic directly from the railroads to a large extent but, by increasing the use of oil in place of coal as fuel, they reduce the coal tonnage upon which the railroads so largely rely. Finally, the rates that railroads can charge upon the oil and the coal that they still carry are kept down by the competition of pipe lines carrying crude oil and gasoline and, to some degree, by the competition of those which handle natural gas.

Pipe Line and Railroad Rates

It would seem that the pipe line, as compared with the railroad, is definitely a superior facility for the transportation of oil under conditions adapted to its peculiarly inflexible manner of operation. The staff of the Federal Coordinator gave some attention to this matter, and reported that pipe line rates were only 31 percent of rail rates on crude petroleum

By tank car and truck		
Intrastate	28.2	18.3
Interstate	8.5	15.5
Total	36.7	33.8
Grand total	1,163.3	2,193.0

SOURCE: *Minerals Yearbook,* 1949, p. 107; American Petroleum Institute, *Petroleum Facts and Figures,* 1952, p. 159.

[13] United States Interstate Commerce Commission, Bureau of Transport Economics and Statistics, *Fluctuations in Railway Freight Traffic Compared with Production, 1928–1946,* June, 1948.

[14] Up to the present time most gasoline which is pumped through pipe lines is transported for proprietary refining companies and a large proportion of the tonnage is distributed from pipe line termini direct to local dealers in motor tank trucks. This method is proving so efficient that it captures railroad tonnage consigned to points within a reasonable distance of the ends of the pipe line routes. But the difficulty is that there are many markets for refined oils, widely dispersed; that there are few pipe line termini; and that there are limitations to the efficiency of long-distance motor hauls. There are conditions under which railroad service may be, definitely, the least expensive means of carrying gasoline to its final destination.

between points in Eastern territory in 1934. The pipe line rates for all territories in 1934 were approximately half of the rates by rail.[15] Before World War II, comparative costs per ton-mile for the transportation of petroleum were approximately 8.3 mills by rail, 1.2 mills to 3.2 mills by pipe line, and 1.2 mills by tank vessel. In the movement of refined products by tank truck, the prewar rates were about 5 cents per ton-mile for short hauls, and from 1.5 to 2 cents per ton-mile on average hauls of 150 to 200 miles.[16]

How successful any particular pipe line will be in earning a profit at rates like these will depend upon how nearly it is worked at full capacity. The cost of operating a pipe line is largely independent of the amount of traffic handled. If the investment is fully utilized, costs to the shipper may be made low and profits will, nevertheless, be earned. If the plant is partly idle even high rates will not produce an adequate return. The income of pipe lines has, actually, been high, although it has declined, in recent years, relatively to investment in the property. In 1949, pipe lines reporting to the Interstate Commerce Commission earned a net operating income of $63,801,677 upon an investment, after deducting accrued depreciation, of $873,869,578, or approximately 7 percent. This is to be compared with earnings of 28 percent in 1937 and of 19 percent in 1941.[17]

Ownership of Pipe Lines

Most, though not all, pipe lines are controlled by parent corporations engaged in the production and refining of petroleum. In some instances, as in that of the Great Lakes Pipe Line Company, several corporations unite in the control of a single pipe line system.[18] Whether so controlled or not, most pipe lines operate as common carriers,[19] accepting oil or products from nonrelated producers or refiners at the same rates and under the same regulations which apply to oil offered by proprietary interests. The actual practice is, however, complicated, and the relative volume of shipments by nonrelated producers or refiners is relatively small.[20]

---

[15] United States, Office of the Federal Coordinator, *Freight Traffic Report,* vol. 2, p. 104.

[16] P. Harvey Middleton, *Oil Industry and Transportation,* Chicago, Railway Business Association, 1943, p. 19.

[17] United States Interstate Commerce Commission, *Statistics of Railways,* 1949, p. 219.

[18] See Temporary National Economic Committee, *Investigation of Concentration of Economic Power,* Hearings, vol. 14, 76th C., 2d S., 1939, pp. 7646, 7885–8001.

[19] 234 U.S. 548, 1914.

[20] The pipe lines formerly took title to the oil which they transported. This is no longer required. The ownership of crude at the time of shipment is now generally vested in the refiner who buys oil in the field and takes possession at the valve between the producer's tank and the pipe line. The refiner-purchaser is usually affiliated with the producer so that this shift is not a matter of importance.

REFERENCES

General Treatises

Bengston, N. A., and Royen, W. V., *Fundamentals of Economic Geography*, New York, Prentice-Hall, 1936.

Johnson, Emory R., *Transport Facilities, Services and Policies*, New York, Appleton-Century-Crofts, 1947.

Locklin, D. Philip, *Economics of Transportation*, Chicago, Irwin, 1947.

Landon, Charles E., *Transportation, Principles, Practices, Problems*, New York, Sloane, 1951.

Uren, Lester Charles, *Petroleum Production Economics*, New York, McGraw-Hill, 1950.

The evidence is that most of the crude oil passing through pipe lines belongs to the producer-refining interests of the major companies and these also own, directly or indirectly, most of the pipe lines. It is difficult to estimate the percentage of ownership in these cases but it certainly exceeds 60 percent and maybe is greater than 90 percent. The concentration of ownership in the case of product lines is also great.

It is charged that the owners of pipe line, who are also shippers, make it difficult for independent producers or refiners to ship oil or products by keeping pipe line rates at high levels, by requiring large minimum shipments or by other practices. (See William Beard, *Regulation of Pipe Lines as Common Carriers*, New York, Columbia University, 1941. See also George S. Wolbert, *American Pipe Lines*, Norman, Okla., University of Oklahoma, 1952; Roy A. Prescott, "The Operation and Regulation of Crude Oil and Gasoline Pipe Lines," *Quarterly Journal of Economics*, February, 1942.) On the other hand, while these charges are denied, it is observed that producers and refiners may be badly located with respect to the existing pipe line system, that they may not have adequate terminal facilities for storage, and that there are other difficulties which can be pointed out.

Pipe line ownership is the subject of a violent debate in which one side advocates and the other opposes a forced separation of pipe line and producing-refining ownership. This could be done by the amendment of what is known as the "Commodity Clause" of the Interstate Commerce Act, passed in 1906. (See chap. 29. See also Forrest R. Black, "Oil Pipe Line Divorcement by Litigation and Legislation," *Cornell Law Quarterly*, June, 1940.)

Pipe line divorcement might stimulate competition, not only in transportation but also in petroleum refining; this would be because it might enable independent refiners who purchased crude oil in the field and needed transportation to obtain service at rates comparable with those which their competitors enjoyed. These rates would presumably provide a fair return upon pipe line investment; but except for this offset they would be the same to independent refiners and to the owners of pipe lines where the service was the same. There are, however, arguments upon the other side. Independent producers would suffer from the separation of oil production and transportation unless the segregated pipe lines continued (1) to offer a gathering service in the field which the present pipe lines are accustomed to provide, and (2) to maintain the usual rate of pipe line extension to meet the needs of newly developed fields. There are reasons to believe that this would not be done. It is also possible that the destruction of present integration might impair efficiency and increase costs in oil production as well as in oil carriage. It has been asserted that integration as practiced by the oil companies contains the germs of monopoly and is not a normal method of industrial development which would be permitted by the Sherman Act if the question were properly raised, but this is a matter for additional discussion.

Periodicals

Emerson, H. N., "Salient Characteristics of Petroleum Pipe Line Transportation," *Land Economics,* February, 1950.

Prewitt, W. A., "The Operation and Regulation of Crude Oil and Gasoline Pipe Lines," *Quarterly Journal of Economics,* February, 1942.

Special and Miscellaneous

American Petroleum Institute, *Petroleum Facts and Figures.*

Automobile Manufacturers' Association, *Automobile Facts and Figures.*

Joint Committee on the Economic Report, *Highways and the National Economy,* 81st C., 2d S., 1950.

National Resources Planning Board, *Transportation and National Policy,* Part II, Section V, *Petroleum Pipe-Line Transportation,* by G. Lloyd Wilson, 1942.

Temporary National Economic Committee, *Hearings on the Petroleum Industry,* 79th C., 2d S., 1940, Parts 14 and 15.

United States Department of Commerce, Bureau of Mines, *Transportation of Gasoline by Pipe Lines,* Technical Paper 517, by C. P. Bowie, 1932.

United States Department of Commerce, Bureau of Public Roads, *Highway Statistics,* annual.

United States Department of Commerce, Civil Aeronautics Board, *Airline Travel Distances,* December, 1948.

United States Department of Commerce, Civil Aeronautics Board, *Airline Traffic Survey,* March, 1949.

United States Department of Commerce, Civil Aeronautics Administration, *Effective Community Air Traffic Potential,* June, 1950.

United States Department of Commerce, Civil Aeronautics Authority, Bureau of Economic Regulation, Accounts and Analyses Division, *Station to Station Airlines Traffic Survey, August, 1939,* September, 1940.

United States Interstate Commerce Commission, *Statistics of Railways,* annual.

United States Interstate Commerce Commission, Bureau of Transport Economics and Statistics, *War-Built Pipe Lines and the Post-War Transportation of Petroleum,* prepared by Sam G. Spal, August, 1944.

Railroad Routes

Railroad Routes

The map which follows divides the United States into a number of territories. Reference to these territories will help the reader to understand the discussion in the present chapter.

FIGURE 22.   Freight Rate Territories.

Extent of Local Railroad Business

A large part of the railroad traffic of the country is local, and much of it is concentrated in the Eastern states because of the volume of business and the concentration of population in that area. These facts might be inferred. The conclusion may be fortified, however, by statistics drawn from an accumulation of waybills collected by the Board of Investigation and Research and analyzed by a bureau of the Interstate Commerce Commission. These statistics refer to all the territories depicted upon the preceding map.

The information which the waybill study supplies is summarized in Table 12. The statistics used in Table 12 are on a 1 percent basis.

TABLE 12.   Railroad Carload Movements, 1950

Commodities	Tons Originated	Tons Terminating in Territory of Origin	Percent
All commodities	13,072,222	11,347,890	87
Products of agriculture	1,216,028	982,812	81
Animals and products	145,372	88,396	61
Products of mines	7,337,023	6,817,909	93
Products of forests	799,084	594,664	74
Manufactures and miscellaneous	3,537,793	2,864,109	81

SOURCE: United States Interstate Commerce Commission, Bureau of Transport Economics and Statistics, *Carload Waybill Analyses, 1950, Territorial Distribution, Traffic and Revenue by Commodity Classes,* June, 1951.

The compilation shows that 87 percent of rail shipments, during the year 1950, both originated and terminated in a single traffic district, the districts or territories being those designated upon the printed map. The national average of 87 percent is exceeded on all commodities in Official territory and in some instances elsewhere; the average of different areas and of different classes of commodities is, very generally, above 70 percent, except in the case of animals and products, where it is somewhat lower. It is true that the table does not, for several reasons, establish the fact that the population in the various territories is self-sufficient to the extent of the percentage which locally consigned shipments bear to the total of freight handled; [1] the figures quoted do, however, suggest the importance of the intraterritorial work which railroads of the country are called upon to do. To the extent that goods are produced in the same area as that

[1] The volume of intraterritorial movements reported in the table is swollen by repeated point-to-point shipments within each territory which are associated with the manufacture of materials and with their preparation for consumption. Interterritorial totals are not subject to this inflation. The predominance of local traffic is also heavily influenced by a few commodities, namely, coal, iron, iron ore, and steel. (See Edward L. Ullman, "The Railroad Pattern of the United States," *The Geographical Review,* April, 1949. See also Edward L. Ullman and others, *Maps of State-to-State Rail Freight Movement for 13 States of the United States in 1948,* Office of Naval Research, Contract N5 OR1-07633, Report no. 3, Cambridge, Mass., Harvard, June, 1951.)

in which they are consumed, the task of the railroad is to make relatively short movements possible that assemble materials at convenient points, facilitate processing, and distribute finished products to consumers. Questions of choice of route and of the location of producing and processing points will arise, but on the whole the task will be one of local adjustment. The greater number of railroad shipments are obviously of this sort.

Significance of Long-Haul Movements

Most railway traffic seeks a destination which is as close as business conditions will permit, and this is natural, for transportation costs money, and whatever may be true of passengers, tons of freight have little "wanderlust" and take no pleasure in watching scenery go by. At the same time we must not forget that important types of railway carriage travel long distances. This must be so because the areas of primary production in this country are widely separated from the manufacturing centers, and because factories are often far removed from the large markets which they serve. We know that it is so also because of facts of common knowledge relating to the commodities which we daily use, and because of the recorded average length of hauls which, for some commodities, largely exceed the averages for the United States. Thus, in 1950, the average haul of sugar was 593 miles; of cattle, 614 miles; of lumber, 1,055 miles; and of oranges and grapefruit, 1,727 miles. The railroads and their long-ranging routes are of first importance for transactions of this kind. It is these routes which the following pages will distinguish and describe.

Distribution of Railroad Mileage

The map printed on page 168 indicates the distribution of the railroad mileage of the United States.

Major Railroad Routes in the United States

The long-distance routes into which railroad mileage in this country can be divided may be listed as follows:

1. Trunk Line route.
2. New York–Atlanta route.
3. Chicago–Atlanta route.
4. Mississippi Valley route.
5. Western Grain route.
6. Southwestern Gulf route.
7. Northern Transcontinental route.
8. Central Transcontinental route.
9. Southern Transcontinental route.
10. Pacific Coast route.[2]

[2] Cf. Sidney L. Miller, *Inland Transportation,* New York, McGraw-Hill, 1933, p. 296.

FIGURE 23.   United States Railroad System, 1951. (Association of American
Railroads.)

These routes connect, in general, areas of unlike economic interest.
Thus routes 2 and 3 join together the cotton-, lumber-, and tobacco-
producing South with the manufacturing states of the North Central and
the Northeast. Route 1, with its extension, route 5, connects the North-

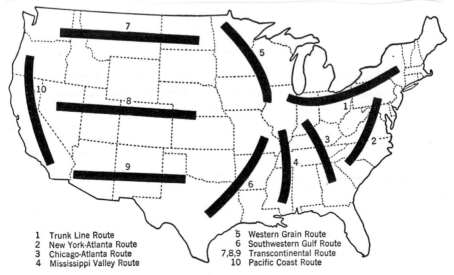

1   Trunk Line Route
2   New York-Atlanta Route
3   Chicago-Atlanta Route
4   Mississippi Valley Route

5   Western Grain Route
6   Southwestern Gulf Route
7,8,9   Transcontinental Route
10   Pacific Coast Route

FIGURE 24.   Major Railroad Routes in the United States.

eastern states with the grain fields of the Northwest. Routes 6, 7, and 8 terminate on the east in the grain belt; and, together with route 9, they tap, on their western end, the petroleum and livestock districts of the Southwest and the mineral, livestock, lumber, and fruit regions of the Rocky Mountains and the Pacific Coast. Route 10 joins the lumber and deciduous fruit sections of the Northwest with the citrus and vegetable districts of southern and central California.

Generally speaking, the nature of traffic over any route can be inferred from the industry of the territory which it serves. It is desirable, however, not to rely upon inference alone; therefore the characteristics of the different routes will be discussed in this chapter in detail.

Route 1. Trunk Line

The most important route in the United States is that between the North Atlantic Seaboard and the state of Illinois.

The larger railroads on the Trunk Line route, outside of New England, are the Pennsylvania, the New York Central, the Baltimore and Ohio, the Chesapeake and Ohio, the Erie, the Norfolk and Western, the Wabash, and the New York, Chicago, & St. Louis. New England territory is occupied for the most part by the New York, New Haven & Hartford, the Boston and Maine, the Maine Central, the Grand Trunk, and the Boston and Albany. Four of the first-named group of carriers have termini at both Chicago and New York and three of these four reach both Chicago and St. Louis. The Wabash and the New York, Chicago, & St. Louis enter Chicago and St. Louis but their lines terminate upon the east at Toledo and Buffalo. The Wabash operates as far west as Kansas City.

The Trunk Line route originally owed its importance to the facilities for communication offered by the Great Lakes, the Ohio River, and later by the Erie Canal. We have already alluded in chapter 4 to the conditions under which railroads entered this territory. The purpose of the railroad companies which built along the Trunk Line route in the 1850's was, in a large way, to share in the outbound grain trade of the northern Mississippi Valley, and at the same time to promote the movement of manufactured goods from the industrial centers of the North Atlantic coast to the farming communities of the West. Their success, the intensive use of the Lake waterways, the rich stores of coal and iron which have been exploited in Pennsylvania, and the extraordinary development of manufactures along the Northeastern seaboard of the United States have made the Trunk Line route the busiest avenue of traffic in the United States, as well as one of the most important in the world.

The route passes from Chicago and St. Louis along the southern shore of the Great Lakes, benefiting from the easy grades and open character of the Great Lakes basin, crosses the Appalachian in Pennsylvania, Maryland, or New York, and reaches the Atlantic seaboard on a line which touches the port of Norfolk on the south and the cities of New York and Boston on the north. For some purposes the whole of New England may be considered as part of the eastern terminus of the Trunk Line route. The southern boundary of this route is the Chesapeake and Ohio Railroad, and its western boundary is the Mississippi River.

On the west the Trunk Line route receives the grain traffic of Kansas, Illinois, Missouri, Nebraska, and the Dakotas, the wool and meat and livestock of the Rocky Mountain states, the copper and iron of Lake Superior, the fruit and sugar and vegetables of California, and the lumber of the Pacific Northwest. A major part of the export trade of the United States is conducted over the Trunk Line railroads. As will appear later, Western routes tend to focus in the territory occupied by the states of Illinois, Missouri, and Iowa; and the Trunk Lines are in an advantageous position to receive and to carry forward such of the Western products as are not locally consumed in the northern Mississippi Valley states. In recent years, however, the competition of the railroads running south from Chicago and St. Louis to the Gulf of Mexico has been increasing, particularly as regards import and export traffic.

RELATION OF NEW ENGLAND TO THE TRUNK LINE ROUTE. New England is located on the northeastern rim of Trunk Line territory. This busy manufacturing region imports large quantities of raw materials—coal, cotton, iron, and steel; it brings in and consumes foodstuffs; and it exports a great variety of manufactured products, many of them of a highly specialized sort. While some of the New England traffic, such as cotton and some fruit, comes from the Southern states, and while a considerable volume of New England manufactures finds a market in the South, most of the trade of New England states goes to swell the east- and west-bound traffic of the Trunk Line systems. Naturally this results in a large influx of cars owned by railroads outside of New England, with important consequences for the New England lines. On September 15, 1951, for instance, the two principal New England railroads, the Boston and Maine and the New York, New Haven & Hartford counted 14,413 boxcars upon their tracks as compared with a total of 9,360 cars which they owned. Such an accumulation of equipment is an advantage to the New England carriers in times of active business; but when traffic is slack it is a disadvantage because the rentals which the New England railroads have to pay for outside cars exceeds the earnings derived from their possession. This matter will be further discussed in chapter 23. The disproportion between eastbound and westbound business makes it necessary to haul many empty cars westbound, but there seems to be no way to prevent this empty-car movement short of changing the entire character of New England industry.

Route 2. New York, Atlanta, New Orleans

Meeting the Trunk Line route on the Northeast but diverging promptly from it in a southwesterly direction is what may be called the New York, Atlanta, and New Orleans route. This route runs roughly parallel with the Appalachian Mountains, between the mountain barrier and the sea, through New Jersey, Pennsylvania, Maryland, Virginia, North and South Carolina, and Georgia.

The largest railroads in this section are the Southern Railway, the Seaboard Air Line, and the Atlantic Coast Line.

The cities along the New York–Atlanta route may be classified in three groups: first, seaports such as Norfolk, Wilmington, Charleston, Savannah, Brunswick, and Jacksonville; and second, a series of towns at the head of navigation of rivers that empty into the Atlantic Ocean or the Gulf. Cities of this type include Richmond, Welden, Columbia, Augusta, and Macon. A third group includes cities along the upper edge of the Piedmont, such as Charlottesville, Lynchburg, Greensboro, Charlotte, Spartanburg, and Atlanta. The southern railways connect towns in these groups with one another and with the coast, while their location enables them to accommodate the current of traffic which flows northeast and southwest between the Southern and the Northeastern states. The northern terminus of Southern railways is Washington, D.C., where connection is made with the Pennsylvania and the Baltimore and Ohio railroads, both characteristically Northern lines. At Atlanta, the New York–Atlanta lines meet railroads leading to the Ohio River gateways on the north. While all three of the lines described end on the south in the state of Georgia, a natural extension takes traffic across the states of Florida, Alabama, and Louisiana to the Gulf ports about the mouth of the Mississippi River.

The topography of the New York–Atlanta route is favorable to railroad traffic in that there is no mountain range to cross. The railroads swing along a series of benches with no great rises or descents. The principal natural obstacle is found in the necessity of traversing a number of east-and-west flowing streams, some of them of considerable magnitude.

Like the Trunk Line route the Southeastern route benefits by a sharp differentiation between the interests and resources of the populations at either end. The Southern states, as has been pointed out, form a region of specialized agriculture. On the other hand, the industrial activity of the Southern region is slight as compared with that of the states in the Northeast, although it is increasing, so that manufactures of all sorts and coal move southbound over the New York–Atlanta route, while northbound the principal traffic consists of cotton, lumber, citrus fruits, and fresh vegetables. In both value and bulk the northbound traffic predominates.[3]

Route 3. Chicago-Atlanta

This route begins in the territory north of the Ohio River and stretches southeast, cutting the New York–Atlanta route at Atlanta, and continuing southeast to the Gulf and to the South Atlantic coast. Over this route pour the grain and flour of the northern Mississippi Valley and the manufactures of Chicago, St. Louis, and the cities of Ohio, Indiana, and Illinois. Northbound the principal commodities are similar to those which leave the Southern states for the Atlantic Seaboard. That is to say, they include cotton, fruit, lumber, and fresh vegetables. The preponderance of traffic is southbound.

At one time railroads operating over the Chicago–Atlanta route engaged in vigorous competition with railroads on the New York–Atlanta route. This competition was especially active after the close of the Civil War and closely followed the establishment of transportation lines and through rates into the South. Corn from Chicago was actually carried at this time via Boston to Atlanta and Chattanooga, while Eastern manufactures were not infrequently brought west via Cincinnati and Louisville, or via Chicago and Cairo, for delivery to Southern destinations.[4]

Agreement between carriers put an end to this form of circuitous competition. There still remained a species of market competition between the routes east and west of the Allegheny Mountains, the ones seeking to supply the Southern states with Eastern manufactures, and the other striving to promote the sale of manufactured products of the Middle West. Even today cities like Atlanta enjoy advantages by access to two competing sources of supply, although some of the rate discriminations which Atlanta, and other cities similarly situated, once enjoyed have been suppressed.

Formerly the Southern railroads west of the Appalachian Mountains were sharply separated from those in the East. The development of great systems south of the Appalachians has tended to make the states of Alabama, Georgia, and Florida a common market and a common source of supply for both New York and Illinois, and to lead the Eastern and the Western railroad systems to interlace their Southern extremities. However, the northeast-southwest route remains distinct from the northwest-southeast route.[5]

[3] National Geographic Society, *The Physiography of the United States,* New York, American Book, 1896.

[4] 6 I.C.C. 195, 216, 1894.

[5] Commodity movements over the New York-Atlanta and the Chicago-Atlanta routes reflect, of course, broad conditions of interterritorial exchange. It is the belief in the South that industrial development in the Southern states has been hindered by rela-

There are no railroad companies which handle traffic over their own rails all the way from Chicago to Atlanta and the Southeast. The nearest approach to this is the Illinois Central line from Chicago to Birmingham. The Southern Railway, however, has a direct route from Cincinnati to southern and southeastern points; and the Louisville and Nashville not only operates between Cincinnati and Atlanta and between Louisville, St. Louis, and Birmingham, but, by virtue of its control of the Atlantic Coast Line, has a reliable connection with most points on the South Atlantic Seaboard. In most cases freight is carried between Chicago and the Ohio River by railroad companies which also serve the Trunk Line route.

Route 4. Mississippi Valley

The products of the northern Mississippi Valley not only press into the old South for local consumption, but they follow the river to Mobile and to New Orleans and pass through these cities on their way to foreign markets. Tropical fruits such as bananas, as well as coffee, potash, guava, sugar, nitrates, and a great variety of other products from South and Central America enter the United States at ports in Texas, Louisiana, and Alabama and travel northward to points beyond the Ohio and Missouri rivers. There is good railroad service, both on northbound and on southbound movements. The Illinois Central carries fruits and vegetables from Hazlehurst, in the Mississippi producing area, to Chicago (772 miles) in 46 hours. Its dispatch freight schedule from New Orleans to Chicago (921 miles) allows 45 hours, and there is a banana train schedule of 39½ hours between the same points of origin and destination. Southbound trains carry merchandise, packing house products and other perishables from Chicago to Memphis (527 miles) in 15 hours, to Birmingham (690 miles) in 22½ hours, and to New Orleans in 34½ hours. Competition between the Mississippi Valley route and the Trunk Line route is very keen, since many products can enter or leave the country equally well by way of the North Atlantic Seaboard or by way of the Gulf.

The Mississippi River is itself a large carrier of freight, as we have seen in chapters 1 and 3. The chief rail carriers south of St. Louis and the Ohio River are the Missouri Pacific on the western side of the river and the Illinois Central, Mobile and Ohio, and Louisville and Nashville on the east. The territory between St. Louis, the Ohio River crossings, and Chicago is served by a number of railroads, including the Illinois Central, the Wabash, the Chicago and Eastern Illinois, the Chicago, Indianapolis & Louisville, and others.

tively high freight rates. (See David M. Potter, "The Historical Development of Eastern-Southern Freight Rate Relationships," *Law and Contemporary Problems,* Summer, 1947, Interterritorial Rates.)

Route 5. Western Grain

West of the Mississippi the general direction of traffic is east and west, and the principal lines of communication reach out toward the Pacific Coast. Common parlance does not, however, speak of these lines of traffic as "transcontinental" until they have crossed the Missouri River; and, as a matter of fact, railroads even some distance west of the Missouri have important movements of freight and passengers to accommodate which are not usually associated with transcontinental business. Such, for instance, is the grain trade of the North Central states and the livestock of the Southwest. It is true, at least of the northern trans-Mississippi railroads, that they represent at their eastern ends rather a western extension of the trunk lines than an eastern extension of the transcontinental properties. The railroad lines serving the grain states of North Dakota, Kansas, Minnesota, Nebraska, South Dakota, and Missouri were referred to in chapter 4 as the "Granger" railroads. The function of the Granger railroads is to collect grain at country elevators and to transport it to primary markets where it is cleaned, mixed, inspected, graded, and weighed. Subsequently that portion of the crop that is not needed for local consumption passes out of the grain districts over connecting routes to more distant markets.

The most important Granger lines are the Chicago and Northwestern; the Chicago, Milwaukee & St. Paul; the Chicago, Burlington, & Quincy; the Chicago, Rock Island, & Pacific; and the Minneapolis, St. Paul, & Sault Ste. Marie.

The largest portion of the Northwestern grain crop handled by these companies empties into the Trunk Line route or takes advantage of the facilities for water transportation offered by the Great Lakes, the St. Lawrence River, and the Erie Canal. Some of it, however, passes south along the Mississippi Valley route for Southern consumption or for export at Galveston or New Orleans. This grain movement will be mentioned in chapter 10. In addition to grain, the Granger roads transport farm and ranch products eastward, including livestock and meat; westward, they carry coal, automobiles, farm machinery, and a variety of manufactured products.

Route 6. Southwestern Gulf

Another route which transports a large amount of freight is the Southwestern Gulf route. This route reaches from Missouri, Iowa, and Illinois southwest and south across Missouri, Oklahoma, Arkansas, and Texas to the Gulf of Mexico. The country traversed is flat except for the Ozark Mountain range and its foothills extending from southern Missouri across Arkansas to the Red River Valley on the southern boundary of Oklahoma. The railroads pass on either side of the Ozarks with an occasional bridge line across them. The important lines have their base in Kansas City and St. Louis, depending for their prosperity upon the markets which they serve in these cities and the connections made there with the larger traffic routes beyond. In this area are east-west channels which connect Memphis and Amarillo and New Orleans and Baton Rouge with Dallas, Fort Worth, Houston, and El Paso. These channels accommodate traffic from Atlanta and points east of the Mississippi when consigned to destinations in the Southwest.

The Southwestern railroads handle a variety of products, including lumber, cotton, sulfur, livestock, wool, grain, fruits, and vegetables.

The largest railroad systems in the Southwest are the Missouri Pacific, the St. Louis and San Francisco, the Southern Pacific, the Atchison, Topeka & Santa Fe, and the Chicago, Rock Island & Pacific. There are, however, a number of smaller companies in this district which are, in the aggregate, of considerable importance. Only two companies, the Santa Fe and the Rock Island, enter Chicago on their own rails; but the Missouri Pacific reaches St. Louis and Kansas City, and the Rock Island, besides Chicago, serves St. Louis and has a branch to Minneapolis. The Southern Pacific, also, through the St. Louis Southwestern, controls a line to St. Louis. Traffic to points east of St. Louis and most business to destinations north of Kansas City is handled by Trunk Line carriers or by the Granger railroads.

Routes 7, 8, 9. Transcontinental

The Trunk Line, Mississippi Valley and Chicago–Atlanta routes converge in the state of Illinois and in eastern Missouri. Here they meet the far-ranging transcontinental routes stretching in narrowing lines from the Mississippi River to the Pacific coast.

The principal transcontinental routes which center in Illinois are three. One, made up mainly of the Chicago, Burlington & Quincy, the Chicago, Milwaukee & St. Paul, the Great Northern, and the Northern Pacific railroads, runs northwest from Chicago to St. Paul and thence west between the fortieth and forty-eighth parallels of latitude to Portland and Seattle on the North Pacific coast. This may be called the Northern route.

The Central Transcontinental route goes nearly due west from Chicago to Omaha. From there it proceeds via Denver and Salt Lake City to Sacramento and San Francisco Bay, with branches in western Colorado and Utah which reach diagonally northwest to Portland and southwest to Los Angeles. The principal railroads involved are the Chicago and Northwestern, the Chicago, Rock Island & Pacific, and the Chicago, Burlington & Quincy on the eastern end; and the Union Pacific, the Denver and Rio Grande, the Southern (Central) Pacific, and the Western Pacific in the center and in the west.

A third transcontinental route, the Southern route, extends from the southern part of California through New Mexico, Arizona, and Texas to a junction with the southern end of the Mississippi Valley and the New York, Atlanta, and New Orleans routes, affording an indirect connection with Chicago and a more direct one with the cities of the Atlantic Seaboard. The principal carrier on this route is the Southern Pacific Company.

In addition to the three transcontinental routes just mentioned there is the route of the Atchison, Topeka & Santa Fe Railway Company, which is partly southern and partly central in its location. This railroad is, with the exception of the Chicago, Milwaukee & St. Paul, the only carrier which connects Chicago with the Pacific Coast over its own rails. Its lines run from Chicago to Kansas City, thence west to Colorado, and thence southwest into New Mexico. Since 1909 the Santa Fe has also operated a more direct route from Kansas City southwest through Wichita and the Panhandle of Texas to a point upon its main line near Albuquerque, New Mexico. From Albuquerque the Santa Fe proceeds westerly through New Mexico and Arizona to California, where its tracks turn to the north and reach a terminus on San Francisco Bay. A branch provides connection with Los Angeles.

The transcontinental routes are very long, and they cross regions which differ widely from one another in climate, natural resources, and density of population. On their eastern end the transcontinental railroads do a considerable local business, multiplying their feeder lines and serving intensively a wealthy agricultural population. Further west, these railroads enter the range country, more arid in character and used chiefly for the pasturage of cattle and sheep. Finally, upon the Pacific Coast, the transcontinental railroads again find an agricultural community, which produces little grain but a vast amount of lumber and a great variety of vegetables and fruits.

The commodities which move in largest volume westbound over the transcontinental routes are steel products, automobiles and automobile parts, and manufactured products of many sorts. Eastbound, the principal shipments are of fresh fruits, vegetables, lumber, canned goods, sugar, wines and brandies, and dried fruits.

Most citrus fruit from California goes by way of Arizona because the southern route from the major producing areas to points of destination is shorter than a route through central or northern states. Deciduous fruits, on the other hand, are shipped through Utah because the orchards lie farther north. Fresh vegetables grown in northern California move through Ogden; those grown in the south, through Arizona. A large proportion of canned goods uses the central route, somewhat because of climatic conditions, but mainly because of the northern location of the canneries. More of the beans go out by way of Arizona: first, because of heavier production in the south and, secondly, because Southern and Southwestern states are large consumers of beans. Dried fruit, centering around Fresno and San Jose, moves in about equal proportions through Utah and Arizona. Roughly 50 percent of the sugar traffic goes through Arizona. Formerly the percentage was lower, but the production of sugar beets in the Imperial Valley and in the southern part of the San Joaquin Valley has increased. Moreover, additions to the output of beet sugar in Colorado, Utah, and in Montana and the Dakotas have caused increasing amounts of California beet sugar to move south into Oklahoma and Texas; while direct shipments of cane sugar from Hawaii through the Panama Canal have removed some of the traffic upon which the central route relied. Most of the infusorial earth produced in the state of California comes from Lompoc in the southern part of the state, and is consumed by sugar refiners in Texas, Louisiana, Cuba, and along the Atlantic Seaboard. The natural route is through the South.

Westbound traffic originating north of the Ohio River and the southern boundary of Missouri and Kansas moves by way of Utah when destined to points north of the Tehachapi but otherwise by way of Arizona. Products originating south of this described line, on the whole, prefer the Arizona route, even to destinations in central California.

Normally, eastbound transcontinental traffic should exceed westbound because of the large volume of fruit, vegetables, and lumber moved out of the Pacific Coast. During World War II the relationship was disturbed by heavy government shipments to the West; but since 1945 something like the normal balance has been resumed. On the Southern Pacific lines, in 1948, 61.6 percent of the average daily carloads through El Paso and Ogden moved eastbound and 38.4 percent westbound. As between Utah and Arizona, roughly 60 percent of the eastbound and 47 percent of the westbound used the Utah route.

Route 10. Pacific Coast

There is continuous rail connection north and south along the Pacific coast from Puget Sound in the north to San Diego in the south. The nearness of the ocean causes competition between rail and water carriers to be keen upon this route. Indeed, rail rates from San Francisco to Los Angeles and Portland have been, until recently, less than those to some intermediate points because of the depressing effect of water service upon the charges for through service between points connected by water lines. But freight moves all-rail between northern and southern California cities in spite of water competition, and between central and southern California, taken as a whole, and the states of Washington and Oregon.

This list of railroad routes is not, of course, a complete enumeration of the paths followed by the long distance traffic of the United States, omitting as it does the many minor routes contained within the larger ones, although these minor routes are frequently clearly marked and carry a considerable burden of traffic. It will serve, however, to indicate the major flows of long-distance traffic, and will show the railroad groups over which these flows take place.

REFERENCES

General Treatises

Haney, Lewis H., *The Business of Railway Transportation,* New York, Ronald, 1924.

Johnson, E. R., Huebner, G. G., and Wilson, G. L., *Transportation, Economic Principles and Practices,* New York, Appleton-Century-Crofts, 1940.

Landon, Charles E., *Transportation, Principles, Practice, Problems,* New York, Sloane, 1951.

Miller, Sidney L., *Inland Transportation,* New York, McGraw-Hill, 1933.

Other Books

McPherson, Logan G., *Railroad Freight Rates in Relation to the Industry and Commerce of the United States,* New York, Holt, 1909.

National Geographic Society, *The Physiography of the United States,* New York, American Book, 1896.

Spearman, Frank Hamilton, *The Strategy of Great Railroads,* New York, Scribner's, 1906.

Van Cleef, Eugene, *Trade Centers and Trade Routes,* New York, Appleton-Century-Crofts, 1937.

Periodicals

Potter, David M., "The Historical Development of Eastern-Southern Freight Rate Relationships," *Law and Contemporary Problems,* Summer, 1947.

Ullman, Edward L., "The Railroad Pattern of the United States," *The Geographical Review,* April, 1949.

Special and Miscellaneous

Ullman, Edward L., and Others, *Maps of State-to-State Rail Freight Movement for 13 States of the United States in 1948,* Office of Naval Research, Contract N5 OR1-07633, Report No. 3, Cambridge, Mass., Harvard, June, 1951.

United States Interstate Commerce Commission, *Consolidation of Railroads,* 63 I.C.C. 455, 1921.

United States Interstate Commerce Commission, Bureau of Transport Economics and Statistics, *Carload Waybill Analyses, 1949, Distribution of Freight Traffic and Revenue Averages by Commodity Classes and Rate Territories,* July, 1950.

United States, Office of the Federal Coordinator of Transportation, *Freight Traffic Report,* vol. 3, 1935.

Commodity Movements: Coal, Steel, Grain, Livestock

The routes described in the three preceding chapters provide the principal highways over which goods move from their localized sources of production in the United States to widely distributed and often distant markets. The general view which the description of these routes presents may now be supplemented by examination of the movement of a few selected commodities. The articles chosen will be coal, iron and steel, lumber, grain, livestock, sugar, and fruit. These commodities all rank among the principal groups that furnish tonnage with which railroads are concerned, and some of them move in quantities over inland waterway routes or highways also. Their transportation is important from the point of view of volume, and it is convenient, also, to discuss these commodity flows because they will serve as text or illustration for later explanations of rates and competition.

Coal

The accompanying map indicates the location of the coal fields of the United States. Most of the bituminous coal in the United States is produced in what is known as the Appalachian region, extending from Pennsylvania in the North to Alabama in the South, and including the states of Pennsylvania, Ohio, Virginia, West Virginia, eastern Kentucky, Tennessee, Alabama, and Maryland. The so-called eastern region comes next in importance, covering the states of Illinois, Indiana, and western Kentucky. Other important sources of coal are in the western region, with Iowa, Missouri, Oklahoma, Kansas, and Arkansas; in the mountain region, chiefly Colorado, Wyoming, Utah, and Montana; and in New Mexico and Texas. Out of a total production of 529 million tons in 1951 the Appalachian produced 403, the eastern region 96, the mountain region 20, and the western region 10 million tons. Most of the anthracite coal was mined in Pennsylvania.[1]

[1] *Minerals Yearbook,* 1951.

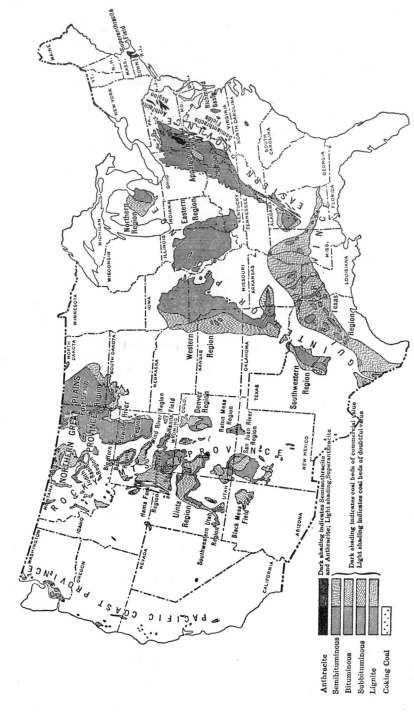

FIGURE 25. Coal Fields of the United States. (J. G. Glover and W. B. Cornell, *The Development of American Industries,* Prentice-Hall, New York, 1932. Adapted from map by Marius R. Campbell of the United States Geological Survey.)

Direction of Movement

Much coal is locally consumed, principally to produce electric power, to drive railroad engines, and for general manufacturing and domestic use; but the demand for these purposes in the various coal mining districts is, naturally, not enough to absorb the supply in all areas, so that a large tonnage passes from sections with surplus production to sections where coal is insufficiently or not at all produced.

The most important surplus districts for bituminous are in West Virginia, Pennsylvania, and Kentucky, and, to a less degree, in Illinois, Alabama, and in the western states of Colorado, New Mexico, Utah, and Wyoming. Of these, the first three much exceed all others in exportable production.

The direction of bituminous coal movements can be followed, in a general way, with the aid of details provided in a map of production districts as set forth in the Bituminous Coal Act of 1937.[2]

In the map reproduced upon page 182 origin districts for bituminous coal are indicated by numbered areas from 1 to 23. The all-rail movements from these districts to three large consuming areas were, in 1939, in the volume shown in Table 13. If we examine the movements indicated in Table 13 with reference to locations shown upon the map we find that rail transport of bitumnious coal produced, in 1939, the following pattern:

Bituminous coal from areas 1 to 6, or from the northern part of the

[2] The districts indicated upon the map are the following:

1. Central Pennsylvania, Maryland, and part of northern West Virginia.
2. Western Pennsylvania.
3. Northern West Virginia.
4. Ohio.
5. Michigan.
6. West Virginia "Panhandle."
7. Southern West Virginia and Virginia "Smokeless."
8. Southern West Virginia, east Kentucky, part of Virginia and Tennessee.
9. West Kentucky.
10. Illinois.
11. Indiana.
12. Iowa.
13. Alabama.
14. Arkansas and Oklahoma.
15. Missouri, Kansas, Oklahoma field.
16. Northern Colorado.
17. Western and southern Colorado, northern New Mexico.
18. Arizona and New Mexico.
19. Wyoming, Idaho.
20. Utah.
22. Montana.
23. Washington, Oregon.

The source is United States Board of Investigation and Research, *The Economics of Coal Traffic Flow,* 79th C., 1st S., Sen. Doc. 82, September 20, 1944.

TABLE 13.   All-Rail Movements of Bituminous Coal for Industrial
and Domestic Uses to Market Areas

Districts of Origin	Areas of Destination		
	Area East of the Mississippi and North of the Ohio and Potomac Rivers (tons)	Area East of the Mississippi and South of the Ohio and Potomac Rivers (tons)	Area West of the Mississippi (tons)
Districts 1–6	45,292,540	8,065	65,780
Districts 7, 8, 9	39,449,800	27,164,744	2,839,618
District 13	51	3,675,186	26,576
Districts 10, 11	27,477,569	49,702	9,420,064
Districts 12, 14–20, 22, 23	146,612	2,880	13,941,977
Total	112,366,572	30,900,577	26,294,024

SOURCE: United States Board of Investigation and Research, *The Economics of Coal Traffic Flow*, 79th C., 1st S., Sen. Doc. 82, September 20, 1944, p. 70. The distribution of coal is also given, for 1944, in the *Minerals Yearbook, 1944*, pp. 838–839.

Appalachian field, found its markets north of the Ohio and east of the Mississippi rivers. The movement included shipments into New England and eastern New York. The reliance of the Northeastern states upon Appalachian coal is of long standing; the increase in the use of fuel oil,

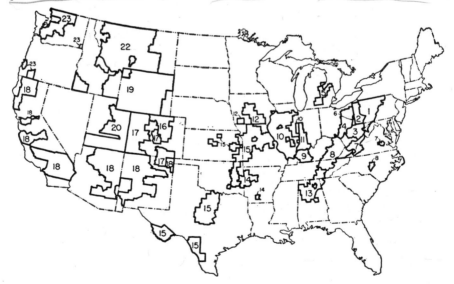

FIGURE 26.   Bituminous Coal Producing Districts. (Board of Investigation and Research, *The Economics of Coal Traffic Flow*, 79th Congress, 1st Session, Sen. Doc. 82, 1944.)

natural gas, and water power, however, and the more effective employ-ment of coal have somewhat reduced the volume of shipments in recent years, and there has been a tendency for more southerly mines in the Appalachian territory to improve their position in competition with northern mines for coastal business. Little coal from areas 1 to 6 crossed the Ohio River to the south or the Mississippi River to the west, by rail. Mines in these districts did, however, contribute largely to the Lake move-ment which began at Lake Erie ports.

Areas 7, 8, and 9 shipped into Ohio, Indiana, and Illinois. Their coal also moved into the northwestern states of Michigan, Wisconsin, and Iowa, where coal was used for manufacturing but also largely for domestic purposes. Carloads from the ranges moved north to Lake Erie and thence by boat to harbors on Lakes Superior or Michigan where they were re-shipped to ultimate destinations.[3] These were the notorious "Lake cargo" shipments. Or they moved directly west by rail without making use of lake facilities. Areas 7, 8, and 9 were also the principal reliance of the states south of the Ohio and east of the Mississippi. Indeed, except for district 13, in Alabama, there was no other area which shipped, in quan-tity, to Southern consuming points. Some coal, in addition, reached New England and New York in the northeast by way of South Atlantic ports such as Baltimore, Hampton Roads, and Charleston, and some moved west across the Mississippi.[4]

Areas 10 and 11 found their chief outlet east of the Mississippi and north of the Ohio, as one would expect. Illinois, however, borders upon the Mississippi and its mines shipped in larger quantities to Western markets than did any other of the numbered districts upon the map. Its markets included Missouri, Iowa, Kansas, Nebraska, and the Dakotas. Here the Eastern mines competed with each other and with coal from the Southwest and from the Rocky Mountains. In Nebraska, which may serve as an illustration, coal was sold from all adjoining states except possibly South Dakota, and also from Illinois, Indiana, Kentucky, West Virginia, Arkansas, and Oklahoma, and a small amount arrived from Utah. In earlier years coal from Colorado and Wyoming had been distributed as far east as the Missouri River but the volume of this tonnage declined because of competition from other producing fields, particularly from those in Oklahoma, Arkansas, and Illinois. Coal consumption in Kansas and Nebraska has been somewhat reduced, however, by the increasing availability of natural gas.[5]

[3] 201 I.C.C. 271, 1934.

[4] 201 I.C.C. 271, 1934. The lake cargo controversy is discussed in Harvey C. Mans-field, *The Lake Cargo Coal Rate Controversy,* New York, Columbia University, 1932.

[5] 218 I.C.C. 693, 697, 1936. An interesting analysis of market regions in the coal industry, arranged in a somewhat different manner from that presented in the text, is given in a volume published by the National Industrial Conference Board in 1931

It is evident from the preceding analysis that coal movements are complicated, spreading out from the two great sources of supply in the Appalachian and in the Illinois–Indiana fields, and are interrupted by the presence of local supplies with which the principal coal-producing areas find it necessary to compete. Differences in the quality of coals in different districts, the physical limitations of some areas, and a freight rate system which facilitates long-distance competitive transportation make it possible for the principal regions to ship around and beyond their rivals in minor fields, although competition with these producers as well as with other forms of fuel limits the price which they can charge.[6]

(*The Competitive Position of Coal in the United States,* New York, pp. 142–143). This analysis is as follows:

"The primary market regions (for coal) are:

"1. The market region of the northern Appalachian group of coal fields, which comprises the northeastern United States as far south as Tennessee and North Carolina and westward over Ohio and Michigan and the states that make up the Lake Dock territory—Wisconsin, Minnesota, the Dakotas, and a small portion of Iowa, and, in addition, adjacent provinces of Canada.

"2. The eastern interior market region, supplied by coal from Illinois, Indiana, and western Kentucky, which is confined to the states of production, to a considerable movement into the states west of the Mississippi River, and to a smaller outlet in the Lake Dock territory and southward into Tennessee and Mississippi.

"3. The southeastern market region, dominated by the Alabama coal field. The coal from this region meets competition in the east from northern rail and coastwise coal shipments and in the west from western Kentucky and Illinois coals.

"4. The large market region west of the Mississippi River, which consists of a number of local markets, small in comparison with the great eastern markets, and competing with fuel oil, natural gas, and water power.

"Between these more or less well-defined market territories are certain areas that are common grounds for competition between widely separated coal production provinces. Most important of these is the Lake Dock Territory, the market of which is sought by both the Illinois-Indiana producers and those in the Appalachian states. . . .

"Of less importance are the competitive zones between the Appalachian field and Alabama in the southeastern Atlantic Coast states, in Iowa and Missouri, where Illinois coal competes with local coals, and in the intermediate western states, which receive supplies from both the Illinois fields and the Rocky Mountain states."

[6] The emphasis in the text has been upon rail shipments of bituminous coal. There are, of course, large shipments of anthracite, especially from Pennsylvania eastward. There are also coal shipments by water and by truck. On the whole, coal movements are predominantly by rail because coal fields are not located upon water routes, and railroads have advantages over trucks in long hauls of a low grade commodity such as coal. The water route participates, however, in the transportation of coal which is brought from the Appalachian fields to Lake Erie ports by rail or truck, thence shipped by water to harbors on Lake Michigan and Lake Superior, and there again transhipped for delivery in Wisconsin, Minnesota, and in other western states (see chap. 7).

Trucks share in the carriage of coal to Lake ports from the mines. They also handle a good deal of anthracite to eastern destinations. In 1939 about 12 percent of the anthracite coal traffic from Pennsylvania fields was carried by truck as against 85 percent by rail, mainly to destinations in the New England states and in the Middle Atlantic states of New York, New Jersey, and Pennsylvania. Minor tonnages of anthracite went south into Delaware, the District of Columbia, and westward into Illinois, Michigan, and into other states as far as Minnesota. Trucks played no part, however, in dis-

Geographers point out the importance of the fact that coal in the United States is found in the interior of the continent, instead of near the seaboard as in the case of other continents. Had there been coal along the coasts but not in the interior, say Bengston and Van Royen, the cost of hauling agricultural products to seaboard markets would have been prohibitive and agricultural prosperity could not have been achieved. Without agricultural prosperity, industrial growth in the interior would have been impossible. Without the great markets of the Middle West and the Rockies, the industrial progress of the East would have been seriously curtailed.[7]

Steel

The manufacture of steel requires two principal raw materials, iron ore and coal. The supply of each material is localized. We have just seen that coal is abundant in certain sections of Pennsylvania and Illinois, and that the coal of this region happens to have the characteristics most serviceable in the production of steel. As for ore, 81 percent of the iron ore of the country is mined near the shores of Lake Superior, and the Great Lakes supply a route which brings this ore at minimum expense to eastern points. Ore and coal must meet, preferably at some intermediate place where the transportation costs are not too great, and this fact, along with the pull of the market, explains the industry's position.[8]

Distribution of Steel-Producing Points

Most steel, because of the conditions mentioned, is produced in the four states of Pennsylvania, Ohio, Indiana, and Illinois, with lesser amounts in New York, Maryland, Alabama, West Virginia, and other

tribution to the west except where hauls were relatively short. (United States Board of Investigation and Research, *The Economics of Coal Traffic Flow,* 79th C., 1st S., Sen. Doc. 82, September, 1944.

[7] Nels A. Bengston and Willem Van Royen, *Fundamentals of Economic Geography,* New York, Prentice-Hall, 1938.

[8] According to data collected by the United States Board of Investigation and Research, 2.196 long tons of iron ore and 1.506 tons of coking coal are required, on the average, with other materials, to produced one long ton of finished steel (*Report on the Economics of Iron and Steel Transportation,* 1945).

Iron ore usually moves toward coal, although the weight involved is somewhat greater, both because of low costs of transport and because the most desirable ore fields are further removed from consumption areas than are good coking coal fields. Coal is relatively more important to iron and steel mills than the ratio of coal to ore consumption in the production of pig iron would indicate, because it is a source of power as well as of heat throughout the entire production process in the industry; this fact, however, would not explain its relative immobility (Temporary National Economic Committee, *Investigation of the Concentration of Economic Power,* Hearings, vol. 18, 76th C., 2d S., 1939, p. 115. See also United States Board of Investigation and Research, *The Economics of Iron and Steel Transportation,* Sen. Doc. 80, 79th C., 1st S., 1945).

states.[9] More definitely, the two great centers of the industry are in the Pittsburgh district, which may be extended for our present purpose to include the Lake Erie cities from Buffalo to Detroit and the plants of eastern Ohio, and the Gary–South Chicago mills at the foot of Lake Michigan. Both can obtain ore from Lake Superior at moderate cost, and both have easy access to the coal of Pennsylvania and Illinois.

FIGURE 27.   Geographic Distribution of Steelmaking Capacity. (C. R. Daugherty, M. G. de Chazeau, and S. S. Stratton, *The Economics of the Iron and Steel Industry,* Vol. 1, McGraw-Hill Book Company, Inc., 1937.)

The establishment of a steel industry in the vicinity of Chicago has been, in part, responsive to changes in the distribution of population and to the consequent enlargement of the consuming power of the Central West, and in part it has been the outgrowth of changes in mining and manufacturing techniques. In particular, technical improvements have reduced the attractiveness of sites near the coal fields. Among these improvements may be classed the better utilization of gases thrown off in the process of reducing coal to coke and the reduction in the amount of

[9] American Iron and Steel Institute, *Annual Statistical Report,* 1950.

heat required for steel manufacture by the maintenance of continuous high temperature in the ingot between the furnace and the rolls. If these advances in the art continue, and if, also, ores are mined with a smaller percentage of metallic content, so that more ore will necessarily be moved in order to secure a given quantity of iron, the position of the Central Western districts will become increasingly secure.[10]

Consumption of Semiprocessed Steel

These facts relating to the iron and steel industry are so well known that we may pass on without discussion. What is not so well understood is that the consumption of steel, as well as its production, is localized. In one sense iron and steel products are among the most widely distributed of all articles. Food, clothing, and hardware are the three staples which are found in both city and village stores. But the demand for heavier steel products such as wire rods, plates, shapes, bars, etc., which generally require further processing, is by no means so dispersed. Such articles are delivered to industries that produce finished goods, and since these industries are geographically concentrated, movements of steel are, for this reason, circumscribed.

The principal consumers of semiprocessed steel are the following: automotive industries, building and construction, food containers, railroads, industrial and electrical machinery, domestic appliances and cutlery, and agricultural industries. The concentration among these and other consumers of steel products was considered by de Chazeau on the basis of figures of the value added by manufacture in 1927. His conclusions were that 90 percent of the motor vehicles, 82.8 percent of the agricultural implements, 72.1 percent of the engines, turbines, and wheels, 68.5 percent of the electrical goods, 59.7 percent of the machine tools, and 61.1 percent of the railroad cars of the United States were then produced in the five states of Illinois, Ohio, Pennsylvania, New York, and Michigan, all lying in a territory bounded on the west by the Mississippi River, on the south by the Ohio River and the southern boundary of Pennsylvania, and on the east by New Jersey and the line of the Hudson River. Almost half of the value added by manufacture in the agricultural implement industry was contributed by Illinois; about the same percentage in the

---

[10] It is possible that future developments may change the location pattern of steel production in the United States in still other ways, altering the optimum locations for the manufacture of steel and products of steel intended for the major markets. The exhaustion of the easily mined ore deposits of the Lake Superior District and the increase in Canadian production would be important factors. It has been suggested that Pittsburgh may lose ground to Detroit, Birmingham, and to the Far West. (Walter Isard and W. M. Capron, "The Future Locational Pattern of Iron and Steel Production in the United States," *Journal of Political Economy*, April, 1949, pp. 118–133). The forecast is still only an estimate, and its accuracy cannot be assumed. See chap. 3.

railroad car industry by Illinois and Pennsylvania; 65 percent in the motor vehicle industry by Michigan, and 27 percent in the machine tools industry by Ohio. These industries are purchasers of semiprocessed steel. It is obvious that iron and steel products must move to the places where such customers of the industry are to be found; and that, since the location of these customers is predominantly in five states, shipments must go to these states in greatest quantity.[11]

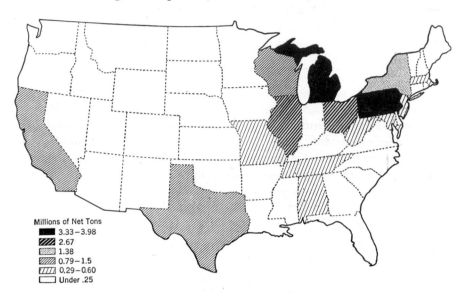

Millions of Net Tons
- 3.33–3.98
- 2.67
- 1.38
- 0.79–1.5
- 0.29–0.60
- Under .25

FIGURE 28. Purchases of Semi-Processed Steel by Consuming States. (Adapted from map of Board of Investigation and Research, *The Economics of Iron and Steel Transportation*, 1945.)

Handling of Steel Manufactures

The remarks in the preceding paragraphs have been directed to the movement of steel, semifinished or finished, but in most cases to steel which requires some further processing before it can be delivered to the ultimate consumer. The forms which this steel takes when it has been processed or assembled into a consumers' good has been indicated to some

[11] The movement of steel products from mills to consumers is adequately explained, at any moment, by the location of consuming industries, and this is the circumstance referred to in the text. This location is itself, however, controlled by the possibilities of cheap transportation. According to McCarty (*The Geographic Basis of American Economic Life*, New York, Harper, 1940, p. 500) this location is upon natural transportation routes connecting New York and Philadelphia with Buffalo, Detroit, Chicago, and Lake Erie points. There are other elements, of course, which influence the locational pattern (United States Board of Investigation and Research, *The Economics of Iron and Steel Transportation*, op. cit., 1945, pp. 106–113).

extent by the list of industries which use rolled steel. These forms may be automobiles or engines, machines, tools, pipes, hardware, electrical equipment, or any of thousands of articles used in the railroad, construction, petroleum, agricultural, or other industries; or they may be goods used by the domestic consumer in and about the home. In the case of many types of consumable products the final distribution follows the spread of population. These steel shipments are not restricted to movements within the producing area; they occur also between the centers of production in Pennsylvania, Indiana, Illinois, and elsewhere, and a great range of destinations in other parts of the United States.

Characteristics of Transportation

Steel hauls are of moderate length, on the average, for reasons which have been given, although some consumer goods move long distances and some semifinished products cannot be locally produced in all territories.[12] On the whole the traffic is desirable from the railroad point of view because the movement is heavy, concentrated, and steady; and rates, though low, can be made substantially higher than the cost of the service rendered.[13] The average loading exceeds that in the major railroad commodity classes except in that of products of mines, and loss and damage claims are relatively small. These same characteristics make steel business attractive to water carriers. There is competition upon the Great Lakes where the destination points permit, and there is competition upon the Mississippi River, although the major steel movements cannot easily resort to river hauls.[14]

To some extent even trucks are used to carry iron and steel. The Interstate Commerce Commission has remarked that trucks desire steel traffic because of its greater weight, space considered, than that of other business,[15] but highway facilities are hardly adequate to carry steel long distances except in the case of shipments of comparatively small units.

[12] Analysis of waybills filed with the Interstate Commerce Commission on a sample basis, in 1950, showed that out of a total of 777,758 tons of steel articles arriving at destinations in the United States, 615,084 tons, or 79 percent, originated in Official Classification Territory. It showed further that out of the 615,084 tons originating in Official Classification Territory, 514,041 tons, or 83 percent, terminated their movement in the same territory. The average haul for all steel shipments originating in Official Territory was 418 miles; that of steel shipments both originating and terminating in the territory was 248 miles. (See United States Interstate Commerce Commission, Bureau of Transport Economics and Statistics, *Carload Waybill Analyses, 1950,* Statement no. 5131, 1951.)

[13] It was the position of the railroads, in 1945, that, in the absence of effective competition by other forms of transport, iron and steel articles constituted a traffic which would move freely on relatively high rates (263 I.C.C. 361, 383, 1945).

[14] 210 I.C.C. 281, 1935. See also United States Board of Investigation and Research, *Report on the Economics of Iron and Steel Transportation,* 1945, p. 48.

[15] 213 I.C.C., 797, 799, 1936.

Competition of Producing Areas

In 1929 the Interstate Commerce Commission had occasion to review the characteristics of the rate structure applying to iron and steel articles. In doing this it divided steel producing territory into three parts: western, including mills in Chicago and western Ohio, Indiana, Michigan, Kentucky, and Wisconsin; middle, including eastern Ohio, West Virginia, western Pennsylvania, and the Buffalo district in New York; and eastern, including New England, eastern New York, New Jersey, Maryland–Delaware, and eastern Pennsylvania. It concluded that each of these districts had surplus capacity, but that except in the middle district, not much cross-shipping occurred. Producers in the western district, according to the Commission, did not reach east of Pittsburgh to any great extent, nor did New England or eastern mills ship to points west of that city. The middle district mills, however, competed actively in eastern territory as far as New England, and in western territory in the direction of Chicago.[16] But in the case of shipments from the principal sources of production to outside areas—and these exist—rate structures are delicately balanced and competition appears to be severe. Thus producers in Trunk Line territory compete actively with those in the Pittsburgh district on shipments to Texas and Louisiana points,[17] and to destinations in Utah, Colorado, and Wyoming.[18] Chicago and Pittsburgh compete at St. Paul; [19] Chicago, Birmingham, and Pittsburgh compete on traffic to the Pacific Coast.[20] These are illustrations of a large variety of contacts in which the rivalry of sources of production, of different types of transport, and of competing centers of distribution is expressed. The effect of rate differences in the steel industry has been obscured, until recently, by the so-called "basing point" system of steel price fixing. This has, however, been modified because of decisions by the Supreme Court of the United States.

Wheat

Most American wheat, and especially most wheat beyond the needs of local consumption, is grown in the range of states west of the Mississippi from North Dakota to Texas.[21] To this should be added a large production in Washington and Montana and lesser crops in Colorado, Idaho,

---

[16] 155 I.C.C. 517, 544, 1929.

[17] 226 I.C.C. 298, 1938; 245 I.C.C. 640, 1941.

[18] 245 I.C.C. 569, 1941; 268 I.C.C. 281, 1947.

[19] 263 I.C.C. 361, 377, 1945.

[20] 255 I.C.C. 739, 1943; 264 I.C.C. 503, 1946; 266 I.C.C. 689, 1946. The transcontinental rate from Birmingham is the same as that from Chicago. The controlling rate in this case, however, is a combination of the rail rate from point of origin to an Atlantic or Gulf port and the water rate from the seaboard to the Pacific coast or, in Far Eastern business, the water rate direct to a Far Eastern destination.

[21] The states referred to in the text are Kansas, North Dakota, Nebraska, Oklahoma, South Dakota, and Texas, in the order named.

and Oregon. Wheat is grown in states east of the Mississippi and north of the Ohio, but the output in this area is insufficient to satisfy the local demand. Table 14 gives, for 1950, the acreage harvested and the number of bushels produced in the Western states in the North Dakota range; it also compares the production of this group with that of the entire United States.

TABLE 14.   Wheat Acreage and Production,
United States, 1951

State	Acreage Harvested (000 acres)	Production (000 bushels)
North Dakota	10,485	150,975
Kansas	9,701	126,113
Nebraska	4,005	58,073
Oklahoma	4,095	38,902
South Dakota	3,839	57,260
Texas	1,923	17,307
Total	34,048	448,630
Other	27,376	538,844
Total	61,424	987,474

SOURCE: United States Department of Agriculture, *Agricultural Statistics,* 1952. p. 4.

Concentration of Grain at Country Elevators

The first step in the transportation of grain is its carriage from the farm to the country elevator close to railroad tracks. This haul was once accomplished by horse and wagon and is now performed by auto truck. The country elevator stores the grain which it receives for subsequent rail shipment and, frequently, cleans, mixes, and dries it in order to improve its grade.

Shipments of Grain from Country Elevator to Primary Markets

Most grain reported by country elevators and warehouses is shipped to large terminal markets. A small proportion is forwarded to less important centers, and the balance is sold to mills, feeders, interior brokers, retailers, etc. The leading terminal markets for wheat are Minneapolis, Duluth, Kansas City, Hutchinson, Omaha, St. Louis, Wichita, Toledo, Chicago, St. Joseph, Peoria, Indianapolis, Sioux City, and Milwaukee, in the order given.[22]

[22] Board of Trade of the City of Chicago, *Annual Report for the Year Ended December 31, 1951.*

It will be noticed that the majority of primary wheat markets and milling centers are located within or adjacent to the areas of largest wheat production. These markets are also important terminals of grain-carrying Trunk Line railroads. Duluth, Chicago, Toledo, and Milwaukee occupy positions on the Great Lakes, and Kansas City, Chicago, and St. Louis have facilities or potential facilities for shipping by river. Minneapolis is near enough to Duluth to make the Lake route available.

Functions of Primary Markets. Reshipment to Secondary Markets

At primary markets grain is inspected, graded, cleaned, mixed and conditioned, and stored in terminal elevators. From these elevators much grain is withdrawn for local consumption, including milling.

There is little movement from one primary market to another, but grain proceeds from concentrating points in the grain-producing districts toward centers of consumption in the East and South. The export trade is variable. During the middle 1930's and again from 1939 to 1943 most wheat produced was consumed within the United States. Prior to 1931, however, the export trade in wheat was much more considerable, and during the last few years it has become again of major magnitude. In 1949, 314 million bushels or their flour equivalent left this country, out of a total production of 1,027 million bushels.[23] In general, the surplus of the Mississippi Valley distributes itself in the states east and south of Indiana, Illinois, and Ohio. This movement is facilitated by the development of secondary markets which provide facilities for local distribution or spring up where a break in transportation occurs, as at Buffalo or at points on the Ohio River.

Competition

Carriers compete vigorously for participation in the carriage of wheat, and difficult rate problems arise because of the rivalry of different lines and of the communities which these lines serve. The competitive movements begin with the transportation of the wheat from farm or country elevators to the primary market and end with its delivery at Liverpool or at the domestic destination where it is finally consumed. Out of the price obtained at the terminal all prior costs are met, including farm, transportation, and commission expense. It follows that the higher the rate into any market and, also, the higher the charge from primary market to ultimate destination, the lower the price which millers can pay for grain upon the farm and the smaller the volume of business which dealers in any city can transact, especially if the transportation rate upon any alternative route through any alternative transshipping place amounts to less than it does by way of the city with which we suppose ourselves to be

[23] United States Department of Agriculture, *Agricultural Statistics*, 1950.

concerned. Very small differences in cost will cause the diversion of wheat from one route to another, and rates are intricately balanced to accommodate, insofar as possible, the divergent interests of all competing groups.

Once collected in the primary markets, wheat may be milled and reshipped as flour, or it may be forwarded, after having been inspected and graded, to the more important centers of consumption farther east. Grain differs from coal and iron in that it is not a material to be used in further production, except as milling may be regarded as a manufacturing process, but a commodity which is to be consumed. It is not, therefore, attracted to any particular area because of the presence of factories at such a spot, nor does it need to be combined with any other commodity before it becomes a good fit for human use. Grain differs also from a product such as coal or steel in that the location of the industry is mostly upon the outskirts of instead of in the center of the densely settled sections of the United States. This location is partly the result of soil and climatic conditions; to a considerable degree it is, besides, a consequence of the fact that wheat farming uses land less intensively than does manufacturing or even some other forms of agriculture and cannot earn a profit on high-priced acreage such as other forms of use are able to control. Whatever the cause, grain-producing districts are not, by and large, great grain-consuming districts. Grain is consumed where there are people to eat it; grain is grown where natural and price conditions are favorable to agriculture; and these two conditions are not, at the same places, generally fulfilled.

Wheat Routes

From the point of view of traffic geography the problem is to trace the flow of wheat from the numerous milling centers mostly west of the Mississippi River, where it is collected from the farms, to its principal destinations in the East. This flow takes place over several routes.

One such route is by way of the Great Lakes. We have already described the character and extent of Lake movements of grain in chapter 7. Lake channels run from west to east; they begin near an important wheat-growing section of the country; and they terminate in an area of dense population. They offer an obvious and an advantageous facility for the carriage of grain.

A second important pathway is built up by a combination of the Western Grain route and the Trunk Line route described in chapter 9. The service on this line is railroad service; neither motor vehicle nor pipe lines, indeed, play an important part in moving grain. Wheat lends itself to efficient railroad transport. It is comparatively uniform in character, it moves in large volume, it can be unloaded and loaded by mechanical devices, and it is not easily damaged. For these reasons grain traffic has long been a chief reliance of a number of Western railroads, and it still is a large contributor to the business of the Trunk Line route. We may perhaps add that in former years the trunk lines carried most of the grain business. The chief commodity about which the railroad wars of the 1870's and 1880's were waged was grain, and the question of the relative rates on grain from Western points to the cities of Boston, New York, Philadelphia, and Baltimore has not been decided yet to the complete satisfaction of all the parties concerned. This controversy will be again referred to in chapter 19.

A third route for the carriage of wheat is the Mississippi Valley route. This is primarily a railroad route, but some grain moves by river instead of by rail to destinations in the South. It will be obvious, upon reflection, that the Mississippi Valley route is less well placed for the transportation of wheat from Western fields to Eastern cities than are either the Great Lakes or the Trunk Line routes. This is because its southern terminus is in a comparatively sparsely settled region. The Southern states offer an inferior, though large, market to the grain growers. Wheat may be re-shipped at Galveston or New Orleans to boats and carried by water to New York, but this route is roundabout. On export business, however, the Southern route can compete, for the reason that most export grain is grown in Kansas and Oklahoma. Railroad rates from this district to Galveston are much lower than to New York, and the shippers' connections from Gulf ports to European cities are reasonably satisfactory.

We shall consider the complicated structure of wheat rates in later pages of the present work.

Livestock

Livestock is widely grown as a farm crop; it is also produced upon the ranges and in the mountain districts of the Far West. In August, 1948, the Bureau of Agricultural Economics of the Department of Agriculture published figures upon the production and consumption of meat in the United States from which some general information can be obtained. These data are summarized in the accompanying table, which shows that the major surplus area in the livestock industry is to be found in the West North Central states of Minnesota, Iowa, Missouri, North Dakota, South Dakota, Nebraska, and Kansas, while the major deficit districts are in New England and in the Middle Atlantic and South Atlantic states. The East North Central states of Ohio, Indiana, Illinois, Michigan, and Wisconsin are large meat producers; but they are also large meat consumers, so that their surplus is not great. These general relationships are to be remembered in considering livestock routes and flows. There are also, however, complications which affect livestock movements apart from the general influences which determine the direction which they take.

Meat Production, 1947, Meat Consumption, January-March, 1944, and Civilian Population, July 1, 1944, as a Percentage of the U.S. Total

States	Meat Production (percent)	Meat Consumption (percent)	Civilian Population (percent)
Northeast (Me., N.H., Vt., Mass., R.I., Conn.)	1.70	6.39	6.30
Middle Atlantic (N.Y., N.J., Pa.)	8.36	21.64	20.40
East North Central (Ohio, Ind., Ill., Mich., Wis.)	24.31	22.14	20.41
West North Central (Minn., Ia., Mo., N.D., S.D., Neb., Kan.)	34.98	9.45	9.80
South Atlantic (Del., Md., Va., W. Va., N.C., S.C., Ga., Fla.)	6.79	12.32	13.64
East South Central (Ky., Tenn., Ala., Miss.)	4.35	6.58	7.91
West South Central (Ark., La., Okla., Tex.)	8.02	8.93	9.66
Mountain (Mont., Idaho, Wyo., Col., N.M., Ariz., Utah, Nev.)	3.41	2.77	3.09
Pacific (Wash., Ore., Calif.)	8.08	9.78	8.79
Total	100.00	100.00	100.00

Source: United States Department of Agriculture, Bureau of Agricultural Economics, *Livestock and Meat Situation,* August, 1948.

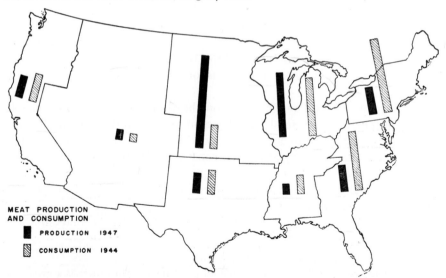

MEAT PRODUCTION AND CONSUMPTION

■ PRODUCTION 1947

▧ CONSUMPTION 1944

Figure 29. Meat Production and Consumption. (Data from United States Department of Agriculture, Bureau of Agricultural Economics, *Livestock and Meat Situation,* August, 1948.)

Feeder Cattle and Sheep

Cattle and sheep from Arizona, New Mexico, and in lesser degree from Utah, Colorado, and some other Western and Southern states, are known as feeders and stockers. Feeders are matured animals which will be held and fed during a period of 2–4 months before they are slaughtered, in order to increase their weight. Stockers are usually immature cattle. They will be kept longer, perhaps 6–9 months, before they are killed. Such animals are reshipped upon arrival at a livestock market into the corn states for feeding. From some districts of origin the proportion of feeders and stockers to total livestock shipments is very high. The movement from other states is less important because the local food supplies available for stock are greater, but in the aggregate it is very large. The traffic is recognized by the Interstate Commerce Commission, which has ruled that railroad rates for the carriage of feeder or stocker livestock should not exceed 85 percent of the rates upon the same kind of livestock when fit for slaughter, in view of its lesser value.[24]

It follows that livestock transportation in the United States may involve first, a local gathering movement; then a concentrating movement to packing centers which we shall presently consider; then, for a certain percentage of the product, an in-and-out movement to fattening fields and return; and finally, after slaughtering, the transportation of meat products to final destination.

Livestock Markets

In New England, in the South, and in the Northwestern states of Oregon, Washington, and Nevada, a relatively large proportion of the product is sold to local butchers for the retail market trade. Livestock so disposed of does not enter into transportation either as animal or as product.

In the corn belt and range states, on the contrary, the proportion sold to local butchers is very small. These communities produce a surplus, and are exporters rather than importers and consumers. Instead of selling to local butchers, farmers and stockmen consign their animals to commission men or dealers at the livestock markets, where animals can be slaughtered and from which products can be shipped. They may also sell to coöperative associations; or they may sell at local shipping points to agents of the packers, who themselves undertake shipment to the primary markets with similar results.[25]

[24] 176 I.C.C. 1,103, 1931; 238 I.C.C. 425, 1940.

[25] Not all livestock, of course, go through all these stages. Thus there is a good deal of direct selling of cattle and sheep from range to feeding areas, reducing movements into and out of livestock centers. Direct sales of livestock by country shippers for slaughter at decentralized killing establishments also tends to bypass facilities at public stockyards.

The principal livestock markets are Chicago, South St. Paul, St. Louis, Omaha, Kansas City, Sioux City, Fort Worth, Denver, and South St. Joseph, Missouri. The rank of the different markets varies with the kind of livestock dealt in.[26] These markets have stockyards where livestock can be conveniently unloaded, inspected, and exposed for sale; they have large slaughtering and packing houses; and they have access to good transportation facilities for forwarding in every direction the products into which the incoming cattle, calves, hogs, and sheep are transformed.[27] Actually,

[26] Rank of Livestock Markets on Basis of Receipts in 1950.

Cattle	Calves	Hogs	Sheep
Chicago	St. Paul	Chicago	Denver
Omaha	St. Louis	St. Louis	Fort Worth
Kansas City	Fort Worth	St. Paul	Kansas City
Sioux City	Kansas City	Omaha	Omaha
St. Paul	Chicago	Sioux City	St. Louis
Denver	Omaha	St. Joseph	St. Joseph
St. Louis	Denver	Denver	Chicago
St. Joseph	Sioux City	Kansas City	St. Paul
Fort Worth	St. Joseph	Fort Worth	Sioux City

SOURCE: United States Department of Agriculture, *Agricultural Statistics,* 1951.

[27] On shipments moving into the Union Stockyards at Chicago a charge per car is assessed against the shipper in addition to the line haul rate. Stockyard terminal charges vary at different markets, but outside of Chicago they are entirely or for the most part absorbed by the railroads. This refers, of course, to the charges connected with transportation. The stockyard is a common carrier if it operates facilities for or performs the service of loading and unloading, and its rates are subject to the control of the Interstate Commerce Commission insofar as they are concerned with transportation, although other services are regulated by the Secretary of Agriculture. There is sometimes a question as to when the service of transportation ends, but the presumption is that transport ceases when the animals reach the unloading pens. Mr. Eastman believed that the railroad rate should cover delivery at public stockyards into suitable pens in all cases (176 I.C.C. 1,122, 158–159, 1931; 245 I.C.C. 241, 1941).

Perishable products of packing houses are distributed to points of consumption in two general ways: (1) by direct movement to point of consumption in less-than-carload lots, generally in what are called "peddler cars," and (2) by carload movement to branch houses and distribution thence either by truck or in less-than-carload rail service.

Branch houses are located at places where the density of population requires a constantly available supply of products. A peddler car is a refrigerator car, owned and loaded by the packer at his packing house with less-than-carload shipments, usually consigned to a number of stations. Consignments are placed in the car in station order, that is, in the order in which the destinations for which they are intended will be reached, so that they may be unloaded by the crews with the least trouble and delay. The shipper precools the car and fills the bunkers with ice and salt at his own expense; when reicing en route is necessary he pays for that also. The car is usually returned empty to the packing house from which shipped, and the carriers pay the owner 1 cent a mile for both loaded and empty movements. Carriers charge shippers the published less than carload rates on the commodities transported; they insist upon a minimum lading outbound, usually 10,000 or 12,000 pounds. The shipper has exclusive use of the car.

extensive direct sale of fresh meats in distant markets as well as of less perishable products of the packing industry is made possible by refrigeration. Whether shipments will be of livestock or of processed articles will depend, in large degree, on the relative costs of transportation. On the whole, and in spite of some exceptions, slaughtering occurs more frequently in the areas where meat animals are raised than in the areas of largest meat consumption.[28]

Conclusion

Coal, steel, grain, and livestock are all commodities which originate in the Mississippi Valley or in the ranges of mountains which border the Valley on the East, and which move outward from the places where they are produced to the manufacturing and population centers of the United States in various directions. In some cases it will be necessary to return to the subject of these traffic movements in order to explain further the transportation rates which are applied and the balancing of advantage between the routes which compete in carrying the goods; but the preliminary picture is, perhaps, supplied. We shall supplement this discussion, in the following chapter, by examining the location and distribution of lumber, fruit, and sugar—commodities which originate upon the outskirts of the country and which reach common markets in converging flows from the outside.

REFERENCES

General Treatises

Bengston, Nels A., and Van Royen, Willem, *Fundamentals of Economic Geography,* New York, Prentice-Hall, 1938.
Glover, J. G., and Cornell, W. B., *The Development of American Industries,* New York, Prentice-Hall, 1932.

This service has attractive features both for the shipper and for the railroad. The shipper likes it because his goods reach destination more quickly and with less handling. The railroad finds it advantageous because peddler cars are loaded by the shipper, shipments are confined to a certain day each week, thus concentrating the offering of less-than-carload lots and adding to the efficiency of operation, and the movement is reasonably steady (191 I.C.C. 257, 321–322, 1933; *Freight Traffic Red Book,* 1948, pp. 947–951).

On the whole, observers notice a tendency toward decentralization of the packing industry, due partly to railroad rate adjustments, partly to improved motor truck operation, and partly to changes in marketing methods encouraged by widespread market news service and increased standardization of grades. See Edward A. Duddy and David A. Revzan, *The Changing Relative Importance of the Central Live Stock Market,* Chicago, University of Chicago, 1938.

[28] United States Department of Agriculture, Bureau of Agricultural Economics, *The Livestock and Meat Situation,* August, 1948, p. 17.

Healy, Kent T., *The Economics of Transportation in America*, New York, Ronald, 1940.
Huebner, Grover G., *Agricultural Commerce*, New York, Appleton-Century-Crofts, 1921.
McCarty, H. H., *The Geographic Basis of American Economic Life*, New York, Harper, 1940.

Other Books

Clemen, R. A., *The American Livestock and Meat Industry*, New York, Ronald, 1923.
Daugherty, C. R., de Chazeau, M. G. de, and Stratton, S. S., *The Economics of the Iron and Steel Industry*, New York, McGraw-Hill, 1937.
Duddy, E. A., and Revzan, D. R., *The Changing Relative Importance of the Central Livestock Market*, Chicago, University of Chicago, Studies in Business Administration, 1938.
Mansfield, Harvey C., *The Lake Cargo Coal Rate Controversy*, New York, Columbia University, 1932.
National Industrial Conference Board, *The Competitive Position of Coal in the United States*, New York, 1931.
Pickett, Victor G., and Vaile, Roland S., *The Decline of Northwestern Flour Milling*, Minneapolis, University of Minnesota, Studies in Economics and Business, No. 5, 1933.
Van Hise, C. R., and Leith, C. K., *The Geology of the Lake Superior Region*, United States Geological Survey Monograph, vol. 52, 1911.
Weld, L. D. H., *Private Freight Cars and American Railways*, New York, Longmans, 1908.

Periodicals

Hartshorne, R., "The Significance of Lake Transportation to the Grain Traffic of Chicago," *Economic Geography*, April, 1926.
Hines, L. G., "The Lake Erie Iron Ore Market," *American Economic Review*, September, 1951.
Isard, W., and Capron, W. M., "The Future Locational Pattern of Iron and Steel Production in the United States," *Journal of Political Economy*, April, 1949.
Predohl, Andreas, *"Die ortliche Verteilung der Amerikanischen Eisen und Stahlindustrie,"* *Weltwirthschaftliches Archiv*, April, 1928.
Voskuil, W. H., "Bituminous Coal Movements in the United States," *Geographical Review*, January, 1942.

Special and Miscellaneous

American Iron and Steel Institute, *Annual Statistical Report*.
Chicago University, School of Commerce and Administration, Institute of American Meat Packers, *The Packing Industry: A Series of Lectures Given under the Joint Auspices of the School of Commerce and Administration of the University of Chicago and the Institute of Meat Packers*, Chicago, University of Chicago, 1924.

National Livestock Producers' Association, *Annual Report*.

Temporary National Economic Committee, *Investigation of the Concentration of Economic Power*, vol. 18, 76th C., 2d S., 1939.

United States Department of Agriculture, *Distribution of the Varieties and Classes of Wheat in the United States in 1934*, Circular no. 424, by J. Allen Clark and K. S. Quisenberry, April, 1937.

United States Board of Investigation and Research, *The Economics of Coal Traffic Flow*, 79th C., 1st S., Sen. Doc. 82, September, 1944.

United States Board of Investigation and Research, *The Economics of Iron and Steel Transportation*, 79th C., 1st S., Sen. Doc. 80, 1945.

United States Department of Agriculture, *Agricultural Statistics*, annual.

United States Department of Agriculture, Bureau of Agricultural Economics, *Livestock and Meat Situation*, August, 1948.

United States Department of the Interior, Bureau of Mines, *Minerals Yearbook*, annual.

Commodity Movements: Lumber, Citrus Fruit, Sugar

This chapter is concerned with the location and distribution in the United States of lumber, oranges, and sugar.

Lumber

The character and direction of lumber shipments have greatly changed in the course of the last century. Short hauls from Maine to Boston (225 miles), from the upper Hudson to New York City (200 miles), and the Pennsylvania river traffic to Philadelphia illustrate the nature of lumber movements up to the time of the Civil War.

When the pine of the Lake states came to be drawn upon, the average length of haul increased. The Department of Agriculture points out that prior to 1860 a lumber haul of 500 miles was exceptional, and even half this distance much above the average; but a large part of the Lake states' cut, even to the Middle Western markets, moved more than 500 miles, and New York is 1,000 miles by water from Saginaw, one of the nearest points of manufacture in the Lake states territory.

Beginning of Southern and Western Shipments

Southern pine shipments began on the Atlantic coast after the Civil War, although rail shipments to the interior were in small volume until after 1890. Water distances ranged from a minimum of 300 miles from Norfolk to Philadelphia to 2,000 or more from Gulf ports to Boston. Aside from purely local markets, the distances by rail were ordinarily in excess of 750 miles, and frequently exceeded 1,000 miles, as illustrated by the distance from Hattiesburg, Mississippi, to Boston, more than 1,000 miles, or to Pittsburgh, 1,100 miles.

Finally, the lumber cut from the Pacific Coast moved the greatest distances of all. By water, Puget Sound is nearly 7,000 miles from New

York. By rail, Omaha is nearly 2,000 miles from Portland, Oregon; Chicago is 2,300 miles, and New York is 3,200 miles.

Consuming and Producing Areas

Seventy-eight percent of lumber shipped in 1943 was softwood—mostly pine, fir, hemlock, and redwood. There are two great areas of surplus lumber production in the United States from which these shipments are obtained. One of these is in Oregon and Washington, in the Northwest, with minor additions from Montana and Idaho; the other, in the Southeast, includes the states of Arkansas, Louisiana, Mississippi, Alabama,

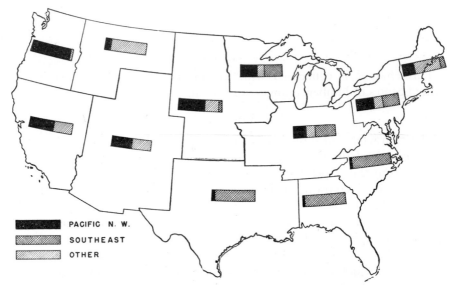

FIGURE 30. Sources of Lumber Consumption, 1943. (U.S. Department of Agriculture, Forest Service and U.S. Department of Commerce, Bureau of the Census, *Domestic Lumber Distribution, 1943,* A. H. Pierson and R. H. Blythe, Jr., 1945.)

Georgia, Florida, South Carolina, and North Carolina. All other states receive more softwood than they ship, although there is a limited amount of interchange. The direction of movement is eastward from the Pacific Coast and northward from the Southern states to the treeless plains of the central and northern Mississippi Valley and to the industrial districts of the North and the Northeast.

Source of Lumber Consumed in Different Regions

Figure 30 indicates the proportion of consumption of softwood lumber which was supplied by Northwestern and Southeastern producers in the United States in the year 1943 in each of 12 indicated districts. (The proportions are based on figures showing the movement of lumber from the point of production to its first destination.) The black segments in each parallelogram show the percentage of lumber received in the specified district from the forests of Oregon and Washington. The cross-hatched segments show the percentage supplied from the Southeastern forests, and the shaded sections indicate the proportion of other sources of supply.[1]

The map shows that in the South and Southeast, as one would expect, most lumber consumption is of Southern pine. This predominance of Southern lumber extends into the central states (Missouri, Illinois, Indiana, Kentucky, Tennessee, Ohio, and West Virginia), although the proportion of Southern pine used in this district has somewhat decreased in recent years. In the prairie, Rocky Mountain, and Pacific Coast regions consumers either use local supplies or import from Oregon and Washington. Southern and Western lumber compete actively in the Lake states, the North Atlantic states, and to some extent in New England, although in this last district local supplies are relatively large. In these areas the importance of Western lumber has been growing.

Importance of Transportation Costs

Lumber is cheap and it is bulky. It is, therefore, a commodity which

[1] SOURCE: United States Department of Agriculture, Forest Service and United States Department of Commerce, Bureau of the Census, *Domestic Lumber Distribution, 1943*, by Albert H. Pierson, Associate Forester, and R. H. Blythe, Jr., Senior Forester, Division of Forest Economics, Washington, D.C., June, 1945.

States	Total Receipts, 1943	Percentage Received from			
		North Pacific	South-east	Other	Total
	(Units of 10,000 board feet)				
Ore., Wash.	394	93	—	7	100
Calif., Nev.	372	55	—	45	100
Mont., Idaho	59	17	—	83	100
Ariz., Utah, Colo., N.M., Wyo.	87	47	—	53	100
N.D., S.D., Neb., Kan., Iowa	123	65	11	24	100
Wis., Mich., Minn.	180	42	18	40	100
Mo., Ill., Ind., Ky., Tenn., Ohio, W.Va.	321	27	50	23	100
Okla., Tex., Ark., La., Miss.	295	8	90	2	100
Ala., Ga., Fla.	256	2	98	—	100
N.C., S.C., Va.	215	3	96	1	100
Pa., N.Y., Md., Del., N.J., D.C.	282	40	34	26	100
Mass., N.H., R.I., Vt., Conn., Me.	125	25	8	67	100
Total	2,709	39	38	23	100

Softwood Lumber Receipts, 1943

one might expect to see produced in the vicinity of the place where it is consumed. Indeed, von Thünen assigned forest culture to the second of the zones which encircled his "Isolated City"—a location nearer to the market than he thought suitable for the growing of grain or the raising of cattle. We may be surprised, therefore, to find the principal sources of American lumber supplies in remote corners of the United States. The reasons for the apparent anomaly are two. In the first place, it is a geographical fact that forests exist in the South and, above all, in the Northwest. Man did not select these locations; he utilizes today a condition for which he is not responsible. In the second place lumber, though cheap and heavy, can be readily transported. It is easy to handle, it is hard to damage, and it moves in large quantities. Such characteristics make lumber desirable freight from the point of view of railroad, shipping, and even trucking companies. Competition for the carriage of lumber is keen, and rates are low. It is therefore enabled to move long distances to market. Yet still, because of the high proportion which the cost of carriage bears to the total of its production costs,[2] lumber is sensitive to conditions of transportation, and the transportation charge, to an unusual degree, determines both the type of vehicle that will be used to carry lumber from mill to market and the boundaries of the territory in which the product of any district can be sold.[3]

Water Route to Eastern and Middle Western Markets

There are three routes by which lumber can be brought from the out-

---

[2] The average revenues received by railroads on the total originated tonnage of lumber, laths, and shingles ranged from 31.6 percent in 1929 to 55.6 percent in 1932 of the average mill price. To Chicago, most important single lumber market, on November 20, 1937, the ratio of freight cost to mill price varied widely according to length of haul and species and grade of lumber, from 12 percent on clear birch from Wausau, Wis., to 121 percent on Douglas fir from Seattle (226 I.C.C. 41, 112, 1938).

A statement submitted to the Interstate Commerce Commission showed that lumber rough plank cost $17 per 1,000 board feet at Puget Sound in 1941. Ocean freight to the Atlantic coast was $16, marine and war-risk insurance 50 cents, and cost of placing lumber of the dock $1. The transportation cost was, therefore, for water movement, 103 percent of the local price at Puget Sound (251 I.C.C. 217, 1942).

[3] It is not to be assumed that transportation costs are the only factors which determine lumber movements. Inequality in production costs between competing areas affects the form and size of the territory which each controls and there are generally other influences also which must be considered. In the case of lumber the production cost of Douglas fir is less than that of Southern pine. A recent study (R. J. Sampson, *The Relationship Between Railroad Freight Rates and the Domestic Distribution of Southern Pine and Douglas Fir Lumber,* 1948) concludes that the average production costs of western lumber (Douglas fir) and of southern lumber (Southern pine) were respectively, in 1948, $55.73 and $67.58 per 1,000 board feet. This relative cost advantage enables Western producers to dominate a larger market than relative transportation charges by themselves would have defined. Transportation differentials should be examined in the light of this and of other facts. But with all appropriate allowance, the statement in the text which emphasizes the importance of the transportation charge will hardly be denied.

side into the lumber markets of the Northeastern and Middle Western states.

The first of these routes is the water route from the Pacific Coast by way of the Panama Canal to ports upon the Atlantic or Gulf seaboards of the United States. From Atlantic ports waterborne lumber moves west by truck, by rail, over the New York Barge Canal, or by way of the Great Lakes. Trucking service has been of increasing importance in recent years. From the Gulf, lumber is shipped by truck or rail or by barge up the Mississippi River as far as Chicago, St. Louis, and Cincinnati. The cargo rate of the intercoastal lines from Pacific points of origin to Atlantic or Gulf destinations is less than the railroad charge, and the volume of movement is large. In 1933, 72 percent of the total lumber movement from the Pacific Coast to points east of the Indiana–Illinois state line used the water service. The relative importance of water shipments has, however, declined. Thus the average movement of lumber through the Panama Canal from the West Coast was, for the two years 1939 and 1941 combined, 1,167 million board feet as compared with total receipts from the Pacific Coast in Illinois, Indiana, Ohio, Pennsylvania, New York, New Jersey, and New England of 2,454 million board feet. This was a proportion of approximately 43 percent. In later years, intercoastal carriage of lumber by ships was insignificant during World War II, and shipments from West Coast to East Coast ports of the United States had not, by 1951, regained a level as high as the figures for 1939 or 1941.

All-Rail Route from the Pacific Coast

It was the all-rail route across the continent which felt the first impact of the stimulated water movement by way of the Panama Canal that occurred at the close of the First World War. In 1935, to check an increasing loss of traffic to the water lines, rail carriers extended the 72-cent rate, formerly applied to Chicago, to destinations extending through Central, Trunk Line, and New England territories to the Atlantic Coast.[4] The consequent reduction in charge ranged up to 20 percent. The result was a sharp increase in lumber shipments from the Far West.[5] The 72-cent rate was increased, in 1936, to 78 cents[6] and, in later years, it went still higher, but the Eastern blanket was maintained.

All-Rail Route from the South

The third route is that from Southern producing points north and northwest into the upper Mississippi Valley. Southern points of origin may

[4] The 72-cent rate was quoted from the Inland Empire as well as from the Pacific coast, thus removing an advantage which the former had enjoyed.

[5] 226 I.C.C. 41, 1938; 245 I.C.C. 67, 1941.

[6] 227 I.C.C. 189, 1938.

be divided into three sections. One section, known as southeastern territory, lies east of the line of the Mobile and Ohio Railroad extending through the eastern portion of the state of Mississippi to Mobile, Alabama. It includes, therefore, most of Alabama, Georgia, and Florida, with some part of Mississippi. Much of the lumber from the southeast moves to Trunk Line and New England territories.[7] Rates are such as to give Southern lumber producers an advantage over their Western competitors that enables them, with Eastern producers, to dominate the Northeastern market.

West of Southeastern territory, but east of the Mississippi River, is what is known as Mississippi Valley territory. West of this again is the so-called southwestern blanket. This blanket includes all lumber-producing points south of the Arkansas River in Arkansas, all of Louisiana west of the Mississippi River, a few points in the southeastern part of Oklahoma, and eastern Texas. The rate from each point in the southwestern blanket territory is the same as that from any other point in the territory to any given destination. Mississippi Valley lumber producers compete actively with those in the blanket territory in the sale of lumber in the northern Mississippi Valley,[8] and both dispute the market with producers in the Far West.[9]

It is sufficient for our present purposes to point out that the competition of Southern and Western lumber shippers has been for many years a factor in controlling the rates on lumber from the South to the Northeast and to points in the northern Mississippi Valley. In May, 1918, the rates from Goldsboro, North Carolina, to New York were 26⅔ percent of the rates from north Pacific coast points to New York. When, by 1923, this percentage relationship rose to 34.4 percent, Southern shippers earnestly complained.[10] When, also, the rail carriers in 1935 reduced rates from the Pacific Coast to the Atlantic Seaboard, Southern shippers again protested. It was true enough that rail rates from the South were still lower to Eastern destinations than were all-rail rates from the West. But Southern lumbermen believed that the difference that had existed before 1935 should not be reduced. Although there had never been a fixed relationship between the rates from the South and those from the West Coast, carriers from each producing section had endeavored to maintain

---

[7] Rates from the Southeast were established to meet water competition along the Atlantic seaboard (85 I.C.C. 270, 272, 1923; 157 I.C.C. 280, 1929). At present, the great majority of Southern pine producers are not located where water routes are available to official territory, at least without a trucking haul (226 I.C.C. 41,117, 1938).

[8] 34 I.C.C. 652, 682, 1915; 36 I.C.C. 137, 1915; 42 I.C.C. 548, 1917. Mississippi Valley points of origin are divided into groups, but there is no single group comparable with that west of the Mississippi River.

[9] 255 I.C.C. 149, 1943.

[10] 85 I.C.C. 270, 281, 1923.

rates so adjusted as to permit free movement of lumber from each, and this condition reductions from the West would destroy.[11] Rates, it was said, should be lower from the South, partly because average distances to market were less, partly because Southern mill costs were higher than in the West, and partly because Southern lumber weighed more than Western lumber per 100 board feet.

Finally, the South felt itself especially threatened by the blanket rate of 72 cents which all-rail carriers were making applicable to New England and New York. She was especially vulnerable to such a change because her own rates to Northern points were not grouped in so comprehensive a way. Southern rates were quoted, that is to say, from areas in the South which have already been described to groups of destinations north of the Ohio River, but there were many areas and groups, and charges increased as shipments moved from west to east. Southern lumber rates were not proportionate to distance, but the schedule of charges used reflected the influence of distance more than did the rates on Western lumber, and so placed Southern shippers at a comparative and increasing disadvantage as lengths of hauls increased.[12]

In spite of Southern objections, the Interstate Commerce Commission approved blanket rates on Western lumber in 1936. These blankets have since been maintained. General rate decisions have, moreover, been of such a character that the position of Southern producers is now even less favorable than it was in 1935.[13]

Oranges, Lemons, and Grapefruit

The principal citrus fruits are oranges, lemons, and grapefruit. Most domestic lemons are grown in California, and most grapefruit in Florida and Texas. Of the oranges, in 1950–51 California produced about 37 percent of the national crop; Florida about 59 percent; and the balance was grown in smaller amounts in Texas, Louisiana, Arizona, Alabama, and Mississippi. California, Florida, Arizona, and Texas are the principal orange-growing states and the influence of other sources of production may, in the case of this product, be ignored.

From the point of view of the student of transportation, citrus fruit

[11] 210 I.C.C. 317, 1935.

[12] The situation was complicated from the point of view of Southern railroads, although not, perhaps, from the point of view of shippers, by the development of trucking service (245 I.C.C. 67, 1941).

[13] See 226 I.C.C. 41, 1938; 248 I.C.C. 545, 1942; 264 I.C.C. 695, 1946; 266 I.C.C. 537, 1946; 269 I.C.C. 33, 1947; 270 I.C.C. 93, 1948; 272 I.C.C. 695, 1948; 276 I.C.C. 9, 1949. See also Sampson, *op. cit.*, pp. 143–151.

As of September 1, 1949, the rate from Hattiesburg, Mississippi, was 62 percent of the rate from Portland to New York although the distance was more than 2½ times as great.

movements in the United States possess a number of interesting characteristics. If we examine the case of oranges as an illustration, the following facts are obviously true:

1. The production of oranges is highly concentrated in the South and West. Consumption, on the other hand, follows the distribution of population, and is most important in the densely settled areas of Central and Eastern United States.

2. The average haul of oranges is long and transportation costs are relatively great. In the season 1950–51 the average transportation cost on a box of California oranges was $1.67. The cost of growing such a box was $1.15 for navel and $1.10 for valencia oranges and the cost of picking, hauling, selling, and advertising was $1.53; so that transportation costs accounted for 38 percent of the total outlay. The cost of transport from Florida points to New York was $1.14, costs of growing were $.57, and the costs of picking, hauling, etc., were $1.40. The proportion of transportation costs to the New York market to total costs was 33 percent.[14]

3. As in the case of lumber, market competition is more important to carriers of oranges than is the competition of parallel transport lines. To this there has been an exception along the Atlantic Seaboard, where coastwise carriers at one time captured the bulk of the citrus tonnage from Florida points to Baltimore, Boston, New York, and Philadelphia. This water service ceased during World War II and has not yet, in comparable volume, been resumed.[15] Truck competition is important in the gathering and short-haul movements of oranges in producing territories generally, and it has been significant, also, in the carriage of oranges from Florida into all the Eastern states and from Texas as far north and east as Chicago.[16] California shippers, however, make no use of trucks for transcontinental movements, and such records as are available indicate that even from the South, most interterritorial shipments move by rail.

[14] California Fruit Growers Exchange, Marketing Research Department, *Statistical Information on the Citrus Fruit Industry. Oranges, Lemons, Grapefruit,* May, 1952.

[15] Coastwise carriers began to operate refrigerated service from Florida points to New York in 1929. So successful were the boat lines in attracting traffic that by the end of 1935, 93.5 percent of the citrus fruit carried from Florida to Baltimore, Boston, New York, and Philadelphia traveled by boat and only 6.5 percent by rail (218 I.C.C. 637, 643, 1936). The rail carriers cut their rates in an attempt to regain the diverted business, and the Interstate Commerce Commission coöperated by granting the carriers relief from prohibitions in the Interstate Commerce Act which would have hampered them in competition (211 I.C.C. 535, 1935; 218 I.C.C. 637, 1936; 226 I.C.C. 315, 1938; 237 I.C.C. 245, 354, 1940). The new rail rates averaged about 63 percent of normal rates. This brought enough traffic back to raise the proportion of citrus fruit carried by rail to 35 percent in 1936–37 and to 56 percent in 1940–41 (266 I.C.C. 627, 641, 1946). Steamship service was restricted in 1941–42 and was unavailable during the three years 1942–45. The result was withdrawal of the Commission's permissive orders under Section 4 of the federal law. High shipping costs are still handicapping water carriers during the postwar years.

[16] 248 I.C.C. 25, 1941.

Relative Sales of California, Florida, and Texas Oranges in Competitive Markets

Table 15 shows the proportions in which the producing areas of California, Florida, and Texas supply selected markets in different sections of the United States.

TABLE 15. Carlots of Oranges Unloaded in Selected Markets, 1951

Market	Origin of Unloads (percent)			
	California	Florida	Arizona and Texas	Other
Western				
Los Angeles	100	0	0	0
San Francisco	100	0	0	0
Portland	97	2	0	1
Seattle	98	1	1	0
Denver	88	10	2	0
North Central				
Minneapolis	92	6	2	0
Kansas City	86	9	5	0
St. Louis	65	31	4	0
Chicago	59	39	1	1
Detroit	70	27	0	3
Cleveland	61	37	0	2
Cincinnati	49	49	0	2
North Atlantic				
Pittsburgh	74	24	2	0
Boston	61	38	1	0
New York	49	51	0	0
Philadelphia	45	55	0	0
South Atlantic				
Baltimore	34	65	1	0
Washington, D.C.	22	78	0	0
Atlanta	6	94	0	0
South Central				
New Orleans	21	79	0	0
Dallas	71	13	15	1
Oklahoma City	82	1	16	1

SOURCE: United States Department of Agriculture, Production and Marketing Administration, *Carlot Unloads of Certain Fruits and Vegetables in 100 Cities, Calendar Year 1951,* March, 1952. The percentages in the text table cover, in all cases, railroad carlots unloaded and, where possible, they include truck deliveries also. The Department of Agriculture reports truck unloads in a number of cities, including Los Angeles,

San Francisco, St. Louis, Chicago, New York, Baltimore, and Washington. The text assumes that truck unloads in California consist of California oranges and that truck unloads in the Eastern and Southern states consist of Florida oranges. Whether the figures are reported or not, truck shipments are important in and near producing areas. On the other hand, oranges are perishable, and the long-distance transport of oranges requires special handling and organization. For the year 1946–47, 85 percent of Florida fresh fruit shipments moved by rail, 4 percent by boat, and 12 percent by truck. Truck movements of California oranges were undoubtedly less than this, at least on interterritorial shipments. (See T. C. Bigham and M. J. Roberts, *Citrus Fruit Rates,* Gainesville, Fla., University of Florida, 1950, p. 42.)

Division of the Market

Few Florida oranges are sold west of the Mississippi River because of competition from California, Texas, and Arizona. On the other hand, Florida oranges dominate the markets east of the Mississippi and south of the Ohio rivers. Competition between the sources of supply is keenest in the North Central and Northeastern regions of the United States. Along the Atlantic Seaboard, Florida has an advantage in towns such as Norfolk, Baltimore, Philadelphia, and New York because of steamship service, although the cost of water carriage has increased. This advantage may be extended inland by motor trucks which deliver oranges to steamship piers in the South and carry them from coastal harbors to interior towns in the Northern states.

The special advantages that Florida producers enjoy decrease or disappear in the case of shipments to North Central states. In southern Ohio and Indiana, California and Florida divide the markets on fairly equal terms; but, in 1951, California supplied 59 percent of the shipments of oranges unloaded at Chicago, 86 percent of those unloaded at Kansas City, and 92 percent of those unloaded at Minneapolis. These are annual figures. It is obvious that Florida producers must find it increasingly difficult to sell as they seek more and more distant markets because the railroad rates which they pay increase with distance.[17] It should be said, however, that the annual proportion of their shipments to the total available supply does not accurately express the success of Southern producers in competing with growers in the West. This is because almost no Florida oranges are unloaded during the months of July, August, and September, and relatively few in June and October. During these months, therefore, California oranges occupy the field. From November to May, on the other hand, competition is keen. In 1951, California oranges represented 89 percent of all shipments in the United States between June and October, but only 56 percent between November and May. Such variations greatly affect the annual distribution of carload deliveries at particular points.

[17] This is not universally true. There is some grouping of points of origin in the Southern states and some allowance for competitive pressures at points of destination. But the text statement is substantially correct.

Railroad Rates on California Oranges

Because of the great differences in distances between different producing areas and the common markets, rates which increase in the same ratio as the distance hauled are inappropriate to the orange industry. Such rates, at least, would restrict the sale of Western fruit. Western carriers use, therefore, a system of blanket charges under which the same rates are charged on California oranges for hauls of varying lengths. Thus in 1918 the rate on oranges from California was the same—$1.15—to all points east of the Rocky Mountains and north of the Ohio River. In 1920 a rate of $1.44 per 100 pounds was charged to the same destinations.[18] By 1928 the rate had risen to $1.55 but the blanket system was retained except that a rate of $1.58 was applied on shipments to New York and to points in New England.[19] In 1946 the rate system was more complicated, but there were still three large zones in Eastern territory. One of these, with a rate of $1.31, included stations in Southeastern states except Florida and large portions of the Mississippi and Missouri river basins; and another, with a rate of $1.35, covered the Northeast. Most stations in Florida were charged $1.51; but this rate was, doubtless, little used because a combination of the competition of Florida producers and seasonal fruit quarantines made shipments from the West difficult during most of the year.[20]

This system of uniform charges is important, not only because it tends to equalize the advantages of different points of origin, but because it facilitates the handling of consignments from the Pacific Coast. Only a small proportion of orange shipments is sold before the freight starts to move. Most cars are "blind billed" to some Middle Western point, and are subsequently redirected before delivery to the destination at which the shipper finally decides to sell his fruit. This close control, based upon up-to-date knowledge, increases the aggregate price at which the annual crop of California oranges can be sold. It is also much simpler to administer, from the carriers' point of view, because the rate to the various destinations from which the shipper can select is likely to be the same.

Railroad Rates on Florida Oranges

Generally speaking, the rates on oranges from Southern to Northern and Western destinations are based upon class scales, and vary in some relation to distance. While destination points are to some extent grouped,

---

[18] 58 I.C.C. 373, 376, 1920.

[19] 144 I.C.C. 603, 622, 1928; 237 I.C.C. 313, 334, 1940.

[20] Stuart Daggett and John P. Carter, *The Structure of Transcontinental Railroad Rates,* Publications of the Bureau of Business and Economic Research, Berkeley and Los Angeles, University of California, 1947, pp. 64–65.

the practice is by no means as extensive as in the California traffic.[21] Absolutely, the Florida rates are lower than those from California to destinations east of and including Kansas City, Missouri, Omaha, and St. Paul. They are, however, higher to Denver and to points in the Southwest. In 1948 the line of equality extended from stations in the vicinity of Fargo, North Dakota, through central Nebraska and Kansas and eastern Texas.[22]

The existing rate adjustment gives the Florida producer a steady advantage in a long list of major markets in competition with his California rivals. This, along with lower costs of orange culture and approximately the same expense for picking, hauling, packing, and selling, has allowed Florida production to increase more rapidly than that in California. The proportion of Florida shipments to those from California has, also, been considerably enlarged in recent years.[23] The present position of California would be still less favorable if rates were changed so as to reflect more accurately differences in distance from the two sources of supply to their common destinations.[24]

[21] Shippers in 1928 suggested that a single rate of 95 cents be applied from all points in Florida to the whole of official territory, following the California practice. The Commission replied that it would never have been justified in establishing the California rate blanket and that it did not propose to extend it (144 I.C.C. 445, 1933; 194 I.C.C. 593, 1933).

[22] In August, 1948, the railroad rates on oranges from Lake Wales, Florida, and from Los Angeles, California, were as follows:

Destination	From Lake Wales (cents)	From Los Angeles (cents)	Lake Wales Rate Under or Over Los Angeles Rate (cents)
Charleston, S.C.	48	166	− 118
Washington, D.C.	94	170	− 76
New York, N.Y.	94	170	− 76
Boston, Mass.	108	170	− 62
Cincinnati, O.	105	166	− 61
Chicago, Ill.	119	166	− 47
St. Paul, Minn.	144	166	− 22
Kansas City, Mo.	133	151	− 18
Omaha, Neb.	140	151	− 11
Fargo, N.D.	165	168	− 3
Dallas, Tex.	149	127	+ 22
Dodge City, Kan.	153	127	+ 26
North Platte, Neb.	171	137	+ 34
Amarillo, Texas	153	115	+ 38
Denver, Colo.	182	127	+ 55
Albuquerque, N.M.	182	112	+ 70

[23] California oranges sell for higher prices than Florida oranges. Bigham and Roberts (*Citrus Fruit Rates*, Gainesville, Fla., University of Florida, 1950) conclude that this offsets the disadvantage of a higher production cost.

[24] Florida producers argue that present rate adjustments should be changed on

Need for Refrigeration

Generally speaking, the development of long-distance transportation of fruit and vegetables is due to the perfection of refrigerating equipment and to the expedited service which railroads have been able to provide for this class of traffic. Fruit and dressed meat resemble each other in their liability to deterioration and in the special attention they require. In neither case would the concentration in production and the character of the movements indicated in preceding pages have been possible without the elaboration of an allied technique of very great importance.

It would be a fascinating exercise in economic history to trace the growth of the packing industry in the Middle West, and to observe the use which Chicago packers made of methods of refrigeration in transit in their struggle with competitors in Cincinnati and other Eastern points. The history of the fruit industry, also, shows that in the period preceding the Civil War the lack of proper methods for conserving fruit caused the loss of enormous quantities of excellent food supplies, in addition to limiting the area in which fruit could successfully be grown. W. A. Taylor, writing in the *Yearbook* of the United States Department of Agriculture for 1900, says of the decades from 1850 to 1870:

The stimulus of planting afforded by the improved facilities for transportation . . . soon resulted in disastrous overproduction in some sections. Large orchards, vineyards, and small-fruit plantations were planted farther from their prospective markets than their products could be transported. This was notably true in the Southern United States, where the added incentive of high prices for early fruits in markets farther north caused large planting of the more perishable fruits, such as strawberries, blackberries, raspberries, peaches, and plums. The planters demonstrated that they could produce these fruits in large quantity and of high quality at a relatively low cost, but the product could not, with the then existing facilities, be delivered to the distant consumer, for whom it was intended, in sound and wholesome condition. Thus, the truckers near Norfolk, Va., demonstrated as early as 1860 that the strawberry could be grown in large quantities and ripened long in advance of the northern crop. But as repeated shipments spoiled in transit, its culture was abandoned until the development of more durable varieties and improved transportation brought the New York market within reach of the growers. The early peach industry of South Carolina and Georgia suffered a similar experience about 1850–1870, and practically ceased to exist for a period of fifteen to twenty years; then suddenly, with the origination of a variety (Elberta) better adapted to long shipment, and the development of a car service adequate for

---

grounds of general policy. The points made are: (1) low competitive rates from California encourage production in a high cost territory; (2) low rates tend to deprive Florida of its natural advantages of location; (3) low rates, as charged, are close to and possibly below a noncompensating level (Bigham and Roberts, *op. cit.*). They object to market competition as a determinant of transportation rates.

fruit transportation, that region sprang into a leading place among the peach-producing sections of the country.

The losses of Northern growers from overproduction were also excessive. In favorable seasons the local markets often failed to take a fair price more than a small portion of the crop, and as it was short lived at best, the prospective profits of the grower vanished through low prices during the period of ten days or two weeks in which his crop was handled. Earlier and later in the season the supply was short and the price remunerative, but neither the grower nor the dealer had fruit to sell. It was a condition of "feast or famine," with but little opportunity for profit to the average producer in either case. Though more marked in the case of the summer fruits, the same condition was true at times with the apple, which has ever been, and promises to continue to be, the most largely grown and most popular of fruits in the temperate zones. In summer and autumn the fruit lay rotting upon the ground for lack of demand at prices that would even reimburse the owner for the expense of harvesting. By midwinter the dwellers in cities and towns were unable to secure fruit at prices within the reach of average incomes. The abundance returned to the earth from whence it came, leaving the consumer hungry and the producer poorer than before.

Introduction of the Refrigerator Car

Shipments of fresh meat eastward from Chicago under refrigeration were made early in the 1860's, over the Michigan Central Railroad. Ordinary boxcars were used, with bins for ice built in both ends. These cars could be iced only from inside, and there was no provision for circulation of air; the results, therefore, were hardly satisfactory. In 1867 a man named Sutherland, of Detroit, took out the first patent for a refrigerator car; and in the late 1860's and 1870's some fruit was shipped in cars of various designs from Illinois points to Chicago, and from Michigan to New York and Boston. The considerable development of the refrigerator car occurred, however, in the 1880's, when certain Chicago packers and dealers in fresh meats became sufficiently interested in the icing problem to build refrigerator cars at their own expense. According to the Federal Trade Commission, the pioneer in this enterprise was Gustavus Swift, and the object was to place fresh meat in eastern markets.[25] Swift obtained technical advice about 1880, and built cars upon principles which have since proved generally successful. His example was followed by Armour, Nelson Morris, Schwarzchild and Sulzberger, and other Chicago packers. These meat cars were also used for the shipment of fruit; and later, after the shipment of meat under refrigeration had proved definitely successful, Armour built several thousand cars especially for the fruit trade and

[25] Federal Trade Commission, *Report on Private Car Lines,* Washington, D.C., Government Printing Office, 1920. See also J. O. Armour, *The Packers, the Private Car Lines and the People,* Philadelphia, Henry Altemus, 1906.

organized a private car line for their operation. Railroad companies at this time were still reluctant to invest the necessary money in what they regarded as an experiment; so that for many years shippers who desired refrigeration equipment continued to build their own rolling stock or to rely upon private car lines such as those of the Swift and Armour companies, controlled by meat packers with headquarters at Chicago. At a later date railroads entered the field and now dominate it.

Refrigerator Car Ownership

On December 31, 1950, the total number of refrigerator cars in use in the United States was reported as, approximately, 125,000 cars. Of these 19,000, in round numbers, were owned directly by the railroads, 80,000 by companies whose stock was held by railroads or groups of railroads, and the balance was owned by independent organizations.[26]

Payment for the Use of Cars

A shipper who uses a refrigerator car usually pays a stated charge or combination of charges in addition to the freight rate. The railroad retains these payments if it is the owner of the car; if the car is owned by a shipper the railroad collects and holds the freight rate and refrigerator charge and pays the owner an agreed sum per mile for the use of the equipment both on loaded and empty trips. Much the same procedure is followed when the car is owned by a private car line. The railroad retains

[26] The railroad controlled companies referred to in the text were the following: American Refrigerator Transit (Missouri Pacific, Wabash); Burlington Refrigerator Express (Burlington), Fruit Growers Express (19 companies); Merchants' Despatch Corporation (New York Central); Northern Refrigerator Line (New York Central); Pacific Fruit Express (Union Pacific, Southern Pacific); Western Fruit Express (Great Northern). See United States Interstate Commerce Commission, Bureau of Transport Economics and Statistics, *Selected Statistics from Annual Reports of Private Car Owners,* Washington, D.C. A separate organization for the operation of refrigerator cars is advantageous because it can more easily provide for the shifting of equipment when the demand in any territory declines. This and the special requirements of the service explain the organization of railroad subsidiary companies.

It is possible that railroads might go still farther with advantage by transferring the title to all their refrigerator equipment to a single operating company, receiving in return stock in this company in reasonable proportions and dividing the net revenue among themselves. Present arrangements with the Railway Express Agency might supply the model for the relationship which would ensue. Under the Railway Express Agency contract, 85 percent of gross rail haul revenue is paid directly to carriers on whose lines such revenues accrue; the balance of income, after deduction of expenses, is divided monthly, among participating carriers (*Moody's Manual of Investment, Industrial,* 1945, p. 843). As of December, 1945, the stock of the Railway Express Agency was held by 70 participating railroads. The Agency also conducted express business on a number of nonstockholding lines. Doubtless such a contract would not fit the refrigerator car business without some change; but it is likely that, with modifications, it would represent a considerable improvement over the organization which now exists.

the freight rate and the price which the shipper pays for protective service. Railroads are responsible for the provision of this service and publish tariffs which name the rates. Car-line companies bill each individual railroad for the services which the companies render to that railroad, upon a unit cost basis, at reasonable rates. They are also entitled to a reasonable rental for the use of their cars.[27]

Transportation in refrigerator cars has been considered by the Interstate Commerce Commission on many occasions, and the use of private car lines in the packing industry was the occasion of a severely critical report by the Federal Trade Commission in 1919.[28] The general position of the Interstate Commerce Commission is that the charge for refrigeration should be based on cost, and that the cost to be ascertained is the expense incurred because cars are iced, which would not be incurred if no icing took place. This excess cost is due, in part, to the cost of the ice, its weight, to the increase in the number of trains which the weight of the ice requires to be hauled, and to the terminal investment and terminal services called for in connection with the icing process. The computation upon which the refrigeration rate is based should not, according to the Commission, take into account the increased speed at which refrigerated trains are hauled, because this is already provided for in the freight rate; nor should it include any portion of constant costs, except those occasioned by the icing service,[29] because the rates on perishable traffic moving without refrigeration already cover this expense. The theoretical basis for this last position is not, perhaps, beyond attack, but the subject need not be argued.

Refrigeration charges may sometimes be too high, and the use of privately owned cars may lead, on occasion, to undesirable results. There is no doubt, however, but that the development of efficient refrigeration alone has made possible a large part of the fruit and meat transportation with which this chapter is concerned.

Motor Truck and Air-Line Refrigeration

Refrigeration has its longest history in railroad operation, but it is, of course, adaptable to motor truck and aircraft service. Like railroads, trucks have experimented with a number of refrigerants, but mechanical

[27] 246 I.C.C. 145, 1941; 246 I.C.C. 737, 1941; 256 I.C.C. 196, 1943; 256 I.C.C. 455, 1943. Car lines may supply ice and salt, fill bunkers and generally supervise the refrigeration, and make repairs to refrigerating devices. They may also assume additional responsibilities, but these must be separately described and paid for; they may not be offset by inflation of the amounts paid for standard operations.

[28] United States Federal Trade Commission, *Report on Private Car Lines*, 1920.

[29] 151 I.C.C. 649, 1929; 172 I.C.C. 3, 1931; 215 I.C.C. 684, 1936; 222 I.C.C. 245, 1937. See also 56 I.C.C. 449, 1920; 50 I.C.C. 652, 1928; 29 I.C.C. 653, 1914; and cases cited.

refrigeration offers them peculiar advantages because of space and weight limitations.[30] There were said to be some 18,000 trucks and 10,000 trailers adapted to refrigeration in 1939. In 1947 there were trucks in production capable of maintaining temperatures as low as —10° F. with outside temperatures of 110° F., and with push button operation and automatic control which required little attention from the driver.[31] Attention has also been paid to refrigerated air transport. Early plans for the cooling of air cargoes have included the use of insulated fiberglas bags with dry ice, and similarly insulated and cooled compartments in planes. More recently, experiments have considered the carriage of refrigerated cargoes in plane load cargoes. The need for refrigerated service is evident in air-line operation, but the volume of such service is still small.[32]

Sugar

Approximately 60 percent of the sugar used in the United States is consumed in the household, the balance being taken by manufacturers of soft drinks, candy and confectionery, bakery goods, ice cream, canned and preserved foods, and miscellaneous minor products.[33] Fifty-seven percent of the total consumption is in New England and in the Middle Atlantic and the Southern States, supplied mainly by Cuban and Puerto Rican sugar. Thirteen percent more is accounted for by the Pacific Coast and the Western mountain states which use, predominantly, cane sugar from Hawaii and the Philippines and domestic beet sugar. The balance, or something less than one-third of the country's sugar consumption, is distributed in the region between the Rocky Mountains and their extensions and the Allegheny Mountains; and it is in this area that the competition of various sources of supply is most intense.[34]

[30] M. V. Stagg, "Low Temperatures on the Highways," *Refrigerating Engineering,* March, 1948; D. Albert, "Truck-Trailer Refrigeration," *ibid.,* January, 1948, pp. 31–35.

[31] *Refrigerating Engineering,* November, 1947.

[32] Don Emery Cox and Henry W. Rahn, "Refrigeration for Air-Borne Perishables," *Refrigerating Engineering,* May, 1947.

[33] United States Department of Agriculture, Bureau of Agricultural Economics, *The World Sugar Situation,* December, 1950.

[34] United States Department of Agriculture, Production and Marketing Administration, *Sugar Report,* August 22, 1950.

The groupings referred to in the text are as follows:

1. *New England states:* Maine, New Hampshire, Vermont, Massachusetts, Rhode Island, and Connecticut.
2. *Middle Atlantic states:* New York, New Jersey, Pennsylvania.
3. *Southern states:* Delaware, Maryland, District of Columbia, Virginia, West Virginia, North Carolina, South Carolina, Georgia, Florida, Kentucky, Tennessee, Alabama, Mississippi, Arkansas, Louisiana, Oklahoma, Texas.
4. *Western states:* Montana, Idaho, Wyoming, Colorado, New Mexico, Arizona, Utah, Nevada.
5. *Pacific Coast states:* Washington, Oregon, California.

Inasmuch as almost all the cane sugar consumed in the United States is either imported or grown in the state of Louisiana, the principal points of origin for domestic cane sugar movements are to be found in the refineries on the Atlantic, Gulf, and Pacific seaboards. Of these, the most important are the refineries scattered throughout Louisiana and those at or near the cities of New York, Philadelphia, Baltimore, Boston, Savannah, Houston (Sugarland), and San Francisco.

In addition to the cane sugar producers, there are manufacturers of beet sugar located in the Western and Middle Western states. In 1950 there were 16 factories for the manufacture of beet sugar in Colorado, 13 in Michigan, 11 in California, 6 in Nebraska, 6 in Idaho, 5 each in Wyoming, Utah, and Montana, 4 in Ohio, 3 in Minnesota, and 1 each in Iowa, Kansas, South Dakota, Washington, and Wisconsin. In terms of daily capacity, 74 percent of the factories were in the six states of Colorado, California, Michigan, Idaho, Nebraska, and Montana; and 18 percent more were to be found in the four states of Wyoming, Utah, Minnesota, and Ohio.[35]

The distribution of beet sugar factories is determined by the agricultural area devoted to the growing of sugar beets, because of the cost of shipping this raw material. The average haul of beets is short but the manufactured product can bear the cost of transportation, and it moves long distances where, as in the Rocky Mountain region, local supply exceeds the consuming capacity of the neighboring population.

Division of Markets

Generally speaking, Cuban and Puerto Rican cane sugar, with local production, dominates Louisiana and Arkansas, the Southern markets east of the Mississippi, and the Northeastern markets as far west as Buffalo and Pittsburgh. On the other hand, Hawaiian sugar is the principal resource in California and Arizona, and beet sugar supplies the Western mountain and prairie states. But in New Mexico, Texas and Oklahoma, and in the states of Indiana, Illinois, Michigan, Iowa, and Missouri, cane sugar from the West Indies and Louisiana competes with cane sugar from Hawaii, and both with beet sugar from Colorado, Utah, and Idaho and with local sources of beet sugar production.

Balance Between Rates from New Orleans and Rates from Points in Colorado

Rates on beet sugar, as from points located in Colorado, determine to a considerable extent the distribution of the product of western factories.

[35] United States Beet Sugar Association, *American Beet Sugar Companies,* 1950–51. See also *Sugar Reference Book and Directory,* New York, 1949.

Speaking of shipments to Oklahoma and Texas, the Interstate Commerce Commission said, in 1942:

Refining companies operating plants in Colorado, California, and other western states generally offer to deliver sugar at the Oklahoma and Texas points here under consideration at prices which are the same for a given grade as the delivered price quoted by the Sugar Land [Houston] operator. This competitive marketing practice requires the more distant refiner to absorb the difference in freight rate, and, partly for this reason, railroads which transport sugar frequently maintain, from the refining points, rates which are differentially or otherwise related. They also publish rates from Houston, New Orleans, and other ports, which are related to those in effect from the northeast refining point. For these reasons, any material change in the carload rate from Sugar Land, the base point of origin for shipments billed to destinations in Oklahoma and northern Texas, usually affects the rate level maintained to the same points from New Orleans and Houston and from refining points in Colorado, Nebraska, Wyoming, Utah, Idaho, Oregon, and California.[36]

Colorado rates to Chicago are also balanced against rates from New Orleans. Thus, in 1933, the sugar rate from Colorado points was made 41 cents on minimum carloads of 60,000 pounds and 36 cents on carloads of 80,000 pounds. The rates from New Orleans were 39 and 34 cents. On these hauls, as in movements to the Southwest, Colorado rates may be lower to a distant point, such as Chicago, where competition is especially severe, than to less remote intermediate markets.[37] In approving a rate structure of this sort in 1933 the Interstate Commerce Commission spoke of the importance of sugar beet production to the welfare and prosperity of Colorado and other sugar beet producing sections, and of the necessity of marketing the bulk of the sugar produced there in the more populous areas in the East.[38]

Competition of Cane Sugar Refineries in the Northern Mississippi Valley

We have already observed that cane sugar is locally grown—mostly in Louisiana—or it is imported through some seaboard port. It follows that the cane sugar supply seeks its domestic market from points situated upon the outside edges of the United States, and that from these origins shipments converge upon interior destinations.

Prices of Refined Sugar

The basic price of refined cane sugar at all refining points is substan-

[36] 253 I.C.C. 111, 112, 1942.
[37] 210 I.C.C. 675, 1935.
[38] 195 I.C.C. 127, 161, 1933.

tially the same. At other than refining points, the price is generally the New York price plus the lowest freight rate via the standard all-rail lines from any Eastern refining point, or, in eleven Far Western states, the San Francisco price and the rates from that point. Costs of production are not the same at all points; but at a given moment the ability of any refining district to enlarge, or even to maintain, its distributing area depends upon the relation of the railroad rate it pays to the railroad rate of its competitors.

The Conflicting Interests of New Orleans and of New York, Philadelphia and Baltimore

The critical rates on cane sugar are: (1) from New York, Philadelphia, and Baltimore to Chicago; (2) from New Orleans to Chicago; and (3) from San Francisco to Chicago. In 1931 the rates from New Orleans to Chicago (919 miles) and from Baltimore to Chicago (796 miles) were 54 cents per 100 pounds. From New York to Chicago (896 miles) the rate was 56.5 cents. This adjustment was the result of a somewhat complicated history, influenced by the tradition that rates from Philadelphia and New York should be greater than rates from Baltimore, for reasons that will be discussed in explaining the differential rate controversy,[39] and influenced also by the desire of New Orleans to compete with New York in the northern Mississippi Valley. In 1932 the Eastern carriers put into effect a rate of 42 cents from New York and 39 cents from Baltimore to Chicago.[40] A provoking cause was the loss of sugar tonnage to the New York State Barge Canal and to the St. Lawrence River. The Southern carriers, to meet this competition as well as to reduce the tendency of sugar shipments to take advantage of the Mississippi River service, countered with rates of 34 and 39 cents from New Orleans to Chicago on minimum carloads respectively of 80,000 and 60,000 pounds. The Eastern railroads did not at once meet the lower of these rates on the larger minimum, and so gave up for the moment the carriage, in large lots, of sugar intended for Chicago consumption. In 1933, however, the Eastern lines adopted a 34-cent rate from Baltimore to Chicago and 37 cents from New York to Chicago, with minimum carloads of 80,000 pounds, thus reëntering the field.

Chicago rates from Gulf refineries are blanketed back almost to St. Louis, to Ohio River crossings and into Kentucky, in order to avoid the necessity of charging more to intermediate than to terminal destinations. The general policy of the Eastern lines is to meet New Orleans rates from the North Atlantic ports to Cincinnati, to Chicago, and to points west and north of Chicago. The specific relationship is between the Baltimore–Chicago rate and the New Orleans–Chicago rate with 3 cents added in

[39] See chap. 18.
[40] 195 I.C.C. 127, 1934.

fixing the tariff from New York. In 1950 the rate was 72 cents from Baltimore and New Orleans on a minimum of 60,000 pounds.[41] To Cincinnati, in 1950, the rate from Baltimore was 60 cents and from New Orleans it was 64 cents on a minimum of 60,000 pounds. Carriers were applying, however, for permission to quote a rate of 56 cents on a minimum of 80,000 pounds to Chicago and Cincinnati from Baltimore, Savannah, and New Orleans. Equalization does not extend into Official Territory east of Cincinnati.

The Rivalry of San Francisco with Refiners in the East and South

San Francisco is relatively distant from Mississippi Valley markets, but she desires a rate adjustment which will enable her to participate in the Valley trade. Her need for special consideration becomes more pressing as her shipments push farther east, because the competition of New York and New Orleans refiners is more effective as the Atlantic and Gulf seaboards are approached. This peculiar circumstance led the railroads serving California to ask the Interstate Commerce Commission in 1914, to approve a rate from San Francisco to Chicago of 46 cents per 100 pounds, while at the same time they desired to charge 55 cents at the Missouri River and at points west thereof. This was in spite of the fact that sugar consigned to Chicago necessarily crossed the Missouri River on its way to destination. The proposed 46-cent rate was 23 cents higher than the rate charged from New Orleans at the time, but it was believed to be sufficiently low to enable Western lines to share in the sugar traffic. The Interstate Commerce Commission acceded, in substance, to the request.[42]

As a matter of fact, the new adjustment did largely increase sugar shipments from the Pacific coast. Before the new rates took effect, some 270,000 tons of sugar annually had gone direct from Hawaii by water and across the Isthmus of Tehuantepec to the Atlantic seaboard, there to be refined and shipped inland. After the new rates were introduced, all of this raw sugar, except under unusual circumstances, was brought to San Francisco. There it was refined and shipped out, largely in competition with sugar refined in the East. Meanwhile the Middle Western sales of

[41] The adjustment to Chicago from Baltimore and New Orleans extended, in 1950, throughout that portion of Illinois on and north of the line of the Baltimore & Ohio from St. Louis through Olney to the Illinois-Indiana state line and west as far as the Monon Railroad from Louisville to Chicago, also to Indianapolis.

[42] 31 I.C.C. 511, 1914. The Western lines asked permission, specifically, to charge rates from San Francisco to points in Missouri east of the Missouri River, and to points in Iowa and in Illinois, which should be 23 cents per hundred pounds less than the rates from New Orleans to the same points of destination. Since the rates on sugar from New Orleans to points in the three states named graded upward from east to west, the effect was to request authority to establish a rate of 46 cents to Chicago while continuing a rate of 55 cents at the Missouri River and points west thereof. The Commission authorized rates from San Francisco to Chicago that might be 25 cents higher than rates to corresponding points from New Orleans, and rates from San Francisco to the Missouri River that might be 23 cents higher than rates from New Orleans.

Eastern refiners declined. Discussing the situation in 1923, the Interstate Commerce Commission pointed out that the American Sugar Refining Company, the largest seaboard refiner, and its subsidiary, the Franklin Sugar Refining Company, with their plants from 1,000 to 1,400 miles nearer the market than those of the San Francisco dealers, sold in 1920, in Illinois, Iowa, and Missouri, 28,000 tons less than the California and Hawaiian Sugar Refining Corporation, and nearly 77,000 tons less than they had themselves sold in these three states in the year 1914. The Commission accordingly refused, in 1923, to permit Western carriers to continue to charge less to more distant points such as Chicago than they charged to destinations upon the Missouri River which were nearer to San Francisco.[43]

After 1914 the general level of sugar rates increased, but the San Francisco rate was maintained at a subnormal figure, in order to meet competition from Eastern and Southern points; and it is worth mentioning that the differential between the San Francisco rate and the rate from New Orleans to Chicago was less than the differential of 23 cents which the Commission had thought reasonable in 1914. In 1935 Western railroads were given permission to reduce the then existing rate of 65 cents to the sum of 60 cents to Chicago and 63 cents to St. Louis on minima of 80,000 pounds.[44] Carriers did not take full advantage of the permission granted in 1935; the rate to Chicago was, however, reduced to 65 cents. Rail charges from California subsequently rose to 76 and 80 cents (minima of 80,000 and 60,000 pounds). They were lowered in 1940 to 70 cents and 74 cents; by 1948 they had risen to 107 cents. The reduction in 1940 was the direct result of competition by private and contract barge lines operating upon the Mississippi River. The present transcontinental rate of 108 cents exceeds the New Orleans rate by a greater absolute difference but by a smaller percentage than the difference earlier approved. Permission to quote lower rates from the Pacific Coast to Chicago than to intermediate points has been allowed.[45]

APPENDIX TO CHAPTER 11

Note on Railroad Refrigerator Car Technique

Refrigerator Car Construction. In its simplest form, a refrigerator car is a boxcar with ice in it. Some cars used by the Pennsylvania Railroad in the early days contained a box filled with ice, which was placed upon the floor of

[43] 81 I.C.C. 448, 457, 1923.
[44] 211 I.C.C. 239, 1935.
[45] 270 I.C.C. 699, 709, 1948.

the car. Later equipment employed by the same company made use of two chests filled with ice, one at each end of the car, hung by wire bands from the roof. The first Michigan Central cars provided fixed bins at each end of the car in which the ice was stored. The development that has taken place since the construction of these initial and primitive types has been in four principal directions. There has been, first, intelligent study of the circulation of air in refrigerator cars. The theory of construction of such equipment is that air, striking an ice chamber, will lose heat. It will then drop to the bottom of the car, circulate through the lading, gradually rising as it absorbs heat from the cargo, and will finally come again in contact with the refrigerant, when it will again start upon its round. To facilitate this regular movement, boxes of ice should be placed high rather than low in the car, in order to obtain full benefit from the melting ice; and the partition which separates the ice compartment and the lading should be insulated, in order to prevent the escape of cold air into the lading space except through the bottom opening. There will be circulation of air in a vehicle so designed. Some modern equipment, accepting the construction just described, increases the circulation by mechanical power. The improvement consists of the installation of fans at the floor level which force air into the bottom opening of the ice compartment, thus reversing the flow. The air is cooled by its passage upward through the bunker; when it issues at the top it falls and circulates through the lading until it is again caught by the fan and forced to repeat its round.[46] Power to operate the fan is obtained by connection with the car axles except when the car is stationary. At this time an electric generator and storage batteries can be employed.[47] There were, in 1946, about 8,500 cars that had fans driven by belts from car axles.

Whichever alternative is employed, proper stowage of freight, as well as proper location and construction of the ice chambers, is necessary in order to obtain satisfactory results. Thus, best results are secured when the air channels between boxes and crates in the lading are unobstructed from the floor to the top of the load, so that cooled air may pass around each and every commodity container.

Another improvement has been in insulation. Early cars used double walls filled with sawdust. Modern practice uses a considerable variety of materials. Almost any degree of insulation can be obtained; but the limiting factors are weight, expense, and the fact that refrigerator cars are frequently used for the shipment of miscellaneous freight in return movements. Construction that is easily damaged should not be employed.

Precooling.   It is interesting to observe that under modern practice less heat will be gained by leakage through the walls, ends, roof, and floor of a standard refrigerator car—assuming a difference of 30° F. between inside and outside temperature—than will be generated in a carload of peaches by the

[46] A variation is to circulate a portion of the cold air in a space between a false wall and the wall of the car instead of freely through the car itself (*Refrigerating Engineering*, December, 1950, p. 1161).

[47] Paul H. Montgomery, "Railway Transportation of Perishable Freight," *Refrigerating Engineering*, August, 1945.

process of ripening.[48] It is this large amount of heat generated by fruit cargoes themselves that has suggested the possibility of "precooling." In the "precooling" process, fruit is packed, placed in cold storage rooms, and cooled to between 32° and 34° F.[49] It is then loaded directly into iced refrigerator cars.[50] Lower car temperatures attained by thorough precooling make it possible to load more fruit into a car. This is because the air in the upper layers of a car that is not precooled is apt to become warm in spite of ordinary refrigeration.

When freight is precooled and the car well insulated standard refrigeration can often be dispensed with; and in any case the amount of icing is notably reduced.

Other Improvements in Refrigeration Technique. A fourth subject which has engaged the attention of refrigerating engineers is the use of some substance or technique in refrigerator car operations which will be cheaper or more efficient than ice. For instance, recent experiments have been made with what is known as "dry ice," or solid carbon dioxide at a temperature of — 109° F., or much below the temperature of water ice. Refrigeration on a different principle has been accomplished by the use of a material known as "silica gel," which has the property of absorbing relatively large quantities of vapor. Used in connection with a refrigerant, silica gel lowers the temperature of the latter by evaporation, and so produces a reduced temperature in the refrigerator car. The ingenious process by which the absorbent power of the silica gel is maintained by recurrent heating need not be here described.[51]

No one of these methods is yet in general use, probably because of the expense involved. It is to be remembered that a railroad refrigerator car is used only during a limited number of days per year, and that it receives severe treatment while in use. The second fact increases the cost of maintenance, while the first limits the revenue which the car can earn. Hence costly and perishable improvements are slow to be introduced.

REFERENCES

General Treatises

Bengston, Nels A., and Van Royen, Willem, *Fundamentals of Economic Geography,* New York, Prentice-Hall, 1936.

[48] Lon A. Hawkins, "Governing Factors in Transportation of Perishable Commodities," *Refrigerating Engineering,* November, 1929.

[49] J. R. Marshall and H. M. Hendricksen, "Refrigeration of Oranges in California," *Refrigerating Engineering,* September, 1947.

[50] Freight may also be precooled by hauling loaded refrigerator cars to a central plant built along the track at a point en route, and causing air to be blown through the iced compartments in each car. See E. L. Overholser and E. D. Moses, *Precooling of Fresh Fruits and Temperatures of Refrigerator Cars and Warehouse Rooms,* Bulletin no. 496, University of California, College of Agriculture, Agricultural Experiment Station, 1930; also C. P. Goree, Jr., and L. R. Graves, "Recent Application of Refrigeration for Precooling," *Refrigerating Engineering,* August, 1929, and J. C. Reer, "Precooling Practices in California," *Refrigerating Engineering,* June, 1947.

[51] See also E. A. Gorman, "Produce Protection in Rail Transit," *Refrigerating Engineering,* July, 1950, p. 668; J. M. Carbert and W. H. Cook, "Special Ice-Salt Mixtures," *ibid.,* March, 1948, p. 25.

Healy, Kent T., *The Economics of Transportation in America,* New York, Ronald, 1940.

Huebner, Grover G., and Johnson, E. R., *The Railroad Freight Service,* New York, Appleton-Century-Crofts, 1926.

Other Books

Bigham, Truman C., and Roberts, Merrill J., *Citrus Fruit Rates,* Gainesville, Fla., University of Florida, 1950.

Daggett, Stuart, and Carter, John P., *The Structure of Transcontinental Railroad Rates,* Berkeley and Los Angeles, University of California, 1947.

Dalton, John E., *Sugar: A Case Study of Government Control,* New York, Macmillan, 1937.

Duddy, E. A., and Revzan, D. A., *The Physical Distribution of Fresh Fruit and Vegetables,* Chicago, University of Chicago, 1937.

Sampson, R. J., *The Relationship Between Railroad Freight Rates and the Domestic Distribution of Southern Pine and Douglas Fir Lumber, 1951,* unpublished Ph.D. Dissertation, Department of Economics, University of California, Berkeley, Cal.

Thompson, J. M., *The Orange Industry: An Economic Study,* Berkeley, Cal., University of California, Agricultural Experiment Station, Bulletin No. 622, 1938.

Periodicals

Cox, Don Emery, and Rahn, Henry W., "Refrigeration for Air-Borne Perishables," *Refrigerating Engineering,* May, 1947.

Goree, C. P., Jr., and Graves, L. R., "Recent Application of Refrigeration for Precooling," *Refrigerating Engineering,* August, 1929.

Gorman, E. A., "Produce Protection in Rail Transit," *Refrigerating Engineering,* July, 1950.

Hawkins, L. A., "Governing Factors in Transportation of Perishable Commodities," *Refrigerating Engineering,* November, 1929.

Montgomery, Paul H., "Railway Transportation of Perishable Freight," *Refrigerating Engineering,* August, 1945.

Roberts, J. W., "Economic Factors in Handling Perishables by Rail," *Refrigerating Engineering,* October, 1929.

Special and Miscellaneous

Association of American Railroads, Railroad Committee for the Study of Transportation, Subcommittee for Economic Study, *Lumber,* 1945.

National Resources Committee, *Regional Planning,* Part I, *Pacific Northwest,* Washington, D.C., Government Printing Office, 1936.

National Resources Planning Board, *Regional Planning,* Part XI, *The Southeast,* Washington, D.C., Government Printing Office, 1942.

National Resources Planning Board, *The Structure of the American Economy,* Washington, D.C., Government Printing Office, 1939–1940.

United States Department of Agriculture, Bureau of Agricultural Economics,

Car-lot Unloads of Certain Fruits and Vegetables in 66 Cities and Imports in 4 Cities and Canada, compiled periodically.

United States Department of Agriculture, Bureau of Agricultural Economics, *The World Sugar Situation,* December, 1950.

United States Department of Agriculture, Forest Service, *Lumber, Distribution and Consumption, 1934,* by R. V. Reynolds and A. H. Pierson, 1936. (See also 1938, 1940, 1941.)

United States Department of Agriculture, Forest Service, *Distribution of Lumber from Sawmills in Western States,* 1945, by Gordon D. Merrick, 1947.

United States Department of Agriculture, Forest Service, *Trends in Lumber Distribution, 1922–1943,* by Gordon D. Merrick, 1948.

United States Department of Agriculture, Forest Service, and United States Department of Commerce, Bureau of the Census, *Domestic Lumber Distribution,* 1943, by A. H. Pierson and R. H. Blythe, Jr., 1945.

United States Department of Commerce, Bureau of Foreign and Domestic Commerce, *Transportation of Pacific Coast Perishables,* by A. Lane Cricher, 1924.

United States Department of Commerce, Lumber Survey Committee, Forest Products Section, *National Survey of Lumber Demand and Supply,* Quarterly Reports nos. 49–75 (1943–1950).

United States Farm Credit Administration, Cooperative Division, *Commercial Trucking of Fruits and Vegetables in Nine Atlantic Coast States,* Bulletin no. 17, September, 1937, by Neptune Fogelberg and Herbert W. Mumford.

United States Farm Credit Administration, Cooperative Division, *Use of Motor Trucks in Marketing Fruits and Vegetables: An Analysis of the Experiences of Growers Cooperative Associations, and Others in Nine States Tributary to the New York Market,* Bulletin no. 18, September, 1937, by Marius P. Rasmussen.

Part

IV

Relations Between the Carriers and the Users of Transportation Service

The Duty of Service

We have discussed in previous chapters two principal aspects of the transportation system of the United States. The first group of chapters in the present book, collected in Parts I and II, has been devoted to a description of the machinery of transport by land, by water, and by air. The second group, in Part III, has considered the major commodity movements which our machinery of transport has made possible. We now turn, in Part IV of this treatise, to the relations between carriers and shippers suggested by the titles "service," "carrier liability," and "equality," and later, in Parts V and VI, we shall again deal with problems of rates and competition with which carriers and shippers are concerned. These new relations and problems are conditioned by facts of technique and geography, as were matters discussed in Parts I, II, and III; but they are also molded by business practice, by customary and by statute law, and by decisions upon economic policy which commissions and courts have handed down. Let us now begin the discussion of these topics by stating simple principles drawn from the law of carriers.

There are two kinds of carriers from the point of view of legal obligation: private carriers and common carriers. Private carriers may, themselves, be divided into three groups: namely, private, in the traditional sense, incidental, and contract carriers. Common carriers are to be separately considered.

Private Carriers

The traditional aspect of private carriage is that the owner of the vehicle also owns the goods which are transported. There can be no obligation with respect to service in such a case because both parties to the act of transport are the same.

Incidental Carriers

Carriers which carry goods which they do not own may, in some instances, escape the legal obligations associated with common or contract carriage. This may occur when the individual or corporation does not engage in transport as a business but only as an incident to a noncarrier operation. There would be such an instance when a manufacturer or dealer sold goods to a customer with agreement to deliver upon the premises of the customer. Title might pass at the factory, so that the manufacturer who owned the vehicle might not own the articles which were transported, or it might pass upon delivery. In either case the manufacturer might make a profit upon the delivery operation by an appropriate adjustment of the quoted price or by the collection of a fee. The Interstate Commerce Commission has been willing to classify the carriage as private when it was not the primary interest of the corporation by which it was performed. It is convenient to refer to this as "incidental" carriage.[1]

Contract Carriers

The third type of private carriage is "contract" carriage. All carriage for hire is controlled by contract, but contract carriers operate under contracts of a somewhat special type. Thus the Interstate Commerce Commission has ruled that all contract carriers of property by motor vehicle shall transport under contracts or agreements which shall be in writing, which shall provide for transportation for a particular shipper or shippers, which shall be bilateral and impose specific obligations upon both carrier and shipper or shippers, and which shall cover a series of shipments during a stated period of time in contrast to contracts of carriage governing each a single shipment. Copies of these contracts must be preserved by the carriers parties thereto so long as the contracts or agreements are in force and for at least one year thereafter.[2] It may be assumed that the same principles apply to contract air and water transportation. There are, however, still

---

[1] 42 M.C.C. 193, 1943; 46 M.C.C. 303, 1946; 48 M.C.C. 737, 1948. The position explained in the text is defended by the Commission. Yet it is not entirely certain how a company will fare which undertakes delivery in its own vehicles with purpose to profit from the transportation operation as such, when the transportation is still a minor factor in the business of the firm. The conclusion apparently is that the carriage will be incidental if it is not undertaken for the purpose of the profit, but that it may be common or contract carriage if the company plans and intends to realize a profit. The Commission cautiously concluded, in the Woitishek case (42 M.C.C. 193, 1943) that each case must be decided upon its own particular facts.

The volume of incidental carriage is very great. Commissioner Rogers, of the Interstate Commerce Commission, testified before a committee of Congress that, as of February 1, 1950, there were 130,000 incidental carriers in the United States, operating 550,000 power units (United States House of Representatives, Committee on Interstate and Foreign Relations, *Transportation Study,* Hearings before a subcommittee, 81st C., 2d S., 1950, testimony Rogers).

[2] 1 M.C.C. 628, 632, 1937.

some difficulties in distinguishing contract from common carriage, as will presently be explained.

Common Carriers

Common carriers differ from private, incidental, and contract carriers in that they offer to serve the public generally. It has been said that "anybody who undertakes to carry for anyone who asks him is a common carrier." [3] The essential difference between a common and a contract carrier is that the one serves all shippers indiscriminately under substantially similar arrangements and the other renders a specialized service meeting the particular needs of a particular shipper. Between these two extremes each case is classified according to the extreme which it most nearly resembles, by the application of secondary tests. Among these tests is that of the number of customers supplied. Thus a company which served 10 customers has been held, in one case, to be a contract carrier, and in another case a company which served 24 customers or more has been held to be a common carrier. Other tests have been those of specialized equipment, or the training of employees in the handling of particular commodities, or the number of kinds of articles transported, or the use or nonuse of regular routes,[4] or the observance or nonobservance of standard charges. No single secondary test is determinative. The characterization of an enterprise is the result of a judgment as to the nature of the business in the light of its main characteristics and of the principles laid down.[5] Of course, no carrier can serve the entire public, for cus-

---

[3] 177 Atl. 343, 1935; 252 N.W. 251, 1934.

[4] In some cases common carriers cannot do business over regular routes because of controlling circumstances. They operate, instead, within an area and not between designated points. An extreme example is that of some motor common carriers in oil fields. These carriers make general offerings, but they serve where needed, at varying locations and frequently off the hard-surfaced roads.

The question of irregular common carriage has been considered by the Interstate Commerce Commission in a number of cases. (See 2 M.C.C. 703, 1937, and 47 M.C.C. 23, 1947). There is sometimes conflict of interest between common carriers on regular routes and common carriers in the same area which have certificates for irregular service, radial or nonradial. It may become necessary in such cases to determine the exact extent of the privileges of each. This is a problem for a regulatory commission (United States Senate, Committee on Interstate and Foreign Commerce, *Domestic Land and Water Transportation,* Hearings on bills relative to domestic land and water transportation, 82d C., 2d S., 1952, pp. 523–565).

[5] The Interstate Commerce Commission summarized a report of its own Division 5, in 1941, as follows:

"It was pointed out that while the statute clearly contemplated that all for-hire motor carriers should be divided into only two classes (common and contract) the line of demarcation between the two was indistinct, and that the two classes graded into each other so gradually as to make the proper classification of some particular carriers very difficult. At one extreme there was visualized those carriers serving all shippers indiscriminately under substantially identical arrangements, and, at the other, those who under individual contracts rendered only a specialized service meeting the peculiar

tomers are limited by place, requirements, ability to pay, and other facts. But speaking for the field of motor freight transport, in which the question of classification has been, latterly, most urgent, the Interstate Commerce Commission has said that "where a diversity of wholly unrelated commodities, not requiring any degree of specialization in their handling, are shown to have been transported for a number of different shippers who have no peculiar needs not found more or less regularly among shippers generally, it is apparent . . . that the service rendered is that of a common carrier." [6]

A considerable proportion of the transport with which we have been concerned in previous chapters, whether by rail, water, highway, or air, is being accomplished by corporations or individuals who are engaged in the business of common carriage. These are bailees, offering their service to all who apply. This is not, it is true, equally the fact in all the different forms of undertaking. Most passenger automobiles are operated by their owners, and, indeed, there is no contract of bailment in passenger transportation. Probably most freight highway movements are by owner-operated trucks and may be classed as private or incidental, or they are covered by contracts of private carriage. But nearly all rail, most air, and a substantial preponderance of water transport is conducted under conditions of common carriage. [7]

Responsibilities of Carriers

All classes of carriers are subject to the general principles of common law and to such statutes as bear upon their transactions. The responsibility of private (including incidental) carriers is to conduct their opera-

---

needs of a particular shipper. The classification of the constituents of these extreme groups, of course, was no problem. The former were clearly common carriers and the latter, contract carriers. Between these two extremes, however, the division recognized a confused assemblage of carriers, each of whom, to a greater or less degree, possessed some attributes of each of the extremes; and it concluded that, since the act, with exceptions not here important, contemplates the regulation of all for-hire motor carriers as either common or contract carriers, each such carrier of uncertain status must be classified according to the extreme which it most closely resembles" (31 M.C.C. 705, 707–708, 1941).

See also 24 M.C.C. 11, 1940; 41 M.C.C. 295, 300, 1942; 43 M.C.C. 33, 1943; 43 M.C.C. 511, 516, 1944.

The distinction between common and contract carriers is discussed in Marvin L. Fair and Ernest W. Williams, *Economics of Transportation,* New York, Harper, 1950; and in D. Philip Locklin, *Economics of Transportation,* Chicago, Irwin, 1947. The operations of contract carriers are well described in testimony before the Senate Committee on Interstate and Foreign Commerce in 1952 (Hearings on bills relative to domestic land and water transportation, March 3 to April 9, 1952, 82d C., 2d S. See chap. 33 for contract carriers in air operation).

[6] 28 M.C.C. 629, 639, 1941. See also 23 M.C.C. 691, 1940; 23 M.C.C. 697, 1940.

[7] English railways are authorized to make special contracts with shippers for the carriage of freight. This may be regarded as a kind of "contract" carriage. See Chap. 14.

tions under rules which apply to business generally and, in particular, to conform to regulations which governments devise in order to protect the public safety, to facilitate movement, and to control wear and breakage upon structures which the public provides. Contract carriers are subject to these same prescriptions; but as bailees, contract carriers must, in addition, recognize the principles of the law of bailment—a special branch of the common law that deals with the relations of bailor and bailee, with possession, title, delivery, reasonable care, compensation, and other matters. Contract carriers, more than incidental carriers, are affected by special statute. Common carriers, finally, as a particular class of bailees, are burdened with still further responsibilities and are governed by a large mass of special laws. The remainder of this chapter and the two following chapters will deal with the law of common carriage. This is the most distinctive segment of jurisprudence with which carriers are concerned.

Responsibilities of the Common Carrier

Legal students are not entirely agreed upon the reasons which originally led to special treatment of the business of common carriage. We characterize the treatment as "special," but we have to remember that certain other business is also subjected to peculiar rules, though not the same as those applied to common carriers, so that an inquiry which starts with common carriage soon expands into an investigation of the nature of "public business." In the larger category place is found for enterprises such as telephones, cotton gins, and milk distributors, which are not necessarily bailees. Whatever may have been true in the past, in the United States today the tendency is strongly to impose special obligations where and when, from the point of view of public policy, these obligations seem to be desirable. And it has been pointed out that in early years in England, before production for a market was the rule, duties were associated with a much wider spread of undertakings than is the practice at the present time.

We may state the traditional duties of the common carrier simply, however, without regard to first origins and without attempting to explore the entire concept of public business. They are, in substance, four: (1) the duty of service; (2) the responsibility of safe delivery of goods intrusted to the carrier's charge; (3) the duty to treat all customers without discrimination; and (4) the duty to charge a reasonable and only a reasonable price for the service that is performed. We shall deal further with the duty of service in this chapter, leaving the other obligations to the chapters which are to follow.

Common-Law Duty of Service

The common carrier's duty of service has been expressed in one of the standard legal treatises as follows:

It is the common-law duty of a common carrier, on being tendered a reasonable compensation, to receive at reasonable times and carry all goods offered to it for transportation, within the line of its business or of the kind which it undertakes to transport. Having room or the facilities for transporting the goods, and holding itself out to the public as ready and willing to carry goods for all persons indifferently, the law imposes upon it the duty of receiving and carrying them over its established route.[8]

Why, one may ask, should a carrier ever desire to refuse to serve? Why, to follow the wording of the preceding paragraph, should it decline, having facilities and being tendered compensation, to transport goods of the kind which it has offered to transport? The answer in most cases is to be found in some angle of business policy. In commercial life, for instance, it is common practice for a wholesaler to refuse to place his goods with a retailer who handles competing lines, or for a retailer to refuse to handle the wares of a wholesaler who sells directly to the consumer. Sometimes, also, a manufacturer, such as a maker of shoe machinery, will refuse to sell one type of machine to a shoe factory unless the factory equips itself completely from the same source of supply. These policies are intended to increase sales and, therefore, production in the long run, but they work at the beginning by means of partial refusals to serve. Policies of this type are not permitted to common carriers.

Memphis News Publishing Co. v. Southern Railway

One of the best-known instances in which a railroad refused to serve, for reasons that it thought satisfactory, occurred in Tennessee in 1902. It appeared that the Southern Railway had at this time a contract with the publishers of a daily newspaper, the *Commercial Appeal,* at Memphis, under which it undertook to carry papers from Memphis out into the country each morning on an early train. The value of the service to the newspaper was increased by making it exclusive, and so the Southern Railway also agreed to refuse, as far as it might lawfully do so, to carry upon this train newspapers of any other publishing company. In return, the publishers of the *Commercial Appeal* guaranteed a minimum revenue for the train in question, and offered certain other considerations which it is not necessary to explain.

The arrangement described operated without apparent friction until the year 1902, when the Memphis News Publishing Company began the publication in Memphis of the *Memphis Morning News.* The *News* secured several thousand subscribers in the territory reached by the early train of the Southern Railway, and demanded the right to ship its papers

---

[8] D. C. Moore, *A Treatise on the Law of Carriers,* Albany, Bender, 2d ed., 1914, pp. 116–117.

by this train to stations where the train was scheduled to stop. This demand was refused because the Southern Railway felt bound by its contract.

But the Supreme Court of Tennessee properly held that the contract constituted no defense. The railroad was a common carrier, said the Court. As a common carrier it must treat all alike. Granting that goods not dangerous in their nature and not unfit for shipment were offered at a proper place and time, and that the cost of carriage was tendered and the railroad had facilities for shipment, then it must accept and transport the articles presented. The failure of the railway to satisfy this elementary duty, as well as the discrimination inherent in the different treatment of the two publishing companies, was sufficient to control the case.[9]

Chicago and Akron v. Suffern

Another case of refusal to serve came before the courts in 1889. Here the offending carrier took up a switch which connected its main line with a certain coal mine, in violation of a plain provision of the constitution of the state of Illinois, in which the mine was located. The coal company sued, and the railroad did not deny the statement that the switch was removed because the coal mine had allowed a switch to be built from its mine to the line of a second and competing railroad, the Atchison, Topeka, & Santa Fe. This removal of a switch was an emphatic method of refusing service, and was held illegal when the case came to trial.[10]

Bennett v. Dutton

Still another, older case involved two competing stage lines in New England—common carriers equally with the railroads which later supplanted them. One of these lines ran from Lowell, Massachusetts, to Nashua, New Hampshire. The other also ran from Lowell to Nashua, but at Nashua connected with a third line, making a through route from Lowell, through Nashua, to Amherst and Francestown. The three stage coaches thus referred to may be designated as the Tuttle, French, and Dutton lines, respectively, from the names of their owners.

Inasmuch as the Dutton and French lines were operating as a single route, Dutton insisted that passengers from Lowell who desired to continue beyond Nashua in his line should come to Nashua by the French stages. Indeed, Dutton would not receive into his coaches, at Nashua, passengers for places above Nashua who had come up from Lowell to Nashua on the same day in Tuttle's vehicles.

There was complaint of refusal to serve. The French-Dutton interests declared that their policy did not really constitute a refusal, but that it was merely a regulation of the place at which passengers would be re-

9 75 S.W. 941, 1903.
10 21 N.E. 824, 1889.

ceived. Persons going from Nashua to Francestown were received at Nashua; persons going from Lowell to Francestown were received at Lowell. The policy was, however, more fundamental than Dutton or French admitted, and was so interpreted by the court. It was not for Dutton, said the judge, to inquire whether intending passengers came to Nashua by one stage or by another. If Dutton had room, he was bound to accept passengers without inquiry as to their antecedents.

As a result of these and many other cases, the duty of common carriers to serve is so clearly understood today that there is little controversy over the principle involved. Disputes which arise concern rather the limitations to and qualifications of the duty of service than its essential character. These limitations include the following:

Carrier Owes Duty Only to Its Public

It is inherent in the nature of the case that the carrier will limit the public which it undertakes to serve. The railroad business is transportation, and it owes no duty save to travelers or to shippers. This fact is generally recognized, although occasionally there are circumstances which give rise to litigation.

Thus, in Minnesota in 1914 there was clearly an attempt to impose upon a carrier obligations toward an outside public. In this case the Minnesota Railroad and Warehouse Commission required the Great Northern Railway to install a 6-ton scale at one of its stations for the weighing of cattle. The scale was not essential for any transportation purpose; but it was convenient to dealers and stock raisers in buying and selling cattle. The Minnesota Commission saw fit to insist upon its installation; but the United States Supreme Court held that the railway had no obligations to dealers in livestock, apart from the transportation of their goods, and refused to sustain the disputed order.[11]

According to the same rule, a carrier is under no obligation to provide facilities for the sale of newspapers, fruit, and candy upon its trains. Nor has a person the right to travel to and fro upon a railroad for the purpose of soliciting passengers, for the railroad does not offer its services as a traveling newspaper stand or as a location for the sale of merchandise. Its public consists of persons who seek change of location either for the pleasure of travel or because they desire to move from one place to another. This group does not include newspaper venders or express men or others of this type, and the railroad may refuse to serve such persons, or may discriminate between them at will.

---

[11] *Great Northern Railway v. State of Minnesota,* 35 Sup. Ct. Rep. 753, 1915. See also *Great Northern Railway v. Cahill,* 40 Sup. Ct. Rep. 457, 1920.

Carrier Need Not Carry All Classes of Goods

To a reasonable extent a carrier may also restrict the classes of goods which it proposes to transport. For example, a man named Honeyman presented himself in 1886 at the station of the Oregon and California Railroad at Portland with four dogs and sought transportation to a town further along the line. The railroad did not profess to carry dogs, did not wish to carry dogs, and its rules forbade the acceptance of such animals. The station agent explained all this to Honeyman. After some argument, however, the agent allowed Honeyman, as an acccommodation, to put the dogs in the baggage car of the train and to give the baggageman a gratuity to take care of them. Subsequently, one of the dogs was injured. The railroad successfully defended itself from liability on the ground that it was not a common carrier of dogs.[12]

In another instance, the treasurer of a California county boarded a train in California with satchels containing $91,952 in gold coin. The county treasurer was on his way to the state capitol at Sacramento, where he was to pay over the money which he carried to the state treasurer. Carrier's employees offered no objection when the county treasurer entered the train at San Jose, California; but all passengers were obliged to change trains at Niles, California, a way station, and the conductor of the second train refused to allow the treasurer to enter with his gold. Instead, he required that the funds be entrusted to a Wells Fargo Express agent who was on board. The treasurer objected. He asserted his right to go into one of the passenger cars with his satchels, or if not into a passenger car, then into the train baggage car. He offered at the same time to pay extra charges for the transportation of his money.

The railroad officer replied that money was not baggage and could not be taken into a baggage car. For the rest, he declared that the treasurer's ticket gave him no right to travel in a baggage car, and finally, that the railroad was not a common carrier of money, except through the medium of the Wells Fargo Express. This position the courts later sustained.[13]

These are two cases in which the carrier was shown to have restricted its public offering by excepting named classes of commodities. Moreover, livestock and valuables are only two out of many articles which carriers may decline to transport. A railroad may refuse explosives, or glass, or other commodities requiring special care or specially subject to damage. It may refuse shipments which result in violation of law. Some carriers carry passengers only, some freight only, and neither type is required to accept traffic of the other sort if it has never undertaken to handle it. On the other hand, a carrier may not make fine distinctions. If it carries

[12] 57 Am. Rep. 20, 1886.
[13] 70 Cal. 169, 1886.

fruit, it must carry vegetables. If it carries horses, it must carry cows. If it accepts one article of a class, it must take other articles of the same class.[14]

Miscellaneous Qualifications of the Duty of Service

Other qualifications of the carrier's duty to serve are to be found in the principle that goods, to be carried, must be offered to the carrier at reasonable times and under reasonable conditions. It is sometimes against the public interest to require common carriers to keep their stations open 24 hours in the day, and the principle may be further extended. Not only must goods be tendered to the carrier at a proper time, but they must be presented at a proper place and be properly packed for carriage. If the carrier desires, it may even insist that the freight charges be prepaid. If conditions are such at any time that delivery at destination is impossible, a carrier may announce an embargo; indeed, if it does not, the carrier, having accepted a shipment, may be liable for delay. A carrier may not, however, refuse to accept articles except when moving entirely on its own line;[15] and it has been held that a carrier cannot refuse to accept freight from connecting lines whose employees have gone on strike, even on the demand of its own personnel.[16]

Carriers Must Supply Facilities

In addition to its obligation to accept freight, a common carrier is required to supply proper facilities. This duty has both a qualitative and a quantitative side.

On the side of quality, plant and equipment must be in good condition, so as to transport safely the commodities which the carrier accepts for transportation. This means that the roadbed must be solid, if the carrier provides it, and the equipment without damaging defect. Thus, if a carrier

[14] The following extracts are from Consolidated Classification No. 19, effective February 28, 1950.

RULE 3

"Unless otherwise provided in this Classification, the following property will not be accepted for shipment nor as premiums accompanying other articles:

"Bank bills, coin or currency, deeds, drafts, notes or valuable papers of any kind; jewelry; postage stamps or letters and packets of letters with or without postage stamps affixed; precious metals or articles manufactured therefrom; precious stones; revenue stamps; antiques; or other related or unrelated old, rare, or precious articles of extraordinary value.

RULE 4

"Carriers are not obligated to receive freight liable to impregnate or otherwise damage equipment or other freight. Such freight may be accepted and receipted for 'Subject to delay for suitable equipment,' or may, for lack of suitable equipment, be refused."

[15] 111 S.E. 166, 1922; 54 S.W. 193, 1899.
[16] *Transport Topics,* February 16, 1942.

offers to carry paper, it may not provide vehicles with protruding nails or bolts; if it transports food, the cars or trucks must not be contaminated, as by prior shipment of livestock, so that they impart an odor to the food. It may be, in certain cases, that special equipment must be built, and this will be the carrier's duty, except that the obligation will be reasonably interpreted, and special equipment will be required only when there is a sufficient amount of traffic to justify the expense.

It has been argued that a shipper who knowingly accepts a defective vehicle assumes responsibility for its defects. This is sometimes true; it should appear, however, either that there is a distinct agreement by the shipper to assume the risk of the sufficiency of the car furnished,[17] or that the shipper does not leave the selection of the car to the carrier but assumes that duty himself.[18] And it has been held that a consideration is necessary in order to make a contract of the character under consideration valid.[19] The mere fact that a shipper has inspected a vehicle will not exempt the carrier from the liability caused by such defect.

Quantitatively, a carrier must supply facilities which are sufficient to accommodate a normal volume of traffic. If business increases, the plant must be enlarged. Doubtless this obligation, like others, must receive a reasonable interpretation. Thus a railroad is not held responsible for failure to meet sudden and unexpected demands. Nor, when traffic is seasonal, must it at all times provide facilities to handle the peak load, knowing that these facilities will remain unused during the greater portion of the year. Its duty in both instances is to provide facilities which will meet normal demand, and to divide its services, when temporarily insufficient, between applicants upon some reasonable and nondiscriminatory basis. But normal traffic each common carrier must accommodate, or surrender its franchise to some other and more capable group of businessmen.

Carrier's Duty Limited to Its Established Routes

It is to be inferred from the fact that a carrier owes duty only to its public that it need supply facilities or render service only in its established routes. It has been argued that a common carrier can be compelled to undertake service in an area which it has not formerly supplied; but this is not the law. The leading case upon the point concerned a dispute in the Northwest in which the Interstate Commerce Commission was overruled.

CONTROVERSY IN EASTERN OREGON. The controversy in the Northwest concerned the state of Oregon. Western Oregon was served, in 1929,

[17] 111 S.W. 358, 1908; 61 S.E. 524, 1908.
[18] 111 S.W. 358, 1908.
[19] 80 S.E. 211, 1913.

by north-and-south lines operated by the Southern Pacific Company. Northeastern Oregon was crossed by the Oregon Short Line, a subsidiary of the Southern Pacific and the Union Pacific in east central Oregon; but there was no railroad, except for a branch of the Oregon Short Line which extended 127 miles in a westerly direction, between the eastern and the western portions of the State. A gap of 185 miles remained to be filled in this section.

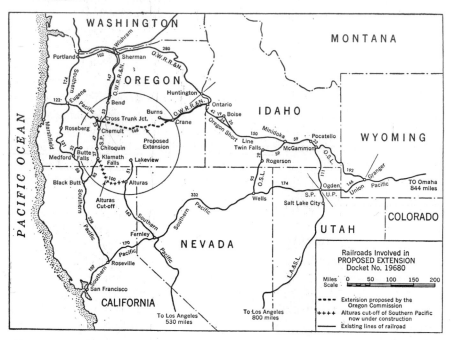

FIGURE 31.   Oregon Extension Case, 1929. (Data from 159 I. C. C. 630, 1929.)

The Public Service Commission of the State of Oregon desired the unoccupied area in the eastern part of the state to be supplied with railroad service, partly for the sake of the people who lived or could live therein, and also because a line across the state from west to east would provide residents of western Oregon with a more direct route to Ogden, Utah, and to points farther east. In 1927 the Public Service Commission petitioned the Interstate Commerce Commission to compel the railroads to build 185 miles of line from Crane on the Oregon Short Line branch to a point on the Southern Pacific near Crescent Lake. In 1929 the Interstate Commerce Commission issued the requested order.[20] But in 1933

[20] 111 I.C.C. 3, 1926; 159 I.C.C. 630, 1929. The Transportation Act of 1920 granted the Interstate Commerce Commission authority to order any carrier by railroad to ex-

the Supreme Court of the United States declared the order void. This litigation established a precedent to which subsequent actions of the Commission have conformed.[21]

Withdrawal from Service

It is a principle at common law that corporations which offer to perform common carriage place themselves, by the acceptance of a franchise or a charter and the enjoyment of privileges such as that of eminent domain, in relations with the state which cannot be dissolved save with the consent of all of the parties which are concerned.[22] This does not, as

tend its lines if it thought that the extension was reasonably required in the interest of public convenience and that the expense would not impair the carrier's ability to perform its duties to the public.

[21] 288 U. S. 14, 1933. The question at issue before the Supreme Court in 1933 was, directly, one of statutory construction. The Commission believed that the Interstate Commerce Act gave it authority to require the construction of a railroad between Crane and Crescent Lake. The Court held that the law did not confer this power, and pointed out that the area between Crane and Crescent Lake was one which the carrier had never undertaken to serve. The Court did not believe that Congress had intended by the Transportation Act to force carriers to spread beyond the field of their commitments, nor did it think that it would be constitutional for Congress to do this. States, remarked the Supreme Court, which had ordered carriers to make extensions beyond their undertakings had always been held to violate due process, and the decisions of the Court would be searched in vain for the announcement of any principle which would support the Commission's decision. In this case the undertaking of the carriers was measured by the lines of railroad which they had already built.

Insofar as the Court's ruling was based upon its construction of the statute, the conclusions arrived at have no permanent significance, for laws can easily be changed. But the principle that the responsibilities of a railroad are to be limited to the operation of the lines which it has laid down and to the construction of minor additions to these lines presents difficulties from the point of view of public policy that deserve thoughtful consideration. In the Oregon case the company had a franchise which permitted it to build the disputed extension. The system had even at one time expected to construct the line, supplying some incidental evidence that the project was a normal one. And what is more important, it could be argued with force that the carriers in the territory were in the position of public agencies, to which a broad responsibility for adequate public service in their area could be ascribed. Although the public is not usually dependent upon a single railroad to the same extent that the users of electric power are dependent upon a single system, nevertheless it was evident in 1929 that eastern Oregon would be served by the Union Pacific or by the Southern Pacific Company or not at all. To the degree that a railroad occupies and encircles a territory so as to make the district its own, to that degree it should be held accountable for service that the appropriate public agency may think proper, subject only to the limitation of "reason" and to the need of adequate payment for what it is asked to do. This was the view of the minority of the Supreme Court in the Oregon case, and it is to be hoped that such an interpretation of the underlying law will ultimately prevail.

[22] One of the many cases in which the law on the matter has been laid down is that of *State v. Dodge City* (36 Pac. 747, 1894), in which the county attorney of Gray County, Kansas, sought to restrain a railroad from tearing up part of its roadbed in that county. In this case, the Supreme Court of Kansas said:

"While the title to a completed railroad is vested in the corporation, it is only private property in a qualified sense. Railroads, like all other public thoroughfares, are public instrumentalities. The power to construct and maintain railroads is granted to

a matter of fact, prevent a carrier from surrendering its charter and salvaging its dismantled property.[23] But it would be idle to make such an attempt. This is because surrendered charters are usually unprofitable and unprofitable business can continue only when there is someone to pay the bills. Nor is there any way to force an owner to contribute earnings which do not come from property which he has dedicated to public use. The rule, however, does restrict partial abandonments. Thus a carrier which earns a fair return on its entire operations under a public charter may not withdraw some of its facilities and concentrate on the more successful portions of its service. At least, it cannot do this without permission from an appropriate public body.[24] Under current procedure the appropriate public authority is usually a commission acting under authority conferred by statutory law.

Additional Statutory Regulation

The foregoing pages list the principal obligations which an individual or a corporation assumes under the common law when it enters upon the business of common carriage, and they consider particularly the service obligation which common carriers must accept. It will be understood, however, that common carriers today, and to a less extent contract carriers also, are subject to a mass of statutory enactments which direct or limit their operation. These statutes relate to service, to rates, to the entry into and withdrawal from the work of carriage, to the conditions under which the carrier may obtain capital and organize its service, and to the relations between any carrier and other carriers with which it may connect or compete. Any intelligent discussion of carrier operations must consider, not only the simple rules of the common law, but the elaborate and often specific requirements of legislation or of administrative prescriptions

corporations for a public purpose. The right to exercise the very high attributes of sovereignty, the power of eminent domain, and of taxation to further the construction of railways could not be granted to aid a purely private enterprise. The railway corporation takes its franchises subject to the burden of a duty to the public to carry out the purposes of the charter. The road, when constructed, becomes a public instrumentality, and the roadbed, superstructure, and other permanent property of the corporation are devoted to the public use. From this use neither the corporation itself, nor any person, company, or corporation deriving its title by purchase, either at voluntary or judicial sale, can divert it without the assent of the state. It matters not whether the enterprise, as an investment, be profitable or unprofitable. The property may not be destroyed without the sanction of that authority which brought it into existence. Without legislative sanction, railroads could not be constructed. When once constructed, they may only be destroyed with the sanction of the state. . . ."

The legal principles stated in the previous paragraph are given expression in decisions based on common law and in the statutes of many American states. Since 1920 they have been also embodied in the Act to Regulate Commerce.

[23] 251 U.S. 396, 1920; 264, U.S. 79, 1924.
[24] 244 U.S. 574, 1917.

formulated and enforced by commissions under the authority of law. This type of regulation will be examined in later chapters of this book.

REFERENCES

General Treatises

Bigham, Truman C., and Roberts, Merrill J., *Transportation, Principles and Problems,* New York, McGraw-Hill, 1952.

Elliott, B. K., *A Treatise on the Law of Railroads,* Indianapolis, Bobbs-Merrill, 1922.

Fair, Marvin L., and Williams, Ernest, *Economics of Transportation,* New York, Harper, 1950.

Frederick, J. H., *Commercial Air Transportation,* Chicago, Irwin, 1951.

Hutchinson, Robert, *Treatise on the Law of Carriers,* Chicago, Callaghan, 3d ed., 1906.

Locklin, D. Philip, *Economics of Transportation,* Chicago, Irwin, 1947.

Moore, D. C., *A Treatise on the Law of Carriers,* Albany, Bender, 1914.

Wilson, G. Lloyd, *Interstate Commerce and Traffic Law,* New York, Prentice-Hall, 1947.

Wyman, Bruce, *The Special Law Governing Public Service Corporations,* New York, Baker, Voorhis, 1911.

Other Books

Mosher, W. E., and Crawford, F. G., *Public Utility Regulation,* New York, Harper, 1933.

Sharfman, I. L., *The Interstate Commerce Commission,* Part III, vol. A, New York, Commonwealth Fund, 1935.

Periodicals

Burdick, C. K., "The Origin of the Peculiar Duties of Public Service Companies," *Columbia Law Review,* June, 1911.

Needham, C. W., "The Rights of the States and Adjacent Owners of Property in the Maintenance and Operation of a Railroad," *Yale Law Journal,* January, 1923.

Rosenbaum, Irwin S., "The Common Carrier—Public Utility Concept," *The Journal of Land and Public Utility Economics,* May, 1931.

Sparr, W. A., "The Case for the Common Carrier in Trucking," *Land Economics,* August, 1948.

Trumbower, H. R., "Railroad Abandonments and Additions," *Journal of Political Economy,* February, 1926.

Common Carrier Liability

The second duty of the common carrier is to deliver safely the goods intrusted to its care. This responsibility is frequently referred to as the liability of an insurer. That is to say, a railroad is regarded as an insurer of the commodities which it transports, and is asked to make loss or damage good, whether or not the injury is the result of its own fault.

Railroad Is Not Technically an Insurer

Strictly speaking, a railroad is not an insurer. This point was decided by the United States Supreme Court a number of years ago in a case in which suit was brought against the Nashville and Chattanooga Railroad Company to recover the value of a consignment of cotton destroyed by fire while in the railroad's hands.

The cotton in question had been insured by an insurance company, and this company, having paid the loss, sued the railroad in the name of the shipper. The railroad refused to pay, alleging that it stood in relation to the owner at most in the position of double insurer, and that the owner, being indemnified, could not thereafter sue or permit suit in his name against the carrier.

In reply to this argument the court ruled that the railroad was not an insurer, although often loosely so called. Its contract, the court said, was not one of indemnity, independent of the care and custody of the goods shipped; it was not entitled to a cession of the remains of the property, or to have the loss adjusted upon principles peculiar to the law of insurance. The insurance company which had originally paid the shipper for the loss was therefore allowed to maintain suit in the shipper's name, and eventually to recover the value of the cotton from the railroad.[1]

[1] 80 U.S. 367, 1871.

Nature of the Carrier's Liability

While the railroad is not, therefore, technically an insurer of the articles it transports, it is nevertheless subject to peculiar liability with regard to them. Where injury or loss occurs, the presumption is that the railroad is at fault. Though there are exceptions which will presently be mentioned, the general rule is that proof that goods are delivered to a carrier in good condition and received by the consignee in bad condition is sufficient to support a claim for recovery.[2]

The common law liability of carriers in old England was stated many years ago to be that if "a delivery to carry or otherwise manage . . ." is made "to one that exercises a public employment . . . and he is to have a reward, he is bound to answer for the goods at all events. . . . The law charges this person," said Lord Holt, "thus intrusted to carry goods, against all events, but acts of God, and of the enemies of the King. For though the force be never so great, as if an irresistible multitude of people should rob him, nevertheless he is chargeable. And this is a politic establishment," the judge continued, "contrived by the policy of the law, for the safety of all persons, the necessity of whose affairs obliges them to trust these sorts of persons, that they may be safe in their ways of dealing; for else these carriers might have an opportunity of undoing all persons that had any dealings with them, by combining with thieves, etc., and yet doing it in such a clandestine manner as would not be possible to be discovered. And this is the reason the law is founded upon in that point." [3]

It would be unjust to our railroad managements to argue that they are

[2] A practical difficulty is to determine what shall be accepted as proof and, particularly, how far a carrier is committed when it signs a receipt for a shipment which it cannot or does not enumerate and inspect. There are statutory provisions and court decisions which bear upon this subject; the difficulties are, however, very far from having been removed.

[3] The history of carrier liability has been studied by competent scholars. Holmes, in particular, traces the extraordinary responsibility of the common carrier back to the early position of bailees such as the drovers of cattle on the Scotch-English border. These drovers took charge of cattle which other people owned. It is easy to see why the owners needed a rule for their protection; their difficulties were not, however, unique, and the principle that governed their case was applied, at one time, to all bailments. Doubtless the bailee's warranty was not, in any case, against all kinds of loss; and the courts seem to have accepted some excuses. The bailees were nevertheless responsible, irrespective of negligence, over a wide field. This responsibility was later both expanded and restricted. It was expanded in that the bailees came to be held in cases of damage as well as for loss. It was restricted to cover only instances in which there was a common occupation or where liability was assumed.

The quotation in the text is from *Coggs v. Bernard* (2 Ld. Raymond 919, English Reports, Full Reprint, vol. 92, pp. 107–115), an important case decided in 1703. The case which is usually referred to as establishing the position of a common carrier "as in the nature of an insurer" was decided by Lord Mansfield in 1785 (I.T.R. 27, 1785). The reader may consult O. W. Holmes, *The Common Law*, Boston, Little, Brown, 1881, and Joseph H. Beale, Jr., "The Carrier's Liability: Its History," *Harvard Law Review*, October, 1897, pp. 155–168.

prone today to conspire with thieves to the disadvantage of shippers; but the policy of the common law as it was formulated in medieval England still finds justification by reason of the shipper's inability to determine, in most cases, the cause of loss or damage to goods when loss or damage occurs. The injury commonly happens at a distance from the shipper's place of business. He has no representative upon the ground, nor any means of obtaining information from the carrier's servants. Not only is the carrier the better-informed party, but it is usually in a better position than the shipper to prevent repetition of the loss in later cases by adopting proper safeguards. Even under changed economic conditions, therefore, the legal rule imposing liability upon the carrier irrespective of negligence remains a "politic establishment" and is consistently enforced by the courts.

Excepted Causes

We have now stated the common-law principle which controls the assignment of responsibility as between carriers and shippers. There are, however, certain exceptions to the rule laid down, as there are to most rules. The carrier's peculiar liability does not extend to loss or damage due to acts of God or acts of the public enemy. In case of all such losses the carrier is liable only if shown to be negligent; it is not liable from the mere fact that goods have been lost or damaged while in its custody.

The carrier may also enter other exceptions in the contract of shipment subject to statutory provision or to the authority of any regulatory body on which authority has been conferred. In the United States, many state legislatures have defined by statute the kinds of loss for which railroad companies shall be exempt except where negligence is shown. These statutes normally include losses due to acts of the shipper himself, to public authority, and to the inherent vice or nature of the goods carried to the exemptions mentioned in the preceding paragraph. The best-known provisions which derive their authority from statute are, however, not state, but federal. They are to be found in the clauses of the standard bill of lading and in the standard livestock contract prescribed by the Interstate Commerce Commission under authority of Congress.

The provisions of the standard bill of lading with respect to "excepted causes" are as follows:

No carrier or party in possession of all or any of the property herein described shall be liable for any loss thereof or damage thereto or delay caused by the act of God, the public enemy, the authority of law, or the act or default of the shipper or owner, or for natural shrinkage. The carrier's liability shall be that of warehouseman, only, for loss, damage, or delay caused by fire occurring after the expiration of the free time allowed by tariffs lawfully on file . . . after notice of the arrival of the property at destination or at the port of export (if intended for export) has been duly sent or given, and after placement of the property for delivery at destination, or tender of delivery of the property to the party entitled to receive it, has been made. Except in case of negligence of the carrier or party in possession (and the burden to prove freedom from such negligence shall be on the carrier or party in possession), the carrier or party in possession shall not be liable for loss, damage, or delay occurring while the property is stopped and held in transit upon the request of the shipper, owner, or party, entitled to make such request, or resulting from a defect or vice in the property, or for country damage to cotton, or from riots or strikes.

A briefer statement, though on some points more explicit, is printed in the uniform livestock contract.

Except in the case of its negligence proximately contributing thereto, no carrier or party in possession of all or any of the live stock herein described shall be liable for any loss thereof or damage thereto or delay caused by the act of God, the public enemy, quarantine, the authority of law, the inherent vice, weakness, or natural propensity of the animal, or the act or default of the shipper or owner, or the agent of either, or by riots, strike, stoppage of labor or threatened violence.

Unless caused by the negligence of the carrier or its employees, no carrier shall be liable for or on account of any injury or death sustained by said live stock occasioned by any of the following causes: Overloading, crowding one upon another, escaping from cars, pens, or vessels, kicking or goring or otherwise injuring themselves or each other, suffocation, fright, or fire caused by the shipper or the shipper's agent, heat or cold, changes in weather or delay caused by stress of weather or damage or to obstruction of track or other causes beyond the carrier's control.

Let us consider a few instances which will illustrate the nature and limitation of a carrier's liability according to the foregoing principles and qualifications thereof.

Illustrative Cases

One quite simple case once concerned the shipment of two pieces of granite from Minneapolis, Minnesota, to Waseca in the same state. The evidence tended to show that the blocks of granite were in good condition when delivered to the carrier, and that when they arrived at Waseca they were broken and had to be replaced. The damage was not due to one of the excepted causes, and the carrier was held liable, although it was not known that the injury was the result of the carrier's fault.[4]

But the decision of the court was different in a case some years earlier which involved the loss of two trunks. These trunks were delivered to a railroad at Cincinnati for transportation to Washington, D.C. There was

---

[4] 102 Atl. 940, 1918.

continued and heavy rainfall while the trunks were enroute, so much so that the carrier feared washouts and exercised great care in the handling of the train on which the trunks were loaded. Eventually, the carrier even withdrew the train from its main track and placed it in a yard at Conemaugh, near the Conemaugh River. While the carrier's equipment was supposedly safe at this point, a dam that held back a reservoir on a tributary stream gave way, and a wave of water, descending a narrow valley, destroyed both the train at Conemaugh and its contents. The catastrophe was known as the Johnstown flood. It caused loss, but the loss was due to an excepted cause, namely, an act of God, and the carrier was not held liable.[5]

An illustration of another excepted cause, the inherent vice of the article shipped, may be found in a case where a shipper forwarded a hogshead of molasses on one of the warmest days of summer. The molasses fermented and the hogshead burst while being unloaded, but the carrier was not held responsible.[6] Cases where cattle gore each other in course of transportation or mules kick, or hogs or horses become sick, are similarly treated by the courts. The carrier is not required to make an extraordinary effort to protect livestock. Thus a railroad which transported a valuable stallion could not be compelled, when the horse fell ill, to attach the car in which the stallion traveled to a passenger train.[7] A railroad must not, however, contribute to such injuries by any negligent act of its own.

Acts of the public enemy include damages due to acts of war. During the Civil War, railroads were not held liable for goods seized by the Confederate Army,[8] and the same rule would have been applied in World Wars I and II had articles within the jurisdiction of American courts been seized by German armies.

Loss due to the action of a shipper occurs, *inter alia,* when a shipper loads freight upon a railroad car and secures it improperly or when a shipper delivers a package or a sealed car to a carrier when the freight is badly stowed. The courts have held that a man who fastened a wagon on a railroad flatcar could not recover because the wind blew the wagon off the flatcar while in transit.[9] And a shipper who loaded a car with furniture, sealed it, and delivered the car to a railroad for transportation, could not complain when the furniture, upon arrival, was found to be in a state of complete confusion.[10]

A carrier is not liable for delay caused by a strike, if it uses due diligence

[5] 147 Pa. St. Rep. 343, 1892.
[6] 38 Atl. 1002, 1895.
[7] 133 N.W. 128, 1911.
[8] 98 Am. Dec. 454, 1869.
[9] 37 Wis. 190, 1875.
[10] 109 S.E. 219, 1921.

in counteracting the strike's effects; but it must advise the shipper when goods are tendered for transportation as to any cause within its reasonable knowledge which will be likely to cause delay. There is some difficulty, as one might expect, in interpreting the phrase "due diligence" in its application to strike conditions. It should be remembered, generally, that a carrier is not required to transport and deliver goods within any special time after receiving them for transportation. It need only deliver them within a reasonable time. Nor can it assume liability by special contract.[11]

The illustrations given and the statements in the preceding section of this chapter cover the principal types of exception to common carrier liability which protect common carriers at the present time. We may repeat that these exceptions may be multiplied by authorized contracts between the parties, or they may be laid down by statute or prescribed by state or federal commissions, and the new conditions will be sustained by the courts.

Beginning of Common Carrier's Liability

We may now return to the general rule imposing responsibility upon common carriers for safe delivery of persons and property intrusted to their care. Out of these principles grows a substantial part of the law of common carriers. We shall not, in this chapter, attempt to state the whole of carrier law, but we shall call attention to a few of the matters which are frequently in dispute.

One important question is as to the moment at which a carrier's liability begins. Is the issue of a bill of lading necessary to fix responsibility upon the railroad? Must the shipper deliver freight at the carrier's depot? Must the freight be boxed or marked in any particular way? What, in brief, constitutes acceptance by the carrier?

In the case of *Meloche v. Chicago, Milwaukee, & St. Paul Railway Company*, the plaintiff was the survivor of the firm of Meloche Brothers, who, prior to August 25, 1896, carried on a drug business in the village of Ontonagon, Michigan. Some days before August 25, the firm closed its drugstore and packed the contents. The goods were properly marked for shipment to Ishpeming, Michigan, and were placed inside the defendant's freight depot for immediate shipment.

Because the railroad had no car by which to ship on the day of delivery, the freight was held until the following morning. In the afternoon of August 25, before the goods had been shipped and before a bill of lading had been issued, a fire occurred in Antonagon which destroyed almost the entire village, including the goods of Meloche Brothers. On these facts, the railroad was held liable.[12]

[11] 225 U.S. 155, 1912.
[12] 74 N.W. 301, 1898.

On the other hand, the railroad was not held liable in the case of *Burrowes v. Chicago, Burlington, & Quincy Railroad Company*.[13] In this case the plaintiff testified that just prior to May 12, 1907, he had given a tent show in the village of Loup City, Nebraska. He desired to move his show to the village of Ashton, some 12 miles distant on the line of defendant's railroad. May 12 was Sunday. On that day the railroad placed a car on its side track at the plaintiff's disposal, and he was notified of its position. On Sunday afternoon, plaintiff and his employees took possession of the car and placed therein his main tent with its poles, stakes, ropes, and so forth, together with a gas machine which he used to manufacture gas and thus supply light for his evening performances. When he had partly loaded his outfit he or one of his men closed the car door. The remainder of his plant, which included his cook tent, his sleeping tents and bedding, together with some personal baggage, his gasoline stove, and cooking utensils, were kept out for use overnight. These were to be loaded the following morning, and plaintiff was then to furnish a statement of weights and contents to the railroad agent, who would then seal the car and fix the charges for transportation. The car was to go forward with the company's 9:30 passenger train.

On Monday morning at about five o'clock it was discovered that the car which contained plaintiff's goods was on fire. In spite of all efforts to extinguish the blaze, the car with its contents was totally destroyed. No notice was given to the defendant or to its agent that plaintiff had commenced to load the car, and the railroad agent had no actual knowledge of the fact of loading until the car was discovered to be on fire.

In neither of these cases did the goods start upon their journey to destination. In neither case was a bill of lading issued. In the one case, however, the shipper had completed his share in the transaction. He had packed the freight, marked it, and placed it in the carrier's depot ready for transportation. The carrier's agent was aware that the freight was on hand. The delivery was complete. In the other case, the shipper delayed the completion of loading for his own convenience. The consignment was not ready to move, for something still remained to be done by the shipper before transportation could be begun. The deliver was incomplete, and the shipper, not the carrier, was still responsible for the safety of the goods.

Ending of Liability

Another important question is as to when the liability of a common carrier ceases. Until this liability is at an end, the carrier must make loss good, irrespective of the cause of the loss, unless "excepted causes" are responsible. After liability ceases the common carrier is liable only for the negligence of its agents.

[13] 123 N.W. 1028, 1909.

On this point two contradictory rules are to be found in the common law.

NORWAY PLAINS CASE. One of these rules is known as the "Massachusetts rule," and springs from a decision in the leading case of *Norway Plains v. Boston and Maine Railroad Company.*

The Norway Plains case involved two parcels which were shipped from Rochester, New Hampshire, to Boston, Massachusetts. One parcel arrived on Saturday, November 2, and was ready for delivery at least as early as November 4. The other parcel reached Boston late on Monday, November 4. The consignee knew on Monday that his goods had arrived, but he did not take them. During a night in November, 1850, the railroad station at Boston burned down and the parcels were destroyed.

In this case the judgment was for the carrier. The court held that the responsibility of the railroad as common carrier continued until the goods were removed from the cars and placed upon the platform. If it was not possible to deliver the goods at once, because the consignee was not at hand or for any other reason, the carrier was required to keep the freight safely, but its liability was only for loss or damage due to its own negligence.[14]

MOSES V. BOSTON AND MAINE RAILROAD COMPANY. The other rule is known as the New York or New Hampshire rule. It is in substance that the peculiar liability of the railroad continues after arrival of the goods until consignee shall have had a reasonable time to remove them from the carrier's premises.

The leading case which supports this principle is *Moses v. Boston and Maine Railroad Company.*[15] Here it appeared that the Boston and Maine Railroad carried 10 bags of wool from Exeter to Boston, Massachusetts, between November 2 and 4, 1850. The wool reached the railroad's Boston depot between one and three o'clock in the afternoon of November 4. From two to three hours were required to unload from cars to warehouse, and the warehouse closed at five o'clock. The wool was still in the warehouse at five and during the night of November 4 it was destroyed by fire.

Under the decision in the Norway Plains case the carrier would not have been liable on the foregoing facts, for the wool had certainly arrived and had been unloaded from the cars before the fire occurred. But in the Moses case the court held that arrival was not enough. The consignee was entitled to a reasonable time in which to remove his goods, and during that time the railroad was liable as common carrier for loss irrespective of negligence. It is this rule which today is followed by the courts.

MARK OWEN CASE. It is of some interest to observe that the carrier's

[14] 61 Amer. Dec. 423, (Supreme Court of Massachusetts), 1854.
[15] 64 Amer. Dec. 381, (Supreme Court of New Hampshire), 1856.

liability continues for the time specified in the tariff or bill of lading, even though the consignee has commenced to unload. This principle was laid down by the United States Supreme Court in 1921, in the case of *Michigan Central v. Mark Owen & Company.*[16]

In this case four carloads of grapes reached Chicago at different times. Upon the arrival of each car, it was placed upon a public delivery track of the railroad company. The consignee accepted each car, breaking the seals thereof; and both parties agreed that at the time the consignee started to unload, each of the cars contained all the grapes which had been originally given to the railroad for transportation.

Subsequent to the beginning of unloading, 126 baskets of grapes disappeared. The shipment moved under a bill of lading which continued carrier's liability for 48 hours after arrival of freight, but carrier maintained that its special liability had been terminated, nevertheless, by consignee's access to and partial removal of the goods. This the Supreme Court refused to concede, and the railroad was held responsible for the loss incurred.

To Whom Delivery May Be Made

Delivery of freight to the proper person is an obvious duty of the common carrier, and this obligation is strictly enforced by the courts. Unless there are special circumstances which permit the delivery to be made otherwise, the delivery must be made to the consignee of the goods, or to his duly authorized agent, and the carrier is responsible for goods delivered to any other person. Likewise, if the carrier does deliver to the designated party it is free from further liability, and this is the fact even though while the shipment is in transit the consignor may have changed his mind. What constitutes an agent of the consignee is to be determined by the ordinary principles of the civil law. Who the consignee may be is usually a simple question of fact, although careless shippers sometimes lose the protection which the law intends to convey by mistaking the identity of persons with whom they are in correspondence and to whom goods are shipped. Contracts of carriage, in these respects, are enforced with great strictness, just as banking law protects the owner of an account from unauthorized charges even when made on plausible excuse. In general, carriers know their responsibilities and pay for their mistakes.

There is one variation in practice, however, which, because of its importance, deserves special mention. It sometimes happens that a shipper intends to cause goods to reach a certain person but does not desire the delivery to be complete until some act has been performed such as the payment of the purchase price of the goods consigned or, at least, a formal

[16] 41 Sup. Ct. Rep. 554, 1921.

acknowledgment of the debt. Or what amounts to the same thing, the shipper desires to borrow upon his consignment, and the bank which makes the loan wishes to retain control over the goods shipped, as security for its advance, until some equivalent security has been put in place of these commodities upon which the bank relies for its protection. The needs of the parties under such circumstances are met by the use of what is known as an "order" bill of lading. A shipper who makes out an "order" bill consigns the goods not to the person who is expected ultimately to acquire possession of them but to himself. The same name appears upon the bill as consignor and consignee, just as a bank check may be payable to the man who signs it. Such an order, indorsed in blank and accompanied by a draft upon the purchaser of the articles, may be sent by the shipper to an agent at point of destination; or the bill and draft may be sold to a bank which will forward them to the bank's agent. In either case the agent will call upon the prospective recipient of the goods and will either collect the purchase price or obtain acceptance of the draft. Proper arrangements having been made, the agent will then deliver the endorsed order bill to the purchaser who will, in turn, present the order bill to the railroad and receive the goods. It is, of course, essential to the success of this mode of dealing that the freight be delivered by the railroad to the holder of the bill and to no one else. Neither the original shipper, therefore, who is both consignor and consignee, nor the purchaser of the articles shipped, nor any other party whatsoever, can obtain goods shipped upon an order bill of lading without presentation and surrender of the bill, and courts will hold carriers strictly to account to see that this condition is fulfilled. The complexity and the possibility of error in this course of business is justified by the very great convenience which it offers to many shippers.

Measure of Damage

When goods are not delivered the carrier must make the loss good by a money payment. This requires a valuation, and in spite of the need for precision, only general indications can be given as to what the valuation is likely to be. The place where the value of the lost goods is to be estimated is always the point of destination, and the time is the moment when the goods should have arrived; so much, at least, is settled. And there is reasonable agreement that sentimental and speculative damages are not to be recovered, although Bonbright points out that such a rule cannot be literally applied. In its simplest form this reduces the process of valuation to the ascertainment of the market value which the articles would have possessed at the specified time and place, and this method is, in fact, frequently employed. It presents, however, two difficulties. One is that the goods in question may not be currently bought and sold at the place of destination and so may have no market value, at least at that place. This may be because they are unique, as a work of art of which there is no duplicate, or because customers are few and the goods are usually brought in from outside. There is another possible difficulty, however, and that is that the practice of valuing at market price at point of destination may yield a figure that includes profits and does not accurately measure loss. In the case of *Illinois Central Railroad v. Crail*,[17] for instance, a Minneapolis coal dealer had bought a carload of coal weighing 88,700 pounds and, on its delivery at the railroad siding, had discovered a shortage of 5,500 pounds. He sued to recover the value of the 5,500 pounds at the current retail price of coal at Minneapolis; but he actually replenished his supply from subsequent imports bought at wholesale rates in other places. In the Crail case the demand of the Minneapolis dealer for the use of retail price in valuation was denied, and recovery was awarded on the basis of the wholesale price. Courts dislike to commit themselves to following a rigid rule, and cases are apt to be decided by taking into consideration the circumstances surrounding the purchase, sale, and transportation of goods and by seeking to ascertain the loss which the disappointed shipper has suffered in each instance. It is unfortunate that such a practice may lead to distinctions in the treatment accorded different manufacturers, dealers, and consumers who may fail to receive identical shipments at a single place and time.[18]

Special Damages

A curious feature of the law of recovery in rail transport is the rule of "special damages." This is a rule which attempts to provide indemnity in cases where failure to deliver causes special loss to the shipper while it protects the carrier from large claims when there is no notification of the need for special care. It declares that a shipper who loses an unusually advantageous sale, or who is subject to penalty provisions in a contract, or who for any other business reason will suffer extraordinary loss by failure of the carrier to deliver his consignments promptly and in good condition may recover more than the usual indemnity, to cover this special loss, provided always that he has advised the carrier of the circumstances in advance. Such a rule appears to do equity without imposing an extraordinary burden upon the party whose responsibilities are increased. As a matter of fact it probably works more injustice than justice. It is unfair, for example, to the carriers for they are not compensated in the rate for their liability to special damage. Goods are classified and rates fixed with an eye to the likelihood of normal damage incident to transport, and this

---

[17] 281 U.S. 57, 1930.
[18] James C. Bonbright, *The Valuation of Property*, New York, McGraw-Hill, 1937. See especially the excellent discussion in chap. 13.

classification is not changed when a single shipment moves under conditions which increase the carrier's liability in case of loss. The carrier, therefore, receives no payment for the extra risk which it assumes. The rule is discriminatory because it does not require that the special payment shall be made in case of loss to all who ship a given quantity of a given article between two specified points at a stated time but only to certain persons whose business arrangements are such that they can anticipate more than the usual loss from carrier dereliction. And finally, the law of special damages abandons the policy of uniform and published rates to the extent that it contemplates an indemnity not based upon average conditions but one which varies from individual to individual as the circumstances in each case may seem to require.

Limitation of Liability

In any ordinary transaction either party may stipulate in the contract for a limitation of his liability. This the common carrier may also do, within limits. Although he may not avoid responsibility for losses due to his own negligence, he may add, as we have seen, to the list of losses for which he is to be liable as warehouseman only. Moreover, the carrier may quote rates which are dependent upon the value of the articles shipped. If the shipper fails to declare what the value is, then the carrier will charge a minimum rate, and if loss or damage occurs, may refuse to be responsible for more than a minimum amount, which will be stated in the bill of lading. If the shipper declares a value that is above the minimum, the carrier's responsibility will be greater, but he will be entitled to a higher rate.

An example of successful limitation of liability by a common carrier may be found in the American Express Company case of 1917.[19] Here a colt was shipped under a so-called livestock contract. The contract contained spaces in which the freight was described. It further stated the rate to be charged, and that the rate was dependent upon the value of the goods. This was followed by clause 3. This clause contained enumerations of various classes of animals and fixed a primary valuation for each class; for instance, "For . . . horses . . . $100"; "For . . . colts . . . $50." The fourth and fifth clauses provided that, after ascertaining the rate to be charged for all classes of animals embraced in clause 3 by applying to those classes the rate provided by the tariff sheets filed with the Interstate Commerce Commission, there should be added to such rate a stated percentage of the amount by which the declared valuation of the shipper exceeded the primary valuation fixed by the terms of clause 3. The fifth clause also concluded with the declaration that the shipper, in order to

[19] 244 U.S. 58, 1917.

avail himself of the alternative rates, had declared a value as follows, and contained blanks for the insertion of such a valuation.

In this case the shipper made no declaration of value. The colt moved at the lowest rate. The animal was lost. The owner sued to recover $1,916.70, the colt's full value, but recovered instead $50.00, or the limited value stipulated in the livestock contract summarized above.

A contract limiting liability need not, under the common law, be signed by the shipper—it is not even necessary that the shipper read it. It is sufficient that he forward freight under a bill of lading that contains limiting clauses. On the other hand, the limitation must take place by contract, express or implied. A newspaper or bulletin board notice disclaiming responsibility, for instance, will not protect the carrier, and the railroad must give a consideration in return for the benefit which it secures. All these and still other matters have been discussed by the courts.

In actual practice, the extent to which carriers may limit their liability for loss or damage to freight is controlled by statute, so that it is necessary to consult the laws of the different states in order to determine finally the carrier's responsibility in any given case. On interstate shipments, and particularly with regard to losses which are the result of carriers' negligence, the relations between carrier and shipper are governed by the following acts:

Carmack Amendment

The material provisions of the Carmack amendment to section 20 of the Act to Regulate Commerce, approved June 29, 1906,[20] are as follows:

That any common carrier, railroad, or transportation company receiving property for transportation from a point in one state to a point in another state shall issue a receipt or bill of lading therefor and shall be liable to the lawful holder thereof for any loss, damage, or injury to such property caused by it or by any common carrier, railroad, or transportation company to which such property may be delivered or over whose line or lines such property may pass, and no contract, receipt, rule, or regulation shall exempt such common carrier, railroad, or transportation company from the liability hereby imposed: *Provided,* That nothing in this section shall deprive any holder of such receipt or bill of lading of any remedy or right of action which he has under existing law.

The Carmack amendment permits a shipper to recover from an initial carrier for loss or damage, occurring anywhere in the course of shipment, to a commodity which passes over several railroads on its way to final destination.

This may be illustrated by the following diagram:

[20] 34 Stat. L. 595, 1906.

A	B	C	D

Let the lines *AB, BC,* and *CD* represent distinct, but connecting, rail-roads. Let us suppose that a shipment originates at *A* and is consigned to *D.* Let us suppose, further, that this shipment is damaged at some point between *C* and *D.* Under the Carmack amendment, the consignor may sue either the initial line *AB,* or the line *CD* upon which the damage occurred. Before the passage of the Carmack amendment, the shipper could sue line *CD,* but he could not sue *AB* unless *AB* had specifically agreed to carry over the whole route and had so adopted roads *BC* and *CD* as its agents. Such agreements *AB* was careful to avoid. Speaking in legal terms, the Carmack amendment construed the mere receipt of property for transportation to a point beyond the line of the receiving carrier as an agreement for through transportation, and therefore it logically deprived the initial carrier of the power to limit its responsibility to the class of accidents which occurred upon its own line.

Stated in another way, the liability of an initial carrier for loss or damage which takes place anywhere between the point of origin and the point of destination of a shipment is exactly the same, when several connecting carriers are concerned, as it would be if the initial carrier owned and operated the entire railway between the points selected. The privilege granted to the shipper by the Act of 1906 is a considerable convenience to him, and it involves no real hardship to the railroad because the initial carrier may in its turn proceed against connecting carriers if these carriers are liable under general principles of common or of statutory law.

In addition to the provisions which gave shippers the right of recovery against initial carriers, the Carmack amendment declared that an initial railroad might not make a valid contract exempting itself from liability for loss or damage which it, or its connections, might have caused. This meant, in plain language, that a railroad may not stipulate for immunity from the results of its own negligence.

AGREED VALUATION UNDER CARMACK AMENDMENT. However, even after the Carmack amendment was passed, it remained possible for carriers to escape the results of their negligent acts by the device of a restricted valuation, such as that mentioned on page 255. This was because the United States Supreme Court held that agreements for restricted valuation were not in a technical sense contracts which avoided responsibility for negligence. It is true that such agreements actually reduce the amounts which shippers can collect when they are damaged by the negligent acts of carriers, but the court was disposed to disregard this aspect of the question. Indeed, the chances that agreements of this type would stand were improved by the new law for the reason that the passage of the Carmack amendment was regarded by the courts as an exercise of federal power which made invalid state laws relating to the liability of carriers for loss or damage to interstate shipments of freight.

First Cummins Amendment

There is reason to believe that Congress did not expect that limited valuation agreements would be considered legal after the legislation of 1906. At any rate, this legislation was supplemented in 1915 by the so-called Cummins amendment to the Act to Regulate Commerce. The first Cummins amendment was approved on March 4, 1915.[21] This new law had three parts:

The Cummins amendment extended the territorial application of the provisions of the Carmack amendment to the transportation of goods within the territories of the United States and the District of Columbia, and to goods exported to adjacent foreign countries.

The Cummins amendment also fixed, definitely and rigidly, the liability of the common carrier by making it liable for the full actual loss, damage, or injury caused by it or by any of its connections to the goods which it transported. The language of the amendment on this point was as follows:

. . . and any such common carrier, railroad, or transportation company . . . shall be liable to the lawful holder of said receipt or bill of lading or to any party entitled to recover thereon, whether such receipt or bill of lading has been issued or not, for the full actual loss, damage, or injury to such property caused by it or by any such common carrier, railroad, or transportation company to which such property may be delivered or over whose line or lines such property may pass within the United States or within an adjacent foreign country when transported on a through bill of lading, notwithstanding any limitation of liability or limitation of the amount of recovery or representation or agreement as to value in any such receipt or bill of lading, or in any contract, rule, regulation, or in any tariff filed with the Interstate Commerce Commission; and any such limitation, without respect to the manner or form in which it is sought to be made, is hereby declared to be unlawful and void: *Provided, however,* That if the goods are hidden from view by wrapping, boxing, or other means, and the carrier is not notified as to the character of the goods, the carrier may require the shipper to specifically state in writing the value of the goods, and the carrier shall not be liable beyond the amount so specifically stated, in which case the Interstate Commerce Commission may establish and maintain rates for transportation, dependent upon the value of the property shipped as specifically stated in writing by the shipper. . . .

The third part of the first Cummins amendment was a provision forbidding a carrier to provide a shorter period for giving notice of claim

21 38 Stat. L. 1196, 1915.

than 90 days, for filing claims a shorter period than 4 months, and for the institution of suit a shorter period than 2 years.

The first Cummins amendment passed Congress by a substantial majority, in spite of the opposition of some legislators who feared that it would result in an increase in railroad rates. It struck particularly at the agreements for restricted valuation which, as has been pointed out, continued even after the passage of the Carmack amendment.

Second Cummins Amendment

The second Cummins amendment was passed on August 9, 1916.[22] This law eliminated the proviso of the first Cummins amendment relating to goods hidden from view by packing, etc., and added the following important clause:

Provided, however, That the provisions hereof respecting liability for full actual loss, damage, or injury, notwithstanding any limitation of liability or recovery or representation or agreement or release as to value, and declaring any such limitation to be unlawful and void, shall not apply, first, to baggage carried on passenger trains or boats, or trains or boats carrying passengers; second, to property, except ordinary live stock, received for transportation concerning which the carrier shall have been or shall hereafter be expressly authorized or required by order of the Interstate Commerce Commission to establish and maintain rates dependent upon the value declared in writing by the shipper or agreed upon in writing as the released value of the property, in which case such declaration or agreement shall have no other effect than to limit liability and recovery to an amount not exceeding the value so declared or released, and shall not, so far as relates to value, be held to be a violation of section ten of this Act to regulate commerce, as amended; and any tariff schedule which may be filed with the commission pursuant to such order shall contain specific reference thereto and may establish rates varying with the value so declared or agreed upon; and the commission is hereby empowered to make such order in cases where rates dependent upon and varying with declared or agreed values would, in its opinion, be just and reasonable under the circumstances and conditions surrounding the transportation. The term "ordinary live stock" shall include all cattle, swine, sheep, goats, horses, and mules, except such as are chiefly valuable for breeding, racing, show purposes, or other special uses.

The second Cummins amendment was an acknowledgment that the first legislation bearing this name had gone too far, and a return to the conditions of 1906. Its effect was to permit carriers once more to make agreements limiting their liability for loss or damage by their negligence to everything except ordinary livestock. The only qualification attached was that the agreed valuation should be accompanied by rates, authorized by the Interstate Commerce Commission, which should vary with the

[22] Stat. L. 441, 1916.

released value of the property transported. Even this qualification was omitted in the case of baggage carried on passenger trains or boats.

The restoration of the old procedure was made on representations of the Interstate Commerce Commission, backed by shippers who preferred to take the chance of loss rather than pay high rates, or to insure in outside companies.

Summary Statement with Respect to Limitation of Liability

At the present time, therefore, the situation with regard to the limitation of their liability by common carriers is as follows:

All questions relating to the limitation of liability on interstate shipments are controlled by federal law. Controversies arising with respect to intrastate shipments are settled according to the principles of the common law or by state statute.

It is permissible for a carrier to restrict its liability for loss or damage by contract with the shipper, provided it does not seek to escape the effects of its own negligence. In actual practice, however, the Interstate Commerce Commission prescribes the terms of the bill of lading which must be used on interstate shipments, and so determines the contract to which shippers and carriers subscribe.

In the case of baggage carried on passenger trains, carriers and shippers may agree upon a valuation which will limit the amount that may be recovered in case of loss. This agreement upon a restricted valuation is not regarded as a limitation of liability, and holds good even in case of losses due to carriers' negligence. The shipper must, however, receive a consideration for any concession which he is asked to make.

In the case of other property, not including ordinary livestock, an agreement upon a limited valuation may be consummated and enforced if the carrier has been authorized or required by the Interstate Commerce Commission to establish rates dependent upon the value which the shipper declares. Such agreements protect the carrier even when the loss or damage is due to carriers' negligence.

Liability of Common Carriers Other Than Railroads

The common law is no respecter of persons, so that the principles which have been explained in this chapter apply to carriage by air, water, and motor vehicle as well as to railroad carriage. The case is different, however, with respect to statutory and to some degree with respect to contractual provisions. The Carmack and the Cummins amendments are made applicable to motor transport by the Motor Carrier Act of 1935. They do not govern shipments by air. These mostly move under contracts of carriage used by the Railway Express Agency which contain the usual common-law exemptions from liability and limit recovery to specified maximum amounts.[23] Water carriage is subject to several different federal statutes and, in general, is so different from land and air carriage in the details of its statutory and contractual regulation that this treatise will make no attempt to discuss the liability of carriers for the loss of shipments that are waterborne.

REFERENCES

General Treatises

Elliott, B. K., *A Treatise on the Law of Railroads*, Indianapolis, Bobbs-Merrill, 1921–22.

Fair, Marvin L., and Williams, Ernest, *Economics of Transportation*, New York, Harper, 1950.

Holmes, Oliver Wendell, *The Common Law*, Boston, Little, Brown, 1881.

Hutchinson, Robert, *Treatise on the Law of Carriers*, Chicago, Callaghan, 3d ed., 1906.

Landon, Charles E., *Transportation, Principles, Practices, Problems*, New York, Sloane, 1951.

Moore, D. C., *A Treatise on the Law of Carriers*, Bender, Albany, 1914.

Other Books

Bennett, W. P., *The History and Present Position of the Bill of Lading as a Document of Title to Goods*, London, Cambridge University Press, 1914.

Bonbright, James C., *The Valuation of Property*, New York, McGraw-Hill, 1937.

Colton, Richard C., *Practical Handbook of Industrial Traffic Management*, New York, Funk & Wagnalls, 1953.

Hotchkiss, E. W., *A Manual on the Laws of Bills of Lading and Contracts of Shipments*, New York, Ronald, 1928.

Knorst, William J., *Transportation and Traffic Management*, Chicago, College of Advanced Traffic, 1950.

Lust, H. C., *The Law of Loss and Damage Claims*, Chicago, Traffic Law Book, 1931.

Van Metre, Thurman V., *Industrial Traffic Management*, New York, McGraw-Hill, 1953.

Wilson, G. Lloyd, *Freight Shipping: Documents, Routing, and Claims*, Washington, Traffic Service Corporation, 1952.

Periodicals

Beale, Joseph, "The Carrier's Liability: Its History," *Harvard Law Review*, October 25, 1897.

Hughes, J. D. I., "The Evolution of the Liability of the Common Carrier in Modern Railway Law," *Law Quarterly Review*, April, 1931.

[23] The limits are $50 for any shipment weighing 100 pounds or less and 50 cents per pound for shipments weighing over 100 pounds.

Special and Miscellaneous

Association of American Railroads, Accounting Division, *Railway Accounting Rules,* annual.

Association of American Railroads, Treasury Division, *Uniform Rules and Regulations Covering Issuance, Handling, and Disposition of Bills of Lading,* annual.

Equality of Charges

Equality of Rates

The simplest statement which can be made concerning transportation rates is that carriers should treat all alike who apply to them for service. Inasmuch as this prescription is too vague and indefinite to serve as a general rule, the statute states more specifically that "if any common carrier shall . . . demand . . . from any person . . . a greater or less compensation for any service rendered . . . than it demands . . . from any other person . . . for . . . a like and contemporaneous service in the transportation of a like kind of traffic under substantially similar circumstances and conditions such common carrier shall be deemed guilty of unjust discrimination which is . . . prohibited and declared to be unlawful." [1]

Permissible Rate Patterns

It follows from the law, as quoted, that it is not necessary to charge the

[1] Interstate Commerce Act, Sec. 2. There was, apparently, no common law in the United States forbidding discrimination before the late 1850's. The English acts incorporating railroads, however, frequently contained clauses providing for equality of treatment and these expressed a very general policy after the passage of the Railway Clauses Consolidation Act of 1845. The rule was effective earlier, therefore, in England than in the United States. As late as 1859 an American judge could say that "the principle derived from [the common law] is very plain and simple. It requires equal justice to all. But the equality which is to be observed in relation to the public and to every individual consists in the restricted right to charge, in each particular case of service, a reasonable compensation and no more. If the carrier confines himself to this, no wrong can be done, and no cause afforded for complaint . . ." There were, however, expressions of a contrary view as early as 1870, and the early state railroad statutes went emphatically beyond the principle just described (B. M. Kline, "The Origin of the Rule Against Unjust Discrimination," *University of Pennsylvania Law Review*, February, 1928, pp. 123–156.) Wyman says that the change in the position of the courts was inevitable, as public opinion was aroused (Bruce Wyman, *The Special Law Governing Public Service Corporations,* New York, Baker, Voorhis, Part X, chap. 37, 1911).

same rate to all persons for transportation, in order to avoid undue discrimination, for the transportation, even for stated distances, may not always be the same. If one examines the statute further, it will appear that carriers need not even treat all persons identically when the distances and the conditions of transport are the same because of exceptions which have not yet been mentioned, but which are present in the law.

Equality Between Passengers

A passenger is a person. Section 22 and Section 1 (7), as well as Sections 2 and 3 of the Interstate Commerce Act deal with passenger discrimination.[2]

The law requires equality in the treatment of passengers. The exceptions are, however, numerous. There can hardly be a greater difference than to transport one individual free and to require another to pay a fare, and yet Sections 1 (7) and 22 devote pages to the listing of categories of passengers to whom carriers may issue passes or grant reductions in rates if the carriers so desire.[3] Tolerance of such variations transforms the

---

[2] There are also minor provisions in other statutes. Section 22 goes back to the original act of 1887; it has been amended from time to time. Section 1 (7) was introduced in 1906. The two sections partially overlap. They are not, however, contradictory.

[3] Under Section 22 and Section 1 (7) carriers may grant free service or service at reduced rates to the following classes of people or in the following circumstances:

1. Carrier employees and their families.
2. Government employees.
3. Persons connected with charitable or religious organizations.
4. Miscellaneous. Carriers are allowed to give free transportation to persons injured in wrecks and to physicians and nurses accompanying such persons. They may carry goods to and from fairs and expositions free or at reduced rates. And they may give free transportation to employees on sleeping cars, linesmen of telegraph and telephone companies, and caretakers of livestock, poultry, and fruit.

The exceptions summarized in the preceding paragraphs apply to motor and water carriers subject to the Interstate Commerce Act as well as to railroads [Secs. 217 (b) and 306 (c)]. The provisions with respect to property apply to freight forwarders 405 (c). The Civil Aeronautics Act permits free or reduced rate passenger transportation in a similar, although more limited, set of cases except in foreign air transportation where the Authority may prescribe any rules that it thinks proper [Civil Aeronautics Act, Secs. 403 (c) and 405 (m)]. It is to be understood that the provisions of the Interstate Commerce Act and of the Civil Aeronautics Act in these matters are permissive and not mandatory.

The burden which passes impose upon the issuing railroads cannot be calculated because a large proportion of the passes are for terms and not for trips. A person who holds a term pass may not travel at all; on the other hand, he may travel a great deal. He is useless as a statistical entity. The Interstate Commerce Commission reports that, in 1951, 125 Class I railroads issued 2,397,301 term passes and 2,800,883 trip passes, or a total of 5,198,184 passes. The record showed that one half of a pass was issued for each $1,000 of railway operating revenue, 24 passes for each 1,000 revenue passengers, and 4.1 passes per employee.

Commission statistics show, more particularly, that the major category to which railroads gave passes, in 1951, was that of employees and their families. The issue was not, apparently, in "line of duty"; this can be inferred because a great many of the

principle of equality in transport between passengers from a moral rule
to a statement of public policy. The content of classes that may be set up
will be determined by courts or by regulative authorities. When there is
no exempted category, passenger rates must be the same to all except
when services are not "like and contemporaneous" or performed under
"substantially similar circumstances and conditions." If services are not
alike or similar, then carriers may charge different persons different rates.
A common distinction is that between coach and Pullman accommodation, or between standard and commuter traffic.

Equality Between Shippers

A shipper is also a person. Carriers must charge the same rates to different shippers when the service rendered is substantially the same. The
same language covers carrier-shipper that governs carrier-passenger relations, except that there are no statutory exemptions in the former case.
Here too, however, there are difficulties. This is because the services which
carriers render shippers often vary. Indeed, no two freight services, as a
practical fact, are ever quite alike. It requires judgment to determine the
point when they cease to be "like and contemporaneous." And for the
most part the decisions depend upon more than factual distinctions.
Qualitative elements enter in. In practice, commissions insist upon literal
equality if too easy recognition of individual differences in operation
causes the rates charged to be secret, unstandardized, and subject to
change at will; if unequal rates confer benefits upon persons or groups
which public policy does not approve; if inequality promotes monopoly;

employee passes were granted to persons who were not employees of the issuing railroad, although they were employees of a railroad somewhere, or they served transportation companies which were not railroads at all. And, of course, employee dependents
would have no service responsibility. Passes of this sort may be interpreted as an addition to a money wage. Railroads evidently feel that the concession costs them very little.
The concession is, however, irregular, the amount is not revealed, and there is no
obvious reason why it should be allowed.

The next largest class was no. 4 above. It cannot be easily described because it is
heterogeneous in character. A considerable number of passes were issued to groups 2
and 3 in 1951, although less than to other groups (I.C.C. Bureau of Transport Economics and Statistics, *Free Transportation Issued, Etc., for Use in the Year Ending December 31, 1951,* Statement no. 5224, 1952).

The public in a democratic country is apt to feel that all human entities are alike
for all purposes and should be so treated, under all circumstances. This is probably a
mistake; the opinion is, nevertheless, practically convenient, because it throws a burden
of proof on persons who wish to have distinctions made.

As an alternative it is still argued that a carrier should be free to make concessions
by granting a pass or by quoting a preferential rate when no injury to a third party
can be shown, although it has been at the same time suggested that the amount which
a carrier sacrifices by granting preference should be added to the carrier's net revenue
in determining whether or not the company is earning a fair return (I. S. Lake, *Discrimination by Railroads and Other Utilities,* Raleigh, N.C., Edwards & Broughton,
1947). But this definitely is not the public view.

and if it produces an effective rate structure which is believed to be unsound.[4] But these are policy decisions. They cannot be confidently forecast, although they can be reasonably discussed.

Competition and Price Differences

Large questions of principle arise in connection with personal discrimination when competition or volume of shipment is offered as an excuse for lower rates to a particular shipper in a particular case. So far as competition is involved, the rule is clear. In the United States the Supreme Court decided more than fifty years ago that public carriers might not grant price concessions to one shipper and deny them to another merely because the two parties differed with respect to the alternatives which they could command. This decision was handed down in the leading case of *Wight v. United States,* decided in 1897.[5]

Wight v. United States

The Wight case arose under a clause in the Act to Regulate Commerce which specifically forbade a carrier to charge one shipper less than another for the transportation of a like kind of traffic under similar circumstances and conditions. The litigation concerned a teaming allowance in the city of Pittsburgh. The facts are illustrated in the accompanying diagram.

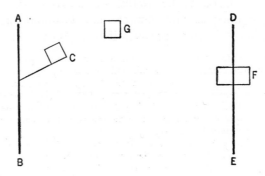

FIGURE 32.   Wight v. United States.

In the diagram, the lines *AB* and *DE* indicate two competing rail-

---

[4] General business discriminates on the basis of the elasticity of demand of different groups and even of different individuals. It expects to gain by restricting sales in markets with the least elastic demand and increasing them in markets where the demand is relatively elastic. As a matter of fact, carriers discriminate in the same fashion, as we shall see in chapters on rates and classification. Whether this is illegal or not will depend upon the government's view of public policy. (See Arthur Robert Burns, *The Decline of Competition,* New York, McGraw-Hill, 1936, chap. 6.)

[5] 167 U.S. 512, 1897. See also *Richmond Chamber of Commerce v. Seaboard Air Line,* 44 I.C.C. 455, 1917.

roads running into Pittsburgh. *F* is a freight house belonging to railroad *DE;* and *C* and *G* are two privately owned warehouses, one located on a spur of the railroad *AB* and the other located in the city of Pittsburgh but not on any railroad line.

The favored shipper in the Wight case was a man named Bruening, who had a beer warehouse at *C,* and who, because of this advantageous position, received his freight without the necessity of paying a drayage charge. In order to share in Bruening's traffic, railroad *DE* offered, if Bruening would ship over its line, to team his freight across the city of Pittsburgh from *F* to *C* without charge, thus making the same delivery at *C* as railroad *AB* was already prepared to make, and at the same expense. Later, Bruening, who had accepted the offer, proposed that he should do the city hauling himself, and that railroad *DE* should pay him 3½ cents per 100 pounds to cover the expense. This was done.

The rate on beer from Cincinnati to Pittsburgh was 15 cents, whether freight moved over *AB* or *DE.* But under the arrangements between Bruening and carrier *DE,* Bruening enjoyed an advantage over the owner of a warehouse located as was the warehouse at *G.* For *G* had to pay 15 cents and accept delivery at *F,* while Bruening paid only 15 cents less 3½ cents, or 11½ cents, for delivery at *F,* the difference being used to cover the teaming cost to *C.*

The discrimination in Bruening's favor was defended on the ground that Bruening's warehouse, by reason of its location, had the benefit of competition. This made conditions, it was said, dissimilar at *C* from those at other warehouses, such as those at *G,* and justified a lower rate to Bruening than was given to his competitors.

The United States Supreme Court ruled, however, that railroad rates must be the same to all unless conditions were dissimilar, and further, that the presence or absence of competition did not make conditions dissimilar in any sense which would justify a difference in rate between two persons shipping a like commodity from the same point of origin to the same city of destination. Translated into language generally applicable to industry, this was equivalent to saying that a railroad might not absorb costs so as to put two unequally situated customers upon an equal basis.[6]

[6] The doctrine of *Wight v. United States* is generally accepted. Lake, however, in his treatise of "Discrimination" (*supra*) maintains that the Supreme Court in the Wight case unduly limited the railroad's effort to obtain traffic. He argues that *G* suffered no damage by the carrier's original action and gained no advantage by the Court's decision.

It may well be that the objection in the Wight case should have been that the railroad was secretly departing from its published rate. It would probably be legal today for a railroad to pick up and deliver freight within a terminal area without an addition to the line haul rate if the total charge was reasonable and the same service was offered to all by provision in the published tariff.

The English rule is less severe than the American in its attitude toward concessions

Rates and Volume of Shipment

Another debatable question is whether a common carrier should be permitted to quote lower rates on relatively large shipments than on smaller shipments. This is the problem of quantity discounts.

There are two kinds of quantity discounts: one which has been called "cumulative" and the other "noncumulative." [7] In a cumulative system a lower rate is quoted in consideration of shipments which exceed a stated minimum in a specified time period, as in a year, or which yield during a given period a minimum revenue. Thus in *Providence Coal v. The Providence and Worcester R.R. Co.*,[8] one of the earliest cases decided by the Interstate Commerce Commission, a New England railroad announced a discount to any consignee receiving 30,000 tons of coal within a year at any station. And in *Books, Drugs, and Cotton Goods,*[9] a much later case, a certain freight forwarder proposed to reduce the rate on books from 139 to 124 cents, subject to the proviso that rates should apply only when the consignee had received 150,000 or more pounds of freight from New York to Chicago in three full calendar months preceding the month in which any shipment was made under these rates.[10] Commutation passenger rates express a similar principle, as does the so-called Air Travel Card Plan in which a subscriber deposits $500 with an air carrier and draws against the deposit for the cost of airplane travel, enjoying a discount of 15 percent if his use aggregates $25 a month or fraction thereof.[11]

The noncumulative, like the cumulative system, quotes lower rates for quantity shipments, but requires that the enlarged volume be shipped at a single place and at a single time. The simplest case is that supplied when relatively low rates are quoted for carload or truckload shipments and relatively high rates for shipments of smaller quantities. In some instances in railroad practice low rates have been allowed for trainload movements, as for molasses sent from Louisiana to points in Illinois and subject to river competition,[12] and for coal from Arkansas to St. Louis. A comparable case in motor transport, but with a different outcome, was decided in

---

made under the pressure of competitive conditions. (See Ministry of Transport, *Report of the Rates Advisory Committee on the Interim Revision of Railway Rates, Tolls, Fares, and Charges,* July and October, 1920, Part III, "Fares Lower Than Ordinary and Services Rendered Free or at Nominal Charges," *British Sessional Papers,* vol. 17, 1921, Cd. 1148.)

[7] W. H. S. Stevens, "Some Laws of Quantity Discounts," *Journal of Business of the University of Chicago,* October, 1929.

[8] 1 I.C.R. 363, 1887.

[9] 256 I.C.C. 85, 1943. See also 264 I.C.C. 225, 1945.

[10] See also 29 M.C.C. 335, 337, 1941, in which trucking companies proposed rate reductions based upon minima of 100,000 and 200,000 pounds with no requirement that the entire minimum quantities should be tendered at one time.

[11] 3 C.A.B. 242, 1942.

[12] 235 I.C.C. 485, 1939.

1941 when the Interstate Commerce Commission disapproved low rates on linoleum based on minimum shipments of 30,000 pounds, a quantity which could not possibly be loaded into a single truck.[13] In the passenger field a "party rate" as distinguished from a commutation rate would illustrate noncumulative rate making.

Comments on Quantity Rate Making

There is little objection to quantity ratemaking in the case of passenger transportation, probably because the indirect effects are unimportant. But there is some opposition to concessions in freight rates that are based upon volume. It is argued that large corporations should not be allowed to force or to buy any better treatment from common carriers than is enjoyed by the small producer.

"Capital," said Judge Baxter of a United States District Court in a leading case,[14] "needs no such extraneous aid. It possesses inherent advantages, which cannot be taken from it. But it has no just claim, by reason of its accumulated strength, to demand the use of the public highways of the country, constructed for the common benefit of all, on more favorable terms than are accorded to the humblest of the land; and a discrimination in favor of parties furnishing the largest quantity of freight, and solely on that ground, is a discrimination in favor of capital, and is contrary to a sound public policy, violative of that equality of right guaranteed to every citizen, and a wrong to the disfavored party, for which the courts are competent to give redress."

The basic excuse for noncumulative discounts in rate making is found in conditions affecting cost. It is assumed, in many cases correctly, that a large volume can be transported more cheaply by the carrier than can a smaller volume if offered at a single time and place. The basic difficulty is that noncumulative discounts may encourage exclusive purchasing, at least when the quantity to be shipped is less than twice the minimum required, and that they may lead to monopoly if they are granted on conditions that only a few shippers can meet. But this last objection loses force when the minimum shipment specified is reasonably low. And it is not compelling when the minimum volume required and the discount offered by one form of transport, as a railroad, merely matches opportunities offered by another form of transport, as a ship or barge. This last circumstance appears in many cases involving railroad trainload rates.[15]

Cumulative discounts are less closely associated with savings than are

---

[13] 31 M.C.C. 193, 1941; 34 M.C.C. 641, 1942.

[14] 12 Fed. 309, 1882.

[15] G. L. Wilson reviews the Commission cases on cumulative and noncumulative discounts in his *New Departures in Freight Rate Making*, New York, Simmons Boardman, 1948, chaps. 8 and 9. See also Spal, S. G., "Agreed Charges in Railway Freight Rates Abroad," *Journal of Business*, April, 1913.

noncumulative allowances. It is hard to see, indeed, why 30 carloads, offered one each day by a single shipper, should be less expensive to transport than 30 carloads offered one each day by 30 successive shippers. Moreover, the tendency of cumulative discounts to promote exclusive patronage is greater than in the case of noncumulative discounts because the minima are higher and the sacrifice which the shipper makes when he divides his patronage is likely to be more considerable. In general, then, American courts and commissions approve noncumulative and disapprove cumulative discounts, although the former may also be condemned if the minima are thought to be unreasonably high.[16]

Additional Types of Unjust Personal Discrimination

Complainants allege unjust discrimination when they attack concessions that result from competition or when they question the propriety of quantity discounts. There are other forms of personal discrimination, however, which have additional defects. In some instances the discrimination takes the form of a conscious and deliberate departure from the published rate or of a manipulation of the published rate to the advantage of one or more selected shippers. In other cases the irregularity consists in the rendering of extra transport services not properly to be associated with the published rate. In still other cases, and these more often than the others are classified as discriminatory only after a balanced assessment of the facts, they occur when shippers and carriers have relations with each other that are not, or are only indirectly connected with transportation, but which provide the shipper with an advantage which to some extent offsets the burden of his transport costs. These practices produce a system in which rates are secret, unstandardized, and unstable. They are objectionable for this reason: they are to be condemned also to the degree that they create a pattern in which competition and volume are recognized in a way which public policy condemns.

Rebates

Rebates and rate manipulation are examples of the first of the types of discrimination mentioned in the preceding paragraph. The rebate has become notorious in the United States because it has been a method for meeting the pressure of competition in a semisecret way. Strictly speaking, to grant a rebate is merely to repay a shipper a portion of the rate which he has in the first instance paid for the transportation of his freight.

---

[16] The problems of quantity discounts, cumulative and noncumulative, are not limited to railroads. See W. H. S. Stevens, "Some Laws of Quantity Discounts," *Journal of Business of the University of Chicago,* October, 1929; E. L. Thorndike, "The Relation between the Quantity Purchased and the Price per Unit," *Harvard Business Review,* Winter, 1939; W. A. Lewis, *Overhead Costs,* New York, Rinehart, 1948, pp. 74–78.

Usually the repayment is accomplished through some part of the carrier organization other than that which collected the original charge. It may or may not be true that the balance which the carrier retains constitutes a fair compensation for the service rendered, and so one cannot say without additional information how far the carrier has lost by the transaction. But rebates are objectionable in railroad work for the reason that they represent a return to the practice of individual bargain as contrasted with a one-price system of rate making, making unreasonable discriminations easy if the carrier wishes to indulge. Moreover, rebating involves departures from rates which railroads in the United States publish and file with the Interstate Commerce Commission, and so is directly contrary to statute law.[17]

There are probably two reasons why railroads have preferred to charge a high rate and repay a portion of it rather than to charge a lower rate in the beginning. In the first place, it is easier to keep a concession concealed when the published rate is actually collected, because the shipping papers, such as the bill of lading, the waybill, and the freight bill, bear the published charge, while the partial repayments of this charge are known to few persons, even of those in the railroad's employ. Concessions will ultimately become known; yet for a time a rebating company will divert traffic from competitors who charge an effectively higher rate.

Another reason is that the rebate lends itself to the system of exclusive contract. An exclusive contract is an agreement under which a shipper gives his entire business to some one carrier for a certain period in return for a reduction in rates. Such a contract was that concluded in the 1870's and early 1880's between the Southern Pacific and Pacific Coast shippers. At this time the Southern Pacific was anxious to meet the competition of the water route between San Francisco and New York in the way least expensive to itself. To do this, it examined the books of shippers to determine the exact cost in individual instances of shipping over the water lines. Having learned shipping costs, the Southern Pacific then offered a rail rate which made the advantages of shipping by rail at least as great as those shipping by sea. These low rates were accorded only to persons who would agree to ship nothing by water and everything by rail. This was the exclusive contract feature. The system was administered by rebate, and violation of the contract made it impossible for the shipper to collect

---

[17] 209 U.S. 509, 1909. Walker, a good many years ago, contended that rebates, historically, were the wholesome result of shippers' initiative (Guy Walker, *Railroad Rates and Rebates,* New York, 1917). It is probably true that rebates were originally in many cases paid to shippers who devised new means of reducing carrier costs. When the new methods were generally adopted the rebates might become absorbed into reductions in the open rate. Walker asserts that "all rate reduction in the United States has been by means of rebates." This statement deserves to be recorded, although it is difficult to defend.

his rebate. Since no rebate was paid on any business until the expiration of the period for which the contract was concluded, the position of the railroad was secure.[18]

The common law does not permit common carriers to enter into exclusive contracts, and the fact that rebates facilitate arrangements of this type is a strong argument against the practice of rebating.[19]

Other Conscious Departures from the Published Rate

There may be conscious and deliberate departure from the published rate analogous to that accomplished by the rebate when shipments are underweighed or misdescribed; when carriers fail to collect for demurrage, switching, icing, pumping, and reconsignment; when passes are issued to shippers not authorized by statute to receive them; when tariff minima required for the application of carload rates are not enforced; when improper claims are made and accepted for loss and damage; and when credit in payment of freight charges is extended to shippers in contravention of rules which the Interstate Commerce Commission has laid down. There may also be discrimination, in still other ways, when a shipper obtains lower rates or greater privileges than those to which he is entitled. Sometimes the preference may result from loose or careless interpretation of a tariff, as when rates on livestock which apply to shipments in double-deck cars only are applied to shipments in single-deck cars, or from neglect of tariff restrictions, as when a shipper is permitted to load and unload cars at transit points and to substitute commodities in ways which the transit tariff does not recognize. There are instances, also, in which the irregularity appears to be intentional. This is obviously the case when a shipment, actually originating at one point, is billed as originating at an-

[18] Stuart Daggett, Chapters on the *History of the Southern Pacific,* New York, Ronald, 1922.

[19] Exclusive contracts are permitted under English, though not under American, law. Under the British Act of 1933, a railroad and a shipper may enter into a contract. The railroad may agree to carry all or a specified portion of the shipper's goods for a stipulated rate during a specified period of time. The rate may be a single sum per unit, sometimes without attention either to the commodity or to the distance over which the commodity is hauled. The figure is often based upon the average transport cost which the shipper has previously incurred. For his part, the shipper usually agrees to ship all or a specified portion of his traffic via the carrier's line. This is also the general principle of the illustrations of American practice given in the text. The British contract or "agreed rates," are, however, public. They require the approval of the Railway Rates Tribunal. Other shippers may object before the Tribunal or ask for similar agreements for themselves. After "agreed rates" have been in effect for a year, nonparticipating shippers may apply for cancellation or modification. (See G. Lloyd Wilson, *New Departures in Freight Rate Making,* New York, Simmons-Boardman, 1948; Gilbert Walker, *Road and Rail,* London, Allen & Unwin, 1947; M. R. Bonavia, *The Economics of Transport,* New York, Pitman Publishing Co., 1947.) There are no rebates under the British plan. Agreed changes were authorized in Canada by the Transport Acts of 1938.

other point from which the rate is lower. It is, probably, also the case when goods are billed to a point short of actual destination, and in the state of origination, and there rebilled to the actual destination in another state. This last may be done because the through rate from point of origin to final destination is more than the combination of a local and an interstate rate. And there would seem to be deliberate evasion of the published rate when a railroad company sells coal to a terminal company for less than the price which the railroad paid for the coal at the mines where it was bought, plus the published freight charge to point of destination.

Changes in Published Rates

Without allowing rebates, carriers may favor selected persons by means of sudden advances or reductions in published rates. If a railroad changes rates on short notice, and a few but not all shippers have advance knowledge of what is to be done, the shippers who are forewarned will have an advantage over other shippers who are not informed. They will be able either to delay their shipments in order to take advantage of a promised reduction in rates, or hasten them in order to anticipate an increase. And they will be able to conclude contracts for future work with a precision and confidence which less favored persons cannot possess.

Moreover, rate changes may be so arranged in point of time as to benefit particular businesses. How this may work was shown in 1892, when complaint was made of discrimination in favor of the Standard Oil Company. It was then alleged that the Central Pacific Railroad, running from Ogden, Utah, to Sacramento, California, was lowering oil rates from $1.25 per 100 pounds to 82½ or 90 cents when the Standard Oil Company desired to make shipments from eastern refining points to the Pacific Coast, the rates being subsequently raised when the shipments had been completed. A letter to a vice-president of the Standard Oil Company, bearing upon an episode of this sort, written under date of December 4, 1888, got into the public press, and seems to establish the fact that transactions of this nature were going on. The letter follows and is self-explanatory:

San Francisco, December 4, 1888

W. H. Tilford, Vice-President,
Standard Oil Company
26 Broadway, New York

Dear Sir:

I herewith hand you copy of a letter I have just received from Mr. _____, Assistant General Freight Agent of the Southern Pacific Company, this city.

This letter I interpret to mean the 90-cent rate is for us to stock up from time to time, and that the $1.25 rate will be in effect whenever we may desire. This $1.25 rate is what Mr. _____ refers to in the latter portion of his letter, as my offer of 90 cents to Mr. Stubbs was on condition that he has the rate of $1.25 put into effect when we might ask him. This letter also reads as if the 90-cent rate and the $1 rate was to be put in effect January 1st. No doubt Mr. Stubbs was unaware that we were stocked up at the present rate of 82½.

The Transcontinental Association adjourned at Chicago yesterday, and I understand that Mr. Stubbs is now on his way home. I will see him on his arrival here, and if Chairman Leeds of the Transcontinental Association has been notified to put the 90-cent rate in effect January 1st I will have the same corrected by wire and the $1.25 rate put in. As soon as Mr. Stubbs reaches home I will telegraph you whether it is intended that the 90-cent rate should be put in effect January 1st or the $1.25.

Yours truly,

E. A. TILFORD [20]

Personal discrimination by means of sudden changes in open rates is now impossible because the Act to Regulate Commerce requires 30 days' notice of all changes, either up or down. Moreover, the Interstate Commerce Commission has the power to suspend changes for 7 months, and may be relied upon to exercise this power when it has reason to believe that such a change will work discrimination or be otherwise improper.

Rendering of Extra or Noncarrier Service

Undue personal discrimination may occur when a carrier performs extra transportation service for a shipper which is not offered to the public generally and compensated by a published charge, or when a carrier allows a shipper credit for services which are not within the carrier's duty to supply.

An instance of the first sort would arise if a carrier should agree to transport a consignment for a particular shipper within a stipulated time or to handle it in a particular way without providing the same service to all shippers who paid the same rate for movements of the same commodity between the same two points.[21]

Recent illustrations of the second sort may be found in practices in intraplant movements of railroad cars by main line railroad companies.[22] Thus in the case of *Chicago By-Product Terminal Company v. The Interstate Commerce Commission*, it was held that a railroad might not make

---

[20] Stuart Daggett, *op. cit.,* pp. 244–245.
[21] See 225 U.S. 155, 1912.
[22] 216 I.C.C. 8, 1936. See also 209 I.C.C. 11, 1935, and 59 Sup. Ct. Rep. 415, 1939.

an allowance to an industry for performing a "spotting" service.[23] In these proceedings the industry occupied an area approximately 2,200 feet wide and 3,200 feet long, in which there were some 35 tracks and a number of unloading points. There were also so-called interchange tracks to which the main line railroad delivered cars. The industry, with its own power, moved cars between the interchange tracks and loading and unloading points located on tracks within the plant. The main line railroad allowed the industry the actual cost of this spotting service, subject to a maximum of $1.85 per spotted car. The Commission found that the transportation duty which the railroad was required to perform, began and ended at the interchange tracks and that an allowance paid for additional service constituted an undue and unreasonable preference and advantage to the favored industry and worked an undue and unreasonable prejudice and disadvantage to shippers in the same business who were not the beneficiaries of such allowance.[24]

Industrial Railroads

If a carrier may not allow a shipper credit directly for services which it is not the carrier's duty to supply, it may not, of course, accomplish the same result indirectly. The so-called industrial railroad cases afford illustrations of attempts at such evasion of the law.

In the industrial railroad cases, manufacturing plants sometimes incorporated trackage within their plants to form a railroad company and then asked that an adjacent main line railroad join with the industrial railroad in quoting through rates to outside destinations of which the industrial railroad was to receive a share. In some but not in all cases it happened that part of the industrial railroad extended beyond the plant and that some other shippers were served. This was illegal, either if the share of the industrial railroad was too great, or if the line carrier, by the arrangement, contributed to the cost of local movements within the plant.[25]

---

[23] "Spotting" or spotting service is service beyond a reasonably convenient point of interchange between road haul or connecting carrier and loading or unloading locations or industrial plant tracks (209 I.C.C. 11, 16, 1935).

[24] 216 I.C.C. 8, 1936. See also 209 I.C.C. 11, 1935; 59 Sup. Ct. Rep. 415, 1939; and 70 Sup. Ct. Rep. 537, 1950.

[25] In the International Harvester Case (10 I.C.C. 385, 1904) testimony showed that, in 1901, the McCormick Company of Chicago operated an extensive plant for the manufacture of agricultural implements. As part of this plant, it had constructed and was maintaining within the limits of its ground 17 miles of railroad track. It used two steam locomotives and several electric motors upon these tracks in the various operations connected with its business.

Cars were delivered to the McCormick Company by the Santa Fe system, the Burlington system, and the Chicago Junction Railway, one of the switching lines in Chicago. These railroads sent their locomotives upon the McCormick Company's tracks in the course of delivery of cars, and performed there certain switching services which, although rendered free of charge, caused the manufacturer some congestion and embarrassment.

Tap Lines

So-called "tap lines" sometimes raise problems similar to those arising out of the operation of industrial railroads. A tap line is a railroad operated in the lumber industry. Lumber companies own or lease extensive areas of timber land. Somewhere in these tracts they erect sawmills, and at least until trucking became common, they have laid track and have used locomotives (1) to pick up logs at points near where the logs are felled, (2) to transport these logs from point of origin to mill, and (3) to carry lumber products from the mill to a junction with a main line railroad somewhere outside the timber area. On occasion, the track has been incorporated as a railroad company and the company has joined with the main line carrier in quoting through rates for transportation from the mill or possibly even from the forest to the final consumer, receiving for its services a portion of the total rate. This situation is similar to that which industrial railroads sometimes exploit, as in the cases in salt and machinery production. There is undue discrimination when the lumber railroad, serving as a plant utility, and owned and controlled by lumber producers, receives compensation for services which the main line railroad has no duty to perform or when its compensation for legitimate operations is unreasonably high.[26]

Overpayment for Transport Service or Facilities Supplied by Shippers

There may be effective discrimination when a shipper is overcompen-

---

Being dissatisfied with existing conditions, the McCormick Company organized the Illinois Northern Railroad. The new railroad acquired, maintained, and proceeded to operate the 17 miles of track formerly owned by the McCormick Company, together with about 5 miles of track that connected the McCormick switch with the line of the Santa Fe. The McCormick Company and its successor, the International Harvester Company, absolutely controlled the Illinois Northern, besides supplying it with a large and probably the major portion of its traffic.

In the ordinary course of business the Illinois Northern Railway now received cars from the main-line railroads at Chicago, switched them 4 miles or less, and delivered them either at the McCormick plant or at one of the industries along the 5 miles of track acquired from the Santa Fe. At first it demanded and received from $1 to $3.50 per car from its connections for the switching service. The Interstate Commerce Commission was of the opinion, when it considered the matter, that $3.50 was a reasonable charge. But following this, the Illinois Northern demanded that its connections allow it not a switching charge but a division of the through rate amounting to 20 percent of the rate on business destined to the Missouri River. Inasmuch as the rate on farm machinery to the Missouri River was $60 per car, the payment to the Illinois Northern for its work suddenly increased from $3.50 to $12. The Commission found that companies like the Sante Fe and the Burlington assented to the increase demanded in order to secure traffic from the International Harvester Company. It therefore concluded that the railroads connecting with the Illinois Northern were using their relations with that company as a means of giving unlawful favors to the International Harvester Company, to whose benefit the earnings of the Illinois Northern ultimately accrued.

[26] 23 I.C.C. 277, 1912; 209 Fed. 244, 1913; 234 U.S. 1, 1914. See also 31 I.C.C. 490, 1914.

sated for contributing facilities or performing operations which improve the quality or lessen the cost to a carrier of rendering a common carrier service. A carrier may pay an individual or a corporation in cases of this kind; but when the payment is unreasonably high the effect will be to reduce the net cost to the shipper of moving goods which the carrier transports. This is unjust discrimination. Illustrations may be found in disputes involving elevation allowances and payments for the use of private cars.

Elevation Allowances

The so-called elevation of grain is a process by which grain is unloaded from wagons or railway cars, taken into a warehouse, cleaned, graded, stored, and subsequently redelivered, perhaps for local consumption or perhaps for further transportation. Elevation greatly facilitates trading in grain, and is also convenient for the railroad, since it allows the consolidation into heavier carloads of small consignments received at country stations. For this reason, railroads sometimes pay part or even the whole cost of elevation. The practice has some reasonable basis, but it may lead to discrimination, as may tap line operation.[27]

Private Cars

Payment for the use of a freight car is payment for the use of a facility which the shipper supplies.

One of the earliest complaints with respect to private cars originated with a New York dealer in livestock back in 1890. This gentleman was accustomed to buy cattle in the West and to ship them to New York. He complained of an arrangement between the railroad and one of his com-

[27] The propriety of elevation allowances has been before the courts and the Interstate Commerce Commission in a number of cases. In a leading case in 1904, it appeared that the Union Pacific Railroad desired to have all of its grain cars unloaded into elevators at the Missouri River, partly to keep these cars upon its line and partly to secure a heavier average loading per car by a subsequent reloading. The company accordingly conveyed land in Council Bluffs and Kansas City to a man named Peavey, and agreed to pay Peavey, if he would construct a grain elevator, the sum of $1\frac{1}{4}$ cents per 100 pounds on grain passing through the elevators. Peavey was an extensive buyer and shipper of grain on his own account, as well as an operator of elevators. At one time, indeed, he handled 60 percent of all the grain shipped from Union Pacific stations. By virtue of the arrangement described, he of course received $1\frac{1}{4}$ cents per 100 pounds on the greater part of his material. This raised the question as to whether or not Peavey was receiving a special favor.

In 1904 the Interstate Commerce Commission considered the Peavey contract, and pronounced it legal (10 I.C.C. 309, 1904). In 1907, however, it cut down Peavey's allowance to $\frac{3}{4}$ cents per 100 pounds (12 I.C.C. 85, 1907), and the following year it declared that even this concession was improper (14 I.C.C. 317, 330–331, 1908).

The principle of paying elevation companies a reasonable sum for transportation services which they perform was later approved by the Supreme Court (176 Fed. 409, 1910; 222 U.S. 42, 1911. See also 24 I.C.C. 197, 1912), but in 1915 the carriers voluntarily discontinued all such payments in the principal cities where the discussion had taken place (34 I.C.C. 442, 1915).

petitors, the firm of Schwarzchild & Sulzberger, under which this firm supplied yard facilities at New York for cattle which were consigned to it and also, through a company organized for the purpose, supplied 250 stock cars for the loading of its livestock. The carrier (Delaware, Lackawanna & Western Railroad Company) paid Schwarzchild & Sulzberger 3½ cents per hundredweight on cattle passing through for the use of yardage facilities; and for the use of the stock cars, a mileage allowance that amounted to $13.71 per round trip between Chicago and New York. The yardage money went directly to the parties mentioned, while the mileage payments were made to a so-called express company which Schwarzchild & Sulzberger controlled. These payments were discriminatory, because they were unreasonable in amount.[28]

Shippers still frequently build cars for the transportation of special types of commodities. Tank cars, refrigeration cars, and coal cars are illustrations of this practice. A shipper who owns cars is more likely to have cars at his disposal when he needs them than a shipper who relies entirely upon the railroad, and the cars are also more likely to suit his special requirements.

But while a shipper may build cars and even rent them to the railroad for a price, his revenue from this source may not exceed a reasonable return upon his investment. He may not, directly or indirectly, secure a reduction in rates as a result of his car ownership, nor may he ask for special service except in the respect mentioned. What is true of railway cars is also true of other railroad facilities.[29]

Underpayment by Shippers for Use of Carrier Facilities

The word "underpayment," in this sense, does not refer to failure by the shipper to pay the established rate but to shipper occupation and use of carrier property for inadequate consideration. Thus it is illegal for carriers,

---

[28] Speaking of this arrangement, the Interstate Commerce Commission said:

"The mileage paid by the railroad companies pursuant to the contract as compensation for the use of the cars, from September 1, 1888, to September 1, 1890, was $205,582.68. The entire expenses of the Express Company, including car repairs and salaries of its officers and manager, for the same period, were $34,050.48, leaving a net profit of $171,532.20. To this must be added the yardage charge paid Schwarzchild & Sulzberger. The amount of this is not shown by the testimony, but at three and one-half cents per hundredweight for a carload of 22,000 pounds it amounts to $7.70 per car, and if the shipments amounted to 100 carloads per week it amounts to $770 per week, or $40,040 per year . . .

"To put the matter in another form, the effect may be looked at upon a single carload shipment. The car mileage for the round trip of a car is $13.71. The yardage paid is $7.70—total, $21.41. Assuming a round trip to be made in a week, the interest on the cost of the car for that period at 6 per cent is 72 cents, leaving a net profit of $20.69. This represents substantially the advantage Schwarzchild & Sulzberger receive over other shippers on a single carload shipment, and they either have so much more profit if their cattle are sold at the market price, or they can sell at a correspondingly lower price than their competitors who are not so favored, and command the market" (3 I.C.R. 502, 1891).

[29] 50 I.C.C. 652, 1918.

without an appropriate charge, to supply shippers with wharf frontage, buildings, and machinery for car loading, or to allow them free storage space on carrier land, or to provide them with office space and telephone service. Such action is discriminatory, even though there is no direct connection between an accommodation and a particular shipment. It was in accordance with this principle that the Interstate Commerce Commission, in 1937, directed certain carriers serving the port of New York to cease to permit shippers in interstate commerce to occupy space by lease or otherwise in warehouses, buildings, on piers owned or controlled by the carriers involved at rates and charges which failed to compensate said carriers for the cost of providing said space. This order was sustained by the Supreme Court of the United States.[30]

Reciprocity in Purchasing

The question has been raised whether it is legitimate for a manufacturer who sells supplies to a railroad to insist that the railroad distribute its patronage in proportion to the commercial tonnage which the manufacturer routes over the purchasing railroad's lines. Some of the larger shippers of railway supplies send periodically to each of various carriers a list or summary of the shipments which they have routed over each carrier's line. Still more generally, it is the practice of shippers who desire to make sales to railroads to appeal directly by correspondence or personal interview to the carriers' traffic departments, in an effort to cause these departments to intercede in their behalf with the purchasing departments. Shippers have usually been successful in securing such intercession; and traffic departments frequently urge purchasing departments to favor particular shippers in awarding contracts because of the routing of traffic which such shippers control. In some instances manufacturers and dealers have threatened to divert, and sometimes have diverted, their business from one carrier to another because the first carrier made purchases from other concerns. On the other hand, railroads have used their purchasing power as a club with which to influence the routing of traffic. Sometimes the result of all this has been that carriers have paid higher prices or have accepted an inferior quality of merchandise, although this has not always been the case. The net effect of the practice is difficult to determine. Looking at the relations between supply houses and carriers as a whole, it does not seem likely that the carriers as a group buy more or that the railway supply houses ship more because of their bargaining than would have been bought and shipped if "reciprocity" had been eliminated from the negotiations. It may, however, be true that insistence on reciprocity makes it more difficult for new and relatively small supply houses to establish themselves. Small carriers may also be at a disadvantage. The system of bargaining, moreover, involves a certain expense with no clear result-

[30] 305 U.S. 507, 1939. See also 216 I.C.C. 291, 1936.

ing gain. Opinions differ as to whether "reciprocal buying" leads to what may properly be termed personal discrimination. The examiner for the Interstate Commerce Commission who heard the testimony relating to the practice was sufficiently impressed with its disadvantages to recommend that the Commission ask Congress to rescind the provisions of the law under which shippers have the right to specify the routes over which their goods are transported, and to vest authority in the Commission to require carriers to purchase, after competitive bidding, from the bidder whose bid was most favorable to the carrier. The Commission did not adopt this recommendation, preferring to leave the matter, for a time, to the carriers and shippers, in the hope that abuses might be corrected on the initiative of those concerned.[31]

Conclusion

The public objection to discrimination is in essence the democratic one that it deprives the individual of that equal chance for the pursuit of liberty and happiness which is conceived to be his inalienable right. It does this directly, by means of a difference in charge and indirectly, by its tendency to concentrate business in a few hands. The margin upon which success in business depends today is so narrow that few concerns can resist the pressure of a competitor who enjoys a constant though perhaps a small advantage such as he can secure by a preference in carrier rates. Discrimination also produces fluctuations in rates, interfering with the forecasting of costs that lends stability to business enterprise. And, finally, by substituting the individual bargain for the fixed price it recurs to a method of marketing which even private business finds wasteful.

Discrimination between persons is forbidden by the laws of most states and, as we have seen, by federal statutes also. Not only this, but certain specific practices have been examined and, under described conditions, these practices have been denounced. It is probable that most real progress in regulation has come from studies of this latter sort. Cases of discrimination today frequently result from complex arrangements, the final result of which is not always clearly perceived even by the parties most concerned. There will always be the possibility of illegality, indeed, so long as shippers and carriers have business relations, and these relations require payments between the parties which can be challenged as excessive or inadequate in any given case. It follows that the problem of personal discrimination will be always with us. But it is the clear duty of both public and private management to enforce fairness and equality in shipper-carrier negotiations and to eliminate improper variations as fast as cases are observed.

[31] 188 I.C.C. 417, 1932.

REFERENCES

General Treatises

Bigham, Truman C., and Roberts, Merrill J., *Transportation Principles and Problems,* New York, McGraw-Hill, 1952.

Bonavia, M. R., *The Economics of Transport,* New York, Pitman, 1947.

Burns, Arthur Robert, *The Decline of Competition,* New York, McGraw-Hill, 1936.

Fair, Marvin L., and Williams, E. W., *Economics of Transportation,* New York, Harper, 1950.

Lake, I. S., *Discrimination by Railroads and Other Utilities,* Raleigh, N.C., Edwards & Broughton, 1947.

Locklin, D. Philip, *Economics of Transportation,* Chicago, Irwin, 1947.

Ripley, W. Z., *Railroads: Rates and Regulation,* New York, Longmans, 1916.

Sharfman, I. L., *The Interstate Commerce Commission,* Part III, vol. B, New York, Commonwealth Fund, 1936.

Wyman, Bruce, *The Special Law Governing Public Service Corporations,* New York, Baker, Voorhis, 1911.

Other Books

Daggett, Stuart, *Chapters on the History of the Southern Pacific,* New York, Ronald, 1922.

Lewis, W. A., *Overhead Costs,* New York, Rinehart, 1948.

Parsons, Frank, *The Heart of the Railroad Problem,* Boston, Little, Brown, 1908.

Tarbell, Ida Minerva, *The History of the Standard Oil Company,* New York, Macmillan, 1933.

Walker, Gilbert, *Road and Rail,* London, Allen and Unwin, 1949.

Walker, G. M., *Railroad Rates and Rebates,* Cleveland, A. H. Clark, 1917.

Wilson, G. L., *New Departures in Freight Rate Making,* New York, Simmons-Boardman, 1948.

Periodicals

Kline, B. M., "The Origin of the Rule Against Unjust Discrimination," *University of Pennsylvania Law Review,* February, 1918.

Newcomb, H. T., "Rebates," *Yale Review,* August, 1907.

Stevens, W. H. S., "Some Laws of Quantity Discounts," *Journal of Business of the University of Chicago,* October, 1929.

Thorndike, E. L., "The Relation between the Quantity Purchased and the Price per Unit," *Harvard Business Review,* Winter, 1939.

Special and Miscellaneous

United Kingdom, Minister of Transport, *Report of the Rates Advisory Committee on the Interim Revision of Railway Rates, Tolls, Fares, and Charges,* British Sessional Papers, vol. 24, Cd. 857, 1920.

Rates

The Total Return for the Service of Transportation—
Fifth and Fourteenth Amendments

In the three preceding chapters we have examined the duties of common carriers under the general heads of service, liability, and the obligation to treat all users equally. We have now to consider the requirement that common carriers must charge a reasonable rate. This is a logical inference from the duty to render service, for a carrier which demands an unreasonable payment for its service can, in so doing, effectively avoid the necessity of rendering any service at all. We shall not, however, in the following chapters, deal solely with the carriers' public obligations with respect to the level of their charge. The problem of carrier pricing is necessarily complex and will be treated from the private as well as from the public point of view. In the present part or section of the text, which will deal with rates, we shall be concerned principally with three matters: first, what is the aggregate return which the owners and operators of the transportation system of any country should expect to receive for their services; second, in what proportions this return should be collected from each of the many users of the transportation service or, if this cannot be determined definitely, what peculiarities in the demand for and in the supply of the service should be regarded in the allocation; and, third, how can the process be simplified and a tariff system be made to work? In Part VI of this book we shall consider more largely the nature of the competition to which common carriers are subject and the rate structures which this competition has helped to form. Our discussion will be based principally upon railroad experience because illustrations in this field are relatively abundant and thought is more mature. It is also true that the railroads carry the bulk of the nation's freight if tonnage and mileage are both reckoned in.

Aggregate Return Should Be Low

It is not possible to state in advance the net return which the railroad or any other form of transportation should receive in any given year. The aggregate which the owners and operators of a transport system obtain in compensation for their services is at the same time the cost of the function of transport to all other members of society. It should, therefore, be as low as possible from the point of view of the last-named groups. This principle, indeed, holds for all services which the public buys. The less that is paid for one thing, the more is left for another. The less paid for transportation, the more remains for production, or the more time can be reserved for purely pleasurable activities. From the point of view of the general public, the smaller the aggregate revenue of the carriers the better, assuming always that the services supplied remain the same.

The last sentence in the preceding paragraph suggests, however, some important qualifications to the doctrine that the best standard of total carrier revenues is the lowest one. Whatever the aggregate carrier revenue may be, it must be sufficient to maintain the plant in as good condition as the needs of the community demand and, ultimately, to replace it when the equipment is worn out. Nothing short of this will render a carrier system truly self-supporting.

Efficiency Should Be Required

It is also reasonable to assume, in considering the aggregate return, that carriers should demonstrate reasonable efficiency in operation. Efficiency is difficult to measure. The term can best be understood, however, as a favorable relation of output of service to input of energy, involving both a proper choice and a coördinated use of related parts in an enterprise which is composed of a variety of units, including the employment of personnel associated with the plant.

The most elaborate published measurements of efficiency in these terms are, probably, those reported by the railroads, in which these carriers apply tests such as the average speed of trains, the number of tons per train, the gross ton-miles per freight train hour, the consumption of fuel per 1,000 gross ton-miles, the cost of repairs per locomotive-mile or per car-mile, the percentage which loss and damage payments bear to freight and switching revenue, and other indexes of the same general sort. The averages show notable improvement in recent years in almost every case and are doubtless made public for this reason. It is to be remembered, however, that many changes of these sorts, while apparently signs of efficiency, can be produced in railroad service by the employment of heavier trains, drawn by more powerful locomotives, and operating over a strengthened track. Between 1929 and 1950, the average tractive power of steam freight locomotives on Class I railroads in the United States increased from 51,368 pounds to 62,647 pounds, not including still more powerful electric engines, and the average capacity of cars, which was 46.6 tons in 1930, had grown to 52.6 tons in 1950. During the period from 1930 to 1950, the percentage of rails weighing 100 pounds to the yard or more, grew from 18 to 56 percent, while at the same time railroads introduced the use of power in track work, improved their signaling and communication practice, and mechanized their operations in still other ways. A special incentive to make these changes was doubtless found in the relatively large increase in the level of railroad wages that occurred in these and in previous years, leading to an attempt to maximize the capital factor and to minimize the labor factor in railroad operation. More machines and relatively fewer men were used, and the averages reflect the operating result. This is efficiency in a sense. It may or may not, however, include an element of increased skill in operation and it depends for its justification upon comparisons of price.[1]

Relative Importance of Factors

From the point of view of the users of transportation the efficiency of transport and the cost of the transportation function should be discussed in terms of the compensation paid to all of the factors which join in supplying transport.

According to figures compiled by the Interstate Commerce Commission, railway expenses in the year 1951 were as shown in Table 16.

Expenditures for Labor

Table 16 shows that compensation to employees is the largest expenditure which a railroad has to make. The fact would be even more evident than it is were we to take account of the large part which the cost of labor plays in the price of materials and in determining the sums which governments find it necessary to collect in taxes.

INFLUENCES WHICH AFFECT THE AMOUNT PAID IN RAILROAD WAGES. Railroad train employees are strongly organized in four great brotherhoods or orders—those of the locomotive engineers, the locomotive firemen and engineers, the conductors, and the trainmen. Telegraphers, signal men, dispatchers, stewards, carmen, maintenance of way employees, and clerical employees are members, principally, of railroad craft unions affiliated with the American Federation of Labor. Machinists, brakemen, blacksmiths, and sheet metal workers belong to national organizations but

---

[1] See United States Board of Investigation and Research, *Technological Trends in Transportation,* Sen. Doc. 76, 79th C., 1st S., September 24, 1944. See also Association of American Railroads, *Transportation in America,* Washington, 1947; and Thor Hultgren, *American Transportation in Prosperity and Depression,* New York, National Bureau of Economic Research, 1948, pp. 207–209, 216–217.

TABLE 16. Distribution of Railway Operating Expenses and Taxes, 1951

Expenditure	Amount (dollars)	Percent	
Compensation to employees	5,011,996,175	62.33	54.21
Materials and supplies other than fuel and miscellaneous	1,699,583,994	21.14	18.38
Fuel	560,855,916	6.97	6.07
Depreciation and amortization of defense projects	460,325,026	5.72	4.98
Loss and damage, injuries to persons and insurance	222,744,139	2.77	2.41
Other	85,771,787	1.07	.93
Total	8,041,277,137	100.00	
Tax accruals	1,203,276,574		13.02
Grand total	9,244,553,711		100.00
Operating revenues	10,382,800,831		

SOURCE: United States Interstate Commerce Commission, *Statistics of Railways, 1951,* Tables 100, 103, 105.

not to organizations peculiarly associated with the railroad industry.[2] The level of pay of these organized employees reflects the bargaining power exerted by their unions.[3] When prices rise, unions are inclined to demand pay sufficient to provide a minimum budget or, more generally, what is called a decent or American standard of living. When prices are stationary

[2] United States National Mediation Board, 14th *Annual Report,* 1948, pp. 55–57. See also United States Department of Labor, Bureau of Labor Statistics, *Directory of Labor Unions in the United States,* Bulletin no. 937, June, 1948.

[3] The average hourly compensation paid to Class I railroad employees from 1940 to 1951 was as follows:

Year	Average Compensation per Hour	Index
1940	$0.751	100
1941	.780	104
1942	.852	113
1943	.923	123
1944	.965	128
1945	.970	129
1946	1.148	153
1947	1.204	160
1948	1.345	179
1949	1.464	195
1950	1.597	212
1951	1.770	235

SOURCE: United States Interstate Commerce Commission, *Statistics of Railways, 1951,* Table 63.

or declining, they seek rather to relate wages in the railroad industry to wages in other comparable lines of work or to utilize the power which their semimonopolistic position creates. These are obviously arguable principles, met with contradictory contentions upon the other side.[4]

In view of the large proportion of railroad expenditures which goes for the payment of wages and salaries, we may fairly say that the aggregate revenue which railroads collect from the shipping and consuming public depends more upon the level of wages which the public consents to have paid to railway labor and, incidentally, to labor producing supplies for railroad use, than upon any other element in railroad operation. This relationship is generally recognized; it has, indeed, been decisive in recent cases proposing increases in railroad rates. The large share of carrier outlay which goes to labor not only aligns the railroad labor group in favor of demands for increases in railroad rates, but it has a bearing also upon issues that affect the efficiency with which transportation service is conducted and so, ultimately, upon the level of the railroad charge. Generally speaking, the practical result, under present conditions, of any increase in the efficiency of the railroad plant which is not accompanied by an offsetting increase in the demand for transport or by a shift of traffic from other agencies will be a decrease in the employment of labor or a lowering of the average wage of railroad employees. This is why railroad labor is resolutely opposed to plans for railroad consolidation, without contesting the assertion that a reduction in the number of operating systems may reduce the cost of carrying passengers and freight. The problem of railroad rates at any time, and also, in a measure, the selec-

[4] The general wage increases granted railroad employees between 1941 and 1949 were as follows:

Effective Date	Increase per Hour Nonoperating Employees (cents)	Operating Employees (cents)
December 1, 1941	10	9½
February 1, 1943	4–10	—
April 1, 1943	—	4
December 27, 1943	5[a]	5
January 1, 1946	16	16
May 22, 1946	2½	2½
September 1, 1947	15½	—
November 1, 1947	—	15½
October 1, 1948	7	—
October 16, 1948	—	10
September 1, 1949	23½	—

[a] 5-day week with no loss in pay.

SOURCE: United States Senate, Committee on Interstate and Foreign Commerce, *Study of Domestic Land and Water Transportation,* Hearings before the Subcommittee on Domestic Land and Water Transportation, pursuant to S. Res. 50, 81st C., 2d S., 1950, testimony Parmelee, p. 57.

tion of methods by which transportation work shall be carried on is always partly a question of the payments to and the standard of living of that part of the community which is engaged in railroad work. This is a social matter, but we must not forget that in the railroad industry it has a vital bearing both upon methods of operation and upon the level of railway rates. The danger is that the monopolistic or semimonopolistic organization of railroad labor may improperly increase the total cost of public transportation service for the benefit of special groups.

Expenditures for Material

Railroads spend approximately one dollar in the purchase of materials and fuel for every three dollars which they invest in labor. The sum involved is, therefore, very large, although it does not represent the largest of the expenditures which the carriers have to make.

The level of payments for material depends largely upon general industrial conditions, and partly also upon the relative bargaining skill of representatives of the railroads as compared with that of representatives of the manufacturers of railroad supplies. Generalization with regard to such matters is difficult and dangerous. Railway materials are bought upon the best terms which railway purchasing agents can secure—persons whose jobs depend on their success in buying at the bottom of the market. Men acquainted with these agents are likely to credit them with average shrewdness and interest in their work. Cases of collusion between supply men and railroad men are so rare as to be negligible, and the presumption is that the railway pays the going price, and not more than the going price, for the material which it has to buy. On the other hand, the fact that prominent industrialists serve as railroad directors and that bankers become interested both in transportation and in the business of railroad supply indicates the possibility that carriers pay prices which are not always as low as they might, under other conditions, be forced to be.

RAILROAD PURCHASES LARGEST IN TIMES OF ACTIVE BUSINESS. It perhaps deserves mention, however, that the going price for railroad material is swelled by the fact that railroad purchases are largest in times of active business when prices generally are high, and smallest during times of general depression when prices are low. Railroads buy heavily when prices are high because their income increases as well as their needs in periods of prosperity, and also because it is easier, then, to borrow money in order to anticipate requirements of a more or less distant future. In this railroads are not unique. All types of business enterprise are apt to spend more liberally in times of rising prices and to curtail their expenses when prices fall, uneconomical as the practical may seem to be. But the magnitude of the railroad industry and the large proportion which its purchases bear to the total production of certain articles give prominence to a policy, when followed by railroad managements, which might escape notice in the case of less important concerns. If it were possible for railroads to purchase more heavily in the trough and less extensively at the peak of the business cycle, they would not only save money for themselves but they would exert a general stabilizing effect upon industry that would be of national advantage.[5]

Payments for the Use of Capital

In the year 1951, the sums credited to owners of railroad capital, including dividends, interest, and rentals, amounted to $1,206,000,000.[6] This was, roughly, one quarter of the sums paid directly to railroad labor and a little more than half of the expenses for material and fuel.

Rate of Return

The rate of return with which railroads are credited upon their investment is a calculated ratio that varies with the figure of earnings used and upon the capital amount to which earnings are applied. On both of these matters there are differences of opinion, although the variations are less than we might suppose. This is because the Interstate Commerce Commission and the carriers base their judgments upon the same fundamental figures—the annual reports of the railroads to the Commission. But the rate, on any usual basis, is not high. The most competent discussion of rates of return earned by railroads in recent years concludes that Class I line haul carriers in the United States obtained an average of 4.2 percent upon their investment between 1941 and 1949, in a range which spread between 6.48 in 1942 and 2.78 in 1946. Some estimates are higher than this and some lower; but the difference is not great. This is a modest return.[7]

[5] See Thor Hultgren, *American Transportation in Prosperity and Depression,* Studies in Business Cycles, no. 3, National Bureau of Economic Research, 1948.
[6] United States Interstate Commerce Commission, *Statistics of Railways,* Table 110.
[7] See the following table.

Rates of Return
Class I Line-Haul Railways

Year	Miller-Cover Percent	Association of American Railroads Percent
1941	4.37	4.28
1942	6.48	6.34
1943	5.92	5.75
1944	4.79	4.73
1945	3.83	3.77

On the general subject of railroad earnings, we may add that the railroads of the United States need for their development and in order to keep pace with the needs of an expanding population, an annual addition to their capital which, in the past, has been estimated at from $740,000 to $1,000,000,000. To obtain such funds they must offer inducements comparable with those obtained in other fields into which capital may flow. The rate of return which railroads are obliged to offer may be comparatively low, but it should be certain, and it cannot be indefinitely reduced. Unlike the question of wages, the matter of payments to owners of capital is not, at least in current discussions, complicated by the consideration of standards of living. This is partly because the individual who owns railroad stock or bonds is not so obviously and publicly associated with the railroad business as is the railroad employee and partly because the former is not usually dependent upon the income from his securities for his entire support.

Railroad Valuation and Fair Return

The question of payments for the use of capital in railroad operation may be raised when a legislature or a commission seeks to reduce railroad rates and the carrier objects on the legal ground that the proposed reduction will infringe rights conferred by the Fifth or Fourteenth Amendments to the Constitution of the United States. It may also be raised when a

1946	2.78	2.75
1947	3.48	3.41
1948	4.28	4.24
1949	2.87	2.86
1950	—	4.23
1951	—	3.69
1952	—	4.10

SOURCE: (1) The Miller-Cover study of rates of return (Sidney L. Miller and Virgil D. Cover, *Rates of Return. Class I Line-Haul Railways of the United States, 1921–1948,* Pittsburgh, University of Pittsburgh, 1950); (2) Association of American Railroads, Bureau of Railway Economics, *Statistics of Railways of Class I, United States, Calendar Years 1939 to 1951,* Washington, 1952.

A rate of return may be taken as the ratio of net railway operating income to a capital sum consisting of depreciated capital investment plus some or all of a working capital consisting of materials and cash.

There is, generally, no difference between the Interstate Commerce Commission and the carriers on the subject of depreciated capital investment and net income. There is, however, some difference in the handling of working capital in the ratio computation. As to this, the carriers insist that the entire accumulation of cash and of materials shall be taken into the account. But the Commission reduces the total investment, when it calculates a ratio, by eliminating obsolete materials in stock, materials to be used for additions and betterments, materials purchased beyond current need, and some other items. The Commission also refuses to include cash on the theory that the railroads need no cash reserve because they collect their revenues in advance of their needs for cash.

The Interstate Commerce Commission does not, itself, compile "rates of return" although it has frequently discussed the subject.

carrier seeks an increase in rates in order to secure net earnings which, it believes, are necessary in order that it may earn a fair return. Or a carrier may ask for higher rates in order to increase or to insure the continuation of payments to capital so that it may render adequate public service. Frequently then, though not always, discussions of "fair return" in litigated cases leads to some form of railroad valuation. A brief reference to the subject is, therefore, necessary at this point.

Valuation is one step in a process designed to protect invested capital in its right to earnings.[8] This right has a constitutional as well as an economic basis, because of the Fifth and Fourteenth amendments to the United States Constitution which forbid federal and state governments to take property without "due process of law." By court decision "due process," in the constitutional sense, refers to formal procedure; but the phrase is also interpreted—and this is significant in the present connection—so as to restrain government from unreasonable and unfair takings whatever procedure may be followed. Under the rule of "due process," restrictions applied to the earnings of business property are equivalent to takings of the property itself.

The doctrine of "due process" in constitutional law does not guarantee a return to capital; it does, however, imply that there is a minimum which owners of capital must be permitted to earn. The practical problem in any controversy in which the point is raised is to determine how much of the business earnings of a utility or carrier is privileged in the sense that it cannot be taken away or how much additional earnings may be secured without interference by the state. One method of solving this problem employs two steps. One of these steps is to ascertain the customary percentage return to capital in a community at a given time, with special attention to categories which resemble utility operation with respect to risks involved. The second requires an estimate or calculation of a "value" or "rate base" or "principal sum" for the litigating enterprise. Once these data are available simple multiplication will indicate the minimum payment of which the owners of capital may not be deprived.

There is considerable literature and a long series of decisions devoted to the elaboration of valuation technique. A general question of principle is as to whether valuation, in the sense of rate base, shall reflect past investment in a carrier or public utility or whether it shall express the cost of reproducing the property which is valued. Another possibility is that the rate base shall be ascertained by cumulating estimates of future earnings discounted according to their remoteness from the date of valuation. This is clearly inappropriate when a valuation is to be used to measure the level of earnings that is to be allowed. And there are secondary problems in conducting either an original cost or a cost of reproduction valuation

[8] This, of course, is not the only use of "valuation."

which have to be considered. There are, finally, difficulties in the whole concept, regarded in the light of the purposes which it is supposed to serve.

In the field of motor and of air transport, valuation is uncertain because a large part of carrier investment goes to the establishment of business relationships and not to the acquisition of fixed assets. In the railroad business, valuation is highly complicated and expensive, and it has been evident for some years also that carriers are unlikely to earn, in fact, sums sufficient to provide a return of 5 or 6 percent upon the cost valuations that have been set up, although they may, at times, operate with what appears to be a measure of prosperity.

Railroad Revenues and Adequate Service

A shift in legal attitude toward the whole subject of valuation was expressed by the United States Supreme Court in 1944 when, in the Hope case, it remarked: "Rates which enable the company to operate successfully, to maintain its financial integrity, to attract capital, and to compensate its investors for the risks assumed certainly cannot be condemned as invalid, even though they might produce only a meager return on the so-called 'fair value' rate base." [9]

The pronouncement of the Supreme Court in the Hope case recognized the necessity of providing reasonable payments for the use of capital in adjusting the general level of railroad rates. It did not endorse the technique of valuation in determining what these payments should be.

Even prior to the Hope case the procedures of valuation were neglected in railroad controversies and the essentials of a reasonable level of rates were stated in other terms. Thus, in the Act of 1933,[10] Congress declared that "in the exercise of its power to prescribe just and reasonable rates the Commission shall give due consideration, among other factors, to the effect of rates on the movement of traffic by the carrier or carriers for which the rates are prescribed; to the need, in the public interest, of adequate and efficient railway transportation service at the lowest cost consistent with the furnishing such a service; and to the need of revenues sufficient to enable the carriers, under honest, economical, and efficient management to provide such service." [11] The same principles are now restated, in other parts of the Interstate Commerce Act, with reference to other forms of transportation.[12] Doubtless because of these prescriptions as well as because of the inherent difficulties in regulating the levels of carrier charges so as to adjust them to a valuation, most general rates cases which have reached the Interstate Commerce Commission in recent years have

---

[9] 320 U. S. 591, 1944.

[10] 48 Stat. 220, 1933.

[11] Interstate Commerce Act, Part I, Section 15a (2).

[12] Interstate Commerce Act, Part II, Section 216 (i); Part III, Section 307 (f); and Part IV, Section 406 (d).

been so-called "revenue cases" in which carriers have alleged that inadequate earnings and high operating costs have impaired their ability to continue adequate and efficient transportation service and to compensate their investors for the risks assumed. This is a sound method of attack, on the whole consistent with the analysis with which this chapter is concerned.

Increases in Railroad Rate Levels

The average receipts per ton per mile on American railroads fell from .757 cents in 1900 to .719 cents in 1916. Between that year and 1921 the average rose to 1.275 cents, after which there was a more or less steady decline to a figure of .932 in 1942. After 1942 average receipts again rose to .978 cents in 1946 and to 1.336 cents in 1951.

The spectacular increases in railroad receipts between 1916 and 1921 and again between 1942 and 1951 were, of course, due to equally spectacular increases in price levels. Intermediate reductions are principally to be explained by motor vehicle competition. Increases in costs, reflected in greater payments for labor and materials, led carriers to ask the Interstate Commerce Commission for higher rates in order to earn larger revenues to meet expense and, if possible, to permit the payment of a return upon invested capital comparable with that obtained in other lines. These applications brought out a series of important Commission decisions in which the financial condition of the American railroad system was repeatedly discussed.[13]

[13] The following table summarizes the results of these decisions during the period 1946 to 1952:

Dates of Increase and Charges Authorized Between
June 30, 1946 and April 11, 1952

Date of Interstate Commerce Commission Report	Effective Date of Rate Increase	Percent Increase over	
		Rates in Effect on June 30, 1946, Cumulated	Rates in Effect Immediately Prior to Increase Shown
June 30, 1946	July 1, 1946	6.5	6.5
December 5, 1946	January 1, 1947	17.6	10.4
October 6, 1947	October 13, 1947	28.1	8.9
December 29, 1947	January 5, 1948	37.8	7.6
April 13, 1948	May 6, 1948	42.8	3.6
July 27, 1948	August 21, 1948	44.2	1.0
December 29, 1948	January 11, 1949	51.7	5.2
August 2, 1949	September 1, 1949	57.3	3.7
March 12, 1951	April 4, 1951	61.1	2.4
August 2, 1951	August 28, 1951	67.6	4.0
April 11, 1952	—	78.9	6.8

Over the entire period, from 1920 to 1952, there have been four questions involved when the Commission has been asked to increase railroad rates. These may be stated as follows: (1) Will increased rates yield increased revenues? (2) Do railroads need increased revenues? (3) May the public properly be asked to pay higher rates because of railroad necessities? (4) If rail rates are to be advanced, according to what method shall this be done?

The position of the Interstate Commerce Commission in the various advanced-rate cases has been that advances in rates can be relied upon to produce additional revenue when first introduced, although in the long run they may have a contrary effect.[14] As for the need, the difficulties which the railroads faced in 1920 were great, and those which the carriers faced in later years were also serious. There was no public disposition in either period to question this plain fact. On the third point there is a difference in opinion. In times of depression, it may be argued that railroads can secure genuine relief only from general business recovery. From this point of view high rates, which impede the flow of commerce, defeat the very purpose for which they are installed. This is a variation of the argument that higher rates do not produce greater earnings. And at any time shippers may insist that rates adjusted to produce a fair return to capital may become unreasonable and illegal when conditions are such that a return to capital in railroading is inconsistent with a return to capital invested in business which makes use of railroad service. This is usually expressed by saying that rates which exceed the value of the service rendered are improper whether or not they provide the carrier with revenue with which to meet its costs. The answer to question three is not obvious because it involves public policy with respect to the distribution

SOURCE: United States Interstate Commerce Commission, Bureau of Transport Economics and Statistics, *Monthly Comment on Transportation Statistics,* April 16, 1952.

The Bureau of Transport Economics and Statistics of the Interstate Commerce Commission estimates that as a result of authorizations of the Commission in major rate cases, railroad freight rates as of April 11, 1952 and also as of March 16, 1953 averaged 78.9 percent above those in effect on March 28, 1938. For purposes of this calculation the rates in effect on March 28, 1938, may be taken as 100. (*Monthly Comment,* etc., March 16, 1953.)

The period covered by the table may be extended backward by reference to the Fifteen Percent case, 1937–38, in which the Interstate Commerce Commission allowed advances amounting generally to 10 percent, with certain exceptions, and to the decision of March 18, 1942, when the Commission permitted increases averaging 4.7 percent. The next increase became effective on July 1, 1946, as stated in the table (*ibid., Monthly Comment on Transportation Statistics,* January 14, 1953).

[14] The Commission said in 1931: "There are elements of plain peril to the railroads in such an increase in freight rates as they propose at the present time. The chief dangers are: (1) that . . . it will stimulate new competitive forces already rapidly developing, (2) that it will alienate or impair . . . friendly feeling . . . and (3) that it will disturb business conditions . . . and accelerate the tendency toward a localization of production . . ." (178 I.C.C. 539, 575, 1931).

of the burden of cyclical variation. There is some reason to urge that carriers, like other factors in industry, should in times of stress bear a share of the general load, although it is highly important that the essential structure of the carrier industry shall be maintained. The answer to the fourth question is still more difficult, if only because general rate advances, framed in terms of absolute increases in rates per ton per mile or in terms of percentage increases in existing rates will change territorial relationships established under a former system. Such advances will affect, differently, the marketing outlets of different commodities because of diverse elasticities in demand and they will alter the relative position of carriers which rely upon differently constituted traffic. On the other hand, complete maintenance of the status quo after an increase in rates will require an impossible complexity of adjustment, even if it should be thought wise to undertake the task.

It cannot be said that the decisions of the Interstate Commerce Commission have supplied us with much thoughtful analysis of the conflicting claims of carriers and shippers where the interests of the two diverge, although something has been done in considering territorial rivalries. These decisions have, however, brought the importance of capital payments into relief and have shown, on the whole, a recognition of the necessity of allowing a return to the investor if new capital is to be attracted to the railroad industry and the work of transport is to remain in private hands. In the long run, the total return for the volume and character of transportation which the community requires must be such that capital, material, and labor costs will be recognized and supplied.

REFERENCES

General Treatises

Bigham, Truman C., and Roberts, Merrill J., *Transportation, Principles and Problems,* New York, McGraw-Hill, 1952.

Fair, Marvin L., and Williams, Ernest W., *Economics of Transportation,* New York, Harper, 1950.

Locklin, D. Philip, *Economics of Transportation,* Chicago, Irwin, 1947.

Parmelee, J. H., *The Modern Railway,* New York, Longmans, 1940.

Sharfman, I. L., *The Interstate Commerce Commission,* Part III, vols. A, B, New York, Commonwealth Fund, 1935, 1936.

Westmeyer, Russell E., *Economics of Transportation,* New York, Prentice-Hall, 1952.

Other Books

Bauer, John, and Gold, Nathaniel, *Public Utility Valuation,* New York, McGraw-Hill, 1934.

Bonbright, J. C., *The Valuation of Property,* New York, McGraw-Hill, 1937.

Dearing, Charles L., and Owen, Wilfred, *National Transportation Policy,* Washington, D. C., Brookings Institution, 1949.

Grunsky, C. E., *Valuation, Depreciation, and the Rate-Base,* New York, Wiley, 1927.

Hultgren, Thor, *American Transportation in Prosperity and Depression,* Studies in Business Cycles, no. 3, New York, National Bureau of Economic Research, 1948.

Miller, Sidney L., and Cover, Virgil D., *Rate of Return, Class I Line-Haul Railways of the United States, 1921–1948,* Pittsburgh, University of Pittsburgh, 1950.

Pegrum, D. F., *Rate Theories and the California Railroad Commission,* Berkeley, University of California, 1932.

Smith, N. L., *The Fair Rate of Return in Public Utility Regulation,* Boston, Houghton Mifflin, 1932.

Whitten, R., *Valuation of Public Service Corporations, Legal Economic Phases of Valuation for Rate Making and Public Purchase,* New York, Banks Law Publishing, 1928.

Periodicals

Adelman, M. A., "Interest Rates and Fair Return," *Land Economics,* November, 1948.

Blachly, Frederick F., "The Role of Smyth v. Ames in Federal Rate Regulation," *Virginia Law Review,* March, 1947.

Bryan, R. F., and Lewis, B. W., "The 'Earning Base' as a 'Rate Base' " (with reply by M. G. de Chazeau), *Quarterly Journal of Economics,* February, 1938.

de Chazeau, M. G., "The Nature of the Rate Base in the Regulation of Public Utilities," *Quarterly Journal of Economics,* February, 1937.

Ferguson, S., "Cost as a Substitute for Value in Utility Rate Base Determination," *Yale Law Journal,* September, 1944.

Goddard, E. C., "The Problem of Valuation: The Evolution of Cost of Reproduction as the Rate Base," *Harvard Law Review,* March, 1928.

Harbeson, R. W., "The Demise of Fair Value," *Michigan Law Review,* April, 1944.

Solterer, Josef, "Ethico-Economic Characteristics of Transportation," *Social Science,* October, 1945.

Special and Miscellaneous

Federal Power Commission v. Hope Natural Gas Company, 315 U.S. 575, 1942; 320 U.S. 591, 1944.

United States Board of Investigation and Research, *Technological Trends in Transportation,* 79th C., 1st S., Sen. Doc. 76, 1944.

United States Senate, Committee on Interstate and Foreign Commerce, *Study of Domestic Land and Water Transportation,* Hearings before a subcommittee, 81st C., 2d S., 1950, testimony Parmelee.

CHAPTER 16

Rates on Particular Hauls—The Theory of Pricing

The Relation of Total Return to the Rates upon Particular Hauls

The total return which a community will pay for labor, fuel, materials, and capital used in transportation will depend upon the intensity of the need for transportation, the competitive, monopolistic, or semimonopolistic position of the industry, and the limitations enforced by public policy. This total return will, of course, be obtained from a great variety of transactions. Under most assumptions there will be alternatives in distributing the burden of what may be considered a fair or necessary return among the competent services for which the return is made, as well as alternatives with respect to the total volume of service which is to be supplied. In the former class the range may be from nothing to the extreme upper limit which the presence or absence of competition and the attitude of public bodies may permit. It is hardly possible in the text to attempt a rounded theory of carrier rates, assuming that there is such a theory and that it has principles which are to be distinguished from those which govern prices as a whole.[1] We shall deal, however, in the present chapter, with some peculiarities in the demand for and in the cost of supplying carrier service which both carriers and the public have recognized in fixing rates upon particular hauls.

Demand for Transport

The demand for transportation is "derived" except in some instances of passenger travel where the wish to move is inspired by the direct

[1] The reader may be referred to T. C. Bigham and M. J. Roberts, *Transportation, Principles and Problems*, New York, McGraw-Hill, 1952, chap. 3, for a discussion, with diagrams, of the effect of increases or decreases of rates upon price with various assumptions with respect to the constancy and variability of costs and to the elasticity and inelasticity of demand. The explanation also distinguishes between cases in which the transportation service is competitive and those in which it is subject to monopoly control.

pleasure afforded by a journey. And almost always, in the case of freight, the shipper's motive is to profit by the increase in the price of selected articles that may follow a change in their location. Freight may move, under exceptional conditions, where the service has no calculable value, but only when nonbusiness considerations enter in, or as a result of policies which look to an ultimate rather than to an immediate reward.[2]

Intensity of Demand

Now the demand for the service of carriage referred to in the previous paragraph may, of course, be analyzed. It has characteristics which may be considered and discussed. We may speak, for instance, of relative intensity of demand. Thus it has been contended that the demand for the transportation of goods of high value is more intense than the demand for the transportation of low-priced goods. Some German writers have maintained that this is the case [3] because, they say, a greater gain usually results from the movement of valuable than from the movement of low-priced goods. If all that is meant by this is that a higher rate per 100 pounds can generally be charged for the transportation of an article worth $5 from A to B than for an article worth 50 cents, then the statement may be true and possibly convenient to remember in drawing up a tariff, though it would have no great theoretical significance. The conclusion would rest on the use of two unlike units—price in dollars and rates per 100 pounds—units which should be reduced to a common basis before laws regarding them should be announced. There is no reason why we should suppose that differences in value in different markets should be

[2] The usual comparison is that between the cost of acquiring a commodity at point A and the price which can be obtained for the article at point B.

Locklin points out that there may be cases in which an article shipped from A to B can be produced at B at less cost than at A but in which goods are nevertheless forwarded from A to B because it is more profitable to devote A's energy to other kinds of work. This is the familiar case of "comparative cost" often referred to in foreign trade. It is not really an exception to the rule mentioned in the text.

A peculiar condition in transport arises when the same type of articles are shipped, contemporaneously, from A to B and from B to A. It is difficult to explain the existence of a demand for transport both ways in cases of this sort. Probably the following conditions are influential:

1. Shippers may, by trademark, label, or by other device, so distinguish their products that articles produced at A become, for selling purposes, separable from those shipped from B to A although, by physical tests, they are the same.

2. Sellers in a restricted market may desire to broaden their area of sales for the sake of stability, or to exploit special opportunities.

3. An increase in the volume of output may reduce production costs. As far as the individual shipper is concerned, this may give transportation service value. It has to be assumed: (a) that the increased volume cannot be sold on the local market without a prohibitive reduction in price; and (b) that the reduction in production costs offsets the transport charges which the shipper pays.

[3] Emil Merkert, "Theoretische Abhandlung über die Preisbildung im Verkehrswesen," Archiv für Eisenbahnwesen, November–December, 1931.

proportionate to the values of the articles considered. Values and differences in value are, after all, different things. It would be an accident if they were equivalent in any case.[4]

Elasticity of Demand

The demand for the service of transportation may be more intense in one case than another. It may, that is to say, have a greater exchange value in terms of goods or other services. The demand may also, for a given kind of service, be more elastic or inelastic. This characteristic is important; but if we are to consider the elasticity of the demand for transport we must imagine several possibilities.

One possibility is that the transport agency has a monopoly insofar as transportation is concerned. If this is the case, an increase in the transport rate will raise the cost of supplying goods to the consumer at points of destination. This will normally affect the selling price of the article sold in degrees depending upon the character of the article, the presence of substitutes, and the proportion which the cost of transportation bears to the aggregate of production costs. It is therefore likely to reduce the number of sales and the transport revenues derived, although the gross revenues from transport may conceivably be maintained and the net revenues in many cases will be increased. The elasticity of the demand for transportation is determined, under such conditions, by the elasticity of the demand for goods.[5] This, at least, is a preliminary assumption. The reader should be reminded, however, that the effect of changes in carrier rates upon the demand for service are difficult to trace because rate

---

[4] Cf. William H. Joubert, *Southern Freight Rates in Transition,* Gainesville, Fla., University of Florida, 1949, p. 13.

The Interstate Commerce Commission has prepared tables that show, for selected periods, the percentages which freight rates on the principal classes of commodities shipped by rail bear to the wholesale values of these commodities at points of destination (United States Interstate Commerce Commission, Bureau of Transport Economics and Statistics, *Freight Revenue and Wholesale Value at Destination of Commodities Transported on Class I Steam Railways in the United States, Calendar Year 1946 and July-December, 1946,* July, 1948). The figures show that the percentages are lowest in the case of high-valued goods, although these goods pay the highest rate per ton. The relationship is interesting. Some caution should be observed, however, in interpreting these conclusions because the distances shipped are not given and because both high- and low-valued goods have characteristics that are independent of their value. See M. L. Fair, and E. W. Williams, *Economics of Transportation,* New York, Harper, 1950, chap. 18, and Sidney L. Miller, *Inland Transportation,* New York, McGraw-Hill, 1933, chap. 30.

[5] It has been said that the demand for the transportation of articles of high value is inelastic and that for the transportation of low valued goods is elastic. There is, probably, no sufficient evidence for this generalization. It is, of course, true that if two articles sell, respectively, for $10 and $100, and if the freight rate on each is $1, then an equal increase of $1 in the rate applied to each will have differing effects on consumption and upon the demand for transportation. But so explained, this is an incident to the method of quoting rates and has no real relation to the principles with which we are here concerned. See p. 300.

changes do not necessarily raise or lower the demand for transportation. The burden may instead be shifted to members of society who are neither shippers nor consumers,[6] and it may be divided between buyers and sellers in varying proportions.[7]

Competition and Elasticity

This brings us to the question of the elasticity of the demand for transportation under conditions of transport competition. When there is competition between carriers, an increase in rates by the original carrier from A to B will not decrease supply at B or alter the spread between prices at A and B, provided that a second carrier operates between A and B and will perform the old transport at the old price. The result will merely be to eliminate the carrier which increases rates from a share in the described transportation.

Nor is the case essentially different when we imagine a second source of supply, C instead of a second carrier from A to B, if the second source can and will supply the market at B when A withdraws. If the production costs at C are the same as those at A and if the transport costs between C and B are, initially, the same as between A and B, then an increase in the rate from A to B will not decrease the supply of goods at B. It will not, therefore, change the market price of goods at B nor affect the value of the service of transport between A and B. It will, however, change the source from which the goods are drawn. If, of course, C cannot supply B with goods at the same overall cost, production and transport combined, then an increase in the rate from A to B may lead to some alteration in the supply at B and to some increase in the value of the service of transportation from A to B, limited by the degree of competition which C is able to provide.[8]

In actual practice, in the United States, carriers are likely to encounter some degree of competition. This is obvious in motor carriage. Insofar

---

[6] An increase in rates may not reduce the volume of shipments or raise the price of goods at the consuming market because it may be absorbed by the owners of land or fixed capital or taken out of shippers' profits. An increase may also produce shifts in the location of commercial and manufacturing centers that will partially offset the change in rates.

See Bureau of Railway Economics, *A Study of the Economic Effects of Reductions in Freight Rates on Export Wheat—1929*, Washington, D.C., 1930; M. R. Benedict, *Freight Rates and the South Dakota Farmer*, Bulletin no. 269, Brookings, S.D., South Dakota State College, Agricultural Economics Department, February, 1932; H. R. Trumbower, "The Incidence of Freight Charges on Agricultural Products," *Journal of Political Economy*, June, 1925.

[7] D. P. Locklin observes correctly that the full effect of rate changes takes time to develop (*Economics of Transportation*, Chicago, Irwin, 1947, chap. 2). This fact should be remembered in analyzing results.

[8] See H. G. Brown, *Transportation Rates and Their Regulation*, New York, Macmillan, 1916. It is assumed that the goods referred to in the illustration cannot be produced at B.

as rail carriage is concerned, the number of alternative railroad routes under separate control between named shipping stations is relatively few, although the number is substantially increased by the participation of indirect, circuitous routes on hauls of substantial length. It is also true that towns connected by only one railroad have recourse to other sources of supply; because of this rail carriers are frequently unable to control quantities shipped and the value of their service without a broad area of agreement. On the whole railroad rates tend to be stable and uniform, when only rail carriage is involved, although railroads may, by emphasis upon the quality of service, seek to attract, each to itself, larger parts of a comparatively unchanged total volume. It is rare that competition is so keen that an addition to the rate will deprive a carrier entirely of its market.[9]

Costs and Transportation

The schedule of demand for carrier service enables us to calculate what, with any volume of transport, will be the price which can be charged, or what volume, at any price, can be expected. The decision as to price or volume is made, of course, in the light of knowledge concerning costs of service that will be incurred and of objectives which it is desired to obtain.[10] Thus a railroad man who appreciates the necessity of finishing the accounting year with a surplus will naturally attempt to fix rates so as to cover, in the case of every shipment, the operating cost of handling that shipment, together with such a percentage of profit as will, on the expected volume of business, take care of the overhead expense. We shall not, in this text, attempt to cover all the difficulties that he will meet. We shall deal only with two special questions, of which the first concerns the relations of cost to volume of traffic, and the second the method of seg-

[9] Some information with respect to the elasticity of demand for railroad passenger service was collected in a study made at Yale University in 1940 and published in *Railway Age* in 1948 (*Railway Age,* January 24, 1948, pp. 218–223). The results were, however, indefinite.

[10] Shippers sometimes demand that rates be adjusted to value of service without regard to cost, on the ground that they should never be asked to pay for transportation more than the service is worth. But it is obvious that an enforced conformity of rates to value of service without regard to cost would encourage production at geographically unfavorable locations and that it would, generally, tend to lower the efficiency of productive enterprise. It would maximize ton-miles although the efficiency of a carrier system is not to be measured by the number of ton or passenger miles which it produces, but by the decrease in the entire cost of production or the enhancement of the value of the product that its operations bring about. It would develop movement for the sake of movement, because it would lower the barrier of rates whenever and to the extent that these barriers hamper traffic. It would absorb costs due to either natural or human disorganization. A poorly managed or badly equipped enterprise can bear only low rates; and these, on a "value of service" principle, would be all that it would have to pay. (See M. H. Robison, "Railway Freight Rates," *Yale Review,* August, 1909.) These are not consequences which a sound price system should produce. The policy would not, of course, be possible in a private economy.

gregating costs when a single expenditure makes possible the rendering of several kinds of service. These problems are clearly, though they are not exclusively, encountered in railroad service.

Costs and Volume of Traffic

There is no sufficient evidence to show, for railroad enterprise at least, that costs steadily decline, per unit output, as the volume of traffic is enlarged. A recent study of railroad expense in prosperity and depression reaches the conclusion that railroad costs are relatively low when the volume of traffic is relatively high. Thus it is said that "under comparable conditions as to morale of labor, quality of fuel and materials, efficiency of management, prices and wage rates paid, a large volume of traffic would always be accompanied by a unit cost lower than that which would accompany a smaller volume of traffic." [11] It is, however, probably impossible to demonstrate statistically that low railroad costs are the characteristic accompaniment of a high volume of traffic as such. We interpret the term "large volume" to be here equivalent to the phrase "high density," or a relatively large number of traffic units (ton-miles and passenger-miles) per mile of road within a given period of time.[12] If we look at the matter in sequence, experience seems to be irregular after a minimum density has been reached. Further increase in density and more intensive use of main line roadway causes certain expenses to fall off, but other costs become higher because of more complex assembling, switching, and interchange services and the use of more costly terminals. If we examine and compare the total record at any given time, we find that railroads with high density sometimes report low costs, but other roads of high density experience high costs.[13] Nor is there any sufficient reason to believe, as a matter of principle, that the optimum scale of operation of a railroad company is to be found at a high rather than at a moderate

[11] Thor Hultgren, *American Transportation in Prosperity and Depression,* Studies in Business Cycles, no. 3, National Bureau of Economic Research, 1949.

[12] Fair and Williams agree with the statement in the text. They say: "We conclude that density, as a separate and distinct long run factor affecting profitableness of operation, is of little significance except as it relates to the utilization of the carrier. A railroad, motor, air, or water carrier may so adapt its plant and facilities to the requirements of traffic as to achieve much the same unit cost whether it is a line in sparsely populated territory and having a low density or one serving a built-up area where the demands of traffic are great" (Marvin L. Fair, and Ernest W. Williams, *Economics of Transportation,* New York, Harper, 1950, p. 312). See also Kent T. Healy, *The Economics of Transportation in America,* New York, Ronald, 1940, p. 169.

[13] In 1946, the operating expense of the Pennsylvania Railroad, with 7,895,000 traffic units per mile of road, was .93 cents per traffic unit while that of the Illinois Central, with 3,648,000 traffic units per mile of road, was .74 cents per traffic unit. One difficulty in the problem is the lack of a standard measure of output. Tons are by no means uniform and the same can be said of miles except as to one characteristic in each case. The combination of tons and passengers to make traffic units gives still less reliable results.

level of size.[14] It can, however, be shown that wherever there is unutilized capacity an increase in the volume of railroad traffic can be handled without a proportional change in total carrier expense. Elaboration of this point leads us to the distinction between constant and variable costs.

Constant and Variable Costs

There is unutilized capacity when a carrier's plant or organization can handle a greater volume of transport than it is called upon to provide. This is a frequent, if not a normal condition in any industry which employs large units of capital, either because investment anticipates future growth or because traffic declines after facilities have been installed.[15] Once a scale of operation has been decided, then the cost of facilities appropriate to this scale is incurred once and for all for a period equal to the life of the investment, at least in the sense that no more investment will be required until capacity is reached and none can be recovered as traffic declines. This cost is, in the aggregate, constant, and it is to be contrasted in this respect with variable expense which changes in amount with alterations in the volume carried.[16]

[14] The same conclusion has been reached with respect to air-line operation (H. D. Koontz, "Domestic Air Line Self-sufficiency: A Problem of Route Structure," *American Economic Review,* March, 1952). See also United States Interstate Commerce Commission, Bureau of Economics and Statistics, *Rail Freight Service Costs in the Various Rate Territories of the United States,* 70th C., 1st S., Sen. Doc. 63, 1943, p. 46.

The problem is more or less at the bottom of the controversy over the relative railroad rates in Official and in Southern Classification Territories. The density of traffic is admittedly greater in Official Territory, but the Interstate Commerce Commission finds that the costs are much the same (262 I.C.C. 447, 576–612, 1945). See also T.V.A., *Regionalized Freight Rates: Barrier to National Productiveness,* 78th C., 1st S., House Doc. 137, 1943, p. 8.

[15] For a distinction between "unutilized" and "excess" capacity, see L. G. Reynolds, "Cutthroat Competition," *American Economic Review,* December, 1940, pp. 736–747. See also Healy, *op. cit.,* chap. 11.

[16] Locklin and others distinguish between constant expenses which represent the return on capital invested and general expenses such as the salaries of executive officers which, although constant, must be regularly incurred if operations are to continue. Doubtless there are degrees in "constancy," but it may be suggested that the significant difference between capital investment and expenditures for the salaries of general officers is only in the time during which the enterprise is committed to reliance upon the apparatus secured by its expenditure. A machine which is leased for a term of five years and a president hired under a five-year contract fall from the corporation's point of view into the same category. This matter of classification may have more than an academic interest if railroad employees successfully maintain, as they seem to desire to do, that a railroad company is under obligation to provide continued employment for its personnel in service even when improvements in technique or decline in business would enable it to handle traffic with fewer men.

Apart from the matters mentioned in the preceding paragraph of this note, the discussion of constant cost, particularly in railroad operation, has taken many forms.

It was common, at one time, to guess at the proportion which general costs bear to the total costs in railroad operation. The estimates ranged from half to two-thirds of total railway expense. The guesses meant little, however, because they were generally made without reference to the length of the period which was assumed. Moreover, the

To the extent that constant costs are really constant and variable costs are proportional to business done, it is simple arithmetic to calculate that the average costs of a carrier will decline as the volume of traffic grows when there is any element of constant cost in the aggregate of expense. We may say that, under such conditions, average costs will fall as volume increases when any usable part of the plant is insufficiently employed.[17] Indeed, we may generalize still farther by introducing the idea

proportion of constant to total costs varies with changes in volume of traffic, assuming that the capital investment over any period remains the same.

In any case, it was believed to be important that railway expenses, in the long run, did vary in reasonably close proportion to the volume of traffic handled. This fact could be established by statistics. The argument could have been expanded. It is always to be remembered that a carrier requires a variety of equipment. The units are of unequal size and have unequal lengths of life. Renewals and additions occur, and it is possible that these may develop into a steady stream even though each individual unit has a separate service period and an unchangeable cost. This stream may swell when traffic increases and shrink when the volume falls, although the response is not likely to be as prompt or as exact as it would be upon another base. Experience indicates, nevertheless, that over short to moderate periods of time, costs may vary little in many segments of a carrier's operations in spite of the fact that volume has gone up or down. The constancy of costs is therefore real in spite of the allowances which should be made.

Finally, it is argued that constant costs are not in any case price determining. According to Wiedenfeld (Kurt Wiedenfeld, *Grundriss der Socialökonomik,* Transportwesen, Tubingen, Mohr, V. Abteilung, III. Teil, 1930) these costs consist mostly of payments for the use of railroad capital. But the investment in a railroad, once made, can neither be withdrawn nor diverted. Thus failure to pay a return on capital does not decrease the amount of capital in use nor, consequently, the output of the plant, with the result that prices for service are not affected. The compensation received by investors is said to be a consequence of price, not a cause of it.

From a long-time point of view it cannot be successfully maintained that the general costs of an undertaking do not affect the prices which that concern will charge. This is, first, because it is not completely true that the capital in a railroad enterprise is irrevocably committed to that business. Terminal lands can in part be put to other use; machine shops may engage in nonrailroad work; equipment may be allowed to deteriorate and the money normally used for maintenance may be invested elsewhere. Operations of this sort may to a certain extent reduce the amount of capital in a railroad business, and so decrease the output, until the price of the produce has been raised. It is to be remembered in this connection that a small withdrawal of railroad capital may produce a considerable effect upon service. It is not necessary, therefore, that the entire capital be withdrawable in order that constant costs should exert an influence upon price. What is more important still, railroads normally require new capital each year so that they may expand their facilities to care for the needs of expanding business. Unless the aggregate return from railroad service promises to cover interest on new investment, such additional capital cannot continue to be raised. Doubtless it is the interest on the new investment, not that paid on previous capital outlay, that is essential from the point of view of prospective investors; but it will be obvious that failure to provide a return upon investments previously made will check the inflow of new capital. For this reason a community must be prepared to pay the constant as well as the variable costs of railroad operation.

It does not seem necessary to embody all of this discussion in the text.

[17] The statement in the text is correct. It is true, however, that variable costs per unit may increase as the limit of a plant's physical capacity is approached. There may well be a period during which traffic may be moved at increasing average costs even

of balance with reference to any part of a carrier's organization. Such an organization may be in or out of balance. When out of balance, with surpluses in certain fields and deficits in others, a company can deal with increments of traffic without additions to its facilities in those departments where there happens to be an excess. The costs connected with these facilities will, then, be constant during the period in which the excess exists and they will be less, per unit of volume, as business is enlarged. Average costs will fall unless the decline in constant costs per unit is offset by changes in variable expense.[18]

The Nature of Out-of-Pocket Costs

The concept of out-of-pocket costs is a further refinement of conclusions which we have just reached. We have mentioned "average" costs. Out-of-pocket costs may be defined as costs which may be segregated, which are first incurred when a particular article is offered for shipment and which disappear when that article ceases to move. What this means is that out-of-pocket costs may be calculated by comparing total costs incurred by an undertaking when a described service is accomplished with total cost when that service is not performed. The relation varies with conditions but out-of-pocket costs will ordinarily be less than average costs per unit except when new investment is required.[19]

though an element of constancy remains because the upward trend in variable expense per unit offsets the decline in constant cost per unit. Bigham and Roberts meet the difficulty by asserting that, during such a period, there is no unutilized capacity. They explain that there is no unutilized capacity, in the economic sense, after the lowest cost combination has been attained even though a plant may provide additional service without new investment (T. C. Bigham, and M. J. Roberts, *Transportation, Principles and Problems,* New York, McGraw-Hill, 1952, p. 168). It is as simple, perhaps, to define capacity in physical terms and to allow for irregularities in variable costs.

[18] Over a period of time and with changes in traffic, facilities which are for a while unutilized may move into the deficit area. Statistics show that expenditures which appear to have been made once for all have to be repeated, so that year by year or decade by decade the outlays become roughly proportionate to traffic (p. 305). Moreover, expenses which are listed as variable develop elements of constancy in that they do not actually change in strict proportion to ton or passenger miles. For short periods, however, and for significant changes in volume, there is, in an important sense, unutilized capacity and there are constant costs. (See Ford Edwards, "Cost Analyses in Transportation," *American Economic Review,* May, 1947.)

[19] Out-of-pocket costs, as the text says, are ordinarily less than average costs. Assuming no new investment, they will be the same as average variable costs when the latter vary in strict proportion to traffic; they will, however, be less than average variable costs when these averages become smaller per unit of traffic as volume grows and they will be more than average variable costs when average variable costs per unit of traffic rise. Assuming average variable costs which are proportional, they will always be less than variable plus constant costs divided by the number of units handled.

See United States Interstate Commerce Commission, *Rail Freight Service Costs in the Various Rate Territories of the United States,* 78th C., 1st S., Sen. Doc. 63, 1943; and Interstate Commerce Commission, Bureau of Transport Economics and Statistics, *The Meaning and Significance of the Out-of-Pocket, Constant, and Joint Costs in*

The direct conclusion from a consideration of out-of-pocket costs is that a carrier may sometimes, with advantage, transport for rates which do not compensate for average expense. Competition may tempt carriers to fix rates at such lower levels, when the market for a given service is separable from the other markets which are served. Indeed, it is possible to argue that a carrier will always maximize earnings if it accepts all freight increments on which the additional revenue secured exceeds the extra costs which are incurred and that it will benefit by retaining business on which the revenue received is greater than the saving that the surrender of the traffic would permit. It is clear, however, that additional or specially considered service makes use of the facilities which serve other transportation; there is some reason to insist that customers who receive such service should contribute to the cost of providing and maintaining the installation that is employed in their behalf. It is also clear that if out-of-pocket costs are less than average costs, a carrier will ultimately fail unless some customers, on some business, pay enough to make the difference good, or unless an outside subsidy can be obtained.

The Interstate Commerce Commission looks askance at rates based upon out-of-pocket costs, although it has approved such rates, or at least rates which have not much exceeded out-of-pocket costs when the public interest did not seem to be sufficiently involved.[20] When the Commission has disapproved rates of the character here discussed, it has been, generally, upon the ground that they disrupt an existing rate structure, that they improperly divert traffic from one carrier to another or from one type of carrier to another, or that they threaten the carrier which quotes them with a loss. "There are many dangers," the Commission has said, in this method of making rates, and the dangers increase the more extensively it is used. "Out-of-pocket cost" is an elusive and shifting thing. When traffic can be added in this way without any increase in truck-miles or man-hours, such cost is one thing, but if sufficient traffic is attracted so that more truck-miles or man-hours are required, it becomes a very different thing. Furthermore, it is always necessary to bear in mind

---

Motor Carrier Operation, 1946. Out-of-pocket or marginal costs may, of course, be greater than average costs when new investment is needed.

Expenses which are included in out-of-pocket costs have sometimes been referred to as "escapable" on the ground that they can be avoided by refusal to undertake an operation. (See W. A. Lewis, *Overhead Costs,* New York, Rinehart, 1949.)

[20] The Commission set down certain requirements to be satisfied by a rate based on out-of-pocket costs as long ago as 1922 (74 I.C.C. 48, 69, 1922). They were as follows:

1. The rate must cover, and more than cover, the extra or additional expenses incurred in handling the traffic to which it applies.
2. The rate must be no lower than necessary to meet existing competition.
3. The rate must not be so low as to threaten the extinction of legitimate competition by water carriers.
4. The rate must not impose an undue burden on other traffic or jeopardize the appropriate return on the value of carrier property generally.

the fact that the method is not a one-way affair, for competitors can use it as well, and where competition is widespread the result may be to beat down a very large part of the rate structure.[21]

Many carrier rates in the United States today cover less than the total cost which could properly be assigned to the services which they render, in spite of the distrust which the Interstate Commerce Commission has shown. The practice gives flexibility to the rate structure. It can hardly be abandoned although it can easily be abused.

Joint Costs

Carrier costs may be characterized as constant, variable, and out-of-pocket costs, but they may also be classified, in part, as joint and common costs. Traditional economic theory recognizes "jointness" when two distinguishable products inevitably emerge out of a single process.[22] The articles so produced are called joint products. A common illustration is that of beef, hides, and horns, all of which are produced together in the process of cattle raising. A peculiarity of this jointness is that an increase in the demand for one of the articles jointly produced may raise the price of the product to which the demand applies, but that it will at the same time oversupply the market with and reduce the price of the other articles which are necessarily and contemporaneously produced. Transportation may be regarded as a single process. The question is as to whether the various services which constitute its product are joint in the sense in which economists employ the word.

The argument that the term "joint product" should not be applied to carrier service rests upon two assumptions or assertions: (1) that a carrier which supplies service of a described sort, say freight service, does not inevitably and contemporaneously also provide another service, such as passenger transportation; and (2) that because of the carrier's freedom of decision, an increase in demand for one type of transport will not necessarily result in an oversupply of other types for which no additional demand exists.

The view of those who believe that the analogy is valid, at least over a

[21] 4 M.C.C. 187, 189, 1938; 21 M.C.C. 86, 88, 1939. See also 236 U.S. 585, 596, 1915. Earlier cases are considered in G. L. Wilson and J. R. Rose, "Out-of-Pocket Costs in Railroad Freight Rates," *Quarterly Journal of Economics,* August, 1946; and in T. C. Bigham, "Regulation of Minimum Rates in Transportation," *Quarterly Journal of Economics,* February, 1947.

Wilson and Rose observe that the Interstate Commerce Commission in rate cases, has usually taken "out-of-pocket cost" as equivalent to "average variable cost." They point out that rates fixed at the level of average variable cost will be less than marginal cost when average variable cost is increasing. The carrier will lose, rather than gain, if it accepts business at this level.

[22] To be "distinguishable" products must have different markets and command different prices.

considerable range of experience, is based upon observations of the following sort:

1. It is not inevitable that a single productive process in any field will produce any named and described group of products or, at least, the inevitability is overstressed. Cattle may be grown without horns, if time is allowed for selection and adaptation; moreover, if the ox is more elaborately described, there will almost certainly be variation in the items which the process yields.

2. Inevitability, in any case, can be determined only by observed coincidence. If it should appear to be the case that every railroad everywhere carried both passengers and freight, just as every ox has both beef and hides, there would be as good ground in the one case as in the other to speak of the products as joint. And there is no reason to refuse to admit degrees of jointness when the evidence is less complete.

3. There may be many reasons why two or more products are developed by a single process. The reasons alleged in the case of the ox are biological, although the concept is not as simple as it appears. The reasons in a carrier case may be financial, in the sense that adequate revenues may be obtained only from the sale of a group of services and not from one service by itself. Either of these reasons, in appropriate cases, may explain results. In speaking of "jointness," however, reasons are unimportant in the classification if the fact exists.[23]

4. It is true in many cases that an increase in the demand for railroad service of a given type affects the supply of other services which have been commonly rendered in close association with the first. Attempts will be in such instances to adjust relative supply or to develop new characteristics in the product, but this is done also when cattle are bred for the sale of beef or for the sale of hides. The flexibility of adjustment and substitution is probably much greater in carrier than in any agricultural and, perhaps, than in most manufacturing operations, but the fundamental principle may be much the same.[24]

---

[23] The cost of handling return loads by railroads is often referred to as a joint expense. It is clear that the provision of facilities for transportation in one direction involves making available roughly the same capacity for carriage in the opposite direction, but there is no physical necessity that the facilities be so used. The car may be returned empty or it may not be returned at all. If a return load is accepted, this may be regarded, with the outgoing load, as a joint product or service; but this is only because it is desirable to join the two services together for reasons of business profit. There are many cases of this sort, of which the return loading of railroad cars is only one. They all serve as illustrations of conditions mentioned in the text. For a contrary view, see Kent T. Healy, *The Economics of Transportation in America*, New York, Ronald, 1946, p. 162, and M. R. Bonavia, *The Economics of Transport*, New York, Pitman, 1947, pp. 103–111.

[24] McDonald suggests that instead of employing the term "joint costs" we might say that any two products are complementary in production if an increase in the quantity of one will lower the separable costs of the other, and competitive if the reverse is true. He adds that "generally one would expect products to be complementary until the

Common Costs

Many carrier costs may be considered joint. The question is largely one of terminology. It is certain, however, that many of them are also common. There are common costs in any process when factors are so combined that the cost of creating one product cannot be separated from that of creating another except by allocation.

In transportation, common costs are incurred when cars are loaded with commodities of different types. This has been called "process jointness." Another kind of jointness, which has been called "time jointness," arises when a machine is used successively in a series of productive efforts, as when a switching tower is operated for the direction of trains which follow each other over a period of time. There is a single investment which contributes to the performance of a number of services, temporally related. A third illustration of commonness has been called "risk jointness," as when two or more products are produced together in order to spread the risks of an enterprise; but this last form is less important in transport than, say, in agricultural production.[25]

Apportionment of Common Costs

Where there are common costs in a productive process it is important that the total outlay be covered by the total price. It is not, however, necessary that the allocation, in transportation, be in proportion to weight and distance carried or in any proportion based upon the physical peculiarities of the various movements. While these should be considered, it is usually possible to show that an allocation on the basis of demand will produce a greater revenue than could be secured by allocation upon another basis. It is also usually possible to show that a distribution on the basis of demand will make it possible for a carrier to supply a larger service for the same total cost. It follows, therefore, that the demand factor should be given weight.[26] There is, however, no accepted basis for the distribution of common costs in transportation nor, indeed, in any other

capacity of plant (track, motive power, and rolling stock) is approached, when they become competitive." In the former case it is quite conceivable that the separable cost of product B may fall to zero when the quantity of product A is increased (J. A. McDonald, "Some Notes on the Economics of Transportation," *Canadian Journal of Economics and Political Science,* November, 1951, pp. 515–522).

There is an elaborate discussion of "joint cost" by D. P. Locklin in the *Quarterly Journal of Economics,* February, 1933, p. 167, entitled "The Literature on Railway Rate Theory."

[25] S. V. Ciriacy-Wantrup, "Economics of Joint Costs in Agriculture," *Journal of Farm Economics,* November, 1941.

[26] Thus Morrison, discussing the handling of outbound and return movements in transportation, contends that the services should be priced according to the relative elasticity of demand in order to maximize net revenue (Hunter Morrison, "Rate Policy of the Interstate Commerce Commission for Back Haul of Trucks: Pricing and Joint Costs," *Journal of Land and Public Utility Economics,* August, 1942, pp. 329–338).

multiple purpose enterprise. There is even question as to whether an accounting basis is possible. On this point Olmstead has well characterized attempts at distribution in the following words:

Such computations consist of two processes. One is an *allocation* to a particular traffic of costs attributable to it; the other is an *apportionment* between the particular traffic and other traffic of costs jointly caused by both kinds of traffic. . . . Allocation is the assignment of facts; apportionment is the determination of policy. The former concerns itself with what is; the latter with what should be. One process consists of untwisting the intertwined but separate and distinct strands of a particular causation; the other of splitting the homogeneous fibres of a single cost jointly caused. Allocation aims to find out what each service *costs;* apportionment aims to determine what each service *ought to pay* . . . Combining the two figures seems like adding quarts to feet. The desirable course would seem to be to resolve the total "cost" into its constituent elements, one marked "Matter of Fact—Allocated Cost of Service" and the other labeled "Matter of Opinion—Mathematical Photograph of Witness's Sense of Justice." [27]

Whatever the fundamental basis of distribution, the following methods of allocation or, as Olmsted prefers to say, of apportionment, have been used in the assessment of common costs:

1. *Distribution of common costs on the basis of ton- and passenger-miles.* This is equal apportionment per unit of traffic with weight and distance used to describe the unit. The practice assigns a large proportion of common costs to low-grade articles, for these move in largest volume, and it burdens long hauls in relation to short hauls because it neglects the importance of terminal expense.

2. *Distribution by uniform addition to direct costs incurred.* This addition may be by fixed amounts or by fixed percentages, as when a dealer adds 10 percent to handling costs to cover overhead expense. Out-of-pocket costs are relatively high on less than carload and on light carload traffic, so the method places a relatively heavy burden upon these groups. It may be, however, that relatively high out-of-pocket costs per 100 pounds is a concomitant of high ability to pay.

3. *Distribution according to ability or willingness to pay.* We come back here, unexpectedly, to the value of service principle. The basic argument for using consumers' demand as the foundation for the distribution of carrier cost is that rates fixed upon this principle will maximize ton and passenger miles, that it will yield the largest revenues, and that it will provide most effectively for the coverage of carrier costs. The practice involves an application of price policy rather than a true allocation of expense.

4. *Distribution according to social benefit.* Social benefit, as the phrase

[27] *Annals of the American Academy of Political and Social Science,* January, 1916, Pub. no. 973.

is here used, is an equivalent to public policy. It may take a multitude of forms, from the simple practice of relieving shipments to distressed areas from the burden of common costs, to the encouragement of the export trade, the stimulation of shipping or of agriculture, or the relief of urban congestion. In some instances distribution may be such as deliberately to discourage types of shipment which, for one reason or another, it is desired to restrain. This type of distribution may be permitted by public agencies; it cannot be required under present law, nor may carriers employ the practice on their own account.[28]

General Comments on the Theory of Carrier Pricing

Returning now to the statement made at the beginning of the present chapter, the fixing of rates on particular hauls in transport service proceeds as does price fixing in other industries except, first, for the general presence of indivisible units of capital and labor and the necessity of allocation, and except to the extent that objectives other than the maximization of profit are more frequently introduced. The pressure in the latter case is sometimes applied in cost allocation and sometimes by direct regulatory control. It is important, partly because of the weight which government bodies can exert, and partly because of the flexibility of the organization to which pressure is applied. Neither government regulation nor private price making can be understood, however, without some knowledge of the complexities to which the present chapter has been addressed.

REFERENCES

General Treatises

Bigham, Truman C., and Roberts, Merrill J., *Transportation, Principles and Problems,* New York, McGraw-Hill, 1952.

[28] The list of methods for allocating common costs is not, of course, complete as stated in the text. The reader who is interested in this general subject may be referred to J. S. Ransmeier, *The Tennessee Valley Authority,* Nashville, Vanderbilt University, 1942, for an elaborate discussion of the alternatives for cost allocation in the case of a major utility enterprise. G. Lloyd Wilson has also enumerated alternatives which might be used in air transportation in an article in the *Traffic World,* September 16, 1950.

The subject is complicated—or perhaps simplified—by the broad contention that prices should be set to cover only out-of-pocket costs and that the balance should be provided by public contributions made possible by taxation. This would make allocation unnecessary. (See Nancy Ruggles, "The Welfare Basis of the Marginal Cost Pricing Principle," *Review of Economic Studies,* vol. 17, no. 42, 1949–50; "Recent Development in the Theory of Marginal Cost Pricing," *ibid.,* vol. 17, no. 43.) This suggestion has received the attention of a number of economists over a number of years. The proposal would require the grant of subsidies to all producers who operated under conditions of decreasing cost. The basic contention is that, by following this principle, the general welfare could be increased. It is hardly necessary to pursue the subject in the present text.

Bonavia, M. R., *The Economics of Transport,* New York, Pitman, 1947.
Brown, H. G., *Transportation Rates and Their Regulation,* New York, Macmillan, 1916.
Colson, C., *Transports et Tarifs,* Paris, Laveur, 1908.
Daniels, W. M., *The Price of Transportation Service,* New York, Harper, 1932.
Fair, Marvin L., and Williams, Ernest W., *Economics of Transportation,* New York, Harper, 1950.
Healy, Kent T., *The Economics of Transportation in America,* New York, Ronald, 1940.
Landon, Charles E., *Transportation, Principles, Practices, Problems,* New York, Sloane, 1951.
Locklin, D. Philip, *Economics of Transportation,* Chicago, Irwin, 1947.
Pigou, A. C., *The Economics of Welfare,* London, Macmillan, 1938.
Ripley, W. Z., *Railroads: Rates and Regulation,* New York, Longmans, 1912.

Other Books

Clark, J. M., *Studies in the Economics of Overhead Costs,* Chicago, University of Chicago, 1923.
Hultgren, Thor, *American Transportation in Prosperity and Depression,* Studies in Business Cycles, no. 3, National Bureau of Economic Research, New York, 1949.
Lewis, William Arthur, *Overhead Costs, Some Essays in Economic Analysis,* London, Allen & Unwin, 1949.
Ransmeier, J. S., *The Tennessee Valley Authority,* Nashville, Tenn., Vanderbilt University, 1942.

Periodicals

Ashton, H., "Railroad Costs in Relation to the Volume of Traffic," *American Economic Review,* June, 1940.
Ciriacy-Wantrup, S. V., "Economics of Joint Cost in Agriculture," *Journal of Farm Economics,* November, 1941.
Edwards, Ford, "Cost Analyses in Transportation," *American Economic Review,* May, 1947.
Locklin, D. Philip, "The Literature on Railway Rate Theory," *Quarterly Journal of Economics,* February, 1933.
Lorenz, M. O., "Constant and Variable Railroad Expenditures and the Distance Tariff," *Quarterly Journal of Economics,* February, 1907.
Lorenz, M. O., "Cost and Value of Service in Railroad Rate-Making," *Quarterly Journal of Economics,* February, 1916.
McDonald, J. A., "Some Notes on the Economics of Transportation," *Canadian Journal of Economics and Political Science,* November, 1951.
Merkert, Emil, *"Theoretische Abhandlung über die Preisbildung im Verkehrswesen,"* Archiv für Eisenbahnwesen, November–December, 1931.
Reynolds, L. G., "Cutthroat Competition," *American Economic Review,* December, 1940.
Ruggles, Nancy, "The Welfare Basis of the Marginal Cost Pricing Principle," *Review of Economic Studies,* vol. 17, no. 42, 1949–1950.

Ruggles, Nancy, "Recent Development in the Theory of Marginal Cost Pricing," *Review of Economic Studies,* vol. 17, no. 43, 1949–1950.

Stamp, Lord, "The Weight of Consignments in Transport," *Economic Journal,* June–September, 1940.

Taussig, F. W., "Contribution to the Theory of Railway Rates," *Quarterly Journal of Economics,* July, 1891.

Taussig, F. W., "Railway Rates and Joint Cost Once More," *Quarterly Journal of Economics,* February, 1913. (For subsequent discussion between Taussig and Pigou see the same journal, May and August, 1913.)

Trumbower, H. R., "The Incidence of Freight Charges on Agricultural Products," *Journal of Political Economy,* June, 1925.

Vaile, R., "Some Effects on Certain Agricultural Products of Uniform Percentage Increases in Freight Rates," *Quarterly Journal of Economics,* August, 1922.

Wallace, D. H., "Joint and Overhead Costs and Railway Rate Policy," *Quarterly Journal of Economics,* August, 1934.

Wilson, G. L., and Rose, J. R., "Out of Pocket Costs in Railroad Freight Rates," *Quarterly Journal of Economics,* August, 1946.

Special and Miscellaneous

Benedict, M. R., *Freight Rates and the South Dakota Farmer,* Bulletin no. 269, Brookings, S.D., South Dakota State College, Agricultural Economics Department, February, 1932.

Bureau of Railway Economics, *A Study of the Economic Effects of Reductions in Freight Rates on Export Wheat, 1929,* Washington, D.C., 1930.

United States Board of Investigation and Research, *Comparison of Rail, Motor, and Water Carrier Costs,* 79th C., 1st S., Sen. Doc. 84, 1944.

United States Federal Trade Commission, *Relative Efficiency of Large, Medium-Sized and Small Business,* TNEC Monograph no. 13, 1941.

United States Interstate Commerce Commission, *Out-of-Pocket Cost as a Factor in Determining Freight Rates,* by M. O. Lorenz and B. T. Elmore, I.C.C. Statement no. 3352, 1933.

United States Interstate Commerce Commission, *Territorial Rail Costs Based on a Separation of the Out-of-Pocket and Constant Expenses, 1939,* Washington, D.C., September, 1942.

United States Interstate Commerce Commission, Bureau of Transport Economics and Statistics, *The Meaning and Significance of the Out-of-Pocket, Constant, and Joint Costs in Motor Carrier Operation,* Washington, D.C., June, 1946.

United States Interstate Commerce Commission, *Freight Revenue and Wholesale Value at Destination of Commodities Transported in Class I Steam Railways in the United States, Calendar Year 1946 and July–December, 1946,* Washington, D.C., 1948.

United States Senate, *Rail Freight Service Costs in the Various Rate Territories of the United States,* by F. K. Edwards, 78th C., 1st S., Sen. Doc. 63, 1943.

Classification Practice

Need for Simplicity in Rate Quotation

Carriers which quote rates seek to make their statements regarding price simple enough to be easily understood and condensed enough to be disseminated at reasonable cost. A second and obvious requirement is that these rates shall conform to whatever theory of pricing the carrier may approve, and a third is that the total return recovered from the traffic shall be satisfactory. These objectives they attempt to attain through their published tariffs with a success which varies in different places and at different times. We shall be principally concerned in this chapter with questions of railroad rate technique, although the principles which the carriers currently recognize will have also to be considered.

Development of the Uniform Classification

It is the need for simplicity which leads to classification. To classify commodities is merely to divide them into groups, separating items in such a way that the units assigned to each group are sufficiently similar to justify uniform treatment. A freight classification arranges items so that in each group they may be accorded uniform treatment with respect to the price of transport.[1]

Carriers have grouped the articles which they have carried, more or less, since the practice of carrying for hire began; but the earlier varieties of classification were relatively so simple that they throw little light upon the practices and problems of the present time. In the United States, therefore, most business history that deals with the subject describes only the development of the uniform railroad classification which is now used,

---

[1] Carriers sometimes quote "all-freight rates" which neglect the assignment of articles in the classification. These and other simplifications are described in Stuart Daggett and John P. Carter, *The Structure of Transcontinental Railroad Rates*, Berkeley and Los Angeles, University of California, 1947. No great volume of freight moves under these arrangements and they will not be dealt with in the text.

and for the same reason we shall limit our historical reference to the modern period.

The origins of the uniform classification are to be found in the groupings worked out by individual railroads. These became numerous before the Civil War; indeed, it has been estimated that there were as many as 138 distinct classifications at one time in what is now termed Eastern Trunk Line territory.[2] Each of these had been built up independently of the others. The number of classes varied in the different publications, and there was little or no relation between the groupings in one classification and those in another.

FIGURE 33. Freight Classification Territories.

This lack of correlation which prevailed in the early period between different groupings of commodities for rate purposes was inconvenient when freight originating upon one railroad found its ultimate destination upon another, because the variety of treatment often made it impossible for a shipper to learn in advance the charges on a consignment that utilized the facilities of several lines. The first result was that special classifications for through shipments were set up, and the second that more general groupings were substituted for the classifications of individual companies. Notable examples of this were the Joint Western Classification, prepared in 1882 and generally adopted by most lines west of Chicago by 1889; the Official Classification, made effective in 1887 for the terri-

[2] H. H. Shannon, "History of Freight Classification," *Traffic World,* January 31, 1931, p. 283.

tory east of the Mississippi and north of the Ohio and Potomac rivers; and the classification of the Southern Railway and Steamship Association, adopted in 1889 by the Southern roads.

Efforts to substitute a single classification for those which still existed in the 1880's met, for many years, with only partial success. The number of minor classifications which persisted after the emergence of the general agreements of the years 1882 to 1889 was, however, decreased, step by step, until only a few state and local classifications remained. During World War I, also, the descriptions of articles listed in the principal classifications and the rules and regulations which these documents contained were unified and the three major classifications—Official, Southern, and Western [3]—with that of the State of Illinois, came to be published in a single volume. This made it possible to find in one source of reference the rating of any selected article in any part of the United States. The volume was known as the *Consolidated Classification*. In 1939 the Interstate Commerce Commission instituted proceedings looking toward still further standardization. The result was an order, in 1945, requiring rail carriers (1) to establish a single comprehensive classification to replace the four classifications that were still preserved in the Consolidated Classification; (2) to provide, in this new classification, for a large increase in the number of class groupings; and (3) to set fixed and reasonable relations between rates applied to the various classes.[4] The new *Uniform Classification* became effective in all territory east of Mountain-Pacific territory on May 30, 1952.[5] This concluded the argument for uniformity,

[3] An exact definition of the Official, Southern, and Western Classification territories was always difficult, but in general terms the territories were as follows:

Official Classification territory: The United States north of the Ohio and Potomac rivers and east of the Mississippi River, except (1) the northern peninsula of Michigan; (2) the states of Wisconsin and Minnesota, and (3) that portion of the state of Illinois lying north or west of a line drawn from Chicago to East St. Louis.

Southern Classification territory: The United States south of Official Classification territory and east of the Mississippi River.

Western Classification territory: The northern peninsula of Michigan, the states of Wisconsin and Minnesota, that portion of the state of Illinois lying north or west of a line drawn from Chicago to East St. Louis, and all United States territory west of the Mississippi River.

Illinois Classification territory: The state of Illinois and border points in adjacent states, excluding points assigned to Official and Western Classification territories.

It was necessary to consult the railroad tariff in order to know with certainty the classification that applied in any given case. Ordinarily the application could be guessed but this was, particularly, not the case when a shipment originated in one classification territory and was delivered in another. Joint rates in such cases were always governed by one classification, which might be that of the territory of origin or, more frequently, that of the territory of destination; when the charge was made up by combining two local rates, however, two classifications might be used.

[4] 262 I.C.C. 447, 1945; 264 I.C.C. 41, 1945; 331 U.S. 284, 1947.

[5] At the date of writing (July, 1952) the Uniform Classification was not effective within or to or from Mountain-Pacific territory pending the completion of Interstate

although the question of the classes to which articles should be assigned will always provoke debate.[6]

Classifications Used by Water and by Motor Carriers

Freight classifications are used by other carriers than railroads, including motor truck lines and water carriers operating in inter-coastal, coastwise, Great Lakes, and inland waterway service. Domestic carriers by water, if publishing class rates at all, make use of the Consolidated and Uniform Classifications. Motor carriers, to a much greater extent, rely upon classifications of their own. Immediately after the passage of the Motor Carrier Act of 1935, carriers and groups of carriers throughout the country were confronted with the problem of providing for classifications to be used in connection with class motor rates. The types of classification which were presently proposed were so various that American Trucking Associations, Inc., a national organization of motor carrier members of affiliated organizations, was asked to prepare a document that the entire industry might use. This work was accomplished in three stages: first, a committee of the Associations was appointed to consider the problem; second, carriers and shippers expressed their views at an annual convention of the national association; and third, a second committee of ap-

---

Commerce Commission investigations into Mountain-Pacific and Transcontinental railroad rates.

[6] Railroad representatives have agreed, for more than 40 years, that carriers should operate with uniform rules, uniform descriptions, uniform packing regulations, and uniform minimum rates. They have never believed—and many shippers agree with them—that articles should be assigned to the same classes in all sections of the country. The argument is that a policy of uniform rating ignores commercial and competitive and to some extent physical conditions which are bound to differ as between different regions. The Commission's reply is, essentially, that carriers may meet special cases by seeking exceptions to the Classification or by proposing commodity rates, but that the broad structure of the Classification should not be impaired (262 I.C.C. 447, 504–505, 1945).

The Commission may be disposed to permit adjustments of the sort referred to; it is to be determined how much flexibility it will allow. In listing the distinctions between commodities from a transportation standpoint the Commission has expressed the opinion that the transportation characteristics of most articles are substantially similar irrespective of the territory in which the shipment occurs (ibid., p. 509).

On the other hand the Commission included the following finding in its decision of 1945: "That it is not intended that the foregoing findings with respect to uniformity shall prevent the making of exceptional classification ratings when required either by the provisions of the Interstate Commerce Act or for commercial or competitive reasons, provided such exceptional ratings may be justified individually upon their own merits, and shall not have the effect of creating a violation of some provision of the Interstate Commerce Act or of being inconsistent wtih the national transportation policy, and shall not tend to impair the general requirement of uniformity of classification hereby found to be just and reasonable" (ibid., p. 511).

No one can predict from these statements what the ultimate policy of the Commission will be. It would be unfortunate, however, if the Commission laid too great emphasis upon uniform ratings in all parts of the United States in view of the variation in the factors of supply and demand which should properly be considered in fixing a railroad charge.

proximately a hundred members, representing motor carriers in more than forty states, met to work out details incident to the compilation of a classification based upon principles which the convention had approved. The final result bears the name "National Motor Freight Classification." It has not, like the railroad classification, been adopted by all companies which might employ it, but it was characterized by the Interstate Commerce Commission as predominant, as early as 1937, although minor classifications, in special territories, were also used.[7]

The National Motor Freight Classification resembled the Consolidated Classification in many respects. Notably, its less-than-truckload ratings corresponded with the less-than-carload ratings of the Consolidated, and its volume ratings with the carload ratings of the railroad issue. The reason was that motor carriers felt that competition with the rails would not permit the maintenance of ratings which differed materially from those of their competitors. Lower minimum weights were, however, generally provided, because the railroad minima were likely to be greater than the weights which it was possible for trucking companies to transport, or greater than they desired to transport, in a single truck or unit.[8] Speaking broadly, the principles employed in most motor classifications are similar to those applied by the railroads,[9] but the variety of shipments is less and, in particular, the classes to which the railroads assign goods of high specific gravity and low value per unit of weight have less importance. For this reason the number of groupings in motor classifications is apt to be smaller than the number which the railroads find necessary. Because of differences in the technique of handling shipments the rules in motor differ also from those in railroad classifications. In general, the practice of classification in motor service is still in process of development, both because of the new and relatively unorganized condition of the industry and because of the recent development of regulatory control.

Classification Listings

Turning now to the construction of a classification, and using the Uniform Railroad Classification as the document with which it is desirable to

[7] Examples are the Official Motor Freight Classification and the Coordinated Motor Freight Classification, both in use by motor carriers in New England.

[8] 24 M.C.C. 501, 519, 1940.

[9] This is not true of the New England classifications, which emphasize motor costs and pay little attention to competitive railroad rates. The ratings in these classifications, in conjunction with New England class rates, are designed to produce approximately the same revenue return per truckload on all commodities transported (8 M.C.C. 287, 291, 1938). The Commission has been asked to apply this principle elsewhere (44 M.C.C. 501, 1945; 47 M.C.C. 601, 1947; 48 M.C.C. 195, 1948). It has refused to do this, although it has approved the New England classification for local use. This is because the Commission believes that value and all other characteristics of an article should be given appropriate consideration, along with density, in determining a rating (49 M.C.C. 233, 238, 1948; 47 M.C.C. 215, 219, 1947).

Item	ARTICLES	Less Carload Ratings	Carload Minimum (Pounds)	Carload Ratings
5	**ABRASIVES:**			
10	Abrasive cloth or paper, including emery or sand paper, in packages...............	60	36,000	37½
15	Alundum, corundum, emery or other natural or synthetic abrasive material consisting chiefly of aluminum oxide or silicon carbide:			
20	Crude or lump, LCL, in bags, barrels or boxes; CL, in bulk or in packages............	55	50,000	27½
25	Flour or grain, in packages.........................	60	36,000	35
30	Refuse, consisting of broken wheels, wheel stubs or wheel grindings, loose, see Note, item 35, or in packages...................	55	50,000	20
35	Note.—LCL shipments may be loose only in lots of 10,000 lbs., subject to minimum charge as for 10,000 lbs.; shipments to be loaded by shipper and unloaded by consignee; shipper to furnish and install all dunnage and packing material; freight charges to be assessed on basis of gross weight of article and all dunnage or packing material.			
40	Wheels, other than pulp grinding, in barrels, boxes or crates, or on skids if weighing each 300 lbs. or over; also CL, loose packed in packing material............	60	30,000	40
45	Wheels, pulp grinding, in boxes or crates, or on skids............	60	30,000	40
50	**ACIDS (see also item 15502):**			
55	Abietic, in barrels or in package 84...............	55	40,000	22½
60	Acetic, glacial or liquid:.			
	In carboys, other than package 800...............	100	30,000	45
	In glass in barrels or boxes or in package 800............	77½	30,000	40
	In bulk in barrels or in packages 595 or 597; also CL, in tank cars, Rule 35............	70	30,000	35
65	Acetylsalicylic, in barrels or boxes............	85	30,000	45
70	Acids, noibn, dry:			
	In glass or in cans or cartons in barrels or boxes............	92½	30,000	55
	In bulk in barrels, boxes, steel pails or 5-ply paper bags............	85	30,000	50
75	Acids, noibn, liquid:			
	In carboys............	100	30,000	60
	In glass in barrels or boxes............	92½	30,000	55
	In bulk in barrels............	85	36,000	50
80	Arsenic, fused, in barrels or boxes, or in bars wrapped in paraffined paper in wooden boxes only..	70	36,000	37½
85	Arsenic, other than fused:			
	In carboys............	100	30,000	45
	In barrels; also CL, in tank cars, Rule 35............	70	36,000	37½
87	Azelaic, from animal or vegetable fats, in bags, barrels or boxes............	77½	30,000	40
90	Boric (boracic):			
	In glass in barrels or boxes............	85	30,000	45
	In cans or cartons in barrels or boxes, or in bulk in bags, barrels, boxes or steel pails; also CL, in double-wall paper bags or in bulk............	70	36,000	37½
95	Carbolic (phenol):			
	In carboys..	100	30,000	55
	In glass or in metal cans in barrels or boxes............	77½	30,000	40
	In bulk in barrels, or in metal drums in barrels or boxes, or in package 598; also CL, in tank cars, Rule 35...	70	36,000	37½
100	Chlorosulfonic:			
	In bulk in barrels; also CL, in tank cars, Rule 35............	60	36,000	35
105	Chromic:			
	In glass or in metal cans in barrels or boxes............	85	30,000	45
	In bulk in steel barrels..	70	36,000	37½
110	Cresylic (cresol):			
	In glass or in metal cans in barrels or boxes............	77½	30,000	40
	In bulk in barrels; also CL, in tank cars, Rule 35............	70	36,000	37½
115	Electrolyte, containing not to exceed 47% sulphuric acid:			
	In carboys...	100	30,000	45
	In glass in barrels or boxes............	70	30,000	40
	In lined barrels or rubber drums..	60	36,000	35
120	Formic:			
	In carboys, other than package 800............	100	30,000	45
	In glass in barrels or boxes or in package 800............	85	30,000	35
	In bulk in barrels .	70	30,000	35
125	Hydrocyanic, in glass or metal cans in barrels or boxes, or in steel cylinders............	85	30,000	45
130	Hydrofluoric:			
	In containers in barrels or boxes, or in steel jacketed lead carboys............	85	36,000	45
	In bulk in barrels or rubber drums, or in steel cylinders; also CL, in tank cars, Rule 35......	70	36,000	37½
132	Hydrofluoric and sulphuric, mixed, in bulk, in metal barrels; also CL, in tank cars, Rule 35....	70	36,000	35
135	Hydrofluosilicic:			
	In carboys............	100	36,000	45
	In containers in barrels or boxes............	85	36,000	45
	In bulk in barrels or rubber drums; also CL, in tank cars, Rule 35............	70	36,000	37½
137	Hydroxy acetic, in bulk in barrels; also CL, in tank cars, Rule 35............	70	30,000	30
140	Lactic:			
	In glass bottles each packed in rattan or willow basket or hamper............	200	30,000	85
	In carboys............	100	30,000	55
	In glass in barrels or boxes............	77½	30,000	40
	In bulk in barrels; also CL, in tank cars, Rule 35............	70	30,000	35
145	Maleic or maleic anhydride:			
	In metal cans in barrels or boxes............	85	36,000	45
	In bulk in barrels; also CL, in tank cars, Rule 35............	77½	36,000	45
150	Monochloroacetic, in bulk in barrels............	70	36,000	37½

FIGURE 34.   Uniform Freight Classification Number 1. (Consolidated Classification Committee, Chicago.)

become familiar, we have to observe that this classification is divided into two parts. One part contains rules and regulations which relate to the documentation, packing, and handling of shipments, and to the assessment and collection of charges; the other is filled with a list of articles bordered with columns in which there are numbers indicating a class to which each article is assigned. To illustrate this arrangement, a page of the listing in Uniform Freight Classification No. 1, Effective May 30, 1952, is reproduced on page 321.

A few explanations will make it easy to understand this simple form.

In the Classification listings the columns are headed "Less-Than-Carload Ratings," "Carload Minimum," and "Carload Ratings." The numbers in the first and third columns show the percentages of Class 100 assigned to each article upon the list. There are thirty alternatives, or classes, which the Interstate Commerce Commission prescribed in 1945. These are as follows: Classes 400, 300, 250, 200, 175, 150, 125, 100, 92.5, 85, 77.5, 70, 65, 60, 55, 50, 45, 40, 37.5, 35, 32.5, 30, 27.5, 25, 22.5, 20, 17.5, 16, 14.5, and 13. The classes recognized are probably more numerous than those which were previously available, although the change may not be great if allowance is made for the percentage classes which carriers were using before 1952. The effect of entries in the first and third columns is to determine the relationship between the rates paid upon any rated article and the rates on articles in Class 100. By derivation this also shows the relationship between the rates paid upon any one article and the rate upon any other article covered by the Classification. The separate columns for less-than-carload and carload ratings express the accepted view that shipments in carload quantities can be handled at less expense than shipments in smaller quantities and should, therefore, be carried at relatively lower rates, and the fixing of carload minima for each commodity serves, in part at least, to locate the dividing line between large and small shipments insofar as this particular problem is concerned.[10]

It will be noticed that the classification lists and distinguishes articles according to the form in which they are presented for shipment as well as by the nature of the goods themselves. Thus arsenic takes one rating when shipped in carboys and another when shipped in barrels or tank cars; and lactic acids have separate ratings according as they are presented (1) in glass bottles packed in rattan baskets, (2) in carboys, (3) in glass in barrels or boxes, or (4) in bulk in barrels or in tank cars in

_____

[10] We shall refer again to the definition of a carload. The Classification does not recognize variations in quantity within the LCL categories, although this might be done. It has been suggested that railroads should provide LCL ratings dependent upon whether goods are shipped in quantities of less than 5,000, 10,000, or 20,000 pounds. Such a practice would supply an incentive for concentrated shipments and it would help the railroads to meet motor competition. (See *Traffic World*, May 20, 1950, part 2, p. 30; *ibid.*, June 24, 1950, p. 19.)

carload quantities. One effect of this is to multiply by several times the number of listings with which the classification is concerned.

Classification Committees

The Classification list is a considerable document. In 1943 the Consolidated Freight Classification contained ratings on approximately 7,800 articles or groups of articles. The actual number of ratings was greater, for in most instances several ratings were assigned to a commodity, dependent upon the method of packing and upon the type of movement—in carload or in less than carload quantity. It may well be imagined that the initial distribution among classes and the continued adjustment of the ratings of so large a variety of goods accepted for railroad transport to the changing conditions of business is a large and important task.

The carriers entrust the administration of their Classification to a committee or committees. Until 1952 they operated through four committees, one for each of the major classifications—Official, Southern, Western, and the State of Illinois—which functioned at the time. These committees had headquarters at New York, Atlanta, and Chicago. They received evidence, and heard arguments for and against applications by shippers and carriers for changes in rules and regulations and requests for the classification of new articles presented for shipment in new forms. There was, in addition, a Consolidated Committee composed of the Chairmen of each of the local organizations. The Consolidated Classification Committee published the Consolidated Classification. It did not establish ratings, for there were no ratings beyond those provided in the Official, Southern, Western, and Illinois classifications or in authorized exceptions thereto, and it had no power, other than that of publication. Each of the committees made recommendations, periodically, to the Executive Committee of the Traffic Association in its area. Individual carriers might protest any recommendation. The appropriate classification committee would then reëxamine the recommendation. If the committee maintained its view, the Executive Committee of the Traffic Association of the territory of the recommending classification committeee would make the final recommendation. As publishers, members of the Consolidated Classification Committee acted as agents for a long list of rail carriers beginning with the Aberdeen and ending with the Yreka Western Railroads. A number of motor carriers and of freight forwarders also participated.

The organization described in the preceding paragraph continued to operate after 1945 because the effective date of the Interstate Commerce Commission's order requiring the adoption of a single Uniform Classification for the United States was several times postponed. The carriers now have, beginning in 1952, the task of remodeling their earlier system of administration. The details of the changes which are being made have not been announced at the present writing. There is no reason to suppose that the carriers will fundamentally change their methods of operation. Their machinery will, however, be altered, in what respects it is not yet possible to say.

Principles Governing the Classification of Freight

We have dealt so far with the purely formal aspects of classification, such as name, uniformity of application, physical appearance, and controlling personnel. The subject can hardly be left, however, without some reference to the principles which guide the carriers, through their representatives, in distributing articles among the classification groups and without some mention of the more important rules which the Uniform Classification contains.

A well-known traffic man, some years ago, divided the considerations which governed the classification of freight into five general classes, of which two related to transportation only, one to insurance, and two to commercial requirements. These five considerations were the following:

1. Weight per cubic foot, with special attention to cases of extraordinary size, shape, or weight.
2. Value per 100 pounds, associated by railroad men with the concept of what the traffic will bear.
3. Liability to loss or damage from pilferage, breakage, leakage, spontaneous damage or decay, and likelihood that the article will damage other freight.
4. Competition and commercial necessity.
5. Volume of traffic.[11]

[11] A more recent statement by the Railroad Classification Committees in 1945 listed the following principles or factors according to which articles were then being assigned to classification classes: weight per cubic foot of the article as packed, liability to damage, liability to damage other goods with which loaded, the value per pound in comparison with competitive articles, possible movement in carloads, character of the article and of the packing to determine extent to which the capacity of cars can be used, commercial conditions and units of sales, trade conditions, and value of the service (262 I.C.C. 447, 481, 1945).

The Commission's own list, in the same decision, contained these items: weight per cubic foot and value per pound as packed for shipment; liability to loss, damage, waste, or theft in transit; likelihood of injury to other freight with which it may come in contact; risks due to hazards of carriage; kind of container or package as bearing upon the matter of liability or risk; expense of, and care in, handling; ratings on analogous articles; fair relation of ratings as between all articles; competition between articles of different description but largely used for similar purposes; commercial conditions and units of sales; trade conditions; value of service; volume of movement for the entire country in either less than carloads or carloads; adaptability to movement in carloads; and carload minimum weights just to carriers and shippers.

There is little difference between the railroad calssification committees' enumeration and that given in the text. The additions suggested by the Interstate Commerce Commission include "ratings on analogous articles," "fair relations as between all articles," "volume of movement for the entire country in either less than carloads or carloads," and "carload weights just to carriers and shippers." The Commission's emphasis upon these matters reflects its responsibility as a regulating body.

Illustrations of how these considerations influence classification today may be found in descriptions given below and in the ratings which, in various instances, have been assigned. The ratings are drawn from Uniform Classification no. 1, which was in force when this summary was made. Lumber, veneer, forest products, and furniture are the articles which are examined. For our purposes, these may be divided into the following groups:

1. Common lumber, in carloads.
    a. Common lumber has a weight per cubic foot that permits heavy loading, and it is not of extraordinary size, shape or weight.
    b. Its value per 100 pounds is low.
    c. Common lumber is but slightly liable to loss or damage in any of the specified ways.
    d. Lumber moves long distances in competition with other timber moving short distances, and it is one of the chief necessities of life.
    e. The volume of movement is extremely large.

Common lumber is therefore entitled to and receives a low rating in the Uniform Classification, or 25 percent.

2. Lumber made of foreign woods, in carloads.
    a. The weight per cubic foot is still entirely satisfactory.
    b. Its value is greater; hence its share of the transportation burden ought to be greater, other things equal.
    c. While it is no more susceptible to damage than lighter wood, it is more valuable; hence the loss, if the freight is damaged, is greater and, all things considered, the insurance risk is greater.
    d. Competition and commercial necessities vary, but the competition of other commodities is less severe than in the case of common lumber.
    e. The volume of traffic is less.

The rating of foreign lumber in the Uniform Classification is slightly higher than that of common lumber, or 27½ percent.

3. Common furniture parts in carload quantities, such as chair seats and backs, school desk or seat parts, wooden cots or couches without legs. These items are, normally, "knocked down flat."
    a. The articles mentioned furnish much less weight per cubic foot than lumber but, since they are "knocked down," they weigh more per cubic foot than do most articles of furniture.
    b. They are, of course, more valuable than lumber, but they are cheap

---

It is interesting to observe that the Commission will not admit that relatively heavy movements in a single territory provide reason for the assignment of an article to a class which is lower than the class which the article occupies elsewhere. The Commission thinks that this would constitute an undue preference. The Commission presumably believes that a favorable classification in such a case would create or perpetuate a difference in volume which would not otherwise exist.

articles of necessary use and their value is low when compared with other furniture.

c. Common furniture parts, K.D., are more liable to damage than lumber, but since they are packed flat they are not excessively liable to damage; and because they are cheap articles, the amount of risk is not great.

d. Competition is keen, though less so than on lumber, and trade necessities require a moderate rate.

Articles in this group are rated 45 percent.

4. Certain kinds of furniture of slightly greater value, and less compactly packed, which have a rating of 55 percent. The list includes sofa arms, table tops covered with plastic, and chairs with upholstered seats.

5. A number of articles of varying values and weights per cubic foot which take ratings in carloads ranging from 60 to 85 percent.

6. Still further along we reach articles such as "setup" furniture in less-than-carload quantities which are rated 100, 125, 150, and 175 percent.

7. Finally there are special kinds of shipments that take a rating of 200 percent. The list includes bamboo and rattan furniture, barber chairs, cradles, outdoor chairs that are painted or varnished, and portable fireplaces.

Alternative Suggestions

Essentially a classification based upon the factors indicated in the preceding pages represents an attempt to relate railroad charges to the two elements of cost and value in ways that can be simply understood and applied in the day-to-day conduct of railroad affairs. Businessmen are not much interested in pure abstraction, and the principles involved in current classification are discussed with less subtlety than economists are sometimes disposed to display. There is some disposition, nevertheless, to consider whether cost and value concepts are properly combined by existing practice. There have been classifications, such as those used by the old canal undertakings and by the Stockton and Darlington Railroad in England in its early days, which laid greater stress on value; [12] and there have been systems such as the *Wagen-Raum* or "space" method used by

---

[12] J. F. Strombeck, *Freight Classification*, Boston, Houghton Mifflin, 1912, pp. 18–28.
Bonavia recalls that the early English canals provided a "way" but did not act as carriers. The total transportation charge paid by the shipper thus fell into two parts: (1) a haulage charge paid to the individual or firm who worked the canal boats. Charges of this sort were kept near to cost by competition; (2) a toll levied by the canal. The toll was designed to yield the maximum contribution to maintenance and interest on capital. It was kept low enough to let traffic pass, but it had no direct relation to the distance over which goods were moved. The toll approximated, rather, the canal company's estimate of the value of the canal's service to the shipper under conditions of at least partial monopoly. For this, the value of the goods provided a sufficient test (M. R. Bonavia, *The Economics of Transport*, New York, Pitman, 1947, p. 130).

many European railroads in the 1870's in which the only distinctions, or almost the only distinctions, were those based upon cost.[13]

It was argued in one of the reports of the Federal Coordinator of Transportation, in 1935, that all cost elements should be eliminated in setting up a classification, and that only value of service elements should be considered.[14]

The context suggests that value of the commodity, not value of the service, was really meant. In elaboration of the plan it was stipulated that no traffic should be handled at a loss, which introduced an uncertain limitation. But the desire to emphasize demand elements rather than cost was clear. If this argument were accepted it would still remain to be determined whether the exaction of higher freight rates on articles of higher value should proceed proportionately, or whether the influence of the value factor should diminish as the classification dealt with goods of higher and higher selling price.[15] If the qualification with respect to "loss" were taken seriously, the whole question of cost calculation and distribution would be reintroduced.

On the other hand, another report of the same federal agency presented the view that the value of articles should not affect their rating, but that the carrier should protect itself against liability by a separate insurance charge.[16] This would leave the cost of transport as the determining factor in classification. Where cost is regarded as predominant, emphasis has been sometimes laid upon density so that it is proposed to assign commodities of high density to lower, and those of low density to higher, groups in the classification.[17] The assumption is that variations in

[13] One form of the "space" system recognized only four classes: (1) fast freight; (2) less-than-carload freight; (3) traffic in carloads of 5000 kg.; (4) traffic in carloads of 10,000 kg. The classification system introduced into Alsace-Lorraine after the Franco-Prussian War was but little more complicated. It contained only seven classes, two for fast freight and less-than-carload freight, four for half and full carloads in open and in covered cars, and a special class for certain raw materials shipped in carload quantities (Albert Pauer, *Lehrbuch der Eisenbahntarifwesen,* Wien, 1900).

[14] United States, Office of the Federal Coordinator of Transportation, *Freight Traffic Report,* 1935, pp. 33–34.

[15] M. O. Lorenz, "Commodity Values and Freight Rates," *Traffic World,* March 8, 1930, p. 649.

[16] United States Office of the Federal Coordinator, *Merchandise Traffic Report,* 1934, p. 7.

[17] In Trunk Line Territory Motor Carrier Rates (24 M.C.C. 501, 522, 1940), the Interstate Commerce Commission was asked to approve the following formula for motor classification in Trunk Line Territory:

All Commodities, Weight per Cubic Foot	Proposed Rating Class	Relation to the Basic Fifth-Class Rating Percent
0 to 2.99 pounds	A	1,330
3 to 5.99 pounds	1	445
6 to 9.99 pounds	2	250
10 to 14.99 pounds	3	160

density cause or are at least positively related to variations in cost. Yet it should be clear that goods of high density are not, necessarily, low-cost articles from the point of view of transportation.[18] Moreover, there are different optimum densities in rail, water, motor, and air transport, and for each type of equipment in each category.[19] Classification according to density would load cars to the best advantage only if the load factor of each facility were separately concerned. Full discussion of these points leads back into the general theory of rate making, in which we have no further time to engage.[20]

Classification Rules

Classifications render their greatest service in grouping large numbers of articles into small numbers of categories so that the process of rate quotation may be simplified; this same grouping stabilizes the relations between the rates on goods in any class and, to some extent, between the rates in different classes. Not all goods, it is true, are shipped under the classifica-

15 to 19.99 pounds	4	115
20 to 39.99 pounds	5	100
40 pounds and over	6	90

Ratings in the above formula did not vary in exact proportion to differences in density, because some other factors, such as susceptibility to damage in transit, risk of damage to other commodities, value of the commodity as reflected in the claim hazard, and perishability were given recognition in ratings higher than density alone would warrant. But no consideration was given to rail or other carrier competition, value of service, or what the traffic would bear. The Commission did not accept the proposals made.

See in this connection the general revision of its railroad classification which the French government accomplished in 1944. One feature of this revision was an increase in the emphasis upon cost of carriage as distinguished from value of service and a stress upon density as a factor affecting costs (G. L. Wilson, "French Railroads Develop New Freight Rate System," *Railway Age,* April 24, 1948).

[18] The critical test is whether the stowage factor of a given commodity is the same as the stowage factor of the vehicle in which the commodity is carried. If a railroad car has a cubic capacity of 2,926 cubic feet and a weight supporting capacity of 40 tons, its carrying capacity will be completely utilized when it is loaded with articles which occupy slightly more than 73 cubic feet per ton of weight. Any lower or higher density will cause a waste. (Cf. United States Board of Investigation and Research, *Transportation Act of 1940,* "Comparison of Rail, Motor, and Water Costs," 1944, pp. 22–23.)

[19] The Bureau of Economics and Statistics of the Interstate Commerce Commission has collected statistics which indicate that commodities of high density are, characteristically, also commodities of low value (United States Interstate Commerce Commission, Bureau of Transport Economics and Statistics, *Weight Density and Value as Factors in Freight Classification,* March, 1946).

[20] A current practical problem is, however, presented by the use of containers in railroad and motor vehicle service. A container is a steel box, packed by the shipper and offered to the carrier as a closed unit. Much of the economy expected from its use depends upon its acceptance as a unit. The container may, nevertheless, hold a variety of articles, of various values and variously rated in the classification. The question is whether container shipments should be assigned to a single class, irrespective of the contents of the box, or whether the contents of each container should be sorted out and the items assigned to different groups for the purpose of rate making.

tion, for when the volume of any movement is very large it may be desirable to treat it separately and not as part of a class which must contain freight of somewhat different characteristics. Rates which are quoted on individual commodities are known as "commodity rates"; if there is an effective commodity rate on a given shipment, that rate, indeed, must be applied even though the article involved may also be mentioned in the classification as belonging to a certain class.

Classifications do more, however, than group the articles which carriers transport. They contain a number of deliberately adopted rules which express the carriers' judgment with respect to many practices connected with the shipment of freight. Some of these rules are highly technical. Thus the Uniform Classification permits goods to be shipped both in wooden and in fiberboard containers, and specifies what the minimum thickness of the sides and ends of these containers shall be. These pronouncements hardly raise questions of principle, although it is to the common interest that adequate packing restrictions be observed. Other pages reproduce standard forms of shipping contracts designed partly to limit carriers' liability in case of loss and partly to promote the orderly and efficient conduct of transportation; or they indicate, for instance, how C.O.D. shipments shall be handled and what the carriers' charges shall be when it collects the sales price of the consignment at destination and remits the proceeds to the consignor. In these and in similar matters the Classification defines and describes a considerable variety of operating and commercial transportation practices in ways which employees of carriers are expected to know and to apply.

There are rules in the Classification, however, which are of a somewhat broader sort, or which, at least, embody conclusions that have been considerably discussed. Certain of these rules (published in the Uniform Classification, effective July 1, 1948) are reprinted for the reader's information.

RULE 7

Section 1. The name of only one shipper, one consignee and one destination shall appear on a shipping order or bill of lading, except that the shipping order and bill of lading may specify the name of a party at the same destination to be notified of the arrival of shipment. . . .

Section 3. Surrender of original order bill of lading, properly endorsed, is required before delivery of the property therein described, but such property may be delivered in advance of surrender of the bill of lading to a party who states to the carrier in writing (or orally if promptly confirmed in writing) that he is the owner or is lawfully entitled to the possession of the property, and that the bill of lading has been lost, delayed, destroyed, or otherwise is not immediately available at a bank or other source, and who presents to the carrier as a substitute for the bill of lading, security in the form of

Substitute 1. Currency, certified check or bank cashier's check in amount equal to 125% of the invoice or value of the property; or at carrier's option.

Substitute 2. A specific bond of indemnity with surety in amount equal to twice such invoice or value; or at carrier's option.

Substitute 3. A blanket bond of indemnity with surety.

Substitute 4. An open-end bond of indemnity, with corporate security duly authorized to write surety bonds and regularly engaged in such business.

Comment: This rule reminds employees of their duty to "take up" order bills of lading before the delivery of property, but permits the acceptance of other security. The use and importance of order bills of lading has been considered in chapter 13.

RULE 10

Section 1. Except as otherwise provided in this Classification or in tariffs governed thereby, when a number of articles for which the same or different ratings or rates are provided when in straight carloads, are shipped at one time by one consignor to one consignee and destination in a carload . . . they will be charged at the straight carload rate (not mixed carload rate) applicable to the highest classed or rated article contained in the carload and the carload minimum weight will be the highest provided for any article in the carload. Where the applicable carload rate, rating and minimum weight are the same on all articles in the shipment, such rate, rating and minimum weight will apply on the mixture.

Section 2. Subject to the conditions of Section 1, when the aggregate charge upon the entire shipment is made lower by considering the articles as if they were divided into two or more separate carloads, the shipment will be charged accordingly. . . .

Section 3. When the aggregate charge upon the entire shipment is less on basis of carload rate and minimum carload weight (actual or estimated weight to be charged for if in excess of the minimum weight) for one or more of the articles and on basis of actual or authorized estimated weight at less than carload rate or rates for the other article or articles the shipment will be charged for accordingly. On articles included in carload shipments on which less than carload rates are applied, carload package requirements will apply . . . Charges on articles in packages shall not be higher than on the same articles loose.

Section 4. If a lower charge would result under the application of Sections 1, 2 or 3 of this rule than under the provision for a specific carload mixture, such lower charge will apply. This rule will not apply upon articles for which carload ratings or rates are not provided nor upon shipments of livestock. . . .

Comment: This is an important rule governing carload mixtures—that is to say, cases in which goods with different classification ratings and with different minimum weights are combined into a single carload. The text gives the rule which appears in the Uniform Classification. The same rule was in the Standard Classification that governed practice before 1952. Prior to 1952, however, the phrasing was replaced, by "exception" in Official and Southern Classification territories and in Western Trunk Line and Southwestern Freight Bureau territories by more liberal wording given in the note below.[21] These exceptions presumably lapsed with the adoption of the Uniform Classification. It is not certain whether or not they will be restored.

RULE 12

Unless otherwise provided for and subject to minimum charges provided in Rules 13 and 29.

Section 1.   Single LCL shipments of one class will be charged for at actual or authorized weight and at rating applicable.

Section 2.   Except as provided in Rule 20, single LCL shipments of two or more classes, when each class is in a separate package, will be charged at actual or authorized estimated weight, and at the rating applicable to each class.

Section 3.   The charge for a package containing articles classed or rated differently shall be at the rating or rates provided for the highest classed or rated article in the package and on shipments subject to CL rating or rate, the highest minimum weight provided for any article in the package will apply. All the articles need not be specified on shipping order or bill of lading but on LCL shipments only one of the articles taking the highest rating or rate, and on CL shipments one of the articles taking highest CL minimum weight; in such instances following notation must also appear on shipping order and bill of lading: "And other articles classified or rated the same or lower."

· · · · · · ·

RULE 10

[21] As applied in Official Classification Territory, Southern Classification Territory, Western Trunk Line Territory, and Southwestern Freight Bureau Territory.

Section 1.   Except as otherwise provided, when a number of different articles for which ratings or rates are provided when in straight carloads are shipped at one time by one consignor to one consignee and destination, in a carload . . . they will be charged at the actual or authorized estimated weight and at the straight carload class or commodity rate (not mixed carload rate) applicable to each article . . . The carload minimum weight will be the highest provided for any article in the mixed carload, and any deficit in the minimum weight will be charged for at the highest carload rating or rate applicable to any article in the mixed carload.

Comment: The form used in transcontinental traffic, before 1952, differed from the standard rule in certain particulars, especially in the case of eastbound freight and in commodity tariffs.

The Commission was asked, in 1945, to prescribe for Western territory something which was the substantial equivalent of the rule given in this note. It held, however, that the change would reduce the carriers' revenue and increase their operating costs; and that the standard form of Rule 10, as used in the West, was not unjust or unreasonable (262 I.C.C. 227, 1945. See also 54 I.C.C. 1, 1919).

Comment: This is a "mixing" rule for LCL shipments. It tends to reduce damage by penalizing the packing of light and fragile articles and heavy articles in the same package.[22]

RULE 13

Unless otherwise provided in this Classification:

Section 1. The minimum charge for a single LCL shipment from one consignor to one consignee on one bill of lading shall be:

(a)   If classified class 100 or lower, for 100 pounds at the class or commodity rate applicable thereto; or

(b)   If classified higher than class 100, for 100 pounds at the class 100 rate; or

(c)   If shipment contains different articles, and no article is rated higher than class 100, for 100 pounds at the class or commodity rate applicable to the article taking highest rate; or if any one of the articles is rated higher than class 100, for 100 pounds at the class 100 rate; but

(d)   In no case shall the charge on a single shipment be less than 143 cents.

When a LCL shipment moves under a rate made by a combination of separately established rates in the absence of joint through rate, whether such separately established rates are governed by same or different classifications published herein, the minimum charge of 143 cents will apply to the continuous through movement and not to each of the separately established factors.

Section 2.   The minimum charge for CL shipments shall be $28.60 per car.

Comment: Because of Rule 13 it is ordinarily cheaper to ship consignments of less than 100 pounds by express than by freight. Paragraph (c) of Section 1, applying to mixed shipments, is of obvious importance.

RULE 14

Section 1.   Carload ratings or rates apply only when a carload of freight is shipped from one station, in or on one car, . . . in one calendar day from midnight to midnight, by one shipper for delivery to one consignee at one destination and is loaded by shipper and unloaded by consignee. Only one bill of lading from one loading point and one freight bill shall be issued for such CL shipment. The minimum CL weight provided is the lowest weight on which the CL rating or rate will apply.

Section 2.   Carload ratings or rates also apply on carload shipments (as described in Section 1), which, under tariffs lawfully on file with the Interstate Commerce Commission (on interstate traffic) and State Commissions (on interstate traffic) are accorded additional services or privileges described below:

(a)   Loading by the carrier, under provisions of the tariff, applicable at shipping station or stopover station.

[22] 251 I.C.C. 461, 1942.

(b)   Unloading by the carrier, under the provisions of the tariff applicable at shipping station or stopover station.

(c)   "Split deliveries" (delivery to more than one party) at destination by the carrier, under provisions of the tariff applicable at destination station.

(d)   Stopover privileges to complete loading or to partly unload while en route under provisions of tariffs or carriers serving the stopover station. . . .

Section 3.   When freight is loaded in or on a car by shipper and such car is not fully loaded but is tendered as a CL shipment, and car is forwarded without other freight in or on it, the shipment will be charged for as a carload.

Comment: The duty of issuing appropriate bills of lading rests on the carriers—the instructions in Rule 14 apply to them. The rule also lists the conditions under which a shipment is entitled to a carload rate.

RULE 15

Section 1.

(a)   Except as provided in Section 2, the charge for a LCL shipment must not exceed the charge for a minimum carload of the same freight at CL rate, subject to CL minimum weight; the charge for a car fully loaded must not exceed the charge for the same lot of freight if taken as a LCL shipment.

(b)   Except where otherwise provided in tariffs of individual carriers, the provisions of this rule will not apply on shipments on which pick-up or delivery service has been performed, or on which an allowance has been made in lieu of pick-up or delivery service.

Section 2.   If a shipment tendered as LCL freight and loaded by carriers or transported and unloaded by carriers is found to be subject to the carload rate, and the carriers' tariffs do not provide that cost of loading or unloading is included in the CL rate, a charge of 8 cents per 100 pounds will be made for such loading and a like charge for unloading, such charge to be based upon actual weight of shipment. The CL minimum weight to be applied on such shipment will be that applicable to car of size required for shipment in the condition tendered for transportation.

Comment: It is reasonable that the rate on a shipment of packages which do not fill a car should not exceed the rate upon a full carload; this conclusion does not follow, however, when the carrier supplies a service to the shipper of the packages which it does not render to the shipper of carload freight. Rule 15 does not apply to mixed carloads.[23]

RULE 16

Section 1.   When both CL and LCL ratings are provided for the same article, the term LCL covers shipments in quantities less than the minimum

23 147 I.C.C. 271, 273, 1928.

weight provided for carloads, subject to Rule 15; also all shipments regardless of weight upon which pick-up or delivery service is performed, or on which an allowance has been made in lieu of pick-up or delivery service, not subject to Rule 15.

Section 2. A single shipment of less than carload freight is a lot received from one shipper, on one shipping order or bill of lading, at one station, at one time, for one consignee and one destination.

Section 3. Two or more single shipments shall not be combined and way-billed as one shipment, but must be carried as separate shipments and at not less than the established minimum charge for each shipment.

Comment: This is a description of LCL ratings, comparable to that provided in Rule 14 to cover carload freight.

Rule 17

When articles not specifically provided for, nor embraced in the classification as articles "noibn," are offered for transportation, carriers will apply the classification provided for articles which, in their judgment, are analogous; in such cases agents must report facts to proper officer of Freight Department in order that rating applied may be verified and necessary classification provided. This rule will not apply in connection with ratings or rates published in Exceptions to the Classification or in commodity tariffs.

Comment: The abbreviation "noibn" is in lieu of the phrase "not otherwise indicated by name." A classical case of classification by analogy was discussed by Ellis Parker Butler in "Pigs is Pigs." It is hard to see how something of this sort can be avoided, but the practice should not be abused. Incomplete listing produces uncertainty; it may lead to different treatment of the same kind of article in different places because carrier agents may not agree.

Rule 20

Parts or pieces constituting a complete article, received as one shipment, on one bill of lading, will be charged at rating or rate provided for complete article.

Comment: A shipment of tables and of marble tops for tables, moving as one shipment but in separate packages, will be classified as "tables" if the goods are shipped on a single bill of lading; but if the shipper is willing to take the trouble to pack and bill the marble tops separately, these "tops" will be classified by themselves and assigned to a lower group.[24]

Rule 24

Section 1. When CL freight, the authorized minimum weight for which

[24] 251 I.C.C. 311, 1942.

is 30,000 pounds or more, is received in excess of the quantity that can be loaded in or on one car, the following shall apply:

The shipment must be made from one station, by one shipper, in one calendar day running from midnight to midnight, on one shipping order or bill of lading, to one consignee and destination.

Each car, except car carrying excess, must be loaded as heavily as loading conditions will permit, and each car so loaded charged at actual or authorized estimated weight, subject to established minimum CL weight, and at CL rate or rating applicable. . . .

Section 2. The excess over quantity that can be loaded in or on one car shall be charged:

If loaded in one closed, at actual or authorized estimated weight and at CL rate or rating applicable on entire shipment, subject to a minimum weight of 6,000 pounds.

If loaded on one open car, at actual or authorized estimated weight and at CL rate or rating applicable on entire shipment, subject to a minimum charge of 4,000 pounds at class 100 rate.

Section 3. Carriers may handle excess through their freight stations and may load other freight in or on car carrying excess, but unless otherwise provided by tariff where two cars are furnished to accommodate load, no different service will be performed in placing two cars for loading and unloading than would be performed were one car furnished and loaded, except that when trackage disabilities existing at place of loading or unloading make it necessary, cars furnished may be placed at different but adjacent locations, or at the same location at different times.

Section 4. The waybill for each car, whether for excess or full load, must give reference to waybill for each other car used in shipment.

Section 5. This rule will not apply when specific items in this Classification provide otherwise; nor on bulk freight or live stock; nor on freight the character of any portion of which at time of transportation requires and is loaded in either heated, refrigerator, insulated, ventilator or tank cars, or cars specially prepared either by carrier or shipper; nor on freight the authorized minimum CL weight for which is less than 30,000 pounds, nor on freight the minimum CL weights for which are subject to Rule 34, nor on freight subject to Rule 29.

Section 6. Freight in excess of full cars must be marked as required for LCL freight.

Comment: The carload rate per 100 pounds should, normally, apply upon an entire shipment even though the goods cannot all be loaded into a single car. This rule applies the principle, with provisions to prevent abuse.

RULE 27

Section 1. Owners are required to load into or on cars freight for forwarding by rail carriers, and to unload from cars freight received by rail carriers, carried at CL ratings or rates, except when tariff of carriers at point of origin or destination or stopover station (as the case may be) provide for loading or unloading of CL freight by carrier.

Section 2.   Owners are required to load into or on cars heavy or bulky freight for forwarding by rail carriers, and to unload from cars heavy or bulky freight received by rail carriers, carried at LCL or any quantity rates or rating which cannot be handled by regular station employees or at stations where carrier's loading or unloading facilities are not sufficient for handling.

Comment: Shippers and consignees usually must load and unload freight shipped in carload quantities. See Rule 14. There are, however, exceptions. This rule is explicit. If the carrier does load or unload freight it is entitled to make a reasonable charge for the service.[25]

Rule 38

Unless otherwise provided in the governing tariffs, if there is an effective commodity rate on a given shipment that rate and not the class rate must be applied, except that rates (either class or commodity) specifically designated as applicable only on import, export, coastwise or inter-coastal shipments must be applied on such shipments to the exclusion of all other rates not so designated.

Comment: Commodity descriptions are applied strictly, and only articles clearly embraced within a commodity description will be treated as removed from the classification. Thus a commodity description "cotton goods in the piece" does not include "cotton plush," although plush is made from cotton and is sold "in the piece." [26]

The classification rules reprinted in the preceding pages are among those most frequently consulted by railroad employees. The reader will observe that the rules do not follow each other in an orderly fashion according to the subject treated. This is because they were not all prepared at a single time but have evolved as the need for them has become apparent. For the same reason some rules, such as Rules 14 and 15, or Rules 10 and 12, are general in scope while others, such as Rules 20 or 38, would seem to have been provoked by arguments which had not been foreseen.

The way problems of interpretation may accumulate may be illustrated by the rules related to carload freight. In general, carload rates are much lower than are rates for shipments in smaller quantities, so that it is advantageous to shippers to cause their consignments to be classed as "carloads." This the carrier will do, but only on certain conditions, the chief of which is that a minimum quantity is offered. But this condition raises at once a number of problems. What, for example, is a fair minimum? Is a minimum always unfair when the article is so bulky that the specified amount cannot be loaded into a standard car? Suppose that a shipper

[25] 269 I.C.C. 25, 1947.
[26] Cf. 225 I.C.C. 556, 557, 1937.

orders a car of a certain size and that the carrier supplies a larger car. Shall the shipper be held to the minimum on the car which he ordered, or to the minimum on the car which he uses? Must the goods in a carload shipment all be presented to the carrier at one time? Must they all be owned by a single shipper, or may a number of shippers combine and offer their goods together? May shippers of carloads require the railroad to deliver to several consignees or only to one consignee? May a number of differently classified articles be placed in a carload to make up the minimum weight, and if this is permissible, what rate and what minimum will apply when the various articles are subject to different classification requirements? Does a shipment become a carload merely because it is shipped in carload quantities, or are there other differences between carload and less-than-carload consignments, such, for instance, as that shippers load and unload the freight in the one case and the carriers load and unload it in the other? What happens when enough freight is offered to fill a carload and a half? Does the first carload pay a low rate and the remaining half carload a higher rate, or does the entire shipment take the carload rating upon a poundage basis? These are only some of the problems which present themselves in connection with carload shipments. The rules reproduced in the text do not answer all the questions which have been asked, but they do attempt to settle some possible disputes and to do this in advance before transportation shall have taken place. So do the rules which relate to less than carloads, to order shipments, to the relative precedence of class and commodity rates, and to other questions of these sorts.

REFERENCES

General Treatises

Bigham, Truman C., and Roberts, Merrill J., *Transportation, Principles and Problems,* New York, McGraw-Hill, 1952.

Fair, Marvin L., and Williams, Ernest W., *Economics of Transportation,* New York, Harper, 1950.

Healy, Kent T., *The Economics of Transportation in America,* New York, Ronald, 1940.

Landon, Charles E., *Transportation, Principles, Practices, Problems,* New York, Sloane, 1951.

Locklin, D. Philip, *Economics of Transportation,* Chicago, Irwin, 1947.

Pauer, Albert, *Lehrbuch der Eisenbahntarifwesen,* Wien, K. K. Hof- und staatsdruckerei, 1900.

Westmeyer, Russell E., *Economics of Transportation,* New York, Prentice-Hall, 1952.

Other Books

Colton, R. C., *Practical Handbook of Industrial Traffic Management,* New York, Funk and Wagnalls, 1953.

Knorst, William J., *Transportation and Traffic Management,* Chicago, College of Advanced Traffic, 4 vols, 1949.

Strombeck, J. F., *Freight Classification,* Boston, Houghton Mifflin, 1912.

Van Metre, Thurman W., *Industrial Traffic Management,* New York, Mcgraw-Hill, 1953.

Wilson, G. Lloyd, *Railroad Freight Classification, Rates, and Tariffs,* Washington, D.C., Traffic Service Corporation, 1950.

Periodicals

Barton, F. L., "Uniform Freight Classification and the Interstate Commerce Commission," *Journal of Land and Public Utility Economics,* August, 1942.

Shannon, Homer H., "History of Freight Classification," *Traffic World,* January 31, 1931.

Special and Miscellaneous

The Freight Traffic Red Book, New York, Traffic Publishing.

The Motor Truck Red Book, New York, Traffic Publishing.

United States Interstate Commerce Commission, Bureau of Transport Economics and Statistics, *Weight Density and Value as Factors in Freight Classification,* March, 1946.

Freight Tariffs—Mileage Scales

Freight Tariffs

We may now pass from the subject of classification to that of tariffs. In most instances the tariff is a separate publication, varying in size from a single sheet to a volume equal in magnitude to the Uniform Classification itself. Tariffs may be of several kinds, but we will here distinguish between "class" and "commodity" tariffs.[1] The former state rates per 100 pounds which will be charged for the transportation of groups of articles which the classification has set up, between points of origin and destination that the tariff names or for distances which the tariff specifies. Thus a rate will be quoted on all articles in Class I from A to B but not, separately, on each article described. Articles in Class I or in any other class may be diverse and they need not be related to or be in competition with each other, but they will have common characteristics to the extent mentioned in discussing the principles of classification. The commodity tariff differs from the class rate publication. Each commodity tariff quotes rates, characteristically, on a list of articles, but on a restricted list. There may be a commodity tariff on canned goods, another on dried fruits and vegetables, another on automobile bodies and parts, and another on clothing. For any article it is still possible, though not always without effort, to find a class rate, in appropriate tariffs on any commodity, for

[1] There is enough variety in tariff publication to encourage somewhat extensive listing. Thus tariffs may be distinguished according to the source of issue, as "individual line" and "agency" tariffs. Another distinction is between publications which quote rates—"rate tariffs,"—and those which provide only bases and rules for the quotation of rates. Rate tariffs include issues which quote class rates, issues which quote commodity rates, few or many, and issues which cover both class and commodity rates. Both class and commodity tariffs may be further subdivided according as the rates which they contain are local, joint or interline, proportional, or some combination of these types. In a technical sense a classification is itself a tariff in that it provides a basis for quoting rates. See Glenn L. Shinn, *Freight Rate Application*, New York, Simmons-Boardman, 1948.

shipment between any two stations in the United States. But when the volume of movement is great or the competition severe there will also be a commodity tariff, covering a selection of articles which are commercially alike. The rate in the commodity tariff will, generally, be lower in such instances and it will, therefore, be used in preference to the class rate.[2] Most tonnage, though not necessarily most shipments, move on commodity rates. On September 28, 1942, 77 percent of the intraterritorial carload traffic originating in Official Territory moved on such rates, as did more than 90 percent of the intraterritorial carload traffic originating in other parts of the United States.[3]

Tariffs are prepared according to rules laid down by regulatory commissions.[4] They must be filled with appropriate regulating bodies. Once printed and filed, the rates in a tariff must be adhered to; and the statutory rule which requires adherence to the published price is enforced by severe penalties.

Tariff Bureaus and Traffic Associations

Tariffs may be prepared and printed by individual railroads or motor carriers; most tariffs, however, are published by agents or by associations working for carrier groups; and this is convenient because it makes it likely that, at any time, carriers which serve the same localities will charge the same rates.[5]

[2] Commodity tariffs, like class tariffs, distinguish between carload and less-than-carload rates and state the minimum weight which must be shipped if the lower carload rate is to be applied.

[3] United States Board of Investigation and Research, *Transportation Act of 1940,* "Report on Interterritorial Freight Rates," Table 31, p. 57. See also United States Interstate Commerce Commission, *Class Rate Investigation* (262 I.C.C. 447, 564, 1945). The predominance of commodity ratings will probably be decreased by the adoption of the Uniform Classification. See chap. 16.

[4] These rules may be very elaborate. The most extensive are those prepared by the Interstate Commerce Commission for the guidance of railroads. These rules specify the size of the tariff, the contents of the title page and of the index, the order in which information is to be presented, the symbols to be used, the number of permitted supplements, the method of amendment or cancellation, and they contain page after page of other directions intended to insure clarity and completeness in tariff publication. Motor vehicles engaged in interstate commerce are also subject to Interstate Commerce control, and other commissions, state and federal, issue tariff orders within the limits of their jurisdiction.

[5] The principal freight associations are the following:

1. The New England Freight Association
2. The Trunk Line Association
3. The Central Freight Association
4. The Illinois Freight Association
5. The Southern Freight Association
6. The Western Trunk Line Committee
7. The Southwestern Freight Bureau
8. The Texas-Louisiana Freight Bureau
9. The Transcontinental Freight Bureau

Tariff bureaus and traffic associations not only publish tariffs, but they provide place, time, and established procedure for the consideration of rate changes. For this purpose several levels of committees are organized in each of a number of railroad "rate bureau territories." Thus in Trunk Line territory, in 1943, shippers might file application with a member railroad for a change in rate. This application would be docketed, making the proposal public. Likewise a member carrier might suggest a change on its own initiative and this, also, would be docketed. If no objection was received within 12 days from either the public or from other railroads, the new rate would be published. If there were objections, the matter would be referred to a so-called "General Freight Committee," made up of general freight agents of member lines. Such agents would be the lowest grade of general officers in the various railroad traffic departments. If the decision of the General Freight Committee should not be satisfactory, then each shipper or carrier could appeal to a "Freight Traffic Managers' Committee," and again to a "Traffic Executive Association," made up, in this last instance, of vice-presidents of railroads. This would be the final phase except in the rare case when there was appeal to railroad presidents.[6] The organization of motor and inland water associations is, on the whole, simpler than that of railroad associations, but there is generally provision for discussion of rate changes at several levels with opportunity for carrier and sometimes for shipper appeal. In all cases, members of traffic associations reserve the right of independent action if they choose to disregard the final decision reached through association machinery.

Traffic associations, finally, consider other matters ranging from trivial cases to issues of considerable scope and importance. Problems of the latter

---

10. The Pacific South Coast Freight Tariff Bureau
11. The North Pacific Coast Freight Tariff Bureau
12. The Pacific Southwest Freight Bureau
13. The Montana Lines Committee
14. The Northern Lines Committee

The principal passenger associations are the following:

1. The New England Passenger Association
2. The Trunk Line Association—Passenger Department
3. The Central Passenger Association
4. The Southern Passenger Association
5. The Southwestern Passenger Association
6. The Western Passenger Association
7. The Transcontinental Passenger Association

In addition to these leading associations, passenger and freight, there are a number of minor or local associations, sometimes with jurisdiction over a state or over some other small defined sections, as in the case of the Utah Freight Bureau or the Texas Freight Bureau, sometimes limited to a single city or to a single class of traffic, as in the case of the Buffalo Freight Committee, the Cincinnati Freight Committee, the Ohio Coal Traffic Association, or the Gulf Foreign Freight Committee.

[6] United States Senate, Committee on Interstate Commerce, 78th C., 1st S., Hearings on S. 942, May, 1943, testimony Franklin.

sort have included the publication of rates over circuitous routes, the technique to be followed in reducing railroad rates in order to meet truck competition, and the establishment of joint rates between rail and motor carriers. Carriers also confer through their associations when they have to deal with orders of the Interstate Commerce Commission, such as those combining classifications or requiring large-scale adjustments of territorial rates, or when they study similar questions upon their own initiative.

Litigation and Legislation on the Subject of Traffic Associations

Early traffic association agreements were more exacting than those effective at the present time. They provided, among other things, for actual fixing of rates by a committee or by an executive officer of the association and for the pooling or division of the revenues obtained. There was a somewhat elaborate staff and penalties for infringement. The association performed certain service functions for its members and had machinery for the arbitration of disputes.[7] The powers of these bodies were, however, reduced in the late 1880's and during the 1890's by legislation and by court decision.

Antipooling and Antitrust Legislation

The two laws which most affected the activity of traffic associations until quite recent years were the Interstate Act of 1887 and the Antitrust Act of 1890. The first of these forbade pooling;[8] the second prohibited combinations in restraint of trade or commerce. As a result of the former, pooling clauses disappeared from traffic association agreements. As for combinations, the carriers did not at first believe that the Antitrust Act applied to railroads. The Supreme Court took the opposite position,[9] with the result that associations were compelled to emphasize their service functions and to minimize their coercive powers. These powers were, indeed, greatly weakened when the Interstate Commerce Commission secured authority to fix through rates and shippers obtained the right to route. On the other hand, later Supreme Court decisions in the Standard Oil and Tobacco cases were interpreted as permitting agreements in furtherance of the Act to Regulate Commerce so long as these agreements preserved the right of independent action and were not apparently coercive. Moreover, there was a tendency to neglect the implications of court decisions of 1897 and 1898 and of the failure of Congress to grant exemptions to railroads in the acts of 1910 and 1914,[10] because of an expanding

[7] Henry Hudson, "The Southern Railway and Steamship Association," *Quarterly Journal of Economics,* October, 1890.

[8] 24 Stat. 529, 530, 1887.

[9] 166 U.S. 290, 1897; 171 U.S. 505, 1898.

[10] In 1910 a bill which ultimately became the Act of 1910 included, at one time, a section which declared that agreements between common carriers specifying or related

and intelligent commission regulation of matters with which traffic associations were normally concerned and because of the tendency of Congress, in special areas, to relax the antitrust laws.[11]

It is probably not surprising that traffic associations multiplied instead of disappearing, in the light of the tendencies just referred to. According to testimony presented by the Department of Justice in 1943, there were then sixty committees and conferences in the railroad field concerned with the making of railroad rates, in addition to the Association of American Railroads, which then represented approximately 98 percent of the Class I railroads in the country. Mr. Wiprud, special assistant to the Attorney General, has referred to these conferences as the private rate making machinery of the United States. The record does not show the number of associations in different years. The Transcontinental Freight Bureau was, however, investigated in 1923, traffic organizations generally were the subject of criticism in 1929, the Western Commissioner agreement was effective in 1932, and the Association of American Railroads became operative in 1934, at which time it established relations with preëxisting territorial rate bureaus in different parts of the United States. We may fairly assume that traffic associations functioned continuously, at least

---

to classifications of freight and the rates, fares, and charges for the transportation of passengers and freight should not be unlawful under the Antitrust Act if filed with the Interstate Commerce Commission within twenty days after being made, but that the rates, fares, and charges provided in the agreement should be subject to the Interstate Commerce Law (61st C., 2d S., H. R. 923, April 1, 1910, Ser. 5592, pp. 75–76).

Likewise the Clayton antitrust bill of 1914 at one time provided that nothing in the antitrust laws should be construed to forbid associations of traffic, operating, accounting or other officers of common carriers for the purpose of conferring among themselves or of making any lawful agreement as to any matter which was subject to the regulatory or supervisory jurisdiction of the Interstate Commerce Commission. The Chairman of the Interstate Commerce Commission approved this clause (63d C., 2d S., vol. 51, pt. 10, p. 9585).

Neither of the sections mentioned was included in the laws as passed.

[11] Congressional exemptions cover labor and agricultural organizations, and associations engaged in export trade.

A slightly different example is the relief from the antitrust laws stipulated in the National Industrial Recovery Act of 1933 (48 Stat. 195, 1933) and in the Bituminous Coal Act of 1937 (50 Stat. 72, 1937). These statutes protected producers in the promulgation and administration of industrial codes. A third group consists of public utility and carrier companies which are permitted to coöperate under the supervision of some regulative agency. Most common carriers, under existing laws, are now permitted to consolidate with other common carriers if the government agency which controls them finds the consolidation to be in the public interest. The permission extends to telephone companies (48 Stat. 1064, 1934, Sec. 221), to air companies (52 Stat. 973, 1938, Sec. 408B), and to rail, motor, and water companies (I.C.A. as amended, Sec. 5, pars. 1, 2, and 11). But in addition to consolidation, the Shipping Act of 1916 (39 Stat. 728, 1916, Sec. 15), the Civil Aeronautics Act of 1938 (52 Stat. 973, 1938), and the Interstate Commerce Act authorize agreements, not involving consolidation, and these are exempted from the antitrust laws. The exemptions in the Civil Aeronautics Act are especially complete.

during all these years, and also that they became increasingly active after the depression of the 1930's had set in.

The Reed-Bulwinkle Act

In 1927, in the Trenton Potteries case [12] and again in 1940 in the Socony-Vacuum case [13] the Supreme Court of the United States handed down decisions based upon a strict interpretation of the Antitrust Act of 1890. Neither of these decisions directly affected common carriers; but both encouraged critics to believe that traffic associations were more vulnerable than they had latterly been supposed to be. Among the results were the initiation of suits, one by the State of Georgia,[14] and another by the United States Department of Justice. The latter particularly attacked the Association of American Railroads and a long list of co-conspirators, alleging combinations in restraint of trade and attempts to monopolize. For their part, the carriers sought new legislation. Their efforts terminated successfully in June, 1948, with the passage of the so-called Reed-Bulwinkle bill.[15] This statute, at least for the moment, makes the position of traffic associations secure.

The principal provisions of the Reed-Bulwinkle bill are as follows:

1. The Act applies to common carriers by rail, highway, and inland water routes and to freight forwarders, which are subject to the Interstate Commerce Act.

2. Carriers of these various sorts which are parties to certain types of rate agreement may apply to the Interstate Commerce Commission for its approval of these agreements.

3. The Commission may approve the agreement which is submitted or it may disapprove. The Act supplies standards for approval and also indicates applications which the Commission is directed to disapprove.[16]

---

[12] 273 U.S. 392, 1927.

[13] 310 U.S. 150, 1940. See also 288 U.S. 344, 1933.

[14] See 324 U.S. 439, 1945.

[15] 62 Stat. 472, 1948.

[16] The significant language relating to approval is as follows:

"Sec. 5a (2) Any party to an agreement between or among two or more carriers relating to rates, fares, classifications, divisions, allowances, or charges (including charges between carriers and compensation paid or received for the use of facilities and equipment), or rules and regulations pertaining thereto, or procedures for the joint consideration, initiation, or establishment thereof, may under such rules and regulations as the Commission may prescribe, apply to the Commission for approval of the agreement, and the Commission shall by order approve any such agreement (if approval thereof is not prohibited by paragraph (4), (5), or (6) if it finds that, by reason of furtherance of the national transportation policy declared in this Act, the relief provided in paragraph (9) should apply to the making and carrying out of such agreement, otherwise the application shall be denied. The approval of the Commission shall be granted only upon such terms and conditions as the Commission may prescribe as necessary to enable it to grant its approval in accordance with the standard above set forth in this paragraph."

4. Parties to any agreement approved by the Commission and other persons under certain circumstances are relieved from the operation of the antitrust laws with respect to the making and carrying out of the agreement.

5. Bureaus, etc., set up by agreement must maintain accounts and files which shall be open to inspection by the Interstate Commerce Commission and shall make such reports as the Commission may require.

The Reed-Bulwinkle bill assumes (1) that tariff bureaus and associations provide an efficient procedure for the discussion and coordination of carrier rates, rules, and regulations; (2) that associations do, upon the whole, encourage constructive consideration of the larger problems of the carrier industry, but that, in their operation, they should be subject to public control; and (3) that some limitation of competition is involved, but that the regulatory authority of the Interstate Commerce Commission can and will protect the public interest. These assumptions are, probably, correct. Carriers would not cease operating if they were forbidden to make use of association machinery, but their efficiency would be impaired.[17]

Simple Forms of Rate Quotation

The tariff is the price list of the carrier industry. Its construction, like that of the classification, is designed to present in intelligible form the information concerning rates which shippers of freight require. For this the foundation has been laid in the classification. Thanks to this last-named publication the tariff is able to quote rates, to a considerable extent, on groups of articles and not on named commodities, though it will quote them on specified commodities whenever the importance of the article and the need of special treatment justifies the practice. In any case, it has to provide rates to and from specific stations, a problem with which the maker of the classification has not been concerned (see Table 17). As the size of the tariff increases the devices for condensation multiply. Instead of quoting a separate charge in the case of every pair of towns, points of origin and destination are grouped and the same schedule of rates is applied from every town in one group to every town in another. Lists of towns in the various groups may be published in a separate section of the tariff or in a publication such as a directory. Sometimes the rate to or from a given point is quoted as an arbitrary over the rate charged to or from another point. Sometimes a tariff attaches a letter or number to each point of origin and another to each point of destination.

---

[17] Stuart Daggett, "Railroad Traffic Associations and Antitrust Legislation," *American Economic Review*, May, 1948, no. 2, pp. 452–464; A. C. Wiprud, *Justice in Transportation*, New York, Ziff-Davis, 1945; United States Senate, Committee on Interstate and Foreign Commerce, 78th C., 1st S., Hearings on S. 942, 1943; United States House of Representatives. Committee on Interstate and Foreign Commerce, 80th C., 2d S., Hearings on H. R. 2536, 1946.

FREIGHT TARIFFS

(Part I. I. C. Act.)

(Form prescribed by I. C. C. Tariff Circular No. 20, effective October 1, 1928, and as amended, also in harmony with Tariff Circular—A. A. R. No. 4, dated August 15, 1940—W. J. Kelly, Chairman.)

Subject to Tariff of Increased Rates and Charges No. X-162-B and X-166-C, Agent C. W. Boin's I. C. C. No. A-882, Agent I. N. Doe's I. C. C. No. 572, supplements thereto or successive issues thereof and to Tariff of Increased Rates and Charges X-168-A, Agent C. W. Boin's I. C. C. No. A-890, Agent I. N. Doe's I. C. C. No. 581, supplements thereto or successive issues thereof.

(Temporarily to be shown on issues that contain rates which do not include the increase granted under Ex Parte General Increased Rates and Charges.)

No Supplement to this Tariff will be issued except for the purpose of canceling the Tariff, unless otherwise specifically authorized by the Commission.
(To be shown on tariffs of less than 5 pages and on tariffs issued in loose-leaf form.)
(Rule 3a, Circular 20.)

I. C. C. No. ——.
(Cancels I. C. C. No. ——.)
(Rule 3b, Circular 20.)

N. & S. R. R. TARIFF No. ——.
(Cancels Tariff No. ——.)
(Use of Road's Tariff No. Optional. If used, tariffs should be assigned a serial number and as reissued be given a *letter suffix.*)
(Rule 3b, Cir. 20 and Rec. 30, Tariff Cir. A. A. R. No. 4.)

NORTH & SOUTH RAILROAD

(Rules 3c and 4b, Cir. 20.)

IN CONNECTION WITH

(Rules 3c and 4b, Cir. 20.)
Full corporate names of carriers must be shown.

BALTIMORE & OHIO R. R. (FX4-No.——.)
CENTRAL R. R. CO. OF NEW JERSEY (FX5-No. ——.)
EAST & WEST R. R. (FX4-No. ——.)
NEW YORK CENTRAL R. R. (FX4-N. Y. C. No. ——.)
PENNSYLVANIA R. R. (FX4-No. ——.)
(AND OTHER RAILROADS AS SHOWN ON PAGE 2.)

LOCAL and/or JOINT and/or PROPORTIONAL and/or EXPORT and/or IMPORT

FREIGHT TARIFF

(Rule 3d, Cir. 20.)

CLASS AND COMMODITY RATES

OF

' Rule 3d, Cir 20 '

FROM STATIONS ON THE *(Rule 3e, Cir. 20.)*	TO STATIONS ON *(Rule 3e, Cir. 20.)*
NORTH and SOUTH RAILROAD (AS NAMED WITHIN)	EAST and WEST RAILROAD (AS NAMED WITHIN)

(Points of origin and destination to the number of 12 (each) may, if practicable, be shown on Title Page—Rules 3e, and 4d, Cir. 20.) [Form of Origin and Destination Stations, as per Recommendation 13 (a), Tariff Circular—A. A. R. No. 4. dated August 15, 1940.]

	Tariff No.	I. C. C. No.	Issued by Agent
Governed, except as otherwise provided herein, by:			
Official Classification	CFC-18	OC-62	A. H. Greenly
Exceptions to Official Classification	90-K	A-848	C. W. Boin
Miscellaneous Rules and Regulations	515-E	3939	B. T. Jones
and by supplements to or successive issue of said publications.			

This tariff contains rates that are higher for shorter than longer distances over the same routes. Such departures from the terms of the amended Fourth Section of the Interstate Commerce Act are permitted by authority of Interstate Commerce Commission Fourth Section Order No. 10090. (Rule 28, Circular 20.)

Transportation service in connection with The East and West R. R. is subject to restoration and discontinuance as indicated on page 4. See bottom of pages for tariff page numbers. (Rule 12, Circular 20.)

Issued December 26, 1949.   Effective February 1, 1950.

(Except as otherwise provided herein.)

(Rules 3g, 14a and 54, Cir. 20. If tariff is to be effective on less than 30 days' notice, Rules 3h, 9d and 14a of Tariff Cir. No. 20 will have to be observed.)

RICHARD ROE,
General Freight Agent,
———————— City.

JOHN JONES,
Ass't General Freight Agent,
———————— City.

JOHN SMITH,
Division Freight Agent,
————————, N. Y.

Issued by
JOHN DOE,
Chief of Tariff Bureau,
922 John Street,
———————— City.
(Rule 3i, Cir. 20.)

(Showing different Officials is optional with carrier, however, discouraged by the Commission. The Division Freight Agent to be shown is the one from whose territory the rates apply, if a road desires to adopt such plan.)

(1000)
(Indicates supply printed.)

RECEIVED		
Month	Day	Year

(File ——————)

Must be shown on title page   Order of I. C. C. June 7, 1915. effective July 15, 1915.
Tariffs should be printed from type of size not less than 8 point bold or full-face, on hard-calendered paper or No. 1 machine-finished book paper of durable quality, except that 6 point bold face type may be used for reference marks, and for explanation of reference marks when appearing on same page that such reference marks appear and for column headings and other places when only a few words are used continuously. (Rule 1, Cir. 20.)

FIGURE 35.   Sample Tariff Title Page.   (Courtesy of *Freight Traffic Red Book,* Traffic Publishing Company, New York.)

TABLE 17. Rate and Classification Practice

Two simple forms of rate quotation may provide an elementary illustration of tariff-making technique.

I

Class Rates Between Northville and Southville, U.S.A.
(Rates in cents per 100 pounds)

Classes	1	2	3	4	5	6	Rule 25	Rule 26
Rates	20	17	15	11	10	8	15	12

II

Rates Between Points in Kansas and Kansas City, St. Joseph, Omaha, and Sioux City
(Rates in cents per 100 pounds)

Point in Kansas	City	1	2	3	4	5
Meriden	Kansas City	36½	30	24	19	12½
	St. Joseph	36½	30	24	19	12½
	Omaha	75	56½	44	34	27½
	Sioux City	100	81½	56½	44	34
Lang	Kansas City	59	49	39	32	25
	St. Joseph	59	49	39	32	25
	Omaha	84	71½	57½	47	37½
	Sioux City	109	90	70	57	46½
(etc.)	(etc.)	(etc.)				

Assembly of these symbols leads to the discovery of the number of a scale and this in turn to the identification of a schedule which supplies rates for each class covered by the tariff. This practice makes it unnecessary to present a complete set of rates in connection with every movement. Sometimes general rules are published. Thus rates to certain cities may be recognized as maxima in the case of hauls on stated routes from named points of origin. Air, water, and motor tariffs are usually less complicated than railroad tariffs because of the smaller number of prices which they have to express. The variety of expedients is considerable; it must be admitted that shippers often find it difficult to interpret a tariff in the form in which it is presented unless they become familiar with the document by extensive use. Simplification in such instances contributes to brevity of statement but not to ease of understanding.

The main difference between the problems presented in classification

making and those presented in tariff making is that the latter deal with
relations in space and the former do not. But the reverse is not true,
namely, that classifications deal with questions of cost and of value while
tariffs do not. This is partly because tariffs are quoted for the transportation of articles which are not classified; but it is also because the rates
applied to different classification groups, no less than the groupings themselves, follow variations in cost, competition, value, and other circumstances of which the classifications take note. But while influences which
affect classification have their bearing upon rates, we shall discuss mileage
rates in the present chapter, and these principally with regard to space
relations, with such other comments as it may seem proper to inject.[18]

Mileage Tariffs

Strictly speaking, a tariff is a mileage tariff when its rates increase in
some systematic relation to the distance hauled. Tariffs in new or noncompetitive territory or on noncompetitive traffic may be of this sort.
There are two types of tariffs, namely, those which name specific rates
from A to B and from C to D, and tariffs which quote rates of so much
a mile, irrespective of point of origin or destination. We shall call the last-
named, "mileage scales." Federal rules in the United States require that
tariffs specify the stations between which rates are charged, and carrier
schedules, accordingly, are only of this sort. On the other hand, commission decisions frequently set up scales to which mileage tariffs must conform, and any tariff can be translated into a scale for purposes of analysis.
We shall refer to scales rather than to tariffs in the balance of this chapter
in order to discuss with the greatest possible clarity certain problems which
mileage rate making presents.

Forms of Mileage Scales

We have said that a mileage scale provides a basis of rates which increase in some systematic relation to the distance hauled. The unit of
distance need not be the single mile. Thus for convenience in constructing
schedules American scales usually make use of zones. That is to say, class
rates are established for blocks of 5 miles up to a distance of 100 miles,
then in blocks of 10 miles up to a distance of 240 miles, then in blocks of
20 miles until the 800-mile point is reached, then in blocks of 25 miles
for distances over 900 and up to and including 2,200 miles, and in blocks
of 50 miles for distances over 2,200 and up to and including 3,000 miles.
In the case of commodity scales there are likely to be zones of greater

---

[18] The reader who is interested in the subject may be referred to Clark's discussion
of mileage rates and consumers and producers' surplus (J. M. Clark, *Standards of
Reasonableness in Local Freight Discriminations,* New York, Columbia University,
Studies in History, Economics and Public Law, vol. 37, no. 1, 1910, chap. 9.

length in the shorter distances although, in scales prescribed by the Interstate Commerce Commission, the breadth of a zone rarely exceeds 50
miles. Schedules on such a basis may still be treated as mileage scales
since the zones form part of a consistent scheme, uniformly applied.

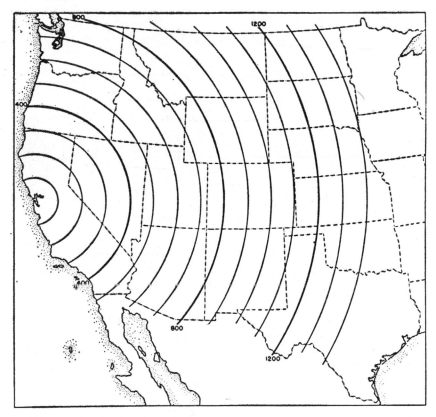

FIGURE 36.   Air Distances from San Francisco at Intervals of 100 Miles.

The form which a governing railroad scale may take can be illustrated
by the basic scale of first-class rates prescribed by the Interstate Commerce
Commission in 1951 for ultimate application in all rate territories in the
United States. The rates in this scale for distances up to and including
50 miles were as follows:

Distances	Rate (cents per 100 pounds)
5 miles and under	58
10 miles and over 5 miles	64
15 miles and over 10 miles	69
20 miles and over 15 miles	73

25 miles and over 20 miles	76
30 miles and over 25 miles	80
35 miles and over 30 miles	83
40 miles and over 35 miles	86
45 miles and over 40 miles	89
50 miles and over 45 miles	91

SOURCE:　281 I.C.C. 213, 1951.

Technical problems to be solved in constructing a mileage scale include the following:

CALCULATION OF DISTANCES.　It is by no means easy to determine

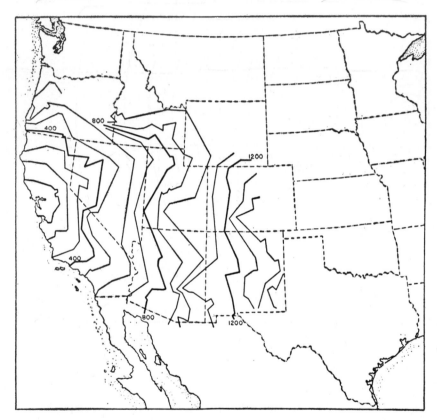

FIGURE 37.　Rail-Route Distances from San Francisco at Intervals of 100 Miles.

the distances to which mileage scales shall be applied. Contrary to ordinary assumption, distance is an elusive thing. Distances by air are different from distances by rail and motor between given points, because of irregularities in surface terrain. This fact can be inferred from Fig. 37 which shows the rail distances from San Francisco, California, at intervals of 100

miles. Rail mileages in one direction may be greater than in the other because a route may follow a shorter line on descending than on rising grades.
Rail and motor mileages, for tariff purposes, are sometimes replaced by
"constructive" or "arbitrary" mileages to allow, partially, for conditions
of cost due to physical obstacles, or to scarcity of traffic. And finally, it
will always be necessary to choose one out of several possible routes when
there is more than one line between point of origin and point of destination. The principles of selection in this last case have been the subject of
extended discussion. The shortest route over which carload traffic can be
moved without transfer of bill of lading is, however, the route which the
Interstate Commerce Commission will now approve.[19]

Terminal Charges

Mileage tariffs require the elaboration of still other practices besides
those relating to the form of rate quotation and to the determination of

[19] In the Central Freight Association case the carriers ordinarily used the shortest
workable routes in presenting their proposals for revision of rates, and the rates calculated over the shortest workable routes were applied to shipments over longer routes
between the same destinations. There were, it is true, some exceptions. Thus, if a short
route involved a two-line haul it was not used if either of the lines composing it had
a longer but reasonably direct route of its own between points of origin and destination. Routes via two or more lines in the same railway system were given preference
over routes by way of railroads which had no corporate connection with one another,
and practicable routes which a shipper would expect to use were taken in preference
to unused or theoretical routes. The Commission assented to these methods except in
certain matters of detail.

The Central Freight Association case was decided in 1917. Eight years later, in the
Southern Class Rate case, the Commission considered routing practice once more in
connection with mileage tariffs, and now required the use of the shortest possible route
in fixing rates instead of the shortest workable route, embracing as a maximum, however, the lines of not more than three carriers for distances up to 200 miles, four
carriers for distances from 200 to 500 miles, and five carriers for longer distances. One
year afterward, in 1926, on petition of the carriers, it restored the old requirement of
using the shortest workable route, but defined the phase to mean the shortest route
that was, irrespective of existing traffic arrangements, physically adapted to the movement of traffic without plain and serious sacrifice of economy and efficiency. Again, on
further representation that the determination of an "economical distance," as contrasted
with an absolute short-line distance, involved the use of informed judgment and
opened the door for endless argument as to the correctness of the results reached, the
Commission redefined the term "shortest workable route" in a new proceeding as the
shortest route over which carload traffic could be moved without transfer of lading.
This final formulation was the one used in the Western Trunk Line case, in the Eastern
Class Rate investigation, and in the Class Rate Investigation, 1939; it is the one which
may be deemed finally approved. The ultimate solution is not entirely satisfactory to
the carriers, some of which, at least, argue that the Commission's rule produces rates
based on routes that are uneconomical and never used, and that it deprives the
originating carrier of its statutory right to use the whole length of its line. The failure
to allow an arbitrary amount to cover the added cost of shipments that require a two-
or-more-line haul is also the subject of criticism. However, the simplicity of the prescribed rule and the objective character of the tests applied have convinced the
Commission of its merit, while the added cost of two-line hauls is provided for in determining the level of the general scale.

distance. There is, for instance, the question of the terminal charge. The cost of moving shipments may be analyzed into terminal and conveyance costs, and both types of expense must be provided for in the rates. English scales do this in one way, and American in another. Thus in England there is a separate schedule for terminals, apart from the haulage rate. The English list of terminal charges includes a payment for the use of the terminal and, in addition, charges for loading and unloading, and covering and uncovering, where these services are rendered. On the other hand, American railroads normally weigh, load, and unload piece goods without separate charge, covering the expense involved by an addition to the general rate, or at least partially covering this expense; for it is probable that, in the United States, some of the terminal outlay is provided from the conveyance rate of the first few miles.

Terminal costs include at least platform costs, clerical costs, switching, and car detention, and a return upon the value or cost of physical facilities that are used. These expenses are partly dependent upon volume of business, but not entirely so. The Interstate Commerce Commission, in 1942, examined the platform costs incurred in handling less than carload tonnage at 22 cities, mostly located in California, and found that the total platform expense per ton ranged from 29 to 160 cents as of the year 1938, and that the largest costs per ton were at San Francisco and Los Angeles, where the volume of business was greatest.[20] The interesting suggestion was that platform costs increase with volume. However, it may not be true, even in California cities, that, at a given terminal, an increase in volume will result in larger unit costs. This will certainly not be true if initial terminal capacity is incompletely utilized.

A second Commission study, published in 1943, stated conclusions with respect to the level of terminal and line haul costs for various railroad loadings and for various sections of the United States as of the year 1939.[21] Table 18 presents certain facts drawn from this report.

The data reproduced in Table 18 constitute only a small portion of the Commission's report. But they show that, according to the Commission's calculations, terminal costs on railroad less than carload movements in box cars were 40 cents for each 100 pounds on loads of 5 tons and approximately 36 cents on loads of 10 tons. On carload shipments the terminal cost was 16.881 cents per 100 pounds on loads of 5 tons, 9.276 cents on loads of 10 tons, and 4.206 cents on loads of 30 tons. Such terminal costs, which are independent of the distance over which freight,

[20] United States Interstate Commerce Commission, Bureau of Transport Economics and Statistics, *Territorial Rail Costs Based on a Separation of the Out-of-Pocket and Constant Expenses, 1939,* September, 1942, p. 35.

[21] United States Senate, *Rail Freight Service Costs in the Various Rate Territories of the United States,* 78th C., 1st S., Sen. Doc. 63, 1943.

TABLE 18.   Rail Terminal and Line Costs, United States, for
Shipments Moving in Boxcars, 1939

Load (tons)	Terminal (cents per 100 pounds)		Line Haul (cents per 100 pounds per mile)	
	C.L.	L.C.L.	C.L.	L.C.L.
5	16.881	40.325	.098179	.10529
10	9.276	35.605	.060499	.06255
15	6.741	34.025	.047938	.04829
20	5.474	—	.041659	
25	4.713	—	.037891	
30	4.206	—	.035380	

when loaded, will ultimately pass, must be provided for in any mileage scale.[22]

Rate of Progression

The rate of progression in a mileage scale may be determined by the necessity of fitting the particular schedule into some larger structure. Thus in the Southern Class Rate Investigation the carriers proposed to build a scale around three so-called "peg" points: first, an initial rate of 30 cents, to be justified by studies of terminal costs; second, a rate of 145 cents for 330 miles, which was the rate and distance from Cairo to Birmingham; and third, a rate of 160 cents for 460 miles, which was the rate and distance from Atlanta to the Ohio River. The second and third pegs were derived from rates previously established by the Interstate Commerce Commission. Similarly, in constructing a scale for use in Central Freight Association territory, the carriers assumed as a rule that the sixth-class rate for the distance of 475 miles between Chicago and the western termini of the trunk lines should not exceed 16 cents, because any greater sum would exceed the existing rate from Chicago to Rochester, New York—that is, to a point which lay outside of the Central Freight Association area and was presumably unaffected by the pending revision. Again, in the Eastern Class Rate investigation, the carriers started with a fifth-class rate of 34 cents for 440 miles, the distance from Pittsburgh to New York. Thirty-four cents was the existing rate between Pittsburgh and New York, and it was desired to leave this rate unchanged because of the immense volume of iron and steel which moved at this price from the Pittsburgh district. On a fifth-class rate of 34 cents, the

[22] Motor truck terminal costs are lower than rail terminal costs because of the simpler character of motor carrier installations. An Interstate Commerce Commission study, conducted in 1945, showed for 95 Western Trunk Line motor carriers an average cost of 10.039 cents per 100 pounds for platform handling, billing and collecting for all weight brackets up to 6,000 pounds. Costs were relatively high for small shipments and relatively lower for heavy shipments, within the range mentioned. Above the maximum of 6,000 pounds, however, there was some tendency for costs to increase (*Traffic World*, February 16, 1946).

carriers built a first-class rate of 97 cents, and a general scale in which the first-class rate increased from an initial 30 cents to the amount of 97 cents in the course of the first 440 miles. It happened in all these cases that the Commission was able to find a way to avoid the compulsion of these outside adjustments, yet even the Commission in the Western Trunk Line case of 1930 felt itself controlled in a general way by its own decisions in Southwestern and in Trunk Line territories, and was compelled to fit the new Western Trunk Line scale somewhere in between the levels in effect on the south and on the east.

The basic principle of a mileage scale is that rates, like costs, increase as distance grows, after provision has been made for terminal expense. The average cost per mile in such a tariff will decline, because the terminal expense chargeable to each distance unit will grow less and less as the number of units multiply while the line haul increment will be constant.[23] We may illustrate this principle by the following table:

[23] It may be impossible to collect rates that cover full terminal costs on shipments moving short distances because of the competition of other forms of carriage. This is a condition which motor vehicle competition can easily bring about. Let us assume that terminal expense is 40 cents, but that the most that shippers can be made to pay on a less than 5-mile movement is 20 cents for loading and nothing for the haul. Let us also suppose that shippers will pay 25 cents toward terminal expense at 10 miles, 30 cents at 15 miles, 35 cents at 20 miles and 40 cents at 25 miles, plus in all cases a line-haul rate of 1.0529 cents per mile. These, then, will be the rates that will be charged.

Mileage Rate Structure

1	2	3	4	5	6	7
Distance (miles)	Terminal Cost (cents)	Terminal Allowance (cents)	Line Haul Cost (cents)	Total Cost (cents)	Total Charge (cents)	Accumulated Deficit (cents)
0	40	20	0	40.00	20.00	20
5	40	25	.53	40.53	25.53	35
10	40	30	1.05	41.05	31.05	45
15	40	35	1.58	41.58	36.58	50
20	40	40	2.11	42.10	42.10	50
25	40	45	2.63	42.63	47.63	45
30	40	50	3.16	43.16	53.16	35
35	40	55	3.69	43.69	58.69	20
40	40	60	4.21	44.21	44.21	0
45	40	40	4.74	44.74	44.74	0

They will, however, result in deficits of varying amounts, reaching an accumulation of 50 cents by the time when shipments have been made to each distance up to a maximum of 30 miles. It will be necessary, subsequently, to recover this accumulation by raising the terminal charge above 40 cents in the case of shipments sent 25 miles and over. By this method total rates and total costs will balance at 20 miles; and after 20 miles rates will exceed costs until the accumulated deficit has been wiped out. The terminal component in the case of hauls that are longer than 40 miles may then revert to the sum of 40 cents.

The particular method of compensation illustrated in the table in this note has the inconvenience that the total rate for a distance of 45 miles is less than that for a

Mileage Rate Structure

Distance (miles)	Terminal Rate Element (cents)	Line Haul Rate Element (cents)		Total (cents)	Average Cost per Mile (cents)
0	40	0	.0	40	—
5	40	5 × .10529 =	.52645	40.526	8.10
10	40	10 × .10529 =	1.0529	41.053	4.10
15	40	15 × .10529 =	1.57935	41.579	2.77
20	40	20 × .10529 =	2.1058	42.101	2.10
25	40	25 × .10529 =	2.63225	42.632	1.71

Average rates per 100 pounds per mile will normally decline, as distance grows greater, in mileage scales which recognize the distinction between terminal and line haul costs, because the fixed terminal charge will be spread over a progressively larger number of mileage units.[24] In the table above the average falls off, for this reason, from 8.10 cents per 100 pounds per mile at 5 miles to 1.7 cents at 25 miles. There is also the possibility that average rates will decline because the line haul cost per mile will become less as the length of haul increases. This is not allowed for in the table.

There is no obvious reason why operating costs should fall, once the carrier has made a separate allowance for loading and unloading freight. After these last expenditures have been absorbed the line haul expense should remain the same, mile by mile, except as the cost may be raised or lowered by peculiarities of terrain, or increased by the necessity of service at intermediate terminals.

But this does not mean that the transportation of goods to relatively

distance of 40 miles. The defect can be remedied, however, by prolonging the area over which the 50-cent deficit is recovered. But it will be necessary to change the rate of progression after 40 miles in any case, in order to prevent unreasonable additions to the rates for longer hauls.

There are a variety of ways in which deficits occurring in one portion of a mileage scale may be offset by surpluses derived from other portions, differing in their selection of the groups which are to bear the extra charge. But with proper attention, the total rate for shorter distances may be kept below the rate for longer distances and the average rate per 100 pounds per mile may even continue to decline. It is also true that competition may cause carriers to hold rates below normal levels on any section of a line—not only on the initial section. This will always lead to complications similar to those analyzed in this note.

[24] It is possible, however, that terminal costs may recur on hauls beyond a certain length. The previous discussion assumes that the only terminal costs are those which are incurred at the beginning and ending of a movement. But carriers sometimes find that long hauls require a continuing succession of expensive services at intermediate stations. If and when this is true, the task of compensation becomes more difficult and the profile of a mileage scale is hard to anticipate. It was the opinion of the English Railway Rates Tribunal that average rates, based upon cost, will not, in fact, decrease after the length of haul exceeds 100 miles. (See C. E. Sherrington, *Economics of Rail Transport in Great Britain,* New York, Longmans, vol. 2, 1928, p. 102.)

remote destinations cannot be so organized that, as a category, it is cheaper than the transportation of goods to nearby points. There can be, that is to say, a distinction between "through" and "way" service. Evidence submitted by an officer of the St. Louis and San Francisco Railway for the period March 1 to March 20, 1938, was to the effect that during this period and on this railroad the wages of train and engine crews were more than twice as great on "way" freight; fuel costs were almost twice as great; maintenance, servicing, and depreciation of locomotives was about 70 percent greater in way service because of the less effective utilization of motive power; the portions of car repair and depreciation expenses attributable to time elements was nearly twice as great; track maintenance expenses assignable to way freight were greater than corresponding through-freight expenses in main line operations because of the relatively greater weight in proportion to the trailing loads; and items of expense which are considered to be variable in proportion to train-miles or train-hours, such as train dispatching, maintenance and operation of signals and interlockers, and maintenance and depreciation of cabooses, were three or four times as great in way service.[25] It is reasonable to believe that conveyances costs are greater for shorter than for longer hauls because the business is handled in a different way. It is doubtful that this difference can explain a mileage scale with a steadily declining rate of progression. It may, however, justify a scale with several rates, each constant within limits, but with lesser rates in segments that govern hauls of relatively extended length.

Current Class Scales

An examination of major class rate scales prescribed by the Interstate Commerce Commission shows a high initial rate for the first 5 miles, followed by a sharp decline. Rates per mile then continue to decline rapidly, though less rapidly, during the first 150 miles, substantially during the next 200 miles, and slightly, though continuously, to the maximum distance covered by the scale. Table 19 shows the average rate per mile to destinations in the first block and average rates per mile to destinations which are more remote, in basic scales prescribed by the Interstate Commerce Commission in 1945 and in 1951.

It is clear from Table 19 that Commission class scales provide for terminal costs, principally, in the charges published for the first few miles, although not entirely in charges for the first mileage group. The continued decline in average charges as hauls increase in length suggests that the Commission also believes that line haul expense becomes less as distances grow greater, although the form of the scale does not reflect, probably,

[25] United States Board of Investigation and Research, "Comparison of Rail, Motor, and Water Carrier Costs," 1944, pp. 290–291.

TABLE 19. Average Rates per Mile in Basic Scales,
1945 and 1951 (in cents)

Scale	Distances from Point of Origin							
	2½ miles	7½ miles	52½ miles	155 miles	350 miles	510 miles	987½ miles	1487½ miles
Basic scale, 1945	16.00	5.73	1.16	.55	.34	.28	.21	.19
Basic scale, 1951	23.2	8.54	1.79	.88	.56	.46	.34	.29

SOURCES: 262 I.C.C. 447, 1945; 281 I.C.C. 213, 1951. Distances are taken to midway points in the rate groups.

the manner in which the decline occurs. It may be added that Commission scales do not produce a declining mileage rate by decreasing the increment of charge from zone to zone. Increments actually tend to rise. It is the enlargement of zones from units of 5 to units of 20 or 25 miles which, in spite of these increases, causes mileage rates to become less.[26]

Orders of the Interstate Commerce Commission

The American type of mileage scale has been rapidly displacing older class rate structures in the United States during the past 30 years. This has been due to the persistent efforts of the Interstate Commerce Commission. The first large case in which the Commission prescribed a mileage scale was the Central Freight Association Scale case in 1917. Following this, the Commission took advantage of an application by the New England railroads for an increase in rates to extend the mileage system into

[26] The Interstate Commerce Commission, in constructing mileage scales, has insisted that the rate of progression of a mileage scale, whatever it may be, shall conform to a regular pattern. Speaking with reference to regular progression at a declining rate, and criticizing certain irregularities in the Eastern class-rate scale effective in 1938, the Commission further remarked that a criterion of smooth progression in a rate scale is that each successive percent of increase, at each 100 miles interval, for example, shall be less than the percent of increase in the period immediately preceding; and also, that the difference between successive increments of increase shall not progress upon an ascending scale (262 I.C.C. 447, 643, 1945).

The pronouncement summarized in the preceding paragraph gives formal approval to progression at a declining rate. We have already seen that average rates per mile in the Commission's basic scale follow this principle. It is not, however, true that the differences in successive percents of increase, from group to group, never rise. There is no particular reason why they should not occasionally increase, and they do so increase even in the Commission's own basic scale. It is to be remembered that the Commission uses groups of different lengths, and that the zones are broader in the case of longer hauls. A comparison of rate increases is likely to show a relatively greater rise at transition points where the increased rate begins to apply to a longer distance. A scale can be constructed in which differences in percentage increases as well as percentage decreases grow steadily less, but such a scale will be complicated, and it may not be superior to the schedule which the Commission adopted in its decision of 1945.

New England. The use of a mileage scale was proposed by the carriers in the New England case, in order to avoid protracted discussion of particular rates and to hasten the relief which they hoped to secure, but the Commission readily assented for more general reasons. A third extensive proceeding in which a mileage scale was prescribed was that of the Southern Class Rate investigation of 1925. Then came decisions in the Mountain-Pacific area, in the Southwest, in what is known as Western Trunk Line territory, and in Official and Trunk Line territory. The Class Rate Investigation of 1939 dealt with all the areas which have been mentioned. No scale has yet been applied to transcontinental traffic. American rates are far from being uniformly on a distance basis, first, because the Interstate Commerce Commission scales do not cover the entire United States; second, because even where effective they do not apply to all commodities; and lastly, because the federal rulings do not govern intrastate traffic, and not all state commissions have followed the federal lead. It is substantially correct to say, however, that class rates in the United States are upon a mileage basis. In traffic governed by commodity tariffs, formal scales are less representative and more difficult to apply.

Arguments in Favor of Mileage Scales

Most people would be inclined to admit that Commission scales represent an improvement on past practice. Certainly American rates were frequently so confused as to defy analysis, and this needed to be changed; and American rate making was on a sectional basis, with sharply defined lines between territories, based on accidents of historical development. This, also, was a condition which required revision. The Interstate Commerce Commission has worked patiently and constructively at these and other rate problems. In its own eyes the great advantage of the new dispensation is to be found in the relative simplicity of mileage rates as compared with the structures they have replaced, and in the fact that charges in a mileage scale are consistent with each other. Simple structures are not necessarily better than complicated ones, in rates any more than in biology, but they are easier to understand, and the first step in conscious human progress is understanding. Rates in a mileage system are more likely to be consistent with each other because distance is easier to measure than, say, competitive advantage. Speaking of the advantages of a mileage scale in eliminating discrimination, the Commission has quoted a League of Shippers as follows:

Granting perhaps that the costs of railroad service may not vary in ratio to increasing distance, yet costs are not ascertainable and it seems generally to be agreed that no system of class rates could or properly should be constructed with reference to variations of the details of costs even if they were available. But there is one standard at least readily available by which to measure and unify all class rates and that is the standard furnished by the quantity of service rendered expressed in terms of miles. In other words, the measure of service furnishes an inflexible yard stick to which all charges could be made to conform without discriminations. Every community would then find its place automatically fixed by the accident of its location and there would be no room for attempting to equalize natural advantages and disadvantages.[27]

Besides the advantages of simplicity and orderliness, mileage rates have other merits. They are, for instance, relatively stable. They may be expected to change less frequently than rates based, for example, upon the value of the service. Business and settlement can adjust themselves to any long-continued practice. Mileage scales are an approximation, as the League of Shippers said, to a measurement of the quantity of service that shippers are securing. Mileage rates tend to check wasteful transportation. It is not always true that the shortest route is the most economical, but it does seem probable that a community will save money if it ships, in general, over direct ways. And finally, mileage rates tend to diffuse population because they deprive the larger towns of the bargaining advantages which are connected with their superiority in numbers and in wealth.[28]

The Commission summed up these and other considerations affecting the policy of mileage rate making in its decision in the Eastern Class rate investigation.

What alternatives [asked the Commission] are offered by those who oppose such a basis? The fact is that with certain exceptions . . . the only alternatives which are here offered are (1) adherence to rates which have the sanction of long-established custom, and (2) the adjustment of rates so that more remote producers can compete in a common market to better advantage with their nearer rivals.

Long-established custom is a matter to be considered in the revision of rates, but certainly it cannot justify rates which are unreasonable, unduly prejudicial, or otherwise unlawful. Doubts may be resolved in favor of what has long existed, and the acquiescence of shippers in such an adjustment may tend to show that it is free from undue prejudice; but otherwise custom is of little weight. And clearly we are without power to adjust rates for the purpose of neutralizing the geographical disadvantages of producers.[29]

---

[27] 100 I.C.C. 513, 567, 1925.

[28] See J. H. Alldredge, in *Traffic World*, October 11, 1930, p. 882, and C. E. Cotterill, *ibid.*, November 8, 1930, p. 1163, for a discussion of the advantages and disadvantages of mileage rates.

[29] 164 I.C.C. 314, 382, 1930. American defenders of mileage scales argue, as the text points out, that rates in these scales vary with distance. The fact that American scales make use of zones and that the rate of progression declines is regarded as an incident. It is interesting to compare with this position the defense of mileage scales, or *Staffeltarife*, by German writers, based upon the contention that zone tariffs with declining rates of progression eliminate distance. Thus Giese takes pains to demonstrate that the decline in the kilometric rate in the German "normal tariff" amounts to a shrinkage in distance, so that a haul of 1,600 kilometers becomes equivalent to one of only 610

Arguments Against Mileage Scales

In opposition to the favorable views set forth in the preceding paragraphs, there is a respectable opposition to the principle of mileage tariffs. Mileage rates are not simple, it is contended, or at least they are not more simple than other rates can be made. They encourage an undesirable localization of industry, injuring the carriers by reducing the ton-miles of service performed and injuring the nation by restraining the healthy growth of great cities. It is argued that mileage does not measure cost, not only because of differences in topography and in density of traffic but also because distance charges do not reflect the costs of handing an intermediate terminal yards and gateways. Still more important, distance does not measure the value of the service. Specifically, mileage rates do not give adequate recognition to competitive factors. Business must be carried on under competitive conditions. Competition does not follow geographical lines or conform to variations in distance, and consequently a system of rates which adheres rigidly to distance frequently resists the normal flow of traffic. While the Interstate Commerce Commission has shown a weakness for mileage rates, another branch of the government, the Post Office Department, has defended proposed increases in the rates on first-class mail by observing that the controlling factor in fixing rates is not the relative cost of the different classes of mail matter and service, but the relative amount which the traffic will bear in view of competition without reduction of organization and facilities which contribute to the integrity of the organization as a whole. This, say the critics of mileage scales, expresses the policy which should be followed in determining carrier rates.

REFERENCES

General Treatises

Bigham, Truman C., and Roberts, Merrill J., *Transportation, Principles and Problems,* New York, McGraw-Hill, 1942.

Bonravia, M. R., *The Economics of Transport,* New York, Putnam, 1947.

---

kilometers. This is because the charge for 1,600 kilometers in the "normal tariff" is only what would be exacted for a haul of 610 kilometers if the unit rate did not decline as the length of haul increased. Giese even declares that this practice in rate-making is to be ranked with the great technical inventions that have had the effect of shortening distance by improving means of communication (K. Giese, *Hauptfragen der Reichsbahnpolitik*). Whether a mileage scale characterized by the use of zones and with a declining unit rate is to be thought of as abolishing or as recognizing distance will probably depend on the system which the scale displaces. Such a scale conforms less to distance than a mileage tariff with no zones and with a constant unit rate. It conforms more to distance than do the American group and basing point systems. At best, the analogy with the great technical inventions increasing the speed and lessening the cost of supplying transportation is very slight.

Fair, Marvin L., and Williams, Ernest W., *Economics of Transportation,* New York, Harper, 1950.

Healy, Kent T., *The Economics of Transportation in America,* New York, Ronald, 1940.

Huebner, G. G. and Johnson, E. R., *The Railroad Freight Service,* New York, Appleton-Century-Crofts, 1926.

Johnson, E. R., Huebner, G. G., and Wilson, G. L., *Transportation, Principles and Practices,* New York, Appleton-Century-Crofts, 1940.

Landon, Charles E., *Transportation, Principles, Practices, Problems,* New York, Sloane, 1951.

Locklin, D. Philip, *Economics of Transportation,* Chicago, Irwin, 1947.

Ulrich, Franz, *Das Eisenbahntarifwesen in Allgemeinen,* Berlin, Guttentag, 1886.

Westmeyer, Russell E., *Economics of Transportation,* New York, Prentice-Hall, 1952.

Wilson, G. L., *Freight Service and Rates. Water, Highway, Air, Pipeline, Forwarder,* Washington, The Traffic Service Corporation, 1952.

Wilson, G. L., *Railroad Freight Rate Structure,* Washington, The Traffic Service Corporation, 1951.

Other Books

Alldredge, J. H., *Rate-Making for Common Carriers,* Atlanta, Harrison, 1929.

Daggett, Stuart, and Carter, John P., *The Structure of Transcontinental Railroad Rates,* Berkeley and Los Angeles, University of California Press, 1947.

Daniels, W. M., *The Price of Transportation Service,* New York, Harper, 1932.

Sherrington, C. E., *Economics of Rail Transport in Great Britain,* New York, Longmans, 1928.

Shinn, Glenn L., *Freight Rate Application,* New York, Simmons-Boardman, 1948.

Van Metre, Thurman W., *Industrial Traffic Management,* New York, Mc-Graw-Hill, 1952.

Wilson, G. L., *New Departures in Freight Rate Making,* New York, Simmons-Boardman, 1948.

Wiprud, A. C., *Justice in Transportation,* New York, Ziff-Davis, 1945.

Periodicals

Alldredge, J. H., "Railroad Mileage Freight Rates," *Annals of the American Academy of Political and Social Sciences,* January, 1934.

Daggett, Stuart, "Mileage Rates and the Interstate Commerce Commission," *Quarterly Journal of Economics,* February, 1932.

Daggett, Stuart, "Traffic Associations and Antitrust Legislation," *American Economic Review,* May, 1948.

Locklin, D. Philip, "A Reorganization of the Railroad Rate Structure," *American Economic Review,* May, 1946.

Spiess, W., *"Der Eisenbahngütertarif in der Volkswirthschaft,"* *Archiv für Eisenbahnwesen,* March–April, 1941.

Special and Miscellaneous

The Freight Traffic Red Book, New York, Traffic Publishing.

United States Board of Investigation and Research, *Comparison of Rail, Motor, and Water Carrier Costs,* 1944.

United States, Federal Coordinator of Transportation, *Merchandise Traffic Report,* 1934.

United States, Federal Coordinator of Transportation, *Freight Traffic Report,* 1935.

United States Senate, Committee on Interstate Commerce, *Hearings on S. 942,* 78th C., 1st S., May, 1943, testimony Franklin.

Part

VI

Competition

Varieties of Competition

The last chapter dealt with the elementary technique of railroad rate making and with the subject of mileage scales. We cannot dismiss the subject of rates, however, without some further explanation of the influences which determine carrier charges and some additional discussion of rate structures to which these influences give rise. For this our earlier excursions into the theory and the economic geography of transport now give us some support. In particular, we must, once more, consider the nature of competition in the carrier industry and its effect upon the price of transport.[1]

Competition of Parallel Lines

Competition which controls the rates for shipments of commodities may be of several sorts. The simplest form of competition is that between transportation agencies which operate on parallel routes. That is, there may be two parallel railroads, or a railroad and a waterway, or a railroad and a motor vehicle service, or any combination of agencies which offer themselves simultaneously to the public as media by which a transportation service may be performed. When two or more independent agencies seek traffic which either one can transport, the rates charged are likely to be lower than when a single carrier bargains with the shipping public. This statement of the probable effect of the competition of carriers operating upon parallel routes would seem to require no proof other than appeal to well-known experience. It should be said, however, that some students of transportation question it, at least in so far as the operation of parallel railroads is concerned. The argument that parallel railroads do not compete is based upon two assumptions. One is that competition between enterprises which employ large amounts of fixed capital, as railroads do,

[1] See National Resources Planning Board, *Transportation and National Policy,* Part I, section VI, by Burton N. Behling, pp. 238–249. This contribution contains a note on the subject of monopolistic competition. See also chap. 15.

is so disastrous that the managers of such companies refrain from competition on grounds of general policy. It is admitted that parallel railroads competed in former years, as during the trunk line rate wars between carriers connecting Chicago and New York, but this kind of rivalry is said to belong to the experience of the distant past. The other assumption is that rates of all railroads connecting any two points must be the same. It is clear that they should be the same, unless one line is prepared to relinquish all traffic which its rival is able to carry; and observation will show that rates for equal service usually are the same between the same two points. Where rates are the same, it is said, there can be no competition. The answer to this denial of the reality of competition between parallel railroads is that equality of rates does not preclude competition; for first, there may be competition in speed, reliability, and care, even when rates are equal. And if this answer is objected to on the ground that equality of service is assumed in the argument, it may be pointed out that the level of rates, where there are two railroads, may be lower than the level would be were there only one; and if this is true, there is evidence of competition, even though all railroads concerned charge the same rates. William R. Wheeler, one-time traffic manager of the San Francisco Chamber of Commerce, once described the sort of competition which results from the rivalry of modern railroad companies so clearly that his testimony deserves citation:

It is a popular fallacy, I think [said Mr. Wheeler], that because there is not a rate war . . . following the advent of a new road into a territory . . . therefore, there is no competition. There is competition in the service and that is what we desire. There is also competition in this respect . . . if you have two roads who have a voice in the rate question, you stand double the chance of gaining tariff concessions that you do if there is only one road to deal with; if there are three roads, you stand three times the chance of getting your concessions; in other words, you do not find—are not as apt to find—three men of one mind as you are of two men of one mind and so on as the number grows. We already have had an example of that here in San Francisco: there was a proposition something more than a year ago to advance rates between San Francisco and Stockton . . . and the fact that it required the consent of three roads instead of two was the only thing that prevented that advance going into effect at that time; we were successful in convincing one of the roads that it was unfair to us to raise those rates and they declined to join in the advance.[2]

Indirect Routing

It is not, however, necessary for routes to be parallel for competition to exist between them. One of the striking features of the operation of the American transportation plant is that it offers service, at equal rates, over

[2] Stuart Daggett, "Later Developments in the Union Pacific Merger Case," *Quarterly Journal of Economics,* August, 1914.

routes which differ greatly in length. Thus traffic between Chicago and New York moves over the Baltimore and Ohio Railroad (920 miles), over the Pennsylvania Railroad (908 miles), and over the New York Central Railroad (974 miles). But it also moves by water from New York to Newport News and thence west over the Chesapeake and Ohio Railway, or it may travel north to Canada and thence west over the Grand Trunk. The facts developed in the differential rate controversy described in the appendix to this chapter, and the struggle between the Great Lakes carriers and the railroads which compete with them, mentioned in chapters 3 and 7, afford illustrations of the competition of routes of unequal length. In the West, freight from Chicago may be carried directly over the Chicago and Northwestern, Union Pacific, and Central Pacific to San Francisco, or it may travel 921 miles to New Orleans before it starts its journey west.[3] Shipments from Portland, Oregon, may move 945 miles by way of the Union Pacific line or 1,487 miles by way of the Southern Pacific lines to a common destination at Ogden, Utah. Testimony in the Union Pacific merger case showed that the Southern Pacific Company solicited freight destined to the Pacific Coast from points almost as far west as Pittsburgh, hauled these goods to the Atlantic Seaboard, thence transported them on vessels to New Orleans, and from that point hauled them in railway cars through El Paso to San Francisco. These illustrations are selected from instances of very long hauls because the routes mentioned can be easily traced and the roundaboutness of the routings readily perceived; but the same practice, though less conspicuous there, is to be found in local business also.

Carriers which compete with direct lines by means of circuitous routing have been accused of promoting waste in transportation. The charge is, to some extent, justified. Ripley declares that indirect routing produces the following evil effects: the amount of transportation in the United States is unnecessarily increased; net railway profits on the traffic are reduced to the vanishing point; industrial conditions are made more rigid; and centralization of population and industry is encouraged.[4] It may be added, however, that direct routes are not always the most economical, for these

---

[3] Stuart Daggett, "The Decision on the Union Pacific Merger," *Quarterly Journal of Economics,* February, 1913.

[4] W. Z. Ripley, "Economic Wastes in Transportation," *Political Science Quarterly,* September, 1906. J. M. Clark observes that every time any place is especially and markedly favored in the matter of railway rates, the way is laid open for uneconomical transportation (*Standards of Reasonableness in Local Freight Discrimination,* New York, Columbia University Press, 1910). During World War I the Railroad Administration in the United States insisted upon direct routing in so far as this lay within its power; and in the case of coal, producers were even forbidden to market their product outside assigned areas. The coal regulations were defended on the ground that elimination of cross-hauling prevented waste, as well as because the policy furnished an incentive to the use of local coal supplies which would not otherwise have been worked in competition with higher grades from outside districts.

routes may be congested; or there may be empty cars on the roundabout line which can be used at no great expense; or some other circumstance may make it desirable to depart from the strait and narrow way. Whatever may be the conclusion with respect to the justification of indirect routing, the fact remains that circuitous routes as well as direct routes compete, and that they thus affect, as we have said, the development of producing centers and the prosperity of cities engaged in the work of distribution.[5]

Market Competition

The competition of two or more carriers which connect the same points of origin and destination is easy to understand. The principal questions are whether it is, in fact, active and whether, when active, it causes waste. Carriers may compete, however, when they do not connect the same points of origin and destination, and there may be competition of a sort when only one carrier is involved. The phrase used to describe variations of this sort is "market competition." This has been repeatedly illustrated in previous pages.

LOCAL SELF-SUFFICIENCY. This is a form of market competition which appears when the movement of freight over a carrier's line, as from A to B, is limited by the availability, at B, of local sources of supply. The necessary condition for shipment in such a case is, normally, that the price of carriage from A to B, added to the cost of production at A, shall not exceed the cost of production at B. More accurately, the price of carriage plus costs of production paid by producers at A may not exceed the costs which producers are willing to incur at B. This rephrasing allows for the possibility that alternative uses for labor and capital may exist at B which are more advantageous than would be production of the articles which A desires to ship although B's costs for these last-named goods may be relatively low.[6]

[5] The Interstate Commerce Commission has gathered information indicating that the extent of circuity in America railroad transport in 1939 was, approximately, 13 percent (United States Interstate Commerce Commission, Bureau of Transport Economics and Statistics, *Monthly Comment of Transportation Statistics*, November, 1947). This compares with an estimate of 12 percent based upon evidence submitted in I.C.C. Docket No. 28,190 (*Rail Freight Service Costs in the Various Rate Territories of the United States*, 78th C., 1st S., Sen. Doc. 63, pp. 29–31, 1943), an estimate of 12.7 percent by the Federal Coordinator of Transportation in 1933, and one of 13.8 percent by the Office of Defense Transportation in 1944.

The problem of circuity in its relation to through railroad rates and to the administration of Section 4 of the Interstate Commerce Act is discussed in chaps. 20 and 21.

[6] A curious complexity occurs when unused capacity for production exists at both A and B. It is not inconceivable that costs of production at both A and B plus cost of transport to the other center may be less than the price currently maintained in each place, under conditions of partial monopoly. Producers at A may, under these circumstances, attempt to dispose of additional output at B and producers at B may try to sell additional output at A rather than risk a general lowering of the price level in

RIVALRY OF PRODUCING CENTERS. Another form of competition appears where several geographically distinct producing centers seek to supply a single market. The commodity movements described in preceding chapters illustrate the competition of producing centers and, consequently, of the lines that serve them. It is evident, for instance, that Florida competes with California in the markets of Chicago and that railroads from Florida to the North compete, in consequence, with railroads stretching from California to the East, although the two groups of lines touch only at one extremity. An equally clear case is presented by the movements of lumber from the South and from the Northwest.

Brown says that the competition of producing centers shipping to a common market is likely to be relatively unimportant in reducing railroad rates.[7] The loss, he says, will fall on the owners of favorably situated land in the producing areas. It is doubtless true that, when a source of supply which has hitherto monopolized a given market meets the competition of a new area of production, the revenue of land and also the returns to fixed capital which has been contributing to the supply shipped to the market will decrease. If there is no alternative use to which this land and capital can be put, then the market value of these agencies will decline. Since the railroad connecting the older source of supply with the market is one of the forms of capital which cannot, in many cases, be withdrawn, the revenue of the carrier will decline as well as the revenue of other forms of production. But it cannot be assumed that this will not provoke a change in rates. Such a reduction is, on the contrary, extremely likely, for reasons which are given in chapter 16.

COMPETITION OF DIRECTIONS. When a single producing center serves two or more markets, we have a case which is slightly different from that considered in the preceding section. Such a situation would be illustrated by the shipment of Georgia cotton to North Carolina or to New England mills, or by the shipment of California peaches to Portland, Oregon, or to Denver, Colorado. The problem in this case may be depicted as in Fig. 38.

Let us suppose a producing center A and two markets, B and C, connected with A by the railroads AB and AC. These two markets may be said to be in competition with each other, because each is bidding at A for a portion of a single supply. If the markets compete, then the railroads which serve them will compete. A reduction in the rate from A to C is

their own home town. Identical articles may, therefore, move from B to A and from A to B. Carriers which connect the two towns will benefit from the practice. It is hard to see how producers at A and at B will gain, in the long run, except that each will be able to operate in a broader and, presumably, in a more stable market. If, of course, producers in the two locations are able to differentiate their products, the total quantity sold may be increased. See chap. 16.

[7] H. G. Brown, *Transportation Rates and their Regulation*, New York, Macmillan, 1916.

likely to be followed by a cut in the rate from *A* to *B*. Just when and how far the rate from *A* to *B* will fall in order to protect the interests of the line *AB* will depend upon the assumptions made, and the facts present a problem to which economic theory may be applied with interesting results. If, for instance, the production at *A* cannot be much increased, and if a slight reduction in price at *C* or *B* will cause a considerable expansion of the quantity consumed at each of these places, then conditions are ripe for active competition between interested lines. Other assumptions may lead to different conclusions. When a single producing area thus serves several markets, the resultant rivalry has been characterized as "competition of directions," and is contrasted with the "competition of locations" which occurs when several producers ship to a single market.

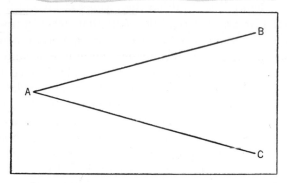

FIGURE 38.   Competition of Directions.

Competition Between Commodities

There is still another form of competition, which bears the infelicitous name of "competition between commodities." This term refers to the competition that takes place for the business of hauling articles that may be manufactured or processed at the point of production or at the market or somewhere between the place of production of the raw material and the place where the finished product is sold to the ultimate consumer. In a sense, all manufactures fall within this class; but the issue is especially controversial when production areas of the raw material are far removed from the consuming areas of the finished goods, when the values of the completed products are not greatly in excess of the value of the materials from which they have been derived, and when fabricating plants have been located in proximity to the materials and others near to the consuming region.[8]

Such a case is that of grain. Wheat is produced as grain but it is con-

[8] L. C. Sorrell, "Transportation Charges and the Market Area," *Traffic World,* June 7, 1930, pp. 1517 ff. See also chap. 22.

sumed as flour. The business is considered a desirable asset to any community. Where the milling industry will actually locate will depend largely upon the relative railroad rates on grain and those on flour. If there is a difference, and if the rates on grain are high and those on flour are relatively low, grain will be milled near the place of production; if the rates on grain are low and those on flour are high, grain will be milled near the place of consumption.

What may be true of grain is also true of rice. Thus, in 1941, rice millers in Louisiana alleged that high railroad rates on rough rice from California to Louisiana were relatively high as compared with rates upon clean rice and rice products, and that this unduly favored milling upon the Pacific Coast. For their part, millers in California objected to lower rates upon rough rice because this threatened their material supply, while rice growers in Louisiana, Texas, and Arkansas also opposed the application on the ground that a reduction in rates upon rough rice would bring the California product into competition with rice locally produced in Southern states and hitherto sold to Southern mills.[9]

Still another business in which the competition of commodities has been important is the packing house industry. The contentious question here is where the livestock shall be slaughtered and converted into forms which can be directly consumed.[10] Eastern and Western cities compete for the location of packing houses. The result of this struggle between East and West is largely determined by the relation between the rates on finished products and those on raw material. If the rates on livestock are low and the rates on dressed beef are high, then the tendency will be for the packing business to establish itself near the great consuming centers of the Atlantic Seaboard. If the rates on livestock are high and the rates on dressed beef are low, then slaughter in the East will be only sufficient to supply special markets such as those furnished, for instance, by the New York "kosher" trade. It is one of the industrial victories of the Middle West that a rate relationship has been established that permits the concentration of the packing industry at Chicago, St. Louis, Omaha, St. Paul, and other cities listed in chapter 10. But controversies still continue; and in 1928 and again as late as 1937 the Interstate Commerce Commission rendered decisions which tended to improve the position of the East.[11] In partial compensation, a highly interesting case in 1945, which ranged the Midwest packers against those in Mountain-Pacific territory, led to the conclusion that rates on fresh meat and packing house products from Illinois, Wisconsin, Minnesota, Missouri, Iowa, Kansas, Nebraska, Colorado, and South Dakota to points in Montana, New Mexico, Utah, Idaho, Arizona,

[9] 248 I.C.C. 427, 1942.
[10] See chap. 10.
[11] 144 I.C.C. 731, 1928; 220 I.C.C. 677, 1937.

Nevada, California, Oregon, and Washington should be reduced. The Interstate Commerce Commission declared, in 1945, that existing rates did not permit free movements of meats from the Midwest to the Pacific Coast; in the case of hogs it found the difficulty to be almost entirely due to the fact that rates on meat were excessive as compared with rates upon live animals. The decision was, of course, highly distasteful to packers in the Far West.[12]

Importance of Carrier and Market Competition

The result of competition in the carrier industry is that the practice of quoting rates upon a strict mileage scale gives way to a process of balancing in which the carrier weighs the likelihood of losing business to other lines as well as the cost of carriage. The loss is easily visualized when the competition is between carriers alone; it is none the less real when competition of markets and of commodities exists. Most great rate structures are the result, indeed, of both carrier and market competition; for except where two carriers lie side by side and serve identical communities, both types of rivalry are sure to be involved.

This balancing of rates is easily observed when rate systems covering important commodities are examined. We have already discussed the adjustment of rates on lumber, oranges, and sugar in describing the traffic flows of these articles, and we have just mentioned the subject of livestock in considering the relationship between rates on finished goods and charges upon material. And, indeed, the effect of competition in the livestock industry is far from adequately described when the rates on livestock and on packinghouse products have been compared, for the rates on each of these articles from different marketing centers to common points of destination have long been set competitively and with a general picture of the industry in view. The tendency in commodity adjustments generally is to arrange rates so that charges from competing towns to common points of destination shall be the same, or at least so that the costs of shipment, including the rates on gathering hauls into handling centers and the charge for the subsequent outgoing movement of the products shall be approximately equal on different routes and by way of different towns between the points of origin and the place where the goods are finally consumed. Or, if the charges are not equal, a relationship is agreed upon or is forcefully maintained.

---

[12] 263 I.C.C. 9, 1945.

APPENDIX TO CHAPTER 19

I

Transit Rates

So-called "transit rates" permit intermediate towns upon a route to share in the advantage which carrier or market competition confers upon points of origin or destination. Under a transit arrangement it is possible to stop a consignment short of destination and then, ultimately, to reship, paying the balance of the through rate. In the case of livestock, shippers use their privilege to rest their stock, to sort and consolidate it with other shipments of the same kind, and to test the possibilities of local sale. Other industries rely upon "transit" to a still greater degree. Thus shippers stop grain consignments for storing, cleaning, sorting, mixing, and milling. A carload of wheat may be converted into flour and reshipped; the total rate collected will be that which the shipper would have paid if he had sent the grain through without a stop. Likewise cotton may be stopped for compression, lumber products for milling, iron and steel for fabrication, and agricultural products for storage. (The general practice of "transit" is well described in R. V. Hobbah, *Railroad Transit Privileges*, Chicago, University of Chicago, 1944. See also E. S. Lynch, *The Influence of Transportation on the Location of Economic Activities*, in the National Resources Planning Board's *Transportation and National Policy*, and R. W. Ernst, "Thought Provoking Transportation Privileges Granted Receivers and Shippers," *Traffic World*, May 10, 1952.)

Transit allowances may sometimes, unfortunately, interfere with competitive balancing instead of simplifying its technique. When transit arrangements are effective over one route but not upon another, the difference in treatment may influence the direction of traffic, or it may stop certain movements altogether.

In a more general way, transit systems sometimes disturb rate adjustments which the Interstate Commerce Commission has built on other principles. A good deal of attention has been paid to this aspect of the practice in the case of grain. Ordinarily, under the Interstate Commerce Commission methods, grain rates from local Western points to Eastern territory are made by adding the outbound rates to primary markets such as Kansas City, Omaha, and Minneapolis, to what are known as "proportional" rates from these primary markets to ultimate destinations. The proportional rate from Kansas City or Omaha to a town which we may call X would usually be less than the rate upon an identical shipment which had originated at Kansas City or Omaha and was consigned to X. Primary markets from which this is the custom bear the additional name of "rate break" points. Proportional rates are applied to all outbound grain which has originated back of the rate break cities, whether the previous haul has been long or short, whether there has been a prior use of several or only of one railroad line, and whether or not the various carriers have concurred in publishing the charge. Most rates quoted in explaining the relative adjustment of rates out of competing grain markets are proportional rates. Such tariffs are balanced in accordance with Commission policy. But it sometimes happens that the transit balances payable on grain which leaves a primary market for further transportation are less than the proportional rates which the Commission has prescribed. When this is true the rate adjustments in the territory are disturbed, and it is possible that the position of some markets, especially secondary markets, may be changed. The Commission sought to avoid this possibility by ruling, in 1930, that transit balances should be disregarded where proportional rates applied. This ruling is still effective, although it has been amended in detail. It does not prevent the quoting and use of transit rates as such. These rates are, on the contrary, extremely common. But it does prevent the alternative use of transit and proportional rates in a single market. Primary markets have protested against this limitation, but without result.

The Commission's first decision in the transit-proportional rate controversy was in 1930 (164 I.C.C. 619, 645, 1930). Exceptions were made to the rule as at first announced, but the principle of the first decision was affirmed in a number of later cases (175 I.C.C. 511, 1931; 205 I.C.C. 301, 333–342, 1934; 215 I.C.C. 83, 90–93, 1936). In 1937, carriers were permitted to file tariffs which authorized departures from the rule of 1930, for a limited period of time, to the extent determined by the best judgment of carriers and shippers (225 I.C.C. 235, 246, 1937). This was approved as an experiment, and the option was terminated in 1938 (231 I.C.C. 793, 1939). The question was taken to Congress in 1939, but without result (United States Senate, Committee on Foreign and Interstate Commerce, Hearings before a subcommittee on S. 2444, *To Prohibit Discriminatory Practices in Granting of Transit Privileges,* 76th C., 1st S., 1939).

II

Seaboard Differentials

The Seaboard Differential Controversy is of sufficient illustrative and historical importance to deserve mention in an appendix to the present chapter. This particular competition was primarily (a) between the cities of New York, Philadelphia, and Baltimore for a share in the export trade in grain originating in the northern Mississippi Valley; and (2) between the railroads which were especially interested in these seaboard towns.

Origin of Seaboard Differentials. The relationship between the New York, Philadelphia, and Baltimore rates on grain had its origin as far back as the seventh and eighth decades of the nineteenth century, when the New York Central Railroad, identified with New York City, the Pennsylvania Railroad, identified with Philadelphia, and the Baltimore and Ohio Railroad, representing Baltimore, as well as other railroads in Trunk Line territory, established rates to Atlantic Seaboard cities designed to distribute eastbound business among the various towns upon the Seaboard, and thus indirectly among the great railroad systems which served these towns.

When the Baltimore and Ohio Railroad reached Chicago in 1874, no one knew how much Mississippi Valley traffic each of the Seaboard cities could fairly hope to attract. The roads serving these cities were young, ambitious, and led by aggressive men. When the Baltimore and Ohio opened its Chicago branch, the company was heralded all over the Northwest as a relief for the farmers and as the Grangers' friend. President Garrett declared at this time that upon completion of his lines he would, like another Samson, pull down the temple of rates upon the heads of the other carriers. The attitude of the Baltimore and Ohio led to retaliation, and the so-called trunk line rate wars were the result. Of these, the first continued from January, 1874, to December, 1875; the second, from April, 1876, to April, 1877; the third, from June, 1881, to January, 1882; and the fourth and last from March, 1884, to November, 1885.

Trunk-Line Rate Wars, 1874–1885. It is difficult to measure the extent of the rate reductions which the railroad wars of the 1870's and 1880's brought about, because rates were not required to be published in these times, and even published rates were not uniformly charged. But it appears that before November 25, 1874, a shipper was required to pay 45 cents per 100 pounds in order to ship a consignment of fourth-class freight from Chicago to New York, while it cost a passenger $19 to travel between these cities. Fourth-class rates are quoted as examples because these included grain rates, and in 1881 grain was said to have constituted 73 percent of the total tonnage carried by the trunk lines to the principal Atlantic ports. On March 25, 1874, the fourth-class rate was cut to 30 cents, or a reduction of one-third, while the passenger rate fell to $9, a reduction of more than one-half. Nor were these the lowest limits reached. In the conflict that raged between April, 1876, and April, 1877, the fourth-class rate fell to 20 cents, which was the lowest grain rate ever in effect up to that time except for one month in 1873; and in 1881 the rate was reduced to 12½ cents, and in 1885 to 10 cents, for brief periods of time. Meanwhile, passenger fares of $7 per person were quoted in 1881 from New York to Chicago, and in 1884 immigrant business westward between these termini was handled at $1 a head. Since the distance was approximately 1,000 miles, this meant a charge of about a mill per passenger per mile.

Rates quoted during the trunk-line rate wars were clearly too low to yield profits to the carriers, and they were, probably, less than the out-of-pocket costs occasioned by the traffic. They were published as war measures, each company hoping that by imposing losses upon its competitors it could make its point of view prevail.

Opposed Rate Making Principles. The immediate issue in the rate wars was the relative rate which should be charged from Chicago to the Seaboard cities of Baltimore, Philadelphia, New York, and Boston. The distances to these four cities from Chicago were, respectively, 802, 823, 900, and 1,009 miles. Baltimore and Philadelphia, being nearer Chicago than was New York, thought that they were entitled to relatively lower rates than New York; and this view was adopted by the Baltimore and Ohio and by the Pennsylvania railroads, in the hope of attracting traffic from the other trunk lines. Mr.

Garrett declared that his principal object was to make Baltimore the principal outlet for the products of the Great West, and he expressed the opinion, in support of a rate adjustment which should reflect differences in distance, that water could be as easily made to run uphill, by natural law, as the laws of trade and of all experience could be ignored. The two cities, however, did not rest upon their nearness to Chicago alone. Inasmuch as New York was nearer Europe than was either Philadelphia or Baltimore, and since, also, New York possessed the advantage of more numerous sailings and better banking facilities, her competitors felt that they needed concessions in railroad rates in order to compete on equal terms. New York, of course, stood out for equal rates to all four Seaboard cities, contending that the easy grades from the West by way of the Mohawk and Hudson valleys offset her handicap of greater distance, and arguing also that steamship lines quoted the same ocean rates to Boston, New York, Philadelphia, and Baltimore, so that no one of these cities was at a disadvantage on the water side.

Attentive readers will observe that arguments in the differential rate controversy rested, on each side, upon two different and opposing principles. The city of Baltimore and the Baltimore and Ohio Railroad desired relatively low railroad rates from the interior (1) because Baltimore was nearer to Chicago than other towns, and her advantage should be recognized, and (2) because Baltimore was farther from Europe and less well equipped with steamships than her rivals, and her disadvantages should be compensated. New York, which bore the chief burden of the opposition, was no more consistent than Baltimore, for at one time she insisted upon the advantages which she possessed, and at another time denied that she enjoyed facilities superior to those of her chief rivals. It would be possible to enlarge upon the argument by enumerating contentions discussed during the sixty years after 1874, but during this entire period the original contradiction persisted unimpaired.

Early Agreements on Differentials. Originally, in 1869, the rate on eastbound class traffic, including grain, was made 10 cents less to Baltimore and 7 cents less to Philadelphia than it was to New York. In 1870 these figures were changed to 5 and 3 cents on grain, though the differentials on higher classes remained unchanged. In 1876 Messrs. Vanderbilt, Scott, King, and Jewett, representing the various trunk lines, conferred at length in an attempt to settle the relationship which should exist. Vanderbilt then agreed that the rates on all freight billed from competitive points in the interior to foreign ports should be the same by all the lines, and hence the same through all the competing Seaboard cities, and the other companies, in turn, agreed that the rates on freight not intended to be shipped to foreign ports should be the same to Baltimore, Philadelphia, New York, and Boston. This particular arrangement seems never to have become effective; but in December, 1876, the carriers put a modified version into effect. According to this later plan, the rates to Europe by way of New York, Philadelphia, and Baltimore were to be the same, while freight intended for local consumption at port cities was to be charged 10 percent less to Philadelphia and 13 percent less to Baltimore than it was to New York. Westbound freight took the same basis as freight not exported. To carry out the agreement, a committee was subsequently appointed, composed of the foreign freight agents of the different lines. The committee met in New York weekly to determine what the ocean rates had been during the preceding week. These ocean rates, added to the established inland rates—presumably the rates to New York—were telegraphed to the West on the last day of each week, and formed the basis, during the week following, for the rates from inland points to foreign ports through all the North Atlantic Seaboard cities.

Agreement of April, 1877. The agreement of December, 1876, broke down, less because of dissatisfaction with its terms than because of alleged rate cutting. Thus the New York Central, the Erie, and the Pennsylvania companies joined in charging the Baltimore and Ohio with making contracts for freight from the West to Baltimore at less than the rates agreed upon, and with making them, too, in many cases and for large amounts, as if in accordance with instructions from headquarters. In April, 1877, nevertheless, the compact was replaced by another agreement, set forth in the following terms:

"Memorandum of agreement made this 5th day of April, 1877, between New York Central and Hudson River R.R. Co., Erie Railway Co., by H.J.J., receiver, the Pennsylvania RR. Co., and the Baltimore & Ohio RR. Co., witnesseth:

"To avoid all future misunderstandings in respect to geographic advantages or disadvantages of the cities of Baltimore, Philadelphia, and New York, as affected by rail and water transportation, and with the view of effecting an equalization of the aggregate cost of rail and ocean transportation between all competitive points in the West, Southwest, Northwest and all domestic and foreign points reached through the above cities, it is agreed:

"First—That in lieu of the percentage differentials heretofore agreed upon, there shall be 'fixed differentials' upon the rates of all eastbound traffic from all competitive points beyond the western termini of the trunk lines, whether on freight shipped locally and afterwards exported or shipped for direct export. These differentials shall be as follows: Three cents per 100 to Baltimore, and 2 cents less per 100 to Philadelphia than the agreed rates established from time to time to New York, and all such traffic shall be billed at the rates thus fixed, and no export or other drawback shall be paid thereon; it being further agreed that the cost to the shipper of delivering grain at each port, from the terminus of each of the roads to the vessel on which it is exported, as well as the number of days free storage allowed thereon, shall be the same.

"Second—That the rates to Boston shall at no time be less than those to New York on domestic or foreign freight.

"Third—Should rail and ocean steam through bills of lading be issued, neither of the parties hereto will accept, as its proportion, less than its current local rates to its seaboard termini. But no joint rail and ocean rail bills of lading shall be given or recognized by the parties hereto.

"Fourth—That on all westbound traffic passing over the roads of the parties hereto from competitive points at or east of their respective eastern termini to all competitive points west, northwest, or southwest of their western termini, the differences in rates from Baltimore and Philadelphia below New York shall on 3d class, 4th class and special, be the same as the differences fixed on eastbound business, and on 1st and 2d classes 8 cents less per 100 from Baltimore and 6 cents less per 100 from Philadelphia than the agreed rates from New York, and that after existing contracts governing foreign business can be terminated, neither of the parties hereto will accept as its proportion of this ocean steam and rail rate less than the established local rates."

Later History of Differential Rates. The agreement of 1877 is given at length because its main provisions remained in force until quite recent years. Until 1899 there was no change at all. In this year the differentials of Baltimore and Philadelphia on export grain were cut in half, becoming 1½ cents and 1 cent instead of 3 cents and 2 cents. In 1903 the differentials on export iron and steel were also cut in half, and in 1905 the differentials on export flour were reduced to 2 cents and 1 cent. Finally, in the Eastern Class Rate Investigation of 1930, all differentials on local business, east or westbound, were eliminated, leaving only the differentials on export traffic.

This does not mean that the agreement of 1877 escaped criticism. On the contrary, the whole matter was referred to Albert Fink, one-time Commissioner of the Southern Railway and Steamship Association and at the time executive officer of the Trunk Lines Joint Executive Committee, as early as 1881 for fresh examination and report. Fink reported that the principal purpose of any adjustment was to give all competing carriers a fair share of the business, and that the differentials of 1877 did this well enough. Again, in 1882, consideration was secured from a board created for the purpose, composed of Messrs. Thurman, Washburn, and Cooley—three eminent gentlemen from legal and political circles. The opinion of this board also reaffirmed the differentials, observing that they seemed to find their reason in competitive forces. Still later, the differential rate adjustment was brought before the Interstate Commerce Commission, and was discussed in a number of Commission decisions. The most important of these were in 1898, in 1905, and in 1930. Rulings of the Commission were responsible for the reduction of the differentials allowed Philadelphia and Baltimore on export flour, and for the elimination of differentials on local traffic to and from the ports; but the differentials of 3 and 2 cents on export business through Baltimore and Philadelphia which represented the central principle of the arrangement of 1877 still remain. In 1933, it is true, a decision of the Supreme Court denied the authority of the Interstate Commerce Commission to prescribe export differentials between ports, but Congress subsequently amended the Interstate Commerce Act, and the Commission's power in such matters is now unquestioned. It is, perhaps, fair to say that the export differential system, as described in previous pages, embodies a working compromise, and that it is stable because the parties to the compromise cannot agree upon any alternative which they would prefer.

REFERENCES

General Treatises

Bigham, Truman C., and Roberts, Merrill J., *Transportation, Principles and Problems,* New York, McGraw-Hill, 1952.

Brown, H. G., *Transportation Rates and Their Regulation,* New York, Macmillan, 1916.

Fair, Marvin L., and Williams, Ernest W., *Economics of Transportation,* New York, Harper, 1950.

Landon, Charles E., *Transportation, Principles, Practices, Problems,* New York, Sloane, 1951.

Locklin, D. Philip, *Economics of Transportation,* Chicago, Irwin, 1947.

McPherson, L. G., *Railroad Freight Rates in Relation to the Industry and Commerce of the United States,* New York, Holt, 1909.

Ripley, W. Z., *Railroads: Rates and Regulation,* New York, Longmans, 1912.

Other Books

Clark, J. M., *Standards of Reasonableness in Local Freight Discrimination,* New York, Columbia University, 1910.

Daish, John B., *The Atlantic Port Differentials,* Washington, Lowdermilk, 1918.

Hobbah, R. V., *Railroad Transit Privileges,* Chicago, University of Chicago, 1944.

Knorst, William J., *Transportation and Traffic Management,* Chicago, College of Advanced Traffic, 1950.

Oppenheimer, Saul Chesterfield, *The National Transportation Policy and Intercarrier Competitive Rates, Legislative History and Legal Interpretation,* Harrisburg, Pa., Evangelical Press, 1945.

Periodicals

Brown, H., "The Competition of Transportation Companies," *American Economic Review,* December, 1914.

Daggett, Stuart, "The Decision on the Union Pacific Merger," *Quarterly Journal of Economics,* February, 1913.

Daggett, Stuart, "Later Developments in the Union Pacific Merger Case," *Quarterly Journal of Economics,* August, 1914.

Ernst, R. W., "Thought Provoking Transportation Privileges Granted Receivers and Shippers," *Traffic World,* May 10, 1952.

Harbeson, R. W., "Transportation Developments and the North Atlantic Ports," *Harvard Business Review,* October, 1933.

Nelson, J. C., "Pattern of Competition and Monopoly in Present Day Transport and Implication for Public Policy," *Land Economics,* August, 1950.

Ripley, W. Z., "Economic Wastes in Transportation," *Political Science Quarterly,* September, 1906.

Roberts, Merrill, "Economic Aspects of Southern Grain Rates," *Southern Economic Journal,* July, 1949.

Sorrell, L. C., "Transportation Charges and the Market Area," *Traffic World,* June 7, 1930.

Wilson, G. L., "Are Railroad Freight Rate Structures Obsolete?," *Harvard Business Review,* January, 1935.

Wilson, G. L., "French Railroads Develop New Freight Rate System," *Railway Age,* April 24, 1948.

Special and Miscellaneous

National Resources Planning Board, *Transportation and National Policy,* Part I, section VI, *The Nature and Control of the Transport Market,* by Burton N. Behling, 1942.

National Resources Planning Board, *Transportation and National Policy,* Part I, section III, *Rates and Rate Structure,* by D. Philip Locklin, 1942.

United States Senate, Committee on Foreign and Interstate Commerce, *To Prohibit Discriminatory Practice in Granting of Transit Privileges,* Hearings before a subcommittee on S. 2444, 76th C., 1st S., 1939.

Group and Basing Point Rates

We have seen in the two preceding chapters that rates may be made upon a distance basis. We have also observed that they may be and are made to meet the exigencies of competition produced by the clash of interests of rival carriers and by the demand of producers and distributors for connection with a market upon relatively favorable terms. The first practice is expressed in the mileage scale; the second in some form of differential or balanced rate system in which the emphasis is upon relationships rather than upon the absolute amount of the carrier charge, and in which the element of distance is subordinated to that of commercial necessity. We may now consider the second practice further and discuss the group or blanket rate; and we may examine a third possibility in rate making, namely, that a carrier may ask less to haul freight to a more distant than to a nearer point upon its line. If this last alternative seems to resemble the policy of selling two eggs for less than the price of one, which Alice found puzzling in her trip behind the looking glass, it may nevertheless, sometimes, be defended with arguments of considerable strength.

Group Rates

Group or blanket tariffs quote identical rates from a given origin to destinations which are successively more remote or they quote the same rates from points of origin which are unequally distant from the destinations to which freight or passengers will move. Something very similar often happens in general business. It occurs when a retail store delivers without charge or at the same charge to all points in a described area, when an electric corporation fixes rates that are uniform within a district, and when steel mills quote the same price for deliveries at near and at more distant towns.

The recognition of blocks or zones in mileage tariffs is an instance of group rate making. So is the practice of charging a single transport price to factories or mines which are in competition. It is true that carriers may, as in the grain and livestock adjustments, use a scheme of differential or related charges, and this may be a preferable solution for the difficulty if the producing units which compete are far apart; but not infrequently it will be feasible for them to erect a group that is sufficiently extensive to include all the competing plants. While this nullifies the advantages of location which some establishments possess, it permits a scattering of production which may conform to public policy. Carriers also group points of destination, for reasons which will, presently, be more fully explained.

Grouping of Producers

Among the earliest cases which came before the Interstate Commerce Commission were those in which carriers serving Jersey City charged the same rates on milk and cream from points of supply over distances which ranged as high as 200 miles. The Commission refused to interfere with this practice of grouping, in spite of the complaints of producers near Jersey City.[1] Among later cases were the "Lake Cargo Coal Cases," in which the relative rates from coal-producing districts in the Appalachians to Lake Erie ports were matters of dispute,[2] and the more recent controversy in which groups in Indiana and other groups in Illinois were parties.

Speaking in the Indiana-Illinois litigation, the Supreme Court said:

Bituminous coal is produced in great quantities in Indiana, Illinois and western Kentucky. In each State there are producing areas that have long been grouped for rate-making purposes. These groups or districts are the Brazil-Clinton, the Linton-Sullivan, the Princeton-Ayrshire, and the Booneville in Indiana; the Northern Illinois, the Fulton-Peoria, the Springfield, the Belleville, and the Southern in Illinois; and the Western in Kentucky. Group rates have been established by the carriers so that all mines within each producing area are accorded the same rates to the same consuming destinations. The result is that comparative distances of the mines in one producing area from a particular consuming destination are commonly disregarded in fixing the group rate.

The Commission followed that method in this case because in its opinion such a rate structure was necessary to afford consumers, coal operators, and carriers a fair opportunity to compete in the purchases, sale, and transportation of coal from the mines in the various groups or districts to the destinations in question. The Commission's power so to act is not challenged here.[3]

In addition to the foregoing, lumber producing points in the South are distributed among groups for the purpose of ratemaking, and Chicago and

[1] 2 I.C.C. 272; 2 I.C.R. 162, 1888.
[2] 46 I.C.C. 159, 1917; 101 I.C.C. 513, 1925; 126 I.C.C. 309, 1927; 139 I.C.C. 367, 1928. See chap. 10.
[3] 69 Sup. Ct. Rep. 278, 1949.

Birmingham are accorded the same rate in shipments to the West. A long list of other producer groupings could easily be supplied.

Grouping of Points of Destination. Texas Common Point System

The grouping of points of destination is even more common in railroad practice than is that of grouping of points of origin. One of the older structures, now broken down, was that of the Texas common point system. In this system a line was drawn through the western portion of Texas, roughly separating the grazing region of the extreme west from the area devoted more exclusively to agriculture. This line began just west of Acme, Texas, near the northern boundary of the state, and ran in a southeasterly direction through the state to Corpus Christi on the Gulf of Mexico. Most of Texas, therefore, lay east of the line. The rates from points of origin outside of Texas to all Texas points in this eastern or common point territory were made the same, with the exception of a small group of points in the vicinity of Houston and Galveston, and another small group near Texarkana. The Texas common point territory extended a maximum distance of 500 miles north and south, and 465 miles east and west. Under the common point arrangement a St. Louis businessman might ship to Corpus Christi on the Gulf for the same rate he would have paid to San Antonio, 159 miles less distant, or to Denison, on the northern boundary of Texas, 375 miles closer than San Antonio. A New York businessman reaching the market through Galveston might ship to Denison or to Fort Worth for the same rate which he would pay to San Antonio or to Waco.[4]

The Texas grouping was the result of competition between routes entering Texas from Kansas City and St. Louis in the north, from Memphis and Vicksburg in the east, and from Galveston in the south. If there had been no group rate, the St. Louis lines would have met the competition of the water route at Galveston, so that rates from the North would have been less to Galveston than from St. Louis to interior Texas cities such as Waco. Likewise, the rail-steamship lines operating through Galveston would have met the competition of the all-rail route from St. Louis at the northern boundary of the state, so that rates from the Gulf would, in turn, have been lower to destinations near the northern boundary such as Denison than they were to Waco or to other interior Texas towns. Instances of lesser charges for longer hauls would have occurred on both movements. Rates of this sort were avoided by the establishment of the Texas group system, to the general satisfaction of shippers and carriers for a number of years.

[4] H. B. Vanderblue and K. F. Burgess, *Railroads: Rates-Service-Management,* New York, Macmillan, 1923.

Trunk Line Rate System

Akin in some respects to the Texas system, though different in others, was the structure that prevailed in Trunk Line territory at one time.

The Trunk Line system was used in that part of the United States which lies north of the Ohio and Potomac and east of the Mississippi River.[5] Its main principles were adopted for eastbound traffic on June 12, 1879, at a meeting of the joint executive committee of the lines in trunk line territory. Seven years later a similar system was adopted for westbound rates. Eliminating as many complications as possible, the substance of the arrangement was as follows: In calculating rates between New York and points in Central Freight Association territory[6] the initial operation was to determine for each destination a governing percentage of the rates from New York to Chicago. In obtaining this percentage the following procedure was adopted: First, a rate of 25 cents per 100 pounds from New York to Chicago was assumed. Second, 6 cents per 100 pounds was deducted from this assumed rate to allow for terminal expenses at the two ends of the haul. Third, the remainder of 19 cents was divided by 920, representing the distance in miles from New York to Chicago. Fourth, this quotient or rate per mile was multiplied by the distance from New York to the point for which a governing percentage was desired, and 6 cents was added to the product to cover terminal expense. Lastly, the figure arrived at by means of the fourth operation was divided by 25 in order to secure a percentage relationship with the New York–Chicago rate. Having arrived at this percentage, then those interested could henceforth always obtain the actual rate from New York to point "X" by multiplying the current New York–Chicago rate, whatever it might be at any time, by the percentage which the calculation produced.[7]

---

[5] W. Z. Ripley, "The Trunk Line Rate System: A Distance Tariff," *Quarterly Journal of Economics,* February, 1906.

[6] Roughly speaking, Central Freight Association territory is bounded on the east by an irregular line running from near Buffalo, N.Y., to Parkersburg, W.Va. It is bounded on the south by the Ohio River; on the west by the Mississippi River from Cairo to Dubuque; and on the north by a line drawn from Dubuque to Milwaukee, and by the Great Lakes from Milwaukee to Buffalo. The territory includes a limited area, also, lying north of Lake Ontario.

[7] The method of making rates to points west of Chicago did not altogether conform to the method used in computing rates to points further east. It is true that percentages, varying from 100 to 117, were assigned to western cities; but these particular percentages were not those which the trunk line formula would produce. In these cases, the influence which determined rates was the competition of carriers to upper Mississippi River crossings with carriers to St. Louis and, still more generally, the competition of the cities of Chicago and St. Louis and of the carriers which served them. The distance from New York to St. Louis was 116 percent of the distance to Chicago, and St. Louis was originally given class rates on a 116 percent basis. In 1908, when the St. Louis and the East St. Louis rates were made the same, this was increased to 117 percent, and the bridge toll to St. Louis was abolished (33 I.C.C. 673, 1915). Competition between the lower and the upper Mississippi River crossings extended the 117

The Trunk Line system, so far described, was a modification of a mileage tariff. But the group principle was also involved, in that rates were not computed for each city in the area but only for key towns, and the charges established for these towns were applied to districts of different sizes and shapes for reasons unconnected with distance.

Figure 39 shows the number and location of trunk line groups in 1925.

FIGURE 39.   Trunk Line Rate Zones.

Study of the map will show that the shape and alignment of the zones in the Trunk Line tariff varied according to competitive conditions. Thus the 78 percent zone, which included the important cities of Columbus, Toledo, and Detroit, extended farther west than the 81 percent zone, which had no town of equivalent importance; and the 93 percent group, in which Indianapolis was located, extended farther west than the groups

percent group as far north as Dubuque, and the difference between 117 percent and the 100 percents which expressed the Chicago rate was eliminated by degrees in the area between the river and Chicago. No allowance was made for terminal costs in these adjustments.

to which the percentages 94 and 95 were assigned. It is also noticeable that the percentages allotted groups in the northern Michigan peninsula rose much more rapidly than increasing distances from New York would justify; and the effect of ferry services across Lake Michigan was reflected in the extension of the Chicago, or 100 percent group, far to the north on the Lake's western shore. Ripley pointed out, as early as 1906, that the zone boundary lines in the Trunk Line scheme lay, in general, immediately west of large cities. The obvious reason was that there was competition at these cities which depressed rates. Transition from one level to another occurred only when the zone had reached so far beyond the compelling city that the force of competition had been weakened. Ripley noticed also that the zone boundaries frequently followed the lines of important transverse railways. This was because it was advantageous for such railways to remain, as far as possible, within a single group. To illustrate this point, let us suppose that two groups were involved, one taking 82 percent of the Chicago rates, and the other 83 percent; and that a north-and-south railroad, connecting with east-and-west lines in this area, desired to deliver freight to destinations in these groups. Such a transverse carrier might have received freight from a junction in the 82 percent group for delivery in the 83 percent group; but it could hardly have accepted consignments in the 83 percent group for delivery in the 82 percent group without making a greater charge for a shorter than for a longer haul. Transverse lines crossing two zones could be worked only one way unless they secured special dispensation from the Interstate Commerce Commission under the provisions of Section 4 of the Interstate Commerce Act, a section which we shall discuss in chapter 21. These zones are the feature of the Trunk Line System which allows it to serve as an illustration of group rates.

Transcontinental Rates

Current practice in the groupings of points of destination may be still further illustrated by transcontinental railroad tariffs. In constructing transcontinental rates, carriers distribute cities from Colorado to the Atlantic coast into groups and charge the same rates to all towns listed in each group. This method of rate making began, apparently, as early as 1887 when the railroads recognized Missouri River common points, Chicago common points, and New York common points. It was expanded to include Cincinnati–Detroit common points and Pittsburgh–Buffalo common points and, later, was further enlarged to cover areas in the south and west. In 1943 the rate zones in Transcontinental Freight Bureau territory applicable to traffic to and from the South Pacific coast were those set forth on the accompanying map.

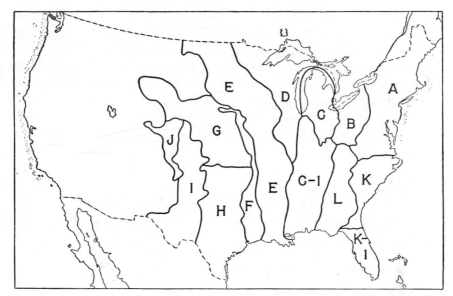

FIGURE 40. Rate Zones in Transcontinental Freight Bureau Territory. From Stuart Daggett and John P. Carter, *The Structure of Transcontinental Railroad Rates*, Berkeley and Los Angeles, University of California, 1947, p. 53.)

Rates from San Francisco, in 1943, were the same to all points listed in zone A, to all points listed in zone B, and so for other zones indicated upon the map. In fact, the groupings were more extended than the map implies because the same rate was sometimes applied to several groups, even in the relatively simple class quotations. Thus, in 1943, first-class rates were those set forth in the following table:

First-Class Rates Between California Terminals
and Points Taking Group Rates, 1943

Group	Rate (cents per 100 lbs.)
A, K, K-1	611
B, L	594
C, C-1	578
D	561
E	545
F	495
G, H, I	462
J	403

SOURCE: Stuart Daggett and John P. Carter, *The Structure of Transcontinental Railroad Rates*, Berkeley and Los Angeles, University of California, 1947, p. 57.

In the case of some commodities, the grouping was still more extreme. This can be illustrated by another map, which shows rates upon dried fruits and vegetables from Fresno, California, to Eastern destinations, again as of the year 1943. It appears in this map that, in the lettuce tariff, the same rates were charged from Fresno to most U.S. destinations.

The foregoing instances, selected out of many, present examples in which carriers have charged identical rates for shipments to destinations unequally distant from a common destination of commodities transported. Group rates, in this sense, are standard in rail, water, and to a less extent in air communication. They are less common in motor vehicle transport.

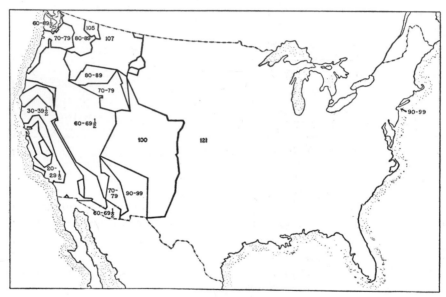

FIGURE 41.   Rates on Dried Fruits and Vegetables from Fresno, California.

Reasons for Group Rate Making

A list of reasons for quoting rates by groups instead of by individual points of origin or destination would include the following:

1. Small differences in mileage and in cost may be disregarded on long hauls.

2. Zones in the direction of movement may be explained by competitive pressure.

The reader's attention is directed to the following chart which illustrates the grouping of destinations in the direction of movement.

Let us suppose that on a direct line *ABCDE* there is pressure at *B* and at *D* but not at *C* or at points, generally, between *B* and *D;* then the rate of progression of a mileage tariff will be steady until *B* is passed. But

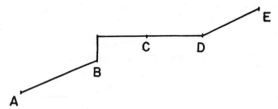

FIGURE 42.   Diagram Illustrating the Grouping of
Destinations in the Direction of Movement.

immediately after *B* the rate may jump to a level appropriate to *D*, and
be held at this new level until *D* is overrun. Professor Ripley noticed this
condition in describing the Trunk Line system. The effect would be to
produce a group between *B* and *D*.

It is conceivable that conditions may be such as to prevent any further
increase in the rates to stations beyond *D*, although in the chart it is
assumed that, at *D*, normal progression will be resumed. If this is true,
the blanket which begins in the vicinity of *B* may be indefinitely enlarged.
Figure 43 presents an illustration of such a case.

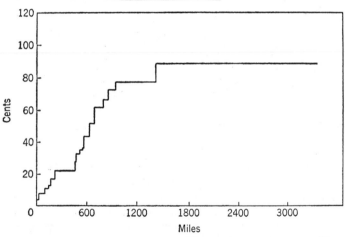

FIGURE 43.   Rates on Canned Goods from San Francisco to Charlotte, via Atchison, Topeka and Santa Fe, Wabash, Pennsylvania,
and Southern. From Stuart Daggett and John P. Carter, *The
Structure of Transcontinental Railroad Rates,* Berkeley and Los
Angeles, University of California, 1947, p. 102.)

The preceding diagram presents the profile of canned goods rates from
San Francisco to Charlotte, via St. Louis, as it existed in 1943. The
diagram shows a more or less regular progression from San Francisco to
the New Mexico–Texas state line, which is also the point where the ter-

ritory of the Transcontinental Freight Bureau begins. At the state line the rate is raised from 78 to 88 cents, and this same rate is thenceforth charged to all subsequent stations upon the route. This is a notable, though not at all a unique instance of a zone in the direction of movement, although the mileage progression is not in the later stages resumed.[8]

3. Competition may also explain zones which transverse to the direction of movement.

Let *A* in the accompanying diagram be a point at which shipments of goods originate; and let *B, C,* and *D* represent markets, connected with *A* by the carriers *ABCD* and *ADCB.* It is evident that the two carriers which have been named compete for traffic. Moreover, their competition is especially severe at *B* and at *D;* for at *B* the roundabout route *ADCB* meets the competition of the short line *AB,* while at *D* the roundabout route *ABCD* meets the competition of the direct route *AD.* Under such conditions it will be conceivable that both railroads may quote low rates to *B* and to *D,* where competition is most intense, and higher rates to *C;* and if they do this, each will charge lower rates to a more distant than to a nearer point upon its line, in violation of Section 4 of the Act to Regulate Commerce. But neither road may adopt the policy suggested. Instead, the same rates may be quoted to *B, C,* and *D* alike. If this is done, *B, C,* and *D* will be within what railroad men would term a "rate group," because the charge from the common point of origin to all places

[8] Lynch has pointed out that groupings of destinations in the direction of movement may give a key city a special advantage when the grouping is applied in both directions and material from several sources must be combined.

Lynch suggests the following illustration:

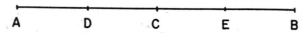

FIGURE 44.   Special Advantages of Key Cities in Group Arrangements.

The explanation is as follows:

"Let us assume that *C* is a 'key' city and *A* and *B* are sources of raw materials. *D* and *E* are other points served by the railroad concerned. On traffic from *A,* charges to all points between *D* and *C,* inclusive, are the same; on traffic from *B,* charges to all points between *C* and *E,* inclusive, are the same. On traffic from *A* charges to *E* are higher than those to *C* while charges on traffic from *B* are higher to *D* than to *C.*

"It can readily be seen that a manufacturing enterprise that requires raw materials from both *A* and *B* will find *C* a more advantageous location, so far as assembly costs are concerned, than either *D* or *E.* Furthermore, *E* is in no more favorable position than *C* for sales to *B,* while its position is inferior in marketing to *A.* A similar relationship obtains between *C* and *D.* Thus a system of grouping, which in every direction favors a 'key' city, affords manufacturers and traders located there decided advantages in transportation charges over competing cities in its territory" (National Resources Planning Board, *Transportation and National Policy,* Part I, Section II, "The Influence of Transportation in the Location of Economic Activities," 1942, by E. S. Lynch, p. 75).

in the area will be the same, although the distances traversed by different shipments may vary.

The transcontinental freight tariff provides an excellent example of this type of rate making. Transcontinental service is supplied by parallel railroad lines reaching the Mississippi Valley in the Southern, Central, and Northern states. Northern companies can not compete with Southern lines in the Southern states nor Southern companies with Northern lines in the Northern states without charging less for longer than for shorter hauls unless, as is the fact, the railroads recognize groups, stretching from north to south, within which all rates from the Pacific Coast are made the same. Nor would it be possible for local lines which connected Northern and Southern points in this same territory to participate in transcontinental business unless these groups were organized. Similar, but older, situations in the Texas and Trunk Line districts have already been described.

4. Grouping of rates may put producers upon an equal basis with respect to a single destination or it may enlarge the area which a producer or group of producers may reach on a single charge. These problems have been discussed. It may be added, however, that grouping introduces a certain flexibility into routing, because a shipment, consigned to a named destination, may be diverted to another destination without a change in the line haul rate.

Generalized Blanket Rates

We have discussed group rates, so far, as a technique which railroads apply under particular conditions, for competitive reasons, or to stabilize industrial relations with which they are concerned. Such rate making has been also advocated upon a more extended scale.

Postal Tariffs

An extreme case of blanket rate making is to be found in the postal tariff, in which the same charge is collected for the carriage of first-class mail from any authorized starting point to any post office within the United States. A similar plan was advocated for railroad service as early as 1898. In his book, *A General Freight and Passenger Post*, J. L. Cowles urged that railroads should be controlled by the United States Post Office and that fares and rates should be introduced as follows:

Passengers	*Fares per Trip*
Way trains, ordinary or second-class cars	$.05
Palace or first-class cars	.20 to .30
Baggage, per piece per trip	.05
Baggage, domicile to domicile	.10 to .30

Freight	*Rate per Car*
Standard cars (flat)	$6.00
Boxcars, oil cars, etc.	8.00

The uniform freight rate was to apply regardless of amount of load up to the car's capacity, and regardless of classification. The time limit for loading and unloading was not to exceed 8 hours.[9]

Hastings Plan

A more recent suggestion, the so-called Hastings plan, has received some attention. This last proposal was submitted to the Senate Committee on Interstate Commerce in 1935 by John A. Hastings, formerly a state senator of New York. As originally introduced, it proposed to divide all rail-

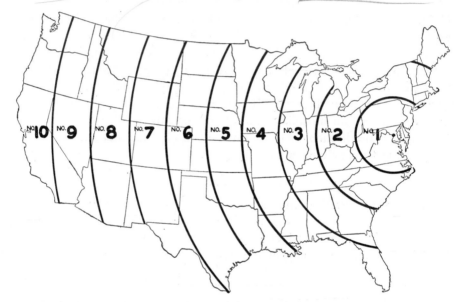

FIGURE 45.   Postalized Coach Fare Regions Under the Hastings Plan.

road passenger traffic into three general classes: namely, short distance, up to 50 miles or thereabouts; regular service other than short distance; and express or limited train service. The fare for the short distance was to be

[9] "The advantages of this reform [says Cowles] ought, it seems to me, to be patent to everyone. Every station, and every man at every station in the country, would be on a par with every other as to passenger and freight rates. Discriminations between individuals and between places would be forever at an end. The great cities would no longer grow at the expense of the intervening country. . . . There would be no more rebates, no more deadheads. Great armies of soliciting agents would disappear. Freight stamps (for freight taxes would be paid in advance) and baggage stamps and passenger tickets would be on sale at drug stores, hotels, and other convenient places, as ordinary postage stamps are today.

15 or 20 cents. The regular train coach fare, other than for short distance, was to be $1.00 for each railroad system which the haul traversed.

In the plan's later form, Mr. Hastings substituted a series of zones, each with a radius of 250 miles, for the original conception of zones each of which comprised the lines of a single railroad system. These zones, starting from any point where transportation might begin, were bounded by concentric circles; thus for service beginning at Washington, D.C., the arrangement might be that shown upon the accompanying map.

The fares to be charged for purely local service were not stated in the revised version of the Hastings plan, but for suburban trips not exceeding 50 miles in length the coach fare was to be 15 cents. For interurban trips, longer than 50 but not exceeding 250 miles, the fare would be $1.25, and for still longer hauls the fare would be a multiple of $1.25 depending upon the number of zones traversed. Thus the coach fare from Washington, D.C., to San Francisco, traversing ten zones, would be $12.50. Higher fares, still calculated on the zone principle but not necessarily increasing every 250 miles, were to be charged per zone for parlor cars ($3.00), for local sleeper cars ($5.00), for regular reserved trains ($10.00), and for de luxe trains ($15.00). Parlor car seats and sleeping berths were to be charged for separately. The Hastings plan as published was confined to passenger service, although an eventual extension to freight movements was foreseen.[10]

Criticism of Plans for Extended Groupings

The postal service earns a profit on first-class rates in spite of extreme blanketing, first, because these rates are extremely high, and second, because the law prohibits competition. Its policy of uniformity of charge, irrespective of distance, is defended upon social grounds. Most simplified plans for group rates or fares promise rate reduction and have attracted support for this reason. It is argued that, in spite of the reduction, lower rates will so increase the volume of traffic that a fair profit will still be obtained. These plans do have, also, social implications. Thus it is contended that equality in rates, irrespective of distance, will distribute industry, eliminate rent, and increase competition. "With a flat rate the manufacturers of the Pacific Coast could meet the shoe manufacturer in Massachusetts on equal terms in every city and village in the United States. The battle would be one of business skill and quality of goods. Monopoly of the shoe trade would pass from a few hands to many." [11]

It is probably true that any rate or fare reduction to the extent proposed by Cowles or Hastings would increase the volume of transportation,

---

[10] Hastings appeared again before a Senate Committee, in 1950, presenting another, slightly changed, version of his plan.

[11] P. W. Francis, *The Pack-Asses of Privilege*, 1911.

whether prices were fixed according to a postal or according to any other system, although the amount of such an increase can be estimated only in a general way. It is also likely, however, that the increase in volume would involve a considerable addition to operating expense, and perhaps some additional capital investment. In these matters the analogy between mail service and general transportation service must not be pushed too far, as the proportion of terminal to total cost in handling first-class mail is greater than in the transportation of passengers or of freight. The imposition of any uniform rate for transportation based upon the average cost of performing service would, moreover, tend to divert short-distance traffic, upon which the rate or fare under a postal service would be relatively high, to private carriage or to types of transport to which the group system was not applied, leaving to the postalized revenues from the remaining business the task of covering the expenses of long distance transport, which would exceed, for the typical ton, the average upon which rates were originally based. Finally, a rate system which freed producers and distributors from the necessity of considering cost of transport in selecting their location, although differential costs of transport would still actually be incurred, would seem likely to decrease the efficiency with which the total process of production and distribution was carried on. For these and other reasons, proposals for postalized rate making have never been approved.

Basing Point Rates

We now pass from group rate making to the more extreme case where lesser rates are charged for longer and greater rates for shorter hauls. This has been often, though inaccurately, referred to as basing point rate making.[12] Strange as it may seem, the practice of charging less for shorter hauls results as naturally from competition as does the practice of a group rate. Let us consider again the situation presented by the diagram of page 390. Here carriers *ABCD* and *ADCB* compete for traffic at points *B, C,* and *D*. We have seen that, in so doing, the contestants may establish a rate group which will provide *B, C,* and *D* with a single, uniform rate, presumably based upon the short-haul costs from *A* to *B* and from *A* to *D* of the respective carriers. But another possibility is that carrier *ABCD* will meet its rival's rate at *D,* without changing its rates at *C* and *B,* and that carrier *ADCB* will similarly reduce its charge at *B* without change in the tariff to *C* and *B*. In this event each carrier will collect a lower rate for a longer than for a shorter haul over its line. This will represent an alteration in the system of carrier charges, but at least for the moment each community concerned will pay the same rate as that

[12] Basing points may be used in systems which do not include examples of lower charges for longer hauls.

collectable under a mileage system, although *B* and *D* will now be served effectively by two railroads and not, each, by only one. Whether the communities will pay less under the basing point or under a group system will depend upon the level at which group rates are fixed. If costs are averaged and rates adjusted to secure the same net return to the carriers in either case, *C* will probably pay less under a group and *B* and *D* less under a basing point method of rate making. It may be assumed that this will be a matter of indifference to the carriers, although under some circumstances they may be affected by a change in the relative importance of the various towns.[13]

The Hillsdale Case

Competition is usually present when carriers charge lower rates for longer than for shorter hauls, but facts vary. We will, therefore, present two specific and two more general illustrations, drawn from actual experience, in order to make the matter clear.

The Hillsdale case was argued before the Interstate Commerce Commission in 1903.[14] The controversy concerned rates on ice shipped from Hillsdale, Michigan, to Springfield and Columbus, Ohio. The following diagram shows the relative position of the towns involved.

In the Hillsdale case the Lake Shore and Michigan Southern Railway operated a line from Hillsdale through Toledo to Sandusky. There were two direct connections between Toledo and Columbus, the Hocking Valley and the Toledo and Ohio Central railroads, and one direct connection between Sandusky and Columbus, over the Columbus, Sandusky, & Hocking Railroad. A fourth route reached Columbus by way of Sandusky and Springfield, over the C. C. C. & St. L. Railroad. There was active competition at Columbus because of this distribution, but there was no carrier competition at Springfield. The distance over the short line route from Hillsdale to Columbus, via Toledo and over the Hocking Valley Railroad was 190 miles; the distance over the shortest route to Springfield was 219 miles. The C. C. C. & St. L. could, however, and did, carry freight, originating at Hillsdale, through Springfield to Columbus over a route whose total length was 264 miles. Because of differences in distance, the standard

---

[13] The minimum which line *ABCD* can defend as a charge to *D* or the line *ADCB* as a charge to *B* will be that price which will cover out of pocket cost. There is no competitive reason, in the conditions given, why either carrier in fixing rates to *C* will charge less than fully allocated cost. The fact that one line or the other collects less than full costs to *B* or *D* may be regarded as an absorption or, what is essentially the same, a distribution of common costs according to the purchasers' willingness to pay. This possibility was examined in chap. 16. The policy will maximize profit, under proper assumptions, including that of the stability of the conditions under which the decision is first made. The questions of public policy involved will be discussed in chap. 21.

[14] *Ulrick & Williams v. L. S. & M. S. Ry. Co.*, 9 I.C.C.R. 495, 1903.

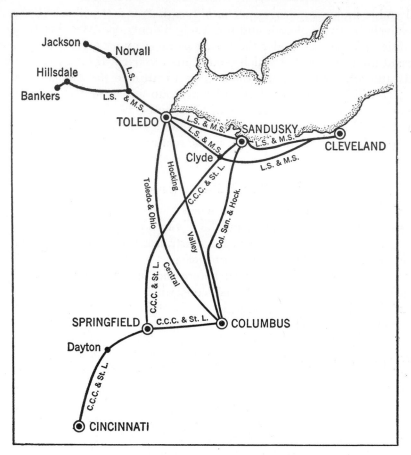

FIGURE 46. The Hillsdale Case.

rate from Hillsdale to Columbus was 80 cents and that to Springfield was 100 cents. The C. C. C. & St. L. maintained the latter late, but it met short line competition by quoting a rate of 80 cents to Columbus. This meant that the C. C. C. & St. L. charged Springfield, a nearer point upon its line, more than it charged Columbus, a more distant point upon its line; but on no other condition could it participate in the haul.

Florida Citrus Case

A relatively recent example of charging lower rates for longer than for shorter hauls has been presented by citrus rates from Florida to Northeastern points. The facts are illustrated by the following map.

Citrus moves by rail from Florida points such as Fort Pierce in eastern Florida to Baltimore, Philadelphia, New York, and other Northern destinations. It also moves by truck from Florida growing centers to ports upon

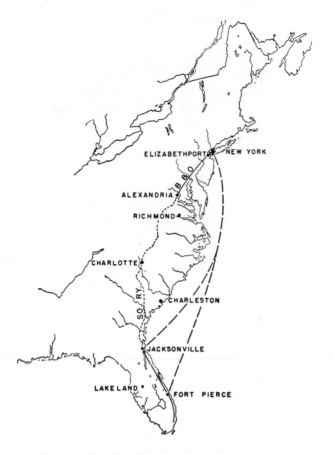

FIGURE 47. The Florida Citrus Case.

the Seaboard and thence by boat to Northern cities. The distances, by rail, from Fort Pierce are 1,269 miles to New York, 1,248 miles to Elizabethport, New Jersey, 1,027 miles to Alexandria, Virginia, and 655 miles to Charlotte, North Carolina. The water rate from Fort Pierce to New York was, in 1935, 56 cents per 100 pounds, in addition to which truck charges of 3 or 4 cents had to be incurred. The rail lines proposed, in 1935, and were allowed to charge 59 cents from Fort Pierce to New York, while quoting at the same time rates of 60 cents to Charlotte, 80 cents to Alexandria, and 81 cents to Elizabethport, all intermediate towns.[15]

[15] 211 I.C.C. 535, 1935; 218 I.C.C. 637, 1936; 226 I.C.C. 315, 1938; 229 I.C.C. 63, 1938; 237 I.C.C. 245, 1943; 246 I.C.C. 615, 1941; 266 I.C.C. 627, 1946. The permission granted in 1935 was withdrawn in 1946.

Southern Territory

The two preceding cases illustrate the principle of charging more for a shorter than for a longer haul in individual instances. The same practice, developed into a system, once characterized rate structures in the Old South and, for transcontinental traffic, on the Pacific Coast.

When railroads began to operate in the Southern states, they found that rail movements from New York or Washington to Atlantic Seaboard cities, such as Wilmington, Charleston, or Savannah, were subject to the competition of steamship lines engaged in the coasting trade. It was necessary for railroads to meet the low rates which the steamers charged; but these rates were effective only to the steamship ports of call, and rates to points intermediate between the Seaboard towns could be, and were, made higher than to the ports themselves. In this fashion Southern railroads treated the principal cities on the South Atlantic Seaboard as basing points. Normally, the rates to interior cities were made by combining the rates to Seaboard basing points with a local rate beyond. But this brings us to a second characteristic of the Southern system. In the development of Southern rates, there emerged a second set of basing points at the head of navigation upon rivers emptying into the Atlantic Ocean or into the Gulf of Mexico. Such points were Richmond, Virginia; Columbia, South Carolina; and Augusta, Macon, and Columbus, Georgia. All of these competitive river centers were in existence before the beginning of the railways, and were places at which shipments were received from the Seaboard or collected from the surrounding country and from which goods were distributed by wagon or pack animals. Railroad rates to the "Fall Line Cities" were made something less than the combination of the rail rate to the Seaboard basing points and of the local rate inland, responding to the possibility of river carriage. Pushing farther west, still another condition was revealed. At Atlanta, the carriers which brought goods from New York and New England into the Southeastern states met the competition of other carriers connecting the Southeast with the manufacturing cities of the northern Mississippi Valley. Because of market competition, Atlanta was made a basing point. Finally, in the course of time, additional basing points were set up where intensive railway competition compelled low rates, or where some rate concession seemed desirable for reasons of railroad policy.

Characterization of the Southern Rate System

The peculiarity of the old Southern basing point system was that it constructed rates to noncompetitive communities by adding locals to basing point rates. The combination was generally high, and in many cases the system produced a greater charge for a shorter than for a longer haul. How this could occur is shown in Figure 48.

Let *B* in this diagram indicate the point of origin of a shipment. Let *A* be a basing point and *X, Y,* and *Z* local centers of population dependent upon *A.* Under a basing point scheme of rate making, the rate from *B* to *X, Y,* or *Z* will be the rate to *A* plus the local rate *AZ, AY,* or *AX,* as the case might be. It follows as an incidental result that the rate *BX* will exceed the rate *BA,* although the traffic to *A* from *B* will pass through *A* on its way to destination. This condition raises difficulties which we have to consider.

It is evident that the old Southern basing point system was a highly selective kind of rate making in which the influence of competition was recognized, when and to the degree in which it was felt, and in which noncompetitive localities received slight consideration. In the whole terri-

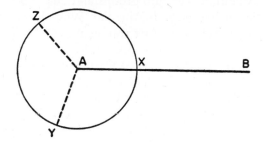

FIGURE 48.   Basing Point Rate-making.

tory east of the Mississippi, and south of the Ohio River and the line of the Chesapeake and Ohio Railway through Lynchburg, Richmond, and Norwolk News within which this method of making rates was used, the policy produced an irregular rate landscape, with summits and depressions which reflected the absence or presence of competition, but which conformed but slightly to the distances over which freight was hauled. For instance, it was possible in the South that the rate on a given commodity might be $1.00 for a haul of 80 miles, 90 cents if the haul was extended to 100 miles, $1.10 for a distance of 120 miles, and 75 cents for a shipment carried 150 miles, all in one continuous line, if the goods passed through local communities and also through basing points where competition existed to a greater or less degree.

Such irregularity made the system unpopular with regulatory authorities, as well as difficult for the general public to understand. It seemed, at best, unrelated to the service which the railroad performed. On the other hand, the basing point system was defended on the following grounds: (1) it was said to diminish the costs of transportation by encouraging a certain concentration of traffic; and (2) it enabled small dealers in the basing cities to compete with wholesale merchants in the large metropolitan areas, for low rates were paid by all residents of basing point towns, and these low rates were, to a considerable degree, independent of the quantities which were shipped.

Since 1910 the Southern system of rate making has been the subject of a number of Interstate Commerce Commission investigations and decisions,[16] the effect of which has been to substitute, in the main, a mileage tariff for the basing point system long characteristic of the Southern states.

Transcontinental Rate Structure

For a second considerable example of the use of basing points in railroad rate making we may return to the transcontinental tariff. We have observed that carriers, in constructing these tariffs, distributed cities from Colorado to the Atlantic Coast into groups and charged the same rates to all towns listed in each group. In the Far West, however, the original practice was different. When the first transcontinental railroads were built they found, on the Pacific Coast, communities which had for some time been supplied by ships that had circled Cape Horn or which, in coöperation with the Panama Railroad, had established a rail and water route by way of the Isthmus of Panama. The lowest rates charged for water transportation were, naturally, those between New York and the Pacific ports, of which the most important was San Francisco. The railroad was compelled to meet the shipping rates, but it saw no reason why it should charge interior cities as little as it charged seaboard towns. Collis P. Huntington later related a conversation about this matter which took place at Carson City, Nevada, in 1861, between Stanford, Dr. Strong, Mr. Crocker, and himself, representing the railroad, and some twenty representative men of Nevada. The Nevada people observed that Huntington kept a pretty good hardware store, but that he was likely to leave it in the mountains if he started to build a railroad in Nevada. Huntington replied that he would look out for that; but, he continued, when the road was built he proposed to charge through rates which, while less than the Nevada people were paying for goods which then came to San Francisco by boat and were subsequently teamed across the mountains, would be materially greater than the rates to San Francisco. "We shall charge you for bringing back," he said, "almost as much as we shall charge from New York." After the road was built, Huntington says he met one of these same men with whom he had talked in 1861. "Said I: 'You recollect that talk we had in the Curry House in 1861?' 'Yes, oh yes.' Well, we talked about that. He said: 'You've got me there, Huntington.' 'Well,' said I, 'I said you would grumble. Now,' said I, 'you shut up.' " [17]

[16] See especially 30 I.C.C. 153, 32 I.C.C. 61, 1914; 100 I.C.C. 513, 1925; 109 I.C.C. 300, 1926; 113 I.C.C. 200, 1926; 128 I.C.C. 567, 1927; 262 I.C.C. 447, 1945.
[17] Stuart Daggett, *Chapters on the History of the Southern Pacific,* New York, Ronald, 1922, pp. 283–284.

The Western system of basing points differed from that in the South in that the same rates were charged to all terminals. It resembled the Southern structure, however, in that rates to local points, even when intermediate, were higher than to terminals. Thus it was important to a town that it be named a terminal, and many disputes arose over the inclusion or exclusion of particular cities. At the beginning the only terminal was San Francisco. As the system developed, additional towns were given terminal privileges, of which the principal, although not the only, cities were Seattle, Tacoma, Portland, Los Angeles, and San Diego. All of these were accessible to ships, although in the case of Los Angeles, the accessibility was more formal than real. The reason for the inclusion of Los Angeles in the list of terminals was the desire of the Santa Fe Railroad to encourage the growth of a distributing center in southern California which might compete with San Francisco farther north. Some towns, like San Jose, once enjoyed but later lost terminal privileges. Others, like Santa Clara, sought them in vain. The test which determined the classification of a Pacific Coast point was the presence or absence of effective water competition; and this test was applied with fair consistency.

Relation Between Terminal and Intermediate Rates

Transcontinental rates were thus molded by competitive influences. However, the cities which ranked as noncompetitive in this system included important centers east of the Pacific Coast such as Reno, Nevada, and Spokane, Washington; and the protests of such towns were much more vigorous and sustained than those of local communities in Southern territory. It probably never was true, unless perhaps at the very beginning, that intermountain cities were uniformly charged the terminal rate plus the local back. Yet the difference was often large, and when rates were reduced to comparable units such as mills per ton per mile the relationship between terminal and intermediate rates appeared difficult to defend. Speaking of the rates on iron and steel in 1918, a representative of the Traffic Bureau of Utah called attention to the fact that the rate on iron and steel articles for export from Chicago territory to Pacific Coast terminals was 40 cents per hundredweight, or 3.54 mills per ton per mile. He continued:

They take an identical carload of the same commodity, and when it is going to the Pacific coast for domestic consumption the rate is 65 cents a hundred, or 5.76 mills per ton-mile. If they were to apply that rate at the Utah common points—the same 65-cent rate—it would pay 8.65 mills per ton-mile. But they say, "We cannot afford that; you must pay 10.84. We haul it for a man in Russia for 3.54, but that is only the out-of-pocket cost. We will make you a rate of 10.84, which is a lower rate than you are entitled to.

I think any article, whether it is transportation or anything else, that could be produced at some profit at a price of 3.54, when you pay 5.76 for it you are paying a handsome profit; and if you pay 8.65 for it you are paying an abnormal profit; and if you pay 10.85 for the same thing you are being outrageously imposed upon, which is what we are doing.[18]

This apparent injustice to the plateau, or intermountain, towns led the Interstate Commerce Commission to scrutinize very carefully the presumptions upon which transcontinental rates at different times were based. One result of this examination was the conclusion, in 1911, that the difference between terminal rates and those to intermediate towns should be less on shipments which originated at cities in the interior of the United States than on shipments which originated at points upon the Eastern Seaboard. This was because the justification for any difference at all was to be found in water competition; and clearly, shippers who were distant from the ocean could not use the sea as easily as could merchants resident upon the coast.[19] In the Nevada case the Interstate Commerce Commission laid down a general rule. Transcontinental carriers were to apply no higher charge to any article carrying a commodity rate from Missouri River points such as Omaha and Kansas City (Group I) to Reno and other points upon the main line of the Central Pacific than to Coast terminal points. Traffic originating at Chicago and in Chicago territory (Group II) moving under commodity rates might have a rate 7 percent higher than that imposed on freight originating in Chicago and Chicago territory and destined for Coast terminals. From Buffalo–Pittsburgh territory (Group III) the rates to intermediate points might rise above those demanded from the same points to the Coast terminals to the extent of 15 percent, while from New York and Trunk Line territory (Group IV) the rates charged to intermountain destinations were not to exceed terminal rates by more than 25 percent.

Opening of the Panama Canal

When the Panama Canal was opened, carriers to and from the Pacific Coast asked that the spread between terminal and intermediate rates be increased because of the intensified competition which the Canal was sure to permit; and this was allowed on westbound shipments of a list of articles especially adapted to water transportation. The list was known as Schedule C. Further adjustments were made on certain specified commodities, eastbound, particularly on asphaltum, barley, beans, and canned goods.[20] The spread was not increased on other articles, and on some goods not suited to water movement no greater charge was allowed to intermountain points than was made to terminal cities. Under the transcon-

[18] Stuart Daggett, *op. cit.*
[19] 21 I.C.C. 329, 1911.
[20] 32 I.C.C. 611, 1915; 33 I.C.C. 480, 1915.

tinental tariffs in force in 1916, commodities were thus divided into three groups, listed in Schedules A, B, and C. Schedule A included commodities which either were not adapted to water transportation or which originated in territories so far removed from the Atlantic Seaboard as to make their transportation by water unlikely. Upon these items the rates to the Pacific Coast were not lower than to intermediate points. Schedule B included about 350 items comprising articles which were more or less adapted to water transportation, upon which the carriers had been authorized to continue rates to intermediate points higher than those to Pacific Coast terminals by the percentages previously mentioned in the text. In Schedule C were articles which originated in large volume on or near the Atlantic Seaboard, were particularly adapted to water transportation, and moved at relatively low rates. The list included about 90 items. The difference between terminal and intermediate rates was greater on these items than in the case of articles described in Schedule B.

War and Post-war Adjustments

Conditions during the First World War were unfavorable to water competition, and this weakened the argument for especially low rates to Western basing points. For this reason the Commission withdrew, in 1916, its permission for preferential rates on Schedule C commodities,[21] and in 1917 it declared generally that rates on shipments from the East to Pacific Coast terminals should not be less than rates to intermediate points.[22] The railroads advanced their terminal rates, in consequence, to the level of their intermediate charges, producing a blanket which extended several hundred miles from the Pacific Coast.

Subsequent to the war carriers applied for at least a partial restoration of the basing system but for the most part without success. In 1922 the Interstate Commerce Commission allowed railroads to quote lower rates on asphalt, barley, beans, canned goods, and rice from California terminal to New York City and on sulfur from Texas and Louisiana mines to California and North Pacific terminals than were charged to intermediate stations,[23] but denied permission on other articles. In 1926 it denied fourth-section relief on a selected list of commodities, westbound, of which iron and steel was the most important.[24] In 1932 it refused to permit the Southern Pacific to establish lower rates between California terminals and the company's Atlantic Seaboard piers at New York and Baltimore than were collected on intermediate hauls. The application in this case covered substantially all carload traffic that was competitive with the intercoastal

[21] 40 I.C.C. 35, 1916.
[22] 46 I.C.C. 236, 1917.
[23] 74 I.C.C. 48, 1922.
[24] 107 I.C.C. 421, 1926.

steamship lines operating through the Panama Canal.[25] In 1907, however, it approved lower rates on soya bean meal from certain transcontinental groups westbound to Pacific terminals than to intermediate destinations in order, partly, to meet competition from the Orient.[26]

Reasons Which Have Influenced the Interstate Commerce Commission

The reasons which explain the Commission's reluctance to authorize the reinstallation of prewar practices in the Far West include the following:

1. Lower rates to and from Pacific terminals appear to restrain, improperly, the development of intermediate localities.

2. These rates divert or threaten to divert substantial tonnage from the intercoastal water lines. It has been the announced policy of Congress to foster and preserve both rail and water transportation. There was some reason to believe, in the thirties, that water service, of the two, was the cheaper to supply.

3. The lower rates actually proposed to and from terminals are likely to yield the railroads little profit and may, in particular cases, be "noncompensatory."

The general rule now is that transcontinental rates between eastern points of origin and destination and Pacific terminals are applied as maxima on shipments to and from intermediate destinations, except in the few cases where special treatment is allowed. The transcontinental rate system no longer illustrates the practice of charging less for longer than for shorter hauls; during its development in the West, however, it afforded an excellent example of a peculiar rate policy, for a time generally applied.[27]

REFERENCES

General Treatises

Bigham, Truman C., and Roberts, Merrill J., *Transportation, Principles and Problems,* New York, McGraw-Hill, 1952.

Brown, H. G., *Transportation Rates and Their Regulation,* New York, Macmillan, 1916.

Healy, Kent T., *The Economics of Transportation in America,* New York, Ronald, 1940.

Johnson, E. R., Huebner, G. G., and Wilson, G. L., *Transportation, Economic Principles and Practices,* New York, Appleton-Century-Crofts, 1940.

McPherson, L. G., *Railroad Freight Rates in Relation to the Industry and Commerce of the United States,* New York, Holt, 1909.

[25] 182 I.C.C. 770, 1932.
[26] 225 I.C.C. 51, 1937; 231 I.C.C. 411, 1939.
[27] Stuart Daggett and John P. Carter, *The Structure of Transcontinental Railroad Rates,* Berkeley and Los Angeles, University of California, 1947.

Ripley, W. Z., *Railroads: Rates and Regulation,* New York, Longmans, 1912.
Vanderblue, H. B., and Burgess, K. F., *Railroads: Rates—Service—Management,* New York, Macmillan, 1923.

Other Books

Bigham, Truman C., and Roberts, Merrill J., *Citrus Fruit Rates: Development and Economic Appraisal,* Gainesville, Fla., University of Florida, 1950.
Cowles, J. L., *A General Freight and Passenger Post,* New York, Putnam, 1898.
Daggett, Stuart, *Chapters on the History of the Southern Pacific,* New York, Ronald, 1922.
Daggett, Stuart, and Carter, John P., *The Structure of Transcontinental Railroad Rates,* Berkeley and Los Angeles, University of California, 1947.
Joubert, W. H., *Southern Freight Rates in Transition,* Gainesville, Fla., University of Florida, 1949.

Periodicals

Ripley, W. Z., "The Trunk Line Rate System: A Distance Tariff," *Quarterly Journal of Economics,* February, 1906.

Special and Miscellaneous

Eastman, Joseph B., Federal Coordinator of Transportation, *Letter to Hon. Burton K. Wheeler,* Chairman of the Senate Committee on Interstate Commerce, relative to "A Plan for Postalizing Passenger Transportation," proposed by John A. Hastings, July 15, 1935.
National Resources Planning Board, *Transportation and National Policy,* Part I, section II, *The Influence of Transportation on the Location of Economic Activities,* by E. S. Lynch, 1942.
United States Senate, Committee on Interstate Commerce, *Investigation of Feasibility and Desirability of Fixing Railroad Rates on the Basis of Zones,* Hearings before a subcommittee on S. J. Res. 58, 76th C., 1st S., 1939.

Local Discrimination—The Long- and Short-Haul Clause of the Act to Regulate Commerce

Mileage rates, differential rates, group rates, basing point rates—to say nothing of other variations—all are intended to maximize carrier profit under monopolistic or competitive conditions as the case may be. Any one of the systems is admissible, providing (1) that it does not yield the carriers an unreasonably high return and (2) that it does not establish a pattern of relationships which is contrary to public policy. There are no legal principles which enable courts to decide whether relative rates to competing producing and distributing centers are fair or whether these rates should be changed. The duty of considering disputed cases of certain types, so that the public interest as well as the private interests of contending parties shall be served, is vested in regulatory commissions, of which the Interstate Commerce Commission is the most important. The branch of regulatory law which is applied is known as the law of local discrimination. This is the subject of the present chapter.

Section 3 of the Interstate Commerce Act forbids discrimination between persons, natural or legal, and it prohibits carriers from subjecting groups of individuals, referred to as localities, ports, regions, districts, etc., and particular descriptions of traffic, to preference or disadvantage.[1] Prior to its passage, litigants appeared separately and each was required to show damage. Since the enactment of the statute states or municipalities or chambers of commerce have become independent litigants and have instituted proceedings without proof that prejudicial rates have been paid

---

[1] Section 3 thus bars local discrimination and what is sometimes called "discrimination between commodities." There is discrimination between commodities whenever there is an improper relationship between the rates charged upon articles that can be substituted for each other in a common market. A special illustration is often provided by rate relationships between finished products and the raw materials out of which these products are made. (See chap. 11, meat-livestock; chap. 18, grain-flour.) Relationships of this sort influence the location of processing activity.

by any shipper.[2] The words "port, port district, gateway, and transit point" were added to Section 3 in 1935,[3] because of a Supreme Court decision holding that the word "locality" did not include towns through which traffic moved to destination, but only points of origin and destination.[4] The words "region, district, territory" were inserted in 1940,[5] with the controversy between the Southern and the Northeastern states in mind, and with the effect of changing somewhat the conception upon which the law of local discrimination depends.

Administration of Section 3

While Section 3 goes beyond the common law in important respects, its administration is controlled by legal principles. Thus, when complaint of undue prejudice is made, injury to complainant must be shown, and the burden of proof is upon complainant. A mere showing of inconsistent carrier practice in rate making is not enough. Injury will occur only when there is a competitive relationship between the parties, so that this, also, must be established. Since the charge is always brought against a named carrier, and the complaint is one of discrimination, it is generally necessary to show that the accused company is responsible for both rates, the higher rate and also the lower rate with which comparison is made. "A carrier," the Interstate Commerce Commission has said, "can not discriminate within the meaning of the statute except as between those whom it serves or whom it may lawfully be required to serve. . . . The law does not deal in these matters with all carriers collectively as a single unit or system, but its commands are directed to each, with respect to the service which it is required to perform." Thus [6] in the eye of the law there is no discrimination if a carrier simply declines to treat its customers as handsomely as does some other carrier. A carrier is not guilty of discrimination, even if it serves two communities and connects them with a common market at unequal rates, if outside competitive conditions are such that the objectionable rate relationship will persist whatever the carrier may do.[7] All this is less important, however, than it sounds. For while the

---

[2] Isaac Beverly Lake, *Discrimination by Railroads and Other Public Utilities,* Raleigh, N.C., Edwards & Broughton, 1947, p. 208. See also 311 U. S. 284, 308, 1947.

[3] 49 Stat. 607, 1935.

[4] In the case of *Texas and Pacific v. United States* (289 U.S. 627, 1933) the Galveston Chamber of Commerce complained that export rates by way of Galveston were unduly prejudicial to New Orleans. The traffic in question passed through Galveston or New Orleans on its way to a foreign destination. The Court held that ports were not "localities" within the meaning of Section 3 with respect to export traffic and could not rely upon this section for relief, although they could allege prejudice with respect to commodities shipped to ports for local consumption.

[5] 54 Stat. 902, 1940.

[6] 16 I.C.C. 323, 332, 1909.

[7] The rules referred to in the text are more fully discussed in I. L. Sharfman, *The Interstate Commerce Commission,* Part III, vol. B, pp. 552 ff. and D. P. Locklin,

Interstate Commerce Commission may not, under such conditions, issue an order directing a carrier to remove a discrimination which the carrier has no power to correct, the Commission may eliminate the discriminatory practice by prescribing a just and reasonable rate under authority conveyed to it by Section 15 (1) of the Interstate Commerce Act upon the principle that the Commission would be powerless to protect regions and territories from discrimination unless all rates involved in the rate relationship were controlled.[8]

It was on this ground that the Supreme Court upheld an order of the Interstate Commerce Commission requiring rail carriers in Official Classification Territory to raise their rates in order to remove discrimination between the Southern and the Northeastern states.

Distance, Cost, and Competition

As a practical matter the pattern of rate relationships which the Interstate Commerce Commission treats as just is defined in what is meant to be simple transportation terms. The initial assumption is that rates from any two points to a given destination should bear the same relation to each other as do the distances traversed. When the nature of the terrain or the conditions of transport are different an equivalent equation is set

Economics of Transportation, Chicago, Irwin, 1947. See also R. W. Harbeson, "Economic Implications of the Railway Class Rate Case," *American Economic Review,* March, 1950.

[8] 331 U.S. 284, 342, 1947. Section 15 (1) of the Interstate Commerce Act as effective November 1, 1951, reads as follows:

"Sec. 15 (1) That whenever, after full hearing, upon a complaint made as provided in section 13 of this part, or after full hearing under an order for investigation and hearing made by the Commission on its own initiative, either in extension of any pending complaint or without any complaint whatever, the Commission shall be of opinion that any individual or joint rate, fare, or charge whatsoever demanded, charged, or collected by any common carrier or carriers subject to this part for the transportation of persons or property as defined in the first section of this part, or that any individual or joint classification, regulation, or practice whatsoever of such carrier or carriers subject to the provisions of this part, is or will be unjust or unreasonable or unjustly discriminatory or unduly preferential or prejudicial, or otherwise in violation of any of the provisions of this part, the Commission is hereby authorized and empowered to determine and prescribe what will be the just and reasonable individual or joint rate, fare, or charge, or rates, fares, or charges, to be thereafter observed in such case, or the maximum or minimum, to be charged, and what individual or joint classification, regulation, or practice is or will be just, fair, and reasonable, to be thereafter followed, and to make an order that the carrier or carriers shall cease and desist from such violation to the extent to which the Commission finds that the same does or will exist, and shall not thereafter publish, demand, or collect any rate, fare, or charge for such transportation other than the rate, fare, or charge so prescribed, or in excess of the maximum or less than the minimum so prescribed, as the case may be, and shall adopt the classification and shall conform to and observe the regulation or practice so prescribed."

Comparable provisions are to be found, as to motor carriers, under Part II of the Interstate Commerce Act, Secs. 216 (e) and 218 (b); water carriers, under Part III, Secs. 307 (b), (h), and 315 (b); freight forwarders, under Part IV, Sec. 406 (b).

up in terms of fully allocated cost. The essential complaint which is then presented in cases alleging local discrimination is that carriers do not adjust their charges according to length of haul or according to cost. The essential defense, if the facts sustain the charge, is apt to be that departure from a distance or fully allocated cost basis in the case is justified by the presence of competition. By competition in such instances is meant the rivalry of parallel lines, the competition of directions, of locations, or possibly of commodities also. We have said something in previous chapters about the advantages and disadvantages of a scheme of rates which associates rates and distance. We have also seen in examining rates applied to lumber, fruit, sugar, and other commodities, and rates charged generally in the South and West that railroad rates, at least, have not always conformed to this criterion and do not always so conform at the present time. Are rates discriminatory in such cases and, if they are, is the discrimination unreasonable or undue?

The answer of the Interstate Commerce Commission appears to be that carriers may depart from the distance and cost rule to a considerable extent in fixing rates to and from competing places, if the necessities of competition compel them, and if they can vary the price of their services without increasing the burden which noncompetitive traffic has to bear. This condition, of course, forbids carriers to quote rates which do not cover out-of-pocket costs. If, indeed, the Commission did not take this view the various forms of competition mentioned in the text, while they might still exist, would have little influence on rates.

In permitting carriers to adjust their rate systems to meet the pressure of competition, the Interstate Commerce Commission has prescribed certain limitations. One such limitation is that a rail line must be at a genuine disadvantage in competition before it may be allowed to quote rates which do not approximately reflect the influence of distance and of cost. When, for example, two lines of equal length touch at their termini, the fact of competition at the ends should not justify a departure from the usual standard of ratemaking between these points. Thus the rate from A to B in the diagram should bear a relation to the rates from A to C and from A to D which can be explained by differences in the cost of transport. The fact that there is competition at B and not at C and D is not controlling, because neither railroad is at a disadvantage as compared with the other in competition at the more distant point. This much is relatively simple. But there are other limitations, less obvious, which seem to be based upon very general conceptions of public interest. It is when carrier rates not based on distance or cost run counter to these concepts that commissions are likely to declare that undue preference exists; when, on the contrary, the attempt of the carriers to meet competitive pressure takes a form consistent with the commission's view of public advantage, proposed rates are likely to be approved.

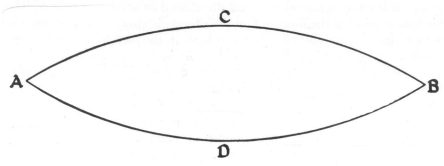

FIGURE 49.   Competition Between Lines of Equal Length.

Concepts of Public Interest in Local Discrimination

The explanation of the term "local discrimination" in the foregoing pages follows closely the analysis of Sharfman in his monograph upon the work of the Interstate Commerce Commission. Rates which discriminate unduly between localities, according to this view, have two characteristics: (1) Such rates are not based on costs but, usually, on competition. (2) In deviating from the amount of charge which a fully allocated cost calculation would justify, these rates produce results which are contrary to the public interest. These conclusions are not always consistent with views which economists entertain,[9] but the formulation leaves some ground for the judgment of a regulating body; as a matter of fact, the regulatory interpretation of the words "undue prejudice" can only be understood from the point of view of policy formation. Simple transportation terms are not sufficient. Nor does the occasional use of a slogan alter the fundamental situation with respect to local discrimination. When the Interstate Commerce Commission refuses to allow a railroad to meet competition at a junction with other carriers because of "undue circuity," it merely registers the opinion that the use of excessively roundabout routes in transportation is contrary to the public good. When it insists upon the recognition of "natural advantage" it generally means that the existing distribution or productive effort should not be disturbed by the attempt of particular carriers to increase their net returns. When it approves a rate not based on distance because it offers shippers a large choice of routes or consumers a wider choice between sources of supply, or producers a larger variety of markets, in spite of the opposition of towns whose charges are not at the same time reduced, it sets up an objective of public policy in terms of active competition and in the light of the larger

[9] See chap. 16.

purposes which, it believes, Congress entertains.[10] Comments such as these will not aid the student in forecasting the outcome of particular litigation in which there is complaint of local discrimination, but they will indicate the background to cases in which the rates to or from competing markets are discussed.

Section 4 of the Act to Regulate Commerce

There is only one section in the Interstate Commerce Act which lays down a specific rule with reference to local discrimination, and that is Section 4. This paragraph, which prohibits charging more for a shorter than for a longer haul, has a long and important history.

Section 4 of the Federal Act of 1887 read, when first enacted, as follows:

That it shall be unlawful for any common carrier subject to the provisions of this act to charge or receive any greater compensation in the aggregate for the transportation of passengers or of like kind of property, under substantially similar circumstances and conditions, for a shorter than for a longer distance over the same line, in the same direction, the shorter being included within the longer distance; but this shall not be construed as authorizing any common carrier within the terms of this act to charge and receive as great compensation for a shorter as for a longer distance: Provided, however, That upon application to the Commission appointed under the provisions of this act, such common carrier may, in special cases, after investigation by the Commission, be authorized to charge less for longer than for shorter distances for the transportation of passengers or property; and the Commission may from time to time prescribe the extent to which such designated common carrier may be relieved from the operation of this section of this act.

Interpretation of the Law

The phrases quoted in the preceding paragraphs were more specific than the general provisions of Section 3, but they left a considerable area for interpretation. This was because Section 4 did not prohibit all railroad charges which were greater for shorter than for longer distances, but only greater charges (1) for the transportation of passengers or of like kind of

---

[10] The Interstate Commerce Commission said, in 1947:

"In the long history of transportation in this country, rate structures have been evolved which have been expressive of the economic needs of carriers, producers, traders, and consumers. . . . Shippers have constantly manifested a desire to reach out farther and farther into distant markets. Congress has recognized the importance of this factor in the rule of ratemaking. . . . In no other country has there been such a degree of freedom of movement of commodities over great distances. Failure to recognize these characteristics in shaping the form, contour, and substance of rate structures would be destructive of the interests of all concerned. We have taken steps from time to time . . . to bring more order and balance into structures developed over a span of many years, but we have recognized and, so far as possible, have preserved the historic spirit and purpose of rates and rate structures . . ." (270 I.C.C. 403, 1947).

property; (2) for a shorter than for a longer distance over the same line; (3) in the same direction; (4) the shorter being included within the longer distance; (5) under substantially similar circumstances and conditions. It was eminently proper to put these qualifications into the law. Indeed, if the legislature had not inserted them, the courts would have supplied most of them by interpretation. But it was none the less difficult to apply them to concrete cases.

In interpreting Section 4 of the original Act of 1887, the Commission began by holding that the burden of proof was on the railroads to justify apparent noncompliance with the law. Without much concerning itself with the first four qualifications mentioned in the preceding paragraph, it then ruled as to the fifth, that:

1. The fact that local traffic was more expensive to handle than long-distance traffic might justify a greater proportional but not a greater absolute charge for the shorter movement.

2. The desire to build up industries at the more distant point did not excuse the continuance of charges to the more distant terminal which exceeded those to intermediate points.

3. When one place enjoyed the advantage of water competition and another did not, or when one place was served by carriers not subject to the Interstate Commerce Act (i.e., Canadian carriers), conditions at the two places were dissimilar.

4. Mere railroad competition by carriers subject to the act did not make conditions dissimilar in the sense in which the words were used in Section 4, even though one city was served by several railroad lines, and another by only one.[11]

The Supreme Court Overrules the Interstate Commerce Commission

These rules provided a basis for the administration of Section 4, but in 1897 the Supreme Court overruled the last one stated, and this action hampered the Commission's developing program. The leading case was *Interstate Commerce Commission v. Alabama Midland*,[12] in which the Supreme Court decided that the provisions of the Interstate Commerce Law were not so stringent as to exclude even railroad competition from consideration in the administration of Section 4. It followed from this decision and from the Commission's views on other points that the law allowed greater charges for shorter than for longer hauls whenever there was either rail or water or foreign carrier competition at the more distant point. The Court held, moreover, that carriers need not ask the Interstate Commerce Commission in advance to determine when dissimilarity existed. They might judge for themselves, subject to appropriate penalties

[11] 1 I.C.R. 278, 1887.
[12] 168 U.S. 144, 1897.

if they misjudged the facts; but they were not required to obtain preliminary authorization for rates which might seem to depart from the
statutory rule. For a while the Commission maintained, even after the
Alabama Midland case, that it had authority, even when conditions at
two points were dissimilar, to compare the extent of discrimination with
the difference in conditions which might be found to exist; [13] but in 1901
the Supreme Court held that the carriers were not subject even to this
restraint.[14] This virtually suspended the operation of Section 4 until legislative alterations could be made.

Amendment of 1910

Legislation in 1910 made four changes in Section 4.

The first and most important was the elimination of the words "under
substantially similar circumstances and conditions." The effect was to
allow comparisons of long- and short-haul rates, even when conditions
were not similar, and to force carriers to rely upon the dispensation of
the Interstate Commerce Commission as a condition of continuance of
greater charges for shorter than for longer distances. Henceforth it was to
be the Commission which was to decide when the law should be suspended, not the courts.

The second change was the insertion of words in the section which
made the law clearly applicable to routes made up of several connecting railroad lines as well as to rate relations on a single railroad. This
had not been the original intention of the framers of the Act of 1887,
but in the course of time the amendment came to seem both natural and
desirable.

The third addition was a clause forbidding carriers to charge any
greater compensation for transport on a through route than the aggregate
of the intermediate rates subject to the provisions of the act. The burden
of proof had been already placed upon railroads to defend the reasonableness of through rates of this description,[15] but an unqualified prohibition
was now inserted in the law.

Finally, the act provided that when a railroad reduced rates to or from
competitive points in competition with a water route, it should not be
permitted to increase them again unless the proposed increase could be
shown to rest upon changed conditions other than the elimination of water
competition.

Of these changes, the widening of the law to include routes as well as
single railway lines raised no questions of principle, and the clause relat-

---

[13] 8 I.C.R. 409, 1900; 8 I.C.R. 503, 1900.
[14] 181 U.S. 1, 1901.
[15] 269 U.S. 1, 1925.

ing to the subsequent increase of rates reduced to meet water competition has never been enforced.

The effect which the Act of 1910 produced by eliminating the words "under substantially similar circumstances and conditions" from Section 4 was, however, very great. It enabled the Interstate Commerce Commission to lay down rules with reference to the administration of the long- and short-haul clause; and, in particular, it enabled the Commission to make its original view prevail, that railroad competition at a more distant point did not necessarily justify neglect of the general prohibition of the law. It was this change which permitted the Commission to revise the basing point system of rate making in the Southern states, as well as to correct a great many local situations with which it had previously been unable to interfere. The Commission does not interpret the law as conferring arbitrary authority. It takes the position that the modified language of Section 4 requires it to grant relief when, in its opinion, the resulting rates will not be unjust or unreasonable, in violation of the first section of the Interstate Commerce Act, or unduly discriminatory, in violation of the third section.[16] But lest this may seem to imply too receptive an attitude towards applications for relief from Section 4, we may add that the Commission has also declared: (1) that it must be affirmatively shown by carriers seeking relief that injustice will not be done to intermediate points by allowing lower rates at the more distant points; and (2) that the intent of the law is to make its prohibition of the higher rate for the shorter haul a rule of well-nigh universal application, from which the Commission may deviate only in special cases, and then to meet transportation circumstances which are beyond the carriers' control. That is to say, a carrier shall not prefer the more distant point by giving it the lower rate because of any policy of its own initiation; but if at the more distant point it finds a condition to which it must conform under the imperious law of competition if it would participate in traffic to that point, it may discriminate against the intermediate place without violating the law, provided it establishes such necessity before the Commission. The discrimination may not be such as to offend the reasonable standards of the law, for it is said that the Commission may from time to time prescribe the extent to which such designated common carrier may be relieved from the operation of the section.[17]

Amendment of 1920

In 1920 Section 4 was once more amended, so that this portion of the statute then read as follows:

That it shall be unlawful for any common carrier subject to the provisions

[16] *Annual Report of the Interstate Commerce Commission,* 1911, pp. 19 ff.
[17] 21 I.C.C. 329, 1911.

tion relating to circuitous routes which the Act of 1920 had contained, thus considerably simplifying administration of the law.

Summary of Present Restrictions

Under the law as it now stands the Commission recognizes the following restrictions in granting exemptions from the rule of Section 4 to rail and water and, by analogy, to motor carriers. First, the rates to the more distant point must be reasonably compensatory. Second, permission to depart from the provisions of the long-and-short clause may not be granted because of potential water competition. Water competition must be actual—in existence—and not merely proposed or possible before it may be recognized. Third, railroad rates reduced by carriers to meet water competition may not be raised without Commission approval, and in giving its consent the Commission must find that the proposed increase rests upon conditions other than the elimination of water competition or that continuance of railroad rates at the lower level is discriminatory or unreasonable. Fourth, all rates must be reasonable and nondiscriminatory. All of these limitations have been mentioned in previous paragraphs or are contained in the various forms of Section 4 which have been printed in the text. It may be added that Section 500 of the Transportation Act of 1920, declaring it to be the policy of Congress to promote, encourage, and develop water transportation, service and facilities, makes the Commission less liberal in dealing with departures from the long- and short-haul rule than it would have been if the Act of 1920 had not been passed.

Attempts to Secure Further Legislation

Section 4 still does not forbid the Interstate Commerce Commission to approve departures from the long- and short-haul rule which rest upon actual and effective water competition. For this reason the law was deemed incomplete by Western congressmen so long as transcontinental rates to the Pacific Coast were lower than rates to intermediate destinations. Senator Gooding of Idaho and Senator Pitman of Nevada introduced amending bills, but none of these were passed. On the other hand there was sentiment in the 1930's behind proposals for legislation which would have repealed the clauses in Section 4 which hamper carriers in charging greater sums for shorter than for longer hauls. Mr. Pettengill, of Indiana,

a joint through rate that exceeded the aggregate of intermediate rates between the same points over the particular route. See Patterson v. Louisville & Nashville Railroad, 269 U.S. 1. The same principles that governed rail rates under such circumstances prior to the 1910 amendments are applicable to similar conditions involving motor-carrier rates. Therefore, the assailed joint rates are presumed to have been unreasonable to the extent that they exceeded the corresponding aggregate of intermediate rates."

introduced bills of this character and they were twice passed by the House of Representatives although the Senate was not willing to concur.

The House vote on the Pettengill bill is shown upon the following map.

The Pacific Coast was for the Pettengill bill in 1937 because its lumber and citrus moved long distances by rail and it was in their interest to strengthen railroad service. Atlantic Seaboard cities, and especially New York, felt that their future depended more largely upon the water route and were disposed to continue some limitation on the freedom of railroad

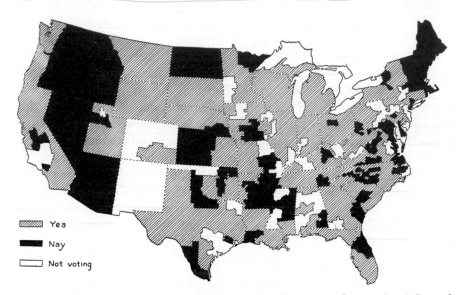

Yea

Nay

Not voting

FIGURE 51.   Vote on the Pettingill Bill, 1937. (Data from *Congressional Record*, 75th Congress, 1st Session, April 14, 1937, p. 3489.)

competition. The northern Mississippi Valley voted to repeal the restrictions in Section 4, but portions of the southern Mississippi Valley feared that this would imperil barge traffic upon the Mississippi River. The so-called "intermountain" states were strongly against repeal. They were the states principally responsible for the Gooding bill of 1925. But some Colorado districts which hoped for low rail rates on beet sugar to certain territories and on steel to the Pacific Coast and Texas either voted for the Pettengill bill in 1937 or did not vote at all. The outcome was the result of sectional and industrial conflict; it was hardly a judgment on principles of legislation. It should be said that the Pettengill bills would not by themselves have rendered lower charges for longer hauls permissible, for action could still have been brought under Sections 1, 2, or 3 of the Interstate Commerce Act if rates should be thought to be unreasonable or discriminatory and the burden of proof would have been upon carriers

circumstance that some markets or producing centers gain by increased carrier competition does not satisfy communities which do not enjoy these benefits. Nor do the competitive policies of railroads, or their accounting practices in calculating costs, impress critics who believe that the problem should be solved on the basis of large national considerations. Freer competition may reduce rates, but it is probably impossible to say, in any case, how far section 4 rate making reduces or increases the transport charges which the whole body of shippers pay as distinguished from the transport costs which carriers incur.

Public Policy and Local Discrimination

Section 4 rate cases, like those under section 3, are often decided according to ideas of public policy based upon the end results which lesser charges for longer hauls seem likely to produce. This is, indeed, the basis upon which any pattern of rates must ultimately stand.[24] If one dignifies these ideas by referring to them as "theories," then at least two can be distinguished which are pertinent, of which the first is the theory of equalization and the second is the theory of natural advantage.

The Theory of Equalization

The assumption of the theory of equalization is that rates should be so adjusted as to admit a maximum number of producing centers into any market, and so also as to give every locality a maximum number of sources

[24] Mr. Eastman, in 1925, classified the grounds upon which relief had been sought under section 4 as follows:
1. Where a circuitous line or route is in competition with a shorter line or route.
2. Where rail lines are in competition with water or rail-water routes between the same points.
3. To meet commercial or market competition where a carrier serving a section desires to establish rates to a common market which will enable producers on its line to compete in that market with producers in other sections.
4. To carriers in poor financial condition whose cost of operation due to conditions over which they have no control are usually high.
5. To carriers operating under disadvantages due to conditions other than circuity, as for example, where carriers forming a joint route are in competition with a carrier having the single line haul between competitive points.
6. To meet emergency situations due to drought, flood and other abnormal conditions.
7. Where a rail line serving one port desires to establish rates from and to said port to and from a common point on the same basis as, or with relation to, rates in effect from or to other ports so as to place the port reached by its lines on a rate equality with other ports.
8. Where rates have been established for many years on a group basis and one or more carriers parties to the adjustment operates through a higher-rated group in reaching points in a lower-rated group.
9. Where temporary relief has been sought to make effective promptly general changes in rates.
   Problems of public policy were evidently involved in many of these applications. (See proposed statement before the House Committee on Interstate and Foreign Commerce on bill to amend section 4 of the Interstate Commerce Act, 1925.)

from which to draw its supplies. Still another illustration of the same principle is the demand of distributing centers for rates which will place them on an equality with one another in handling trade between important sources of production and the markets in which supplies are sold.

The contention just referred to explains a number of American rate practices which would otherwise be hard to understand. Such is, for instance, the quotation of export rates from the Middle West through the Atlantic Seaboard cities of New York, Philadelphia, Baltimore, Boston, and Newport News, in inverse proportion to the cost of ocean transportation from each town to the European markets in which all of the cities named sell their wares. The purpose clearly is to give each of the towns mentioned a share of the through business. Is this fair? Is it wise? Is it in accord with public policy? Or should rates be based upon cost, distance, or some other physical fact, and business be allowed to go where it will?

The same question may be asked when a number of coal mines are assigned to a rate group in which each producer pays the same rate to market as his competitor, in spite, sometimes, of considerable differences in the distances hauled. Steel plants, fruit ranches, cotton mills, and many other types of producers as well are often treated in this way. Indeed, study will show that the equalization principle is widely recognized in American rate making, and that it receives some, though perhaps less complete, application in the rate systems of European states. The advantage of the practice is that it decentralizes industry. Its disadvantage is that it tends to increase the volume of transportation required in the production and distribution of goods.

The Principle of Natural Advantage

An alternative contention which is advanced in cases involving relative rates between different places is that rate structures should recognize natural advantages, not seek to counteract them. This theory is opposed to the principle of equalization. It tends to preserve and to emphasize inequalities, not to cover them over. Its influence is rather, therefore, to concentrate industry.

According to the Interstate Commerce Commission, cities may possess the following natural advantages connected with transportation:

1. *Nearness.* Obviously, nearness to market is a natural advantage, as is nearness to source of supply.

2. *Low cost of operation.* The effect of low cost is analogous to the effect of nearness. The simplest case is that of a route between two towns which is devoid of natural obstacles, such as mountains or streams. A city which reaches its markets over such a route possesses a natural advantage which may be recognized in the rate.

3. *Competition.* In addition to nearness and ease of access, a town

which is located at the junction of a railway and a waterway or of two railways, or, indeed, of any two routes over which shipments can be made, has a natural advantage. This is essentially the argument upon which the transcontinental rate structure was built up, and also that upon which the Section 4 cases are decided. Not only direct competition should be considered under this head, but market competition also. When a town can buy from several markets, or when it can sell in several markets, although there may be but one route from or to each destination, it enjoys a bargaining advantage which is important.

The theory of natural advantages is reasonably easy to understand and to apply as long as the advantages contemplated are expressed only in terms of cost of transportation. So interpreted, it becomes a doctrine justifying relations of rates based upon relative costs, as contrasted with the equalization theory in which competition is given greater weight. The introduction of competition into the concept of natural advantage cannot easily be explained.

Comparative Costs and Established Interests Standards

Forty years ago Professor J. M. Clark stated the problem of relative carrier rates in words which still require consideration.

The standard of reasonableness [said Professor Clark], so far as it has been unearthed, is the expression of the right of any market to the services of those producers who will satisfy its wants at the lowest social expense. That is, rates should be such as to give the competitive markets to the most efficient producers, including in the calculation of efficiency the actual cost of any transportation involved. This we may call the *comparative cost standard* of reasonableness. Another has also been suggested, which we may call the *established interests standard,* and which requires in its mildest form that producers' markets shall not be so limited as to destroy the value of actual invested capital, if such a result can possibly be avoided. Sometimes the vested-interest idea is extended to cover the expectation or an average rate of growth. The latter standard is comparatively easy to apply, while the former or comparative cost standard is difficult if not impossible.[25]

The comparative cost standard is an extension of the natural advantage principle with the omission of competition as a factor. The theory would, presumably, call for the use of full allocated cost; for the acceptance of allocation, especially allocation on the basis of demand would reintroduce the element of competition which it is desired to exclude. The reference, in this connection, to an established interests standard, merely recognizes the unnecessary waste caused by too rapid a rate of change.

[25] John Maurice Clark, *Standards of Reasonableness in Local Freight Discriminations,* New York, Columbia University, 1910, pp. 68–69.

Miscellaneous Standards

Under some conditions as in Russia and, to a less extent in England today and in Germany before the First World War, factors other than economic efficiency or controlled obsolescence may enter into the discussion of rate relationships, including social, political, and military objectives, and in any case potentialities as well as actual developments must be held in mind.

Conclusion

The difficulties of purposive transportation policies in a community such as the United States are, first, that there is no general agreement with respect to the relative net efficiency of production in different areas; second, that public sentiment favors diffusion and parallel sectional development even at the expense of efficiency; and, third, that there is no disposition to give an administrative body such as the Interstate Commerce Commission the extensive authority over national development which constructive control of national transportation would involve. The Commission, indeed, is already criticized for arrogating to itself legislative discretion in carrying out regulative functions assigned to it by law.[26] The result is that arguments alleging local discrimination are directed in the first instance to disparities between relative rates and relative costs without much regard to principle and that they then develop problems of transportation equity and public policy which the Commission has no express authority to consider but which it must recognize before its decisions are handed down.

REFERENCES

General Treatises

Bigham, Truman C., and Roberts, Merrill J., *Transportation, Principles and Problems,* New York, McGraw-Hill, 1952.

Brown, H. G., *Transportation Rates and Their Regulation,* New York, Macmillan, 1916.

Clark, J. M., *Standards of Reasonableness in Local Freight Discriminations,* New York, Columbia University, 1910.

Fair, Marvin L., and Williams, Ernest W., *Economics of Transportation,* New York, Harper, 1950.

[26] Calvin Crumbaker, *Transportation and Politics,* Eugene, Ore., University of Oregon, 1940.

The Supreme Court ruled in *Texas and Pacific v. United States* (289 U.S. 627, 637, 1933) that "a tariff published for the purpose of destroying a market or building up one, of diverting traffic from a particular place, or in aid of some other, is unlawful; and obviously. What the carrier may not lawfully do, the Commission may not compel." See also 331 U.S. 284, 362, 1947. But most tariffs, as a matter of fact, have one or other of the effects mentioned in the quotation.

Lake, I. B., *Discrimination by Railroads and Other Public Utilities*, Raleigh, N.C., Edwards & Broughton, 1947.

Locklin, D. Philip, *Economics of Transportation*, Chicago, Irwin, 1947.

Ripley, W. Z., *Railroads: Rates and Regulation*, New York, Longmans, 1912.

Sharfman, I. L., *The Interstate Commerce Commission*, Part III, vol. B, New York, Commonwealth Fund, 1936.

Vanderblue, H. B., and Burgess, K. F., *Railroads: Rates—Service—Management*, New York, Macmillan, 1923.

Other Books

Crumbaker, Calvin, *Transportation and Politics*, Eugene, Ore., University of Oregon, 1940.

Dewey, Ralph, *The Long and Short Haul Principle of Rate Regulation*, Columbus, Ohio State University, 1935.

Shinn, Glenn L., *Freight Rate Application*, New York, Simmons-Boardman, 1948.

Periodicals

Barton, Frank L., "Economic Effects of Discriminatory Freight Rates," *Law and Contemporary Problems*, Summer, 1947.

Daggett, Stuart, "Interterritorial Freight Rates and the Pacific Coast," *Law and Contemporary Problems*, Summer, 1947.

Locklin, D. Philip, "Discrimination Between Places under Section 3 of the Interstate Commerce Act," *Journal of Political Economy*, October, 1934.

Ripley, W. Z., "Local Discrimination and Transportation," *Quarterly Journal of Economics*, May, 1909.

Vanderblue, H. B., "The Long and Short Haul Clause Since 1910," *Harvard Law Review*, February, 1923.

Wilson, G. L., "Leading Cases on the Fourth Section," *Traffic World*, September 4, 1943.

Special and Miscellaneous

United States House, Committee on Interstate and Foreign Commerce, Hearings before a subcommittee on H. R. 3263, 3610, 5362 and 8364 to amend the Fourth Section of the Interstate Commerce Act, 74th C., 1st S., 1935.

United States Senate, Committee on Interstate and Foreign Commerce, *Study of Domestic Land and Water Transportation*, Hearings before a subcommittee pursuant to Sen. Res. 50, 81st C., 2d S., 1950.

Theories of Location

We conclude the section of this treatise which deals with railway rates and the movement of traffic with some consideration of what is called the "theory of location." The treatment will be condensed, with emphasis upon the relationship of transportation to the subject as a whole.

Location and Unit Development

The study of location has been undertaken with several purposes in mind. Some writers have discussed it as part of a general theory of unit distribution. In its simplest form, the location of any phenomenon is a function of age. Given, at least, an area everywhere equally favorable to the development of a unit chosen for study, and assuming that the first example of the phenomenon occurs at a given point, then the spread of the unit may be expected to occur continuously and the units most distant from the point of greatest concentration will be those of most recent occurrence.[1] This observation has been of some importance in zoological studies, but its application to industry is relatively slight.

Location and Economic Progress

Other students who have considered economic progress have laid down laws according to which the location of industries has, as they believe, changed from time to time in the course of social growth, and have divided history into periods according to the variety and sequence of arrangements which have been observed. Much weight is given in such analyses to improvements in transport, although other influences are also given place. It is possible to argue that production, in comparatively undeveloped societies, is primarily for the local market, and that, as the costs of transport and other impediments to movement are reduced, specialized centers for production occur which distribute over considerable areas.

[1] James Small, "Age and Area Development," *Scientific American Supplement,* June 1, 1918, p. 338.

Economic history can be written, if this is true, in terms of change from a world where the self-sufficing and self-centered group is successively the village, the city, the territory, and the entire world, or in terms of stages of human economy marked by whatever patterns are conceived to occur in ordered sequence. Such a history is likely to be at least more interesting than one which concerns itself primarily with the succession of kings. There is no close agreement among historians in arranging and accounting for sequences of economic types, nor always in weighing the influence of improved transport upon the forms of economic structure; but a theory of location may serve as a guide in historical analysis, and even Alfred Weber, to whom we shall presently refer, has his summary of tendencies of development couched in "location" terms.

Location and the Distribution of Industry

Still another purpose of a theory of location is to determine the causes which, at any moment, account for the form and distribution of industry. Knowledge of the causes of distribution makes for more intelligent social control and more efficient operation; it also points the way for future development. There has been much talk of location in recent years in the United States in connection with plans for industrial advance, public and private. Individual problems are, of course, intensively considered by enterprises which wish to shift or to expand.

Factors of Location

Whether or not a large proportion of a given product is produced in a defined district and whether or not an unusual proportion of the labor force in the segment will be occupied in producing such a product will depend upon conditions which can be defined and evaluated, more or less correctly. These conditions are referred to as factors of location and they are assembled in factor lists.[2]

[2] An industry may be said to be concentrated when a large proportion of the total industry product is produced in a limited section of a total defined area. The fact that over 50 percent of the value added in the manufacture of automobiles in the United States is contributed by the State of Michigan or that 67 percent of the iron ore is mined in Minnesota are examples of this type of concentration. These circumstances are highly significant for some purposes.

Relative concentration may, however, be of a different character. There may be concentration when an exceptionally large proportion of the labor force in any given area is devoted to one or to a few products in comparison with the proportion in the same area employed in producing other products. This kind of concentration is also important; it may be, indeed, more significant in the life of a community than the mere fact that a large fraction of the national output comes from a selected source.

The measurement of economic balance which has occupied the public mind during recent years has dealt with the second of these types of concentration rather than with the first, and procedural techniques for the purpose have been elaborately evolved. A popular method requires first, a calculation of the percentage of persons gainfully

Among the multitude of factor lists which might be described we select two, for purposes of illustration. One of these is chosen because of its early importance, and the other because of its relatively elaborate design.

The first list consists of a much quoted summary prepared by Frederick S. Hall, and printed in the United States Census for 1900. Hall summarizes the factors of production under seven heads:

1. Nearness of raw materials.
2. Nearness to markets.
3. Nearness to water power.
4. Favorable climate.
5. Supply of labor.
6. Capital available for investment in manufactures.
7. The momentum of an early start.[3]

The second list may be found in the report of a survey conducted in 1926 and 1927 by the Metropolitan Life Insurance Company in coöperation with the National Electric Light Association. This report was based upon returns from 2,084 communities, representing 75 percent of the total urban population of the United States and two-thirds of that of Canada. The final summary of the investigation published by the Metropolitan gives the following list and rating of the principal factors of location (Table 20). The Metropolitan survey not only enumerates factors of production but estimates the relative importance to be attached to each in the industries which are examined.

Lists such as those published by the Census or prepared by the Metropolitan Life Insurance Company—and there are many of them—focus attention upon problems and relationships which affect the success of enterprises at selected locations.[4] There seems to be agreement that the prin-

---

employed in a total area in each of a number of occupations; second, knowledge of the percentages gainfully employed in these same occupations in selected divisions of the total area; and third, a comparison on one percentage with another in each case to secure a "location quotient." Thus, if Michigan had 63.87 percent of all workers in automobile factories and only 6.62 percent of the nation's manufacturing wage earners, the location quotient for automobile factories in Michigan would be 9.65, an unusually high ratio. If the national percentage of 6.62 is deducted from the Michigan percentage of 63.87 the remainder, or 57.25, would be Michigan's "coefficient of specialization" in so far as automobiles were concerned (P. S. Florence, W. G. Fritz, and R. C. Giles, "Measures of Industrial Distribution," National Resources Planning Board, *Industrial Location and National Resources*, 1942, chap. 5; P. S. Florence, "Economic Research and Industrial Policy," *The Economic Journal*, December, 1937; P. S. Florence, *Investment, Location and Size of Plant*, Cambridge, Mass., National Institute of Economic and Social Research, University Press, 1948.

[3] 12th United States Census, *Manufacturers*, Part 1, 1902, p. cxc. Cf. E. M. Hoover and C. P. Wood, "The Selection of Locations," Report of the National Resources Planning Board, *Industrial Location and National Resources*, 1942, chap. 20.

[4] There is an excellent general discussion by G. T. Renner, "Geography of Industrial Localization," *Economic Geography*, July, 1947. See also W. S. Tower, "Some Factors Influencing the Location and Migration of Industries," *Bulletin of the Geographical*

TABLE 20. Ratings of Principal Factors of Location

Factor		Industry Group				
	Food	Textiles	Lumber	Machinery	Leather	Chemicals
1. Markets	1	2	1	1	3	1
2. Materials	2	6	4	6	4	4
3. Transportation	3	4	3	3	6	2
4. Labor	4	1	2	2	2	3
5. Living conditions	5	7	6	7	7	6
6. Available factory building	6	3	5	4	2	5
7. Power	7	5	7	8	—	7
8. Near related industries	8	—	8	—	—	8
9. Financial aid	—	8	—	5	8	—

SOURCE: Metropolitan Life Insurance Company, New York, in cöoperation with the National Electric Light Association, *Industrial Development in the United States and Canada, A Cooperative Survey, 1926 and 1927.*

cipal factors of location are markets, raw materials, fuel or power, labor, and transportation, although minor factors are also recognized and the promoters of enterprise will consider all circumstances which influence revenue or costs. There is less general agreement upon the relative importance of factors. This is because industries vary. The mobility of factors and the degree of their distribution is, moreover, significant. Labor and materials may be everywhere essential; but labor and material which are widely distributed or mobile may exert little pulling force.

Transportation and Mobility

Transportation affects location because it increases the mobility of factors. It enlarges the mobility of power because coal can be shipped long distances at relatively slight expense. It makes raw material such as ore, grain, cotton, lumber, and the like, more easily accessible. It reduces, although it does not eliminate, the advantage of geographical nearness to a market. Where there is no transportation there is, as a matter of fact, little industry, and neither an abundance of labor or of materials can remedy the defect.[5] We have seen in previous chapters how even slight

Society of Philadelphia, April, 1911; and E. A. Ross, "The Location of Industries," *Quarterly Journal of Economics,* April, 1896. Renner distinguishes between extractive, reproductive, facilitative, and fabricative industries and notices the differences between them. He also considers the influence of industrial interrelationships and problems of growth and trend.

[5] Whether land, labor, and capital, as such, are mobile depends upon the period of time allowed as well, of course, upon a variety of other considerations. The subject of location is sometimes discussed in these terms. The usual comment is that labor and capital are relatively mobile but that land is fixed. As Bonravia says (*The Economics of Transport,* p. 8), "No amount of improvements in transport can render it mobile."

differences in the cost of transportation to users may provoke controversy in areas which are, in general, well supplied. And since production is flexible, variations in the character and efficiency of transport may change the nature as well as the distribution and the kind of commodities produced. The functional importance of transportation among the factors of production is, therefore, very great.[6] The following pages will refer to several general, schematic analyses, in which the working of a transport system, under assumed conditions, is described.

Johann Heinrich von Thünen

In the nineteenth century a German writer upon agricultural economics and farm practice named J. H. von Thünen treated the subject of location and transportation from an original point of view. Von Thünen was intensely concerned with the methods of land cultivation in the Germany of his time. Toward the end of the eighteenth century what was known as the three-field system was common German practice. A native economist, Albrecht Thaer, argued strongly for the adoption of another type, which substituted for the use of fallows the alternate cultivation of grain and fodder crops. We have today little concern with the details of this controversy, except through the fact that it led von Thünen to write an elaborate treatise in which he maintained, in general, that the method of cultivation which should be preferred in Germany, as well as the crops to be sown in different places, depended in each case upon the distance of any given farm from its market. Von Thünen's own interest was primarily in the question of type of cultivation; his reputation rests upon the careful methods which he employed in his research and upon his conclusions with respect to the distribution of crops.[7]

It is doubtless true that it is difficult to shift a piece of land in terms of its geographical position in ways which a geographer would recognize. But if one cares to measure space relationships in terms of transfer costs—and this is both defensible and interesting—then one piece of land can draw near to another with all the implications which this implies.

[6] Renner says that transportation facilities follow rather than precede industrial location. The major lineaments of the American transportation pattern, he remarks, have been the result of building roads and railways from one industrial locus to another. He concludes, therefore, that transportation has been a result rather than a cause. The essence of the comment is that transportation is mobile to the extent that it will be found anywhere, if other factors are at hand. But this is certainly not true for the short run and the statement is probably exaggerated for the long run of industrial experience.

[7] Von Thünen was born in Oldenburg, Germany, in 1783, and died in 1850. He received a systematic education in the theory and practice of agriculture, as well as a more liberal training at the University of Gottingen. In 1810 he bought a landed estate from his brother-in-law which he cultivated for forty years. It was here that he kept the records and conducted the experiments upon which his scientific work was based. The first volume of his monumental treatise *Der Isolierte Staat* was published in 1826; the second and third volumes appeared between 1850 and 1863. In 1830 von Thünen received an honorary degree from the University of Rostock. In 1848 he was

Der Isolierte Staat

In simplifying his problem, von Thünen produced one of the first theoretical discussions of the effect of transportation upon location. He imagined, that is to say, a single city in the midst of a fertile plain without navigable rivers or canals. All the land in the plain was assumed to be equally fertile and equally workable. At a distance from the city the plain ended in an uncultivated wilderness, cutting the territory completely off from the rest of the world. All manufactured goods were produced in the city, and the city was exclusively supplied with food products coming from the plain.[8] Given these assumptions how, asked von Thünen, would agriculture be carried on in the plain and how, in particular, would greater or less distance from the city affect production?

The proposition with which von Thünen started his analysis of the question at issue was that the price of grain at any point in the isolated state would be the town price less the cost of transport to the town. Since the city was assumed to be the only market and since all grain was disposed of in the city except that used locally on the farm, this was bound to be the case. Taking a city price of 1,500 thaler per 1,000 bushels as a base, von Thünen was able to work out from his own experience of farming costs the proper price at all points outside his central city until points were reached so distant that the price of grain was zero. Similarly the price of products of the farm other than grain would be the city price less costs of transport.

Because of the effect of transport costs upon price, products would be grown near the city, von Thünen said, which were heavy in proportion to their value, because transportation costs on such articles would be so high as to prevent a distant culture. Products that were easily spoiled and must be consumed fresh would also be grown near the city. Thus vegetables, fresh milk, and timber would be produced close to town, but grain and cattle farther away.

Von Thünen's next principle set forth a theory of rent. Since the price of farm products declined with distance from the city, the gross selling price of the products of a distant farm was less than the product of a nearer farm producing the same volume. Assuming that costs were paid in the produce of the land itself—that is to say, in grain—then the net yield of a more distant grain farm would be less than the yield of a nearby

offered the position of representative in the German Parliament meeting at Frankfort au Main, and in the same year he was made honorary citizen of the town of Teterow.

[8] Still other assumptions were implicit or explicit in the Thünen illustration. These included the following: (1) All farms on the plain were of the same size. (2) The fertility was such as to yield a stated number of bushels of grain under a described system of cultivation, and was maintained without diminution. (3) Climate did not vary. (4) Operations were intelligently conducted with the object of obtaining a maximum net money income.

property in the same proportion that its gross yield was less. But since some farm costs would be paid in money,[9] and since these costs would be much the same on all farms, near and far, the net yield of farming land, and therefore its rent, would decrease more rapidly than its distance from the market increased. The theory underlying this treatment was similar to that of Ricardo, but with primary emphasis upon location rather than upon differing qualities of the land.

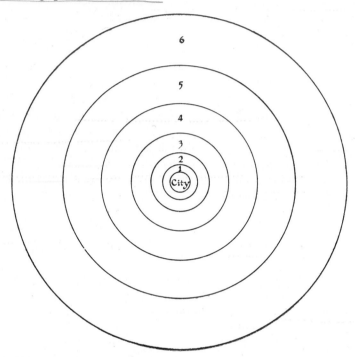

FIGURE 52.   Von Thünen's "Isolierte Staat."

Lastly, distance from the city would affect the use of land. Extensive methods would become profitable at a distance and intensive methods would be more profitable in the vicinity of the city. Von Thünen relied largely upon his own farming experience to establish the truth of this observation, but he also made use of the law of declining price set up in the first of his generalizations to establish his point. To his own complete satisfaction he proved that there was no one single method of cultivation that was best. Thaer was wrong and the earlier German practice was wrong. Methods should vary with conditions, and the farther land was from the market, the less labor and capital per acre should be applied.

[9] Von Thünen estimated that, in general, one-quarter of farm costs had to be met in money.

Von Thünen's conclusions are illustrated in the accompanying diagram. This diagram shows von Thünen's "Isolated City" surrounded by concentric rings, which divide the plain into zones. Within the first zone, and nearest the city, he described cultivation as "free." A market, that is to say, was close, and fertilizers were abundant. This was the zone devoted to dairy products and fresh vegetables. In zone 2, forests were grown for firewood and building purposes. Zones 3, 4, and 5 were mostly devoted to grain, and zone 6, to cattle. Of the intermediate zones, the third—zone 3—was cultivated under a rotation system with alternate grain and fodder crops but no fallow; zone 4 was less intensively worked with alternations of grain, pasture, and fallow; in zone 5, the least intensively cultivated of the three, one-third of the land was left continuously in meadow and one-third of the plowed land was left fallow each year.

Criticism of von Thünen's Theory

Von Thünen's contributions to the theory of location have been the subject of extravagant praise. The so-called "Thünen's Law"—that maximum net earnings are attained when the intensity of cultivation is proportioned to the price of the gross product—has been hailed as supplying a key at once to agricultural economy, to history, and to comparative economic geography. It has been characterized as equally important in its way as Newton's law of gravitation for astronomy, the concept of the atom for chemistry, or the theories of Darwin for the biological sciences.[10] On the other hand the formalized character of von Thünen's exposition has been distasteful to some; certain gaps in his scientific equipment have been pointed out, especially in agricultural chemistry; and much of the definiteness of his theory of location has been removed by later expansion and modification.

Perhaps the points at which the von Thünen picture diverge farthest from present reality are the following:

1. Von Thünen's assumption of the equal availability of all lands for all products is almost never true to fact, and for this reason alone the actual distribution of forms of agriculture and industry seldom, if ever, resemble closely the picture which he presents. Our previous discussion of the orientation of commodities such as sugar and lumber must make us conscious of the divergence from von Thünen's scheme in the case of products of this type.

2. Von Thünen, of course, failed to anticipate the enormous increase in the mobility of goods which has occurred during the past 100 years. This increase has been so great as to widen the zones concentric to the "Isolated City" until, in some instances, they embrace the entire world.

[10] Max Büchler, *Johann Heinrich von Thünen und seine nationalökonomischen Hauptlehren*, Bern, Haller'sche Buchdruckerei, 1907.

Not only this but, in general, improvements in transport increase the influence of natural conditions, as against conditions arising out of the cost of carriage, and profoundly alter an adjustment predicated upon transport costs alone.

3. Our author does not sufficiently consider the interdependence of economic operations. There is such interdependence in simple agriculture, as when groups of plants are cultivated together because they make different demands upon the soil and so permit a fuller use of the soil's fertility, or because they have different times for seeding, plowing, and harvesting, which equalize the seasonal demands upon agricultural labor and equipment. Another example is that of livestock, which may be raised, or at least fattened, in districts of intensive grain cultivation, either for the sake of fertilizer or because the livestock consumes and transforms products such as corn into goods more easily shipped to market.

4. Again, it is to be observed that the selection of products is influenced by requirements for capital and labor. If a given fruit requires much hand labor, it will tend to locate near centers of population, not only because it may be perishable but because it seeks a labor supply. Hoe crops may be found close in because of the need for tools and machines. Flax, for instance, can stand transportation very well but needs much labor; hence it is found in the middle distances.[11] In all problems that involve industrial location the importance of available supplies of labor is especially great.

5. The assumption of a single city reduces the value of the von Thünen analysis for the most numerous problems of modern economy. Current discussions have most frequently to deal with the location of points, not with the characterization of areas, and the rivalry of many competing cities presents situations which von Thünen was not interested in explaining.[12]

The System of Alfred Weber

In von Thünen's illustration there was but one city upon the plain. His interest was in the changes in crops and in methods of cultivation which occurred as distance from this city increased. But let us suppose that several cities exist upon the plain, that each of these cities may engage in manufacturing operations for the benefit of whatever consumers may be

[11] Friedrich Aereboe, *"Ursachen und Formen wechselnder Betriebsintensität in der Landwirthschaft,"* *Thünen Archiv,* vol. 2, 1907–1909, pp. 362–394.

[12] Ritschl makes the interesting suggestion that if there are several cities in a "Thünen" plain, the circles around them will intersect. Assuming growth, they must intersect. But a given area cannot at the same time be in zone 3 of city I and in zone 7 of city II. Ritschl remarks that certain of Thünen's zones will be driven, in such an event, from their original position encircling special cities and will resolve themselves into zones encircling the whole group of cities taken into the calculation. This, he thinks, is the significance of areas such as those in Russia, South Africa, Argentina, and Canada, which serve Europe as a whole (*Schmoller's Jahrbuch,* vol. 51, p. 813).

persuaded to buy its wares, and that the raw materials for manufacturing processes as well as fuel or other sources of power are obtainable from many, though fixed, points. Where, under these assumptions, will production—primarily manufacturing production—occur, and also from what parts of the plain will the raw materials of industry be drawn? These are the questions which occupied Alfred Weber.

Terms and Assumptions Used by Weber

Weber was a German economist, born at Erfurt in 1868. He taught at the University of Prague from 1904 to 1907 and at the University of Heidelberg from 1907 to 1933. In 1909 he published a treatise upon the location of industry which is still the standard reference for certain aspects of the subject. The treatise laid great emphasis upon the factor of transportation.[13]

In order to understand Weber's analysis we need to familiarize ourselves with the assumptions upon which his argument is based and with the meaning of certain terms which he employs. The formal assumptions are as follows:

1. Weber postulates a single country, with uniform climate and technique, inhabited by a population of a single race.

2. He proposes to deal with a single product, or at least to consider a single product at a time. Goods of different quality, though of similar type, are treated as different products.

3. The position of sources of raw material is stated, and is assumed to be known.

4. The position of points of consumption is stated, and is assumed to be known.

5. Labor is geographically fixed. Weber assumes that there exists a number of places where labor at definite, predetermined wages can be had in unlimited quantities.[14]

6. Transportation costs are a function of weight and distance. Differences in topography are allowed for by appropriate additions to distance and differences in transportability by additions to actual weight.

Among the terms which Weber uses are the following:

1. *Ubiquities.* These are materials available practically everywhere, and presumably at the same price everywhere.

---

[13] Alfred Weber, *Über den Standort der Industrien,* Erster Teil, *Reine Theorie des Standorts,* Tübingen, Mohr, 1909. An English translation was published by the University of Chicago in 1929. See Alfred Weber, *Theory of the Location of Industries,* Chicago, University of Chicago, 1929 (English translation by C. J. Friedrich). Prior to Weber a German mathematician named Launhardt anticipated some of the conclusions at which Weber arrived.

[14] Tord Palander, *Beiträge zur Standortstheorie,* Uppsala, Almquist & Wiksells, 1935, p. 173.

2. *Localized materials.* These are materials obtainable only in geographically well-defined localities.

3. *Pure materials.* These are localized materials which enter to the extent of their full weight into the finished product. Thread to be woven into cloth is perhaps an example of this category.

4. *Gross materials.* Under this head are assembled localized materials which impart only a portion or none of their weight to the finished product. Fuel is the extreme type of gross material, for none of its weight enters into the product.

5. *Material index.* Such an index indicates the proportion which the weight of localized materials bears to the weight of the finished product. A productive process which uses pure material has an index of 1.[15]

6. *Locational weight.* This is the total weight to be moved per unit of product. An article made out of ubiquities would have a locational weight of 1 because only the product itself would be moved; if it were made from pure material the locational weight would be 2 because transportation of both the product and an equivalent weight of materials would be required.

7. *Isodapane.* This is the locus of points of equal transportation cost. The meaning of the term will appear more clearly in the discussion.

Working with these assumptions, employing these terms, and seeking in the first instance to measure the effect of transportation upon location, Weber now imagines certain cases and announces the conclusions at which he arrives.

Case I. One Market and One Source of Raw Materials

The first case supposes a raw material to be produced at *A* and the finished product made out of the material to be consumed at *B*. The problem in the case illustrated by the diagram is to determine where the manufacture or processing is to take place. Weber states that four possibilities exist:

A ———————————————————— B

FIGURE 53.   Alfred Weber—Case I.

1. If ubiquities only are used, the processing will occur at point of consumption *B*, because the selection of *B* will make transportation unnecessary.

2. If one pure material is used, processing may occur at *A*, at *B*, or at any point between *A* and *B*. This conclusion is based upon the fact that

---

[15] The distinction between pure and weight-losing materials is now fully recognized in discussions of location, although Weber's names are not always used, and Weber's writings may not be responsible. It must always have been made in practical operation. It was not, apparently, understood by writers of many of the older books.

the weight to be transported and the distance to be covered is the same in all instances. It has been pointed out in criticism of Weber's statement that manufacture at an intermediate point will require an extra handling of the goods, and that the through rate from A to B may be less than the sum of the rail or motor rate from A to the intermediate point and from that point to B. The first of these difficulties Weber disregards, and the second is probably eliminated by the sixth of the assumptions that we have earlier set down.[16]

3. If pure material plus ubiquities is used the processing will occur at the point of consumption B, because the pure material will be without influence, and the ubiquities will govern.

4. If one weight-losing material is used, processing will occur at point of production, because if this decision is made the weight which is lost will not have to be transported.

Case II. One Market and Two Sources of Materials

Weber's second case supposes raw materials which are available at two places, A and B, at equal prices. The finished product is to be consumed at C and the problem as before is to determine where manufacture or processing is to take place. Three possibilities are now considered:

1. If ubiquities alone are used, manufacture will occur at the point of consumption for the same reasons which governed when only two points were involved.

2. If several pure materials are employed, manufacture will also take place at point of consumption. On this supposition the weight of materials exactly equals the weight of the product. All weights, whether in the form of materials or in the form of product, have to be moved from their deposits to the place of consumption. They should not deviate unnecessarily; therefore each material will proceed along the straight line which leads from the place of its origin to the point of its consumption. Unless the way of one should lead by chance through the deposit of another, all of these ways will meet for the first time in the place of consumption. Since the assembly of all materials at one spot is the necessary first condition of manufacture, the place of consumption is the location where manufacturing will be carried on; a productive enterprise, using several pure materials alone, will always locate at the place where its products are consumed.

3. The conclusion is different if several localized weight-losing materials

---

[16] Ohlin says that if the product which may be processed at A is also shipped to other places than B, then B cannot be as favorable a point for its manufacture as A. But (1) this suggestion is contrary to Weber's hypothesis that the entire product is consumed at B; and (2) it assumes advantages of large-scale production which are outside the field of discussion at this point.

are used. In analyzing this case Weber sets up what he calls a "locational figure," which is a triangle in the simpler illustrations with which we are concerned. Let us suppose a process which uses two weight-losing materials produced at A and at $B,$ and let us suppose that the product is to be consumed at $C.$ Manufacture will not take place at C because it is undesirable to transport from A and B to C the material weight which does not enter into the weight of the finished product. It will not, according to Weber, occur at A or at B unless the importance of one material happens to be so great as to overcome the influence of all other elements. It will,

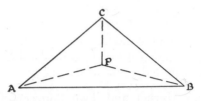

FIGURE 54.   Alfred Weber—
Case II.

usually, be found somewhere within the triangle—as at point $P.$ To this point the raw material will be brought, there it will be manufactured, and from P the finished product will be sent on. Let us imagine, says Weber, a process of production which uses two localized materials, ¾ ton of one and ½ ton of another being necessary in order to produce one ton of the product. These weights will represent the force by which the corners of the locational figure will draw the location toward themselves. Suppose a frame to be set up, with corners placed at the corners of the locational figure. Over these corners run threads, the threads being loaded with weights proportional to the amounts indicated. In the inner part of the figure these threads are connected at some point. Where this connecting point comes to a rest, there will be the location. It will be the place which, if selected, will cause the industry to be burdened with the smallest number of ton-miles.[17]

Introduction of the Labor Factor. The Isodapane

An isodapane, as Weber uses the term, is a line which is the locus of points of equal, though not of minimum transportation cost. The essential result of the part of Weber's location theory which we have so far described is that it indicates where, upon a plain, intelligent businessmen will manufacture an article whose market and sources of raw material have been stated, when they are influenced only by conditions of trans-

[17] Weber considers the possibilities of using localized pure materials with ubiquities, localized weight-losing materials with ubiquities, and localized weight-losing materials with pure materials, but these combinations introduce no new principles.

portation. For any commodity at any time the decision will fix upon a point. Manufacture at any other location than this point will involve an increase in total transportation costs. How much this increase will be will depend upon the position of the alternative location. It should be possible to list all points at which aggregate transportation costs in connection with a given volume of output will exceed aggregate transportation costs at the ideal location by 1; in another list may be placed all points at which the excess is 2; in still another the points at which the excess is 3, and so on. If all the plus-1 points are indicated upon a map and there joined together by a line, the line will unite points of equal transportation costs. It will, therefore, be called an isodapane. A second isodapane may unite the plus-2 points, and a third, the plus-3 points. Every point of optimum location from the point of transportation alone may be surrounded by a series of isodapanes by which the increase of transportation cost may be measured which deviation from the optimum will produce.

The accompanying illustration, adapted from Palander,[18] will show the method of constructing an isodapane. Let us suppose a raw material to be available at a point in the diagram indicated by the letter M. The product made from this raw material is to be consumed at N. The circles surrounding N measure the cost of shipping a single unit of the finished product. It is assumed that the necessary raw material weighs twice as much as the product, and to show this fact upon the diagram the successive circles concentric to M are drawn close together and those concentric to N are drawn relatively far apart. According to Weber's rule, the optimum point for manufacture under these circumstances—transportation conditions alone being taken into account, and rates for material and finished product being the same per pound—is M, and the truth of this principle under the assumptions with which we work can be demonstrated by a little calculation.

It is, however, possible to manufacture at other places. If the processing is done at M, the finished product can be shipped to N at a cost of 8 and there will be no cost for shipment of material. If the point B is selected, the cost of forwarding the finished product will be the same, but there will be an expense of 4 incurred in the course of assembling material at B. The total transportation expense will be 12. If the point D is chosen, the cost of forwarding the finished product will be 6 and the cost of assembling raw material also 6, or again a total of 12. The same total will result if manufacture occurs at A, B, C, E, or F. A line drawn through these various points—an isodapane—will connect points of like shipping costs, in all cases in excess of the minimum possible by the amount of 4.

[18] Tord Palander, *Beiträge zur Standortstheorie*, Uppsala, Almquist & Wiksells, 1935, p. 312.

So long as transportation conditions alone determine the location of manufacturing activity isodapanes supply no useful information. But if labor or other costs are different in different locations the entrepreneur may sometimes find it advisable to abandon the spot which is most suitable from the point of view of transport in favor of a site where labor is less

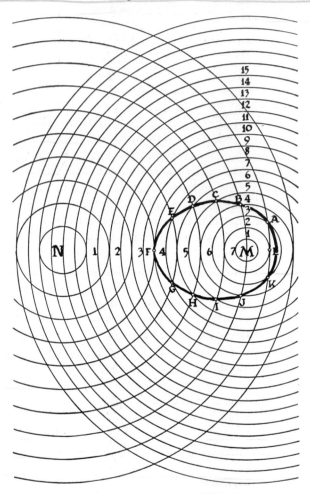

FIGURE 55. Construction of an Isodapane.

expensive. Whether he will do so will depend upon the amount which he will lose by such action and upon the amount which he will gain. If the labor advantage at a given site is to be measured by the figure 4 he will profit by a shift if the new point lies within the area bounded by the isodapane which indicates a transportation disadvantage of 4. If it lies without this area he will lose. The isodapane of 4 in this case will be called the "critical isodapane." Weber's use of isodapanes adds nothing to our knowledge of the effect of labor upon industrial location. The material assembled in the preparation of "factor lists" is much more informative in this regard. But it provides a technique for the systematic introduction of a new variable into a theoretic scheme which the extreme complexity of the data considered seems to demand.[19]

Weber's Generalizations

Although Weber did not invent the locational triangle, it forms the basis of much of his exposition and by the use of this device, along with the concepts of pure materials, weight-losing materials, and ubiquities, he threw light upon questions of location which some authors of factor lists never understood. He also drew, out of his abstract discussion, a number of conclusions, also abstract. These included the following:

1. The orientation of industry is independent of the general level of transport costs. This conclusion properly emphasizes the relative character of problems of location. Critics have pointed out, however, that changes in the general level of transport costs may cause new sources of material to be employed and old ones to be abandoned; these changes may also affect location by altering the relative importance of transport and other costs.

2. Pure materials can never bind production to the place where pure materials are produced. This is logical, but only on Weber's assumption that transport cost varies strictly with weight and distance and that interruption of movement is not expensive.

3. Weight-losing materials draw industries toward the sources of production. Production will be located at any source if the weight of a given material is equal to or greater than the sum of other materials plus the weight of the product. The concept of weight-losing materials is important.

4. Industries with a high material index are drawn toward the source of supply of raw material; these with low material index are drawn toward the place of consumption. As stated, this appears to be true.

5. Given a single market and two weight-losing materials located at different points the place of production will be found in a triangle the lines of which connect the market and the material sources. The exact location will depend upon the relations of the weight components to each other. It will be near a given corner if the weight component of that corner is high. This is again true under the assumptions which Weber makes. But Hoover later reasoned that the resultant calculation will place the processing point at the market or at one of the other corners of the triangle in more cases than Weber seems to have supposed.

[19] Weber also allows for a second variable, which he calls "agglomeration." This is described in the appendix to the present chapter (p. 449).

Criticisms of Weber's Analysis

There have been numerous criticisms of Weber's theories, centering, generally, about three points.

First, it is objected that transportation costs do not vary with distance. Weber's assumption that they do so vary is essential to his analysis; it compelled him, however, to work with constructive rather than with actual miles. As a matter of fact he was required to assume, also, a standard size of shipment always and a standard speed; at least we must imagine that these conditions were in his mind. Such simplifications, together with a refusal to recognize the possible effects of competition, provided him with a basis for his conclusions; they likewise limited the application of the principles which he announced. His conclusions need much interpretation before they are used in any concrete case.

A second criticism is that the choice between locations in the Weberian triangle is not in modern practice free but is, instead, restricted to the selection of points upon established routes. Processing can occur, that is to say, only at locations accessible to rail, highway, air, or water lines. This observation is more or less significant according to the density of the transport network which is in place.

A third comment is that Weber does not examine the relative importance of transport as compared with other factors in determining location, nor does he analyze these factors by themselves. It is pointed out, moreover, that factors, including materials, are more or less mobile, instead of stable as Weber represents them. In addition, one material or factor can be substituted for another, depending upon relative price.[20]

Still another observation is that industries are often linked together so that an optimum location cannot always be determined by separate reference to one industry alone. These and other facts affect the use of Weber's theories—they do not impair their logic under circumstances which correspond to the assumptions which Weber makes.

Finally, critics assert that Weber concerned himself solely with "orientation," which is defined as the type of location which is attractive to an individual producer under various conditions.[21] He does not discuss the

---

[20] Predohl takes the position that Weber's theory is essentially, or can be stated in terms of, a theory of substitution in which optimum combinations of production and transport factors are combined at different places, the lowest optimum at any place being the location which the entrepreneur will approve (Andreas Predohl, "Theory of Location in Its Relation to General Economics," *Journal of Political Economy*, June, 1928, p. 372).

[21] See Edgar M. Hoover, *Location Theory and the Shoe and Leather Industries*, Cambridge, Mass., Harvard, 1937; and his *The Location of Economic Activity*, New York, McGraw-Hill, 1948. These two volumes provide the most comprehensive and critical discussion of location which has been published in English up to the present time.

extent and shape of the areas which established producers can command
under conditions which can be described. This criticism, if it may be
termed such, has undoubted force. We shall next turn to this subject of
area control. It is that which has most occupied students in recent studies
of location. We shall also deal with some questions of transport pricing—questions which arise naturally in this kind of a survey.

The Law of Market Areas

We have considered two formal analyses dealing with transportation
and location. The purposes of these inquiries were different. Von Thünen
sought to explain how distance and consequent cost of transport would
affect methods and distribution of agricultural production when the
market and the limits of a producing area were known. Alfred Weber
attempted to show where manufacturing would occur when the sources of
material and the location of the market were assumed. If, now, we proceed on the supposition that multiple points of production or distribution supply an area in which a total product is consumed we have a third
problem, namely, that of determining the division of this consuming area
between the enterprises which serve it. There are many situations in which
the answer to this question is more immediately important than is a theory
which explains the distribution of producing points themselves. This, indeed, will always be true for short periods and for instances in which
points of production are irrationally selected and are not subject to
change. And, in any case, it is as logical to assume that production is
fixed and that the market to be served by each producer is the thing to
be delimited as it is to proceed upon the basis that the market is fixed and
that the location of producing points is the fact to be ascertained.

There is no single name which is associated with the study of market
division in any dominating sense. But a number of recent writers have
concerned themselves with what we may call the law of market areas.
The main outlines of this law are simple. Let us begin with a simple set
of facts. Let us suppose, that is, two producing points and consider the
division of the market that lies between them. The problem is the one
which the previous paragraph has defined. There are several possible
cases:

Case I. Assumption of Equal Manufacturing Costs

In the accompanying diagram the two manufacturing points in the
illustration are indicated by the letters A and B. We may suppose that the
cost of producing a unit of product at A is the same as that of producing
it at B. We may suppose, also, that transportation rates exactly cover
carrier costs and that they are the same per ton per mile from each point
of origin, in whatever direction the goods may move. As drawn, each

arc in the diagram indicates a given distance from the point about which it is described. The intersection of any two arcs of the same order—the seventh arc, for example, of those encircling A and the seventh arc of those encircling B—fixes the location of a point equally distant from A and from B and equally expensive to reach in terms of production and transport cost. On our assumptions all such intersections will occur upon the line XY. We can, therefore, venture the general conclusion that under

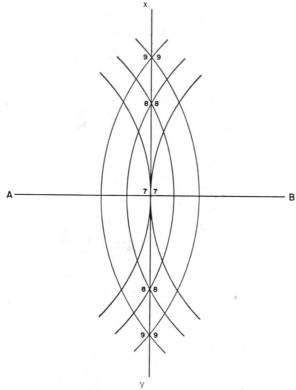

FIGURE 56. Law of Market Areas—Case I.

the specified conditions the boundary between the area in which A has a selling advantage and that in which B has an advantage is a straight line at right angles with the shortest line connecting the two supplying points.

Case II. Assumption of Unequal Manufacturing Costs

Let us now alter the hypothesis by supposing that costs of production at A are higher than those at B. If costs at B are X and costs at A are $X + 6$, then the line of equal total costs will pass through points that are nearer to A than to B by 6 so that the disadvantages of manufacture under which A labors may be offset by savings in transportation expense.

It remains, therefore, to find the locus of all places which are 6 units nearer A than B. This, also, may be illustrated by a diagram.

It is to be especially observed that in this case, where production costs or base prices at A are higher than at B, the boundary between the territories respectively tributary to A and B is not a straight line, but a curve bent around the center with the higher production cost. The curve is not, however, a segment of a circle but a hyperbola, the open ends of which, we may assume, will never meet.[22]

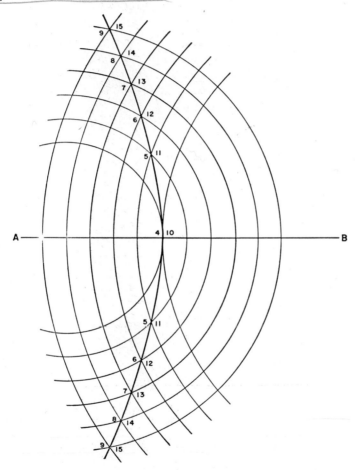

FIGURE 57. Law of Market Areas—Case II.

[22] Hoover properly points out that the same reasoning which applies to the measurement of market areas also applies in the reverse to the measurement of supply areas. A market area is the district in which a producer distributes his goods. A supply area is the district from which a purchaser obtains his goods. Both are shaped by conditions of transport and by transport costs. (See E. M. Hoover, *The Location of Economic Activity*, New York, McGraw-Hill, 1948, p. 48.)

Case III. Variation in the Level of Transportation with Respect to Production Costs

The shape of market areas controlled respectively by *A* and *B* may be changed when the transport cost goes up and down, provided that the production costs in the two localities remain the same.

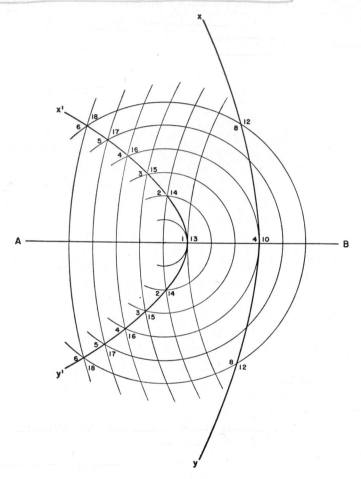

FIGURE 58. Law of Market Areas—Case III.

Let us assume that the cost of transportation per ton per mile which we have relied upon in previous diagrams is cut in half. Let us suppose that the reductions apply to all shipments regardless of point of origin or destination. The question is whether this will affect, in any way, the division of the market between *A* and *B*. To this there are two answers, depending upon the varied assumptions made in Cases I and II.

1. In Case I the cost of producing a unit of product at A was stipulated to be the same as that of producing it at B. If this continues to be the fact, then the division of the market beween A and B will not be changed by a change in the general level of transport cost.

2. In Case II the cost of producing a unit of product was stipulated to be higher at A than at B and equilibrium was established upon this basis. The disadvantage under which A labored in production was, that is to say, offset, up to a designated line, by an advantage in transportation. Community A yielded distance to compensate for excess production cost. If now, A's cost disadvantage remains the same and the value of A's distance concession is diminished, then the previous adjustment must be reviewed. Figure 58 illustrates this case.

In the preceding diagram the line XY is identical with the line separating market areas in Fig. 57. It is the locus of all points where, assuming costs of transport to be 1 cent per mile, the combination of production and transport costs is the same for A and B. The present diagram, however, allows for a change in rates. The line $X'Y'$ is now the locus of all points where, assuming costs of transport to be $\frac{1}{2}$ cent per mile, the combination of transport and production costs are the same for A and B. It will be observed that the amount of distance which A concedes has increased from 6 to 12 miles; point A can continue competition but only in a narrower field.

It is a general principle, illustrated by the diagram, that a decline in the general level of transport costs will increase the area dominated by communities which enjoy a relative advantage in production costs and will decrease the area controlled by communities which work at a production disadvantage. This is the reason why relatively handicapped communities frequently impose restrictions that are intended to provide protection for the local group. It is also the reason for the tendency of production to be centralized, in spite of local efforts, as the technique of carriage is improved.[23]

Case IV. Use of Transport Rates Which Are Not Proportional to Distance

The shape of market areas will also be changed if it is assumed that transport costs and rates are not proportional to distance.

Let us suppose that carriers arbitrarily establish rates which progress regularly up to a certain distance—12 miles—but which cease to increase

[23] Landon explains that an increase in prices, rates remaining the same, will encourage concentration, while a decrease in the price level will encourage decentralization. This is the same phenomenon as that to which the text refers (C. E. Landon, *Transportation,* New York, Sloane, 1951). For a mathematical statement of this and of other elements in the Law of Market Areas, see C. P. Hyson and W. P. Hyson, "The Economic Law of Market Areas," *Quarterly Journal of Economics,* May, 1950, pp. 310–324.

after the 12-mile point has been passed. The rate at 12 miles is assumed to be the maximum for any distance.

Figure 59 illustrates the effect of a rate schedule of the kind described upon the division of the market between *A* and *B*, with the understanding that production costs at *A* remain 6 points higher than at *B* and have to be allowed for. The critical line is here the locus of all points at which

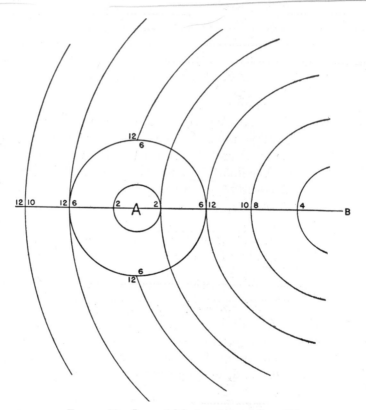

FIGURE 59. Law of Market Areas—Case IV.

the transport rates from *A* are 6 units higher than from *B* under the conditions which have been described. The area which *A* will dominate, on this hypothesis, is restricted to points within the circle bounded by this line. It is to be remarked that *B* now controls the territory beyond A as well as a portion of the territory between *A* and *B*. This is, indeed, a frequent consequence of blanket rates.[24]

[24] Case IV suggests the great variety of conclusions which may appear when a student departs from preliminary and simple assumptions. The use of a blanket rate, which Case IV assumes, amounts to the absorption by a carrier of costs which the shipper would normally bear and which would usually determine the areas in which he would conduct

Conclusion

We conclude our discussion of the theory of location at this point in order to keep the present chapter within bounds. The reader will be familiar with the character of thinking which the subject has provoked. The theory of location has a considerable literature, in which the formalized discussions of von Thünen, Weber, Fetter, and many others form a not undistinguished part. Its principles can be expanded and refined and integrated into economic theory as a whole. Meanwhile the problems raised have their own importance. Something is being done with "location" in the field of marketing at the present time, and a systematic study of locational relations is an activity in which the serious student of transportation can be encouraged to indulge.

APPENDIX TO CHAPTER 22

I

Note on "Agglomeration"

Agglomeration is a word used by Alfred Weber to cover three distinct situations. There is, first, the case of simple enlargement of plant, bringing into existence the advantages of large scale production. There is, second, the local association of several plants, presumably in the same industry, which encourages the development of technical equipment and facilitates the sale of finished product. And there is, third, the case in which the mere aggregation of manufacturing activities, of unrelated as well as of related types, leads to conditions which are on the whole more favorable than any single plant or group of related plants could develop for itself.

Points for agglomeration differ from locations where sources of raw materials or supplies of capable labor are to be found in that they depend for their existence upon the decision of the undertakings which agree to create them. A competent prior survey will reveal deposits of coal and iron. Proper inquiry will bring to light efficient groups of laborers. Weber assumes that labor is geographically fixed. But an agglomeration point is merely a place to which a number of persons engaged in industry decide to resort. Without

---

his operations. His field of operation, that is to say, is now altered in shape and size. It may equally well happen that a shipper will be content to accept less than average profit on sales in a certain district. He may do this because of generous emotion, which is unlikely, or because of overall or long-term conditions with which he feels that he has to deal. One type of shipper variation is discussed in the appendix to this chapter. Possibilities of these kinds are not a proper basis, however, for the criticism of location theory. This theory is far from perfect, but simplification is a useful device in the processes of thought.

the decision, it does not exist; after the decision, it is there. Looked at from another point of view, a point for agglomeration is not one to which it is to the advantage of any single producer to transfer his plant. While it may be to the advantage of two producers to come together, neither will gain unless the other also acts. It is in spite of these conditions that the location of industry is influenced by advantages arising out of the association of manufacturing enterprises.

Weber takes four steps in absorbing the factor "agglomeration" into his conceptual scheme. In the first place, he puts aside for the moment variations resulting from geographical differences in the supply of labor. We start again from locations determined by transportation conditions alone. Secondly, he

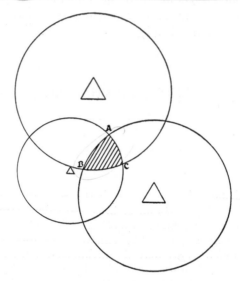

FIGURE 60.   Diagram Illustrating
"Agglomeration."

assumes a gain which is to result from agglomeration. This gain may be progressive, increasing with the extent of agglomeration, or it may be fixed, emerging when a definite amount of concentration has been attained. In our explanation of Weber's theory we shall restrict ourselves to the latter, more simple case. A third assumption is that an enterprise which shifts from the best available location, from the point of view of transportation, incurs a loss which has to be balanced by gains from agglomeration. And lastly, there is recognition of the fact that there can be no gain from concentration unless the opportunity for association is presented to several enterprises at once.

Figure 60 shows how these suppositions are applied.

Let us suppose three locational triangles within each of which there is a manufacturing point. We are already familiar with the method by which such points are selected. Around the optimum points in each triangle let us draw isodapanes. Let us imagine a fixed gain from agglomeration measured by the

figure 5, and let the isodapanes upon the chart, on the other hand, connect the points where manufacture is more costly than at the optimum, in terms of transportation expense, by the amount of 4. On these assumptions it may be profitable to move an enterprise, in order to obtain the advantages connected with agglomeration, from any optimum location within a triangle to another location within the area bounded by the encircling critical isodapane. Actually to induce movement there must be an area which is within the critical isodapanes encircling two or more producing points, for the advantages of agglomeration appear only when two or more points are involved. Such an area is the shaded figure ABC. Industries will locate within this space, rather than at points within the various locational triangles, if their directors are alert to seek the most favorable positions for their enterprises. There have been some criticisms of this analysis but the method used is consistent with that which Weber elsewhere employed.

II

Basing Points and Market Areas

Market area boundaries are not marked by physical barriers. Shippers may always sell in a market area which they are not expected to invade. When they do this they are said to "absorb" rates or costs because they supply goods to customers for less than the sum of their mill or base price and the transportation charge. Of course this interferes with market area design.

There are many reasons why shippers may desire to cross market boundaries. The most obvious is that they may wish to expand their sales. Absorption is, in its simplest form, a kind of price reduction, commonly limited to new territory, and to destinations which are relatively remote. So used, it enables a shipper to participate in the supply of an area from which he has been formerly excluded. This may be advantageous because of temporary excess capacity and also when conditions of production suggest that the producer's scale of operation can be economically enlarged. Absorption may be regularized in the sense that an individual firm may absorb freight costs at all points where the firm desires to compete.

Now rate absorption may be the independent act of an individual shipper. Or, on the other hand, it may be part of a general plan in which many or all shippers participate. Such a plan may establish what is called a uniform delivered price or it may set up a kind of basing system in which all concur.

Under the first of these arrangements the delivered price of a commodity is made everywhere the same or everywhere the same within a described zone or zones. The probable actual fact will be that the base price of supplying mills plus the normal carrier charge will be greater at some destinations than at others so that different prices should normally emerge. But under a uniform price system some shippers will absorb some costs and these costs will not be collected from the customer or reflected in the price. Uniform delivered prices are common when delivery costs are low. They have some marketing advantage. One collateral effect is that the purchaser is no longer dependent upon nearness to his sources of supply because, with a uniform delivered price, he can obtain material at the same expense whether the haul be short or long.

Under the second arrangement, the basing point system, location is equalized in the sense that all producers accept or agree upon a common principle in calculating the price which they will charge. It is stipulated (1) that this price shall be equal to mill price plus a transportation charge, and (2) that this transportation charge will not be the transport rate from point of shipment, as a general rule. It will rather be the rate from some selected point of origin which is called a basing point; or it may be the lowest of the actual rates from any of a listed number of competitive centers, referred to as multiple basing points. The shipper "absorbs" when he pays the carrier a higher rate from point of shipment than the rate which he uses in quoting his sales price. It is conceivable that the shipper may pay the carrier less than the calculated rate; if he does this there is no absorption; on the contrary, his net profit is increased. Under such a circumstance the shipper is said to assess "phantom freight" in making up his price. This is most likely to occur on shipments to locations near the producer's mill. It gives him a measure of protection on his local operations. A basing point rate system will not, by itself, produce a uniform delivered price. It will tend to equalize the transport charge on which price is partly based, but it will not equalize the price which producers fix as the base price at their mills.

The use of basing points, and particularly the use under a general plan, has been violently criticized from a number of points of view. Some of the objections are based upon general economic reasoning, and some refer to immediate effects. In most cases a basing point rate system is alleged to have, at least, the following defects:

1. It is a part of a program to fix and maintain commodity prices. The fundamental fault of a basing point system is that it lessens competition by establishing and publicizing a method of determining price.
2. It results in unnecessary cross-hauling.
3. It discriminates in the sense that some purchasers are charged for transport costs which are not incurred—"phantom freight"—while other purchasers are charged prices which do not properly provide for transport expenses which the shipper has been compelled to meet.[25]
4. The system, as a whole, benefits the large firm as against the small.

Extreme critics prefer a system in which prices are quoted for delivery at the point of production (f.o.b. mill pricing) and the cost of transport is then added for carriage to the point of use.

On the other hand, it is maintained that

1. The logical alternative to a basing point system is f.o.b. pricing at the various producing points. The tendency of such a practice is to lessen competition by dividing the country into districts, each dominated by a few producers, unless individual absorption is assumed.
2. Individual cost absorption in any case leads to piecemeal cost erosion, carrying prices to bankruptcy levels when capacity is excessive.[26]

[25] Fritz Machlup, *The Basing-Point System*, Blakiston, Philadelphia, 1949.
[26] See J. M. Clark, "Law and Economics of Basing Points," *American Economic Review*, March, 1949.

3. The amount of cross-hauling which takes place is exaggerated. It has been said that it is measurable by the amount of rates absorbed, but this is by no means the case.
4. A basing point rate system can be framed which does not permit of phantom freight. There are reasons, however, for continuing the practice so referred to. Other kinds of discrimination are justified by the general results.

General plans for basing point rate making have been declared illegal by the courts.[27]

R E F E R E N C E S
General Treatises

Black, John D., *Introduction to Production Economics*, New York, Holt, 1926.

Bonavia, M. R., *The Economics of Transport*, New York, Pitman, 1947.

Hoover, E. M., *The Location of Economic Activity*, New York, McGraw-Hill, 1948.

Hoover, E. M., *Location Theory and the Shoe and Leather Industries*, Cambridge, Mass., Harvard, 1937.

Landon, Charles E., *Transportation, Principles, Practices, Problems*, New York, Sloane, 1951.

Locklin, D. Philip, *Economics of Transportation*, Chicago, Irwin, 1947.

Ohlin, B. G., *Interregional and International Trade*, Cambridge, Mass., Harvard, 1933.

Palander, Tord, *Beiträge zur Standortstheorie*, Uppsala, Almquist & Wiksells, 1935.

Sombart, W., *Der Moderne Kapitalismus*, München und Leipzig, Duncker & Humblot, 1928. See especially vol. II, Part II, chaps. 47, 54.

Thünen, J. H. von, *Der Isolierte Staat in Beziehung auf Landwirthschaft und Nationalökonomie*, Berlin, Wiegand, Hempel and Pavey, 1875.

Weber, Alfred, *Über den Standort der Industrien*, Erster Teil, *Reine Theorie des Standorts*, Tubingen, Mohr, 1909.

Weber, Alfred, *Theory of the Location of Industries*, Chicago, University of Chicago, 1920 (English edition with introduction and notes by Carl Joachim Friedrich).

[27] The critical Supreme Court decision in the basing point controversy is *Federal Trade Commission v. Cement Institute* (68 Sup. Ct. Rep. 793, 1948. See also *Federal Trade Commission v. A. E. Staley Mfg. Company* (65 Sup. Ct. Rep. 971, 1945). The Court held, in this case (1) that the basing point delivered system was an unfair method of competition prohibited by the Federal Trade Commission Act and (2) that the system had effected discriminations which were in violation of the Clayton Act.

Congress subsequently passed a so-called "freight absorption" bill in 1950 (S. 1008). The President vetoed this bill on June 16, 1950, on the ground that it was capable of widely conflicting interpretations. (See also United States Senate, Committee on Interstate and Foreign Commerce, Hearings on S. 236 before a subcommittee, 81st C., 1st S., 1949.)

There is still some question whether individual freight absorption is or will be held to be illegal and whether and on what conditions uniform delivery prices will be allowed. It is not necessary, however, to pursue the subject further at this point.

Other Books

Bressler, R. G., *City Milk Distribution,* Cambridge, Mass., Harvard, 1952.

Büchler, Max, *Johann Heinrich von Thünen und seine nationalökonomischen Hauptlehren,* Bern, Haller'sche Buchdruckerei, 1907.

Fetter, Frank A., *The Masquerade of Monopoly,* New York, Harcourt, Brace, 1931.

Florence, P. S., *Investment, Location, and Size of Plant,* Cambridge, National Institute of Economic and Social Research, Cambridge University, 1948.

Kautz, Erich A., *Das Standortsproblem der Seehafen,* Jena, Fischer, 1934.

Garver, F. B., Boddy, F. M., and Nixon, A. J., *The Location of Manufacturers in the United States, 1899–1929,* Minneapolis, University of Minnesota, 1933.

Holmes, W. G., *Plant Location,* New York, McGraw-Hill, 1930.

Machlup, Fritz, *The Basing Point System,* Philadelphia, The Blakiston Company, 1949.

Sage, G. H., *Basing-Point Pricing Systems Under the Federal Anti-Trust Laws—A Legal, Business, and Economic Analysis,* St. Louis, Thomas Law Book, 1951.

Seedorf-Seraphim, *Johann Heinrich von Thünen zum 150 Geburtstage,* Rostock, 1933.

Periodicals

Aereboe, Friedrich, *"Ursachen und Formen wechselnder Betriebsintensität in der Landwirthschaft,"* Thünen Archiv, 1907–1909, pp. 362–394.

Borkiewicz, L. V., *"Eine geographische Fundierung der Lehre vom Standort der Industrien,"* Archiv für Socialwissenschaft, 1910, pp. 759–785.

Clark, J. M., "Law and Economics of Basing Points," *American Economic Review,* March, 1949.

Cunningham, W., "The Localization of Industry," *Economic Journal,* December, 1902.

Englander, O., *"Kritische und Positives zu einer allgemeinen reinen Lehre vom Standort,"* Zeitschrift für Volkswirthschaft und Socialpolitik, 1925–1927, pp. 435–505.

Fetter, F. A., "The Economic Law of Market Areas," *Quarterly Journal of Economics,* May, 1924.

Florence, P. S., "Economic Research and Industrial Policy," *Economic Journal,* December, 1937.

Helburn, S., "Location of Industry," *Journal of Land and Public Utility Economics,* August, 1933.

Hyson, C. P., and Hyson, W. P., "The Economic Law of Market Areas," *Quarterly Journal of Economics,* May, 1950.

Isard, Walter, "The General Theory of Location and Space-Economy," *Quarterly Journal of Economics,* November, 1949.

Keir, Malcolm, "Economic Factors in the Location of Manufacturing Industries," *Annals of the American Academy of Political and Social Science,* September, 1921.

Kryzanowski, Witold, "Review of the Literature of the Location of Industries," *Journal of Political Economy,* April, 1927.

Launhardt, W., *"Die Bestimmung des Zweckmassigsten Standortes einer gewerblichen Anlage,"* Zeitschrift des Vereines deutscher Ingenieure, 1882, pp. 105 ff.

Predohl, Andreas, "The Theory of Location in Its Relation to General Economics," *Journal of Political Economy,* June, 1928.

Renner, G. T., "Geography of Industrial Localization," *Economic Geography,* July, 1947.

Ross, E. A., "The Location of Industries," *Quarterly Journal of Economics,* April, 1896.

Salin, *"Der Isolierte Staat, 1826–1926,"* Zeitschrift für die gesamte Staatswissenschaft, 1926, pp. 410–431.

Small, F. S., "Age and Area Development," *Scientific American Supplement,* June 1, 1918.

Special and Miscellaneous

Florence, P. S., Fritz, W. G., and Gilles, R. C., *"Measures of Industrial Distribution,"* in National Resources Planning Board, *Industrial Location and National Resources,* 1943, chap. 5.

Hall, F. S., *The Localization of Industries,* 12th United States Census, Manufactures, Part I, 1902, pp. cxc–ccxiv.

Hoover, E. M., and Wood, C. P., "The Selection of Locations," National Resources Planning Board, *Industrial Location and National Resources,* 1942, chap. 20.

Lynch, Edward S., "Influence of Transportation on the Location of Economic Activities," in National Resources Planning Board, *Transportation and National Policy,* Part I, Section II, pp. 71–86.

Metropolitan Life Insurance Company, New York, in coöperation with the National Electric Light Association, *Industrial Development in the United States and Canada, A Cooperative Survey,* 1926 and 1927.

P.E.P. (Political and Economic Planning), *Report on the Location of Industry,* London, P.E.P., 1939.

Schumacher, Hermann, "Location of Industry," *Encyclopedia of the Social Sciences,* 1933, vol. 9, pp. 585–592.

Tower, W. S., "Some Factors Influencing the Location and Migration of Industries," *Bulletin of the Geographical Society of Philadelphia,* April, 1911.

Relations of Carriers
with Each Other

Coöperation Between Railroad Companies

Problems of Administration

There are two characteristics of a transportation system such as that in the United States which impress even the casual observer. One is that this system is geographically diffused; the other is that it is administered by a large number of separate companies without centralized control or direction except that supplied by government authority under the provisions of regulative law. If, as is the case with street railway companies, the units of the system had only local functions to perform, the decentralization of executive authority might seem natural; but since waterways, railroads, pipe lines, and, to a lesser degree, automobile carriers engage in interstate and foreign traffic and necessarily have relations with one another, it would be unfortunate if somehow or other these agencies did not manage to coöperate in national service.

Internal Organization

The fact that transportation companies operate in space and under conditions which make detailed supervision of personnel difficult has caused them to pay more than usual attention to questions of internal organization. This is, at least, true of railroads, which have had the most experience and the longest history among the operative units in the transportation field. While railroads have not engaged in time studies or applied the principles of scientific management as fully as industrial plants, they have worked out in detail alternative relationships of authority between their various officers and they have experimented in the field of employee organization, particularly in recent years. We shall discuss neither railroad internal organization nor the relationship of transportation companies to their employees, but the reader is reminded that common carriers have something to contribute in the field of industrial relations.

459

American Railroad Pools

Early types of agreements between railroad companies included many and various arrangements looking toward the abatement of competition. The more important of these contracts were known as railroad pools. As used in railroad discussion, the term *pool* implies an agreement to divide business of a described kind, moving between specified termini, between parties who subscribe to the agreement, on terms that have been agreed upon. The methods of dividing the business vary. Sometimes two railroads agree each to confine its operations to a certainly described territory. This automatically produces a division of the business in the area. Sometimes the railroads agree that each will handle only a certain percentage of all the tonnage and sometimes a percentage distribution is settled in advance, not of the tonnage itself, but of the revenue from that tonnage. The difference between the two last forms is unimportant.

The railroad pool originally provoked public opposition because this sort of undertaking seemed likely to raise rates. It was accordingly forbidden in the Act of 1887, and in a revised form it was held subject to the Antitrust Act of 1890. In 1920 the prohibition was removed, probably because, during the 33 years after 1887 the level of railroad rates had been brought under government control. As a matter of fact, little use has been made of the liberalized clauses of the Interstate Commerce Act. Railroad conditions are more nearly stable, discriminations or departures from the published rates are subject to extreme penalties, and organizations have been built up within the law sufficient to provide the indispensable minimum of business cooperation without recourse to pooling.

Operating Agreements Between Transportation Companies

Operating arrangements between transportation companies are easier to enforce than agreements regarding price or the division of business because there is less difference in interest between the parties, and also because they are less likely to arouse public opposition. On the continent of Europe, a number of governments had reached a general agreement on such matters before the last World War. No government action has been needed in the United States. Coöperation in this country has been accomplished by private initiative, but it has been none the less widespread and important.

The most striking instances of operating coöperation between railroads in the United States are in the field of accounting, in the establishment of through rates and routes, in the common use of cars, and in the development of standard practice through the activity of committees of the Association of American Railroads (formerly the American Railway Association). There is little comparable to these achievements in the activity of other transportation agencies. Taken in connection with the statutory extension of the liability of the initial carrier to the shipper for loss or damage occurring anywhere enroute, when several successive carriers participate in transportation, they have done much to transform the variously owned properties of the country into a single operating system. This is a decidedly fortunate outcome, for the reason that traffic in this country constantly tends to pass beyond the lines of the transportation system upon which it originates, and coöperation between carriers both improves service and relieves the shipper of expensive responsibility for the distant handling of his goods.

Let us examine some of the forms of operating coöperation which contribute to the functioning of American railroads as a single transportation system.

Through Billing

One simple method by which railroads coöperate in interline hauls is by the use of through or interline waybills. A waybill, in American practice, is a document representing the freight and traveling with it.[1] The form below is mandatory under the rules of the Association of American Railroads.

Examination of this waybill will show that it contains spaces for the insertion of the names of shipper and consignee, description of goods, weight, rate (per 100 pounds), freight charges (weight multiplied by rate), advances, and amount prepaid. The meaning of these terms is obvious except, perhaps, that of the term *advances,* which refers to expenses incurred or payments made by the billing carrier, in connection with shipments, that are to be collected in addition to freight charges from the consignee. The waybill has also places for routing instructions, for the identification of the car in which the shipment moves, for the name of the station where the bill is made out, for a billing date and number and for instructions with respect to icing, ventilation, weighing and the like. It is an operating paper, which accompanies freight from the beginning of its journey to the end. A bill is a "through bill" if it covers a movement which begins upon the line of one carrier and ends upon the line of another carrier. It is a local bill if the points of origin and destination are both upon one road. In either case the waybill serves the freight train conductor as a memorandum of freight which is on his train; it informs the station agent of the charges which must be collected from the consignee; and it supplies the general auditor with a record and a basis for records which enable him to check the accounts of station agents, to

---

[1] The airlines use a document called the "airbill," which is a combination of the waybill and the bill of lading.

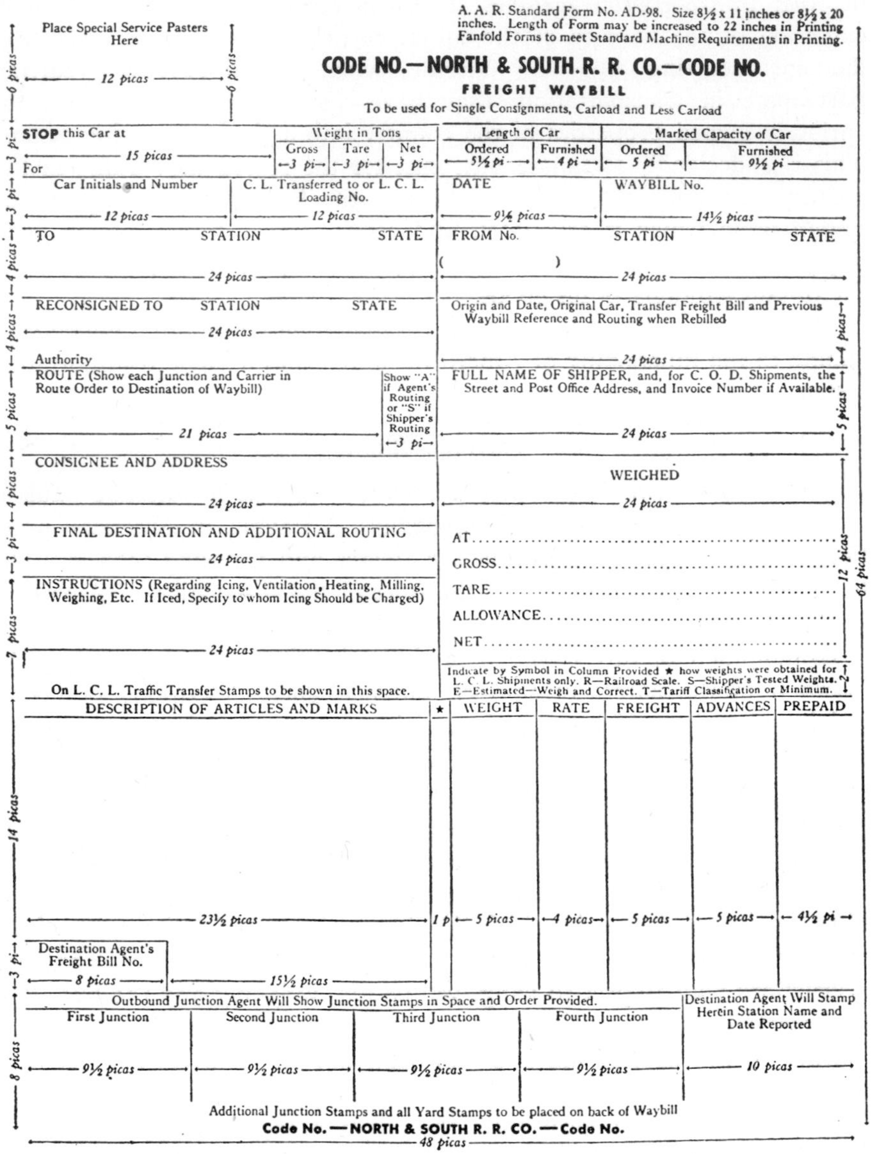

A. A. R. Standard Form No. AD-98. Size 8½ x 11 inches or 8½ x 20 inches. Length of Form may be increased to 22 inches in Printing Fanfold Forms to meet Standard Machine Requirements in Printing.

Place Special Service Pasters Here — 12 picas — 6 picas

CODE NO.—NORTH & SOUTH. R. R. CO.—CODE NO.

FREIGHT WAYBILL

To be used for Single Consignments, Carload and Less Carload

STOP this Car at — 15 picas — For

Weight in Tons: Gross —3 pi— | Tare —3 pi— | Net —3 pi—

Length of Car: Ordered — 5½ pi — | Furnished — 4 pi —

Marked Capacity of Car: Ordered — 5 pi — | Furnished — 9½ pi —

Car Initials and Number — 12 picas — | C. L. Transferred to or L. C. L. Loading No. — 12 picas — | DATE — 9½ picas — | WAYBILL No. — 14½ picas —

TO STATION STATE — 24 picas — | FROM No. ( ) STATION STATE — 24 picas —

RECONSIGNED TO STATION STATE — 24 picas — Authority | Origin and Date, Original Car, Transfer Freight Bill and Previous Waybill Reference and Routing when Rebilled — 24 picas — 4 picas

ROUTE (Show each Junction and Carrier in Route Order to Destination of Waybill) — 21 picas — | Show "A" if Agent's Routing or "S" if Shipper's Routing —3 pi— | FULL NAME OF SHIPPER, and, for C. O. D. Shipments, the Street and Post Office Address, and Invoice Number if Available. — 24 picas — 5 picas

CONSIGNEE AND ADDRESS — 24 picas — | WEIGHED — 24 picas —

FINAL DESTINATION AND ADDITIONAL ROUTING — 24 picas —

INSTRUCTIONS (Regarding Icing, Ventilation, Heating, Milling, Weighing, Etc. If Iced, Specify to whom Icing Should be Charged) — 24 picas —

AT.......... GROSS.......... TARE.......... ALLOWANCE.......... NET.......... — 12 picas

On L. C. L. Traffic Transfer Stamps to be shown in this space.

Indicate by Symbol in Column Provided ★ how weights were obtained for L. C. L. Shipments only. R—Railroad Scale. S—Shipper's Tested Weights. E—Estimated—Weigh and Correct. T—Tariff Classification or Minimum.

DESCRIPTION OF ARTICLES AND MARKS	★	WEIGHT	RATE	FREIGHT	ADVANCES	PREPAID
23½ picas	1 p	5 picas	4 picas	5 picas	5 picas	4½ pi

Destination Agent's Freight Bill No. — 8 picas — | — 15½ picas —

Outbound Junction Agent Will Show Junction Stamps in Space and Order Provided.

First Junction	Second Junction	Third Junction	Fourth Junction	Destination Agent Will Stamp Herein Station Name and Date Reported
9½ picas	9½ picas	9½ picas	9½ picas	10 picas

Additional Junction Stamps and all Yard Stamps to be placed on back of Waybill

Code No.—NORTH & SOUTH R. R. CO.—Code No.

— 48 picas — 64 picas — 14 picas — 8 picas — 7 picas — 3 pi

FIGURE 61. Freight Waybill. The word *pica* is an indication of size: it is one-sixth of an inch.

divide revenues among all companies that are interested, and to prepare statistical reports descriptive of the business done.

ADVANTAGES OF THROUGH BILLING. Before the practice of through billing was introduced, a carrier customarily "billed" only to a junction point with a connecting road. That is to say, the point of destination indicated on the waybill was the end of the first carrier's line. At the junction point, the connecting carrier made out a new waybill, showing the junction point as the place of origin and the place to which the freight was going as the destination unless, indeed, more than two carriers were involved, when the arrangements become still more complicated.

Local billing of this type was and is expensive. It requires a multiplication of clerical work. Moreover, it increases the chances of mistake. Still again, the tendency of local billing is to break up a through shipment into a series of local hauls. It is evidence that a carrier seeks to limit its responsibility for loss or damage to accidents occurring upon its own lines, and refuses to employ connecting carriers for delivery at a point beyond its own terminus, thus endeavoring to place the shipper in direct contractual relation with each carrier over whose lines his goods may pass.

It needs no argument to prove the convenience, in an interline transaction, of using a single waybill from point of origin to final destination on whatever railroad line that destination may be. Although through billing cannot be said to be universal, in the majority of cases railroads recognize the advantage of acting as a unit in the matter of billing, and operate in this respect with little attention to the dividing lines created by the diversity of ownership of separate railroad systems.

Through Routes and Rates

The fact of through billing creates a through route because it indicates the intention of the carriers to deal with a shipment as a single transaction although several companies may contribute to the service.[2] When a through route has been set up in this or in any other way, carriers will quote through rates which will apply on shipments from a station on one road to a station upon another. These rates will be usually, although not always or necessarily, less than the sum of local rates. This practice makes it unnecessary for shippers to consult a succession of local tariffs to learn the amount that they will pay.[3]

[2] Through billing is not, however, the only admissible evidence. See, on this subject, 245 U.S. 136, 139, 1917. See also D. P. Locklin, *Economics of Transportation,* Chicago, Irwin, 1947, p. 616; T. C. Bigham and W. J. Roberts, *Transportation, Principles and Problems,* New York, McGraw-Hill, 1946.

The Commission has said: "Existence of a through route is to be determined by the incidents and circumstances of the shipment, such as the billing, the transfer from one carrier to another, the collection and division of transportation charges, or the use of a proportional rate to or from junction points or basing points. These incidents named are not to be regarded as exclusive of others which may tend to establish a carrier's course of business with respect to through shipments (United States Interstate Commerce Commission, *Annual Report,* 1907, pp. 75–76).

The fact of rail connection does not, alone, constitute a through route; carriers must hold themselves out as offering through transportation service (72 Sup. Ct. Rep. 978, 983, 1952).

[3] There are, inevitably, complications in this matter. Carriers publish through rates from points on the line of one railroad to points upon the line of another. These rates

Division of Revenue on Interline Business

A through rate which covers services rendered by several connecting carriers must, in practice, be collected from the shipper at the beginning or at the ending of the haul. This requires a considerable amount of additional intercarrier coöperation. The efficiency of the methods employed by American railroads in making quick and accurate division of the revenues derived from through business, and the extent to which these methods require coöperative action between interested carriers, are seldom appreciated by the general public.

In dividing interline revenue, the percentage of total receipts to be assigned each carrier which participates in a through movement is determined by agreement.[4] The carrying out of division agreements is a func-

---

may be available (1) over any combination of lines operated by the two carriers; (2) over a specified and limited sequence of lines; or (3) the tariff may not establish any rule with respect to the selection of movements to which through rates will be applied. In the last case, the Interstate Commerce Commission will interpret the tariff so that it will apply over any combination of the lines of the participants which is not unnecessarily circuitous and over which operating conditions are not unduly adverse. This is a matter of judgment. (See Glenn L. Shinn, *Freight Rate Application,* New York, Simmons-Boardman, 1948.) Somewhat similar problems arise in the interpretation of Section 4 of the Interstate Commerce Act. See chap. 20.

[4] Agreements in the past have reflected the relative bargaining powers of the parties. They have been much regularized, however, under Interstate Commerce Commission control. The principal variations are the following:

1. Mileage prorate. On this basis carriers divide revenues in proportion to the share of each in the total mileage covered. The practice is simple when the parties use a mileage figure which is that of the routes over which commodities travel. It may be indefinitely complicated by substitution or inflation. Mileage prorates provide each participant with the same earnings per ton-mile. This may not be fair (a) when the terminal costs of one carrier are higher than those of the other, and (b) when the length of haul of one carrier is much greater than that of the other. Mileage prorates are most satisfactory when the total haul is long and the participating carriers contribute each approximately the same number of miles of line.

2. Rate prorate. The division, here, depends upon local charges. The practice is to add the local rates of the respective carriers from origin to interchange point and from interchange point to destination, to determine the percentage which each local rate is of the total, and to divide the joint revenue on the basis of the percentages so obtained. In most cases the first class rate is used in the computation. Unlike the mileage prorate, rate prorates favor the carrier with a short line. They are criticized (a) because the technique used employs local tariffs which are built to cover four terminal operations although there are only two terminals in the through movement to which the division is applied; and (b) because the scale may not recognize differences in costs. This last is particularly likely when a first-class rate prorate is applied to all shipments.

The Interstate Commerce Commission has developed a special formula for rate prorates which can be used when the origin of a movement is in one district and the destination in another, and when the rate levels in the two areas are not the same. This has been referred to as a "factor" division. It is described in the Southwestern-Official case of 1939 (234 I.C.C. 135, 166, 1939). See also 269 I.C.C. 765, 1948; 278 I.C.C. 89, 1950.

For reference to the whole question of divisions, including the division of revenues between motor carriers, see United States Interstate Commerce Commission, Bureau of Transport Economics and Statistics, *Practices of Motor Carriers of Property in the Division of Revenues of Joint Hauls,* Statement no. 451, January, 1945.

A. A. R. Standard Form No. AD-104.
Size 8½ x 11 inches or 11 x 8½ inches.

CODE NO.   NORTH AND SOUTH RAILROAD

NO._____

ABSTRACT OF INTERLINE WAYBILLS RECEIVED

	FROM STATION ON THE		DIVISIONS	PROPORTIONS	
MONTH OF 19 No.		R. R.			
		ARB'Y			
VIA	&	R. R.			
VIA	&	R. R.			
VIA	&	R. R.			
VIA	&	R. R.			
VIA	&	R. R.			
		ARB'Y			

FROM ( )			TO ( )			COMMODITY ( )	
NO.	STATION	STATE	NO.	STATION	STATE	ICC NO.	DESCRIPTION

WAYBILL		CAR		WEIGHT	FREIGHT	ADVANCES	PREPAID	DIVISIONS OVER	ARB'Y
DATE	NUMBER	INITIALS	NUMBER						

CODE NO.   NORTH AND SOUTH RAILROAD

NOTE.—Number of lines for Roads and Routes, Station From or To and Commodity may be increased or decreased and space for particulars of waybills correspondingly decreased or increased as considered advisable.

FIGURE 62.   Abstract of Interline Waybills Received.

tion of the accounting departments of the carriers which are concerned. In this matter the initiative is taken by the destination railroad, because the original waybill, upon which the accounting depends, is in the hands of the agent of the destination railroad at the time when the act of transportation is completed.

ABSTRACTS OF INTERLINE WAYBILLS. The process of interline settlement

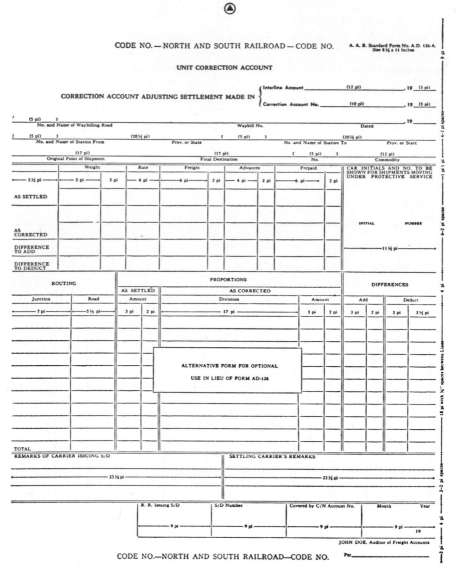

FIGURE 63.   Correction Account.

begins with the forwarding of waybills by a station agent to the auditor of his railroad. This is done at regular intervals, generally daily, and the bills are accompanied by report sheets upon which the most essential items of information on the bill—consignor, consignee, nature of shipment, weight, rate, advances, and prepaid—are set forth. These reports are known as abstracts, and are in the form shown on page 465.

Abstracts of interline freight received are checked in the auditor's office against the accompanying waybills.

DIVISION STATEMENT. The division statement is made out from the abstract. This is a statement sent by the receiving railroad to all railroads from which freight has been received during the preceding month.

The division statement reproduces the information contained in the abstract, although in slightly different form, owing to the fact that it represents the accumulation of reports from many receiving stations on the reporting railroad line. The division statement also contains one thing which the abstracts do not, namely, a calculation of the proportion and amount of revenue to which each railroad that has participated in interline movements is entitled as its share. The basis of such a calculation is found in agreements previously entered into by the parties interested.

CORRECTION ACCOUNT. For purposes of monthly settlements between carriers, the division statement rendered by the receiving road is accepted as accurate. This statement is, however, checked by the carriers to whom it is sent; the receiving road is notified of errors; and the latter, through a so-called "correction account," adjusts the mistakes which have been discovered.

It should be added, to make the description of the process of interline settlements complete, that when a railroad has a balance to pay to another railroad on received business and a balance to receive on forwarded business, or vice versa, only the difference between the two amounts is remitted or collected. This fact, as well as the circumstance that every carrier is a receiver as well as a forwarder of freight, and so initiates part of the settlements in which it is interested, has done much to convince American railroads of the fairness and economy of the interline accounting methods which they pursue.[5]

Railway Clearing Houses

Before the introduction of the plan of audit office settlement between railroads on a "received" basis, most railroads followed what was known as the "junction settlement" plan—a system which called for an accounting at each junction point between railroads at the time when freight passed from one to the other. This was an altogether clumsier and less effective method than the one now in force. An alternative with more promise might be a clearing house operation, following banking practice. This last-named system has received the attention of railroads in the United States and formed the subject of a memorandum released by the Federal Coordinator of Transportation in March, 1934.[6]

[5] See Association of American Railroads, *Railway Accounting Rules,* Washington, D.C., for forms and instructions relative to interline railroad settlements.

[6] United States, Federal Coordinator of Transportation, *Memorandum on the Ap-*

A railway clearing house would replace the system of interline accounting which we have described to a greater or less degree according (1) as the clearing house undertook to calculate the divisions due each member railroad on interline business, or (2) as it served merely as a facility for the clearing of claims separately and independently ascertained by the carriers party to the plan. The old Railway Clearinghouse of the British railroads was an organization of the former sort. It received monthly reports from station agents of all traffic interchanged between British railway lines. It audited these accounts to determine their correctness, calculated divisions, and collected from or paid to individual lines the sums which each owed or was entitled to receive.

In contrast to the British organization, the American Railway Clearinghouse, set up in 1907 to handle per diem accounts, was a system of the second kind. This clearing house received statements from member railroads showing amounts for which these railroads acknowledged liability to each company whose cars had operated upon a reporting railroad's line. These statements enabled the clearing house to set up for each member an account showing the gross sums which that railroad was obligated to pay or to receive to or from all carriers party to the plan. Carriers with a debit balance paid the appropriate amount to the clearing house; carriers with a credit balance received a payment from the clearing house. One single payment in each case was substituted for the multiplicity of drafts required before the clearing house mechanism was in use. The American Railway Clearinghouse was discontinued in 1912.

Mr. Eastman believed that there were possibilities of economy and efficiency in the adaptation of the clearing house plan to conditions confronting American railroads, and there is reason to think that some saving in the accounting cost of handling interline transactions could be secured even if the proposed organization were limited to clearing balances between carriers. To make the economy really significant, however, it would be necessary to entrust the calculation of balances also to the central accounting agency; and carriers will be slow to do this, or, if they consent, they will probably insist upon such checking as will offset any saving that centralization may produce. Further reduction in the cost of interline accounting is more likely to occur through the simplification of the bases for the division of rates between carriers and from a shrinkage in the volume of interline business as a result of railroad consolidation than from a general adoption of the clearing house device. Whether by clearing house operation, however, or by the efficient system at present in use, interline accounting provides an example of the coöperation of carriers in transportation within the United States.

plication of the Clearinghouse Principle to the Business of the American Railways,
March, 1934.

Free Interchange of Cars Between American Railroads

There is another form of operating coöperation between railroads which is even more important than through billing or through rate making or well-devised methods of interline revenue settlement. This consists of the free circulation of freight cars with little or no regard for ownership.

It is very important that freight cars move readily from one railroad system to another because if they did not the expense and delay incident from a point on the line of one carrier to a point on the line of another carrier would be intolerable. All freight would necessarily be transferred from car to car at every junction. There would be labor costs to pay, there would be loss and damage as a result of handling, and consignments would have to wait whenever the supply of cars to receive them at a junction happened to be too small to accommodate the volume of goods accumulated there for transportation. At the same time the efficiency in utilization of rolling stock would be less than it is now, as there would be many instances in which empty cars would stand idle at junction points while waiting for a load.

If we except narrow-gauge equipment, all freight cars in the United States are built to conform to general specifications which make it certain that any car can be used upon any railroad in the country, in conjunction with any other freight car or locomotive. The same is true, one may add, of passenger cars and of locomotives, passenger or freight. On this physical basis, two sorts of operating arrangements have grown up.

Private Cars

The first has to do with the privately owned car. We have already described, in chapter 11, the introduction of the private refrigerator car for the carriage of fresh meat and fruit. In December, 1951, there were 268,722 freight cars of all sorts in the United States owned by private interests, not including corporations separately organized but controlled by one or more railroad companies. This was in the neighborhood of 13 percent of all freight car equipment then in use.[7]

[7] On or about December 31, 1951, the number of freight carrying cars not directly owned or leased by steam railways in the United States was as follows:

Class of Car	Number
Box	3,097
Flat	306
Stock and poultry	1,558
Gondola and hopper	8,437
Tank	146,636
Refrigerator	107,371
Other	1,117
Total	268,722

The origin and development of the use of private cars is succinctly described by the Interstate Commerce Commission as follows:

In the development of freight traffic in the different sections of the country it became evident that many commodities might be transported to much greater advantage in certain kinds of cars especially adapted to the character and peculiar qualities of the particular articles, than in the ordinary cars furnished by carriers. The latter were slow to respond to the demand for improved cars of special pattern, and frequently failed to provide them. Hence, by agreement between shipper and carrier, the former undertook to provide his own cars for the transportation of his particular articles. In analogy to the custom that prevailed between connecting carriers in respect to the use of each other's cars, the railway company became the hirer of the shipper's cars, paying for their use on the basis of a certain amount per mile on the loaded, or loaded and empty, movements. Initiated in a small way with respect to a few articles, the development has been in the direction of rapidly expanding use of private cars. It became necessary that some industries should have a constant and adequate supply of cars in order to conduct business on a large and economical basis. Articles of a perishable nature required prompt movement; some of such articles moved during short periods of each year; and there were demands for cars of special type from many different sections of the country which the carriers could not, or did not, supply. It has also come about that private cars now in use are not owned by shippers alone. They are owned in large numbers by separate corporations, who make their arrangements for the use of the cars with shippers, and procure from the

SOURCE: United States Interstate Commerce Commission, *Statistics of Railways,* 1951, Table 25.

Legislation was proposed in 1940 which would have authorized shippers to provide cars for the transportation of fresh meats, packing house products, or dairy products as they might desire and would have made it unlawful for railroads to refuse to accept such cars upon their lines. The railroads, however, successfully opposed the bill (United States House of Representatives, Committee on Interstate and Foreign Commerce, *Shippers' Refrigerator Cars,* 1940, Hearings before a subcommittee on H. R. 7466 and H. R. 8242, 1940). Some packing companies, such as Armour and Co. and Wilson and Co. own cars but their equipment is a relatively small proportion of the refrigerator cars in use.

Most private oil tank cars are owned by corporations such as the General American Transportation Co., the Union Tank Car Co., and the North American Car Corp., which build or buy cars for the purpose of leasing them to shippers, or they are owned by oil companies. In 1951 the Warren Petroleum Corporation, the Sinclair Refining Company, the Mexican Petroleum Company, the Gulf Oil Corporation, the Tidewater Associated Oil Company, the Socony-Vacuum Oil Company, and the Sun Oil Company each owned more than 1,000 cars apiece.

In addition to the foregoing, the Allied Chemical and Dye Corporation, the Du Pont de Nemours Company, the Dow Chemical Company, and some others own cars for the transport of liquids other than oil. There are many private car owners of stock and refrigerator cars, and the International Harvester Company, the United States Sugar Corporation, the Ford Motor Company, and other corporations own private cars of other types. (United States Interstate Commerce Commission, Bureau of Transport Economics and Statistics, *Selected Statistics from Annual Reports of Private Car Owners,* Washington, 1951.)

railroads the payment of mileage. Many of these companies lease cars to railroad companies, receiving only the mileage allowance for their use; others lease their cars to carriers for an agreed monthly rental, requiring the carriers to keep the cars in repair; still others lease to shippers at an agreed rental per month, and credit the mileage earnings to the latter. Many of these concerns are car builders, who supply cars of special design to shippers on order. They have facilities for repairing their cars located at convenient points in different parts of the county.[8]

Inasmuch as private cars are not owned by railroad companies, there is no reason why any railroad should wish to prevent the passage of such cars from its own to the lines of a connecting carrier. Private cars, therefore, move with complete freedom over the railroads of the country without regard to system boundaries. Indeed, because of the excellent organization of some of the large car-owning corporations and the close supervision which the operation of private cars receives, these cars probably move more rapidly and on the average with lighter loads than the equipment owned by the railroads themselves.

Cars Owned by Railroad Companies

In addition to their arrangements concerning private cars railroads have perfected practices which permit railroad-owned cars to leave their owners' tracks.[9] As a matter of fact, large railroads often have more foreign than home owned cars upon their lines. The relation varies from time to time. During the period of federal operation of American railroads (December 28, 1917 to March 1, 1920) the excess was very large. Indeed, on November 1, 1920, 9 months after the relinquishment of federal control, only 31 percent of the cars reported by large railroads as on their lines were owned by the railroads which reported them. Under restored private management the percentage rose rapidly, until by July 1, 1921, 74 percent of the cars on line were owned by reporting railroads. At the present writing (December, 1950) the proportion has again fallen to 36 percent. Cars from California may be found any day in New England, and cars owned in New York may travel to Texas and back before they again reach the railroad to which they belong. A yard clerk in a busy Eastern

---

[8] *In the Matter of Private Cars,* 50 I.C.C. 652, 657, 1918. Major car owning companies such as the General American Transportation Company and the Union Oil Tank Car Company still follow the practices which the Interstate Commerce Commission described in 1918, except that in the second case the lessor received both a rental from the shipper and a mileage payment from the railroad over which the equipment moves. Mileage rates vary with the type and class of car; but a tariff charge of 2½ cents per mile for refrigerator and 2 cents per mile for tank cars is not unusual. (See also 201 I.C.C. 323, 1934.)

[9] The Interstate Commerce Commission may require railroads to permit their equipment, in the operation of through routes, to be carried beyond their own lines (284 U.S. 80, 91, 1931). The present practice is, however, the result of railroad initiative.

terminal is likely to see, in the course of a month's experience, specimens of the freight equipment of every large railroad in the United States.[10]

Carriers properly insist upon three things in connection with the use of their cars. The first condition attached to the free interchange of equipment is that reasonable attention shall be paid to the repair of railroad cars while in foreign service. A second condition is that cars shall be returned to the home road as rapidly as is consistent with the economical handling of through freight and with the restriction of empty car-mileage to a reasonable figure. The third condition is that a fair rental shall be paid to the road which owns equipment by each other carrier which uses that equipment. These three conditions are expressed respectively in what are known as the master car builders' rules, the car service rules, and the per diem rules.

Interchange Rules of the Association of American Railroads

The code of rules governing repairs to freight cars interchanged between railroad companies is published by the Association of American Railroads, Mechanical Division. It defines the conditions under which railroads may refuse to receive cars from their connections,[11] locates the responsibility for repairs as between owning and using companies, and contains a detailed list of prices at which different sorts of repairs may be charged.

In general, owners of cars are responsible for repairs made necessary by ordinary wear and tear. This includes, for instance, the repair of defects due to excessive wear of couplers and to worn flanges or treads of wheels. It also includes the repair of air hose burst from air pressure, the replacement of missing or worn-out parts of brakes which have failed under fair treatment, and the cleaning of triple valves that have not been cleaned within the previous 15 months.

The using road, on the other hand, is responsible for damages of any kind to body, truck, brake apparatus, etc., of the car due to unfair usage, derailment, or accident; for damaged sills, flat wheels caused by sliding; for material missing from trucks offered in interchange except journal-box lids and nuts; and for other repairs and replacements of this general class.

It is evidently desirable for carriers to agree upon the allocation and cost of repairs, as well as upon procedure for the settlement of disputes

[10] The proportion of home to foreign cars on line varies when we compare different portions of the year. It is highest in January and February and lowest during the months from August to December. The changes affect all parts of the country: east, west, and south. Seasonal traffic is likely to be interregional. It is best handled when cars move freely without regard to ownership.

[11] Railroads maintain car inspectors at interchange points to pass upon the physical conditions of cars tendered. (See Charles F. Landon, *Transportation. Principles, Practices, Problems,* New York, Sloane, 1951.)

regarding repairs. This is, indeed, an essential part of a policy looking to the free interchange of equipment between connection carriers.

Code of Car Service Rules

In addition to the rules relating to repairs, railroads have agreed upon what is known as a code of car service rules. These rules relate to the handling of cars and include the following provisions:

1.   Home cars shall not be used for the movement of traffic beyond the limits of the home road when the use of other suitable cars under these rules is practicable.

2.   Foreign cars at home on a direct connection must be forwarded to the home road loaded or empty.

If empty at junction with the home road and loading at that point via the home road is not available, they must, subject to Rule 6,[12] be delivered to it at that junction, unless an exception to the requirement be agreed to by roads involved. When holding road has no physical connection with the home road and is obliged to use an intermediate road or roads to place the car on home rails under the provisions of this paragraph and the car has record rights to such intermediate road or roads, it may be so delivered.

If empty at other than junction points with the home road, cars under this rule may be—

(a)   Loaded via any route so that the home road will participate in the freight rate, or

(b)   Moved locally in the direction of the home road, or

(c)   Moved locally in an opposite direction from the home road, or delivered to a short line or a switching road, if to be loaded for delivery on or movement via the home road, or

(d)   Delivered empty to home road at any junction point, subject to Rule 6, or

(e)   Delivered empty to road from which originally received under load at the junction where received if such road is also a direct connection of the home road, or

(f)   Returned empty to the delivery road when handled in switching service.

3.   Foreign cars at home on other than direct connections must be forwarded to the home road loaded or empty. Under this rule cars may be—

(a)   Loaded via any route so that the home road will participate in the freight rate, or

(b)   Loaded in the direction of the home road, or

(c)   Moved locally in an opposite direction from the home road, or delivered to a short line or a switching road if to be loaded for delivery on

---

[12] "Rule 6.   If a movement of traffic requires return of empty cars to home road via the junction at which cars were delivered to interchange under load, the home road may demand return of empty cars at such junction, except that cars offered a home road for repairs, in accordance with the Interchange Rules of the Mechanical Division, must be accepted by owners at any junction point."

or movement via the home road, or to a point in the direction of the home road beyond the road on which the cars are located, or

(d)   Delivered empty to road from which originally received, at the junction where received, if impracticable to dispose of them under paragraphs (a), (b) or (c) of this rule.

4.   Cars of railroad ownership must not be delivered to a steamship, ferry, or barge line for water transportation without permission of the owners, filed with the Car Service Division.

5.   Empty cars of indirect ownership (Rule 3) to the road requesting the service may be short-routed at a reciprocal rate of five cents (5¢) per mile, plus bridge and terminal arbitraries, with a minimum of one hundred (100) miles for each road handling the car, the road requesting the services to pay the charges.[13]

The purpose of car service rules is to secure the return of cars to owning roads. Railroads which allow their cars to travel freely to distant destinations believe that compliance with these rules is a reasonable condition to be attached to foreign use. It is difficult, however, to enforce car service rules in times of car shortage, because the return to an owning road may, at a given moment, constitute an inefficient handling of a car. Car service rules are largely disregarded by both carriers and shippers under these circumstances. If and when rules are disregarded cars will accumulate on individual railroads and in districts which receive more freight tonnage than they originate, particularly on railroad lines and in states eastward from Pittsburgh and Buffalo. At this stage the Car Service Division of the Association of American Railroads will issue relocation orders transferring cars to points where the supply is relatively small.[14] The Interstate Commerce Commission also has authority to issue orders under powers conferred by Section 1 of the Interstate Commerce Act. The Commission's powers are designed and interpreted, however, to meet emergency situations;[15] current traffic problems are handled by the carriers themselves.[16]

[13] E. W. Caughlin of the Car Service Division of the Association of American Railroads has published a series of excellent articles describing the handling of railroad cars under the car service rules which the text summarizes. The series also discusses other problems of car handling. (See *Railway Age,* 1952, February 11, p. 57; March 24, p. 39; April 21, p. 58; May 26, p. 24; June 23, p. 73; July 28, p. 40.)

[14] The Code of Per Diem Rules reads, in part, as follows:

"Rule 19.   The Board of Directors of the Association of American Railroads shall appoint a Car Service Division composed of a Chairman and the requisite number of members, territorially representative, invested with plenary power to—

(d)   Transfer cars from one railroad or territory to another when necessary to meet traffic conditions, with due regard to car ownership and requirements.

[15] The Commission has exercised its authority upon occasion, most notably in times of preparation for national defense, but also in other years. During World War II and again, beginning in 1950, it worked in coöperation with a federal Office of Defense Transportation. (See chap. 33.)

[16] On the general question, it may be noted that a bill was introduced into Congress in 1947 which proposed to transfer the active direction of car service to a Bureau of

Code of Per Diem Rules

The code of per diem rules is published by the Car Service Division of the Association of American Railroads. The rules provide that a road which uses a foreign freight car shall pay a rental to the owner of the car which it employs. This is reasonable enough as a matter of principle. It will bring in no net revenue to any company if every railroad has as many foreign cars upon its line as it has system cars abroad; but it will yield something when this equivalence does not occur, and inequality is not unknown.[17] The practice of per diem payment also influences carriers to return foreign cars to their owners when these cars are not actively in use. The owning company desires this, first, because it is interested in checking maintenance; and, second, because the cars which a carrier has bought and owns are, presumably, better suited to its local needs than are foreign cars which might take their place.

PER DIEM RATE. There is no objection today to the payment of a rental by a using to an owning road for the service which the latter's cars supply. Parties differ, however, with respect to the amount and with respect to the manner of calculation.

Service within the Interstate Commerce Commission but independent of the Commission to some degree (United States House of Representatives, Committee on Interstate and Foreign Commerce, Hearings before a subcommittee on H.R. 3140, 80th C., 1st S., June 17 and 18, and July 18, 1947). The principal objections raised were: (1) that the bill would change the character of the Interstate Commerce Commission from that of a quasi-judicial regulatory body to that of an active administrative agency, and (2) that no increase in general efficiency was to be expected.

[17] Under conditions of perfect equilibrium, every carrier should have upon its line at all times the same number of cars that it owns, in spite of the fact that a substantial portion of its equipment can always be expected to be on the lines of other carriers. While some of its cars will be away, this number will be balanced by the foreign cars on hand. Unfortunately, this state of perfect equilibrium does not always exist. In the Northwest, carriers at critical times have had relatively few cars upon their lines. Thus on March 1, 1947, the Great Northern had on its lines but 58.6 percent as many boxcars as it owned and the Northern Pacific 65.6 percent. The relationships in the Central West were better but still unsatisfactory to many central western carriers. The Burlington, for instance, had upon its lines boxcars equal only to 65.4 percent of its ownership and the Santa Fe had 85.6 percent. On the other hand, many Eastern railroads reported more cars on their lines than they owned. An extreme case was that of the New York, New Haven & Hartford which, on February 15, 1947, owned a total of 3,719 boxcars. It had on its lines, on February 15, 12,290 boxcars, or more than three times its ownership. The New Haven owned 6,450 freight carrying cars of all kinds, and the number on its lines was 17,190, or 266.6 percent of ownership (268 I.C.C. 687, 692–696).

An excess of equipment operated over equipment owned is an advantage to a carrier because the revenue obtainable from a foreign car is, on the average, greater than the per diem rental. Thus the average gross freight revenue per freight car day (serviceable) loaded and empty for all class I railroads was $9.33 in 1945 and $8.47 in 1946. Net operating income assignable to freight service per freight car day is less than this—there are no general figures available—but, in 1946, figures submitted to the Interstate Commerce Commission showed a net income of $1.58 for the Santa Fe, $1.80 for the Burlington, and $2.12 for the Great Northern railroads (268 I.C.C. 659, 671, 1947).

The per diem rate used by American railroads began at 20 cents a day in 1902, when the system was inaugurated; to this sum was added a penalty of 80 cents on cars held on any road for more than 30 days. The penalty rate was discarded in 1907. In that year the straight rate was raised to 50 cents. In 1908 it was lowered to 25 cents, but by a series of subsequent increases it rose to 100 cents in 1920. This dollar rate persisted until February 1, 1945. It was then increased, first to 115 cents, then to 125 cents, and recently to 240 cents, where it now stands. An interesting experiment in the machinery of assessment was made, during a part of this period, but without permanent result.[18]

CALCULATION OF RENTAL. The per diem rate is based, as the name implies, upon time. The charge is a given amount per car per day. The alternative would be a charge per mile for the distance traveled upon a foreign road.

The advantage of calculating rental upon a time basis is that it lessens the temptation to use cars as warehouses. The great merit of the per diem system is that it tends to keep cars moving. The objection to the time basis is that the advantage of car possession is a function of distance

---

[18] The experiment referred to in the text was known as the "frozen per diem system" or the "average per diem system"; it was a modification of the per diem arrangements which the text has described. The peculiarity was that each railroad under the scheme paid for the use of boxcars of any other railroad, each month, a sum based upon the average detention of such cars during the same month of a selected previous period, not upon the actual detention in the month for which the payment was made. As adopted in 1935, the test period comprised the years 1932, 1933, and 1934. To illustrate its working we may assume that railroad A had detained the cars of railroad B during the month of June in 1932, 1933, and 1934, an average of three days each. It would follow that railroad A would pay railroad B a per diem for the month of June, 1936, a sum calculated by multiplying the number of B's cars on the lines of A during June, 1936, by the factor three, irrespective of the actual detention in the latter month (Report of General Committee, Transportation Division, American Railway Association, on Empty Freight Car Mileage, 1934).

This departure from the strict per diem rule was expected to have two beneficial results. In the first place, it somewhat simplified the accounting between railroads. Second, and more important, was the fact that it reduced the penalty for failure to return cars promptly. In practice it amounted to a selective reduction of the per diem charge, at the expense of car-owning roads, in the belief that this reduction would decrease the forced movement of empty freight cars and so redound to the advantage of the railroad system as a whole.

The frozen per diem plan was put into general effect on May 1, 1935. Records subsequently kept by the Association of American Railroads indicated that a reduction in empty car mileage occurred during 1935 of nearly 443,000,000 and during 1936 of nearly 808,000,000 empty car miles, representing a saving of $12,000,000 in 1935 and of $22,222,850 in 1936 (*Traffic World*, June 5, 1937, p. 1239). Whether the saving was or was not due to the new system was, of course, a matter of opinion. Difficulties arose, however, because of the alleged excessive detention of cars away from home and of failure to obtain a general observance of the car service rules. There was also some feeling that "frozen per diem" reduced the incentive to acquire new cars or to make replacements (*Traffic World*, November 28, 1936, p. 1066. The plan was suspended on July 1, 1937, and has not been, so far, revived.

traveled and not of time consumed, and that costs vary with distance as well as with time.[19] These facts suggest the use of both time and mileage as bases in the calculation of per diem rates. The change has not been made; there is, however, no proposal to go back to the original practice of an exclusive mileage charge.[20]

[19] Owning roads support two types of cost in connection with their equipment. One kind of cost is fixed (investment) and can be charged out upon a time basis. But the other kind (repairs) is at least partially responsive to use. The Office of the Federal Coordinator calculated, in 1936, that the fixed cost of an average freight car was then 31.4 cents per day, and that the cost of repairs was 1.52 cents per mile. A simple calculation with these factors shows that a per diem rate of 150 cents would cover owner costs only when the mileage of a car did not exceed 78 miles per day. With this or a lesser mileage the owner would make money; with a higher mileage he would lose (United States, Office of the Federal Coordinator, Section of Car Pooling, *Study of Freight Car Ownership Costs as Related to Car Hire, 1935*). An offshoot of this argument is the contention of Western railroads that Western cars are more severely treated in the East than are Eastern cars in the West.

[20] The text describes arrangements for the free movement of railroad freight cars. Other types of carriers interchange equipment with each other, but not so freely.

Motor companies. The amount of motor equipment interchanged is relatively small because of the local character of most motor movements and because equipment is not generally standardized. Interchange is, however, essential in the carriage of heavy objects and machinery that requires special vehicles and it is highly convenient for the transportation of household goods.

Interstate Commerce Commission regulations permit carriers to interchange although the process is not as simple as with railroad cars, for a number of reasons. Equipment interchanged usually consists of trailers. The arrangement provides for the interchange of loaded trailers or the receiving company supplies a vehicle that can be used by the tendering company while the loaded vehicle is hauled to destination. The balance in equipment is thus maintained. In some parts of the country trucks are also exchanged. When vehicles pass from one company to another the practice is for the receiving company to lease the trailer or the truck or truck and trailer. According to Interstate Commerce Commission rules the receiving company must supply a driver or place the former driver on its payroll. There are other requirements also. Thus the charge for the use of the equipment must be kept distinct from divisions of the through rate between participating companies. The company acquiring equipment is responsible for inspection. Finally, the contract providing for interchange must describe the equipment to be interchanged, the points of interchange, the use to be made of the equipment, and the consideration for such use (16 Fed. Reg. 4806, May 23, 1951).

The Interstate Commerce Commission has recently commented upon the fact that trailer interchanges are growing. According to an estimate quoted in the Commission's *Annual Report for 1951*, there are between 600 and 800 motor carriers which now regularly engage in the practice of interchange.

Air companies. The number of equipment units involved is much less in the case of air than in the cases of rail or motor travel. Air lines do, however, interchange planes to a limited extent under agreements which the Civil Aeronautics Board approves. These agreements permit planes of carrier A to proceed through an interchange point and make deliveries at stations on carrier B; they give the same privilege to planes of carrier B in the reverse direction. The pilots of the delivering company operate planes between interchange point and destination; the delivering carrier pays a rental for plane use. There is no balancing of the number of planes exchanged; sometimes, indeed, only one of the two agreeing carriers sends its equipment beyond its terminus, although this is unusual. The interchanged planes will, of course, return to the owning road.

Among the first interchange agreements were those between the Capital Airline and

Car Pooling

Plans for car pooling differ fundamentally from car service and per diem regulations because they abandon the principle that freight cars shall be returned to their owners. A pool suggested by the Federal Coordinator proposed, in place of this, that a corporation be set up to which railroads should assign all their freight cars of types and classes which were to be pooled. The corporation was thenceforth to allocate these cars among five

---

the National Airlines (10 C.A.B. 231, 1949) and between the Delta Airlines and the American Airlines (10 C.A.B. 757, 1949). There is also an interchange arrangement between National Airlines and Eastern Airlines at New Orleans for Houston traffic (United States Senate, Committee on Interstate and Foreign Commerce, *Air-Line Industry Investigation,* 81st C., 1st S., Hearings pursuant to S. Res. 50, 1949, testimony Landis) and one between Delta Airlines and the T.W.A. under which the former leases aircraft to the latter for flights from Cincinnati to Detroit, thus permitting passengers arriving at Cincinnati on Delta equipment to continue without change of planes (8 C.A.B. 857, 1947). Before the war, Western Air Express, operating from Los Angeles to Salt Lake City, and United Airlines, operating thence to the East Coast, entered into an interchange agreement which provided for through plane service between Los Angeles and eastern points. This arrangement was terminated during the war. More recently, Pan American Airways, operating from the Canal Zone to Miami and Pan American–Grace Airways, operating from the Canal Zone down the west coast of South America to Buenos Aires agreed upon through operation of Panagra airplanes from Miami to Buenos Aires (C.A.B. Docket no. 3785, 3787, Order Serial E-5282, 1951; Order Serial E-5541, 1951). Likewise the Continental and the American Airlines provide through planes between Houston and San Antonio, Texas and points west of El Paso served by American Airlines (C.A.B. Docket no. 1102, Orders Serial E-5531, 1951); Midcontinent and Continental operate a through service between St. Louis, on the one hand, and Colorado Springs and Denver, on the other (*Annual Report of the C.A.B.,* 1952, pp. 4–5); and the T.W.A., Braniff, and Eastern companies have requested permission to operate a single-plane service from Miami to Los Angeles and San Francisco via Houston, Dallas, Fort Worth, Amarillo, and Phoenix (*Traffic World,* February 16, 1952, p. 17). Doubtless more agreements will be registered in the years to come.

The Civil Aeronautics Board recognizes the advantage of airplane interchange as such. The Board is sometimes reluctant, nevertheless, to approve proposals because interchange may create additional competition (T.W.A.-Delta, C.A.B. Docket no. 2346, Order Serial 3016, 1949). In an attempt to state a governing principle the Board has said that interchange should "cause minimum interference with the existing route pattern . . . should leave substantially undisturbed the historic participation of existing carriers in the traffic served, and should not cause undue diversion" (*Southern Service to the West* case, C.A.B. Docket no. 1102, Order Serial 5090, 1951). It is rather curious that these considerations should be allowed to interfere with an improved operating practice in air transportation.

Water lines. Water lines rarely, if at all, exchange equipment with each other. There are, however, water lines which carry cars and may be considered railroad operators in a certain sense. These water lines have arrangements with railroads which are somewhat analogous to interchange. Thus a railroad may haul a car to a rail-water terminal and there deliver it, without unloading, to a vessel for completion of the movement. The shipping company will deliver the car to another water terminal, paying the railroad a rental charge for the railroad car while the car is in the possession of the ship. The Interstate Commerce Commission has authority to require such arrangements (323 U.S. 612, 1945. See also 195 I.C.C. 215, 1933; 206 I.C.C. 328, 1935; 226 I.C.C. 7, 1938; 237 I.C.C. 97, 1940; 243 I.C.C. 199, 1940; and 248 I.C.C. 109, 1941).

districts—New England, Eastern, Southeastern, Western, and South-western—according to need, and district managers appointed by the corporation were to distribute the allocations among the railroads in each district. Each railroad which enjoyed the use of a pool car in any district was to be charged a rental based partly on time held and partly on the mileage which the car should run. The corporation was to care for repairs to pooled equipment out of the proceeds of the rental charge, and from the same source was to compensate owners for the so-called fixed costs of ownership, made up of interest, taxes, insurance, and depreciation. The corporation was to be managed by a board of control consisting of two members from each district and one representative designated by the Federal Coordinator or by the Interstate Commerce Commission.[21]

In pressing the car pooling plan the Federal Coordinator criticized the existing per diem system, both on the ground that it failed to distribute cars efficiently in times of industrial activity, and because it occasioned an abnormal amount of empty car mileage when traffic slackened. He believed that carrier attempts to shift the burden of car hire by hauling cars empty tended to increase the operating cost of the American railroad plant; and he felt that inefficient distribution of equipment not only resulted in unnecessary local shortages and surpluses of equipment, but on the whole caused the production of a mass of equipment larger than was necessary to do the work. Such conditions, the Coordinator thought, could be cured by a central administration of the use of railroad cars.

Railroads objected to car pooling at this time because they thought that efficient maintenance of cars required that equipment be owned by individual carriers and brought back to these carriers from time to time for inspection and repair. It seemed to them that cars owned by an organization representing all railroads might be in the position of the children in Plato's *Republic* who called every citizen "father," but who had no effective claim on the interest of anyone. Common control would discourage the construction of cars suitable to special needs. It would, in particular, deprive a well-run railroad of the advantage in traffic solicitation which might come from the assurance that patrons would be supplied with cars. Carriers said that the possibilities of saving in empty-car mileage under pool administration was exaggerated, and that any saving which occurred would be offset by the slowing down of car movements and by the overhead expenses of pool management. Objections of this type were offered by a general committee of the Association of American Railroads in 1934 and called forth a sharp reply from Mr. Castle of the Coordinator's staff.

While car pooling is not, today, practiced in any general sense, it is

21 United States, Office of the Federal Coordinator of Transportation, *Report on Freight Car Pooling with Plan for Proposed Box Car Pool,* 1934.

true that railroad systems, made up of a number of lines with separate corporate identities, pool their cars for purposes of operation. Thus the Santa Fe system operates cars with several different ownerships and markings in a single fleet. The Gulf Coast Lines operate cars of the Beaumont, Sour Lake & Western, the New Orleans, Texas & Mexico, the Orange and Northwestern, and the St. Louis, Brownsville & Mexico as a single group. The New York Central has cars bearing markings of 6 different lines comprising the system and the Southern Railway cars have 11 different markings.

There is also what amounts to car pooling when a number of railroads combine in the organization of a corporation which maintains a fleet of cars for common use. The Fruit Growers' Express is an example. This company is owned by 23 railroads and provides cars to take care of the perishable traffic originating upon the lines of its owners as well as the traffic of some other lines with which contracts have been made. This makes it unnecessary for the railroads involved to own refrigerator cars individually. It makes also for economy because the peak movement of perishables comes at different times on the lines of the carriers parties to the agreement. The practice has been earlier referred to in discussing private cars and the problems of refrigeration.

Summary of Forms of Operating Coöperation Between Railroads

We have now mentioned through billing, through rate making, current practices in interline revenue settlements, the use of private cars, regulations regarding the repair of railroad equipment upon foreign lines, and per diem and car service rules. These practices all imply extensive coöperation between independent American railroads; and while the list of instances might be extended, enough examples have been presented to justify the statement made at the beginning of this chapter that the railroads of the country operate, to a noteworthy extent, as a single railroad system in spite of the diversity of ownership of the different parts. There is, of course, something to be said on the other side. Thus there is much wasteful cross- and roundabout hauling which might be avoided if railroads were actually under a single ownership, and there is frequently uneconomic use of terminals. There is, again, costly duplication of service by competing companies, involving the running of two or more trains between identical termini when only one is needed. Yet in spite of such qualifying facts, railroad operation in the United States is characterized, in general, by a smooth and willing coöperation between railroad lines which is a distinct achievement in American practice. For technical and competitive reasons this achievement is not duplicated in degree by other types of carriage or in relations between rail, water, motor, and air transport. Some progress has been made in vehicle interchange and in the establishment of through routes and rates on shipments handled by different kinds of transportation; even in this area the development is slight.

Association of American Railroads

The largest formal operating organization of railroads is the Association of American Railroads. This society includes in its active membership 116 of the 127 Class I line haul railroad companies of the United States, operating 219,071 out of 226,101 miles of road; it takes in, also, companies representing more than half of the switching and terminal trackage of the country. By special arrangement, the Pullman Company and the Railway Express are members. Outside of the country, the Canadian Pacific, the Canadian National, and the National Railways of Mexico are on the list as well as some smaller organizations. The Association has, finally, a large number of nonvoting associate members, including small railroads, independent of or controlled by larger railroads; short lines owned by steel, coal, lumber, petroleum, copper, paper, and other industries; and terminal companies such as those at Cincinnati and Detroit and the city tracks at New Orleans.[22] Among the associate members are the British Railways, the Chilean State Railways, the Ministry of Railways of the Government of India, and the National Railways of France.

The present name of the Association of American Railroads dates from 1934. The organization itself goes back to the so-called "time conventions" which met at least as early as May, 1872. Time conventions were conferences of connecting or competing railroads to consider changes in train schedules that affected more than one line, or to regulate "speed wars." There were changes and consolidations among these conventions, resulting finally in the combination, in 1886, of the two largest conventions, the General Time Convention of the northern roads, and the Southern Time Convention operating south of the Ohio and Potomac, into an inclusive "General Time Convention," comprising roads both north and south. In 1891 this became the American Railway Association. In 1934 the Railway Association combined with the Association of Railway Executives, the Presidents' Conference Committee, the Railway Accounting Officers' Association, the Railway Treasurers' Association, and the Bureau of Railway Economics under its present name.

Departments of the Association of American Railroads

The work of the present association is carried on through seven major

---

[22] The principal Class I railroads which are not members of the Association of American Railroads are the New York, Chicago & St. Louis (1,687 miles), the Pere Marquette (1,950) miles, the Chesapeake & Ohio (5,062 miles), the Denver & Rio Grande Western (2,464 miles), and the Alton (959 miles). For the most part these abstentions result from conflicts of personalities. Abstaining companies coöperate with members of the Association in certain operations.

departments assisted by or functioning through a number of divisions, sections, bureaus, and committees. These departments and their divisions and sections are as follows:

LAW DEPARTMENT. This department deals with questions of law and legislation of common concern to the railroad industry. It represents the industry in litigation and other legal matters, in proceedings before the Interstate Commerce Commission and other governmental bodies. Within the Law Department is the Patent Division, which deals with matters of patent law in which railroads are interested.

OPERATIONS AND MAINTENANCE DEPARTMENT. This department is organized in seven divisions, one bureau, and two special committees.

1. Operating-Transportation Division. This division, through nine sections, concerns itself with standard codes of rules for train operation; car service, demurrage and per diem; methods of freight station work; improved containers; physical standards for railroad employees; police protection of railroad property and shipments; reduction of accidents; improved communications; and fire protection and insurance. The Communications Section of the Operating-Transportation Division has developed a Manual of Recommended Practice for all aspects of the railroad communication plant.

2. Engineering Division. This division, through three sections, considers the design, construction, and maintenance of track, the institution and use of electrical apparatus, and the design, construction, and maintenance of railway signals. The American Railway Engineering Association, a professional group, functions as the Construction and Maintenance Section of the Engineering Division. The A.R.E.A. publishes a Manual of Standard Practice which is amended from time to time by action taken by members of this group. The Signal Section has also issued a manual as well as a series of pamphlets intended as handbooks for signal employees.

3. Mechanical Division. This division deals with design, building, maintenance and repair of locomotives, cars, and other railroad mechanical equipment. It is responsible for mechanical rules governing interchange of freight cars among railroads. Through its electrical section it examines problems involved in the use of electricity on electrical equipment and mechanical devices. This has resulted in a manual for use in the mechanical departments of individual railroads.

4. Purchases and Stores Division. This division studies problems raised by the purchase, storage, and distribution of materials.

5. Freight Claim Division. This division publishes a code of Principles and Practices for the Investigation and Disposition of Freight Claims, and a code of Freight Claim Rules to cover the interline apportionment among carriers of amounts paid to claimants. It recommends practices to be followed in loss and damage prevention activities. Much of its work is carried on in cooperation with receivers and shippers of freight.

6. Motor Transport Division. This division acts as a clearinghouse for information and material in connection with the use of railroads of motor transportation in perfecting their services, freight and passenger.

7. Car Service Division. This division deals primarily with the flow of freight and passenger cars from railroad to railroad, and with the distribution of cars between railroads. Under agreements signed by the railroads, the Car Service Division has wide powers to work with the Interstate Commerce Commission in all car service matters on and between all railroads, to supervise the application of Car Service and Per Diem Rules, to suspend or permit departure from the mandatory provisions of Car Service Rules and to transfer cars from one railroad or territory to another if necessary to meet traffic conditions.

8. Bureau for the Safe Transportation of Explosives and Other Dangerous Articles. This bureau makes inspections, investigates accidents, and develops appropriate rules for safety.

9. Committee on Automatic Train Control and Signals. Since the enactment of the Signal Inspection Act, this committee is the unit of the Association dealing with the Interstate Commerce Commission on matters brought about by this act.

10. Joint Committee on Grade Crossing Protection. This committee has published recommended practices with respect to railroad-highway grade crossing protection. It investigates proposed devices and coöperates with regulatory bodies.

TRAFFIC DEPARTMENT. This department deals with governmental departments and agencies on behalf of member roads with respect to matters of a traffic nature; it serves as a medium for the discussion of general traffic problems among member roads; it conducts studies and advises member roads with respect to such matters as the publication and simplification of tariffs. It has no authority in rate matters but has interested itself in traffic policies. The department has set up a permanent Tariff Simplification Committee.

FINANCE, ACCOUNTING, TAXATION, AND VALUATION DEPARTMENT. This department works through an Accounting Division, a Treasury Division, and a Valuation Division. The Accounting Division issues mandatory rules and recommended practices, and adopts standard forms for railroad accounting. The Treasury Division deals with methods of collecting transportation charges, handling order-and-advise shipments, collection of shippers' invoices, collection of undercharge freight bills, etc. The Valuation Division cooperates in collecting and analyzing yearly prices paid for materials entering into railroad construction and in developing methods for keeping valuations current.

RESEARCH DEPARTMENT. This department, organized in 1944, is engaged, through fifteen subcommittees in the study of both technical and general aspects of the railroad problem and in the direction of research sponsored by the Engineering Division. It is headed by a Research Engineer who supervises laboratory and field work, directs the preparation of reports, assists committees in planning new projects, and keeps abreast of research projects in other fields.

BUREAU OF RAILWAY ECONOMICS. This bureau is a fact-finding agency and the statistical and economic clearing house for the railroads. Its library is now the largest transportation library in the United States.

PUBLIC RELATIONS DEPARTMENT. This department seeks to make available, and to distribute in convenient form, a great variety of information about American railroads.

Operations of the Association

The permanent staff of the Association of American Railroads is comparatively small. While some departments, such as the Law and Public Relations departments, are centralized, most work is done through divisions and sections. These are directed by representatives of member roads of the Association who control the activities of each unit through elected officers, and by committees of direction who are themselves officers of member roads. The secretaries of divisions and of sections, however, and the executive vice-chairmen, when these officers exist, are employees of the Association. Departments of the Association of American Railroads, as such, do not hold annual meetings; but certain of the divisions and sections do hold such meetings, elect officers, create committees, and approve reports. Reports and recommendations of divisions and sections are not considered at annual meetings of the Association itself. They are, in appropriate cases, made the subject of letter ballot by member roads.

All this means that the Association coördinates and directs but does not criticize or control the conclusions reached by the elements in its organization. For the most part these conclusions take the form of recommendations with respect to practice which member roads may accept or reject individually as they choose. But in some cases the member roads agree that they shall be mandatory, as in the case of rules issued by the Treasury Division; and in other cases, as in that of freight claim rules, they set up codes of minor law to which reference is currently made.

Railroads need and the Association can provide three distinct forms of service. In the first place, railroads need development and wide dissemination of technical information with respect to railway engineering and commercial equipment and procedure. The Association has been reasonably successful in this field. The opportunities before it are very large. In the second place, they need standardization of material and practice when common action by separate carriers is required. Uniformity of accounting forms, uniformity of train rules and of freight claim rules, uniformity of car design to the extent that cars can be interchanged, and many other kinds of standardization facilitate carrier cooperation. Some of these matters have been discussed in the present chapter. It is hard to see how the railroads could have reached their present standards or their present degree of cooperation without the assistance of the American Association. Generally, though not always, the interests of all carriers in these matters is the same.

The third type of service is that of protection against outside attack. The Association's powers in this direction are limited by the antitrust acts and by certain paragraphs in the Act to Regulate Commerce. It is presently accused of having overstepped the limits set by this restrictive legislation. The Association accepts the position of representative of the railroad industry before the general public and before regulating bodies, and it interests itself, less publicly and directly, in the relations between the railroads and other transport agencies. In these activities it is constantly alert to suggest, to criticize, and to explain, in the interests of the rail carriers as a whole.

REFERENCES

General Treatises

Bigham, Truman C., and Roberts, Merrill J., *Transportation, Principles and Problems,* New York, McGraw-Hill, 1952.

Fair, Marvin L., and Williams, Ernest W., *Economics of Transportation,* New York, Harper, 1950.

Huebner, G. G., and Johnson, E. R., *The Railroad Freight Service,* New York, Appleton-Century-Crofts, 1926.

Johnson, E. R., *Transport Facilities, Services, and Policies,* New York, Appleton-Century-Crofts, 1947.

Landon, Charles E., *Transportation, Principles, Practices, Problems,* New York, Sloane, 1951.

Locklin, D. Philip, *Economics of Transportation,* Chicago, Irwin, 1947.

Van Metre, T. W., *Industrial Traffic Management,* New York, McGraw-Hill, 1953.

Westmeyer, Russell E., *Economics of Transportation,* New York, Prentice-Hall, 1952.

Other Books

Colton, Richard C., *Practical Handbook of Industrial Traffic Management,* New York, Funk & Wagnalls, 1953.

Loree, L. F., *Railroad Freight Transportation,* New York, Appleton-Century-Crofts, 1929.

Morris, Ray, *Railroad Administration,* New York, Appleton-Century-Crofts, 1930.

Parmelee, Julius H., *The Modern Railway,* New York, Longmans, 1940.

Shinn, Glenn L., *Freight Rate Application,* New York, Simmons-Boardman, 1948.

Van Metre, T. W., *Industrial Traffic Management,* New York, McGraw-Hill, 1953.

Periodicals

Hudson, Henry, "The Southern Railway and Steamship Association," *Quarterly Journal of Economics,* October, 1890.

Special and Miscellaneous

Association of American Railroads, *Railway Accounting Rules,* Washington, D.C., annual.

The Freight Traffic Red Book, New York, Traffic Publishing, annual.

The Motor Traffic Red Book, New York, Traffic Publishing, annual.

United States House of Representatives, Committee on Interstate and Foreign Commerce, *Shippers' Refrigerator Cars,* Hearings before a subcommittee on H.R. 7466 and H.R. 8242, 76th C., 3d S., 1940.

United States House of Representatives, Committee on Interstate and Foreign Commerce, *Through Rates,* Hearings on H.R. 3400, 76th C., 1st S., 1939.

United States Interstate Commerce Commission, Bureau of Transport Economics and Statistics, *Practices of Motor Carriers of Property in the Division of Revenues of Joint Hauls,* Statement no. 451, January, 1945.

United States, Office of the Federal Coordinator of Transportation, *Memorandum on the Application of the Clearinghouse Principle to the Business of the American Railways,* 1934.

United States, Office of the Federal Coordinator of Transportation, *Report on Freight Car Pooling with Plan for Proposed Box Car Pool,* 1934.

United States, Office of the Federal Coordinator of Transportation, *Study of Freight Car Ownership Costs as Related to Car Hire,* 1935.

United States Senate, Committee on Interstate and Foreign Commerce, *Airline Industry Investigation,* Hearings pursuant to Sen. Res. 50, 81st C., 1st S., 1949, testimony Landis (air equipment interchange).

Terminals

General Character of the Terminal Problem

The terminal problem is dealt with at this point because of the close relations which carriers have with each other at terminal points and the desirability of some understanding between the transportation lines which serve a terminal if maximum efficiency in operation is to be obtained. The terminal problem has, however, many aspects, and we shall permit ourselves some freedom in discussion.

Generally speaking, the peculiarities of the terminal situation arise first, out of the difficulty and expense incurred in conducting traffic into, through, and around great cities, and second, in the monopoly power which the possession of a unique and nonreproducible location gives to the common carrier which is so fortunate as to enjoy it.

In the large city, the service of transportation competes for space with other uses of land in two ways: first, it must displace other facilities in order to maintain the station and the yard, storage, or industrial tracks requisite for rail service, or the garages, hangars, warehouses, and stations required for bus, truck, and airplane operation; and second, it must occupy the city streets in seeking access to and egress from the points where the road haul begins. It is a common error to assume that transportation is finished when the "terminal" is reached. This is true only when the word is understood to mean place of utilization; the point usually called "terminal" marks rather a change in the character of the conveyance than a cessation of movement.

Competition for space is difficult for the transportation agency because, on the whole, the carrier requires facilities which are at the level of the ground and, except for office and warehouse space, can less readily utilize construction built high into the air than can banks, stores, and factories. The airplane, requiring large level tracks of ground for landing—tracts which are extensively rather than intensively employed—is the most obvious example of an agency which needs terminal land but cannot afford to bid for centralized city accommodation. The airport, accordingly, even when financed from city funds, is apt to be located at some distance from the center of population and must rely upon the motor vehicle to bring air passengers to their homes. Bus, auto, and truck services still largely use the city streets but railroads, only less than airplanes, spread out in city territory to find storage space for their cars, tracks, stations where freight may be handled, and facilities to attract and to protect passengers. Rail passengers need to complete their journeys on foot or by some other means of transport, and rail freight also, though to a less degree, is handled by some form of local transport other than the rail.

In the present chapter we shall discuss the terminal problems of air and or railroad transportation, omitting the less developed motor terminals [1] and the highly specialized water terminals. Both motor and water terminals are important in certain areas, especially in some large cities and along the Great Lakes and the Mississippi River, but they are generally less significant for inland transportation than are terminals for railroad and for air.[2]

Airports and Landing Fields

The term *airport* means any area of land or water which is used, or intended for use, for the landing and take-off of aircraft, and any appurtenant areas which are used, or intended for use, for airport buildings or other airport facilities or rights of way, together with all airport buildings and facilities located thereon.[3] Distinction is sometimes made between the fully organized airport with hangars, repair facilities, salesrooms, stores, restaurants, and the like and the air park or airstrip. The air park is a field with only one or two landing strips, few or no hangars and no special installations. The flight strip is a strategically located landing and take-off strip, preferably along a highway and adjacent to a gasoline service station.[4]

On January 1, 1951, there were 4,601 commercial and municipal airports in the United States available for public use, to which were to be added 1,802 airports or landing fields, privately or publicly owned, which supplied no public services and were open to the public only when

[1] An example of a large trucking terminal is the New York Union Motor Truck Terminal, built and operated by the Port of New York Authority, and opened in 1949 (*Traffic World,* November 5, 1949, pp. 33–35).

[2] Pipe line terminals are not a feature of petroleum transportation in the usual sense.

[3] 60 Stat. 170, 1946, Sec. 2, par. 2. See United States Department of Commerce, Civil Aeronautics Administration, *Airport Terminal Activities and Space Utilization,* Airport Planning Series, July, 1950.

[4] Charles Froesch and Walter Prokosch, *Airport Planning.* New York, Wiley, 1946, p. 43.

emergency occurred.[5] The number of paved airports capable of serving modern transport planes is, of course, much less than this. It is a contentious question as to how far and by what agency the smaller fields are to be built up and how far attention is to be centered upon the larger installations. The answer depends upon the anticipated character of airplane use. If, as the Department of Commerce guessed in 1945, there will be 400,000 private aircraft in the United States in ten years from the close of World War II,[6] this will mean a heavy call for the development of smaller fields. The transport industry, which requires more elaborate accommodation, operated only 1,061 aircraft in 1949, and will contribute less importantly to the demand.[7] If, on the other hand, the technical obstacles to the development of personal air transport are greater than some people suppose, the emphasis should be placed on large airports, well equipped and carefully spaced to meet the commercial and military needs of public transport operation.

Area Required for Airports

In the air industry the competition for terminal space is more than usually acute because of the large area required for terminal operations. Light aircraft, weighing less than a ton, with a take-off distance of 300 to 700 feet and a safe runway length of 2,000 to 3,000 feet [8] can be accommodated by fields of moderate cost and size. In contrast with landing fields required for local and personal use, air terminals for general transport service are of more impressive dimensions. The planes for which these fields were designed ranged, in 1948, from the Douglas DC-3 with a gross weight of 25,200 pounds to the Douglas DC-7 with a gross weight of 162,000 pounds. Such planes may easily need 2,000 feet for a take-off, and the safe runway length has been calculated at 4,020 feet for the DC-3 and at 10,452 feet for the DC-7.[9] Since take-off and landing strips must be laid to face in several directions, the aggregate space required is multiplied. In 1944, the average size of all airports in the United States

[5] United States Department of Commerce, Civil Aeronautics Administration, *Statistical Handbook of Civil Aviation,* January, 1950.

[6] United States House of Representatives, Committee on Interstate and Foreign Commerce, Hearings on H.R. 3170, 79th C., 1st S., 1945, testimony Burden, p. 98.

[7] *Aviation Week,* February 28, 1949, p. 83; United States Department of Commerce, Civil Aeronautics Administration, *Statistical Handbook of Civil Aviation,* 1948.

Mr. Boeing, speaking for the Personal Aircraft Council of the Aeronautical Chamber of Commerce, urged in 1945 that every community in the United States, 16,752 in all, should be encouraged to provide convenient and economical landing facilities immediately, and that each should receive some degree of federal aid (Hearings on H.R. 3170, *sup. cit.,* testimony Boeing, p. 403. See also testimony Geuting, p. 409).

[8] The Civil Aeronautics Administration multiplies the take-off distance by 15 in calculating a safe runway length.

[9] Charles Froesch and Walther Prokosch, *Airport Planning,* New York, Wiley, 1946, p. 43. See also United States Department of Commerce, Civil Aeronautics Administration, *Airport Design,* April 1, 1944, and *Airport Survey,* 1939.

was 368 acres. Class I airports averaged 117 acres each; Class II airports, 151 acres; Class III airports, 426 acres; Class IV airports, 762 acres; and Class V airports, 1,050 acres.[10]

Airport Location

Air carriage requires the selection of a site which is conveniently located with respect to the center of the community served and with respect to existing highway systems and other forms of transportation. Time taken in traveling or in transferring freight between the airport and the office or warehouse must be added to the elapsed time of airplane movement in determining the average speed of transit. It may be decisive in determining the relative advantage of air and land or water travel. Freedom from obstructions, both actual and potential, and possibilities for a real expansion are, also, important.

There is little generalized information with respect to airport location. A few studies, however, have given the matter some attention. One such study, published in 1930, was conducted by the School of City Planning of Harvard University.[11] It collected information from 81 airports. Forty-five of these were located more than 5 miles and 10 additional were located more than 3 miles from the business centers of the communities to which they were attached. The transportation time from the business center to the airport, for distances of 5 miles and over, ranged from 11 to 90 minutes.

A second inquiry was directed by the Civil Aeronautics Authority in 1938 and 1939. Out of 206 airports used by scheduled air carriers in 1938, 95 were found to be located from 3 to 6 miles from the centers of towns served, 50 from 6 to 10 miles, 13 from 10 to 15 miles, and one was over 15 miles away. Only 47 were as near as 3 miles from the city center. Transit time was not reported in this inquiry.

Still a third summary, based upon 179 airports and published in 1946, concluded that 55 percent of the airports considered required a half hour or more for travel to the community center.[12]

The view of the Civil Aeronautics Authority in 1946 was that small airports of the private flier type should lie within 5 miles of the community served.[13] This estimate, however, has little bearing upon the needs of public transport. The various figures given suggest the handicap which confronts airplane operation. Air carriers frequently provide local automobile service between hotels and flying fields. There is also occasional

[10] Charles Froesch and Walther Prokosch, *op. cit.,* pp. 61–62.

[11] Henry V. Hubbard, Miller McClintock, and Frank B. Williams, *Airports, Their Location, Administration, and Legal Basis,* Cambridge, Mass., Harvard, 1930.

[12] Sherman P. Voorhees, *Air Transport,* July, 1946, p. 33. See also John H. Frederick, *Airport Management,* Chicago, Irwin, 1949, p. 21.

[13] United States House of Representatives, Committee on Interstate and Foreign Commerce, Hearings on H. R. 3170, 79th C., 1st S., 1945, testimony Donaldson, p. 59.

discussion of the possibility of using helicopters for communication between air termini and business or residential centers. Such expedients, however, if and when feasible, provide no real answer to the passenger problem and do not meet at all the difficulty of moving freight. In general, the shorter the haul, the more important convenient access to an airport terminal becomes.

Airport Finance

Of course the need for area alone will not keep the area from the center of a town, but airplanes cannot utilize land as intensively as other types of business and so are barred from central locations by considerations of expense. Indeed, there is a pessimistic assumption that air terminals, even at a distance from population centers, cannot be made to pay. As a matter of fact, they do not pay, although it is a question whether this is a necessary condition of their operation. In 1937, out of 1,675 airports, 278 reported a profit to the Civil Aeronautics Authority, 914 a loss, and 483, by what was possibly wishful accounting, an exact balance of income and outgo. Amortization, interest, and depreciation were excluded from these figures. The average net loss was $1,012 annually for all the airports concerned, and $16,148 for airports near cities of over 500,000 population.[14] In 1940, it was reported that of the estimated 650 municipal airports in the country, less than 15 percent were paying their own way or breaking even on operating costs without regard to the cost of maintaining airport runways and facilities.[15] Rates for the use of airports are not raised because there is a public sentiment in favor of subsidizing airplane operations, and the practice of municipal airports in keeping charges low prevents terminal companies which might like to experiment from making a compensatory charge.

Under the conditions which have been described, most of the investment in airports has come from public authorities. Up to 1933, it is true, funds were derived in approximate equality from municipalities and from private investors, with small contributions from state and federal governments. After 1933 private investment became negligible, and federal contributions were, up to 1945, the principal resource.[16] In 1946 federal

[14] United States Department of Commerce, Civil Aeronautics Authority, *Airport Survey*, 1939, 76th C., 1st S., House Doc. 245, p. 55. See also *Proceedings of the National Airport Conference*, December 6 and 7, 1937, for similar results.

[15] American Municipal Association, Report no. 143, p. 11. See Charles S. Rhyne, *Airport Lease and Concession Agreements*, Washington, D.C., National Institute of Municipal Law Officers, 1948, p. 30. Rhyne is of the opinion that municipalities grant the right to airlines to use municipal airport facilities upon unreasonably favorable terms.

[16] Federal expenditures from 1933 to 1944 were as follows:

Civil Works Administration	$11,503,267
Federal Emergency Relief Administration	16,239,554

subsidies for airports were regularized under the provision of the Federal Airport Act.

Federal Airport Act of 1946

The Federal Airport Act directs the Administrator of Civil Aeronautics to prepare, annually, a national plan for the development of public airports in the United States, including the Territory of Alaska, the Territory of Hawaii, Puerto Rico, and the Virgin Islands.[17]

The act prescribes a basis for the apportionment of money which Congress may appropriate as a federal contribution to this plan. Seventy-five percent of Congressional appropriations, less not to exceed 5 percent for planning, research, and administration expense, is to be apportioned by the Administrator for expenditure among the several states, one-half in the ratio which the population in each state bears to the total population of all the states, and one-half in the proportion which the area of each state bears to the total area of all the states. The balance is to be made available for projects in the several states which the Administrator may deem most appropriate for carrying out the national airport plan.[18]

Actual federal contributions for airport development take place within the limits indicated by the previous paragraph. The initiative is federal in each case in the sense that development occurs under a national plan.[19]

Public Works Administration	14,773,080
Works Projects Administration	331,089,971
CAA Defense Landing Area Program	367,099,299
Total	$740,705,171

SOURCE: United States Department of Commerce, Civil Aeronautics Administration, *Civil Aviation and the National Economy*, September, 1945. See also United States House of Representatives, Committee on Interstate and Foreign Commerce, Hearings on H. R. 3170, 1945, testimony Bayard, p. 65; and Civil Aeronautics Authority, *Airport Survey*, 1939, 76th C., 1st S., House Doc. 245, p. 13.

The federal act of 1946 authorized the expenditure of $500,000,000 by the federal government for airport development in the United States, to be spent over a 7-year period from July 1, 1946, to July 1, 1953. Federal appropriations under this act amounted, by 1950, to $157,000,000, of which $60,700,000 had been paid out. The total federal expenditures to 1950 were, therefore, in excess of $800,000,000.

State and municipal expenditures on airports are not easily calculable. It has been estimated that approximately 72 percent of all capital outlays for civil airports were, through 1944, from federal funds. Maintenance and administration is a local charge (United States Senate, Committee on Interstate and Foreign Commerce, *Study of Domestic Land and Water Transportation*, Hearings before the Subcommittee of the Committee on Domestic Land and Water Transportation, pursuant to S. Res. 50, 81st C., 2d S., 1950, testimony Alderman, pp. 113–114).

[17] 60 Stat. 170, 1946; 62 Stat. 173, 1948; 62 Stat. 1,111, 1948.

[18] Special provision is made for Alaska, Hawaii, Pureto Rico, and the Virgin Islands (60 Stat. 170, 1946. U.S.C., 1947, Suppl., Title 14, Part 550).

[19] In the case of large projects (Class IV and higher) the Administrator submits a request for authority to Congress at least two months before the close of each fiscal

The initiative is local in the sense that progress on any specific project in the national plan requires a sponsor. A sponsor may be a state, territory, possession, municipality, county, or government agency, or public corporation. It may not be a private party and, with some exceptions, it may not be the United States. The sponsor may submit a project application for some airport development included in the current revision of the national airport plan and the Administrator may approve the application if certain conditions appear to have been met, including a guarantee of maintenance.[20]

If and when a project application is made and approved, the Administrator transmits to the sponsor an offer to pay a portion of the allowable project cost.[21] This offer, when accepted, becomes a "grant agreement." The proportion of the allowable cost of an approved project which the United States will assume varies with the size of the installation and its locality but in general, within the United States, the federal government will pay 50 percent of allowable project costs, other than the costs of land acquisition, for the development of Class 3 or smaller airports and, a varying portion, never exceeding 50 percent, according to a stated formula, which the Administrator may deem expedient in carrying out the provisions of the Act. The United States' share of land acquisition costs is 25 percent for smaller and not to exceed 25 percent for larger airports.[22]

---

year, in order to enable Congress, if it so wishes, to object by law or by concurrent resolution.

[20] Section 9 (d) of the Federal Airport Act reads as follows:

"(d) All such projects shall be subject to the approval of the Administration, which approval shall be given only if, at the time of approval, funds are available for payment of the United States share of the allowable project costs, and only if he is satisfied that the project will contribute to the accomplishment of the purposes of this Act, that sufficient funds are available for that portion of the project costs which is not to be paid by the United States under this Act, that the project will be completed without undue delay, that the public agency or public agencies which submitted the project application have legal authority to engage in the airport development as proposed, and that all project sponsorship requirements prescribed by or under the authority of this Act have been or will be met. No project shall be approved by the Administrator with respect to any airport unless a public agency holds good title, satisfactory to the Administrator, to the landing area of such airport or the site therefor, or gives assurance satisfactory to the Administrator that such title will be acquired."

Section 11 of the Act lists a series of assurances which are required with respect to future operation. These include assurances that the airport will be available for public use on fair and reasonable terms and without unjust discrimination, that it will be suitably operated and maintained, and that its facilities will be available for military and naval aircraft.

[21] The Act lists certain types of cost as "allowable." The overall requirement is that costs shall be necessarily incurred and reasonable in amount.

[22] Section 10 of the Federal Airport Act contains the following paragraphs:

"(b) In the case of any State containing unappropriated and unreserved public lands and nontaxable Indian lands (individual and tribal) exceeding 5 per centum of the total area of all lands therein, the United States' share under subsection (a) (1) and the maximum United States' share under subsection (a) (2), shall be increased

Comments on Federal Airport Policy

The policy of the Federal Airport Act is to place the planning for airports squarely in the hands of the federal government except in the case of large communities such as New York and Chicago where the necessary expenditure is very large relative to possible federal aid, and in the case of minor ports and landing fields which the national plan will not include. The degree to which federal control will be effective will depend, of course, upon the size of the appropriations that Congress will be willing to provide.[23] Under the federal government the Federal Airport Act strengthens the municipalities as compared with state governments because cities, as well as states, are permitted to apply directly to the Civil Aeronautics Administration; and cities, rather than states, have been and are most likely to be interested in promoting airport plans. Whoever the sponsor, federal contributions will lessen the cost of airports to users because sponsors receiving federal aid will be unlikely to include this aid in the capital expenditures for which they expect a return. Airports for general use, under these circumstances, will hardly be built with private funds. From the point of view of users there will be an advantage in that municipally owned ports will be opened to all planes, or at least to all planes of stated types, irrespective of ownership. This will avoid many of the perplexities which harass the users of railroad terminals. The danger is that federal funds will be disbursed extravagantly in response to political pressure or on overoptimistic expectations of local use.[24]

---

by whichever is the smaller of the following percentages thereof: (1) 25 per centum, or (2) a percentage equal to one-half the percentage that the area of all such lands in such States is of its total area. [Actual United States percentages in 1947 ranged from 51.39 to 62.50.]

"(c) The United States' share payable on account of any approved project in the Territory of Alaska shall be such portion of the allowable project costs of the project (not less than 50 per centum in the case of a class 3 or smaller airport, and not to exceed 75 per centum in the case of an airport of any class) as the Administrator may deem appropriate for carrying out the provisions of this Act.

"(d) To the extent that the project costs of an approved project represent the cost of acquiring land or interests therein or easements through or other interests in air space, the United States share (1) in the case of a project for the development of a class 3 or smaller airport, shall be 25 per centum of the allowable costs of such acquisition, and (2) in the case of a project for the development of a class 4 or larger airport, shall be not to exceed 25 per centum of the allowable costs of such acquisition."

[23] The Act of 1946 authorized appropriations up to the amount of $500,000,000 during a period of seven years with a maximum of $100,000,000 annually, to which was added $20,000 for airports in Hawaii, Alaska, and Puerto Rico. In September, 1950, the life of the 7-year program was extended another 5 years, without the authorization of additional funds. Congressional appropriations were $45,000,000 in 1947, $32,500,000 in 1948, $3,000,000 in 1949, $14,500,000 in 1950, $36,436,476 in 1951, $28,700,000 in 1952, and $14,321,154 in 1953 (United States Bureau of the Budget, *Annual*).

[24] The official analogy is between federal expenditures for airports and those for highways (United States House of Representatives, Committee on Interstate and Foreign Commerce, Hearings on H.R. 3170, 79th C., 1st S., 1945, testimony Wallace, pp.

Railroad Terminals

The second type of transport agency for which the terminal problem is of prime importance is the railroad. A rail terminal consists of many parts. There is a building or buildings and a complex of tracks used for the receipt and delivery of passengers. There are inbound and outbound freight houses, and specially placed tracks, accessible to shippers, where goods in carload quantities can be loaded into and unloaded from railroad cars by consignor or consignees. There are side tracks and spurs running to private warehouses and factories. Cars are placed upon these private lines to be loaded or unloaded at the convenience of the shipper. There is a multitude of tracks used for switching operations and for the storage of cars. There may be facilities for servicing and repairing cars and locomotives, water pumping and electric power plants, ice manufacturing plants, and installations of still other sorts. This aggregate of buildings, tracks, and appurtenances is known as a railroad terminal. For many purposes it is not necessary to distinguish between its elements.

Character and Importance of Terminal Operations

All railroad traffic has to pass to, from, or through some terminal, more or less of the character just described. The process constitutes a substantial portion of the total haul from the point of view of time and cost, though not, of course, from the point of view of the distance over which goods or passengers are carried. The federal Board of Investigation and Research estimated, in 1944, that the operating cost of less than carload shipments moving in the lower Mississippi Valley, in boxcars, with net loads of 5 tons, for distances of 200 miles was 59.6 cents per 100 pounds. Of this 38.25 cents or 64 percent was for terminal expense. In the case of carload traffic, supposing a net load of 40 tons, the cost was 44.06 cents. Of this 16.54 cents or 38 percent was the result of terminal handling.[25] With respect to time consumed, freight cars moved, in 1952, at an average speed of 17.6 miles per hour when in motion. They accomplished, however, an average mileage of only 46.2 miles per day. Terminal time is

25, 27; testimony Burden, p. 31). An analogy between airports and harbors is also drawn (*ibid.*, testimony Tipton, p. 239). Government officials refuse to admit, however, any analogy with the railroad situation (*ibid.*, testimony Wallace, p. 27; testimony Tipton, p. 239). The result is that railroads opposed the enactment of the Act of 1946 (*ibid.*, testimony Souby, p. 217; testimony Corbett, p. 369).

[25] United States, Board of Investigation and Research, *Comparison of Rail, Motor, and Water Carriers' Costs* (79th C., 1st S., Sen. Doc. 84, 1945). The Office of the Federal Coordinator estimated, in 1935, that as much as 53.67 percent of the cost of freight transport was due to terminal operation, including the cost of intermediate yardings and interchange as well as the costs at origin and destination terminals (United States, Office of the Federal Coordinator, *Report on Economy Possibilities of Regional Coordination Projects,* 1935, prepared by the Section of Regional Coordination).

spent in loading and unloading cars, in arranging cars into trains, in fitting locomotives to the loads, in inspecting equipment, and in other similar operations. Freight is not only delayed in cars, but it may remain in freight houses, coming or going, for additional periods.[26] There are no estimates for passenger traffic comparable to those just mentioned, but passenger termini are responsible for a large part of the cost of passenger transport, although they may not retard passenger movements to an equivalent degree. Terminal time is unproductive in the sense that it brings in no important revenue. It is important that it be controlled. At least, this is true up to the point where the costs of greater speed will offset the advantages that result from lessened time.

Passenger Terminals

The simplest form of rail terminal service is that provided for passengers—a statement which holds true in spite of the elaborate structures erected for advertising purposes in some cities or to gratify the aesthetic sense or the civic pride of the communities in which the terminals are placed. Passenger terminal service is simplified by the fact that passengers load and unload themselves, and also by the circumstance that intramural systems of local transportation are more fully developed for the carriage of people than for the carriage of goods.

In the case of passenger movements, the fact that the terminal of the line haul carrier is not the final destination of the traffic which flows into it is more than ordinarily obvious; and this, perhaps, is the matter of most importance in determining the location and administration of such facilities.

The so-called passenger terminal marks a change in the method of conveyance, as from rail to electric car or bus, or from motor bus to pedestrian locomotion. The point at which this change takes place should be chosen so as to produce the greatest speed and economy for the passenger with respect to the total transit. In large cities it is generally impossible for the machine which accomplishes the road haul to deposit the individual within, say, a quarter of a mile of his local destination. Rather than to attempt this, it is desirable to carry suburban passengers into the regular channels or arteries of the intramural scheme of transportation. It has been suggested in Chicago that all suburban trains should pass through a subway loop instead of stopping at any passenger terminal or, which

[26] The Federal Coordinator of Transportation dealt with the distribution of freight car time between placement for loading and release at destination. His information covered all freight cars which terminated their movement on December 13, 1933. His conclusion was that out of an average of 144 hours of average elapsed time per car, 68 hours were consumed by shipper and consignee in loading and unloading, 26 hours were spent in terminals at points of origin and destination, 27 hours were spent at intermediate terminals, and 23 hours were occupied by movement in road trains (*Freight Traffic Report*, 1935, vol. 2, p. 71).

would accomplish the same purpose, that suburban steam trains should be transferred to city elevated tracks at the circumference of the elevated system. It is to be doubted whether either of these suggestions offers a complete solution to the Chicago problem; but the fact that they are made, as well as the present success of the electric, motor bus, and of some rail lines which bring passengers into the city and deposit them at a great variety of unpretentious but convenient stations, indicates the character of the suburban service which gives satisfaction in a congested district.

Through passenger transportation differs from suburban in that the convenience of outgoing passengers demands a longer time to board the train and to get settled therein with baggage than is required for suburban traffic. The ideal arrangement, when this has been provided, is the through car from point of origin to final destination, even when the movement passes over the lines of several roads. When traffic is insufficient for such service, the best alternative is probably the union terminal, used by all through lines, with easy transfer from incoming to outgoing trains.[27] In weighing the advantages of through cars and union terminals it must be remembered that very many passengers may wish to stop temporarily when cities like Chicago, St. Louis, or New York lie upon their route. These passengers will make use, before they leave, of surface, elevated, or subway cars, cabs, buses, automobiles, or other conveyances. Through passenger stations should be convenient to these facilities and to the business or hotel or theater district to which the passengers resort, but they need not be located with regard to the center of population of the city as a whole.

Recent Changes in the Design and Use of Passenger Terminals

In comparing different passenger terminals, adequacy of installation, accessibility of the station from all portions of the city and its suburbs by private vehicles, buses, and interurban lines, and the consonancy of the development with the character and civic plans of the community should be regarded as well as the expense of construction and operation.[28] These tests are standard and have been applied for many years. During the last two decades, however, certain changes in utilization of passenger terminal facilities have taken place which have had interesting results upon terminal location, design, and management. A study by a committee of the American Railway Engineering Association discussed these changes under the following heads:

[27] A good example of a union passenger terminal is the union station opened in Cincinnati in 1933. This terminal is jointly owned and used by all of the railways serving the city; it permitted the carriers to abandon five existing passenger stations (*Railway Age,* April 22, 1933, p. 575). The so-called "Union Terminal" at Chicago is not used by all the railroads which serve that town.

[28] See Los Angeles Passenger Terminal cases, 100 I.C.C. 421, 435, 1925.

1. *Increase in the importance of terminals in large urban centers.* Relative reductions in local and increases in long-distance travel have produced a tendency to reduce and to consolidate facilities in the small stations and to place increased demands on many of the important terminals located in the larger cities.

2. *Increased use of automobiles by patrons arriving at and departing from the station.* This has intensified the need for ample parking space and buses, taxicabs, and private autos, with convenient auto approaches to the station and "short-cut" exits from platforms to auto-loading sections. It has reduced the area necessary for waiting room within the terminal, although more attractive and comfortable waiting accommodation has been provided.

3. *The tendency to replace trunk baggage with hand baggage.* This has led to an increase in parcel checking facilities and to a decrease in the provision for heavy baggage. Central parcel windows are being supplemented with coin-operated lockers distributed throughout the station.

4. *Increased length of trains.* Longer trains require longer station platforms and better arrangements for the quick ingress and egress of passengers. The old train shed is relatively inflexible in this respect and is giving way to other structures.

There have also been changes in terminal administration policy which are less to be attributed to alterations in the character of use than to the desire to attract clients and at the same time to derive revenue from facilities which are provided. In the first category one may place all those improvements and enlargements which make rail passenger stations more attractive, such as more elaborate furnishing and decoration, moving stairways, and the use of the electric eye to open and to close doors. To the latter may be assigned the greater use of "concessions." Thus, in an apparent attempt to increase their earnings, carriers have sold to "concessionaires" the right to operate station facilities such as restaurants, lunch rooms, parcel checking locations, and toilet rooms which the railroads formerly provided free or directly managed. The use of pay toilets has become general, and in the larger stations there are more pay than free toilets. This enumeration may suggest matters to which attention is currently directed in the construction and operation of passenger terminal railroad plants.

Analysis of Freight Traffic

Freight terminals are called upon to handle:

1. Through traffic.
2. Carload local traffic.
3. Less-than-carload local traffic.

During the year 1948 the carloads of freight handled by the Terminal Association at St. Louis were as follows:

Number of Carloads of Freight Handled by the Terminal Railroad Association at St. Louis During the Year 1948

	Number of Cars
Cars loaded on tracks and at freight houses of other railroads on the west side served by Terminal motive power	62,465
Cars unloaded on tracks and at freight houses of other railroads on the west side served by Terminal motive power	37,752
Cars loaded at industries and team tracks on west side located on Terminal rails	82,244
Cars unloaded at industries and team tracks on west side located on Terminal rails	117,725
Cars loaded at industries and team tracks on east side located on Terminal rails	72,933
Cars unloaded at industries and team tracks on east side located on Terminal rails	89,606
Through carloads and carloads having either origin or destination, or both origin and destination in the St. Louis and East St. Louis switching districts on the rails of other railroads	973,143
Total	1,435,868

The terms "west side" and "east side" in the table indicate position with respect to the Mississippi River. The table shows that 462,725 cars or 32 percent of the cars handled were loaded or unloaded on tracks or at freight houses served by Terminal motive power or were loaded or unloaded at industries and team tracks on Terminal rails. This traffic began or ended at St. Louis. The balance of 973,143 cars, or 68 percent, consisted of through traffic together with cars with points of origin or destination in the St. Louis and East St. Louis switching districts which were not on Terminal rails and were not served by Terminal motive power.[29] Available information does not disclose the volume of through traffic, taken by itself. The amount, nevertheless, was certainly very large.

Traffic in the Chicago switching district is estimated at 45,000 cars per day. This movement can be broken down as follows:

Car Movements in Chicago Switching District, 1949

1.	Inbound loads from beyond Chicago	9,600 per day
	To freight houses	14%
	To team tracks	10%
	To industries	76%
2.	Outbound local loads to points beyond Chicago	5,960 per day
	From freight houses	24%
	From team tracks	3%
	From industries	73%

[29] Courtesy Terminal Railroad Association of St. Louis.

3. Through loaded traffic originating at points
      outside Chicago   5,000 per day
4. Empty cars into, out of, and through Chicago   20,000 per day

The balance of the 45,000-car movement per day is made up of loaded cars moving between industries in the Chicago District, between industries and freight houses and freight houses and industries in the District.[30] Approximately 11 percent of the grand total consists of cars which neither originated in nor were finally destined to points within the district.

Through Traffic

The data just presented suggest that the through freight traffic of our large cities constitutes a substantial proportion of the whole which they receive. Of the three types of traffic mentioned, it is the one which presents in principle the least difficulty. This is for the reason that through freight traffic makes no characteristic use of the facilities of an intermediate terminal, although, of course, it may sometimes be the subject of some manufacturing or commercial operation which has to be regarded. Through traffic comes to a terminal because lines of communication lead through that terminal, not because the latter has any drawing power in so far as through traffic is concerned. The best way to treat it is to keep it out of the terminal altogether, which is, perhaps, best accomplished by the belt line, a railroad that encircles the town at some distance from the center, intersecting the converging main routes and making it possible to transfer freight from one route to another without entering the area of greatest congestion. The sorting of incoming and outgoing freight under such a system is accomplished at one or more "clearing yards," where trains are broken up and cars are regrouped according to the railroads to which they are to be delivered. Unfortunately, freight is not always kept out of the congested area even when belt lines exist. In Chicago, a 2-day test showed, in 1934, that 40 percent of the through traffic was taken into the downtown district instead of passing over switching lines around the city; this through traffic was then moved back through different switching lines to the outer belts where it was delivered to outbound lines. The congestion which results where this practice is pursued is increased by the manner in which the freight is usually handled. It is the preponderant custom throughout the country for each carrier to deliver its through cars to the yards or facilities of other carriers. The delivering engine then returns with a light load or with no load at all. This further obstructs the terminal with a multiplicity of movements which would be avoided if the traffic were better organized.[31]

[30] Courtesy of the Chicago & Western Indiana Railroad Company.

[31] United States, Office of the Federal Coordinator of Transportation, *Report on Economy Possibilities of Regional Coordination Projects,* 1935, pp. 3, 4. See also excellent

Carload Local Traffic

Local traffic cannot be kept out of the terminals. A main function of the terminal is, indeed, to enable shippers to receive and forward traffic which has destination or origin in the terminal town. At a city such as Chicago or St. Louis, where many lines enter the switching district, each has a train yard for receiving and dispatching trains. These yards are usually some distance from the downtown business district. Incoming cars are switched in the outlying yard, and from this point they move to freight houses, team tracks, warehouses, grain elevators and the like, where they are delivered to consignees. The volume of movement in a large terminal is very great. Thus, in Chicago, the Office of the Federal Coordinator observed a daily operation from the train yards to the stockyards district alone of 239 separate trains or switching cuts, and corresponding moves from the stockyards district to the train yards. These trains or yard cuts consisted of from 1 to 35 or 40 cars. More or less similar movements took place to and from produce terminals, potato marts, and other downtown destinations.

Railroad freight cars originating at or destined to a terminal in carload quantity may be placed upon a public track accessible to trucks where they are loaded or unloaded by shipper or consignee. This is, however, a clumsy method. In the greater number of cases, the cars containing freight are placed upon private tracks built at the industries' expense and operated sometimes by the carrier and sometimes by locomotives owned by the industry.

Switch Connections with Private Side Tracks

Paragraph 9 of Section I of the Interstate Commerce Act reads as follows:

Any common carrier subject to the provisions of this Act, upon application of any lateral, branch line of railroad, or of any shipper tendering interstate traffic for transportation, shall construct, maintain and operate upon reasonble terms a switch connection with any such lateral, branch line of railroad, or private side track which may be construed to connect with its railroad, where such connection is reasonably practical and can be put in with safety and will furnish sufficient business to justify the construction and maintenance of the same; and shall furnish cars for the movement of such traffic to the best of its ability without discrimination in favor of or against any such shipper. If any common carrier shall fail to install and operate any such switch or connection as aforesaid, on application therefor in writing by any shipper or owner of such lateral, branch line of railroad, such shipper or

articles by E. W. Coughlin, Manager, Railroad Relations Car Service Division, Association of American Railroads, in *Railway Age,* April 21, 1952, p. 58, and May 26, 1952, p. 44.

owner of such lateral, branch line of railroad may make complaint to the Commission, as provided in section thirteen of this Act, and the Commission shall hear and investigate the same and shall determine as to the safety and practicability thereof and justification and reasonable compensation therefor, and the Commission may make an order, as provided in section fifteen of the Act, directing the common carrier to comply with the provisions of this section in accordance with such order, and such order shall be enforced as hereinafter provided for the enforcement of all other orders by the Commission, other than orders for the payment of money.

This paragraph of the Interstate Commission Law gives to the Commission power to require a rail carrier to install a switch track connection under certain circumstances and subject to certain limitations. It does not enable the Commission to force a carrier to build a side track upon private land, even when the shipper is prepared to share in the expense,[32] but it does make it possible for an industry which builds a spur track up to a railroad right of way to demand a connection with the main track and a reasonable operating service. In most cases, however, no compulsion is needed, for the carrier which uses a spur thereby enlarges its terminals at slight expense; while at the same time it attaches the industry to itself in such a way as to give it a great advantage in soliciting the industry's traffic, both inbound and outbound.

Traffic delivered at an industry spur or siding is covered by the published rate, except that delay in loading or unloading cars in excess of a period of free time, usually 48 hours, makes shipper or consignee subject to a demurrage charge. Traffic delivered on private tracks does not make use of city streets and does not, therefore, give rise to the peculiar problems which characterize team track or less-than-carload railroad service.

Less-than-Carload Local Traffic

Cars used for less-than-carload traffic, like full carloads, must be sorted into trains; and insofar as possible all freight consigned to a given destination must be loaded into a single car. In this case also handling is easier if the operations can be accomplished outside of the congested area. It was with this in mind that the Chicago and Northwestern established a yard at Proviso, 13 miles west of Chicago. Before this yard was placed in service, cars were received and dispatched at each of 26 stations in the Chicago district. The building of a less-than-carload freight transfer at Proviso made it possible for the Northwestern to consolidate the loading and classification of outbound cars for the entire system at one point. All outbound less-than-carload freight from the 26 stations mentioned was sent by freight car or by motor truck directly to Proviso for loading into outbound cars. The results are said to have been: (1) a substantial ac-

[32] 22 I.C.C. 354, 1912.

celeration in the movement of freight from Chicago and adjacent territory; (2) the saving of between 100 and 150 cars out of the equipment required to handle traffic, due to concentrated and heavier loading of outbound equipment; (3) a reduction in loss and damage claims; and (4) a diminution in the amount of overtime payments.[33]

Generally speaking, the appliances for the intramural transportation of less-than-carload freight include the belt line, the subway, and the motor truck. In New York, the presence of considerable bodies of water between Manhattan Island and the New Jersey and Brooklyn shores permits the use of barges or lighters for a portion of the intramural haul, thus relieving the city streets. In Chicago, some use is made of the Chicago River, but more of the tunnel property of the Chicago Warehouse and Terminal Company. This independent company operates a narrow-gauge railroad system through a tunnel, 7½ feet high and 6 feet wide, which extends under nearly all of the streets of the downtown district, and is connected by elevators with the freight floors of the railroad stations, as well as with a number of commercial houses and industries, and with surface stations maintained by the tunnel company. The subway has never been profitable, but it performs a notable service in carrying freight in the most congested areas of the city.

Trap Cars

The name "trap" or "ferry" is applied to a car placed at an industry or commercial house having a private siding and there loaded by a shipper with less-than-carload shipments of various sorts and hauled by a carrier to a local freight or transfer station for the handling and forwarding of contents. It is also applied to a car loaded with less-than-carload shipments which is hauled to and placed upon the private track of an industry or commercial house from a local freight or transfer station. Service of this sort is usually rendered free of charge if a prescribed minimum weight is loaded into the car; if the stipulated minimum is not loaded, charges are named, usually upon a per car basis.

Trap car service was originally instituted in order to enable carriers to compete for the less-than-carload business of firms which were at a distance from their freight houses in a city, although near to the freight house of some competing line. It has been continued partly because of the indirect advantage of relieving congested main freight stations, and the practice has been extended in certain instances. Such an extension occurs, for example, when carriers establish freight substations at convenient points within their switching limits, from which less-than-carload shipments are transported to main freight stations, or transfer stations, for the

[33] *Railway Age,* October 28, 1933, pp. 616, 618.

rehandling and forwarding of contents, thus multiplying the points at which railroad service ends and other forms of transportation begin.[34]

Truck Service in City Streets

The greater part of local less-than-carload freight makes use of city streets, and it is there that carriers create most congestion. The crowding occurs, in the first place, because city thoroughfares are not planned to accommodate an extensive vehicular traffic and cannot be easily widened as such traffic grows. It occurs also because the business of city freight transportation is usually directed by a large number of independent and uncoördinated trucking companies. This leads to duplication of facilities and overoccupation of street space, and also to irregular and unplanned arrival of trucks at the rail freight houses. Railroad freight terminals must be larger under such a system than they would need to be if the rail carriers were not required to find storage space for a portion of their inbound freight, although this disadvantage is partially offset by the reduction in warehouse space which consignees might otherwise be forced to provide. There is no question but that motor truck service is immensely more efficient than the service that the old horse-drawn vehicles could supply for the handling of traffic to and from the rail; and the efficiency of modern service has grown with the adoption of special types of trucks, such as those equipped with demountable bodies, or trucks fitted to handle so-called "unit containers" to be transferred directly between motor vehicle and railroad car without rehandling of the contents, or trucks with cranes for hoisting, or other special operating machinery.[35] It is highly doubtful,

---

[34] Trap or Ferry Car Service Charges, 34 I.C.C. 516, 1915. See also 246 I.C.C. 332, 1941.

[35] What is known as a "container" is a steel box, approximately as wide and about one-fifth as long as the platform of a railroad flat car. Containers used by the Pennsylvania Railroad, which may serve as illustrations, are 7 feet wide, 9 feet long, and 8 feet high. Their capacity is 440 cubic feet, the average weight is 3,000 pounds, and the load capacity is 10,000 pounds. Five such containers, clamped on a flat car, will completely occupy the floor. One container will provide a complete load for a truck of reasonable dimensions. The advantage to the railroad from the use of such equipment is that it reduces the amount of station handling. Empty containers are brought to the shipper's door by motor truck. They are loaded by the shipper, sealed, and then hauled by truck to the rail terminal. The railroad has only to swing the container from truck to flat car and then make it fast. There is no checking, no record is made of the container's contents, and the packages in the container are not separately handled. From the shipper's point of view, the first advantage is that the necessity for carting or boxing small pieces of freight is reduced. Losses from pilferage become almost impossible. The shipper loads at his convenience, because the container is left at his place of business. And beyond this, the cartage and railroad rates on less-than-carload shipments in containers may be expected to be less than the rates on the contents of containers when presented to the railroad as separate consignments. There are, on the other hand, disadvantages. A valuable study of freight transport equipment, including a section on containers and demountable bodies, was completed for the Federal Coordinator of Transportation in 1935. See *Report of Mechanical Advisory Committee to the Federal Coordinator of Transportation*, December 27, 1935. The Board of In-

nevertheless, whether the most efficient appliances that can be devised, within the limits of reasonable expenditure, will serve to meet the physical requirements of less-than-carload terminal handling in our largest cities, without an improved organization of intramural freight transportation. Fortunately, some steps have been taken toward this end, and more may be expected.

Off-Track and Constructive Stations

Among the devices for accomplishing a better control of city movements are what are known as "off-track" and "constructive" stations.

An off-track station is a station not reached by the line of any carrier. The railroad will accept at or will deliver freight to such a location at the published rate without addition for the haul from rail terminus to the off-track location. In St. Louis the trucking movement is performed by the Columbia Transfer Company, which is paid by the railroads for the service. A constructive station is a point in a city up to which the railroad is willing to absorb a trucking charge. It may not be associated with a structure of any kind. The local shipper or consignee hauls his own freight and the railroad repays him a portion of the cost. Both off track and constructive stations have a history, and one or both still exist in cities like St. Louis and New York. But their importance has declined with the developing practice of pickup and delivery. We do not need to describe them at any greater length.

Pickup and Delivery

Under both the trap car and the off-station system, the rail carrier accepts responsibility for delivery of freight at points considerably removed from freight houses where the line haul ends. The system of pickup and delivery is an extension of this practice.

Pickup and delivery has been standard in England for all except the heavier classes of goods—coal, iron, cement, etc.—for many years. Inbound freight is checked from car to platform, trucked to dray loading section, loaded and checked into railway drays or motor trucks, and then sent out, over scales, into the town for delivery. Outbound freight is col-

---

vestigation and Research, created by the Transportation Act of 1940, also discussed the merits and demerits of containers at considerable length. (See *Report on Technological Trends in Transportation*, 79th C., 1st S., Sen. Doc. 76, Ser. 10,951, September 20, 1944.)

A recent variation, using the principle of the container, is the so-called "speedbox." A speedbox is a small aluminum container, 48 inches high, 48 inches wide, and 34 or 40 inches deep. Consignees load their freight shipments at their own place of business, lock and seal them. Speedboxes are transported between towns by boxcars or trucks and are delivered, without opening, to the consignee. It is estimated that 60 percent or more is saved in time of handling, when speedboxes are used, as compared with the time used in handling when less than carload shipments are forwarded in the customary way (*Traffic World*, January 20, 1951, pp. 79–84).

lected at consignee's door and follows a reverse procedure until loaded into the railway car. The railway companies' cartage vehicles collect and deliver most of the miscellaneous goods traffic passing through their terminals.

In Canada, a similar service is operated by the rail carriers under contracts or agreements with teaming companies acting as their agents. This service applies to traffic rated in the Canadian classification as fifth class or higher, less-than-carload and carload, with the exception of bulk freight or articles weighing 2,000 pounds or over per piece or per package.[36]

In the United States, pickup and delivery service has long been standard for parcel post and for express service; and pickup and delivery has been available to shippers of a limited number of commodities through the activities of "forwarding companies" which collect less-than-carload shipments, consolidate them into carloads, present them to line haul carriers at the railroad terminals for carriage at the carload rate, and receive and distribute them at destination.[37] Prior to 1930, however, it was the general practice of railroads to transport freight in less-than-carload quantities only from and to their regularly constituted freight stations, which were usually in buildings adjacent to their tracks.[38]

Introduction of Pickup and Delivery

In 1932 the principal New England lines established pickup and delivery service, following the example of the Boston and Maine. The same year the Pennsylvania, the Erie, and several other Eastern railroads published tariffs providing for pickup and delivery service at substantially all their stations for less-than-carload freight moving 260 miles or more. Railroads in Southern and Western territories established the service throughout their areas in 1936. In this year, also, substantially all standard railroads in official territory and many short lines and electric railways became parties to tariffs similar to those filed by the Pennsylvania in 1932. The practice is, therefore, general though not universal in the United States.

Provisions of Pickup and Delivery Tariffs

The peculiarities of the pickup and delivery system are as follows:

1. Pickup and delivery service is authorized by tariffs filed with the Interstate Commerce Commission.

2. Tariffs provide for the delivery of freight by railroad companies at shippers' receiving rooms, platforms or doorways directly accessible to

[36] *Railway Age,* July 5, 1924, p. 30.

[37] 258 I.C.C. 547, 1944. Pickup and delivery service is also provided by air carriers, through their subsidiary, Air Cargo, Inc., although the arrangements are recent. In 1949 the air lines had pickup and delivery contracts at almost 200 cities (United States Senate, Committee on Interstate and Foreign Commerce, Hearings on S. Res. 50, 81st C., 1st S., *Air-Line Industry Investigation,* Part I, testimony Ramspeck, p. 416).

[38] 218 I.C.C. 441, 1936.

trucks at a warehouse, factory, store, place of business, or private residence, or for the acceptance of freight at these locations.

3. The service is available only on shipper's application.

4. The service is rendered only for commodities and at stations specified in the published tariff.

5. Only one tender of goods will be made. If delivery of shipment cannot be effected, freight will be returned to the railroad freight house and will be held subject to disposition by the owner or consignee.

6. Freight delivered at or accepted at shippers' premises is carried by the railroad at the line haul rate.[39]

7. Pickup and delivery will be accomplished by trucks owned by the railroad or it will be performed under contract by agencies which the railroad employs. The consignor or consignee may, however, provide his own transport and may deliver or accept freight at the railroad station. If he so elects, the railroad will make him an allowance for this local carriage. The sum of 5 cents per 100 pounds has been often paid.[40]

Reasons for the Development of Pickup and Delivery Service

The reasons for railroad offer of pickup and delivery service are to be found (1) in the expectation of economies in the handling of less-than-carload freight at terminals and (2) in the pressure of competition.

The advantages of pickup and delivery, from the point of view of terminal operation, are two: first, it enables the railroad to clear its freight houses promptly of incoming freight, and possibly to reduce the provision of yard storage tracks; and second, it may make it possible to obtain a higher load efficiency in road vehicles by scientific loading and routing, with the result that traffic congestion upon the streets is likely to be reduced. A third advantage sometimes mentioned is that railroad pickup and delivery will permit the railroad to distribute less-than-carload freight by truck from inexpensive locations on the outskirts of the congested area instead of bringing freight of this description to freight houses in the heart of town. The shipper who furnishes his own cartage naturally wishes his freight accepted at the station which is nearest to his industry. With rail pickup and delivery, the shipper cares less where his traffic leaves the rail. This third advantage, however, is a somewhat doubtful one from the com-

[39] An extra charge is made, under some tariffs, when the line haul exceeds a stated distance, such as 260 miles.

[40] A considerable number, amounting possibly to a majority of shippers, do their own carrying. This is either because these shippers are located so that their terminal transport is relatively inexpensive, or because railroad service offered is inconvenient or inadequate. Such service, for instance, may be rendered at inconvenient hours of the day. For certain commodities specialized equipment, not owned by the railroad, may be needed, etc. (E. S. Lynch, "Railroad Pick-Up and Delivery," *Journal of Land and Public Utility Economics*, May, 1938).

munity standpoint, as the traffic formerly moving to the center of the city by rail is now thrown upon the city streets.

The most important reason for the introduction of railroad pickup and delivery has been competition—first, the competition of railroads with motor transport and, to a less degree with water carriage, and, secondly, the competition of railroads with each other. Lynch is of the opinion that one railroad followed another in adopting the new policy. "Were it not," he says, "that the nation's railroad market is of the chain-competitive type, there is little likelihood that many systems would have extended their hauling beyond their railheads." [41] On the other hand, the Interstate Commerce Commission has observed that the carrier's object in establishing pickup and delivery was to arrest the decline in their less-than-carload traffic which they believed to be due to the development of motor transportation.[42] Pickup and delivery, when the service is performed by railroad carriers, constitutes an improvement in service. If performed by consignor or consignee, under an allowance, it brings about a reduction in the rate. In either case it is an aggressive action designed to bring back traffic to the rail. One can only speculate as to how far it has been successful, but there is some evidence, at least in particular situations, where it has produced results.[43]

Specialized Terminals

Some rail carriers have devoted thought and money to the construction of special facilities for particular kinds of freight, hoping in this way to attract traffic to their lines for reasons other than those connected with a purely transportation service. There is considerable variety in these special facilities which railroads supply to patrons. Some carriers, for instance, which handle large quantities of express provide vaults for the protection of money and valuables, bonded rooms for imported articles, and frostproof and refrigerator space for perishable commodities.[44] At Port Reading, New Jersey, the Philadelphia and Reading Railway operates a terminal with special reference to the needs of jobbers who supply New York City with coal. For this purpose it provides facilities for the prompt

[41] Edward S. Lynch, *op. cit.*

[42] 218 I.C.C. 441, 447, 1936.

[43] See 248 I.C.C. 385, 1942; 251 I.C.C. 549, 1942. Cf. 238 I.C.C. 671, 1940.

Certain technical questions may arise in connection with pickup and delivery service. There may be dispute, for instance, as to whether platforms or driveways are really accessible to trucks (225 I.C.C. 516, 1937). Shippers may not make seasonable application for service (253 I.C.C. 64, 1942). The rail rate, after deduction of the calculated cost of delivery service, may be noncompensatory (237 I.C.C. 741, 1940). And shippers may demand the installation of pickup and delivery (243 I.C.C. 17, 1940), or resist its withdrawal. The Interstate Commerce Commission has held that evidence in each case should determine whether pickup and delivery service should be supplied (258 I.C.C. 697, 1944).

[44] *World Ports,* June, 1930, pp. 554–558.

railroad's standpoint, a joint produce terminal has the advantage of cheapness, not only because the first investment is less for each participating carrier but also because the peaks of traffic come at different times on different railroads, and the capacity of a joint terminal is better utilized than is the capacity of a terminal serving a single railroad line.[51]

Air Rights

When structures can be erected above railway yard or main line tracks there is an important saving in space, and a more intensive utilization of the most expensive part of the railway's real estate. The thought that what are known as "air rights" can be developed is recent, and the practice is still limited. An example of successful air rights development is the large terminal warehouse which the Reading built at Philadelphia, using space formerly entirely occupied by two railroad freight houses and their appurtenant tracks.[52] Another illustration may be found in the "Merchandise Mart" erected above the Chicago and Northwestern Railway in Chicago. The building in which the Mart is located is 18 stories high and is said to be the largest building in the world, measured by floor area. It is constructed on property formerly occupied by the Northwestern's Wells Street passenger station. When the railroad's Madison Street passenger station was built, the Northwestern sold the air rights over its tracks to Marshall Field and Company. On the lower level, which it retained, the railroad built a modern freight terminal, which now has also space for the accommodation of motor trucks. Above, and spanning the terminal, Marshall Field constructed a wholesale mercantile center. It occupied part of this structure itself and leased space to many other firms as well. The location was convenient to wholesalers, and especially to the mail-order house, because of its convenient access to transportation. On the other hand, the railroad benefited, because the revenue derived from the sale of the air space was almost a net addition to its income.[53]

More important than any of these illustrations has been the development of the New York Central terminals in New York City. Extensive construction in the Grand Central terminal zone in the neighborhood of Forty-second Street and Fifth Avenue was first made possible by the substitution of electricity for steam as motive power in the New York terminal district. When this had been done, the railway tracks were depressed; and over the space once entirely devoted to tracks the railway built revenue-producing buildings, including apartment houses and luxurious hotels. The Grand Central Station was also enlarged, and store space was rented

---

[51] American Railway Engineering Association, *Proceedings,* vol. 33, 1932, p. 116.

[52] *Railway Age,* July 19, 1930, p. 103.

[53] *Railway Age,* September 26, 1931, p. 471. See also *Civil Engineering,* February, 1944, p. 50.

in the building. The result was a large increase in income to the railway; and in this case the city also benefited by the restoration of streets across the railway property and by the enlargement of the space in the restricted Manhattan district which could be used for business and residential purposes.[54] Part of the gain accrued to the city government by virtue of the enhancement of realty values in the district and the consequent increase in tax revenues.

Open vs. Closed Terminal

A pressing current problem with respect to rail freight terminals and carload traffic is one of administration. The question is whether such terminals in our large cities shall be operated as a unit or whether, in each city, the individual and competitive advantages of each carrier shall be preserved.

In a sense, all rail terminals are open, in that a line-haul carrier will deliver at any point within a terminal with which its tracks connect. They are closed, or partially closed, in that delivery may be made at the published rates only at stations or spurs which the line haul carrier may own. For delivery at other points the shipper may be required to pay an extra switching charge.[55]

Open Terminals and Reciprocal Switching

Under current practice the rate charged by a railroad pays for the expense of the line haul and for delivery at the railroad's terminal at point of destination. There is no extra collection for placement of cars upon team tracks or upon spurs. But there will be an extra switching charge when a car which has been hauled to a terminal upon the line of Carrier A is there transferred to railroad B and placed for delivery at a point upon the tracks of this second carrier. This is the operation contemplated in the arrangements previously described. Carrier B has no responsibility to the shipper and will assess the cost of its terminal haul to carrier A. If carrier A, in turn, recovers from the shipper, then the shipper's outlay from point of origin to final destination will be greater when A performs the line haul service than it would have been if the line haul carrier had been B, assuming that either could have accomplished the movement between termini. This fact will influence the shipper's choice, for interterminal transport, between carriers A and B.

In order to equalize the attractiveness of the routes of A and B, under

---

[54] W. D. Pence, "Railway Terminal Air Rights Developments and Movements of Local Land Values," *Journal of Land and Public Utility Economics,* May, 1929. It has been suggested that railroad air rights might be used in the development of terminal facilities for airplanes.

[55] See the two Interstate Commerce Commission reports on railway consolidation: 63 I.C.C. 455, 483–484, 1921; and 159 I.C.C. 522, 1929.

these conditions, railroad A may absorb the switching cost of the terminal service performed by B, making the net cost to the shipper from point of origin to final destination the same by either route. If this practice is generalized it will place all terminal industries upon A's lines insofar as the shipper is concerned. If all carriers adopt the plan, convenience in the location of individual terminal facilities will cease to be an element in attracting traffic.

The policy of switching cost absorption is referred to as "reciprocal switching" although no formal agreement between carriers is required. It is a policy which opens terminals in a cost sense in addition to opening them in an operating sense. Actually, the practice is sufficiently frequent to be of considerable importance. Thus it is customary for carriers reaching Chicago to treat connecting-line switching charges on all carload traffic as included in the line haul rate.[56] In the Southwest, the method is referred to as "general," [57] and abundant examples can be found in other sections of the United States. Sometimes absorption occurs only in the case of competitive traffic. Often it does not extend to outbound cars loaded on carrier team tracks as distinguished from cars loaded on industry spurs. Sometimes it spreads over a considerable area. Thus, in 1940, the Illinois Central absorbed truck charges within a 10-mile rural area in the case of freight which was to move out over its lines.[58] Where, as at Chicago, there is a developed system of belt line railroads the effect of reciprocal switching is very great.[59]

Reciprocal switching is restricted to carload traffic. With belt lines it is possible to operate, also, "universal freight stations" which extend, to a limited extent, the advantages of the open terminal to less-than-carload freight.

A universal station is one at which freight is accepted for delivery upon the line of any connecting carrier. At Chicago the Belt Railway Company operates two universal less-than-carload freight stations, one at Cragin and one at Clearing, which handle both inbound and outbound freight for all railroads; the Chicago Junction Railway operates two less-than-carload stations, and the Manufacturers' Junction and the Illinois Railway operate one apiece. These facilities are in addition to the lighters of the Merchants' Lighterage Company and to the tunnnel system of the Chicago Warehouse and Terminal Company referred to in earlier pages of this chapter.

[56] 241 I.C.C. 207, 214, 1940.
[57] 255 I.C.C. 633, 1943.
[58] 238 I.C.C. 671, 1940.
[59] Irregular adoption of reciprocal switching, as where carriers absorb switching charges on some hauls but not on others, may disrupt relations between communities which the Interstate Commerce Commission has established. The Commission may interfere, in such instances, on grounds of public policy (241 I.C.C. 207, 1940).

Unified Terminals

Reciprocal switching is, of course, unnecessary when terminals at any city are "unified." To unify a terminal the operation and, perhaps, also the ownership of terminal properties is placed in the hands of a separate corporation [60] which may be municipally controlled, as in the case of the belt railroads at San Francisco and New Orleans, or jointly controlled by rail carriers which enter the city, as at St. Louis and Kansas City. The best-known organization of the latter sort is probably the Terminal Railroad Association of St. Louis. This Association operates a passenger station used by all trunk line railroads operating into and out of St. Louis, together with extensive interchange freight yards, less-than-carload freight facilities, and ample team yards for carload freight, which supplement the terminal yards and facilities of the individual roads.

OPERATION AND OWNERSHIP OF THE ST. LOUIS TERMINAL. The Terminal Railroad Association of St. Louis has two bridges across the Mississippi River at St. Louis and has access over a third bridge owned by the City of St. Louis. At the present time the railroads break up their inbound trains after arrival at East St. Louis and St. Louis, and classify freight traffic in their own yards for delivery: (1) on their own rails; (2) on other railroads with which they have direct connection; (3) to the Terminal Railroad Association; or (4) to other transfer agencies located within the St. Louis-East St. Louis switching district. Only a few railroads have direct connection with each other, so the Terminal Railroad Association handles most of the intermediate and transriver movements between the various lines.

Except in the case of freight interchanged in St. Louis and East St. Louis proper that does not cross the river, the Terminal Railroad Association takes the cars from its connections on the west side of the river to its principal clearing or classification yards on the east side, or vice versa, where the cars are again classified for delivery to other roads and to industries located upon Terminal's rails. Cars are then handled in direct transfer movement between the yards and the interchange tracks of the individual railroads, where they are again classified for movement beyond in road trains and for local delivery. The Terminal Railroad Association of St. Louis is owned and controlled by 15 Trunk Line railroads serving the St. Louis gateway. These companies agree under contract to pay sufficient tolls to cover interest, taxes, rentals, and other charges, each company contributing its proportion in the event of deficiency.

LEGALITY OF UNIFIED TERMINALS. There is, of course, some question as to the legality of terminal unification of the St. Louis type, but after consideration this consolidation has been approved by the courts. The first case was in 1904, when the Supreme Court of Missouri ruled

[60] See 159 I.C.C. 522, 547, 1929.

that the consolidation of the Terminal Railroad Association of St. Louis with the Merchants' Terminal Company—a merger which consummated the control over St. Louis terminal facilities which the former now enjoys—was not contrary to the constitution or statutes of the state of Missouri.[61]

In 1912, the Supreme Court of the United States held that the unification of the terminal facilities of railroads centering at St. Louis was in violation of the Sherman Antitrust Act of 1890, but it took pains to say that this decision was based upon certain peculiarities in the terms upon which the St. Louis terminal properties were held together, not upon the inherent illegality of the whole arrangement; and it prescribed only a reorganization, and not a dissolution, to satisfy the law. According to the Supreme Court, the reorganization should provide:

1. For the admission of any existing or future railroad to joint ownership and control of the combined terminal properties, on just and reasonable terms.

2. For the use of the terminal facilities by any other railroad not electing to become a joint owner.

3. For the elimination of any provision in the agreement between the Terminal and its proprietary companies which should restrict any of the latter to the use of the facilities of the Terminal Company.

4. For the removal of certain specified abuses in the administration of the St. Louis Terminal and the judicial settlement of future disputes between the Terminal and proprietary companies and new applicants who desired terminal privileges.[62]

The specifications of the highest court were met by a reorganization agreement dated September 21, 1914, so that the useful life of the Terminal Association was continued.

DISADVANTAGES OF UNIFIED TERMINALS. The arguments against the establishment of unified terminals are the following:

1. A single terminal will not, as is sometimes assumed, enable any shipper to deliver his freight at the nearest freight station, no matter what its final destination may be, as he is able, for instance, to drop a letter into the nearest mail box. The cost of switching and of handling and rehandling freight would be so great under such a system as to compel some classification of receiving stations according to the destination of freight which leaves the terminal.

2. Joint operation may be inefficient operation. It is argued that railroads which now own terminal facilities cannot transfer title to a new company because such properties are usually covered by a variety of longterm mortgages. The most that can be accomplished, according to this point of view, will be a series of long-term leases, and the joint selection

[61] 81 Southwestern 395, 1904.
[62] 224 U.S. 383, 1912; 236 U.S. 194, 1915.

by the interested parties of a manager to operate as an agent for all the railroads entering a given city. This, it is said, will make for extravagance, because of the relative indifference of each participating road to economies, the results of which are divided among a number of carriers.

3. Unification of terminals deprives companies which have acquired ample and well-placed terminal properties of the advantage due to their foresight.

4. The merger of terminals will reduce competition because a large portion of this competition takes the form of rivalry between carriers in offering good terminal facilities and in prompt handling of traffic through terminals.

ADVANTAGES OF CONSOLIDATED TERMINALS. The advocates of unified terminals argue that they are not a device for restraining competition, but a most effective method of promoting competition, as well as of minimizing the expense of handling city freight business. Speaking of the St. Louis situation, the Supreme Court of Missouri observed:

We gather from the information that all along the lines of the terminal tracks intersecting the city from north to south, from east to west, and belting it on the west, there are manufacturing and other business concerns with switch tracks or spurs into their premises which enable the shipper to load the cars on the switch tracks on his premises, and have them delivered to any railroad that reaches the city. A more effectual means of keeping competition up to the highest point between parallel or competing lines could not be devised. The destruction of the system would result in compelling the shipper to employ the railroad with which he has switch connection, or else cart his product to a distant part of the city at a cost possibly as great as the railroad tariff.

St. Louis is a city of great magnitude, in the extent of its area, its population, and its manufacturing and other business. A very large number of trunk-line railroads converge in this city. In the brief of one of the well-informed counsel in this case it is said that St. Louis is one of the largest railroad centers in the world. Suppose it were required of every railroad company to effect its entrance to the city as best it could, and establish its own terminal facilities; we would have a large number of passenger stations, freight depots, and switch yards, scattered all over the vast area, and innumerable vehicles employed in hauling passengers and freight to and from those stations and depots. Or suppose it became necessary, in the exigency of commerce, that all incoming trains should reach a common focus, but every railroad company provide its own track; then not only would the expense of obtaining the necessary rights of way be so enormous as to amount to the exclusion of all but a few of the strongest roads, but, if it could be accomplished, the city would be cut to pieces with the many lines of railroad intersecting it in every direction, and thus the greatest agency of commerce would become the greatest burden.[63]

The arguments for a unified terminal are clearly expressed in the quota-

[63] 81 Southwestern 395, 398, 1904.

tion given above, as far as the economies of terminal location and operation are concerned. It may be added that the large accumulation of cars on the Terminal rails at St. Louis makes a car supply available for outbound loading that is greater than any individual line could hope to furnish.[64] Still another advantage is that a unified terminal prevents the discrimination which exists when the interchange of cars between industries on the same switching road is made at a single service charge, while the charge is higher for industries on separate switching roads for the reason that the cars pass over two or more railroads and the rates reflect what is apt to be a higher cost.

Authority of the Interstate Commerce Commission to Require the Opening of Terminals

Prior to 1920 the Interstate Commerce Act imposed upon railroads the obligation to afford all reasonable, proper, and equal facilities for the interchange of traffic between their respective lines and for the receiving, forwarding, and delivering of passengers and property to and from their several lines and those connected therewith.[65] The mandate was, however, qualified by the proviso that the law should not be construed as requiring any common carrier to give the use of its tracks or terminal facilities to another carrier engaged in like business. It is possible that this proviso should have been interpreted to apply only to the physical use of one carrier's tracks or terminal facilities by the power, equipment, or employees of another carrier. Commissioner Hall argued at one time for such an interpretation,[66] and there was some support for his position,[67] but he was unable to convince his colleagues.

Under the Interstate Commerce Act as it stood before 1920 the Commission was able to declare that there was nothing sacred about a railroad terminal. The terminal tracks of a railroad might be put to the purpose of legitimate transportation for the benefit of the public just as its main line was so employed.[68] A belt line might not close its line on the theory that it was private property,[69] nor might a railroad interchange traffic with one connection and refuse to do so with another when conditions were substantially the same.[70] The Supreme Court also distinguished between the case in which a railroad insisted upon its statutory immunity and that in which it voluntarily threw its terminal open to many branches of traffic. When the railroad followed the latter policy, it was obligated to avoid discrimination between its patrons.[71]

[64] H. J. Pfeifer, "Improvements of St. Louis Terminals," *Proceedings of the St. Louis Railway Club,* May 10, 1929. See also T. M. Pierce, "The St. Louis Plan of Unified Terminals," *ibid.,* February 10, 1928.

[65] Section 3.

[66] 40 I.C.C. 679, 693, 1916.

[67] 231 U.S. 457, 1913; 236 U.S. 351, 1915. See *contra,* 212 U.S. 132, 1909.

[68] 28 I.C.C. 621, 1913.

[69] 26 I.C.C. 226, 1913.

[70] 33 I.C.C. 76, 85, 1915.

Yet these were general phrases; and when the Commission was confronted in 1916 with a refusal of the Louisville and Nashville Railroad to switch traffic, originating at or destined to points on the Louisville and Nashville, which was offered by connecting lines at Louisville, Kentucky, or was intended for delivery to connecting lines at Louisville, it declined to interfere. "We cannot believe," said the Commission, "that the law was intended to mean that a competing rail line may now be built between important commercial centers, served by a railroad long established and possessing adequate and valuable terminals at both points, and 'by making a physical connection . . . at an arbitrary point near its terminus' be accorded the right of access to those terminals for originating and delivering freight hauled by it and which the carrier owning the terminals is not only prepared but anxious to carry at rates and under rules and regulations that are subject to all of the requirements and restrictions of the act.[72]

Amendment of 1920

It is only since 1920 that the power of the Interstate Commerce Commission over railroad terminals has been enlarged by the elimination of the qualifying proviso to Section 3 and by the addition to the act of the following explicit grant of authority:

If the Commission finds it to be in the public interest and to be practicable, without substantially impairing the ability of a carrier owning or entitled to the enjoyment of terminal facilities to handle its own business, it shall have power to require the use of any such terminal facilities, including main-line track or tracks for a reasonable distance outside of such terminal, of any carrier, by another carrier or other carriers, on such terms and for such compensation as the carriers affected may agree upon, or in the event of a failure to agree, as the Commission may fix as just and reasonable for the use so required, to be ascertained on the principle controlling compensation in condemnation proceedings. Such compensation shall be paid or adequately secured before the enjoyment of the use may be commenced. If under this paragraph the use of such terminal facilities of any carrier is required to be given to another carrier or other carriers, and the carrier whose terminal facilities are required to be so used is not satisfied with the terms fixed for such use, or if the amount of compensation so fixed is not duly and promptly paid, the carrier whose terminal facilities have thus been required to be given to another carrier or other carriers shall be entitled to recover, by suit or action against such other carrier or carriers, proper damages for any injuries sustained by it as the result of compliance with such requirement, or just compensation for such use, or both, as the case may be.[73]

The amendment of 1920 strengthened the Commission's authority by giving the Commission power to require a carrier to give the use of its

[71] 238 U.S. 1, 1915.
[72] 40 I.C.C. 679, 690, 1916.
[73] 41 Stat. 456, 479–480, 1920. The Act of 1940 altered the text of the Act of 1920

terminal facilities to another carrier engaged in like business provided only (1) that the grant should be in the public interest; (2) that reasonable compensation should be paid; and (3) that the requirement should not impair the ability of the grantee to handle its own business. This was a reversal of the policy which the statute had formerly expressed. The new phrasing enabled the Commission to interfere in terminal administration in a substantial number of cases.[74] Its success in so doing was, doubtless, made easier by its view that the term *facilities* in the law covered the machinery for and the process of terminal switching, as well as terminal tracks and buildings, whether the switching was actually performed by the applying or by the possessing road. Direct operation by one railroad

---

to make it clear that the Commission's authority was restricted to carriers by railroad only (54 Stat. 898, 904, 1940).

[74] The Interstate Commerce Commission construed the term "public interest" with some caution. It had to deal with cases in which railroads with favorable terminal locations endeavored to retain the competitive advantages which they possessed. A prospective gain to an applicant, in such instances, had to be balanced against a probable loss to another railroad. The Commission made large use of general phrases in its decisions, emphasizing the interests of shippers and of the general public, as well as those of the carriers. As between railroads, the Commission was slow, at least upon occasions, to allow the incursion of a competing line. This was the case, for example, when the Commission was asked to require the Pennsylvania to afford the use of its terminal facilities to the Western Maryland at York, Pa., a use which would have divided between the two carriers traffic naturally tributary to the Pennsylvania (73 I.C.C. 40, 1922). It also declined to compel a carrier to turn a warehouse into a freight station and operate it jointly with a competitor when both carriers already operated stations and the request for Commission action was intended to remove handicaps suffered by the inferior line (195 I.C.C. 289, 1933). The Commission did, however, take affirmative action in a number of cases. It ordered a carrier to grant to a competitor the use of a terminal connecting track, holding the record open for 60 days to enable the parties to agree upon the compensation to be paid (161 I.C.C. 699, 1930). On one occasion, the Commission allowed a carrier whose main track terminated 12 miles away from a certain city to use the main-line track of a second carrier into that city in order to reach the property operated by a union terminal. In this case the carrier which owned the 12-mile stretch offered to enter into through rate and routing arrangements with the petitioner, but this was not enough (93 I.C.C. 3, 1924; 146 I.C.C. 171, 1928). At another time, when carrier A owned a track connecting two terminal segments of carrier B, and was willing to allow carrier B to operate over this track as a bridge line, the Commission did not force A to permit B to serve shippers located upon the connecting track (148 I.C.C. 653, 1928). And the Commission has held that it has no authority to require carriers to construct a union station (100 I.C.C. 421, 1925).

The recognition of a carrier's right to compensation is necessary under the Constitution of the United States. It is doubtful if the 1920 amendment added anything to the constitutional protection. The nearest thing to a rule which the Interstate Commerce Commission has announced is that, in determining just compensation, the decisive fact is the loss which the opening of a terminal causes to the owning railroad—not the use value to the nonproprietary corporation. In computing this loss, the Commission will include damages from all actual and direct injuries resulting from the entry of an additional carrier, a share of maintenance costs, and interest charges on the value of the facilities which the incoming railroad uses; for the new use will occupy a part of the premises which the proprietor himself might otherwise have employed (107 I.C.C. 208, 1926).

upon the tracks of another is almost certain to impair the ability of the owning carrier to conduct its business. An order that an owning railroad switch the cars of a connection within a terminal area can be complied with at much less cost.[75]

Emergency Transportation Act of 1933

The Emergency Transportation Act of 1933 declared it to be the purpose of the law, *inter alia,* "to avoid unnecessary duplication of services and facilities of whatsoever nature and permit the joint use of terminals and trackage incident thereto or requisite to such joint use." Regional coördinating committees created by the act were enjoined to carry out these purposes insofar as the carriers had legal powers to accomplish such results. If carriers were unable to proceed because of legal or other difficulties, they were to recommend to the Federal Coordinator that he issue appropriate orders, and the Coordinator was authorized to give these orders and to enforce them. If the regional committees did not recommend, the Coordinator might proceed on his own responsibility. He was hampered, however, by the coincident requirement that his action should not reduce the employment nor impair the compensation of railroad employees.[76]

Armed with these powers, the Coordinator undertook studies of terminal operation at a number of selected cities and published estimates of savings which, in the judgment of his staff, terminal unifications could produce at these selected points. In all, nearly 5,000 projects were considered, including suggested changes at Chicago, St. Louis, and New York, and a number of drastic proposals for reorganization were advanced. Thus at Chicago the Coordinator indicated that the number of major yards might be reduced from 21 to 8, the number of industrial yards from 60 to 18, the number of freight stations from 72 to 12 and the number of passenger stations from 6 to 4. The net saving was set at $10,502,245.[77] Total annual economies of $50,000,000 were believed by the Coordinator's staff to be possible if a thoroughgoing policy of terminal unification were put in force.[78]

[75] According to the Interstate Commerce Commission, the word *facility* may be defined as everything necessary for the convenience of passengers and the safety and prompt transportation of freight. Depots, platforms, spur and side tracks, station grounds, and elevators are parts of facilities. A switch engine used only and entirely for handling freight at a terminal is clearly a terminal facility. A railroad with terminal tracks, signaling devices, and all other necessary instrumentalities but lacking motive power to operate over such tracks, cannot be said to have complete and adequate terminal facilities (69 I.C.C. 489, 494, 1922).

Under this definition the Commission has required a carrier to switch a competitor's cars into its terminals against its will (69 I.C.C. 489, 1922; 112 I.C.C. 125, 1926; 136 I.C.C. 597, 1928; 263 I.C.C. 287, 1945). It has, of course, also sometimes refused to issue such an order (80 I.C.C. 314, 1923; 73 I.C.C. 361, 1922; 73 I.C.C. 40, 1922).

[76] See chap. 30.

[77] *Traffic World,* February 15, 1936.

On the whole, these estimates and suggestions were coldly received by both the railroad management and the labor groups, and they failed to attract much popular interest, probably because of the technical character of the problems with which the Coordinator's reports were concerned. Railroad executives objected to terminal unification in the hands of separate operating companies in general and to the changes which the Coordinator proposed in particular because they feared that simplification might slow down operation and lead to loss of revenue. They objected also to interference with the direct contacts which had been built up between carriers and shippers over many years; and carriers with advantageously located termini were unwilling to surrender the competitive advantages which they enjoyed because of their position. The fundamental advantages of competition were emphasized in contrast to the disadvantages incident to common control. If rail termini were to be consolidated, why not combine also liquor taverns, drugstores, beauty parlors, and churches? [79]

Even more emphatic was the reaction of railroad labor, inspired by the fear that unification would reduce the number of available jobs.[80] This led to public criticism of the activity of the Coordinator and to public defense upon his part. Mr. Eastman argued that normal attrition of the railroad working force would provide a margin that would permit economies without damage to the employees at work at any time, and that reasonable negotiations between labor and management might provide for any additional safeguards that public policy might require,[81] but without effect. The fact that he could secure little voluntary coöperation from either management or labor and the limitations which the law placed upon his initiative prevented the Coordinator from achieving tangible results.

Conclusion

There is reason to believe that the terminal problem will assume even greater importance in the future than in the past, for all types of transport, with the increasing concentration of population in our great cities, the growth in volume of traffic which must be handled, the generally rising level of terminal expense, and the ever keener competition for the occupation and use of city land.[82] It is by no means clear what the final solution will be, or even when immediate steps should be taken to maintain an

[78] United States, Office of the Federal Coordinator of Transportation, *Report on Economy Possibilities of Regional Coordination Projects,* 1935. See also reports on terminal grain elevators made public in 1934 and in 1936.

[79] *Traffic World,* February 23, 1934, p. 326.

[80] In Birmingham, Alabama, for instance, 21 railroad labor organizations formed a central organization to oppose the unification of rail terminals in that city. The unions estimated that unification would throw 820 men out of jobs in the Birmingham terminals and that it would cause an annual payroll loss to Birmingham of $750,000 (*Traffic World,* September 7, 1935, p. 390).

[81] *Ibid.,* December 14, 1935, p. 1025.

equilibrium which threatens to be generally disturbed. The fundamental division at present, insofar as rail carload traffic is concerned, is between those who advocate the continuance of multiple ownership of terminal facilities with cooperation only with respect to noncompetitive business, and those who demand unified terminals, either controlled by an agent of the main line carriers as at St. Louis, or entirely independent, or operated by the state. A compromise suggestion is that freight houses and industry spurs be left to individual control, but that belt lines be constructed at each large city and operated either by the municipality itself or by an independent "system," recognized as such in a consolidation program, and disassociated from any standard railroad control.

Perhaps no single plan will prove everywhere the best, but instead, a variety of remedies may be applied to a highly complicated and varying complaint.

REFERENCES

General Treatises

Droege, John A., *Freight Terminals and Trains,* New York, McGraw-Hill, 1925.

Fair, Marvin L., and Williams, E. W., *Economics of Transportation,* New York, Harper, 1950.

Frederick, J. F., *Commercial Air Transportation,* Chicago, Irwin, 1951.

Landon, Charles E., *Transportation, Principles, Practices, Problems,* New York, Sloane, 1951.

Wilson, G. L., *Coordinated Motor-Rail-Steamship Transportation,* New York, Appleton-Century-Crofts, 1930.

Wilson, G. L., and Bryan, L. A., *Air Transportation,* New York, Prentice-Hall, 1949.

Other Books

Bollinger, Lynn L., Passen, Alan, and McElfresh, Robert E., *Terminal Airport Financing and Management,* Boston, Harvard Business School, Division of Research, 1946.

Frederick, John H., *Airport Management,* Chicago, Irwin, 1949.

Froesch, C., and Prokosch, W., *Airport Planning,* New York, Wiley, 1946.

Hubbard, H. V., McClintock, M., and Williams, F. B., *Airports, Their Location, Administration, and Legal Basis,* Cambridge, Mass., Harvard, 1930.

Periodicals

Bollinger, L. L., "Private Versus Public Management of Airports," *Harvard Business Review,* Summer, 1946.

---

[82] The Interstate Commerce Commission revived the controversy when it remarked, in its annual report for 1947, that present legislation does not give the Commission sufficient power to deal with terminal situations. This provoked a reply that terminal difficulties were now caused by disproportionately high labor costs and by congestion due to high volume of traffic and inadequate facilities. Neither of these causes, it was said, would be removed by unification (*Railway Age,* March 6, 1948, pp. 459, 460).

Cunningham, R. M., "The Steel Container as a Method of Handling Freight," *Harvard Business Review,* April, 1930.

Fagg, Fred D., "The Problem of Airport Size," *Journal of Air Law,* October, 1937.

Fair, Marvin L., "The Interstate Commerce Commission and the Railroad Terminal Problem," *Quarterly Journal of Economics,* May, 1930.

Lynch, E. S., "Railroad Pick-Up and Delivery," *Journal of Land and Public Utility Economics,* May, 1938.

Mayer, H. M., "Localization of Railway Facilities in Metropolitan Centers as Typified by Chicago," *Journal of Land and Public Utility Economics,* November, 1944.

Pence, William D., "Railway Terminal Air Rights Developments and the Movements of Local Land Values," *Journal of Land and Public Utility Economics,* May, 1929.

Wales, H. G., "The Kansas City Wholesale Fruit and Vegetable Market," *Journal of Business,* July, 1946.

Special and Miscellaneous

American Railway Engineering Association, *Proceedings,* vol. 33, p. 117, 1932, vol. 47, pp. 102–104, 1946.

Rhyne, Charles S., *Airport Lease and Concession Agreements,* Washington, D.C., National Institute of Municipal Law Officers, 1948.

United States Department of Commerce, Civil Aeronautics Administration, *Airport Terminal Activities and Space Utilization,* Airport Planning Series, July, 1950.

United States Department of Commerce, Civil Aeronautics Administration, *Civil Aviation and the National Economy,* 1946.

United States Department of Commerce, Civil Aeronautics Administration, *Legislative History of the Federal Airport Act,* vol. 1, Senate Action; vol. 2, House Action, April, 1948.

United States House of Representatives, Committee on Interstate and Foreign Commerce, *Federal Aid for Public Airports,* Hearings on H. R. 3170, 79th C., 1st S., 1945.

United States House of Representatives, *Conference Report to Accompany S. 2, the Federal Airport Act,* House Rep. 1828, 79th C., 2d S., Ser. 11,023, 1946.

United States, Office of the Federal Coordinator, *Container Report,* 1936.

United States, Office of the Federal Coordinator, *Freight Traffic Report,* 1935.

United States, Office of the Federal Coordinator, *Report on Economy Possibilities of Regional Coordination Projects,* 1935.

United States, Office of the Federal Coordinator, *Report of Mechanical Advisory Committee,* 1935.

United States Senate, Committee on Interstate and Foreign Commerce, Hearings before a subcommittee pursuant to Sen. Res. 50, *Airline Industry Investigation,* 81st C., 1st S., 1949.

United States Senate, Committee on Interstate and Foreign Commerce, *Study of Domestic Land and Water Transportation,* 81st C., 2d S., 1950.

Consolidation

The discusion of terminal unification leads naturally to the subject of consolidation. Consolidation may mean, in certain connections, any action, by previously independent companies, which concentrates policy control. It may also mean combination of independently managed units for purposes of operation. We shall consider railroad, motor, and air experience in this chapter. We shall omit inland waterways because the material in the field is relatively slight,[1] and pipe lines because of the peculiar conditions which units of this industry present.

Railroads

The distribution of railway mileage among operating companies in the United States, in 1951, is shown in Table 21.

Persistence of the Short Line Railroad

There are two facts which stand out prominently from the statistics in the preceding table. One is the persistence of the short line railroad. Nearly half of all the companies that operate railroads in this country control, each, 30 miles of line or less, and 76 percent operate not more than 150 miles apiece. Carriers of this type, of course, do a strictly local business. Their costs are high, their revenues are frequently not large, and their number is decreasing, yet many of them perform a service which it would be inconvenient to replace.[2]

[1] But see chap. 32, "Inland Water Regulation."

[2] The problem of the short line railroad deserves more attention than can be given in the text. Some of these carriers are private lines, serving, principally, the lumber and mining industries; others have been constructed primarily to serve the general public. Almost all connect with and some belong to a larger carrier. Generally speaking, short line railroads operate with light rails, over hilly, rolling, or mountainous country, and have heavy grades and sharp curves to overcome. They own their own

TABLE 21. Railroad Mileage in the United States, 1951, Classified According to
Mileage Operated by Companies Reporting to the Interstate
Commerce Commission

Class	Number	Mileage	Cumulative Number (percent)	Cumulative Mileage (percent)
Over 10,000	4	44,611	.88	18.62
9,000.1 to 10,000	1	9,867	1.18	22.74
8,000.1 to 9,000	3	25,284	1.88	33.30
7,000.1 to 8,000	2	15,831	2.22	39.91
6,000.1 to 7,000	5	32,869	3.33	53.63
5,000.1 to 6,000	1	5,117	3.55	55.77
4,000.1 to 5,000	5	27,110	4.67	67.84
3,000.1 to 4,000	1	3,242	4.89	68.43
2,000.1 to 3,000	7	16,752	6.44	75.43
1,000.1 to 2,000	13	19,073	8.93	83.40
500.1 to 1,000	20	14,757	13.78	89.55
150.1 to 500	52	13,952	25.33	95.38
30.1 to 150	122	8,225	52.44	98.81
30 or less	214	2,845	100.00	100.00
Total	450	239,535		

SOURCE: Interstate Commerce Commission, *Statistics of Railways,* 1951.

locomotives but are largely, though not entirely, dependent upon Class I railroad connections for their freight train cars.

During the last 20 or 30 years the importance of the short line railroad has declined.
The extent of the reduction in their number is shown in the following table:

Railroads Reporting to the Interstate Commerce Commission
Which Operated 150 Miles or Less in 1951

Year	Number of Companies	Mileage	Percent of the Number of All Companies Reporting to the I.C.C.	Percent of the Mileage of all Companies Reporting to the I.C.C.
1926	772	24,825	83.10	9.55
1930	630	20,132	81.71	7.68
1951	336	11,070	74.67	4.62

The preceding table shows that between 1930 and 1951 the number of short line
railroads reporting to the Interstate Commerce Commission fell from 630 to 336 and
that the mileage operated decreased from 20,132 miles to 11,070 miles, declines of 47
and 45 percent.

There are a number of explanations for the change referred to, but a list of reasons
would include the following:

Large Operating Units

The other fact which the table presents with striking force is the concentration of mileage for purposes of operation in the hands of a relatively small group of companies. The short line railroads use very little track, numerous as they are and important as they may be from some points of view. On the other hand, 15 companies, with properties ranging from 6,000 to a little over 13,000 miles, operate more than half of the mileage of the country. These are the great enterprises of the railroad world. The list includes the Atchison Topeka & Santa Fe, the New York Central, the Chicago, Milwaukee & St. Paul, the Pennsylvania, the Union Pacific, the Chicago, Burlington & Quincy, the Great Northern, The Southern Pacific, the Chicago and Northwestern, and a number of other companies. The average mileage operated by these companies in 1951 was 9,742 miles, although a few departed widely from this norm.

Control of Subsidiary Companies

If we take into account conditions of control, the concentration is still more noticeable. This is because many large American railroads own a controlling interest in a substantial amount of auxiliary or subsidiary mileage. They are systems, containing several operating units, although subject to a centralized control. The central direction in a system formulates policy and selects the higher personnel. It seldom interferes in operating detail. Among American systems we may mention the Southern Pacific which operated, in 1950, only 8,142 miles but controlled other companies by lease and stock ownership so that the total mileage under

1. Short line railroads have participated in a general shrinkage in the number and operated mileage of all railroads.

2. The passenger business of short line railroads has almost disappeared.

3. Short line railroads have been affected by the diversion of less-than-carload and carload traffic to motor carriers.

4. The exhaustion of natural resources has reduced the traffic of short line railroads which were dependent on particular supplies of timber, ore, coal, sand, gravel, limestone, and other commodities.

5. An appreciable number of short lines have been absorbed into larger systems. Some of the lines so absorbed have been later abandoned, with or without a substitution of motor service.

It is hardly possible to predict the future of short line railroads in the face of these various conditions. The Federal Coordinator of Transportation considered the matter in a report published in 1937, but he was able to offer little in the way of helpful suggestion (United States, Office of the Federal Coordinator, Section of Research, *Report on Short Line Railroads,* reproduced and distributed by the American Short Line Railroad Association, August, 1937). The short line railroads have an association of their own which is active in advocating legislation and in discussing possibilities for future adjustment. There are a number of ways in which aid may be given to short line railroads, if this should be thought desirable. The subject is well discussed in J. M. Herring, *The Problem of Weak Railroads,* Philadelphia, University of Pennsylvania, 1929; and in D. Philip Locklin, *Economics of Transportation,* Chicago, Irwin, 1947. See also W. W. Splawn, *Consolidation of Railroads,* New York, Macmillan, 1925.

its direction was 14,358 miles. The corresponding figures for the Atlantic Coast Line system were 5,505 and 12,545; for the Missouri Pacific 6,948 and 11,324, and for the Pennsylvania 10,117 and 13,154. Such interests are commonly acquired by company funds directed by aggressive management.

Banking and Personal Connections

Finally, concentration may be increased by associations which do not rely upon intercorporate ownership but upon personal holdings and friendships and the prestige of businessmen. These groups may be spoken of as systems, although the word is here used in a somewhat looser sense. The old Huntington, Hill, Harriman, Gould, and Morgan groupings rested largely upon personal ownership. The Van Sweringen system seems to have been a similar example, with individual variations. Probably the importance of such connections has much decreased. Facts brought out by an elaborate congressional investigation and published in 1931 showed that concentrated individual holdings did not, then, amount to a large part of the total stock outstanding in the case of the major railroad corporations, and there is no reason to suppose that this condition has since been changed. Nor are institutional holdings relatively great.[3] What happens still is that small groups of men exercise great influence because of inertia and lack of organization on the part of stockholders and because of personal prestige. Bankers can be influential because railroads must look constantly to the sources of capital funds and must consider the views of persons and organizations through which these funds are sought,[4] and corporation management can maintain itself in power for a number of years, aided by its facilities for proxy solicitation. It would be unlikely that rail carriers, otherwise independent, would be linked by personal and external stock holdings of men who are neither managers nor bankers.

Minimum and Maximum Limits to the Size of Operating Units

From the point of view of operation, a railroad should be large enough to permit of proper division of labor, as most railroads over 1,000 miles in length probably are; and it should connect, if possible, economic areas of different characteristics. For instance, it should join agricultural and manufacturing, or lumber and fruit, or steel- and cotton-producing dis-

[3] The percentage of voting power held by the first and second largest interests in 13 of the largest railroads in the United States never, in 1929, exceeded 10½ percent (United States House of Representatives, *Regulation of Stock Ownership in Railroads,* House Rep. 2789, 71st C., 3d S., 1931, Part I, Ser. 9328).

[4] Among the banks, J. P. Morgan and Co. and Kuhn Loeb and Co. are known to have exerted influence over railroads in which they were interested, although the exact character of this influence is difficult to determine (See National Resources Committee, *The Structure of the American Economy,* 1939–40, appendix 13, pp. 310–312).

tricts, and should not allow itself to be confined within an area where economics, products, and conditions are uniform.

The maximum advisable size of a railroad from the point of view of operation is not easy to define; but the limiting factor is probably the capacity of the supervising personnel. A railroad should not be so great that the controlling officer is unable to inspect it at reasonable intervals and unable to establish personal contact with divisional chiefs and officers in charge of construction projects, if not with men still further down in the line of authority. Sir Henry Thornton, once president of the Canadian Government Railways, has said that one man cannot effectively manage a railroad which is more than 20,000 miles in length. Capacities and conditions, of course, differ; but this limit is not exceeded in the United States nor, with private railroads, in any country of the world.[5]

Optimum Size of Systems

A railroad system should not, presumably, be smaller than the minimum unit referred to in the previous section, but its maximum size need not be controlled by the same considerations. Most legislation in the United States during the past 30 years has dealt with systems, not with operating units. This is mainly because the structure of an operating unit is more difficult to change.

HISTORY OF LEGISLATION. The sequence of federal laws dealing with railroad consolidations between 1920 and 1940 was as follows:

1. *Act of 1920*. Section 5, paragraphs (4) and (6) of the Interstate Commerce Act as amended in 1920, read in part as follows:

(4) The Commission shall as soon as practicable prepare and adopt a plan for the consolidation of the continental United States into a limited number of systems . . .

(6) It shall be lawful for two or more carriers by railroad, subject to this Act, to consolidate their properties or any part thereof, into one corporation for the ownership, management, and operation of the properties theretofore in separate ownership, management, and operation, under the following conditions:

(a) The proposed consolidation must be in harmony with and in furtherance of the complete plan of consolidation mentioned in paragraph (5) and must be approved by the Commission.

2. Section 1, paragraph 18, of the Interstate Commerce Act, as amended in 1920, gave to the Commission power to grant or to deny

---

[5] The limit set forth in the text relates to the geographic extension of a railroad. It is probable, also, that there are limits with respect to the scale of operations. It is entirely possible that a given railroad may reach a condition of increasing costs and decreasing returns as the volume of traffic which it handles grows larger. A carefully prepared study published in 1949 (Thor Hultgren, *American Transportation in Prosperity and Depression*, Studies in Business Cycles, no. 3, National Bureau of Economic Research, 1949) came to a contrary conclusion. This opinion is, however, open to criticism.

certificates of convenience and necessity to cover the extension, new construction, or acquisition and operation of lines of railroad. Literally interpreted, the language of the paragraph covered the case of consolidation or merger, and in a few instances the Commission relied upon its power to grant certificates in authorizing a consolidation.

3. Section 5, paragraph 2, of the Interstate Commerce Act as amended in 1920, read as follows:

Whenever the Commission is of opinion, after hearing, upon application of any carrier or carriers engaged in the transportation of passengers or property subject to this Act, that the acquisition, to the extent indicated by the Commission, by one of such carriers of the control of any other such carrier or carriers either under a lease or by the purchase of stock or in any other manner not involving the consolidation of such carriers into a single system for ownership and operation, will be in the public interest, the Commission shall have authority by order to approve and authorize such acquisition, under such rules and regulations and for such consideration and on such terms and conditions as shall be found by the Commission to be just and reasonable in the premises.[6]

Most mergers between 1920 and 1929 were actually approved under Section 5, paragraph 2. The essential difference between the language in Section 5, paragraph 2 and that in Section 5, paragraphs 4 and 6 of the Interstate Commerce law was that the latter did and the former did not require conformity to any general plan when the two railroads desired to come together. Such conformity was, of course, impossible until a general plan had been announced, and this was not done until 1929. Approval under Section 5, paragraph 2, was admissible, however, when the proposal did not involve consolidation. Generally speaking, plans for the merger of two or more railroad properties take one or the other of the following forms: (1) purchase of all or of a majority of stock; (2) lease; (3) operating agreement; (4) purchase of properties and franchises, except the franchise of the selling company to be a corporation; (5) surrender of franchise by the seller, dissolution of the selling corporation, and acquisition of title to all assets by the purchasing company. Frequently two or more of these methods are employed at the same time, such as lease and purchase of stock; and within each category there is, of course, a considerable variety as to terms. From the point of view of effective control, all five of the methods indicated are alike in that they vest in the acquiring corporation power to dictate the policies of the railroad line that is acquired. The legal difference between the first three and the last two is that in the first cases the corporate identity and the legal title to property of the vendor corporation are both preserved, while in the latter cases corporate identity and legal title to property of the vendor are not both preserved. Cases one to three

[6] 41 Stat. 456, 477, 481, 1920.

do not, and cases four and five, do, constitute "consolidations." Such distinctions are technical and narrow, especially when leases run for several hundred years and stock purchases cover practically all outstanding shares; moreover, there is an advantage in dealing with all five types of merger under a single set of rules. This the Act of 1920 did not do.

Amendment of 1933

By 1933 the Commission had published a general plan and this fact, together with a realization of the defects of existing practice, caused the law to be amended so as to bring all types of merger under a single rule. Hence the Act of 1933, which repealed Section 5, paragraph 2, of the Interstate Commerce Act as it stood in 1920. This amendment now authorized the Commission to approve any consolidations, mergers, purchases, leases, operating contracts, or acquisitions of control which it found (1) to be in harmony with and in furtherance of its general plan for the consolidation of railway properties and (2) to be promotive of the public interest. Congress subjected holding companies to control in so far as they served as agencies for railroad consolidation by the insertion of carefully selected phrases in the law. The same act created the temporary position of Federal Coordinator of Transportation. The Coordinator was empowered to make studies and to issue orders looking, among other things, to the avoidance of waste and preventable expense in railroad operation. This might include orders requiring consolidation. The Coordinator might not, however, issue orders which reduced the number of employees in service or worsened employees' compensation.[7]

Amendment of 1940

Finally, in 1940, the statute was once more changed. These last mentioned alerations had continued the authority of the Interstate Commerce Commission over consolidations, mergers, and the like, but had simplified procedure by permitting the Commission to act when it believed that the consolidation would be in the public interest, without reference to any predetermined plan. To these provisions the Act of 1940 added three interesting paragraphs:

1. The Commission shall have authority in the case of a proposed transaction . . . involving a railroad or railroads, as a prerequisite to its approval of the proposed transaction, to require, upon equitable terms, the inclusion of another railroad or other railroads in the territory involved, upon petition by such railroad or railroads respecting such inclusion, and upon a finding that such inclusion is consistent with the public interest.

The authority conveyed by the preceding paragraph had been, in fact, exercised by the Commission, but it was now for the first time embodied

[7] 48 Stat. 211, 214, 1933.

in the law. Carriers may always refuse to enlarge the terms of a proposed consolidation but, if they do so, the proposal fails.

2. No transaction which contemplates a guarantee or assumption of payments or of fixed charges, shall be approved by the Commission . . . except upon a specific finding by the Commission that such guaranty or assumption is not inconsistent with the public interest. No transaction shall be approved . . . which will result in an increase of total fixed charges, except upon a specific finding by the Commission that such increase would not be contrary to public interest.

This paragraph was inserted, with a minimum of debate, to guide the practice and protect the financial position of consolidating companies.

3. As a condition of its approval . . . of any transaction involving a carrier or carriers by railroad . . . the Commission shall require a fair and equitable arrangement to protect the interests of the railroad employees affected. In its order of approval the Commission shall include terms and conditions providing that during the period of four years from the effective date of such order such transaction will not result in employees of the carrier or carriers by railroad affected by such order being in a worse position with respect to their employment, except that the protection afforded to any employee pursuant to this sentence shall not be required to continue for a longer period, following the effective date of such order, than the period during which such employee was in the employ of such carrier or carriers prior to the effective date of such order. Notwithstanding any other provisions of this Act, an agreement pertaining to the protection of the interests of said employees may hereafter be entered into by any carrier or carriers by railroad and the duly authorized representative or representatives of its or their employees.

These labor clauses were the result of a compromise which the railroad brotherhoods finally accepted as sufficient to induce them to support the new law. By this time the office of Federal Coordinator of Transportation had been abolished and the employees had lost such protection as they had enjoyed under the Act of 1933. The carriers and other advocates of the Act of 1940 agreed to the labor compromise because the pending bill could not be passed without the labor vote.[8]

The Policy of Railroad Consolidation

The highly condensed summary in the preceding pages shows that the subject of railroad consolidation was actively discussed in the United States for at least twenty years, between 1920 and 1940. Some of the debate centered upon particular groupings which were proposed and some turned around large questions of public policy.[9] Speaking generally, the amount

[8] 54 Stat. 898, 906, 1940. See 70 Sup. Ct. Rep. 530, 1950.

[9] The act of 1920, in particular, was an invitation to prepare plans for the consolidation of all railroads in the United States into a limited number of systems.

of railroad consolidation which conformed to the systematic outlines that were published from time to time was very small. Leonard, in his study of railroad consolidations, declares that it was negligible.[10] The reason was, doubtless, first, that railroad consolidation was never compulsory under the federal statute and, second, that large suggestions for reorganization usually ran counter to the interests and ambitions of major established railroad corporations. A large railroad in the United States reacts, through its management, as a territorial group might be expected to behave. It has its loyalties, its sense of power, its hopes for growth, and its antagonisms. These influences are difficult to overcome. What has occurred is some moderate increase in average system size and a more noticeable enlargement of the average size of operating railroad units. Thus in 1920, to cite one illustration, 4.02 percent of the railroad companies in the United States operated 18.36 percent of the mileage while in 1950, 3.62 percent of the companies operated 58.48 percent of the mileage. But this change was rather the result of the disappearance of a number of small companies than the consequence of an increase in absolute size of the companies at the head of the railroad list.

Consolidation and Monopoly

Congress did not endorse a railroad consolidation policy in 1920 because the legislature preferred monopoly to the carrier competition which had characterized rail history. How remote, indeed, was the idea of monopoly from the legislative mind in 1920 is shown by the injunctions which the statute laid upon the Commission to guide the latter in the

---

Those actually formulated include a plan reported by Professor Ripley to the Interstate Commerce Commission in 1920–21 and a revision of this suggestion that the Commission worked out and published in 1921 (63 I.C.C. 455, 1921). They include also a plan finally adopted by the Commission in 1929 (159 I.C.C. 522, 1929) with the reservation that changes might be made. Other plans have been submitted by private parties, such as the Oldham plan (*Railway Age*, November 5, 1921), the Prince Plan (See United States, Office of the Federal Coordinator, *Report on Regulation of Railroads*, 73d C., 2d S., Sen. Doc. 119, 1934), and the so-called Four-Party plan submitted by Eastern railroads to the Interstate Commerce Commission in 1931 and approved with a few changes.

In these plans, the Commission and the Ripley reports proposed to distribute the rail mileage of the United States among 19 systems. The Oldham suggestion set up 14 systems, and the Prince plan, 7 systems. The Four-Party plan dealt only with railroads in Eastern territory; the others were nation-wide. The Prince plan was strictly regional in character; the rest provided competitive systems in the different territories. The Prince plan allocated all railroads in the United States to its 7 systems, except Class I switching and terminal companies that were unassigned and several important terminal properties, such as those at Chicago and St. Louis, which were to be owned jointly by several systems. The Ripley, Oldham, and Four-Party rearrangements considered major systems; the Commission plan of 1929 included a large number of minor companies as well. Since 1940 no general plan for railroad consolidation has been prepared.

[10] William Norris Leonard, *Railroad Consolidation Under the Transportation Act of 1920*, New York, Columbia University, 1946.

formulation of a comprehensive plan. These injunctions required that competition should be preserved as fully as possible, and that wherever practicable the existing routes and channels of commerce should be preserved.[11] It may seem paradoxical to require consolidation and to expect competition to be preserved, but the opposition is more apparent than real, and both policies may be enforced.

The Support of Railroad Credit

Congress did believe that consolidation might make it easier to support railroad credit by the manipulation of railroad rates. The Act of 1920 directed the Interstate Commerce Commission to establish rates so that carriers as a whole, or as a whole in each of such rate groups or territories as the Commission might designate, would earn a fair return upon the value of their property used in the service of transportation. The legislature was committed to this policy, but it understood that an increase in rate levels which would enable railroads on the average to earn a fair return would permit some carriers to earn more than a fair return while others still failed to collect a reasonable amount. Senator Cummins was the most influential man in the Senate at this time, so far as railroad legislation was concerned, and it was his view that consolidation which brought all systems to something like an average earnings level would remove this obstacle to a promising method of control. The logic of this opinion can be disputed, but it was accepted at the time.[12]

[11] 41 Stat. 456, 1920, Sec. 5 (4).

[12] The weakness of the theory upon which Senator Cummin's view was based lay in the fact that consolidation does not prevent excess profits, but only conceals them. Let us suppose, for example, that four railroad corporations exist, each with an investment of $50,000,000, all charging the same rates, with earnings as follows:

Corporation A	$5,000,000
Corporation B	4,000,000
Corporation C	2,000,000
Corporation D	1,000,000

Let us suppose further than $3,500,000 constitutes a fair return upon a capital of $50,000,000. If there are 1,000 stockholders in each corporation, and if every stockholder holds the same number of shares as every other, then each stockholder in Corporation A will receive $5,000, in Corporation B, $4,000, in Corporation C, $2,000, and in Corporation D, $1,000. Since a fair return is assumed to be $3,500,000, or $3,500 per stockholder, we may suppose that the facts justify Corporations C and D in requesting an advance in rates. Or, what amounts to the same thing, we may suppose that Corporations C and D will be unable to attract new capital unless their revenues are increased.

Senator Cummins delighted to argue that an advance under the conditions given would be denied, for the advance would benefit Corporations A and B as well as Corporations C and D and would cause the dividends to stockholders of A and B to rise as well as dividends to stockholders of C and D. What the corporations should do, he said, was to consolidate, A with D and B with C, thus producing two corporations, each with an investment of $100,000,000, and with earnings of $6,000,000, or $1,000,000 less than a fair return. This income could then be raised to $7,000,000 by

Diffusion of the Resources of Strong Railroad Companies

Is it ever desirable to unite two railroad properties, one weak, one strong, when the union only conceals and does not remove the fact of weakness? Putting the Cummins argument aside, the answer to the question depends on whether it is legitimate to draw upon the resources of strong railroads to improve service or to lower rates in territories which weak railroads formerly supplied. This is one possibility that grows out of consolidation. If it is realized, shippers in one section will be called upon to contribute for the benefit of shippers in another section. Evidently some persons will gain but, on the other hand, some persons will lose. Certainly it will be easier for New England to secure fresh capital for rail construction if the Pennsylvania Railroad owns her railroad lines than if she is served by an independent company, for the Pennsylvania can draw upon the resources of the states of Pennsylvania and Ohio, while the New Haven relies upon the industries of New England alone. But the Pennsylvania may have less left for Ohio if she puts her credit at the service of the New England states. If it is the duty of government to promote a certain equality in the rate of development of all parts of its domain, or even if a government desires results which will not flow from the uncontrolled processes of industry, then mergers may be encouraged for the very reason of the shifts in funds which they permit. This is one advantage of government ownership of all of a country's railroad lines, for in such a system the resources drawn from rail operations constitute a disposable surplus to be applied wherever government policy directs. The

a rate advance without impropriety; for there would be neither weak nor strong roads, and no one would be overpaid.

But it is clear enough that if the terms of the imagined merger have been controlled by the relative earning power of the corporations concerned—and this would be a reasonable basis in a voluntary negotiation—the proceeds of an advance in rates after consolidation would be distributed to the same persons and in the same proportions as before. For on such a basis the old stockholders of Corporation A will hold 5/6 of the stock of Corporation AD, and the former stockholders of Corporation B will hold 4/6 of the stock of Corporation BC. The effect of a 16 percent increase in rates before consolidation would have been to give the stockholders of Corporation A an advance of $800,000, or 16 percent of $5,000,000. The effect of the same advance after consolidation will be to give them 5/6 of an advance of $960,000, which is the same amount.

Locklin says, generally, that Congress was not particularly concerned with what happened to stockholders when it passed the Act of 1920. It was interested, he says, in preserving the existence of weak lines which were thought to be worth saving, and in creating systems of equal earning power in order to facilitate rate making. This was doubtless true. But the fact that made rate making really difficult, as Congress looked at the problem, was the circumstance that some corporations needed more money and other corporations did not. Congress objected to any policy which gave additional revenue to companies with adequate earning power. It can hardly be argued that, when Congressmen spoke of companies in this connection, they did not ultimately have in mind the individuals who owned the companies. Congressional reasoning does not separate corporate and human entities in such a remote and abstract way.

danger is that the processes of politics may prove to be as uncontrolled as those of industry, and as little promotive of the general good.

Economies in Operation

Consolidation may enable the consolidating companies to operate at less expense. This may be true when weak and strong lines get together and it is likely when there is a merger of efficient lines. The combined savings which may result from railroad consolidation are variously described, but they may include the following:

1. *Reduction in overhead expenses.* Consolidation lessens clerical work in railroad offices because it cuts down the number of intercompany transactions and makes it possible to combine tax returns and statistical reports required by state and federal governments. Frequently, also, the supervisory personnel which a single consolidated company employs will be smaller than the personnel needed by two or more separate organizations; indeed, the general offices of a small railroad are sometimes entirely closed when the road is taken over by a large connecting line.

2. *Saving in operating costs.* The Chicago, Milwaukee & St. Paul bought the Chicago, Terre Haute & Southeastern in order to obtain coal on more favorable terms. Another sort of saving may be secured by simplification of procedure at junction points of the consolidating systems. It may be possible, also, to close some shops on a system or, if all shops are continued in use, the carriers may be able to confine certain shops to particular types of work. Again, division points may be changed and terminals may be consolidated. It is true that operating savings may lead to the discharge of employees, and that rearrangements of methods of operation may cause other workmen to shift their residences and so impose upon them a considerable expense, but this is, perhaps, inevitable, and the gain may outweigh the loss. Another saving may result from the fact that freight cars of a consolidated system will be "at home" on all parts of it, so that they can be put at the public service without limitation and when in need of repair can be fully repaired where they are, instead of being sent back to a home line.

3. *More effective use of plant.* This is a matter which can be discussed from many points of view, some of which bear upon subjects mentioned in the preceding paragraph. The operating advantages which may follow when several railroads combine in the ownership or operation of a terminal are well known. It is also true that two companies may supplement each other's terminal facilities, as when one railroad has well-placed terminals in one city, while another railroad has special terminal advantages in another town. Passing from the question of terminals, we find instances where the acquisition of a particular piece of line may be of considerable importance to an acquiring system. Thus a railroad may be

able to use a well-placed track for detour purposes in the event of a break in its own line. Or a subsidiary may be used regularly as double track. The Southern Pacific, to cite an example, expected in 1924 to secure the advantage of double-track operation between Tucson and El Paso by acquiring the line of the El Paso and Southwestern. If the purchased mileage is well located, the advantages are, of course, increased. The purchase of the Chicago, Milwaukee & Gary by the St. Paul enabled the latter company to handle through traffic between its Eastern connections and all points on its system in the Northwest without passing it through the congested switching district of Chicago; the value of the Gary for this purpose was thought to justify the responsibilities incident to its acquisition.

It sometimes happens that two systems may be described as "complementary"; and where this is true, consolidation may lead to very great improvements in the effective use of plant. In general, if freight produced upon the lines of one railroad is marketed upon the lines of another or customarily passes over the tracks of another on its way to market, the companies participating in the haul regard themselves as complementary; but it does not necessarily follow that such is the case. Two railroads may, however, be specially fitted to work together, either because one possesses certain facilities such as refrigerator cars or stock cars or special types of locomotives that the other needs, or because the lines of one company afford more direct routes than lines of other carriers for interline movements to and from the territory served, or because the peak loads of the two systems do not coincide in time or in space.

Economies of the nature described in the foregoing paragraphs may follow consolidation; but they do not, of course, necessarily occur, especially when companies which are already large increase the scale of their operations.

Summary of Arguments in Favor of Railroad Consolidation

The general character of the arguments for railroad consolidation is apparent from the discussion in this chapter. It is asserted, in brief, that mergers will simplify the task of regulation by reducing the number of companies with which the government has to deal. This will be administratively convenient, and it will be of particular advantage when the government addresses itself to the regulation of railroad rates. Consolidation will diffuse the resources of prosperous railroad lines, and it will permit operating economies of a great variety of kind.

Arguments Against Consolidation

Opponents of consolidation believe that the policy, rightly understood, is of no help in supporting railroad credit. They take occasion, moreover, to object to the philosophy implicit in much consolidation discussion, by asserting bluntly that prosperous railroads have no more reason to take over embarrassed railroads than prosperous bankers or farmers or manufacturers have to contribute to the support of business which does not pay. It is denied that consolidation will produce economies or, at least, if economies are admitted it is contended that they will be offset by the decreased efficiency inherent in the operation of large properties, widely scattered, by a small number of centralized organizations.

The policy of establishing large systems is further criticized on the ground that it will retard the abandonment of ill-judged enterprises; that it will make for rigidity, prematurely forcing traffic into channels which may not suit the industrial development of future years; that it will lessen competition; that it will reduce employment; that it will require expensive financial and corporate reorganization; and that it will be highly difficult of accomplishment in a country where dissatisfied minorities can resort to judicial process to enforce their real or supposed constitutional rights.

Generally speaking, railroad executives oppose compulsory railroad consolidation because it systematizes the industry and limits the field for imagination and initiative. The exercise of these qualities, they believe, is essential to efficiency in transportation service. Rail labor opposes consolidation, also, but principally upon the ground that it will reduce employment. As Mr. Willard of the Baltimore and Ohio once said, it is not human nature for a man to want to consolidate himself out of a job. Of the two types of opposition, that of the labor group is the more effective. It can be allayed in one of two ways, if at all. The first is to attach to the approval of each specific consolidation the condition that the employees of consolidating railroads shall continue to be employed in the same or in equivalent jobs. With such a rule the pay roll of any railroad system might be gradually cut down but the process would be slow. The other solution is some form of dismissal wage. This was the policy agreed to by the railroad labor organizations and by the greater part of the rail managements of the United States in 1936. Arrangements of these sorts have imposed considerable expense upon the railroads, but probably not more than public policy should require.

Motor Consolidation

Motor and air mergers have attracted less attention, during the past 30 years, than have railroad consolidations. This is doubtless due to the fact (1) that no general policy has been announced by Congress; and (2) that private proposals have been of a narrower range.

Motor Transportation. Carriers of Property

Only a beginning has been made in the consolidation of independently owned trucking companies. In 1951 there were 1,737 Class I common and 215 motor contract carriers of property engaged in intercity service reporting to the Interstate Commerce Commission.[13] The operating revenues of motor carriers of property in intercity service totaled, in 1951, $2,500,719,375. (Excluding companies which carried both property and passengers.) There were, however, only 17 carriers whose revenues exceeded $10,000,000. The six largest carriers of property in intercity service were, in sequence: The Associated Transport, with operating revenues, in round numbers, of $37,000,000; the Roadway Express, with revenues of $29,000,000; the Consolidated Freightways, with revenues of $28,000,000; the Allied Van, with revenues of $25,000,000; Riss & Co. and the Interstate Motor Freight, each with revenues of $21,000,000; and the Pacific Intermountain Express, with revenues of $20,000,000. No other intercity motor carriers, common or contract, earned as much as $15,000,000 in 1951, and only one, the United Parcel Service of New York, earned as much as this in local service. The average operating revenue of all Class I motor common carriers in 1951 only slightly exceeded $1,000,000. This indicates a very moderate degree of concentration.[14]

Legislative and Administrative Regulation of Motor Truck Consolidation

It is safe to say that the relatively small size of trucking units is due to the newness of the industry, to the small investment required of entrants, and to the lack of an established connection with the capital market. It is not the result of legislative or administrative repression.[15] As a matter of fact, the statutory law makes the consolidation or unification of operation of motor trucking companies relatively easy, and the Interstate Commerce

[13] Excluding carriers engaged in local and suburban service, and 26 companies carrying both freight and passengers.

Class I motor carriers, up to and including 1949, were those which reported an annual operating revenue of at least $100,000. The limit was changed to $200,000 in 1950. Class I carriers of property, in 1949, received about 76 percent of the total of revenues of interstate and local carriers of property reported by Classes I, II, and III. Class I carriers of passengers accounted for about 89 percent of the total of revenue reported by all classes.

[14] Interstate Commerce Commission, Bureau of Transport Economics and Statistics, *Statistics of Class I Motor Carriers, 1951.*

[15] The Interstate Commerce Act relieves carriers that may desire to consolidate from any regulatory control of the process when the aggregate number of motor vehicles owned by the parties does not exceed 20 [Sec. 5 (10)]. And it also relieves all consolidations from the prohibitions of the antitrust laws in cases of consolidation which the Interstate Commerce Commission has approved [Sec. 5 (11)]. The United States Department of Justice has argued that it was the intent of Congress in enacting Section 5, in which these provisions appear, that the Commission should approve only transactions which would not result in "unreasonable" restraint of competition within the meaning of the antitrust laws, regardless of benefit that might occur or the adequacy of remaining competition. But the Commission has refused to accept this view. It has remarked that such an interpretation would render the provisions of Section 5 largely meaningless (38 M.C.C. 137, 150–151, 1942).

Commission, which has authority, is friendly.[16] Thus the Commission said, in the Associated Transport case of 1932:

Consolidation of these carriers into one unit would present many opportunities for greater economy and efficiency of operation. It would permit of more efficient and greater utilization of equipment, and corresponding reduction in consumption of motor fuel and tires. Many carriers are now finding it difficult to provide adequate equipment to meet the needs of the shipping people. Consolidation of the tonnage of the carriers would result in a higher load factor on vehicles used in over-the-road service, and there would be a large reduction in the number of trucks required for peddler runs and for pick-up and delivery service at terminal points. Extension throughout the proposed system, as planned, of scientific maintenance and safety programs, which the carriers involved have been unable to undertake to the extent which would be possible to applicant with the combined facilities and resources, would add to the average life of equipment and result in more economical and safe operation and in fewer road failures. The experience and the garage and testing facilities of Consolidated and Horton would be of material assistance in carrying out such a program. Vehicles could be readily shifted from one part of the system to another to meet peak demands and extraordinary needs, and by reason of that fact less reserve equipment in the aggregate would be required.[17]

The economies in scale referred to in the quotation from the Associated Transport decision should not, the Commission thinks, be denied motor truck companies merely because unification with other companies would make them large. Large motor carrier systems have a place in the industry as well as small. And the danger of monopoly is small. Mr. Eastman once remarked that, under existing transportation conditions, monopoly was the thing which was least to be feared. However, he added, if a monoply on any route should develop, the Commission could grant operating authority to a new concern and comparatively little investment would be required to establish competition.[18]

The position of the Interstate Commerce Commission and its power to implement its views has led to a multiplicity of applications for approvals of mergers, acquisition of stock control, leases, purchase of property and operating rights and other forms of intercarrier relationships between motor truck concerns. Most of these applications, however, have involved small unifications in areas of active competition. The principal problems have been financial; or they have concerned the degree of economy to be

[16] The regulation of motor vehicle consolidation by the Interstate Commerce Commission will be again discussed in chap. 31.

[17] The Associated Transport Company had applied, in 1932, for permission to acquire control by purchase of stock of eight corporations doing business in New Jersey, North Carolina, Massachusetts, Connecticut, New York, Virginia, and Georgia (38 M.C.C. 157, 1932. See also 40 M.C.C. 557, 595, 1941, and 45 M.C.C. 309, 321, 1946).

[18] 36 M.C.C. 61, 1940.

expected; or sometimes, when consolidation seemed to threaten more intensive development of a given route and this was opposed by other carriers in the territory, the alleged equities of established lines have been invoked.[19] The net result of the Commission's attitude in these matters should be, in time, an increase in the number of relative large motor truck corporations. But the tendency has not yet produced a striking change.

Motor Buses

In 1951 there were 166 motor companies, reporting to the Interstate Commerce Commission, which carried passengers in intercity service in the United States. Of these 61 earned, each, more than $1 million. The total revenue from intercity passenger transport was $392,578,888.

For one reason or another, consolidation of motor bus services in this country has progressed further than has the consolidation of motor trucking companies. The largest companies are three: The American Bus, the Transcontinental Bus, and the Greyhound companies.[20] The most im-

[19] In one interesting case the Commission refused to permit the consolidation of two connecting motor organizations which proposed, together, to offer a transcontinental service. The decision was based, in part, upon the probable diversion of traffic from rail to truck. The Commission observed, in this litigation, that railroads had an inherent advantage in their ability to transport freight in large volume, for long distances, at low operating cost; it held that the motor applicants had not shown that they possessed a comparable advantage in handling the traffic that was expected. (57 M.C.C. 341, 1950; 57 M.C.C. 467, 1951.)

[20] The American Buslines operates between New York, Philadelphia, and Washington, D.C., at one end and Los Angeles and San Francisco via Pittsburgh, Chicago, St. Louis, Dallas, El Paso, and Phoenix, Arizona, at the other. In 1951 it merged with the Burlington Transportation Company, operating between Chicago and St. Louis and Los Angeles and San Francisco via Omaha and Lincoln, Nebraska, Denver, and Salt Lake City (50 M.C.C. 299, 300, 1947; 55 M.C.C. 305, 1948; 57 M.C.C. 673, 1951), and in 1953 it was taken over by the Transcontinental Bus.

The Transcontinental Bus was organized in 1947 to take over certain operating rights and property of the Santa Fe Trails Company, the Dixie Motor Coach Corporation, and the Continental Company, along with a number of less important lines. Of these, the Santa Fe Trails had been controlled by the Atchison, Topeka & Santa Fe Railroad and its operations were conducted largely over routes parallel to that company's lines (See 45 I.C.C. 653, 655, 1947). The Dixie Motor operated chiefly in eastern Texas, although also in Arkansas, Louisiana, and Oklahoma; the Continental operated almost entirely in Texas. The Transcontinental now owns all of the stock of Continental, all of the motorbus operating rights and property of the Santa Fe Transportation Company, and all of the motorbus operating rights and certain property of Dixie. It also owns stock in some other companies. Its own stock is, mainly, held by the interests which formerly controlled the interests now vested in Transcontinental Bus.

It may be noticed that one result of the consolidation of 1947 was that the Atchison, Topeka & Santa Fe Railroad, which formerly controlled the Santa Fe Trails Company, came to hold 39.1 percent of the Transcontinental Bus, or less than a controlling interest. The Santa Fe Trails Company ceased, therefore, to be "controlled by or affiliated with" a railroad, under the interpretation used in the Greyhound cases (50 M.C.C. 193, 1947; 50 M.C.C. 305, 447, 1947).

The Transcontinental and other carriers are members of a nation-wide association of independent motorbus companies known as National Trailways Bus System, which

portant, the Greyhound, is a group held together by the Greyhound Corporation, which is a holding company, incorporated in Delaware in 1926. By 1951 the Corporation had become a stockholder in companies that furnished a coördinated intercity bus service extending into 46 states and the District of Columbia and into 7 Canadian provinces. It operated 6,280 buses over 89,585 miles of line.[21] This extraordinary development can be at least partly accounted for by three things: first, efficient overall planning; second, successful organization; and third, the acquisition of bus lines in certain sections of the country which railroads had developed. With respect to the first, the efficiency of planning may, probably, be assumed from the results. On the second point, the Corporation has managed to combine centralized general control with decentralized operation. What happened was that the corporations which formed part of the Greyhound system in increasing number, as the system grew, were grouped on regional bases. There was a parent company in each region. This parent company might operate directly in any case. Where there was more than one company in a region, as might occur, the companies were distinct but the officers were usually identical and policy and management were determined by the parent which was itself controlled in a general way by the Greyhound Corporation of Delaware. This seemed to provide a degree of operating decentralization which was satisfactory to the company's local clientele.

As for the railroad interest, there were bus corporations in certain regions, as in the Northwest, which railroads had previously set up. These corporations had not been too profitable; they were, moreover, handicapped by statutory rules which applied to motor corporations affiliated with a railroad. The railroads were persuaded or they seized the opportunity to transfer their bus properties to some Greyhound "parent." The railroad bus lines became subsidiaries of the parent and the railroad acquired a stock interest in the parent, in no case exceeding 50 percent, with managment committed by contract to the Greyhound Corporation.[22] From the railroad point of view this accomplished two things. First, the joint interest between the railroad and Greyhound in the local companies had the practical effect of transforming an operating deficit into an operating profit. And secondly, the domination of the Corporation re-

was organized for purposes of national advertising and coördination of schedules with a view to competing more effectively with the Greyhound system. The Trailways organization is relatively strong in the Southeastern section of the United States and along the Atlantic seaboard extending into New England. It is weaker in the inland area north of Tennessee and Virginia and east of Cincinnati and Columbus, Ohio (United States House of Representatives, Committee on Interstate and Foreign Commerce, *Transportation Study*, Hearings before a subcommittee, 81st C., 2d S., 1950, testimony Rogers, p. 144).

[21] *Moody's Manual*, 1952, p. 521.

[22] 1 M.C.C. 77, 1936; 1 M.C.C. 342, 1936.

lieved the regional enterprises from the statutory rules which have been mentioned. Specifically, a "parent" company in a group was not considered to be controlled by or affiliated with a railroad even though the railroad owned a portion of the parent's stock. The parent could, therefore, apply for certificates or for the approval of purchase of new motor properties without the limitations imposed by Section 213 (later Section 5) of the Interstate Commerce Act.[23] From the point of view of the Greyhound Corporation, railroad participation provided, in effect, a new source of capital, and at the same time encouraged railroad coöperation in operation.[24] Undoubtedly these relationships contributed greatly to the Greyhound system's growth.

Concentration in Motor Bus Operation

There may be some question whether the Greyhound Corporation, by itself, is in a position to exercise monopoly control of intercity motor bus operation in the United States. The size of the organization is, however, very great. In 1936 there were 7 regional companies in the system, with Greyhound ownership in 5 ranging from 50 percent to 66.66 percent.[25] The sixth company was completely owned. In 1951 the Corporation reported 12 regional companies. In 6 of these Greyhound owned 100 percent of the stock; in 2 it owned 50 percent; and in the rest its proportion of ownership lay in between.[26] Current figures do not permit overall comparisons; but in 1949 the Greyhound System owned 38 percent of all the buses owned by Class I motor carriers of passengers engaged in intercity service which reported to the Interstate Commerce Commission, and the System earned 49 percent of the total revenues derived from this service. This by itself was a considerable concentration. If we add the American Bus and the Transcontinental Bus the concentration is still greater. In dealing with this situation the Interstate Commerce Commission has permitted consolidation to develop in the motor bus field because of the greater efficiency of coördinated operation. Representatives of Greyhound have gone further. They have argued that the terms of the Transportation Act of 1940 indicate a national policy to favor unifications of motor carriers, as well as of rail carriers, if these unifications produce a public benefit. The Commission has refused to accept this principle.[27] It is

---

[23] See chap. 26.

[24] 45 M.C.C. 33, 1946.

[25] 1 M.C.C. 342, 1936.

[26] The railroads interested in the regional companies included the Great Northern, the Southern Pacific, the Pennsylvania, the Richmond, Fredericksburg and Potomac, and the St. Louis and Southwestern. The Pennsylvania, in 1951, owned 50 percent of the common and preferred stock of the Pennsylvania Greyhound. In all other cases the railroad holdings were less than 50 percent (*Moody's Manual, Public Utilities*, 1952, p. 500).

[27] 45 M.C.C. 83, 91–92, 1946.

not, however, averse to large-scale operation in the carriage of passengers by bus.

Air Transportation

Air-line corporate history, up to 1938, was confused. The period of the late 1920's and early 1930's was characterized by absorptions or consolidations of competing lines, the bidding for and acquisition of new routes, reorganizations, and extensions. It was during these years that the American Air Lines (originally organized as American Airways), the Transcontinental and Western Air, the United Air Lines, the Northwest Airways, and the Eastern Air Lines had their beginning. The important influence in the development of the airline structure was the mail contract. Consolidation as a technique received no special attention, either before or after the cancellation of air contracts in 1934,[28] although some amalgamations occurred. The fact that an air line consisted of little more than an organization, a given number of planes, and a right to operate kept the situation fluid, as well as the circumstance that the distribution of rights became the subject of violent political dispute.

Concentration in Ownership

Air-line ownership in the United States is concentrated, in spite of the lack of much unification of independent enterprises, in the sense that a few large companies do most of the air-line business. Table 22 supplies the statistical basis for this last statement. It shows that four companies

TABLE 22. Domestic Air-Mail Carriers: Scheduled Operations, 1950

Companies	Revenue Passenger Miles	Ton-Miles (Mail, Express, Freight, Excess Baggage)	Operating Revenue
			(thousands of
	(000)	(000)	dollars)
American, United, T.W.A., Eastern	5,484	156,853	360,962
Northwestern, Braniff, Capital, Chicago & Southern, Delta, Western	1,708	52,146	117,311
Colonial, Continental, Inland, Mid-Continent, National, Northeast	573	7,932	44,811
Total	7,765	216,931	523,084

[28] Henry Ladd Smith, *Airways: The History of Commercial Aviation in the United States*, New York, Knopf, 1944.

handle more than 70 percent of the air passenger and freight business of the country and earn 69 percent of the operating revenues. Three of these, American, Transcontinental and Western Air (now Transworld), and United connect the Atlantic and Pacific coasts and also serve the populous area between Chicago and New York. One, the Eastern, operates between Boston, New York, New Orleans, and Houston, Texas. The spread of these companies is, therefore, nation wide.

Consolidations, Agreements, Interlocking Directorates

Since 1938 the consolidation of air-line companies has been subject to the control of the Civil Aeronautics Board. In the present context the term includes consolidation, mergers, acquisitions of control, agreements, interlocking directorates, and pooling arrangements. The Civil Aeronautics Board must control these activities in order to make its certificate policy effective, as well as for more specific reasons.

The provisions of the Civil Aeronautics Act which relate to consolidation in its various forms may, for convenience, be separated into three parts:

1. *Consolidation.* The Act distinguished four operations:

    a. Consolidation of two or more air companies.

    b. Consolidation of rail, water, or motor common carriers with air common carriers.

    c. Consolidation of foreign with domestic air companies.

    d. Consolidation of aircraft manufacturing companies with companies engaged in common carriage.

Persons seeking approval of a consolidation, merger, purchase, lease, operating contract, or acquisition of control must apply to the Civil Aeronautics Board. There is a public hearing. The Board may approve the application unless it finds that the proposal will not be consistent with the public interest; except that it cannot approve a merger which will result in monopoly or jeopardize an air carrier not party to the plan. Consolidations which have been approved are immune from attack under the antitrust laws.[29]

2. *Agreements.* Air carriers must file with the Board copies of contracts or agreements affecting air transportation; and these may be approved or disapproved according to the relation to the public interest.[30]

---

[29] C.A.A., Sec. 408 (b), provides "that the Authority shall not approve a consolidation, merger, purchase, lease, operating contract, or acquisition of control which would result in creating a monopoly or monopolies and thereby restrain competition or jeopardize another air carrier not a party to the consolidation, merger, purchase, lease, operating contract, or acquisition of control . . ."

[30] The clause referred to in the text reads as follows:

"Sec. 412 (a). Every air carrier shall file with the Authority (Board) a true copy

The language of the Act is broad enough to cover an agreement for the simple exchange of equipment in through service,[31] pooling agreements,[32] and agreements for soliciting traffic.[33] It would doubtless cover the instance of the "traffic association" which has, in rail and motor transport, occasioned controversy.

3. *Interlocking directorates.* Section 409 of the Civil Aeronautics Act reads, in part, as follows:

(a) . . . it shall be unlawful, unless such relationship shall have been approved by order of the Authority upon due showing . . . that the public interest will not be adversely affected thereby—

(1) For any air carrier to have and retain an officer or director who is an officer, director, or member, or who as a stockholder holds a controlling interest, in any other person who is a common carrier or is engaged in any phase of aeronautics.

This may be regarded as a variant of the prohibition of consolidation. However, most of the cases have involved relations between air carriers and airplane manufacturing companies and not between competing air carriers.[34]

. . . of every contract or agreement . . . affecting air transportation . . . between such air carrier and any other air carrier . . . for pooling or apportioning earnings, losses, traffic, service, or equipment, or relating to the establishment of transportation rates, fares, charges, or classifications, or for preserving and improving safety, economy, and efficiency of operation, or for controlling, regulating, preventing, or otherwise eliminating destructive, oppressive, or wasteful competition, or for regulating stops, schedules, and character of service, or for other cooperative working arrangements.

"(b) The Authority (Board) shall . . . disapprove any such contract or agreement . . . that it finds to be adverse to the public interest, or in violation of this Act, and shall . . . approve any such contract or agreement . . . that it does not find to be adverse to the public interest, or in violation of this Act . . ."

[31] 1 C.A.B. 723, 1940. See chap. 23.

[32] There have been relatively few pools in air operation, in the formal sense. An interesting illustration, however, which the Board approved, involved two Alaskan air companies, one with a base at Juneau and another with a base at Katchikan, Alaska. These two companies arranged to install a service, with alternate flights, using each others' termini as necessary. The Board gave its temporary approval (8 C.A.B. 127, 1947).

A variation which was not, strictly, a pool, occurred in 1940 when the Pan American Airways, the Matson Navigation Company, and the Inter-Island Steam Navigation Company proposed to set up a joint corporation to conduct air transportation between the West Coast of the United States and the Hawaiian Islands. The Board disapproved, on the ground that this arrangement would impair competition (3 C.A.B. 540, 1942).

[33] In 1947 the Pan American Airways appointed the United States Lines—a steamship corporation—its general agent in a number of European countries. The United States Lines was given a commission, in return for which it solicited traffic for Pan American and furnished meteorological and other data which were of service to Pan American in its transatlantic operations. The parties argued that there was no real competition between the air and the steamship lines in this case. The Board ruled, however, that the agreement was not in the public interest (8 C.A.B. 609, 1947).

[34] Joint relations between air carriers and manufacturers may cause the former to pay

The sections of the Act which relate to consolidation, agreements, and interlocking directorates show some anxiety for the promotion of competition among air lines and for the protection of air carriers against control by other forms of carriage.[35] It will be observed that these sections deal with other questions also, such as the relations between domestic and foreign air companies and that between people who fly airplanes and people who build them. The Board's power over agreements is particularly comprehensive. The consolidation sections supplement those which deal with the use of certificates. They are less effective in maintaining competition, because it is easier to encourage competition by granting new certificates than by supervising contracts which airlines may wish to make.

Air-Line Consolidations Since 1938

In 1938 there were 15 domestic air trunk lines reporting to the Civil Aeronautics Authority, in addition to the Hawaiian lines. Three more, All American Aviation, Marquette, and the Colonial Lines, were added in 1939 and 1940. In 1950, fourteen of the original 15 lines were still in operation, as were the Colonial Lines. Two companies, the Catalina Air Transport and the Marquette, with a combined route mileage of 576 miles (in 1938) had disappeared; and one company, the All American Aviation, had concentrated from the beginning upon local and pickup business. In addition, one company, the Inland Airlines, had joined with another, the Western Airlines, although it retained its separate corporate existence.[36]

---

excessive prices for equipment or to be unduly limited in choosing the types of planes best suited to its operations (1 C.A.B. 498, 1939; 1 C.A.B. 547, 1940; 7 C.A.B. 27, 41, 1946; 7 C.A.B. 863, 898, 1947; 8 C.A.B. 672, 1947). Manufacturing companies are regarded as engaged in a phase of aeronautics. The Board has refused to permit a person to serve as director of an air line and a steamship line on the ground that the latter was another common carrier (8 C.A.B. 617, 619, 1947). On the other hand, the Board has allowed officers of air lines to act as directors of Air Cargo, a corporation organized to formulate a program for the development of air cargo and air express (3 C.A.B. 711, 1942).

[35] See chap. 33.

[36] The Catalina Air Transport operated planes between Avalon, in Santa Catalina Island near the California coast, and Wilmington, Long Beach, and Los Angeles. Most of its traffic was summer business. The company was not profitable and was, apparently, glad to sell to the United Airlines (2 C.A.B. 798, 1941).

The Marquette, operating between St. Louis and Detroit, was bought by the Transcontinental and Western Air in 1939 (3 C.A.B. 111, 1941). There was some question at the time as to the validity of the grandfather proceedings under which the company had been allowed to do business. The property was, in any case, small, and not too apparently successful.

Control over the Inland Airlines, operating between Cheyenne, Wyo., Huron, S.D., and Great Falls, Mont., was acquired by Western Airlines in 1943 in a deliberate attempt to expand the latter system. The two services had little in common. The Western, however, had a superior record of efficiency, and the Civil Aeronautics Board approved the purchase, although the decision of the Board was not unanimous (4 C.A.B. 654, 1943).

During later years there were some changes in name, some transfers of property, and some actual or attempted sales,[37] but up to the present writing there have been no important consolidations, unless the merger of the Mid-Continent and the Braniff Airlines, can be counted as such. There are several, however, in process of consideration.[38]

General Proposals for Air Consolidation

There have been proposals to encourage air-line consolidation, for varying purposes.

Thus Mr. Fred Gardner testified before a Senate Committee in 1949:

This policy (of the C.A.B.) has resulted in an air-line system similar to a tree which grew too fast and now needs material pruning for permanent shaping and to insure continued survival.

There should be a wholesale consolidation of airlines, with the thought in mind of cutting to a minimum the duplication in stand-by costs which are . . . $160,000,000 a year, one-third of present costs, a substantial element in the cost of operating the airlines.

These consolidations must be based on a hard-boiled, impartial, practical solution to the problem of merging and integrating our domestic air-line systems. The prime purposes should be to cut down excessive competition and provide the most efficient network for profitable service and for national defense requirements.[39]

[37] One instance was the transfer, by Western Airlines to United Airlines, of a route between Denver and Los Angeles. The segment had enabled Western, at one time, to participate in traffic between Los Angeles and Eastern points. But the development, particularly, of a nonstop service by United Airlines between Los Angeles and Chicago had deprived the Western route of much of its importance. Transfer from Western to United was a reasonable result (6 C.A.B. 298, 1947).

A second problem concerned the disposition of the Mid-Continent Airlines. This company had suffered financially from war conditions in the early 1940's, and its owners desired to sell. The first proposal was to consolidate Mid-Continent with the American Airlines. The Civil Aeronautics Board refused permission for this merger because it found little advantage from the point of view of operation. In 1952 Mid-Continent was consolidated with Braniff Airways, more than doubling the size of the latter system.

There have also been a few minor operations or suggested plans. These include a proposal by National Airlines to acquire stock of Caribbean-Atlantic Airlines, doing business in the West Indies, which the Civil Aeronautics Board disapproved (6 C.A.B. 671, 1946); an application by the Braniff Airway to buy control of a Mexican corporation (6 C.A.B. 947, 1946); and an application by certain carriers in Alaska (6 C.A.B. 110, 1947). The Board acted favorably on the last two applications. Neither were significant from the point of view of air-line consolidation. See also Orlando Airlines (7 C.A.B. 429, 1946) and T.W.A.-Arizona Airways (7 C.A.B. 787, 1947).

[38] The purchases or mergers currently proposed concern Delta Air Lines and Chicago & Southern, and Eastern Air Lines and Colonial.

Consolidation and transfer up to 1948 are discussed in an article by Louis E. Black in the *Journal of Air Law and Commerce*, Autumn, 1948, pp. 409–433; and Winter, 1949, pp. 20–39.

[39] United States Senate, Committee on Interstate and Foreign Commerce, *Air-Line Industry Investigation*, Hearings pursuant to S. Res. 50, 81st C., 1st S., 1949, p. 877.

In 1951 it was suggested, with a somewhat different emphasis, that the larger companies other than the Big Four should be brought together. Here the proposal was that the 12 minor organizations should be merged so as to create organizations which were comparable in size to the larger air lines. It was further stipulated that these companies should be arranged so that two carriers of equal strength should compete in every market capable of supporting a single line.[40] This was not markedly different from the consolidation legislation applied to railroads in 1920. It would be subject to similar criticisms, although it might be easier to introduce.

Some rearrangements of the routes served by the more important air-line companies may take place during the next few years; the effect may be to improve load factors and, in some cases, perhaps, to provide a broader basis for the support of air-line overhead expense. But it may well be that the regulatory authorities will find it easier to adjust service, if this should be desirable, by the grant or transfer of certificates than by corporate consolidation. The reasons are that air-line operation is relatively fluid because no route investment is needed for a change and that air-line organizations can be changed with speed as airplane traffic grows.

Conclusion

Looking at the different agencies of transport, the general conclusion seems to be that consolidation of carriers has occurred within the United States, but that, except in the case of railroads and motor buses it has not been specially emphasized as a device. Concentration in the transport industry is, nevertheless, considerable. Summarizing the information presented in this chapter, it appears that 1 motor bus system out of 166 received approximately half of the operating revenues earned by bus lines reporting to the Interstate Commerce Commission in 1951, and that two other corporations earned a substantial proportion of the rest. In air transport, four companies out of sixteen earned 69 percent of the operating revenues of all trunk line domestic air companies. And among the railroads, 15 out of 450 corporations operated more than half and 10 companies more than one third of the total mileage.

There is no evidence to establish the fact that either consolidation or concentration has established a monopoly of transport in the United States. Rivalries between and within the various agencies continue; moreover, the wide extent of what is technically known as "private carriage" and the supervision of regulatory commissions seems to have kept any possibility of any general monopoly successfully in check. It is possible, though not certain, that the growth in the size of operating units, up to a certain point, has improved efficiency by transforming what would be

[40] "Public Regulation of Domestic Airlines," *Yale Law Journal*, November, 1951, pp. 1196–1217.

otherwise a problem of intercarrier coordination into a task of intrasystem management. This is most likely where the objectives of the parties has been focused upon expense. The case for the continuation and expansion of consolidation, in the public interest, rests upon the assumption that such an improvement in efficiency will commonly occur.

REFERENCES

General Treatises

Bigham, Truman C., and Roberts, Merrill J., *Transportation, Principles and Problems*, New York, McGraw-Hill, 1952.

Chapman, John W., *Railroad Mergers*, New York, Simmons-Boardman, 1934.

Fair, Marvin L., and Williams, E. W., *Economics of Transportation*, New York, Harper, 1950.

Grodinsky, Julius, *Railroad Consolidation, Its Economic and Controlling Principles*, New York, Appleton-Century-Crofts, 1930.

Leonard, W. N., *Railroad Consolidation Under the Transportation Act of 1920*, New York, Columbia University, 1946.

Locklin, D. Philip, *Economics of Transportation*, Chicago, Irwin, 1947.

Miller, S. L., *Inland Transportation*, New York, McGraw-Hill, 1933.

Parmelee, J. H., *The Modern Railway*, New York, Longmans, 1940.

Puffer, C. E., *Air Transportation*, Philadelphia, Blakiston, 1941.

Smith, Henry Ladd, *Airways. The History of Commercial Aviation in the United States*, New York, Knopf, 1944.

Splawn, Walter M., *Consolidation of Railroads*, New York, Macmillan, 1925.

Other Books

Daggett, Stuart, *Railroad Consolidation West of the Mississippi River*, Berkeley, University of California, 1933.

Herring, J. M., *The Problem of Weak Railroads*, Philadelphia, University of Pennsylvania, 1929.

Sharfman, I. L., *The Interstate Commerce Commission*, Part III, vol. A, New York, Commonwealth Fund, 1935.

Simnet, W. E., *Railway Amalgamation in Great Britain*, London, Railway Gazette, 1923.

Periodicals

Baker, G. P., "The Possibilities of Economies by Railroad Consolidation and Coordination," *American Economic Review*, March, 1940.

Black, Louis E., "Realignment of the Domestic Airline Route Pattern," *Journal of Air Law and Commerce*, Autumn, 1948 and Winter, 1949.

Daggett, Stuart, "Judicial Proceedings for the Separation of the Central Pacific and Southern Pacific Railroad Lines," *University of California Chronicle*, October, 1922.

Daniels, W. M., "Economic Purposes and Limitations of Consolidation," *American Economic Review Supplement*, March, 1924.

George, John J., "Supreme Court Views, Federal Authorization and Merging of Motor Carriers," *Land Economics,* May and August, 1950.

Koontz, H. D., "Domestic Air Line Self-Sufficiency: A Problem of Route Structure," *American Economic Review,* March, 1952.

Leonard, W. N., "The Decline of Railroad Consolidation," *Journal of Economic History,* May, 1949.

Nelson, J. C., "Economics of Large Scale Operation in the Trucking Industry," *Journal of Land and Public Utility Economics,* February, 1941.

Oldham, J. E., "The Problem of Railroad Consolidation," *Harvard Business Review,* January, 1923.

Ripley, W. Z., "Geographical Limitations of Consolidated Systems," *American Economic Review Supplement,* March, 1924.

Simpson, S. P., "The Interstate Commerce Commission and Railroad Consolidation," *Harvard Law Review,* December, 1929.

Special and Miscellaneous

National Resources Committee, *The Structure of the American Economy,* Appendix 13, 1939–1940.

United States House of Representatives, Committee on Interstate and Foreign Commerce, *Transportation Study,* Hearings before a subcommittee, 81st C., 2d S., 1950, testimony Rogers (discussion of motor vehicle consolidation).

United States Interstate Commerce Commission, *Report to the Interstate Commerce Commission on Consolidation of Railways,* 63 I.C.C. 455, 465, 1921.

United States Interstate Commerce Commission, *In the Matter of Consolidation of Railroads,* 159 I.C.C. 562, 1929; 185 I.C.C. 403, 1932.

United States Interstate Commerce Commission, *Railroad Coordination and Consolidation: A Review of Estimated Economies,* prepared by B. N. Behling, Statistical Analyst, Bureau of Statistics, 1940.

United States, Office of the Federal Coordinator of Transportation, *Report on Regulation of Railroads,* 73d C., 2d S., Sen. Doc. 119, 1934.

Coördination

Meaning of Coördination

"Coördination," like "appeasement," is a word of inclusive meaning. Mostly, however, it refers to the complementary and harmonious use of, or the selection between, different tools or different techniques in rendering a given service or in producing a given good. These tools or techniques may be under a common administrative control, which determines the kind and the amount of each which shall be employed and the spatial and other relations which shall exist between the various units. We have discussed problems of this sort in the chapter on "Coöperation." The work of adjustment in such cases becomes a rather common form of business or of military or government activity. It presents a certain novelty in the field of transport only when carrier management handles some tools or uses some methods that are relatively new. Or, in the second place, different tools and techniques may be under different administrative direction. Here there is a clash of contending interest and the setting up, perhaps, of competing tests of merit. Tools and techniques are now represented by spokesmen, and we hear of railroad interests and motor vehicle interests and air interests and water interests. Governments which attempt to mediate set up on their part indirect controls, and coördination becomes the name attached to a somewhat confused attempt to prevent unnecessary waste when several rivals each insist upon the superior facility with which either can perform a job. The comments in this chapter are mainly, though not entirely, addressed to situations of this sort.[1]

[1] The term *coördination* has been employed, according to Peterson, to indicate:

1. Coöperative or joint action by two or more independent operating agencies of a single type in performing acts of transportation. The phrase "single type" here refers to assemblies of techniques and apparatus which have customarily functioned under a common control.
2. Coöperative or joint action by two or more independent agencies of different types in performing acts of transportation.

Joint Action of Independent Agencies

It is frequently possible for agencies under independent administrative control to join in performing an act of transportation. Thus one carrier may haul from A to B and a connecting carrier may haul from B to C in the case of a shipment which originates at A and comes to rest at C. This is coördination, and there is a good deal of it today, especially in cases where transportation requires services which one of the carriers involved may find it inconvenient to supply. Interagency transfers and through routes supply obvious examples.

1. *Interagency transfers.* The physical participation of two or more types of carrier in a single movement is facilitated when goods must, in any event, be unloaded from the vehicles in which they were first installed, at some agency meeting point; as in the case of articles received in a railroad car at a city terminal and necessarily reshipped to a local consumer or destination. We have here the basis of much rail-motor coördination.

Joint hauls are relatively easy when goods are shipped in packages that are conveniently interchangeable. The reader is referred to the use of "containers" and of "speedboxes" which were described in chapter 24. The demountable truck trailer is only an extension of the idea expressed in the container. In this case the entire body of the truck is used as a container; this body is shifted from the truck chassis to a railroad flat car at a convenient place of interchange. A less elaborate method is to load a trailer, chasis and all, upon railroad equipment. This can be done when demountable truck bodies are not available.[2] It saves a good

3. Use by a single operating agency, in performing acts of transportation, of machinery or techniques which have, customarily, been independently controlled.
4. Arrangements or agreements by two or more independent operating agencies of different types for the division of traffic, so that each will do that work for which it is inherently best fitted. The arrangements may cover (a) a field which is already occupied; or (b) a field which it intended to invade.

Peterson adds that persons who discuss coördination sometimes emphasize the elimination of waste, reduction in transport cost, and precise adjustment of service to demand which coördination can bring about. They sometimes consider the conditions, such as free competition, integrated control, or government regulation which, in their judgment, make coördination likely. (See G. Shorey Peterson, "Transport Coordination," *Journal of Political Economy,* December, 1930, pp. 661–681.)

[2] The New York, New Haven & Hartford Railroad provides what it calls "trailer-on-flatcar service." Motor carriers and shippers of various classes of freight, located in Boston, bring motor trailers, loaded with freight, into Yard 5 of the railroad. The trailers are detached from motor tractors, then lifted upon and fastened to a railroad flatcar and thereafter transported to New York. Trailers, similarly transported, come into Boston from New York, and trailer-on-flatcar service is provided at other points in the New Haven system.

Labor union teamsters picketed the described service, in 1952, on the ground that it eliminated over-the-road truck drivers. The union was, however, permanently enjoined from interfering with the railroad's trailer-on-flatcar operations (*Traffic World,*

deal of handling cost. Similar practices are used by specialized steamships that are equipped to take railroad cars aboard at one terminal and deliver them at another. These operations approximate equipment exchange, although the analogy is not complete.

2. _Through routes._ We have a somewhat more elaborate form of coördination when rail and motor or rail and water agencies agree upon through routes and rates. The nature of a through route was described in chapter 23. It is a familiar device in railroad practice. The operational advantages to the participating carriers are of the same kind when agencies of different types take part, if the parties are equally responsible, as they are when arrangements are made by agencies of a single type. On the other hand, an extended system of through routes may divert traffic from lines which are more direct. This is unimportant when only one administrative unit is concerned. It arouses controversy when there are several operating and owning units. The law requires some interagency through route arrangements, but it is not general upon this point.[3] Different agencies of transport have made little use of through routes and rates in their relations with each other except in the case of rail-water operations, where the authority of the Interstate Commerce Commission has been compelling.[4]

March 28, 1953, p. 283). In Italy, there are contrary cases in which a railroad freight car is hauled upon a truck trailer (_Traffic World,_ February 6, 1954, p. 34).

[3] The establishment of through routes in which agencies of different sorts coöperate is required by statute to the following extent:

1. Common carriers by railroad. Railroad common carriers must establish through routes and rates with water common carriers upon reasonable request. They may set up through routes and rates with motor carriers, but they are under no obligation to provide such routes and rates.

2. Common carriers by motor vehicle. Motor common carriers may establish through routes and rates with common carriers by railroad and by water. They are under no obligation to provide such routes and rates.

3. Common carriers by water. Water common carriers must establish through routes and rates with rail common carriers. They may establish such routes and rates with carriers by motor vehicle.

4. Common carriers by air. Air common carriers may establish through service and joint rates, fares, and charges with other common carriers.

[4] Interagency through route practice may be summarized as follows:

Air and rail. Air carrier service was effectively coördinated with rail service on long hauls in the period before night flying became common. Passengers flew by day and they were then transferred to railroads for the continuance of their movement during the night. This technique was abandoned when airplanes began to travel both day and night. Passengers and freight still arrive at air termini by rail or motor, but there are few or no examples of through routes and rates between surface and air agencies in the formal sense.

Motor and rail. Motor-rail coördination exists to some extent but it is limited by the unwillingness of railroads, for competitive reasons, to join with motor carriers in the establishment of through routes and rates. The Association of American Railroads declared, in 1937, that it was not desirable for railroads to enter into joint billing arrangements with, or to advance charges to, motor carriers except where the services of the motor carriers were within a terminal district. The United States Department of

Advantages of Joint Action of Independent Agencies

The advantages of joint action by independent agencies are obvious, when this is possible. Through routes are a convenience to the shipper and generally to the participating carriers. There is a clear gain also when connecting carriers coöperate with integrated schedules, interchangeable equipment, and special arrangements or facilities for freight transfer. It is to be hoped that coördination of agencies under independent administrative control will steadily increase. There is certainly no public sentiment which will discourage progress toward this result.

Integrated and Multiple-Type Carriers

There is controversy, however, when a single agency, in performing acts of coördination, itself uses machinery or techniques which, previously, have been independently controlled. It would be an illustrative case if a railroad carried traffic by truck or by airplane as well as over rails; or if a steamship accommodated its passengers, in part, by planes. Such arrangements might be perfected for some service over the entire route of a railroad or a steamship company, or they might be developed only on portions of a route or at times when the advantages seemed to be the most pronounced.

A railroad which chooses between rail and motor units and fits either or both into its operating scheme makes technical decisions which are the same in nature as decisions between standard and Diesel locomotives or

Justice charged that this declaration violated the Antitrust Act, and the resolution was withdrawn (*Transport Topics,* July 21, 1941). There is little evidence, however, that the policy of the railroads has changed. Mr. Knudsen, Defense Transport Administrator, has urged that railroads should, at least, develop through rail-motor routes to and from points which are not located upon a railroad line (*Traffic World,* July 5, 1952, p. 22).

Air-motor-water. Some water carriers have joined with trucks as well as with railways in joint arrangements, but on the whole little progress has been made (United States Board of Investigation and Research, *A Report on the National Traffic Pattern,* Sen. Doc. 83, 79th C., 1st S., 1945, pp. 100, 103, Ser. 10, 944).

Rail and water. The principal rail-water movements are as follows:
1. By rail from interior points to coastal cities and thence to destination by a water line.
2. By water from a point of assembly on the Great Lakes to a receiving point elsewhere upon the Lakes and thence to destination by rail; and
3. By water to the Mississippi River system to a river port and thence by rail to destination.

It is understood that reverse movements may occur in these various cases.

Carriers frequently quote through rates from point of origin to point of destination upon these movements. It is possible, however, to obtain substantially the same result by a combination of local and proportional rates. The proportional rate has been explained in chap. 19. In 1945 the Interstate Commerce Commission refused to require the establishment of joint rates on grain reaching Chicago by barge, but fixed instead reasonable proportional rates to cover the cost of further movements by rail (262 I.C.C. 7, 1945). This was still, however, a form of coördination.

between coal and oil as a source of power. It coördinates in either case in the sense that it selects the most effective equipment for its work.

There are new problems, however, if two assumptions are introduced.

The first assumption is that an organization which adopts a new technique may proceed in such a way as to hinder the improvement of the technique and not so as to develop it to the fullest possible extent. It is conceivable, for instance, that a railroad may add to its equipment by the purchase of competing independent motor companies and that it may, subsequently, make only incidental use of the facilities which these companies had actively employed. There is no proof that this would happen, but the suspicion is entertained.

The second assumption is that sound public policy requires the independence of techniques and, especially of motor and air techniques, whatever may be the effect, at any moment, upon the efficiency of the transport organization as a whole. There are those who hold this view, in these cases, because, in their opinion, (1) independent motor and air companies deserve protection because they have been innovators in their field. This is a position with ethical implications. It is also maintained (2) that the quality of carrier operation will improve more rapidly if there are companies whose existence depends entirely upon their specialized success; and (3) that competition will be more active between one-type enterprises than between companies which employ expedients of many sorts.

The arguments for and against the development of multiple transport agencies have been vigorously presented during recent years, and particularly in connection with rail-motor, rail-air, and again with reference to water-air transportation. In the former case the objections to expansion of these organizations have been emphasized by the wide-spread motor industry. There is, on the other hand, a substantial demand for freedom in transport organization by persons interested in railroad and in water shipping and by those who hesitate to impose limitations upon combinations of methods of operation which seem likely to produce good technical results. The subject will be better understood if more detail can be supplied.

Rail-Motor Coördination

There are several reasons, specifically, why a railroad may wish to operate motor trucks.

1. A railroad may desire to pick up and to deliver freight at terminals. When the practice was first introduced, the rail carriers contracted with independent trucking companies; but, later, they operated trucks themselves in a majority of cases. There is not much objection, at present, to this procedure.

2. A railroad may wish to penetrate an area which its tracks do not

reach. This is an expansion, but one which can be accomplished at little cost if motor vehicles are used. There is little opposition if the territory is not already occupied by other railroad or trucking companies.[5]   There will be opposition if the territory is occupied and the regulatory body will be asked, in such a case, to judge the public need. Strictly speaking, the railroad is not, in this instance, only selecting machinery with which to meet an established responsibility. It is asking for a new certificate. Its request is therefore complicated in principle by its proposed use of new apparatus for the performance of new service, and this may prejudice its application.

3. A railroad may propose to introduce a bus or truck service and, simultaneously, to withdraw a railroad line. These are cases of railroad abandonment, mitigated by a partial replacement. The question of principle in such cases is whether the railroad bus or truck service is to be regarded as a new operation in the area concerned or whether it is to be taken as the old service in another form. The Interstate Commerce Commission may here require the railroad to apply for a certificate of public convenience and necessity on the theory that the railroad motor vehicles are new entrants into a territory made vacant by the rail withdrawal.[6] Such a certificate will, obviously, be difficult to obtain if the rail line is being abandoned because traffic has shifted from rail to road, for in this case motor service will be already available. The result is that the railroad will be prevented from adopting its competitor's technique in an attempt to retain business which the railroad once possessed.[7]

4. A railroad may propose a trucking service in the area which its rail line serves; it may wish, at the same time, to operate its railroad line. What often happens is that the railroad intends to substitute trucks for local way-freight trains. The railroad is frequently allowed to use trucks for such a purpose, but upon conditions which limit the efficiency with which its motor vehicles can be employed.[8] The railroad not only objects

---

[5] The Interstate Commerce Commission has granted many railroad applications for permission to install motor service in unoccupied territories. (See 1 M.C.C. 225, 1936; 3 M.C.C. 711, 1937; 15 M.C.C. 296, 1938; 15 M.C.C. 427, 1938; 15 M.C.C. 691, 1939; 21 M.C.C., 725, 1940; 25 M.C.C. 96, 1939; 25 M.C.C. 171, 1939; 31 M.C.C. 643, 1942; 33 M.C.C. 759, 1942.)

[6] United States House of Representatives, Committee on Interstate and Foreign Commerce, *Transportation Study,* Hearings before a subcommittee on Transportation Problems, 81st C., 2d S., 1950, testimony Rogers, p. 150.

[7] There are, of course, instances where the issue of a certificate is not opposed and where the promise of motor service allays objections to the withdrawal of a railroad line (217 I.C.C. 511, 1936. See also 34 M.C.C. 599, 1942; 41 M.C.C. 219, 221, 1942).

[8] The conditions which the Interstate Commerce Commission imposes in the case mentioned in the text are the following:

1.   That a railroad may not serve, with motor trucks, stations which are not stations upon its railroad line. This prohibition holds even though the highway route between railroad stations passes through off-railroad communities.

to these conditions, but it desires to go much further than the Interstate Commerce Commission is willing to permit.

Reasons for the Attitude of the Interstate Commerce Commission

The reluctance of the Commission to encourage the coördination of rail and motor service under railroad direction in cases where its consent is refused or qualified is partly the result of statutory construction. Thus the Commission finds support for its position in the preamble to the Transportation Act of 1940,[9] and also in Section 213 of the Motor Carrier Act

---

2. That railroad-owned vehicles must follow routes parallel and adjacent to the railroad. This enforces the provision in the preceding paragraph.

3. That shipments carried by a railroad motor service must be limited to freight which the motor organization receives from or delivers to the controlling railway under a through bill of lading covering, in addition to the motor movement, a previous or subsequent movement by rail. The application of this principle may be illustrated by the following diagram.

Kansas City	A	B	Texar-kana	Port Arthur

Let the above diagram represent a section of the Kansas City Railroad. All places indicated are stations upon this railroad. Let it be supposed that the Kansas City Southern proposes to establish motor carriage between Kansas City and Port Arthur. Such an application was actually made to the Interstate Commerce Commission in 1938 (10 M.C.C. 221, 1938). Under the decision rendered by the Commission in the Kansas City Southern case the railroad was allowed to introduce motor transport, but its trucks could serve no off-line stations. They could pick up and deliver freight only at Kansas City, towns A and B, Texarkana, and Port Arthur. Moreover, the company could carry no freight to or from stations on its line unless this freight had received or was to receive, railroad transportation. It could not, that is to say, accept freight originating at A and destined to B, or freight originating at B and destined to Texarkana.

4. That a rail-owned motor service may transport goods between points upon its line even though these goods have not previously moved and will not subsequently move upon the railroad. This is a qualification of or an alternative for the rule stated in paragraph (3). But where this qualification is allowed, a substitute restriction is introduced. It is that the Commission may name certain key points upon the railroad line; it is also stipulated that the rail-owned motor carrier shall not transport shipments between, or through or to or from more than one of the key points designated. In this version the restrictions in paragraphs (1) and (2) are retained.

Under the provisions here stated, and assuming that Kansas City, Texarkana, and Port Arthur are key points, it becomes possible for a railroad-owned motor company to carry (1) freight between A and B in the diagram; and (2) freight between A or B and Kansas City or between A or B and Texarkana. It is not permissible for a railroad owned motor company to transport (1) freight between Kansas City and Texarkana, Texarkana and Port Arthur, or Kansas City and Port Arthur; or, (2) freight between A or B and Port Arthur. (See 40 M.C.C. 457, 1946; 42 M.C.C. 586, 1943; 43 M.C.C. 470, 1944; 43 M.C.C. 767, 1944; 44 M.C.C. 401, 1945; 46 M.C.C. 69, 93, 1946; 47 M.C.C. 433, 1947.)

[9] The Act of 1940 sets forth the National Transportation Policy as follows:

"It is hereby declared to be the national transportation policy of Congress to provide for fair and impartial regulation of all modes of transportation subject to the provisions of this Act, so administered as to recognize and preserve the inherent advantages of each . . . all to the end of developing, coordinating, and preserving a national trans-

covering purchase and consolidation.[10] It also, however, expresses a wish to protect the independent motor carrier from intensified competition. This position is clearly stated in a leading case in 1936, cited with approval in 1946,[11] in which the Commission said:

We are not convinced that the way to maintain for the future healthful competition between rail and truck service is to give the railroads free opportunity to go into the kind of truck service which is strictly competitive with, rather than auxiliary to, their rail operations. The language of Section 213 is evidence that Congress was not convinced that this should be done. Truck service would not, in our judgment, have developed to the extraordinary extent to which it has developed if it had been under railroad control. Improvement in the particular service now furnished by the partnership might flow from control by the railroad, but the question involved is broader than that and concerns the future of truck service generally. The financial and soliciting resources of the railroads could easily be so used in this field that the development of independent service would be greatly hampered and restricted, and with ultimate disadvantage to the public.

The details of the situations given show how the selective use of carrier machinery may, with this spirit, and under certain circumstances, be limited and controlled.

Air-Water Coördination

Interagency coördination problems are considered by the Civil Aeronautics Board as well as by the Interstate Commerce Commission. The principles followed by the Board are similar to those which we have discussed in previous pages. The technical rule is differently worded, but the substance is the same. When a carrier other than an air carrier desires to buy or to consolidate with an air carrier the Board will approve only when the purchased company's operations are auxiliary and supplemental to the operations of the acquiring company.[12] The Board applies sub-

---

portation system by water, highway, and rail, as well as other means, adequate to meet the needs of the commerce of the United States, of the Postal Service, and of the national defense. All of the provisions of this Act shall be administered and enforced with a view to carrying out the above declaration of policy."

[10] Now Part I, Sec. 5 (2) of the Interstate Commerce Act.

[11] 1 M.C.C. 101, 111, 1936; 40 M.C.C. 457, 467, 1946.

[12] This is the Board's interpretation of Section 408 (b) of the Civil Aeronautics Act of 1938. The Act provides for hearings in consolidation cases. It then continues:

"Unless, after such hearing, the Authority finds that the consolidation, merger, purchase, lease, operating contract, or acquisition of control will not be consistent with the public interest or that the conditions of this section will not be fulfilled, it shall by order approve such consolidation . . . upon such terms and conditions as it shall find to be just and reasonable and with such modifications as it may prescribe: *Provided,* That the Authority shall not approve any consolidation . . . which would result in creating a monopoly or monopolies and thereby restrain competition or jeopardize another air carrier not a party to the consolidation . . . *Provided further,* That if the applicant is a carrier other than an air carrier, or a person controlled by a carrier other

stantially the same policy when a surface carrier proposes to install rather than to purchase an airplane operation.[13] It justifies its unwillingness to grant air certificates to surface carriers by two arguments:

In the first place, the entrance of surface carriers into the field of air transport will, the Board believes, threaten the solvency of existing air carriers.

The Board would not be justified [said the Civil Aeronautics Board in 1947], in closing its eyes to the potential threat which the entry of surface carriers

---

than an air carrier within the meaning of section 5 (8) of the Interstate Commerce Act as amended, such applicant shall for the purposes of this section be considered an air carrier and the Authority shall not enter such an order of approval unless it finds that the transaction proposed will promote the public interest by enabling such carrier other than an air carrier to use aircraft to public advantage in its operation and will not restrain competition."

[13] Strictly speaking, installation air cases are governed by Section 401 of the Civil Aeronautics Act. This section reads as follows:

"Sec. 401 (a) No air carrier shall engage in any air transportation unless there is in force a certificate issued by the Authority authorizing such air carrier to engage in such transportation.

"(d) (1) The Authority shall issue a certificate authorizing the whole or any part of the transportation covered by the application, if it finds that the applicant is fit, willing, and able to perform such transportation properly, and to conform to the provisions of this Act and the rules, regulations, and requirements of the Authority hereunder, and that such transportation is required by the public convenience and necessity; otherwise such application shall be denied."

Section 401 (d) (1) requires only a showing of public convenience and necessity. The Board originally held that a surface carrier applying for a certificate should also show that the proposed air service was auxiliary and supplemental to its surface operations (3 C.A.B. 619, 1942; 6 C.A.B. 857, 1946). This, in effect, applied the Sec. 408 (b) rule to Sec. 401 (d) (1) cases.

In 1947 the Civil Aeronautics Board reconsidered its first opinion to the extent of holding that restrictions enumerated in Sec. 408 (b) were not legally controlling in cases under Sec. 401 (d). It still maintained, however, that the language in Sec. 408, as well as all other indications of the intent of Congress, could and should be considered in appraising the public convenience and necessity required for favorable action under the regulatory law (7 C.A.B. 799, 1947). This decision reduced the rigidity of the Board's position by abandoning the unqualified conclusion that no surface carrier should be permitted to engage in air transportation except when this transportation was auxiliary to its own surface operations, but it left the Board free to consider the policy expressed in Sec. 408 as one of the standards which might be applied in the Board's decisions under Sec. 401. Admiral Landis, in a concurring opinion, emphasized the importance of flexibility in handling questions of this sort. It is not clear, however, that the Board's position was really changed.

The Civil Aeronautics Board does not recognize the possibility of "restricted" air operations. While it does not assert that it will never grant a certificate to a water carrier, it has felt compelled to refuse such a certificate when the only applicant was a water carrier and to prefer an air line to a shipping line when these companies competed for the privilege of operating over a given route. The Civil Aeronautics Board does not follow the practice of foreign governments upon these points. Nor is it influenced by the opinion expressed in Congress that its policy may be too severe.

Cases before the Civil Aeronautics Board which raise questions considered in this note and in the text have mostly dealt with water-air relations. In 1944, however, the Board applied its interpretation of Sec. 401 to a proposed operation of helicopters by the Greyhound Corporation (6 C.A.B. 1, 1944).

into this field would in many cases offer to independent air carriers. . . . Surface carriers engaging in air transportation would at times be under a strong incentive to act for the protection of their investment in surface transportation interests. Again, by reason of their superior resources and extensive facilities for solicitation, such carriers would often be the possessors of powerful competitive weapons which would enable them to crush the competition of independent air carriers. This threat is not peculiar to air transportation, as will be apparent from those decisions of the Interstate Commerce Commission which have sought to safeguard the development of motor transportation against the unrestricted entry of rail carriers into the motor carrier field.[14]

Somewhat illogically the Board also maintains that there will be less competition if surface carriers operate air lines, because a transportation company engaged in both sea and air transport will be slow in developing the latter service. If this is true, the new air line, if owned by a surface carrier, will compete less rather than more strongly with independent air carriers. A reduction in competition the Board believes, in this case, to be disadvantageous.

In the second place, the Board has argued that the grant of certificates to surface carriers will retard the development of air transportation as such. It explained a refusal to permit certain shipping companies to operate an air line between New York and San Juan, in 1946, by observing that the Board was expressly charged with a public responsibility for the development of an air transportation system adequate to the needs of our commerce, our postal service, and the national defense. Then it continued:

A major objection to reliance upon the claimed advantages of the combined sea-air service plan under a single management and ownership in determining the comparative public interest in the selection of a carrier to render an air service is that at times it will be incompatible with the promotional and competitive objectives which have been made the subject of an express mandate of the Congress to the Civil Aeronautics Board. It can hardly be doubted that an indifference on the part of management to the question of whether a prospective traveler uses the company's boats or its airplanes would not be consistent with the fullest development of the potential air travel market. The proposed combined air-sea service would seek the sale of air transportation on the plan of 'one way by air—one way by boat.' The applicants who propose such a plan are here confronted by independent air carrier applicants dedicated solely to the advancement of air transportation and bent on selling air travel not one way but both ways on the proposed route.[15]

The result of all this has been a policy very similar to that which the Interstate Commerce Commission has endorsed elsewhere, but without the relaxations which it has been possible for the Commission to allow.

[14] 7 C.A.B. 799, 803, 1947.
[15] 6 C.A.B. 857, 903, 1946.

Rail-Air Coördination

Railroads and air lines coöperated before night flying became common, as has been previously observed. Present problems in coördinating rail-air service resemble, however, those of air-water transportation.

Railroads desire to have the right to operate airplanes in order to complete their existing service. It is expected that rail-operated air lines may be useful in feeder and pickup service. More generally, railroads would like to establish air lines which would serve in a general way the territory that the railroads occupy so that they would be in a position to offer the public, as transportation companies, whatever transport the public might require.

Rail carriers have made few definite plans, although they have filed some applications. This is doubtless because of the attitude of the Civil Aeronautics Board in air-water cases, and because of the explicit statement by the Board in one of the railroad decisions that the Civil Aeronautics Act expresses a well-established policy that the various forms of transport should be mutually independent.[16]

Principles Involved in the Restriction of Multiple-Type Transportation

The rulings of the Interstate Commerce Commission and of the Civil Aeronautics Board have restrained the operations of multiple-type transportation. This has restricted selective use and has controlled one form of interagency coördination. It is fair to ask what general principles are involved and whither these restrictions lead. The principles may be summarized as follows:

1. Neither the Commission nor the Board are prepared to accept the rule that the organization of carriage should be based upon the types of machinery or upon the methods used. Endorsement of this principle would be a logical extension of the record; it would be obviously unreasonable, in spite of such a fact. It would produce an unwieldy number of transport companies. It would also disrupt the organization of any company which was successful in discovering new methods and new tools.

2. The regulative bodies will, however, attempt to maintain the separate integrity of certain organizations which have been independently developed and which possess political and industrial power. The stated reasons are: (a) that these companies have rights as pioneers in their fields; (b) that they have peculiar skills; (c) that the public is peculiarly interested in the rapid developments of their techniques; and (d) that independent organization will, in the various cases, stimulate competition. These reasons have been previously referred to.

3. The support which is given independent organizations may be, but is not always, modified or withdrawn when a carrier that characteristically

---

[16] C.A.B. Docket nos. 556, 562, Order Serial no. 2417, 1943.

uses one method or one tool can promote economy in operation or improve the quality of its service in an undertaking to which it is committed, by the addition of another method or another type of equipment. Action in such cases is, however, safeguarded by special rules.

Effects of Restrictions

Restrictions on multiple-type organizations tend to decrease the overall efficiency of transport because they hamper the impartial assignment of machinery to the tasks which each unit can best perform. Technical knowledge can be employed by any management, and executive ability and experience is not monopolized by any group. But an organization with a broad outlook should be able to judge the possibilities of a given manner of providing service better than a management which is committed to a single method or to equipment of a single kind. This is the basic argument for the common control of the elements used in a coördinated enterprise.

It is true, of course, that multiple management may be biased. This is the offsetting danger. Direction may, that is, cling to old techniques or it may try to protect branches of a business in which its greatest investment has been made. Of these two possibilities, the former, under present conditions, would seem to be unlikely. The second exists in all businesses because old equipment in a growing industry will normally be greater at any moment than the experimental investment in new equipment which it is proposed to substitute for old. How far it will be realized in transport will depend upon the optimism of management and the pressure of competition. If multiple agencies can drive single agencies from the field by lowered costs or by discriminatory practice and if these enterprises can then combine, there will be less competition than there was before and new techniques will be more slowly introduced. If agencies employing multiple techniques compete with each other and with unit types at a new level and with greater power, there will be vigorous competition and all possible innovations will be employed. There is no present agreement with respect to the probable result.

Suggestions for Coördination Policy

It would be an improvement upon the practice of the Interstate Commerce Commission and of the Civil Aeronautics Board, in the author's judgment, if the following policies were approved.

1. Certificates for the installation of new service should be freely granted to applicants of any type when the new services are to operate on routes and between stations which the applicant is, with any equipment, authorized to serve. The use of motor or air carriage by a railroad or by a shipping line, under this principle, would be treated as identical with the introduction of new and improved units of the equipment which

the applicant was already permitted to employ. Orders allowing the acquisition of one carrier by another should be issued when no monopoly or reduction in competition was reasonably to be expected as a result.

2. Certificates for the installation of new services which are not covered by applicants' existing rights would be granted when the services to be installed meet a public need. It would be well on such occasions if all applicants were examined and rated according to their demonstrated ability, willingness, and resources for the task on hand; and if the association of applicants with one technique or with another should be considered pertinent only as it bore upon the efficiency that they would show in handling the new work which they would have to do. The public convenience and necessity should be the controlling guide. Orders permitting the acquisition by one carrier of a carrier of another type, operating outside the area in which an applicant was authorized to operate, likewise, should be issued without special reference to the equipment of the applicant or to the type of operation to be acquired. In considering these cases, however, the regulatory body should be alert both to the effects of acquisition by the applicant upon the service which the public is likely to receive and to the possibilities of monopolistic control.

The adoption of the policies suggested in the foregoing paragraphs would offer opportunities for economy through multiple operation. This would be of advantage to the public. The author does not believe that the advantage would be offset by the unwillingness of management to realize its opportunities. He thinks that competition is more likely to be encouraged than to be discouraged in the transport field. It is assumed that the wording of existing legislation would need amendment to make these policies effective; existing laws designed to prevent monopoly should, however, be preserved.

REFERENCES

General Treatises

Bigham, Truman C., and Roberts, Merrill J., *Transportation, Principles and Problems,* New York, McGraw-Hill, 1952.

Fair, Marvin L., and Williams, Ernest W., *Economics of Transportation,* New York, Harper, 1950.

Landon, Charles E., *Transportation, Principles, Practices, Problems,* New York, Sloane, 1951.

Locklin, D. Philip, *Economics of Transportation,* Chicago, Irwin, 1947.

Wilson, G. Lloyd, *Coordinated Motor-Rail-Steamship Transportation,* New York, Appleton-Century-Crofts, 1933.

Other Books

Fenelon, K. G., *Transport Coordination,* London, King, 1929.

Mance, H. Osborne, *The Road and Rail Transport Problem,* New York, Pitman, 1940.

Oppenheim, S. C., *The National Transportation Policy and Intercarrier Competitive Rates, Legislative History and Legal Interpretations,* Harrisburg, Pa., Evangelical Press, 1945.

Periodicals

Ashton, Herbert, "The Meaning and General Aspects of Integration," *Social Science,* October, 1945.

Davies, Ashton, "The Coordination of Transport," *Journal of the Institute of Transport,* April, 1930.

Hickey, E. J., Jr., "Surface Carrier Participation in Air Transportation Under the Civil Aeronautics Act," *Georgetown Law Journal,* January, 1948.

Lawrence, J. V., "Problems of Integration in Highway Transportation," *Social Science,* October, 1945.

Locklin, D. Philip, "Transport Coordination and Rate Policy," *Harvard Business Review,* Summer, 1937.

Moulton, H. G., "Fundamentals of National Transportation Policy," *American Economic Review Supplement,* March, 1934.

Peterson, G. S., "Transport Coordination: Meaning and Purpose," *Journal of Political Economy,* December, 1930.

Sauvy, A., *"À propos de la Coordination des Transports: Repartition d'un Objectif—Production entre Deux Activités,"* *Revue d'Economie Politique,* Jan.–Feb., 1949.

Sorrell, Lewis C., "Problems of Integration in Air Transportation," *Social Science,* October, 1945.

Walker, G., "The Economics of Road and Rail Competition," *Economic Journal,* June, 1933.

Special and Miscellaneous

American Railway Engineering Association, *Coordination of Facilities at Rail and Water Terminals,* Proceedings of Annual Convention, vol. 36, 1935.

American Railway Engineering Association, *Coordinated Traffic,* Proceedings of Annual Convention, vol. 46, 1945.

Dewey, R. L., "Transport Coordination," in National Resources Planning Board, *Transportation and National Policy,* 1942, pp. 140–160.

Hultgren, Thor, "The Nature of an Economical Division of Traffic," in National Resources Planning Board, *Transportation and National Policy,* 1942, pp. 129–139.

International Railway Congress Association, "Application of Rational Organization to the Transport of Goods," *Bulletin,* October, 1936.

International Railway Congress Association, "Competition by Roads, Waterways, and Airways," *Bulletin,* October, 1938.

International Railway Congress Association, "General Observations on the Effect of Motor Transport," *Bulletin,* September, 1935.

Nelson, J. C., "New Concepts in Transportation Regulation," in National

Resources Planning Board, *Transportation and National Policy,* 1942, pp. 197–237.

United States House of Representatives, Committee on Interstate and Foreign Commerce, *Transportation Study,* Hearings before a subcommittee on Transportation Problems, 81st C., 2d S., 1950.

United States House of Representatives, Committee on Merchant Marine and Fisheries, Hearings before a subcommittee on the Merchant Marine in Overseas Aviation, 78th C., 2d S., 1944.

United States Interstate Commerce Commission, *Coordination of Motor Transportation,* 182 I.C.C. 263, 1932. See also 72d C., 1st S., Sen. Doc. 43, 1932.

United States Interstate Commerce Commission, *Railroad Coordination and Consolidation, A Review of Estimated Economies,* Prepared by B. N. Behling, Statistical Analyst, Bureau of Statistics, 1940.

United States Interstate Commerce Commission, Bureau of Transport Economics and Statistics, *Historical Development of Transport Coordination and Integration in the United States,* April, 1950.

United States, Office of the Federal Coordinator of Transportation, *Regulation of Transportation Agencies,* Sen. Doc. 152, 73d C., 2d S., 1934.

United States Senate, Committee on Commerce, Hearings on S. 1814, a bill to amend the Civil Aeronautics Act, 79th C., 2d S., 1946.

Part

VIII

Problems and Practice
of Regulation

The Legal Basis for Regulatory Control

The Legal Basis for Regulatory Control

Both federal and state agencies regulate transportation in the United States. Of these two, the former is the more important, but the latter cannot be ignored.

Source of State Power

State powers over transportation are drawn, broadly, from the sovereign authority of the original thirteen states—enjoyed also by states which have been subsequently admitted to the Union—with the deduction of powers which the states have transferred to the national government. To these may be added certain rights and privileges of control in areas in which transfers have been made. These last rights and privileges are extremely difficult to define. They will be considered in individual categories and examples in later chapters.

Source of Federal Power

Federal authority over transportation is derived from the national constitution.[1] There are several pertinent clauses in this document;[2] the

[1] It is not to be stated, without qualification, that federal authority, in its totality, is derived from the Constitution. Thus the federal power to control tidelands has been upheld, not because it is provided for in the constitution, but because the United States government is said to have the right and responsibility to exercise whatever power and dominion it needs, as a sovereign state, to protect the country against external danger (332 U.S. 19, 1947). The exclusion of aliens and the acquisition of new territory have likewise been justified as a legitimate exercise of authority recognized by the law of nations (George Sutherland, *Constitutional Power and World Affairs*, New York, Columbia University, 1919). The regulation of inland transportation, however, appears to depend upon a delegated power conferred by and limited by clauses in the constitution.

[2] Article 1, section 8, gives Congress power to regulate commerce with foreign nations, among the several states, and with the Indian tribes. It also gives Congress authority to define and punish piracies and felonies on the high seas and offences against the law of nations.

basic provision, however, from the point of view of transportation, is that which gives Congress power to regulate commerce among the several states and with foreign nations. This is because the term *commerce* includes transportation in all its various aspects. Congress, then, has the power to regulate transportation, provided that the transport is among the several states or with foreign nations.

In attempting to define the authority of the Interstate Commerce Commission the Interstate Commerce Act refers to the transportation of passengers or property "from one State or Territory of the United States, or the District of Columbia, to any other State or Territory of the United States, or the District of Columbia, or from one place in a Territory to another place in the same Territory, or from any place in the United States through a foreign country to any other place in the United States, or from or to any place in the United States to or from a foreign country, but only so far as such transportation takes place within the United States." To this enumeration, which includes foreign as well as interstate commerce, we may add the case of transportation between two points in a single state, where the movement passes out of the originating state in the course of its journey. Thus a shipment from Arkansas through Indian Territory to another point in Arkansas has been held to be interstate commerce,[3] and similarly a shipment from New York City through New Jersey and Pennsylvania to Buffalo, New York.[4] But the concept of interstate commerce, so defined, does not extend to commerce with which one state only is concerned.

Division of Authority Between State and Federal Governments

Federal officials, in regulating transport, have to determine in given cases whether a movement is or is not to be regarded as interstate. The previous section has mentioned one, though by no means the only question of this type which arises in commerce cases.[5] But a significant question

---

Article 2, section 2, gives Congress power to make and enforce treaties.

Article 3, section 2, provides that the judicial power of the United States shall extend to all cases of admiralty and maritime jurisdiction. The courts have held that this provision vests power, by consequence, in the federal legislature.

Article 4, section 3, gives Congress power to dispose of and to make all needful rules and regulations concerning territory or other property belonging to the United States.

[3] 187 U.S. 617, 1903.

[4] 152 Fed. 269, 1907.

[5] One of the most difficult problems is that of establishing "continuity of movement." Thus a shipment is not, necessarily, entirely interstate because it is offered to a carrier at a point in one state and ultimately arrives at a point in another state. For the movement may resolve itself, when closely examined, into two or more operations, some of which are local in character. The fundamental test is that of intent; and intent is not always easy to discover. (See 204 U.S. 403, 1907; 233 U.S. 334, 1914; 40 Sup. Ct. Rep. 93, 1919; 43 Sup. Cit. Rep. 643, 1923; 50 Sup. Ct. Rep. 51, 1929; 61 Sup. Ct. Rep. 881, 1941.) A further complication in the field of transportation arises from

from the point of view of constitutional law is, also, whether the federal power over interstate commerce, derived from the national constitution, is exclusive or nonexclusive. If the former, the result will be to deprive state governments of any rights of control over movements which have been identified as interstate. If the latter, both federal and state governments will participate in regulation, with presumable priority to federal rules in case of conflict.

Exclusive Power

We may assume that federal authority over interstate commerce, exerted within the limits of the Constitution, overrides all local and conflicting rules. There is no dissent from this principle in any constitutional controversy.

Federal power is exclusive, in the controversial sense, when it can be exerted only by the federal government. Under this principle, state governments cannot regulate interstate commerce even when their regulations do not conflict with federal rules. Chief Justice Marshall's decision in *Gibbons v. Ogden* [6] is usually referred to as an expression of the "exclusive" view. This was a case in which the Supreme Court held that the State of New York lacked power to grant rights of exclusive navigation in New York waters as against vessels coming from New Jersey and licensed under the laws of the United States. So stated, the reach of the decision was only moderate. But Marshall also stated, and enlarged upon the point, that he was not convinced that the argument denying to the state any authority whatever over a subject the regulation of which had been entrusted to the federal government had been refuted. According to Marshall, the state might exercise "divisible" powers in such a case; thus, it might tax, and its taxes might affect interstate commerce. The taxes would be valid if they did not "burden" interstate commerce. Or it might exercise police powers of various sorts. But the power to regulate interstate commerce as such was indivisible and exclusive. Complete authority had been transferred to the federal government by the adoption of the Constitution, and the states retained no share. [7]

---

the fact that a federal regulatory statute may not cover all shipments which, from the point of view of constitutional law, are shipments in interstate commerce (298 U.S. 170, 1935; 44 M.C.C. 419, 1945. But see 34 M.C.C. 233, 1942 and 48 M.C.C. 171, 1948).

[6] 9 Wheaton 1, 1824.

[7] Mr. Justice Frankfurter thinks that the broad view stated in the text was the view which Marshall really held. In Frankfurter's opinion, Marshall felt that the time was not ripe, however, for such a contraction of state sovereignty. He therefore accepted a narrower basis in *Gibbons v. Ogden* for decision of the case. But his larger position was enormously influential, in spite of his restraint (Felix Frankfurter, *The Commerce Clause Under Marshall, Taney and Waite,* Chapel Hill, N. C., University of North Carolina, 1937).

Concurrent Power

If states have concurrent power over interstate commerce they may exercise authority, provided that they avoid conflict with the national government. A substantial number of people believed, at one time, that states possessed a general jurisdiction of this sort.[8] The doctrine was never accepted in an uncompromising form, but the Supreme Court approved a variant in the *Cooley v. Board of Wardens* case, decided in 1851.[9]

The facts in the Cooley case were somewhat complicated. The litigation involved an act of the legislature of Pennsylvania in 1803 which required vessels of a described type, entering or leaving the port of Philadelphia, to take a pilot or, in the alternative, to pay half-pilotage. It appeared that similar though not identical regulation had been effective in Pennsylvania before the federal constitution had been approved. Congress, by act of 1789, had declared that all pilots in ports of the United States should continue to be regulated in accordance with the existing laws of the states or with such laws as the states might, respectively, later enact until further legislative provision should be made by Congress. This declaration seemed to adopt the Pennsylvania law of 1803. However, if the federal constitution excluded the state from the regulation of interstate commerce, as was contended, the federal, as well as the state, law was without effect. For Congress could not regrant or in any manner reconvey to the state an authority which the state did not constitutionally possess. The argument in favor of this view was based upon the theory of "exclusive" power. If the Constitution really vested this kind of power in the nation, then neither Congress nor the states could modify the fundamental rule.

In a decision written by Justice Curtis, the Supreme Court held:

1. That regulation of pilotage was a regulation of interstate commerce.
2. That Congress had power to control pilotage.
3. That Congressional power over interstate commerce was compatible, however, with the retention of some power by the states.
4. That the power of Congress was exclusive when the subjects of power were in their nature national or admitted only of one uniform system of regulation.
5. That when the subjects of power demanded diversity of regulation, then the states might legislate until Congress should find it necessary to act.
6. That pilotage regulations were and should be diverse with respect

[8] J. E. Kallenbach, *Federal Cooperation with the States Under the Commerce Clause,* Ann Arbor, Mich., University of Michigan, 1942.
[9] 12 Howard 298, 1851.

to different ports. The evidence could be found in known facts; the conclusion was also supported by the declaration of Congress in the Act of 1789 and by continuous practice between 1789 and 1851.

Neither the majority nor the dissenting opinion in the Cooley case mentioned the fact that the vessels involved held federal licenses, although this circumstance had been important in *Gibbons v. Ogden*. The Court there apparently believed that a federal license did not grant a general right to navigate without a pilot in state waters although it did grant a right to navigate in areas which a state, for commercial reasons, might desire to restrict.

Congressional Direction

After 1851, states might take action affecting interstate commerce on either of two grounds. They might, in conformity with Marshall's distinctions, exercise their various police powers or powers which they possessed concurrently with Congress, including the power to tax. Or, so long as Congress had not acted they might, in conformity with the Cooley rule, regulate interstate commerce when the subjects involved were not national and did not require one uniform system of regulation.

If the exercise of state power was to take place under the Cooley rule the states must show that the proper conditions prevailed. There were two possibilities: one, that the problem was jurisdictional and should be handled by a court; the other, that it could be settled by a policy determination, in which case the expressed or inferred will of Congress would prevail. The Cooley case treated the matter as, on the whole, judicial. The court examined evidence; although it referred to Congressional action it considered this action to discover the nature of the activity which was being regulated and not to find an authoritative basis of control. But in the course of time the other possibility has been given increasing weight. In many instances Congress, as a matter of policy, has specified in its legislation the degree to which state regulation may be effective. In other instances it has specifically waived authority in favor of state legislation. In still other instances, as in liquor legislation, it has fitted federal enactments into schemes of state law.[10] In any event the authority of local bodies has been judicially sustained when its exercise conforms to federal purpose. Where there is no persuasive indication of the intent of Congress the principles of the Cooley case have been applied.[11] The net result

[10] See generally, Kallenbach, *op. cit.* and F. D. G. Ribble, *State and National Power over Commerce*, New York, Columbia University, 1937.

[11] The Supreme Court summarized its position in 1948 as follows:

"Certain first principles are no longer in doubt. Whether as inference from congressional silence, or as a negative implication from the grant of power itself, when Con-in these cases has been to replace the concept of an interstate commerce which, by its nature, demands diversity of control, by inquiries into the intent of Congress. The intent can be specifically stated in a federal law or it can be inferred. This tends to transfer the conflict between local and federal authorities, in the matter discussed, from the judicial to the political sphere. Here is where it probably belongs.

Federal Power and Intrastate Commerce

We have pointed out that federal power over interstate commerce in the United States, exerted within the limits of the Constitution, overrides all local and conflicting rules. It remains to explain that this authority carries with it the power to regulate intrastate commerce, if such action is necessary for effective regulation of the interstate transport with which the federal government is primarily concerned. This is an extremely important principle. It can be broken down, for analysis, into several parts.

Safety Regulations

The Interstate Commerce Act vests in the Interstate Commerce Commission the authority to require the installation of appliances, methods, and systems intended to promote the safety of railroad operation.[12] It may also establish reasonable requirements for common, contract, and private motor carriers with respect to the qualifications and maximum hours of service and for the safety of operation and equipment.[13] The Civil Aeronautics Authority may likewise prescribe standards, rules, and regulations in air transport in the interest of safety. It may issue or refuse airman, aircraft, and air carrier operating certificates and establish minimum

---

gress has not specifically acted we have accepted the Cooley case's broad delineation of the areas of state and national power over interstate commerce. Absent congressional action, the familiar test is that of uniformity versus locality; if a case falls within an area in commerce thought to demand a uniform national rule, state action is struck down. If the activity is one of predominantly local interest, state action is sustained. More accurately, the question of whether the state interest is outweighed by a national interest in the unhampered operation of interstate commerce.

"There is no longer any question that Congress can redefine the areas of local and national predominance, despite theoretical inconsistency with the rationale of the Commerce Clause as a limitation in its own right. The words of the Clause—a grant of power—admit of no other result. When Congress enters the field by legislation, we try to discover to what extent it intended to exercise its power of redefinition . . .

"But whether Congress has or has not expressed itself, the fundamental inquiry, broadly stated, is the same: does the state action conflict with national policy? The *Cooley* rule and its later application, Southern Pacific Co. v. Arizona [325 U.S. 761, 1945], the question of congressional "occupation of the field," and the search for conflict in the very terms of state and federal statutes are but three separate particularizations of this initial principle" (*California v. Zook,* 336 U.S. 725, 728–729, 1949).

[12] Sec. 25 (b).
[13] See chap. 30, "Railroad Regulation."

standards for operation.[14] These provisions will be again referred to in the chapter on air regulation.

Federal regulations of the sort just listed are applicable in the first instance to interstate carriage. But it is obvious that safety rules which are limited to interstate transport will not protect interstate carriage unless intrastate carriers conform. A defective railroad car loaded with intrastate consignments will endanger interstate traffic carried in the same train. And an incompetent pilot or a poorly designed or constructed airplane will be a menace to all airplanes upon a route.

In these cases the federal power is applied, with a minimum of opposition, to intra- as well as to interstate transactions. The railroad statutes go back to 1893. They have been abundantly interpreted in the sense stated. The constitutionality of the motor laws is not questioned. The air laws are more recent, but it has already been held in the lower courts (1) that the operation of an airplane without a federal pilot's license, airman's certificate, and certificate of airworthiness between two points in California is illegal, even though the airplane avoids established airways; [15] and (2) that it is illegal to operate an aircraft within a state without a federal certificate of airworthiness, on a federally designated airway, even though a state certificate has been obtained.[16] It should be added that a state law identical with the federal law is not, apparently, destroyed by coincident federal action. Thus proceedings can be brought in a state court, on this assumption, for violation of the state statute.[17] But the state cannot prescribe standards inconsistent with the federal rule.

Federal Control of Intrastate Railroad Rates

The federal government may not only enforce safety practices in intrastate transportation but it may exercise power over intrastate railroad rates, upon the same underlying principle. It could, constitutionally, also regulate some intrastate motor and water rates if Congress had not withdrawn this power in later laws.[18] This power over railroad rates has been

---

[14] The Civil Aeronautics Board promulgates flight rules and, in general, air traffic rules in the interest of safety. These regulations govern rights of way, minimum safe altitudes, flight over congested areas, operations with restricted liability, acrobatic flights, careless or reckless operation, etc. (*Code of Federal Regulation of the United States of America*, "Supplement," 60.00 to 60.90.)

[15] 55 Fed. Suppl. 151, 1944.

[16] 131 Fed. (2d), 932, 1942.

[17] 336 U.S. 725, 1949.

[18] The pertinent clause in the Motor Carrier Act is as follows:

"Sec. 216 (e) . . . That nothing in this part shall empower the Commission to prescribe, or in any manner regulate, the rate, fare, or charge for intrastate transportation, or for any service connected herewith, for the purpose of removing discrimination against interstate commerce or any other purpose whatever."

The provisions of Sec. 303 (k), relating to water transportation, are substantially identical.

practically developed along two lines. One of these has been given
prominence by the so-called Shreveport decision of the Interstate Commerce Commission, in 1912, and the other is supported by court and
commission opinions rendered subsequent to 1920.

The Pensacola Fish Case

The facts presented in *Houston, East and West Texas v. United States,*
commonly known as the Shreveport case, can best be understood if two
prior bits of litigation are first discussed. One of these is selected because
of its simplicity, and the other because the Shreveport ruling followed
close upon it.

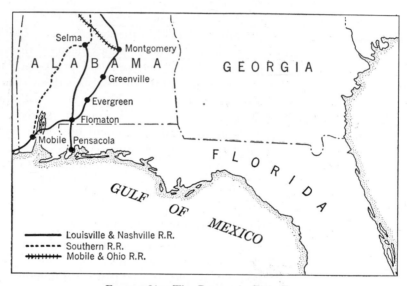

FIGURE 64.   The Pensacola Fish Case.

Figure 64 shows the relative position of the states of Florida and Georgia
and the location of the cities of Pensacola and Mobile. In a case brought
before the Interstate Commerce Commission in 1910 [19] it appeared that
both Mobile and Pensacola were centers for a considerable fishing industry. Swift fishing vessels cruised in the Gulf of Mexico, and their catch
was brought back to these mainland towns, whence it was shipped to
interior cities in Alabama and in other states. Just before September 15,
1907, the railroad rate from both Pensacola and Mobile to Birmingham,
Alabama, was $1.00 per 100 pounds. With equal rates Pensacola secured

___

See chap. 33, "Air Regulation," for discussion of federal control of rates on intrastate
air carriage.
[19] 18 I.C.C. 415, 1910.

more business than did Mobile, because it had slightly better fishing equipment, was a little nearer the market, and was more active in pushing sales.

In order to regain for Mobile business which Pensacola had taken away, the Railroad Commission of Alabama, on September 15, 1907, established a mileage rate scale in Alabama, under which the rate on fresh fish from Mobile to Birmingham was reduced from $1.00 to 55 cents per 100 pounds. This rate did not apply from Pensacola, because the haul from Pensacola to Birmingham was interstate and the rate not subject to the Alabama Railroad Commission's control. In consequent proceedings, the reasonableness of the $1.00 rate from Pensacola to Birmingham was not attacked; and the Interstate Commerce Commission, when appealed to, observed that no reduction which it could fairly require would do more than modify, without removing, the discrimination of which Pensacola complained. Here, then, was a state rate, properly under the control of a state railroad commission by the principles of constitutional law, and yet this state rate affected interstate commerce. For so long as it was possible to ship fish from Mobile to Birmingham more cheaply than from Pensacola to Birmingham, the traffic over one route was sure to dwindle and that over the other route would increase.[20]

Minnesota Rate Cases

The second preliminary litigation which should be mentioned centered on two orders of the State Railroad Commission of Minnesota and two acts passed by the legislature of that state. These orders and laws prescribed 2 cents a mile as the maximum fare for passengers, except for persons under 12 years of age, for whom the maximum rate was to be 1 cent a mile. Maximum class rates were set for general merchandise, and maximum commodity rates in certain cases. In opposition, suits were brought by stockholders of the Northern Pacific Railway, the Great Northern Railway, and the Minneapolis and St. Louis Railroad Companies, seeking to enjoin the enforcement of the orders and of the legislation which has been described.

[20] The Commission stated its view as follows:

"It may be . . . that the Congress may constitutionally protect interstate commerce, as well as the carriers that are engaged in interstate transportation, by requiring that any state traffic moved by such a carrier shall bear its just proportions of the cost of operation and yield its proper proportion of profit to the carrier; and that with such an end in view it may authorize the Commission to fix minimum rates, at least, for state traffic when moved by carriers engaged also in interstate transportation; or that it may provide that no carrier engaged in the transportation of passengers or property may at the same time carry state traffic at rates that are less than the rates exacted by it for interstate carriages of like distance and under like transportation conditions. It has, however, not attempted any such legislation, and whether such an enactment would stand the test of scrutiny by the courts under the constitution as it now stands, and if so, whether it would be desirable from the standpoint of a broad public policy, are questions that must ultimately be determined by the legislative power and therefore cannot profitably be discussed by the Commission in this proceeding."

The Minnesota rate cases were decided in 1913, one year after the Pensacola controversy. The evidence showed beyond a shadow of a doubt that the action of the state legislature and of the State Railroad Commission in Minnesota had produced profound effects upon interstate rates in the entire Northwest territory. At the same time, the action, in form, related entirely to traffic within the state of Minnesota; and it was not clear that the indirect effect of state action upon interstate business was enough to invalidate the orders of the local bodies. The critical character of the problem was so far appreciated that the railroad commissioners of eight states filed their brief as *amici curiae,* in support of the view that the Minnesota legislation should be sustained. Possibly even the Supreme Court was moved to an unusual degree of caution, for if the Minnesota maximum rate laws were declared void, it was evident that other similar laws might share the same fate, and that a considerable part of the structure of state railroad legislation might be destroyed. Whether or not it was influenced by such considerations, the Court did actually sustain the Minnesota legislation, and insofar approved the position of those who stood for local rights. Yet the careful reasoning by which the Supreme Court here justified its opinion contained suggestions more in accord with national than with state ideas. Federal authority over interstate commerce, said the Court, is paramount. States cannot regulate interstate commerce, nor can they place burdens upon it. They can, however, take certain action which affects interstate commerce, because our system of government is a practical adjustment by which the national authority as conferred by the Constitution is maintained in its full scope, without unnecessary loss of efficiency. To this extent states have concurrent authority with the federal government. Concurrent authority is not equal authority. It yields when the federal government has itself acted. Yet in the absence of federal action some state laws affecting interstate commerce are good; and among these are laws regulating the internal commerce of a state, even when such legislation affects the flow of commerce between the states.[21] The Court's opinion only restated well-known law. It contained an intimation, however, which the Interstate Commerce Commission was not likely to overlook.

Shreveport Case

We now come to the so-called "Shreveport" litigation, in which the hints thrown out by the Supreme Court in the Minnesota cases were acted upon, and the kind of problem presented by the Pensacola case was fully resolved.[22]

Shreveport, Louisiana, is about 40 miles from the Texas state line, and 231 miles from Houston, Texas. In 1911 the Railroad Commission of

[21] 184 Fed. 765, 1911; 230 U.S. 352, 1913.
[22] 23 I.C.C. 31, 1912.

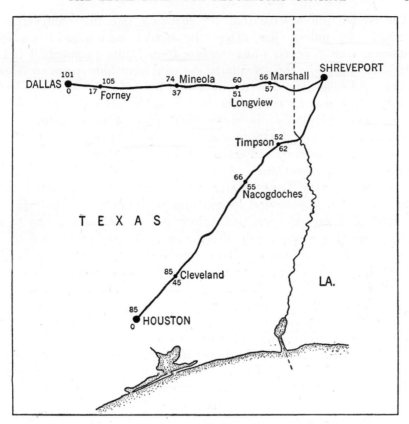

FIGURE 65. The Shreveport Case.

Louisiana complained to the Interstate Commerce Commission that the railroads serving Shreveport were charging unreasonable rates from Shreveport to various points in Texas, and likewise that these railroads were discriminating against Louisiana in favor of Texas traffic. The accompanying map, drawn from data submitted to the federal commission, shows the foundation for the complaint.[23]

[23] Distances between Shreveport, Dallas, and Houston, 1912.

Shreveport and Dallas

To	From	
	Shreveport (miles)	Dallas (miles)
Shreveport	0	189.7
Marshall	42.0	147.9
Longview	65.7	124.0
Mineola	111.5	78.2
Forney	169.4	20.3
Dallas	189.7	0

The reader will observe that the first-class rate from Shreveport to Marshall (42 miles), just across the border separating Texas from Louisiana, was 56 cents; while the rate from Dallas to Marshall (147.9 miles) was only 57 cents. Similarly the rate from Shreveport to Nacogdoches (92.4 miles) was 66 cents while that from Houston to Nacogdoches (138.3 miles) was 55 cents. The two Texas points enjoyed a rate advantage over Shreveport in most intermediate Texas territory, until destinations close to the state boundary had been reached. These illustrations could be multiplied and extended to include other stations and commodity as well as class rates.

POSITION OF THE TEXAS RAILROAD COMMISSION. When the Interstate Commerce Commission looked into the matter, it found that the low level of Texas rates was not entirely due to voluntary action by the carriers, but that it was partly also the result of pressure exerted by the Texas Railroad Commission. This commission believed in protecting Texas shippers. It wished to encourage local jobbing and manufacturing establishments, in order to increase population in Texas, enlarge the yield of taxes, and afford to Texas farmers an improved market for their goods. It sought to accomplish this purpose, moreover, by ways which included attention to the relationships of railroad rates. "This Commission," said the *Fifth Annual Report of the Texas Railroad Commission,* "has always had in mind the securing of relatively just state and interstate rates, with a view of enabling Texas merchants and manufacturers to do business in competition with outsiders." Speaking particularly of Shreveport, the Texas commission argued that Shreveport enjoyed low carload rates from Northern and Eastern points. Such rates, in combination with local rates from Shreveport into Texas, were said to give an advantage to Shreveport jobbers which only a contrary adjustment of the scheme of local rates could possibly correct. Like Alabama and Minnesota, and even in greater degree, the Texas commission was alive to the desirability of protecting local interests.

POSITION OF THE INTERSTATE COMMERCE COMMISSION. The Interstate Commerce Commission, with the Supreme Court decision in the

To	*Shreveport and Houston*	
	From	
	Shreveport (*miles*)	Houston (*miles*)
Shreveport	0	230.7
Timpson	63.9	166.8
Nacogdoches	92.4	138.3
Cleveland	187.5	43.2
Houston	230.7	0

Minnesota cases behind it, was ready to take action, in 1913, which had seemed impossible in 1910. It did this in three ways:

1. The Commission prescribed scales of maximum class rates between Shreveport and stations on the Texas and Pacific and the Houston, East and West Texas Railways between Shreveport and Dallas and Houston, Texas. These maxima were appreciably lower than the interstate rates then in force;

2. The Commission directed the carriers mentioned to establish and maintain class rates which were no higher than the scale maxima prescribed above;

3. The Commission ordered the Texas and Pacific and the Houston, East and West Texas Railways to cease from charging higher rates upon any commodity from Shreveport into Texas than were contemporaneously charged for the carriage of such commodity from Dallas or Houston toward Shreveport for an equal distance.

These orders were subsequently supported by the courts.[24]

Legal Importance of the Shreveport Rule

The Shreveport decision did not expound new law, nor were the facts in the case novel. The Commission acted (1) to enforce the provisions of Section 3 of the Interstate Commerce Act and (2) to override local and conflicting orders which interfered with this enforcement. The Commission did not attempt, generally, to supersede state legislation. It is true that, in some subsequent cases, it extended its own orders beyond the limits which could be justified in proceedings which charged local discrimination.[25] But these extensions were corrected by the courts. What the decision of the Interstate Commerce Commission in the Shreveport case and the court opinions which endorsed it did do was to establish the power

[24] 205 Fed. 380, 1913; 234 U.S. 342, 1914, 284 U.S. 125, 1931.

[25] The Supreme Court has declared, more than once, that an Interstate Commerce Commission decision, under the Shreveport rule, must have a definite field of operation. The Commission must locate areas of discrimination between intra- and interstate traffic and must limit its action to the remedy of abuses which have there appeared. For the power of the Commission is dominant only to the extent that its exercise removes a discrimination against interstate traffic. Thus the Commission could not compel a railroad, generally, to charge rates for intrastate hauls of lumber on its lines which were the same as interstate rates from points in the northern portion of Florida to destinations in Georgia, when the only competition between intra- and interstate movements was in a limited area in the north (282 U.S. 194, 1930). Nor could the Interstate Commerce Commission require an increase in all intrastate passenger fares in Illinois to eliminate discrimination against interstate movements from St. Louis and Keokuk to Illinois points (245 U.S. 493, 1918). Nor could it compel an increase in express rates between certain points in South Dakota and all other stations in that state when its findings showed discrimination only in the case of traffic commercially tributary to a limited number of cities (244 U.S. 617, 1917). And in every instance the findings of the Commission must be clear and supported by evidence with respect to each element essential to the exercise of its power (325 U.S. 507, 1945).

of the federal government, acting through an authorized commission, to regulate intrastate railroad transportation charges when this regulation was necessary to protect protesting localities against undue rate discrimination which interfered with their relations with points situated in other states. Until 1920 this Commission was subject to two handicaps: (1) It could not initiate a "Shreveport" investigation. It could act only upon complaint. And (2) it could not prescribe an intrastate rate for the purpose of eliminating discrimination. It could only order that discrimination should cease. But in that year both difficulties were removed.

Transportation Act of 1920

The Transportation Act of 1920 gave the Commission power to investigate on its own motion, on petition of the carrier concerned, and on complaint of a state commission. It also gave the Commission power to prescribe an intrastate rate in order to remove discrimination. Rates so prescribed were to be observed by the carriers, the law of any state or the decision or order of any state authority to the contrary notwithstanding.[26] The new provisions strengthened the Commission in its application of the Shreveport rule. According to some of its sponsors this was all that the law proposed.[27] There was on the other hand reason to suppose that at least some elements in Congress desired to go farther and to prohibit not merely state action which discriminated against specified localities, as in the Shreveport case, but also action that discriminated against interstate commerce as a whole.[28] As a matter of fact the law as passed mentioned

[26] Interstate Commerce Act, Sec. 13 (4). The Commission, in its investigations, might confer with State regulatory bodies, hold joint hearings, and avail itself of the coöperation of State authorities.

[27] Senator Cummins, in presenting the legislation to the Senate, said:

"The committee has attempted simply to express the decision of the Supreme Court of the United States. We have not attempted to carry the authority of Congress beyond the exact point ruled by the Supreme Court in the cases to which I have referred [Shreveport, Minnesota rate, and Illinois cases] and the only thing we have done in the matter has been to confer upon the Interstate Commerce Commission the authority to remove the discrimination when established in a proper proceeding before that body —an authority which it does not now have" (*Congressional Record*, December 4, 1919, p. 141).

[28] Thus Mr. Esch, after pointing out the relations of the Act of 1920 to the Shreveport decision, went on to say:

"We have incorporated into law the decision of the court. When by reason of the low level of the intrastate rates an undue burden is cast upon the interstate traffic the citizens and the shippers of other States would have had to pay higher interstate freight rates than they would have had to pay had that State enacted or put into force and effect proper intrastate rates. We give this power of determination to the Interstate Commerce Commission . . ." (*Congressional Record*, November 11, 1919).

And Senator Cummins was still more explicit. He said:

"I may say, for the benefit of the Senate . . . that the House bill originally proposed another element; that is, it proposed that we should declare that if the rates in force in any State did not sustain a fair share of the burden which the interstate carrier

the two things separately, so that it was hard to suppose that no distinction could be made.[29] Moreover the Transportation Act directed the Interstate Commerce Commission to fix such rates as would yield railroad carriers a reasonable return, and this created a situation in which the relative earnings on intrastate and interstate railroads would be important. It was in spite of this that some Congressmen contended that no new power over intrastate commerce had been conferred.

Interpretation of Section 13

The Supreme Court, in 1922, held that Section 13 of the Interstate Commerce Act as amended in 1920 did go further than the Shreveport rule. In the case which the Court considered, the Interstate Commerce Commission had ordered carriers to increase intrastate railroad passenger fares in Wisconsin so as to correspond with increases in interstate fares which the Commission had prescribed. The state authorities would not cooperate because of a state statute fixing the maximum railroad fare on intrastate passenger business in Wisconsin at 2 cents per mile. On these facts the Supreme Court held (1) that the Commission order went beyond any authority recognized in the Shreveport litigations; (2) that the Commission's order was nevertheless valid under Section 13 of the Interstate Commerce Act as amended in 1920; and (3) that Section 13 was constitutional.[30]

must bear, then the Federal authority should have the jurisdiction to take possession of the entire field and lift the rates so that the carriers should receive from intrastate business a proper share of the revenues which it must have in order to pay for maintenance and operation and a fair return upon the value of the property. That is the contention, and there is a great deal of merit in it. We have not thought, however, that we were justified in going to that extent. But I predict that it will not be many years before Congress will be compelled to go to that length" (*Congressional Record,* December 4, 1919).

[29] The pertinent language of the Transportation Act of 1920 was as follows:
"Whenever in any such investigation the Commission . . . finds that any such rate . . . causes any undue . . . prejudice as between persons or localities in intrastate commerce on the one hand and interstate or foreign commerce on the other hand, or any undue . . . discrimination against interstate or foreign commerce, which is hereby forbidden and declared to be unlawful, it shall prescribe . . ." etc.

[30] The Court distinguished specifically between the phrase in Sec. 13 (4) which condemned any rate which caused "undue preference as between persons or localities in intrastate commerce on the one hand and interstate or foreign commerce on the other hand" and the following phrase which made illegal "any undue . . . discrimination against interstate or foreign commerce." Of these, it said that the former could be justified by the reasoning of the Shreveport decision. The latter could not be justified by this reasoning but it was nevertheless a legitimate exercise of the constitutional powers of Congress over interstate commerce (257 U.S. 563, 1922).
The Supreme Court took notice, in the Wisconsin case, of the fact that the general policy of the Transportation Act of 1920 was to enable the railroads of the United States to maintain an adequate railway service, and it summarized Sec. 15a of the Interstate Commerce Act as amended in 1920 to make this conclusion clear. Its decision did not depend, however, upon the wording of Section 15a of the act of 1920. In 1933,

Section 13 (4) is still in the Interstate Commerce Act. It does not, like the Shreveport rule, deal with particular railroad rate relationships, but it is important in what are known as "revenue" cases. These are usually general proceedings concerned with the need of railroads for additional earnings. They may involve all the passenger rates or all the freight rates in a given area. In the initial case, in 1920, the Commission authorized railroads to advance rates 40 percent in the states north of the Ohio and east of the Mississippi and different percentages in other areas.[31] In 1931 the Commission permitted a general increase in interstate freight rates throughout the country of 10 percent;[32] and in later years a number of increases were allowed because of advances in railroad costs. Section 13 (4) empowers the Interstate Commerce Commission to require changes in state rates to conform with national policy on such occasions. The section is constitutional, because its provisions are incidental to the regulation of interstate commerce and necessary to the efficiency of this regulation.[33] The basic assumed fact is that interstate commerce, as a whole, will be unduly burdened if intrastate business does not contribute a fair proportion to the reasonable compensation which carriers should earn. Proceeding from this conclusion, commission orders have repeatedly required railroads to advance their rates on intrastate transportation, without regard for local laws, and the courts have sustained these orders.

Federal authority under Section 13 (4) is, however, limited to the protection of interstate commerce. It does not replace state jurisdiction in any general sense. The federal agency does not exercise, over intrastate railroad transport, a jurisdiction comparable to that which it possesses over interstate commerce. The mere fact that a local rate is lower, mile for mile, than an interstate rate does not justify a federal commission in increasing the former, upon revenue grounds. For it is possible that a particular state rate is already contributing generously to carrier profits and, if so, it should not be raised.[34] Nor should it be raised, of course, if the increase will not produce more revenue.[35] State railroad rates, therefore, do not follow the interstate prescriptions of the Interstate Commerce Commission in detail. They are forced to conform sufficiently, however, to make national policies effective. The statutory clauses which make this necessary do not apply to motor or to inland water carriage.[36]

Sec. 15a was later amended by excision of the reference to a fair return (48 Stat. 211, 220, 1933). But the Court then held that the change did not affect the Commission's responsibilities or powers insofar as the protection of interstate commerce was concerned (292 U.S. 1, 1934; 325 U.S. 507, 1945).

[31] 58 I.C.C. 220, 1920.

[32] 178 I.C.C. 539, 1931; 179 I.C.C. 215, 1931.

[33] 257 U.S. 563, 1922; 257 U.S. 591, 1922; 318 U.S. 675, 1943.

[34] 325 U.S. 507, 1945.

[35] 234 I.C.C. 331, 1939. An increase in local railroad rates may easily divert traffic to motor carriage.

[36] The Interstate Commerce Commission will not protect intrastate commerce against

Conclusion

The final conclusion with respect to the control of transport in the United States is this. Insofar as intrastate transportation is concerned, the states have regulatory powers. But this authority is limited by the rights of federal boards or commissions to regulate intrastate transport, either when such regulation is required to make interstate control effective, as in the case of safety devices or methods of operation or, in the case of railroads, to protect interstate commerce along the lines specified in the Shreveport cases and in the cases under the federal laws of 1920 and those of later years. On the other hand, state power may be expanded to cover phases of interstate transport when the federal government has not prescribed a rule and the activity regulated is of a local sort or when, and this is important, the federal government gives consent. We shall consider this possibility further in our discussion of motor and of water regulation.

On its side, the federal government has full control over interstate commerce in principle, and can and does regulate this commerce in great detail. With some techniques, as in air and in railroad transport, and increasingly with the growth of long distance carriage, interstate transportation is of primary importance. And the power of the federal agencies is enlarged, as that of state government is restricted, by the extension of federal authority over local transport whenever this seems necessary to regulate or to protect the carriage with which the federal government is principally concerned. The net result is a growing predominance of federal over state direction. This, in turn, reduces the power and prestige of state transport administrations and increases that of national bodies, leaving to the former, in the main, besides some strictly local movements, only those areas of authority from which the federal government intentionally withdraws. We shall deal in succeeding chapters with the statutory

---

interstate commerce when intrastate rates are relatively high. The Shreveport rule and the so-called Transportation Act of 1920 rule do not apply in cases of this sort. In the Mutual Creamery case of 1927 the Commission said:

"The coexisting Federal power over the relationship of interstate and intrastate rates may be exercised in direct operation upon intrastate rates only to the extent necessary for effective regulation of interstate or foreign commerce . . . Only in a strained sense could it be said that the removal of undue prejudice to or unjust discrimination against intrastate commerce resulting from a difference in levels of interstate and intrastate is necessary for the effective regulation of interstate commerce, and certainly the effective protection of interstate commerce calls for no such action" (132 I.C.C. 207, 211–212, 1927). The Commission has repeatedly refused to consider complaints which alleged that low interstate rates unduly prejudiced resident producers who shipped from local points of origin to the same ultimate destinations (177 I.C.C. 285, 286, 1931; 223 I.C.C. 179, 182, 1937; 238 I.C.C. 569, 570, 1940; 264 I.C.C. 593, 595, 1946). Control of intrastate rates in these various instances lies with state and not with federal authority.

basis, the administrative organization, and the major problems with which state and federal regulation of transport is concerned.[37]

R E F E R E N C E S

General Treatises

Bigham, Truman C., and Roberts, Merrill J., *Transportation, Principles and Problems,* New York, McGraw-Hill, 1952.

Corwin, Edward S., *The Commerce Power Versus States Rights,* Princeton, Princeton University, 1936.

Frankfurter, Felix, *The Commerce Clause Under Marshall, Taney, and Waite,* Chapel Hill, University of North Carolina, 1937.

Locklin, D. Philip, *Economics of Transportation,* Chicago, Irwin, 1947.

Reynolds, G. G., *The Distribution of Power to Regulate Interstate Carriers Between the Nation and the States,* New York, Columbia University, 1928.

Ribble, F. D. G., *State and National Power over Commerce,* New York, Columbia University, 1937.

Sharfman, I. L., *The Interstate Commerce Commission,* Part II, New York, Commonwealth Fund, 1931.

Sutherland, George, *Constitutional Power and World Affairs,* New York, Columbia University, 1919.

Other Books

Melder, F. E., *State and Local Barriers to Interstate Commerce in the United States,* Orono, Me., University of Maine, 1937.

Periodicals

Beck, J. M., "Federal Power over Intrastate Railroad Rates," *University of Pennsylvania Law Review,* November, 1922.

Coleman, W. C., "The Evolution of Federal Regulation of Intrastate Rates: The Shreveport Rate Cases," *Harvard Law Review,* November, 1914.

Sheppard, J. S., "Another Word About the Evolution of Federal Regulation of Intrastate Rates and the Shreveport Rate Cases," *Harvard Law Review,* January, 1915.

[37] *Wickard v. Filburn* (317 U.S. 111, 1942) is an extreme case which illustrates the scope of federal power, although this case does not deal with transportation.

The Supreme Court held, in this litigation, that a farmer who produced, for his own use, 239 bushels of wheat in excess of the quota allotted to him under the federal Agricultural Adjustment Act of 1938 was liable to penalty unless the excess was stored according to regulations promulgated by the Secretary of Agriculture or delivered to the Secretary without compensation. The Court said:

"That an activity is of local character may help in a doubtful case to determine whether Congress intended to reach it. The same consideration might help in determining whether in the absence of Congressional action it would be permissible for the state to exert its power on the subject matter, even though in so doing it to some degree affected interstate commerce. But even if appellee's activity be local and though it may not be regarded as commerce, it may still, whatever its nature, be reached by Congress if it exerts a substantial economic effect on interstate commerce."

State Regulation

State regulation of transportation in the United States is exercised within the limits which the previous chapter has discussed. It is exerted over intrastate carriage except when the federal authorities have established a right to intervene, and over interstate carriage where the activity is of a local sort or when the federal government indicates consent. In the early years the initiative in regulation was, actually, taken by the states; in later years the federal administration became dominant, although the distribution of influence varied with the types and circumstances of transport with which governments found themselves concerned. The machinery used was also different at different times.

Railroads. Regulation by Charter Provisions

The story of transport regulation in this country begins with the railroad, and the first action of state legislatures with respect to railroads was to issue charters. A charter is a grant of power by sovereign authority which enables a corporation to exist for described purposes and to do certain things.[1] Evidently the fact that a railroad cannot function without

[1] Meyer enumerates the leading features of railway charters in the United States as follows:

"The leading features which are common to railway charters of the several states may be associated with the following points, every charter having one or more provisions, relating to some or all of these points: name of company; number of commissioners; number on board of directors; the amount of capital stock, size and number of shares; the amount and payment per share at the time of subscription, and the maximum assessment per share, together with the number of days' notice required; systems of voting; the time limit as to beginning and completing construction, junctions, branches, and extensions; route; expropriation and methods of valuation, together with the manner in which disputes are settled; the amount of land which may be held; the number of miles to be constructed before traffic may be opened; the power to borrow money and the rate of interest; the distribution of dividends, liability of stockholders, annual reports; passenger and freight rates. In every state charters may be found which contain provisions on only a few of these points, while in most states charters were granted containing provisions on all of them, and perhaps others not here

a grant of power from the state affords the latter a convenient opportunity to insist that the railroad accept certain principles of conduct as a condition of operating at all. Some early charters, for instance, contained clauses requiring publicity of rates, fixing maximum scales of charges, calling for annual reports, and forbidding discrimination, besides the phrases conveying powers immediately necessary to the corporate organization.

Defects of Charter Regulation

Unfortunately, the practice of regulating railroad companies through charter provision presents difficulties. In the first place, a railroad charter affects one corporation only. Secondly, charters not infrequently conflict, one with another, and where they do not, differences in their terms cause controversy. This was true even in England before 1945, in spite of the fact that English railroad charters were all issued by Parliament and might, therefore, be expected to have been consistent with one another. In France, where there were few important private railways and one charter-issuing authority, the government was able to standardize charters and to use them effectively; but in the United States, where there are many railway companies and where each state government has authority to issue charters, the chance for variety is much greater, and the attempt to regulate through charter provision has led to futility and confusion. Lastly, charters are difficult to amend, at least unless the right to amend is reserved when the charters are first granted, because a charter is a contract and cannot, therefore, be changed without the consent of both parties concerned. These facts have led American jurisdictions to give up the attempt to regulate through charter provision and to act through other forms of law.

Early General Laws and Constitutions

In addition to regulation through charters, the state may act by general law. That is, it may prescribe rules of conduct for all railroads subject to its authority. Sometimes this is done through constitutional provision and sometimes through simple statute. Probably the difference is less than is supposed. Certainly in the West today constitutional amendments resemble ordinary statutes in the detailed character of their provisions, differing from them mainly in the fact that they can be altered or repealed only by popular vote.

It is now over a hundred years since American states began to regulate railroad carriers by constitutional or statute law. The first general law was passed as early as 1833. In this as in subsequent statutes the states

indicated . . ." (B. H. Meyer, *Railway Legislation in the United States*, New York, Macmillan, 1903, pp. 53–54).

dealt with applications for railroad charters, the safety of travel, the taxation of railroad companies, subscriptions to and transfer of stock, annual reports, and a variety of other items. It will be perceived that the subject of the early laws resembled that of the charters. In but few cases was an attempt made at the beginning to fix maximum rates for the carriage of passengers or freight; and although some of the laws set up commissions, these bodies were concerned rather with matters of safety than with rates. Early general legislation in this country marked an advance in the direction of standardized treatment of railroad companies; but it accomplished little in the way of effective control.

State Commissions

Finally, the state may regulate through a general law implemented by a Board or Commission. Such a commission will act in an administrative or semijudicial capacity. It will interpret the provisions of a controlling statute and will apply them to specific cases, proceeding on its own initiative or on complaint. It will even set up regulations of its own within the framework of the legislative purpose and the power which the law conveys. The advantages of a commission are its flexibility and its expertness, due (1) to the concentration of its members upon the task of regulatory control and, (2) to the presence of a technical staff which a commission will be interested to provide. A commission can make effective contact with the parties concerned in any controversial situation and it can accumulate facts rapidly—neither of these possibilities is open to a legislative body. It is true that a commission may blunder if it is poorly staffed or if it is inadequately equipped. But experience seems to show that it is the best type of administrative machinery that has been so far devised.

Granger Movement

Experiments with charters, general laws, and commissions began in the several states. Among these was the law that set up the Massachusetts Railroad Commission of 1869.[2] The development was accelerated by the

---

[2] The Massachusetts statute of 1869 created a railroad commission of three men appointed by the governor for 3-year terms, with power to prescribe the form of annual reports rendered by railroad corporations, to supervise the railroads "with reference to the security and accommodations of the public," and to undertake certain duties of inspection, investigation, arbitration, and report. The commission was subsequently given authority to prescribe a system of accounts which every corporation operating a railroad was required to follow. No railroad could be opened for use until the board had examined it and certified that the laws relating to its construction had been observed, and that it appeared to be in a safe condition. No railroad could be constructed across another at the same grade or across navigable waters without the consent of the commissioners. No railroad corporation might locate or construct its road until a sworn estimate of the cost of construction had been submitted to the board and the board had been satisfied that a certain amount of the stock subscriptions had been paid in.

The commission had supervision of the relocation of freight and passenger stations.

so-called "Granger movement" of the 1870's. The nature and effect of this experience needs to be discussed.

The Granger agitation proposed to organize the farmers of the South and of the Middle West for the improvement of their economic condition. The granges were farmers' organizations, nonpolitical, and intended to encourage diversification of crops, systematization of farm work, coöperation in buying and selling, and other sound agricultural policies. The idea seems to have been conceived by a government clerk named Kelley. Kelley's duties led him through the Southern states in the year 1866, where he was impressed by the unprogressive spirit which the farmers there displayed. In 1867, aided by five other government clerks and a fruit grower of Wayne, New York, he worked out a ritual, framed a constitution, adopted a motto and a schedule of fees, and launched an organization bearing the name of "Patrons of Husbandry," which was destined to enjoy an extraordinarily influential career.

An energetic man can always make converts in the United States if equipped, as Kelley was, with a constitution, a motto, a ritual, and a set of fees. Such symbols make an irresistible appeal to American citizens. It so happened, however, that the Grange organization benefited in its early years by a very great agricultural depression. Between 1866 and 1876 the

---

It could revise the tariff for the care and carriage of milk. It could regulate the fares established by street railroad companies, but not so as to reduce their profits below a certain percentage upon the cost of the road. It could make rules regulating the transportation of explosives, the violation of which subjected a corporation to heavy penalties. It could approve of the use of certain mechanical appliances and by written notice revoke such approval. It could fix the route of a railroad in a city or town where the town or city authorities could not agree, in the matter of a route, with the directors of the railroad.

The Massachusetts Railroad Commission could not, however, fix a rate, except as specified, or require a railroad to change its methods of operation or add to its equipment; nor could it generally enforce existing laws, except by investigation and presentation of facts to the state attorney general for such action as he might deem expedient or by inclusion of its conclusions in an annual report to the legislature. These characteristics of the law earned for the Massachusetts Commission the name of a weak, or advisory, commission, as contrasted with commissions exercising mandatory powers over railroad rates, such as the later boards in Wisconsin and in Illinois.

The Massachusetts Commission is credited with causing the introduction of improvements and economies in the railroads of Massachusetts, such as the automatic block system, continuous or train brakes, and gradual elimination of grade crossings; with the reform of the system of railroad bookkeeping in the state, and with bringing about a steady decline in the average passenger- and ton-mile receipts of Massachusetts railways. Doubtless it had some influence in these matters. It should be observed, however, that much of the Commission's achievement lay in the fields in which it possessed positive authority; and that the tendency to rate reductions in Massachusetts during the seventies and eighties, to which its friends allude and which it had no authority to enforce, was by no means confined to the railroads which lay within its jurisdiction and probably resulted from causes over which it had little control. The trend of regulatory development in the United States has been in the direction of the strong rather than in that of the weak commission, and the Massachusetts type did not maintain itself even in the state whose name it bears.

price of wheat dropped from $1.52 per bushel to $.96 per bushel, the price of corn from $.47 to $.34, and the price of cotton from $97.54 to $47.31 per bale. This decline, which was the result of overproduction, aggravated by poor marketing methods and by a disturbed state of the currency, predisposed the farmers to joint action of some kind and partly accounts for the rapid growth of the Grange during the ten years that have been mentioned. The most rapid development of all came after the Panic of 1873. On May 19, 1873, granges in the United States numbered 3,360; on March 1, 1874, 14,365; and on January 1, 1875, there were 21,697 of these farmers' organizations. This was the high point of the movement. In July, 1876, the number of granges had declined to 15,127, although the membership in the order still amounted to 588,525.[3]

Illinois Railroad Legislation, 1869–1871

Out of the seething discontent west of the Allegheny Mountains came several interesting experiments in legislation. The states principally affected were Illinois, Minnesota, Iowa, and Wisconsin.

In Illinois, a law was passed in 1869 declaring in general terms that railroads should be limited to just, reasonable, and uniform rates. This was followed in 1870 by an amendment to the constitution of Illinois declaring railroads to be public highways, forbidding stock watering and consolidations of competing lines, requiring railroads to make annual reports to a state officer, and directing the legislature to pass laws to correct abuses and to prevent unjust discrimination and extortion by railroad carriers in the state.[4]

Acting under the mandate of the constitution, the Illinois legislature, in 1871, promptly passed a series of supporting laws. One of these, relating to passenger fares, divided the railroads of the state into classes based upon their gross earnings per mile and fixed a sliding scale of maxima for the different classes, ranging from 2½ cents to 5½ cents per mile. Another act, applying to freight rates, forbade discrimination and, more particularly, provided that:

No railroad corporation . . . shall charge or collect for the transportation of goods, merchandise or property on its said road, for any distance, the same nor any larger or greater amount as toll or compensation than is at the same time charged or collected for the transportation of similar quantities of the same class of goods, merchandise or property over a greater distance upon the same road.

Section 3 of the same act provided that:

No railroad corporation shall increase its rates of toll or compensation to be

[3] S. J. Buck, *The Granger Movement,* Cambridge, Mass., Harvard, 1913, p. 58.
[4] F. N. Thorpe, *American Charters, Constitutions, and Organic Laws, 1492–1908,* Washington, D.C., Government Printing Office, 1909.

charged for the transportation, receipt, handling or delivery of any property from any point on its line of road to any other point on its line of road by reason of any decrease in its rates which may be required to be made under the first section of this act.

The normal or maximum rates, above which no increase was to be made, were fixed as the rates of the year 1870. It followed in practice that the law established the actual rates in effect in 1870 on any railroad in Illinois as the maximum rates for that railroad, as far as the transportation of the same class of goods for equal distances was concerned. This drastic rule was based upon the assumption that the rate voluntarily charged by a railroad could be assumed to be a reasonable rate.

Still another law in 1871 established a board of railroad and warehouse commissioners of three men, appointed by the governor for terms of two years, with salaries of $3,500 each. The commissioners had no power to fix rates; but the railroads were required to supply them with statistical and other information, and it was their duty to report to the governor annually and meanwhile to cause prosecutions to be brought for any violations of the law which they might discover.

Finally, an act regulating the receiving, transportation, and delivery of grain by railroad corporations forbade discrimination between shippers and warehouses in the handling of grain.

Illinois Act of 1873

There was difficulty in enforcing the Illinois Act of 1871, partly because there were no adequate penalties for charging more than the maximum passenger fares provided by the law and partly because the clauses relating to discrimination were unenforceable by reason of their rigidity. Indeed, when a case under the freight-rate law reached the state supreme court, that tribunal ruled that the effect of the law was to prohibit all discrimination, not merely unjust discrimination, and that this was impossible under the state constitution because it forbade an act which might be shown to be perfectly innocent.

Hence in 1873 the law relating to freight rates was repealed, and a new act was substituted for it. This new law forbade unjust discrimination and unreasonable rates. With respect to the particular measure of discrimination, the statute now declared that a difference in charge between persons and places for the same service in the same direction made a *prima facie* case of unjust discrimination, and that in attempting to justify such discrimination the railroad might not allege competition as an excuse.[5] The words "in the same direction" were new in this connection, while the reference to a *prima facie* case meant that the carriers might

[5] *Third Annual Report of the Illinois Railroad and Warehouse Commission,* 1873, p. 162.

now submit evidence in justification of a discrimination and that their practices would not be condemned offhand.

Still more important, the new act provided substantial penalties for extortion, or for making any unjust discrimination as to passenger or freight rates, and directed the Railroad and Warehouse Commission of Illinois to make a schedule of reasonable maximum rates and fares for the transportation of passengers and freight and cars upon each railroad within the state. This legislation remained upon the statute books until supplemented by the law of 1913.

Other Granger Legislation

Laws similar to, although not identical with the Illinois statutes were passed, in the 1870's, in Minnesota, Iowa, and Wisconsin.[6] Not only this, but between 1870 and 1886 restrictive laws were enacted in Missouri, California, Nebraska, Kansas, and Oregon, as well as in a number of Southern states. We shall not describe this legislation, but we may comment upon the laws of the four states in which the Granger movement began.

Economic Effect of the Granger Laws

The prompt repeal or substantial amendment of most of the Granger laws, and the difficult economic conditions in the Granger states at or about the period when this legislation was made effective, have led to the general assumption that these laws were ill-devised and destructive. Moreover, the best-informed study of the Granger legislation which has been published confirms this assumption by declaring that the maximum rates prescribed in Iowa and Wisconsin during the Granger period were lower than conditions warranted, that the work of the railroad commission in Minnesota was unsatisfactory, and that the Illinois schedules failed to cause trouble largely because litigation postponed their effectiveness until the natural development of business had brought railroad charges below the maxima prescribed by law.[7]

There is, however, another side to the picture. For one thing, there is little evidence that the Granger laws actually caused serious losses to the carriers. Indeed, the Illinois law was not enforced until 1880, and a prolonged contest in Wisconsin seriously interfered with the administration of the new law in that state. Detrick has shown that railroad construction in the Granger states compared favorably with construction during the 1870's in other states in the West, South, and East, and that the rate of increase in net earnings in these states was well above the average of neighboring

---

[6] R. Saby, *Railroad Legislation in Minnesota, 1849–1897*, St. Paul, Volkszeitung Company, 1912.

[7] S. J. Buck, *op. cit.*

commonwealths. Even in Wisconsin, the state which is popularly supposed to have been most unfavorably affected by maximum rate legislation, the increase in average net earnings during the period from 1873 to 1876 was greater than in Indiana, Michigan, or Missouri, and also greater than the average for the Middle states of New York, New Jersey, Pennsylvania, Delaware, Maryland, and West Virginia, or the average for ten selected Southern states ranging from Tennessee to Florida.[8] If the Granger legislation was unduly drastic, at least it was innocuous because only partially enforced.

Nature of Experiments Undertaken by the Granger States

The real significance of the Granger laws is not to be found in their effect upon conditions in the states which passed them, but in the fact that they made certain experiments and provoked certain statements of principle from the courts which proved of great importance in the development of railroad legislation.

The experiments referred to in the preceding paragraph include the following:

1. The establishment of schedules of maximum rates by direct legislative enactment.
2. The creation of commissions with authority to draw up schedules of maximum rates.
3. The attempt to prevent discrimination between places by "pro rata" or "short haul" clauses in the law.
4. The attempt to preserve competition by forbidding the consolidation of parallel lines.
5. The prohibition of the granting of passes to public officials.

Not all of these experiments have been mentioned in the text and by no means all of them proved successful enough to become standard practice in the legislation of the American states. On the contrary, the establishment of rates by direct legislative enactment has been generally unsuccessful in this country, and the enforcement of uniform or pro rata rates without regard to local conditions has seldom made for the best interests either of the railroad which is subject to them or of the community which the railroad serves. On the other hand, the railroad commission has proved an increasingly useful device, and the prohibition of consolidations between parallel railroad lines at least marked a way which American legislatures followed for many years.

[8] C. R. Detrick, "The Effects of the Granger Acts," *Journal of Political Economy*, March, 1903. The Southern states referred to in the text were the following: Virginia, Kentucky, North Carolina, Tennessee, South Carolina, Georgia, Florida, Alabama, Mississippi, and Louisiana.

Attitude of Railroad Managements Toward State Railroad Control

Still more important than the experiments which the Middle Western states launched in the 1870's through the medium of the Granger laws was the fact that these statutes, when they reached the courts for review as to their constitutionality, called forth such emphatic declarations of the public nature of railroad employment and of the consequent public responsibility of carriers and their subjection to public control as to provide a foundation upon which later railroad regulation could securely rest.

Old and clearly formulated as is the law of common carriage, railroad companies in the United States did not, in 1871, recognize the right of the public to control their affairs. Speaking of the railroads' attitude as late as 1882, Judge Reagan of Texas enumerated the pretensions of leading railroad officials and their lawyers as follows:

1. They assume that the railroads are private property.
2. They deny that they are bound by the law of common carriers.
3. They deny that their roads are public highways.
4. They assume that their charters constitute a contract between them and the state which amounts to a prohibition against future interference with their management of these corporations by the legislative authority,
5. They deny, some of them wholly, and some in a qualified manner, the constitutional power of Congress and of state legislatures to regulate and control the terms on which they shall carry merchandise [9]

This position of the railroad companies to which Judge Reagan referred was contrary to the general theory of the law, even at the time when the Granger acts were passed; but it was nevertheless an important step in advance when the new state legislation led courts to reaffirm the fundamental doctrine that railroad companies are subject to public control.[10]

[9] United States House of Representatives, 47th C., 1st S., House Misc. Doc. 55, 1882, Ser. 2047, p. 238.

[10] The leading Supreme Court decisions were handed down in 1876. They were as follows:

Munn v. Illinois (94 Stat. 113, 1876). This case dealt with a section of the constitution of Illinois relating to warehouses and, more particularly, with an act of the legislature of Illinois, passed under the authority of the constitution of 1870, which required the managers of public warehouses in that state to obtain licenses from the circuit court of the county in which the warehouse was located and to observe certain stated maximum rates for the storage and handling of grain. Munn and Scott were lessees of elevators in Chicago who continued to do a warehouse business without taking out a license and who charged higher rates than those stated by the act. The question at issue in the case was whether the state legislature had authority to pass the law which Munn and Scott refused to obey and whether the fixing of maximum rates for the storage of grain deprived the plaintiffs of their property without due process of law, contrary to the Fourteenth Amendment to the Constitution of the United States.

Addressing itself to the question of constitutionality, the United States Supreme Court stated and elaborated upon the principle that there were certain businesses "affected with a public interest" which the public had a right to control. "When," said

Later State Developments

By the end of 1876 there had been enacted in the United States a respectable body of state law, attempting the regulation of railroad companies in various ways, and the constitutionality of this legislation had been upheld by the federal courts. During later years states broadened their statutes and perfected their administrative techniques. By 1947, 47 states and the District of Columbia had commissions with jurisdiction over common carriers. Such commissions, typically, were authorized to regulate rail and motor service. They had, in most cases, power to prescribe rates, to grant or to refuse certificates conveying the right to operate, to supervise service, and to authorize consolidations. Sometimes they regulated capitalization also. This was progress from the days of the Granger laws. The effectiveness of this state control over transport was not, it is true, uniform. It depended and will continue to depend upon the character of the facility which is regulated and upon the size and financial resources of the state which any given commission undertakes to represent.

The following pages of this chapter will discuss problems of state regulation of railroad, motor, and air transportation in some detail. State control of water transport is relatively unimportant.

---

the Court, "one devotes his property to a use in which the public has an interest, he, in effect, grants to the public an interest in that use, and must submit to be controlled by the public for the common good, to the extent of the interest he has thus created. He may withdraw his grant by discontinuing the use; but, so long as he maintains the use, he must submit to the control."

It seemed obvious to the Supreme Court that a public grain warehouse was affected with a public interest, and that the legislature therefore had authority to make regulations regarding its use. It was not necessary to the decision in *Munn v. Illinois* to extend the principle of the decision to railroads although, as a matter of fact, common carriers were mentioned as illustrations of public business in the course of the court's discussion.

Chicago, Burlington & Quincy v. Iowa (94 U.S. 155, 1876). In this case the Supreme Court ruled that railroad companies were engaged in a public employment affecting the public interest and were, therefore, subject to public control under the doctrine of *Munn v. Illinois*. The court therefore dismissed a bill filed by the Chicago, Burlington & Quincy Railroad Company asking for an injunction to restrain the attorney general of the state of Iowa from enforcing the Iowa railroad legislation of 1874.

Peik v. Chicago and Northwestern Railway Company (94 U.S. 164, 1876. See also 94 U.S. 179, 1876 and 94 U.S. 181, 1876). This case differed from the foregoing in that the bill was filed by first mortgage bondholders of the Chicago and Northwestern Railway Company in order to restrain the railroad company from conforming to, and the Railroad Commission of Wisconsin and the attorney general of Wisconsin from enforcing, the Wisconsin law of 1874 limiting the rate of charges for transporting passengers and freight on the railroads in that state. The suit was somewhat summarily dismissed, because the principle involved was regarded as settled by previous decisions.

Winona and St. Peter Railroad v. Blake (94 U.S. 180, 1876). In this case the Supreme Court upheld the legislation of Minnesota as it had already upheld that of the other Granger states.

Railroads

State regulatory laws now invariably apply to railroads. These laws are somewhat less than moderately effective, for several reasons. On the organizational side, most railroad systems are distributed over several states, so that it becomes difficult for a company to comply with state requirements unless the rules and regulations of all states in which it operates happen to be the same. And there must be correlation in operating control unless the several states are willing to isolate themselves to a considerable degree. In addition to this, there is federal intervention, upon grounds which have been explained in chapter 27. The practical result is that state railroad regulation is seriously circumscribed. It is not, however, completely abolished. The Interstate Commerce Commission has tried to collaborate with State commissions, so that States may have some voice in the administration of federal railroad laws.[11]

[11] Voluntary state-federal coöperation in railroad regulation was proposed, after the Shreveport case, by B. H. Meyer, chairman of the Interstate Commerce Commission (National Association of Railroad Commissioners, *Proceedings,* 1916, pp. 7–8). The state commissions did not at first respond; but representatives of the state and federal bodies agreed, in 1922, upon a coöperative plan (National Association of Railroad and Utilities Commissioners, *Proceedings of the 34th Annual Convention,* 1922, pp. 426–431. See also United States Interstate Commerce Commission, *Annual Report,* 1922, Appendix H). This agreement was revised in 1925 and again in 1937 (*ibid., Proceedings of the 37th Annual Convention,* 1925, pp. 43–48; *Proceedings of the 44th Annual Convention,* 1937, pp. 49–56).

The present arrangement provides for the following steps:

1. A state, or group of states, or the Interstate Commerce Commission may propose coöperation in a given case.

2. If fewer than eight states are involved, the individual states will appoint their representatives.

3. If more than eight states are involved, the state representatives will be selected by the president of the National Association of Railroad and Utilities Commissioners from a panel which the Association will have established on the basis of certain rules.

4. Selected members of the coöperative panel will sit with a division of the Interstate Commerce Commission during the hearing of a case and with the full Commission during oral argument. A preliminary draft of the Commission's decision and order will ordinarily be made available, with request for comment, before the Commission issues its final report, although this is not always done. The responsibility for decision will lie with the Commission. Panel members may transmit their own conclusions to the interested state commissions; these views are not incorporated in the Commission's report; the federal commission is required, however, to state the concurrence or nonconcurrence of the state representatives in the decision which it has reached (*ibid., Proceedings of the 61st Annual Convention,* 1949, pp. 242–251).

Coöperative proceedings, according to one or another of the approved plans, have now occurred over a period of approximately 30 years in railroad cases where the rate making authority of a state is or may be affected by action of the Interstate Commerce Commission. There has always been some difficulty. State commissioners are busy men and cannot easily leave their local work to sit in controversies which they have no power to decide. There is question whether a commissioner should appear when his state is a contending party. When state representatives have participated they have sometimes complained that they have not been furnished with transcripts of the record and that the federal commission has given little attention to their views. We may believe that

Motor Vehicles

State legislatures and commissions have been and are active in regulating the use of motor vehicles. This is currently much more significant than the state control of railroad operations. State regulation of motor transport seemed an obvious necessity when vehicles began to occupy the public roads. It was important to determine the types of auto carriers that might be employed and the conditions of their operation in order to protect the public and to protect highways which, for the most part, had been locally financed. Hence a variety of state and local rules which specified the speed, weight, and size of motor cars; the kinds of brakes; the number, color, and position of lights, gongs, and whistles; the location of gasoline tanks; the strength of chassis frames; the use of signals; and the relative priority of vehicles at intersections. Later federal regulation was to deal with some of these same subjects.[12]

State Economic Regulation of Motor Vehicles

In addition to safety control, motor regulation early sought to eliminate abuses resulting from operating and pricing policies in the motor industry. Speaking with respect to the operation of motor carriers in California before the period of regulation, Mr. Howell, Vice-President and General Manager of the Motor Transit Company of California, has testified:

It was a chaotic condition, without responsibility, without inspection, a great menace to the public health and morals and to the pocket book of the community. Anybody who could make the first payment down on a second-hand car would go into the business. The car would break down and the passengers were left stranded wherever they happened to be, and the driver disappeared. If there happened to be a fire and the car burnt up, that was all there was to it. He lost his investment, his first payment on the car, and under the contract the seller had no recourse for any salvage from the fire loss.

The game got so bad that cigar stores, bootblacks, newsboys, were selling tickets over stage lines, taking a commission of 10, 15, 20 or 30 per cent on the sale, and if the car which was to carry the passenger didn't show, the pas-

---

these proceedings have been of value because they have provided state authorities with additional opportunity to present their views and because they have given the federal commission the benefit of some local knowledge. There is little reason to suppose that they have affected general policies where state and federal views have clashed.

It may be added that state commissions now participate in cooperative plans with the Federal Communications Commission, the Federal Power Commission, and with the Securities and Exchange Commission as well as with the Interstate Commerce Commission. The Act to Regulate Commerce also requires the Interstate Commerce Commission to give notice to governors of states in the case of applications for the issue of certificates [Sec. 1 (19)]; for railroad consolidation [Sec. 5 (2) (b)]; for valuations [Sec. 19a (b)]; and for the issue of securities [Sec. 20 (a) (6)]. The purpose of these notices is to enable local interests to state their opinions.

[12] See the appendix to the present chapter for a list of the state safety requirements which were effective in 1949.

senger had no recourse. . . . Some of these people found it was cheaper to have tickets printed and sell them over some fictitious name of a stage line and never make any attempt to find transportation for the passenger, and when he [*sic*] had collected several hundred dollars or a thousand or more he would close his cubby-hole window and go off with the proceeds, leaving the tickets lying around. . . . The City [of Los Angeles] passed an ordinance finally making it a misdemeanor to sell tickets over any stage line except through a permit of the Board of Public Utilities and the filing of a bond to protect the public against such misuse.

And it was by different little things day after day that we finally got the carriers down to responsibility and regularity, open fares, published fares, and schedules, and later that spread to the State when the State laws were passed.[13]

State Economic Regulation

In an attempt to straighten out the situation which these criticisms reveal, the District of Columbia and 47 states had statutes regulating the business of common and contract carriers by motor vehicle by January, 1950. These were in addition to laws regulating common carriers by railroad. Most of the states that had regulatory laws vested in a board or commission the power to grant or to withhold certificates of convenience and necessity for motor carriage, to fix rates, fares, charges, and classifications, to regulate service and safety to operation, and to require the filing of reports. In a number of states the commission prescribed or supervised the carriers' accounting systems. In California and New York the railroad or public utility commission supervised the fiscal affairs of motor vehicle common carriers. The right to inspect books and, generally, to make rules and regulations, was a common feature of state laws, while less frequently the right to order improvements was specifically reserved. Such systems of control attempted to secure more than safety of operation; they sought to eliminate discrimination, unreasonableness of charge, the irresponsi-

---

[13] United States Interstate Commerce Commission, *Motor Bus and Truck Investigation,* I.C.C. Docket 18,300, vol. 8, testimony Howell, pp. 1780–1782.

Miller has also, but more generally, listed the abuses believed to be found in the practice of motor carriage in 1933 as follows:

1. Motor vehicle owners discriminated between shippers. This was accomplished by rebates, by sudden changes in rates, by secret rates, or by simple differences in the rates charged different patrons.

2. Motor rates were unstable. This made for uncertainty in business operations even when, at any moment, all shippers paid the same charge.

3. Truck operations disturbed marketing machinery and interfered especially with existing systems for the distribution of vegetables, fruits, and livestock.

4. The multiplication of trucks congested the highways. Unorganized competition also led to the wasteful use of motor equipment, as when an excessive number of vehicles operated between termini.

5. Motor vehicle owners were financially irresponsible.

From S. L. Miller, *Inland Transportation,* New York, McGraw-Hill, 1933.

bility of motor operators, and excessive and wasteful competition. These were the abuses which we have enumerated; most of the control work that was not concerned with safety may be classified under one or the other of these heads.

Private Carriers Make Motor Regulation Difficult

State motor regulation suffers from the presence of the private carrier. It is true that the private carrier can be and is compelled to comply with safety rules and with regulations designed to protect the public roads. Some states even once thought that they could require all persons who transported passengers or property in motor vehicles upon their highways to operate as common carriers. But this proved not to be the case.[14]

From 70 to 80 percent of motor trucks and the great predominance of passenger automobiles are to be classed as private.[15] It follows that State economic regulation is currently directed to a very small proportion of a large competitive field. Moreover, if government requirements become too burdensome within this area, operators shift from common to contract carriage, or shippers buy and use trucks or automobiles of their own. The traffic is not regulated, although some carriers may be.

Relations Between State and Federal Control

State economic regulation of motor carriers is also partially ineffective because it is limited to intrastate commerce. This restriction, while always important, is less significant in motor than in railroad or air transport because of the typically shorter haul and local character of motor operation.[16] And the authority of state commissions over motor carriers is enlarged by the willingness of Congress to recognize the appropriateness of local control of interstate motor commerce in some instances and to allow state participation in other cases where ultimate power is reserved to a federal board. Thus the federal law does not apply to intrastate motor carriers which handle relatively small amounts of interstate commerce,[17]

[14] See 266 U.S. 570, 1925; 271 U.S. 583, 1926. A state may, however, require a private carrier to apply for a permit and it may refuse to issue this permit under certain conditions (287 U.S. 251, 1932; 286 U.S. 374, 1932).

[15] See chap. 2.

[16] See chap. 2.

[17] To quote from the Interstate Commerce Act:

"Sec. 204 (a) It shall be the duty of the [Interstate Commerce] Commission . . .

"(4a) To determine, upon its own motion, or upon application by a motor carrier, a State board, or any other party in interest, whether the transportation in interstate commerce performed by a motor carrier or class of motor carriers lawfully engaged in operation solely within a single State is in fact of such nature, character, or quantity as not substantially to affect or impair uniform regulation by the Commission of transportation by motor carriers engaged in interstate or foreign commerce in effectuating the national transportation policy declared in this Act. Upon so finding, the Commission shall issue a certificate of exemption to such motor carrier or class of motor carriers or to motor transportation solely within a municipality,[18] it is modified with respect to States which have State regulatory boards,[19] and it recognizes the need for joint local and federal action when both interests are involved. The nature and extent of state-federal coöperation in the case of railroads has been mentioned on pages 595–597. In motor vehicle legislation the federal law authorizes the Interstate Commerce Commission to hold joint hearings with state authorities in matters arising under the Interstate Commerce Act, much as is done in that part of the statute which applies to railroads. But the Motor Law goes further. It requires,

which, during the period such certificate shall remain effective and unrevoked, shall exempt such carrier or class of motor carriers from compliance with the provisions of this part, and shall attach to such certificate such reasonable terms and conditions as the public interest may require . . . In any case where a motor carrier has become exempt from the provisions of this part . . . it shall not be considered to be a burden on interstate or foreign commerce for a State to regulate such carrier with respect to the operations covered by such exemption . . ."

Legislation originally proposed by the National Association of Railroad and Public Utility Commissioners would have granted exemption to all motor carriers not operating across state lines ("Annual Convention," *Proceedings,* 1941, p. 184). But Congress would not go so far. Comparatively few cases have arisen under Sec. 204 (a) (4a), because of the expense of Interstate Commerce Commission hearings (*ibid.,* 1942, p. 115).

[18] See chap. 33.

[19] Again quoting from the Interstate Commerce Act: "Sec. 206 (a) . . . No common carrier by motor vehicle shall engage in any interstate . . . operation . . . unless there is in force a certificate of public convenience and necessity issued by the Commission . . .

"*And provided further,* That this paragraph shall not be so construed as to require any such carrier lawfully engaged in operation solely within any State to obtain from the Commission a certificate authorizing the transportation by such carrier of passengers or property in interstate or foreign commerce between places within such State if there be a board in such State having authority to grant or approve such certificates and if such carrier has obtained such certificate from such board. Such transportation shall, however, be otherwise subject to the jurisdiction of the Commission under this part."

The general rule is that a motor carrier may haul freight or passengers, when the points of origin and destination are within a single state, under a certificate granted by a State authority. It is possible, however, that a carrier whose lines are entirely within a state's boundaries may desire to participate with connecting carriers by the receipt or delivery of traffic which has an origin or destination at a point in another state. This would be a participation in interstate commerce; it would, ordinarily, require an application for a federal certificate or permit. Section 206, however, makes it possible for a carrier which holds a state certificate for local operation to haul traffic on its lines within a state that could be classed as interstate because it had a point of origin or destination elsewhere, and to do this without applying to the Interstate Commerce Commission for the grant of a federal certificate. The local state certificate, in such a case, is interpreted as carrying the privilege of participating in a federal operation as an incidental consequence (3 M.C.C. 503, 1937; 36 M.C.C. 659, 1941; 41 M.C.C. 693, 1943).

It is still true, under the conditions stated, that a carrier which itself sends vehicles from one state to another must hold a federal certificate. It is also true that a carrier which engages in interstate commerce on the basis of a state certificate is subject to the provisions of the Interstate Commerce Act with respect to rates and charges, safety, insurance, accounts and reports, issue of securities, unifications, transfers, and other matters.

that is to say, a reference to joint boards when the operations of the carriers or brokers involved cover not more than three states.[20] It specifies the subjects which these boards may consider,[21] and it provides that orders of joint boards shall become orders of the Commission after an appropriate time and in the absence of repeal.[22]

Yet in spite of these concessions and the large volume of local business, the state is not in a position to meet all of the problems of motor transport to which government direction should be applied. The state cannot, more precisely, regulate without federal permission those aspects of interstate motor transport which are national in character and require a uniform system of control. We shall explain in the following chapter that interstate rates are in this category, in discussing the Wabash case. And several Supreme Court decisions held, in 1925, that a state may not refuse a carrier permission to operate in interstate commerce because this, likewise, is a matter which is not primarily of local concern.[23] These and other limitations caused Congress, eventually, to pass a federal motor carrier law. State regulation, however, has been and still is important in the motor carrier field.

State Regulation of Air Transport

State legislation affecting air carriers was classified by the Federal Coordinator of Transportation, in 1934, as follows:

⟨ 1.   Statutes which fix the legal status of all aircraft as to contracts, crimes and torts, define the rights and liabilities of parties affected by aircraft opera-

[20] Joint boards are composed of one member of each state within which the motor carrier or brokerage operations involved are or are proposed to be conducted. The member from any state is to be nominated by the board or such state from its own membership or otherwise and is approved by the Interstate Commerce Commission; or if there is no board in such state or if the state board fails to make a nomination when requested by the Commission, then the Governor of such state may nominate a member. Where only one member of a board participates in a hearing, that member constitutes a quorum and may recommend an order (See National Association of Railroad and Public Utilities Commissioners, *Proceedings,* 1947, pp. 243–245; *ibid.,* 1950, pp. 96–97; *Public Law 185,* 81st C., 1st S., July 26, 1949; Sen. Rep. 1212, 80th C., 2d S.; and Sen. Rep. 81, 81st C., 1st S., 1949). There has been controversy upon this last-named point.

[21] The Commission refers to joint boards applications for certificates, permits, or licenses; applications for the approval of consolidations, mergers, and acquisitions of control or operating contracts; complaints as to the violation of safety and other Commission regulations; and complaints as to rates, fares, and charges of motor carriers or the practices of brokers. Most applications referred are for certificates, permits, or licenses. The reference is mandatory when not more than three states are involved; it is optional in other cases, because the national aspects of the controversy are, then, more apparent. [See Sec. 205 (a) (b).]

[22] Orders of boards are governed by the same rules which apply to orders of an individual Commissioner or of a division of the Commission.

[23] 266 U.S. 570, 1925; 267 U.S. 307, 1925; 267 U.S. 317, 1925.

tions, and require federal registration and licensing as a prerequisite to operations within the state.

2. Statutes of the character above described that also create a supervisory tribunal with authority to make rules and regulations concerning registration, licensing, and operation of aircraft. Such tribunals have a power to enforce the provisions of state laws.

3. Statutes which class aircraft engaged in the transportation of persons or property, for hire, as common carriers and make them subject to the same character of regulation as is applied to other kinds of common carriers.

4. Statutes enabling the state aviation authority, or municipalities, or other political subdivisions of the state to acquire, maintain, and operate airports, landing fields, and other air navigation facilities.[24]

This classification is still serviceable.

In general, state law has the same force with respect to crimes and torts in airplane operation as in the case of like offenses elsewhere. Controversies which require the definition and delimitation of the liabilities of common carriers for loss and damage are usually also decided under state statutes, although it is conceivable that Congress might legislate with respect to air liability as it has in connection with the liability of marine carriers upon the high seas or the liability of rail and motor carriers on land. The authority of local and political units to acquire and maintain airports can only be derived from state legislation. In these fields the states exert unquestioned power. With reference to other matters listed in our preliminary enumeration, the authority of the several states is limited, in varying degrees, by the paramount power of the federal government.

State Safety Regulations

State statutes which provide rules or regulations concerning licensing and other matters affecting air safety yield to predominant federal authority. Most states, therefore, which assert jurisdiction over the technical aspects of air operations follow the federal rules. Federal licenses for aircraft and airmen were required, in 1950, in all states except Colorado; [25] many states, indeed, merely provide that a federal license shall be registered with some agency of the state. Some states demand both a state and a federal license; but when this is stipulated, the state license is, in most instances, only a certificate of registration or recordation of the federal license.[26] Federal operating directions are everywhere accepted, although

[24] United States, Office of Federal Coordinator of Transportation, *Report on Regulation of Transportation Agencies,* 73d C., 2d S., Sen. Doc. 152, pp. 257–258, 1934.

[25] The Colorado Aeronautics Commission and administrative offices were not functioning, on March 1, 1950, because of lack of appropriations. (See *Status of State Aviation Laws,* compiled and printed by the Civil Aeronautics Administration, data assembled by National Association of State Aviation officials from information supplied by member states.)

[26] Charles S. Rhyne, "Federal, State and Local Jurisdiction over Civil Aviation,"

states have passed additional rules.[27] Congress might, if it so desired, set aside areas for concurrent operating state control, but it has not done so in the aeronautics law. State operating regulation is not entirely futile; it has, however, relatively slight importance.

State Economic Regulation of Air Commerce

States are more inclined to seek independent control over the economic aspects of intrastate air transportation than to urge their right to regulate the techniques of flight. By "economic" is here meant the issue, modification, suspension, or revocation of certificates permitting air carriers to fly planes within state boundaries; the regulation of service; the fixing of rates; the filing of reports; and the regulation of accounts.[28]

State regulatory officials of 27 states had, in 1946, authority to provide economic regulation of intrastate air commerce.[29] The powers which

---

Law and Contemporary Problems, Winter-Spring, 1946, pp. 458–487. See also *Status of State Aviation Laws, supra.*

[27] As of May 1, 1950, 38 states prohibited low-altitude flying, 40 states had legislation concerning flight under the influence of liquor, and 17 states regulated air dusting in one way or another. The Uniform State Aeronautics Act, then substantially adopted in 28 states, had some provisions governing flight.

State criminal statutes cover aviation as well as other occupations. Thus a pilot, under certain conditions, may be prosecuted under state laws for manslaughter if he causes the death of an individual within a state.

[28] See text of the Uniform State Air Carrier Bill, approved by the National Association of Railroad and Utilities Commissioners in 1944, *Proceedings, 56th Annual Convention,* 1944, pp. 161–179.

[29] The 27 states were as follows: Alabama, Arizona, Arkansas, California, Colorado, Illinois, Kansas, Kentucky, Maryland, Massachusetts, Michigan, Montana, Nebraska, Nevada, New Mexico, North Dakota, Oklahoma, Pennsylvania, Rhode Island, South Dakota, Tennessee, Utah, Vermont, Virginia, Washington, West Virginia, and Wyoming. In two of these states, Kansas and Montana, the existence of regulatory authority, under state law, was not entirely free from doubt.

The above list was presented to the 58th annual convention of the National Association of Railroad and Utility Commissioners, along with a summary of state laws which read, in part, as follows (*ibid., Proceedings,* 1946, pp. 230–233):

"In all but three of these states, this authority is vested in the public service commission which also has general regulatory jurisdiction over other classes of transportation companies. In Kentucky, South Dakota, and Tennessee, however, this authority is exercised by specially created aeronautics commissions or boards.

"Of the 27 states which provide by law for economic regulation of intrastate commerce, 10 states have done so by special statutes dealing specifically with air commerce. These are the states of Alabama, Arkansas, Kentucky, Massachusetts, New Mexico, Rhode Island, South Dakota, Tennessee, Vermont, and Virginia . . .

"Thirteen state commissions have been vested with this jurisdiction by virtue of the broad definition of the terms 'common carrier' or 'public utility,' or by the inclusion of new terms referring to air carriers, in their general public service laws. These 13 states are: Colorado, Illinois, Kansas, Maryland, Michigan, Montana, Nevada, North Dakota, Pennsylvania, Utah, Washington, West Virginia and Wyoming.

"In most cases these general statutes have not made specific reference to air carriers, but have been construed to apply to such carriers . . .

"In the 4 remaining states . . . this authority is based upon provisions of the state constitution. These are the states of Arizona, California, Nebraska, and Oklahoma."

regulatory boards or commissions possess in these states vary. While the available information is not complete, most seem to have jurisdiction over the subjects mentioned: namely, certificates, intrastate rates, service, and accounts. Some of them have authority to regulate security issues and consolidations. Most state activity has been in the field of certificates of public convenience and necessity. A good many of these permits have been issued to air lines which have desired to operate exclusively intrastate. Sometimes the permit has been general in character. Thus the Pennsylvania Commission granted, in July, 1946, permission to operate a charter service between Du Bois, Clearfield County, and any other airport or landing in Pennsylvania.[30] Sometimes air lines maintain schedules on established routes, as between Ithaca and New York City or between Baltimore and Salisbury.[31] These certificates can exist side by side with authority given interstate carriers by the Civil Aeronautics Board which includes the right to serve more than one community in a given state.

Objections to State Economic Control

The principal conflict between state and federal agencies occurs with respect to situations of the kind last mentioned. For interstate air carriers, the federal board which has jurisdiction believes that the right to do intrastate business is an essential, though incidental privilege of an interstate air line. This is because intrastate traffic improves load factors and supplements interstate earnings. They go even farther than this. Interstate air carriers not only oppose state interference with or jurisdiction over their own right to handle local business, they object also to opening the local field to operators certificated by the states. For the incursion of carriers with state permits, they say, would increase competition. It would interfere with the federal program of balanced and controlled air rivalries, and it might create a pattern of service which was different from that which the federal administration approved.[32] State control over intrastate rates, it is added, might produce results equally objectionable to the federally subsidized undertakings. And in the case of both certificates and rates, multiple responsibility, to state and federal governments, would be inconvenient and expensive.

Argument for State Economic Control

The argument for state control of air transport begins with the observa-

[30] *Ibid., Proceedings,* 1946, p. 41.
[31] *Ibid.,* p. 241.
[32] Oswald Ryan, "Economic Regulation of Air Commerce by the States," *Virginia Law Review,* March, 1945; W. C. Green, "The War Against the States in Aviation," *ibid.,* September, 1945. See chap. 27.

tion that intrastate traffic is, in some areas, important, and that it may well become larger. Fifty percent of the passengers leaving San Francisco by air in September, 1950, were on their way to destinations in California. Comparable percentages in the same month were 35 percent from Houston, Texas; 24 percent from Shreveport, Louisiana; 14 percent from Pittsburgh; 10 percent from Cleveland; 8 percent from Atlanta; and 8 percent from the city of New York.[33]

There is no apparent way of correcting current statistics so as to secure a precise division between interstate and intrastate air traffic. There will, however, be many intrastate passengers when two conditions are met: (1) A state must be large, so that intrastate distances are reasonably long. (2) There must be pairs of cities in a commonwealth which benefit from air communication. Examples of air traffic which meets these two conditions are the exchanges between Los Angeles and San Francisco; between Philadelphia and Pittsburgh; between Cleveland and Cincinnati and Columbus; between Atlanta, Augusta, and Savannah; between New York City and Buffalo, Syracuse, Rochester, and Albany; and between Houston and Dallas, San Antonio, and Austin. Instances of air traffic which does not meet these conditions are those out of Chicago and Boston, where the intrastate business is extremely small.

Advocates of state control over intrastate air traffic ask for state regulation of rates and service on intrastate air carriage.[34] They demand, as a minimum, local authority to establish short line routes which reach points

[33] United States Civil Aeronautics Board, *Airline Traffic Survey*, September, 1950. New York, for the purpose of the calculations, includes Newark, N. J.

The figures quoted in the text are subject to modification, to an uncertain extent, for purposes of interpretation.

1. The fact that a passenger boards an airplane in one state and disembarks at another airport in the same state does not show, necessarily, that he is making a local trip. He may be merely shifting planes at a point where several lines converge.

2. On the other hand, in some instances, as in the case of traffic out of New York City, a considerable portion of local business will pass through a second state on its way to destination. This is, technically, interstate traffic according to rules applied in surface transport. Air traffic of this sort, however, affects intermediate states slightly, if at all. The reason for including it in the interstate category is less persuasive than in the case of surface transportation. The National Association of Railroad and Utilities Commissioners has proposed that, for purposes of regulation, it be classed as interstate (*Proceedings, 59th Annual Convention*, 1947, pp. 147, 206).

3. A third observation may be that the figures in the text are taken from reports to the Civil Aeronautics Board by federally certificated carriers. There is local traffic by noncertificated or state certificated carriers which, if included, would increase the total assigned to intrastate business. This traffic is considerable in California, and may be important elsewhere.

[34] See National Association of Railroad and Utilities Commissioners, *Proceedings, 58th Annual Convention*, 1946, p. 226; *ibid., 60th Annual Convention*, 1948, p. 230.

not covered by main line schedules and which are beneficial to the population of a state. The general position of the states is that the development of a network of local operators cannot come about under centralized federal regulation any more than the development of our national system of motor trucks and bus lines could have come about under exclusive Interstate Commerce Commission regulation. State air traffic is not incidental but a vital part of national transportation. It would be as inconvenient and expensive for intrastate carriers to deal exclusively with Washington as for interstate carriers to accept responsibilities to the separate states. Nor is it clear, say the states, that the competition of state certificated carriers would be a disadvantage to the interstate lines or to the federal government that sudsidized them. The rates on local business would usually be high. But the costs would be also high. The through lines might gain, rather than lose, if they were relieved from the burden of such traffic. This might be especially true of feeder services and of business within or adjacent to municipal areas, if helicopter or small plane service could be arranged, and if this business could be privately financed. It could also be true if air lines connecting distant termini could be spared the burden of some, at least, of the intermediate stops which they are now compelled to make.[35]

Comments on State Economic Air Control

State economic regulation of intrastate air transport is subject to the principles announced in the Shreveport cases and in those which followed the enactment of the Transportation Act of 1920. It is also controlled by court decisions interpreting the certificate provisions of the Act to Regulate Commerce. State powers will be still further limited if the Supreme Court holds that the authority of the Civil Aeronautics Board is promotional as well as regulatory and that states, for this reason, may not interfere with any federal acts which are designed to develop an adequate system of air transportation, no matter what the local application or effect may be.[36] The implication of a Supreme Court ruling based upon this principle and specifically applying it to transport would be far-reaching. It is not impossible, however, that such a principle now represents the law. The result would not be, necessarily, to prevent all state regulation of intrastate commerce. But it would make such regulation entirely dependent upon the statutes which Congress might enact.

[35] See F. C. Hamley, "Appropriate Areas of State Economic Regulation," *Law and Contemporary Problems,* Winter-Spring, 1946, pp. 458–507.

[36] Oswald Ryan, "Regulation of Air Transportation Under Civil Aeronautics Act," *Public Utilities Fortnightly,* November 24, 1949, pp. 695–703. See also 317 U.S. 111, 1942.

APPENDIX TO CHAPTER 28

State Regulation of Motor Vehicle Operation

The variety of local motor regulation may be illustrated by reference to prescriptions in force in 1952 and in 1949.

The following paragraphs summarize state rules, in 1952, with respect to the weight and dimensions of motor vehicles traveling on the public roads.

Weight. Maximum limits of weight are sometimes expressed in a single gross figure; but frequently the law sets a maximum per axle or per inch width of tire or it makes use of a formula containing several elements. The permissible weight varies in some states with the distribution of load upon the wheels, influenced by the spacing of axles; in other states such refinements are neglected.

In 1952, 35 states prescribed a maximum of 18,000 pounds axle load for a single truck (in 5 cases the limit was less on secondary highways), 13 states had limitations from 19,000 to 22,400 pounds, and 1 state (Vermont) had no statutory limitation. Maxima of this sort were relatively high in Pennsylvania, New York, and in the New England states.

The allowable gross weights vary with the type of vehicle and combination and they are different in different states. The state differences embarrass truckers. For the purpose of illustration, it is necessary to assume the use of a selected vehicle—a satisfactory sample might be a 5-axle semitrailer, with one axle under the tractor and four under the vehicle which follows. Such a combination could have left California on a transcontinental trip in 1952, with a gross weight approaching 77,000 pounds. It could have passed without interference until it reached the edge of Colorado, where the permissible gross weight was 77,000 pounds. Further east it would have found that the maximum in Kansas was 64,650 pounds and that it was 60,000 pounds in Missouri. If it had then turned southeast it would have encountered maxima of 42,000 pounds in Kentucky and in Tennessee. The route directly east would have been clear, on the assumption that weights had been reduced to meet the Missouri law but, again, the transit would have been interrupted by maxima of 45,000 pounds in Pennsylvania and of 50,000 pounds in the New England states. These variations would have been less marked in the case of a lighter vehicle but they would still have created difficulties to some extent. (See Association of American Railroads, *Digest of State Laws Pertaining to the Regulation and Taxation of Motor Vehicles, 1952.*)

Variations in requirements can force transfer of lading at state lines. It is also true that the failure of operators to conform to rules damages state highways (United States Senate, Committee on Interstate and Foreign Commerce, *Study of Domestic Land and Water Transportation,* Hearings before a subcommittee pursuant to S. Res. 50, 81st C., 2d S., 1950, testimony MacDonald).

Size. States regulated the width of motor vehicles, in 1952, and many controlled height and length as well. Limitations of automobile dimensions are recognized as an obvious necessity; there is some difference of opinion, however, as to what the limits should be.

The allowable width of motor vehicles in all states is 96 inches, except that Connecticut and Rhode Island permit 102 inches, New Mexico permits 102 inches on highways designated as adequate by the State Highway Commission, and Tennessee and Vermont do not restrict the width of buses.

Most states set a limit of 35 feet on the length of a single unit and of 45 to 50 feet on vehicle combinations. In the West, however, a maximum length of 60 to 65 feet is the rule. The following lengths were permitted in 1952: Arizona, 65 feet; California, 60 feet; Colorado, 60 feet; Idaho, 65 feet; Montana, 60 feet; New Mexico, 64 feet; Oregon, 60 feet; Utah, 60 feet; New Mexico, 65 feet; Oregon, 60 feet; Utah, 60 feet; Washington, 60 feet; Wyoming, 60 feet. In contrast, 19 states limited motor vehicle combinations to 45 feet and 15 states to 50 feet (Association of American Railroads, *op. cit.* See also *Report of Committee on Laws and Ordinances,* The President's Highway Safety Conference, 1949).

Maximum vehicle heights are usually 12½ feet, but sometimes 13, 13½, or 14 feet. There were, in 1952, no restrictions on height in Massachusetts and in Nevada.

The following paragraphs summarize state rules, in 1949, with respect to automobile lights and signals. The data for 1952 are not available.

Lights. Motor vehicle headlights conform to standards set up by the American Society of Automotive Engineers, and these meet the requirements of all states. The rules for clearance lights differ, however. While state laws generally demand clearance lights on equipment exceeding 80 or 84 inches in width, the number of these lights specified varies, as does their color. Thus California prescribed four amber lights, in 1949; Maryland, Minnesota, and Oregon required two amber or white lights at each side in front and two red lights at each side in the rear. Nebraska insisted only on two lights, on the left side; amber or green in front and red in the rear. Rhode Island was satisfied with red reflectors. Taillights must usually be visible at a distance of 500 feet, but the stipulated distance was 300 feet in Maryland and 100 feet in Maine. Spot lights were usually, but not always, permitted; but the direction of the beam was defined differently in different states.

Signals. To indicate an intention to stop or suddenly to decrease speed, 36 states required, in 1949, that the hand and arm should be extended beyond the side of the vehicle, downward. But in 5 states the arm must be horizontal, and in Alabama, Indiana, and West Virginia, the arm must be moved up and down.

An intention to turn left was, generally, to be conveyed to others by extending the arm horizontally. In 6 states the index finger, in addition, was to be pointed, and in Connecticut the hand was to be moved up and down. A forthcoming right-hand turn was to be signaled in some states by extending the hand and arm upward, in some by extending it horizontally, in some by moving the arm upward or forward with a sweeping motion, and in some by extending the arm and rotating the hand.

Uniformity in motor vehicle regulation can be obtained (1) by adjustment of state laws to the provisions of a uniform code or (2) by federal legislation. Real differences in local conditions make the former difficult. It would probably be practically and legally impossible, also, for the federal government to fix motor weights and sizes upon state roads, especially if the federal authorities set standards which the state highways could not bear. But it might not be impossible for the federal government to set size and weight limitations for motor vehicles upon a national system of interstate highways, if maintenance and construction of these highways were provided for by federal funds. The Board of Investigation and Research once recommended something of this sort (*Interstate Trade Barriers Affecting Motor Vehicle Transportation,* 79th C., 1st S., Sen. Doc. 81, Ser. 10,952, 1945. See also D. P. Locklin, *Economics of Transportation,* Chicago, Irwin, 1947, pp. 697–698).

During World War II and again in 1950 the Federal Administrator of Defense Administration appealed to the state governors for some relaxation in the state rules covering the sizes and weights of motor vehicles. In 1942 the governors of all the states agreed to adhere to the terms of a so-called "emergency formula" on the subject of sizes and weights, and to a program of full reciprocity among the states. In 1950 the governors agreed that the states should issue oversize and overweight permits for individual highway freight movements essential to defense production. These were, however, only temporary solutions to the problem that was raised.

R E F E R E N C E S

General Treatises

Bigham, Truman C., and Roberts, Merrill J., *Transportation, Principles and Problems,* New York, McGraw-Hill, 1952.

Fair, Marvin L., and Williams, Ernest W., *Economics of Transportation,* New York, Harper, 1950.

Johnson, E. R., Huebner, G. G., and Wilson, G. L., *Transportation,* New York, Appleton-Century-Crofts, 1940.

Locklin, D. Philip, *Economics of Transportation,* Chicago, Irwin, 1947.

Meyer, B. H., *Railway Legislation in the United States,* New York, Macmillan, 1903.

Miller, S. L., *Inland Transportation,* New York, McGraw-Hill, 1933.

Reynolds, C. G., *The Distribution of Power to Regulate Interstate Carriers Between the Nation and the States,* New York, Columbia University, 1928.

Other Books

Buck, S. J., *The Granger Movement,* Cambridge, Mass., Harvard, 1913.

Kallenbach, J. E., *Federal Cooperation with the States Under the Commerce Clause,* Ann Arbor, University of Michigan, 1942.

Saby, R., *Railroad Legislation in Minnesota, 1849–1897,* St. Paul, Volkszeitung Company, 1912.

Thorpe, F. W., *American Charters, Constitutions, and Organic Laws, 1492–1908,* Washington, D.C., Government Printing Office, 1909.

Periodicals

Adams, C. F., "The Granger Movement," *North American Review,* April, 1875.

Detrick, C. R., "The Effects of the Granger Acts," *Journal of Political Economy,* March, 1903.

Green, W. C., "The War Against the States in Aviation," *Virginia Law Review,* September, 1945.

Nelson, James C., "Joint-Board Procedure Under the Motor Carrier Act," *Journal of Land and Public Utility Economics,* February, 1937.

Rhyne, Charles S., "Federal, State and Local Jurisdiction over Civil Aviation," *Law and Contemporary Problems,* Winter-Spring, 1946.

Ryan, Oswald, "Economic Regulation of Air Commerce by the States," *Virginia Law Review,* March, 1945.

Hanley, Frederick G., "Appropriate Areas of State Economic Regulation," *Law and Contemporary Problems,* Winter-Spring, 1946.

Starr, G. W., "The Position of the State in Economic Control and Regulation of Air Commerce," *Journal of Air Law and Commerce,* Spring, 1948.

Special and Miscellaneous

Purcell, M. R., *Interstate Barriers to Truck Transportation; History and Current Status of Regulations Regarding Size and Weight, Taxes and Other Selected Phases That Affect Trucking,* Washington, D.C., Bureau of Agricultural Economics, 1950.

United States Board of Investigation and Research, *Interstate Trade Barriers Affecting Motor Vehicle Transportation,* 79th C., 1st S., Sen. Doc. 81, Ser. 10,952, 1945.

United States, Office of the Federal Coordinator of Transportation, *Report on Regulation of Transportation Agencies,* 73d C., 2d S., Sen. Rep. 152, 1934.

Federal Regulation—Interstate Commerce Commission: Expenditures and Organization

The addition of federal legislation to the state statutes had been discussed in Congress prior to 1887. Resolutions calling for the investigation of the problem of interstate regulation had, indeed, been presented in the Senate and House of Representatives as early as 1868; and the report of the Windom Committee of 1872, as well as that of a committee of the New York legislature in 1879, known as the Hepburn Committee, had provided members of Congress with authoritative information regarding railroad discrimination and, to a less degree, with data bearing upon the possibility of a lower level of railroad rates. These were the years of the trunk line rate wars, of railroad discrimination which led to the foundation of great private fortunes in coal and in oil, and of the beginning of complaints respecting the transcontinental system of railroad rates. Proposals for legislation appeared in every session of Congress, though none found place upon the statute books. In 1885 the House and the Senate, through the so-called Cullom Committee, undertook an extensive investigation which, in 1886, resulted in still another elaborate report. But there was no effective federal action until 1887, when a Supreme Court decision made it evident that state jurisdiction was insufficient under principles of constitutional law.

Rule of the Granger Cases

The particular question which is referred to in the preceding paragraph concerned the relative powers of state and federal governments over interstate commerce when the federal government had not acted. The Cooley decision had formulated principles for such cases, and the application of these principles seemed for some time to vest satisfactory power in the several states for the control of railroad operation. But this situation later

612

changed. We will state the problem and describe the Supreme Court's reaction in the so-called Granger cases. We will then explain how the Court's position was altered in 1886.

In stating the problem, the reader's attention is directed to Fig. 66.

Let *A* in this diagram represent one, and *B* another, state. Let *ab*, *cd*, and *efg* represent shipments. Of these one shipment, *ab*, begins and ends in state *A;* another, *cd*, begins and ends in state *B*, and the third, *efg*, begins in state *A* and has for destination a point in state *B*.

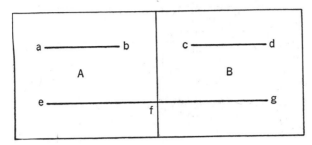

FIGURE 66.   Rule of the Granger Cases.

Now there was no doubt in 1886, and there had been no doubt for years, that state governments in *A* and *B* had jurisdiction over the hauls *ab* and *cd*, or that the federal government might control the haul *efg*. But this statement did not cover all the possible situations. Suppose that the federal government had taken no action, and suppose that state *A* desired to regulate as much of the transportation *efg* as took place between *e* and *f*, and state *B* as much as took place between *f* and *g*. Had the two states authority? Or, taking a still more general case: suppose that state *A* wished to establish a maximum rate per mile to be charged by all railroads within the state. Could a statute fixing such a maximum be enforced as to the portion of the haul *efg* which lay within state *A*, and a similar statute be enforced by state *B* with respect to the portion of the haul *efg* which lay within that commonwealth?

The answer of the Supreme Court in the Granger cases was that the states could exercise jurisdiction if this action did not run counter to any Congressional rule or law. This opinion was delivered in 1876. It appeared to make it possible for state governments, between them, to cover completely the field of interstate as well as that of intrastate railroad transportation.[1]

---

[1] Inspection of the facts of the Granger cases will show that they fell within the class of instances illustrated by the diagram in the text. More particularly, in *Chicago, Burlington & Quincy Railroad v. Iowa* (94 U.S. 155, 1876), the statute at issue divided all the railroads of Iowa into classes according to business, and established a maximum of rates for each of the classes. These maxima applied both to traffic originating and

Wabash, St. Louis & Pacific v. Illinois

In 1886, however, the rule of the Granger cases in the respect mentioned was overturned by a new decision, rendered in the case of *Wabash, St. Louis & Pacific Railway Company v. Illinois*.[2] The facts in this case may be represented by Fig. 67, which is similar to the one already reproduced on page 613.

The complaint in the Wabash controversy arose because a certain person was charged $39 for the carriage of goods from Peoria, Illinois, to

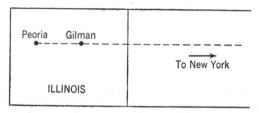

FIGURE 67. The Wabash Case.

New York City, while another person was charged $65 for the carriage of a similar quantity of similar articles from Gilman, Illinois, to the same destination. The reason for this was severe competition at Peoria, and less severe competition at Gilman. A greater charge for a shorter than for a longer haul over the same road being forbidden by Illinois statute, the attorney general of the state brought suit to recover penalty. The railroad

terminating within the state and to traffic which began or ended in other states than Iowa.

In *Peik v. Chicago and Northwestern* (94 U.S. 164, 1876) the nature of the statute complained of was the same as that in Iowa, save that the eighteenth section of the law excepted rates on freight which came from beyond the boundaries of the state to be carried across or through the state.

It is clear that the Iowa and Wisconsin statutes of 1874 both applied, in part, to interstate commerce. It did not follow necessarily that the state legislatures had exceeded their authority in these laws, as Congress had taken no action in regulation of interstate railroad rates; but, none the less, it was necessary for the courts to decide whether rate regulation was a field in which the powers of the state were concurrent with those of the federal government or whether this was a matter calling for uniform national regulation in the sense that states were debarred from acting, even in the absence of provision by the federal body. The Court recognized this and made its opinion clear.

"The law," said the Court in *Peik v. Chicago and Northwestern,* "is confined to State commerce, or such interstate commerce as directly affects the people of Wisconsin. Until Congress acts in reference to the relations of this company [the Chicago and Northwestern Railway Company] to interstate commerce, it is certainly within the power of Wisconsin to regulate its fares, etc., so far as they are of domestic concern. With the people of Wisconsin this company has domestic relations. Incidentally, these may reach beyond the State. But certainly, until Congress undertakes to legislate for those who are without the State, Wisconsin may provide for those within, even though it may indirectly affect those without."

[2] 118 U.S. 557, 1886.

admitted that its practice was contrary to local law, but protested that the state statute was unconstitutional. Now this contention had no basis under the rule in the Granger cases, for Congress had taken no more action to control interstate commerce in 1886 than it had in 1876; and according to Supreme Court doctrine, in the absence of action by Congress, it was proper for a state government to protect its own citizens from discriminatory or unreasonable rates even though it should incidentally regulate interstate commerce in so doing. Nevertheless, the Court accepted in 1886 the argument which it had rejected ten years before, after a review of cases in which the inconveniences of state interference with interstate commerce were described. The Supreme Court did not even now deny that there were instances in which state rules might be applied to interstate commerce in the absence of federal action; but it felt that the regulation of railroad rates on interstate freight must be regarded as exclusively within the field of federal authority and could not safely be remitted to local rule and regulation.

Act of 1887

The moment the Wabash case was decided, it became evident that state legislation with respect to railroads must be supplemented by federal law, or else that a very considerable share of railroad traffic would escape all legislative control. Confronted with this condition, and encouraged by a public opinion which strongly supported regulation, Congress passed the Interstate Commerce Act. The terms of this statute may be summarized as follows:

1. The Act applied to transportation in interstate and foreign commerce.
2. The Act declared that:
   a. All rates must be reasonable.
   b. Undue preference to persons or to localities was forbidden.
   c. It was unlawful to charge more for shorter than for longer hauls.
   d. Tariffs must be filed, published, and adhered to.
   e. Railroads were to supply facilities for the interchange of traffic with connecting lines.
3. A Commission was set up.
4. The Commission was given power to enforce the provisions of the Act. It could require reports from carriers, and had some jurisdiction over accounts.
5. Commission orders were to be enforced through the courts.[3]

Interstate Commerce Commission Expenditures

Figure 68 traces the later expansion of work undertaken by the Com-

---

[3] 24 Stat. 379, 1887; 25 Stat. 855, 1889. See also 25 Stat. 382, 1888; 25 Stat. 505, 1888; 26 Stat. 743, 1891; 27 Stat. 443, 1893.

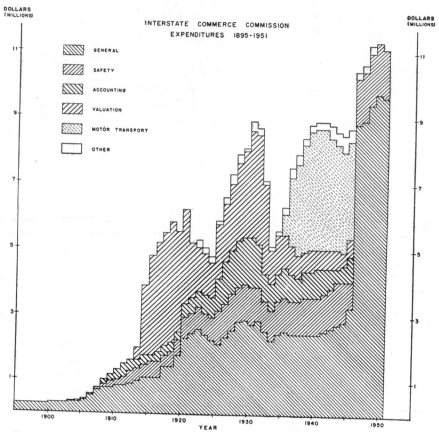

FIGURE 68.   Interstate Commerce Commission Expenditures, 1895 to 1951.
(Annual Reports of the Interstate Commerce Commission.)

mission that was created by the Act of 1887. The expenditures recorded
were made under the authority of the original act and of later laws.[4]

[4] The diagram is based upon figures supplied in the annual reports of the Interstate
Commerce Commission. In the early years the segregations are unimportant, but in
later years they become significant. The amount of the expenditures for any purpose
in any year is measured by the width of the band associated with that outlay. The sum
of all expenditures is indicated, in any year, by the height of the composite column
and for all years by the total of all columns which is the area shown in the chart. After
1946 the Commission ceased to supply details except for safety control and for a few
minor items. This does not mean, of course, that classes of expenditure which had been
made in 1946 were not repeated in 1947, or subsequently. But the lack of detail makes
it impossible to determine the extra cost of particular activities, such as the regulation
of water transport and of freight forwarders. As a matter of fact, the segregation of
expenditures in the Commission reports cannot be used for the purpose of cost analysis in any section, if only because the financial burden of assuming additional or special
duties at any time will necessarily be, to some extent, distributed through the entire

Generalizations Based upon Commission Expenditures

Several facts are evident from the summary of Commission payments which the diagram of Commission expenditures over a substantial period provides. The following generalizations are suggested:

1. It is obvious that the Commission began its work, in the period 1887 to 1891, in a very modest way. Thus, in 1891, its expenses were only $214,844, as compared with a total figure of $11,223,803 in 1949. The difference is not, of course, accounted for by changes in the salaries of the Commissioners themselves, or by increases in their number. The direct cost of employing commissioners has always been small. It began with a sum of $37,500 in 1887 and had grown to only $132,000 in 1949. The growth in the Commission's total outlay was not due to this, but to expansion of the Commission's powers and to the necessary cost of assembling an organization and of meeting the operating costs incident to Commission work.

2. The nonsegregated expenditures of the Interstate Commerce Commission, upon which its reputation has been based, did not rise to any substantial extent until 1906. They then grew rapidly between 1906 and 1921. After 1921 they continued without much change. The latter part of this period included depression years and the years of the Second World War. The apparent large increase after 1946 is due to the inclusion in the nonsegregated category of expenses which had previously been separately described, along with some new, specialized undertakings.

3. The cost of accounting control was not important until 1906. It was not large until the Commission, after the passage of the Act of 1920, attacked problems suggested by the experience of the First World War.

4. The duties of regulating and inspecting railroad equipment, locomotives, and safety devices were assumed at an early date. The Commission spent a noticeable part of its total appropriations for these purposes as early as 1912. Expenditures for railroad safety have not much increased in recent years. The costs of motor safety regulation are not separately stated in the chart. This type of control may always be, but it is not necessarily, a part of Commission regulation.

5. The cost of railroad valuation was very large between 1913 and 1933. It then declined to a more reasonable figure. We shall comment, later, upon this experience.

6. When the Interstate Commerce Commission undertook, in 1935, to regulate motor transportation it entered a new and important field. The addition of jurisdiction over inland waterways and freight forwarders, along

Commission organization. But the detail is informative to the extent that it shows the duties which the Commission has undertaken to perform, the approximate dates when these duties were assumed, and an approximation of the monies devoted to the purpose.

with motor carriage, accounts for the final growth of costs in 1947, 1948, and 1949. This increase was partly offset by a decline in valuation expense.

We will now examine the categories of expenditure which have been mentioned, in the order in which they have been drawn upon the chart. This will provide a somewhat more detailed explanation of growth in federal control. Succeeding chapters will discuss, still further, the regulative structure which has finally emerged.

General Expenditures

Expenditures called "general," in spite of the apparently casual heading, are the outlays which have directly supported federal regulation.[5]

The federal acts of 1906[6] and 1910[7] as we have already said, were first responsible for their increase. It is not too much to say, indeed, that federal railroad regulation began in 1906, not in 1887, in the sense of the initiation of effective control. It was in 1906, for instance, that the Commission first obtained authority to fix a maximum rate and to establish through rates and their divisions. It was the same law of 1906 that made a Commission decision presumptively effective.[8] The well-known "commodity clause" was part of the Act of 1906,[9] and it was the Act of

---

[5] The term *general,* when applied to the distribution of Commission expenditures, covers all nonsegregated items. This meant, until 1946, all outlays except those for safety control, accounting, valuation, motor transport, and miscellaneous or other; since 1946 it has meant all expenditures except those for safety control and miscellaneous or other. The general work of the Commission, so defined, includes its regulation of rates, finance, consolidation, service, and other matters for types of carriers covered by the language of the Act. The Commission has engaged in general regulation, in addition to its special duties, to the extent that this was authorized or directed at any time by the law in force.

[6] 34 Stat. 584, 1906.

[7] 36 Stat. 539, 1910.

[8] Under the Act of 1887 the Interstate Commerce Commission could (1) issue an order and (2) apply to the courts for enforcement of that order.

Under the Act of 1906, where the Commission's order was not for the payment of money, but called upon the carrier for some other action such as the reduction of a rate, the order became effective within the time limit set in the order, unless suspended by court action. The difference between this and the rule under the Act of 1887 was that the carriers, after 1906, were forced to take the initiative in order to prevent the Commission's order from becoming effective.

[9] The commodity clause [I.C.A. Sec. 1 (8)] forbade a railroad to transport, in interstate or foreign commerce, "any article or commodity, other than timber and the manufactured products thereof, manufactured, mined, or produced by it or under its authority, or which it may own in whole or in part, or in which it may have any interest, direct or indirect, except such articles or commodities as may be necessary and intended for its use in the conduct of its business as a common carrier." A somewhat similar restriction was later applied to freight forwarders [I.C.A. Sec. 411 (b)].

This clause has been the subject of a great deal of litigation. (See 213 U.S. 366, 1909; 220 U.S. 257, 1911; 238 U.S. 516, 1915; 253 U.S. 26, 1920; 254 U.S. 255, 1920; 298 U.S. 492, 1936; 333 U.S. 771, 948.)

The legislation in 1906 was provoked by the fact that certain Eastern railroads had engaged in the mining of anthracite coal, acting frequently through the agencies of

1910 which experimented with a Commerce Court to which cases involving the Commission's orders should be brought.[10]

The federal Act of 1920,[11] in addition to the Acts of 1906 and 1910, was responsible for further increases in the Commission's outlays for general purposes after these laws were passed. The Act of 1920 was a statute which instructed the Commission, after the First World War, to fix rates which would yield a fair return upon a fair value on railroad property. This same law of 1920 also gave to the Commission the power to fix a minimum rate,[12] to issue or refuse permission for carrier construction or

subsidiary corporations. The practice was not new (see 3 I.C.R. 460, 1891 and 8 I.C.C. 630, 1901) but independent mining companies complained in 1906 that this double interest led the railroads to discriminate in favor of their subsidiaries in supplying cars and in connecting with mining sidings. It was also alleged that railroads raised transportation rates on coal in order to hamper the competition of independent coal mines with mines in which the railroads had an interest.

The act, as originally passed and as it still stands, was limited to railroads. There have been repeated attempts, however, to extend it to other forms of transportation, especially to pipe lines. (See William Beard, *Regulation of Pipe Lines as Common Carriers,* New York, Columbia University, 1941, and George S. Wolbert, *American Pipe Lines,* Norman, Okla., University of Oklahoma, 1952.)

An analogous case in some but not in all respects is one in which industrial companies, such as steel, automobile, and lumber producers, control common carriers. This relation has operating advantages, if only because the carrier is assured of traffic and the industry of specialized service. It opens possibilities for preference, however, which are not greatly different from those which led to the regulation of rail-mining relationships.

For a general discussion of the subject see Bruce Wyman, "Business Policies Inconsistent with Public Employment," *Harvard Law Review,* May, 1907; T. L. Kibler, *The Commodities Clause,* Washington, D.C., John Byrne, 1916; and I. B. Lake, *Discrimination by Railroads and Other Public Utilities,* Raleigh, N.C., Edwards & Broughton, 1947. The testimony of Mr. Aitchison, Chairman of the Interstate Commerce Commission, before a House subcommittee in 1950 is also informing (United States House of Representatives, Committee on the Judiciary, Hearings before the Subcommittee on Study of Monopoly Power, 81st C., 2d S., Ser. 14, Part 4A, pp. 849–897, 1950).

[10] The Commerce Court was set up in 1910 and was abolished in 1913. It was an interesting experiment which deserved a more patient testing than it received. Supporters of the idea hoped to reduce delay and to develop judicial expertness by substituting a single federal court, below the Supreme Court, for the many circuit courts to which controversies under the Interstate Commerce Act were from time to time referred. Actual experience was too short to determine whether these results were attained during the life of the organization.

In the long run, it is probably undesirable to break down a judicial system by the creation of tribunals which deal each with a special type of problem. Courts are most useful when they apply general standards to a wide variety of situations. Nor is it clear that a single court of appeal, below the Supreme Court, can do much to simplify the task of this last-named tribunal. The Commerce Court was not discontinued, however, because of these reflections. Its life was terminated because of the antagonism of the Interstate Commerce Commission and because of political opposition to President Taft, who was the Court's sponsor. The Court's prestige also suffered from the acts of one of its members who was impeached for misconduct antedating his appointment.

[11] 42 Stat. 456, 1920.

[12] The minimum rate power was granted, in 1920, to protect railroads from the effects of unrestrained railroad competition. Protection to waterways was also men-

abandonment, to regulate railroad securities, and to prepare plans for railroad consolidation. Reference to the diagram of Commission expendi-

tioned in the congressional report. In subsequent years the power expanded as the purposes of the federal law became more complex.

The 1920 amendment accomplished, ultimately, the following:

1. It gave the Commission a direct restraining power over competition in the railroad and, after 1935, in the motor field. The reference here is to competition among railroads and among motor carriers, not to competition between the two types of carriage. This was particularly useful in early motor regulation.

2. It enlarged the general authority of the Commission over rates and discrimination. The Commission could now prevent interference with established rate structures, consequent on rate reductions; it could also handle cases of discrimination with precision and set limits to variations under Section 4.

3. It could limit the competition of one type of carriage with another. This has been, probably, the most publicized feature of this portion of the Act of 1920 since the passage of the Motor Carrier Act of 1935.

For most purposes the Commission has relied upon cost calculations in setting minimum rates for the protection of carrier revenues, although the value of the service rendered has not been entirely neglected. The question in its mind has been whether a carrier would be better off with a given bit of business at a given rate than it would be without it (259 I.C.C. 475, 534, 1945). The Commission has found, however, that even this apparently simple standard has forced it to experiment with a variety of cost calculations and to the discussion of out-of-pocket, fully allocated, and reasonably compensatory charges. (This is well discussed in T. C. Bigham and M. J. Roberts, *Transportation Principles and Problems,* New York, McGraw-Hill, 1952. See also chaps. 16 and 18 of the present treatise.

The problem of regulating interagency competition has introduced additional complications. The Commission has been asked to protect relatively inefficient carriers, when there was active competition between agencies of different types, by fixing minimum rates which would cover the costs incurred by the agency which found itself at a disadvantage (234 I.C.C. 609, 1939; 259 I.C.C. 475, 535, 1945). It has been unwilling to do this, although it has sometimes been able to give a more moderate relief. The fact that the concession could be asked shows the extent to which the minimum rate power may be used in distributing traffic among competing parties.

Objections to the grant of the minimum rate power to the Interstate Commerce Commission and to the Commission's use of its authority have included the following:

1. The issue of a minimum rate order that does not go below the cost of service is a subsidy to the status quo. It is also a public recognition of a vested right in particular carriers to the traffic on which the rate is charged (H. C. Mansfield, "The Minimum Rate Power and the Control of Carrier Competition," *Yale Law Journal,* June, 1936, pp. 1406–1425).

2. A minimum order which prevents a common carrier from lowering rates may preserve that carrier's rate structure, but the Commission cannot control private carriage, and the carrier's traffic may decline.

3. In general, the Commission's exercise of its minimum rate power has served to deprive the shipping public of the inherent advantages of flexibility and low cost afforded by motor (before 1935) and water transportation and to obstruct the introduction of technical improvements into the field (Allen Shrag, "Competing Modes of Transportation and the Interstate Commerce Commission," *University of Pennsylvania Law Review,* July, 1946, p. 391).

In spite of these objections, it would seem that authority to control minimum rates was a reasonable complement to the Commission's power to regulate maximum rates, when it was conferred in 1920, on the assumption that Congress desired to place the responsibility for carrier price fixing upon an administrative body. How far this should be done is, of course, a question of national policy of the most fundamental sort.

tures will show that the imposition of these responsibilities in 1920 increased the general expenditures of the Commission in succeeding years.

Safety Control

Turning from nonsegregated expenditures, we may now pass to other items in the order in which they are depicted on the chart. This brings us to safety control. There was no provision for safety control in the Act of 1887. The annual reports of the Commission did not, indeed, segregate safety expenditures until 1901. The Commission's responsibility for the safety of railroad operation began, however, with the Safety Appliance Act of 1893, which was amended in 1903 and again in 1910.[13] The first of these laws required railroads to install driving wheel and train brakes, automatic couplers, and standard drawbars. The last two laws contained more precise specifications in some cases, and additional provisions for enforcement. The second step was the Hours of Service Act of 1907, which forbade railroads to require or to permit employees to remain on duty during an excessive number of hours.[14] Regulation was extended to locomotives, upon a particular matter, in 1908,[15] and was made general in 1911 and in 1915.[16] Meanwhile, in 1908, the inspection of mail cars had been required.[17] In 1906 the Interstate Commerce Commission was directed to investigate and report on the use and necessity for block signal systems and appliances for the automatic control of railway trains, and in 1908 the direction was extended generally to appliances and systems intended to promote the safety of railroad operation. The power to prescribe train control devices was conferred in 1920.[18] The Commission required reports on railroad accidents as early as 1888, and these were prescribed by statute in 1901 and in 1910.[19] Under the locomotive inspection acts, also, railroads were directed to report all failures of a locomotive boiler or its appurtenances which resulted in death or serious accident.[20]

[13] 27 Stat. 531, 1893; 29 Stat. 85, 1896; 32 Stat. 943, 1903; 36 Stat. 298, 1910. See U.S. Code, Title 45, chap. 1, Secs. 1–16. The federal safety legislation, generally, superseded and excluded state regulation (236 U.S. 439, 447, 1915).

[14] 34 Stat. 1415, 1907. See also the act of 1916, establishing an 8-hour day for railroad operating employees (39 Stat. 721, 1916). This second law was not, entirely, a safety statute.

[15] 35 Stat. 476, 1908. This act required rail carriers to equip locomotives with ash pans which could be dumped or emptied or cleaned without compelling any employee to go under the locomotive.

[16] 36 Stat. 913, 1911; 38 Stat. 1192, 1915; 40 Stat. 616, 1918; 43 Stat. 659, 1924; 54 Stat. 148, 1940; 61 Stat. 120, 1947.

[17] 35 Stat. 324, 1908; 35 Stat. 965, 1909.

[18] 41 Stat. 456, 498, 1920. See also 34 Stat. 838, 1906; 35 Stat. 325, 1908; 50 Stat. 835, 1937.

[19] 31 Stat. 1446, 1901; 36 Stat. 350, 1910.

[20] The railroad safety laws up to 1931 are described in I. L. Sharfman, *The Interstate Commerce Commission*, Part I, pp. 244–281, New York, Commonwealth Fund, 1931.

The duties of the Interstate Commerce Commission under the railroad safety laws now include the following:

1. The collection of information concerning accidents from annual and special reports rendered by the railroads, and by investigation.

2. The formulation of general rules for the promotion of safety in railroad operation. The Commission has established rules and standards for the construction and repair of cars and locomotives and power brakes and for the installation, maintenance, and repair of signal and train control systems, and for the carriage of explosives and other dangerous articles. It considers applications for the modification of these rules.

3. The enforcement of its own rules and of legislative prescriptions, including the hours of service laws, by referring cases of violation to United States attorneys for court proceedings.

4. The Commission's expenditures with reference to motor vehicle safety are not segregated in the diagram on page 616 and they did not begin, in any case, until the passage of the Motor Carriers Act of 1935. Under this statute the Commission has also extensive powers conveyed to it in general terms. The Commission's authority covers the hours and qualifications of drivers, and it has formulated rules which govern some aspects of motor operation and equipment.[21]

In the single year 1949 the Commission spent a total of $1,554,306 for safety control, not including outlays connected with motor vehicle operation.

Accounts

The Act of 1887 authorized the Commission to require annual reports and to fix the time and manner in which such reports should be made. It also authorized the Commission, within its discretion, for the purpose of enabling it the better to carry out the purposes of the Act, to prescribe (if in the opinion of the Commission it was practicable to prescribe such uniformity and methods of keeping accounts) a period of time within which all common carriers subject to the provisions of the Act should have, as near as might be, a uniform system of accounts, and the manner in which such should be kept.[22] This was a hesitant grant of power. Under the original act the Commission created a Division of Statistics whose chief functions were to examine the annual reports of carriers and to compile statistical data based thereon. The Division used its influence to secure uniformity in these reports; it did not, at this time, attempt any general regulation of accounts.[23]

[21] See chap. 31. Motor safety regulation is administered by the Commission's Bureau of Motor Carriers. The railroad rules are formulated and enforced by the Commission's Bureau of Safety. See, in general, U.S. Code, Title 45, Secs. 1–50.

[22] 24 Stat. 379, 1887, Sec. 20.

[23] Sharfman, *op. cit.*, Part III, vol. A, p. 70.

In 1906 Congress somewhat enlarged the Commission's power with respect to carrier reports. It retained the original language with respect to carrier accounts, but it now granted the Commission specific authority to prescribe and to inspect carrier accounts, records, and memoranda and it made it illegal for any carrier to keep any accounts, records, or memoranda other than those prescribed or approved by the Commission. Penalties were attached to any violation of this law.[24]

In 1920 Congress authorized the Commission to regulate the extent to which railroad depreciation might be charged to operating expense; [25] in 1935, accounting regulation was extended to motor carriers and brokers; [26] in 1940, to water carriers; [27] and in 1942, to freight forwarders.[28] Meanwhile, in 1938, the Civil Aeronautics Board received jurisdiction over the accounts of air carriers.[29]

The Commission has used the authority conveyed by the laws which have been mentioned to develop a series of accounting classifications which are now prescribed for all companies subject to its jurisdiction.[30]

[24] The language of the Act of 1906 with respect to carrier accounts was as follows:

"The Commission may, in its discretion, prescribe the forms of any and all accounts, records, and memoranda to be kept by carriers subject to the provisions of this Act, including the accounts, records, and memoranda of the movement of traffic as well as the receipts and expenditures of money. The Commission shall at all times have access to all accounts, records, and memoranda kept by carriers subject to this Act, and it shall be unlawful for such carriers to keep any other accounts, records, or memoranda than those prescribed or approved by the Commission, and it may employ special agents or examiners, who shall have authority under the order of the Commission to inspect and examine any and all accounts, records, and memoranda kept by such carriers. This provision shall apply to receivers of carriers and operating trustees" (34 U.S. 514, 594, 1906, Sec. 20).

[25] 41 Stat. 456, 493, 1920. See also 54 Stat. 898, 917, 1940. The Act of 1920 gave representatives of the Commission access to carrier documents, papers, and correspondence as well as to accounts, records, and memoranda. It included in this material kept during the period of federal control.

[26] 49 Stat. 543, 563, 1935. Authority to regulate the depreciation accounting of motor carriers was not conferred until 1940.

[27] 54 Stat. 898, 945, 1940. The Act of 1940 gave to the Interstate Commerce Commission power to regulate the accounts of railroads, water lines, and pipe lines leased to railroads subject to the Act and the accounts of persons who furnished a railroad or express company with protective service against heat or cold.

[28] 56 Stat. 284, 294, 1942.

[29] 52 Stat. 973, 1938.

Accounting matters were first handled by the Division or Bureau of Statistics and Accounts in the Interstate Commerce Commission organization. Accounting was separated from statistics in 1911 and the present Bureau of Accounts was set up in 1920. This became, in 1948, the Bureau of Accounts and Cost Findings into which were merged (1) the Bureau of Accounts; (2) the Section of Accounts of the Bureau of Motor Carriers; and (3) the Section of Cost Finding of the Bureau of Transport Economics and Statistics. This merger brought together the regulation of accounts maintained by all carriers subject to the Commission and placed the study of transportation costs within the Bureau which formulated and prescribed accounting requirements. (See United States Interstate Commerce Commission, *Annual Report,* 1948, p. 71.)

[30] Interstate Commerce Commission classifications governed, in 1949, the following

These classifications contain each a list of capital, revenue, expense, and other accounts, each numbered and each accompanied by a paragraph describing the entries which are appropriate to the account. Such directions are based upon standard accounting principles. They may, however, represent conclusions on practice concerning which opinions differ. Some of the categories have been the subject of elaborate Commission decisions and some, though by no means all of them, have been carried to the courts. Thus the Commission once ruled, against carrier opposition, that the cost of poles driven into the ground at the end of railroad ties in order to stabilize the track should be treated as an operating expense, not as a capital investment.[31] It successfully defended the opinion that the cost of mines which have been bought to assure a supply of coal should be charged to "miscellaneous physical property" and not carried into the general cost of road account;[32] and it has maintained that a railroad should not write into its property accounts the full cost of improvements made off the railroad's right of way but that it should deduct the estimated replacement cost of the portions of track which were no longer used and charge this item into the operating expenses of the current year.[33] It has had to decide whether or not a carrier's property depreciates and, if it does, how the depreciation shall be reflected in the accounts.[34] These problems are mentioned for purposes of illustration. The solution given, in a particular case, may have a considerable and general importance. If general conclusions are to be drawn from carrier accounts, these accounts should be uniform and carriers should base their practice upon principles of a fundamental sort. The Commission has received coöperation from private carriers, but the initiative and the final responsibility for accounting regulation has been its own.[35] It has enforced compliance with its rules by inspection of carriers' accounts.

---

classes of corporations (*Code of Federal Regulations,* 1949, Title 49, Parts 10–24, 181–182, 323–324):

1. Steam roads.
2. Electric railways.
3. Sleeping car companies.
4. Express companies.
5. Pipe line companies.
6. Persons furnishing cars or protective services against heat or cold.
7. Common and contract carriers of passengers (motor).
8. Common and contract carriers of property (motor).
9. Maritime carriers.
10. Carriers by inland and coastal waterways.

[31] 262 I.C.C. 134, 1945.
[32] 287 U.S. 134, 1932.
[33] 231 U.S. 423, 1913.
[34] 118 I.C.C. 295, 1926; 177 I.C.C. 351, 1931.
[35] The constitutionality of the law which granted accounting powers to the Commission was affirmed in 1912 (224 U.S. 194, 1912).

The Commission has depended upon uniform and elaborated accounts for the intelligent control of rates, service, consolidations, reorganizations, security issues, certificates, extensions, abandonments, and other matters. This tool has enabled it, also, to undertake a number of special tasks. Thus the Commission calculated the payments due individual railroads under the Federal Control Act of 1918. It certified the sums due under this law and under the act of 1920, and it later determined the amount of railroad earnings subject to recapture during postwar years. These assignments explain the considerable increase in accounting expenditures between 1920 and 1932. After 1933 the Commission was relieved from the burdensome task of recapture calculation. It was still called upon, however, by Congress, by the Coordinator of Transportation, and by government departments. Between 1935 and 1939 it assisted the Senate in an extensive congressional investigation of holding companies—the work, in 1936, occupied the time of nearly half of the Commission's field staff. In 1943 it suffered from the transfer of a number of its accountants to other government bureaus. More recently, the Commission has undertaken an increasing number of studies of railroad and motor operating costs. Some of these inquiries have been published separately, and some of them have been introduced as evidence in pending cases; the Commission has also prepared analyses and surveys of a more general type.

The Interstate Commerce Commission reported a total of $24,873,483 under the head of accounting expenditures between 1908 and 1946. It is possible that this figure did not completely cover the outlays made. On the other hand, the total includes sums which were not spent for the purpose of carrier regulation.

Valuation

There was no provision for the valuation of railroad property in the Act of 1887. But Congress, in 1913, added a new section to the law which directed the Commission to investigate, ascertain, and report the value of all the property owned and used by every common carrier subject to the provisions of the Act. The Commission was instructed also to keep itself informed of all extensions and improvements or other changes in the conditions and value of the property of common carriers and to revise and correct its valuations from time to time.[36] Congress amended the valuation law, slightly, in 1922,[37] and in 1933 it made two other changes.[38]

[36] 37 Stat. 701, 1913.

[37] 42 Stat. 624, 1922. The Act of 1913 required the Interstate Commerce Commission to ascertain the original and present cost of lands, rights of way, and terminals owned or used for the purposes of a common carrier, taken as of the time of dedication to public use, and the present value of the same. It was also directed to determine, separately, the original and present cost of condemnation and damages or of purchase in excess of such original cost or present value. The Commission interpreted the Supreme

The first change withdrew street, suburban, and electric interurban railways from the list of properties that should be valued. The second eliminated the direction that the Commission should keep its valuations up to date.[39]

Examination of the chart will show that the valuation activities of the Interstate Commerce Commission under the acts of 1913, 1922, and 1933 may be divided into three periods. The first of these was between 1913 and 1924, the second between 1925 and 1933, and the third between 1933 and the present time.

Speaking generally, the Commission organized its staff in the first period and completed, during these years, the engineering and accounting work necessary for an inventory and appraisal of railroad properties in the United States.[40] During the second period, and notably in 1925, 1926, and 1927, the Commission finished its tentative valuations. By 1933 it had considered carrier protests and had issued final reports. The Commission also defended its views before the courts between 1925 and 1933, and began to give serious attention to the task of bringing its valuations to date. This was evidently necessary because the Commission's completed valuations were based on figures of the years 1914 to 1921, and could hardly be used without some degree of modernization.[41] Moreover, new companies had begun to appear which had not operated in 1933. After 1933 the Commission's problem was to make its valuations useful in the best state in which they could be maintained, with due reference to limitations which the courts were inclined to impose.

USES MADE OF COMMISSION VALUATIONS. One original purpose of the Valuation Act was to enable the Interstate Commerce Commission to protect the public more effectively against extortionate railroad rates. It was on this ground that Senator LaFollette gave the act his full support.[42] The activity of the Commission under the Act of 1913 cannot, however, be satisfactorily described as an attempt merely to prevent extortion; this is because the views of the Commission and of Congress were

Court decision in the Minnesota Rate case (230 U.S. 352, 1913) as relieving it from the duty of ascertaining the costs of condemnation. The Supreme Court later held, however, that the Commission was still required to find excess costs (252 U.S. 178, 1920). Congress ended the controversy, in 1922, by removing the disputed phrases from the law.

[38] 48 Stat. 211, 221, 1933.

[39] The Commission was instructed, instead, to keep track of the cost of additions, betterments, and changes in carrier investment so that it might revise and correct its inventories and valuations when this was deemed necessary. The alteration seemed small, but it was important.

[40] The Commission did some work on telephone and telegraph companies and, later, upon pipe lines, but these were relatively minor problems.

[41] See United States Interstate Commerce Commission, *Annual Report,* 1933, p. 75.

[42] See *Congressional Record,* 62d C., 3d S., pp. 47 (Adamson), 50 (Collop), 3795 (LaFollette). See also 75 I.C.C. 463, 1923.

always broader than this limitation would suggest and partly because new and directive statutes were later passed.[43] The most important of these new laws were the Transportation Act of 1920 and the act amending the federal bankruptcy law approved in 1935. The declarations which these acts made which involved the use of valuations were as follows:

1. That the Interstate Commerce Commision, beginning in 1920, should initiate new rates or adjust existing rates so that carriers should earn a fair return upon the aggregate value of railway property.[44]

2. That the revenues of any railroad which exceeded 6 percent on a fair value should be recaptured.[45]

3. That railroads in the United States should be consolidated into a limited number of systems and that the stock and bond issues of any consolidated corporation should not exceed the value of the consolidated properties.[46]

4. That the Commission should take a constructive part in the process of railroad reorganization and that it should determine railroad values, if and when necessary, in connection with this work.[47]

Whatever the purpose of Congress in 1913, and this is debatable, these statutory provisions contemplated the use of railroad valuations in a considerable variety of ways. It does not, however, appear that the valuation expenditures of the Commission have been of major importance, either as a basis for rate regulation or for the special purposes mentioned in the text. Speaking of the latter, the recapture clauses of the Act of 1920 were found unworkable and they were repealed in 1933,[48] although the Commission's Bureau of Valuation concentrated, at one time, upon this subject. The slow progress of consolidation and the nature of the issues raised made valuations for this purpose of relatively small importance; and the Commission, in working out the details of railroad reorganizations, found it best to use earnings and not valuation as a guide. With reference to rate regulation, the appraisal is more difficult. Undoubtedly the Commission contributed actively to the general discussion of valuation principles and techniques, after 1927, although its views were not always acceptable to the United States Supreme Court. It completed and published a number of estimates or calculations of the fair value of

[43] The Supreme Court held, in 1927 (273 U.S. 299, 1927) that a Commission valuation was a finding of fact and not an order subject to judicial review. The valuation itself was distinguished from the use to which it might be put. The Court, in this opinion, left the way open to the use of valuations for a variety of purposes.

[44] 41 Stat. 456, 488, 1920 [Sec. 15a (2)].

[45] Ibid. [Sec. 15 (a) (6)]. The figure of 6 percent mentioned in the statute was a temporary rate. The critical rate was, in regular course, to be set by the Commission. The Commission later set the rate at 5¾ percent of the valuation.

[46] Ibid., Sec. 5 (4); Sec. 5 (6) (b). See chap. 25.

[47] 47 Stat. 1474, 1933; 49 Stat. 911, 1935; 49 Stat. 1969, 1936 [Sec. 77 (13) (e)].

[48] 48 Stat. 211, 220, 1933.

TABLE 23.   Fair Values Established by the Interstate
Commerce Commission

Case	Carriers Included	Valuation Date	Valuation Established
58 I.C.C. 220, 1921	All railway carriers	Presumably Dec. 31, 1919	$18,900,000,000
226 I.C.C. 41, 1938; 229 I.C.C. 435, 1938	All railway carriers	Jan. 1, 1937	21,020,000,000
226 I.C.C. 41, 1938; 229 I.C.C. 435, 1938	Class I Line Haul	Jan. 1, 1937	19,972,000,000
229 I.C.C. 435, 1938	All railway carriers	Jan. 1, 1938	20,998,000,000
229 I.C.C. 435, 1938	Class I Line Haul	Jan. 1, 1938	19,882,000,000
264 I.C.C. 695, 1946	Class I Line Haul	Jan. 1, 1945	19,571,000,000
269 I.C.C. 33, 1947; 270 I.C.C. 93, 1947; 270 I.C.C. 403, 1948	Class I Line Haul	Jan. 1, 1947	20,622,713,588
276 I.C.C. 9, 1948	Class I Line Haul	Jan. 1, 1948	20,978,646,326

SOURCE: Sidney L. Miller, *Rates of Return—Class I Line-Haul Railways, 1921–1948*, Pittsburgh, University of Pittsburgh, 1950, p. 80.

the railroads of the United States (Table 23) and it accumulated information which was incidentally useful to itself and to other government departments.[49] But the Commission found valuation data less helpful in

[49] The Commission's Bureau of Statistics wrote, in 1937:
"The valuation data contained in the archives of the Commission afford useful guidance in connection with various Government activities. For example, the Postmaster General calls for elements of value for property under consideration for railroad terminal post offices, the fair value of which is required in determining the terms of rentals or leases. The Treasury Department finds valuation data useful in its income-tax work and as a guide in the purchase of public building sites. The War Department calls on the Commission from time to time for valuation records in connection with navigation projects, flood control and soil conservation work. The Department of Agriculture has used the appraisals of the Commission to assist in determining the rates to be charged for use of stockyards, and draws extensively on the Commission's information covering costs of construction and construction materials. The Federal Coordinator of Transportation during his period of office used the Commission's records extensively in connection with technical and budget studies and inquiries concerning aids, gifts, grants, and donations for railroad construction and extension. His recommendations as to certain terminal consolidations and depreciation on fixed property were based on information made available through the Commission" (United States Interstate Commerce Commission, *Activities 1887–1937*, prepared by the Bureau of Statistics with the coöperation of the other Bureaus of the Commission, 1937, p. 152).

rate control than Congress had anticipated for two reasons in addition to the complications which were produced by arguments with the federal courts. One reason was the slowness, doubtless unavoidable, with which the original valuation data were compiled and analyzed. The lapse of time between the passage of the act of 1913 and the completion of the first general valuation was so long that the Commission decided its first and probably its most important case under the Act of 1920 on the basis of a partial valuation record only. Indeed, the value cited in this advance rate decision of 1921 did not greatly differ from the book cost of the railroads which were involved. The other reason was that many of the early and most of the later cases which the Commission handled after 1920 were so-called "revenue" cases in which the solvency of railroad carriers was at stake and not the question of a fair return. Business depression, shipper pressure, and the competition of other carriers made it practically impossible to use valuation as a guide in such a litigation. The Commission, it is true, included valuation data in its reports, even after 1933, and these data may have had some use; but in no case was the valuation said to be controlling nor, in so far as one can judge, was it an important basis for the conclusions which were reached.[50]

VALUATION EXPENDITURES. Congress originally expected that the railroads of the United States could be valued for approximately $3,000,000.[51] The Commission actually spent $55,411,038 up to and including the year 1946, of which $45,983,684 were paid out during the 20 years between 1914 and 1933. The annual average during this last period was $2,-299,184, or more than three-quarters of the total outlay expected in 1913.[52]

Motor Vehicles

There was no provision for motor vehicle regulation in the Act of 1887. There was, indeed, no motor industry to regulate when the original act was passed. Proposals for federal regulation of motor carriage were first presented to Congress in 1925, after Supreme Court decisions in that year had restricted state efforts to control interstate motor service. The first bills were not passed; but similar legislation was laid before Congress in

[50] The Supreme Court does not now insist that a valuation shall be made (320 U.S. 591, 1944). See R. W. Harbeson, "The Demise of Fair Value," *Michigan Law Review*, April, 1944.

[51] Mr. H. C. Adams of the University of Michigan was quoted to this effect (*Congressional Record*, December 3, 1913, 62d C., 3d S., p. 48); and Mr. Delano, President of the Wabash Railway, guessed about the same (Sen. Rep. 1290, 62d C., 3d S., Ser. 6330, p. 48, 1913).

[52] These figures do not include, of course, the accompanying expenditures of the railroad carriers. See B. H. Moore, *The Federal Valuation of the Railroads in the United States,* American Railway Engineering Association, Bulletin 503, September and October, 1952.

each of the next ten successive years.[53] Finally, the submission of a report by the Federal Coordinator of Transportation and the introduction of a bill by Senator Wheeler in 1935 started the train of proceedings which culminated in a federal law.[54] The Motor Carrier Act was published, in 1935, as Part II of the Interstate Commerce Act.[55] It was the first statute, apart from laws regulating the Merchant Marine, in which Congress undertook to regulate forms of transport which did not operate upon rails.

The chart on page 616 makes it apparent that activity under the motor law became immediately responsible for a considerable proportion of the total expenditures of the Interstate Commerce Commission. This was primarily because the Act imposed a comprehensive system of regulation, at one time, upon an extensive industry made up preponderantly of small operators who had had relatively little experience in regulation. And the Act also specifically required motor operators first, to secure certificates or permits as a condition of continued service and, second, to file copies of their tariffs and of the contracts under which contract carriage was carried on. Between the date of the passage of the Act and November 1, 1938, the Commission received 93,364 applications for certificates and permits. It also accepted for filing 189,290 common carrier tariffs, 24,923 schedules of minimum contract carrier rates, and 27,688 confidential contracts for its information. The handling of such material caused some confusion at the beginning and was responsible for a good deal of expense. The Commission soon prescribed accounting classifications for motor carriers, formulated safety rules, and began to hear complaints; by 1939 it was able to settle down to constructive work. We shall consider motor regulation further in chapter 32.

Water Transport and Freight Forwarders

There was no provision for the regulation of water transport and of freight forwarder operations in the Act of 1887, and Commission expenditures for these purposes under later laws are not segregated in its

[53] Federal motor legislation was desired by railroads, by bus operators, by regulating authorities, both state and local, and by shippers who disliked the instability of rates which came from unregulated transportation. Opposition came from motor vehicle manufacturers, motor truck operators, and from shippers who feared that any restriction on the use of trucks would produce higher rates. Action was perhaps hastened by the organization of extracongressional committees and conferences which included recommendations for federal motor control in their programs for railroad reconstruction or transport reorganization (Joint Committee of Railroads and Highway Users, 1931; National Transportation Committee, 1933; National Transportation Conference, 1933–34).

[54] Warren H. Wagner, *A Legislative History of the Motor Carrier Act, 1935,* Denton, Md., Rue Publishing, 1936; United States, Office of the Federal Coordinator, *Report of the Federal Coordinator on Regulation of Transport Agencies,* 73d C., 2d S., Sen. Doc. 152, 1934.

[55] 49 Stat. 543, 1935.

reports. The authority which the Commission possesses will, however, be examined in chapters 31 and 32.

Organization of the Interstate Commerce Commission

It was an inevitable result of the growth of federal regulation that the organization of the Interstate Commerce Commission developed along with the increase in responsibilities which it assumed. This Commission, in 1887, had 5 members, appointed for terms of 6 years at a salary of $7,500. It now consists of 11 members, appointed for terms of 7 years at a salary of $15,000.[56] Not more than 6 commissioners may be appointed from one political party. The tenure of office is reasonably stable. Thus over the total life of the Commission from 1887 to 1949 the average term of service has been approximately 10 years including, out of 49 appointees, 8 cases where the tenure was 3 years or less. Of the commissioners in office on November 1, 1949, one had then served 28 years, two 20 years, one 17 years, one 16 years, and all but two of the remainder a minimum of 10 years each. This continuity doubtless helps to account for the success which the Commission has attained. The personnel covers, of course, a considerable range of ability and experience. Of the membership in 1949, two commissioners had been, before their appointment, members of the Supreme Courts of their respective states. Three commissioners had served on state railroad commissions or on the staff of a state Public Service Commission. One member had been chief of a State Highway Commission and, later, Assistant Secretary of Commerce for the federal government. Two commissioners benefited from previous experience on the Commission's staff as directors of the Bureau of Motor Carriers and of the Bureau of Finance. Of the remainder, one was a former operating employee who had represented the Order of Railway Conductors in rail-labor negotiations and one was a gas and electric engineer.[57]

Internal Organization of the Interstate Commerce Commission

The present organization of the Interstate Commerce Commission contains the following elements:

1. *Chairman.* The chairman of the Commission is elected by its mem-

[56] In 1906 the membership of the Interstate Commerce Commission was enlarged from five to seven, the salaries were increased to $10,000 annually, and the term of office was made 7 years (34 Stat. 548, 1906). Two members were added in 1917 (40 Stat. 270, 1917), and two more in 1920 (41 Stat. 497, 1920), and salaries were raised to $12,000. General reductions in salaries following the depression after 1929 reduced Commission salaries to $8,500, but the cut was restored in later years. The increase to $15,000 occurred in 1949 (Public Law 359, 81st C., 1st S., chap. 695, October 15, 1949).

[57] The rules of practice of the Interstate Commerce Commission are published in the United States Code of Federal Regulations, Title 49, chap. 1, Part 1.

bers. Since 1910, when Chairman Knapp resigned, the position has been rotated annually, except for the years 1940–43, when a 3-year term was used. The chairman has been executive head of the Commission and ex-officio member of Division 1. He has presided at Commission conferences, has reported to the Commission on the progress of the Commission's work, and has acted as correspondent and spokesman for the Commission in its relations with outside parties.[58] There have been proposals to alter the character and the powers of the Chairman of the Interstate Commerce Commission, but these changes have not been all approved.

2. *Divisions*. The Commission functions as a whole when it so desires. But it may also divide its members into "divisions" and refer any part of its work to a division. In case of reference, the senior in service of the commissioners constituting a division acts as chairman, and the division possesses all the jurisdiction and powers of the Commission and is subject to the same duties and responsibilities with respect to the subject or subjects which are assigned.[59] A division, so-called, must have at least three members. But the Commission may also delegate any portion of its work, business, or function to an individual commissioner, with power, or sub-

---

[58] The Interstate Commerce Commission adopted specifications of duties and responsibilities relating to the chairman in 1945. The order read as follows:

"The following duties and responsibilities are delegated to the Chairman (or, in his absence to the Acting Chairman who shall be the available senior Commissioner in point of service) to be exercised in addition to his statutory duties and any other duties that may be assigned or delegated to him:

"1.   He shall be the executive head of the Commission.

"2.   It shall be his duty and responsibility to see that the work of the Commission is promptly and efficiently dispatched. To accomplish this purpose he is specifically authorized and directed (a) to bring to the attention of any Commissioner or division any lagging or failure in the work under his or its supervision, (b) to report periodically —not less than four times a year—to the Commission at regular or special conferences on the progress of all the Commission's work, and (c) to suggest ways and means of correcting or preventing any unusual or unnecessary delays in the disposition of any official matters which he is unable otherwise to have remedied.

"3.   He shall be an ex officio member of Division 1.

"4.   He shall preside at all Commission arguments and conferences and shall exercise general control over the Commission's argument calendar and conference agenda.

"5.   He shall have general supervision of the minutes of the Commission and shall see that they are accurately and promptly recorded.

"6.   Except in instances where the duty is otherwise delegated or provided for, he shall act as the correspondent and spokesman for the Commission in all matters involving relations with the heads of other agencies of Government, and in any other case where an official expression of the Commission is required" (11 Fed. Reg. 10,662, September 21, 1946). These have been the chairman's duties during most recent years.

[59] United States Code, 1946, Title 49, Sec. 17. There were, on May 1, 1950, five divisions as follows:

1.   Administrative;
2.   Rates, Tariff, and Valuation;
3.   Rates, Service, and Safety;
4.   Finance;
5.   Motor carriers.

ject to certain limitations, or to a board made up of specified types of employees. Decisions of a division may be reviewed by the Commission as a whole, and decisions of individual commissioners or of boards may be reviewed by a division or by the entire Commission. The work of the divisions, as is that of the Commission as a whole, is assisted by examiners, a group of valuable employees whose services are not always sufficiently understood.[60]

3. *Bureaus.* The bureaus of the Commission are essential to the Commission's work. In 1950 there were 15 of these bureaus, each charged with a function of administration, enforcement, or research. The list included the Bureau of Accounts, which formulates, interprets, and polices the Commission's accounting regulations; the Bureau of Inquiry, which enforces the criminal and penal provisions of the Act; the Bureau of

[60] An examiner is a Commission employee who conducts hearings and renders reports. He analyzes the evidence in the cases to which he is assigned and prepares tentative decisions. These tentative decisions are submitted to the parties in the case and they are then transmitted to the Commission or to a division of the Commission for such action as this agency thinks wise, after consideration of criticisms or objections which parties may desire to submit. The examiner has no power to decide, but his reports greatly expedite the handling of cases.

Examiners were authorized by the Act of 1906 (34 Stat. 384, 594, 1906) and the manner of their use has developed in the course of time. (See *Interstate Commerce Commission Activities, 1887–1937, op. cit.*) They must be used when the Interstate Commerce Commission desires to delegate the conduct of a hearing to some one other than a Commissioner. This principle was restated in 1951 when the United States Supreme Court overruled the contrary opinion of a District Court (Memorandum no. 479, etc., citing *Wong Yank Sung v. McGrath,* 339 U.S. 33, 1950). Unfortunately the Interstate Commerce Commission had not uniformly followed the required procedure, so that many cases had to be reheard. Legislation was introduced to cover previous litigation, but Congress has not yet passed a validating law (*Traffic World,* June 28, 1952, p. 65).

Examiners are now subject to the Administrative Procedure Act of 1946 (60 Stat. 237, 244, 1946) and to the Classification Act of 1949 (5 U.S.C. (Suppl.), Sec. 1082). They receive a level of compensation set by the Civil Service Commission and are subject to rules which the Civil Service Commission prescribes. This means that the Civil Service Commission and not the agency which uses an examiner—the Interstate Commerce Commission in the present case—sets the salary of his grade, selects him for appointment and promotion when opportunities occur, and controls his discharge. The Interstate Commerce Commission, however, can assign examiners to particular tasks within a grade; it can reduce the number of examiners employed at any time when its organization is, in this respect, overstaffed; and it can request an increase in the number of its examiners when the funds of the Interstate Commerce Commission permit. (73 Sup. Ct. Rep. 570, 1953.) Thus the tenure rights of examiners are limited. The Interstate Commerce Commission has a working control over the examiners which it employs. It is clearly the intention of Congress that these officials shall have an independence which partakes of that of the judiciary; but the Interstate Commerce Commission is permitted, in some respects, to direct their work.

There is an excellent description and discussion of Interstate Commerce Commission procedure, including the contribution of examiners, in a monograph prepared by the the so-called Attorney General's Committee on Administrative Procedure, in 1941 (United States Senate, 77th C., 1st S., Sen. Doc. 10, Ser. 10,563, 1941).

Traffic, which receives, files, and examines freight tariffs, the Bureau of Motor Carriers, and a number of others.

The bureaus as a whole contain a body of approximately 2,000 employees engaged in investigation, litigation, supervision of rate publication, collection and analysis of accounting and statistical data, administration of car service, valuation, administration, and, generally, enforcement of Commission rules and orders of various sorts.[61]

The personnel of bureaus is appointed by the Commission except in the case of the Bureau of Locomotive Inspection where the Chief Inspector and two assistant inspectors are appointed by the President of the United States. Most of the employees of the Commission work in one or another of the bureaus.

Proposals for Reorganization of the Interstate Commerce Commission

There have been a number of suggestions for the reorganization of the Interstate Commerce Commission, the most important of which have contemplated the separation of the Commission's semijudicial from its other functions, or are designed to subject the Commission to some form of executive control. Among the former has been the plan to create a National Transportation Board with power to supervise service and safety, to direct routing, to open terminals, to regulate consolidations, and to issue certificates of convenience and necessity. Or, more simply, it has been suggested that the bureaus of statistics, accounts, service, locomotive inspection,

[61] The personnel of the Interstate Commerce Commission was, as of December 31, 1950, distributed as follows:

Officials and Employees	Office	Field
Commissioners	11	
Commissioners' offices	34	
Secretary and his office	12	
Bureau of Administration	188	
Bureau of Accounts and Cost Finding	68	53
Bureau of Finance	44	
Bureau of Formal Cases	88	
Bureau of Informal Cases	14	
Bureau of Inquiry	10	11
Bureau of Law	30	
Bureau of Motor Carriers	394	322
Bureau of Service and Service Working Fund	24	48
Bureau of Traffic	243	
Bureau of Transport Economics and Statistics	139	
Bureau of Valuation	80	7
Bureau of Water Carriers and Freight Forwarders	14	6
Bureau of Locomotive Inspection	26	84
Bureau of Safety	35	92
Total	1,454	623
Grand Total	2,077	

safety, and finance be transferred from the Interstate Commerce Commission to the Department of Commerce.

Among the latter have been proposals to permit the President to appoint the chairman of the Commission and those to transfer the entire Commission to the Department of Commerce or to a newly created Department of Transportation with results that would vary according to the details of the plan. Such changes would be partly designed to produce economy and efficiency in administration; their more serious intent would be to transfer to the executive branch of the federal government powers of which, it is contended, the President has been improperly deprived.

Still other suggestions have been (1) that members of the Commission shall be drawn, in specified proportions, from geographical districts of the United States or from service groups such as those engaged in motor, air, and water transport; (2) that regional subcommissions should be set up to which cases should be initially referred; [62] and (3) that the internal organization of the Commission should be radically rearranged. [63]

[62] A variation of this is that state commissions should be clothed with federal authority, at least to some extent.

[63] An elaborate report by a firm of management consultants (Wolf Management Engineering Co.) has been considered by the House Committee on Interstate and Foreign Commerce. The most striking proposal in this survey was that the performance of all administrative functions of the Interstate Commerce Commission shall be delegated to a managing director who shall be selected by and should be responsible to the Commission but who should have full authority over all civil service rated personnel. This would keep equipment inspection and functions relating to safety rules and railroad car service within the Commission; it would at the same time provide for a degree of independent administrative control. It is assumed that the position of this Director shall be relatively permanent so as to permit of long-term planning.

If the Wolf plan is accepted, the 15 bureaus of the Interstate Commerce Commission will be replaced by 3 general staff offices (Administration, Law, and Secretary) and by 6 specialized administrative bureaus (Certificates and Finance, Traffic, Hearings, Transport Services, Safety Inspection, and Accounts and Statistics). There will also be an Office for Field Administration which will coordinate the activities of the Commission's field employees organized in six geographical regions under the direction of regional managers. These offices and bureaus will be directly responsible to the Managing Director. Details with respect to these substitutions are elaborately supplied.

The proposals of the Wolf Management Engineering Company relate only to the administrative duties of the Interstate Commerce Commission. They do not contemplate changes in the quasi-judicial, quasi-legislative, and policy making functions of the Commission except that they are intended to release Commissioners from administrative tasks. The report does, however, also suggest that the Commission make greater use of specialized technicians and of accredited independent engineers, and that it delegate its regulatory authority more freely to boards composed of qualified employees. It is expected that this would free the time of commissioners still further for the consideration of broad problems.

The Commission has accepted, in principle, the report of the Wolf Management Engineering Company and has appointed a Managing Director. It is not yet clear how far the specific recommendations of the Company will be adopted. (Wolf Management Engineering Company, *Survey of Organization and Operations of the Interstate Commerce Commission,* Report submitted to the Committee on Interstate and Foreign Commerce on December 22, 1952, pursuant to S. Res. 332, 82nd Congress. 83d C., 1st S., Washington, D.C., Committee Print, Government Printing Office, 1952).

This list by no means includes all ideas for Commission reorganization; but it indicates the character of some plans that have been discussed. The prestige of the Commission and the unwillingness of Congress to increase the power of the President have so far prevented any serious interference with the present Commission's organization or scope of work.

R E F E R E N C E S

General Treatises

Auerbach, Carl A. and Nathanson M., *Federal Control of Transportation,* St. Paul, West Publishing Co., 1953.

Bigham, Truman C., and Roberts, Merrill J., *Transportation, Principles and Problems,* New York, McGraw-Hill, 1952.

Dixon, F. H., *Railroads and Government,* New York, Scribner's, 1922.

Fair, Marvin L., and Williams, Ernest W., *Economics of Transportation,* New York, Harper, 1950.

Healy, Kent T., *The Economics of Transportation in America,* New York, Ronald, 1940.

Landon, Charles E., *Transportation, Principles, Practices, Problems,* New York, Sloane, 1951.

Locklin, D. Philip, *Economics of Transportation,* Chicago, Irwin, 1947.

Meyer, B. H., *Railway Legislation in the United States,* New York, Macmillan, 1903.

Miller, Clarence A., *Interstate Commerce Commission Law and Procedure,* Washington, D. C., National Law Book, 1939.

Parmelee, Julius H., *The Modern Railway,* New York, Longmans, 1940.

Ripley, W. Z., *Railroads, Rates and Regulation,* New York, Longmans, 1912.

Sharfman, I. L., *The Interstate Commerce Commission. A Study in Administrative Law and Procedure,* New York, Commonwealth Fund, 5 vols., 1931, 1935, 1936, 1937.

Van Metre, Thurman W., *Transportation in the United States,* Brooklyn, Foundation Press, 1950.

Westmeyer, Russell E., *Economics of Transportation,* New York, Prentice-Hall, 1952.

Other Books

Beard, William, *Regulation of Pipe Lines as Common Carriers,* New York, Columbia University, 1941.

Bernhardt, Joshua, *The Interstate Commerce Commission: Its History, Activities and Organization,* Institute for Government Research, Service Monographs of the United States Government, no. 18, Baltimore, Johns Hopkins Press, 1923.

Bonbright J. C., *Valuation of Property,* New York, McGraw-Hill, 1937.

Doyle, Wilson K., *Independent Commissions in the Federal Government,* Chapel Hill, N.C., University of North Carolina, 1939.

Kibler, T. L., *The Commodities Clause,* Washington, D.C., John Byrne, 1916.

Lake, I. B. *Discrimination by Railroads and Other Public Utilities,* Raleigh, N.C., Edwards & Broughton, 1947.

Meriam, Lewis, and Schmeckebier, Lawrence F., *Reorganization of the National Government,* Washington, Brookings Institution, 1939.

Miller, Sidney L., and Cover, Virgil D., *Rates of Return, Class I Line-Haul Railways of the United States, 1921–1948,* Pittsburgh, University of Pittsburgh, 1950.

Schultz, Robert, *Depreciation and the American Railroads,* Philadelphia, University of Pennsylvania, 1934.

Wolbert, George, *American Pipe Lines,* Norman, Okla., University of Oklahoma, 1952.

Periodicals

Adams, H. C., "Administrative Supervision of Railways Under the Twentieth Section of the Act to Regulate Commerce," *Quarterly Journal of Economics,* May, 1908.

Aitchison, C. B., "The Evolution of the Interstate Commerce Act, 1887–1937," *George Washington Law Review,* March, 1937.

Dixon, F. H., "The Interstate Commerce Act as Amended," *Quarterly Journal of Economics,* November, 1906.

Dixon, F. H., "The Mann-Elkins Act Amending the Act to Regulate Commerce," *Quarterly Journal of Economics,* August, 1910.

Dunn, S. O., "The Commerce Court Question," *American Economic Review,* March, 1913.

Esch, J. J., "The Interstate Commerce Commission—Its Influence on Legislation," *George Washington Law Review,* March, 1937.

Harbeson, R. W., "The Emergency Railroad Transportation Act of 1933," *Journal of Political Economy,* February, 1934.

Harbeson, R. W., "The Transportation Act of 1940," *Journal of Land and Public Utility Economics,* August, 1941.

Herring, E. P., "Special Interests and the Interstate Commerce Commission," *American Political Science Review,* October and December, 1933.

Jones, Eliot, "The Commodity Clause Legislation and the Anthracite Railroads," *Quarterly Journal of Economics,* August, 1913.

Mansfield, H. C., "The Minimum Rate Power and the Control of Carrier Competition," *Yale Law Journal,* June, 1936.

Margolius, Bernard, "The Interstate Commerce Commission and the Development of Safety Legislation," *George Washington Law Review,* March, 1937.

Marshall, L. C., "The Commodity Clause," *Journal of Political Economy,* July, 1909.

Mortimer, George H., "Should the Interstate Commerce Commission Remain an Independent Tribunal?" *George Washington Law Review,* March, 1937.

Prescott, W. A., "The Operation and Regulation of Crude Oil and Gasoline Pipe Lines," *Quarterly Journal of Economics,* February, 1942.

Whitesel, Theodore L., "Recent Federal Regulation of the Petroleum Pipe Line as a Common Carrier," *Cornell Law Quarterly,* March, 1947.

Wyman, Bruce, "Business Policies Inconsistent with Public Employment," *Harvard Law Review,* May, 1907.

Special and Miscellaneous

Aitchison, C. B., *Organization and Manner of Work of the Interstate Commerce Commission,* 71st C., 1st S., Sen. Doc. 8, 1929.

Moore, B. H., *The Federal Valuation of the Railroads in the United States,* American Railway Engineering Association, Bulletin no. 503, September-October, 1952.

United States, Attorney-General's Committee, *Report of the Attorney-General's Committee on Administrative Procedure—Administrative Procedure in Government Agencies,* Sen. Doc. 10, 77th C., 1st S., Ser. 10,563, 1941.

United States Board of Investigation and Research, *Report on Practices and Procedures of Government Control of Transportation,* H. Doc. 678, 78th C., 2d S., 1944.

United States, Committee on Organization of the Executive Branch of the Government, *Regulatory Commissions: A Report to Congress,* March, 1949.

United States, Committee on Organization of the Executive Branch of the Government, *Task Force Report on Regulatory Commissions* (Appendix N), prepared for the Commission on Organization of the Executive Branch of the Government.

United States Interstate Commerce Commission, *Interstate Commerce Commission Activities, 1887–1937,* Washington, D.C., Government Printing Office, prepared by the Bureau of Statistics with the coöperation of other bureaus of the Commission, 1937.

United States, Office of the Federal Coordinator of Transportation, *Report on Regulation of Transport Agencies,* 73d C., 2d S., Sen. Doc. 152, 1934.

United States, President's Committee on Administrative Management, *Report on Administrative Management in the Executive Branch of the Government of the United States,* 75th C., 1st S., Sen. Doc. 8, 1937, Ser. 10104, January, 1937.

United States, President's Committee on Administrative Management, *The Problem of the Independent Regulatory Commissions,* no. 3 of Studies on Administrative Management in the Government of the United States, by R. E. Cushman, 1937.

Wolf Management Engineering Company, *Survey of Organization and Operations of the Interstate Commerce Commission,* Report submitted to the Committee on Interstate and Foreign Commerce on December 22, 1952, pursuant to S. Res., 332, 82d Congress. 83d C., 1st S., Washington, D.C., Committee Print, Government Printing Office, 1952.

Railroad Regulation

Most of the previous chapter has considered railroad regulation. The present chapter returns to the subject for two purposes. In the first place, the additional pages will make it possible to mention some peculiarities and problems in railroad regulation that have not been sufficiently discussed. In the second place, the text will now adopt a form which, beginning with railroads, will be subsequently used also in explaining the regulation of motor, water, and air transportation. The analysis will, that is to say, be presented in headings, and these will be the same in each of the next four chapters in order to facilitate comparison of government control of different agencies under the provisions of present law. The general plan is not intended to prevent the introduction of special arguments or observations; nor will it cut off digressions when these should be made.

Railroads

The subject of the present chapter is railroad regulation. The text deals with the Interstate Commerce Act and collateral legislation.

Classification of Railroads

Part I of the Interstate Commerce Act concerns itself with railroad and pipe line common carriers that transport passengers or property in interstate or foreign commerce.[1] It covers also rail–water, rail–pipe line, and pipe line–water movements, and motor transportation in terminal areas performed by a railroad line.[2] There is no mention of a separate category of railroad contract carriage.[3]

[1] The act applies to foreign commerce only so far as that commerce takes place within the United States.

[2] As a special case Part I covers the operations of a carrier by water when this carrier absorbs switching, terminal, lighterage, car rental, haulage, handling, or other railroad charges for services within the switching, drayage, lighterage, or corporate limits of a port terminal of district. Such a carrier by water is subject to Part I.

[3] In Great Britain and in Canada railroads do operate upon a contract basis. In

Exemptions

No railroad common carriers are exempted which carry passengers or property in interstate or foreign commerce.

Declaration of Policy

Congress has made several declarations of national transportation policy. The declaration which affects the railroads is to be found as a preamble in the Transportation Act of 1940. It reads as follows:

It is hereby declared to be the national transportation policy of the Congress to provide for fair and impartial regulation of all modes of transportation subject to the provisions of this Act, so administered as to recognize and preserve the inherent advantages of each; to promote safe, adequate, economical, and efficient service and foster sound economic conditions in transportation and among the several carriers; to encourage the establishment and maintenance of reasonable charges for transportation services, without unjust discriminations, undue preferences or advantages, or unfair or destructive competitive practices; to cooperate with the several States and the duly authorized officials thereof; and to encourage fair wages and equitable working conditions;—all to the end of developing, coordinating, and preserving a national transportation system by water, highway, and rail, as well as other means, adequate to meet the needs of the commerce of the United States, of the Postal Service, and of the national defense. All of the provisions of this Act shall be administered and enforced with a view to carrying out the above declaration of policy.

Certificates, Permits, and Licenses

The Commission does not issue permits or licenses to railroad corporations. But the Act of 1920 gave it authority to grant or to refuse certificates

---

England, carriers have contracted with shippers to transport the shipper's goods to all destinations during a given period of time in return for a negotiated rate. The shipper pays something less than normal rates under such agreements; but he is likely to bind himself to send all his goods or at least a specified part of his goods by the line of the contracting carrier. The rate bases in England include: (1) a percentage of the invoice price or value of the goods; (2) a per package or per shipment or consignment basis; and (3) a fixed total amount for a given period of time. In Canada the arrangements are similar in principle to those in England although the rate bases seem to be somewhat different (G. L. Wilson, *New Departures in Freight Rate Making,* New York, Simmons-Boardman, 1948).

An American observer may feel that a grant to a carrier of the right to make individual bargains which trade rate adjustments for exclusive patronage surrenders a great deal of the protection against discrimination which American shippers now enjoy. It is true that the contracts are made public in England and in Canada, that they must be approved by the Railway Rate Tribunal or by the Board of Transport Commissioners as the case may be, and that outside shippers may complain and seek agreements for themselves. But on the other hand, the effective publicity is probably less under English and Canadian than under American practice; the small shipper, moreover, is not likely to negotiate with any great success.

Whatever the merits of the system, English and Canadian railroads may do both a common and a contract carrier business—a privilege which American railroads do not enjoy.

(1) for construction or extension of railroad lines, and (2) for the abandonment of the operation of existing lines. No railroad subject to the Act may now build a new line, or extend or abandon an old one, without the Commission's permission.[4]

The Commission may attach terms and conditions to the issue of certificates, but it may not revoke them, and its authority does not extend to the construction or abandonment of local tracks or to street, suburban, or interurban electric railways which are not operated as a part of a general steam railroad system of operation.[5]

The initial purpose of certificate regulation is to restrict the business of common carriers to persons of financial standing, experience, and reliability, so as to protect users against malpractice and investors against certain types of risk. To this is added the attempt to discourage wasteful duplication of carrier facilities in selected areas and to give preference to existing enterprises against competition. Thus it has been said, particularly, that a new carrier should not be permitted to invade a field where existing carriers are in a position to and are willing to increase their service to the extent necessary to meet the public need. It is conceivable that such a policy may yield good results over a period of time. It has some dangers, however, when indiscriminately applied.[6]

[4] Section 1 (18) now reads:
"After ninety days after this period takes effect no carrier by railroad subject to this part shall undertake the extension of its line of railroad, or the construction of a new line of railroad, or shall acquire or operate any line of railroad, or extension thereof, or shall engage in transportation under this part over or by means of such additional or extended line of railroad, unless and until there shall first have been obtained from the Commission a certificate that the present or future public convenience and necessity require or will require the construction, or operation, or construction and operation, of such additional or extended line of railroad, and no carrier by railroad subject to this part shall abandon all or any portion of a line of railroad, or the operation thereof, unless and until there shall first have been obtained from the Commission a certificate that the present or future public convenience and necessity permit of such abandonment. Nothing in this paragraph or in section 5 (Relating to consolidation) shall be considered to prohibit the making of contracts between carriers by railroad subject to this part, without the approval of the Commission, for the joint ownership or joint use of spur, industrial, team, switching, or side tracks."

[5] Sec. 1 (22). "The authority of the Commission . . . shall not extend to the construction and abandonment of spur, industrial, team, switching or side tracks, located or to be located wholly within one State, or of street, suburban, or interurban electric railways, which are not operated as a part or parts of a general steam railroad system of transportation."

[6] The difficulties which confront any system of certification are of two separate kinds. In the first place, the refusal of certificates may protect existing operators in the exercise of monopolistic powers. This result will never, probably, be intended, but it may occur. On the other hand, the grant of a certificate may be costly, at least in railroad operation, when large investments of capital are required. The commitment of blocks of new capital should sometimes be delayed even when a proposed new service is essentially better than the service rendered. For when new facilities press upon the market at a rapid rate, a community may suffer unnecessary loss through the obsolescence of previously used equipment, the disruption of established methods of doing business, and

Actually, in the case of railroads, the demand for new construction has, in recent years, been comparatively slight. During the 23 years from 1930 to 1952 the Interstate Commerce Commission issued certificates of convenience and necessity authorizing new railroad construction to the extent of 3,218 miles. This was at the rate of some 140 miles a year. It denied or dismissed applications covering 6,166 miles, or at the rate of approximately 268 miles per year. Steam railroads operated approximately 224,000 miles of line in 1952. It would appear that the Commission's decisions on applications for new construction have been of little importance in the railroad field during the past 23 years.

Abandonments

The Commission, under the statute, represents the federal government in its relations with railroads, and has, within its jurisdiction, power to give or to withhold assent for the abandonment of railroad service.[7]

---

the idleness of men at one time employed. There is a gain in these cases from the efficiency of the new device; but there is a loss from the destruction of the old tools and methods. The gain should be preserved and the loss minimized, in so far as possible, but so long as the gain accrues to one set of individuals and the loss is borne by another, no attempt at calculating the balance is likely to be made. This is where a government may properly interfere.

[7] There is, here, a possible clash between state and federal authority. The following remarks are pertinent:

The Commission's authority does not, on general principle, extend to the abandonment of spur, industrial, team, switching, or side tracks located wholly within one state.

The Commission's powers do cover the abandonment of intrastate railroad operations in some cases. With respect to these, the following statement is, probably, correct:

1. The jurisdiction of the Interstate Commerce Commission in the matters here referred to, rests upon its delegated authority over interstate commerce.

2. It follows that the Commission may not authorize or refuse to authorize the abandonment of a railroad which (a) lies entirely within a single state; (b) is independently owned; and (c) does not participate in the handling of interstate or foreign commerce. Nor may it prevent the abandonment of the intrastate business conducted by any railroad whose structure and ownership are such that the cessation of local operations will not affect interstate and foreign commerce (258 U.S. 204, 1922).

In spite of the limitations stated in the preceding paragraphs Commission approval is required for most railroad abandonments for the following reasons:

3. The limitations stated do not qualify the Commission's authority over the abandonment of railroad operation in interstate and foreign commerce.

4. The Commission may authorize the abandonment of a railroad which handles intrastate traffic when the continuance of this service imposes an undue burden upon interstate and foreign commerce.

Thus the Interstate Commerce Commission may permit the abandonment of an unprofitable branch of an interstate carrier even though the branch line lies entirely within a state and devotes itself entirely to local business (254 I.C.C. 745, 763, 1944; 271 U.S. 153, 1926; 320 U.S. 685, 690, 1944). The Commission has justified this conclusion by the following explanation:

"Were railroads not permitted," the Commission has said, "to eliminate the infection of unprofitable operation on short branch lines that infection might continue to spread as a cancerous growth to the main stems and sap the strength of the entire system thereby directly affecting their ability to render adequate service in interstate commerce" (257 I.C.C. 785, 792, 1945).

The most important reason for railroad abandonment is competition, especially highway competition.[8] It is easy to understand that duplication of railroads by motor routes or by water or pipe line facilities may remove the need for certain of the shorter railroad lines. Shippers cease to use railroad service or use it to a relatively small extent and the rail carrier ultimately withdraws. The second most influential cause is the exhaustion of natural resources or industrial relocation. This covers the case of the cutting over of timber lands, the exhaustion of mines, the permanent flooding of agricultural areas, and the shifting of factory position.[9] Withdrawals also result from attempts to secure operating economy. Thus it is sometimes possible for two or more railroads to operate over a single track and to abandon trackage previously employed; or a tunnel may make a detour unnecessary, or a line may be relocated to reduce its grade. Most abandonments are small—the railroad average in the year 1952 was only 45 miles.

Communities frequently, though not always, object to railroad abandonment because it generally means a decrease in service. Even shippers who prefer highway to railroad carriage may wish to use or to be able to use a railroad for part of their business at certain times. Abandonment may lessen the number of competing carriers. In an undetermined number of cases it may leave a community without any carriers at all.

During the 23 years from 1930 to 1952 the Commission authorized the abandonment of approximately 1,500 miles of railroad track per year and denied or dismissed applications covering, in round numbers, 296 miles per year. Most denials were based upon the hope that conditions would improve or upon the feeling that unprofitableness of operation had not been demonstrated.

The general contention of shippers is that railroads should not be allowed to discontinue unprofitable service so long as the railroads, as a whole and including lines rendering this service, earn a reasonable return. The Interstate Commerce Commission, on the contrary, believes that the efficiency of the national transportation system is improved and the railroad industry in its entirety as an instrumentality of the public service is

---

And the Commission may permit the discontinuance of a local subsidiary of an interstate system when the subsidiary incurs deficits which must be made good by a parent company that derives its income from interstate traffic (233 I.C.C. 321, 1939; 242 I.C.C. 20, 1941). It is not practically important in such cases whether the deficits of the subsidiary are the result of local operations or whether they are the result of interstate transactions in which the subsidiary participates, although the Commission sometimes restricts its consent to the abandonment of interstate operations only (261 I.C.C. 794, 1946). More frequently the Commission's decision covers the operations of the subsidiary as a whole.

The final result, in railroad regulation, is that almost all abandonments must be approved by the Interstate Commerce Commission before they can be made effective.

[8] Charles R. Cherington, *The Regulation of Railroad Abandonments*. Cambridge, Mass., Harvard, 1948.

[9] The difficulties of short line railroads were discussed in chap. 25.

fostered and protected by the abandonment of unwanted, unneeded, and uneconomical lines.[10] Of these two views, that of the Commission would seem to be the best.[11]

Federal Safety Regulations

This subject has been discussed in chapter 29.

Service

There are several portions of the Interstate Commerce Act which confer upon the Interstate Commerce Commission power to regulate railroad service. Thus the Commission may require rail carriers to make physical connection with each other or with spurs and sidings owned by shippers, or with docks maintained by water carriers. It may compel carriers, under certain conditions, to admit other railroads to joint use of their terminals. It may establish through routes and it has general authority under other sections of the Act.[12] The chief authority which the Commission has exercised, however, has been over railroad car service, and this should be separately described.

CAR SERVICE. Car service, under the Act, includes the use, control, supply, movement, distribution, exchange, interchange, and return of locomotives, cars, and other vehicles used in the transportation of property, including special types of equipment. Carrier practice in these matters has been described in chapter 23. The power to regulate is, obviously, of great importance.

Under normal conditions the Commission may exercise authority over car service in two ways:

1. It may require railroads to file their rules and regulations.
2. It may establish reasonable rules, regulations, and practices.

Under emergency conditions, the Commission's authority is greatly in-

[10] United States Senate, Committee on Interstate Commerce, *Abandonment of Railroad Lines,* Hearings before a subcommittee on S. 1489, 78th C., 2d S., 1944, p. 107.

[11] One of the advantages of a private and individualistic society is that mistaken or obsolete enterprises are written off at the expense of those who are responsible for them, and not carried at the charge of society. Abandonment is a process by which the writing off may take place. It may even be wise to insist that property be abandoned. Thus, a member of the New England Governors' Railroad Committee declared, in November, 1932, that at least 2,000 out of the 8,000 miles of New England railways had become obsolete since the absorption by trucks of a large portion of the short-haul business of which they had formerly possessed a monopoly; he advocated the transformation of these obsolete lines into modern highways (*New York Journal of Commerce,* November 18, 1932).

[12] The Act directs rail carriers to afford all reasonable, proper, and equal facilities for the interchange of traffic [Sec. 3 (4)]; it also makes it unlawful for a common carrier to prevent the carriage of freight from being continuous from the place of shipment to the place of destination (Sec. 7).

The Commission cannot, however, compel a railroad to extend its lines into an area which it has not undertaken to serve. (See chap. 12.)

creased. It may now suspend the operation of carrier rules and issue orders of its own governing the distribution and use of equipment and the priority to be accorded traffic of various sorts. Emergency conditions are not defined in the Act but the Commission has interpreted the phrase to cover shortages of equipment or congestions of traffic due to a great variety of circumstances, including flood, storms, wrecks, landslides, strikes, seasonal movements of grain and coal, the requirements of foreign relief, and generally the unexpected accumulation of freight waiting to be moved or the special need for receiving a supply.

The Commission supervises railroad car service through its Bureau of Service which, in turn, operates through field agents scattered throughout the country. In 1947 there were 70 such agents: [13] they investigate, hear complaints, offer suggestions to the carriers and make recommendations to the Bureau. The Commission is in a position, with its agents, to fix minimum loads, to reroute traffic, to order priorities, to expedite the return of empty cars to their owners or, in some cases, to distribute empty cars without regard to ownership, to raise or lower demurrage charges, and to correct the failure of carriers to comply with the Commission's general regulations.[14]

The Commission may issue orders with respect to car service, it may authorize its agents to take action, or it may suggest remedial changes to the carriers which these carriers will accept and enforce. The Commission has authority to fix car service rules. It has not done so because it is not disposed to assume a function of railroad management which is now performed by the Car Service Division of the Association of American Railroads. It is, however, active and influential in the distribution of

---

[13] 268 I.C.C. 687, 1947.

[14] The Commission does not, however, have authority to fix per diem rates. This fact appears to have been established in 1947, when the Commission issued an order to increase the per diem rate to 200 cents per day for a period of 6 months in order to bring about greater efficiency in the use of cars (268 I.C.C. 659, 1947). There was a car shortage, in 1947, and the increase was to operate as a penalty to reduce unnecessary car detention. The Office of Defense Transportation filed a brief in the proceedings urging a still higher charge. The District Court of the United States for the District of Columbia issued, however, a restraining order (75 Fed. Suppl. 63, November 20, 1947). The Court held that the Commission had no power to use the per diem charge as a means of regulation. The Court added that prompt return of emptied foreign cars to the owners, regardless of available freight in the direction of the owning road, would decrease rather than increase efficiency in use.

The Commission has asked Congress to amend Sec. 20 (3) of the Interstate Commerce Act so as to enable it to fix payments for the use of foreign cars (United States Interstate Commerce Commission, Annual Report, 1951, p. 151). The argument is that high or penalty charges would discourage a railroad from hoarding or retaining a foreign car for which it did not have an urgent and immediate need (Traffic World, April 19, 1952, p. 62).

In the particular controversy referred to in this note, the carriers voluntarily adopted a $2.00 per diem rate, but not until May, 1952.

railroad cars, and in some other matters made possible by wartime legislation in 1941, 1950, and 1951.[15]

[15] The importance of proper handling of railroad equipment was emphasized by inquiries of the Interstate Commerce Commission in 1907 (12 I.C.R. 561, 1907) and in 1917 (42 I.C.C. 657, 1917). In 1917 Congress gave the Commission authority (1) to establish rules for car service and (2) when necessity appeared, to issue directions with respect to car service which would promote the public interest (40 Stat. 101, 1917). In 1920 (41 Stat. 458, 476, 1920), in 1940 (54 Stat. 898, 901, 1940), and in 1942 (56 Stat. 176, 1942) these powers were enlarged.

At various times since 1917 the Commission's authority over car service has been displaced or supplemented by other federal legislation.

During the First World War the federal government assumed direct responsibility for the use and distribution of railroad equipment.

In 1941, after the outbreak of the Second World War, Congress created the Office of Defense Transportation. This was a branch of the Office of Emergency Management. It was empowered to coordinate and to direct traffic movements, to establish priorities, and to develop measures designed to secure maximum use of existing domestic transportation facilities. It was empowered also to stimulate the provision of additional means of carriage (6 Fed. Reg., December 25, 1941, p. 6725, E. O. 8988). The Office of Defense Transportation had authority over motor and water transport as well as over railroad carriage, and it regulated local in addition to interstate transportation. The most active period of the Office was between 1941 and 1944 although it was not terminated until 1949. Among its pronouncements were orders fixing the minimum loading of railroad cars, assigning designated types of cars for use in designated areas, restricting the number of passenger railroad vehicles in use, directing the installation of improved facilities at interchange points, and controlling the direction of movements in certain instances. This is a representative but not an exhaustive list of the orders which the Office issued. The fact that Mr. Eastman, who was the first, and Mr. Johnson, who was the second, Director of the Office of Defense Administration were also members of the Interstate Commerce Commission helped to prevent friction between these organizations. (See United States, Office of Defense Transportation, *Civilian War Transport: A Record of the Control of Domestic Traffic Operations by the Office of Defense Transportation, 1941–1946,* Washington, D.C., Superintendent of Documents. See also annual reports of the Interstate Commerce Commission, and T. C. Bigham and W. J. Roberts, *Transportation, Principles and Problems,* New York, McGraw-Hill, 1952.)

In 1950, in the course of the country's military defense program, Congress passed the National Defense Act of 1950 (Public Law 774, 81st C., 2d S., chap. 932, 1950). This act authorized the President to determine priorities and to allocate materials and facilities. The President, in turn, delegated his authority in so far as it concerned transport "to that commissioner of the Interstate Commerce Commission who is responsible for the supervision of the Bureau of Service of the Commission with respect to domestic transportation, stowage, and port facilities, or the use thereof (but excluding air transport, coastwise, intercoastal, and overseas shipping)" (E. O. 10,161, 15 Fed. Reg. 6105, September 12, 1950). The arrangement was presently stabilized by the establishment of a Defense Transport Administration under the jurisdiction of this commissioner, who was to serve as Administrator (D.T.A. Organization Order DTA-1, 15 Fed. Reg. 6728, October 5, 1950). In 1951 Congress further created the Defense Production Administration with authority, among other things, over the functions previously delegated to the Interstate Commerce Commission but with instruction that this authority should be redelegated to the parties to whom delegation had previously been made (E. O. 10,200, 16 Fed. Reg. 61, January 4, 1951). Later, the jurisdiction over motor carriers was separately assigned to the Director of the Bureau of Motor Carriers of the Interstate Commerce Commission (DTA-Delegation 2, 16 Fed. Reg. 2046, March 3, 1951).

The result of the legislative and administrative provisions of 1950 and 1951 was to

Consolidation, Merger, and Acquisition of Control

This subject has been discussed in chapter 25. The Interstate Commerce Act permits railroads to combine with each other on condition that the Interstate Commerce Commission shall approve.[16] Applications must, however, be called to the attention of persons interested, including the governor of each state in which any part of the properties of the carriers involved in the proposed transaction is situated, and there must be a hearing in all cases. The Antitrust Act does not apply to consolidations which the Commission has sanctioned.

In rendering its decisions the Commission is no longer required to fix applications into a general plan, but it must give weight to the following considerations: (1) the effect of the proposed transaction upon adequate transportation service to the public; (2) the effect upon the public interest of the inclusion, or failure to include, other railroads in the territory involved in the application; (3) the total fixed charges resulting from the consolidation; and (4) the interest of the carriers' employees.[17] It may require applicants to include railroads which were not originally mentioned in a proposed consolidation as a condition of approval, but it cannot alter a petition and then insist that the proponent accept the revised arrangement.[18]

Control of consolidation is not, presently, a major activity of the Interstate Commerce Commission for reasons which have been previously explained. Between 1943 and 1951 there were 494 applications filed. During these same years the Commission granted 474 applications and denied or dismissed 30. Most proposals were, however, of secondary im-

---

leave the control of car service in the hands of those members of the Interstate Commerce Commission who were, respectively, the heads of the Bureau of Service and, later, of the Bureau of Motor Carriers of the Commission. The jurisdiction of these individuals under their delegated powers was somewhat broader than that of the Interstate Commerce Commission itself because it was based upon the broad provisions of wartime emergency legislation as well as upon the narrower jurisdiction conferred by the Interstate Commerce Act alone. The situation in 1950–51, in this respect, resembled that created by the legislation of 1941.

An executive order, in February, 1953, abolished the Office of Defense Administration and transferred its functions to the Office of Defense Mobilization. It is not apparent that this shift affects the authority of the Office of Defense Administration or the relations of that Office to the Interstate Commerce Commission.

It is possible, however, that the control of car service as a peacetime function may be transferred from the Commission to the Department of Commerce, thus relieving the Commission of an important function which it now, normally, performs.

[16] Sec. 5 (2), Sec. 1 (3b). There are special provisions in the Act which provide for the case (1) where a person who is not a common carrier desires to acquire control of one or more railroad corporations [Sec. 5 (2) (a), (i)]; and (2) for other special cases [Sec. 5 (4), (5), (6)].

[17] Sec. 5 (2) (c).

[18] Sec. 5 (2) (d).

portance.[19] Since 1940, indeed, the Commission has approved only 10 applications involving the purchase or merger of railroad systems which exceeded 1,000 miles in length. Of these instances, 2 applications called for the reincorporation of a railroad under the laws of another state; 2 were the result of receivership and reorganization; and in 6 cases the purpose of the contemplated merger or purchase was to improve the relations between a major company and its subsidiaries.

Rates and Tariffs

This is a major Commission activity. Common carriers by railroad must file and publish their tariffs and must collect the rates which they publish. No change in published rates may be made except after a notice of 30 days. The Commission may, however, modify this last requirement. The Commission may consider the lawfulness of any new rate or schedule, suspending the effective date thereof as long as 6 months,[20] and it may consider any existing charge and determine what shall be the lawful rate or the maximum, maximum or minimum, or maximum and minimum, classification, regulation, or practice to be observed. It may also establish through rates and prescribe divisions of through rates applicable to the transportation of passengers or property by railroad common carriers or by railroads and water lines.[21] These are all standard provisions which have been mentioned in chapter 29 and, by reference, in other chapters of this book.

RATE MAKING RULE. The rate making rule which binds the Commission in regulating rates reads as follows:

In the exercise of its powers to prescribe just and reasonable rates the Commission shall give due consideration, among other factors, to the effect of rates on the movement of traffic by the carrier or carriers for which the rates are prescribed; to the need, in the public interest, of adequate and efficient railway transportation service at the lowest cost consistent with the furnishing of such service; and to the need of revenues sufficient to enable the carriers, under honest, economical, and efficient management to provide such service.[22]

This rule is difficult to interpret. It does not lead to a determinate result unless the supply and demand schedules of railroad service are known and then only for a given time and place. Nor is it clear what weight is to be attributed to the movement of traffic when proposed charges meet the other requirements which the paragraph provides. A reasonable interpreta-

---

[19] The figures given in the text do not cover applications or authorizations for trackage rights, operating contracts or agreements, joint use, etc., which come to the Commissions under the consolidation clauses of the law.

[20] Sec. 15 (7).

[21] Sec. 15 (3).

[22] Sec. 15a (2).

tion might be to construe the rule as a prohibition of monopolistic railroad pricing and a suggestion that over short periods, at least, a railroad might properly expect, sometimes, to do business at a loss. The language employed is probably best understood when it is compared with a somewhat similar paragraph in the Act of 1920 to which attention is given in the note below.[23]

COMMISSION CONTROL. In 1935 there were approximately 500,000 tariffs and supplements on file with the Interstate Commerce Commission,[24] all subject to correction, replacement, and review. A representative of the United States Department of Justice asserted, in 1943, that between 89,000 and 124,000 changes were annually filed with the Commission, not including motor carrier cases.[25] Changes in published tariffs are filed by private carriers. It has been contended that less than 1 percent of the changes are suspended, for investigation, and it is therefore concluded that most become effective without governmental review.[26] It appears to be the fact, however, that (1) all tariff changes receive at least routine scrutiny by the Commission organization; (2) many changes are for editorial reasons or for reasons of convenience; (3) changes which are required by the Commission or are made necessary by Commission order do not need to be delayed; and (4) the Commission will seldom suspend tariff changes which result in lower rates.[27] Problems involved in the ex-

[20] The Act of 1920 required the Interstate Commerce Commission to divide the railroads of the United States into groups. It continued:

"The Commission shall from time to time determine and make public what percentage of such aggregate property value constitutes a fair return thereon, and such percentage shall be uniform for all rate groups or territories which may be designated by the Commission. In making such determination it shall give due consideration, among other things, to the transportation needs of the country and the necessity (under honest, efficient and economical management of existing transportation facilities) of enlarging such facilities in order to provide the people of the United States with adequate transportation . . ."

Finally, the Commission was directed to fix rates which would be sufficient to yield a fair return upon the aggregate value of the railway property in each group. The Commission ultimately declared that a fair return would be 5¾ percent.

The directive phrases of the Act of 1920 which are quoted in this note were repealed in 1933. But the history of the intervening period undoubtedly left the impression that the federal government was supporting a rate system in the railroad interest, without reference to the interests of other parties which were concerned with transportation. This could explain both the elimination of the quoted paragraph and the later substitution of language of a more general sort.

[24] United States, Office of the Federal Coordinator of Transportation, *Freight Traffic Report*, vol. 1, p. 71.

[25] United States Senate, Committee on Interstate Commerce, Hearings on S. 42, 79th C., 1st S., 1943, Part I, p. 75.

[26] *Ibid.*

[27] Mr. Aitchison, Chairman of the Intertsate Commerce Commission, testified elaborately upon this question in 1946 (United States Senate, Committee on Interstate Commerce, 79th C., 2d S., 1946, Hearings on H. R. 2536, pp. 1175 ff.). The Commission itself observed, in its annual report for 1943 (p. 12) that:

ercise of Commission rate authority have been discussed in earlier chapters of the text.

Discrimination

The subject of railroad discrimination has been discussed in chapters 14 and 21. Sections 2, 3, and 4 of the Interstate Commerce Act deal with this matter in general terms.

Securities

The Act of 1920 conveyed to the Commission authority to regulate security issues of common carriers by railroad engaged in interstate commerce, with some exceptions.[28] The Commission's approval was required for the issue of shares, bonds, or evidence of indebtedness or for the assumption of obligations or liabilities as lessor, lessee, guarantor, etc. Notes maturing in not more than 2 years were exempt up to a total of 5 percent of the par value of the securities of the issuing corporation. The Commission's authority extended to corporations incorporated under state laws—most companies, indeed, were in this class.[29]

In addition to its powers over new security issues the Interstate Commerce Commission has functions with respect to the readjustment of outstanding securities and the reorganization of railroad corporations. These derive from the Federal Bankruptcy Act and, latterly, from Section 20 (b) of the Interstate Commerce Act.

Section 77 of the Bankruptcy Act was enacted in 1933 and was amended in 1935 to meet the needs of railroads.[30] Under the Act as

---

"Analysis of the filing of tariffs in a recent year showed that approximately 40 per cent of the total number lodged in our Bureau of Traffic, and reported in our annual report for the year, stated rates which either had been required by us, or had secured our formal approval as justified under the act, or the filing was permitted upon administrative consideration of the applications for special permission."

[28] The Act of 1920 excepted street, suburban, or interurban electric railways which were not operated as part of a general steam railroad system of transportation (41 Stat. 494, 1920). Sleeping-car companies were taken out in 1949 (63 Stat. 483, 487, 1949).

[29] Sec. 20a.

[30] 47 Stat. 1474, 1933; 49 Stat. 911, 1935; 49 Stat. 1969, 1936. Railroads, as a class, were not entitled to the benefits which the Bankruptcy Act provided for voluntary bankrupts.

The legislative history of the Act of 1935 may be followed in the following: 74 C., 1st S., House Doc. 89, pp. 100, 229 (Report of the Federal Coordinator of Transportation, 1934); 74th C., 1st S., H. Rep. 1283, 1935, Ser. 9888; *Ibid.,* Sen. Rep. 1336, 1935, Ser. 9980.

The Supreme Court has characterized the Acts of 1933 and 1935 as follows:

"Both acts are bottomed upon the theory of debtor rehabilitation by adjustment of creditors' claims. Such treatment was essential for embarrassed railroads, as ordinary bankruptcy liquidation or judicial sales were impossible because of the size of their indebtedness and the paucity of buyers. The acts were a part of the relief granted financially involved corporations, public and private, in the depression years of the

amended in 1935 and 1936 a railroad may file a petition and give notice of insolvency to a court, with a copy to the Commission. This accomplished, interested parties, including the railroad, may file plans of reorganization. In the simplest possible case, these plans will be examined by the Commission; one of them or a plan which the Commission itself devises will be certified to the court; the court will approve the plan and return it to the Commission; the Commission will secure the assent of security holders and transmit the plan to the court; the court will confirm the proposed reorganization. Even though the securityholders do not assent, the court may still confirm. Both the Commission and the court hold hearings under this procedure. The Commission plays an important part in determining the kind of reorganization which shall take place and this is true, also, in more complicated and contentious negotiations. It cooperates with, although it does not supplant the federal courts. The results of the act have been somewhat disappointing, but the law remains in force.[31]

Finally, the Commission has authority under Section 20b of the Interstate Commerce Act to allow capital readjustments which fall short of a comprehensive reorganization but which may, nevertheless, afford a carrier considerable relief. Section 20b was added to the Act in 1948.[32]

early thirties. Since railroads could not take advantage of the Bankruptcy Act, their financial adjustments for years had been carried out in equity receiverships under judicial control. These were cumbersome, costly and privately managed with inadequate consideration for the public interest in a soundly financed transportation system" (338 U.S. 468, 1943).

[31] See Sen. Rep. 925, 79th C., 2d S., 1946; Sen. Rep. 1170, 79th C., 2d S., 1946; H. Rep. 1838, 79th C., 2d S., 1946.

The relative functions of the court and of the Commission under the Act of 1935 have, of course, been much discussed. The present act provides for hearings by both agencies. The bill originally presented in 1933 proposed Commission hearings only. Reorganization plans were to be submitted to the court, but the court was to act upon the Commission's record and not upon the basis of hearings of its own (76th Congr. Rec. 2905–2906, January 30, 1933; 72d C., 2d S., H. Rep. 1897, 1933, p. 6, Ser. 9649). This was changed, however, before the bill was passed, to provide for court hearings also (76 Congr. Rec. 4907, 5104–5134, 1933). It is the duty of the Commission to determine whether the corporate structure proposed for a reorganizing company is such that the rehabilitated enterprise may have a reasonable prospect of satisfactory public service. It is for the court to see that, in revising the corporate structure, the relations between various classes of investors are substantially maintained (338 U.S. 468–475, 511–515, 1943).

Under the Act of 1948, to be presently discussed, the Commission may withdraw a plan which it has submitted to a court if the Court has not confirmed it and if changes which have occurred after December 31, 1939, make reconsideration desirable (62 Stat. 163, 168, 1948).

[32] This amendment was preceded by two earlier laws which amended the Federal Bankruptcy Act with the same general purpose. Of these one was passed in 1939 (53 Stat. 1134, 1939) and one in 1942 (56 Stat. 787, 1942). Both were temporary statutes, the first lapsing in 1940 and the second in 1945. Congress also passed a bill in 1946 which amended the Interstate Commerce Act, but this did not receive presidential approval.

It empowers the Commission to consider and approve a change or modification in any class of securities or in the provisions of any mortgage, deed of trust, etc., which a railroad company may care to submit, if the proposal meets conditions specified in the Act; and it may issue an order making the proposal effective at such time as the Commission may select.[33] This rather important grant of power enables the Commission to permit a railroad financial readjustment (1) without the expense and delay of a general reorganization, and (2) without submission of a plan for the review of the federal courts.

Summary

This chapter and the preceding chapter have enumerated and to some extent discussed the regulatory authority exercised by the Interstate Commerce Commission over railroad carriers. They have not followed all the ramifications to which this authority extends. The power to regulate railroads is the oldest of the powers which the Commission holds and in many respects it is the most completely developed. The most important of the duties which the Commission discharges today, in dealing with railroads, is probably the duty of supervising rates from the point of view of reasonableness and the relation of charges to each other. In addition to this, the regulation of railroad finance and the efforts of the Commission to promote the safety of railroad carriage are of first importance. The Commission performs, however, many other functions. The provisions of the Interstate Commerce Act with respect to railroads have served as a model in the preparation of motor vehicle, water, and air laws. The decisions of the Commission in its railroad work have also influenced policies of regulation in other fields.

[33] The provisions of Section 20b are necessarily complicated. Thus the Commission must find that the proposal:

1. Will be in the public interest;
2. Will be in the best interest of the carrier, of each class of its stockholders, and of each class of its obligations affected by the modification or alteration;
3. Will not be adverse to the interests of any creditor of the carrier not affected by the modification or alteration.

If the Commission finds that the requirements of the preceding paragraphs are met it will cause the carriers to submit the proposal to the holders of each class of securities affected for acceptance or rejection. If at least 75 percent of the holders of each class of securities assent, the Commission will issue an order authorizing the change upon the terms and conditions and with the amendments, if any, determined to be just and reasonable. The order will become effective at such time as the Commission may fix.

The described procedure does not apply to carriers who are in equity receivership or in process of reorganization under Section 77 except under special circumstances which the act details.

REFERENCES

General Treatises

Bigham, Truman C., and Roberts, Merrill J., *Transportation, Principles and Problems*, New York, McGraw-Hill, 1952.

Fair, Marvin L., and Williams, E. W., *Economics of Transportation*, New York, Harper, 1950.

Healy, Kent T., *The Economics of Transportation in America*, New York, Ronald, 1940.

Johnson, E. R., *Government Regulation of Transportation*, New York, Appleton-Century-Crofts, 1938.

Jones, Eliot, *Principles of Railroad Transportation*, New York, Macmillan, 1924.

Locklin, D. Philip, *Economics of Transportation*, Chicago, Irwin, 1947.

Ripley, W. Z., *Railroads: Rates and Regulation*, New York, Longmans, 1912.

Sharfman, I. L., *The Interstate Commerce Commission*, New York, Commonwealth Fund, 1931, 1935, 1936, 1937.

Van Metre, Thurman W., *Transportation in the United States*, Brooklyn, Foundation Press, 1950.

Westmeyer, Russell E., *Economics of Transportation*, New York, Prentice-Hall, 1952.

Other Books

Alldredge, J. H., *Rate-Making for Common Carriers*, Atlanta, Harrison Company, 1929.

Bernhardt, Joshua, *The Interstate Commerce Commission*, Washington, D.C., Brookings Institution, 1930.

Cherington, Charles, *Railroad Abandonments*, Cambridge, Mass., Harvard, 1948.

Dixon, F. H., *Railroads and Government*, New York, Scribner's, 1922.

Frederick, John H., Hypps, Frank T., and Herring, James M., *Regulation of Railroad Finance*, New York, Simmons-Boardman, 1930.

Hammond, M. B., *Railway Rate Theories of the Interstate Commerce Commission*, Cambridge, Mass., Harvard, 1911.

Meyer, Hugo R., *Government Regulation of Railway Rates*, New York, Macmillan, 1905.

Schultz, Robert, *Depreciation and the American Railroads*, Philadelphia, University of Pennsylvania, 1934.

Shinn, Glen L., *Reasonable Freight Rates: Tests, Standards, and Practices Explained and Clarified*, Washington, D.C., Traffic Service, 1952.

Van Metre, T. W., *Industrial Traffic Management*, New York, McGraw-Hill, 1953.

Periodicals

Cherington, Charles, "Railroad Abandonments in New England, 1921–1937," *Journal of Land and Public Utility Economics*, February and May, 1938.

Hale, R. L., "Commissions, Rates, and Policies," *Harvard Law Review,* May, 1940.

Huntington, S. P., "The Marasmus of the Interstate Commerce Commission: The Commission, the Railroads, and the Public Interest," *Yale Law Journal,* April, 1952.

Mansfield, Harvey C., "The Hoch-Smith Resolution and the Consideration of Commercial Conditions in Rate-Fixing," *Cornell Law Quarterly,* April, 1931.

Mansfield, Harvey C., "The Minimum Rate Power and the Control of Carrier Competition," *Yale Law Journal,* June, 1936.

Marshall, D. R., "Railroad Certificates of Convenience and Necessity Issued Under the Interstate Commerce Act," *Oregon Law Review,* April and June, 1943.

Sharfman, I. L., "The Interstate Commerce Commission: An Appraisal," *Yale Law Journal,* April, 1937.

Trumbower, Henry R., "Railroad Abandonments and Additions," *Journal of Political Economy,* February, 1926.

Special and Miscellaneous

Locklin, D. Philip, "Rates and Rate Structure," in National Resources Planning Board, *Transportation and National Policy,* Washington, D.C., 1942.

United States, Office of Defense Transportation, *Civilian War Transport: A Record of the Control of Domestic Traffic Operations by the Office of Defense Transportation, 1941–1946,* Washington, D.C., Superintendent of Documents.

United States Senate, Committee on Interstate Commerce, *Abandonment of Railroad Lines,* Hearings before a subcommittee on S. 1489, 78th C., 2d S., 1944.

Motor Vehicle Regulation

Effect of Federal Inaction

Federal inaction, in the late 1920's, left a large area of motor carriage which was not subject to regulation of any kind except with respect to the safety of motor operation. This area was enlarged by evasions. Thus a representative of the United Electric Railways Company of Rhode Island testified, in 1926, to the success with which motor bus lines were avoiding local regulation in that state in traffic between the Rhode Island towns of Woonsocket, near the Massachusetts border, and Providence, in the southern part of the state.

Anyone who sees fit—and there are such—[said the witness] goes to the center of Woonsocket with their busses and stops directly across the street from the . . . street railway terminal, and sign their busses, "Woonsocket-Providence." They load their busses just ahead of the cars and trains right there, and then run one and one-tenth miles to that border [of Massachusetts], go over that border 250 feet where there is a cemetery and a freight yard, and nothing else, turn around and come straight down that highway to Providence with their passengers, and it cannot be stopped because under the law, as interpreted, it is interstate if the wheels of these vehicles go over the soil of another State.

A different procedure seems to have been equally effective on the Connecticut side of Rhode Island. The same witness said:

From Providence to Westerly, at the Connecticut border, is some 38 miles over a brand new State highway. Over this route a lady named Mrs. Mooney invested in four busses and sought permission from the Public Utilities Commission of Rhode Island for an intrastate certificate of public convenience and necessity. She obtained it. She filed her bonds for the protection of her passengers and created a business between those two points and the villages *en route*. After she had created that business, one of these gentlemen said, "Well, how can we get in on that?" Very easily. There is a bridge which is located

655

at the center of the business district of Westerly, which divides Rhode Island from Connecticut, and the middle line of the bridge is the boundary line. The bus of this man is taken to that bridge and is stopped on the Connecticut side of the bridge with the front wheels right at the border line. The man leaves the bus and goes ahead 150 feet where her bus is running on a scheduled time approved by the commission, and to which she holds, and he says: "Bus for Providence, express, right here, leaves at once." The people go down to this express bus and he carries the people from Westerly to Providence, and he is doing an interstate business with no interstate passengers. And you cannot stop it.[1]

This lack of motor regulation in the 1920's recalls the situation which confronted Congress with respect to railroad regulation in 1886.

Motor Carrier Act of 1935

The beginning of federal motor legislation has been mentioned in chapter 29.[2] The Motor Carrier Act was passed in 1935. It was published as Part II of the Interstate Commerce Act. It followed, in general, the forms which Part I of the Act had made familiar; the two parts were not identical either in language or in substance, but the inclusion of motor with railroad regulation in a single statute made it possible to incorporate sections of Part I in Part II without confusion. The problem was further simplified by the fact that both Parts I and II were administered by one functioning commission. At the beginning, motor carrier cases of all sorts were assigned to Division 5 of the Interstate Commerce Commission. This extreme concentration terminated in 1939 when the organization of this commission was revised. The Commission has, however, a Bureau of Motor Carriers, with important administrative duties.

Classification of Carriers

Part II of the Interstate Commerce Act applies to private carriers, contract carriers, brokers, and common carriers engaged in interstate or foreign commerce.

1. *Private carriers.*[3] The Act does not contemplate the regulation of

[1] United States Senate, Committee on Interstate Commerce, Hearings on S. 1734, 1926, testimony Williams, pp. 90–91.

[2] 49 Stat. 543, 1935. Detailed amendments were approved in 1938 (52 Stat. 1029, 1938) and there were changes by reference in the Transportation Act of 1940 (54 Stat. 919, 1940) and in the Freight Forwarder Act of 1942 (56 Stat. 284, 1942). Mention may also be made of the War Powers Acts (56 Stat. 176, 1942; 58 Stat. 827, 1942; and 59 Stat. 658, 1945) and of the Act of 1942 (56 Stat. 746, 1942), which made portions of Section 20 of the Interstate Commerce Act, Part I, applicable to motor carriers.

[3] The term "private carrier of property by motor vehicle" means any person not included in the terms "common carrier by motor vehicle" or "contract carrier by motor vehicle," who or which transports in interstate or foreign commerce by motor vehicle

private carriers, except with respect to the safety of operation, but the Commission can probably regulate such carriers if this is necessary to prevent impairment of the public service of common carriers.[4]

2. *Contract carriers.* The term "contract carrier" has been defined and discussed in chapter 12. Motor contract carriers are more numerous and important than are contract carriers by rail, air, or water.[5]

3. *Brokers.* The recognition of brokers as a class is peculiar to the Motor Carrier Act. Only brokers who deal with transportation are, of course, to be considered.[6] Brokers are intermediaries, but not all intermediaries are brokers. There are at least three possibilities in motor carriage:

a. A motor company may own or lease equipment. It may then solicit traffic and carry passengers or goods in the vehicles which it controls, with or without the assistance of connecting lines.

b. A motor company may not own or lease equipment, or not enough to provide for its needs. But it may arrange with owner-operators under contract, agreeing itself to solicit traffic, provide insurance, pay taxes and certain other expenses, in return for a percentage of the price which the shipper pays. The company will route trucks and assign loads under such a contract. The owner-operator is designated as its agent.[7]

c. A company may seek out persons who desire the service of transport. It may then refer these persons to independent owner-operators and receive a percentage of the tariff which is charged.[8]

The possible variations and gradations in these arrangements is very great. The motor carrier has been held to be a common carrier in the first two of the three instances cited. It has been held to be a broker in the

property of which such person is the owner, lessee, or bailee, when such transportation is for the purpose of sale, lease, rent, or bailment, or in furtherance of any commercial enterprise [Sec. 203 (a) (17)].

[4] 41 Fed. Suppl. 71, 715, 1941.

[5] The Interstate Commerce Act forbids either a motor or a water company to operate both as a common and as a contract carrier, except when the Interstate Commerce Commission declares that dual operation is in the public interest and consistent with the national transportation policy (Sec. 21, 310). This is to discourage discrimination. The thought is that a carrier which performs both functions for a single customer may accomplish a rebate on the common carrier portion by quoting an extremely low contract price. Or a shipper may obtain an advantageous contract by promising a certain proportion of his business to be handled in common carriage. (See 45 M.C.C. 1, 1946; 27 M.C.C. 191, 202, 1940; 260 I.C.C. 783, 790, 1946. For exceptions see 40 M.C.C. 107, 114, 1945; 45 M.C.C. 445, 448–449, 1947.)

[6] Sec. 203 (a) (18). The term "broker" means any person not included in the term "motor carrier" and not a bona fide employee or agent of any such carrier, who or which, as principal or agent, sells or offers for sale any transportation subject to this part, or negotiates for, or holds himself or itself out by solicitation, advertisement, or otherwise as one who sells, provides, furnishes, contracts, or arranges for such transportation.

[7] 32 M.C.C. 719, 1942.

[8] 34 M.C.C. 209, 1942.

third. The distinction is between a person who organizes transport and one who only brings two parties together, makes a transaction possible, and collects a fee for the service which he has performed.[9] It is to be remarked that the first two persons are responsible for the transport which subsequently takes place. The third person is not so responsible.

4. *Common carriers.* The term "common carrier" has its usual meaning.

Exemptions

The Motor Carrier Act does not apply to motor transportation operated by or for railroad, water, or freight forwarding companies in the transfer, collection, and delivery service within terminal areas except in so far as safety regulations are concerned. These operations are regulated, however, in other parts of the Interstate Commerce Act. Apart from this group, Section 203 (b) of the Motor Carrier Act exempts no less than nine separate kinds of motor vehicles. These are not subject to the federal law except in so far as qualifications and maximum hours of service of employees and safety of operation are concerned. Using general terms, we may say that these exemptions include motor vehicles of a distinctly local or urban type, such as taxicabs and hotel automobiles; vehicles used to carry school children or newspapers; vehicles carrying livestock, fish, or agricultural commodities,[10] not including manufactured products thereof, or controlled and operated by a farmer [11] or by a coöperative associa-

---

[9] 8 M.C.C. 211, 224, 1938. For more complicated situations see 46 M.C.C. 159, 1946; 48 M.C.C. 327, 1948.

[10] Horticultural commodities were included in the category of agricultural commodities by amendment to the Interstate Commerce Act in 1952.

[11] The farmer exemption includes only motor vehicles controlled or operated by a farmer when used in the transportation of his agricultural commodities and products thereof, or in the transportation of supplies to his farm. This would be, in most cases, private carriage. But the broad exemption of vehicles carrying agricultural commodities includes cases that might be classified as common or contract carriage (10 M.C.C. 533, 1938; 11 M.C.C. 646, 1938).

The Act was intended to cover specialized for-hire transportation for farmers or for fishermen by persons not engaged in farming or fishing or in livestock management. The Act specified that this should not include transport by vehicles which were used in carrying other property or passengers for transportation, and that it should not include the manufactured products of agricultural commodities.

The result of the exemption of vehicles carrying fish or agricultural commodities has been, however, greater than was anticipated. This is partly because there has been difficulty in deciding what is a manufactured product and partly because the courts have held that vehicles can be used for carrying agricultural commodities and also for hauling other commodities if the two classes of goods are not carried at the same time (166 Fed. 2d, 116, 1948).

According to Commissioner Rogers of the Interstate Commerce Commission there were, in 1950, 20,042 authorized motor carriers of property under the Interstate Commerce Act and 1,596 authorized carriers of passengers, operating an estimated total of 250,000 power units. In contrast to this, there were nearly 40,000 carriers, having an estimated 150,000 power units, exclusively used to transport exempt commodities, for

tion; vehicles in national parks; and transportation by motor vehicle when incidental to transportation by aircraft.[12] Subject to review by the Commission, the Act also exempts transportation in interstate or foreign commerce within a municipality,[13] and casual, occasional, or reciprocal transportation by motor vehicle for transportation.[14] Finally, the Commission does not regulate incidental carriers. This is not because of any reference in the Act but because incidental carriers are private and not subject to regulatory control.

which no authority from the Interstate Commerce Commission was required (United States House of Representatives, Committee on Interstate and Foreign Commerce, *Transportation Study,* Hearings before a subcommittee on Transportation Problems, 81st C., 2d S., 1950, p. 140). These last-named carriers could be substantial companies, organized much as are regulated carriers; they could be so-called gypsy operators traveling in the direction in which available loads led them; or they could even be private shippers who combined for hire transportation with the movement of their own goods. An example of the last would be a Texas packer who shipped meat in his own trucks to California and then returned with a load of fruits and vegetables under the agricultural exemption. Another example, in reverse, would be that of an operator who carried exempt commodities on an outbound trip and who then leased his equipment, with himself as driver, to a certified motor carrier for the movement of nonexempt commodities.

Exempt motor carriers do not need certificates in order to carry on their business, nor are they required to publish rates. It is charged that they do not carry adequate insurance and that they are not responsible in the settlement of claims but these are probably secondary matters. They have taken traffic from the standard motor carriers and from the railroads also. These interests desire to have the scope of the present exemptions reduced (United States Senate, Committee on Interstate and Foreign Commerce, *Study of Domestic Land and Water Transportation,* Hearings before a subcommittee pursuant to Sen. Res. 50, 81st C., 2d S., 1950, pp. 233–242, 725–923).

[12] The aircraft exemption was probably intended to cover local pickup and delivery service. The Commission has, however, ruled that it has no jurisdiction in certificate cases involving the performance of line-haul service for airports over distances ranging up to 100 miles (United States House of Representatives, Committee on Interstate and Foreign Commerce, *Transportation Study, op. cit.,* testimony Idol, p. 172.

[13] This is obviously a special case, although there are some cities in which it may be important. More exactly, the Act exempts motor transport within a municipality, between contiguous municipalities, or within a zone adjacent to and commercially a part of and such municipality or municipalities. The boundaries of zones have to be separately determined in every case. The provision is in addition to the exemption of hotel cabs and of taxicabs and to that of motor vehicle transportation which is incidental to transportation by aircraft. It does not duplicate the exemption of motor vehicles used by railroads and water companies and freight forwarders in terminal delivery because it does not apply to cases where the transportation is under a common control, management, or arrangement for continuous carriage to or from an outside point. The meaning of the words *municipality, contiguous,* and *commercial zone* were considered generally by the Interstate Commerce Commission in 1946 (46 M.C.C. 665, 1946). Commercial zone limits have been set individually in some instances (48 M.C.C. 95, 1948; 48 M.C.C. 441, 1948; 48 M.C.C. 460, 1948).

[14] The words "casual . . ." etc., are difficult to interpret (100 Fed. 490, 1939; 10 M.C.C. 533, 1938). The principal examples which have been considered by the Commission have involved automobile owners who have arranged, through travel bureaus, to carry passengers to agreed destinations for a negotiated price. This has been referred to as a "share-expense" agreement; actually the price has had little to do with the expense incurred. Arrangements of this sort are often convenient; they have been, how-

Regulatory Provisions of the Motor Carrier Act

For convenient reference the terms of the Motor Carrier Act are tabulated below as they apply to the different classes of motor carriers. Only the more important powers of the Interstate Commerce Commission are included in the list.

Summary of Motor Carrier Act Provisions

Common Carriers	Contract Carriers	Private Carriers	Brokers
Declaration of policy. See Railroads—National Transportation Policy.	*Declaration of policy.* See Railroads—National Transportation Policy.	*Declaration of policy.* See Railroads—National Transportation Policy.	*Declaration of policy.* See Railroads—National Transportation Policy.
Certificates, permits, and licenses. Commission may issue or refuse certificates. May suspend, amend, or revoke.	*Certificates, permits, and licenses.* Commission may issue or refuse permits. May suspend, amend, or revoke.	*Certificates, permits, and licenses.* No control.	*Certificates, permits, and licenses.* Commission may issue or refuse licenses. May suspend, amend, or revoke.
Service. Commission may establish reasonable requirements with respect to service accounts, records, and reports, qualifications and maximum hours of service of employees, and safety of operation and equipment.	*Service.* Commission may establish reasonable requirements with respect to accounts, records, and reports, qualifications and maximum hours of service of employees, and safety of operation and equipment.	*Service.* Commission may establish reasonable requirements to promote safety of operation and to that end prescribe qualifications and maximum hours of service of employees, and standards of equipment.	*Service.* Commission may establish reasonable requirements with respect to licensing, financial responsibility, accounts, records, reports, operations, and practices.

ever, subject to considerable abuse. The practice threatened at one time to develop into an unregulated form of carriage of some importance. This was because travel bureaus advertised for customers, established relations with car operators, and collected fees as intermediaries and none of this was subject to the Interstate Commerce Act (33 M.C.C. 533, 1938).

Casual transportation is still exempt but, since 1940, the exemption no longer covers transportation sold by a broker and furnished by a person engaged in transportation under a certificate or a permit. This means that a travel bureau can no longer negotiate a share-expense arrangement between a prospective traveler and a common or contract carrier without becoming subject to the federal law (54 Stat. 808, 921, 1940).

Summary of Motor Carrier Act Provisions

Common Carriers	Contract Carriers	Private Carriers	Brokers
Consolidation, merger, and acquisition of control. Pooling. Commission must approve.	*Consolidation, merger, and acquisition of control. Pooling.* Commission must approve.	*Consolidation, merger, and acquisition of control. Pooling.* No control.	*Consolidation, merger, and acquisition of control. Pooling.* No control.
Rates. Must be filed, published, and adhered to. 30 days notice of change. Commission must approve.	*Rates.* Minimum rates must be filed, published, and adhered to. Commission may prescribe.	*Rates.* No control.	*Rates.* No control.
Discrimination. Issue of passes limited. No rebates or concessions. Undue preference forbidden. Commission may regulate credit to shippers.	*Discrimination.* No rebates or concessions. Minimum rates must not give undue advantage to contract in competition with common carriers.	*Discrimination.* No control.	*Discrimination.* No rebates or concessions.
Security issues. Commission must approve.	*Security issues.* Commission must approve.	*Security issues.* No control.	*Security issues.* No control.

Declaration of Policy

The declaration of national policy in the Interstate Commerce Act governs motor as well as railroad and water transportation.

Certificates, Permits, and Licenses

This subject has been somewhat discussed in chapter 25, and what was there said will not be repeated. No common carrier by motor vehicle may engage in highway operations in interstate or foreign commerce, with exceptions previously considered, without a certificate, no contract carrier without a permit, and no broker without a license. Certificates and permits and licenses are to be granted on a showing (1) that the applicant is fit, willing, and able properly to perform the services proposed and to conform to the provisions of the Motor Carrier Act and to the requirements, rules, and regulations of the Commission thereunder; and (2) that the proposed service will be required by the present or future public convenience and necessity (in the case of common carriers) or will be consistent with the public interest and the national transportation policy declared in the Act (in the case of contract carriers and brokers). Private carriers as defined in the law need no permit. Common and contract carriers, however, who were in bona fide operation on June 1, 1935 (July 1, 1935 for contract carriers), are entitled to certificates or permits upon demonstration of this fact.[15] No person may at the same time hold a certificate as a common carrier and a permit as a contract carrier authorizing operation over the same route or within the same territory unless the Commission finds this dual operation to be consistent with the public interest and with the national transportation policy. The Commission shall, in issuing a certificate, specify the service to be rendered and the routes over which or the territory within which operations shall be conducted and the Commission may attach reasonable terms, conditions, and limitations to the certificate, at the time of issue or thereafter. In issuing a permit the Commission shall specify the business covered and the scope thereof. It may attach to the permit such reasonable terms, conditions, and limitations as are consistent with the character of the holder as a contract carrier. No such terms, conditions, or limitations, however, shall restrict the right of a carrier to add to its equipment and facilities over the routes, between the termini, or within the territory specified in the certificate, as the development of the business and the demands of the public shall require. The Commission, therefore, may regulate the number of organizations engaged in motor transport, but not the amount of the facilities which are supplied. A certificate, permit, or license may be suspended, changed, or revoked for willful failure to comply with any provision of the Act, or with any lawful order, rule, or regulation of the Commission, or with any term, condition, or limitation of the certificate, permit, or license.[16]

[15] These are the so-called "grandfather" applications. Sections 206 and 209 of the Motor Carrier Act direct the Commission to issue certificates to common and permits to contract carriers on a showing that these carriers were in bona fide operation on June 1 (common) and July 1 (contract), 1935, over the route or within the territory for which application is made and that they have so operated between the critical date and the time of application except as to interruptions of service over which the applicant has had no control. Special allowance is made for seasonal services.

[16] But no certificate, permit, or license may be revoked unless the holder willfully fails to comply, within a reasonable time—not less than 30 days, to be fixed by the Commission—with a lawful order of the Commission requiring compliance, issued after notice and hearing. The Commission may, in granting a certificate, reserve the right to impose restrictions (71 Sup. Ct. Rep. 382, 1951; 71 Sup. Ct. Rep. 422, 1951). A certificate, permit, or license may be suspended on reasonable notice of not less than 15 days.

NUMBER OF CERTIFICATES ISSUED. Table 24 sets forth the number of motor carrier certificates, permit, and license applications filed with the Commission between August 9, 1935, and October 31, 1951. The

TABLE 24. Motor Vehicle Applications for Certificates, Permits, and Licenses and for Transfer or Lease of Operating Rights and for Permission to Acquire Control Denied or Granted between August 9, 1935, and October 31, 1951

Type of Application	Number of Applications
Applications based upon prior operation	89,696
Applications for authority to institute new operations	41,889
Brokers' applications	1,526
Applications for recognition of State authority	7,828
Applications for temporary authority to operate	54,408
Applications for the transfer or lease of operating rights or for permission to acquire control	33,455
Total	228,802
Applications disposed of or pending	
Applications approved	105,904
Applications denied, dismissed, withdrawn, or revoked	118,873
Applications pending	4,025
Total	228,802

SOURCE: United States Interstate Commerce Commission, *Annual Report,* 1951.

Commission's published figures show the magnitude of the motor certificate problem with which it has to deal. The situation is also complex because motor carriers are organized in a number of ways to perform a variety of services. Local carriers are different in some respects from through or long distance carriers. Contract carriers are to be distinguished from common carriers. Of the latter, some are common carriers of general freight and some specialize with respect to individual commodities. Some companies supply scheduled service on regular routes, some offer nonscheduled service on regular routes, and some render nonscheduled service, radial or other, on irregular routes. Some motor common carriers operate principally with their own equipment, and others use leased equipment or purchased transportation. All of this occurs in the presence of private motor carriers and of contract carriers which handle traffic within the states. These variations complicate the task which the Commission is expected to perform.

POLICIES AND OBJECTIVES OF THE INTERSTATE COMMERCE COMMISSION. The Commission has sought, in exercising its "certificate" authority, to accomplish two principal results in the regulation of motor carriers.

1. The Commission was originally required to legalize motor transpor-

tation operations which existed in 1935.[17] It did this by the prompt approval of a great mass of "grandfather" applications. It is important to notice, however, that applicants who based their petitions upon prior operation were entitled only to the continuance of the particular services which they had been rendering and over the routes or within the territory which their vehicles had been accustomed to traverse in 1935. For other services and for other routes they had no privilege—for such operations they were required to seek certificates or permits like other people. The Commission made this restriction effective by limiting the kinds of service which holders of "grandfather" certificates could supply and the routes over which they could operate. These limitations reduced efficiency; but the applicants could always secure a regular certificate if they were able to make a case.[18]

2. The Commission is directed to approve applications for authority to institute new operations when a proper showing has been made. Such applications have been fewer than those based on prior operation; but (a) they may be expected to become more numerous in the long run and, (b) they alone offer an opportunity to develop the principles upon which the Commission will rely.

The Commission's policy is guided, in considering new operations, by the language used in certain sections of the statute and by the National Transportation Policy. Some of the tests to be applied are clear. It is obvious, for instance, that unfit applicants are to be rejected. Some of them—referring to the standards of public interest—supply only a basis for administration. Here the Commission must strike out for itself. What it actually does is to decide in each case whether there is a demand for the service offered sufficient to justify the cost and, second, whether the introduction of a new service will so adversely affect carriers which already operate upon a route or in a territory that the resulting increase in competition will be contrary to the public interest as a whole. This is the rule applied in railroad regulation, and here as there it raises the question of controlled monopoly as contrasted with free competition. It is the problem, in other words, as to how far carriers who have rendered good service

---

[17] This problem did not arise in railroad regulation, because Part I of the Interstate Commerce Act requires certificates only for the construction of new lines of railroad or for extensions of existing lines [Sec. 1 (18)]. The wording of the certificate clauses in Part III (water carriers) is, however, substantially the same as that in Part II (motor carriers), and that in the Civil Aeronautics Act is similar. Under Part IV (freight forwarders) persons engaged in the forwarding business when the law was passed were required to apply for a permit, but after this application was filed, they could continue to operate until otherwise ordered by the Commission.

[18] The Supreme Court has held, however, that an applicant which had held itself out as a general carrier of freight and had carried a wide variety of general commodities could not be denied the right to carry other commodities of the same class merely because it had never carried them before (315 U.S. 475, 1942; 315 U.S. 495, 1942).

in the past are to be protected against the intrusion of new and necessarily speculative operations.[19] Actually, the Commission seems moderately inclined toward the second of these alternatives, although it cannot go too far because it controls only a fraction of motor carrier enterprise and because it was forced to recognize, at the beginning, a large motor system which was then at work.[20]

CERTIFICATE RESTRICTIONS. A feature of the Commission's policy which has attracted attention has been the frequent introduction of restrictions in the certificates which it has approved. We have just mentioned these restrictions in referring to "grandfather" applications. The need for limitation was first evident in these cases but the practice was extended, and naturally so, because a motor company with a limited certificate left gaps in service which could be accurately filled only by other companies restricted in a complementary way. And in some cases motor vehicle owners wished to avoid the responsibilities of general service. For whatever reasons, limitations were put into certificates and they have often been embarrassing. Thus motor carriers have been restricted with respect to the kind of commodities which they may carry, the routes which they may follow, and the stations which they are allowed to serve. The restrictions are not necessarily the same in outbound as in inbound movements. The degree of limitation varies but it is frequently severe, especially in the case of special commodity carriers.[21]

---

[19] There are good statements of Commission practice in Marvin L. Fair and Ernest W. Williams, *Economics of Transportation*, New York, Harper, 1950, pp. 516–528, and in D. Philip Locklin, *Economics of Transportation*, Chicago, Irwin, 1947, pp. 717–724. See also chap. 26, *supra*, for the issue of motor certificates to railroads. The Commission said, in 1942: "Existing motor carriers should normally be accorded the right to transport all traffic in the territories served by them, as against any new operator seeking to enter the field, unless the latter would offer a definitely superior service to the shipping public" (41 M.C.C. 165, 170, 1942).

Still again, in 1947, the Commission remarked that reasonable competition was in the public interest (44 M.C.C. 535, 548, 1945), but it said: "The fundamental purpose underlying the certificate and permit requirements of the act, is the protection of existing carriers from unbridled and uncontrolled competition in the form of unneeded services which tend to instability in, and low standards of, service" (47 M.C.C. 23, 39, 1947. See also 44 M.C.C. 131, 140, 1944 and 48 M.C.C. 17, 21, 1948).

[20] Between 1944 and 1949 the number of motor carriers of property which operated subject to the Commission's regulation declined from 21,058 to 20,172.

[21] Under present regulation a company may be allowed to carry livestock but it may not, on the return trip, load feed or farm machinery on its trucks. Another company may haul cotton, but not tobacco; or furniture, but not commodities in general. A carrier may transport freight between specified termini but it may not serve intermediate points. It may operate over a specific route between termini but not over an alternative route which may be shorter. It may, sometimes, be permitted to carry goods in truck loads but not in smaller quantities. These restrictions were elaborately described in a study prepared for the United States Board of Investigation and Research in 1944. (See *Federal Regulatory Restrictions upon Motor and Water Carriers*, 79th C., 1st S., Sen. Doc. 78, Ser. 10,943, prepared under the direction of James C. Nelson, 1945). The authority of the Interstate Commerce Commission to insert limitations in

Are Certificates Justified in Motor Carrier Regulation? The effect of certificate limitation in reducing efficiency and the general peculiarities of motor carriage have convinced some observers that certificate control is not justified in the motor industry. The points made are the following:

1. Free entry will improve efficiency. This is not merely a repetition of the observations in the preceding paragraph. The belief is that new entrants will bring new energy and new ideas.

2. Competition will satisfactorily protect the shipper from carrier exploitation.

3. The limited geographical extent of the service of most motor companies and the relatively small proportion of overhead costs in motor operation will discourage the practice of discrimination.

4. Motor carriage is not, characteristically, a business which depends upon a large and specialized capital equipment. The economic wastes of competition are, therefore, minimized. And a company which does withdraw is likely to find a market for its capital goods among remaining firms or with private users.

5. The present system of certificate limitation is peculiarly inept.[22]

If the federal government were to abandon certificate control the state governments would be compelled to abandon the policy also. It is, of course, impossible to predict the result with confidence. Free entry would increase the flexibility of motor operation and it might, to some extent, lower costs. It would impair the quality of service at the margin. It might or it might not increase the number of operating motor companies, but it would multiply the entrances and exits during any period. Safety regulations would, presumably, be retained, so that there would be no effect along this line. The subject is intriguing, but we should expect no early and radical alteration of the law.[23]

---

motor carrier certificates has been sustained by the Supreme Court (320 U.S. 401, 1943; 319 U.S. 88, 1943; 322 U.S. 1, 1944).

[22] United States Board of Investigation and Research, *Federal Regulatory Restrictions upon Motor and Water Carriers, op. cit.*

[23] The Board of Investigation and Research (*ibid.*, p. 303) made, in 1944, the following recommendations with respect to regulatory restrictions in the case of interstate motor carriers of property:

1. Special commodity restrictions should be limited to carriers whose service is of such specialized nature as to be unsuited to the transportation of general commodities, but such restrictions should not prevent the carrier from using its equipment for transportation of such commodities as are necessary to provide adequate and economical loads, outbound and inbound.

2. Route restrictions which require unnecessary circuitous movements over specified highways or through gateway points or unnecessary movement through congested areas should be eliminated from all certificates and permits.

3. Authorizations which prevent common and contract carriers from rendering service to and from all points within their authorized territories and points through which their vehicles pass in serving presently authorized territories should be abolished.

Abandonment

The Motor Carrier Act (Part II of the Interstate Commerce Act) does not, in terms, forbid abandonment. A motor carrier which holds a certificate must, however, render reasonable service under that certificate so long as the grant continues. It cannot, therefore, cease operation over a portion of its certified route unless an amendment to its certificate is secured.[24] This may be as effective a restraint as a direct prohibition of abandonment.

Federal Safety Regulations

Federal safety rules for motor vehicles operating in interstate commerce are now prescribed by the Interstate Commerce Commission under the authority of the Motor Carrier Act of 1935. They apply to common and to contract carriers and, with a few exceptions, to private carriers of property.[25] These regulations cover (1) qualifications of drivers; (2) rules for driving, including directions for the use of lights and signals; (3) parts and accessories necessary for safe operation (under this head the Commission prescribes the number, character, and position of motor vehicle lights, braking standards, the necessary safety features in fuel systems, and the provision of horns, windshield wipers, safety chains, fire extinguishers, and other things); (4) the reporting of accidents; (5) maximum daily and weekly hours of service for motor carrier employees (the standard for drivers under federal rules is 60 hours a week and 10 hours in any period of 24 hours, with certain exceptions);[26] and (6) inspection and main-

4. Restrictions upon the type of service rendered should be limited to those necessary to confine carriers to common or contract carriage, except where rendition of both types is consistent with the public interest.

[24] 20 M.C.C. 581, 1939.

[25] The Interstate Commerce Commission safety rules were, at first, applied only to common and contract carriers of passengers or property, excepting carriers engaged in transportation within a municipality and casual and occasional transportation. They did not cover private carriers (14 M.C.C. 669, 672, 1939). But the rules were subsequently extended to private carriers of property, with some modifications in their application to farm trucks and in the provisions with respect to the reporting of accidents and overtime (23 M.C.C. 1, 1940).

The language used in the federal statute [Sec. 204 (a)] is not identical in its references to common, contract, and private carriers. Taken literally, the law gives authority to the Commission to establish reasonable requirements in the case of common and contract carriers. But in the case of private carriers it conveys authority to establish reasonable requirements in order to promote safety of operation. The Commission has held, however, that the last limitation is implied in the first two grants of power (3 M.C.C. 663, 1937; 13 M.C.C. 481, 1939); and this view has been approved by the Supreme Court (305 U.S. 534, 1940; 319 U.S. 44, 1943). For a contrary view, see 31 Fed. Suppl. 35, 1939.

[26] The Interstate Commerce Commission has held that its power to fix maximum hours of service extends only to employees whose duties affect the safety of operation (13 M.C.C. 481, 487, 1939; 28 M.C.C. 125, 1941).

tenance. The rules for maintenance are not elaborate, but they require reports at the end of every day and stipulate that equipment shall be maintained in safe operating condition.

Federal safety rules are not intended to preclude states or subdivisions of states from establishing or enforcing state or local laws relating to safety, compliance with which would not prevent full compliance with the federal rules. This is expressly stated in the law.[27] The result is that the Commission has not issued orders with respect to the size and weights of motor vehicles [28] or with respect to the use of signals in interstate or foreign commerce, as these have been described in the appendix to chapter 29. On the subject of speed, the Commission contents itself with the direction that motor vehicles shall be driven at speeds in accordance with the laws, ordinances, and regulations of the jurisdictions in which they are operated.[29] As the law stands, motor carriers must observe all valid regulations and restrictions respecting the use of highways issued by states, counties, and municipalities in the exercise of their police powers, so long as state and federal requirements do not conflict. The Commission has been active without much interference with local regulation, although it has been limited by scarcity of funds.[30]

[27] Sec. 202 (b) of the Interstate Commerce Act reads as follows:
"Nothing in this part shall be construed to affect the powers of taxation of the several States or to authorize a motor carrier to do an intrastate business on the highways of any State or to interfere with the exclusive exercise by each State of the power of regulation of intrastate commerce by motor vehicles on the highways thereof."

[28] Sec. 225 of the Interstate Commerce Act reads as follows:
"The Commission is hereby authorized to investigate and report on the need for Federal regulation of the sizes and weight of motor vehicles and combinations of motor vehicles and of the qualifications and maximum hours of service of employees of all motor carriers and private carriers of property by motor vehicle . . ."

[29] *Code of Federal Regulations,* 1949, Title 49, "Transportation," Parts 190–197, Safety Regulation." See also 14 M.C.C. 669, 1939. A revised set of Interstate Commerce Commission rules became effective on July 1, 1952. See *Federal Register,* May 15, 1952, pp. 4423–4452.

[30] Federal safety regulation has been handicapped by what is known as "trip leasing."

In the case of a trip lease a certificated motor carrier arranges with an independent truck owner to conduct described operations under the terms of a lease contract covering the owner's truck. The arrangement is for a single movement, in most cases. It is advantageous to both parties. Thus the certificated carriers is able, by trip leasing, to enlarge the number of trucks at its disposal without the necessity of capital investment. The independent truck owner secures employment. Moreover, by selecting contracts, the owner is frequently able to obtain a load on a return movement to the base at which it started its initial, outbound haul. There are, however, difficulties from the regulatory point of view. These difficulties include the following:

1. In some cases the certificated carrier has sent the leased truck to destinations outside of the territory which the carrier was authorized to serve. Such evasions have been difficult to detect.

2. Trip lease arrangements have disturbed motor rate structures.

3. Safety regulations have been difficult to enforce. This is partly because the owner-operator has not been, characteristically, an employee of the certificated carrier.

Service

The Interstate Commerce Commission has full authority over the accounts, records, and reports of common and contract carriers and of brokers. It has, also, power to regulate service, although most of the Commission's service regulations, including those which deal with the qualifications and hours of service of employees, are designed to promote safety in operation.

In general, the Commission may require reasonable service for the sake of travelers and shippers.[31] What is reasonable will largely depend upon the certificate under which the carrier operates.

The Commission may require motor common carriers to establish through routes with other motor carriers for the carriage of passengers and it may set the terms and conditions under which these through routes shall be operated. But it has no authority to require through routes for the carriage of property.[32] Nor may it demand through routes, in the case of passengers, between motor common carriers and common carriers by railroad, by water, or by air. It has power, however, to prescribe divisions of rates when such through routes have been established.

Indirectly, the Commission has some power over motor service through its authority to prevent unfair or destructive competition. It has characterized as destructive competition the action by a motor carrier, authorized to operate over "irregular" routes, in operating regularly and character-

---

Certificated carriers, moreover, have had little occasion or incentive to inspect leased equipment, especially in cases where the lease was made without the owner's appearance at the carrier's terminal. They have had even less opportunity to supervise the truck owner's methods of operation.

For these and other reasons the Interstate Commerce Commission has recently adopted a number of restrictive rules applying to "trip leasing." (See 51 M.C.C. 461, 546, 1950; 52 M.C.C. 675, 743, 1951; 16 Fed. Reg. 4805, May 23, 1951; *Traffic World*, May 26, 1951; 73 Sup. Ct. Rep. 307, 1953.) It has required, among other things (1) that equipment lease contracts be reduced to writing; (2) that the life of these contracts shall be at least 30 days when the truck driver is the owner or his employee; (3) that certificated carriers shall inspect and be responsible for equipment; and (4) that the compensation of the owner-operator may not be measured by a percentage of the gross revenue. The Supreme Court has held that the Commission has authority to establish these rules.

The rules referred to have considerably strengthened the Commission's influence in the field of motor safety regulation. They have, however, aroused much opposition. The Commission postponed the application of items 2 and 4 until March 1, 1954, and exempted common carriers in refrigerated trucks from its leasing rules until March 1, 1955.

[31] Sec. 216 (a). "It shall be the duty of every common carrier of passengers by motor vehicle . . . to provide safe and adequate service, equipment, and facilities for the transportation of passengers in interstate or foreign commerce . . ."

Sec. 216 (b). "It shall be the duty of every common carrier of property by motor vehicle to provide safe and adequate service, equipment, and facilities for the transportation of property in interstate or foreign commerce."

[32] 41 M.C.C. 143, 146, 1942; 44 M.C.C. 747, 1945.

istically between fixed termini and in making constant use of certain highways. The operation was illegal, according to the Commission, because it deprived regular route carriers of protection which the Act supplied.[33]

The Commission has no authority over motorcar service comparable with that which it exercises over railroad car service operation. On the whole, it has made little use of its powers to demand improvements in service. Doubtless this is because it can get better results, in most cases, by the grant of a new certificate to a competing motor company.

Consolidation, Merger, and Acquisition of Control

These subjects have been discussed in chapters 25 and 26. Most motor applications for permission to consolidate contemplate the purchase of stock, property, or operating rights. Omitting cases in which railroads are involved and the large bus unifications, they are most frequently presented by small- or moderate-size truck or bus organizations which wish to buy or sell for any of the numerous reasons that cause transfers of ownership in business enterprise. The public interest is rarely affected, and the Commission is ready enough to approve the majority of the requests which are made in instances of this kind. It is frequently possible to show that substantial economies in operation will result. The Commission understands that large-scale motor enterprise may have its disadvantages, but only experience can show how great these offsetting defects will be; meanwhile it may be sound policy to encourage experiment.[34]

There is little danger of monopoly in most motor carrier applications for unification. Consolidation is, indeed, sometimes opposed because it will increase competition. This may easily occur when the vendee is stronger than the vendor and more likely to develop service.[35] On the other hand, the terms of a merger may be ill advised. The Commission will give reasonable latitude to the business judgment of motor operators who wish to buy or sell or merge. But it occasionally disapproves of a sale when the vendee is not likely to be able to meet the obligations which it assumes,[36] or when bankers' or promoters' profits seem too high,[37] or when the Commission objects to some particular feature of a financing.[38] The Commission is particularly sensitive to overvaluations of intangibles in an industry in which physical assets are relatively small.[39] It uses no fixed formula in determining a reasonable purchase price.[40] But it has frequently required

[33] 47 M.C.C. 23, 38, 1947.
[34] 5 M.C.C. 25, 1937.
[35] 40 M.C.C. 499, 504, 1946; 45 M.C.C. 257, 274, 1946.
[36] 45 M.C.C. 220, 1946.
[37] 36 M.C.C. 61, 98, 1940.
[38] 45 M.C.C. 309, 321, 1946.
[39] 5 M.C.C. 201, 206, 1937; 36 M.C.C. 61, 91, 1940.
[40] 45 M.C.C. 393, 399, 1947.

a purchasing company to write off, from its investment account, during a stated period, the amount by which its payment exceeds the net book value of the purchased property exclusive of intangibles.[41]

Rates and Tariffs

Common carriers by highway must file and publish their tariffs and must collect the rates which they publish. Contract carriers must file their contracts and charge at least the minimum rates which these contracts specify.[42] The Commission may, however, grant contract carriers relief from this requirement. Common carriers may not change their rates and contract carriers may not reduce their minima except on 30 days' notice. The Commission may consider the lawfulness of any new rate or schedule, suspending the effective date thereof as long as 7 months, or it may investigate or hear complaints directed against an existing rate or schedule. For common carriers it may determine the lawful rate, fare, or charge, or the maximum or minimum or maximum and minimum thereafter to be charged. In the case of contract carriers the Commission may prescribe the minimum charge but the minimum shall give no undue advantage to any contract carrier in competition with any common carrier by motor vehicle subject to Part II. No authority over rates charged by brokers or by private carriers is vested in the Commission by the Motor Carrier Act. The clauses which we have just summarized, in so far as they relate to common carriers by road do not differ essentially from the provisions of the Interstate Commerce Act, Part I. Rates may be disapproved, of course, either because they are unreasonable or because they are discriminatory.[43]

[41] 45 M.C.C. 337, 346, 1946; 45 M.C.C. 425, 430, 1947; 45 M.C.C. 627, 635, 1947.

[42] Common and contract carriers differ with respect to the proper degree of publicity to be given contract rates.

As for filing, contract carriers are required to file the minimum rates which they actually charge. If, however, they charge more than the minimum in some cases, these charges remain secret. The result is that motor common carriers do not know, with any precision, the extent of the competition which they meet. Another objection is that contract carriers often render accessorial services for which they may or may not collect a charge. Reference to such extra charges is seldom made.

Motor common carriers believe that the practices mentioned in the preceding paragraph, together with the fact that contract carriers sometimes offer a service which is closely similar to common carriage, put common carriers at an appreciable disadvantage (United States Senate, Committee of Interstate and Foreign Commerce, *Study of Domestic Land and Water Transportation*, Hearings before a subcommittee pursuant to Sen. Res. 50, 81st C., 2d S., 1950, testimony McBride, p. 1204). Contract carriers reply that contract carrier rates should not be made public at all, because these rates constitute a cost to the industries using contract carriage and that no such costs should be exposed. They also say that motor common carriers should not be allowed to know the rates charged by contract carriers because they would then use these rates as a target for attack as they use railroad rates today (*ibid.*, testimony Orr, p. 1529).

[43] The Interstate Commerce Commission has no authority to award reparation with respect to motor rates charged on shipments in the past. This is in contrast to its au-

RATE MAKING RULE. The rate making rule which binds the Commission in regulating the rates of common carriers by motor vehicle is identical with that applied to railroads and to domestic water transportation, except that the Motor Carrier Act (Part II of the Interstate Commerce Act) requires the Commission, in prescribing rates, to give due consideration to the inherent advantages of transportation by motor carriage.[44]

RATE POLICY OF THE INTERSTATE COMMERCE COMMISSION. The immediate result of Commission decisions in the late 1930's was the issue of large orders prescribing minimum rates for motor common carriers in Middle Atlantic, Central, New England, and Trunk Line territories.[45] Most of the class rates in these decisions, at least in Middle Atlantic, Central, and Trunk Line territories, were put at the same level as class rates for railroad carriage because railroad competition, at the moment, was of primary importance.[46] The Commission, however, disavowed any intention to force motor carriers to charge rates based upon the price of railroad service.[47] After the outbreak of the Second World War the picture was somewhat changed, with decisions permitting motor carriers to advance their rates because of increased costs.[48]

Apart from its general orders, the Interstate Commerce Commission has regulated motor rates in much the same manner as it has controlled railroad charges, and this is not surprising because the same division considers both price schedules. Thus it has discussed and has prescribed classification ratings, with especial attention to quantities offered [49] and to the weight and space occupying characteristics of the articles shipped.[50] It has interpreted, approved, or disapproved particular class and commodity rates. In doing this the Commission has sometimes acted on complaint of shippers; but often on application of carriers for an increase. It has con-

---

thority in Parts I and II of the Interstate Commerce Act (43 Stat. 337, 340, 1944). The Commission may, however, find that a motor rate was, at a given time in the past, unreasonable to a stated extent, and this finding can be used in a court action seeking damages. (See G. L. Wilson, "Steps for Recovery of Damages Based on Unlawful Motor Rates Outlined," *Traffic World*, October 11, 1952, pp. 40–41.)

[44] See chaps. 30, 32.

[45] Many, though not all, of these decisions were made subsequent to action by groups of carriers or motor carrier conferences. Minimum rate orders protected the rate levels which these conferences approved, subject to differences which the Commission might introduce. (See 4 M.C.C. 68, 1937; 8 M.C.C. 233, 1938; 8 M.C.C. 287, 1938; 24 M.C.C. 501, 1940; 47 M.C.C. 657, 1948.)

[46] 8 M.C.C. 233, 1938; 28 M.C.C. 369, 1941; 42 M.C.C. 425, 436–437, 1943. The motor scales mentioned in the text, along with the New England minima, were suspended or vacated in 1942 and 1943.

[47] 28 M.C.C. 369, 371, 1941.

[48] 46 M.C.C. 513, 1946; 47 M.C.C. 259, 1947; 48 M.C.C. 541, 1948; 48 M.C.C. 733, 1948.

[49] 48 M.C.C. 541, 550, 1948.

[50] 44 M.C.C. 501, 1945.

sidered the extent to which a carrier should be permitted to charge rates which are lower than the prevailing level but which are still reasonably compensatory insofar as the carrier which quotes them is concerned.[51]

Both in the larger and in the smaller cases, the Commission has given weight to cost, but it has also taken other factors into the account. A clear example of this may be found in the California Motor Carrier Rate Case of 1942, in which the Commission fixed rates that were in excess of any of the calculated costs submitted by the parties. To do otherwise, it said, "would necessitate giving controlling weight to density and loading speed of each commodity and little, if any, weight to its ability to bear transportation charges or to the many other factors which should be considered here in fixing lawful minimum rates and charges."[52] The Commission conforms in this to the rate making rule which the statute prescribes. It conforms to the Motor Carrier Act also when it refuses to consider carrier good will, earning power, or the value of an operating certificate as elements of value in determining the reasonableness of a rate.[53] The considered view of the Commission is that motor rates tend to be unreasonably low, not unreasonably high, and its decisions are consistent with this belief.[54]

[51] 32 M.C.C. 339, 1942. The Commission distinguishes, in the motor rate cases a proper minimum from a noncompensatory rate. The Commission will not permit carriers to charge rates which do not cover costs (10 M.C.C. 275, 1938; 24 M.C.C. 794, 1940; 26 M.C.C. 639, 1940; 43 M.C.C. 289, 1911). But a rate may be compensatory in the sense that it covers cost and still be less than the minimum which the Commission thinks that the carrier should collect. Commission "minima" are set at the level of a "reasonable" rate.

[52] 41 M.C.C. 19, 41, 1942. See also 24 M.C.C. 501, 514, 1940, and 47 M.C.C. 215, 219, 1947.

[53] The Commission has not attempted to place a value upon motor carriers either generally or in detail. This is because a valuation would be difficult and because it would be an idle gesture in any case. Carriers have, upon occasion, asked for a fair profit, but in doing this they have argued on the basis of a reasonable operating ratio, not upon that of a fair return. The Commission, in at least one case, has mentioned 93 percent as a reasonable ratio for a motor carrier (42 M.C.C. 633, 650, 1943). The calculation of an operating ratio is, however, only a manner of determining average transaction profit. It is only incidental to the question of a total fair return. There can hardly be such a thing as a reasonable operating ratio in any sense which can serve as a profit limiting factor in a public enterprise, although it is obvious that a business will not continue if its operating ratio exceeds 100 percent.

[54] Like railroad rates, truck rates reflect distance, condition of terrain, special services required, and value of the shipments, with perhaps less attention to differentials and to group arrangements affecting competing producers than railroads are accustomed to display. Truck rates are often lower for larger than for smaller movements, but when this is true the dividing points are not, characteristically, at the railroad carlot level, but take account of smaller differences such as those between 2,000, 4,000, 10,000, and 18,000 pounds. It is to be remembered in this connection that the load factor for a motor truck is not the same as that for a railroad car; hence the relationship of weight and volume which should be encouraged in road shipment is not identical with that which will be desired for railroad hauls.

The Association of American Railroads, in 1945, published tables of comparative

Discrimination

The Motor Carrier Act forbids a common carrier to give undue preference to any particular person or to collect from anyone a compensation difference from the published rate. The formidable list of exceptions to this requirement which is published in Part I applies also to these prohibitions. Tariff rates must be collected when freight is delivered, subject to the rules governing the granting of credit which the Commission prescribes.

The general paragraph in the Motor Carrier Act relating to local discrimination is somewhat shorter than the corresponding paragaph in Part I of the Interstate Commerce Act, but the substance of it is the same. Common carriers are forbidden to give undue preference to any particular port, gateway, locality, region, district, territory, or description of traffic.[55] There is, however, no specific prohibition of rate structures in which more is charged for shorter than for longer hauls.[56] Nor do the discrimination clauses of the Interstate Commerce Act refer to the practices of contract carriers.

---

rail and truck rates, as of March 1, 1944, carload and less-than-carload. These tables indicated that motor class rates were then, for the samples given, generally higher than rail rates between the same points of origin and destination. The comparison did not state whether the rates used were for carload or for less than carload quantities. Rates on specific commodities such as sugar, canned goods, oranges, and the like were also shown to be higher than rail charges both for truckload, carload, and for less than truck and railroad minima (*Highway Motor Transportation,* Report of Subcommittee on Motor Transport of the Railroad Committee for the Study of Transportation, Association of American Railroads, August, 1945). On the other hand, comparisons of motor first-class rates with corresponding rates charged by other agencies which the Department of Commerce published in 1948 concluded that motor first-class rates were lower, in 1948, than first-class rates by rail, parcel post, express, or air. The Department of Commerce did not, however, regard this situation as likely to be permanent and expressed the opinion that motor and rail class rates throughout the nation were on approximately the same general level.

Such estimates as we have suggest that the cost of carriage by truck is lower than that by rail when the size of the consignment is less than 10,000 pounds and the length of haul less than 400 miles; but that the cost by rail is less of goods shipped in carload quantities, and especially on hauls of considerable length (United States Board of Investigation and Research, *Comparison of Rail, Motor, and Water Carrier Coasts,* 79th C., 1st S., Sen. Doc. 84, 1944). This conclusion is not surprising; it follows that if motor and rail carriers charge approximately the same rate on most traffic that both are absorbing costs, under certain circumstances, in order to compete.

On the whole, the greater speed and flexibility of much trucking service and the reduced likelihood of damage should make shippers willing to pay a somewhat higher charge for truck than for railroad carriage in many cases and this, with a cost advantage on some types of business, should provide the trucks with an area within which they should be reasonably secure except for competition among themselves. There is, however, no present stability in motor rate policy unless it be that current trucking practice is to charge the sum, small or large, which the traffic in any case will bear.

[55] The words "region, district, and territory" were inserted by amendment in 1940. Port districts and transit points are not mentioned in the Motor Carrier Act.

[56] This omission is comparatively unimportant because cases of greater charges for shorter hauls can always be attacked by allegation of unreasonableness or of undue preference (43 M.C.C. 145, 146, 1944; 46 M.C.C. 729, 732, 1947).

Few complaints of local discrimination by motor vehicle were brought to the Interstate Commerce Commission in 1936, 1937, and 1938. In general, the Commission was not disposed to lay much stress upon the relative adjustment of motor rates during these early years for reasons expressed in the New England case of 1938.

We are dealing [said the Commission in these proceedings] with a situation very unlike any to be found in the case of railroads . . . The very limited number of railroads jointly operate a homogeneous system of transportation. The motor carriers constitute no such system, but are instead hardly more than a mere aggregation of hundreds of individual carriers whose operations, many of which are very small, are disconnected to a greater extent than they are connected. Because of the number and disassociation of the carriers the apparent incongruities in the proposed rates often furnish no legal basis for a charge of unlawful discrimination, and have their origin in the special conditions surrounding particular carriers.[57]

More instances of alleged local discrimination emerged in later years, and this was inevitable as motor traffic was enlarged. Towns like Sioux City, Iowa, which competed with Omaha, Nebraska, at destinations in South Dakota,[58] and Topeka, Kansas, which shipped to Chicago in competition with Kansas City,[59] complained that rates were not properly related to distance in their cases. And in the reverse direction the rates from Chicago to points in Kansas were said to be relatively unreasonable in comparison with rates from Chicago to points in Oklahoma.[60] Complaints of this sort are always possible. They have, however, attracted much less attention than in the railroad field. And where there is controversy it is rare for any single motor carrier to be responsible for both the higher and the lower rate. So far as this is true, a charge of local discrimination will not lie.

There have been many instances of personal discrimination in motor traffic, more or less deliberate. This is evident from Commission orders. Thus the Commission has held it illegal for a warehouse which furnishes traffic to a trucking company to collect a commission of 30 percent of the line haul transportation rate.[61] A motor carrier may not extend undue credit to a shipper in the payment of freight bills.[62] It is illegal for a carrier to allow a shipper to accumulate goods on the carrier's premises for 10 days prior to shipment without a storage payment.[63] A trucking company may not lease a garage from a shipper for more than a reason-

---

[57] 2 M.C.C. 530, 547, 1937.
[58] 32 M.C.C. 735, 1942.
[59] 46 M.C.C. 513, 1946.
[60] 48 M.C.C. 554, 559, 1948.
[61] 41 M.C.C. 766, 768, 1943.
[62] 2 M.C.C. 365, 1937.
[63] 22 M.C.C. 295, 1940.

able rental.[64] A motor line may not absorb the charge for the handling of goods from a dock, where transportation terminates, to the interior of a warehouse,[65] nor may it assume more than standard liability for loss or damage during transport without extra compensation,[66] rate reductions on certain metal products from East Alton, Illinois, to St. Louis cannot be limited to a small area in St. Louis where only one factory can be found,[67] and a motor company cannot quote a rate between Philadelphia and New York destinations which applies only to petroleum originating at a plant located on a small island in the Delaware River.[68] In brief, a motor carrier, like a railroad carrier, is forbidden to grant a service to any shipper which will distinguish him from other shippers or which will, by indirection, reduce the published charges that he will pay.

Securities

Common and contract motor carriers are subject to Section 20a of Part I of the Interstate Commerce Act—a reference which brings their security issues completely under Commission control. Short-term notes, however, are exempt up to a total of $200,000, and the Commission may not regulate other issues in cases where the par value of the securities to be put out, together with the par value of the securities already outstanding, does not exceed $1,000,000. Motor carrier securities are exempt from the provisions of the Securities Act of 1933.

Motor securities are most frequently issued in order to buy or to rehabilitate equipment, to provide working capital, for expansion on a moderate scale by the purchase of operating rights and property, and for refunding. Of these purposes refunding is relatively rare and the financing of consolidation has been previously mentioned. A very frequent cause for borrowing is the need for working capital to provide for irregular expenditures such as taxes or for regular expenditures during periods when earnings are below the annual average.[69] Small motor carriers also borrow to offset delayed payments from their customers [70] in the expectation that they will cover financing costs by taking advantage of trade discounts.[71] They even borrow for speculative purposes, as when a company issues notes to raise money to buy trucks which are then leased for purposes unconnected with the carrier's transport obligations.[72]

For these and for more substantial purposes also, motor carriers obtain

[64] 4 M.C.C. 657, 1938.
[65] 47 M.C.C. 119, 142, 1947.
[66] *Ibid.*
[67] 30 M.C.C. 297, 1941.
[68] 24 M.C.C. 405, 1940.
[69] 35 M.C.C. 798, 1940; 36 M.C.C. 41, 1940; 40 M.C.C. 172, 1945.
[70] 39 M.C.C. 171, 174, 1943; 39 M.C.C. 258, 262, 1943.
[71] 39 M.C.C. 283, 1943.
[72] 37 M.C.C. 569, 1941.

funds from banks, insurance companies, purveyors of equipment and supplies, and other special sources. They seldom resort to public sale. The sums involved in these transactions are generally small, because the typical motor company has only a limited credit. A great many of the loans are unsecured and are repayable within a few months. Others are for somewhat longer periods but rarely for more than 5 years; in such cases there is apt to be provision for serial repayment. The security given, when there is security, is apt to take the form of a chattel mortgage upon equipment, although other property is sometimes pledged. Where the creditor is a vendor, he may rely upon a vendor's lien or upon a conditional sale; the chattel mortgage is, however, more common.

It is the function of the Interstate Commerce Commission to exercise some general control over motor carrier financing, without too much interference with the relations between motor borrowers and the financial agencies which are willing to risk their funds. It does this, in part, by regulation of the purposes for which obligations may be incurred. Thus it has declared that the issue of short-term notes to finance the construction of a new terminal is improper.[73] It has disapproved of the issue of securities to provide for the payment of accrued dividends on cumulative preferred stock.[74] And the Commission is reasonably of the opinion that the cost of motor license plates and permit tags is chargeable to operating expenses and is not a proper basis for the issue of stock.[75] More rarely, the Commission objects to the kind and volume of securities which are to be put out, as in the cases of consolidation to which we have referred. It has taken favorable notice, however, of occasions in which companies have retired indebtedness by the issue of stock, pointing out that such a substitution strengthened the credit of the company which proposed it and was in the interest of the public which the applicant served.[76] The Commission has refused to allow a carrier to issue stock against intangibles[77] and it has disallowed a "write-up" by reappraisal showing an increase in the value of physical property which had not been realized.[78] The influence of the Commission in these matters has been good. Its actual accomplishment has, probably, been slight.

Summary

It is evident from statements in the preceding pages that the federal government, through the Interstate Commerce Commission, actively

---

73 40 M.C.C. 172, 175, 1946.
74 36 M.C.C. 721, 1941.
75 39 M.C.C. 211, 213, 1943.
76 15 M.C.C. 117, 119, 1938.
77 5 M.C.C. 524, 1938.
78 5 M.C.C. 420, 1938.

supervises motor carrier operation.[79] The most important decisions of the Commission are in the fields of certificates, rates, and consolidation. It also has and exercises authority, however, over securities, accounts, service discrimination, and the safety of motor carriage. State governments participate in the control of motor vehicles; they must do so because intrastate motor transport is of great importance. It is to be remembered that both federal and state regulation is limited by the predominance of private motor business. Public motor regulation differs in this from railroad and air regulation and, in lesser degree, from that of water regulation.

APPENDIX TO CHAPTER 31

Freight Forwarders

Freight forwarder regulation may be discussed as an adjunct to motor regulation although it is also associated with railroad and air regulation. The Interstate Commerce Act, Part IV, provides for freight forwarders. This goes back to the Act of 1942 (56 Stat. 284, 1942). The original act was later amended, notably in 1946 (60 Stat. 21, 1946) and in 1950 (64 Stat. 1,115, 1950) Air regulation of forwarders was authorized by the Civil Aeronautics Act of 1938 (52 Stat. 977, 1938).

Under the Interstate Commerce Act a freight forwarder is defined as a person, not subject to Parts I, II, or III of the Act, which holds itself out as a common carrier of property to the public and (1) assembles and consolidates shipments, (2) assumes responsibility for transportation, and (3) utilizes for transportation the services of carriers subject to Parts I, II, or III [Sec. 402 (5)]. The Act does not undertake to cover all of these persons. Thus it exempts (1) coöperative associations; (2) the handling of ordinary livestock, fish, agricultural commodities, and used household goods; the consolidation or distribution of freight by shippers or groups of shippers for their own advantage; and (4) the operation of warehousemen or other shippers' agents in consolidating or distributing pool cars in terminal areas. The exemptions

---

[79] The Commission complains that its appropriations and its personnel are inadequate. Thus Commissioner Rogers testified in 1949:

"Mr. Thomas, we spoke earlier about the sort of job we were doing, and I said off the record that we were not doing a good job. What I meant by this is, when it takes months and months to get a case decided and when we have authorized certificates to be issued and cannot get them out, and when the violations of the act are wholesale and when the safety work is not effective, with people being killed and hurt, which we can't hope to prevent even though we are working as hard as we can, I will say that we are not doing a good job and we are not doing what the act contemplates in this present situation" (United States Senate, Committee on Interstate and Foreign Commerce, *Study of Domestic Land and Water Transportation,* Hearings before a subcommittee pursuant to Sen. Res. 50, 81st C., 2d S., 1950, testimony Rogers, p. 1506).

are considerable—it has been said that there are almost as many operators claiming to be exempt as there are regulated freight forwarders. The regulatory statute covers, however, a substantial group.

The Interstate Commerce Commission, under the Act, regulates forwarders in substantially the same manner as it regulates other transportation agencies. Thus the Commission has authority over forwarders with respect to permits, service, rates, discrimination, agreements, contracts, accounts, and to some extent, with respect to the relations between forwarders and other parties.

Under the Civil Aeronautics Act the freight forwarders are air carriers (3 C.A.B. 698, 704, 1942) and the term "air carrier" is defined as follows:

Section 1 (2). " 'Air carrier' means any citizen of the United States who undertakes, whether directly or indirectly or by a lease or any other arrangement, to engage in air transportation: *Provided,* That the Authority may by order relieve air carriers who are not directly engaged in the operation of aircraft in air transportation from the provisions of this Act to the extent and for such periods as may be in the public interest."

The Civil Aeronautics Board has also defined freight forwarders in its "Economic Regulations" in the following terms:

"An air freight forwarder shall be defined to mean any person which engages indirectly in air transportation of property only, and which, in the ordinary and usual course of his undertaking, (a) assembles and consolidates or provides for assembling and consolidating such property and performs or provides for the performance of break-bulk and distributing operations with respect to such consolidated shipments, (b) assumes responsibility for the transportation of such property from the point of receipt to point of destination, and (c) utilizes for the whole or any part of the transportation of such shipments, the service of a direct air carrier subject to the act" (C.F.C. Title 49, Part 296).

The Civil Aeronautics Board exempts air forwarders from some of the regulation which is usually applied to air line operation. The most important concession is that air forwarders may file a letter of registration instead of applying for a certificate of convenience and necessity. The letters may be later revoked or suspended but they are granted without a showing of public need. The air forwarder must still, however, file and publish tariffs and provide safe and adequate service at reasonable rates and avoid discrimination. The Board may prescribe accounts, require insurance, prevent unfair competition, regulate agreements, and control consolidations and interrelationships. It regulates with caution, however, in what it regards as an experimental period (9 C.A.B. 473, 1948; 10 C.A.B. 182, 1949).

Functions of the forwarder. The functions of the freight forwarder are indicated by the definitions which have been given. In general, the forwarder accepts goods for shipment, mainly in small quantities. It issues a bill of lading at point of origin and collects a rate for delivery at ultimate destination. It assumes responsibility for the entire movement. The forwarder owns, however, no vehicles and must rely upon other carriers—often on several types of carriers for necessary transportation. But it solicits the freight, performs much and sometimes all of the clerical work, and characteristically relieves the vehicle operator of all duties except those directly connected with the movement of the goods. It also consolidates small shipments into carload or truckload or planeload units, reducing the subsequent costs of handling. Speaking more specifically, and with reference to motor and rail movement, the forwarder takes the following steps in the ordinary course of business. First, it arranges with a motor carrier for the carriage of the goods from their starting point to an assembly point where its representatives receive them and combine them with other shipments. Second, it reships, most frequently by rail but sometimes by motor or air to a distribution point near the consignment's destination. Third, at the distribution point the forwarder arranges for the final movement of the individual shipments to the consignees to which they are addressed. This is a complete and elaborate operation; the forwarder may, of course, operate in a narrower field. The net earnings of the forwarder result from a difference in the rate which the owner pays and the sum of the rates which the forwarder pays to transportation companies for the service rendered plus its own operating expense.[80]

Freight forwarder problems. The problems which the freight forwarder meets vary with the transportation agencies that it employs.

Rail-forwarder relationships. Most freight forwarder payments are made to railroads for line haul operations. The forwarder collects a less-than-carload rate from the owner of the goods and pays the railroad on the basis of a carload rate. There is enough spread between these categories in the railroad tariffs to yield the forwarder a profit. The railroads, at one time, refused to quote carload rates on consignments which forwarders tendered on the ground that these rates applied only to goods which were owned by as well as tendered by a single shipper. This restriction was, however, held to be improper (14 I.C.C. 422, 1908; 14 I.C.C. 437, 1938; 220 U.S. 235, 1911). There was some controversy as to whether the forwarder was to be regarded as a shipper or as a carrier; the Supreme Court took the first alternative in these early cases.

Motor vehicle–forwarder relationships. Motor vehicle tariffs do not, like railroad tariffs, heavily favor quantity shipments. The forwarder must do one of two things if he is to make a profit on assembly and distribution movements or on the minority of line haul shipments which go by road. One possibility is that he may obtain concessions from the motor carrier in the form of special rates. The second possibility is that he may classify himself as a common carrier and claim a division of the total rate. Litigation and legislation during the last few years must be regarded from the point of view of these expedients. The sequence has been as follows:

1. After approximately 1920 and until 1935 forwarders obtained special rates from motor carriers by individual and private negotiation. When the

---

[80] Forwarder operations have been frequently described. See, *inter alia,* 43 M.C.C. 527, 1944; 256 I.C.C. 305, 1943; 259 I.C.C. 277, 1944. See also United States Senate, Committee on Interstate and Foreign Commerce, Hearings on S. 2113, 81st C., 1st S., 1949; and United States House of Representatives, Committee on Interstate and Foreign Commerce, *Freight Forwarders,* Hearings on H. R. 5967, 81st C., 2d S., 1950.

Motor Carrier Act of 1935 was passed this practice was abandoned because it seemed illegal in the light of statutory clauses forbidding discrimination.

2. After 1935 the forwarders filed tariffs with the Interstate Commerce Commission. These tariffs showed joint rates and divisions between forwarders and motor companies. The divisions were such as to burden the forwarders with something less than the payment of a standard rate. The Commission held, however, that a forwarder was not a common carrier by motor vehicle and so was not subject to the Interstate Commerce Act. It followed that a forwarder could not join with motor carriers in tariffs which had been filed (2 M.C.C. 415, 1937; 8 M.C.C. 211, 1938; 309 U.S. 638, 1940). In a later case the Commission added that only common carriers could participate in joint rates (272 I.C.C. 413, 450, 1938). In order to give reasonable chance for adjustment, existing joint rates were allowed to be continued for a time.

3. Failing joint rates, motor carriers then filed tariffs in which they proposed to transport for freight forwarders, at reduced "proportional" rates, packages which the forwarders had consolidated into carload or truckload lots. This was also held illegal (10 M.C.C. 556, 1938; 17 M.C.C. 573, 1939; 310 U.S. 344, 1940). The matter was then carried to Congress.

4. In 1942, Congress added Part IV to the Interstate Commerce Act, regulating forwarders in this as carriers though not as common carriers. In this Act Congress authorized motor carriers to quote special rates for "assembly" and "distribution" for freight forwarders but not special rates for "line haul" motor movements. This was a considerable concession; but it was at least partially canceled out by two restrictions: (a) that the differences between special and standard rates should be justified by differences in cost; and (b) that the special rates should be open to shippers who were not forwarders. As it turned out, motor carriers were unwilling to quote special rates which were generally available. The forwarders secured rates which were generally available. The forwarders secured, therefore, no general relief. Existing joint rates were again continued in 1942, but their status was not improved.

5. In 1946 Congress authorized freight forwarders and motor carriers to make agreements. The Commission was empowered to prescribe the terms of these agreements, subject to the provision that motor carriers might not collect less from forwarders than their published rates in the case of line haul movements unless lower costs of operation could be shown. In this legislation Congress by-passed, without eliminating, the act of 1942. Its chief purpose was to avoid the difficulties which had made the Act of 1942 ineffective and at the same time to obtain considered action by reference to a regulatory board. Congress continued the Act of 1942, but motor carriers might now disregard it and make agreements which, if approved, were not open to shippers who were not forwarders. Existing joint rates were still continued, pending action, although the Commission might set a date when their effectiveness would cease. The Commission regarded the act of 1946 as a reiteration of the purpose of Congress that joint rates should be withdrawn (272 I.C.C. 413, 446, 1948).

6. The Act of 1950, now in effect, was the second and last amendment of the Act of 1942. It was immediately provoked by a decision of the Interstate

Commerce Commission which (a) reviewed the general situation under the act of 1946; (b) declared that existing joint rates should be promptly canceled. The Commission observed that only common carriers could participate in through rates and forwarders were not common carriers. And (c) the Commission ruled that in motor-forwarder agreements the rates charged forwarders for terminal-to-terminal service should not be less than the motor carriers' published rates (*ibid.*, p. 451).

The provisions of the Act of 1950 were as follows:

1. The statute inserted the word *common* in the definition of a freight forwarder. Thus it now defined a forwarder as a person "who holds himself out as a common carrier of property" instead merely as one "who holds himself out as a carrier of property."

2. It declared that nothing in the act should be construed to prevent freight forwarders from entering into contracts with motor vehicles operating under Part II of the Interstate Commerce Act. It could be inferred from the language used that Congress did not intend that charges in these contracts should be compared with or measured by the published rates of motor carriers. They were rather to be compared with standards set in other sections of the Act which dealt with rate divisions.

3. It provided for the filing of contracts and for their regulation by the Interstate Commerce Commission.

4. It instructed the Commission that, in connection with line haul shipments for distances exceeding 450 miles, the forwarders should not pay motor carriers less than the motor vehicle published rate. The implication was that on shorter movements the same tests should be applied that were used in testing assembly and distribution rates.

The Act of 1950 made it clear that freight forwarders were common carriers under the Act to Regulate Interstate Commerce, and that they might, as such, participate in divisions of through rates charged in joint forwarder and motor carrier movements. The arguments for and against this disposition were fully presented in the House and Senate hearings in 1949 and 1950.

Air-forwarder relationships. The air lines make even less distinction in their rates between large and small shipments than do the railroads and they have not quoted special terminal-to-terminal rates for the forwarders' accommodation. The air forwarder, however, like the surface forwarder, can supply assembly and distribution service prior and subsequent to line haul carriage. (See John O. Emery, "The Freight Forwarder and the Development of Air Freight," *Law and Contemporary Problems*, Winter, 1950, pp. 29–36.)

Comments. The freight forwarder specializes upon a particular aspect of carriage in that (1) it deals with shipments that originate and terminate as less than carload freight and (2) characteristically makes use of more than one agency of transport in its operation. Many railroads, some trucking lines, and most certificated air companies oppose the forwarder because they believe that it diverts traffic from the facilities which they offer or because the forwarder absorbs for itself the high rates on small shipments which the standard companies have been able to collect.

It is a curious fact that a railroad, under existing law, cannot establish a motor service which will assemble freight in a district which the railroad does not serve, consolidate these shipments, and bring the goods to a railroad terminal for long-haul transportation while a forwarding company can do exactly this to the advantage of both the railroad and the owner of the goods. (See chap. 26.) It is curious also that a railroad or an air line will object to the consolidation of less-than-carload or less-than-planeload freight. Finally, it is interesting to observe that, after more than 40 years, the parties do not yet agree as to whether the freight forwarder is a shipper or a carrier in its operations. The position of the freight forwarder is not yet firmly established; but there is much evidence that it presently performs a service which the major carriers are not legally or technically in a position to supply.

REFERENCES

General Treatises

Bigham, Truman C., and Roberts, Merrill J., *Transportation, Principles and Problems,* New York, McGraw-Hill, 1952.

Fair, Marvin L., and Williams, Ernest W., *Economics of Transportation,* New York, Harper, 1950.

Johnson, E. R., *Government Regulation of Transportation,* New York, Appleton-Century-Crofts, 1938.

Johnson, E. R., *Transport Facilities, Services, and Policies,* New York, Appleton-Century-Crofts, 1947.

Johnson, E. R., Huebner, G. G., and Wilson, G. L., *Transportation: Economic Principles and Practice,* New York, Appleton-Century-Crofts, 1940.

Locklin, D. Philip, *Economics of Transportation,* Chicago, Irwin, 1947.

Parmelee, J. H., *The Modern Railway,* New York, Longmans, 1940.

Westmeyer, Russell E., *Economics of Transportation,* New York, Prentice-Hall, 1952.

Other Books

Keyes, L. S., *Federal Control of Entry into Air Transportation,* Cambridge, Harvard University Press, 1951.

Stocker, H. E., *Motor Traffic Management,* New York, Prentice-Hall, 1942.

Taff, Charles A., *Commercial Motor Transportation,* Chicago, Irwin, 1950.

Van Metre, Thurman W., *Industrial Traffic Management,* New York, McGraw-Hill, 1953.

Wagner, Warren H., *A Legislative History of the Motor Carrier Act, 1935,* Denton, Md., Rue Publishing, 1936.

Walker, Gilbert, *Road and Rail, An Enquiry into the Economics of Competition and State Control,* London, Allen & Unwin, 1947.

Periodicals

Barton, F. L., and McGehee, R. B., "Freight Forwarders," *Harvard Business Review,* Spring, 1942.

George, J. J., "Authorization of Contract Motor Carriers by the Interstate Commerce Commission," *Cornell Law Quarterly,* June, 1941.

George, J. J., "Emergence of Contract Motor Carrier Regulation," *Journal of Land and Public Utility Economics,* May, 1937.

George, J. J., "The Federal Motor Carrier Act of 1935," *Cornell Law Quarterly,* February, 1936.

George, J. J., and Boldt, J. R., "Certification of Motor Common Carriers by the Interstate Commerce Commission," *Journal of Land and Public Utility Economics,* May, 1941.

Gorenstein, M., "Private Carriage by Motor Vehicle Under Federal Regulation," *Interstate Commerce Commission Practitioners' Journal,* 1944.

Haid, E. A., "Regulation of Motor Carriers," *Washington University Law Quarterly,* December, 1937.

Kauper, P. G., "Utilization of State Commissioners in the Administration of the Federal Motor Carrier Act," *Michigan Law Review,* November, 1935.

Nelson, James C., "Coordination of Transportation," *The Journal of Land and Public Utility Economics,* May, 1938.

Nelson, James C., "Joint-Board Procedure under the Motor Carrier Act," *Journal of Land and Public Utility Economics,* February, 1937.

Nelson, James C., "The Motor Carrier Act of 1935," *Journal of Political Economy,* August, 1936.

Walker, J. L., "Analysis of Motor Carrier Act, 1935," *John Marshall Law Quarterly,* March, 1937.

Westwood, Howard C., and Elpern, George S., "Owen-Operators of Motor Vehicles: Implication for Air Carrier Problems," *Virginia Law Review,* March, 1945.

Special and Miscellaneous

Nelson, James C., "New Concepts in Transportation Regulation," in National Resources Planning Board, *Transportation and National Policy,* Washington, D.C., 1942.

United States Board of Investigation and Research, *Federal Regulatory Restrictions upon Motor and Water Carriers,* 79th C., 1st S., Sen. Doc. 81, Ser. 10,952, 1945.

United States Board of Investigation and Research, *Interstate Barriers Affecting Motor Vehicle Transportation,* 79th C., 1st S., Sen. Doc. 81, 1945.

United States Department of Agriculture, *Motor Vehicle Traffic Conditions in the United States,* 75th C., 3d S., House Doc. 462, Ser. 10,251, 1938.

United States Department of Agriculture, *Interstate Barriers to Truck Transportation: History and Current Status of Regulations Regarding Size and Weight, Taxes and Other Selected Phases That Affect Trucking,* prepared by M. R. Purcell, Bureau of Agricultural Economics, 1950.

United States House of Representatives, Committee on Interstate and Foreign Commerce, *Regulation of Freight Forwarders,* Hearings on H. R. 3684, 1941.

United States House of Representatives, Committee on Interstate and Foreign Commerce, *Service of Freight Forwarders,* Hearings on H. R. 2764, 79th C., 1st S., 1946.

United States House of Representatives, Committee on Interstate and Foreign

Commerce, *Freight Forwarders,* Hearings on H. R. 5967, 81st C., 2d S., 1950.

United States Interstate Commerce Commission, *Federal Regulation of the Sizes and Weights of Motor Vehicles,* 77th C., 1st S., House Doc. 354, Ser. 10,591, 1941.

United States, Office of Federal Coordinator of Transportation, *Report on Regulation of Transportation Agencies,* 73d C., 2d S., Sen. Rep. 152, 1934.

Special References on Freight Forwarders

United States Senate, Committee on Interstate Commerce, *Less-Than-Carload-Freight Traffic and Freight Forwarder Carload Traffic,* Hearings before a subcommittee on Sen. Res. 146, 76th C., 3d S., 1940.

United States Senate, Committee on Interstate Commerce, *Services of Freight Forwarders,* Hearings on H. R. 2764, 79th C., 2d S., 1946.

United States Senate, Committee on Interstate Commerce, *Freight Forwarders,* Hearings on S. 2113, 81st C., 1st S., 1949.

C H A P T E R   3   2

Inland Water Regulation

United States Shipping Board—United States Maritime Commission—Interstate Commerce Commission

Between 1916 and 1940 the principal responsibility for the regulation of rates and traffic upon inland waterways was vested in the United States Shipping Board or in its successor, the United States Maritime Commission. There were also laws which empowered the Interstate Commerce Commission to regulate joint rail and water services and to protect water carriers from destructive attack by railroads which operated under Interstate Commerce Commission control. The situation was changed in 1940. In this year Congress transferred regulatory authority over inland waterways from the Maritime Commission to the Interstate Commerce Commission. The latter Commission was given new powers for the purpose, and these it has since retained.

Accomplishments of Federal Regulation of Inland Waterways Prior to 1940

The system of inland waterways regulation before 1940 had many desirable characteristics. These features may, for convenience, be listed as follows:

1. Maximum and minimum water rates were subject to regulation along the coast and in intercoastal commerce. Maximum rates were regulated upon the Great Lakes. In addition, the rates of water lines controlled by competing railway services were subject to Interstate Commerce Commission regulation to the same extent as the rates of the controlling railroad corporations.[1]

2. The provisions of the Interstate Commerce Act relative to discrimination extended to traffic handled under common management by rail and

---

[1] See appendix to the present chapter, *infra*.

water carriers. The Shipping Act of 1916 and the Intercoastal Act of 1933 also protected shippers against discrimination, to some extent.

3. Water rates were required to be filed and schedules adhered to except by carriers engaged in port-to-port river business.

4. Federal agencies might call for reports from water carriers, although their authority to prescribe accounts was limited.

5. Destructive competition between rail and water routes was restrained in a number of ways, to the general advantage of the water lines. Statutory provisions gave the Interstate Commerce Commission power to compel physical connection between rail and water lines and authority to require joint routes and maximum joint rates on, and a fair division of resulting revenues from, interstate rail-water business. They also placed obstacles in the way of railroad ownership of water services. The Commission could use its general powers to moderate the intensity of railroad competition.[2]

Weaknesses of Federal Inland Waterway Regulation Prior to 1940

We may place alongside of this list of merits ascribed to the system of federal waterway control before 1940 a summary of apparent defects:

1. The federal system provided no control of minimum rates on rivers or on the Great Lakes even when water carriers joined with railroads in the quotation of through rates. In the case of river port-to-port navigation there was no control of rates at all.

2. River lines were not required to publish or to adhere to published tariffs, except tariffs published jointly with rail lines.

3. Contract carriers were not regulated except in intercoastal commerce.

4. There was no adequate governmental control over the accounts of water carriers. Section 21 of the Shipping Act required common carriers by water to file with the federal agency any account appertaining to the business of the carrier which the Shipping Board (later the Maritime Commission) required, in the form and within the time prescribed. This section did not convey the general power to prescribe accounting systems. The authority of the Interstate Commerce Commission over carriers' accounts extended only to the accounts of water carriers which were operated under a common control or arrangement with rail lines for continuous carriage in interstate commerce and to the accounts of railroad-controlled water carriers which came within the terms of the Panama Canal Act of 1912.[3]

---

[2] The Interstate Commerce Commission was given, among other things, the power to fix so-called proportional rates, applicable to the rail segment of a rail-water haul to or from a water port (161 I.C.C. 649, 1930). This was not, strictly speaking, a regulation of water carriage, but it did or might affect the total rate on rail-water or water-rail movements. (See appendix to this chapter, *infra.*)

[3] I. L. Sharfman, *The Interstate Commerce Commission,* New York, Commonwealth Fund, 1931, Part II, p. 37.

5. Water carriers were not required to apply for certificates of convenience and necessity. Water carriers on the Mississippi, Columbia, and Willamette rivers might apply for certificates, but they might operate whether they obtained them or not. Moreover, in granting certificates for river operation and in the establishment of joint rates which ordinarily followed, the Interstate Commerce Commission did not feel itself at liberty to consider the general adequacy of transport facilities in the area to be served because of the implications in statutory language.

6. The regulation of inland waterways in the United States was divided between the Maritime Commission and the Interstate Commerce Commission. The former supervised coastal, intercoastal, and Great Lakes water carriers from port to port; the latter controlled water traffic carried under common arrangement with railroad lines, traffic handled by certain railroad-owned steamship lines, and, in some respects, traffic on the inland rivers. It seemed obvious that the regulation of inland waterway transport would be more effective if this dual administration were removed.[4]

Analysis by the Federal Coordinator of Transportation

In 1934 the Federal Coordinator rendered a report to the Interstate Commerce Commission for transmission to Congress in which he stressed the general lack of prosperity, due to uncontrolled competition, which characterized the water industry, and emphasized the need for reorganization and extension of federal regulation in this field. Government supervision, he thought, should include control over the amount of competitive services afforded, control over minimum charges, control over the operations of contract and private carriers, and the requirement that published rates should be adhered to and unjust discrimination avoided. He proposed that regulatory authority should be vested in the Interstate Commerce Commission for these purposes and that the jurisdiction of other agencies or departments of the government should be at the same time reduced.[5] A bill to make these changes was considered by Congress in 1935, but no serious attempt to pass new waterway legislation occurred until 1939. In this year Mr. Lea in the House and Mr. Wheeler in the Senate introduced general transportation bills which proposed, among other things, to amend existing legislation relating to waterways and to transfer to the Interstate Commerce Commission the responsibility for regulatory control. These bills failed to pass in the second session of the 76th Congress because of the combined opposition of waterway, labor,

[4] See United States, Office of the Federal Coordinator, *Report of the Federal Coordinator of Transportation,* 73d C., 2d S., Sen. Doc. 152, 1934. See also United States House of Representatives, Committee on Merchant Marine and Fisheries, Hearings on H. R. 4307, 76th C., 1st S., 1939, pp. 250–260.

[5] United States, Office of the Federal Coordinator, *op. cit.,* pp. 10–11.

and farming interests; they were reconsidered in slightly altered form when Congress reconvened, and they were quickly passed in 1940.[6]

Act of 1940

Part III of the Interstate Commerce Act was enacted in 1940.[7] It consolidated, revised, and extended the federal laws which provided for the regulation of inland waterways. This Act is now effective, and must be considered at some length.

In general, the Transportation Act of 1940 centralized water regulation by transferring to the Interstate Commission powers which the Maritime Commission had exercised over inland transport. It did not repeal or qualify these powers, or change the authority previously vested in the Commission except to the extent that previous legislation was inconsistent with the rules which were now laid down. It did, however, broaden statutory control and it changed the basis of its administration.[8]

[6] The congressional history of the Act of 1940 is given in the Morgan report, United States Interstate Commerce Commission, *Problems in the Regulation of Domestic Transportation by Water,* Ex Parte no. 165, August, 1946.

[7] 54 Stat. 898, 929, 1940.

[8] Part III of the Interstate Commerce Act (Transportation Act of 1940) was reasonably specific with respect to repeal and to nonrepeal.

The following laws were repealed in part:

1. The Shipping Act, 1916, as amended and the Intercoastal Act, 1933, as amended, insofar as they were inconsistent with any provision of Part III

2. The Shipping Act, 1916, as amended, and the Intercoastal Act, 1933, as amended, insofar as they provided for the regulation of, or the making of agreements relating to, transportation of persons or property by water in interstate commerce which was within the jurisdiction of the Commission under the provisions of Part III.

3. Any other provisions of law insofar as they were inconsistent with the provisions of Part III.

Part III of the Interstate Commerce Act did not repeal earlier legislation in the following respects:

1. The Shipping Act of 1916 and the Intercoastal Act of 1933 remained in force insofar as they provided for the regulation of transportation between continental United States and the noncontiguous territories or possessions of the United States. The Maritime Commission continued to control this type of commerce.

2. The Maritime Commission retained its authority over steamship conferences, including conferences in the intercoastal trade (Act of 1916).

3. The Maritime Commission continued to regulate persons who carried on the business of forwarding or furnishing wharfage, dock, warehouse, or other terminal facilities in connection with a common carrier by water (Act of 1916). This authority, however, did not apparently extend to transportation facilities used in or in connection with transportation by water subject to Part III.

4. The Transportation Act was not to be construed so as to affect any law of navigation, the admiralty jurisdiction of the United States, liabilities of vessels and their owners for loss or damage, or laws respecting seamen, or any other maritime law, regulation, or custom.

5. Certain sections of the Act of 1920 remained in force. These sections related to the application of the coastwise laws and to railroad practice in quoting preferential rates on certain export freight.

6. Part III repealed portions of the Inland Waterways Corporation Act of 1924 as

We may now turn to the provisions which the Act of 1940 positively contains.

Classification of Carriers

The Act of 1940 applies to common and contract carriers by water in interstate or foreign commerce. In the case of foreign commerce the Act controls only such portion of the transportation as takes place within the United States. The definitions of common and contract carrier are of a standard type, with one exception. Thus the statute declares that "the furnishing for compensation (under a charter, lease, or other agreement) of a vessel, to a person other than a carrier subject to this Act, to be used by the person to whom such vessel is furnished in the transportation of his own property, shall be considered to constitute, as to the vessel so furnished, engaging in transportation by the person furnishing such vessel, within the meaning of the . . . definition of 'contract carrier by water.'"

This type of service is not recognized in railroad, motor, and air transportation. The Commission may grant exemption from regulation to a water contract carrier of the sort described if the inclusion is not necessary to effectuate the national transportation policy.

Exemptions

Not all classes of water traffic are subject to regulation under Part III of the Interstate Commerce Act. The principal categories which are exempt are the following:

1. *Commodities in bulk, carried by contract carriers*—except contract carriers engaged in interstate commerce via the Panama Canal—when the cargo space of the vessel in which the commodities are transported is being used for the carrying of not more than three of these commodities.[9]

---

amended, but it provided that certificates which had been issued under this legislation and through rates which had been established should be considered legal.

7. In general, the provisions of earlier laws which were not inconsistent with the provisions of the Transportation Act of 1940 were not repealed.

[9] The statute does not exempt transportation which was subject to the Intercoastal Act of 1933, as amended. The Intercoastal Act covered contract carriers operating through the Panama Canal. The Intercoastal Act also limited its application to common carriers operating through the Panama Canal, but the coverage of the Act was extended in 1938 to cover every common carrier by water in interstate commerce as defined in the Shipping Act of 1916. The Shipping Act defined a "common carrier in interstate commerce" as a common carrier engaged in the transportation by water of passengers or property on the high seas or the Great Lakes. The later result was that the exemptions in the Act of 1940 did not apply (1) to contract carriers engaged in transportation via the Panama Canal, and (2) to common carriers engaged in the transportation of passengers or property on the high seas and the Great Lakes. The subject is further complicated, however, by the fact that common carriage, as defined in the Shipping Act, proved not to be identical with common carriage as understood by the Interstate Commerce Commission. It followed that transportation in bulk by some common carriers was exempt from regulation after 1940—namely, transportation

The statute stipulates that commodities in bulk, to be exempt must be commodities which are loaded and carried without wrappers or containers and received and delivered by the carriers without transportation mark or count. The Commission actually goes further than this in limiting the definition. Thus it has characterized bulk freight as freight which can be poured, scooped, or shoveled.[10] And it has said that the term "in bulk" commonly refers to a loose mass which is poured or thrown into a vessel or vehicle without regard to order, and which is restrained during transportation only by the bottom and sides of the carrying vessel and its bulkheads.[11] This description will cover coal, grain, and iron ore; it will not include pig iron, which is handled piece by piece,[12] nor granite, which must be stowed in orderly fashion.[13]

2. *Liquid cargoes in bulk in tank vessels.*[14] This includes liquid products towed or transported in steel tankers or steel tank barges, but not shipments in open barges in containers. Liquid cargoes consist mainly of petroleum and its products. Other commodities include molasses, chemicals and acids, and tar.[15] The exemption applies both to contract and to common carriage.[16]

3. *Local water transportation in harbors and between contiguous harbors and transportation in small craft.* This exemption covers strictly local common or contract service, independently conducted. The service is not to be operated by or for a rail or a motor carrier or as an agent of these or of coastwise water carriers, nor may the carrier which supplies the service participate in through rates and routing arrangements.[17] The category includes harbor towage and the shifting of barges,[18] and salvage operations. The term "small craft" is defined in the Act; one of the re-

---

by carriers which qualified as common carriers under the Commission definition but not under the definition of the Shipping Act. (See 250 I.C.C. 653, 666, 1943; 260 I.C.C. 15, 1943; 260 I.C.C. 135, 1944.)

[10] 250 I.C.C., 436, 439, 1942.

[11] 250 I.C.C. 101, 103, 1941.

[12] 250 I.C.C. 436, 439, 1942. Other bulk shipments are sand and gravel, sulfur, limestone, and cement.

[13] Bulk commodities are not exempt when they are handled in the same unit as non-bulk commodities (250 I.C.C. 381, 385, 1942; 250 I.C.C. 436, 439, 1942; 260 I.C.C. 329, 1944). This means, among other possibilities, that a common carrier barge line which combines several barges in a tow is subject to regulation upon all the barges even though some of them may contain only bulk shipments (United States Senate, Committee on Interstate and Foreign Commerce, *Study of Domestic Land and Water Transportation,* Hearings before a subcommittee pursuant to S. Res. 50, 81st C., 2d S., 1950, testimony Maclean, p. 1295.

[14] These vessels must be certified under regulations approved by the Secretary of Commerce.

[15] 260 I.C.C. 501, 1945; 260 I.C.C. 681, 1946.

[16] But see page 690, footnote 9.

[17] 250 I.C.C. 441, 1942.

[18] 250 I.C.C. 614, 1943.

quirements is that the vessel must not have a carrying capacity exceeding 100 tons.

Current statistics are not published, but in the prewar period, 1939–41, bulk traffic, including liquid cargoes, accounted for 69 percent of the exempt carriers and about 98 percent of the total exempt vessel tonnage. Most of this transportation was performed by contract carriers.[19]

In addition to these major exemptions, the Act relieved the following transportation from regulation under Part III:

1. *Transportation by water by an express company in the conduct of its business as a common carrier.* This transportation is regulated under Part I of the Interstate Commerce Act.

2. *Water transportation operated by railroads or motor carriers in transfer, collection, or delivery service in terminal areas, or transportation in the performance of floatage, car ferry, lighterage, or towage.*[20] This transportation is considered to be part of railroad or motor service and is regulated as such under Parts I and II of the Interstate Commerce Act. The business is, usually, common carriage.

A clear illustration of the exemption would be presented by a lighterage company which transferred livestock from railroad cars to barges and delivered them to points in New York harbor.[21] Car ferriage for railroad lines is similarly exempt.[22] The provisions of Part III exempting these types of transportation are to be compared with similar exemptions in the Motor Carrier Act.

3. *The carriage of the property of any person who owns substantially all the voting stock of the carrier which does the transportation.* The exemption here covers the case of a manufacturing or mining company which organizes a subsidiary shipping corporation to carry freight which the manufacturing or mining company supplies.[23] To enjoy exemption,

---

[19] United States Interstate Commerce Commission, *Problems in the Regulation of Domestic Transportation by Water,* Ex Parte no. 165, report of C. S. Morgan, Chief Carrier Research Analyst, Bureau of Transport Economics and Statistics, August, 1946, pp. 16–17.

See also United States Senate, Committee on Interstate and Foreign Commerce, *Study of Domestic Land and Water Transportation,* pursuant to S. Res. 50, 81st C., 2d S., 1950, p. 243, testimony Grubbs. According to testimony in these hearings, bulk traffic accounted for 95 percent of the commerce on rivers and harbors of the United States, excepting the Great Lakes, in 1946, and the percentage of bulk traffic on the Great Lakes was somewhat greater.

[20] Water transportation of the kinds described in the text is also exempt when it is performed by an agent or under a contractual arrangement for a railroad, motor, express, or water company. This includes the case where a harbor company docks vessels for a line engaged in coastal service. Whatever regulation is appropriate is here applied to the coastal line and not, directly, to the agent.

[21] 250 I.C.C. 7, 1941; 260 I.C.C. 23, 27, 1943.

[22] Car ferries are to be distinguished from ferries in the ordinary sense (250 I.C.C. 791, 1943; 260 I.C.C. 103, 1943; 260 I.C.C. 430, 1945).

[23] 250 I.C.C. 109, 1941.

however, the subsidiary corporation must engage solely in transporting the products of the parent company.[24] This limits the freedom to cases which are, in reality, instances of private or contract carriage.

4. *Contract carriage by water which, by reason of the inherent nature of the commodities transported, their requirement of special equipment, or their shipment in bulk, is not actually and substantially competitive with transportation by any common carrier subject to Parts I, II, or III of the Interstate Commerce Act.*

This is a very specialized exemption. Among the services which have been held exempt have been the transportation of explosives, ammunition, and ammunition components for the United States Government,[25] the carriage of poles, pipes, iron products, and machinery of unusual sizes and weights,[26] and the towage of floating derricks in the harbor of New York.[27] On the other hand the transportation of sand between points in New York Harbor and points in adjoining streams and harbors,[28] and the towing of logging rafts by contract carriers on the Columbia and Willamette rivers have been held not to be exempt, largely because no special equipment is required.[29] The Commission will take notice of competition by other carriers when this exists, but it may deny exemption when there is, in fact, no competition, if the lack of competition is not the result of circumstances specified in the act.[30]

If we take into account all classes of exemption, and consider also private carriage, which is exempt, figures show that, in 1939–41, 30.3 percent of the capacity of water carriers engaged in inland transportation, including coastal and intercoastal transport, was regulated, 55.9 percent was exempt, and 13.8 percent was private.[31] Later estimates indicate that the present proportion of domestic water transportation that is subject to the Interstate Commerce Commission is still smaller than the previous estimate assumes.[32] The Interstate Commerce Commission has urged that

[24] 250 I.C.C. 677, 681, 1943.
[25] 250 I.C.C. 737, 1943.
[26] 250 I.C.C. 33, 1941; 250 I.C.C. 62, 1941.
[27] 250 I.C.C. 157, 1942; 250 I.C.C. 559, 1943.
[28] 250 I.C.C. 5, 1941.
[29] 250 I.C.C. 525, 529, 1942.
[30] 250 I.C.C. 51, 1941.

[31] United States Interstate Commerce Commission, *Problems on the Regulation of Domestic Transportation by Water, op. cit.,* pp. 19–20.

[32] United States Senate, Commmittee on Interstate and Foreign Commerce, *Study of Domestic Land and Water Transportation,* Hearings before the Subcommittee on Domestic Land and Water Transportation pursuant to S. Res. 50, 81st C., 2d S., 1951, testimony Grubbs, pp. 242–245.

In 1951 there were 578,627,300 tons moved in Lake, coastwise, and internal water commerce in the United States, omitting intraport and local commerce (United States Army, Office of the Chief of Engineers, *Commercial Statistics,* 1951, p. xix). The tonnage reported by carriers subject to the Interstate Commerce Commission, including

the exemption of bulk commodities from regulatory control shall be repealed,[33] but this has not yet been done.

Regulatory Provisions of Part III of the Interstate Commerce Act

For convenient reference the terms of Part III of the Interstate Commerce Act are tabulated below as they apply to common and contract water carriers. Only the most important powers of the Interstate Commerce Commission are included in the list.[34]

Common Carriers	Contract Carriers
Declaration of policy. See Railroads—National Transportation Policy.	*Declaration of policy.* See Railroads—National Transportation Policy.
Certificates of convenience and necessity. Commission may issue or refuse. Commission may authorize transfer. It may not revoke.	*Permits.* Commission may issue or refuse. Commission may authorize transfer. It may not revoke.
Service. Commission may require reports. May prescribe records and accounts. May establish through routes. Is not responsible for safety regulation.	*Service.* Commission may require reports. May prescribe records and reports. Is not responsible for safety regulation.
Consolidation, merger, and acquisition of control. Pooling. Commission must approve.	*Consolidation, merger, and acquisition of control. Pooling.* Commission must approve.
Rates. Must be filed, published, and adhered to. 30 days notice of change. Commission may prescribe.	*Rates.* Must be filed, published, and adhered to. 30 days notice of change. Commission may prescribe.

the commerce of the Mississippi River and its tributaries but excluding other river carriage, was 84,422,294 (*Statistics of Railways,* 1951, p. 213), or 15 percent of the preceding figure. From the Interstate Commerce Commission figures should also be deducted a large but unenumerated tonnage which, while carried by companies reporting, was not subject to the Commission's jurisdiction.

[33] United States Interstate Commerce Commission, *Annual Report,* 1946, p. 35. In 1953 the Commission stated that 52.4 percent of the overall water tonnage was unregulated. *Ibid.,* 1953, p. 14.

[34] The term "contract carrier by water" under Part III of the Interstate Commerce is defined to include any person which, under individual contracts or agreements engages in the transportation by water of passengers or property in interstate or foreign commerce for compensation. This is a standard definition. But Sec. 302 (e) adds a special group to this category in the following terms:

"The furnishing for compensation (under a charter, lease, or other agreement) of a vessel, to a person other than a carrier subject to this Act, to be used by the person to whom such vessel is furnished in the transportation of its own property, shall be considered to constitute, as to the vessel so furnished, engaging in transportation for compensation by the person furnishing such vessel, within the meaning of the foregoing definition of 'contract carrier by water.' " See p. 690.

The Interstate Commerce Commission is given authority, however, to exempt persons in this special group from regulation when the inclusion of the group was not necessary in order to effectuate the national transportation policy.

Common Carriers	Contract Carriers
Discrimination. Issue of passes limited. No rebates or concessions. No discrimination between connecting lines. Undue preference forbidden. No greater charge for shorter hauls. Commission may regulate credit extended to shippers.	*Discrimination.* No rebates or concessions. Minimum rates may not give undue advantage to contract in competition with common carriers.
Security issues. No control.	*Security issues.* No control.

Declaration of Policy

The declaration of national policy in the Interstate Commerce Act governs inland water as well as railroad and motor transportation.

Certificates and Permits

The certificate and permit provisions of Part III are substantially the same as those which govern motor carriers. The limiting date for "grandfather" applications is, however, January 1, 1940. Certificates and permits may be transferred, upon application, but they cannot be revoked.

NUMBER OF CERTIFICATES ISSUED. The routine work of handling water carrier applications is performed by the Bureau of Water Carriers of the Interstate Commerce Commission. From the time when Part III of the Interstate Commerce Act became effective to November 1, 1951, the Commission received and decided 2,846 applications for authority to continue, extend, or institute water carriers operations or for exemption.[35] Most of these applications were handled without formal hearing, and most of them, presumably, were of slight importance. On November 1, 1951, there were outstanding 259 common carriers certificates, 57 contract carrier permits, and 97 freight forwarder permits. Some of these certificates and permits covered substantial fleets; but in a large number of cases the documented carriers operated only a few small tugs, barges, or self-propelled vessels in coastal or inland water transportation.

POLICIES OF THE INTERSTATE COMMERCE COMMISSION. In exercising its powers under Part III the Commission has had, of course, to distinguish between proposals for the continuance of old and the institution of new operations.

1. *Applications for continuance.* Most applications during the early years were, necessarily, for continuance.[36] Under the so-called "grandfather clause" of the Act the Commission has considered technical aspects

---

[35] United States Interstate Commerce Commission, *Annual Report,* November 1, 1951, p. 127.

[36] Companies holding certificates under the Inland Waterways Corporation Act are not required to obtain certificates under the Act of 1940 [Sec. 320 (e)]. See 260 I.C.C. 783, 1946.

of legislation. Thus it has held that the requirement of operation prior to January 1, 1940, means operation within a reasonable length of time prior to that date. An applicant which had ceased service in 1936 or 1937 could not claim the right to continue without a showing of public convenience and necessity. Nor could an applicant which had not operated continuously between 1940 and the date of its application enjoy the privilege accorded by the statute.[37] Somewhat more generally, and in line with decisions in motor carrier cases, the Commission has limited "grandfather" certificates to operations previously performed. Thus a company which had engaged in general towage before 1940 would not be authorized to offer a car ferry service.[38] And a steamship line in the lumber trade which had served six points in Oregon continuously up to 1940 was denied authority to handle freight at three other ports which it had not regularly supplied.[39] On the other hand, a company which had held itself out to accept shipments in an area was permitted to continue its general undertaking and, in doing this, to call at ports at which its vessels had not touched.[40] And a company which had carried a wide variety of commodities was not denied the right to carry other commodities of the same class merely because it had not carried these commodities before.[41] Route restrictions, in grandfather cases, do not seem to have been as annoying in water as they have been in motor regulation. This is probably because there are fewer intermediate stations on a water route or because the grant of area certificates is more usual.

2. *Institution of new service.* This is, of course, the basic task of the Interstate Commerce Commission under the certificate power. The Commission's authority is somewhat less in water than it is in motor cases because it cannot restrict service of water lines by inserting clauses in a certificate or permit and because it may not revoke a certificate which it has once put out.[42] The Commission proceeds, however, to apply the standard tests with some common sense qualifications. Thus it will not grant a certificate to a company which is not prepared to operate,[43] or

---

[37] 260 I.C.C. 515, 519, 1945.

[38] 260 I.C.C. 395, 398, 1944.

[39] 250 I.C.C. 187, 1942.

[40] 250 I.C.C. 219, 222, 1942; 250 I.C.C. 249, 272, 1942; 259 I.C.C. 469, 471, 1942.

[41] 250 I.C.C. 249, 271, 1942.

[42] The Commission has attempted, unsuccessfully, to revoke a water certificate. Thus in the Seatrain case the Commission canceled a certificate which authorized the Seatrain Company to carry commodities generally and substituted a certificate authorizing the company to carry loaded and empty railroad cars and liquid cargo in bulk. The United States Supreme Court held that this exceeded the authority of the Commission (64 Fed. S. 156, 1946, 329 I.C.C. 424, 1947). The principle of the Court's decision would, presumably, cover the case of a permit also. The Commission protests that it will be unable to prevent the accumulation of unused certificates without power of revocation (*Annual Report,* 1947, p. 51). It adds that this will make it difficult for the Commission to determine how far new certificates should be granted.

[43] 250 I.C.C. 469, 472, 1942; 260 I.C.C. 201, 205, 1944.

for a stretch of water which is not yet open for navigation.[44] It will not accept a temporary emergency as a basis for a permanent authorization; [45] there are also cases where it has found that an applicant was not "fit and able," [46] and at least one in which the Commission denied a certificate to a company whose special interests seemed likely to interfere with a common carrier's obligations.[47] On the other hand, the Commission is not disposed to deny a certificate merely because rail and motor carriers are rendering adequate service,[48] nor is it unaware of the Congressional desire to develop water and especially inland water transportation and of the heavy expenditures which the government has made. It has been said that the Commission has been relatively generous in granting certificates for water operations.[49] But on the whole, the number of certificates and permits which the Commission has allowed for the institution of new service has been relatively small, and fewer Class A and B water carriers now (1949) report to the Commission than reported 9 years ago.

Abandonments

The Act of 1940 (Part III of the Interstate Commerce Act) does not forbid abandonment.

Federal Safety Regulations

The Interstate Commerce Commission has no responsibility for the safety of water carrier operation. But there is a great deal of federal legislation, not connected with the Interstate Commerce Act, which relates to ship construction, navigation, and to the loading of commercial vessels.[50]

Service

The Commission has full authority over the accounts, records, and reports of common and of contract water carriers subject to the Act. In granting certificates or permits for the institution of new service we have

[44] 250 I.C.C. 469, 472, 1942.
[45] 250 I.C.C. 550, 1942; 250 I.C.C. 767, 780, 1942; 260 I.C.C. 235, 237, 1944.
[46] 260 I.C.C. 603, 1945.
[47] 250 I.C.C. 291, 1942.
[48] 260 I.C.C. 701, 709, 1946.
[49] Nelson, James C., S. Doc. 78, 79th C., 1st S., p. 266, 1945.
[50] Safety regulations in coastwise and inland waterway transportation are administered by the Coast Guard. Thus the Commandant of the Coast Guard inspects vessels, determines the minimum complement of officers and men, classifies the various officer ratings, including pilots, enforces statutory limitations of hours of service, and is responsible for the fixing of load lines. Navigation rules designed to prevent collisions are set by statute. The Coast Guard also designates, from time to time, the lines which divide the high seas from rivers, harbors, and inland waters. (See *United States Code*, Titles 33 and 46.) State and municipal regulations of pilotage are also recognized as valid (*ibid.*, Title 46, Sec. 215).

said that it has no power to specify the service to be rendered by water carriers although we have seen that it may specify service in issuing certificates and permits to motor carriers. That is to say, it may not determine the kind of goods which may be carried under a certificate. Doubtless the Commission might interfere if a carrier failed to provide service which it had undertaken or held itself out to perform, but its power even here is limited because a water certificate may not be revoked. In any event, the Commission has taken little direct action in such matters.[51]

The Commission retains its power to establish rail-water routes and to require physical connections between rail and water carriers. This is a form of service regulation which did not originate with the Act of 1940. The statute also requires water carriers to afford facilities for the interchange of traffic between their respective lines and connecting lines, and the Commission has authority to enforce this rule.

Consolidation, Merger, and Acquisition of Control

The acquisition of water carriers by competing railroad carriers was partially dealt with in the Act of 1912. Under the present statute, water carriers are subject to Section 5 of the Interstate Commerce Act. This means that they are, equally with railroad and motor carriers, required to obtain Commission consent before pooling traffic. Likewise a water carrier may not, without approval, merge or consolidate with or acquire control of another water carrier or guarantee its earnings, whether directly or through a holding company, investment trust or in any other manner. Approved mergers or consolidations are, however, exempt from the antitrust laws in water as in other cases. Agreements between carriers must be filed. Special provisions which govern the relations between railroad and water carriers are described in the appendix to the present chapter.

There has been a good deal of shifting among the larger companies in the Atlantic and Gulf trade in recent years—although less in intercoastal shipping and in barge transportation upon the Mississippi. There has also been some concentration. If we pick the seven largest companies in each area, we find that these, in 1949, earned 83 percent of the revenue of Class A carriers in the Atlantic and Gulf trade, 68 percent in Pacific and Intercoastal service, and 83 percent upon the Mississippi. These percentages are to be compared with 61, 82, and 78 in 1941. The percentage of the revenues of all Class A carriers earned by the largest company in 1949 was 35 in the Atlantic and Gulf trade, 16 in Pacific Coast and

---

[51] Sec. 305 (a). We have earlier stated that the Commission may attach reasonable terms, conditions, and limitations to the exercise of privileges granted by a certificate. This does not constitute, however, a positive power to regulate service—the authority is rather negative than positive. (See 64 Fed. S. 156, 159, 1946; 219 U.S. 88, 1943; 220 U.S. 401, 1943; 329 U.S. 424, 1947.)

Intercoastal, and 22 upon the Mississippi. Concentration in this last sense declined between 1941 and 1949 except in the Atlantic and in the Gulf marine.

Consolidations and mergers in inland water transport raise few questions of public policy. This is because water companies compete actively among themselves and because they are subject to even greater pressure from rail and motor carriage. Most Interstate Commerce Commission decisions consider minor problems. Sometimes the application is for a minor lease and or for the transfer of a certificate. In some cases a water company desires to acquire new equipment,[52] or to extend somewhat its field of operations.[53] In one instance a company leased its operating rights because the Government had taken over more than half of its coastwise tonnage.[54] In others the object has been merely the simplification of an existing organization.[55]

Rates and Tariffs

Common carriers by water subject to Part III must file and publish their tariffs and must collect the rates which they publish. Contract carriers must file with the Commission, post and keep open for public inspection, and maintain schedules of minimum rates and charges. The Commission may, however, grant contract carriers relief from this requirement. Common carriers may not change their rates and contract carriers may not reduce their minima except on 30 days' notice. The Commission may consider the lawfulness of any new rate or schedule. For common carriers it may determine the lawful rate or charge, or the maximum or minimum, or maximum and minimum thereafter to be charged; it may also establish through routes and prescribe lawful through rates and divisions of through rates between carriers by water or between water and railroad carriers. In the case of contract carriers the Commission may prescribe the minimum charge, but the minimum must give no undue advantage to contract carriers in competition with common carriers by water subject to Part III. Rates may be disapproved either because they are unreasonable or because they are discriminatory. They may be suspended but not for a period which exceeds 7 months. In the case of a through route where one of the carriers is a common carrier by water, the Commission is directed to prescribe such reasonable differentials as it may find justified between all-rail rates and the joint rail-water routes which are set up. These clauses do not differ essentially from the provisions of the Interstate Commerce Act, Part II, except for the reference to dif-

[52] 250 I.C.C. 194, 1942; 260 I.C.C. 5, 1943.
[53] 250 I.C.C. 85, 1941; 260 I.C.C. 39, 1943.
[54] 250 I.C.C. 113, 1941.
[55] 250 I.C.C. 26, 1941; 250 I.C.C. 57, 1941; 260 I.C.C. 355, 1944.

ferentials and some difference in the authority given to the Commission in fixing through rates. They enlarge the power which the Commission exercised before 1940, principally by grant of the authority to fix a specific water rate.[56]

RATE MAKING RULE. The rate making rule which binds the Commission in regulating the rates of water carriers is substantially the same as that applied to railroads and motor carriers. There is, however, no special reference to the "inherent advantages of transportation by water." The tests are (1) the effect of rates upon the movement of traffic by the carrier or carriers for which the rates are prescribed; (2) the need, in the public interest, of adequate and efficient transportation service by such carriers at the lowest cost consistent with such service; and (3) the need of revenues sufficient to enable carriers, under honest, economical, and efficient management, to provide such service. As with motor carriers, the Commission is forbidden, in practice, to consider good will, earning power, or the value of an operating certificate in determining the reasonableness of a water rate.

RELATIVE RAIL AND WATER RATES. The rate responsibilities of the Commission extend to common carrier transportation on the Great Lakes, to intercoastal and coastal water transport, and to water carriage upon the Mississippi River and its tributaries. Between 1940 and the present time, however, Great Lakes shipments have been mainly withdrawn from Commission regulation by the operation of exemptions in Part III of the Interstate Commerce Act and more than half of the companies operating upon the Mississippi River are private carriers not subject to the statute. Although the operating costs of regulated carriers have risen the Commission is hampered by its limited jurisdiction and by railroad competition. Most rate complaints under these conditions are brought by water carriers, not by shippers; they are directed to the relationships between rail and water rates, and they are adjusted by the exercise of the Commission's powers under Part I as well by the use of authority conveyed

---

[56] The clauses in Part III of the Interstate Commerce Act which give the Commission authority over through routes and rates are supplemented by provisions in Part I. Thus Sec. 6 (11) gives the Commission power to establish physical connections between, and proportional rates upon traffic handled by rail and water carriers; and Sec. 1 (4) authorizes the Commission to fix through rates.

Parts I and III may, sometimes, overlap. Thus Part I applies to joint rail-water traffic which, under certain circumstances would be exempt under Part III. In such a case the Commission would exercise jurisdiction. The pertinent clause of the statute is Sec. 303 (a), which reads as follows: "In the case of transportation which is subject both to this part and Part I, the provisions of Part I shall apply only to the extent that Part I imposes, with respect to such transportation, requirements not imposed by the provisions of this part." The situation is not dissimilar from that which arises with respect to motor carriage under Sections 202 (c) and 203 (a) (14) of the Motor Carrier Act.

by Part III of the Interstate Commerce Act.[57] The general rate regulatory powers of the Commission over water transportation have been of some, but not major direct importance. But this is not true of certain special situations, including that which concerns rail-barge relationships upon the Mississippi River.

SPECIAL PROBLEMS UPON THE MISSISSIPPI. There is active competition between rail and water transport in the Mississippi River area. This competition arises in three types of cases:

1. *Local movements between ports on the Mississippi River.* The water route is usually circuitous, and it is frequently more expensive to operate than is direct railroad service.[58] Barge rates are nevertheless systematically lower than railroad rates and were so established before the Commission, in 1940, received the power of control. The typical differential has been 20 percent, based upon competition and upon the lower quality of river service and the extra costs which shippers have to bear.[59] The differential has been fortified by the fact that Congress has committed itself, by liberal appropriations and by direct legislation, to the development of river navigation. It was changed somewhat in amount by the Interstate Commerce Commission in 1948.

2. *Through movements under through rates, using both rail and river transport, but beginning or ending or beginning and ending at a point not accessible to river transportation.* In this case the total rail-barge or rail-barge-rail rate from point of origin to destination is made less than the all-rail rate by deducting the river differential on the river portion of the haul.[60] Railroads object to the practice because it diverts traffic that would otherwise move all-rail and because it is not justified by differences in

---

[57] The postwar condition of water carriers in the United States was usefully analyzed in a Senate report in 1950. See *Merchant Marine Study and Investigation*, Final Report pursuant to S. Res. 50, 81st C., 2d S., Sen. Rep. 2494, pp. 14, 86, 1950.

[58] 270 I.C.C. 591, 606, 1948. See also chap. 34.

[59] The original 20 percent barge-rail differential basis was established in 1919 by the United States Railroad Administration. It later was followed by the Interstate Commerce Commission in a long series of decisions fixing differentials between rail and barge-line rates. By 1946 these were, generally, 20 or 10 percent, depending upon the rail distance beyond the interchange port involved in the barge-rail haul.

Extra costs to shippers in river transport include insurance and excess time in transit. In through hauls requiring both rail and water service there may be also costs of interchange and risks of breakage which would not be equally encountered upon an all-rail route. (See *Problems in the Regulation of Domestic Transportation, op. cit.*, p. 463.)

[60] An example of the application of a 20 percent river differential to a joint through rate would be as follows:

Suppose the all-rail first-class rate from St. Louis to New Orleans to be $1.125. Using a 20 percent differential, the barge rate would then be set at 90 cents, or 22.5 cents less than the all-rail rate between the ports. If the all-rail first-class rate from Chicago to New Orleans were $1.375, then the joint rail-barge rate from Chicago to New Orleans via St. Louis would be 22.5 cents less than the all-rail rate, or $1.15, because of the low barge component.

operating expense. The Interstate Commerce Commission has, however, approved joint rates which are built around a low-priced water segment because it considers the policy to be consistent with the Congressional policy of developing water transportation, whatever may be the facts regarding cost.

Low rail-water rates are accepted as necessary because of the inferior attractiveness of the water service.[61]

3. *Rail-river transportation which employs the device of a "proportional" rate.* This can be an alternative to a through rate with transit or stopover privileges. A railroad quotes a proportional rate when it distinguishes between outbound shipments from a given point which have originated at that point and outbound shipments which have originated elsewhere and pass through the point on their way to a more distant destination. In the first case the rail carrier applies a local and in the second case a lower proportional rate upon the outbound movement. Thus a railroad may quote a local rate on grain from Cincinnati to Southern cities, applicable to shipments which have originated in Cincinnati, and a lower proportional rate on outbound shipments from Cincinnati which have originated in some other town. The purpose is to permit shippers to unload, store, or process goods at Cincinnati, en route, without sacrificing the rate advantage which they would normally secure by an uninterrupted haul. Most proportional rates assume an inbound railroad movement. The inbound carriage to a river port may, however, occur by barge. In this case the connecting railroad may or may not quote a proportional rate on the outbound shipment, and the proportional rate, when quoted, may or may not be the same as the charge which follows an

---

[61] 71 Sup. Ct. Rep. 264, 1951. The Commission has suggested, without requiring it, that the revenue from joint river-rail rates should be divided between the participating carriers on a rate-pro-rate basis. The following calculation illustrates the principle of a rate-pro-rate division:

Let us suppose a haul from Memphis, Tenn., to Fargo, N.D., of which the part from Memphis to Twin Cities is by barge and that from Twin Cities to Fargo is by rail. Suppose the following rates: (1) through rail-barge rate, Memphis to Fargo, 231 cents; (2) local barge rate, Memphis to Twin Cities, 178 cents; (3) local rail rate, Twin Cities to Fargo, 119 cents. On these assumptions, the local barge rate from Memphis to Twin Cities would be approximately 60 percent of the sum of the local rail and water rates, and the barge line would, therefore, be assigned this percentage of the through rate of 231 cents between Memphis and Fargo as a division, or 138 cents. The rail division would be 93 cents.

In the *Rail and Barge Joint Rates* decision of 1948 (270 I.C.C. 591, 620, 1948) the Commission further proposed that the share of the barge line should be reduced by 1 cent because it was more expensive to transfer freight from rail to barge than it would have been to transfer freight from one railroad car to another upon an all-rail haul. If this were done, the divisions would become 137 and 94. This would seem fair under the circumstances, as it throws the burden of the differential upon the water lines which profit most. The alternative of a mileage-pro-rate would allow the barge lines to profit by the windings of the Mississippi River—a result which ought not to be allowed.

inbound railroad haul. Railroads have discriminated against barge lines in these matters; a good deal of controversy has been the natural result.[62]

GENERAL ATTITUDE OF THE COMMISSION TOWARD WATER RATES. The following principles may be derived from the rate decisions of the Interstate Commerce Commission:

1. Water carriers should participate with railroad carriers in the general rate increases which the Commission has approved in postwar years. The Commission has taken notice of the unfavorable prewar financial condition of coastwise water lines, of the large expenditures necessary to replace or recondition vessels requisitioned for war service, and of the increased ship operating and terminal costs due to increased wages and improved working conditions of employees.[63]

2. Water carriers should also be permitted to reduce particular rates in order to recover traffic lost to railroad lines if the lower rates can be shown to cover costs.[64]

[62] It is the contention of the barge lines that ex-barge grain, e.g., forwarded from a river port, should pay the same rate as grain which has reached the port by rail to the same ultimate destination. The railroads reply that the outbound movement from a river port is, essentially, the balance of a through haul. They argue also that the total distance covered by shipments which reach a river port by rail is characteristically longer than that covered by that which comes by barge and they conclude that the outbound rail rate may be lower in the former case, reflecting the lower overall costs of longer as compared with shorter movements, even though the distances from the intermediate river port to final destination may, in both instances, be the same. The problem is not, directly, one of barge line rates, but it is evident that the barge lines and their customers are seriously involved.

The Interstate Commerce Commission has discussed ex-barge proportional rates in a number of cases (246 I.C.C. 353, 1941; 248 I.C.C. 307, 1941; 259 I.C.C. 629, 670, 1945; 262 I.C.C. 7, 1945; 270 I.C.C. 713, 1948). Its present position is controlled by the Supreme Court decision in the *Mechelen Barge Line* case (330 U.S. 567, 1947). In this litigation the Court declared that the railroads from Chicago to the East could not lawfully charge more for carrying ex-barge than for carrying ex-rail grain to identical destinations unless it could be shown that the railroad incurred a greater cost.

The Supreme Court said, in the Mechelen case: "The basic error of the Commission here is that it seemed to act on the assumption that the congressional prohibitions of railroad rate discrimination against water carriers were not applicable to such discrimination if accomplished by through rates. But the assumption would permit the destruction or curtailment of the advantage to shippers of cheap barge transportation whenever the transported goods were carried beyond the end of the barge line. This case proves that. For while Chicago is a great grain center, it cannot consume all barge-transported grain. That grain, like other grain coming to Chicago for marketing or processing, is reshipped to distant destinations. To penalize its transportation in barges by charging discriminatory rates from Chicago to its final destination has precisely the same consequence as would follow from raising barge rates inbound to Chicago. Recognizing that it could not require these barge carriers to raise these inbound rates which it accepted as reasonable, the Commission has here approved an order which would bring about the same prohibited result by raising the railroad rate charged by eastern roads for ex-barge grain shipments east from Chicago. Congress has forbidden this" (*vide supra*).

[63] 264 I.C.C. 695, 1946. See also 266 I.C.C. 537, 614, 1946; 268 I.C.C. 567, 1947; 269 I.C.C. 33, 1947; 270 I.C.C. 93, 101, 1948; 270 I.C.C. 403, 447, 462, 1948.

[64] An example of this practice occurred on the Mississippi River in 1948 when the

3. The Commission will improve the relationship of water to railroad rates in certain instances by refusing to permit railroads to meet competitive water rates at water terminals without corresponding reductions at intermediate destinations.[65]

4. The Commission will even refuse to allow a railroad to increase rates to a river terminal when this increase will divert traffic upon which water lines rely. This is because the destruction of rail-barge movements does not conform to the national transportation policy.[66]

5. But it is not clear to the Commission that water costs, in general, are now lower than the costs of transportation by rail carriers.[67]

6. And the Commission will not require railroads to install increased rates constructed on a basis higher than competing water rates in the absence of a showing that the existing railroad rates are unreasonably low,[68] or for the purpose of permitting water lines to share in traffic.[69] This last decision, in particular, is a disappointment to the water lines—a disappointment which they have vigorously expressed.

Discrimination

The Interstate Commerce Act forbids water common carriers to give unreasonable preference to any particular person or to collect from anyone a compensation different from the published rate. The exceptions set forth

---

Federal Barge Lines proposed to reduce their rate on cotton from 48.2 cents to 24 cents per 100 pounds from Memphis to New Orleans, on a minimum of 50,000 pounds, in an attempt to recover cotton traffic which had been almost entirely transferred to the railroad lines. The suggested rate seemed certain to cover out-of-pocket cost and probably fully allocated cost, although there was some difference of opinion on this point (273 I.C.C. 337, 1948).

[65] 268 I.C.C. 515, 1947.

[66] 274 I.C.C. 637, 670, 1949.

[67] The Commission considered this matter at some length in the Increased Freight Rate case of 1947 and reached the following conclusion (270 I.C.C. 403, 444, 1947):

"Recent large increases in water carrier costs, coupled with difficulties experienced by some branches of the industry in restoring services interrupted by the war, have caused reversal of the competitive position of water and rail carriers. This reversal is, of course, the basis of the problems we now face in adjusting rail and water rates with due regard for the rights of both rail and water carriers and for our responsibilities to the public."

[68] 268 I.C.C. 515, 1947. The Commission said, in this case (p. 536): "The fact that water carriage under the rates of June 30, 1946, was not a profitable business does not of itself make successively increased sums based on such rates a proper criterion for the prescription of the minimum rates of competing carriers."

[69] 266 I.C.C. 624, 635, 1946. The Maritime Commission and the War Shipping Administration petitioned the Interstate Commerce Commission, in 1946, to readjust transcontinental railroad rates so that intercoastal shipping rates might be advanced (268 I.C.C. 567, 569, 1946). The railroads subsequently requested and the Commission approved some advances in transcontinental rates, but not to protect the water lines. The Commission expressed the opinion, instead, that railroad rate structures must be worked out primarily in terms of rail transportation (United States Interstate Commerce Commission, *Annual Report,* 1948, p. 51).

in Part I apply also to water carriers. Tariff rates must be collected when freight is delivered, subject to rules governing the granting of credit which the Commission prescribes.

The language in Part III which deals with local discrimination is identical with that in Part I. Greater rates for shorter than for longer hauls are made illegal except when the Commission has approved. There is no mention of farm commodities, but a special section makes it unlawful for a common carrier by water to attempt to prevent any other such carriers from extending service to any publicly owned terminal located on any improvement project authorized by Congress at the same rates which it charges at its nearest regular port of call. There is also an important section in the statute which directs all common carriers by water to afford all reasonable, proper, and equal facilities for the interchange of traffic with other water and with railroad lines and requires that these carriers shall not discriminate between their connections in their rates, fares, and charges, or unduly prejudice any connecting line in the distribution of traffic which is not specifically routed by the shipper. This is the counterpart of an identical section in Part I, addressed to railroad carriers.

Few cases of personal or of local discrimination in the usual sense have reached the Commission.[70] The question of interchange and the allied problem of relative rail and river rates has, however, been important, especially in the case of water carriers upon and railroad lines reaching the Mississippi River.[71]

Securities

The Interstate Commerce Commission has no power to regulate the issue of securities by companies engaged in inland water transportation.

Summary

The Interstate Commerce Commission has authority to regulate inland

[70] But see 251 I.C.C. 217, 1942, in which a shipper complained of improper allocation of loading space for his cargo. There have also been some, although not many, charges of local discrimination including cases where there has been departure from the rule of Section 4 (Long and Short Haul Clause). Thus, in 1947, the rail-barge rate on iron and steel from Chicago to Houston via New Orleans was 2 cents less than the rail rate from Chicago to New Orleans—a clear departure from the rule which the Commission nevertheless approved (268 I.C.C. 439, 1947). See also the decisions in 264 I.C.C. 551, 1946.

[71] A relatively simple case concerning interchange was brought by the Seatrain lines and reached the Supreme Court in 1945. The question was whether the Commission could direct a railroad to allow the Seatrain Company to receive and carry railroad cars. The Supreme Court held in the affirmative (323 U.S. 612, 1945). Equally simple was a complaint that railroads were imposing a rail switching charge of $23.44 on ex-barge traffic at Knoxville, on the Mississippi, instead of the charge of $9.38 which was applied to ex-rail traffic. The Commission held in this instance that the difference was reasonable (274 I.C.C. 195, 1949).

water transportation which resembles its power to regulate railroad and motor carriage. This might be inferred without detailed comparison, from the fact that the water clauses form a part of the inclusive Interstate Commerce Act. Its regulation is, however, relatively ineffective for two major reasons. The first reason is that the exemptions from Commission control are numerous and important. The second is that water transport, especially on the Mississippi but to a large extent upon the Great Lakes and in intercoastal commerce also, competes actively with rail and motor carriage. This is so evident that the functions of the Commission have been largely protective in its relations with water transport; and its regulation of rail and motor carriers has, probably, been more effective in directing and developing water service than has its regulation of the water carriers themselves. The reader is referred, in this connection, to the appendix to the present chapter.

APPENDIX TO CHAPTER 32

The History of Inland Waterway Regulation

The following account presents details of the development of Inland Waterway Regulation which, for certain purposes, are important.

The first Board provided by Congress was the Shipping Board, set up in 1916. As stated in the text, this Board was enlarged in 1920, and in 1936 it was succeeded by the Maritime Commission. The Shipping Board, in 1916, consisted of five members, appointed by the President for terms of 6 years at salaries of $7,500. Under the Merchant Marine Act of 1920 it became a body of seven members appointed by the President for terms of 6 years at salaries of $12,000. The Maritime Commission, authorized in 1936, was again a commission of five members, appointed for 6 years; but the salary rate of $12,000 was continued. These agencies possessed regulatory powers although they were not set up, primarily, for regulation. These powers included the following:

1. Under the Act of 1916, common carriers engaged in interstate commerce on the high seas or on the Great Lakes were directed to file and to publish maximum rates (39 Stat. 728, 1916). This requirement covered coastal and intercoastal but not river traffic. In 1933, common carriers by water engaged in intercoastal commerce by way of the Panama Canal (47 Stat. 1,425, 1933) and in 1938 all common carriers by water in interstate commerce as defined in the Act of 1916 were compelled to file and publish the actual rates charged—a change of considerable importance.

2. The Act of 1916 did not give authority to the Shipping Board to fix specific rates, and the Act of 1933 specifically denied this power. In 1938,

rates and their relation to each other. It also occasionally discussed the reasonableness of joint rates to which river steamships were parties.

The Commission also considered cases before 1940, where the through rate to final destination on a joint water-rail haul was less than the rate to some intermediate point. Section 4 of the Interstate Commerce Act applied to such instances as it did to similar situations presented by all-rail hauls. Rates which were quoted in 1937 from New York to Southern points by way of New Orleans may serve as an illustration. Evidence before the Commission in these cases showed that water carriers which operated between New York and New Orleans met the competition of direct railroad lines between these points. No conflict with Section 4 was in so far involved. Rail rates from New York to New Orleans increased on southbound movements as shipments proceeded farther and farther from New York. The highest rail rate was that to New Orleans. Lower rail rates were charged to destinations north of that city. When carriers on the water route desired to handle freight consigned to points north of New Orleans, they found it necessary to quote rates, in connection with their rail connections, to these points, and to make these rates, which were less than the rates charged for delivery at New Orleans itself. They charged, that is to say, less for a longer than for a shorter haul. It is curious that the Interstate Commerce Commission approved this type of rate making when proposed by the water lines in the New Orleans and in other cases, on the ground of competitive necessity (123 I.C.C. 203, 1927; 204 I.C.C. 460, 1934; 218 I.C.C. 1936; 220 I.C.C. 1, 1937; 220 I.C.C. 456, 1937), in spite of its critical attitude in Southern cases where only the needs of railroads were involved.

The Commission was on familiar ground in dealing with questions raised in the two preceding paragraphs in this note. It was forced, indeed, to regulate rail-and-water shipments with respect to rate relationships consistently with its action with reference to all-rail carriage—or to do this, at least, in most cases—if any considered policy of relative transportation charges was to be enforced.

3. *Physical connection.* The Panama Canal Act of 1912 (37 Stat. 580, 568, 1912), as amended by the general statute of 1920 (41 Stat. 456, 483, 1920), vested in the Interstate Commerce Commission the authority to require a physical connection to be established between the lines of a rail and those of a water carrier. The language of the Act of 1920 on this point was as follows:

"To establish physical connection between the lines of the rail carrier and the dock at which interchange of passengers and property is to be made by directing the rail carrier to make suitable connection between its line and a track or tracks which have been constructed from the dock to the limits of the railroad right of way, or by directing either or both the rail or water carrier, individually, or in connection with one another, to construct and connect with the line of the rail carrier a track or tracks to the dock. The Commission shall have full authority to determine and prescribe the terms and conditions upon which these connecting tracks shall be operated, and it may, either in the construction or the operation of such tracks, determine what sum shall be paid to or by either carrier: *Provided,* That construction required by the Commission under the provisions of this paragraph shall be subject to the same restrictions as to findings of public convenience and necessity and other matters as is construction required under section 1 of this Act."

Power to require a physical connection enabled the Commission to force rail and water carriers to create conditions which would make it possible to transport "under a common control." It is to be observed that the exercise of this power did not depend upon complaint by a water company which desired to interchange traffic. Nor was the Commission's jurisdiction limited to cases where rail and water companies had previously operated under common control. Thus the State of New York was able to obtain an order directing the New York Central Railroad to operate a connection with the State Barge Canal (95 I.C.C. 119, 1924; 272 U.S. 457, 1926).

Jurisdiction over through routes and rates permitted the Commission to require use of the necessary facilities. As a matter of fact, the Commission's power to require physical connections has been little used, although it is potentially important.

4. *Railroad-controlled water carriers.* The Panama Canal Act of 1912 also enabled the Interstate Commerce Commission to control water carriers in ways which have not yet been mentioned. This statute made it unlawful for any railroad or other common carrier subject to the Act to Regulate Commerce to own, lease, operate, control, or have any interest whatever in any common carrier by water with which it did or might compete except on a favorable Commission finding. If this finding was secured, the interest might continue; but in this case the rates, schedules, and practices of the water carrier must be filed with the Commission and the water carrier became subject to the Act to Regulate Commerce in the same manner and to the same extent, with respect to rates, schedules, and practices, as were the railroads controlling the water carrier or interested in its operations (37 Stat. 560, 566–567, 1912, Sec. 11; 54 Stat. 909, 1940).

The Commission was active in discharging the responsibilities which this law imposed. In many cases, it compelled railroads to surrender control over ocean, lake, or river lines. In other instances, the Commission found that rail-controlled water service was being operated in the interests of the public and was of advantage to the convenience and commerce of the people. It found also, in these last cases, that continuance of rail control would not exclude, prevent, or reduce competition upon the route which was under consideration. This finding made, the Commission thereafter regulated the rates, schedules, and practices of the controlled water line as it regulated the rates, schedules, and practices of the controlling railroad (43 I.C.C. 168, 1917; 45 I.C.C. 505, 1947; 206 I.C.C. 427, 1935; 195 I.C.C. 215, 1933; 206 I.C.C. 328, 1935).

5. *Localized rate reductions.* The clause in the Interstate Commerce Act which attempts to prevent specialized and temporary reductions in railroad rates for the purpose of destroying competing water carriers may be included in this list of Commission powers, although it does not apply to the water

carriers themselves. The clause, adopted in 1910 (36 Stat. 539, 548, 1910), reads as follows:

"Wherever a carrier by railroad shall in competition with a water route or routes reduce the rates on the carriage of any species of freight to or from competitive points, it shall not be permitted to increase such rates unless after hearing by the Interstate Commerce Commission it shall be found that such proposed increase rests upon changed conditions other than the elimination of water competition."

In actual practice, the clause has proved unnecessary, especially since 1920, when the Interstate Commerce Commission received authority to fix a minimum railroad rate. Moreover, the difficulties inherent in its application have been so great that the courts and the Commission have failed to enforce it on several separate grounds.

In the first place, the Interstate Commerce Commission has pointed out that the primary purpose of the law itself is to encourage water competition. This being the case, the carriers are rather to be encouraged to raise their rates at competitive points than to continue them upon a level that makes the competition of boat lines impossible. It follows that a railroad which has reduced its rates at certain stations to destroy a competing water service should be urged to raise them, not prevented from ever doing so.

The Interstate Commerce Commission has also held that rail carriers not only are not required, but are forbidden, to continue low rates to points which have once enjoyed water competition when the competition has ceased, unless, indeed, they reduce their rates to other points so as to preserve a proper relationship, for the continuance of low rates under such conditions produced a discrimination which the Act to Regulate Commerce makes unlawful (40 I.C.C. 35, 1916).

Finally, the United States Supreme Court has ruled that carriers which quoted lower rates to water competitive points than to intermediate destinations with the approval of the Commission may subsequently raise these rates when water competition disappears, in spite of the section now under discussion, because the law does not apply to reduction made under Commission authority (249 U.S. 557, 568, 1919). The result of these various arguments and interpretations has been that the particular piece of legislation just described has proved of negligible importance.

This concludes the enumeration of powers conferred upon maritime boards and upon the Interstate Commerce Commission, before 1940, for the purpose of inland waterway regulation. Of these, the Commission retained its old authority after the new statute had been passed. The Maritime Commission transferred its authority over inland waterways to the Commission. After 1940, therefore, the Interstate Commerce Commission exercised: (1) the powers which it had earlier received; (2) the authority transferred in so far as this was not qualified or withdrawn by the new legislation; and (3) whatever additional authority the Act of 1940 supplied. It is helpful to regard the present situation from this point of view. This is, partly, because a review of legislation calls attention to jurisdiction which the Interstate Commerce Commission has possessed as collateral to its railroad work. An analysis only of the

Act of 1940 might neglect these powers. And it is also true that some clauses in the present law, which relate to authority which has been transferred, require a knowledge of origins before their meaning can be fully understood.

R E F E R E N C E S

General Treatises

Bingham, Truman C., and Roberts, Merrill J., *Transportation, Principles and Problems,* New York, McGraw-Hill, 1952.

Fair, Marvin L., and Williams, Ernest W., *Economics of Transportation,* New York, Harper, 1950.

Johnson, E. R., *Transport Facilities, Services, and Policies,* New York, Appleton-Century-Crofts, 1947.

Locklin, D. Philip, *Economics of Transportation,* Chicago, Irwin, 1947.

Westmeyer, Russell E., *Economics of Transportation,* New York, Prentice-Hall, 1952.

Other Books

Johnson, E. R., *Government Regulation of Transportation,* New York, Appleton-Century-Crofts, 1938.

Sharfman, I. L., *The Interstate Commerce Commission,* Part II, New York, Commonwealth Fund, 1931.

Periodicals

Zoll, E. J., "The Development of Federal Regulatory Control over Water Carriers," *Interstate Commerce Commission Practitioners' Journal,* Vol. 12, pp. 552–576, 1945.

Special and Miscellaneous

National Resources Planning Board, *Transportation and National Policy,* Part II, section II, *Coastwise, Intercoastal and Great Lakes Shipping,* prepared by the Division of Economics and Statistics, United States Maritime Commission, 1942.

United States House of Representatives, Committee on Merchant Marine and Fisheries, Hearing on H. R. 4307, 76th C., 1st S., 1939.

United States Interstate Commerce Commission, Bureau of Transport Economics and Statistics, *Problems in the Regulation of Domestic Transportation by Water,* Ex Parte no. 165, 1946, Appendix A, prepared by C. S. Morgan, Chief Carrier Research Analyst.

United States, Office of the Federal Coordinator of Transportation, *Regulation of Transportation Agencies,* 73d C., 2d S., Sen. Doc. 152, 1934.

United States Senate, Committee on Interstate and Foreign Commerce, Subcommittee on Domestic Land and Water Transportation, Hearings pursuant to Sen. Res. 50, 81st C., 2d S., 1950.

United States Senate, Committee on Interstate and Foreign Commerce, *Merchant Marine Study and Investigation.* Final Report pursuant to Sen. Res. 50, 81st C., 2d S., Report no. 2494, 1950.

Air Regulation

Federal Regulation of Air Transport

The earliest federal connection with air transportation occurred through the Post Office. The first general federal statute was, however, passed in 1926.

Act of 1926

The federal Act of 1926 declared it to be the duty of the Secretary of Commerce to foster air commerce. His immediate obligation was to investigate; but he was also authorized to establish civil airways within the limits of available appropriations. Beyond this, and principally, he was empowered to provide, by regulation, for the registration and rating of aircraft, and for the examination and rating of airmen and of air navigation facilities; he was, further, to establish traffic rules. An amendment in 1934 directed him to provide for the rating of airlines as well as for that of aircraft and airmen.[1] The statute met an obvious need for adequate and uniform safety regulation.

Air Mail Acts of 1934 and 1935

By 1934 it had seemed desirable to regularize the contacts between the Post Office and air companies. This was done through the Air Mail Acts of 1934 and 1935.[2]

These acts gave to the Postmaster General authority to prescribe the number and frequency of air-mail schedules, the intermediate regular stops, and the times of departure of all planes carrying air mail. He was empowered to prescribe a system of accounts for ail-mail contractors. The Secretary of Commerce, under the new statutes, was to determine the speed, load capacity, safety features and safety devices that were to be used in mail carriage. He was directed to prescribe maximum flying hours

[1] 44 Stat. 568, 1926; 48 Stat. 1113, 1934.
[2] 48 Stat. 933, 1934; 49 Stat. 612, 1935.

713

of pilots and safe methods for operation in the case of air-mail lines. The Interstate Commerce Commission was to fix rates for mail transportation, within limits which the law laid down. In common with the Post Office Department the Commission had the right to examine and to audit the books of air-mail contractors. When the Commission conducted an audit it was required to render a full report to the Post Office within 30 days; this report was to specify all instances in which the contractor had failed to comply with provisions of the uniform system of accounts which the Post Office Department had prescribed.[3]

The Acts of 1934 and 1935 supplemented the Act of 1926, but only with respect to one particular type of airplane service.[4]

Defects in the System of Air Carrier Control

The legislation between 1926 and 1935 accomplished a beginning in air regulation, but it was defective in several ways.

1. Authority was vested in too many supervisory organizations.

2. The system did not provide for the regulation of nonmail carriers except with respect to labor conditions and the safety of air operation.

3. Existing statutes made no provision for the control of rates for air passenger and air express, and there was no requirement that air companies proposing to serve as common carriers should demonstrate that public convenience and necessity justified their entrance into the common carrier field.

These and other weaknesses aroused little general public interest. Representatives of the air industry declared, however, that the result of governmental inaction was unbridled competition between air lines, insufficient earnings, and impending financial collapse. According to the president of the Air Transport Association of America, which represented 99 percent

---

[3] The law was objectionable in this last respect because it required one agency of the government to police carriers, accounts, and business transactions prescribed by another agency. The Civil Aeronautics Act of 1938 put an end to this division of responsibility.

[4] The Acts of 1934 and 1935, along with some other legislation, had provisions which affected airline labor. This legislation was complicated. The provisions of the Act of 1934 gave to the Secretary of Commerce authority to prescribe maximum flying hours of pilots on air-mail lines. The same law declared that rates of pay and working conditions of persons employed by air-mail contractors must conform to standards set by the National Labor Board. In 1936 an amendment to the Railway Labor Act of 1926 applied the provisions of this act to common carriers by air engaged in interstate commerce and to carriers transporting mail (48 Stat. 1189, 1936). This extended the jurisdiction of the National Mediation Board, created by the Railway Labor Act, to the adjustment of labor disputes in airline service. These various grants of authority caused confusion, especially with respect to the relative jurisdiction of the National Labor Board and the National Mediation Board; for it could be argued that the Railway Labor Act, as amended in 1936, substituted the processes of collective bargaining for the power of regulation which the National Labor Board had possessed under air-mail legislation. The cancellation of air-mail contracts and the passage of the Civil Aeronautics Act of 1938 clarified the law in these matters.

of all flying done by scheduled air lines, $120 million of private capital
had been invested in air transport, of which $60 million had been lost.
Since the beginning, 100 scheduled lines had been organized, and of these
scarcely more than a score remained. The credit of the air carriers was
gone, just at the time when access to new supplies of money was critically
needed. Antitrust legislation prevented air carriers from agreeing among
themselves. The companies demanded, therefore, legislative restraint
which they were themselves unable to provide, and their complaints attracted congressional attention in due course.[5] The situation was curiously
unlike that which had provoked the extension of government control over
railroad operation, and it differed also from the conditions which had led
to water and motor carrier legislation. In one of these cases the shippers,
and in the other a competing type of carrier had asked for government
protection; the air carriers, on the other hand, asked for federal action
almost entirely to remedy the industry's internal ills.[6]

Civil Aeronautics Act of 1938

Recognized defects in existing statutes, the desire for some limitation of
competition, and the hope of government financial aid led, in 1938, to
the passage of legislation which controls commercial flying at the present
time. The last of the three reasons for federal action has proved the most
important. The statute may, nevertheless, be examined as a regulatory
law.[7]

Organization of Control

The Civil Aeronautics Act created three agencies called, respectively,
the Civil Aeronautics Authority, the Administrator, and the Air Safety
Board.[8] All three formed part of the same organization, but they had in

[5] United States House of Representatives, Committee on Interstate and Foreign
Commerce, Hearings on H. R. 9738, 75th C., 3d S., 1938, testimony Gorrell, pp. 298,
309, 338.

[6] 52 Stat. 973, 1938.

[7] 52 Stat. 973, 1938. See, in connection with the legislative history of the act, the report of the Federal Aviation Commission in 1935 (United States Senate, Doc. 15, 74th
C., 1st S., 1935) and congressional hearings during the 75th Congress on H. R. 9738
and S. 3845. See also Charles S. Rhyne, *The Civil Aeronautics Act Annotated*, Washington, D.C., National Law Book, 1939.

[8] It is a striking fact that the regulation of airplane operation was not, in 1938,
entrusted to the Interstate Commerce Commission. Mr. Eastman was in favor of this
assignment, and the President, at one time, supported the idea. The creation of a new
commission, in 1938, was apparently influenced by the following facts:
1. There was some desire, on the part of the air lines, for a special regulatory
   authority.
2. The new Commission was expected to regulate the safety of air operation. This
   would require, under the circumstances, the regulation of private flights. The Interstate Commerce Commission did not wish to be charged with responsibility for air
   private carriage.

each case, at the beginning, an independent existence. Of the three, the Civil Aeronautics Authority consisted of five members, appointed by the President of the United States for terms of 6 years at salaries of $12,000. In preliminary legislative discussions the House had proposed a board of three and the Senate one of five members; the latter's view prevailed. The Authority exercised general economic control. The Administrator was a single person, appointed by the President at a salary of $12,000 and holding office at the President's pleasure. He was charged with executive and promotional functions.[9] The Air Safety Board consisted of three members, appointed by the President for 6 years at salaries of $7,500. Its duties were confined to the study of accident prevention. It had no power except the power to investigate and to recommend. The establishment of such a board had been urged upon Congress by the Air Line Pilot's Association in 1938.[10]

The tripartite division of the Civil Aeronautics Administration under the Act of 1938 was due, insofar as the Air Safety Board was concerned,

---

3. It seemed desirable to concentrate the direction of airplanes engaged in foreign and airplanes engaged in domestic operations in one regulatory body. The Interstate Commerce Commission had exercised some jurisdiction over international surface transportation, but on a very modest scale.

4. The new Commission was to be assigned promotional duties of the first importance. This was a function which the Interstate Commerce Commission never had assumed except in a few particular cases under statutory instruction.

5. The sum of the duties and responsibilities outlined in the legislation might involve the organization which regulated air operations in relationships with the executive departments of the federal administration which the Interstate Commerce Commission preferred to avoid.

These matters are well discussed by Stuart G. Tipton, Acting Head, Air Transport Association of America, in *Prospects and Problems in Aviation,* published by the Chicago Association of Commerce, 1945.

[9] The duties of the Administrator, as set forth in the Civil Aeronautics Act of 1938, were—

1. To designate and establish civil airways;

2. To certify that projects for the construction of landing areas, with federal funds, or the construction and operation of navigation facilities in such areas were reasonably necessary for use in air commerce or that these projects were in the interest of national defense;

3. To recommend to the Secretary of Agriculture with respect to the provision of meteorological service;

4. To undertake or to supervise developmental work tending to the creation of improved air facilities and equipment;

5. To collect and disseminate information;

6. To make plans for the orderly development and location of landing areas, airways, and all other aids and facilities for air navigation.

Section 301 of the Civil Aeronautics Act provided general instruction in the following words:

"The Administrator is empowered and directed to encourage and foster the development of civil aeronautics and air commerce in the United States, and abroad, and to encourage the establishment of civil airways, landing areas, and other air navigation facilities. . . ."

[10] Hearings on H. R. 9738, *op. cit.,* testimony Behnke, p. 252.

to the desire of Congress to give the Safety Board an independent status for its own protection. Failure to do this, Congress believed, would check the free comment which the Board was expected to provide. The work of the Administrator might have been done by the Civil Aeronautics Authority itself, although there was some advantage in relieving a regulatory organization from administrative and promotional duties. The creation of a separate office in this case was intended to preserve the independence of the Authority. The principle upon which Congress acted was that the President could direct the personnel of a commission charged with executive duties, but that he lacked power to dismiss a member of a commission which had no executive responsibilities. It followed that the Authority must be stripped of executive functions in order to be safe. Hence the device of an Administrator, concededly subject to presidential removal, to whom were assigned those activities, which, if exercised by the Authority, might have placed that body under presidential control. The division of work which the law prescribed might have been defended from the point of view of sound administrative organization; actually, it was inspired by a distrust of the influence of the President and by the wish to maintain congressional prestige.

Presidential Reorganization of 1940

The organization set up in 1938 is to be explained by the reasoning described in the preceding paragraph. Unfortunately for the congressional intent, this somewhat cumbrous machinery attracted the attention of a President who wished to simplify departmental organization and who disliked extradepartmental tribunals which were outside his jurisdiction. It happened also that the President had been granted, in 1939, extensive powers to consolidate and to transfer functions of government agencies which he could use in the given case.[11]

In the exercise of his authority under last-mentioned powers, the Executive presently issued two orders.[12] The first of these transferred the general licensing powers of the Civil Aeronautics Authority to the Administrator. While the Authority was still to prescribe general rules, and while it was to continue to consider applications for certificates of convenience and necessity, the Administrator, now to be known as the Administrator of Civil Aeronautics, was made responsible for the issue and recordation of certificates of registration to owners of aircraft, for the issue of airman certificates to airmen, and of airworthiness certificates for aircraft, engines, propellers, and appliances. The Administrator was also

[11] 53 Stat. 561, 1939.
[12] 54 Stat. 1231, 1235, 1939; House Doc. 681, 76th C., 3d S., 1940.

to perform functions previously vested in the Civil Aeronautics Authority by the Civilian Pilot Training Act of 1939; [13] and he had certain minor duties in connection with the alteration of structures along or near civil airways in the interest of safety in air commerce. The powers and functions assigned to the Administrator under this order have since been further enlarged by laws passed in 1946 [14] and in 1948.[15]

The second order did two things. In the first place, it eliminated the Air Safety Board as a separate organization, transferring its duties to the Civil Aeronautics Authority, now renamed the Civil Aeronautics Board; and in the second place, it transferred both the Administrator of Civil Aeronautics and the Civil Aeronautics Board to the Department of Commerce.[16] Here the Administrator was to perform his functions under the direction and supervision of the Secretary of Commerce. The Civil Aeronautics Board was to exercise its functions of rule-making (including the prescription of rules, regulations, and standards), adjudication, and investigation, independently of the Secretary of Commerce; but its budgeting, accounting, personnel, procurement, and related routine management functions were to be performed under the Secretary's direction and supervision through such facilities as the Secretary might designate or establish.

Reorganization Plan No. 13

The last change in the organization of the Civil Aeronautics Board, up to the present writing, occurred in 1950 when the President transferred the executive and administrative functions of the Board [17] to its chairman. This was an improvement suggested by the Hoover Commission in 1949.[18]

[13] 53 Stat. 855, 1939.

[14] The Federal Airport Act of 1946 directed the Administrator to prepare an annual plan for the development of airports in the United States and gave him authority to approve or disapprove of projects which might be presented (60 Stat. 170, 1946. See chap. 24).

[15] The Act of 1948 authorized the Administrator to designate and to establish such civil airways as he might think were required in the public interest. He was given detailed powers to assist him in this undertaking (62 Stat. 1216, 1948).

[16] The term "Civil Aeronautics Authority" is still sometimes used to designate the entire organization, including both the Civil Aeronautics Board and the Administrator of Civil Aeronautics. But this is for convenience only.

[17] Including (1) the appointment and supervision of personnel employed under the Board, (2) the distribution of business among such personnel and among administrative units of the Board, and (3) the use and expenditure of funds (United States House of Representatives, 81st C., 2d S., House Doc. 517.

[18] See United States, Commission on Organization of the Executive Branch of the Government, *Independent Regulatory Commissions,* March, 1949. See also *ibid., Task Force Report on Regulatory Commissions,* Appendix N, January, 1949. The power to accomplish such a reorganization was conferred upon the President by the Reorganization Act of 1949 (63 Stat. 203, 1949).

Structure of Regulation

The administrative structure which now regulates air transport in the United States is that provided by the Civil Aeronautics Act of 1938 as altered by the Presidential orders of 1940 and 1950.[19] The terms of this act may be analyzed as follows:

Classification of Air Carriers

The Act applies to common carriers and to carriers of the mail, interstate and foreign. But safety regulations may be applied to contract and to private carriers. So much is routine, insofar as regulation is concerned, except that independent contract air carriers are not subject to economic control.[20]

---

[19] There is a good description and discussion of the procedure of the Civil Aeronautics Board and of the Administrator, under legislation up to 1941, in a monograph prepared by the so-called Attorney General's Committee on Administrative Procedure in 1941 (Administrative Procedure in Government Agencies, Monograph of the Attorney General's Committee on Administrative Procedure, Civil Aeronautics Authority, Sen. Doc. 10, 77th C., 1st S., Ser. 10,563, Part 6, 1941).

The Board's power to exercise economic control over air transport is conferred by the enabling act (52 Stat. 973, 1938), and the rules and procedures which it has approved appear in the Civil Air Regulations, subchap. B.

The Board has made an interesting attempt, in this connection, to separate its functions of adjudication and prosecution. For this purpose, the Board has set up a public counsel system under which attorneys from the Board's Bureau of Law appear in all major economic proceedings for the purpose of accomplishing an adequate record and exploring the public interest in the case. It has set up also an enforcement attorney whose duty it is to prosecute all violations of the economics provisions of the Civil Aeronautics Act and Board regulations. These officers are members of the Board's staff; but they are invested with complete independence of action during the proceedings in which they participate and are treated by the Board as counsel for the parties to the proceeding (Traffic World, September 24, 1949, p. 18, testimony Ryan).

[20] Most federal regulatory laws cover contract as well as common carriers, although the requirements are not the same in the two cases. The reader will have observed this in studying the various laws. The air statute does not cover air contract carriers as such; the only pertinent provision is that which permits certificated air common carriers to make charter trips under regulations prescribed by the Civil Aeronautics Authority (Sec. 401f).

The exemption of contract carriers may be explained by the fact that there were few air contract carriers in 1938; it may also have been that Congress wished to give the industry a maximum degree of flexibility in its organization. Conditions have changed, however, and there is some discontent with the existing gap in statutory control. Contract air carriers do not report to the Civil Aeronautics Board; they charge what they please and as they please; they choose between customers and between kinds of business; and they are adaptable in still other ways. Common air carriers, in particular, do not like this kind of competition. It was proposed, in 1948, to amend the existing law. The United States Department of Commerce and some other parties objected to the change, however, and nothing was done (United States House of Representatives, Committee on Interstate and Foreign Commerce, Interstate Contract Carriers by Air, Hearings on H. R. 6149, 80th C., 2d S., 1948; and United States Senate, Committee on Interstate and Foreign Commerce, Regulation of Interstate Contract Carriers by Air, Hearings before a subcommittee on S. 2449, 80th C., 2d S., 1948).

Exemptions

There are no exemptions mentioned in the Civil Aeronautics Act. The Board may, however, exempt air carriers from economic regulation, except for certain labor provisions of the Act.[21] The Board has exercised its power, especially with respect to what have been referred to as "non-scheduled carriers," and this has created difficulties.

NONSCHEDULED OR IRREGULAR OPERATIONS. At the beginning, in 1938, the Civil Aeronautics Board exempted carriers engaged in non-scheduled operations from most of the obligations of Title IV of the Civil Aeronautics Act.[22] This freed such carriers from the need of obtaining certificates, from rate control, and from economic regulation generally except for certain labor provisions and the duty of rendering reports.[23]

In 1938, the "nonscheduled" group consisted chiefly of small operators, engaged in air transport as a by-product of other services, such as aerial photography, advertising, crop dusting, and the like.[24]

Following the close of World War II, however, a number of returning pilots took advantage of the exemption. They bought planes, under veterans' priorities, organized companies, started operations, and acquired experience.[25] Their service developed rapidly and became more and more difficult to distinguish from the operations of standard lines. In fact, as business grew, the number of their flights increased and the casual character of their offerings disappeared. The volume which they attained has been previously described.[26] It included not only incidental transport but carriage for long distances, as from Los Angeles to New York, in large planes, with a high degree of frequency, accompanied by public advertising.[27] This was very different from the incidental service of so-called "fixed base" operators. It was selective, in the sense that it was usually restricted to large cities; it carried no mail and so received no subsidy; and it

---

[21] Sec. 416 (b) (1). "The Authority, from time to time and to the extent necessary, may . . . exempt from the requirement of this title or any provision thereof, or any rule, regulation . . . prescribed thereunder, any air carrier or class of air carriers, if it finds that the enforcement of this title or such provision, or such rule . . . is or would be an undue burden on such air carrier or class of air carriers and is not in the public interest."

[22] 3 Fed. Reg. 2886, 1938; *Code of Federal Regulations of the U.S.A.*, Cum. Suppl. Title 14, Sec. 292.1 (a).

[23] See George C. Neal, "The Status of Non-Scheduled Operations under the Civil Aeronautics Act of 1938," *Law and Contemporary Problems*, Winter-Spring, 1946, pp. 508–23.

[24] 6 C.A.B. 1049, 1946.

[25] United States Senate, Committee on Interstate and Foreign Commerce, *Air-Line Industry Investigation*, Hearings pursuant to S. Res. 50, 81st C., 1st S., testimonies Haney, Landis.

[26] See chap. 6.

[27] 6 C.A.B. 1049, 1946. See also *Air-Line Industry Investigation, op. cit.*, testimonies Fischgrund and Ramspeck.

offered less luxurious accommodations to passengers at cheaper rates and at lower costs. How far it stimulated new business and how far it diverted traffic from the standard lines was a subject of debate.

The standard lines objected to the operation of nonscheduled carriers because they thought that it was competitive and that it was unfair.[28] The growth and apparent success of the new carriers also disturbed the Civil Aeronautics Board, because it created a large volume of traffic outside of the Board's control. This threatened to interfere with the development of a planned air system such as the Board had in mind. There was also the possibility that nonscheduled operations would diminish the revenues of standard lines and so increase the annual subsidies which these lines would need.

Under these circumstances, the reaction of the Civil Aeronautics Board was (1) to revise the Board's existing regulations so as to clarify the restrictions under which nonscheduled air carriers were to operate, and (2) to conduct a campaign of enforcement against those carriers which seemed to be operating in violation of the law.

The campaign of enforcement took the form of notices to individual companies followed, when necessary, by orders to cease and desist.

The rule revision was in two parts:

1. In 1947 the Civil Aeronautics Board revised its regulations by recognizing a class of "cargo carriers" which was to be exempt from certification and from some other obligations pending the receipt of a standard certificate. The group was limited to only those carriers of property who, on May 5, 1947, had applications on file with the Board and were at that date actively engaged in the carriage of air cargo. The list originally included nine cargo lines. Of these, four were later awarded temporary certificates and the rest withdrew. In 1951 the number in operation was still four. All-cargo carriers transport no mail and receive no subsidy. They are still regarded as experimental.[29] Regularly certified air lines have also developed air cargo services, however, and the general practice may expand.[30]

2. At the same time the Board amended its orders by the substitution of the term "irregular" for that of "nonscheduled" carrier, by a more careful definition of the group which, under this name, were entitled to exemption, and by a new specification of the economic regulations from which the group was freed. These amendments were again altered, some-

---

[28] Their argument was that the standard lines were required (1) to serve a relatively large number of stations; (2) to furnish special services to the Post Office; and (3) to comply with burdensome safety regulations. It was contended that the irregular carriers were partly or entirely free from these obligations.

[29] The problem of the "air cargo carrier" was mentioned in chap. 6. Some of these carriers, prior to 1947, had operated as contract and some as nonscheduled carriers.

[30] See p. 109.

what, in 1949, especially by a requirement of individual exemption of large-scale irregular carriers which replaced the grant of general exemption to these carriers as a class, and by the subsequent association of restrictions with these individual exemptions. Letters of registration to irregular air lines were limited to cases where exemption, rather than certification, served the public interest. The result of this action was that some irregular carriers applied for exemption, a few sought temporary certificates, and many withdrew on the ground that they could not operate profitably upon the limited scale which was proposed. The Board's action was, later, carried to Congress. It is, currently, the subject for an elaborate reëxamination by the Board itself.[31]

[31] The definition of "irregular" air transportation can be made extremely elaborate. (See 14 C.F.R. 292, 1, 1949.) The last proposed revision was in 1950 (*Federal Register,* June 8, 1950, p. 3591), but the effective date of the action then taken was later postponed (*Federal Register,* July 4, 1951, p. 6503). Under the regulation in 1949 the test of regularity was periodic recurrence. Under the wording proposed in 1950 (for large irregular carriers) the test was frequency. Thus a large irregular carrier might not engage in more than a total of three flights during any period of four successive calendar weeks between New York and Chicago without forfeiting its status. The second basis was at least administratively feasible, the former probably was not. The difficulty in any definition of regularity is the time element. Successive items in a series which form part of a larger whole may, of course, be observed during a stated period of time. There may be sequences in the arrangement of these items during the period of observation which resemble each other. These sequences may seem to form a pattern and the periodic recurrence of the pattern may be assumed. Such behavior may be called "regular." But sequences which do not repeat themselves within the observed period may also form patterns when the observation is prolonged. As a matter of fact, irregularity, in the sense of purely random occurrence, is extremely rare with respect to actions which involve human relationships.

Irregular air carriers object to the "frequency" test. But they object because they think that regulation on this basis will put them out of business, not because the regulation cannot be interpreted or systematically applied. And they insist that their operations are in the public interest. In this they probably have more political support than have the Civil Aeronautics Board and the standard air lines. (For the C.A.B. point of view see 10 C.A.B. 486, 1949; C.A.B. Order E-4081, April 18, 1950; United States Senate, Committee on Interstate and Foreign Commerce, *Legislative Program and Statement of Policies of Civil Aeronautics Board,* 82d C., 1st S., 1951.)

The real controversy about irregular carriage turns then about the problem of regulatory control. With respect to this matter, distinction is made between smaller and larger carriers.

A small irregular carrier is one which utilizes equipment of less than 12,500 pounds. The Board believes that the small carriers render the equivalent of an air taxi service from points on air-line routes to communities which are not served by air transportation, or a similar service in the reverse direction. There are a great many of these small carriers. The Board is not disposed to restrict this service, even though it may be regularly supplied and no certificates may have been approved.

The large irregular carriers, utilizing equipment of 12,500 pounds or more, form the group which causes controversy. There were 61 large irregular carriers operating at the end of 1952, of which 5 accounted for 34 percent of the total revenues in this group. (Air Transport Association of America, Research Department, Release no. 20, August 26, 1953). They provide for, although they do not limit themselves to, service upon standard routes. Their operations are flexible and cheap. They compete with a list of

Declaration of Policy

The declaration of policy in the Civil Aeronautics Act reads as follows:

In the exercise and performance of its powers and duties under this Act, the Authority shall consider the following, among other things, as being in the public interest, and in accordance with the public convenience and necessity—

(a) The encouragement and development of an air-transportation system properly adapted to the present and future needs of the foreign and domestic commerce of the United States, of the Postal Service, and of the national defence;

(b) The regulation of air transportation in such manner as to recognize and preserve the inherent advantages of, assure the highest degree of safety in, and foster sound economic conditions in, such transportation, and to improve the relations between, and coordinate transportation by, air carriers.

(c) The promotion of adequate, economical, and efficient service by air carriers at reasonable charges, without unjust discriminations, undue preferences or advantages, or unfair or destructive competitive practices;

(d) Competition to the extent necessary to assure the sound development of an air-transportation system properly adapted to the needs of the foreign and domestic commerce of the United States, of the Postal Service, and of the national defence;

(e) The regulation of air commerce in such manner as to best promote its development and safety; and

(f) The encouragement and development of civil aeronautics.

The quoted paragraphs contain clauses similar to those which govern the promotion and regulation of rail, motor, and water carriage. They mention, that is to say, the present needs of the foreign and domestic service of the United States, of the Postal Service and of the national defense. And they emphasize the importance of sound economic conditions and of adequate air service at reasonable charges without discrimination or unfair or destructive competitive practices.

On the other hand, the air declaration differs from the rail, motor, and water statements in several respects. It goes beyond them in its reference to Civil Aeronautics, which is the science of flight as distinguished from airplane operation. It falls short in that it does not direct the Civil

---

standard lines, which the Board desires to support, but they are, in large part, exempt from regulation.

The Civil Aeronautics Board expresses the view that large irregular carriers should be permitted to exist. But it does not believe that any air-line organization should be allowed to perform route-type operations, serving the public, without having first obtained a certificate of public convenience and necessity. The Board is prepared to furnish a list of companies which, it thinks, have been doing just this thing. It remains to be seen whether the Board can make its opinion good. (See United States Senate, Select Committee on Small Business, *Report on Role of Irregular Airlines in United States Air Transportation Industry,* Sen. Rep. 540, 82d C., 1st S., 1951; *ibid.,* Hearings before a subcommittee, April and May, 1951.)

Aeronautics Authority to recognize and help to preserve the inherent advantages of all forms of transportation and not only the inherent advantages of air carriage. In the same spirit it approves coördination between air carriers, but does not recommend interagency coördination in a general sense. Nor does the air formula require the Authority to coöperate with the several States or to encourage fair wages and equitable working conditions. Finally, while the air declaration refers to competition, it measures the proper extent of competition by its effect upon the development of an air system, not by its advantage from the point of view of the public which is being served.

Certificates of Convenience and Necessity

Under the Civil Aeronautics Act the Board has power to grant or to refuse certificates of convenience and necessity. The provisions for issue are, substantially, those which govern the issuance of motor and water certificates. They are not different in principle from those which govern railroads. Foreign air carriers receive permits instead of certificates but have to meet the same requirements.[32]

Applicants who had been continuously operating between May 14, 1938, and the effective date of the Aeronautics Act or who had been carrying mail prior to this last-named date have received certificates when these pertinent facts have been shown. This "grandfather" exemption is, however, highly restricted in its application.

Domestic air carrier certificates may be altered or suspended, if public convenience so requires; or they may be revoked for intentional failure of a holder to comply with their terms, with any provision in the Civil Aeronautics Act relating to air economic regulation, with the Board's economic regulations, or for nonuse.[33] The issuance, suspension, or revocation of a permit to a foreign carrier is, however, subject to the approval of the President of the United States.[34]

---

[32] It is of some interest that an air common carrier may make charter trips or perform any other special service without regard to the points named in its certificate, under regulations prescribed by the Civil Aeronautics Authority (Board). See T. B. Stibolt, "Limitations on Charter Services as Authorized under Section 401 (f) of the Civil Aeronautics Act of 1938," *Journal of Air Law and Commerce,* Winter, 1948, pp. 238–243.

[33] But no certificate shall be revoked unless the holder fails to comply, within a reasonable time, with a lawful order of the Board requiring compliance.

[34] The clauses in the Civil Aeronautics Act which deal with suspension and revocation need authoritative interpretation.

The apparent intention of the law is to make air certificates permanent, once they have been issued. The Civil Aeronautics Board has held, however, that it may require a carrier to suspend service between points on a route for which it has a certificate, in order to make room for another company which the Board desires to protect (9 C.A.B. 534, 546, 1948). Suspension for such a reason or, more generally, for public convenience and necessity as the Board may interpret this phrase in any case, might be freely ordered

CERTIFICATE PROCEDURE. The Board proceeds by hearing applications, usually in contested cases. It will deny an application for a new service where little new traffic is expected or when disproportionately large capital expenditures will be incurred.[35] But when there seems to be a public need a certificate will issue even though the stability of existing carriers may be impaired and government mail subsidies may have to be increased.[36]

The Board operates under a double pressure in these matters. The fact that route mileage, between 1949 and 1952, increased from 72,667 miles to 77,977 miles would seem recently to indicate a conservative point of view. On the other hand, the Board has been reminded of the need for

---

and it would be equivalent to revocation insofar as any particular air line was concerned.

The answer to the question of interpretation raised in the preceding paragraph will determine how far and in what way the Civil Aeronautics Board can act in fixing the air route structure of the United States. If its power to revoke is limited it can act only by approving or denying new applications. This is already the restriction under which the Interstate Commerce Commission now works and which the Board has accepted in most cases. If it can suspend freely it can remodel and redistribute at any time. It has been proposed, for example, that the Board should suspend all route certificates and that, after hearing, it should establish a new route pattern, respecting route segments contained in the suspended certificates only to the extent to which they conformed to the new pattern so arranged (L. E. Black, "Realignment of the Domestic Airline Route Pattern," *Journal of Air Law and Commerce,* Winter, 1949, pp. 20–39). The Board has not, itself, suggested such drastic action; but at least one member has predicted that the Board intends to make increased use of its suspending power (J. J. O'Connell, Jr., "Legal Problems in Revising the Air Route Pattern," *Journal of Air Law and Commerce,* Autumn, 1948, pp. 397–408). The authority which the Board would exercise, if the asserted power were conceded, would be exceptionally great. (See Oswald Ryan, "The Revocation of an Airline Certificate of Public Convenience and Necessity," *The Journal of Air Law and Commerce,* Autumn, 1948, pp. 377–389; L. S. Keyes, "National Policy Toward Commercial Aviation—Some Basic Problems," *Journal of Air Law and Commerce,* Summer, 1949, pp. 280–297.

35 The Board said, in 1940, that it was not sufficient to find that new routes would be of substantial benefit to the users. "It is a necessary prerequisite to a finding of public convenience and necessity," the Board continued, ". . . that it be found that the advantage to the traveling public, the users of the Postal Service, the shippers of goods, and the national defense, would be great enough to justify the expense to the Government that the new service would involve" (2 C.A.B. 63, 86, 1940. See also 7 C.A.B. 599, 600, 1946; 7 C.A.B. 639, 644, 1946; 8 C.A.B. 1, 3, 1947; 8 C.A.B. 152, 156; and 8 C.A.B. 726, 734, 1947 for illustrations).

36 8 C.A.B. 487, 516, 1947. See John H. Frederick, *Commercial Air Transportation,* Chicago, Irwin, 1946, pp. 280–292.

37 James M. Landis, formerly Chairman of the Civil Aeronautics Board, has argued for more comprehensive planning and less adjudication in adversary proceedings in the issue of air certificates. He believes that there will still be a broad gamble to be made by the public, but that the extent of the gamble, and the portion of it that the public, as against private groups, should bear, ought to be capable of being made more precise. Otherwise, he says, a change in public temper may dry up not only private but public funds, and a more serious blow to the future of air transportation cannot be imagined ("Air Routes under the Civil Aeronautics Act," *Journal of Air Law and Commerce,* Summer, 1948, pp. 295–302).

planning [37] and it has recently expressed the view that a maximum may, temporarily, have been attained.[38]

CERTIFICATE POLICY—RESTRICTION IN THE NUMBER OF SYSTEMS.

For line haul operations, the Board early announced and has adhered to the view that the number of operating systems, at least, should not lightly be increased. It is true that 4 companies were added, at one time or another, to the original list of 15 carriers that operated in 1938. But in awarding a certificate for a route between Pittsburgh and Birmingham, in 1940, the Board stated its views in the following terms:

In reaching this conclusion [granting the certificate to an established company] we recognize the fact that the considerations which lead us to this determination would be equally applicable in any case in which an existing air carrier is competing with a company without operating experience for a new route or service. The number of air carriers now operating appears sufficient to insure against monopoly in respect to the average new route case, and we believe that the present domestic air-transportation system can by proper supervision be integrated and expanded in a manner that will in general afford the competition necessary for the development of that system in the manner contemplated by the Act. In the absence of particular circumstances presenting an affirmative reason for a new carrier there appears to be no inherent desirability of increasing the present number of carriers merely for the purpose of numerically enlarging the indusrty.[39]

The policy indicated in the preceding paragraph has been effectively implemented. As a result, the number of domestic air mail trunk lines is, today, approximately the same as the number operating in 1938.[40]

In contrast with the foregoing, the Board has been relatively nonrestrictive in dealing with local traffic. The Board rejected in principle, in an early case, the suggestion that existing carriers should be preferred to new companies in the development of local routes. Such a policy, the Board said, would reserve for existing air lines the privilege of providing all additions to the present air transportation systems of the United States and would be contrary to the public interest.[41] As a matter of fact, the

[38] The Board said, in 1951:

"Since the enactment of the Civil Aeronautics Act in 1938, 117,128 permanently certificated route miles have been added to the domestic trunkline network. The last five years of this expansion were accompanied by a technological revolution which added an enormous increase to the preexisting transport capacity, thereby further accentuating the expansion. When to these developments a third significant event is added —the failure of the post-war traffic to reach the level which was anticipated by the industry and this Board alike—the resulting accumulated experience strongly suggests that we may have reached and, in some cases, even exceeded the optimum number of certificated services that can be economically supported by the available traffic'" (*Southern Service to the West Case,* Serial no. E-5090, 1951).

[39] 2 C.A.B. 447, 480, 1941.
[40] See chap. 6.
[41] 2 C.A.B. 133, 146, 1940.

Board has granted certificates for feeder services to new corporations organized for the purpose in preference to established trunk lines.[42] The reason given is that independent operators will be more likely to develop local traffic than will trunk lines whose main interest is in longer hauls.[43] Most of the large area cases now provide for independent local service, although the period of the certificate is usually limited to 3 years.[44]

CERTIFICATE POLICY. DISTRIBUTION OF ROUTE MILEAGE AMONG EXISTING SYSTEMS. The Board must distribute new routes or route extensions among established systems if the number of line haul corporations is to remain the same, or approximately the same.[45] The facts which the Board considers in this work include the following:

1. *Quality of service offered.* The nature of the service which applicants can render will be, of course, of first importance, as well as the economy and efficiency with which the service can be supplied. The Board usually assumes that service on a new route will be adequate insofar as stations on that route are concerned. But connections between such stations and outside points will vary with the carrier to which the new route will be assigned. Direct service without change of plane may be expected between

---

[42] 6 C.A.B. 695, 737, 1946; 7 C.A.B. 481, 495, 505, 1946.

[43] 7 C.A.B. 863, 879, 1947. There have been, however, exceptions to this rule (8 C.A.B. 360, 391–393, 1947. See also dissenting opinion in the *Pioneer* case, 7 C.A.B. 469, 474–477, 1946).

[44] The Civil Aeronautics Board has been criticized for its readiness to grant certificates to independent feeder lines on the ground (1) that these lines will divert traffic from surface carriers and (2) that the development of heavily subsidized air feeder services will throw little light upon the relative advantage of air and surface carriage in short-haul operation.

The Board refers to its action in feeder line cases as experimental, but it is already convinced that feeder service should be further developed. It suggests that trunk line carriers may eliminate service to certain marginal traffic points which are or can be served economically by the local service carriers.

The amount of local feeder air service is increasing; this is, of course, no evidence that the operations will soon be able to pay their way. (See United States Senate, Committee on Interstate and Foreign Commerce, *Legislative Program and Statement of Policies of Civil Aeronautics Board,* 82d C., 1st S., 1951.)

[45] The competition for these extensions is extremely active because of the flexibility of air operations and because of the fact of government support. The second circumstance reduces the risk which a carrier incurs in seeking a route extension. The first lessens the costs involved. Thus an air carrier which wishes to extend its service anticipates little additional capital expense beyond the cost of additional airplanes, if new equipment is required. Route and terminal accommodation will be already in position for its use. If the flying equipment that it owns is being inefficiently utilized the additional outlay may be very small. The result is that four or five companies may apply at the same time for permission to operate a given route. Cases of this sort are settled by the Board in adversary proceedings.

The Civil Aeronautics Board, in preparing its decisions, may, technically, only approve or reject applications as made. It goes further than this in practice, and sometimes distributes routes in a manner which does not exactly correspond with any application. The Supreme Court allows the Board a good deal of freedom, although the described procedure does not precisely fit the language of the Act (*Civil Aeronautics Board v. State Airlines,* 94 Law Ed. 346, February 6, 1950).

stations on a single system but not between points on two different systems. Hence the emphasis upon so-called "one-carrier" relations.[46] The importance of these relations can, however, be overstressed.[47] Large carriers sometimes make a better showing than small carriers with respect to quality, economy, and efficiency. But the Board will allow for this fact so as not to throttle the growth of smaller enterprises.[48]

2. *Competition.* The Civil Aeronautics Board believes that competition between air carriers is desirable, at least on routes which offer sufficient traffic to support competing services.[49] On the other hand, competition provokes wasteful duplication of service; it diverts traffic from one carrier to another to the disadvantage of weaker companies; and it may interfere with the establishment of a sound air system for the nation as a whole.[50] It is fair to say that the Board recognizes the possible benefits of competition but that it does not respond readily to the argument that competition stimulates more traffic and better service in the individual case.[51] In later years, in fact, the Board appears to have largely abandoned the idea of promoting competition. It now emphasizes the policy of preserving air-line earnings so as to minimize subsidies and, conceivably, to lower air transport rates. This strongly affects its certificate policy.[52]

[46] 7 C.A.B. 27, 35, 1946; 8 C.A.B. 487, 521, 1947; 9 C.A.B. 38, 54, 1948; 9 C.A.B. 414, 431, 1948.

[47] See dissenting opinion by Mr. Landis in 8 C.A.B. 523–526, 1947.

[48] 4 C.A.B. 1, 18, 1942; 4 C.A.B. 546, 548, 1944.

[49] 2 C.A.B. 353, 386, 1940; 4 C.A.B. 254, 264, 1943; 9 C.A.B. 38, 55, 1948. The Board has said:

"The Act has clothed the Board with full power and machinery by which it may require the performance of safe and adequate service. However, service which is just adequate, as that term is used in the Act, will not provide the public with the full advantages which should be expected from the most modern form of transportation nor will it encourage the development contemplated by the Congress. The improvements which flow from a competitive service cannot be obtained by legislative fiat. There is no regulation conceivable which could assure courtesy by a carrier's employees, for example, and it would be extremely difficult to dictate many other matters affecting the quality of the service rendered. A sound competitive system should encourage and give added impetus to the development of each competing air carrier's enterprise to a much greater extent than would a monopolistic system . . . There is a strong, although not conclusive, presumption in favor of competition on any route which offers sufficient traffic to support competing services without unreasonable increase of total operating cost" (4 C.A.B. 552, 555, 1944).

[50] 7 C.A.B. 83, 108, 1946; 7 C.A.B. 481, 498, 1946; 8 C.A.B. 536, 541, 1947.

[51] 8 C.A.B. 487, 517, 1947.

[52] The Board presented an illuminating statement of its views in a decision rendered in 1951. In this decision the Board concluded—

1. That Congress did not require the Civil Aeronautics Board to seek competition merely for the sake of having competition.

2. That Congress had directed the Board to adhere to a policy of competition only "to the extent necessary to assure the sound development" of the air transportation system.

3. That a case for competition may be made out where, in a particular case, an air carrier is failing to attain high standards of public service and where only provision for

3. *Support of weak systems*. The Board has denied an obligation to expand small carriers to the point where all systems are equal in size and opportunity,[53] and it has declared that a carrier's financial difficulties are not by themselves a justification for a certificate award.[54] But the Civil Aeronautics Board uses its certificate powers to strengthen weaker air lines where this can be done without too great cost to the Government or too great impairment of the service which the public will enjoy.[55] It acts very much on grounds of principle in this matter, under its interpretation of Section 2 of the Civil Aeronautics Act. Critics have objected that route enlargement is not necessarily a source of strength, but this argument has not been much regarded by the Board.[56]

---

an economic competitive service would contribute effectively to the assurance of such standards.

4. But that, in considering competition, the sharp fluctuations in earnings which characterize the air industry must be remembered, and the general desirability that carriers should maintain a relatively good position. Only this will lead, in the long run, to good service at low rates.

5. And that, in encouraging competition, competitive services need not everywhere be required. The benefits of a competitive spirit may spread to routes that have no competition.

This revealing exposition of the Board's present views provoked one member to register dissent. (See United States Civil Aeronautics Board, Serial no. E-5090, 1951. See also United States House of Representatives, Committee on Interstate and Foreign Commerce, *Transportation Study*, Hearings before a subcommittee on Transportation Problems, 81st C., 2d S., 1950, "Statement of the Civil Aeronautics Board," p. 18.)

[53] 8 C.A.B. 726, 734, 1947.

[54] 8 C.A.B. 487, 515, 1947. See also 7 C.A.B. 639, 645, 1946.

[55] 4 C.A.B. 633, 635, 1944; 7 C.A.B. 639, 644, 1948. The mere fact that a large established company can operate more cheaply than a weaker line is not sufficient to justify the award of a new route.

[56] Mr. Young, member of the Board, discussed this matter in a dissenting opinion in 1947. He said:

". . . Attention has been called to instances wherein additional routes, or route extensions, were granted to 'weak' carriers as a solution to their economic problems. Such a policy has been referred to as reflecting 'wise industrial statesmanship.' Perhaps it does, but if the idea is premised upon the belief or conclusion that the size of a carrier's route system is the controlling factor affecting its chances of economic success then, in my opinion, it is not well founded. There are other considerations, of equal or greater consequence, that contribute to success or failure.

Furthermore, I believe that, in the absence of circumstances unusually favorable in character, a so-called 'weak' carrier might actually be led into overextending, through a process of route enlargement, thus further weakening its position. Especially would this appear to be a likely result where direct and vigorous competition is involved. To compete effectively with an already established carrier means building up good will, cooperating competitive schedules, and employing flight equipment which equals or exceeds in performance and comfort that which is used by the competitor. It requires time, calls for capital investment, and depletes working capital—and the 'weak' carrier must be able to withstand such an impact, probably for a substantial period, if ultimately it is to be benefited. And if the route happens to be a weak one . . . then the situation becomes more acute, involves the welfare of both carriers, and well may result in the Government's absorbing a cost which should never have been incurred in the first instance" (8 C.A.B. 477, 483, 1947).

What has actually happened in the distribution of new routes and route extensions has been that these additions have been assigned to established companies, but with some tendency to favor the middle-sized and smaller systems against the larger organizations. The expansion of the Northwest Air Lines and of the Pennsylvania Central illustrates the possible result of such a practice.[57] More generally, we may observe that the mileage operated by middle-sized and relatively small domestic air trunk lines more than doubled between 1938 and 1948 while that operated by the four largest systems increased only by approximately 16 percent.[58]

Safety

The authority of the Civil Aeronautics Board over the safety of air flight is very great. Under the Civil Aeronautics Act it has the power to prescribe standards for the construction, inspection, and maintenance of aircraft; to issue rules concerning aircraft flight, and to regulate the hours of service of employees. The Board investigates accidents and conducts special studies and investigations in matters pertaining to safety and accident prevention.[59] The Administrator issues airman certificates, specifying the capacity in which the holders are authorized to serve as airmen; aircraft certificates; and operating certificates which certify that the holder

See also the conclusion of Joseph O'Connell, chairman of the Civil Aeronautics Board, that the Board has gone too far in certifying weak routes and carriers (*Journal of Air Law and Commerce*, Autumn, 1948, pp. 397–408).

[57] The Northwest Air Lines, in 1938, operated only from Seattle and Portland to Chicago. By 1948 they had added a service from Chicago to Washington. They now reach New York. The Western Airlines (then the Western Air Express) operated, in 1938, from San Diego to Salt Lake City and Great Falls, Montana. In 1950 the company was also flying planes from San Diego via San Francisco to Seattle, and from Great Falls to Denver, Minneapolis, and St. Paul, as well as to Edmonton, Canada. The Pennsylvania Central, in 1938, operated from Chicago and Milwaukee through Pittsburgh to Washington, with a side route to Buffalo and Baltimore. In 1950, besides maintaining this route, it had extended its service to New York and, in the South, it operated from Pittsburgh to Memphis, Atlanta, New Orleans, and Mobile.

[58] Dearing and Owen suggest that the relative increase in the group of middle-sized domestic air trunk lines has been due to changes in the technology of the air industry. This is on the assumption that the flying equipment in the earlier period was well suited to regional operations, while afterward, the range and capacity of airplanes increased so that they could not be efficiently handled on a regional basis. This may have presented two alternatives to the Civil Aeronautics Board: (1) to permit the major carriers to absorb regional lines, or (2) to allow the regional carriers to expand. The adoption of the second alternative would explain why the middle group of air carriers became relatively enlarged (C. L. Dearing and Wilfrid Owen, *National Transportation Policy*, Washington, D. C. Brookings Institution, 1949).

See also, on the general question of routes, H. D. Koontz, Domestic Air Line Self-Sufficiency; A Problem of Route Structure," *American Economic Review*, March, 1952.

[59] U.S.C. Title 49, subchapter 6. One of the more recent suggestions is that the promulgation of rules relating to the safety of aircraft operation should be transferred to the Department of Commerce with a right of appeal to the Civil Aeronautics Board (United States Committee on Organization of the Executive Branch of the Government, *A Report to Congress*, March, 1949).

is able to conduct a safe operation between named points in accordance with laws which are laid down. Federal safety rules are not limited to interstate commerce or to interstate carriers in their application. It is obvious that they could not adequately protect interstate operations unless they were generally applied.[60]

Service

The duty is imposed upon air carriers of providing safe and adequate service on reasonable request. This includes reasonable through service in connection with other air carriers. Through service with common carriers which are not air carriers is permitted, but not required.[61] The Board has authority to require reasonably adequate service to all certificated points.[62]

It has made some general observations with respect to "adequacy," [63] but it has not directly interfered with air carrier operations. Adequacy of service has, rather, been considered in connection with the issue of certificates and in the discussion of mail pay compensation. Shippers have not

[60] The burden of enforcement is very heavy. Partly, though probably not entirely for this reason, Congress has discussed legislation which would permit state courts to hear proceedings for the collection of civil penalties and would allow state courts or state agencies to suspend airmen, aircraft, or air operating certificates for violation of federal regulations. This would provide a substantial enlargement of state participation in the enforcement of local rules.

The Civil Aeronautics Board did not, in 1948, object to greater state activity provided. (1) that the states should organize agencies which were competent, and (2) that the rules to be enforced should be federal rules.

The following subjects were also considered at this time: (1) Whether the authority of state agencies should extend to air companies operating under federal certificates of convenience and necessity, or only to non-certificated carriers; (2) Whether the states might impose and enforce local regulations in addition to federal rules.

Congress did not pass the bills that were debated in 1948. (U.S. Congress, Senate, *Local Enforcement of Civil Aviation Safety Regulation.* Hearings before a subcommittee of the Committee on Interstate and Foreign Commerce on H.R. 6147, 80th C., 2d S., 1948.)

[61] Sec. 404 (a) It shall be the duty of every air carrier to provide and furnish interstate and overseas air transportation, as authorized by its certificate, upon reasonable request therefor and to provide reasonable through service in such air transportation in connection with other air carriers; to provide safe and adequate service, equipment and facilities in connection with such transportation.

Sec. 1002 (i) The Authority shall, whenever required by the public convenience and necessity, after notice and hearing, upon complaint or upon its own initiative, establish through service for interstate or overseas air transportation . . . and the terms and conditions under which such through service shall be operated.

[62] 3 C.A.B. 72, 76, 1941.

[63] The Board has said that, as a rule, adequate service requires at least two daily round trips over each segment of a route (7 C.A.B. 469, 473, 1946; 8 C.A.B. 175, 181, 1947). More generally, it has ruled that the problem of adequacy includes, among other factors, both the supply of an adequate frequency of departure, and the provision of a sufficient aggregate of payload to meet the requirements of commerce. The actual determination of the size of equipment that should be used in a given case, or of the point at which a change should be made from small aircraft to larger ones, is a problem of managerial judgment. (1 C.A.B. 275, 284, 1939.)

complained of the facilities accorded them between towns which air carriers have served.

Consolidation

The subject of air line consolidation has been discussed in chapter 25.

Rates and Tariffs

The Civil Aeronautics Board has power to fix the rates which air lines charge for mail and for commercial carriage. The Act requires common carriers by air to file and to publish property and passenger rate tariffs and to collect the prices for transport which they establish. Changes in published rates can be made only on 30 days' notice, except that the Board may permit changes after a shorter interval. The authority of the Board to suspend property and passenger rates and to determine their amount is substantially that possessed by the Interstate Commerce Commission.[64]

RATE MAKING RULE. The Civil Aeronautics Act, like the Interstate Commerce Act, has a rule of rate making for passengers and property; the two rules are substantially, though not exactly, the same. The rates for the carriage of mail are adjusted upon another basis.[65]

RATE POLICY OF THE CIVIL AERONAUTICS BOARD. The Civil Aeronautics Board has issued few, if any, rate orders upon complaint, although it has adequate authority. It differs in this from the Interstate Commerce Commission. But it has issued general orders with respect to rates. These have been promulgated when the earnings of air lines have seemed to be excessive,[66] at other times when earnings have been too low, and in at least one case the Board has fixed minimum rates to check competition between carriers, especially that between regular and nonscheduled lines.[67]

[64] The Interstate Commerce Commission has the power to prescribe rate, fare, or charge, or the maximum or minimum, or the maximum and minimum to be observed. The Civil Aeronautics Board has the same power, conferred in almost the same words, in the case of domestic air transport. On overseas business the Board has only the power to prescribe maximum or minimum, or maximum and minimum rates, fares, and charges. Strictly speaking, there is no difference between these two powers; we may suppose, however, that Congress intended that the Board should recognize an area between the maximum and minimum rates prescribed for overseas transport in which the carriers might adjust charges at their discretion.

[65] See chap. 34.

[66] In 1943 the Board ordered 11 of the 16 carriers then operating to show cause why air passenger fares should not be reduced 10 percent (C.A.B. Order Serial no. 2164, February 27, 1942). No blanket reduction followed, but a number of lower fares were introduced. In 1945, when air profits were high, the Board required the four largest air carriers to show cause why an adjustment should not be made in the air-mail pay they were receiving. This was an obvious alternative to a cut in rates (C.A.B. Order Serial nos. 3350, 3351, 3352, 3353).

[67] For this and for a general discussion of the history of air fares and rates see

The Civil Aeronautics Board is in a peculiar position in these matters. On the one hand, as a government agency, it should have regard for the financial burden which low rates might lay upon the federal administration. It cannot allow unchecked experimentation at government expense. On the other hand, as a promotional organization, it feels obliged to regulate rates, on the whole, with an eye to the development of air commerce, not with attention to government expense. In this dilemma, the Board usually recognizes its promotional responsibilities. It is willing, that is to say, to approve rates which do not cover costs of operation when these rates are likely to increase volume, providing, as a limiting consideration, that the rates are high enough to cover costs when the expected volume shall have been secured.[68] This is in striking contrast to the principles followed by the Interstate Commerce Commission in rail, motor, and water cases. It probably causes excessive diversion of traffic to the air lines as well as some increase in the subsidy account. An incidental result is that shipper complaints are few because shippers cannot establish the unreasonableness of an air-line rate by criteria commonly used in controversies involving other forms of transport. Most parties which appear before the Board are carriers. The users of air service, as we have said, rarely or never initiate a case.

Discrimination

The paragraphs in the Civil Aeronautics Act which concern discrimination are patterned upon those in the Interstate Commerce Act. Rebates are prohibited, as is the carriage of persons or property for less than the published rates. There are categories to which passes may be issued.[69]

Frederick W. Gill and Gilbert Bates, *Airline Competition*, Boston, Division of Research, Graduate School of Business Administration, Harvard, 1949.

[68] 9 C.A.B. 340, 1948. This policy is acceptable to the air carriers because the Government makes carrier losses good. See chap. 34. See also the *Air Forwarder Association* case, in which the Board said: "Present evidence as to cost is not too material. All industry goes through the experience of promotional rates—of rates initially set below costs but with costs falling below that rate if the hoped-for volume is attained. In the light of the vast potential market for air cargo a reasonable promotional rate is not unjustifiable" (8 C.A.B. 469, 473, 1947).

The elaborate study of airline competition published by the Harvard Graduate School of Business Administration observes (1) that neither the Board nor the air carriers knew accurately, as late as 1948, the actual costs incurred in rendering various kinds of airline service, either as to passengers or type of commodity carried, or as to route, segment, or station operated; and, (2) that there was little need for the airlines to know their costs accurately because they would not have been able to use this criterion in setting specific rates, inasmuch as this would have made many fares prohibitively high from the standpoint of rail competition (Gill and Bates, *Airline Competition, op. cit.*).

[69] Passes may be issued, also, to persons who are not in the categories, but only (1) if provision has been made in published tariffs; and (2) if no undue or unreasonable preference results (1 C.A.B. 677, 680, 1940).

And, in general, no air carrier may subject any person, port, locality, or description of traffic to undue prejudice.[70] Complaints of discrimination, like complaints of unreasonable rates, are very few, and those which charge local discrimination, particularly, are nonexistent.[71] The reason is, probably, the comparative simplicity of the air-line tariffs and the small volume of airborne freight.

UNFAIR COMPETITION. The problem of unfair competition may be mentioned in connection with discrimination, although the issues raised are not entirely the same.

The Civil Aeronautics Act gives power to the Civil Aeronautics Board to investigate and determine whether any air carrier or foreign air carrier has been or is engaged in unfair or deceptive practices or unfair methods of competition.[72] The statute does not define the words *unfair* or *deceptive,* nor has the Board rendered decisions which make their meaning clear. There have been cases in which air lines have unsuccessfully attacked mail schedules of their competitors on the ground of unfair competition; [73] and, in 1942, the Civil Aeronautics Board held that air lines did not compete unfairly when they issued annual travel cards to prospective passengers, after a deposit, even though the practice deprived travel agents of their usual commission.[74] On the other hand, the prohibition of "un-

---

[70] This list is less comprehensive than the enumerations found in the Interstate Commerce Act. The differences may be significant under some circumstances.

[71] What might have been a complaint of local discrimination was registered in the Hawaiian case (7 C.A.B. 83, 106, 1946). This controversy involved the award of a certificate for operation from the West Coast of the United States to Hawaii. The certificate was ultimately granted to United Air Lines out of San Francisco. The ports of Seattle and Tacoma contended that the Puget Sound area was being discriminated against in favor of California. The complainants pointed out that Los Angeles and San Francisco were common fare points so that a passenger for Hawaii could board a plane at Los Angeles and travel to San Francisco and thence to Hawaii without extra cost, whereas a passenger from Seattle would pay a full fare from that city to San Francisco and, in addition, a full fare from San Francisco to Hawaii. The argument was actually presented to support the award of a West Coast-Hawaii certificate to a line based in the Northwest. The Board remarked that it might have been the basis of a discrimination charge (7 C.A.B. 83, 106, 1946).

It might also be contended that airlines discriminate in favor of terminal and against intermediate points by failure to stop their planes. This problem is usually disposed of, however, by the terms of the route certificate which the air-line company receives.

[72] Sec. 411. "The Authority may, upon its own initiative or upon complaint by any air carrier or foreign air carrier, if it considers that such action by it would be in the interest of the public, investigate and determine whether any air carrier or foreign air carrier has been or is engaged in unfair or deceptive practices or unfair methods of competition in air transportation. If the Authority shall find, after notice and hearing, that such air carrier or foreign air carrier is engaged in such unfair or deceptive practices or unfair methods of competition, it shall order such air carrier or foreign air carrier to cease and desist from such practices or methods of competition.

[73] John H. Frederick, *op. cit.,* p. 323.

[74] 3 C.A.B. 242, 247, 1942.

lawful operation" in the Motor Carrier Act has been held to protect persons who use transportation facilities, not persons who operate them. We must await further litigation to make this subject clear.

Securities

The Civil Aeronautics Board has no authority to control the issue of air-line securities. It has asked for this authority, but without success.[75]

General Comment on the Civil Aeronautics Act of 1938

It will be observed that the Civil Aeronautics Act sets up a regulatory structure of a type made familiar by the Interstate Commerce Act. The statute is, however, less elaborate than the Interstate Commerce Act and the control which it provides is less intensive. Thus the Act of 1938 has no long and short haul clauses. Part II of the Interstate Commerce Act also lacks this clause; the omission is not, probably, important in either case. The so-called Carmack and Cummins amendments to the Interstate Commerce Act are not extended to air carriers. The Civil Aeronautics Board has no power to regulate the issue of securities. It has none of the operating control which the Interstate Commerce Commission derives from its power over car service and by explicit delegation, although it can require air carriers to organize through service, prescribe through rates, and regulate equipment interchange. It has no jurisdiction over contract carriers, except with respect to safety; and none, explicitly, over carrier documentation. On the other hand, the Board has influence because of its power to grant or to withhold subsidies, and the limits of its authority under general phrases of the law are probably broader than one might suppose.[76]

The Civil Aeronautics Board has been concerned, in practice, with four problems. The first of these has been the definition of its authority; the second, the certification of and the distribution of routes between air carriers; the third, the safety of air operation; and the fourth, the administration of mail pay. It has dealt slightly with rates, service, discrimination, and unfair practices. In other words, it has been more interested in the development of air carriage and in the relations of air carriers with each other than it has been in the protection of the shipping public. As air traffic grows, this situation may change. Meanwhile the Administrator of Civil Aeronautics has performed important functions of an administrative and promotional kind.

[75] See R. F. Murray, "Regulation of Airline Securities," *Harvard Business Review,* May, 1950.

[76] W. M. Wherry and T. E. Wolcott, "Some Discrimination Problems in Air-Freight Service," *Cornell Law Quarterly,* September, 1945, pp. 31–47.

R E F E R E N C E S

General Treatises

Fair, Marvin L., and Williams, Ernest W., *Economics of Transportation,* New York, Harper, 1950.

Frederick, John H., *Commercial Air Transportation,* Chicago, Irwin, 1946.

Johnson, E. R., *Transport Facilities, Services, and Policies,* New York, Appleton-Century-Crofts, 1947.

Locklin, D. Philip, *Economics of Transportation,* Chicago, Irwin, 1947.

Puffer, Claude E., *Air Transportation,* Philadelphia, Blakiston, 1941.

Westmeyer, Russell E., *Economics of Transportation,* New York, Prentice-Hall, 1952.

Wilson, G. Lloyd, and Bryan, Leslie A., *Air Transportation,* New York. Prentice-Hall, 1949.

Wolfe, Thomas, *Air Transportation, Traffic and Management,* New York, McGraw-Hill, 1950.

Other Books

Dearing, C. L., and Owen, Wilfrid, *National Transportation Policy,* Washington, D.C., Brookings Institution, 1949.

Dykstra, Gerald O., and Dykstra, Lillian G., *The Business Law of Aviation,* New York, McGraw-Hill, 1946.

Gill, F. W., and Bates, G. L., *Airline Competition,* Boston, Harvard, Division of Research, Graduate School of Business Administration, 1949.

Keyes, L. S., *Federal Control of Entry into Air Transportation,* Cambridge, Mass., Harvard, 1951.

Rhyne, Charles S., *The Civil Aeronautics Act Annotated,* Washington, National Law Book, 1939.

Periodicals

Ballard, F. A., "Federal Regulation of Aviation," *Harvard Law Review,* October, 1947.

Black, L. E., "Realignment of the Domestic Airline Route Pattern," *Journal of Air Law and Commerce,* Autumn, 1948, Winter, 1949.

Fagg, F. D., "Legal Basis of Civil Air Regulation," *Journal of Air Law and Commerce,* January, 1939.

Frederick, J. F., and Lewis, A. D., "Air Routes and Public Policy," *Harvard Business Review,* Summer, 1941.

Keyes, L. S., "National Policy Toward Commercial Aviation—Some Basic Problems," *Journal of Air Law and Commerce,* Summer, 1949.

King, Harold J., "The Rate-Making Function of the Civil Aeronautics Board," *American Journal of Economics and Sociology,* vol. 1, no. 2.

Koontz, H. D., "Air Line Self-Sufficiency: A Problem of Route Structure," *American Economic Review,* March, 1952.

Landis, James M., "Air Routes Under the Civil Aeronautics Act," *Journal of Air Law and Commerce,* Summer, 1948.

Markham, D. W., and Blair, D. H., "The Effect of Tariff Provisions Filed Under the Civil Aeronautics Act," *Journal of Air Law and Commerce,* Summer, 1948.

Murray, Roger F., "Regulation of Airline Securities," *Harvard Business Review,* May, 1950.

Neal, George C., "The Status of Non-Scheduled Operations Under the Civil Aeronautics Act of 1938," *Law and Contemporary Problems,* Winter-Spring, 1946.

O'Connell, J. J., Jr., "Legal Problems in Revising the Air Route Pattern," *Journal of Air Law and Commerce,* Autumn, 1948.

Rhyne, Charles S., "Federal, State, and Local Jurisdiction over Civil Aviation," *Law and Contemporary Problems,* Winter-Spring, 1946.

Ryan, Oswald, "Economic Regulation of Air Commerce by the States," *Virginia Law Review,* March, 1945.

Ryan, Oswald, "Regulation of Air Transportation Under the Civil Aeronautics Act," *Public Utilities Fortnightly,* November 24, 1949.

Ryan, Oswald, "The Revocation of an Airline Certificate of Convenience and Necessity," *Journal of Air Law and Commerce,* Autumn, 1948.

Spencer, F. A., "The Economic Regulation of Air Transport," *Univeristy of Chicago Law Review,* April, 1938.

Stibolt, T. B., "Limitations on Charter Services as Authorized Under Section 401 (f) of the Civil Aeronautics Act of 1938," *Journal of Air Law and Commerce,* Winter, 1948.

Tipton, Stuart G., "Legislative Program for Aviation," *Law and Contemporary Problems,* Winter-Spring, 1946.

Westwood, H. C., "Choice of the Air Carrier for New Air Transport Routes," *The George Washington Law Review,* December, 1947; February, 1948.

Westwood, H. C., "Procedure in New Route Cases Before the Civil Aeronautics Board," *Journal of Air Law and Commerce,* Summer, 1947.

Wherry, W. M., "Some Discrimination Problems in Air-Freight Service," *Cornell Law Quarterly,* September, 1945.

Special and Miscellaneous

Craemer, J. F., *Local Regulation of Commercial Aviation,* Proceedings of the National Association of Railroad and Utilities Commissioners, 57th Annual Convention, 1945.

Tipton, Stuart G., "The Regulation of Air Transport, State, Federal, and Local," in *Prospects and Problems in Aviation,* Chicago, Chicago Association of Commerce, 1945.

United States, Attorney General's Committee on Administrative Procedure, *Administrative Procedure in Government Agencies,* Sen. Doc. 10, 77th C., 1st S., Ser. 10,563, Part 6, 1941.

United States, Commission on Organization of the Executive Branch of the Government, *Independent Regulatory Commissions,* 1949.

United States, Commission on Organization of the Executive Branch of the Government, *Task Force, Report on Regulatory Commissions,* Appendix N, 1949.

United States Department of Commerce, Civil Aeronautics Administration, *The Development, Operation, and Regulation of the Non-Scheduled Air Carrier*, Office of Aviation Information, Aviation Statistics Division, May 26, 1947.

United States House of Representatives, Committee on Interstate and Foreign Commerce, *Local Enforcement of Civil Safety Regulation*, Hearings on H. R. 6147, 80th C., 2d S., 1948.

United States House of Representatives, Committee on Interstate and Foreign Commerce, *Transportation Study*, Hearings before a subcommittee on Transportation Problems, 81st C., 2d S., 1950.

United States Senate, Committee on Interstate and Foreign Commerce, *Air Line Industry Investigation*, Hearings pursuant to Sen. Res. 50, 81st C., 1st S., 1949.

United States Senate, Committee on Interstate and Foreign Commerce, *Local Enforcement of Civil Aviation Safety Regulation*, Hearings before a subcommittee on S. 2452, 80th C., 2d S., 1948.

United States Senate, Committee on Interstate and Foreign Commerce, *Legislative Program and Statement of Policies of Civil Aeronautics Board*, Hearings, 82d C., 1st S., 1951.

United States Senate, Committee on Interstate and Foreign Commerce, *Prohibition of Free Transportation on Air Lines*, Hearings, 73d C., 2d S., 1934.

United States Senate, Committee on Interstate and Foreign Commerce, *Regulation of Interstate Contract Carriers by Air*, Hearings before a subcommittee on S. 2449, 80th C., 2d S., 1948.

Public Aid

This chapter discusses the public aid given to rail, motor, water, and air transport in the United States as distinguished from the regulation of these enterprises.

Reasons for Public Aid

Government aid to transportation has at least three possible results:

1. It may provide facilities for government use. Postal deliveries, government administration, and military preparation are only three of many government activities which would be impossible without transport.

2. It may accelerate the development of business enterprises that will be, in the long run, adequately supported by user contributions, but which cannot, in the short run, obtain a sufficient quantity of private funds.

3. It may make construction possible in cases where the effect will be socially beneficial, but where the benefit cannot ever or easily be associated with private use.

The following pages describe a fourfold system of public aid which has been intended, we must assume, to achieve some or all of the above named results. It is a system which is intimately linked with the regulatory structure that we have examined and with the construction and operation of the transport organization that is the subject of this book. The principal purpose of this chapter is to describe the manner of grant, to estimate the volume, and, to some extent to explain the basis upon which government assistance to transport in this country has been allowed. The subject is contentious, and there will be digressions and expressions of opinion at certain points.

Railroads

Public aid to railroads in the United States was briefly mentioned in chapter 4. Elaborate studies of this aid were prepared by the Federal Coordinator of Transportation in 1938 [1] and by the Board of Investigation and Research in 1944.[2] In these studies the Coordinator estimated the total aid granted, up to 1918, at the figure of $1,283 million, of which $516 million was credited to federal and state grants of land and rights of way. To this total the Coordinator added $161 million to cover railroad aid from the beginning of the First World War to 1936. The Board of Investigation and Research located aids amounting to $629 million which it thought calculable or significant, of which $495.5 million was credited to land grants and $1 million or $2 million to rights of way. The chief difference between the two estimates was that the Coordinator included and the Board was disposed to exclude from the list of aids such items as stock subscriptions by public and by private parties, grants of banking privileges to railroad companies, and guarantees and endorsements of railroad bonds—mostly by the Southern states before the Civil War or in the reconstruction period. There were differences of some importance also in the monetary value attached to the railroad use of city streets at grade and in the valuation of grants of rights of way. The Board did not regard as subsidies payments made during and following the First World War. As between the two estimates, that of the Board is, probably, to be preferred.[3]

On the basis of the latest official estimates the land grant was, by a considerable margin, the most important form of subsidy in the experience of the United States. The gift of public land, as noted, was mentioned in chapter 4. The grants were of little direct assistance in the construction of the railroads to which they were given because the land or mortgages secured by the land were rarely salable while construction was going on. They provided an incentive to the investment of private capital, however, because of the expectation of later liquidation; they also yielded profits to individuals. The government's gamble in this matter may be regarded as successful, from its own point of view. It is reasonable to believe that the undeveloped West was settled more rapidly than it would have been if the grants had not been made. Moreover, the government was ultimately repaid the value which the railroads realized from the gift.

The railroad experience is not dealt with more fully in the text because

[1] United States, Office of the Federal Coordinator, *Public Aids to Transportation*, vol. 2, 1938.

[2] United States Board of Investigation and Research, *Public Aids to Domestic Transportation*, 79th C., 1st S., House Doc. 159, 1944.

[3] Neither the Coordinator nor the Board was in a position to estimate the net result of government railroad financing during the First World War or that of the Reconstruction Finance and Public Works Administration loans during the depression of the 1930's. The war financing was made necessary by the policies of the War Railroad Administration. It can hardly be regarded as a gift. The depression financing included loans, a large part of which were subsequently repaid.

the present value of past public aids to railroads is negligible, either as a current source of revenue or as a help in competition with other forms of transport enterprise. This is in contrast with government subsidies to other forms of transport enterprise.[4]

Highway Transportation

Government expenditures for road construction and maintenance have been much greater than for railroad building. They are, also, much more recent. The total outlay between 1921 and 1945 has been calculated at $47 billion, of which $26 billion was for construction and improvement and $21 billion was for road maintenance and administration. Since 1945 the annual expenditures have been between $2 billion and $4 billion a year. In 1950, state governments spent $2,156 million on state-administered highways and $752 million on urban and local roads. Of this $425 million was reimbursed to the states by federal appropriation, mostly through the Office of Public Roads.[5] There is nothing on such a scale in the financing of other forms of transportation. Nor is there any reason to expect that the rate of expenditure will be seriously curtailed. On the contrary, a congressional committee which collected information from State Governors and Highway Departments [6] reported that the cost of correcting highway deficiencies would be $41 billion, or approximately four-fifths of the sums that had already been laid out. The American Association of State Highway Officials prepared, in 1951, an estimate of $32 billion. This sum, though less, was still extremely large.[7]

[4] See appendix to the present chapter for a sketch of the history of railroad land grants.

[5] United States Department of Commerce, Bureau of Public Roads, *Highway Statistics, 1950.*

[6] Joint Committee on the Economic Report, *Highways and the National Economy,* Sen. Doc. 145, 81st C., 2d S., 1950.

[7] Proposals for highway reconstruction raise important questions of principle. There is a variety of tests which might be applied. Among them are the following:

1.   Bonavia, an English writer, has defined the ideal quantity of road as the quantity necessary to carry without congestion such a volume of motor traffic as would be produced by perfect competition among road carriers and also between road and rail—each competitor covering his full social costs. This provides for the objection that the demand for highway improvement is increased by uneconomical diversion of traffic from rail to road. It has difficulties from the engineering point of view because it is probably impossible to determine the ideal quantity mentioned from any known state of facts.

2.   The purpose of reconstruction has been generally stated to be "to provide a road and street system brought to acceptable standards for safe, convenient, and economical motor transportation" (Charles L. Dearing and Wilfrid Owen, *National Transportation Policy,* Washington, D.C., Brookings Institution, 1949). This can hardly mean more than a purpose to spend upon highways the share of the national income which the public desires to have spent in the light of all its needs or, more simply, to spend all that the public can be persuaded to approve. This principle is as practical as it is indefinite; the result is likely to depend upon political rather than upon economic and engineering considerations.

STATE LEGISLATION. State assistance to highway building began as early as 1891, when the State of New Jersey passed a law providing for a measure of state participation. The policy, initiated by New Jersey, was followed by other states in one form or another until, by 1917, all of the 48 states had enacted state aid highway laws. This aid constituted an addition to local funds raised by counties, rural road agencies, and city governments, and, in some cases, to toll receipts collected from users.

FEDERAL LEGISLATION. The large scale entry of the federal government into the highway field is the result of the so-called Federal-Aid Road Act of 1916, supplemented and amended by the Federal Highway Act of 1921, the Hayden-Cartwright Act of 1934, the Federal Highway Act of 1944, and the Federal Highway Acts of 1948 and 1950. The principles which have been approved by the federal highway acts and which are now in force may be stated in the following terms:

1. *Responsibility of the federal government.* The federal government accepts the responsibility of contributing to the cost of highway construction of primary interstate and intercounty roads, of urban roads, and of secondary and feeder roads.

2. *Selection of highways.* The highways to be built are selected by agreement between State and federal authorities or, in the case of secondary and feeder roads by agreement between the State and local authorities, subject to general provisions of the law. The older federal legislation provided that each state should designate a system of interstate and intercounty highways eligible for federal aid, such system not to exceed 7 percent of the total mileage in each state. The Act of 1944 contemplated a somewhat larger network. The projects were still, however, to be submitted by the states, with the final approval in the hands of the federal authorities.

3. *Amount of federal contribution.* The overall contribution is deter-

---

3. The purpose may be to permit vehicles of the maximum weight and speed which have been developed in recent years or are likely to be developed to use the roads with something like the facility which smaller and slower cars have hitherto enjoyed. This is a purpose that can be defined with reasonable precision if the period taken is not too long. It is also a proper subject for debate, especially if the emphasis is placed upon trucking operations, in which the largest and heaviest if not the fastest motor vehicles are employed and which have done most damage to our existing roads. It would not occur, for instance, to a railroad organization to allow its motive power or equipment departments to build cars and locomotives of types which the existing track could not support without regard to the expense of reconstructing the railroad track and roadbed and without assurance that the combined outlay would be justified; nor would an industrial establishment develop any one of its productive factors without calculating the effect upon other branches of the undertaking. A well-run private or public business will always exercise judgments of this kind.

If the question is not raised currently, it is because persons who build and operate motor vehicles have only an indirect and uncertain responsibility for the financing of road improvements and because public representatives in state highway departments are professionally committed to the construction of bigger and better highways.

mined by the Congressional appropriation in any year.[8] Federal contributions to any project are limited to 50 percent of the cost of construction, although a somewhat greater proportion is permitted in states where there is a large proportion of unappropriated public land. Highways are maintained by the states or by civil subdivisions of the states.[9]

4. *Division of funds*. Money provided by the federal government is divided in two general ways:

a. According to the character of the improvement. The distinctions made are between projects in the federal aid highway system, projects on secondary and feeder roads, and projects in urban areas.

b. According to the state in which the funds are spent. There is, that is to say, a policy of apportionment of federal highway aid among the states, using population, area, and existing highway routes as a basis of division.

PRINCIPLES OF HIGHWAY FINANCING. Under the present plan of federal legislation, the roads which motor vehicles use in the United States are built and maintained by states and are partly paid for by the federal government. The division of expenditures between state and federal authorities is largely a political matter; and this is also true, to some extent, of other subjects, such as the basis of the distribution of federal funds among the states and the division of revenues between urban and rural areas. The current policy, in addition, raises some economic questions of importance.

The specific economic problem with respect to highway financing is whether or not government practice subsidizes highway traffic and whether, if it does, the policy can be defended. The inquiry develops into a discussion of user charges. A user charge, in this connection, may be a toll, or it may be a tax or other levy including, in the case of highway transport, fuel taxes, registration fees, and motor licenses, which a highway user may be forced to pay. If state and federal governments do not

[8] But the authorization in the federal highway acts is regarded as a commitment. These authorizations in recent statutes have been as follows:

Act of 1944—500 million for each of 3 years.
Act of 1948—450 million for each of 2 years.
Act of 1950—500 million for each of 2 years.

Later appropriations have been: 1952, $387,500,000; 1953, $475,000,000; 1954, $550,000,000.

Not all of the money authorized and appropriated has been spent, but the balance is regarded as a federal obligation, in addition to whatever sums may be provided by subsequent legislation. (See United States Senate, Committee on Public Works, *Federal Aid Highway Act of 1952*, Hearings before a subcommittee on S. 2437 and S. 2585, 82d C., 2d S., 1952, testimony Staats, p. 100.)

[9] There was an unsuccessful attempt, in 1950, to increase the federal share to 75 percent.

impose user charges they must meet their highway obligations by drafts upon general funds.

REASONS FOR RELIANCE UPON GENERAL FUNDS. There are some reasons for charging highway costs to general funds, instead of providing them from special taxes.

1. The expenditure is, it can be argued, general in nature and analogous to outlays for justice and police.

2. Even when the benefits from motor transport are specialized the benefits vary, to some degree, in proportion to taxable value, so that contributions from general funds can be expected to burden taxpayers in some rough proportion to benefits received.

3. User taxes are not always collectable in areas where highways must be built or improved. This is especially true in the case of city streets.

4. It is convenient to finance construction by general taxation in some cases where benefit of transport to the public served is great but where the traffic is small and the cost per vehicle-mile is relatively great. If roads are built from the proceeds of road-user taxes, where such conditions prevail, and the taxes are levied at a standard rate, these roads must necessarily be subsidized by traffic on more frequented routes. If they are built from the proceeds of local taxes they may be financed, more accurately, by the interests which they serve. This explains the belief that the taxpayer should provide for a large part of the expense of constructing local roads.

REASONS FOR REQUIRING USER CONTRIBUTIONS. The reasons for levying taxes which amount to user contributions include the following:

1. There is now a notable body of highway users from which funds can be derived. It is easier to obtain large funds for road improvement from special levies upon these persons than from general taxes. Benefits to the user are also measurable to a considerable degree.

2. A properly adjusted charge protects the highways by penalizing uses which destroy the roadbed or interfere with efficient operation. It also compensates for wear and tear in ordinary operation and for special highway features that have to be supplied.[10]

---

[10] The practical problem is, here, to recognize differences between vehicles with respect to weight, size, and usual speed. Heavy equipment should, presumably, pay more than light equipment for highway use if roads are built to make their operation possible. But the use of highways is common to vehicles of all types. There is, therefore, a problem of allocation, and this presents difficulties. Railroads are particularly interested in the collection of a proper charge from large motor units engaged in long-distance movements, because this business competes with service which the railroad must handle if it is to survive.

The reader is referred to testimony by Mr. McDonald upon this subject before the Subcommittee on Domestic Land and Water Transportation in 1950 and especially to a study filed in connection with this testimony. The matter is also discussed by the Federal Coordinator of Transportation and by the United States Board of Investigation

3. Charges against the user discourage traffic diversions except in cases where the total highway costs, increased by operating expense, are lower than costs by other means of transportation. This is a fundamental difficulty to which we shall again refer.

GENERAL COMMENTS ON USER PAYMENTS. The best information available indicates that motor vehicle operators, who are the principal users of the highway system, have not paid sums equal to the cost which the government has incurred. The deficit has been considerable.[11] The Board and the Coordinator of Transportation concluded, however, that motor vehicle operators paid an equitable proportion of highway costs between 1921 and 1937 or that they nearly did so between 1921 and 1940. The conclusions which these two organizations reached are by no means the only opinions which experts have expressed, for calculations made by students vary, especially with respect to the burden which vehicle operators should bear.

Inland Waterways

Inland waterways, along with railroad and highway systems, constitute a form of surface transportation to which the government has given financial aid.

Most federal aid to inland waterways has been given to projects upon the Mississippi River system and upon the Great Lakes. The total expenditures also include heavy outlays upon seacoast harbors and channels and lesser amounts for intercoastal canals and other waterways, but these are less significant for our present use. Table 25 shows the federal expenditures for all the purposes which have been mentioned.

Great Lakes

Federal money spent upon the Great Lakes has in large part been used for construction in the vicinity of St. Mary's Falls between Lake Superior and Lake Huron and in Lake St. Clair and in the St. Clair and Detroit rivers between Lake Huron and Lake Erie. These improvements were mentioned in chapter 3. They are still continuing. Thus, between 1946

and Research. See Richard L. Neuberger, "Who Shall Pay for Our Roads?" *Harpers,* October, 1952, for an argument in favor of a weight-distance tax on motor trucks.

[11] The Coordinator found that road-use payments made by motor vehicle operators during the period 1921–1937 amounted to only 41 percent of estimated total highway costs (United States, office of the Federal Coordinator, *Public Aids to Transportation,* vol. 4, pp. 158–160); the United States Board of Investigation and Research reported that highway user revenues during the period 1921–1940 amounted to 42 percent of the total costs (*Report on Public Aids to Domestic Transportation,* pp. 244, 294). Mr. MacDonald, Commissioner of Public Roads, testified that road-use taxes and tolls amounted to 56.7 percent of government expenditures on roads and streets in 1948 and 57.3 percent in 1949 (United States Senate, Committee on Interstate and Foreign Commerce, *Study of Domestic Land and Water Transportation,* Hearings before a subcommittee pursuant to Sen. Res. 50, 81st C., 2d S., 1950, pp. 1011–1012).

TABLE 25.   Federal Expenditures for Rivers and Harbors
up to June 30, 1948

Class	New Work	Maintenance	Total
	(millions of dollars)	(millions of dollars)	(millions of dollars)
Mississippi River system	881.9	367.3	1,248.1
Lake harbors and channels	222.9	115.0	336.6
Intracoastal canals and other waterways	197.5	115.2	311.3
Seacoast harbors and channels	789.3	420.4	1,207.4
Miscellaneous	9.0	76.8	85.7
Total	2,100.6	1,094.7	3,189.1

SOURCE: United States Army, *Annual Report of the Chief of Engineers,* 1948, Part I, vol. 1, p. 22. Totals include various adjustments outside of completed outlays for new work and maintenance. The expenditures given for the Mississippi do not include expenditures for flood control. Total federal expenditures for rivers and harbors had risen, by 1952, to $3,895,364,254. The Engineer's later reports do not, however, segregate the details.

and 1950, $91 million was spent in construction and $25 million in maintenance of the Great Lakes route at these locations, besides routine care and development of harbors at other points.[12] The gross total of government expenditures upon the Great Lakes, up to 1948, was stated in Table 25 under the heading of "Lake harbors and channels." There are proposals, as yet unapproved, for the deepening of the St. Lawrence to provide a seaway usable by ocean vessels. If this project is carried through, the government investment in Lake navigation will be enormously enlarged. There are no estimates of the present value of the federal investment in Great Lakes channels and harbors.

Mississippi River

The gross government expenditure upon the Mississippi River system, up to 1948, was $1,248,100,000. This figure, however, like other statistics supplied by the government engineers, is cumulative from the first federal improvement of each waterway; and the Engineers do not attempt to show how much of past expenditures are still useful. Nor is there any entry for depreciation. On the other hand, there is no allowance for interest charges.[13] The present value of the federal investment in the Mississippi is, obviously, a matter for debate.

[12] United States Army, *Annual Report of the Chief of Engineers,* 1950, Part I, vol. 2, pp. 2138–2148.

[13] The Federal Coordinator gave the cost of new federal work on the Mississippi system as $596,246,046 up to June 30, 1936. He calculated the unamortized remainder of the government investment in the same stream as $333,002,847 (United States, Office of the Federal Coordinator, *Public Aids to Transportation,* vol. 3). On a somewhat different basis, the United States Board of Investigation and Research arrived at

The Policy of Government Expenditures upon Inland Waterways

Government expenditures for the improvement and maintenance of the Great Lakes and, especially, of the Mississippi River system have been and are very large, whatever the manner of calculation. Of these, past outlays are irrecoverable. It is not necessary, however, to complete all projects which have been authorized. And for the future, it is not certain that present practice should be continued on the basis adopted by the Army Board of Engineers.[14] The alternatives would be (1) to cease or to curtail largely government expenditures for the improvement of navigation or (2) to shift the financial burden to waterway users by some form of tolls or other user contribution. The problem is most critical with respect to the Mississippi River. Further comments upon this subject may be submitted under the following heads:

COST OF TRANSPORT. The basic difficulty with the federal policy of improvement upon the Mississippi River is that, taken as a whole, the cost of transportation upon the river is more than that upon adjacent railroads, except in the case of relatively short hauls, if we include maintenance and capital investment in the category of cost. This was the conclusion of the Federal Coordinator of Transportation in 1939,[15] of the Board of Investigation and Research in 1944,[16] and of the Interstate Commerce Commission in 1947 and 1948.[17] On the basis of mills per ton per mile the river costs are relatively low on the Ohio and on the Mississippi farther south, although even here the comparison varies with the commodity; but on the basis of rates per ton the river costs are high because of the windings of the stream, even in the favored districts, and upon the Missouri River and the upper Mississippi they are very high indeed.[18] The handicap of the river is magnified when the point of origin or of destination of a movement does not lie upon the river bank. Such cases have, usually, two characteristics. In the first place, the freight requires more handling than would be necessary upon an all-railroad route.

---

an "adjusted total for the Mississippi River system, as of 1940, of $633,251,678" (United States Board of Investigation and Research, *Public Aids to Domestic Transportation,* 79th C., 1st S., House Doc. 159, 1944). No outlays for flood control are included in any of these figures.

[14] See Part II of the appendix to the present chapter.

[15] *Public Aids to Transportation, op. cit.,* vol. 3, 1939.

[16] *Ibid.,* 1944.

[17] 270 I.C.C. 403, 444, 1947; 270 I.C.C. 591, 1948. See chap. 33.

[18] The disadvantage of the river route is easily understood when distances by rail and by water between selected points upon the river are compared. Thus the channel (river) distance from Cairo, Ill., to Vicksburg is 609.7 miles and that from Cairo to Baton Rouge, La., is 846.4 miles, while the corresponding distances over the Illinois Central Railroad are 388.7 and 536.4 miles. The rail distances are approximately 63 percent of the water distances in these illustrations. (See United States Army Corps of Engineers, *The Improvement of the Lower Mississippi River for Flood Control and Navigation,* by Major D. O. Elliott.)

And, second, the haul is longer—not only because of the vagaries of the river itself but also because the Mississippi lies across the current of great streams of traffic and its use frequently requires diversion and detour. We have finally to remember that the quality of water service is inferior (1) in the case where the shipper desires speed and (2) in the case of articles which are liable to damage when transferred from rail to barge or from barge to rail. Barge line rates do not fully reflect these disadvantages, because the barge lines bear neither the costs of maintenance nor of improvements to the stream. Where they do not, the advantage which they may enjoy is a gift by the taxpayer to persons affected by the operation of the plant.

AMENDMENT TO PRESENT PROCEDURE. The main argument for continued government investment in the improvement of the Mississippi for purposes of navigation is that a federal subsidy to inland waterways is consistent with government protective policies in other places and at other times, and that the development of the entire Mississippi area has been accelerated by government outlays upon the stream. It is also argued that the average cost of river shipment will decrease as the volume of river carriage grows. There is enough force in these suggestions to make it unlikely that the policy of improving and maintaining the Mississippi as an instrument of navigation will be abandoned. Congress could modify present difficulties, however, by greater care in the approval of new projects,[19] by the general reduction of expenditures north of Cairo, Illinois, and by the adoption of some system of tolls or river charges. This last alternative is now politically more possible than it was some years ago.[20]

Air Transportation

Air promotion is, presently, the responsibility of the Civil Aeronautics Administrator and of the Civil Aeronautics Board. The Board and Administrator have, that is to say, along with their power to regulate, a duty to encourage and to develop an air transportation system properly adapted to the present and future needs of the United States, of the postal service, and of the national defense. Other phrases in the Act of 1938 emphasize in other ways the promotional elements which these officers are required to bear in mind. No limit is placed upon the rate of growth of air transport. The Act of 1938 makes no mention of other

[19] The Interstate Commerce Commission might be requested to submit its views to Congress on each new project considered as an addition to the national transportation system.

[20] Full user charges would remove the attractiveness of waterway improvements except in cases where the overall cost of transportation by water was less than the cost of transportation by land. Mississippi Valley interests object to this equalization because they wish to retain a subsidy. They also argue that railroad rates do not cover fully allocated railroad costs. River pricing is less flexible. Barges would be at a positive disadvantage if they had to provide for a full user charge.

agencies of transport except as we may find references in the clauses "sound development," the "inherent advantages of air transportation," and the words "public convenience and necessity." The Civil Aeronautics Board and the Civil Aeronautics Administration are, with the Bureau of Public Roads, in the United States Department of Commerce. The Board has no relations, however, with the Interstate Commerce Commission, and the objectives of the Administration and of the Bureau are independently pursued.

Federal Aid to Air Transportation

Federal aid to air transport takes two forms: (1) assistance to air routes, and (2) operating subsidies. These must be separately described.

Federal Assistance to Air Routes

The federal government supports air routes by liberal appropriations. The money is devoted to the establishment of airways and to the building of airports.

AIRWAYS. The establishment of airways requires the location of lighted beacons and of intermediate landing fields. This was the first equipment. To these are now added radio ranges and markers, instrument landing systems, communication stations, despatching, aircraft control towers, weather reporting circuits, and other devices. (The presently proposed use of "omnidirectional" ranges will permit the abandonment of defined airways and will allow navigation between all points in continental United States. The realization of an all-weather airways system with electronic aids will still further facilitate air movement. These improvements will also increase expenses of installation and operation.)

By 1950 there were approximately 70,000 miles of implemented airways in the United States and its territories, all federally owned and operated. The cumulative expenditures for federal airways from 1925 through 1950 amounted to $513 million, of which about one-third was spent for establishing the system and two-thirds for its maintenance and operation. The total annual requirements for construction, maintenance, and operation of these airways had risen to $92 million by 1949.

AIRPORTS. The subject of federal aid to airports was discussed in chapter 24 with special reference to the Federal Airport Act of 1946. It need only be said here that the amounts involved are large. Plans prepared by the Administrator of Civil Aeronautics in 1952 contemplated an expenditure of $650.6 million to satisfy the country's aeronautical needs as estimated for the following three years, of which $335.6 million were to be charged to the federal government as its share and the rest to other public agencies.[21] Up to 1950 the total federal expenditures had exceeded $800 million.[22]

Operating Subsidies

Operating subsidies provide the final feature of aid to air transport which it is necessary to consider. They are, at the same time and of all features, the most contentious. Common carriers by air already receive a kind of aid by virtue of their freedom to use structures provided by the taxpayer without the payment of a user charge. The industry desires more than this, however, and it receives more in ways which may be described at reasonable length.

HISTORY OF AIR-MAIL CONTRACTS. At all times since 1920 financial assistance to American air companies has been given through contracts for the carriage of the mails. This was originally because the Post Office, because of its control over mail shipments, was in a position to supply the first air lines with business. It was also, and more particularly, because the Postal Administration was familiar with the mail contract system by virtue of its relations with ocean shipping. Congress approved the policy of mail subsidy by a series of laws, and of these the last, passed in 1938, is effective at the present time.

AIR MAIL AND THE ACT OF 1938. The procedure under the present controlling statute and the distribution of authority over mail carriage is governed by the following provisions of the Act of 1938, general and specific:

1. The Act creates a Civil Aeronautics Board to regulate air transport in all its public aspects. The general powers and responsibilities of this Board have been examined in chapter 33.

2. The statute approves the practice of granting operating subsidies to air companies by calculated overpayment for the service of carrying the mail.

3. The character and quality of the service offered by the companies are, ultimately, to be determined by the Civil Aeronautics Board and by the Postmaster General. Air carriers notify the Postmaster General by what schedules and between what points they propose to operate. The Postmaster General may change these schedules, subject to appeal to the

[21] United States Department of Commerce, Civil Aeronautics Administration, *Operations under the Federal Airport Act, 1952*. Congressional appropriations for airports in 1950 to 1954 were, actually 94 million.

[22] The staff of the United States Board of Investigation and Research favored, in 1944, the levy of reasonable charges for the use of airports. It doubted the justification of federal appropriations to build low-cost landing fields for essentially local service and private flying. Proposals for airports with prescribed runways as short as 1,800 feet are still, however, included in the national plans (United States Board of Investigation and Research, *Public Aids to Domestic Transportation*, House Doc. 159, 79th C., 1st S., 1944).

Civil Aeronautics Board, but otherwise they become effective. Once the schedules are established, then the Post Office may tender mail for transport by any scheduled planes.

4. The rates to be paid for air-mail carriage are fixed by the Civil Aeronautics Board, either on its own initiative or upon petition by the Postmaster General.

5. Air-mail rates are to be sufficient, together with all other revenues, to enable air carriers "under honest, economical, and efficient management," to "maintain and continue the development of air transportation to the extent and of the character and quality required for the commerce of the United States, the Postal Service, and of the national defense."

6. The Civil Aeronautics Board has general power to require adequate service, equipment, and facilities.

RATE-MAKING ELEMENTS RECOGNIZED IN THE CASE OF AIR-MAIL CARRIAGE. Under Section 408 (b) of the Act of 1938 the Civil Aeronautics Board fixes the rates for mail carriage, as has just been said. It may set rates upon a level determined by air mail costs; but it does not do this in any case where an air carrier, in its judgment, needs federal aid. Its decision is made after consideration of the revenues which a given carrier will require to meet its expenditures of every kind. This is in conformity with the provisions of the Civil Aeronautics Act summarized in the paragraph numbered (5) above.

PROCEDURE OF THE CIVIL AERONAUTICS BOARD IN AIR-MAIL CASES. The procedure of the Board in air-mail cases is deliberate.[23] What it actually does has the following peculiarities:

[23] Mr. O'Connell, Chairman of the Civil Aeronautics Board, described the Board's procedure, in 1949, as follows:

"A mail rate case for a carrier is inaugurated by the filing of a petition by the carrier or by a Board order for an increased or decreased mail rate. In the event that a carrier files for an increased mail rate, which has been the typical case over the last few years, it is entitled to have its mail rate adjusted, when the rate is made final, back to the date of the petition.

"As soon as Board staff can be assigned to a case, a detailed analysis of the carrier's operations, costs, traffic, and revenues is made on the basis both of our routine periodic reports, special audits, and also on the basis of special information which is furnished by the carrier, usually at our request.

"There then follow a series of conferences at which the Board's legal and rate staffs confer with the management of the carrier to determine the facts surrounding the various issues arising out of the staff analysis. Representatives of the Post Office Department also participate in these conferences. It is out of these conferences that the initial decision comes as to whether or not disallowances will be made from the past costs of the carrier or from the estimates of its future needs.

"If, on the basis of the conferences, the carrier management and the Board's staff can reach reasonable agreement as to the facts and the treatment to be afforded the facts surrounding the rate, the case is presented to the Board in the form of a tentative statement of findings and conclusions. This statement contains a proposed rate for the past period back to the date of the carrier's petition and also for the future period. This Board after studying this statement and making such changes as it feels desirable

Where the carrier is relatively self-sufficient and requires no subsidy, the Commission sets a rate upon a ton-mile basis that is calculated to cover the ascertained or the estimated cost of air-mail carriage. This is known as a "service" rate. There are four airlines which receive a service rate of 45 cents, namely: American Airlines, Eastern Airlines, Transworld Airlines and United Airlines. Certain other carriers receive 53 cents, and this is also called a service rate. Six carriers which received 53 cents were allowed, in 1954, to quote a 45 cents rate between points where they were in competition with the Big Four.

Where a subsidy is contemplated, the procedure is more elaborate. In this instance the Board secures the following information:

1. A statement of carrier costs of operation.
2. A statement of revenues from sources other than air mail.[24]
3. A statement of carrier investment.

What the Board refers to as a "break-even" need is the difference between items (1) and (2) above. To this is added a fair return on item (3), figured recently at 7 percent. The general policy of the Board is to set mail rates under the given conditions at a sum per airplane mile which will produce revenue equal to the total so calculated. This is a "need" rate as distinguished from a "service" rate. It embodies the public aid or subsidy which the Board is disposed to give. The rate fixed applies to the transportation of mail between points which an applicant is authorized to serve under the certificate of public convenience and necessity which it holds and under the schedules which the Postmaster General approves.[25] If the sums allowed prove insufficient, the Board may later authorize an additional, retroactive grant.[26]

---

issues the statement to the carrier accompanied by a show cause order as to why the rates proposed should not be made final.

"If the carrier agrees to the rate, there is a brief *pro forma* hearing at which other interested parties may appear and the rate is then formalized. On the other hand, if the carrier does not agree to the rate, or if other parties, such as the Post Office, object, the particular issues on which there is a disagreement are taken to a full public hearing and are subsequently orally argued before the Board which then issues its opinion" (United States Senate, Committee on Interstate and Foreign Commerce, *Air-Line Industry Investigation,* Hearings pursuant to Sen. Res. 50, 81st C., 1st S., 1949, pp. 132. 136, testimony O'Connell).

[24] If a carrier does both a domestic and a foreign business, its profits on the domestic business will be included in category (2) in calculating the need for revenue on foreign business (74 Sup. Ct. Rep. 354, 1934).

[25] 8 C.A.B. 805, 1947.

[26] The arrangement which the Board makes in a subsidy case may be somewhat complicated. The payment is based upon a so-called basic rate applied to basic airplane miles. The basic mileage is the mileage considered necessary by the Board under economical and efficient management. It differs from "scheduled mileage," which represents all mileage offered in the published schedules of the carrier, and from "designated mileage," which concerns the operation only of those flights authorized for the carriage

The revenue per ton per mile which domestic trunk lines received for the carriage of United States mails in 1948 varied from 58 to 1,697 cents. The payments to feeder lines reached a maximum of 9,190 cents. Later figures are not available. It is obvious that the higher rates had no relation to the cost or value of the air-mail service, but only to the need for government support.[27]

HONEST, ECONOMICAL, AND EFFICIENT MANAGEMENT. The Act of 1938 limits its subsidy support to air carriers under honest, economical, and efficient management. Honesty is taken pretty much for granted; the Civil Aeronautics Board does, however, scrutinize the operating statements which carriers render with some care. Its method of enforcing economy is to disallow cost items which it thinks improper. The effect of the disallowance of a cost item is to raise the applicant's net return, to reduce the carrier's "need," and to lower the air-mail rate that is allowed. Examination of the Board's reports shows that the disallowances are usually specific and that they are seldom large. Thus the Board has disapproved air carrier expenditure for travel, entertainment, and publicity.[28] It has disallowed charitable contributions, although the Pan American Company has insisted that this was a normal cost of doing business.[29] It has disallowed expenses for an "executive" plane which a company had used

---

of mail on schedules published by the Post Office Department. The compensation has no relation to the tonnage of mail carried and relates, characteristically, only to basic mileage accomplished by airplane carriers.

Actually, the adjustment works out on the basis mentioned in the preceding paragraph, in most cases, although more or less elaborate formulas are employed. In some instances, however, where the designated miles exceed the basic miles the government will pay for the excess but at a lower rate; and in other instances the scheduled miles are used. This last occurs in contracts with some carriers where the agreement also provides for adjustments according to the load factor reported. The higher the load factor achieved in such operations, the lower the effective mail rate that will be paid.

[27] The various bases which the Civil Aeronautics Board has used in fixing air-mail rates are described in R. W. Porter, "Allocation of Air Transportation Cost in Determining Domestic Mail, Passenger, and Cargo Rates," *Journal of Air Law and Commerce,* Summer, 1948, pp. 354–365.

Because mail rates are applicable to all routes which a designated air line may serve, except when segments are specially recognized, two companies may receive different compensation for the carriage of mail between identical points. There is no possibility of explaining this difference on the ground of differences in operating conditions. It might, it is true, be feasible to set rates by routes. A reasonable method would be (1) to determine the cost of mail carriage on different routes; (2) to fix mail rates at levels which would cover the cost so ascertained; and (3) to permit the carriage of mail at these rates by whatever carriers, with appropriate certification, offered to accept the business. There would be some difficulty in allocating costs, but Mr. Landis, one-time chairman of the Civil Aeronautics Board, thought that these would not be insuperable (United States Senate, *Air-Line Industry Investigation, op. cit.,* p. 321, testimony Landis). It would not, however, be possible to administer such a system within the framework of the present law because it would base mail payments exclusively upon cost without reference to need.

[28] 9 C.A.B. 807, 1948.
[29] 6 C.A.B. 876, 1947.

on nonrevenue flights [30] and those for the operation of 2 out of 13 planes which a company owned when one was of a military type and the other was chiefly employed for the training of personnel.[31] More broadly, it has considered the extent to which a company should be allowed to accumulate a reserve of spare parts and whether equipment should be depreciated in three or in four years.[32] And it has refused, in at least one case, to allow a charge to cover the costs of grounding defective equipment; the Board here reasoned that the costs were peculiar to the industry, but said that they had already been allowed for in calculating a fair return. These are samples of the results of rather minute examinations of carrier accounts. The checking doubtless saves the government some money. It is unlikely that it has much effect upon the quality of management as a whole. The real difficulty in air transport is that there is no yardstick with which to measure the economy or efficiency of air line operation. And if there were a yardstick, it would be constructed out of the experience of a small number of operating units, each of which would be subject to influences which reduced their consciousness of costs.

CRITICISM OF AIR SUBSIDIES.   Criticism of the organization of public aid to air carriage rests, currently, upon facts which have been mentioned in preceding pages, and which can now be summarized, with some additions:

1. Public aid to air transport is supported by a government promotional organization. This body has no responsibility for other forms of transportation and no interest in a "balanced" program. Its prestige depends upon the development of a particular technique.

2. A substantial portion of public aid is given through air-mail payments—a method which was discredited in shipping practice and was abandoned in the Merchant Marine Act of 1936. It was specifically disapproved in the report of the Federal Aviation Commission of 1935.[33] The difference between the air-mail contracts formerly awarded to vessels, and to air-line companies also, and the contracts now employed is not sufficient to justify the persistent use of what should be regarded as an outmoded device.

3. Public aid through air-mail payments conceals the amount of subsidy which air lines receive. The public is entitled to this information. Figures published recently by the Civil Aeronautics Board are estimates only and are subject to review.

[30] 9 C.A.B. 607, 1948.
[31] 8 C.A.B. 825, 1947.
[32] 9 C.A.B. 645, 1948.
[33] United States Federal Aviation Commission, *Report of the Federal Aviation Commission Containing Its Recommendations of a Broad Policy Covering All Phases of Aviation and the Relation of the United States Thereto,* 74th C., 1st S., Sen. Doc. 15, 1935.

4. The present method of fixing air-mail rates provides air lines with a cost-plus guarantee on all their operations in at least a proportion of the cases. It lessens the importance of managerial efficiency. It allows unnecessarily expensive experimentation, setting up services which attract local support and are later difficult to discontinue in spite of their extravagance from the point of view of results that are obtained. Under some circumstances it allows competitive rate reductions to the detriment of nonsubsidized air carriers which might seek to operate in a given field.

5. The cost of air-mail subsidies is charged, in the federal budget, to the Post Office. The Post Office Department is required to solicit funds from Congress for expenditures over which it has no control. This practice, however, is likely to be changed.

The weaknesses listed in the preceding paragraphs are substantial. Some of them can, however, be reduced or even possibly removed.

APPENDIX TO CHAPTER 34

I

Railroad Land Grant Rates

The land grants to railroads in the United States go back to 1850, when Congress granted lands to the State of Illinois in aid of railway construction in that state.[34] Other federal grants followed, up to 1871, most of which were made to railroads west of the Mississippi River; state governments transferred some land also.[35] The total acreage given has been estimated at 183 million acres and the value at time of donation at $178 million.[36] In partial compensation, land grant railroads agreed to carry mail and federal troops and property at less than the normal charge. As finally adjusted, land grant railroads carried the mail at 80 percent [37] and troops and property at 50 percent of the commercial rate.[38]

[34] 9 Stat. 466.

[35] The Federal Coordinator of Transportation discusses the history of land grant legislation, in a good deal of detail, in his report of *Public Aids to Transportation*, 1938.

[36] *Ibid.*, p. 36. Approximately 8,000,000 acres of land granted but not patented were restored to the United States under the terms of the act of 1940.

[37] The federal Act of 1876 (19 Stat. 78, 82, 1876) provided that lines aided in whole or in part by federal land grants requiring transportation at such charges as Congress might impose, should receive only 80 percent of the compensation fixed for railroads in general.

[38] There were three sorts of provision in the land grant acts:

1. **Free toll lines.** Most of the acts provided in substance that the aided railroads

Operation of land grant rates. Federal land grants were more complicated in their operation than Congress originally expected. There is no reason
to suppose that the grants ever provided funds which could be used to build
the railroads for whose construction grants were made. Land grants do not
work that way because they have little value until a road is built. They did,
however, supply an incentive which may have helped to attract outside capital.

It is also unlikely that the government ever received enough rate reductions
from the land grant railroads to compensate for the original subsidy. These
lines were, after all, few in number and the traffic over them for many years
was comparatively slight.

The government did, however, obtain widespread rate concessions from
what were called "equalization agreements" and these should be credited to
the land grant legislation. The agreements were voluntary and were for the
purpose of enabling non-land-grant railroads to capture a share of the traffic
which the land grant railroads might be expected to control. In practice, they
notably increased the railroad mileage over which the government had favorable rates without increasing the contribution which the government was
asked to make.[39]

---

should be public highways for the use of the federal government free from any toll
or other charge for the transportation of its troops or property.

This was interpreted by the Supreme Court to authorize the free use of the railroad's
tracks, the necessary locomotives and cars to be furnished by the government and
operated at its expense (93 U.S. 442, 1876). In actual practice the carriers were first
allowed 66⅔ percent of the rates paid by the public (12 Court of Claims 295, 1876)
and later 50 percent (15 Court of Claims 126, 1879).

2. Congressional rate lines. Some acts required carriers to perform services for the
Government at such charges as the Government might impose.

Statutes in and after 1892 (27 Stat. 174, 180, 1892) placed these companies on the
same basis as the free toll lines.

3. Free grant lines. A few acts provided that federal troops and property should be
transported over the aided roads without any charge to the Government.

Later statutes placed these companies also on the same basis as the free toll lines.

4. Full charge lines. Some acts merely required that the rates which railroads charged
for the transportation of troops and property should be reasonable and not in
excess of those paid by private parties.

(See, on the whole question of railroad land grants, the Reports of the Federal Coordinator (1938) and of the Board of Investigation and Research (1944) on Public
Aids to Transportation.)

[39] By "equalization agreement," railroads which had not received land grants or
which were listed as "full charge" lines equalized their rates with the allowance to land
grant carriers. The arrangements were first made individually and then, after 1914,
they took the form of a collective agreement. The principle was that the government
should pay, as a maximum, the most favorable total combination which could be discovered by combining the whole or parts of land grant and non-land-grant lines between points of origin and destination. In such calculations the land grant element
was taken as 50 percent of the commercial charge. The routes which were developed in
these combinations were often extremely circuitous; they were frequently, indeed, routes
over which the traffic could not be effectively handled. The shipment, however, actually moved over the direct route from origin to destination, and the calculated rate was
divided between participating carriers (United States House of Representatives, Committee on Interstate and Foreign Commerce, *Repeal of Land-Grant Rates on Transportation of Government Traffic,* Hearings before a subcommittee on H. R. 4184, 78th C.,
2d S., 1944, testimony Fletcher, pp. 44 ff).

Looking at the strictly financial benefits which the government obtained from its land grant policy we find that the total rate reductions were small at first, as was natural, and that they continued small for many years.[40] The total reductions for the carriage of troops and government property, up to December 31, 1927, were estimated by the Federal Coordinator as $48 million and by the Board of Investigation and Research at $56 million, in addition to $35 million which the Coordinator included on account of carriage of the mail. This was for a period of 50 years. But the Board of Investigation and Research also summarized the land grant rate reductions of all sorts, as of June 30, 1942, to amount to $341 million; and the Board expected that the total would be $580 million by the end of another fiscal year.[41] This was more than the land grant railroads had ever received from the granted lands and, of course, much more than the value of this land at the time when transfer had taken place. The government's bargain had shown a substantial profit although the profit was one for which the land grant railroads by themselves were only partly responsible. The primary reasons were, first, the increase in size and international and military commitments of the United States government after the land grant acts had been passed; second, the equalization agreements which had expanded the scope, in practice, of the rate reductions contemplated by the land grant laws; and third, the insistence of the federal government upon a highly liberal interpretation of the land grant laws.[42]

Repeal of the land grant rates. There were several reasons suggested to Congress for the repeal of certain provisions of the land grant laws.

1. The government had received, through rate reductions, more than the equivalent of its original gift.

2. The quotation of low rates on government shipments tended to keep railroad rates on other shipments high.

3. Low rate on land grant railroads, extended by equalization, disturbed the relations between communities in the United States, at least so far as government business was concerned. This was because a more distant source of supply might easily have better access to land grant mileage than a city nearer a delivery point that each desired to reach; it would follow that the

[40] Mr. Eastman testified in 1938 that the average up to that time had been less than $2,000,000 per year (United States House of Representatives, Committee on Interstate and Foreign Commerce, *Eliminating Land-Grant Reductions in Compensation for Transportation,* Hearings on H. R. 10,620, 75th C., 3d S., 1938, p. 8).

[41] United States Board of Investigation and Research, *Public Aids to Domestic Transportation,* 79th C., 1st S., H. Doc. 159, 1944, pp. 126–128.

[42] It proved difficult for the parties to agree upon the shipments which were eligible for land grant rate reductions, especially in later years. The land grant laws referred simply to government troops or property; in 1940 the phrase was changed to read "military or naval property of the United States moving for military or naval and not for civil use" (54 Stat. 929, 1940). It had always been somewhat difficult to define government property. It was still harder to distinguish between military or naval and civil use, especially in war time when the resources of the country were being utilized for military advantage in many ways. (See United States House of Representatives, Committee on Interstate and Foreign Commerce, *Repeal of Land-Grant Rates on Transportation of Government Traffic,* Hearings on H. R. 6156, 77th C., 2d S., 1942, testimony J. M. Souby, pp. 45–77).

former would enjoy a lower rate although a longer movement was involved. Land grant adjustments, indeed, sometimes produced rates that were greater for shorter than for longer hauls in direct violation of Section 4 of the Interstate Commerce Act.[43]

4. Land grant rates were not published. This objection was based upon the method by which the government ascertained, for any haul, the maximum rate which it was required to pay. The maximum depended upon a calculation which, in turn, rested upon the quoted rates upon a selected aggregate of routes. It followed that the effective total rate was not and could not easily be published. A result was that a business firm which sought to manufacture and to deliver an article to the government at a given place could not know what competition it would meet at the time it made its bid.

5. The use of land grant rates had an adverse effect upon railroad service. Mr. Eastman testified that they had, in his judgment, the following consequences:

a. They delayed the forwarding of shipments, because of complications with respect to billing.

b. They deprived the Government in many cases of more expeditious service which would have been available except for the attempt to take advantage of land grant reductions.

c. They threatened to restrict and handicap the Office of Defense Transportation in the event that it became necessary to direct traffic for the purpose of avoiding bottlenecks or congestion or in order to clear the way for the movement of military traffic.[44]

As a result of the considerations mentioned, land grant deductions were stopped on government civilian traffic in 1940 [45] and in 1945 they were abolished, effective October 1, 1946.[46] The federal government now pays full commercial rates for railroad service except on traffic covered by voluntary agreements concluded under Section 22 of the Interstate Commerce Act.

II

Procedure of the United States Army Engineers in Handling Waterway Projects

Waterway improvements are initially suggested by local interests for inclusion as a project in a rivers and harbors bill. If so included, the Corps of Engineers of the United States Army makes a preliminary investigation. This is followed by a detailed investigation and estimate of cost if the preliminary

---

[43] United States House of Representatives, Committee on Interstate and Foreign Commerce, *Repeal of Land-Grant Rates on Transportation of Government Traffic,* Hearings before a subcommittee on H. R. 4184, 78th C., 2d S., 1944, testimony Fletcher.

[44] United States House of Representatives, Committee on Interstate and Foreign Commerce, *Repeal of Land-Grant Rates on Transportation of Government Traffic,* Hearings on H. R. 6156, 77th C., 2d S., 1942.

[45] 54 Stat. 954, 1940 [Sec. 321 (a)].

[46] 59 Stat. 606, 1945.

inquiry justifies the step. These estimates are then referred to the Board of Engineers for Rivers and Harbors and then to the Chief Engineer. At this stage the Chief Engineer seeks the views of the governors of the States involved and of federal agencies including the Bureau of the Budget but not including the Interstate Commerce Commission. Finally, if the decisions along the way are favorable, the report of the Chief of Engineers is submitted to Congress by the Secretary of the Army, is embodied in a bill, is referred to a committee, is enacted into law, and is covered by an appropriation. (See United States Senate, Committee on Interstate and Foreign Commerce, *Study of Domestic Land and Water Transportation,* Hearings before a subcommittee pursuant to Sen. Res. 50, 81st C., 2d S., 1950, testimony Prince, p. 216; Report of Federal Coordinator of Transportation, *Public Aids to Transportation,* vol. 3, Appendix F, p. 177, 1939.)

The Board of Engineers for Rivers and Harbors works under general instructions embodied in federal legislation (United States Code, Sec. 541, Title 33). The Board finds it necessary, however, to develop a formula of its own for practical application. The problem is to determine the net public benefit of a proposed expenditure of public funds. The estimate which the Board makes in terms of public gain, in judging the desirability of a new project starts with the figure of cost which has been reached in the detailed investigation. This is reduced to an annual basis by the calculation of interest at 3 percent, a charge for amortization (based upon an assumed 25-year life for movable parts and a 50-year life for fixed parts), and an estimated amount for maintenance. This is the yearly outgo. Against it is placed a presumed public benefit, taken as the difference between the assumed cost of transportation on the project—the yearly outgo—and the ascertained cost by the most economical alternative means of transportation of the volume of traffic carried by the present waterway when this waterway has been developed to a reasonable extent. In most cases the actual alternative is railroad carriage, and in an undetermined number of cases the all-rail rate is used for comparison instead of an estimate of railroad costs. In some other cases the railroad charge has been neglected on the ground that it is unduly low because of rail-water competition (National Resources Planning Board, *Transportation and National Policy,* Part II, Sec. IV, p. 446). If the annual public benefit so computed exceeds the yearly outgo the project is held justified from a public point of view.

The Engineers' calculation of net benefits for the improvement of a waterway, such as the Mississippi River, recalls vividly the attempts to measure the benefits of canals during the middle of the nineteenth century. (See chapter 2.) There were difficulties recognized in the earlier discussions and there are additional complications today which should be mentioned in considering the basis upon which the Board of Engineers proceeds. Among these difficulties and complications the following deserve remark:

1. There is a necessity for judgment when water and rail estimates are influenced by the expected volume of water shipments on the one hand and upon railroad costs or rates upon the other.

2. A substantial diversion of shipments from rail to water routes may in-

crease the unit costs which other railroad shipments have to bear. This would, if it occurred, reduce the net public benefit to be derived from the development of a water plant. There is substance to the complaint that waterway improvements at the present time are not considered by those branches of the administration which are concerned with the direction of the transportation of the nation as a whole, but only by officers interested in a particular device. This objection is intensified by the special character of river transport.

3. The fact that taxpayers, not users, pay the cost of waterway development, distorts the effects of waterway improvements. One may expect a diversion and a change in utilization from this fact which cannot be justified by the calculated reduction in the operating cost of water carriage. In many cases relatively direct and inexpensive routes may be abandoned in favor of indirect rail-water routes which are more expensive in terms of operating cost but less expensive in terms of the expense which the boat owner incurs and the shipper has to pay.

4. It is erroneous, in any case, to assume that the public gain is to be measured by multiplying the decreases in costs which can be attributed to an improvement by the volume of freight carried by the water line after the improvement has been made. It is probably safe to say that a shipper who forwards X tons of freight for 500 cents makes a gain of 100 if the charge is reduced to 400 cents, no other changes in the situation having occurred. But the assumption that a shipper who did not and never would have paid more than 450 cents gains more than 50 is difficult to prove. The further elaboration of this idea has been considered in chapter 2.

III

Separation of Air-Mail Payments and Air Subsidies

There have been a number of Congressional bills and reports which have proposed a separation of air-mail payments and air subsidies. (See United States Senate, Committee on Interstate and Foreign Commerce, Hearings pursuant to S. Res. 50, 1950, testimony Parmalee, for a list covering the years 1949–50.) A bill passed the House of Representatives in 1950 and another bill passed the Senate in 1951, both designed to separate air-mail subsidy from air-mail pay, but neither was approved by Congress as a whole. The House bill authorized the Civil Aeronautics Board (1) to fix an air mail rate at a level governed by air-mail costs and (2) to make subsidy payments to air carriers in the amounts necessary to maintain and develop air service. The air-mail rates were to be paid by the Postmaster General; the subsidies were to be paid by the Board out of sums which Congress should provide. The Senate bill adopted the principle of separation but the Senate found some difficulty in describing a method of allocating costs between air mail and other services which it was disposed to endorse.

The Civil Aeronautics Board published two studies, one in 1951 and the other in 1952 which attempted to measure the amount of subsidy paid in 1951 and to estimate the probable amounts in 1952 and 1953.

The first study divided domestic carriers into seven groups. The Board concluded that the mail payments to the four principal domestic lines, which were $0.45 per mail ton-mile, involved no subsidy and that corresponding "no subsidy" or "service" rates could be calculated for other groups of carriers by comparison of operating costs omitting passenger expense. On this basis it became possible to determine the mail subsidy which any group received by a simple formula $P—MX$ in which P represented total mail revenues which air-line companies in the group received, M the mail ton-miles carried, and X the service rates which were on record for the group. The same method was used in dealing with international lines, although the number of groups was not the same.

The general conclusion reached was that, in 1951, domestic carriers received a subsidy of $34,565,000, or 55.81 percent of the mail revenues paid them, and international carriers received a subsidy of $40,111,000, or 70.2 percent of the mail revenues paid them. According to the Civil Aeronautics Board these percentages should be expected to decline.

The Board's estimates throw some light upon the air subsidy situation. They are, however, subject to technical criticism, and they are insufficient in themselves to justify the methods used and the amounts spent in air subsidies at the present time. Additional attention is likely to be paid to this contentious subject. (See Civil Aeronautics Board, *Administrative Separation of Subsidy from Total Mail Payments to Domestic Air Carriers,* September, 1951; *ibid., Administrative Separation of Subsidy from Total Mail Payments to United States International Overseas and Territorial Air Carriers,* June, 1952.)

R E F E R E N C E S

General Treatises

Bigham, Truman C., and Roberts, Merrill J., *Transportation, Principles and Problems,* New York,, McGraw-Hill, 1952.

Bonavia, M. R., *The Economics of Transport,* New York, Pitman, 1947.

Cleveland, F. A., and Powel, F. W., *Railroad Promotion and Capitalization in the United States,* New York, Longmans, 1909.

Dearing, Charles L., and Owen, Wilfrid, *National Transportation Policy,* Washington, D.C., Brookings Institution, 1949.

Frederick, John H., *Commercial Air Transportation,* Chicago, Irwin, 1951.

Haney, L. H., *Congressional History of Railways in the United States, 1850–1887,* Madison, Wis., Bulletin of the University of Wisconsin, 1908.

Landon, Charles E., *Transportation, Principles, Practices, Problems,* New York, Sloane, 1951.

Locklin, D. Philip, *Economics of Transportation,* Chicago, Irwin, 1947.

Moulton, H. G., *The American Transportation Problem,* Washington, D.C., Brookings Institution, 1933.

Moulton, H. G., *Railways Versus Waterways,* Boston, Houghton, Mifflin, 1912.

Puffer, Claude E., *Air Transportation,* Philadelphia, Blakiston, 1941.

Sanborn, J. B., *Congressional Grants of Land in Aid of Railways*, Madison, Wis., Bulletin of the University of Wisconsin, 1899.

Smith, H. L., *The History of Commercial Aviation in the United States*, New York, Knopf, 1944.

Other Books

David, Paul T., *The Economics of Mail Transportation*, Washington, D.C., Brookings Institution, 1934.

Durrenberger, J. A., *Turnpikes: A Study of the Toll Road Movement in the Middle Atlantic States, 1931*, Valdosta, Ga., Southern Stationery and Printing, 1931.

Gomez, R. A., *Intergovernmental Relations in Highways*, Minneapolis, University of Minnesota, 1950.

Hebden, Norman, and Smith, W. S., *State-City Relationships in Highway Affairs*, New Haven, Yale, 1950.

Owen, Wilfred, and Dearing, Charles L., *Toll Roads and the Problem of Highway Modernization*, Washington, D.C., Brookings Institution, 1951.

Periodicals

Allen, E. D., "The Theory of Highway Costs and the Different Approaches to Their Allocation," *Journal of Land and Public Utility Economics*, August, 1939.

Ellis, David M., "The Forfeiture of Railroad Land Grants, 1867–1894," *Mississippi Valley Historical Review*, June, 1946.

Henry, Robert S., "The Railroad Land Grant Legend in American History Texts," *Mississippi Valley Historical Review*, September, 1945.

Peterson, G. S., "Highway Policy on a Commercial Basis," *Quarterly Journal of Economics*, May, 1932.

Porter, R. W., "Allocation of Air Transportation Cost in Determining Mail, Passenger, and Cargo Rates," *Journal of Air Law and Commerce*, Summer, 1948.

Special and Miscellaneous

Association of American Railroads, *Analysis of Reports of Staffs of Federal Coordinator of Transportation and Board of Investigation and Research* (in United States Senate, Committee on Interstate and Foreign Commerce, Hearings before a subcommittee pursuant to Sen. Res. 50, 81st C., 2d S., 1950).

Joint Committee on the Economic Report, Sen. Doc. 145, 81st C., 2d S., 1950.

National Interregional Highway Committee, *Report Outlining and Recommending a National System of Interregional Highways*, 78th C., 2d S., House Doc. 379, 1944.

United States Board of Investigation and Research, *Public Aids to Domestic Transportation*, 79th C., 1st S., House Doc. 159, 1944.

United States Department of Agriculture, Bureau of Public Roads, *Toll Roads and Free Roads*, House Doc. 272, 76th C., 1st S., 1939.

United States, Department of Commerce, Public Roads Administration, *Highway Development, Administration, and Finance,* compiled by Public Roads Administration and Federal Works Agency, Washington, D.C. Presented at the 45th annual meeting, American Road Builders' Association, Chicago, 1946.

United States Federal Aviation Commission, *Report of the Federal Aviation Commission Containing Its Recommendations of a Broad Policy Covering All Phases of Aviation and the Relation of the United States Thereto,* 74th C., 1st S., Sen. Doc. 15, 1935.

United States House of Representatives, Committee on Interstate and Foreign Commerce, *Air-Mail Subsidies,* Hearings before a subcommittee on H. R. 2908 and H. J. Res. 331, 81st C., 2d S., 1950.

United States House of Representatives, Committee on Interstate and Foreign Commerce, *Separation of Subsidy from Air-Mail Pay,* House Rep. 3041, 81st C., 2d S., 1950.

United States, Office of the Federal Coordinator of Transportation, *Public Aids to Transportation,* 1938.

President of the United States' Air Policy Commission, *Survival in the Air Age,* Washington, D.C., 1948.

United States Senate, Committee on Interstate and Foreign Commerce, *Air-Line Industry Investigation,* Hearings pursuant to Sen. Res. 50, 81st C., 1st S., 1949.

United States Senate, Committee on Interstate and Foreign Commerce, *Study of Domestic Land and Water Transportation,* Hearings before a subcommittee pursuant to Sen. Res. 50, 81st C., 2d S., 1950.

United States Senate, Committee on Interstate and Foreign Commerce, *Separation of Air Mail Pay from Subsidy,* Hearings on Bills, Various, 82d C., 1st S., 1951.

United States Senate, Committee on Public Works, *Federal Aid Highway Act of 1952,* Hearings before a subcommittee on S. 2437 and S. 2585, 1952.

Conclusion

This final chapter will be divided into two parts. Of these the first will summarize current proposals for the amendment of the Interstate Commerce Act and the Civil Aeronautics Act. The second will contain some observations on the subject of National Transportation Policy.

Proposed Statutory Amendments

There is a good deal of interest in transport legislation as this book is being written, and a number of suggestions for federal action have been proposed to congressional committees and have been there elaborately discussed. These proposals have been also debated in conferences in which carriers primarily and shippers to some extent have been represented. There is no unanimous opinion upon the subjects that we shall mention; there is, however, a considerable and favorable sentiment for each of the specific items which will be listed and described. The situation resembles somewhat that which prevailed prior to the passage of the Transportation Act of 1920, except that the likelihood of important statutory changes is much less.

Strengthening of Federal Control

Plans for the correction or amplification of present laws with respect to transport may be divided into two groups. Proposals in the first group would enlarge federal control of transportation. Measures in the second group would weaken this control in some specific way. Those in the first category may be considered in the following order:

1. *Exemptions from regulation.* Current suggestions for legislation contemplate reduction in the exemptions now accorded operators of motor vehicles. The reader may refer, in this connection, to chapter 31. It is suggested in particular:

    a. That motor vehicles which carry exempt agricultural products should not, at another time, be allowed to carry nonexempt commodities.

b. That the transportation of the manufactured products of fish should not be exempt.

c. That the transportation of imported goods should not be exempt.

d. That the Interstate Commerce Commission should have authority to remove exemptions when it found that they were unnecessary.

Still another proposal would limit the exemptions allowed vehicles engaged in the carriage of fish or agricultural commodities to hauls from the area of production to the primary market serving fisherman or farmer.[1]

Some kind of limitation is earnestly desired by motor common carriers and by railroads. This was likewise recommended in the Bricker report.[2] The question of systematic regulation versus flexible operation is involved. As might be expected, the farming interests oppose any limitation of motor exemptions on the ground that it would reduce the facilities which farmers now enjoy and might lessen the efficiency of the trucks which are now employed.

2. *Regulation of contract carriage.* This also raises the problem of flexible operation. Contract carriers are either not regulated, as in the case of air carriers, or they are only slightly regulated, as in the case of carriers operating by highways or by water. The chief problem is that of the motor carrier.

Common carriers desire that the supervision which the Interstate Commerce Commission and the Civil Aeronautics Board exercise over contract carriers be enlarged:

a. By requiring air contract carriers to obtain permits from the Civil Aeronautics Board before engaging in interstate operations.

b. By subjecting contract air carriers to the same kind of economic regulation that is applied to contract motor and water carriers.

c. By requiring common carriers generally to file, adhere to, and make public the rates which they actually charge.

Proposed legislation in Congress goes even further with respect to contract carrier rates by authorizing the Interstate Commerce Commission to prescribe reasonable rates to be charged by contract motor or water carriers, and by making contract carriers subject to the clauses of the

---

[1] Transportation Association of America, *Sound Transportation for the National Welfare,* Report to the Board of Directors by the Public Administration Board, Cooperative Project on National Transportation Policy, Chicago, April, 1952, p. 68.

See United States Senate, Committee on Interstate and Foreign Commerce, *Domestic Land and Water Transportation,* Hearings on bills relative to domestic land and water transportation, 82d C., 2d S., 1952, pp. 661–741.

[2] United States Senate, Committee on Interstate and Foreign Commerce, *Domestic Land and Water Transportation,* Progress Report by a subcommittee pursuant to Sen. Res. 50, 82d C., 1st S., Sen. Rep. 1039, 1951.

Interstate Commerce Act which now forbid discrimination by rail, motor, and forwarder common carriers.

The first two of these proposals listed are intended to place air contract carriers in the same position as that occupied by other contract carriers. The third improves the competitive position of rail, motor, and water common carriers by increasing the amount of information that common carriers can command and by putting contract carrier rates under general regulatory control. The last-mentioned addition would equalize the duties of contract and common carriers with respect to discrimination.

Testimony with respect to the contentions summarized in the preceding paragraphs, and particularly testimony with respect to the proposal that contract carriers shall file and make public the rates which they charge, develops the great flexibility and utility of contract carrier service. The testimony also indicates that common carriers suffer from contract carrier competition and that they will continue to suffer unless Congress stiffens the rules which govern contract carriage.[3]

3. *Federal regulation of the sizes and weights of motor vehicles.* A bill for federal regulation of the sizes and weights of motor vehicles was introduced into the 82d Congress. The bill fixed specific limits and dimensions with the provision that the Interstate Commerce Commission might authorize motor vehicles to operate when not in conformity with such limitations, when the Commission thought that this was vital.

The main conflict in legislation of this sort is between federal and state governments, although motor carriers will take part in the controversy if bills carry provisions which they do not approve. The text has discussed this general subject in chapters 31 and 32.

4. *User charges on inland waterways.* Legislation has been introduced authorizing the Interstate Commerce Commission to prescribe user charges for the use, for commercial purposes, of improved inland waterways. This would bring the Commission into an active controversy.

A corollary of the above is the proposal that the Interstate Commerce Commission should report upon the desirability of proposed inland waterway improvements from the point of view of public convenience and necessity. Only improvements for navigation would be investigated. The Commission report would be submitted to the Chief of Engineers. This would increase the responsibility of the Interstate Commerce Commission but not its power.

5. Regulation of frequency of service and of types of carrier equip-

---

[3] Figures given by one witness, however, are to the effect that the proportion of intercity ton-miles handled by contract motor carriers declined from 24.1 to 8.5 percent between 1939 and 1949 while the proportion handled by common motor carriers increased from 75.9 to 91.5 percent (*Domestic Land and Water Transportation,* 1951, *op. cit.,* p. 590, testimony Wheeler).

ment which may be employed. Neither the Interstate Commerce Commission nor the Civil Aeronautics Board now has this direct authority. The Civil Aeronautics Board, at least, desires the power to place conditions in certificates of convenience which will limit the number of schedules which a company may fly or the types of equipment which it may utilize. This is to avoid subsidies that may result from overexpansion or from the use of planes for purposes for which they are not designed.

There has been some trouble, also, with surface motor carriers operating on a contract basis. Contract carriers receive permits on the theory that they serve, in each case, only a few customers. With a successful business, they may presently serve many customers. The Interstate Commerce Commission cannot and does not restrict this growth; it does, however, sometimes withdraw the contract carriers permit when the growth has taken place, without issuing a common carrier certificate in its stead. The contract carriers feel that they should at least be warned when conditions are such as are described, although they do not ask that the Commission be given power to regulate their internal affairs.

Boards and commissions would have much more power if they could control motor and air operations or the development of operations under a certificate as well as the entrance into a business which a certificate traditionally allows. There is probably no logical or qualitative difference in the two situations. The degree of government interference with private business would be, however, much larger if this particular authority were conferred.

6. *Various.* It has been proposed that the Interstate Commerce Commission be given authority:

    a. To grant or to refuse certificates to freight forwarders. At present, these operators need only a permit.

    b. To revoke water carrier certificates in certain cases. These certificates cannot now be recalled. Many certificates remain in effect, therefore, even though they are not used.

    c. To require railroads to install signal, radio communication, and other safety systems. This would give the Commission power over what has been, for the most part, a managerial responsibility.

    d. To require a railroad to participate in a through route which does not embrace substantially the entire length of it line between the termini of the route.

    e. To require a trucker who operates under a certificate as a common carrier to accept any or all freight for transportation to or from any point upon its line of operation, within the capacity of its equipment.

    f. To consider on appeal cases which involve the abandonment of railroads operating entirely within a single state, or the abandonment of the passenger service of these railroads. The purpose here is to overcome the resistance of State bodies which oppose the abandonment of unprofitable local lines.

7. It has been proposed that the Civil Aeronautics Board be given authority:

    a. To compel air carriers to initiate service to wholly new points. At present the Board may compel this service when it can be interpreted as an amendment to an existing certificate, but not when the route is entirely different.

    b. To fix rates on international flights.

    c. To regulate airline securities.

The statutory amendments in the preceding group do not always instruct the regulatory commissions to do specific things; but the effect of their approval in such cases would, doubtless, be much the same as it would be if this instruction were provided.

Weakening of Federal Control

In addition to the foregoing list there are proposed amendments to existing statutes which withdraw matters from the jurisdiction of regulatory commissions or which direct these commissions to act in certain ways which lessen their efficiency or their independence. These amendments may be said to weaken federal control. They include the following:

1. *Repeal of the long- and short-haul clause.* There are two suggestions with respect to Section 4 of the Interstate Commerce Act. One is that the clause be applied to motor carriage, and the other is that the clause be repealed. There are also two parts of the clause: first, the phrases which make illegal greater charges for shorter hauls and, second, those which forbid through rates that are higher than the aggregate of intermediate rates.

The railroads are the chief advocates of the repeal of the first part of Section 4. They argue frankly that they need a freer hand in competition. They say also that the present prohibition increases the complexity of tariff making and that the public is protected in any case by other sections of the Interstate Commerce Act, including Sections 2 and 3 and that giving the Commission power to set a minimum rate. The motor carriers are indifferent to the long- and short-haul provision, but they anticipate difficulty if they are forbidden to charge more on through traffic than the aggregate of local rates. The water and especially the intercoastal lines are generally opposed.

It seems clear that the railroads expect some relaxation of regulation from the repeal of Section 4. The amount would depend upon the reactions of the Commission. The argument is, in any event, between the proponents of less and those who desire the same amount of regulation.

2. *Repeal of the commodity clause.* As with the long- and short-haul clause, there is opinion favoring repeal and opinion favoring extension. The clause does not now prevent a considerable unification of industrial and transport operations, partly because of the liberal exemptions granted to classes of carriers under the Interstate Commerce Act. Repeal would, however, accomplish a relaxation of control. The contrary view is that the present prohibition should be extended to motor and water carriers, on the general principle that the business of the regulated carrier should be limited to the supply of transportation service.

3. *Rate increase applications.* This proposal has several elements: It provides:

a. That carriers may certify to the Interstate Commerce Commission (1) that they have incurred or that they are about to incur expenses of specified sorts and (2) that an increase in their rates is necessary in order to maintain service in the face of this increased expense.

b. That on the basis of the described certification, carriers may file rate schedules to take effect in 30 days.

c. That the Interstate Commerce Commission, before the 30 days has expired, may find the schedules to be discriminatory or that they will produce excessive revenues.

d. That the Interstate Commerce Commission may not suspend the schedules that are filed. In some forms of the proposal, however, the Commission is permitted to make further investigation within 60 days.

The arrangement thus explained is limited to railroads in some formulations; in others it is extended to all carriers. The purpose is to hasten the disposition of rate increase cases. By eliminating rate suspension in certain situations—a procedure which had been established in 1910—it also establishes the assumption that newly filed rates are reasonable unless the contrary can be proved in 30 days. The previous presumption had been that existing rates were reasonable, at least to the extent that shippers should continue to pay the older charge until the propriety of a change in rates in disputed cases had been shown.

The sums at stake in this particular proposal are considerable. According to railroad testimony, the average elapsed time between applications for rate increases and their effective date was, between 1946 and 1951, a period of 163 days.[4] The total revenues lost during the elapsed periods was not given in this summary for Class I railroads as a whole, but for the railroads in the Southern region it was calculated at $195,981,873.[5] Argu-

[4] *Domestic Land and Water Transportation,* 1952, *op. cit.,* pp. 921–923, testimony Davis.

[5] *Ibid.,* p. 929.

ments for alteration of the law merge into a consideration of the financial condition of railroads generally. From the point of view of National Transportation Policy it is evident that the proposal would put increased pressure upon the Interstate Commerce Commission and would, in that sense, weaken the system of federal control.

4. *Change in the rule of rate making.* It is argued that the Commission should no longer be required to give due consideration, in fixing rates, to the effect of these rates upon the movement of traffic. The removal of the instruction would presumably exclude the Commission from a field in which, it is thought, managerial judgment should control.

5. *Certificates of convenience and necessity.* There are proposals that the Interstate Commerce Commission, at least when it handles applications for authority to institute a new truck operation, shall take into account the effect upon other modes of transportation already in existence. It would be advantageous to the railroads if this principle were systematically applied.

Summary of Suggestions

Most of the suggestions in the preceding pages are submitted by carriers of one type or another which feel themselves at a relative disadvantage under the present system of regulatory control, or they come from regulatory bodies that would like to see their powers complemented or increased. There is very little active "shipper-public" interest. More particularly, there would appear to be three currents with reference to regulation. There is, first, the normal demand of government organizations for a more completely rounded authority. On the other hand, there is a reaction against regulation in some transport fields which is stronger than it has been for many years. And in the third place, interested parties complain that existing policies bear unequally upon different forms of carriage. There are proposals for legislation that are intended to correct the balance.

National Transportation Policy

The preceding pages have summarized immediate proposals for the amendment of existing statutes that provide for transportation control. Are these suggestions consistent with National Transportation Policy? What, in fact, is that policy, how is it framed, and how can it be defined?

Most transport policy in a modern country is a combination of two segments. It generally includes the idea that there shall be a great deal of transportation available, that the people who supply it shall not enjoy a monopoly return, and that the carriers shall not, by price manipulation, change markedly the geographical distribution or industrial organization of population and industry unless the public, in its political aspect, is informed and has approved. It is contained in a number of limited rules and phrases which have become embedded in legislation, more or less experimentally, to meet special situations, and which the public has interpreted and found good. When a large number of these limited rules accumulate it may be possible, if the rules are consistent with each other, to derive from them principles which, in some areas, are relatively precise. If there are enough principles, there will presently be a policy that is sufficiently definite to be applied. This policy will be a growth and not a line of conduct fixed by a definition. It will be based upon a series of recorded actions and will be only imperfectly expressed by a code or by a statutory phrase. While we do have a "Declaration of National Policy" in the Interstate Commerce Act and another in the Civil Aeronautics Act, these pronouncements do little to indicate national purposes or ideals or to govern national procedure. As a matter of fact, they consist merely of broad assertions combined with qualifying words or phrases so as to yield, with respect to every problem, an indeterminate result. And while the declarations do suggest subjects to which the attention of regulatory organizations should be drawn, the list includes items with which commissions have struggled for 80 years; nor are the purposes of selection stated in revealing terms.

Under the circumstances the author will not attempt to state a national policy for the United States or to consider in detail suggestions for present change. He will observe, however, that certain matters should be studied or restudied, in his judgment, as a background for proposals mentioned in this chapter and as a guide to future administration of the federal law.

The Rights of Different Forms of Carriage

A national transportation policy must take account of the fact that, in the United States, our transport system now consists of at least five separate techniques and that these techniques have distinct organizations and claim separate rights and privileges. This is proper; but policy should also recognize the fact that the claims of the special techniques are self-regarding and often exaggerated, and that all are essentially devoted to one common task. It is to be regretted that public recognition of the new machinery in some instances and of the contribution made by the groups which have created it has led to a considerable transfer of attention from the needs of the users of transportation to the needs of the transportation itself. This is not a sound position for a national transportation policy to take. It hampers coördination, it introduces improper standards of regulation, and it interferes with wise promotion in ways in which the text next has previously explained.

The Problem of Promotion

It is interesting to observe that none of the present proposals for the amendment of the Interstate Commerce Act and of the Civil Aeronautics Act relate to the question of carrier promotion. Yet promotion is an essential element of national policy and it is also the field of government activity where the organization is least coördinated, the most wasteful, and the results least carefully considered. The basic reason for this is that the promotion of particular forms of carriage starts with persons who are already connected with or who benefit by the enlargement of facilities of a special kind, and that it is supported by government officials whose reputation depends upon the successful development of agencies for which they are professionally responsible. Thus the competition of interests which operate motor or air or water facilities is carried into the government organization and appears in the form of reports, testimony, and recommendations urging expansion of appropriations for service of one or of another kind. The details which justify these statements were presented in chapter 34. They are noticed by most impartial observers of present practice.

Government expenditures for transport in the United States have had large and desirable results. The independence of the forms of transportation upon which outlays have been made, the disconnected appeals for help, and the variations in the collection of user charges have led, on the other hand, to the waste of public funds. The defects in the system have produced even more serious results. They have distorted the development of the machinery upon which the public relies for service. The country owes much to state and federal administrations for the support which various kinds of transport have received. It is useful to observe, however, that our transportation agencies, except the railroads, do not collect charges from their customers today which are sufficient to cover the cost of the facilities which they use and which for the most part they do not finance. It is also reasonably certain that, in some cases, the effect of subsidy is to divert shipments from routes where the operating costs are comparatively low to routes where the operating costs are relatively high or where low operating costs are the consequence of the liberal expenditure of government funds. There are cases in which, one may well believe, the government transfers capital by taxation and investment from a private use which is or might be productive to a use which, from the point of view of private or social value, is inferior to a marked degree.

It is likely that the overall efficiency of transportation in this country would be increased if the extent and distribution of government aid for carriage were regularly considered by some single government organization to which special organizations might be required to submit their proposals for general examination and control. Some progress has been made in this direction by the transfer of the Administrator of Civil Aeronautics, the Commissioner of Public Roads, and the Inland Waterways Corporation to the Department of Commerce and by the creation of the office of Under Secretary of Commerce for Transportation.[6] It has been further proposed that a separate Department of Transportation be set up and that this Department be authorized, among other things, (1) to facilitate the application of uniform standards in determining the justification of projects involving several forms of transportation; and (2) to provide a continuing and authoritative source of information for the legislative and executive branches of government concerning the financial and operating position of the several transportation agencies and the adequacy of the total transportation plant to meet the needs of commerce and national security.[7]

If a new department were set up, there might, at the same time, be a formal development of the policy of user charges and the new agency might fix the level at which these charges should be made. This would be really part of the same plan, because the special intention would be to prevent the diversion of traffic from relatively economical to relatively expensive routes, as well as to eliminate the subsidization of enterprises for which the public is not willing to pay. The reorganization mentioned would increase the authority of the executive branch of the federal administration. It might admit political considerations that would influence public policy; but present arrangements are not free from these defects. It would not, of itself, produce coördination; but it might create a frame of mind that would be favorable to this result.

[6] The Office of Under Secretary of Commerce for Transportation was set up in 1940. The Under Secretary exercises direction and supervision over agencies in the Department of Commerce, through their respective heads, including the agencies mentioned in the text, the Weather Bureau, the Coast and Geodetic Survey, and to a limited extent, the Federal Maritime Board. He will also exercise a delegated authority in coordinating other transportation programs and responsibilities that are or may be vested in the Department of Commerce. This is the general assignment.

What, if anything, the Under Secretary will be able to accomplish with respect to agencies outside the Department of Commerce is, of course, quite uncertain. In 1952, his office was a modest organization of about 25 people. It regarded itself as a research group, charged with the duty of analyzing the promotional policies of the federal government and their effects. According to the Secretary of Commerce at the time, its studies were expected to lead to recommendations for legislative or administrative action. Its effort was to see that the transportation activities of the federal government were nonconflicting and that they promoted a well-rounded, privately owned and operated transportation industry, furnishing adequate service at the lowest overall cost consistent with that service. It disclaimed any wish for regulatory authority. This was an admirable position for the Office of the Under Secretary to take. There is no evidence as yet, however, that the influence of the Office upon general transportation policies will be great.

[7] Charles L. Dearing and Wilfrid Owen, *National Transportation Policy*, Washington, D.C., Brookings Institution, 1949, p. 388.

Proposals for the reorganization of the apparatus for transport promotion are among the few which are made, characteristically, by outside observers. The development of user charges is advocated also by these observers but especially by railroads. Suggestions with respect to user charges are opposed by water and by air interests and are tolerated by motor carriers on the assumption that highway improvements are already financed by motor vehicle contributions.[8]

The Development of Private Carriage

National policy has also to consider seriously the problem of private carriage. This is, as we have seen, the subject of several of the proposals for amendment of the Interstate Commerce Act and of the Civil Aeronautics Act which we have reported in a summary form. Most of these proposals contemplate an increased control over private carriage, and this is natural, in view of the sources from which the proposals come. But the question of private carriage cannot be so easily dismissed.

There is no doubt but that the percentage which private carriage bears to the total machinery of transport in the United States has been, in recent years, considerably increased. This circumstance with respect to transportation has been surveyed in chapters 31–33. There are several reasons for the change.

The predominance of unregulated private transport upon the Mississippi River and upon the Lakes can be explained by the operations of large industrial companies with whose private ships and barges it has seemed undesirable to interfere. The situation, here, is not new; and public opinion, with respect to private vessels and bulk cargoes, has not been especially adverse. In motor and air transport the explanation is somewhat different.

In the case of motor transport, the principal highway user has been, from the beginning, the private carrier. This has been, quite simply, the result of the small size of the operating unit. The passenger car is, and so far as one can anticipate will remain, the typical highway vehicle. It holds its place because of its flexibility in use, because of the small investment required, and because of the relative simplicity of its operation. The political influence of the enormous body of private owners would, moreover, prevent any serious attempt to introduce government control except with respect to the safety of operation.

To a lesser degree, but still in an important measure, the private motor

[8] The railroad point of view was elaborately presented in United States Senate, Committee on Interstate and Foreign Commerce, *Study of Domestic Land and Water Transportation,* Hearings before a subcommittee, pursuant to Sen. Res. 50, 81st C., 2d S., 1950, pp. 88–231.

truck has maintained an independent position. This independence is partly the result of conditions in the majority of cities except in some urban centers where vehicles must be economical of space. It has also been true of agricultural districts. While the Interstate Commerce Commission would prefer to extend its authority over certain types of agricultural operations as present plans propose, it does not seem likely that the exceptions which we have mentioned in earlier pages will be much reduced. Contributing to this situation is the circumstance that government regulation of motor carrier certificates has not added to the efficiency of motor operation. It may be that more thorough control would eliminate some waste in motor trucking operations. But the motor trucking business does not differ so greatly from other business that is now conducted upon a private basis as to make its regulation necessary for the reasons which appear to make railroad control essential. Nor is it certain that the operating and traffic problems of the motor truck will be, during the next few decades, so similar to those of railroads as to permit the same rules to be applied. There are grounds which may justify a relaxation of government economic control of motor operation, at least in those areas of service where competition with the railroad is least pronounced.

Air carriage differs from motor carriage and resembles railroad transport in that it requires large investment and utilizes equipment which amateurs cannot easily learn to direct. The position of the government is also strengthened by a combination of subsidy with air-line control and by the absence of pleasure use. The present argument for private carriage is not strong. Contract carriage is, however, exempt, and there is a substantial demand for the reduction of Commission control over so-called irregular carriers which may change substantially the scheme of air carrier regulation. In this case private air carriage has achieved considerable success without subsidy and with a minimum of government interference.

All things taken together, an essential decision in determining national policy is whether private carriage is to be eliminated in the United States as far as possible, or whether the policy should be to allow private carriage to expand and to concentrate control upon those branches of the transport system where regulation can be most effectively applied.

Effects of Imperfections in the Present System of Regulation and Promotion

It is unfortunate that conditions which have been mentioned in preceding pages now prevail, and for several reasons.

One major circumstance is that government policies weaken the railroad system, which is the principal carrier of freight in the United States on a ton mile basis. The railroad is the only transport industry which does not benefit from the promotional activity of the federal government. It differs in this from air and water transport; and from the motor business in that it is apparently impossible for the railroad to argue, as the highway carrier has done, that the taxpayer should bear part of its burden in providing a right of way. The railroad differs also from other carriers in that its competitive activities are subject to relatively great control. There is a real possibility that the government may be forced to take the railroads over in order to supply a financial aid which is politically impossible so long as railroad management remains in private hands.

Another difficulty in the present situation is that the position of the Interstate Commerce Commission has become impaired. The damage is not yet serious, but the process has begun. The mere growth of the transport industry has, indeed, weakened the Commission in a certain sense because it has raised a volume of problems which the Commission's standard organization has not been able to solve without a degree of internal delegation of authority which the Commission has never used. The separate functioning of the Civil Aeronautics Board has relieved the Interstate Commerce Commission to some extent, but in other ways it has made the Commission's work more difficult.

The Commission suffers, first, because its tasks have grown in number; second, because its appropriations have been reduced; and third, because a relatively large fraction of the transport industry today, including some of the air and a large part of surface carriage, is relatively free from regulation, but competes with the balance which is controlled. It may also be that the Commission has overreached itself by entering the field of managerial control.

The weakening of the Commission lessens the authority of the only government organization that seeks to reduce waste in transportation in a general way. It is the only one which is not committed to the progress of a single technique, and the only one which has seriously attempted to discover and to apply broad principles in the regulation of transportation.

It is to be hoped that the present disorganization of transport and of regulation will be repaired without the reduction of vigor in either case. There is much to be done, especially in the concentration and reconstruction of the agencies of regulation and in the technique of handling their work. Obviously the coördination of operating agencies has been delayed. It is to be hoped, also, that government promotion will be reorganized on some general basis which will principally regard the public interest and not the interest of the private parties that are concerned. There is no sufficient reason why this cannot be done. How far the particular proposals for statutory amendment which are pending will be approved, there is no present way for anyone to predict.

REFERENCES

General Treatises

Bigham, Truman C., and Roberts, Merrill J., *Transportation, Principles and Problems,* New York, McGraw-Hill, 1952.

Dearing, Charles L., and Owen, Wilfrid, *National Transportation Policy,* Washington, D.C., Brookings Institution, 1949.

Fair, Marvin L., and Williams, E. W., *Economics of Transportation,* New York, Harper, 1950.

Landon, Charles E., *Transportation: Principles, Practices, Problems,* New York, Sloane, 1951.

Westmeyer, Russell E., *Economics of Transportation,* New York, Prentice-Hall, 1952.

Other Books

Oppenheim, S. C., *The National Transportation Policy and Intercarrier Competitive Rates,* Harrisburg, Pa., Evangelical Press, 1945.

Periodicals

Cunningham, William J., "The Transportation Problem," *Harvard Business Review,* Autumn, 1946.

Dewey, Ralph, "The Transportation Act of 1940," *American Economic Review,* March, 1941.

Dewey, Ralph, "Criteria for the Establishment of an Optimum Transportation System," *American Economic Review,* May, 1952.

Eastman, J. B., "The Adjustment of Rates Between Competing Forms of Transportation," *American Economic Review,* March, 1940.

Nelson, James C., "Highway Development, the Railroads, and National Transportation Policy," *American Economic Review,* May, 1951.

Young, Robert R., "A National Transportation Policy," *Law and Contemporary Problems,* Summer, 1947.

Special and Miscellaneous

National Resources Planning Board, *Transportation and National Policy,* Washington, D.C., 1942.

President's Committee to Submit Recommendations upon the General Transportation Situation, *Report of Committee Appointed September 20, 1938,* Washington, D.C., Hayworth Printing, 1938.

Railway Business Association, *Sound Policies in Transportation,* Prepared by P. Harvey Middleton, President, Chicago, September, 1953.

Transportation Association of America, *Sound Transportation for the National Welfare,* Report to the Board of Directors by the Public Administration Board, Cooperative Project on National Transportation Policy, Chicago, April, 1952.

United States, Commission on Organization of the Executive Branch of the Government, *Independent Regulatory Commissions,* 1949.

United States House of Representatives, Committee on Interstate and Foreign Commerce, *Transportation Study,* Hearings before a subcommittee on Transportation Problems, 81st C., 2d S., 1950.

United States, Office of the Federal Coordinator of Transportation, *Regulation of Railroads,* Sen. Doc. 119, 73d C., 2d S., 1934.

United States, Office of the Federal Coordinator of Transportation, *Regulation of Transportation Agencies,* Sen. Doc. 152, 73d C., 2d S., 1934.

United States, Office of the Federal Coordinator of Transportation, *Report,* H. Doc. 89, 74th C., 1st S., 1935.

United States, Office of the Federal Coordinator of Transportation, *Fourth Report,* H. Doc. 394, 74th C., 2d S., 1936.

United States Senate, Committee on Interstate and Foreign Commerce, *Air Line Industry Investigation,* Hearings pursuant to Sen. Res., 81st C., 1st S., 1949.

United States Senate, Committee on Interstate and Foreign Commerce, *Study of Domestic Land and Water Transportation,* Hearings before a subcommittee pursuant to Sen. Res. 50, 81st C., 2d S., 1950.

United States Senate, Committee on Interstate and Foreign Commerce, *Domestic Land and Water Transportation,* Progress Report by a subcommittee pursuant to Sen. Res. 50, 82d C., 1st S., Sen. Rep. 1039, 1951 (Bricker Report).

United States Senate, Committee on Interstate and Foreign Commerce, *Domestic Land and Water Transportation,* Hearings on Bills relative to Domestic Land and Water Transportation, 82d C., 2d S., 1952.

Index

Abandonment, 241–242; of railroads, 640–644; in case of motor carriers, 667; in case of inland water carriers, 697
See also Service
Abstracts of interline waybills, 465–466
Accidents in air transport, in dirigible, 99; in scheduled airline service, 119; comparison with accidents in service by other transport agencies, 120; causes of, 121
Accounting, on interline railroad business, 461–468; regulation of, for railroads, motor vehicles, freight forwarders, and air carriers, 622–625
Ader, Clement, 102
Agglomeration, 449–451
Air mail, beginning in the United States, 104, 106; saving in time by, 106; rates charged for, 106–107; volume and character of, 107; contracts for carriage of, 750–755
Air cargo, 110; organization of Air Cargo, Inc., 111; ton-mileage handled, 111
Air express, beginnings of, 108; character and volume of, 108–109; relation with Railway Express Agency, 108
Air freight, difference between air express and, 109; amount carried by, 110; ton-mileage of, 110; potential volume of business, 110
Air line companies, 152–153; commercial operations of, 1950, 543–544
Air passenger traffic, volume carried, 8–10, 111; coach service, 112; comparative rates by air and rail, 112–114; characteristics of movement, intensity of demand for, 153–155; length of haul, 153–155; feeder services, 155
Air passenger traffic, intercontinental flights, Central and South America, 114; transpacific aviation, 114–115; transatlantic aviation, 115–116; stratosphere flying, 115–116; international agreements, 116–118
Airplanes, developed from gliders, 101; early experiments with, 102; improvements in performance of, 103–104
Airports and landing fields, general character of problems, 488–490; location of, 490–491; finance of, 491; Federal Airport Act of 1946, 492–494
See also Terminals

Air rates, 110
Air rights, *see* Terminals
Air routes, *see* Routes
Air transportation, general discussion of, 98–121; balloons, 98; dirigible airships, 98–99; history of airplanes, 101–102; advantages and disadvantages of, 118–120
See also Consolidation; Public aid; Regulation
Allegheny Portage Railroad, *see* Pennsylvania State Works
Apportionment of costs, 311–313
Association of American Railroads, 481–485

Bailment, contract carriers subject to law of, 233
Balloons, 98
Baltimore & Ohio Railroad, early history of, 61–65; enters Wheeling, 62; and trunk line wars, 375–378
Bankruptcy Act, Sec. 77, *see* Securities, issue of
Basing point rates, general character of, 394–395; illustrations of, 394–397; in Southern territory, 398–399; in Western territory, 400–404
Basing points and market areas, *see* Location
Benefits from transportation, nature of, 12; improvements in speed, 13–15; in cost, 15–16; division of labor, 16–17; competition in prices, 17–18; equalization in supply of goods, 18–19; measure of, 19–20; by differences in cost, 20–21; by total expenditures for transport, 22; by social benefit, 22–23; political and social effects of, 23
See also Transportation
Bills of lading, provisions of standard railroad, 246–247; uniform livestock contracts, 247; carrier must issue, 256; limitation of liability in, 246–247, 255–261; order, 253.
Black Warrior River, 4
Brokers, under Motor Carrier Act, 657, 661–663
Buses, *see* Motor vehicles

Canadian Pacific Railway, 74
Canals and connecting channels, ton-mileage over, 4; New York canals, 4, 32–34; around the falls of rivers, con-

719–722; proposed reductions in, 764–766

Facilities, duty of common carriers to provide, *see* Service
Fort Peck Dam, 42
Freight forwarders, regulation of, 678–683
Frozen per diem, *see* Cars, per diem rates

Gliders, 101
Government ownership, of Pennsylvania State Works, 31; of Erie Canal, 32–34; of Mississippi River service, 42–44; of American railroads, 72
Grain, location of production of in United States, 130; western routes for transport of, 174
    See also Wheat
Granger cases, 612–613
Granger movement, *see* Regulation
Granger railroads, 73, 174
Great Lakes, traffic upon, 4, 9–10, 48–49; shipping companies on, 50–51; increases in tonnage upon, 51; low cost of carriage upon, 51; commodities carried upon, 129
    See also Detroit River; St. Clair River; St. Lawrence River; St. Mary's Falls Canals; Welland Canal
Group rates, 381–382; and grouping of producers, 382; and points of destination, 383; in trunk-line rate system, 383–386; and transcontinental traffic, 386–388; reasons for, 388–391; generalized, and postal tariffs, 390–392; under Hastings plan, 392–393; criticism of, 393–394

Hastings plan, *see* Group rates
Hensen, W. S., 102
Highways, *see* Roads
Hope decision, *see* Valuation
Hoquiam River, 4
Hudson River, 4

Illinois classification, *see* Classification
Illinois waterway, depth of, 38
Incidental carriers, definition of, 230; responsibilities of, 232–233
Inland waterways, varieties of traffic, 3–4, 29–30; ton-miles on, 4, 9; passenger miles upon, 10; commodities handled on, 129–130; regulation of, 686–706
    See also Canals; Great Lakes; Hudson River; Mississippi

River; Missouri River; Ohio River; St. Lawrence River
Inland Waterways Corporation, 42–44
Interchange, of railroad cars, *see* Cars; of motor equipment, 477; of airplanes, 477–478; of water equipment, 478
Intercoastal Waterway, 4
Interline revenue, division of, 461–468
Internal waterways, definition of, 30
Interstate commerce, 569–584
Interstate Commerce Act, *see* Regulation
Interstate Commerce Commission, expenditures of, for general purposes, 615–621; for safety, 621–622; for accounting regulation, 622–625; for valuation, 625–629; for motor vehicles, 629–630; for water transport and freight forwarders, 630–631; organization of, 631–636
Intraport tonnage, 30
Iron ore, location of production, 130; movement on Great Lakes, 136–138; receipts at Lake ports, 138–140; at final destinations, 140–141; exhaustion of Lake Superior deposits, 143; development of Labrador supplies, 144
Iron and steel, distribution of steel producing points, 185–186; consumption of semi-processed steel, 187–188; consumption of steel manufactures, 188–189; characteristics of transportation of, 189; competition of producing areas, 190
Irregular air carriers, 720–723
Isodapanes, *see* Location

James River, 4
Joint cost, *see* Theory of rates

Labor, railroad expenditures for, 287–290; influences which affect amounts paid, 287–289; average compensation per hour, 1940–1950, 288; increases in railroad wages to, 1941–1949, 289
Lakes, *see* Great Lakes
Lakes-to-the-Gulf Waterway, *see* Mississippi River
Land grants, to railroads, 755–760
    See also Public aid
Langley, S. P., 102
Law of market areas, *See* Location
Levassor, 82
Liability of common carriers, carriers not technically insurers, 244; nature of, 245–246; excepted causes, 246–247; illustrative cases, 247–249; beginning of, 249–250; ending of, 250–252; and delivery, 252–253; and measure of